L.W. Nixon Library
Butler Community College
901 South Haverhill Road
El Dorado, Kansas 67042-3280

DISCARD

D1172069

MAXIMUM MINIMUM WAGE

BY BOB FINGERMAN

Also by Bob Fingerman

White Like She
Minimum Wage
Beg the Question
You Deserved It
Recess Pieces
Bottomfeeder
Connective Tissue
From the Ashes
Pariah

MAXIMUM MINIMUM WAGE

BY BOB FINGERMAN

BF
12

MAXIMUM MINIMUM WAGE

ISBN: 978-1-60706-674-3
First printing
March 2013

Published by Image Comics, Inc.

Office of publication:
2001 Center Street, Sixth Floor
Berkeley, CA 94704

Copyright © 2013 Bob Fingerman. All rights reserved.
MINIMUM WAGE™ (including all prominent characters featured
herein), its logo and all character likenesses are trademarks of
Bob Fingerman, unless otherwise noted. Image Comics® and
its logos are registered trademarks of Image Comics, Inc. No
part of this publication may be reproduced or transmitted,
in any form or by any means (except for short excerpts for
review purposes) without the express written permission of
Bob Fingerman or Image Comics, Inc. All names, characters,
events and locales in this publication are entirely fictional. Any
resemblance to actual persons (living or dead), events or places,
without satiric intent, is coincidental. Printed in Korea.

For international rights inquiries, write to:
foreignlicensing@imagecomics.com

IMAGE COMICS, INC.
Robert Kirkman - chief operating officer
Erik Larsen - chief financial officer
Todd McFarlane - president
Marc Silvestri - chief executive officer
Jim Valentino - vice-president
Eric Stephenson - publisher
Ron Richards - director of business development
Jennifer de Guzman - pr & marketing director
Branwyn Bigglestone - accounts manager
Emily Miller - accounting assistant
Jamie Parreno - marketing assistant
Jenna Savage - administrative assistant
Kevin Yuen - digital rights coordinator
Jonathan Chan - production manager
Drew Gill - art director
Monica Garcia - production artist
Vincent Kukua - production artist
Jana Cook - production artist
www.imagecomics.com

"For Michele, the love of my life. Yup."

FOREWORD

Minimum Wage is an important comic. If I were tasked with introducing someone to comics in an attempt to make them love and cherish the medium as much as I do, I'd give them *Watchmen*, *Bone*, *Savage Dragon* and *Minimum Wage*. To me, those are the cornerstones of the foundation of what I read early on that firmly established my love of the comic book medium. In my opinion, those four books show you the wide range of what comics can offer.

I'm a very particular person. I have a lot of little things that bug me, nag at me, rub me the wrong way; one of those things is the term "pet peeves." Another is introductions where the writer tells a story about himself and talks about his life more than the book he is introducing. I think it's ridiculous, and to me it often comes off like the writer doesn't really have a lot to say about the book so he tells one anecdote about his life that somehow involves the book and then call it a day.

It annoys me.

That said, I'm sort of going to do that now. Buckle up and let the self-loathing begin.

I grew up in small town in Kentucky with a sporadically religious upbringing. It wouldn't be too much of a stretch to say I lived a somewhat puritan lifestyle. I guess the easiest way to put this is that I never knew there
was such a thing as "performance art" where someone would cut a cross into their chest with a razor blade and then let a woman urinate on them…until I read *Minimum Wage*. I certainly never would have realized such a thing could be laugh out loud funny.

Years after reading that scene, when I attended a friend's college graduate art show thing, another senior whose focus was performance art did a piece where he stripped down naked and laid on a four foot square patch of grass surrounded by candles, curled in a fetal position, ball sack dangling ever presently between his thighs, while a cassette tape across the room played the sounds of birds chirping. After three minutes, the tape would end, he would stand up… flip the tape and resume the position until the tape needed to be flipped again. We stood politely through three tape flippings before realizing that the point was to see how long you'd stare at his nut sack. As I watched this, rolling my eyes and trying not to laugh, I did think to myself: *at least he's not getting peed on*.

I had the benefit of shopping at a comic shop in my mid-teens that was blissfully lax on the whole "you have to be 18 to buy mature comics" rule. I had no trouble getting *Lobo* or Vertigo comics or the holy-crap-mostly-forgotten *Penthouse Comix*, which had work from Jason Pearson, Dave Johnson, Adam Hughes, and countless other amazing artists including some guy named Bob Fingerman. So I was picking up all that stuff at age 15 and 16.

I was also buying *Minimum Wage* and it was blowing my mind every few months when an issue would (finally) come out.

It would not be a stretch to say that *Minimum Wage* was my first serious look at issues like women's rights, gay rights and other things that most definitely led to me being the Left-leaning disappointment I am to my in-laws. I was certainly aware of those issues. I knew about the existence of abortion. I wasn't an idiot. But I rarely talked to my parents about such heavy issues. My friends and I would play role-playing games or watch movies and it wasn't often we'd chat about anything more than Robert Rodriguez's *Desperado* and how cool that guy with the knives was. *Minimum Wage* was the first time I seen things like poverty and pregnancy explored in a real way. It was a time when I'd watch *Batman: The Animated Series* after school and then read Rob Hoffman contemplating jerking off to two teenagers having sex in a car on the street below his apartment at night.

That guy probably shouldn't have been selling me these comics.

It was the first black and white indie comic I read. It took me from *Amazing Spider-Man* and *Savage Dragon* and opened up my comic reading world to *Too Much Coffee Man*, *THB*, *Reid Fleming*, *Negative Burn*, *Johnny The Homicidal Maniac*, *Cerebus* and *Bone*. All because Bob drew a *Savage Dragon* card in a *Savage Dragon* card set and I recognized his name on *Otis Goes Hollywood* (is that in print?[1]) and then discovered this gem, *Minimum Wage* in ads found in that series. There's something else I owe Erik Larsen.

Minimum Wage was the first time I saw a real relationship between two people depicted in such an honest, heartbreaking and often times hilarious way in comics. It really showed what comics could be and has informed my take on writing comics in truly significant ways. It may not be apparent but I think there's a lot of *Minimum Wage* in *The Walking Dead* and *Invincible* and other things I've done. I owe a lot to Bob, frankly. When people ask, in interviews, what my main influences are, I always say *Savage Dragon* and *Minimum Wage*. My comics are all sexual relationships and amputations; it's all right there in those two books.

So you, dear reader, are in for a treat. You're either getting ready to cozy up with this gem and read it all over again in it's new definitive and painstakingly updated form, or you're going to experience this series for the first time, without having to wait between issues or for the story to be wrapped up separately in a standalone (but equally awesome) graphic novel years later. I'm so jealous.

The story of Rob and Sylvia is near and dear to my heart. It just seems crazy to me that my life has changed over the years to where I'm in a position at Image Comics to help bring this book into your hands, and that I'm somehow the guy writing an introduction to what is without a doubt one of my single favorite comics of all time, is one more example of how cool and insanely awesome my life has become.

This book is important to me, and I hope it will be just as important to you. Enjoy! But I already know you will.

Robert Kirkman
Backwoods, CA
2013

1. Yes, it is, collected in the book *You Deserved It* (Dark Horse, 2005) — Bob.
PS: Jeez, Robert, this foreword got me all choked up. Sincerely. Thanks and thanks again, buddy.

PREFACE

What you hold in your hands could just as easily have been titled *Minimum Wage, the OCD Edition*. Though I can't say I'm crazy about the results he's gotten, I completely understand and empathize with George Lucas's compulsion[1] to go back in and fiddle with his older work. The knowledge that perfection is unattainable doesn't stop certain types from trying to achieve it. Or at least get closer and closer. Over and over again.

Maximum Minimum Wage is what very well might be—emphasis on the qualifying word "might"—the *final* version of this saga. *Or at least this portion of it.* Once again I went back in and retooled some of the art and dialogue. After having written several novels—including the two that actually got published, *Bottomfeeder* (M Press, 2006) and *Pariah* (Tor, 2010)—I flatter myself that my writing skills have improved over the years since the previous edition, which I foolishly redubbed *Beg the Question*. What was I thinking? Let's take the identifiable name/brand, *Minimum Wage*, and toss it away. Oh, and you know what else would be a great idea? Let's *not* feature the main characters on the cover. Or even any art. Let's take an iconic image from the narrative and use a photograph of it.

A photograph.

I was trying to be fancy. I'd not yet published a novel, and I was desperate for some respectability. Years of working for porn mags will do that to one's self-esteem. I also shrank the book from standard comic book size to more standard hardcover novel format. It looked just like a prose novel at first blush; very handsome, but not at all like the comic it was. A seriocomic (though hopefully more *comic* than *serio*) roman à clef set in Brooklyn, New York, before it became oh so fashionable. Actually, the area in which much of its action is set, Bay Ridge, is still refreshingly unhip. That's what you get for being at the ass-end of the borough, a good hour from the lowest tip of lower Manhattan. Or anywhere. It's a good place to look at the Verrazano Bridge[2] and that's about all. Well, maybe a few more things.

Hi, Bay Ridge.

So, this spiffy volume, what's it got? I'm thinking of this as my Criterion Edition, and we all buy those not just for their impeccable prints of the movies but also for the bonus supplemental materials, even if we already have a previous release of the same title. Criterion is always the upgrade[3]. But if you've already got earlier versions of *Minimum Wage* and are either on the fence about buying this one[4] or buying it, then tossing your old ones to make room, prepare for the collector's dilemma: you'll want all of them because they're all different, like snowflakes, only mass-produced.

The guest artist gallery alone is worth the price of admission. In addition to some of the classic back covers and pinups from the original run, there are also loads of all-new contributions. It's a dazzler. Plus there's sketchbook material, a full-color cover gallery and more.

---

1   I suspect part of his selling to Disney was to break the habit of picking at it and letting it get more and more infected. I admire him for it and if anyone wants to pay me four billion dollars for total ownership of *Minimum Wage*, I'm open to discussion. Maybe even a little less than that.

2   See Chapter 7.

3   This isn't an unpaid endorsement for Criterion editions, by the way.

4   Though this seems unlikely. I mean who reads prefaces in the store? Unless it's a Barnes & Noble, where people seem to get *waaaay* too comfortable reading there. Sometimes navigating the aisles there is like stepping through a refugee camp. Okay, cheapskate, c'mon. If you're not only reading the preface, but the footnotes, while still in the store, you're not only weird, but you're a bad person. If you're reading this, like a normal, respectable human being, in the comfort of your own home, carry on. And thank you.

The first book in this series was *Minimum Wage Book One*, and I regard that as the "pilot" episode. Or TV movie. It was the 72-page introduction to these characters and their corner of the world. It was scrappy and low budget, so naturally when it went to series I recast with more attractive actors. In other words, the reason it was not included in the *Beg the Question* version was that the art style was radically different from the way it developed over the course of its serial run. It was kind of the inverse of *Peanuts*, in that it started looser, with a less sure line, and got tighter and slicker as it went on[5]. I couldn't even retouch it, as I did almost every single page of issues 2 through 10. "2 through 10," you say. But what of *numero uno*?

The first regular issue was *also* in that looser style, so it got tossed in favor of redrawing a condensed version of that chapter as well as some scenes from *Minimum Wage Book One* for *Beg the Question*. This book has both *Minimum Wage Book One* and the "lost" first issue, back in print for the first time since 1997.

But here's the part that longtime fans and newcomers (hopefully) will find the *most* intriguing bonus: *the script for the never drawn eleventh issue*. I won't say more, lest I accidentally leak some spoilers, but you'll get a taste of what might have been coming down the road for Rob and Sylvia.

Minimum Wage never drew a big audience, but it drew a smart one. I was as proud of the readers it attracted as the work itself and because of it I made some long-lasting friendships. It was favored by many of my favorite comedians, which was a real compliment. Sorry if that sounds a little boasty, but as a lifelong comedy nerd I think that's super cool.

My feisty little ensemble cast was fun to write and draw, so I'm glad their exploits entertained and sometimes even got under readers' skins. There's more story to tell and hopefully I'll get to it at some point. Sales-willing, maybe sooner than later. Spread the word and keep the faith (and get your friends, family and coworkers to buy this book)! Review it online[6]! Evangelize it and perhaps Rob, Sylvia, et al, will rise again like a flock of phoenixes!

It could happen.

Okay, I don't want to go on too long. This book is a big, fat, dense, read. I'm happy to say it's not a comic you'll plow through in ten minutes. Least of all, *this* edition. Thank you for buying it, especially if it is an upgrade. And seriously, keep the other version (or versions).

None of them are perfect, but I keep trying. We'll get there. Together.

Bob Fingerman
New York City
December 2012

---

5   Or to be more apt, like *The Simpsons*. Picture *The Tracey Ullman Show* era Simpsons versus how they look now. Or the cutout construction paper *South Park* cast and the new digital version. You get the idea.
6   Seriously, do that. It helps.

Chapter One

PATCHOULI VAPOR TRAIL

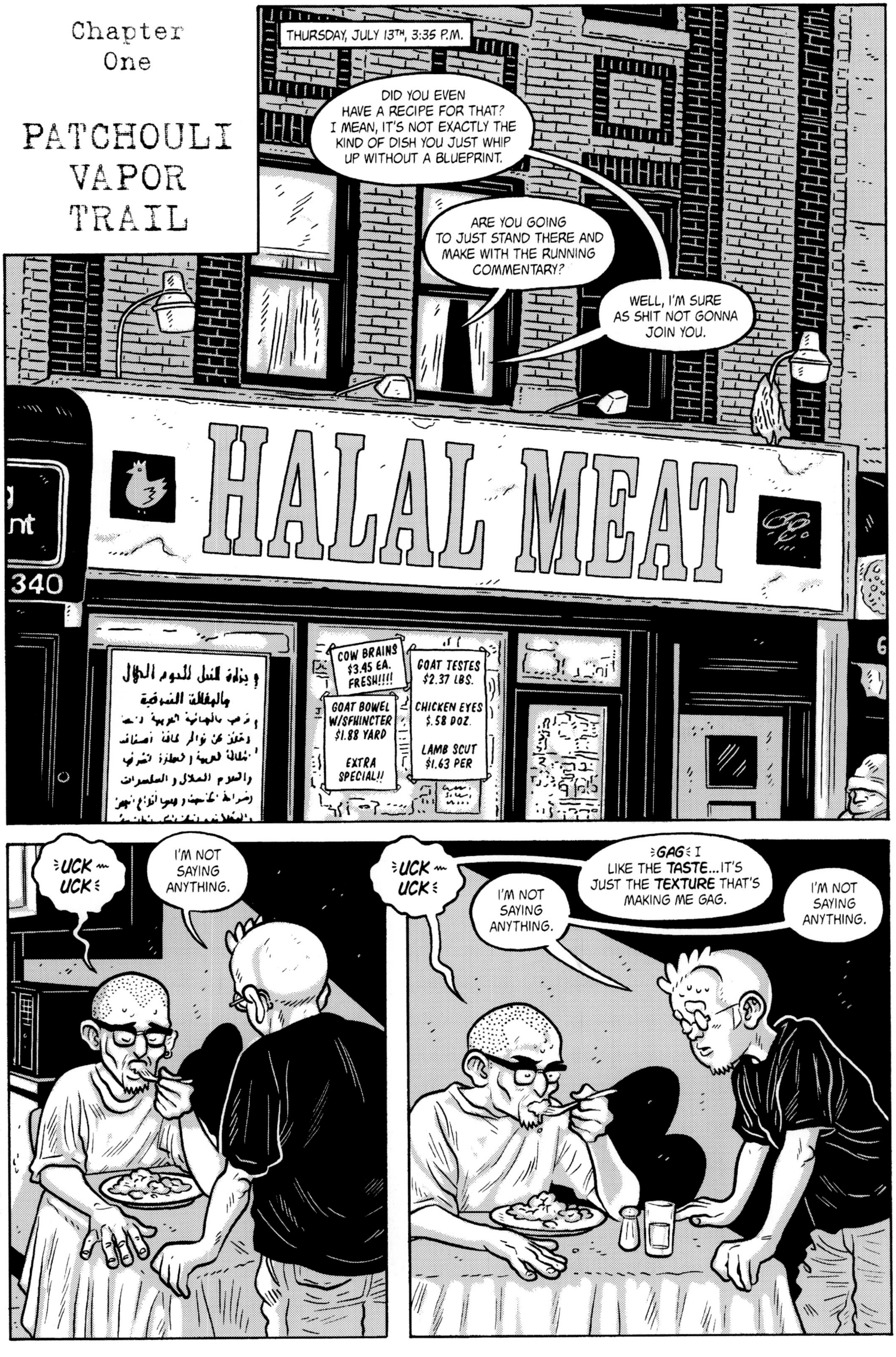

THURSDAY, JULY 13TH, 3:35 P.M.
DID YOU EVEN HAVE A RECIPE FOR THAT? I MEAN, IT'S NOT EXACTLY THE KIND OF DISH YOU JUST WHIP UP WITHOUT A BLUEPRINT.
ARE YOU GOING TO JUST STAND THERE AND MAKE WITH THE RUNNING COMMENTARY?
WELL, I'M SURE AS SHIT NOT GONNA JOIN YOU.
HALAL MEAT
340
COW BRAINS $3.45 EA. FRESH!!!!
GOAT TESTES $2.37 LBS.
GOAT BOWEL W/SFHINCTER $1.88 YARD
CHICKEN EYES $.58 DOZ.
LAMB SCUT $1.63 PER
EXTRA SPECIAL!!
UCK UCK
I'M NOT SAYING ANYTHING.
UCK UCK
GAG I LIKE THE **TASTE**...IT'S JUST THE **TEXTURE** THAT'S MAKING ME GAG.
I'M NOT SAYING ANYTHING.
I'M NOT SAYING ANYTHING.

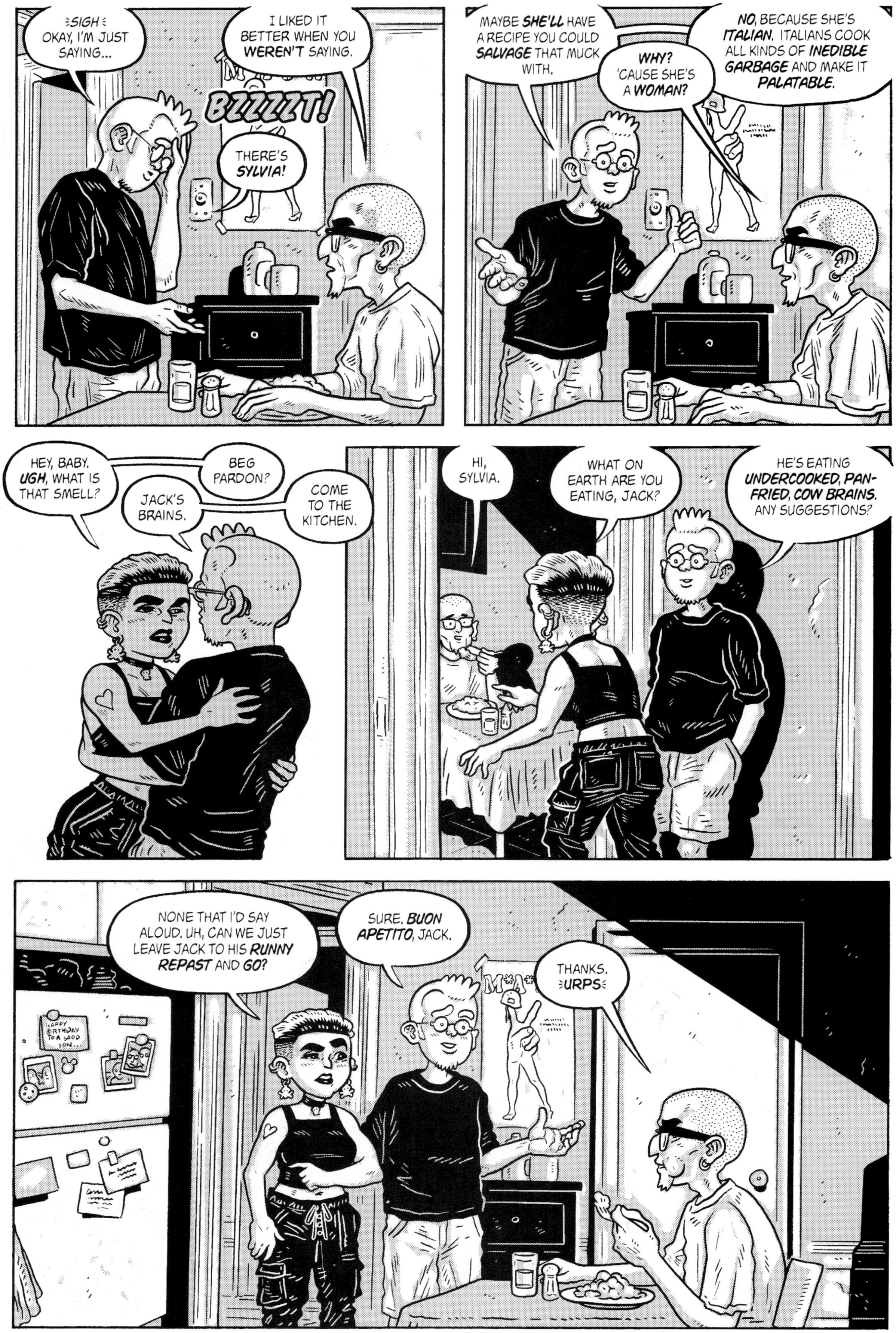
SIGH OKAY, I'M JUST SAYING...
I LIKED IT BETTER WHEN YOU WEREN'T SAYING.
BZZZZT!
THERE'S SYLVIA!
MAYBE SHE'LL HAVE A RECIPE YOU COULD SALVAGE THAT MUCK WITH.
WHY? 'CAUSE SHE'S A WOMAN?
NO, BECAUSE SHE'S ITALIAN. ITALIANS COOK ALL KINDS OF INEDIBLE GARBAGE AND MAKE IT PALATABLE.
HEY, BABY. UGH, WHAT IS THAT SMELL?
BEG PARDON?
JACK'S BRAINS.
COME TO THE KITCHEN.
HI, SYLVIA.
WHAT ON EARTH ARE YOU EATING, JACK?
HE'S EATING UNDERCOOKED, PAN-FRIED, COW BRAINS. ANY SUGGESTIONS?
NONE THAT I'D SAY ALOUD. UH, CAN WE JUST LEAVE JACK TO HIS RUNNY REPAST AND GO?
SURE. BUON APETITO, JACK.
THANKS. URPS
HAPPY BIRTHDAY TO A GOOD SON...

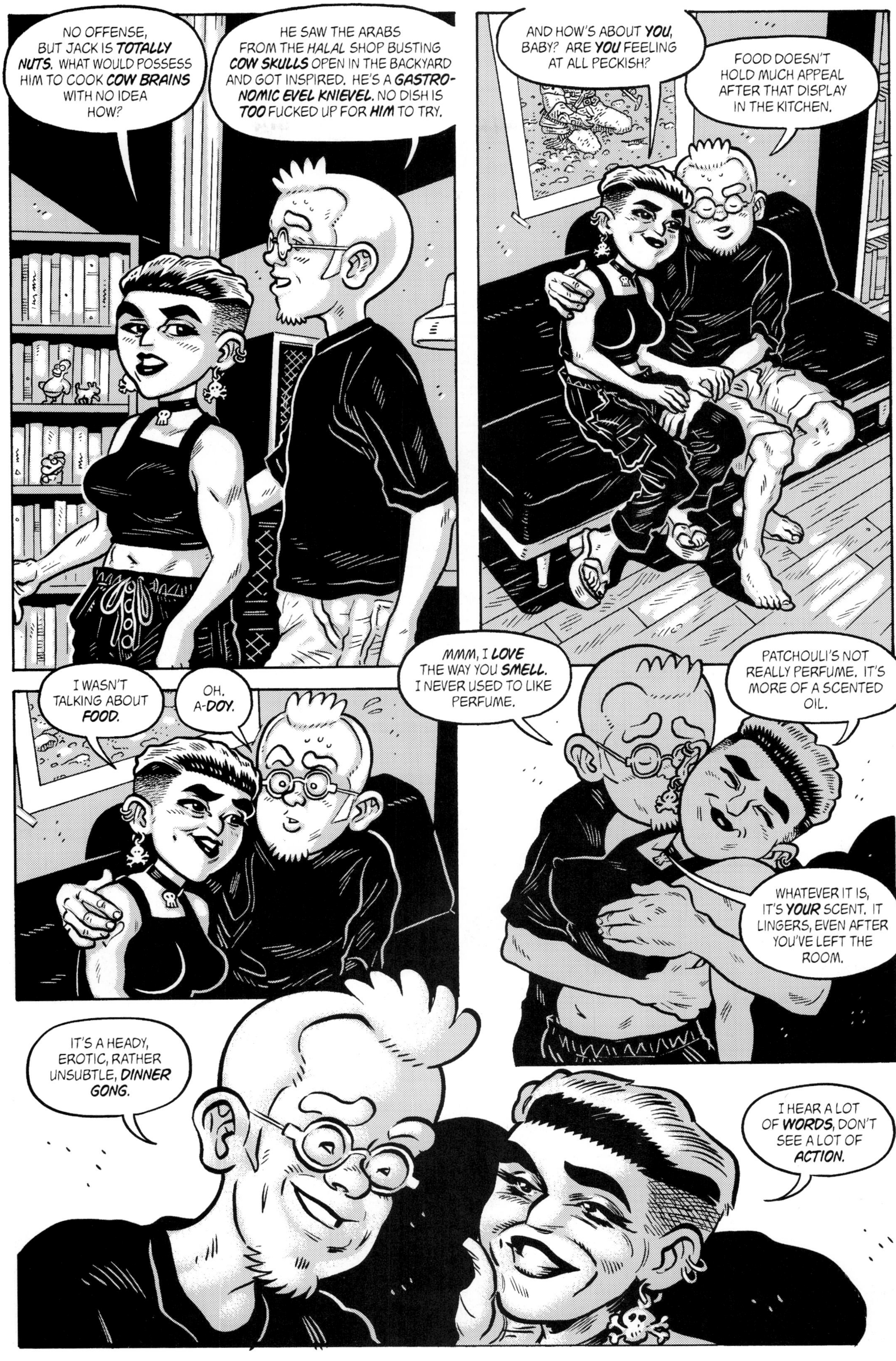
NO OFFENSE, BUT JACK IS TOTALLY NUTS. WHAT WOULD POSSESS HIM TO COOK COW BRAINS WITH NO IDEA HOW?
HE SAW THE ARABS FROM THE HALAL SHOP BUSTING COW SKULLS OPEN IN THE BACKYARD AND GOT INSPIRED. HE'S A GASTRONOMIC EVEL KNIEVEL. NO DISH IS TOO FUCKED UP FOR HIM TO TRY.
AND HOW'S ABOUT YOU, BABY? ARE YOU FEELING AT ALL PECKISH?
FOOD DOESN'T HOLD MUCH APPEAL AFTER THAT DISPLAY IN THE KITCHEN.
I WASN'T TALKING ABOUT FOOD.
OH. A-DOY.
MMM, I LOVE THE WAY YOU SMELL. I NEVER USED TO LIKE PERFUME.
PATCHOULI'S NOT REALLY PERFUME. IT'S MORE OF A SCENTED OIL.
WHATEVER IT IS, IT'S YOUR SCENT. IT LINGERS, EVEN AFTER YOU'VE LEFT THE ROOM.
IT'S A HEADY, EROTIC, RATHER UNSUBTLE, DINNER GONG.
I HEAR A LOT OF WORDS, DON'T SEE A LOT OF ACTION.

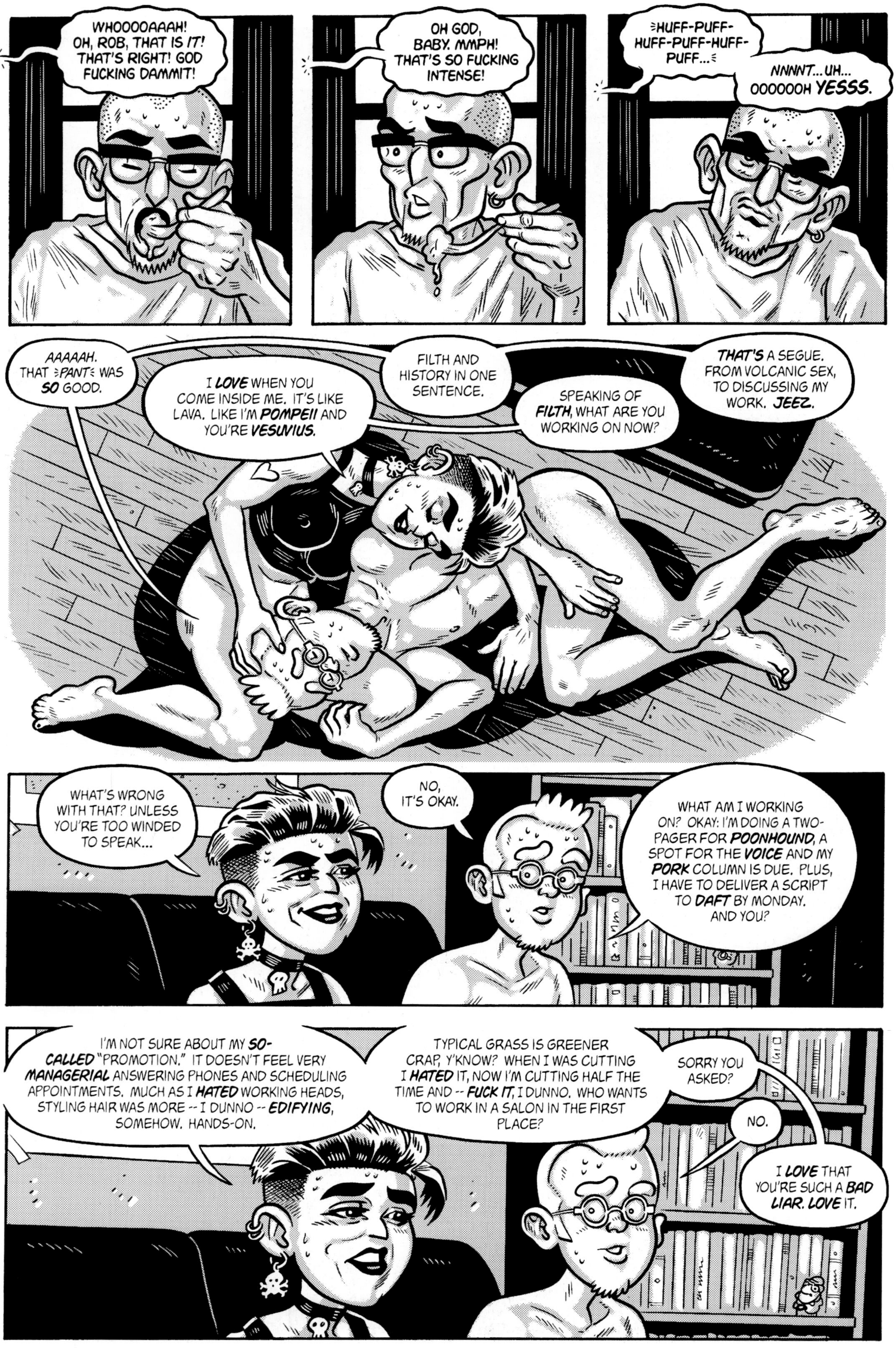
WHOOOOAAAH! OH, ROB, THAT IS IT! THAT'S RIGHT! GOD FUCKING DAMMIT!
OH GOD, BABY. MMPH! THAT'S SO FUCKING INTENSE!
HUFF-PUFF-HUFF-PUFF-HUFF-PUFF...
NNNNT...UH... OOOOOOH YESSS.
AAAAAH. THAT PANT WAS SO GOOD.
I LOVE WHEN YOU COME INSIDE ME. IT'S LIKE LAVA. LIKE I'M POMPEII AND YOU'RE VESUVIUS.
FILTH AND HISTORY IN ONE SENTENCE.
SPEAKING OF FILTH, WHAT ARE YOU WORKING ON NOW?
THAT'S A SEGUE. FROM VOLCANIC SEX, TO DISCUSSING MY WORK. JEEZ.
WHAT'S WRONG WITH THAT? UNLESS YOU'RE TOO WINDED TO SPEAK...
NO, IT'S OKAY.
WHAT AM I WORKING ON? OKAY: I'M DOING A TWO-PAGER FOR POONHOUND, A SPOT FOR THE VOICE AND MY PORK COLUMN IS DUE. PLUS, I HAVE TO DELIVER A SCRIPT TO DAFT BY MONDAY. AND YOU?
I'M NOT SURE ABOUT MY SO-CALLED "PROMOTION." IT DOESN'T FEEL VERY MANAGERIAL ANSWERING PHONES AND SCHEDULING APPOINTMENTS. MUCH AS I HATED WORKING HEADS, STYLING HAIR WAS MORE -- I DUNNO -- EDIFYING, SOMEHOW. HANDS-ON.
TYPICAL GRASS IS GREENER CRAP, Y'KNOW? WHEN I WAS CUTTING I HATED IT, NOW I'M CUTTING HALF THE TIME AND -- FUCK IT, I DUNNO. WHO WANTS TO WORK IN A SALON IN THE FIRST PLACE?
SORRY YOU ASKED?
NO.
I LOVE THAT YOU'RE SUCH A BAD LIAR. LOVE IT.

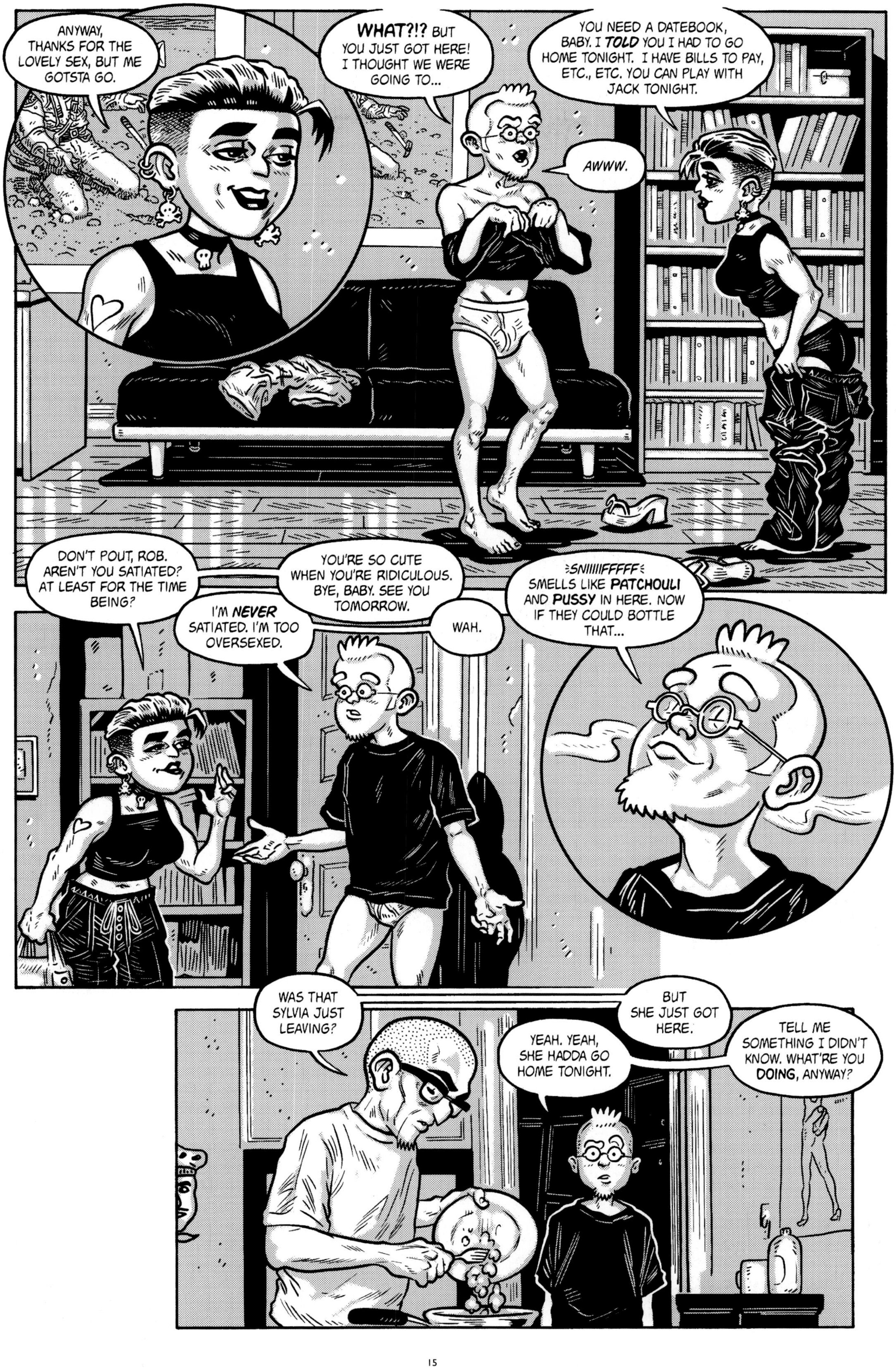
ANYWAY, THANKS FOR THE LOVELY SEX, BUT ME GOTSTA GO.
WHAT?!? BUT YOU JUST GOT HERE! I THOUGHT WE WERE GOING TO...
YOU NEED A DATEBOOK, BABY. I TOLD YOU I HAD TO GO HOME TONIGHT. I HAVE BILLS TO PAY, ETC., ETC. YOU CAN PLAY WITH JACK TONIGHT.
AWWW.
DON'T POUT, ROB. AREN'T YOU SATIATED? AT LEAST FOR THE TIME BEING?
I'M NEVER SATIATED. I'M TOO OVERSEXED.
YOU'RE SO CUTE WHEN YOU'RE RIDICULOUS. BYE, BABY. SEE YOU TOMORROW.
WAH.
SNIIIIIFFFFF
SMELLS LIKE PATCHOULI AND PUSSY IN HERE. NOW IF THEY COULD BOTTLE THAT...
WAS THAT SYLVIA JUST LEAVING?
YEAH. YEAH, SHE HADDA GO HOME TONIGHT.
BUT SHE JUST GOT HERE.
TELL ME SOMETHING I DIDN'T KNOW. WHAT'RE YOU DOING, ANYWAY?

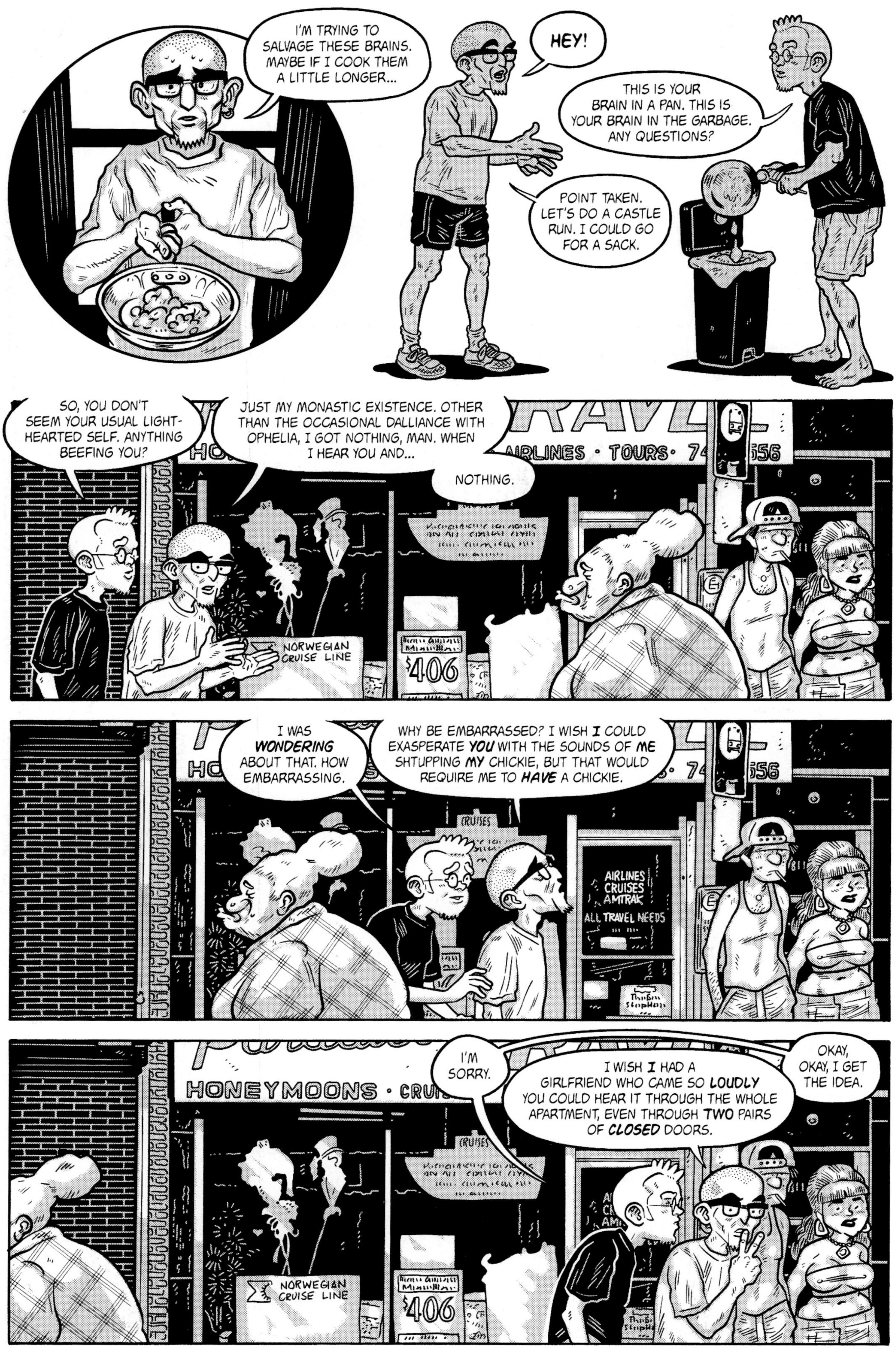

I'M TRYING TO SALVAGE THESE BRAINS. MAYBE IF I COOK THEM A LITTLE LONGER...
HEY!
THIS IS YOUR BRAIN IN A PAN. THIS IS YOUR BRAIN IN THE GARBAGE. ANY QUESTIONS?
POINT TAKEN. LET'S DO A CASTLE RUN. I COULD GO FOR A SACK.
SO, YOU DON'T SEEM YOUR USUAL LIGHT-HEARTED SELF. ANYTHING BEEFING YOU?
JUST MY MONASTIC EXISTENCE. OTHER THAN THE OCCASIONAL DALLIANCE WITH OPHELIA, I GOT NOTHING, MAN. WHEN I HEAR YOU AND...
NOTHING.
AIRLINES · TOURS
NORWEGIAN CRUISE LINE
$406
I WAS WONDERING ABOUT THAT. HOW EMBARRASSING.
WHY BE EMBARRASSED? I WISH I COULD EXASPERATE YOU WITH THE SOUNDS OF ME SHTUPPING MY CHICKIE, BUT THAT WOULD REQUIRE ME TO HAVE A CHICKIE.
CRUISES
AIRLINES CRUISES AMTRAK
ALL TRAVEL NEEDS
I'M SORRY.
I WISH I HAD A GIRLFRIEND WHO CAME SO LOUDLY YOU COULD HEAR IT THROUGH THE WHOLE APARTMENT, EVEN THROUGH TWO PAIRS OF CLOSED DOORS.
OKAY, OKAY, I GET THE IDEA.
HONEYMOONS · CRUI
CRUISES
NORWEGIAN CRUISE LINE
$406

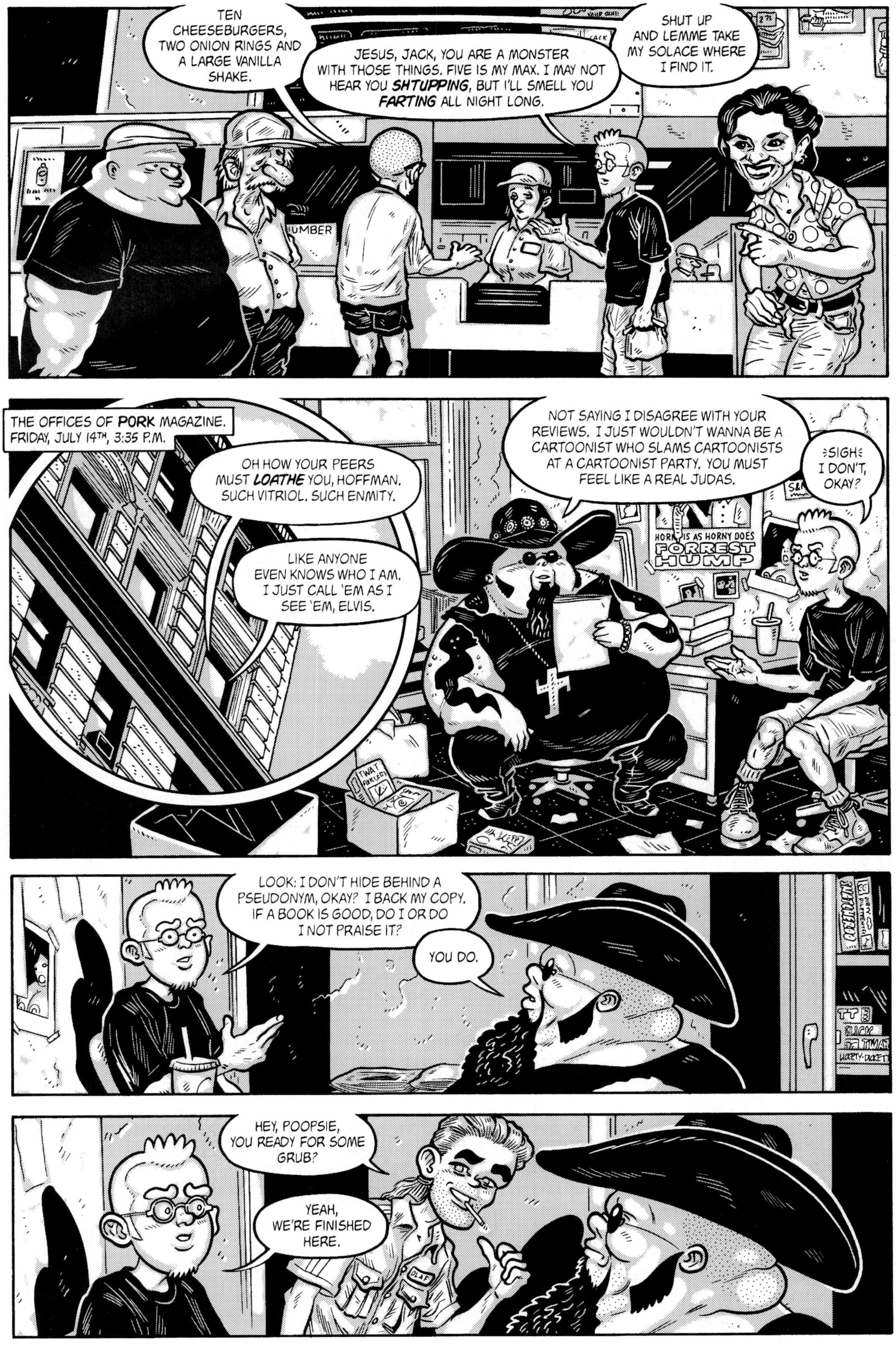

TEN CHEESEBURGERS, TWO ONION RINGS AND A LARGE VANILLA SHAKE.
JESUS, JACK, YOU ARE A MONSTER WITH THOSE THINGS. FIVE IS MY MAX. I MAY NOT HEAR YOU SHTUPPING, BUT I'LL SMELL YOU FARTING ALL NIGHT LONG.
SHUT UP AND LEMME TAKE MY SOLACE WHERE I FIND IT.
THE OFFICES OF PORK MAGAZINE. FRIDAY, JULY 14TH, 3:35 P.M.
OH HOW YOUR PEERS MUST LOATHE YOU, HOFFMAN. SUCH VITRIOL. SUCH ENMITY.
LIKE ANYONE EVEN KNOWS WHO I AM. I JUST CALL 'EM AS I SEE 'EM, ELVIS.
NOT SAYING I DISAGREE WITH YOUR REVIEWS. I JUST WOULDN'T WANNA BE A CARTOONIST WHO SLAMS CARTOONISTS AT A CARTOONIST PARTY. YOU MUST FEEL LIKE A REAL JUDAS.
SIGH I DON'T, OKAY?
HORNY IS AS HORNY DOES
FORREST HUMP
LOOK: I DON'T HIDE BEHIND A PSEUDONYM, OKAY? I BACK MY COPY. IF A BOOK IS GOOD, DO I OR DO I NOT PRAISE IT?
YOU DO.
HEY, POOPSIE, YOU READY FOR SOME GRUB?
YEAH, WE'RE FINISHED HERE.
OLAF

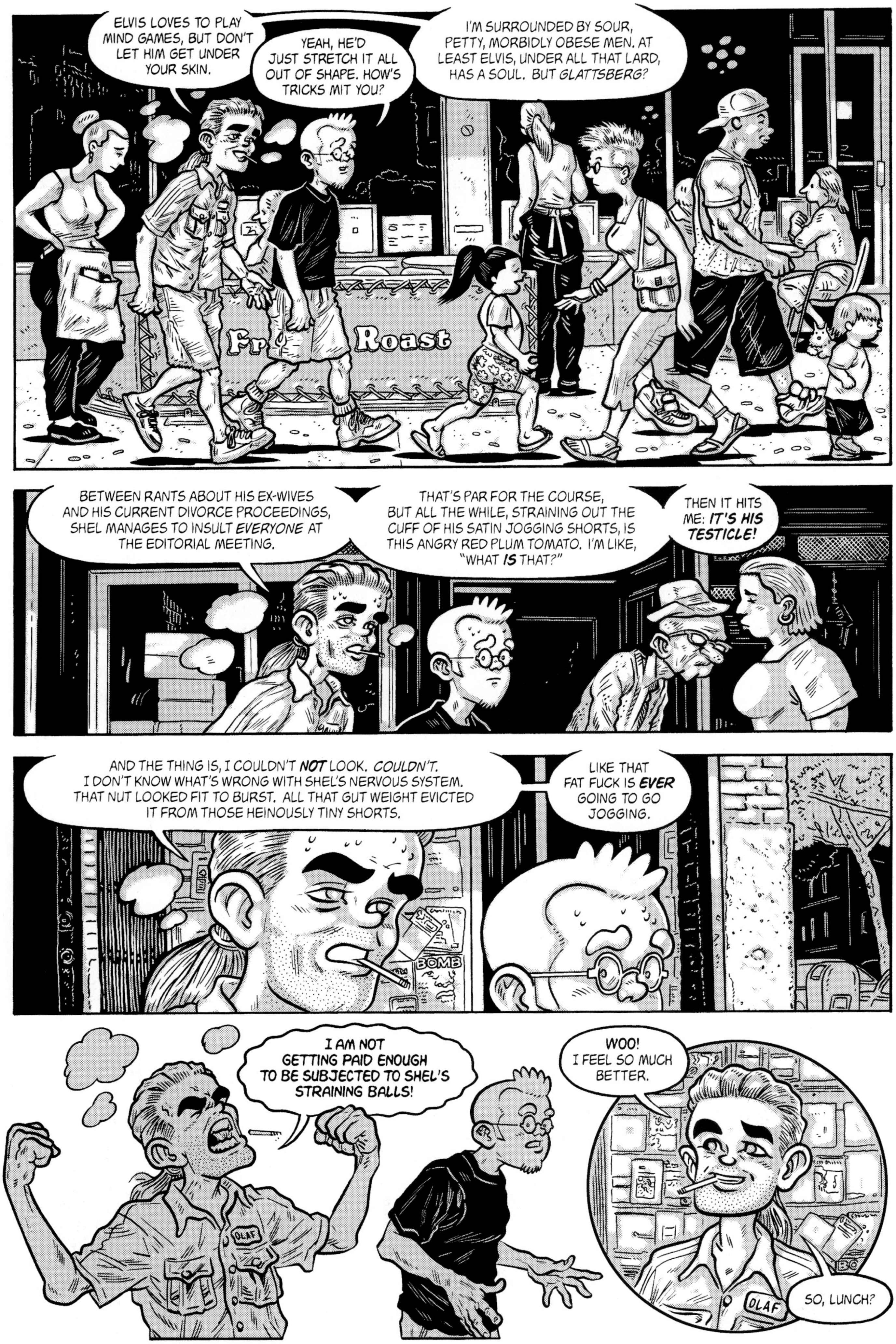
ELVIS LOVES TO PLAY MIND GAMES, BUT DON'T LET HIM GET UNDER YOUR SKIN.
YEAH, HE'D JUST STRETCH IT ALL OUT OF SHAPE. HOW'S TRICKS MIT YOU?
I'M SURROUNDED BY SOUR, PETTY, MORBIDLY OBESE MEN. AT LEAST ELVIS, UNDER ALL THAT LARD, HAS A SOUL. BUT GLATTSBERG?
Roast
BETWEEN RANTS ABOUT HIS EX-WIVES AND HIS CURRENT DIVORCE PROCEEDINGS, SHEL MANAGES TO INSULT EVERYONE AT THE EDITORIAL MEETING.
THAT'S PAR FOR THE COURSE, BUT ALL THE WHILE, STRAINING OUT THE CUFF OF HIS SATIN JOGGING SHORTS, IS THIS ANGRY RED PLUM TOMATO. I'M LIKE, "WHAT IS THAT?"
THEN IT HITS ME: IT'S HIS TESTICLE!
AND THE THING IS, I COULDN'T NOT LOOK. COULDN'T. I DON'T KNOW WHAT'S WRONG WITH SHEL'S NERVOUS SYSTEM. THAT NUT LOOKED FIT TO BURST. ALL THAT GUT WEIGHT EVICTED IT FROM THOSE HEINOUSLY TINY SHORTS.
LIKE THAT FAT FUCK IS EVER GOING TO GO JOGGING.
BOMB
I AM NOT GETTING PAID ENOUGH TO BE SUBJECTED TO SHEL'S STRAINING BALLS!
OLAF
WOO! I FEEL SO MUCH BETTER.
OLAF
SO, LUNCH?

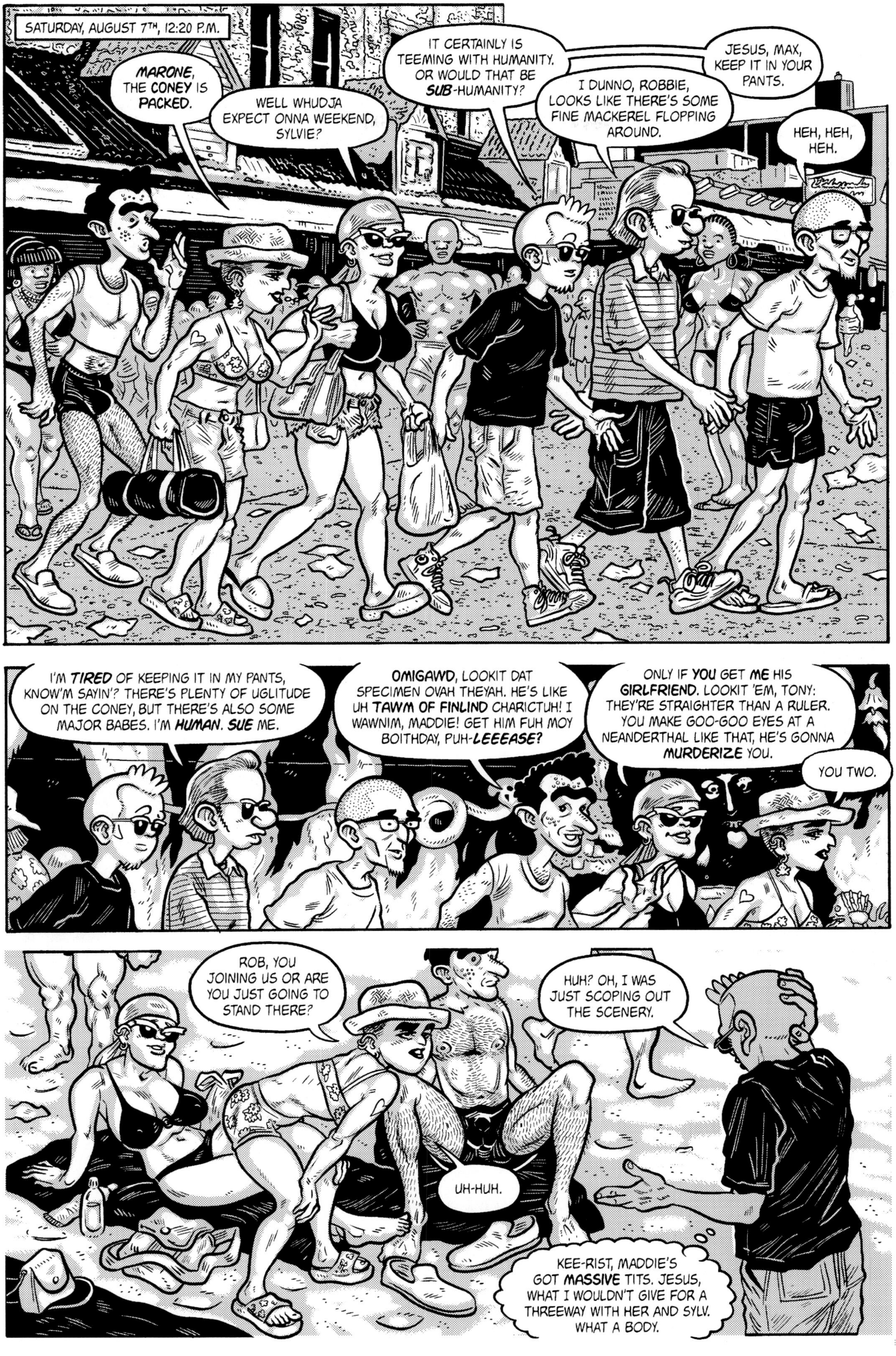
SATURDAY, AUGUST 7TH, 12:20 P.M.
MARONE, THE CONEY IS PACKED.
WELL WHUDJA EXPECT ONNA WEEKEND, SYLVIE?
IT CERTAINLY IS TEEMING WITH HUMANITY. OR WOULD THAT BE SUB-HUMANITY?
I DUNNO, ROBBIE, LOOKS LIKE THERE'S SOME FINE MACKEREL FLOPPING AROUND.
JESUS, MAX, KEEP IT IN YOUR PANTS.
HEH, HEH, HEH.
I'M TIRED OF KEEPING IT IN MY PANTS, KNOW'M SAYIN'? THERE'S PLENTY OF UGLITUDE ON THE CONEY, BUT THERE'S ALSO SOME MAJOR BABES. I'M HUMAN. SUE ME.
OMIGAWD, LOOKIT DAT SPECIMEN OVAH THEYAH. HE'S LIKE UH TAWM OF FINLIND CHARICTUH! I WAWNIM, MADDIE! GET HIM FUH MOY BOITHDAY, PUH-LEEEASE?
ONLY IF YOU GET ME HIS GIRLFRIEND. LOOKIT 'EM, TONY: THEY'RE STRAIGHTER THAN A RULER. YOU MAKE GOO-GOO EYES AT A NEANDERTHAL LIKE THAT, HE'S GONNA MURDERIZE YOU.
YOU TWO.
ROB, YOU JOINING US OR ARE YOU JUST GOING TO STAND THERE?
HUH? OH, I WAS JUST SCOPING OUT THE SCENERY.
UH-HUH.
KEE-RIST, MADDIE'S GOT MASSIVE TITS. JESUS, WHAT I WOULDN'T GIVE FOR A THREEWAY WITH HER AND SYLV. WHAT A BODY.

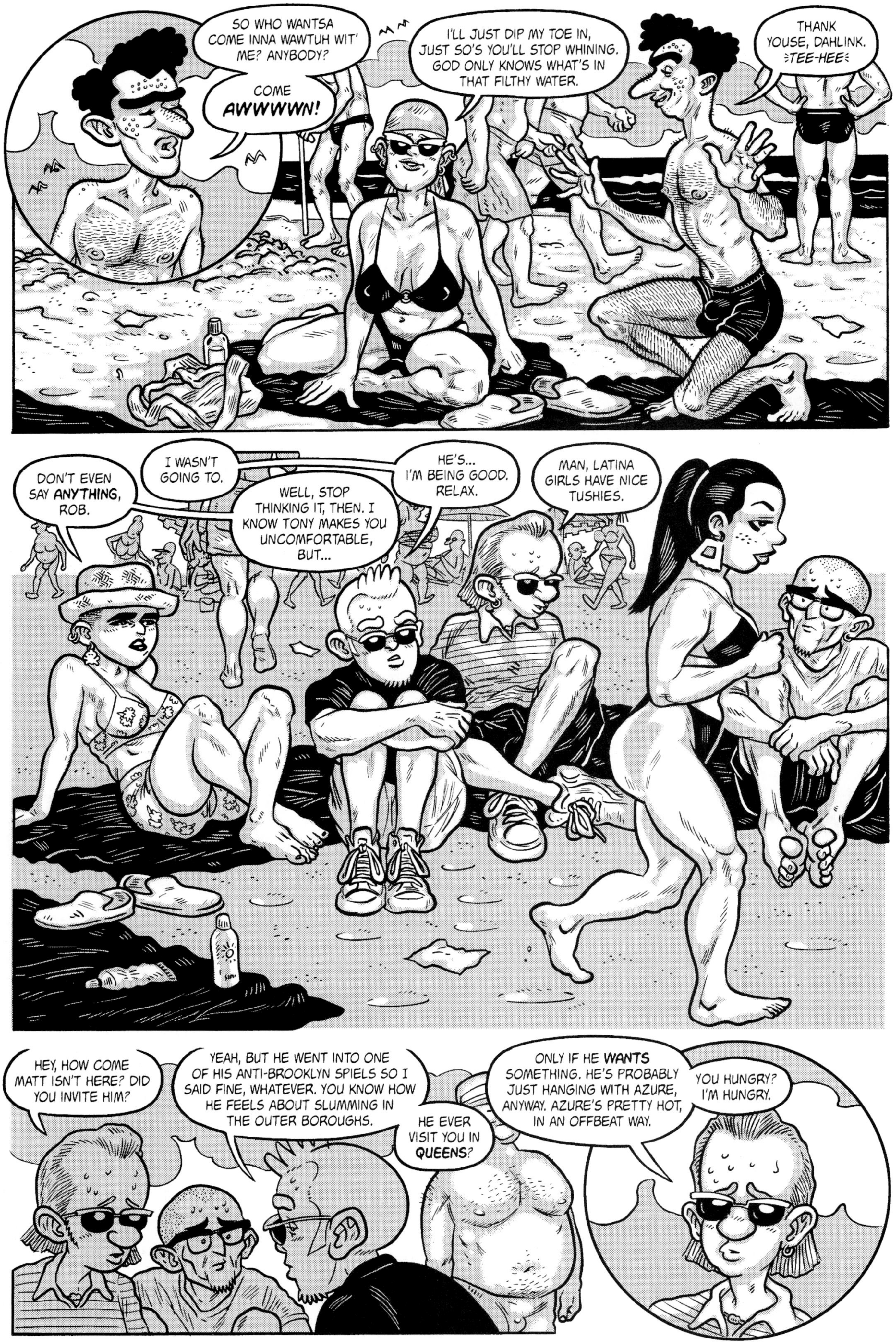

SO WHO WANTSA COME INNA WAWTUH WIT' ME? ANYBODY?
COME AWWWWN!
I'LL JUST DIP MY TOE IN, JUST SO'S YOU'LL STOP WHINING. GOD ONLY KNOWS WHAT'S IN THAT FILTHY WATER.
THANK YOUSE, DAHLINK. TEE-HEE
DON'T EVEN SAY ANYTHING, ROB.
I WASN'T GOING TO.
WELL, STOP THINKING IT, THEN. I KNOW TONY MAKES YOU UNCOMFORTABLE, BUT...
HE'S... I'M BEING GOOD. RELAX.
MAN, LATINA GIRLS HAVE NICE TUSHIES.
HEY, HOW COME MATT ISN'T HERE? DID YOU INVITE HIM?
YEAH, BUT HE WENT INTO ONE OF HIS ANTI-BROOKLYN SPIELS SO I SAID FINE, WHATEVER. YOU KNOW HOW HE FEELS ABOUT SLUMMING IN THE OUTER BOROUGHS.
HE EVER VISIT YOU IN QUEENS?
ONLY IF HE WANTS SOMETHING. HE'S PROBABLY JUST HANGING WITH AZURE, ANYWAY. AZURE'S PRETTY HOT, IN AN OFFBEAT WAY.
YOU HUNGRY? I'M HUNGRY.

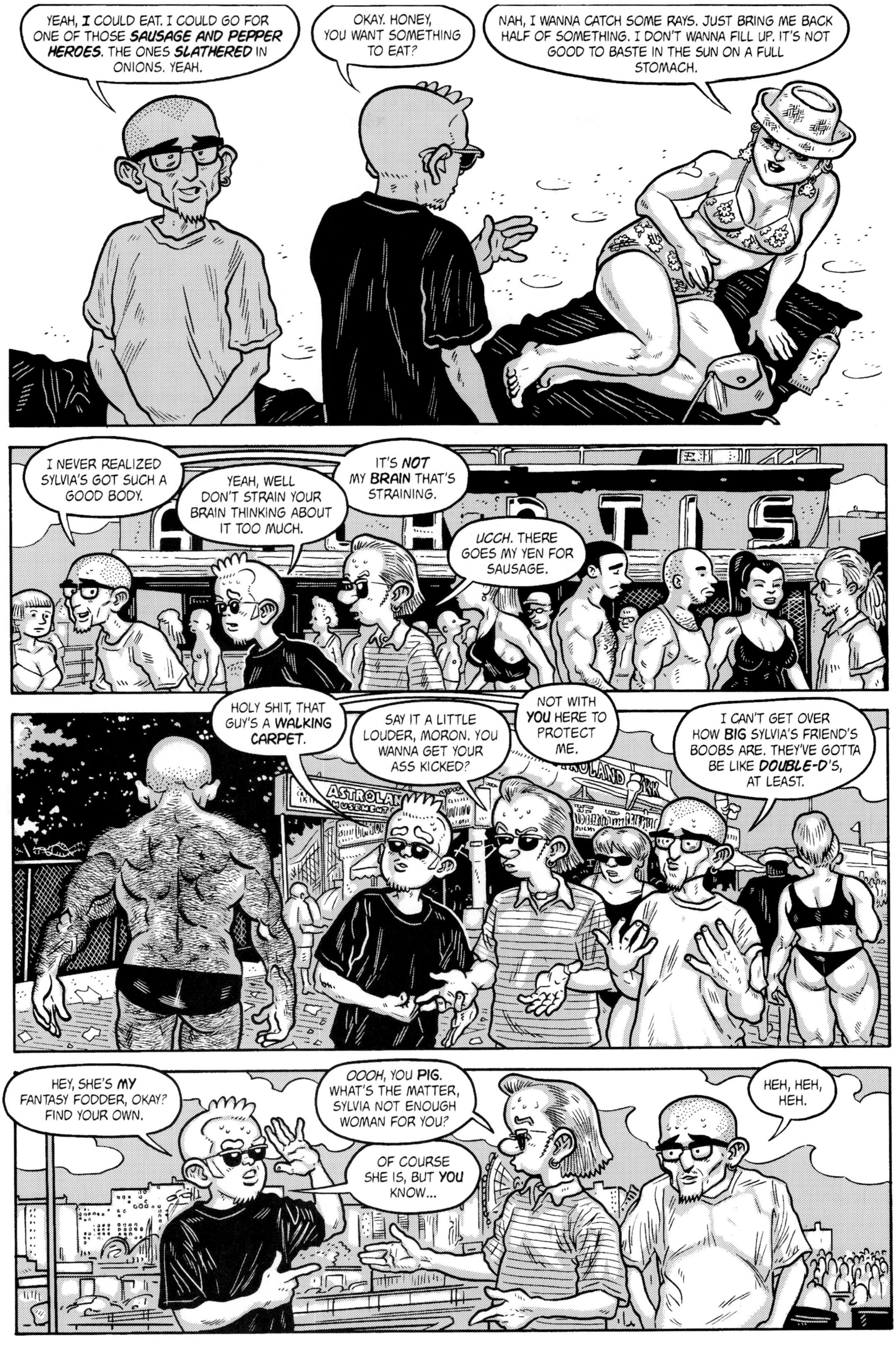
YEAH, I COULD EAT. I COULD GO FOR ONE OF THOSE SAUSAGE AND PEPPER HEROES. THE ONES SLATHERED IN ONIONS. YEAH.
OKAY. HONEY, YOU WANT SOMETHING TO EAT?
NAH, I WANNA CATCH SOME RAYS. JUST BRING ME BACK HALF OF SOMETHING. I DON'T WANNA FILL UP. IT'S NOT GOOD TO BASTE IN THE SUN ON A FULL STOMACH.
I NEVER REALIZED SYLVIA'S GOT SUCH A GOOD BODY.
YEAH, WELL DON'T STRAIN YOUR BRAIN THINKING ABOUT IT TOO MUCH.
IT'S NOT MY BRAIN THAT'S STRAINING.
UCCH. THERE GOES MY YEN FOR SAUSAGE.
HOLY SHIT, THAT GUY'S A WALKING CARPET.
SAY IT A LITTLE LOUDER, MORON. YOU WANNA GET YOUR ASS KICKED?
NOT WITH YOU HERE TO PROTECT ME.
I CAN'T GET OVER HOW BIG SYLVIA'S FRIEND'S BOOBS ARE. THEY'VE GOTTA BE LIKE DOUBLE-D'S, AT LEAST.
HEY, SHE'S MY FANTASY FODDER, OKAY? FIND YOUR OWN.
OOOH, YOU PIG. WHAT'S THE MATTER, SYLVIA NOT ENOUGH WOMAN FOR YOU?
OF COURSE SHE IS, BUT YOU KNOW...
HEH, HEH, HEH.

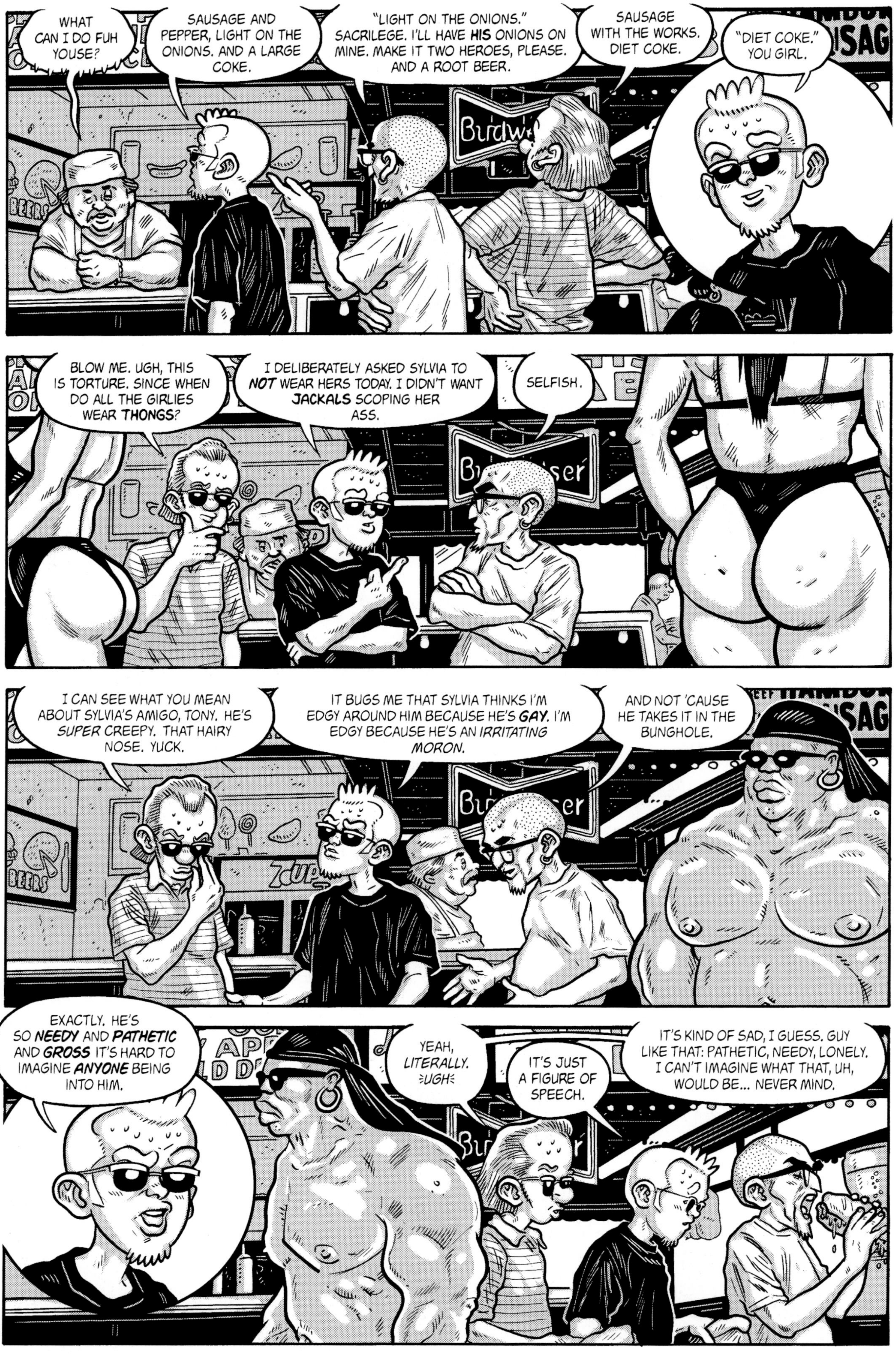
WHAT CAN I DO FUH YOUSE?
SAUSAGE AND PEPPER, LIGHT ON THE ONIONS. AND A LARGE COKE.
"LIGHT ON THE ONIONS." SACRILEGE. I'LL HAVE HIS ONIONS ON MINE. MAKE IT TWO HEROES, PLEASE. AND A ROOT BEER.
SAUSAGE WITH THE WORKS. DIET COKE.
"DIET COKE." YOU GIRL.
BLOW ME. UGH, THIS IS TORTURE. SINCE WHEN DO ALL THE GIRLIES WEAR THONGS?
I DELIBERATELY ASKED SYLVIA TO NOT WEAR HERS TODAY. I DIDN'T WANT JACKALS SCOPING HER ASS.
SELFISH.
I CAN SEE WHAT YOU MEAN ABOUT SYLVIA'S AMIGO, TONY. HE'S SUPER CREEPY. THAT HAIRY NOSE. YUCK.
IT BUGS ME THAT SYLVIA THINKS I'M EDGY AROUND HIM BECAUSE HE'S GAY. I'M EDGY BECAUSE HE'S AN IRRITATING MORON.
AND NOT 'CAUSE HE TAKES IT IN THE BUNGHOLE.
EXACTLY. HE'S SO NEEDY AND PATHETIC AND GROSS IT'S HARD TO IMAGINE ANYONE BEING INTO HIM.
YEAH, LITERALLY. UGH
IT'S JUST A FIGURE OF SPEECH.
IT'S KIND OF SAD, I GUESS. GUY LIKE THAT: PATHETIC, NEEDY, LONELY. I CAN'T IMAGINE WHAT THAT, UH, WOULD BE... NEVER MIND.

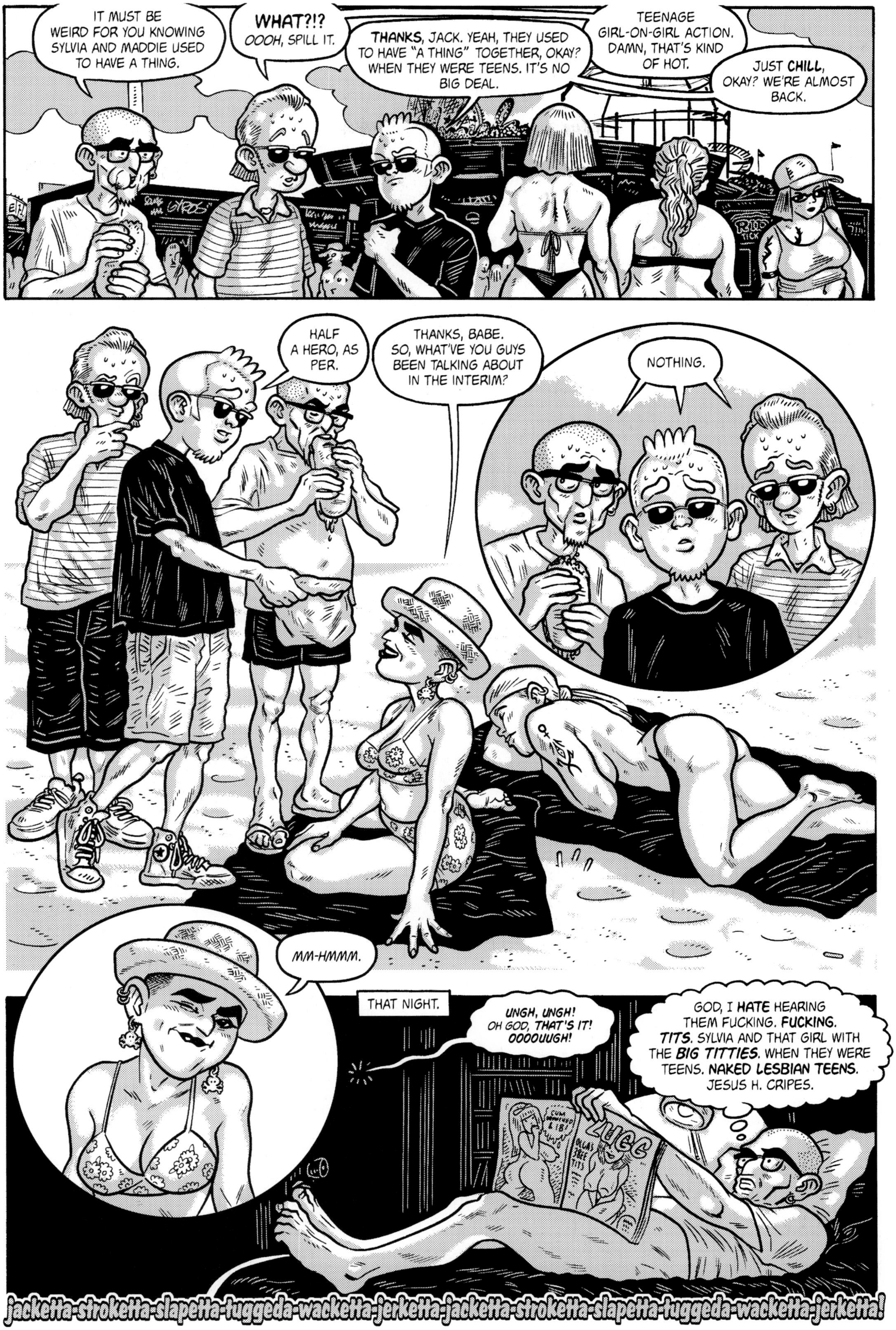
IT MUST BE WEIRD FOR YOU KNOWING SYLVIA AND MADDIE USED TO HAVE A THING.
WHAT?!? OOOH, SPILL IT.
THANKS, JACK. YEAH, THEY USED TO HAVE "A THING" TOGETHER, OKAY? WHEN THEY WERE TEENS. IT'S NO BIG DEAL.
TEENAGE GIRL-ON-GIRL ACTION. DAMN, THAT'S KIND OF HOT.
JUST CHILL, OKAY? WE'RE ALMOST BACK.
HALF A HERO, AS PER.
THANKS, BABE. SO, WHAT'VE YOU GUYS BEEN TALKING ABOUT IN THE INTERIM?
NOTHING.
MM-HMMM.
THAT NIGHT.
UNGH, UNGH! OH GOD, THAT'S IT! OOOOUUGH!
GOD, I HATE HEARING THEM FUCKING. FUCKING. TITS. SYLVIA AND THAT GIRL WITH THE BIG TITTIES. WHEN THEY WERE TEENS. NAKED LESBIAN TEENS. JESUS H. CRIPES.
jackeTTa-strokeTTa-slapeTTa-tuggeda-wackeTTa-jerkeTTa-jackeTTa-strokeTTa-slapeTTa-tuggeda-wackeTTa-jerkeTTa!

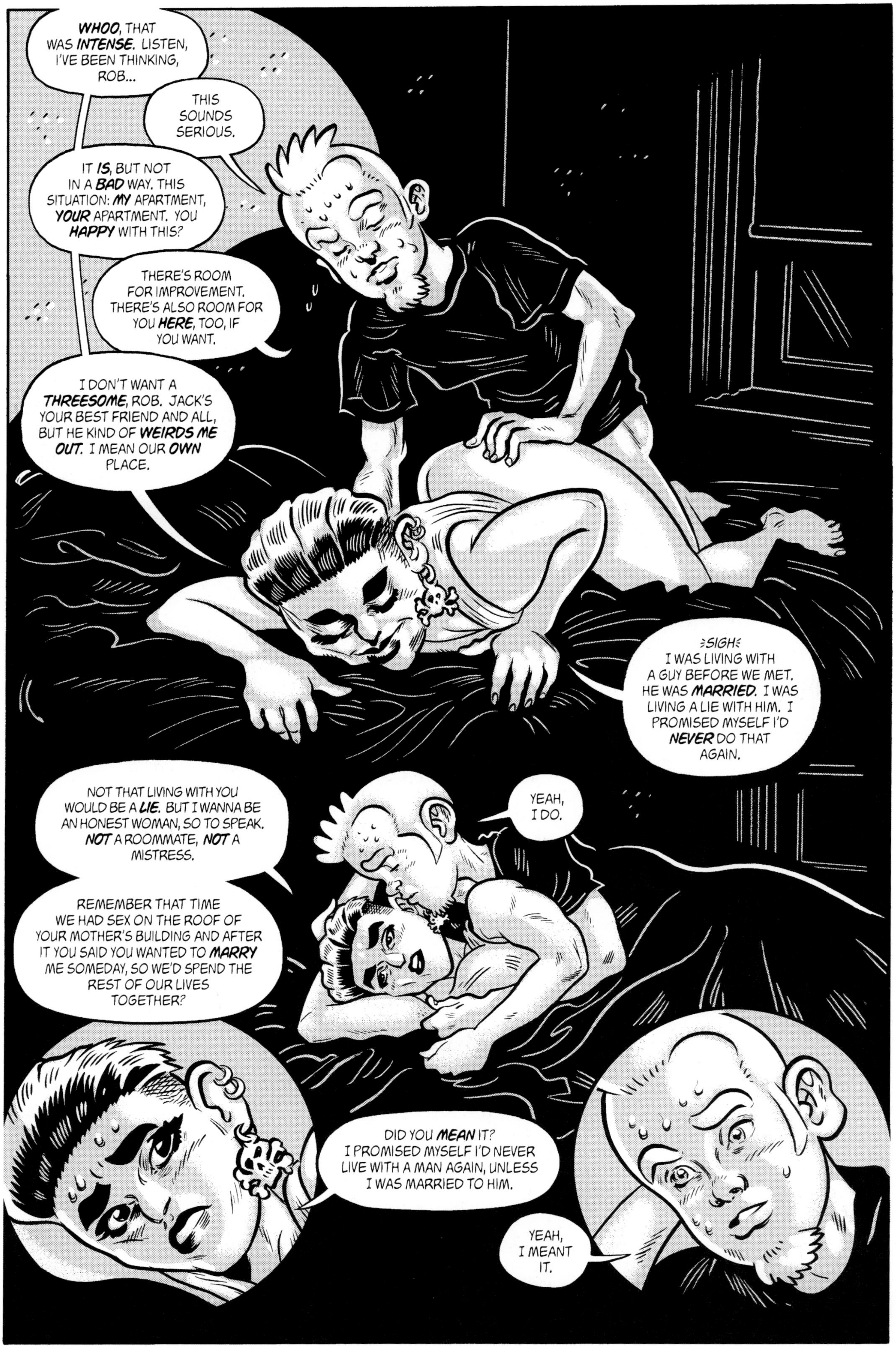
WHOO, THAT WAS INTENSE. LISTEN, I'VE BEEN THINKING, ROB...
THIS SOUNDS SERIOUS.
IT IS, BUT NOT IN A BAD WAY. THIS SITUATION: MY APARTMENT, YOUR APARTMENT. YOU HAPPY WITH THIS?
THERE'S ROOM FOR IMPROVEMENT. THERE'S ALSO ROOM FOR YOU HERE, TOO, IF YOU WANT.
I DON'T WANT A THREESOME, ROB. JACK'S YOUR BEST FRIEND AND ALL, BUT HE KIND OF WEIRDS ME OUT. I MEAN OUR OWN PLACE.
SIGH
I WAS LIVING WITH A GUY BEFORE WE MET. HE WAS MARRIED. I WAS LIVING A LIE WITH HIM. I PROMISED MYSELF I'D NEVER DO THAT AGAIN.
NOT THAT LIVING WITH YOU WOULD BE A LIE. BUT I WANNA BE AN HONEST WOMAN, SO TO SPEAK. NOT A ROOMMATE, NOT A MISTRESS.
YEAH, I DO.
REMEMBER THAT TIME WE HAD SEX ON THE ROOF OF YOUR MOTHER'S BUILDING AND AFTER IT YOU SAID YOU WANTED TO MARRY ME SOMEDAY, SO WE'D SPEND THE REST OF OUR LIVES TOGETHER?
DID YOU MEAN IT? I PROMISED MYSELF I'D NEVER LIVE WITH A MAN AGAIN, UNLESS I WAS MARRIED TO HIM.
YEAH, I MEANT IT.

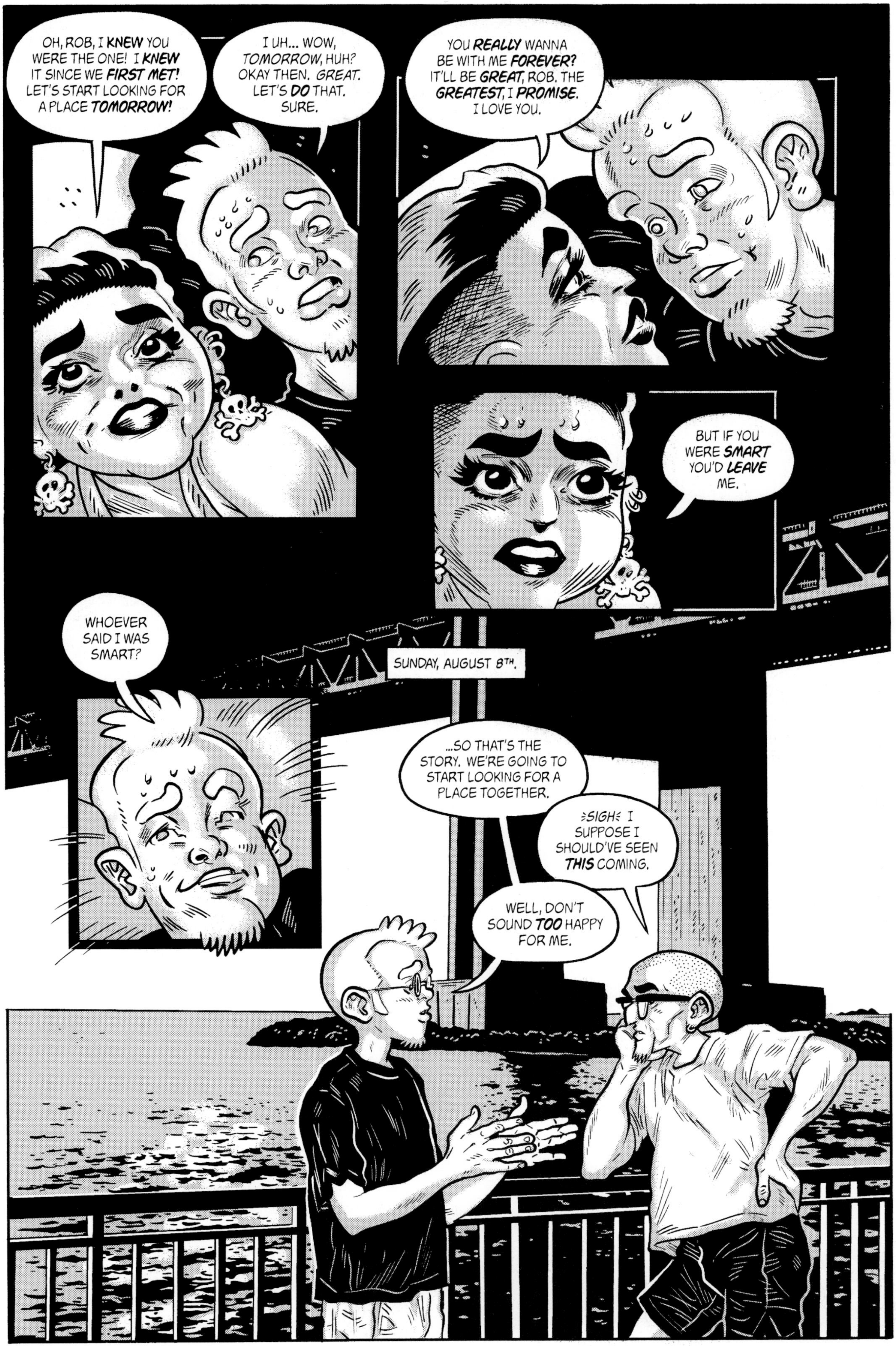

OH, ROB, I KNEW YOU WERE THE ONE! I KNEW IT SINCE WE FIRST MET! LET'S START LOOKING FOR A PLACE TOMORROW!
I UH... WOW, TOMORROW, HUH? OKAY THEN. GREAT. LET'S DO THAT. SURE.
YOU REALLY WANNA BE WITH ME FOREVER? IT'LL BE GREAT, ROB. THE GREATEST, I PROMISE. I LOVE YOU.
BUT IF YOU WERE SMART YOU'D LEAVE ME.
WHOEVER SAID I WAS SMART?
SUNDAY, AUGUST 8TH.
...SO THAT'S THE STORY. WE'RE GOING TO START LOOKING FOR A PLACE TOGETHER.
≷SIGH≶ I SUPPOSE I SHOULD'VE SEEN THIS COMING.
WELL, DON'T SOUND TOO HAPPY FOR ME.

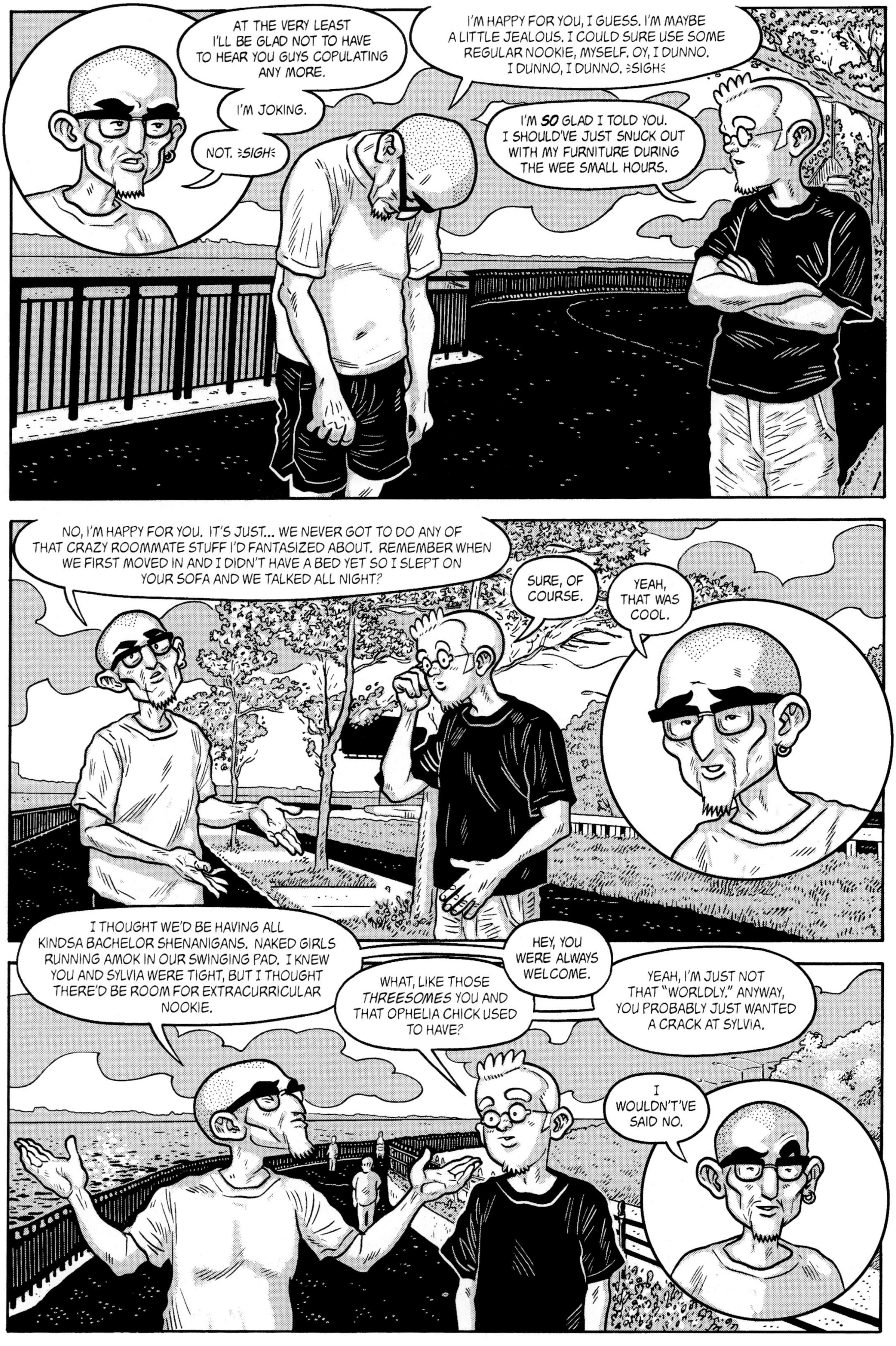
AT THE VERY LEAST I'LL BE GLAD NOT TO HAVE TO HEAR YOU GUYS COPULATING ANY MORE.
I'M JOKING.
NOT. ⪾SIGH⪽
I'M HAPPY FOR YOU, I GUESS. I'M MAYBE A LITTLE JEALOUS. I COULD SURE USE SOME REGULAR NOOKIE, MYSELF. OY, I DUNNO. I DUNNO, I DUNNO. ⪾SIGH⪽
I'M *SO* GLAD I TOLD YOU. I SHOULD'VE JUST SNUCK OUT WITH MY FURNITURE DURING THE WEE SMALL HOURS.
NO, I'M HAPPY FOR YOU. IT'S JUST... WE NEVER GOT TO DO ANY OF THAT CRAZY ROOMMATE STUFF I'D FANTASIZED ABOUT. REMEMBER WHEN WE FIRST MOVED IN AND I DIDN'T HAVE A BED YET SO I SLEPT ON YOUR SOFA AND WE TALKED ALL NIGHT?
SURE, OF COURSE.
YEAH, THAT WAS COOL.
I THOUGHT WE'D BE HAVING ALL KINDSA BACHELOR SHENANIGANS. NAKED GIRLS RUNNING AMOK IN OUR SWINGING PAD. I KNEW YOU AND SYLVIA WERE TIGHT, BUT I THOUGHT THERE'D BE ROOM FOR EXTRACURRICULAR NOOKIE.
WHAT, LIKE THOSE *THREESOMES* YOU AND THAT OPHELIA CHICK USED TO HAVE?
HEY, YOU WERE ALWAYS WELCOME.
YEAH, I'M JUST NOT THAT "WORLDLY." ANYWAY, YOU PROBABLY JUST WANTED A CRACK AT SYLVIA.
I WOULDN'T'VE SAID NO.

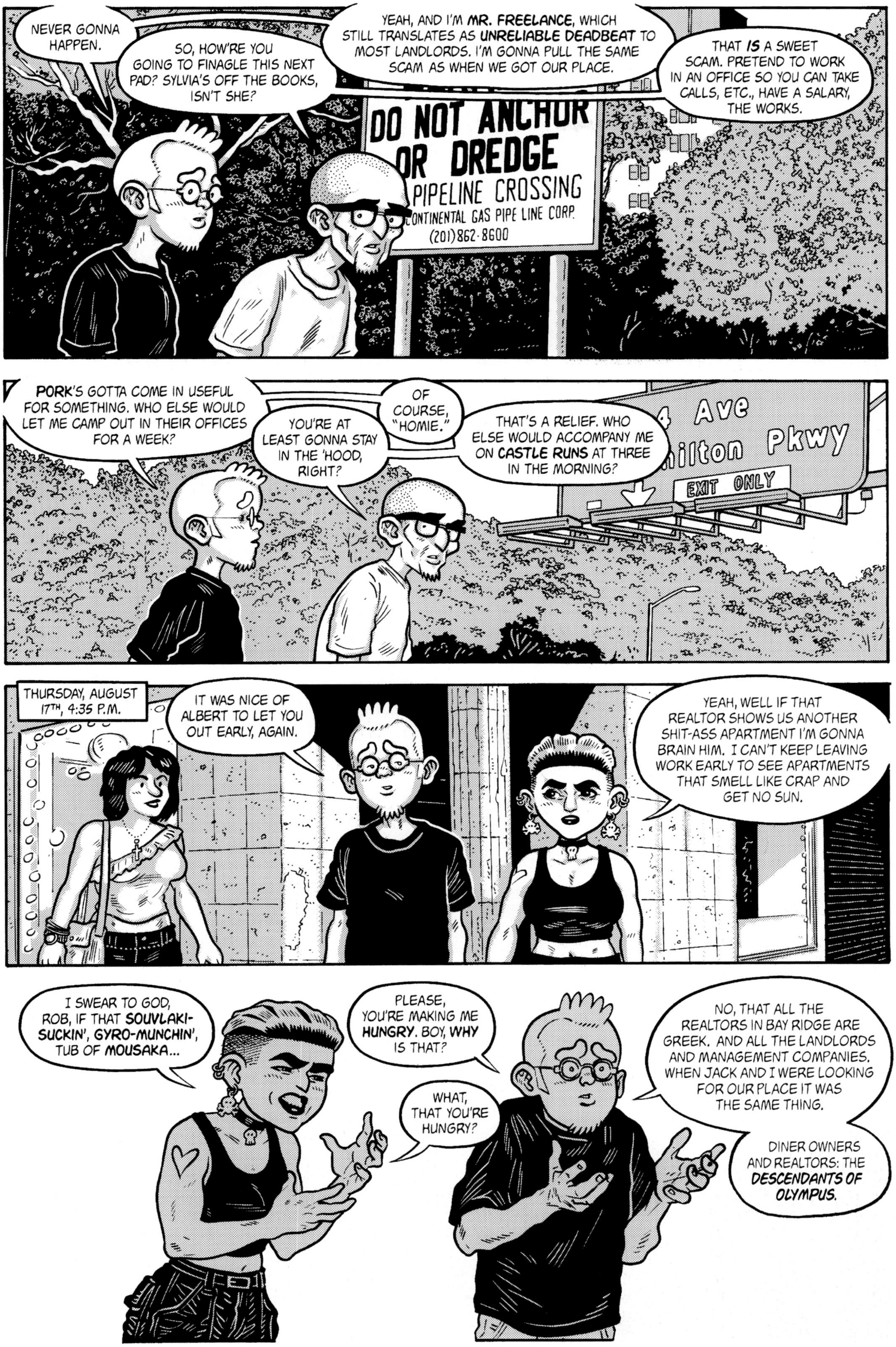
NEVER GONNA HAPPEN.
SO, HOW'RE YOU GOING TO FINAGLE THIS NEXT PAD? SYLVIA'S OFF THE BOOKS, ISN'T SHE?
YEAH, AND I'M **MR. FREELANCE**, WHICH STILL TRANSLATES AS **UNRELIABLE DEADBEAT** TO MOST LANDLORDS. I'M GONNA PULL THE SAME SCAM AS WHEN WE GOT OUR PLACE.
THAT **IS** A SWEET SCAM. PRETEND TO WORK IN AN OFFICE SO YOU CAN TAKE CALLS, ETC., HAVE A SALARY, THE WORKS.
DO NOT ANCHOR OR DREDGE
PIPELINE CROSSING
CONTINENTAL GAS PIPE LINE CORP.
(201) 862-8600
PORK'S GOTTA COME IN USEFUL FOR SOMETHING. WHO ELSE WOULD LET ME CAMP OUT IN THEIR OFFICES FOR A WEEK?
YOU'RE AT LEAST GONNA STAY IN THE 'HOOD, RIGHT?
OF COURSE, "HOMIE."
THAT'S A RELIEF. WHO ELSE WOULD ACCOMPANY ME ON **CASTLE RUNS** AT THREE IN THE MORNING?
EXIT ONLY
THURSDAY, AUGUST 17TH, 4:35 P.M.
IT WAS NICE OF ALBERT TO LET YOU OUT EARLY, AGAIN.
YEAH, WELL IF THAT REALTOR SHOWS US ANOTHER SHIT-ASS APARTMENT I'M GONNA BRAIN HIM. I CAN'T KEEP LEAVING WORK EARLY TO SEE APARTMENTS THAT SMELL LIKE CRAP AND GET NO SUN.
I SWEAR TO GOD, ROB, IF THAT **SOUVLAKI-SUCKIN'**, **GYRO-MUNCHIN'**, TUB OF **MOUSAKA**...
PLEASE, YOU'RE MAKING ME **HUNGRY**. BOY, **WHY** IS THAT?
WHAT, THAT YOU'RE HUNGRY?
NO, THAT ALL THE REALTORS IN BAY RIDGE ARE GREEK. AND ALL THE LANDLORDS AND MANAGEMENT COMPANIES. WHEN JACK AND I WERE LOOKING FOR OUR PLACE IT WAS THE SAME THING.
DINER OWNERS AND REALTORS: THE ***DESCENDANTS OF OLYMPUS***.

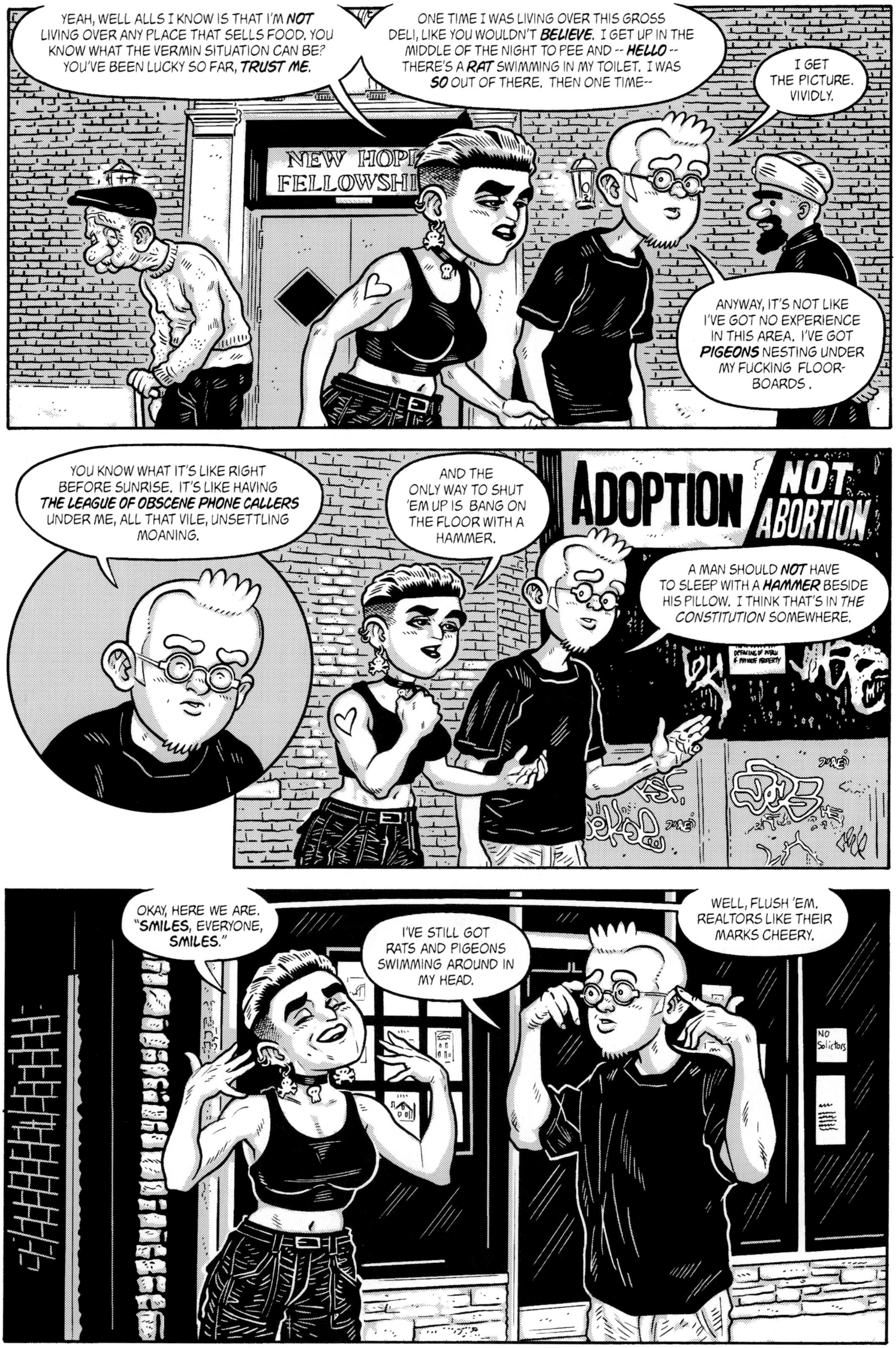
YEAH, WELL ALLS I KNOW IS THAT I'M NOT LIVING OVER ANY PLACE THAT SELLS FOOD. YOU KNOW WHAT THE VERMIN SITUATION CAN BE? YOU'VE BEEN LUCKY SO FAR, TRUST ME.
ONE TIME I WAS LIVING OVER THIS GROSS DELI, LIKE YOU WOULDN'T BELIEVE. I GET UP IN THE MIDDLE OF THE NIGHT TO PEE AND -- HELLO -- THERE'S A RAT SWIMMING IN MY TOILET. I WAS SO OUT OF THERE. THEN ONE TIME--
I GET THE PICTURE. VIVIDLY.
NEW HOPE FELLOWSHI
ANYWAY, IT'S NOT LIKE I'VE GOT NO EXPERIENCE IN THIS AREA. I'VE GOT PIGEONS NESTING UNDER MY FUCKING FLOOR-BOARDS.
YOU KNOW WHAT IT'S LIKE RIGHT BEFORE SUNRISE. IT'S LIKE HAVING THE LEAGUE OF OBSCENE PHONE CALLERS UNDER ME, ALL THAT VILE, UNSETTLING MOANING.
AND THE ONLY WAY TO SHUT 'EM UP IS BANG ON THE FLOOR WITH A HAMMER.
ADOPTION NOT ABORTION
A MAN SHOULD NOT HAVE TO SLEEP WITH A HAMMER BESIDE HIS PILLOW. I THINK THAT'S IN THE CONSTITUTION SOMEWHERE.
OKAY, HERE WE ARE. "SMILES, EVERYONE, SMILES."
I'VE STILL GOT RATS AND PIGEONS SWIMMING AROUND IN MY HEAD.
WELL, FLUSH 'EM. REALTORS LIKE THEIR MARKS CHEERY.
NO Solictors

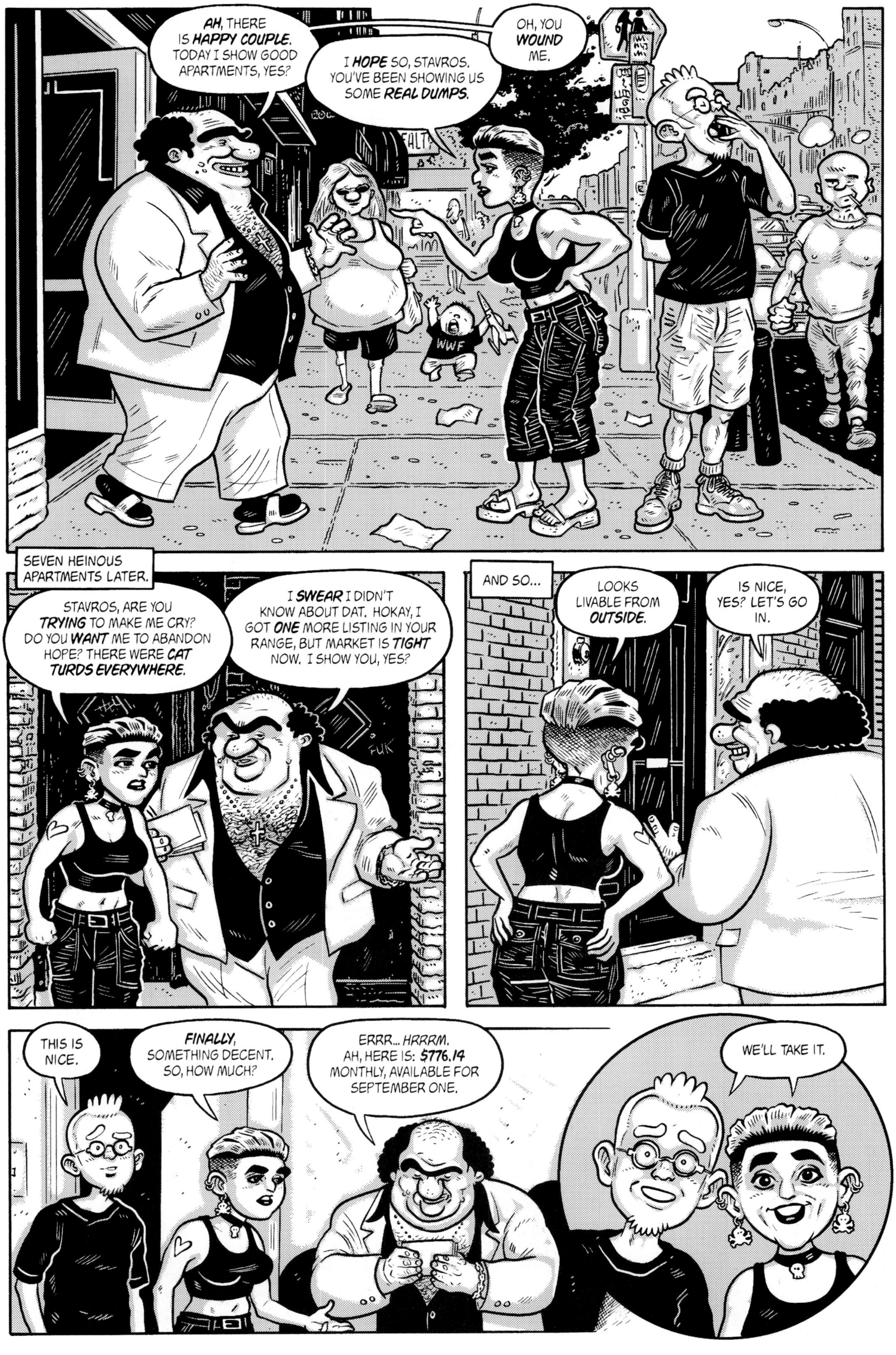
AH, THERE IS HAPPY COUPLE. TODAY I SHOW GOOD APARTMENTS, YES?
I HOPE SO, STAVROS. YOU'VE BEEN SHOWING US SOME REAL DUMPS.
OH, YOU WOUND ME.
SEVEN HEINOUS APARTMENTS LATER.
STAVROS, ARE YOU TRYING TO MAKE ME CRY? DO YOU WANT ME TO ABANDON HOPE? THERE WERE CAT TURDS EVERYWHERE.
I SWEAR I DIDN'T KNOW ABOUT DAT. HOKAY, I GOT ONE MORE LISTING IN YOUR RANGE, BUT MARKET IS TIGHT NOW. I SHOW YOU, YES?
FUK
AND SO...
LOOKS LIVABLE FROM OUTSIDE.
IS NICE, YES? LET'S GO IN.
THIS IS NICE.
FINALLY, SOMETHING DECENT. SO, HOW MUCH?
ERRR... HRRRM. AH, HERE IS: $776.14 MONTHLY, AVAILABLE FOR SEPTEMBER ONE.
WE'LL TAKE IT.

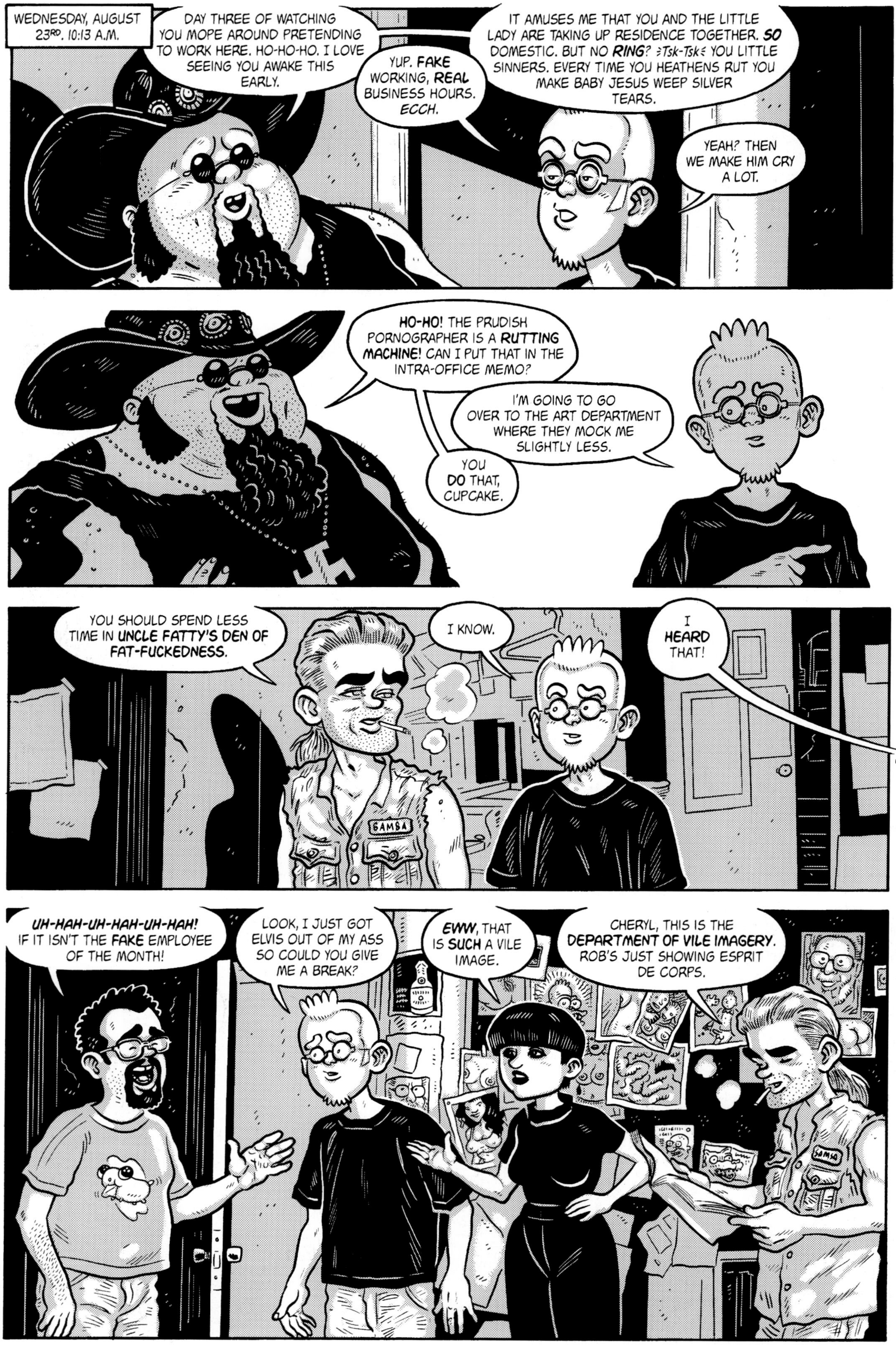

WEDNESDAY, AUGUST 23RD. 10:13 A.M.
DAY THREE OF WATCHING YOU MOPE AROUND PRETENDING TO WORK HERE. HO-HO-HO. I LOVE SEEING YOU AWAKE THIS EARLY.
YUP. FAKE WORKING, REAL BUSINESS HOURS. ECCH.
IT AMUSES ME THAT YOU AND THE LITTLE LADY ARE TAKING UP RESIDENCE TOGETHER. SO DOMESTIC. BUT NO RING? Tsk-Tsk YOU LITTLE SINNERS. EVERY TIME YOU HEATHENS RUT YOU MAKE BABY JESUS WEEP SILVER TEARS.
YEAH? THEN WE MAKE HIM CRY A LOT.
HO-HO! THE PRUDISH PORNOGRAPHER IS A RUTTING MACHINE! CAN I PUT THAT IN THE INTRA-OFFICE MEMO?
I'M GOING TO GO OVER TO THE ART DEPARTMENT WHERE THEY MOCK ME SLIGHTLY LESS.
YOU DO THAT, CUPCAKE.
YOU SHOULD SPEND LESS TIME IN UNCLE FATTY'S DEN OF FAT-FUCKEDNESS.
I KNOW.
I HEARD THAT!
SAMSA
UH-HAH-UH-HAH-UH-HAH! IF IT ISN'T THE FAKE EMPLOYEE OF THE MONTH!
LOOK, I JUST GOT ELVIS OUT OF MY ASS SO COULD YOU GIVE ME A BREAK?
EWW, THAT IS SUCH A VILE IMAGE.
CHERYL, THIS IS THE DEPARTMENT OF VILE IMAGERY. ROB'S JUST SHOWING ESPRIT DE CORPS.
SAMSA

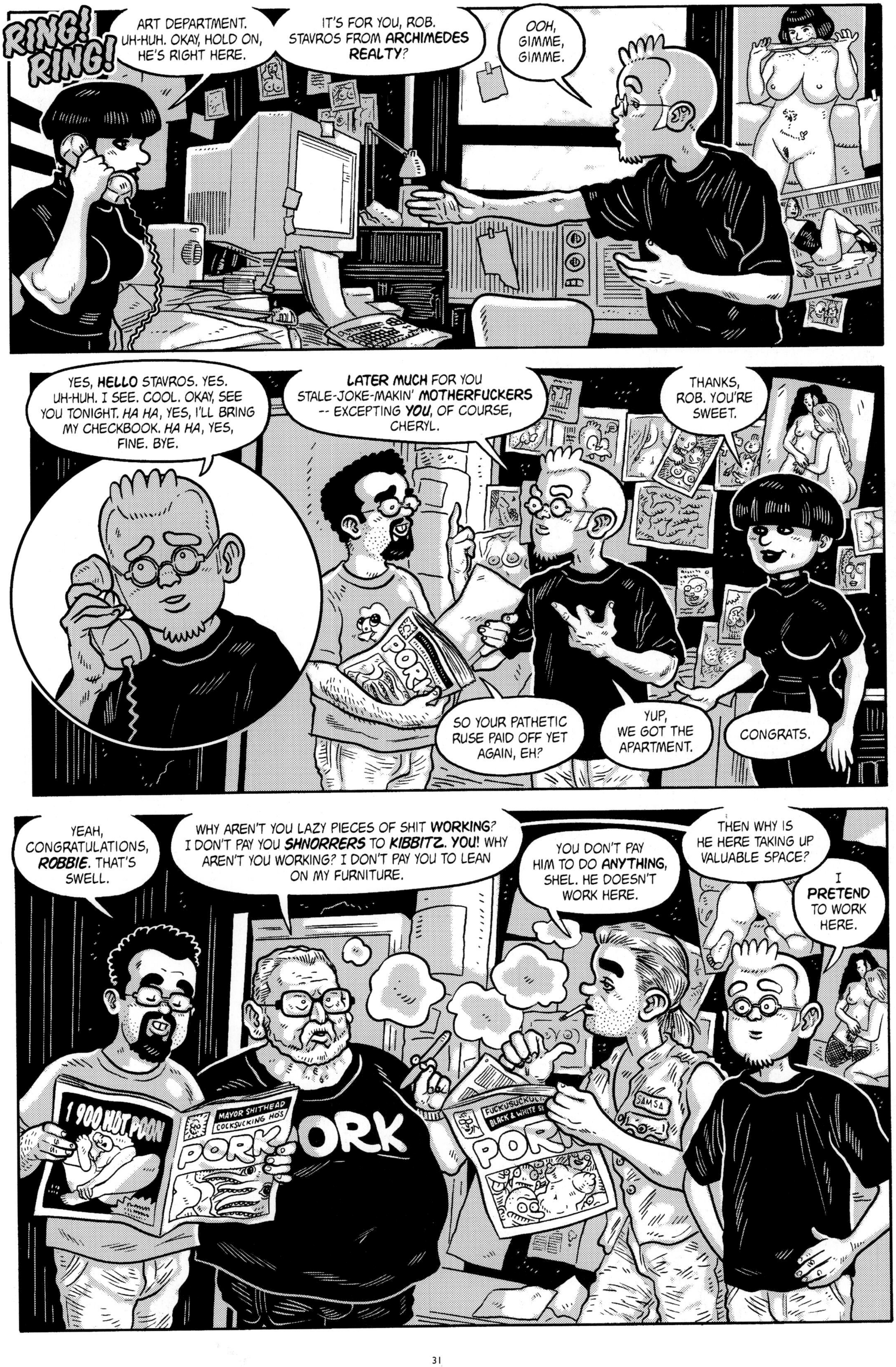
RING! RING!
ART DEPARTMENT. UH-HUH. OKAY, HOLD ON, HE'S RIGHT HERE.
IT'S FOR YOU, ROB. STAVROS FROM ARCHIMEDES REALTY?
OOH, GIMME, GIMME.
YES, HELLO STAVROS. YES. UH-HUH. I SEE. COOL. OKAY, SEE YOU TONIGHT. HA HA, YES, I'LL BRING MY CHECKBOOK. HA HA, YES, FINE. BYE.
LATER MUCH FOR YOU STALE-JOKE-MAKIN' MOTHERFUCKERS -- EXCEPTING YOU, OF COURSE, CHERYL.
THANKS, ROB. YOU'RE SWEET.
SO YOUR PATHETIC RUSE PAID OFF YET AGAIN, EH?
YUP, WE GOT THE APARTMENT.
CONGRATS.
PORK
YEAH, CONGRATULATIONS, ROBBIE. THAT'S SWELL.
WHY AREN'T YOU LAZY PIECES OF SHIT WORKING? I DON'T PAY YOU SHNORRERS TO KIBBITZ. YOU! WHY AREN'T YOU WORKING? I DON'T PAY YOU TO LEAN ON MY FURNITURE.
YOU DON'T PAY HIM TO DO ANYTHING, SHEL. HE DOESN'T WORK HERE.
THEN WHY IS HE HERE TAKING UP VALUABLE SPACE?
I PRETEND TO WORK HERE.
1 900 HUT POON
MAYOR SHITHEAD
COCKSUCKING HOS
PORK
PORK
BLACK & WHITE
PORK
SAMSA

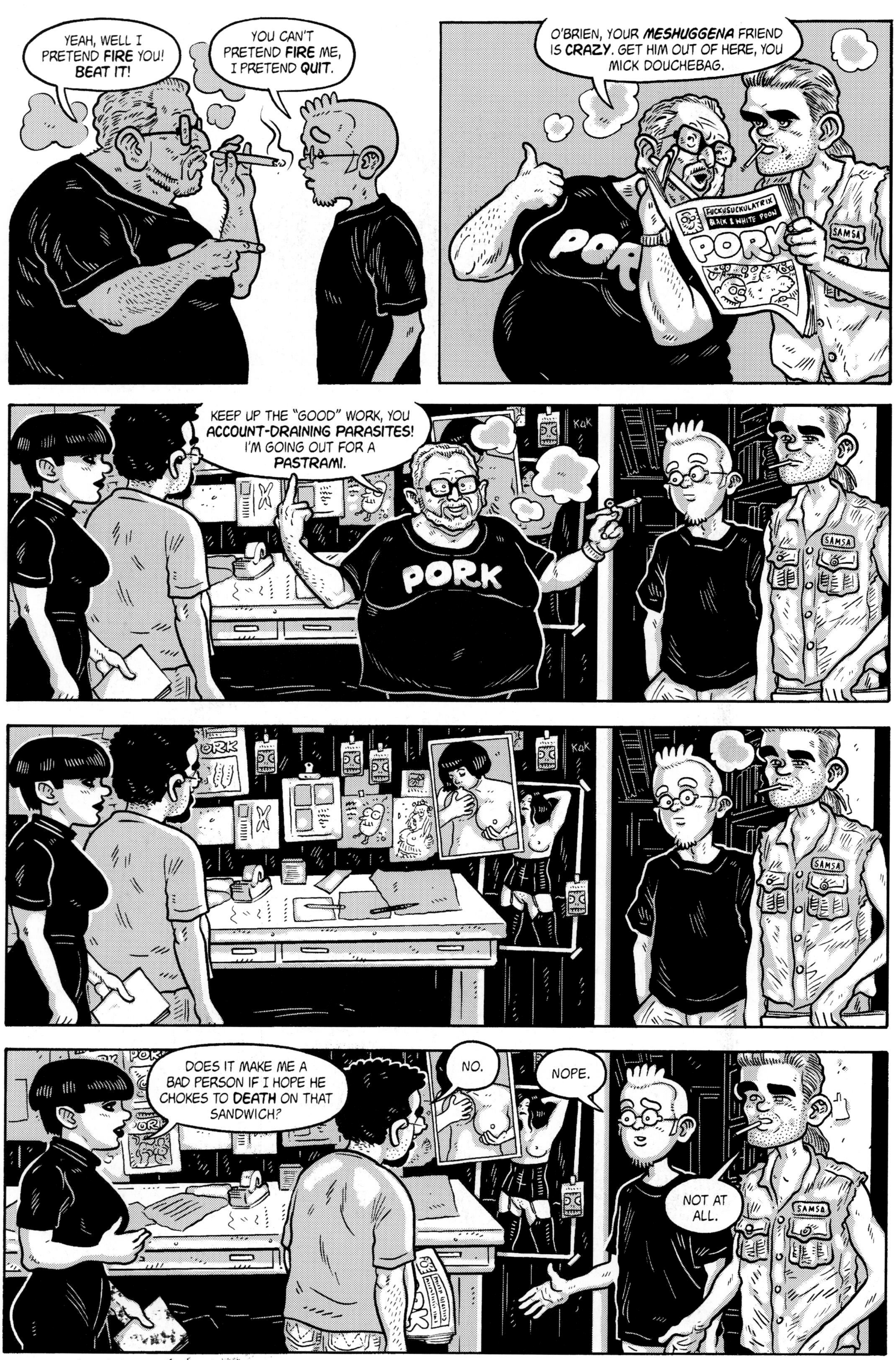
YEAH, WELL I PRETEND FIRE YOU! BEAT IT!
YOU CAN'T PRETEND FIRE ME, I PRETEND QUIT.
O'BRIEN, YOUR MESHUGGENA FRIEND IS CRAZY. GET HIM OUT OF HERE, YOU MICK DOUCHEBAG.
FUCKYSUCKULATRIX
BLACK & WHITE POON
PORK
SAMSA
KEEP UP THE "GOOD" WORK, YOU ACCOUNT-DRAINING PARASITES! I'M GOING OUT FOR A PASTRAMI.
PORK
DOES IT MAKE ME A BAD PERSON IF I HOPE HE CHOKES TO DEATH ON THAT SANDWICH?
NO.
NOPE.
NOT AT ALL.

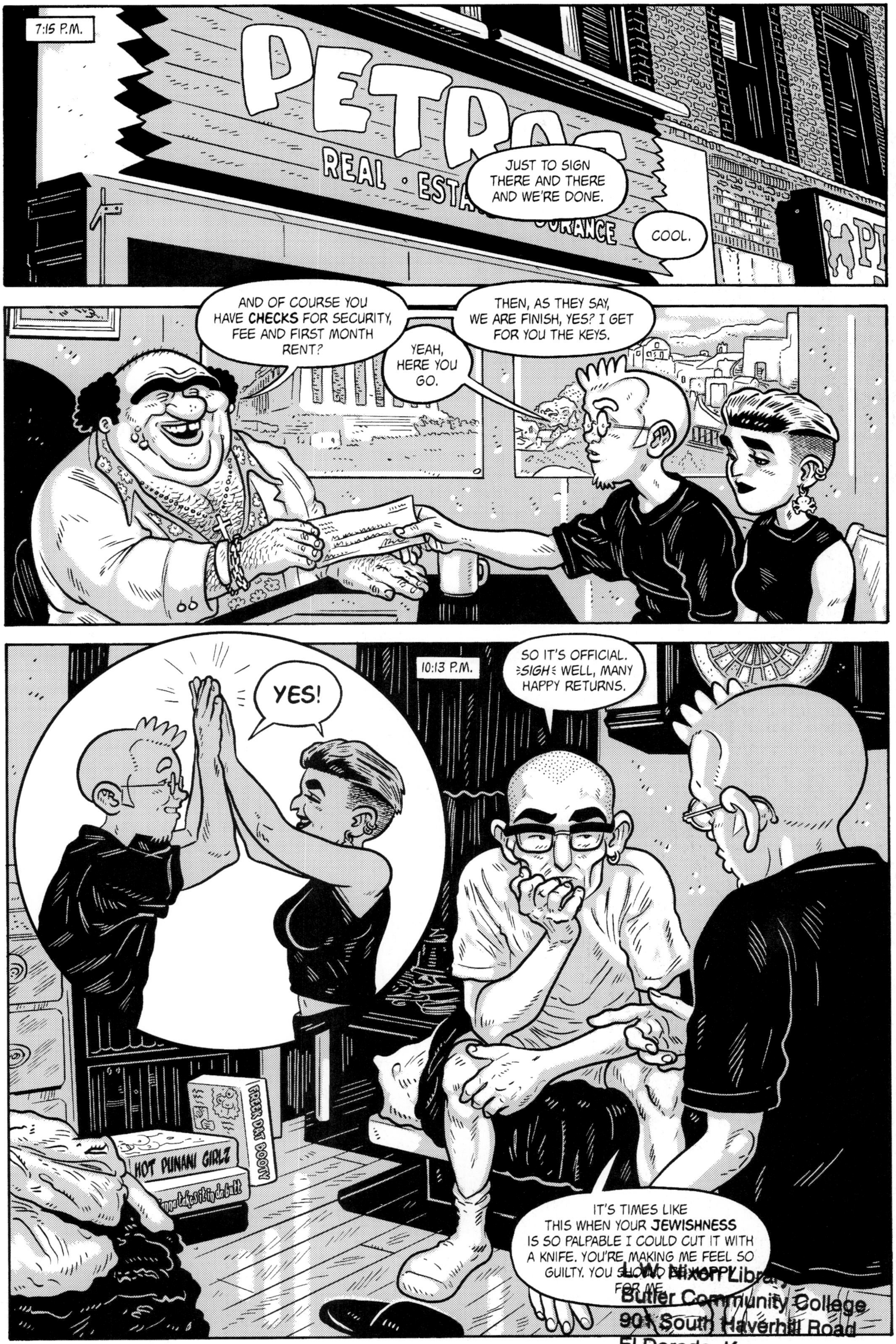
7:15 P.M.
PETROS
REAL · ESTA... ...URANCE
JUST TO SIGN THERE AND THERE AND WE'RE DONE.
COOL.
AND OF COURSE YOU HAVE **CHECKS** FOR SECURITY, FEE AND FIRST MONTH RENT?
YEAH, HERE YOU GO.
THEN, AS THEY SAY, WE ARE FINISH, YES? I GET FOR YOU THE KEYS.
10:13 P.M.
YES!
SO IT'S OFFICIAL. *SIGH* WELL, MANY HAPPY RETURNS.
HOT PUNANI GIRLZ
FREEK DAT BOOTY
IT'S TIMES LIKE THIS WHEN YOUR **JEWISHNESS** IS SO PALPABLE I COULD CUT IT WITH A KNIFE. YOU'RE MAKING ME FEEL SO GUILTY. YOU SHOULD BE HAPPY FOR ME.

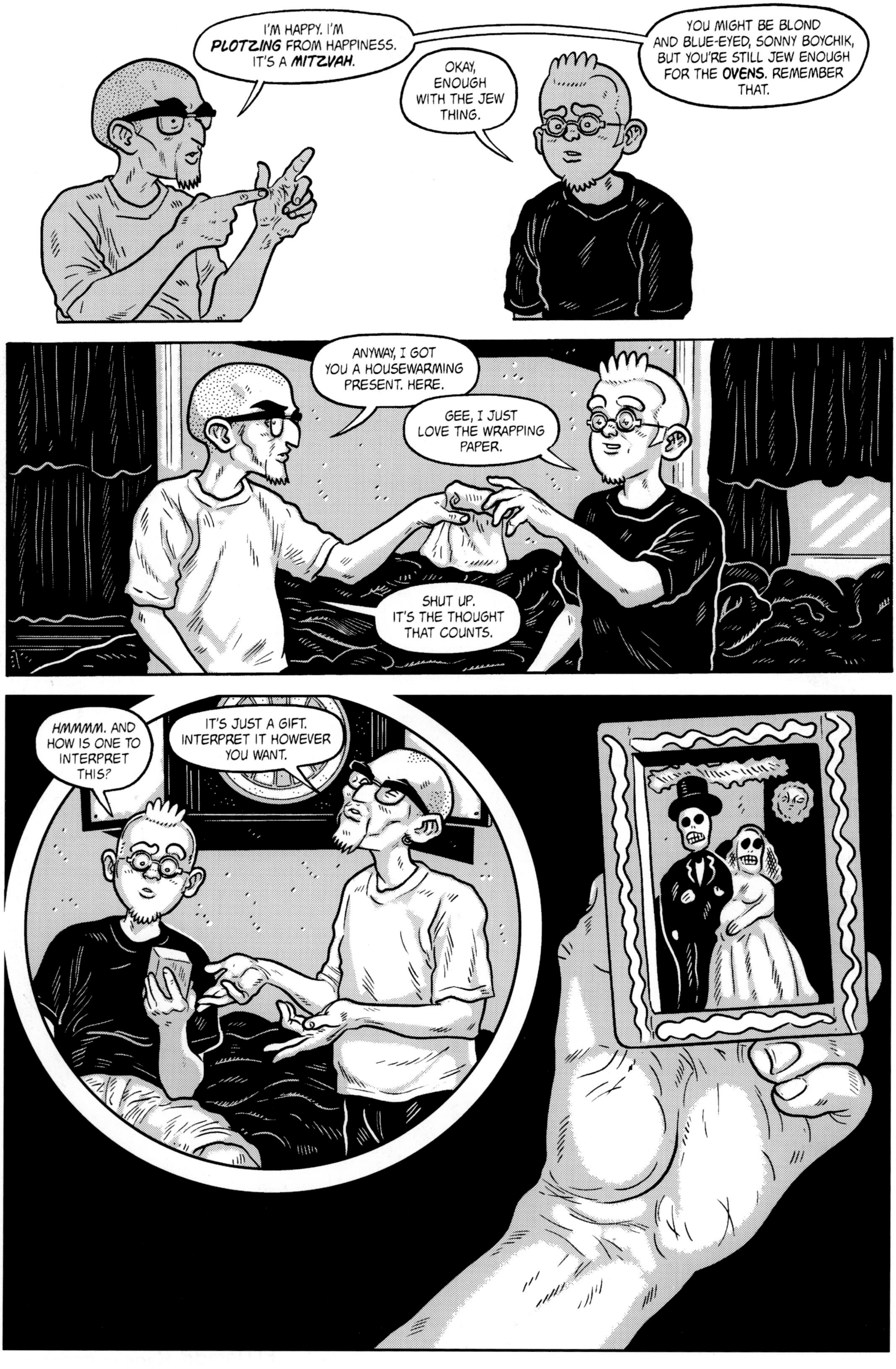
I'M HAPPY. I'M **PLOTZING** FROM HAPPINESS. IT'S A ***MITZVAH***.
OKAY, ENOUGH WITH THE JEW THING.
YOU MIGHT BE BLOND AND BLUE-EYED, SONNY BOYCHIK, BUT YOU'RE STILL JEW ENOUGH FOR THE **OVENS**. REMEMBER THAT.
ANYWAY, I GOT YOU A HOUSEWARMING PRESENT. HERE.
GEE, I JUST LOVE THE WRAPPING PAPER.
SHUT UP. IT'S THE THOUGHT THAT COUNTS.
HMMMM. AND HOW IS ONE TO INTERPRET THIS?
IT'S JUST A GIFT. INTERPRET IT HOWEVER YOU WANT.

Chapter Two

BELABORED DAY WEEKEND

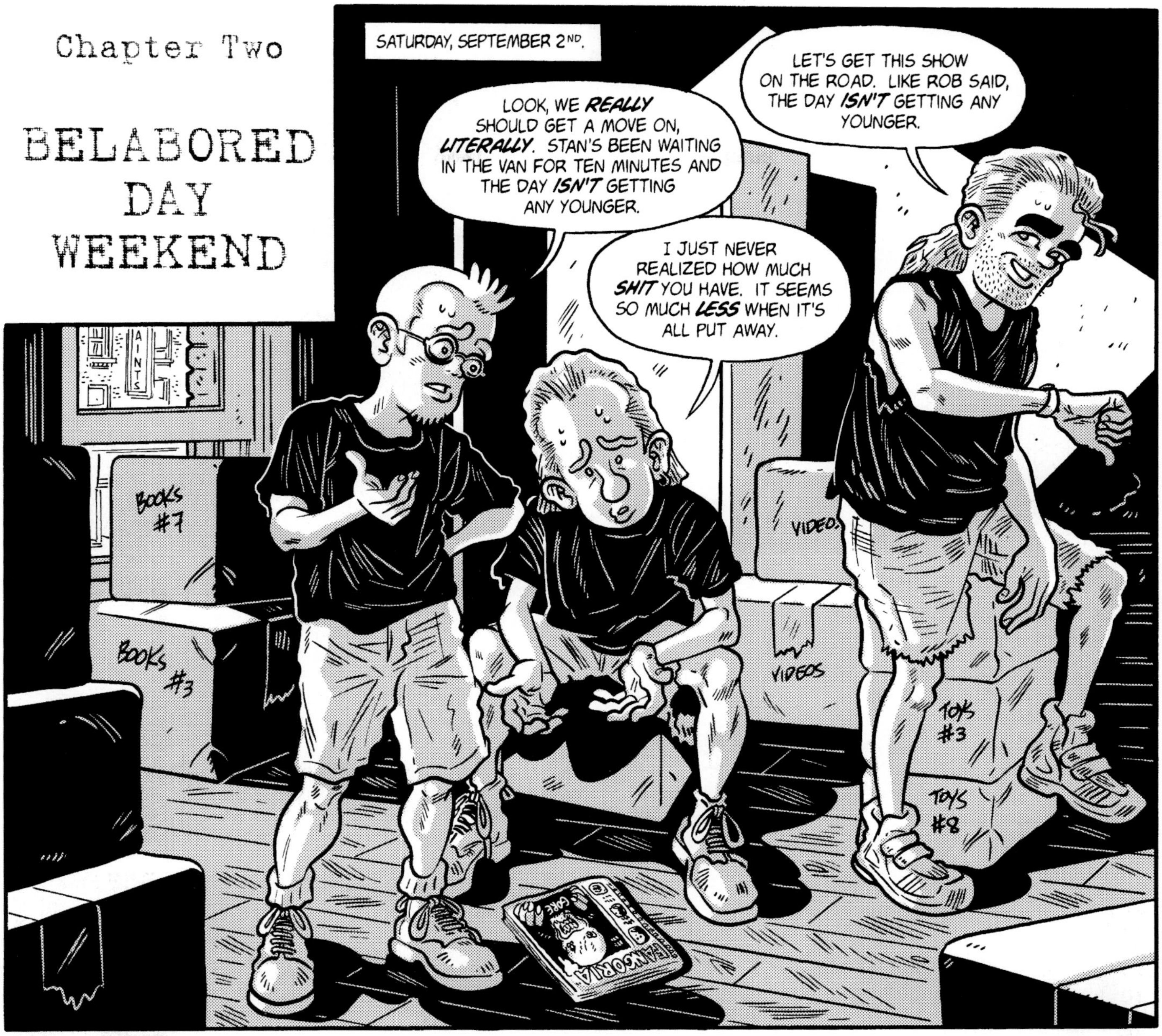
SATURDAY, SEPTEMBER 2ND.
LOOK, WE REALLY SHOULD GET A MOVE ON, LITERALLY. STAN'S BEEN WAITING IN THE VAN FOR TEN MINUTES AND THE DAY ISN'T GETTING ANY YOUNGER.
LET'S GET THIS SHOW ON THE ROAD. LIKE ROB SAID, THE DAY ISN'T GETTING ANY YOUNGER.
I JUST NEVER REALIZED HOW MUCH SHIT YOU HAVE. IT SEEMS SO MUCH LESS WHEN IT'S ALL PUT AWAY.
BOOKS #7
BOOKS #3
VIDEO
VIDEOS
TOYS #3
TOYS #8
FANGORIA

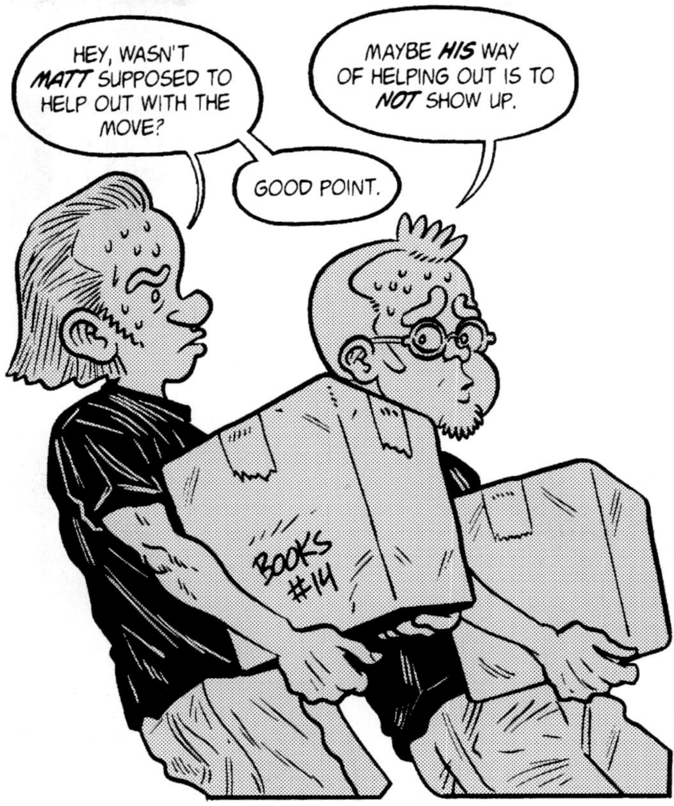
HEY, WASN'T MATT SUPPOSED TO HELP OUT WITH THE MOVE?
MAYBE HIS WAY OF HELPING OUT IS TO NOT SHOW UP.
GOOD POINT.
BOOKS #14

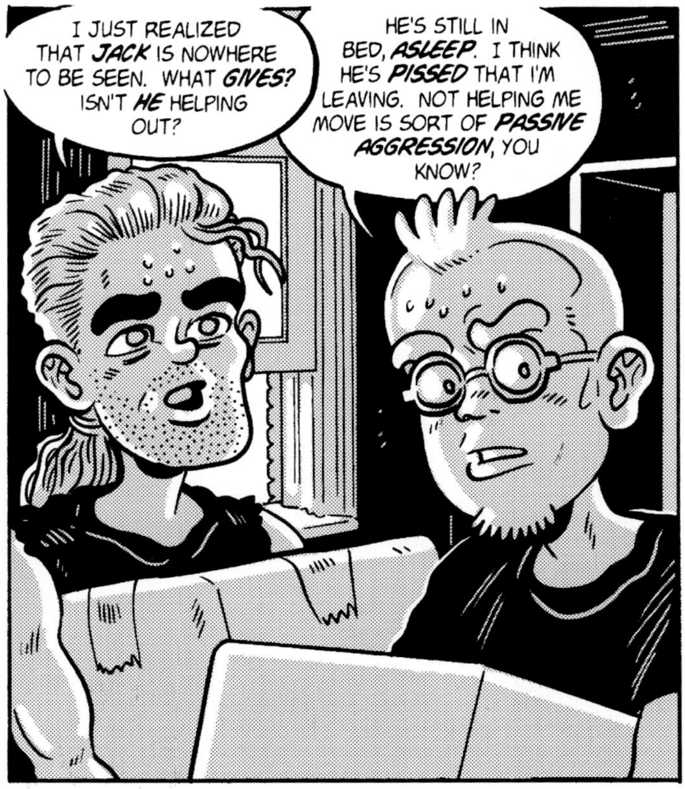
I JUST REALIZED THAT JACK IS NOWHERE TO BE SEEN. WHAT GIVES? ISN'T HE HELPING OUT?
HE'S STILL IN BED, ASLEEP. I THINK HE'S PISSED THAT I'M LEAVING. NOT HELPING ME MOVE IS SORT OF PASSIVE AGGRESSION, YOU KNOW?

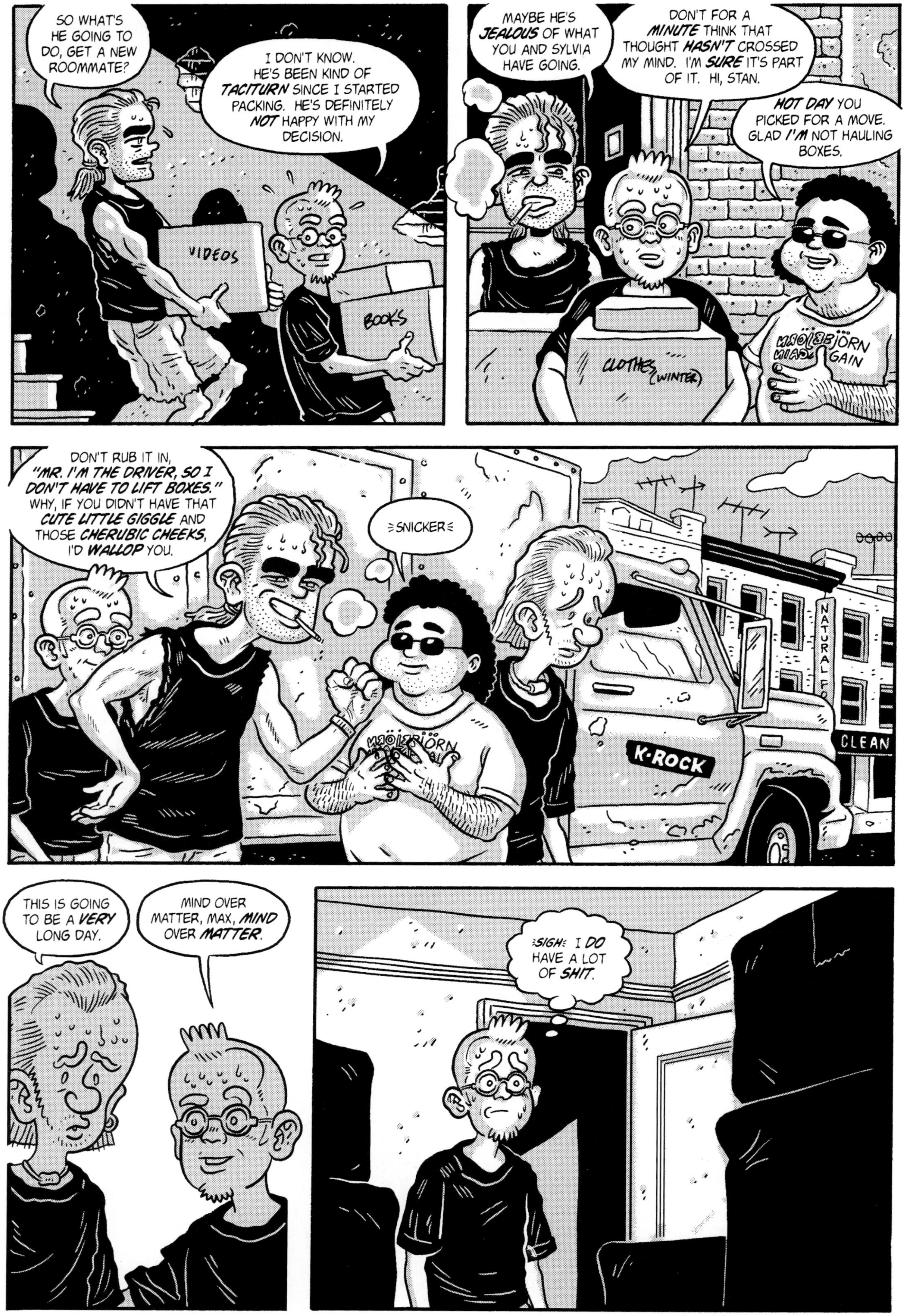

SO WHAT'S HE GOING TO DO, GET A NEW ROOMMATE?
I DON'T KNOW. HE'S BEEN KIND OF TACITURN SINCE I STARTED PACKING. HE'S DEFINITELY NOT HAPPY WITH MY DECISION.
VIDEOS
BOOKS
MAYBE HE'S JEALOUS OF WHAT YOU AND SYLVIA HAVE GOING.
DON'T FOR A MINUTE THINK THAT THOUGHT HASN'T CROSSED MY MIND. I'M SURE IT'S PART OF IT. HI, STAN.
HOT DAY YOU PICKED FOR A MOVE. GLAD I'M NOT HAULING BOXES.
CLOTHES (WINTER)
DON'T RUB IT IN, "MR. I'M THE DRIVER, SO I DON'T HAVE TO LIFT BOXES." WHY, IF YOU DIDN'T HAVE THAT CUTE LITTLE GIGGLE AND THOSE CHERUBIC CHEEKS, I'D WALLOP YOU.
SNICKER
K-ROCK
NATURAL F
CLEAN
THIS IS GOING TO BE A VERY LONG DAY.
MIND OVER MATTER, MAX, MIND OVER MATTER.
SIGH I DO HAVE A LOT OF SHIT.

YAWN! WE NEVER GOT TO DO ANY OF THAT WILD, *BACHELOR BOY* TYPE STUFF TOGETHER. NEVER GOT TO TAKE ADVANTAGE OF THE WHOLE *ROOMMATES THING.*

JACK! YOU *STARTLED* ME. I DIDN'T THINK YOU WERE UP.

VIDEOS #12

TOYS

I COULDN'T SLEEP WITH ALL THE *BANGING* AND *SHOUTING.*

THE *BANGING* AND *SHOUTING* HAVEN'T EVEN GOTTEN INTO *FULL* SWING YET.

NO, I GUESS WE *DIDN'T* DO ANY STUFF LIKE *THAT.* BUT THEN AGAIN, I'M NOT *REALLY* A BACHELOR. THE *MAIN* REASON I LEFT HOME WAS TO PURSUE MY RELATIONSHIP WITH SYLV. YOU *KNEW* THAT.

I GUESS I JUST DIDN'T THINK IT WOULD...

WHAT? *LAST?* I HOPE THAT'S *NOT* WHAT YOU WERE GOING TO SAY.

NO. I DON'T *KNOW,* I JUST WOKE UP. I'LL LET YOU GET ON WITH THE BUSINESS AT HAND.

WAS THAT *JACK* IN HERE I HEARD?

YEAH. YEAH, YEAH, YEAH.

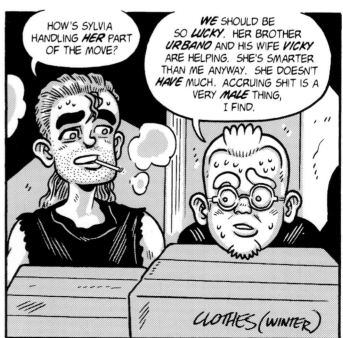

HOW'S SYLVIA HANDLING *HER* PART OF THE MOVE?

WE SHOULD BE SO *LUCKY.* HER BROTHER *URBANO* AND HIS WIFE *VICKY* ARE HELPING. SHE'S SMARTER THAN ME ANYWAY. SHE DOESN'T *HAVE* MUCH. ACCRUING SHIT IS A VERY *MALE* THING, I FIND.

CLOTHES (WINTER)

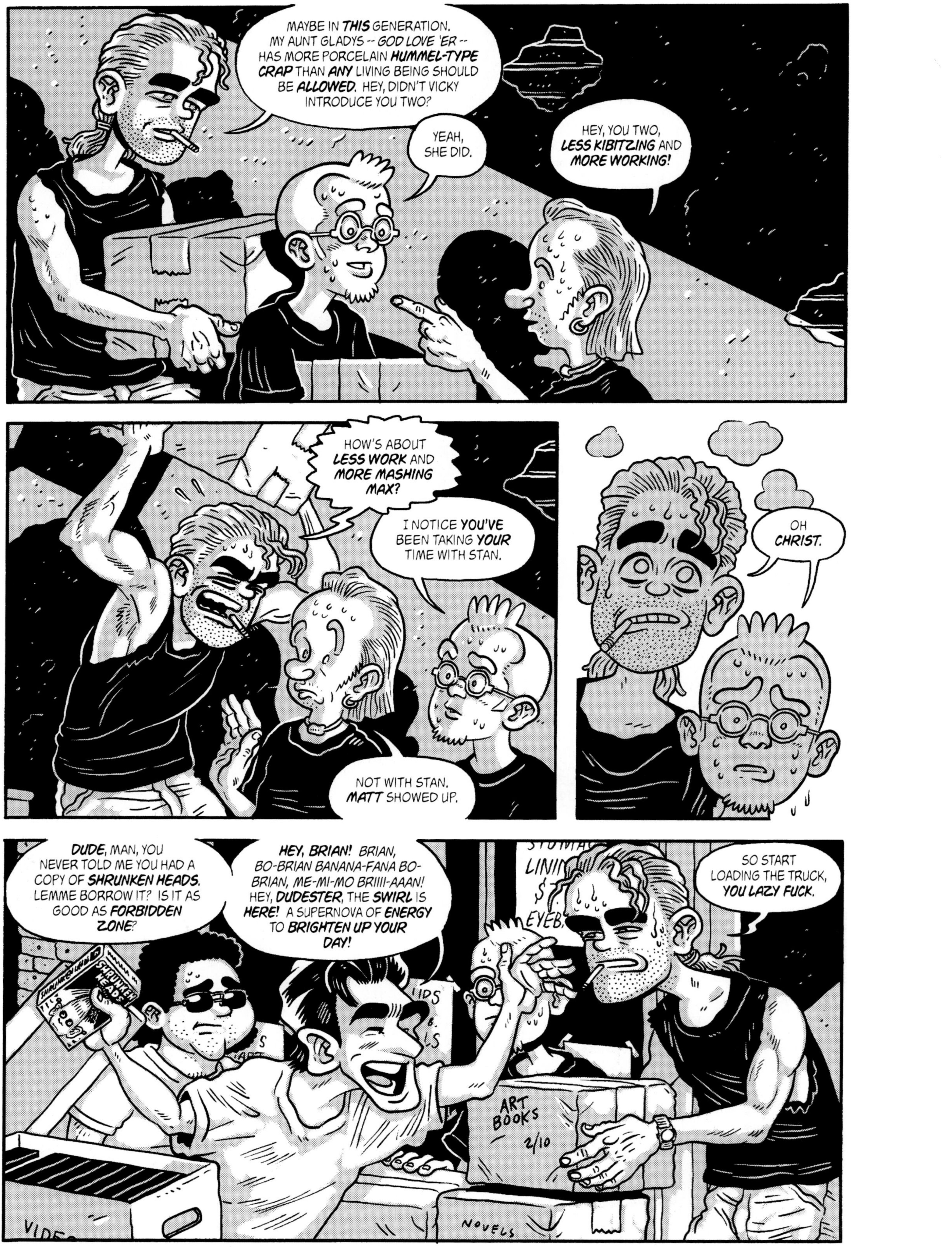
MAYBE IN **THIS** GENERATION. MY AUNT GLADYS -- **GOD LOVE 'ER** -- HAS MORE PORCELAIN **HUMMEL-TYPE CRAP** THAN **ANY** LIVING BEING SHOULD BE **ALLOWED.** HEY, DIDN'T VICKY INTRODUCE YOU TWO?
YEAH, SHE DID.
HEY, YOU TWO, **LESS KIBITZING** AND **MORE WORKING!**
HOW'S ABOUT **LESS WORK** AND **MORE MASHING MAX?**
I NOTICE **YOU'VE** BEEN TAKING **YOUR** TIME WITH STAN.
NOT WITH STAN. **MATT** SHOWED UP.
OH **CHRIST.**
DUDE, MAN, YOU NEVER TOLD ME YOU HAD A COPY OF **SHRUNKEN HEADS.** LEMME BORROW IT? IS IT AS GOOD AS **FORBIDDEN ZONE**?
HEY, BRIAN! BRIAN, BO-BRIAN BANANA-FANA BO-BRIAN, ME-MI-MO BRIIII-AAAN! HEY, **DUDESTER,** THE **SWIRL** IS **HERE!** A SUPERNOVA OF **ENERGY** TO **BRIGHTEN UP YOUR DAY!**
SO START LOADING THE TRUCK, **YOU LAZY FUCK.**
SHRUNKEN HEADS
ART BOOKS 2/10
NOVELS

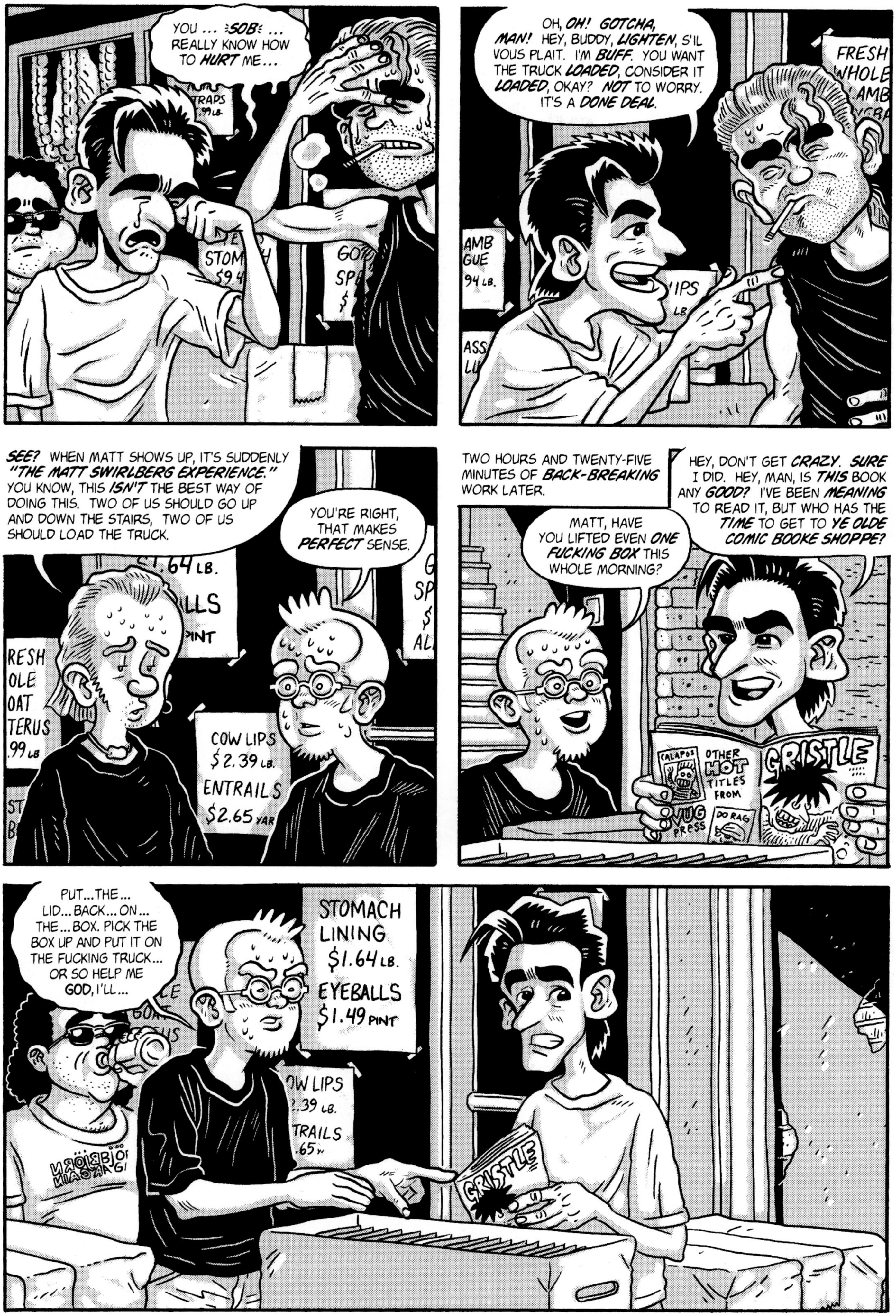
YOU ... SOB ... REALLY KNOW HOW TO HURT ME...
TRAPS 99 LB.
STOM $9.4
OH, OH! GOTCHA, MAN! HEY, BUDDY, LIGHTEN, S'IL VOUS PLAIT. I'M BUFF. YOU WANT THE TRUCK LOADED, CONSIDER IT LOADED, OKAY? NOT TO WORRY. IT'S A DONE DEAL.
FRESH WHOLE LAMB
AMB GUE 94 LB.
SEE? WHEN MATT SHOWS UP, IT'S SUDDENLY "THE MATT SWIRLBERG EXPERIENCE." YOU KNOW, THIS ISN'T THE BEST WAY OF DOING THIS. TWO OF US SHOULD GO UP AND DOWN THE STAIRS, TWO OF US SHOULD LOAD THE TRUCK.
YOU'RE RIGHT, THAT MAKES PERFECT SENSE.
RESH OLE OAT TERUS .99 LB
COW LIPS $2.39 LB. ENTRAILS $2.65 YAR
TWO HOURS AND TWENTY-FIVE MINUTES OF BACK-BREAKING WORK LATER.
MATT, HAVE YOU LIFTED EVEN ONE FUCKING BOX THIS WHOLE MORNING?
HEY, DON'T GET CRAZY. SURE I DID. HEY, MAN, IS THIS BOOK ANY GOOD? I'VE BEEN MEANING TO READ IT, BUT WHO HAS THE TIME TO GET TO YE OLDE COMIC BOOKE SHOPPE?
GRISTLE
OTHER HOT TITLES FROM VUG PRESS
PUT...THE... LID...BACK...ON... THE...BOX. PICK THE BOX UP AND PUT IT ON THE FUCKING TRUCK... OR SO HELP ME GOD, I'LL...
STOMACH LINING $1.64 LB. EYEBALLS $1.49 PINT
GRISTLE

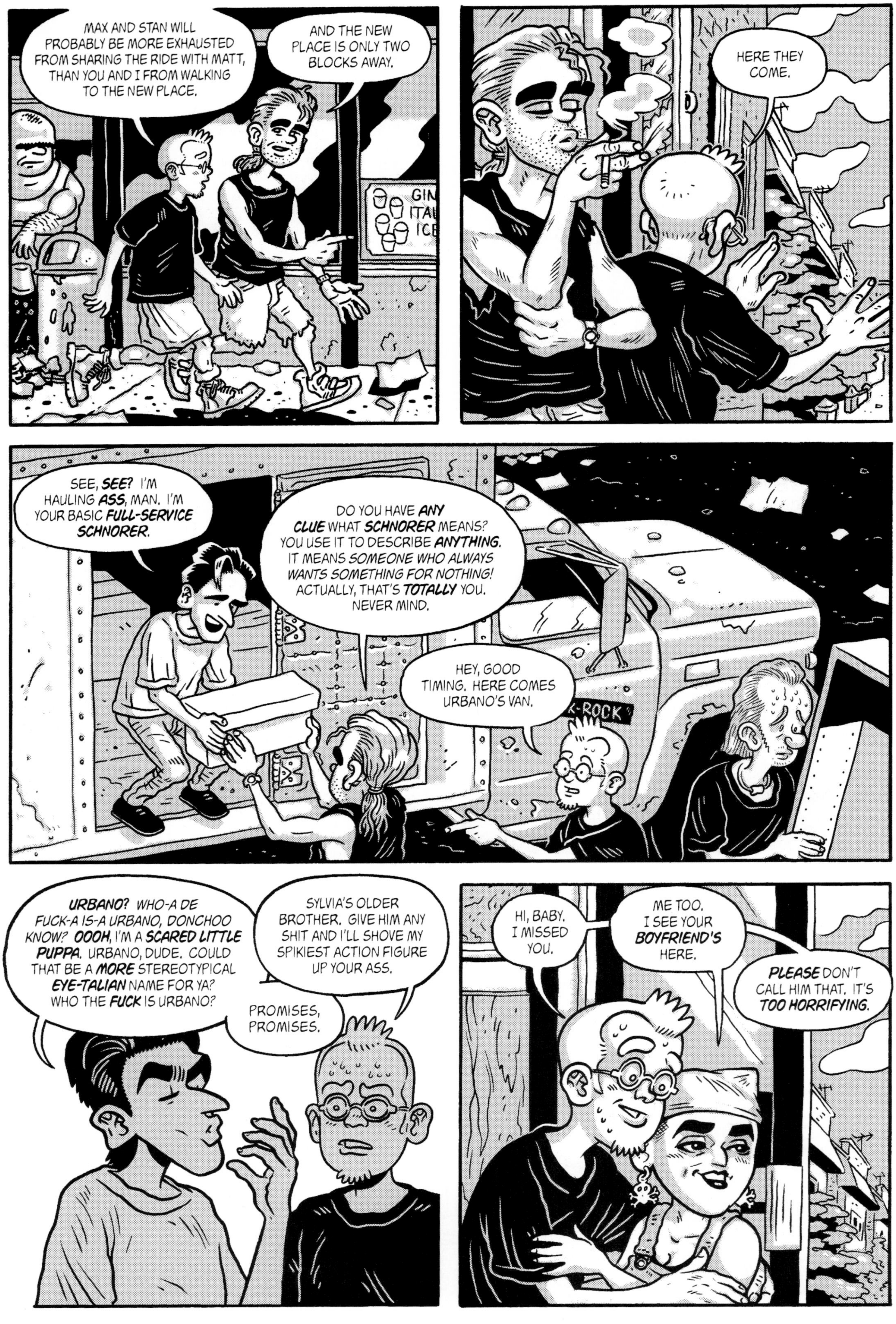
MAX AND STAN WILL PROBABLY BE MORE EXHAUSTED FROM SHARING THE RIDE WITH MATT, THAN YOU AND I FROM WALKING TO THE NEW PLACE.
AND THE NEW PLACE IS ONLY TWO BLOCKS AWAY.
GIN ITAL ICE
HERE THEY COME.
SEE, SEE? I'M HAULING ASS, MAN. I'M YOUR BASIC FULL-SERVICE SCHNORER.
DO YOU HAVE ANY CLUE WHAT SCHNORER MEANS? YOU USE IT TO DESCRIBE ANYTHING. IT MEANS SOMEONE WHO ALWAYS WANTS SOMETHING FOR NOTHING! ACTUALLY, THAT'S TOTALLY YOU. NEVER MIND.
HEY, GOOD TIMING. HERE COMES URBANO'S VAN.
K-ROCK
URBANO? WHO-A DE FUCK-A IS-A URBANO, DONCHOO KNOW? OOOH, I'M A SCARED LITTLE PUPPA. URBANO, DUDE. COULD THAT BE A MORE STEREOTYPICAL EYE-TALIAN NAME FOR YA? WHO THE FUCK IS URBANO?
SYLVIA'S OLDER BROTHER. GIVE HIM ANY SHIT AND I'LL SHOVE MY SPIKIEST ACTION FIGURE UP YOUR ASS.
PROMISES, PROMISES.
HI, BABY. I MISSED YOU.
ME TOO. I SEE YOUR BOYFRIEND'S HERE.
PLEASE DON'T CALL HIM THAT. IT'S TOO HORRIFYING.

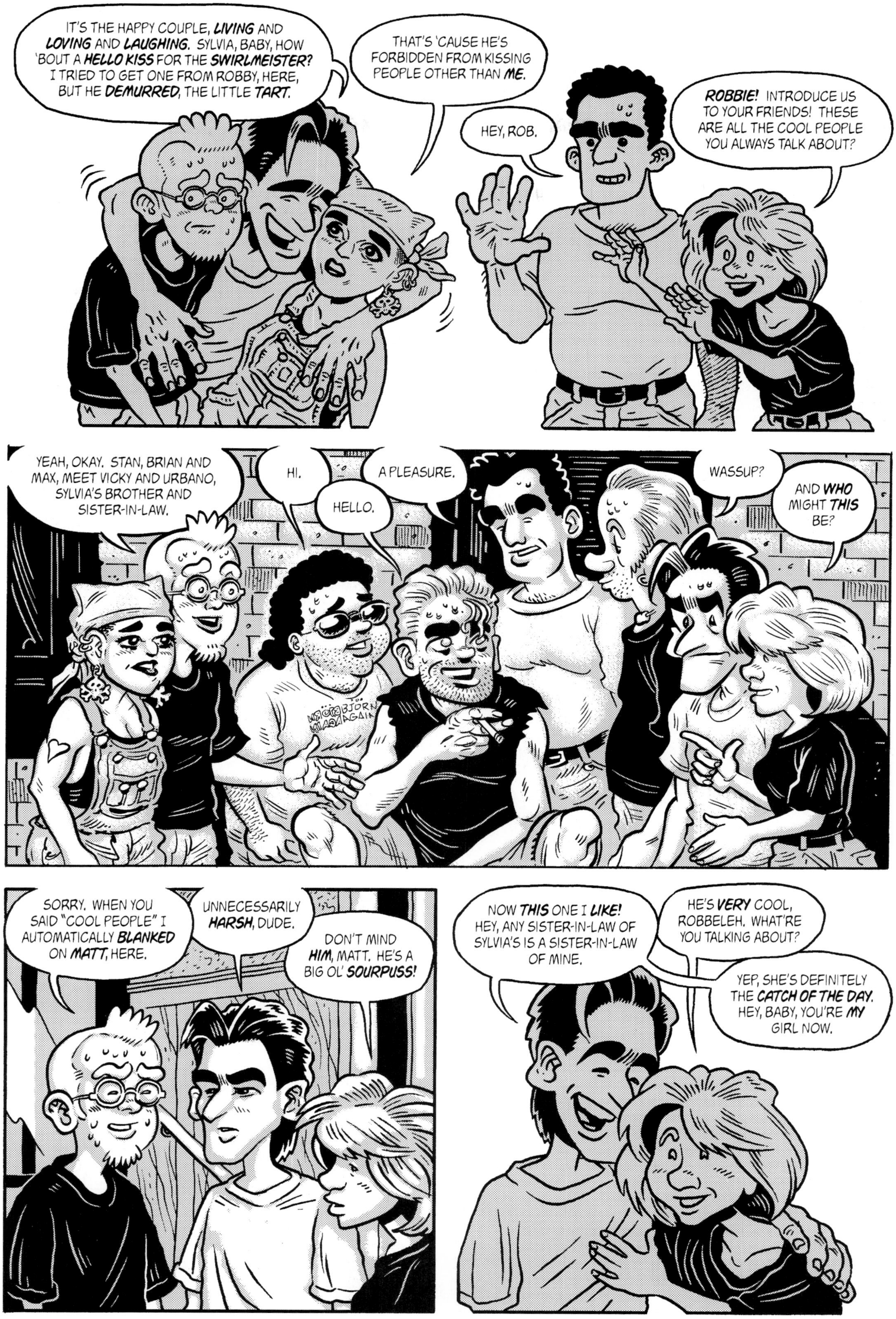
IT'S THE HAPPY COUPLE, LIVING AND LOVING AND LAUGHING. SYLVIA, BABY, HOW 'BOUT A HELLO KISS FOR THE SWIRLMEISTER? I TRIED TO GET ONE FROM ROBBY, HERE, BUT HE DEMURRED, THE LITTLE TART.
THAT'S 'CAUSE HE'S FORBIDDEN FROM KISSING PEOPLE OTHER THAN ME.
HEY, ROB.
ROBBIE! INTRODUCE US TO YOUR FRIENDS! THESE ARE ALL THE COOL PEOPLE YOU ALWAYS TALK ABOUT?
YEAH, OKAY. STAN, BRIAN AND MAX, MEET VICKY AND URBANO, SYLVIA'S BROTHER AND SISTER-IN-LAW.
HI.
HELLO.
A PLEASURE.
WASSUP?
AND WHO MIGHT THIS BE?
SORRY. WHEN YOU SAID "COOL PEOPLE" I AUTOMATICALLY BLANKED ON MATT, HERE.
UNNECESSARILY HARSH, DUDE.
DON'T MIND HIM, MATT. HE'S A BIG OL' SOURPUSS!
NOW THIS ONE I LIKE! HEY, ANY SISTER-IN-LAW OF SYLVIA'S IS A SISTER-IN-LAW OF MINE.
HE'S VERY COOL, ROBBELEH. WHAT'RE YOU TALKING ABOUT?
YEP, SHE'S DEFINITELY THE CATCH OF THE DAY. HEY, BABY, YOU'RE MY GIRL NOW.

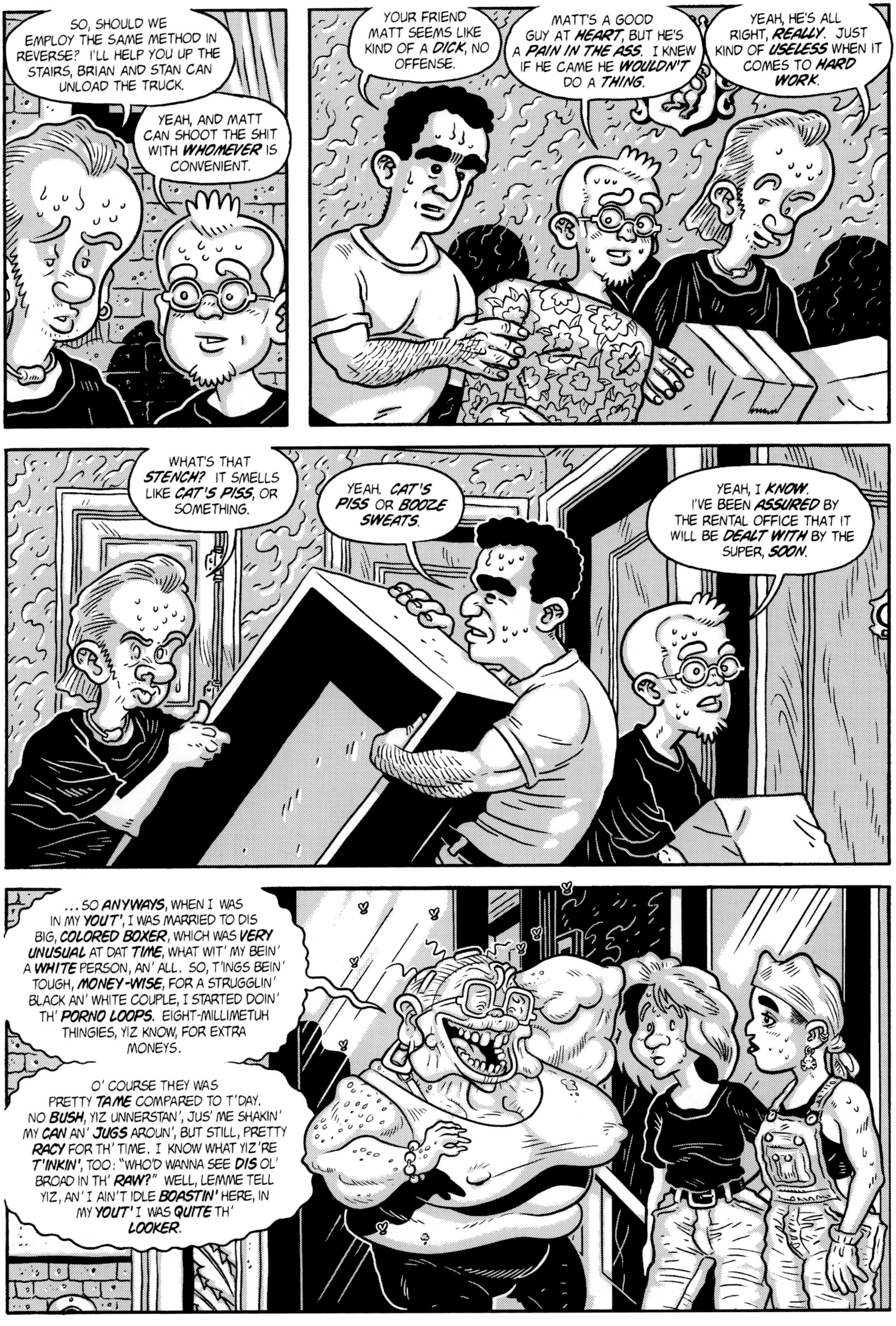
SO, SHOULD WE EMPLOY THE SAME METHOD IN REVERSE? I'LL HELP YOU UP THE STAIRS, BRIAN AND STAN CAN UNLOAD THE TRUCK.
YEAH, AND MATT CAN SHOOT THE SHIT WITH WHOMEVER IS CONVENIENT.
YOUR FRIEND MATT SEEMS LIKE KIND OF A DICK, NO OFFENSE.
MATT'S A GOOD GUY AT HEART, BUT HE'S A PAIN IN THE ASS. I KNEW IF HE CAME HE WOULDN'T DO A THING.
YEAH, HE'S ALL RIGHT, REALLY. JUST KIND OF USELESS WHEN IT COMES TO HARD WORK.
WHAT'S THAT STENCH? IT SMELLS LIKE CAT'S PISS, OR SOMETHING.
YEAH. CAT'S PISS OR BOOZE SWEATS.
YEAH, I KNOW. I'VE BEEN ASSURED BY THE RENTAL OFFICE THAT IT WILL BE DEALT WITH BY THE SUPER, SOON.
...SO ANYWAYS, WHEN I WAS IN MY YOUT', I WAS MARRIED TO DIS BIG, COLORED BOXER, WHICH WAS VERY UNUSUAL AT DAT TIME, WHAT WIT' MY BEIN' A WHITE PERSON, AN' ALL. SO, T'INGS BEIN' TOUGH, MONEY-WISE, FOR A STRUGGLIN' BLACK AN' WHITE COUPLE, I STARTED DOIN' TH' PORNO LOOPS. EIGHT-MILLIMETUH THINGIES, YIZ KNOW, FOR EXTRA MONEYS.
O' COURSE THEY WAS PRETTY TAME COMPARED TO T'DAY. NO BUSH, YIZ UNNERSTAN', JUS' ME SHAKIN' MY CAN AN' JUGS AROUN', BUT STILL, PRETTY RACY FOR TH' TIME. I KNOW WHAT YIZ'RE T'INKIN', TOO: "WHO'D WANNA SEE DIS OL' BROAD IN TH' RAW?" WELL, LEMME TELL YIZ, AN' I AIN'T IDLE BOASTIN' HERE, IN MY YOUT' I WAS QUITE TH' LOOKER.

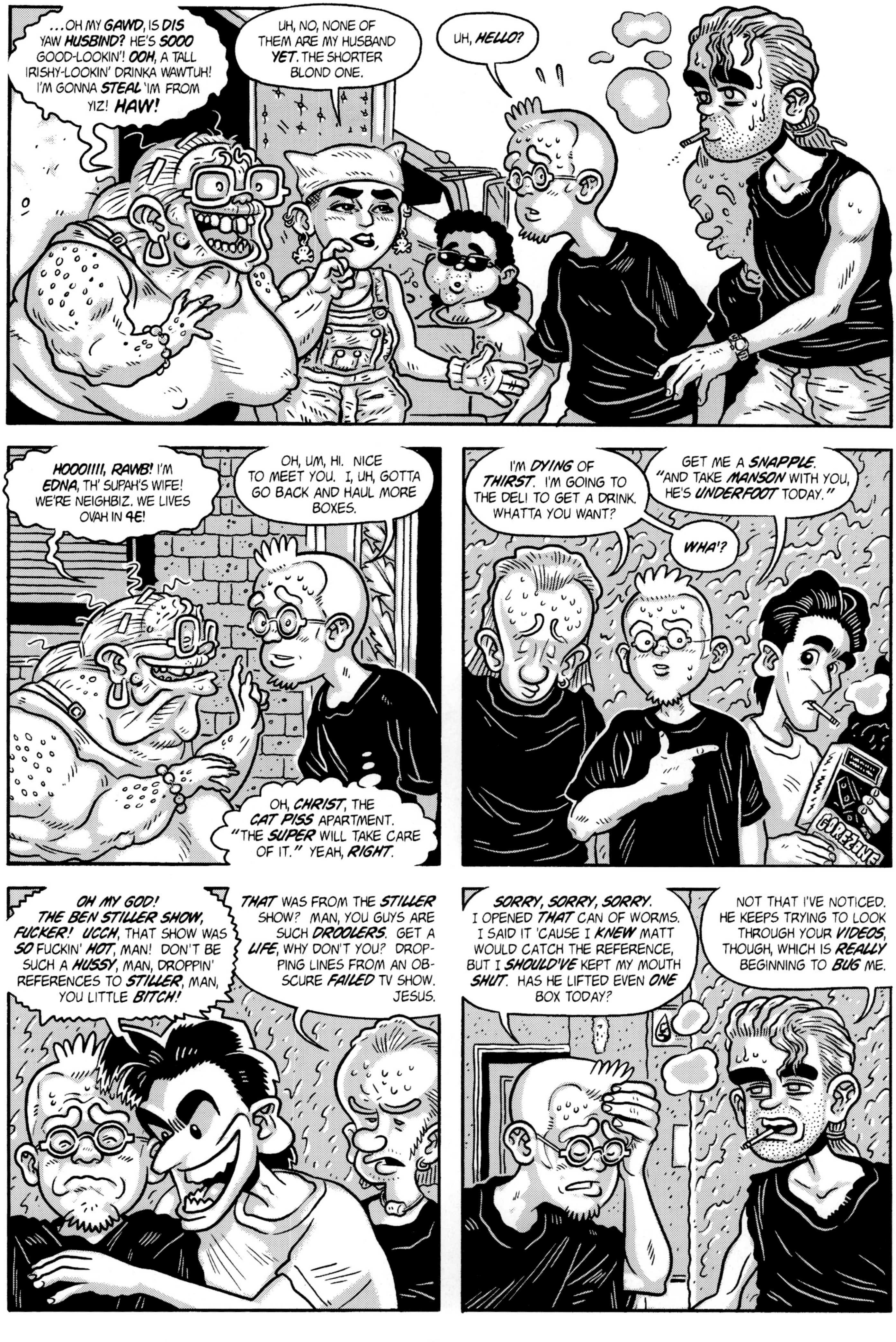
...OH MY GAWD, IS DIS YAW HUSBIND? HE'S SOOO GOOD-LOOKIN'! OOH, A TALL IRISHY-LOOKIN' DRINKA WAWTUH! I'M GONNA STEAL 'IM FROM YIZ! HAW!
UH, NO, NONE OF THEM ARE MY HUSBAND YET. THE SHORTER BLOND ONE.
UH, HELLO?
HOOOIIII, RAWB! I'M EDNA, TH' SUPAH'S WIFE! WE'RE NEIGHBIZ. WE LIVES OVAH IN 4E!
OH, UM, HI. NICE TO MEET YOU. I, UH, GOTTA GO BACK AND HAUL MORE BOXES.
OH, CHRIST, THE CAT PISS APARTMENT. "THE SUPER WILL TAKE CARE OF IT." YEAH, RIGHT.
I'M DYING OF THIRST. I'M GOING TO THE DELI TO GET A DRINK. WHATTA YOU WANT?
GET ME A SNAPPLE. "AND TAKE MANSON WITH YOU, HE'S UNDERFOOT TODAY."
WHA'?
GOREZONE
OH MY GOD! THE BEN STILLER SHOW, FUCKER! UCCH, THAT SHOW WAS SO FUCKIN' HOT, MAN! DON'T BE SUCH A HUSSY, MAN, DROPPIN' REFERENCES TO STILLER, MAN, YOU LITTLE BITCH!
THAT WAS FROM THE STILLER SHOW? MAN, YOU GUYS ARE SUCH DROOLERS. GET A LIFE, WHY DON'T YOU? DROPPING LINES FROM AN OBSCURE FAILED TV SHOW. JESUS.
SORRY, SORRY, SORRY. I OPENED THAT CAN OF WORMS. I SAID IT 'CAUSE I KNEW MATT WOULD CATCH THE REFERENCE, BUT I SHOULD'VE KEPT MY MOUTH SHUT. HAS HE LIFTED EVEN ONE BOX TODAY?
NOT THAT I'VE NOTICED. HE KEEPS TRYING TO LOOK THROUGH YOUR VIDEOS, THOUGH, WHICH IS REALLY BEGINNING TO BUG ME.

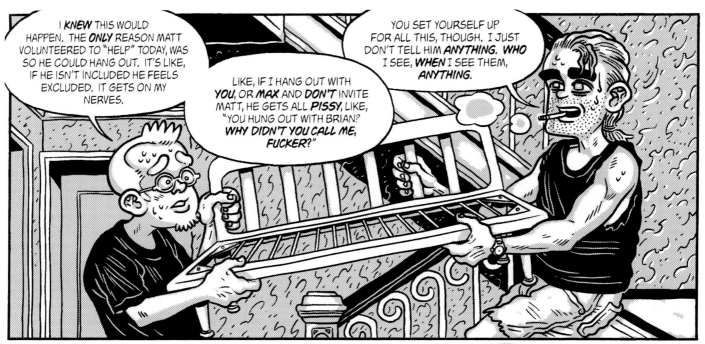

I **KNEW** THIS WOULD HAPPEN. THE **ONLY** REASON MATT VOLUNTEERED TO "HELP" TODAY, WAS SO HE COULD HANG OUT. IT'S LIKE, IF HE ISN'T INCLUDED HE FEELS EXCLUDED. IT GETS ON MY NERVES.

LIKE, IF I HANG OUT WITH **YOU**, OR **MAX** AND **DON'T** INVITE MATT, HE GETS ALL **PISSY**, LIKE, "YOU HUNG OUT WITH BRIAN? **WHY DIDN'T YOU CALL ME, FUCKER?**"

YOU SET YOURSELF UP FOR ALL THIS, THOUGH. I JUST DON'T TELL HIM **ANYTHING**. **WHO** I SEE, **WHEN** I SEE THEM, **ANYTHING**.

"YOU ARE ONE SMART INDIAN..."

MAMET.

FUCK. WE ALL NEED TO STOP THE QUOTE-DROPPING. MAX IS **RIGHT**: I **AM** A DROOLER. AT LEAST I DON'T RUN AROUND QUOTING **PYTHON**, OR **WOODY ALLEN**.

UGH, THAT'S WORSE. **GEEK ELITISM.** LIKE THERE'S A PECKING ORDER OF DROOLER-DOM. IT'S THE **MOVE**. I'M SLIPPING INTO SOME KIND OF SICK REVERIE.

YOU'LL FEEL BETTER WHEN MAX GETS BACK WITH THE DRINKS.

I'LL FEEL BETTER WHEN THIS DAY IS **OVER**.

44

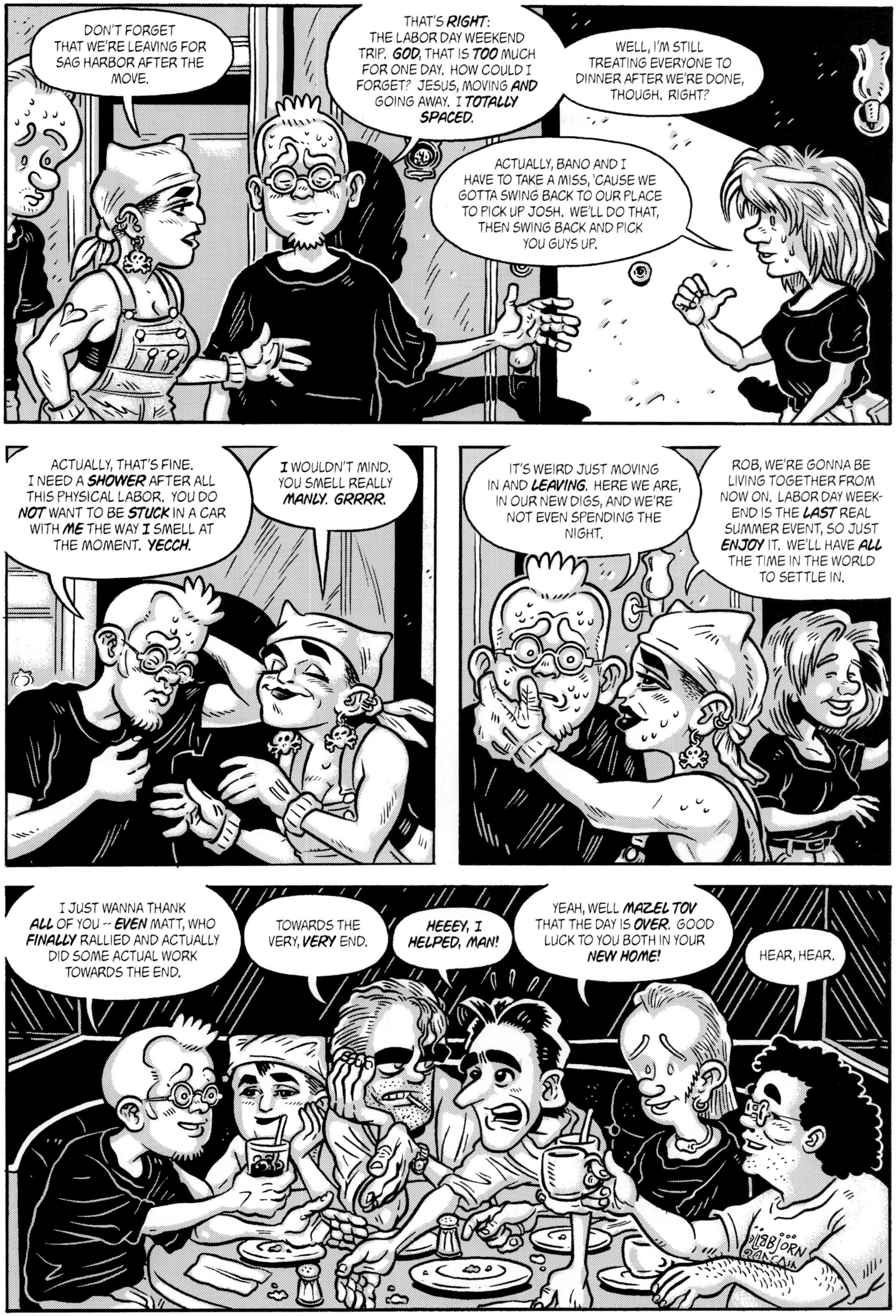
DON'T FORGET THAT WE'RE LEAVING FOR SAG HARBOR AFTER THE MOVE.
THAT'S RIGHT: THE LABOR DAY WEEKEND TRIP. GOD, THAT IS TOO MUCH FOR ONE DAY. HOW COULD I FORGET? JESUS, MOVING AND GOING AWAY. I TOTALLY SPACED.
WELL, I'M STILL TREATING EVERYONE TO DINNER AFTER WE'RE DONE, THOUGH. RIGHT?
ACTUALLY, BANO AND I HAVE TO TAKE A MISS, 'CAUSE WE GOTTA SWING BACK TO OUR PLACE TO PICK UP JOSH. WE'LL DO THAT, THEN SWING BACK AND PICK YOU GUYS UP.
ACTUALLY, THAT'S FINE. I NEED A SHOWER AFTER ALL THIS PHYSICAL LABOR. YOU DO NOT WANT TO BE STUCK IN A CAR WITH ME THE WAY I SMELL AT THE MOMENT. YECCH.
I WOULDN'T MIND. YOU SMELL REALLY MANLY. GRRRR.
IT'S WEIRD JUST MOVING IN AND LEAVING. HERE WE ARE, IN OUR NEW DIGS, AND WE'RE NOT EVEN SPENDING THE NIGHT.
ROB, WE'RE GONNA BE LIVING TOGETHER FROM NOW ON. LABOR DAY WEEK-END IS THE LAST REAL SUMMER EVENT, SO JUST ENJOY IT. WE'LL HAVE ALL THE TIME IN THE WORLD TO SETTLE IN.
I JUST WANNA THANK ALL OF YOU -- EVEN MATT, WHO FINALLY RALLIED AND ACTUALLY DID SOME ACTUAL WORK TOWARDS THE END.
TOWARDS THE VERY, VERY END.
HEEEY, I HELPED, MAN!
YEAH, WELL MAZEL TOV THAT THE DAY IS OVER. GOOD LUCK TO YOU BOTH IN YOUR NEW HOME!
HEAR, HEAR.

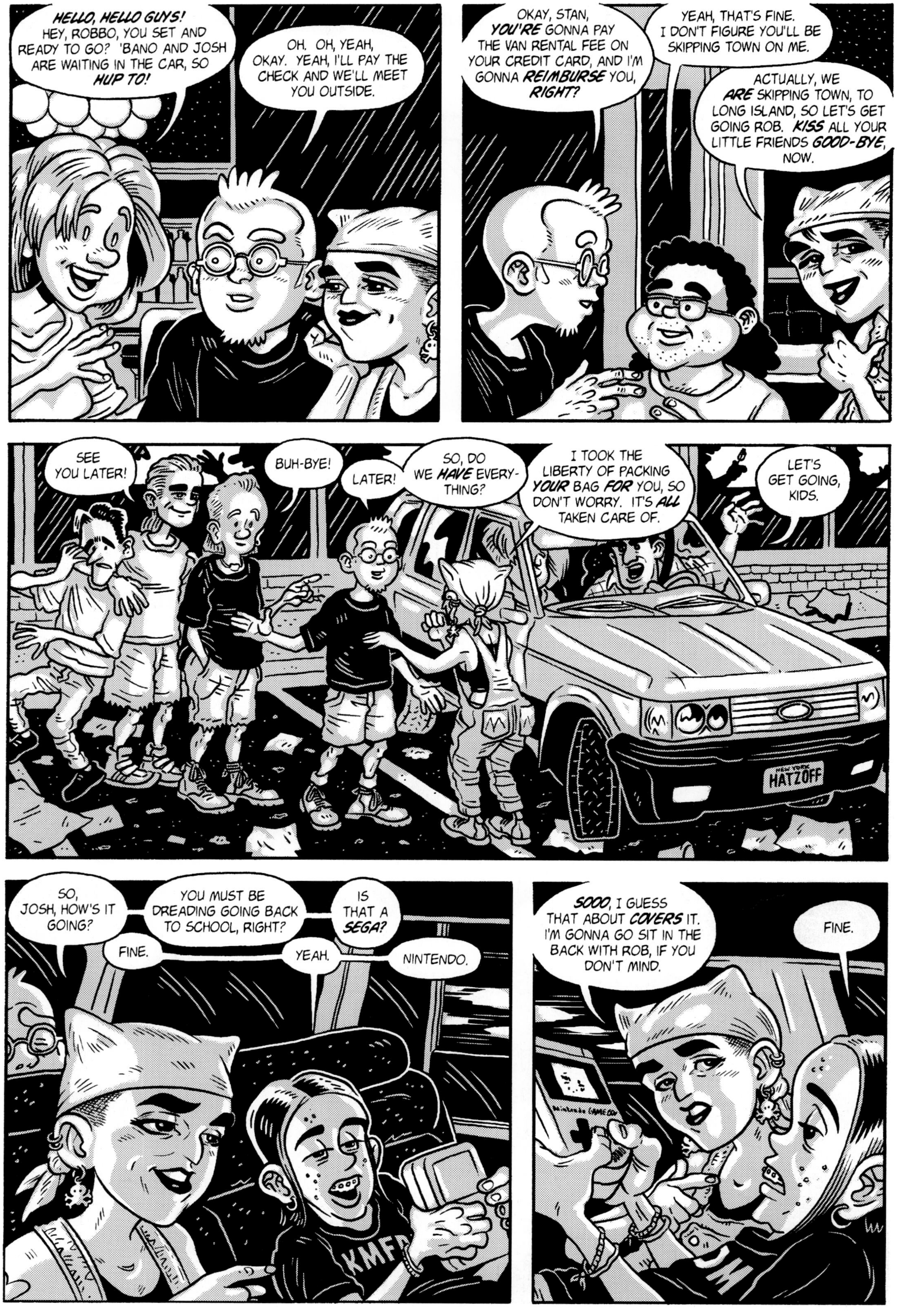
HELLO, HELLO GUYS! HEY, ROBBO, YOU SET AND READY TO GO? 'BANO AND JOSH ARE WAITING IN THE CAR, SO HUP TO!
OH. OH, YEAH, OKAY. YEAH, I'LL PAY THE CHECK AND WE'LL MEET YOU OUTSIDE.
OKAY, STAN, YOU'RE GONNA PAY THE VAN RENTAL FEE ON YOUR CREDIT CARD, AND I'M GONNA REIMBURSE YOU, RIGHT?
YEAH, THAT'S FINE. I DON'T FIGURE YOU'LL BE SKIPPING TOWN ON ME.
ACTUALLY, WE ARE SKIPPING TOWN, TO LONG ISLAND, SO LET'S GET GOING ROB. KISS ALL YOUR LITTLE FRIENDS GOOD-BYE, NOW.
SEE YOU LATER!
BUH-BYE!
LATER!
SO, DO WE HAVE EVERY-THING?
I TOOK THE LIBERTY OF PACKING YOUR BAG FOR YOU, SO DON'T WORRY. IT'S ALL TAKEN CARE OF.
LET'S GET GOING, KIDS.
NEW YORK HATZOFF
SO, JOSH, HOW'S IT GOING?
FINE.
YOU MUST BE DREADING GOING BACK TO SCHOOL, RIGHT?
YEAH.
IS THAT A SEGA?
NINTENDO.
SOOO, I GUESS THAT ABOUT COVERS IT. I'M GONNA GO SIT IN THE BACK WITH ROB, IF YOU DON'T MIND.
FINE.

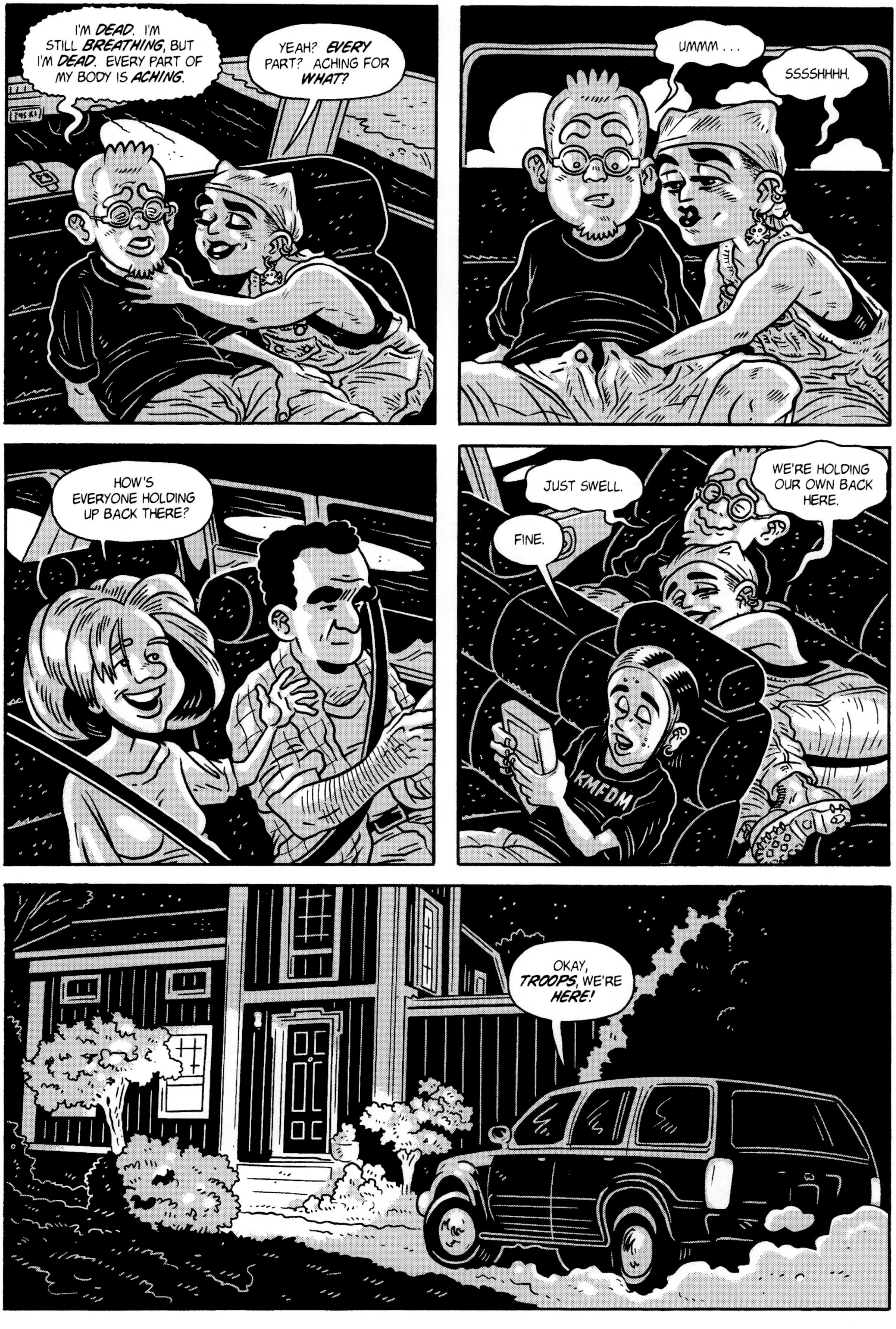
I'M DEAD. I'M STILL BREATHING, BUT I'M DEAD. EVERY PART OF MY BODY IS ACHING.
YEAH? EVERY PART? ACHING FOR WHAT?
UMMM . . .
SSSSHHHH.
HOW'S EVERYONE HOLDING UP BACK THERE?
JUST SWELL.
FINE.
WE'RE HOLDING OUR OWN BACK HERE.
KMFDM
OKAY, TROOPS, WE'RE HERE!

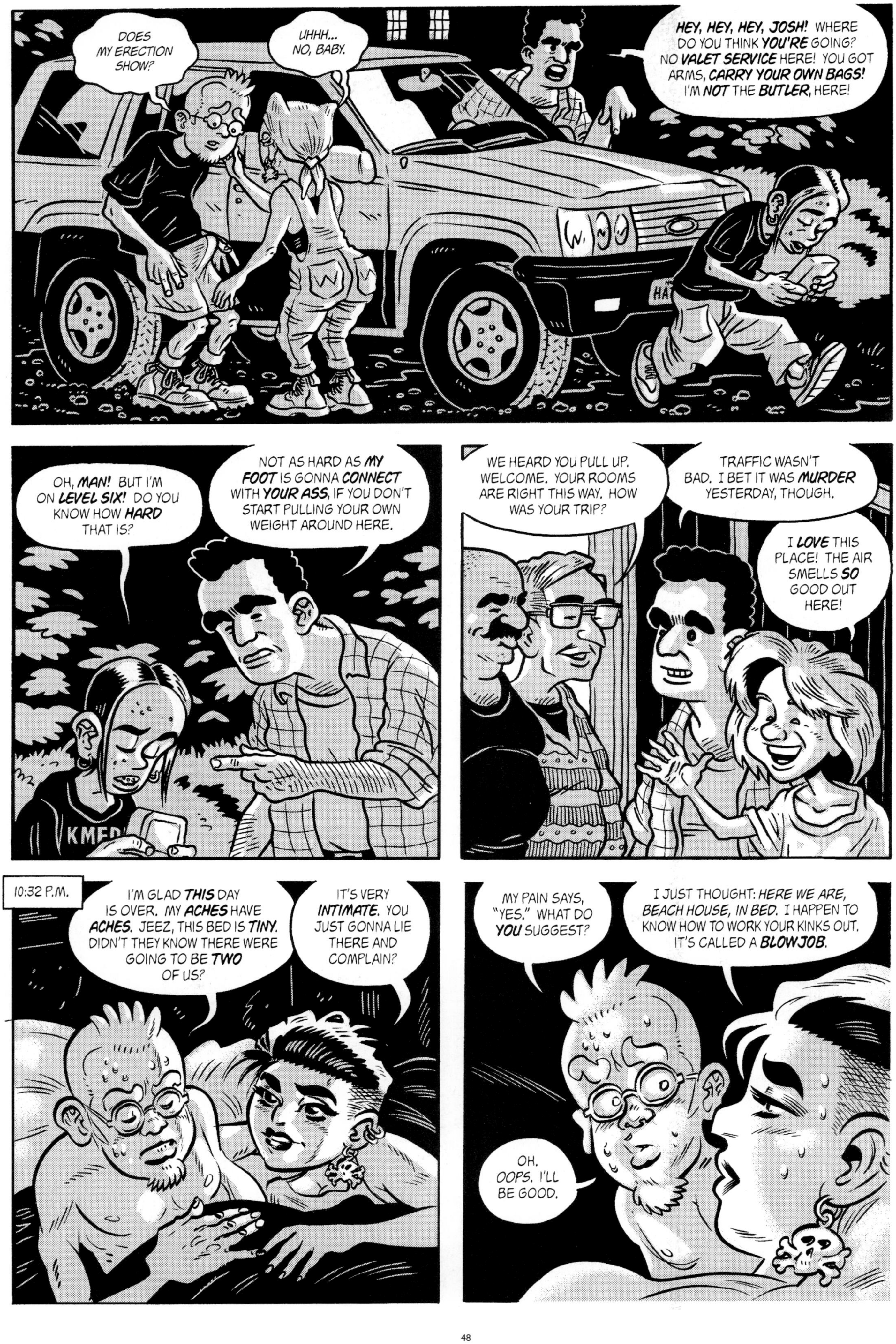
DOES MY ERECTION SHOW?
UHHH... NO, BABY.
HEY, HEY, HEY, JOSH! WHERE DO YOU THINK YOU'RE GOING? NO VALET SERVICE HERE! YOU GOT ARMS, CARRY YOUR OWN BAGS! I'M NOT THE BUTLER, HERE!
OH, MAN! BUT I'M ON LEVEL SIX! DO YOU KNOW HOW HARD THAT IS?
NOT AS HARD AS MY FOOT IS GONNA CONNECT WITH YOUR ASS, IF YOU DON'T START PULLING YOUR OWN WEIGHT AROUND HERE.
WE HEARD YOU PULL UP. WELCOME. YOUR ROOMS ARE RIGHT THIS WAY. HOW WAS YOUR TRIP?
TRAFFIC WASN'T BAD. I BET IT WAS MURDER YESTERDAY, THOUGH.
I LOVE THIS PLACE! THE AIR SMELLS SO GOOD OUT HERE!
10:32 P.M.
I'M GLAD THIS DAY IS OVER. MY ACHES HAVE ACHES. JEEZ, THIS BED IS TINY. DIDN'T THEY KNOW THERE WERE GOING TO BE TWO OF US?
IT'S VERY INTIMATE. YOU JUST GONNA LIE THERE AND COMPLAIN?
MY PAIN SAYS, "YES." WHAT DO YOU SUGGEST?
I JUST THOUGHT: HERE WE ARE, BEACH HOUSE, IN BED. I HAPPEN TO KNOW HOW TO WORK YOUR KINKS OUT. IT'S CALLED A BLOWJOB.
OH. OOPS. I'LL BE GOOD.

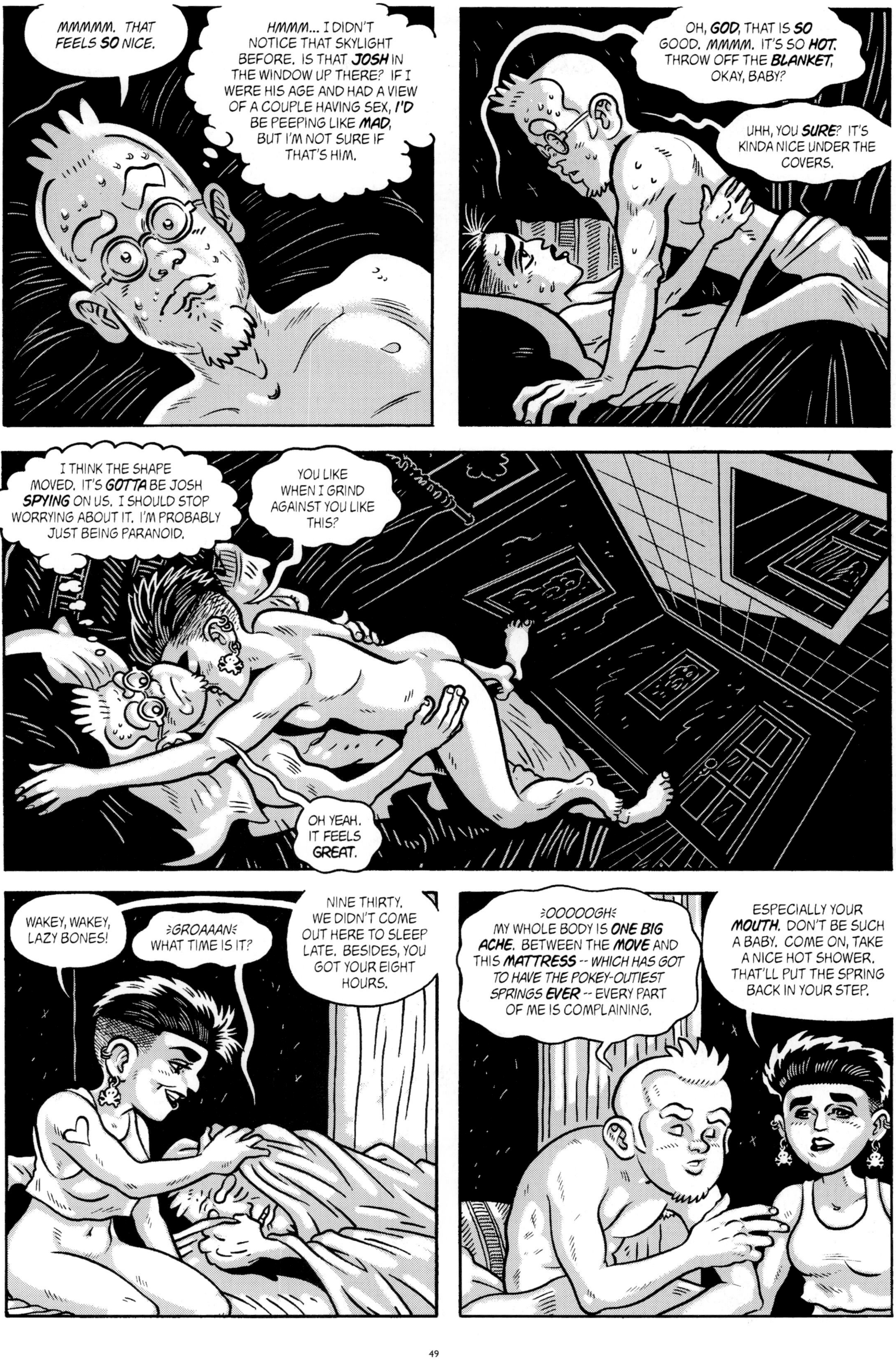
MMMMM. THAT FEELS SO NICE.
HMMM... I DIDN'T NOTICE THAT SKYLIGHT BEFORE. IS THAT JOSH IN THE WINDOW UP THERE? IF I WERE HIS AGE AND HAD A VIEW OF A COUPLE HAVING SEX, I'D BE PEEPING LIKE MAD, BUT I'M NOT SURE IF THAT'S HIM.
OH, GOD, THAT IS SO GOOD. MMMM. IT'S SO HOT. THROW OFF THE BLANKET, OKAY, BABY?
UHH, YOU SURE? IT'S KINDA NICE UNDER THE COVERS.
I THINK THE SHAPE MOVED. IT'S GOTTA BE JOSH SPYING ON US. I SHOULD STOP WORRYING ABOUT IT. I'M PROBABLY JUST BEING PARANOID.
YOU LIKE WHEN I GRIND AGAINST YOU LIKE THIS?
OH YEAH. IT FEELS GREAT.
WAKEY, WAKEY, LAZY BONES!
GROAAAN WHAT TIME IS IT?
NINE THIRTY. WE DIDN'T COME OUT HERE TO SLEEP LATE. BESIDES, YOU GOT YOUR EIGHT HOURS.
OOOOOGH MY WHOLE BODY IS ONE BIG ACHE. BETWEEN THE MOVE AND THIS MATTRESS -- WHICH HAS GOT TO HAVE THE POKEY-OUTIEST SPRINGS EVER -- EVERY PART OF ME IS COMPLAINING.
ESPECIALLY YOUR MOUTH. DON'T BE SUCH A BABY. COME ON, TAKE A NICE HOT SHOWER. THAT'LL PUT THE SPRING BACK IN YOUR STEP.

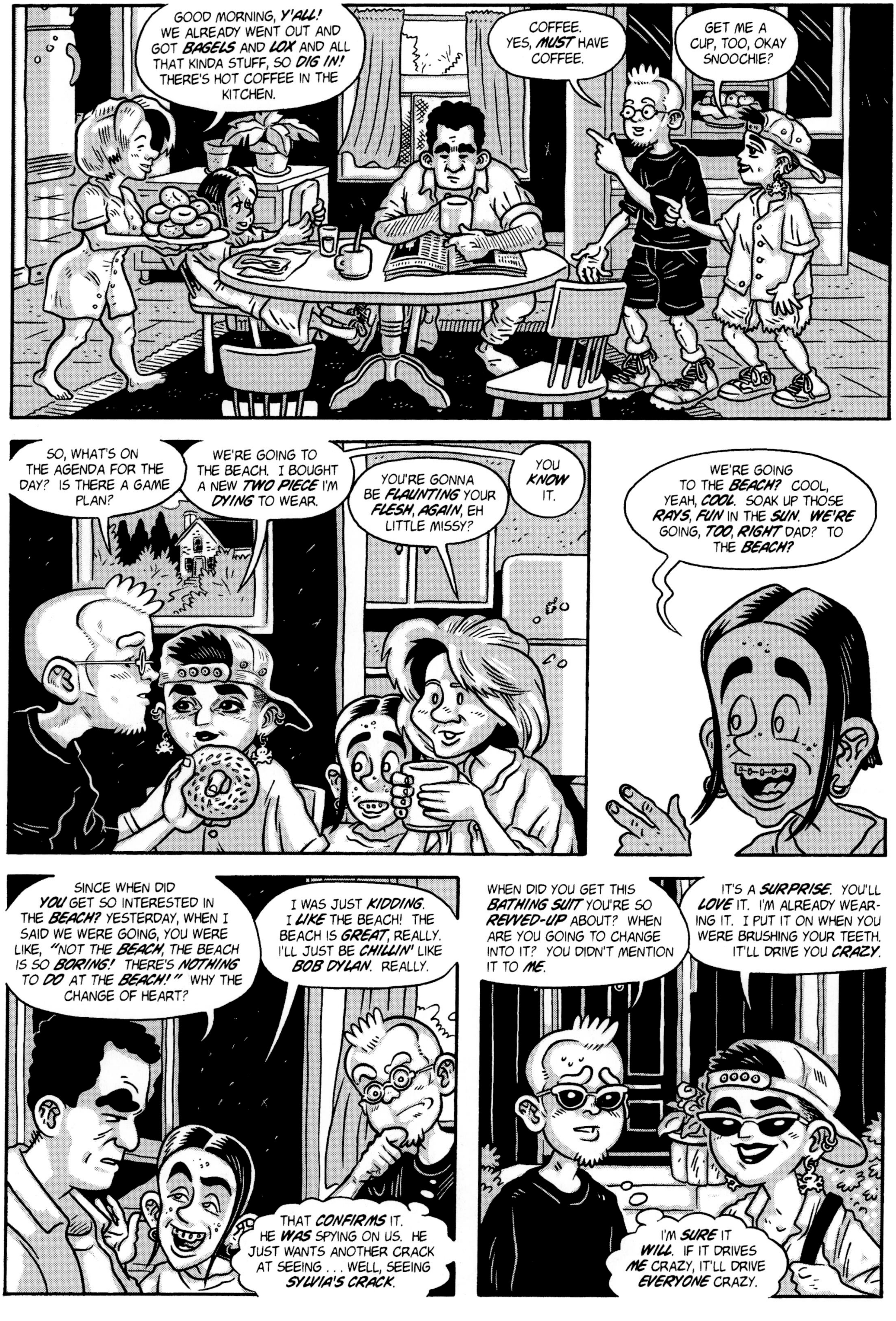

GOOD MORNING, Y'ALL! WE ALREADY WENT OUT AND GOT BAGELS AND LOX AND ALL THAT KINDA STUFF, SO DIG IN! THERE'S HOT COFFEE IN THE KITCHEN.
COFFEE. YES, MUST HAVE COFFEE.
GET ME A CUP, TOO, OKAY SNOOCHIE?
SO, WHAT'S ON THE AGENDA FOR THE DAY? IS THERE A GAME PLAN?
WE'RE GOING TO THE BEACH. I BOUGHT A NEW TWO PIECE I'M DYING TO WEAR.
YOU'RE GONNA BE FLAUNTING YOUR FLESH, AGAIN, EH LITTLE MISSY?
YOU KNOW IT.
WE'RE GOING TO THE BEACH? COOL, YEAH, COOL. SOAK UP THOSE RAYS, FUN IN THE SUN. WE'RE GOING, TOO, RIGHT DAD? TO THE BEACH?
SINCE WHEN DID YOU GET SO INTERESTED IN THE BEACH? YESTERDAY, WHEN I SAID WE WERE GOING, YOU WERE LIKE, "NOT THE BEACH, THE BEACH IS SO BORING! THERE'S NOTHING TO DO AT THE BEACH!" WHY THE CHANGE OF HEART?
I WAS JUST KIDDING. I LIKE THE BEACH! THE BEACH IS GREAT, REALLY. I'LL JUST BE CHILLIN' LIKE BOB DYLAN. REALLY.
THAT CONFIRMS IT. HE WAS SPYING ON US. HE JUST WANTS ANOTHER CRACK AT SEEING . . . WELL, SEEING SYLVIA'S CRACK.
WHEN DID YOU GET THIS BATHING SUIT YOU'RE SO REVVED-UP ABOUT? WHEN ARE YOU GOING TO CHANGE INTO IT? YOU DIDN'T MENTION IT TO ME.
IT'S A SURPRISE. YOU'LL LOVE IT. I'M ALREADY WEARING IT. I PUT IT ON WHEN YOU WERE BRUSHING YOUR TEETH. IT'LL DRIVE YOU CRAZY.
I'M SURE IT WILL. IF IT DRIVES ME CRAZY, IT'LL DRIVE EVERYONE CRAZY.

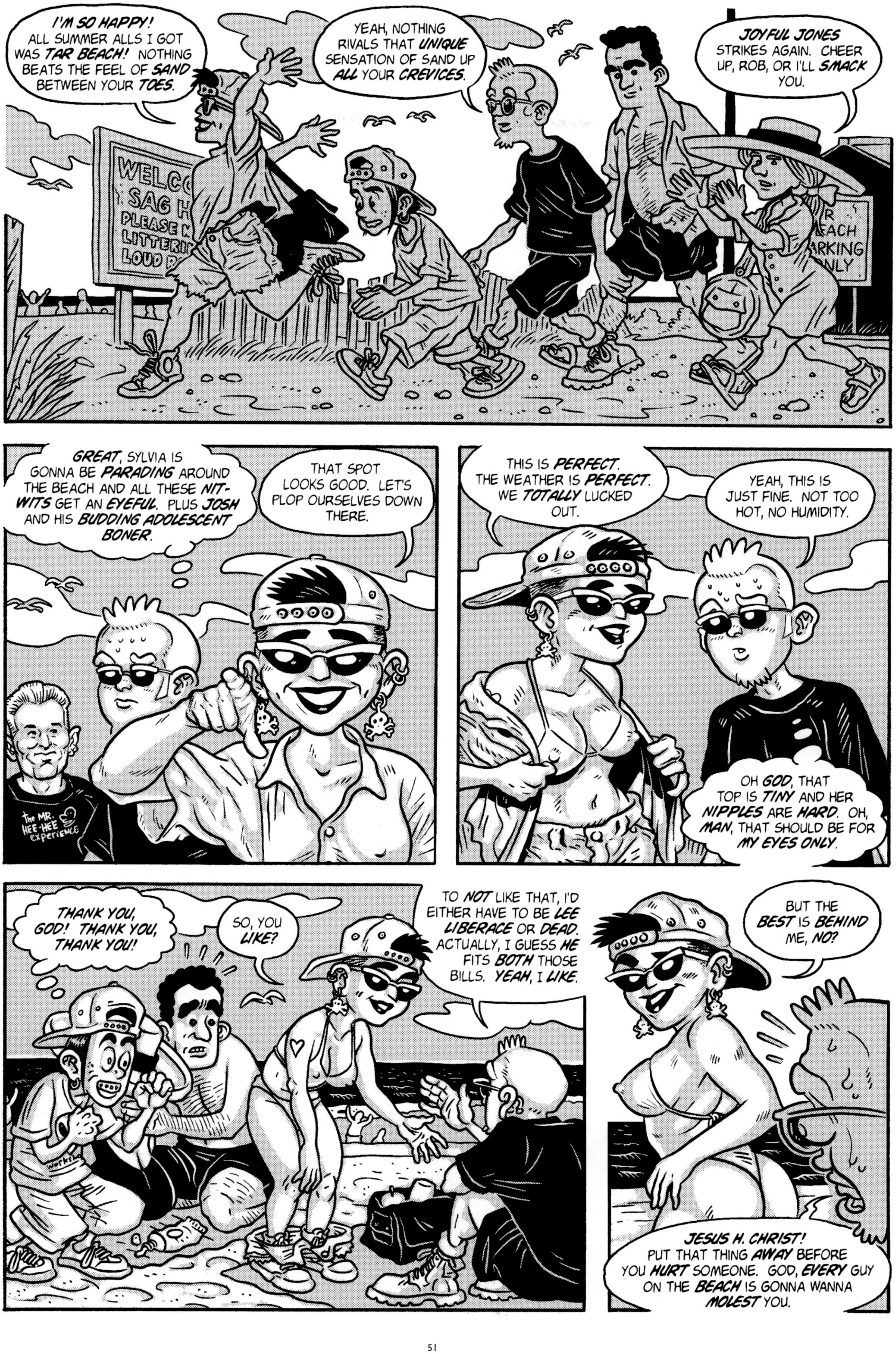
I'M SO HAPPY! ALL SUMMER ALLS I GOT WAS TAR BEACH! NOTHING BEATS THE FEEL OF SAND BETWEEN YOUR TOES.
YEAH, NOTHING RIVALS THAT UNIQUE SENSATION OF SAND UP ALL YOUR CREVICES.
JOYFUL JONES STRIKES AGAIN. CHEER UP, ROB, OR I'LL SMACK YOU.
GREAT, SYLVIA IS GONNA BE PARADING AROUND THE BEACH AND ALL THESE NIT-WITS GET AN EYEFUL. PLUS JOSH AND HIS BUDDING ADOLESCENT BONER.
THAT SPOT LOOKS GOOD. LET'S PLOP OURSELVES DOWN THERE.
The MR. HEE-HEE experience
THIS IS PERFECT. THE WEATHER IS PERFECT. WE TOTALLY LUCKED OUT.
YEAH, THIS IS JUST FINE. NOT TOO HOT, NO HUMIDITY.
OH GOD, THAT TOP IS TINY AND HER NIPPLES ARE HARD. OH, MAN, THAT SHOULD BE FOR MY EYES ONLY.
THANK YOU, GOD! THANK YOU, THANK YOU!
SO, YOU LIKE?
TO NOT LIKE THAT, I'D EITHER HAVE TO BE LEE LIBERACE OR DEAD. ACTUALLY, I GUESS HE FITS BOTH THOSE BILLS. YEAH, I LIKE.
BUT THE BEST IS BEHIND ME, NO?
JESUS H. CHRIST! PUT THAT THING AWAY BEFORE YOU HURT SOMEONE. GOD, EVERY GUY ON THE BEACH IS GONNA WANNA MOLEST YOU.

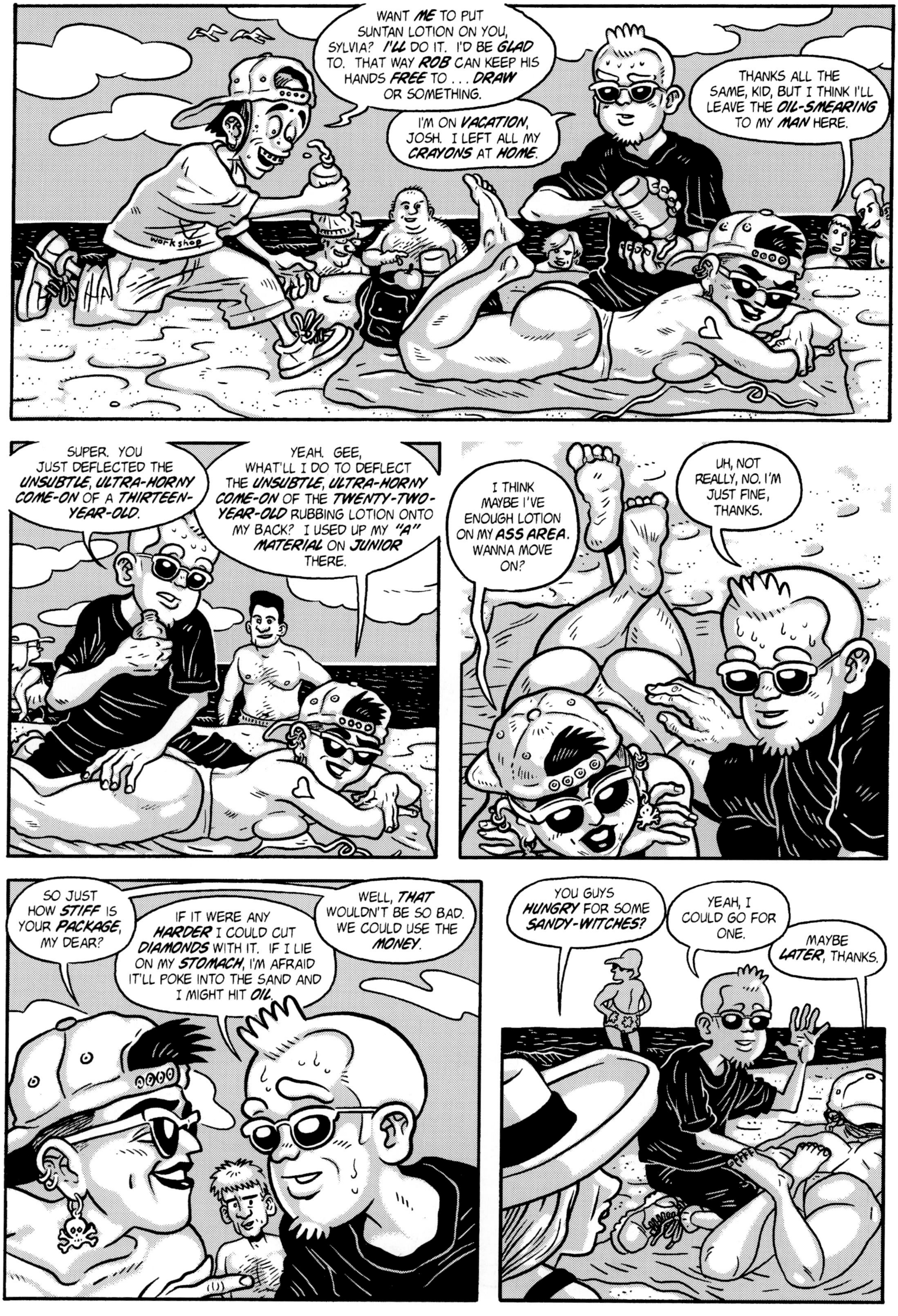
WANT ME TO PUT SUNTAN LOTION ON YOU, SYLVIA? I'LL DO IT. I'D BE GLAD TO. THAT WAY ROB CAN KEEP HIS HANDS FREE TO . . . DRAW OR SOMETHING.
I'M ON VACATION, JOSH. I LEFT ALL MY CRAYONS AT HOME.
THANKS ALL THE SAME, KID, BUT I THINK I'LL LEAVE THE OIL-SMEARING TO MY MAN HERE.
workshop
SUPER. YOU JUST DEFLECTED THE UNSUBTLE, ULTRA-HORNY COME-ON OF A THIRTEEN-YEAR-OLD.
YEAH. GEE, WHAT'LL I DO TO DEFLECT THE UNSUBTLE, ULTRA-HORNY COME-ON OF THE TWENTY-TWO-YEAR-OLD RUBBING LOTION ONTO MY BACK? I USED UP MY "A" MATERIAL ON JUNIOR THERE.
I THINK MAYBE I'VE ENOUGH LOTION ON MY ASS AREA. WANNA MOVE ON?
UH, NOT REALLY, NO. I'M JUST FINE, THANKS.
SO JUST HOW STIFF IS YOUR PACKAGE, MY DEAR?
IF IT WERE ANY HARDER I COULD CUT DIAMONDS WITH IT. IF I LIE ON MY STOMACH, I'M AFRAID IT'LL POKE INTO THE SAND AND I MIGHT HIT OIL.
WELL, THAT WOULDN'T BE SO BAD. WE COULD USE THE MONEY.
YOU GUYS HUNGRY FOR SOME SANDY-WITCHES?
YEAH, I COULD GO FOR ONE.
MAYBE LATER, THANKS.

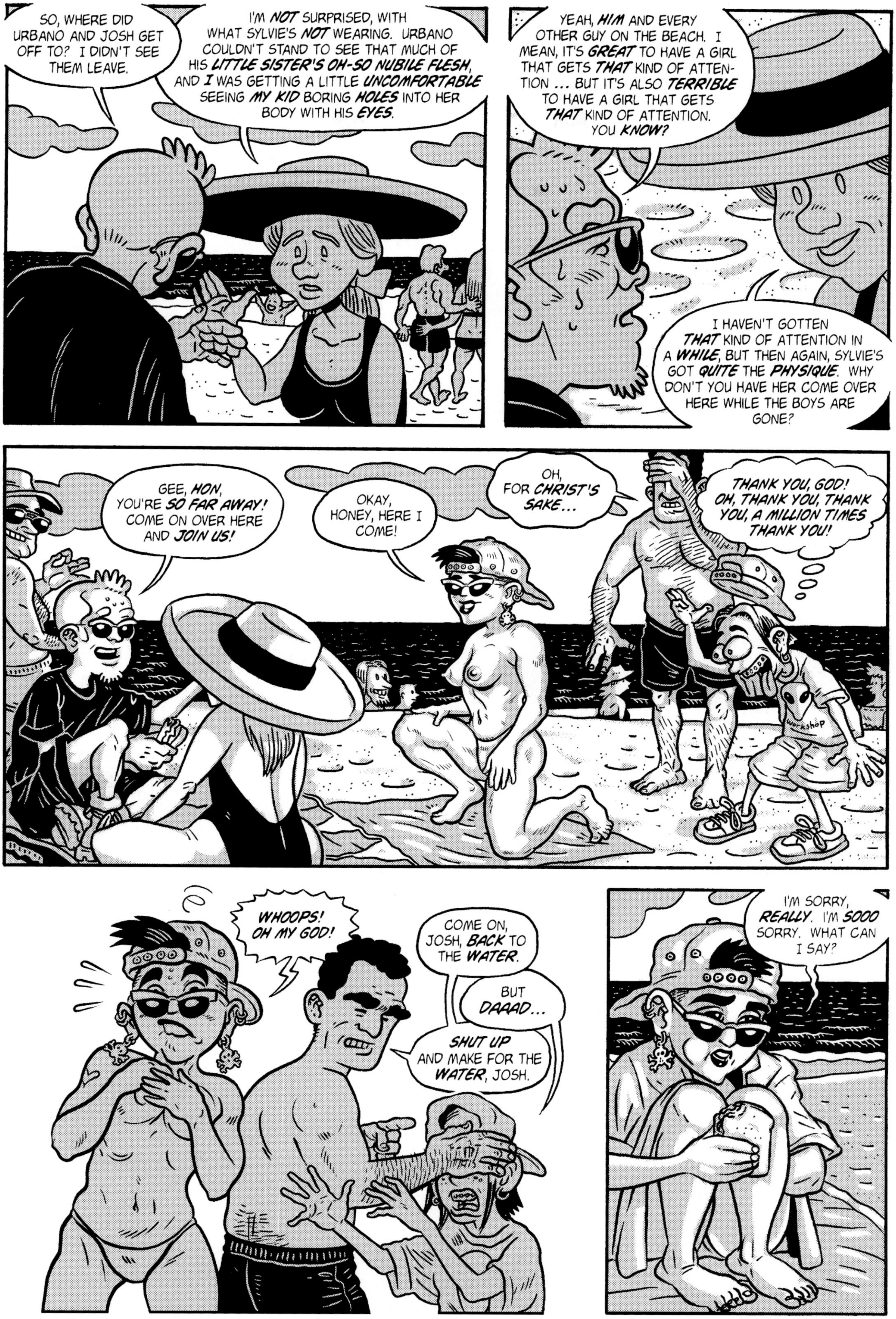
SO, WHERE DID URBANO AND JOSH GET OFF TO? I DIDN'T SEE THEM LEAVE.
I'M NOT SURPRISED, WITH WHAT SYLVIE'S NOT WEARING. URBANO COULDN'T STAND TO SEE THAT MUCH OF HIS LITTLE SISTER'S OH-SO NUBILE FLESH, AND I WAS GETTING A LITTLE UNCOMFORTABLE SEEING MY KID BORING HOLES INTO HER BODY WITH HIS EYES.
YEAH, HIM AND EVERY OTHER GUY ON THE BEACH. I MEAN, IT'S GREAT TO HAVE A GIRL THAT GETS THAT KIND OF ATTENTION ... BUT IT'S ALSO TERRIBLE TO HAVE A GIRL THAT GETS THAT KIND OF ATTENTION. YOU KNOW?
I HAVEN'T GOTTEN THAT KIND OF ATTENTION IN A WHILE, BUT THEN AGAIN, SYLVIE'S GOT QUITE THE PHYSIQUE. WHY DON'T YOU HAVE HER COME OVER HERE WHILE THE BOYS ARE GONE?
GEE, HON, YOU'RE SO FAR AWAY! COME ON OVER HERE AND JOIN US!
OKAY, HONEY, HERE I COME!
OH, FOR CHRIST'S SAKE...
THANK YOU, GOD! OH, THANK YOU, THANK YOU, A MILLION TIMES THANK YOU!
WHOOPS! OH MY GOD!
COME ON, JOSH, BACK TO THE WATER.
BUT DAAAD...
SHUT UP AND MAKE FOR THE WATER, JOSH.
I'M SORRY, REALLY. I'M SOOO SORRY. WHAT CAN I SAY?

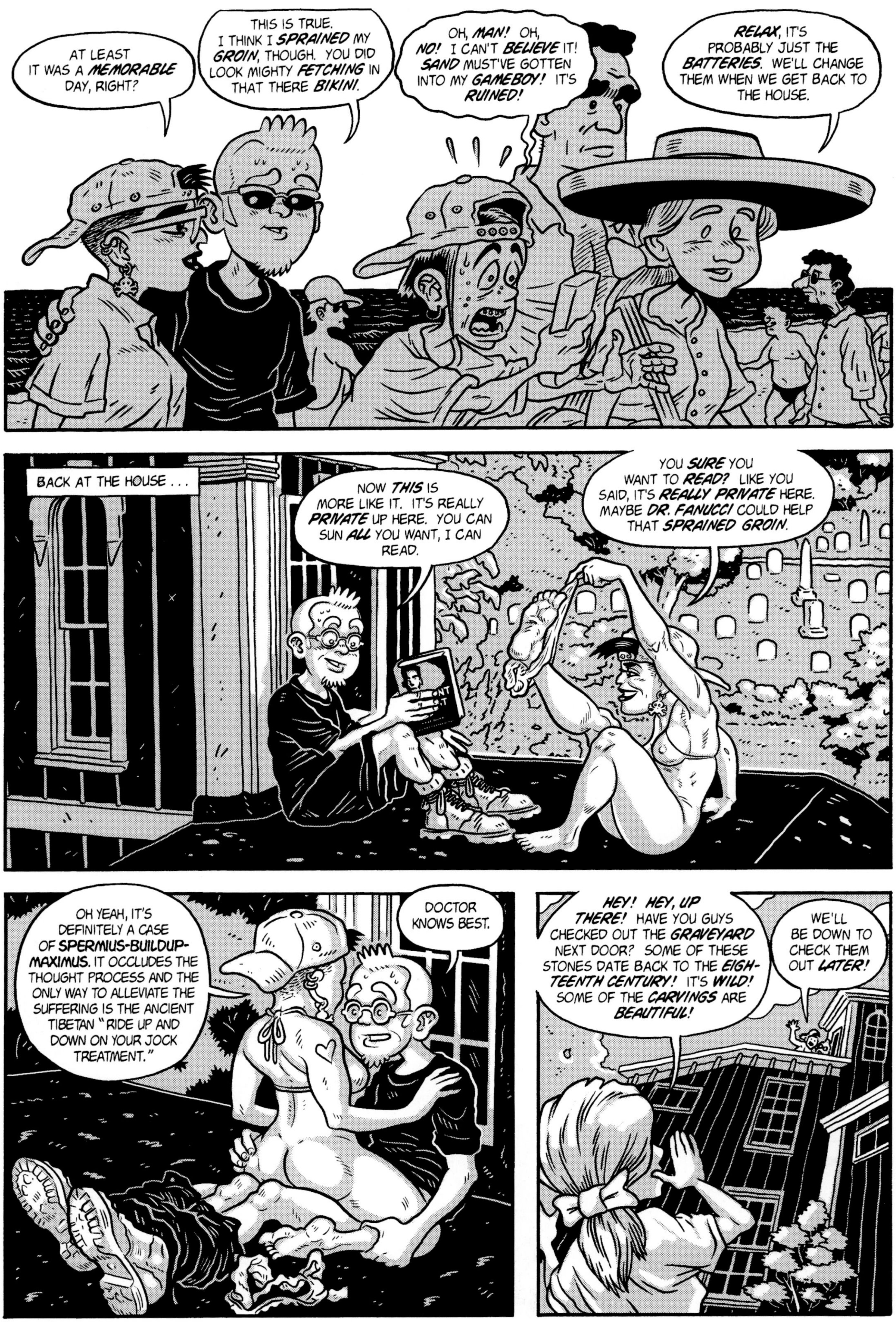
AT LEAST IT WAS A MEMORABLE DAY, RIGHT?
THIS IS TRUE. I THINK I SPRAINED MY GROIN, THOUGH. YOU DID LOOK MIGHTY FETCHING IN THAT THERE BIKINI.
OH, MAN! OH, NO! I CAN'T BELIEVE IT! SAND MUST'VE GOTTEN INTO MY GAMEBOY! IT'S RUINED!
RELAX, IT'S PROBABLY JUST THE BATTERIES. WE'LL CHANGE THEM WHEN WE GET BACK TO THE HOUSE.
BACK AT THE HOUSE . . .
NOW THIS IS MORE LIKE IT. IT'S REALLY PRIVATE UP HERE. YOU CAN SUN ALL YOU WANT, I CAN READ.
YOU SURE YOU WANT TO READ? LIKE YOU SAID, IT'S REALLY PRIVATE HERE. MAYBE DR. FANUCCI COULD HELP THAT SPRAINED GROIN.
OH YEAH, IT'S DEFINITELY A CASE OF SPERMIUS-BUILDUP-MAXIMUS. IT OCCLUDES THE THOUGHT PROCESS AND THE ONLY WAY TO ALLEVIATE THE SUFFERING IS THE ANCIENT TIBETAN "RIDE UP AND DOWN ON YOUR JOCK TREATMENT."
DOCTOR KNOWS BEST.
HEY! HEY, UP THERE! HAVE YOU GUYS CHECKED OUT THE GRAVEYARD NEXT DOOR? SOME OF THESE STONES DATE BACK TO THE EIGHTEENTH CENTURY! IT'S WILD! SOME OF THE CARVINGS ARE BEAUTIFUL!
WE'LL BE DOWN TO CHECK THEM OUT LATER!

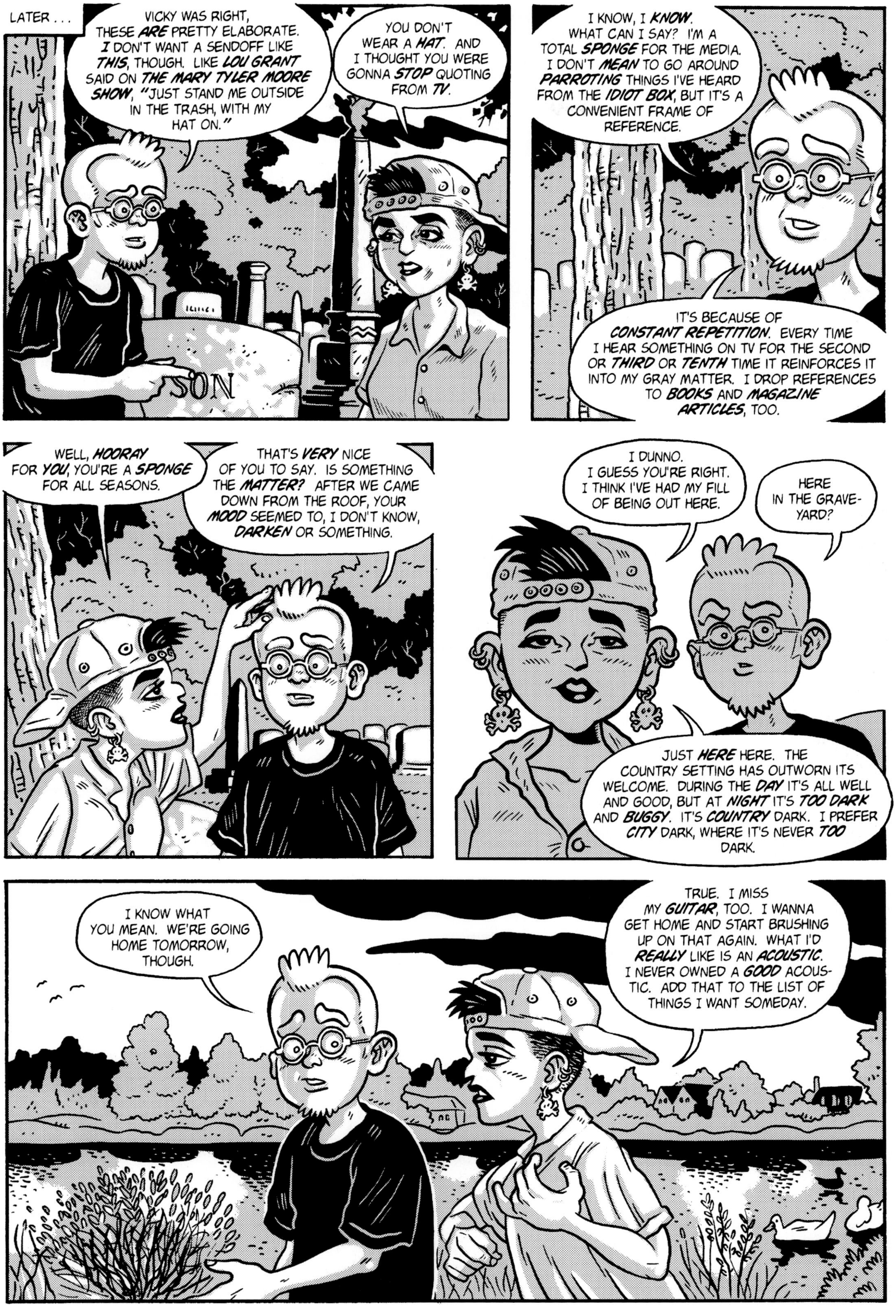
LATER . . .
VICKY WAS RIGHT, THESE ARE PRETTY ELABORATE. I DON'T WANT A SENDOFF LIKE THIS, THOUGH. LIKE LOU GRANT SAID ON THE MARY TYLER MOORE SHOW, "JUST STAND ME OUTSIDE IN THE TRASH, WITH MY HAT ON."
YOU DON'T WEAR A HAT. AND I THOUGHT YOU WERE GONNA STOP QUOTING FROM TV.
SON
I KNOW, I KNOW. WHAT CAN I SAY? I'M A TOTAL SPONGE FOR THE MEDIA. I DON'T MEAN TO GO AROUND PARROTING THINGS I'VE HEARD FROM THE IDIOT BOX, BUT IT'S A CONVENIENT FRAME OF REFERENCE.
IT'S BECAUSE OF CONSTANT REPETITION. EVERY TIME I HEAR SOMETHING ON TV FOR THE SECOND OR THIRD OR TENTH TIME IT REINFORCES IT INTO MY GRAY MATTER. I DROP REFERENCES TO BOOKS AND MAGAZINE ARTICLES, TOO.
WELL, HOORAY FOR YOU, YOU'RE A SPONGE FOR ALL SEASONS.
THAT'S VERY NICE OF YOU TO SAY. IS SOMETHING THE MATTER? AFTER WE CAME DOWN FROM THE ROOF, YOUR MOOD SEEMED TO, I DON'T KNOW, DARKEN OR SOMETHING.
I DUNNO. I GUESS YOU'RE RIGHT. I THINK I'VE HAD MY FILL OF BEING OUT HERE.
HERE IN THE GRAVE-YARD?
JUST HERE HERE. THE COUNTRY SETTING HAS OUTWORN ITS WELCOME. DURING THE DAY IT'S ALL WELL AND GOOD, BUT AT NIGHT IT'S TOO DARK AND BUGGY. IT'S COUNTRY DARK. I PREFER CITY DARK, WHERE IT'S NEVER TOO DARK.
I KNOW WHAT YOU MEAN. WE'RE GOING HOME TOMORROW, THOUGH.
TRUE. I MISS MY GUITAR, TOO. I WANNA GET HOME AND START BRUSHING UP ON THAT AGAIN. WHAT I'D REALLY LIKE IS AN ACOUSTIC. I NEVER OWNED A GOOD ACOUS-TIC. ADD THAT TO THE LIST OF THINGS I WANT SOMEDAY.

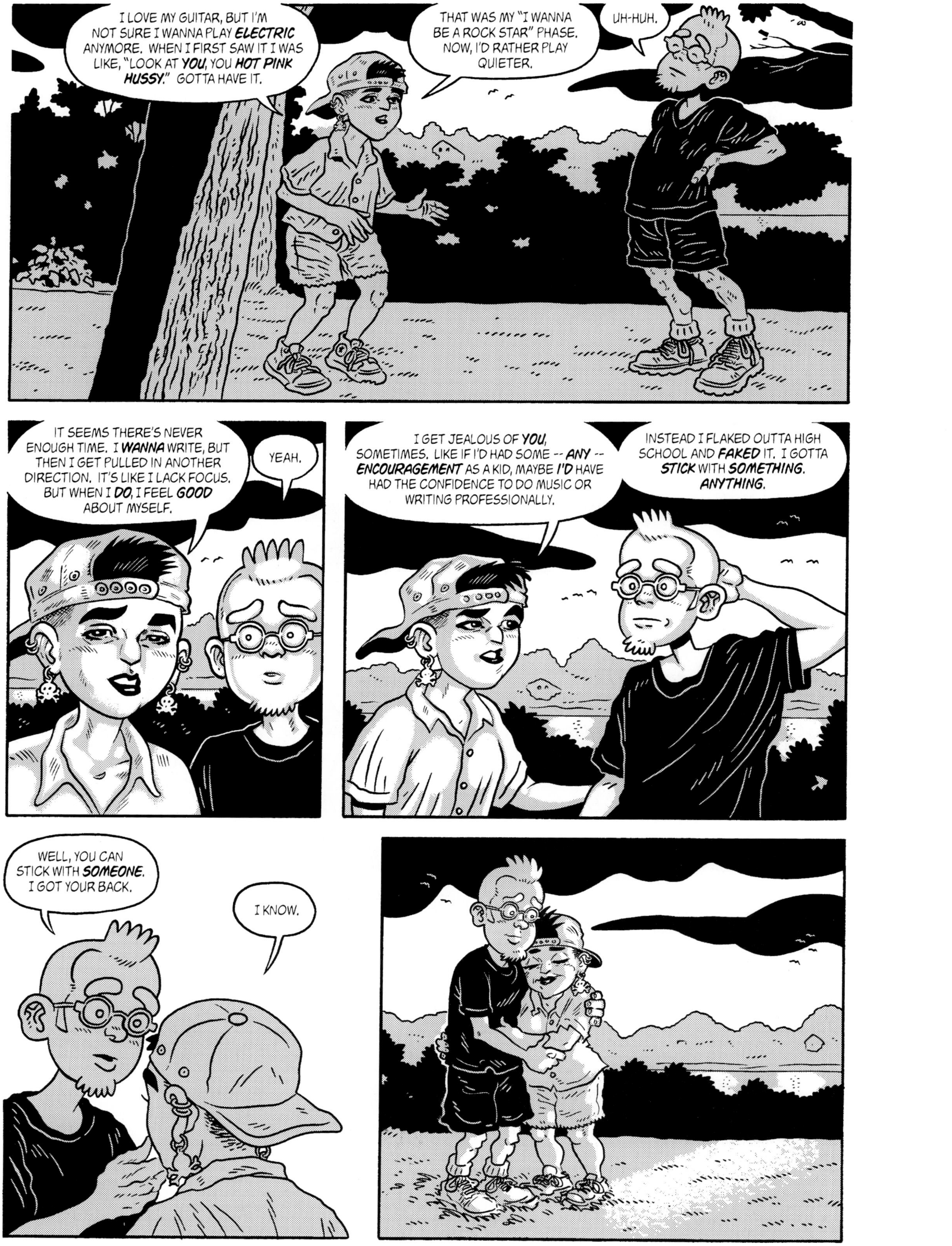
I LOVE MY GUITAR, BUT I'M NOT SURE I WANNA PLAY ELECTRIC ANYMORE. WHEN I FIRST SAW IT I WAS LIKE, "LOOK AT YOU, YOU HOT PINK HUSSY." GOTTA HAVE IT.
THAT WAS MY "I WANNA BE A ROCK STAR" PHASE. NOW, I'D RATHER PLAY QUIETER.
UH-HUH.
IT SEEMS THERE'S NEVER ENOUGH TIME. I WANNA WRITE, BUT THEN I GET PULLED IN ANOTHER DIRECTION. IT'S LIKE I LACK FOCUS. BUT WHEN I DO, I FEEL GOOD ABOUT MYSELF.
YEAH.
I GET JEALOUS OF YOU, SOMETIMES. LIKE IF I'D HAD SOME -- ANY -- ENCOURAGEMENT AS A KID, MAYBE I'D HAVE HAD THE CONFIDENCE TO DO MUSIC OR WRITING PROFESSIONALLY.
INSTEAD I FLAKED OUTTA HIGH SCHOOL AND FAKED IT. I GOTTA STICK WITH SOMETHING. ANYTHING.
WELL, YOU CAN STICK WITH SOMEONE. I GOT YOUR BACK.
I KNOW.

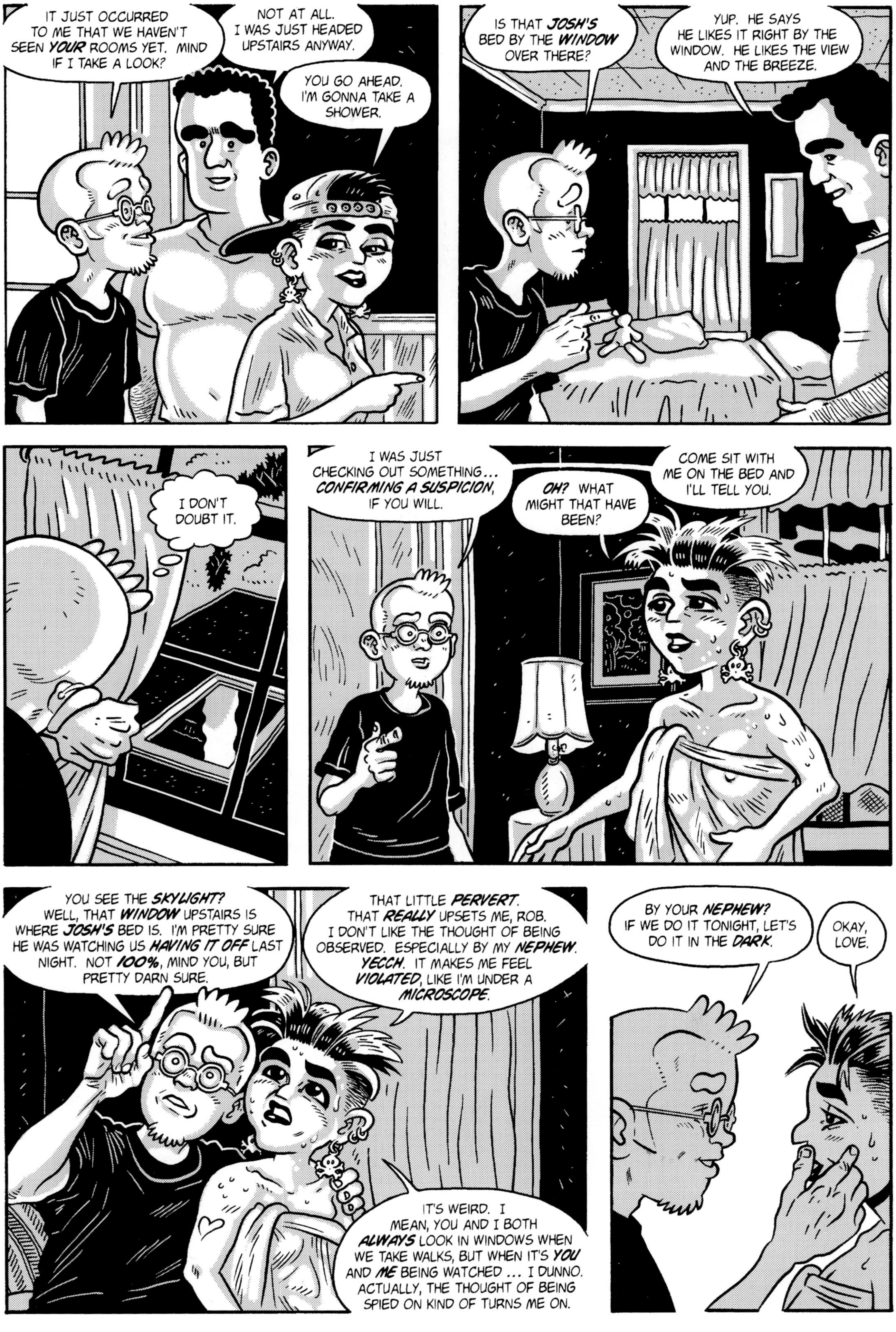
IT JUST OCCURRED TO ME THAT WE HAVEN'T SEEN YOUR ROOMS YET. MIND IF I TAKE A LOOK?
NOT AT ALL. I WAS JUST HEADED UPSTAIRS ANYWAY.
YOU GO AHEAD. I'M GONNA TAKE A SHOWER.
IS THAT JOSH'S BED BY THE WINDOW OVER THERE?
YUP. HE SAYS HE LIKES IT RIGHT BY THE WINDOW. HE LIKES THE VIEW AND THE BREEZE.
I DON'T DOUBT IT.
I WAS JUST CHECKING OUT SOMETHING... CONFIRMING A SUSPICION, IF YOU WILL.
OH? WHAT MIGHT THAT HAVE BEEN?
COME SIT WITH ME ON THE BED AND I'LL TELL YOU.
YOU SEE THE SKYLIGHT? WELL, THAT WINDOW UPSTAIRS IS WHERE JOSH'S BED IS. I'M PRETTY SURE HE WAS WATCHING US HAVING IT OFF LAST NIGHT. NOT 100%, MIND YOU, BUT PRETTY DARN SURE.
THAT LITTLE PERVERT. THAT REALLY UPSETS ME, ROB. I DON'T LIKE THE THOUGHT OF BEING OBSERVED. ESPECIALLY BY MY NEPHEW. YECCH. IT MAKES ME FEEL VIOLATED, LIKE I'M UNDER A MICROSCOPE.
IT'S WEIRD. I MEAN, YOU AND I BOTH ALWAYS LOOK IN WINDOWS WHEN WE TAKE WALKS, BUT WHEN IT'S YOU AND ME BEING WATCHED ... I DUNNO. ACTUALLY, THE THOUGHT OF BEING SPIED ON KIND OF TURNS ME ON.
BY YOUR NEPHEW? IF WE DO IT TONIGHT, LET'S DO IT IN THE DARK.
OKAY, LOVE.

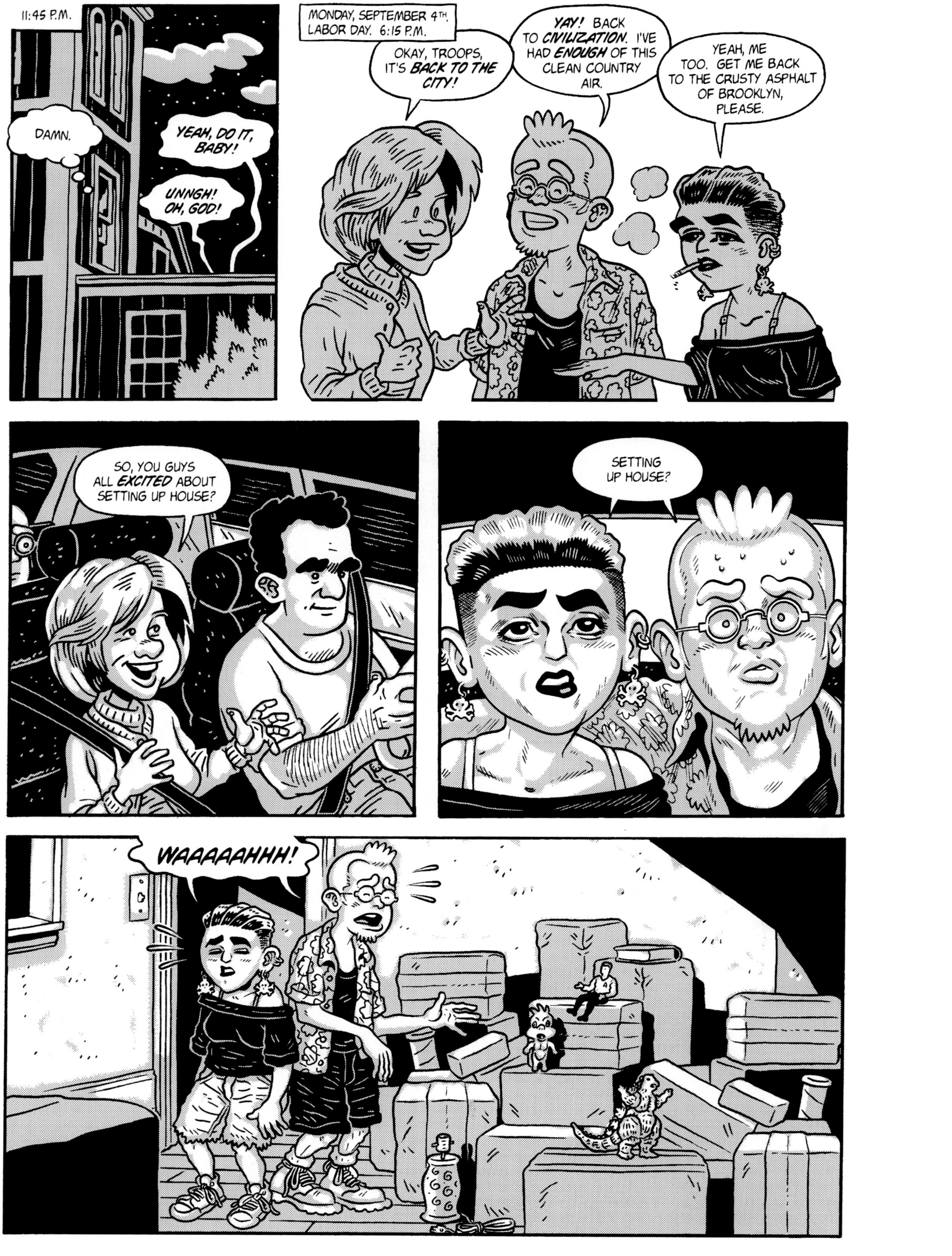
11:45 P.M.
DAMN.
YEAH, DO IT, BABY!
UNNGH! OH, GOD!
MONDAY, SEPTEMBER 4TH. LABOR DAY. 6:15 P.M.
OKAY, TROOPS, IT'S BACK TO THE CITY!
YAY! BACK TO CIVILIZATION. I'VE HAD ENOUGH OF THIS CLEAN COUNTRY AIR.
YEAH, ME TOO. GET ME BACK TO THE CRUSTY ASPHALT OF BROOKLYN, PLEASE.
SO, YOU GUYS ALL EXCITED ABOUT SETTING UP HOUSE?
SETTING UP HOUSE?
WAAAAAHHH!

Chapter Three

GRAVID SITUATION

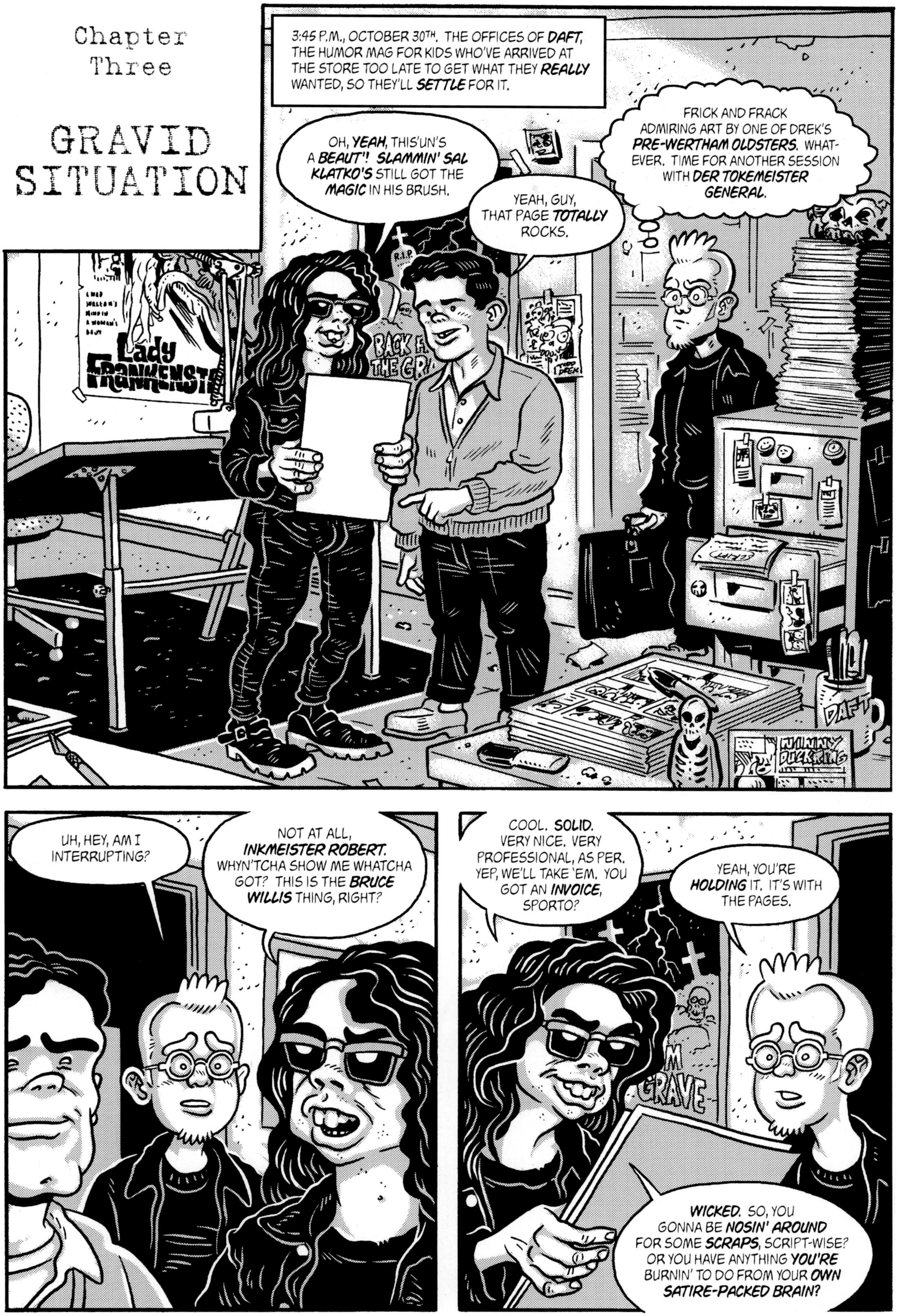

3:45 P.M., OCTOBER 30TH. THE OFFICES OF DAFT, THE HUMOR MAG FOR KIDS WHO'VE ARRIVED AT THE STORE TOO LATE TO GET WHAT THEY REALLY WANTED, SO THEY'LL SETTLE FOR IT.
OH, YEAH, THIS'UN'S A BEAUT'! SLAMMIN' SAL KLATKO'S STILL GOT THE MAGIC IN HIS BRUSH.
YEAH, GUY, THAT PAGE TOTALLY ROCKS.
FRICK AND FRACK ADMIRING ART BY ONE OF DREK'S PRE-WERTHAM OLDSTERS. WHATEVER. TIME FOR ANOTHER SESSION WITH DER TOKEMEISTER GENERAL.
DAFT
UH, HEY, AM I INTERRUPTING?
NOT AT ALL, INKMEISTER ROBERT. WHYN'TCHA SHOW ME WHATCHA GOT? THIS IS THE BRUCE WILLIS THING, RIGHT?
COOL. SOLID. VERY NICE. VERY PROFESSIONAL, AS PER. YEP, WE'LL TAKE 'EM. YOU GOT AN INVOICE, SPORTO?
YEAH, YOU'RE HOLDING IT. IT'S WITH THE PAGES.
GRAVE
WICKED. SO, YOU GONNA BE NOSIN' AROUND FOR SOME SCRAPS, SCRIPT-WISE? OR YOU HAVE ANYTHING YOU'RE BURNIN' TO DO FROM YOUR OWN SATIRE-PACKED BRAIN?

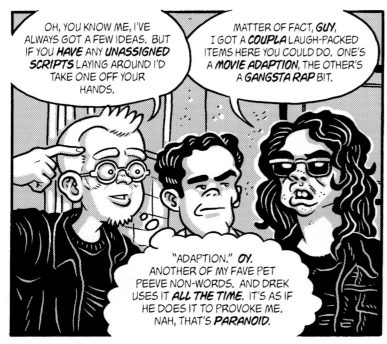

OH, YOU KNOW ME, I'VE ALWAYS GOT A FEW IDEAS. BUT IF YOU **HAVE** ANY **UNASSIGNED SCRIPTS** LAYING AROUND I'D TAKE ONE OFF YOUR HANDS.

MATTER OF FACT, **GUY**, I GOT A **COUPLA** LAUGH-PACKED ITEMS HERE YOU COULD DO. ONE'S A **MOVIE ADAPTION**, THE OTHER'S A **GANGSTA RAP** BIT.

"ADAPTION." **OY**. ANOTHER OF MY FAVE PET PEEVE NON-WORDS. AND DREK USES IT **ALL THE TIME**. IT'S AS IF HE DOES IT TO PROVOKE ME. NAH, THAT'S **PARANOID**.

"'YO, G-MONEY, IT'S D.J. DAFFY DAFT COMIN' **AT CHOO**!' 'GESEUNDHEIT.'" AI-YI-YI, TODD. WHICH OF YOUR **GERIATRIC SCRIBES** PENNED THIS?

WHA'?

FOR YOUR **4-1-1** IT WAS WRITTEN BY **GOLDEN AGE LEGEND SOL GOLDENBERG**. HE'S **STILL** GOT HIS FINGER ON THE PULSE OF AMERICA'S YOUTH CULTURE.

HEY, **LOOKIT**, I GOTTA **IT-SPLAY** AN' MAKE A RENDEZVOUS WITH SOMEONE AT MY **CRIB**.

YEAH, WE GOTTA GO SEE A DOG ABOUT A MAN, Y'DIG?

UH, SURE. LISTEN, THOUGH, ONE THING. I STILL HAVEN'T BEEN PAID FOR THE LAST STUFF, AND I WAS WONDERING --

CALM YOUR **MANTIES**, TH' **CHECK'S IN TH' MAIL**. CATCH YA LATER. CALL ME. HEY, YOU KNOW THE WAY OUT, MAN. **CIAO**! GOTTA **GO GO GO**!

GOTTA GET THERE **QUICK**, MAN. THAT BALE OF WICKED **HIGH-GRADE MARIJAHOOBIE** IS DUE AT THREE PEE-EM!

NO DUH! **HASTE**, BRER DREK, **HASTE**!

IT'S KIND OF TOUCHING THAT DREK KEEPS USING THESE OUT OF TOUCH DINOSAURS. "**MOSH** PIT? MORE LIKE **MESHUGGA** PIT." **YES**, BECAUSE THE KIDS **LOVE** YIDDISH PUNS. KURTZMAN WAS A **GENIUS**, BUT HE HAS A **LOT** TO ANSWER FOR.

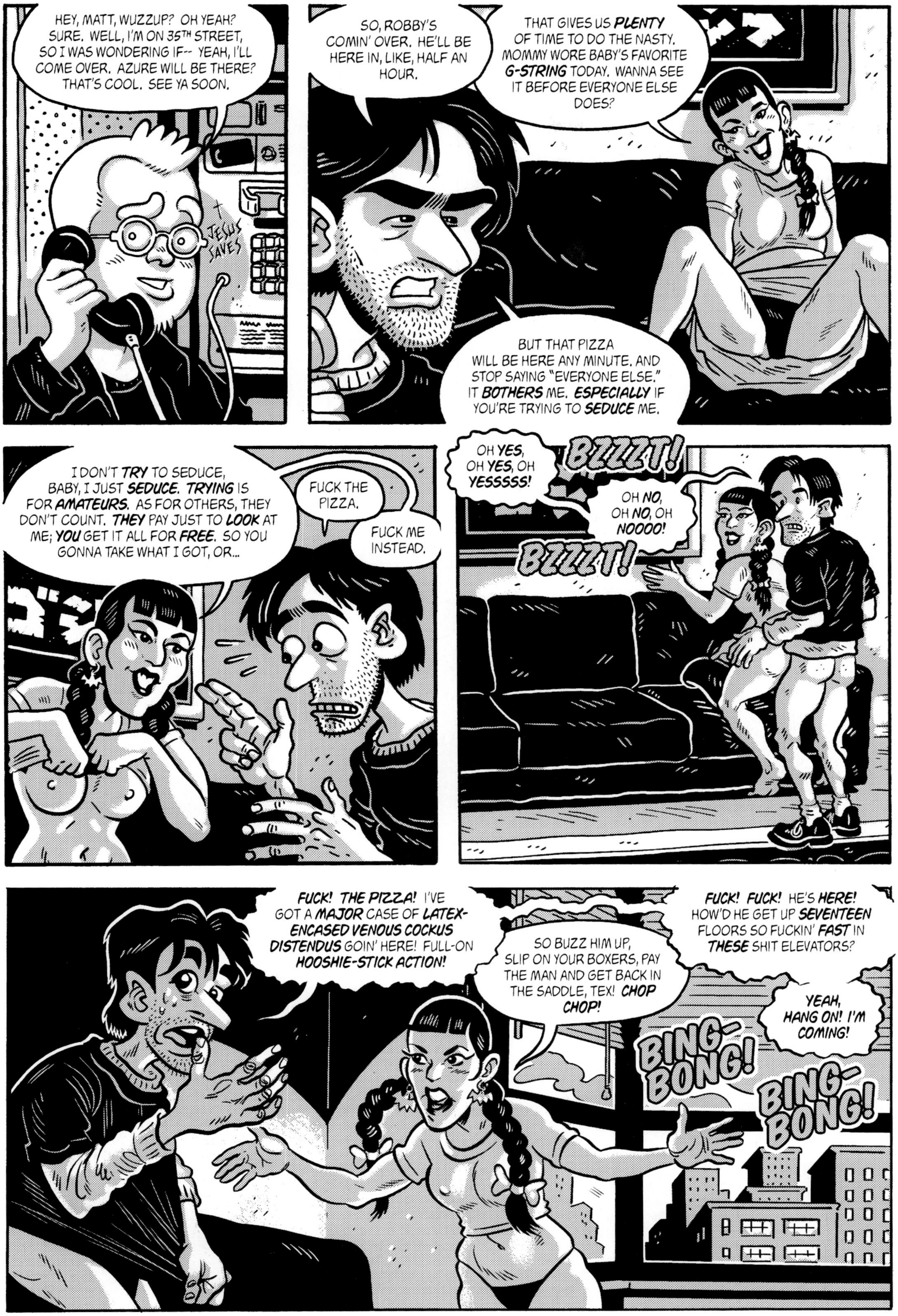
HEY, MATT, WUZZUP? OH YEAH? SURE. WELL, I'M ON 35TH STREET, SO I WAS WONDERING IF-- YEAH, I'LL COME OVER. AZURE WILL BE THERE? THAT'S COOL. SEE YA SOON.
JESUS SAVES
SO, ROBBY'S COMIN' OVER. HE'LL BE HERE IN, LIKE, HALF AN HOUR.
THAT GIVES US PLENTY OF TIME TO DO THE NASTY. MOMMY WORE BABY'S FAVORITE G-STRING TODAY. WANNA SEE IT BEFORE EVERYONE ELSE DOES?
BUT THAT PIZZA WILL BE HERE ANY MINUTE. AND STOP SAYING "EVERYONE ELSE." IT BOTHERS ME. ESPECIALLY IF YOU'RE TRYING TO SEDUCE ME.
I DON'T TRY TO SEDUCE, BABY, I JUST SEDUCE. TRYING IS FOR AMATEURS. AS FOR OTHERS, THEY DON'T COUNT. THEY PAY JUST TO LOOK AT ME; YOU GET IT ALL FOR FREE. SO YOU GONNA TAKE WHAT I GOT, OR...
FUCK THE PIZZA.
FUCK ME INSTEAD.
OH YES, OH YES, OH YESSSSS!
BZZZZT!
OH NO, OH NO, OH NOOOO!
BZZZZT!
FUCK! THE PIZZA! I'VE GOT A MAJOR CASE OF LATEX-ENCASED VENOUS COCKUS DISTENDUS GOIN' HERE! FULL-ON HOOSHIE-STICK ACTION!
SO BUZZ HIM UP, SLIP ON YOUR BOXERS, PAY THE MAN AND GET BACK IN THE SADDLE, TEX! CHOP CHOP!
FUCK! FUCK! HE'S HERE! HOW'D HE GET UP SEVENTEEN FLOORS SO FUCKIN' FAST IN THESE SHIT ELEVATORS?
YEAH, HANG ON! I'M COMING!
BING-BONG!
BING-BONG!

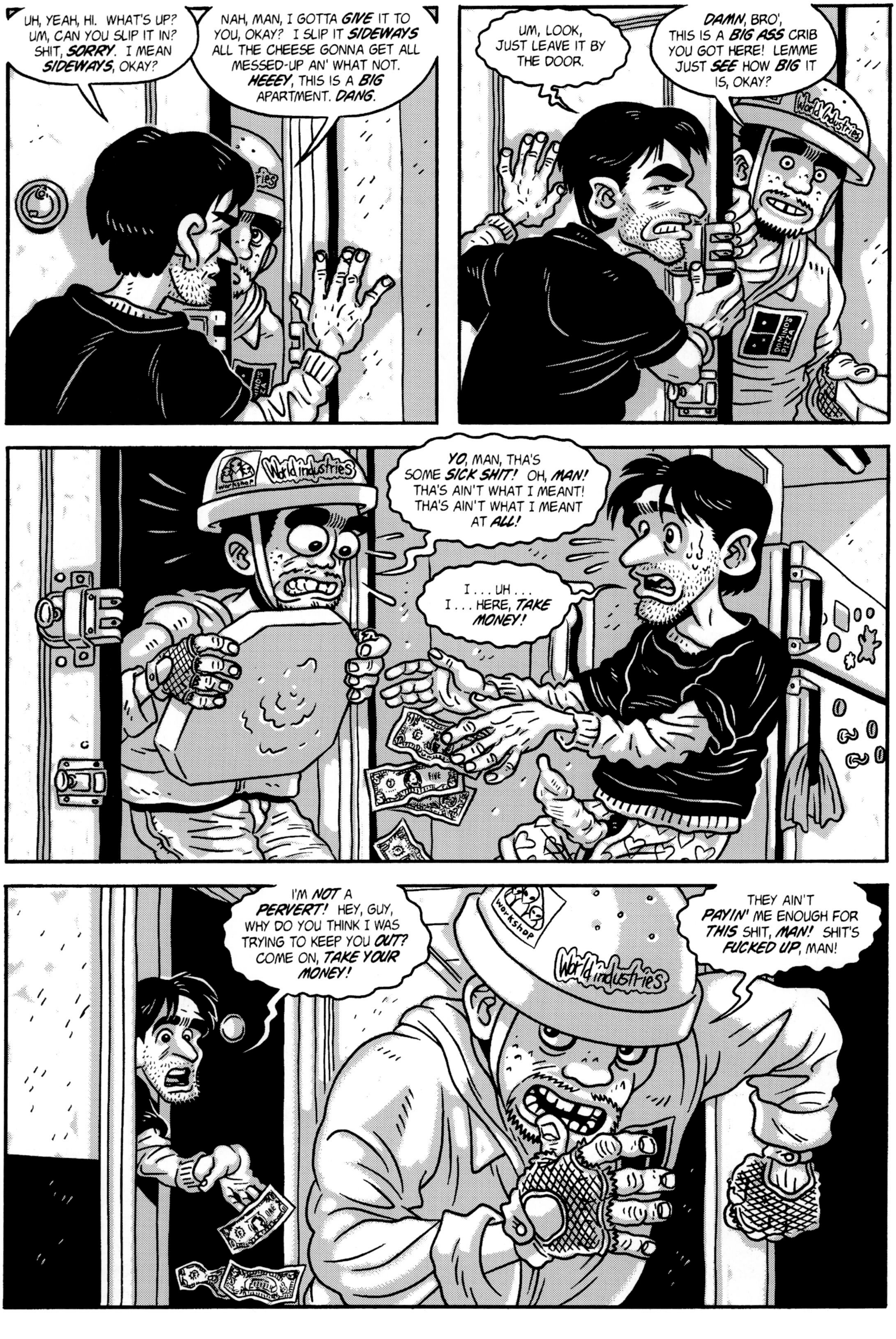
UH, YEAH, HI. WHAT'S UP? UM, CAN YOU SLIP IT IN? SHIT, SORRY. I MEAN SIDEWAYS, OKAY?
NAH, MAN, I GOTTA GIVE IT TO YOU, OKAY? I SLIP IT SIDEWAYS ALL THE CHEESE GONNA GET ALL MESSED-UP AN' WHAT NOT. HEEEY, THIS IS A BIG APARTMENT. DANG.
UM, LOOK, JUST LEAVE IT BY THE DOOR.
DAMN, BRO', THIS IS A BIG ASS CRIB YOU GOT HERE! LEMME JUST SEE HOW BIG IT IS, OKAY?
YO, MAN, THA'S SOME SICK SHIT! OH, MAN! THA'S AIN'T WHAT I MEANT! THA'S AIN'T WHAT I MEANT AT ALL!
I . . . UH . . . I . . . HERE, TAKE MONEY!
I'M NOT A PERVERT! HEY, GUY, WHY DO YOU THINK I WAS TRYING TO KEEP YOU OUT? COME ON, TAKE YOUR MONEY!
THEY AIN'T PAYIN' ME ENOUGH FOR THIS SHIT, MAN! SHIT'S FUCKED UP, MAN!

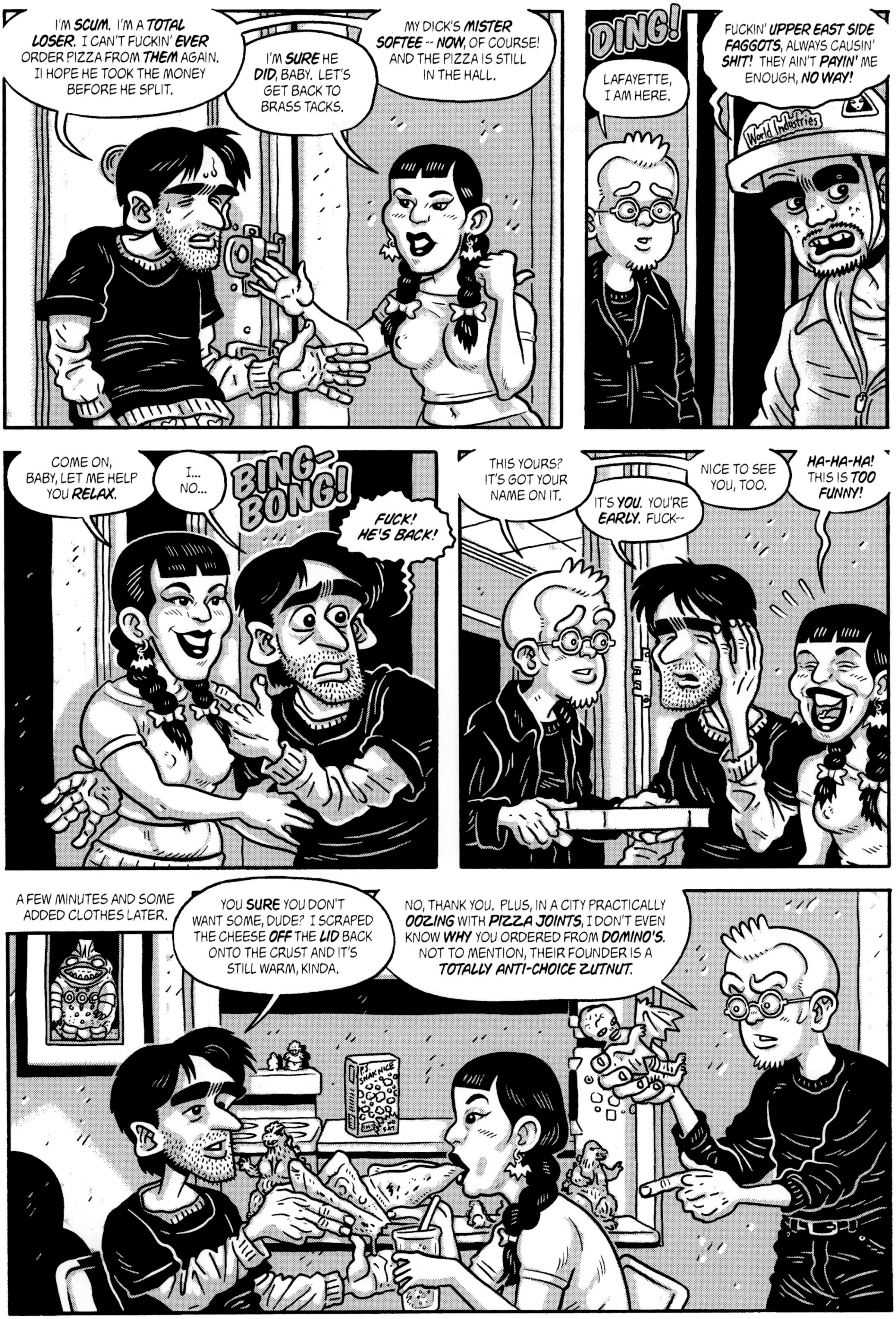
I'M SCUM. I'M A TOTAL LOSER. I CAN'T FUCKIN' EVER ORDER PIZZA FROM THEM AGAIN. I HOPE HE TOOK THE MONEY BEFORE HE SPLIT.
I'M SURE HE DID, BABY. LET'S GET BACK TO BRASS TACKS.
MY DICK'S MISTER SOFTEE -- NOW, OF COURSE! AND THE PIZZA IS STILL IN THE HALL.
DING!
LAFAYETTE, I AM HERE.
FUCKIN' UPPER EAST SIDE FAGGOTS, ALWAYS CAUSIN' SHIT! THEY AIN'T PAYIN' ME ENOUGH, NO WAY!
World Industries
COME ON, BABY, LET ME HELP YOU RELAX.
I... NO...
BING-BONG!
FUCK! HE'S BACK!
THIS YOURS? IT'S GOT YOUR NAME ON IT.
IT'S YOU. YOU'RE EARLY. FUCK--
NICE TO SEE YOU, TOO.
HA-HA-HA! THIS IS TOO FUNNY!
A FEW MINUTES AND SOME ADDED CLOTHES LATER.
YOU SURE YOU DON'T WANT SOME, DUDE? I SCRAPED THE CHEESE OFF THE LID BACK ONTO THE CRUST AND IT'S STILL WARM, KINDA.
NO, THANK YOU. PLUS, IN A CITY PRACTICALLY OOZING WITH PIZZA JOINTS, I DON'T EVEN KNOW WHY YOU ORDERED FROM DOMINO'S. NOT TO MENTION, THEIR FOUNDER IS A TOTALLY ANTI-CHOICE ZUTNUT.
P.J. SNAK NICE

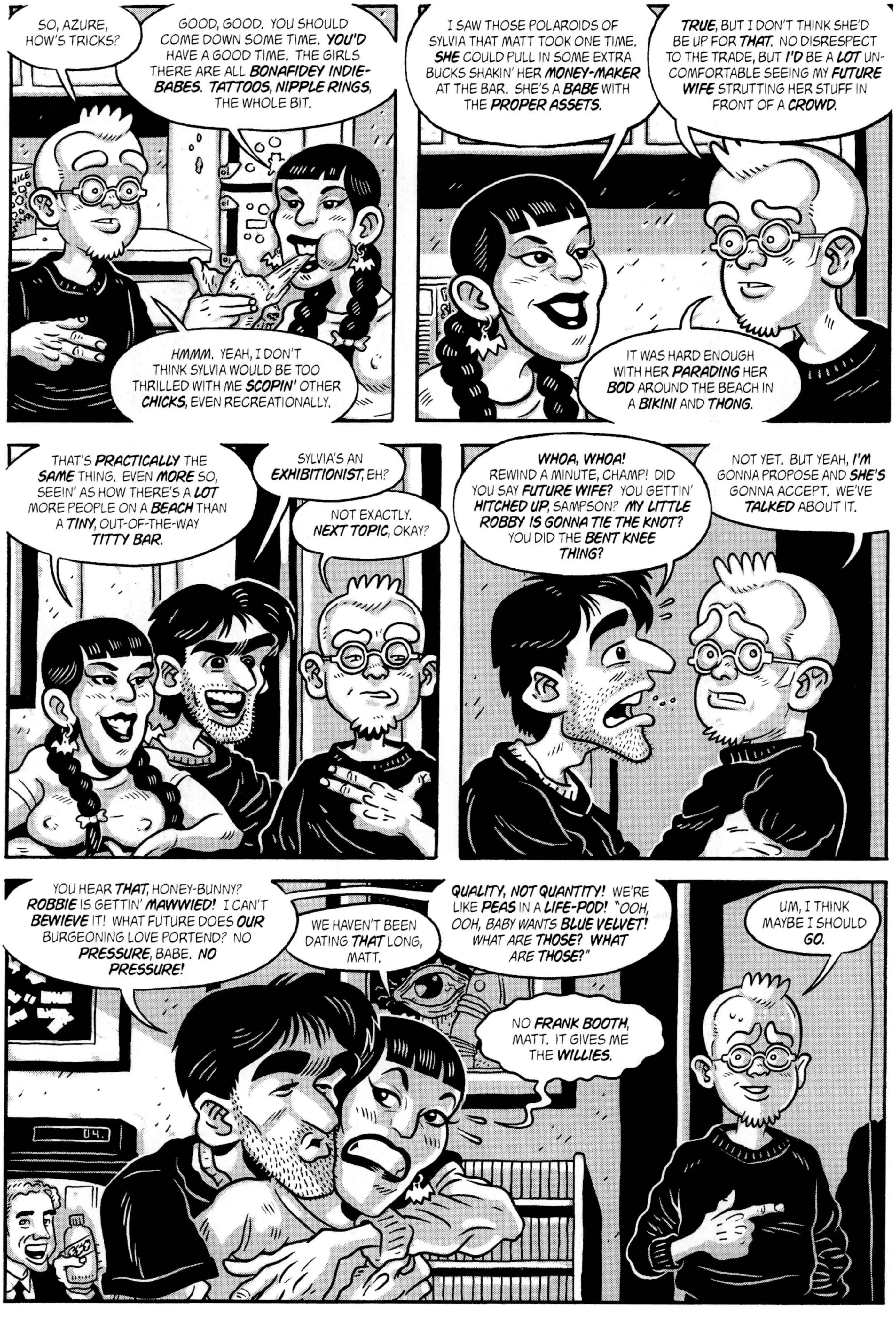
SO, AZURE, HOW'S TRICKS?
GOOD, GOOD. YOU SHOULD COME DOWN SOME TIME. YOU'D HAVE A GOOD TIME. THE GIRLS THERE ARE ALL BONAFIDEY INDIE-BABES. TATTOOS, NIPPLE RINGS, THE WHOLE BIT.
HMMM. YEAH, I DON'T THINK SYLVIA WOULD BE TOO THRILLED WITH ME SCOPIN' OTHER CHICKS, EVEN RECREATIONALLY.
I SAW THOSE POLAROIDS OF SYLVIA THAT MATT TOOK ONE TIME. SHE COULD PULL IN SOME EXTRA BUCKS SHAKIN' HER MONEY-MAKER AT THE BAR. SHE'S A BABE WITH THE PROPER ASSETS.
TRUE, BUT I DON'T THINK SHE'D BE UP FOR THAT. NO DISRESPECT TO THE TRADE, BUT I'D BE A LOT UN-COMFORTABLE SEEING MY FUTURE WIFE STRUTTING HER STUFF IN FRONT OF A CROWD.
IT WAS HARD ENOUGH WITH HER PARADING HER BOD AROUND THE BEACH IN A BIKINI AND THONG.
THAT'S PRACTICALLY THE SAME THING. EVEN MORE SO, SEEIN' AS HOW THERE'S A LOT MORE PEOPLE ON A BEACH THAN A TINY, OUT-OF-THE-WAY TITTY BAR.
SYLVIA'S AN EXHIBITIONIST, EH?
NOT EXACTLY. NEXT TOPIC, OKAY?
WHOA, WHOA! REWIND A MINUTE, CHAMP! DID YOU SAY FUTURE WIFE? YOU GETTIN' HITCHED UP, SAMPSON? MY LITTLE ROBBY IS GONNA TIE THE KNOT? YOU DID THE BENT KNEE THING?
NOT YET. BUT YEAH, I'M GONNA PROPOSE AND SHE'S GONNA ACCEPT. WE'VE TALKED ABOUT IT.
YOU HEAR THAT, HONEY-BUNNY? ROBBIE IS GETTIN' MAWWIED! I CAN'T BEWIEVE IT! WHAT FUTURE DOES OUR BURGEONING LOVE PORTEND? NO PRESSURE, BABE. NO PRESSURE!
WE HAVEN'T BEEN DATING THAT LONG, MATT.
QUALITY, NOT QUANTITY! WE'RE LIKE PEAS IN A LIFE-POD! "OOH, OOH, BABY WANTS BLUE VELVET! WHAT ARE THOSE? WHAT ARE THOSE?"
NO FRANK BOOTH, MATT. IT GIVES ME THE WILLIES.
UM, I THINK MAYBE I SHOULD GO.

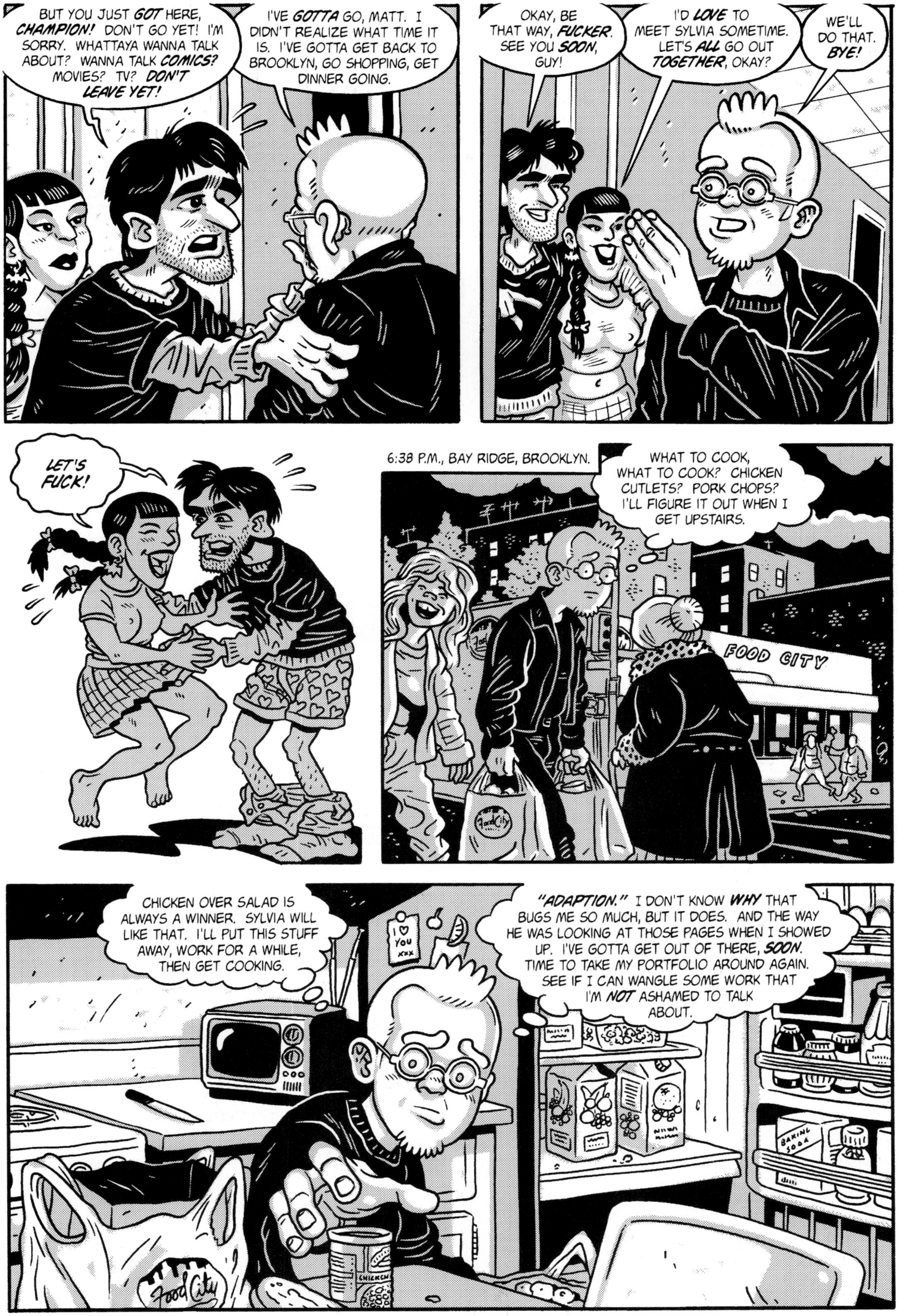
BUT YOU JUST GOT HERE, CHAMPION! DON'T GO YET! I'M SORRY. WHATTAYA WANNA TALK ABOUT? WANNA TALK COMICS? MOVIES? TV? DON'T LEAVE YET!
I'VE GOTTA GO, MATT. I DIDN'T REALIZE WHAT TIME IT IS. I'VE GOTTA GET BACK TO BROOKLYN, GO SHOPPING, GET DINNER GOING.
OKAY, BE THAT WAY, FUCKER. SEE YOU SOON, GUY!
I'D LOVE TO MEET SYLVIA SOMETIME. LET'S ALL GO OUT TOGETHER, OKAY?
WE'LL DO THAT. BYE!
LET'S FUCK!
6:38 P.M., BAY RIDGE, BROOKLYN.
WHAT TO COOK, WHAT TO COOK? CHICKEN CUTLETS? PORK CHOPS? I'LL FIGURE IT OUT WHEN I GET UPSTAIRS.
FOOD CITY
CHICKEN OVER SALAD IS ALWAYS A WINNER. SYLVIA WILL LIKE THAT. I'LL PUT THIS STUFF AWAY, WORK FOR A WHILE, THEN GET COOKING.
"ADAPTION." I DON'T KNOW WHY THAT BUGS ME SO MUCH, BUT IT DOES. AND THE WAY HE WAS LOOKING AT THOSE PAGES WHEN I SHOWED UP. I'VE GOTTA GET OUT OF THERE, SOON. TIME TO TAKE MY PORTFOLIO AROUND AGAIN. SEE IF I CAN WANGLE SOME WORK THAT I'M NOT ASHAMED TO TALK ABOUT.
I ♡ YOU XXX
BAKING SODA
Food City

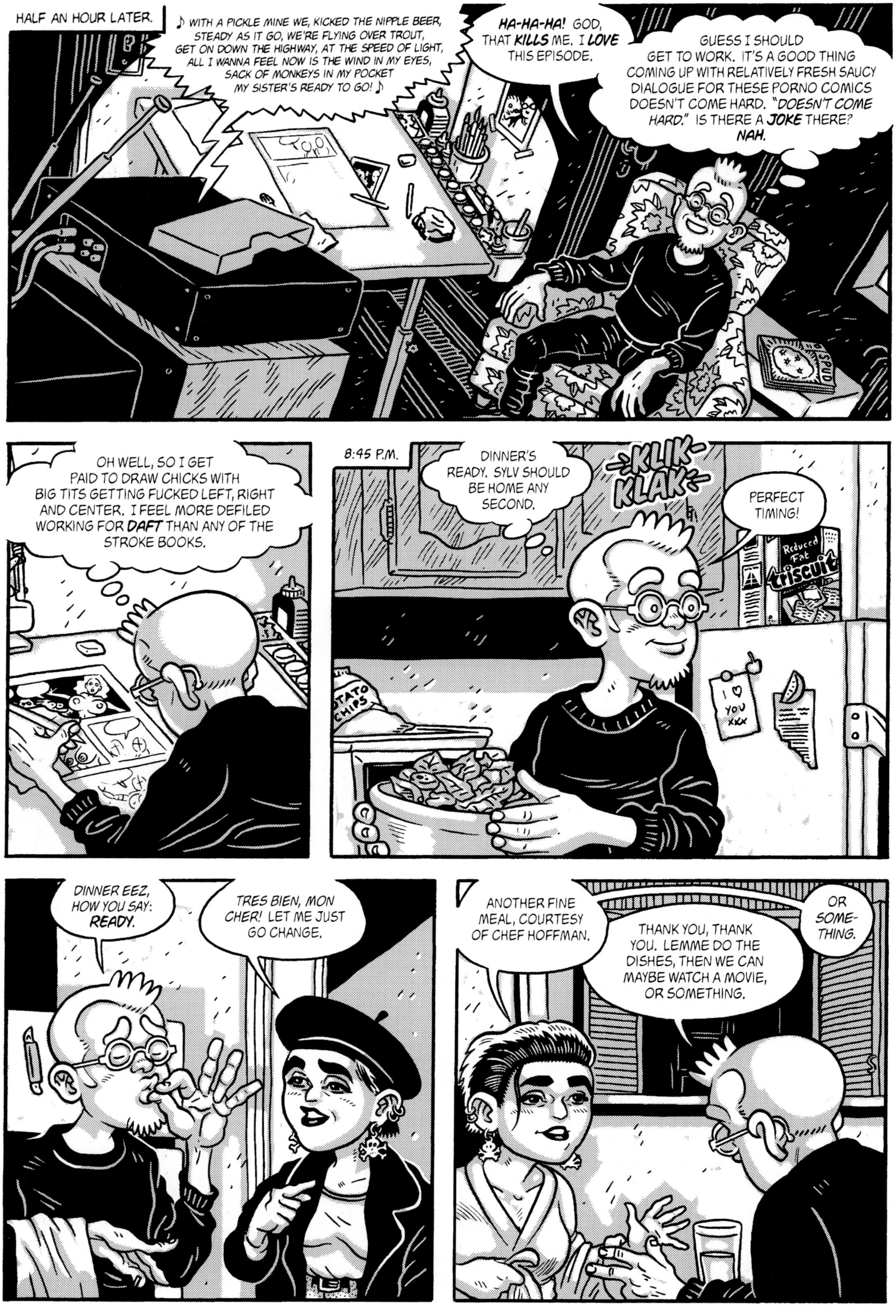
HALF AN HOUR LATER.
♪ WITH A PICKLE MINE WE, KICKED THE NIPPLE BEER, STEADY AS IT GO, WE'RE FLYING OVER TROUT, GET ON DOWN THE HIGHWAY, AT THE SPEED OF LIGHT, ALL I WANNA FEEL NOW IS THE WIND IN MY EYES, SACK OF MONKEYS IN MY POCKET MY SISTER'S READY TO GO! ♪
HA-HA-HA! GOD, THAT KILLS ME. I LOVE THIS EPISODE.
GUESS I SHOULD GET TO WORK. IT'S A GOOD THING COMING UP WITH RELATIVELY FRESH SAUCY DIALOGUE FOR THESE PORNO COMICS DOESN'T COME HARD. "DOESN'T COME HARD." IS THERE A JOKE THERE? NAH.
SPUD
OH WELL, SO I GET PAID TO DRAW CHICKS WITH BIG TITS GETTING FUCKED LEFT, RIGHT AND CENTER. I FEEL MORE DEFILED WORKING FOR DAFT THAN ANY OF THE STROKE BOOKS.
8:45 P.M.
DINNER'S READY. SYLV SHOULD BE HOME ANY SECOND.
KLIK KLAK
PERFECT TIMING!
Reduced Fat Triscuit
POTATO CHIPS
I ♡ YOU XXX
DINNER EEZ, HOW YOU SAY: READY.
TRES BIEN, MON CHER! LET ME JUST GO CHANGE.
ANOTHER FINE MEAL, COURTESY OF CHEF HOFFMAN.
THANK YOU, THANK YOU. LEMME DO THE DISHES, THEN WE CAN MAYBE WATCH A MOVIE, OR SOMETHING.
OR SOME-THING.

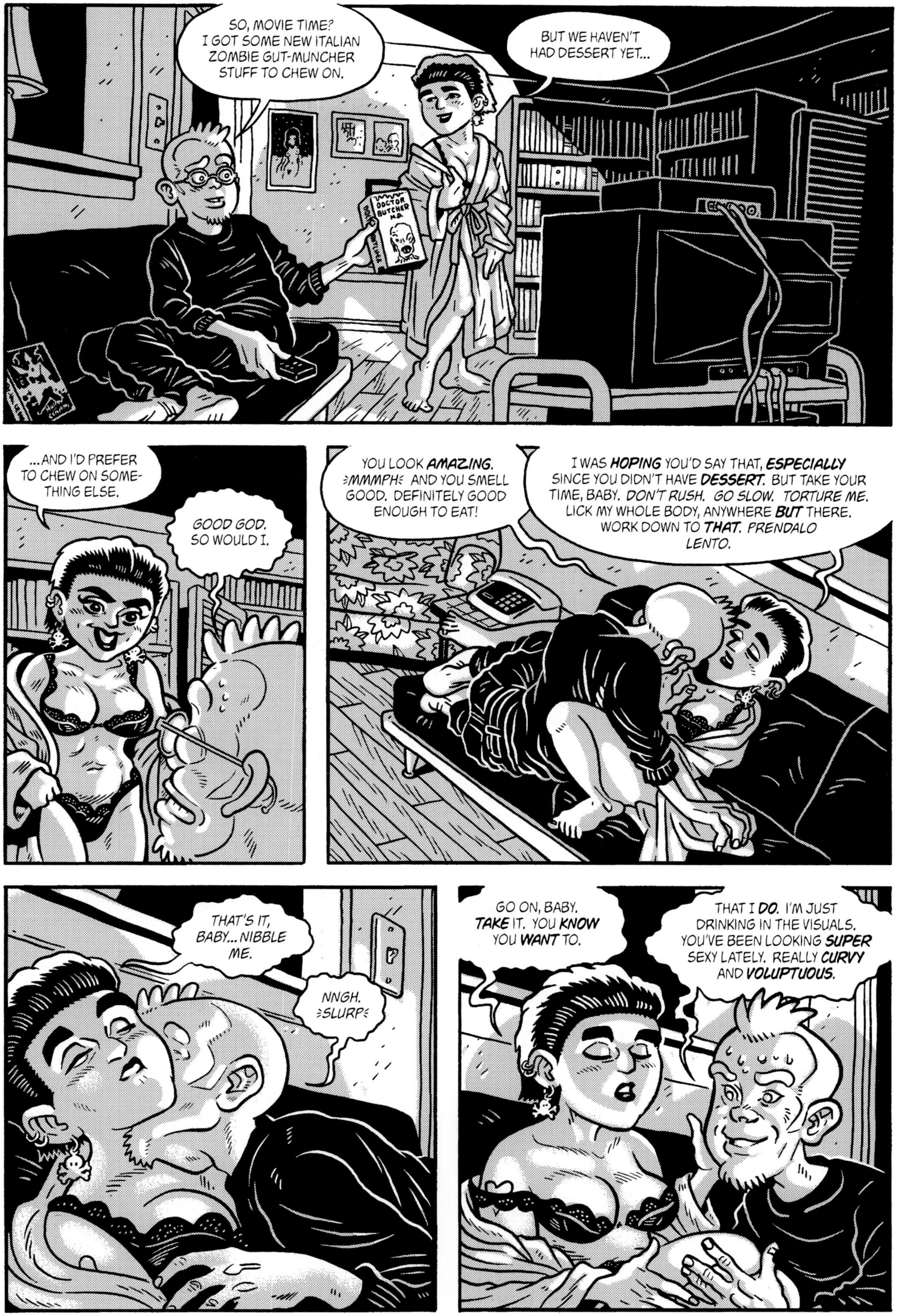

SO, MOVIE TIME? I GOT SOME NEW ITALIAN ZOMBIE GUT-MUNCHER STUFF TO CHEW ON.
BUT WE HAVEN'T HAD DESSERT YET...
DOCTOR BUTCHER M.D.
...AND I'D PREFER TO CHEW ON SOMETHING ELSE.
GOOD GOD. SO WOULD I.
YOU LOOK AMAZING. MMMPH AND YOU SMELL GOOD. DEFINITELY GOOD ENOUGH TO EAT!
I WAS HOPING YOU'D SAY THAT, ESPECIALLY SINCE YOU DIDN'T HAVE DESSERT. BUT TAKE YOUR TIME, BABY. DON'T RUSH. GO SLOW. TORTURE ME. LICK MY WHOLE BODY, ANYWHERE BUT THERE. WORK DOWN TO THAT. PRENDALO LENTO.
THAT'S IT, BABY... NIBBLE ME.
NNGH. SLURP
GO ON, BABY. TAKE IT. YOU KNOW YOU WANT TO.
THAT I DO. I'M JUST DRINKING IN THE VISUALS. YOU'VE BEEN LOOKING SUPER SEXY LATELY. REALLY CURVY AND VOLUPTUOUS.

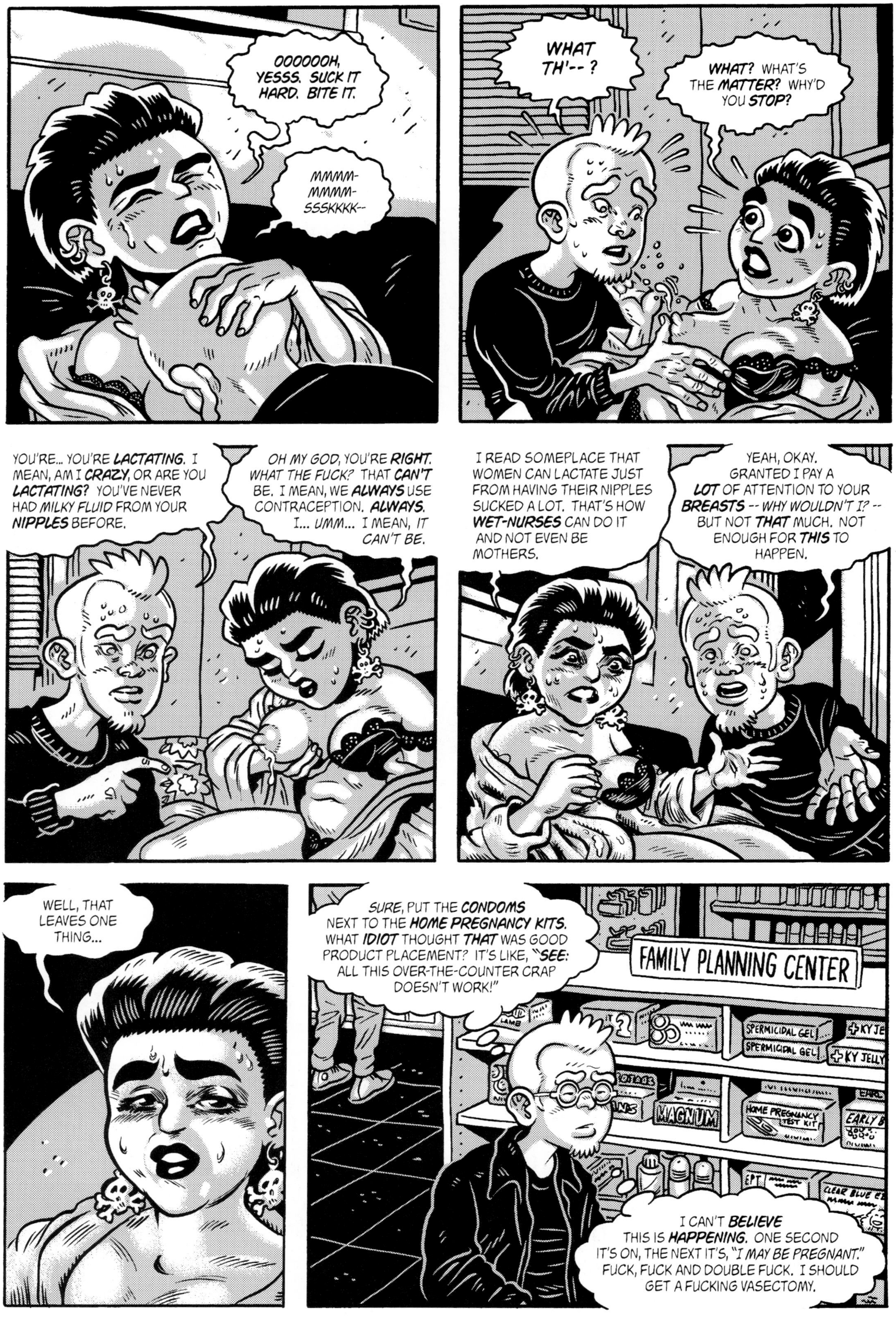

OOOOOOH, YESSS. SUCK IT HARD. BITE IT.
MMMM-MMMM-SSSKKKK--
WHAT TH'-- ?
WHAT? WHAT'S THE MATTER? WHY'D YOU STOP?
YOU'RE... YOU'RE LACTATING. I MEAN, AM I CRAZY, OR ARE YOU LACTATING? YOU'VE NEVER HAD MILKY FLUID FROM YOUR NIPPLES BEFORE.
OH MY GOD, YOU'RE RIGHT. WHAT THE FUCK? THAT CAN'T BE. I MEAN, WE ALWAYS USE CONTRACEPTION. ALWAYS. I... UMM... I MEAN, IT CAN'T BE.
I READ SOMEPLACE THAT WOMEN CAN LACTATE JUST FROM HAVING THEIR NIPPLES SUCKED A LOT. THAT'S HOW WET-NURSES CAN DO IT AND NOT EVEN BE MOTHERS.
YEAH, OKAY. GRANTED I PAY A LOT OF ATTENTION TO YOUR BREASTS -- WHY WOULDN'T I? -- BUT NOT THAT MUCH. NOT ENOUGH FOR THIS TO HAPPEN.
WELL, THAT LEAVES ONE THING...
SURE, PUT THE CONDOMS NEXT TO THE HOME PREGNANCY KITS. WHAT IDIOT THOUGHT THAT WAS GOOD PRODUCT PLACEMENT? IT'S LIKE, "SEE: ALL THIS OVER-THE-COUNTER CRAP DOESN'T WORK!"
FAMILY PLANNING CENTER
SPERMICIDAL GEL
SPERMICIDAL GEL
KY JELLY
MAGNUM
HOME PREGNANCY TEST KIT
EPT
CLEAR BLUE
I CAN'T BELIEVE THIS IS HAPPENING. ONE SECOND IT'S ON, THE NEXT IT'S, "I MAY BE PREGNANT." FUCK, FUCK AND DOUBLE FUCK. I SHOULD GET A FUCKING VASECTOMY.

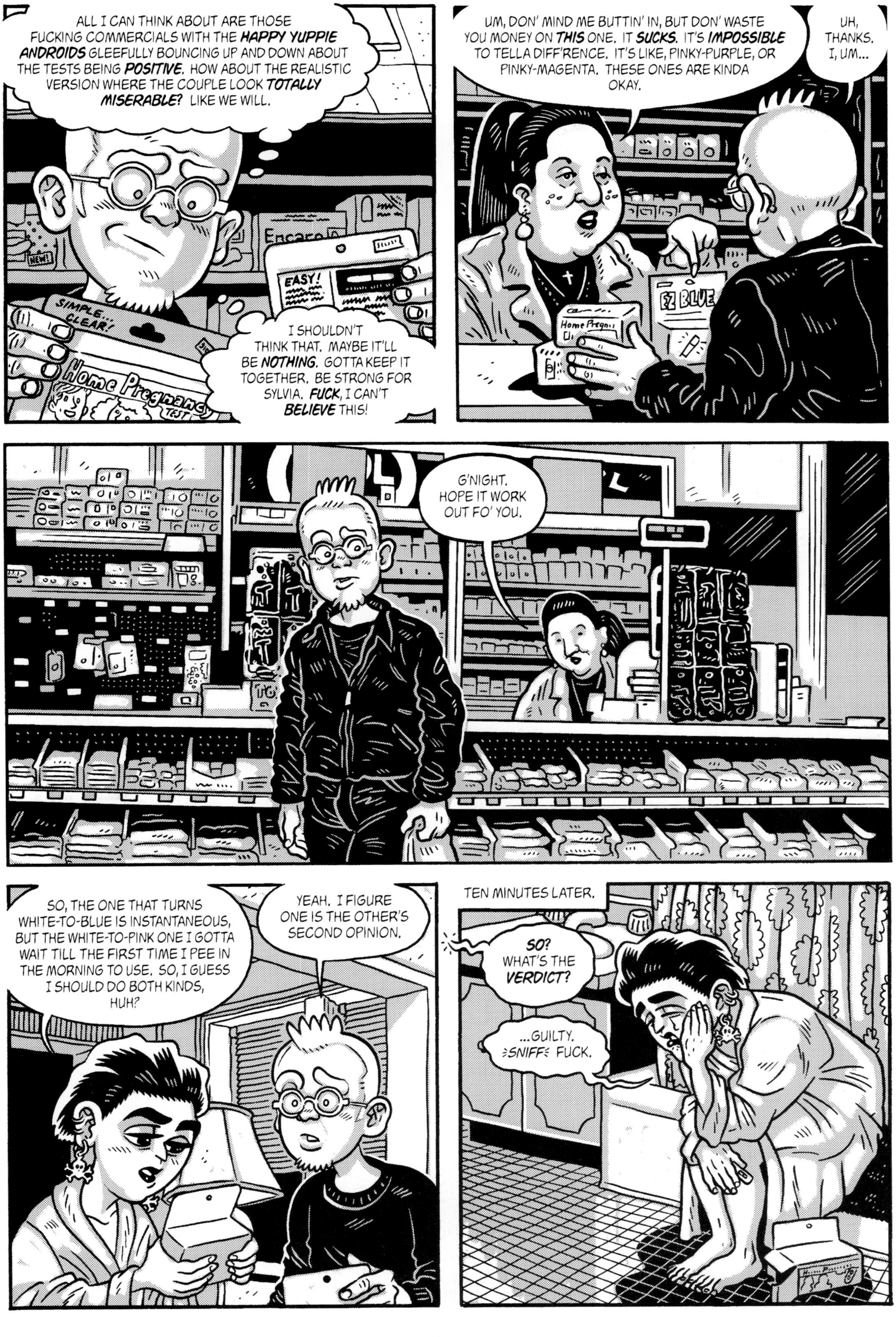
ALL I CAN THINK ABOUT ARE THOSE FUCKING COMMERCIALS WITH THE HAPPY YUPPIE ANDROIDS GLEEFULLY BOUNCING UP AND DOWN ABOUT THE TESTS BEING POSITIVE. HOW ABOUT THE REALISTIC VERSION WHERE THE COUPLE LOOK TOTALLY MISERABLE? LIKE WE WILL.
EASY!
SIMPLE... CLEAR!
Home Pregnancy TEST
I SHOULDN'T THINK THAT. MAYBE IT'LL BE NOTHING. GOTTA KEEP IT TOGETHER. BE STRONG FOR SYLVIA. FUCK, I CAN'T BELIEVE THIS!
UM, DON' MIND ME BUTTIN' IN, BUT DON' WASTE YOU MONEY ON THIS ONE. IT SUCKS. IT'S IMPOSSIBLE TO TELLA DIFF'RENCE. IT'S LIKE, PINKY-PURPLE, OR PINKY-MAGENTA. THESE ONES ARE KINDA OKAY.
UH, THANKS. I, UM...
EZ BLUE
G'NIGHT. HOPE IT WORK OUT FO' YOU.
SO, THE ONE THAT TURNS WHITE-TO-BLUE IS INSTANTANEOUS, BUT THE WHITE-TO-PINK ONE I GOTTA WAIT TILL THE FIRST TIME I PEE IN THE MORNING TO USE. SO, I GUESS I SHOULD DO BOTH KINDS, HUH?
YEAH. I FIGURE ONE IS THE OTHER'S SECOND OPINION.
TEN MINUTES LATER.
SO? WHAT'S THE VERDICT?
...GUILTY. SNIFF FUCK.

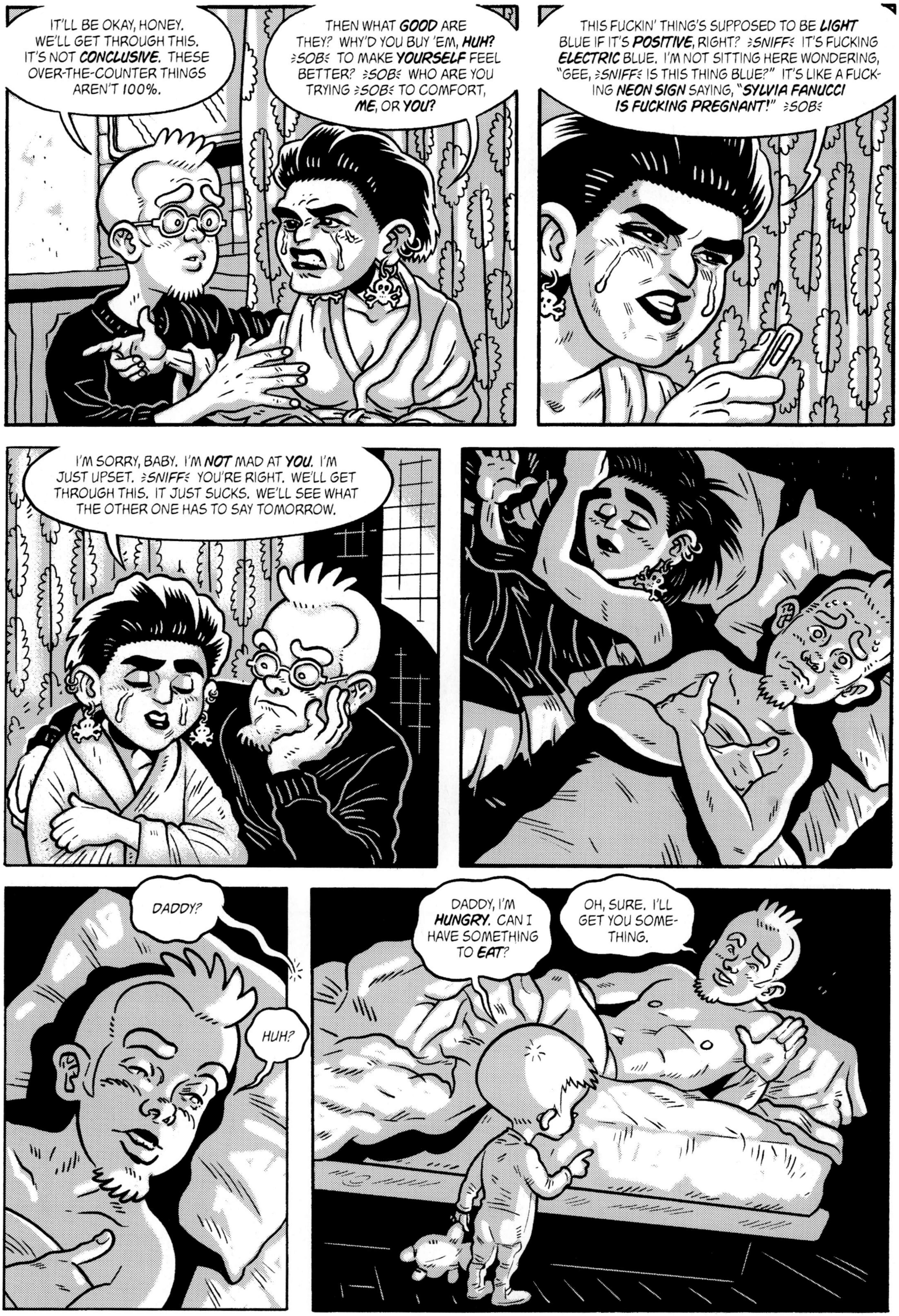
IT'LL BE OKAY, HONEY. WE'LL GET THROUGH THIS. IT'S NOT CONCLUSIVE. THESE OVER-THE-COUNTER THINGS AREN'T 100%.
THEN WHAT GOOD ARE THEY? WHY'D YOU BUY 'EM, HUH? ≷SOB≶ TO MAKE YOURSELF FEEL BETTER? ≷SOB≶ WHO ARE YOU TRYING ≷SOB≶ TO COMFORT, ME, OR YOU?
THIS FUCKIN' THING'S SUPPOSED TO BE LIGHT BLUE IF IT'S POSITIVE, RIGHT? ≷SNIFF≶ IT'S FUCKING ELECTRIC BLUE. I'M NOT SITTING HERE WONDERING, "GEE, ≷SNIFF≶ IS THIS THING BLUE?" IT'S LIKE A FUCKING NEON SIGN SAYING, "SYLVIA FANUCCI IS FUCKING PREGNANT!" ≷SOB≶
I'M SORRY, BABY. I'M NOT MAD AT YOU. I'M JUST UPSET. ≷SNIFF≶ YOU'RE RIGHT. WE'LL GET THROUGH THIS. IT JUST SUCKS. WE'LL SEE WHAT THE OTHER ONE HAS TO SAY TOMORROW.
DADDY?
HUH?
DADDY, I'M HUNGRY. CAN I HAVE SOMETHING TO EAT?
OH, SURE. I'LL GET YOU SOMETHING.

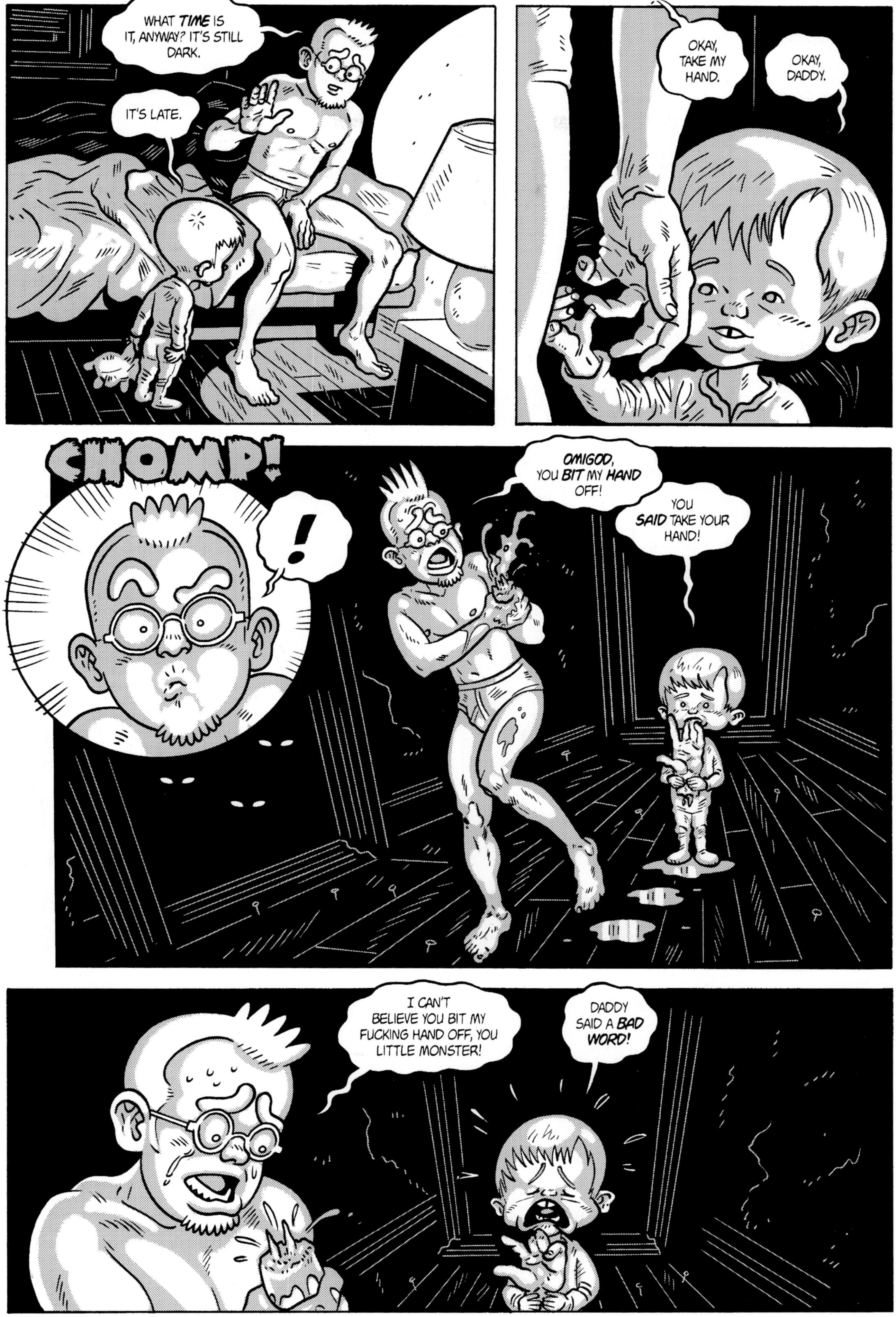
WHAT TIME IS IT, ANYWAY? IT'S STILL DARK.
IT'S LATE.
OKAY, TAKE MY HAND.
OKAY, DADDY.
CHOMP!
!
OMIGOD, YOU BIT MY HAND OFF!
YOU SAID TAKE YOUR HAND!
I CAN'T BELIEVE YOU BIT MY FUCKING HAND OFF, YOU LITTLE MONSTER!
DADDY SAID A BAD WORD!

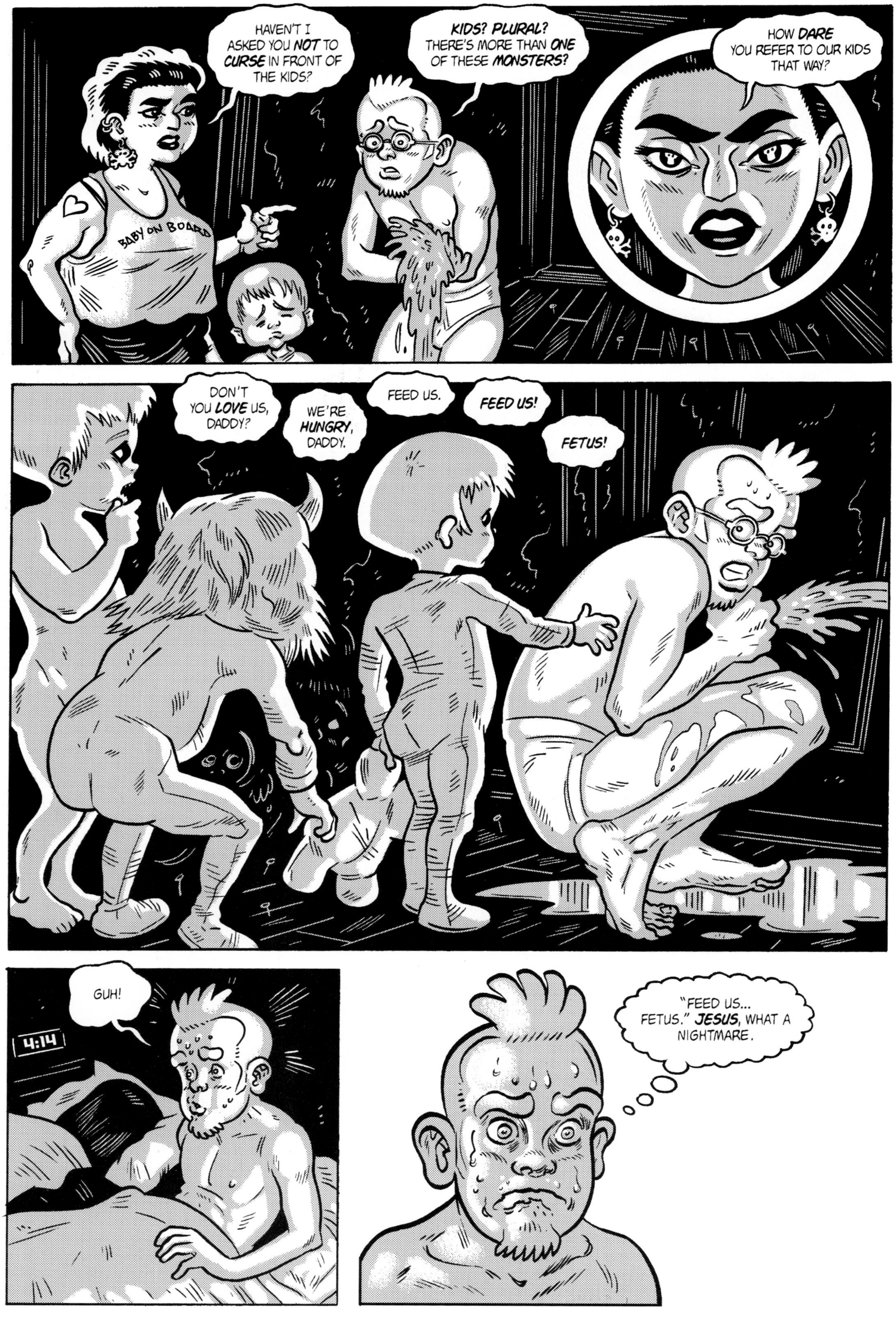
HAVEN'T I ASKED YOU NOT TO CURSE IN FRONT OF THE KIDS?
KIDS? PLURAL? THERE'S MORE THAN ONE OF THESE MONSTERS?
HOW DARE YOU REFER TO OUR KIDS THAT WAY?
BABY ON BOARD
DON'T YOU LOVE US, DADDY?
WE'RE HUNGRY, DADDY.
FEED US.
FEED US!
FETUS!
GUH!
4:14
"FEED US... FETUS." JESUS, WHAT A NIGHTMARE.

6:35 A.M., HALLOWEEN.

ROB. ROB, **WAKE UP.** I'M **PREGNANT.**

HUH? WHAT? WHAT **TIME** IS IT?

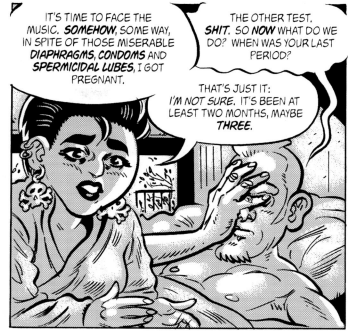

IT'S TIME TO FACE THE MUSIC. **SOMEHOW**, SOME WAY, IN SPITE OF THOSE MISERABLE **DIAPHRAGMS, CONDOMS** AND **SPERMICIDAL LUBES,** I GOT PREGNANT.

THE OTHER TEST. **SHIT.** SO **NOW** WHAT DO WE DO? WHEN WAS YOUR LAST PERIOD?

THAT'S JUST IT: I'M **NOT SURE.** IT'S BEEN AT LEAST TWO MONTHS, MAYBE **THREE.**

WHAT?!? THREE MONTHS! HOW COULD YOU MISS NOTICING IT NOT ONCE, BUT **TWICE?** HOW DOES **THAT** HAPPEN? I'M NOT TRYING TO BE INSENSITIVE, BUT **HOW?**

DON'T RAISE YOUR VOICE, ROB, I'M RIGHT HERE. **HOW?** EASY. MY CYCLE HAS **NEVER** BEEN ALL THAT REGULAR, OR RELIABLE. I'VE MISSED PERIODS BEFORE.

ANYWAY, IF I **HAVE** BEEN PREGNANT FOR A WHILE, WE'VE GOT TO GET THIS TAKEN CARE OF, **LIKE NOW.**

I AGREE, BUT JUST LIKE THAT?

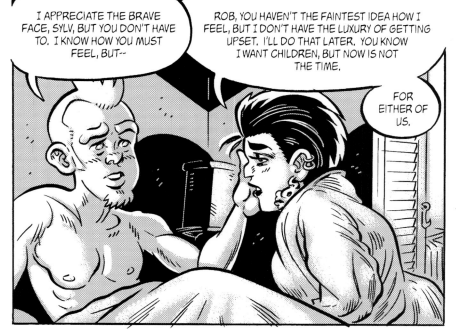

I APPRECIATE THE BRAVE FACE, SYLV, BUT YOU DON'T HAVE TO. I KNOW HOW YOU MUST FEEL, BUT--

ROB, YOU HAVEN'T THE FAINTEST IDEA HOW I FEEL, BUT I DON'T HAVE THE LUXURY OF GETTING UPSET. I'LL DO THAT LATER. YOU KNOW I WANT CHILDREN, BUT NOW IS NOT THE TIME.

FOR EITHER OF US.

TRUE. AND I DON'T THINK I **EVER** WANT TO HAVE THEM. WHAT A MESS.

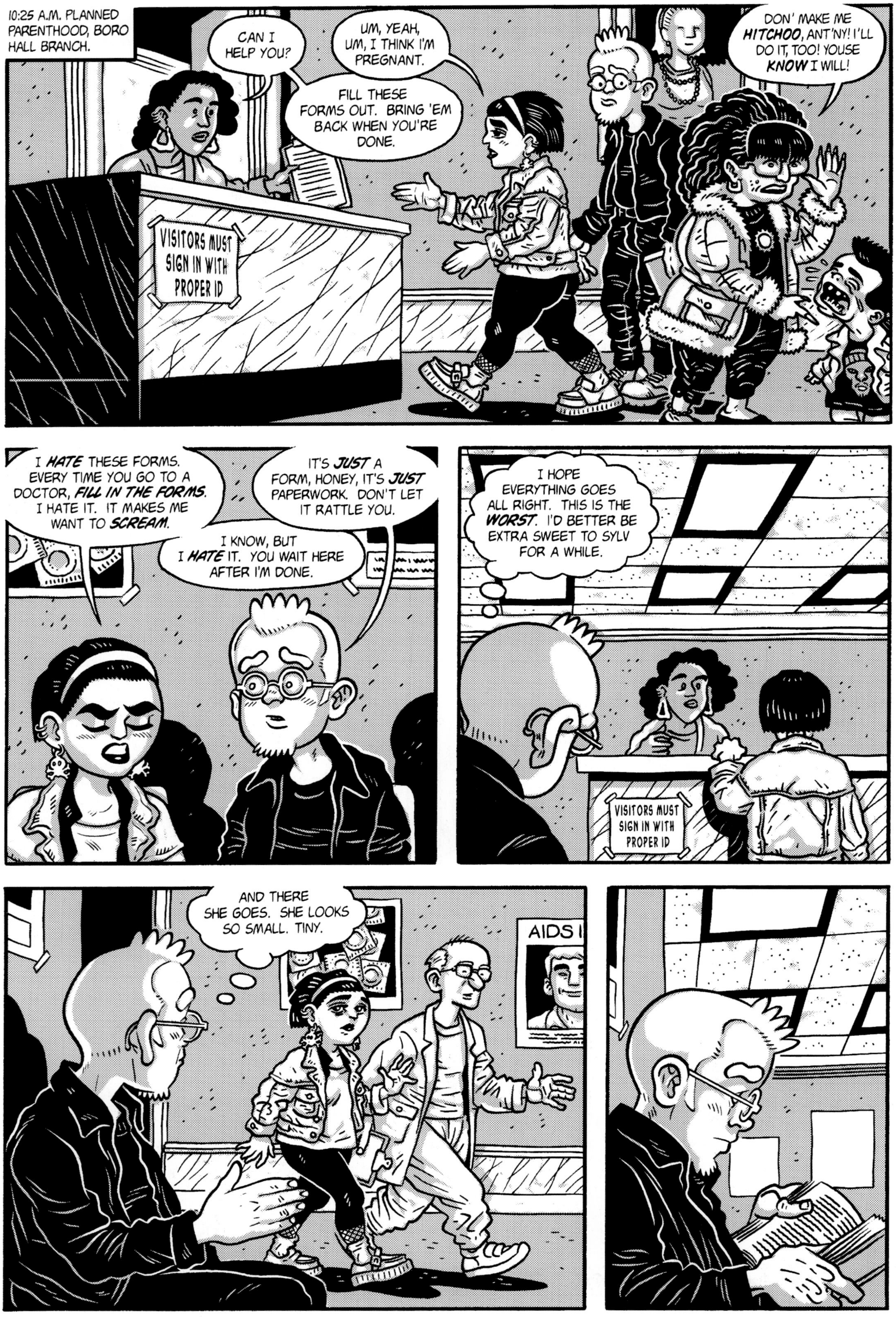
10:25 A.M. PLANNED PARENTHOOD, BORO HALL BRANCH.
CAN I HELP YOU?
UM, YEAH, UM, I THINK I'M PREGNANT.
FILL THESE FORMS OUT. BRING 'EM BACK WHEN YOU'RE DONE.
DON' MAKE ME HITCHOO, ANT'NY! I'LL DO IT, TOO! YOUSE KNOW I WILL!
VISITORS MUST SIGN IN WITH PROPER ID
I HATE THESE FORMS. EVERY TIME YOU GO TO A DOCTOR, FILL IN THE FORMS. I HATE IT. IT MAKES ME WANT TO SCREAM.
IT'S JUST A FORM, HONEY, IT'S JUST PAPERWORK. DON'T LET IT RATTLE YOU.
I KNOW, BUT I HATE IT. YOU WAIT HERE AFTER I'M DONE.
I HOPE EVERYTHING GOES ALL RIGHT. THIS IS THE WORST. I'D BETTER BE EXTRA SWEET TO SYLV FOR A WHILE.
VISITORS MUST SIGN IN WITH PROPER ID
AND THERE SHE GOES. SHE LOOKS SO SMALL. TINY.
AIDS I

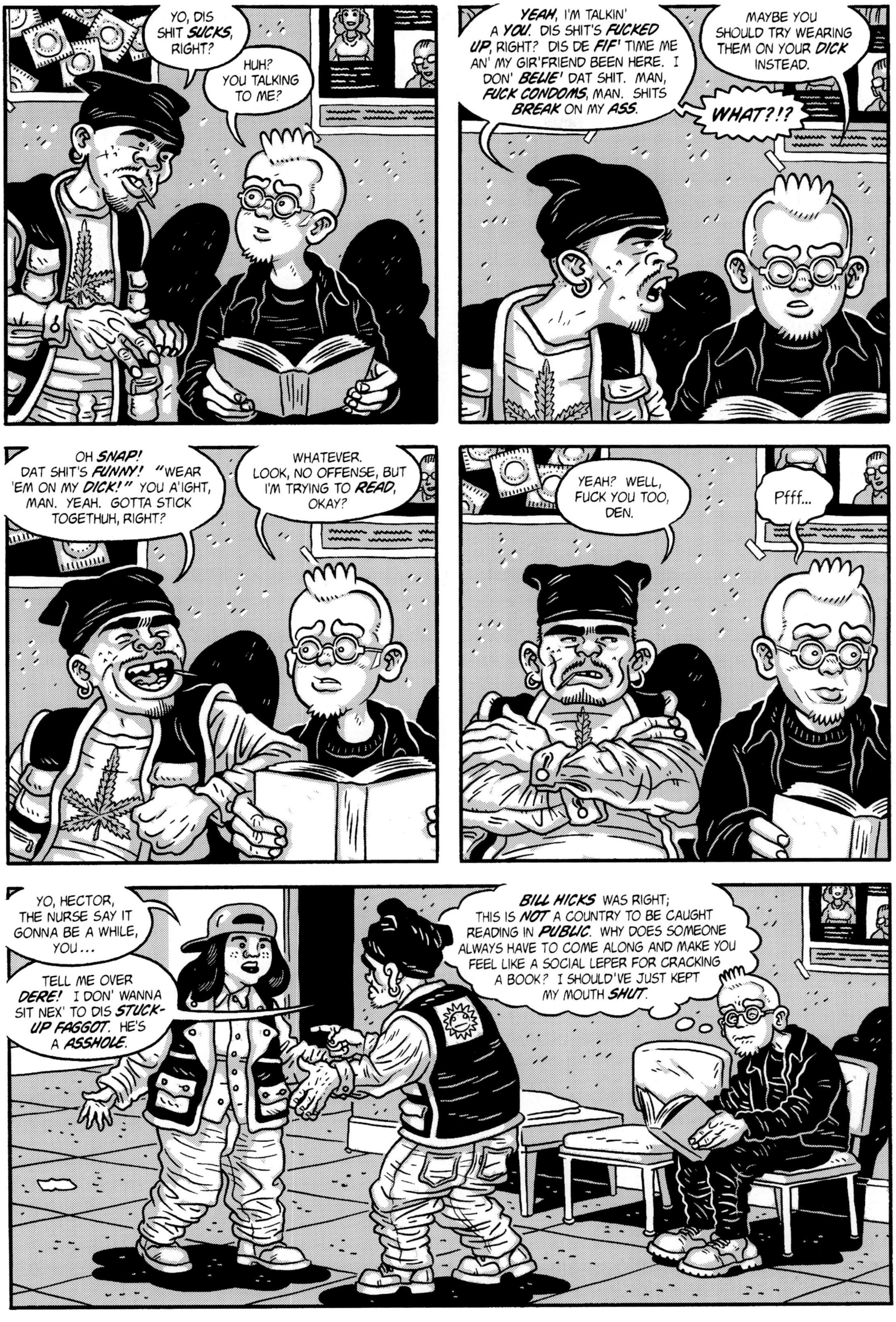
YO, DIS SHIT SUCKS, RIGHT?
HUH? YOU TALKING TO ME?
YEAH, I'M TALKIN' A YOU. DIS SHIT'S FUCKED UP, RIGHT? DIS DE FIF' TIME ME AN' MY GIR'FRIEND BEEN HERE. I DON' BELIE' DAT SHIT. MAN, FUCK CONDOMS, MAN. SHITS BREAK ON MY ASS.
MAYBE YOU SHOULD TRY WEARING THEM ON YOUR DICK INSTEAD.
WHAT?!?
OH SNAP! DAT SHIT'S FUNNY! "WEAR 'EM ON MY DICK!" YOU A'IGHT, MAN. YEAH. GOTTA STICK TOGETHUH, RIGHT?
WHATEVER. LOOK, NO OFFENSE, BUT I'M TRYING TO READ, OKAY?
YEAH? WELL, FUCK YOU TOO, DEN.
Pfff...
YO, HECTOR, THE NURSE SAY IT GONNA BE A WHILE, YOU...
TELL ME OVER DERE! I DON' WANNA SIT NEX' TO DIS STUCK-UP FAGGOT. HE'S A ASSHOLE.
BILL HICKS WAS RIGHT; THIS IS NOT A COUNTRY TO BE CAUGHT READING IN PUBLIC. WHY DOES SOMEONE ALWAYS HAVE TO COME ALONG AND MAKE YOU FEEL LIKE A SOCIAL LEPER FOR CRACKING A BOOK? I SHOULD'VE JUST KEPT MY MOUTH SHUT.

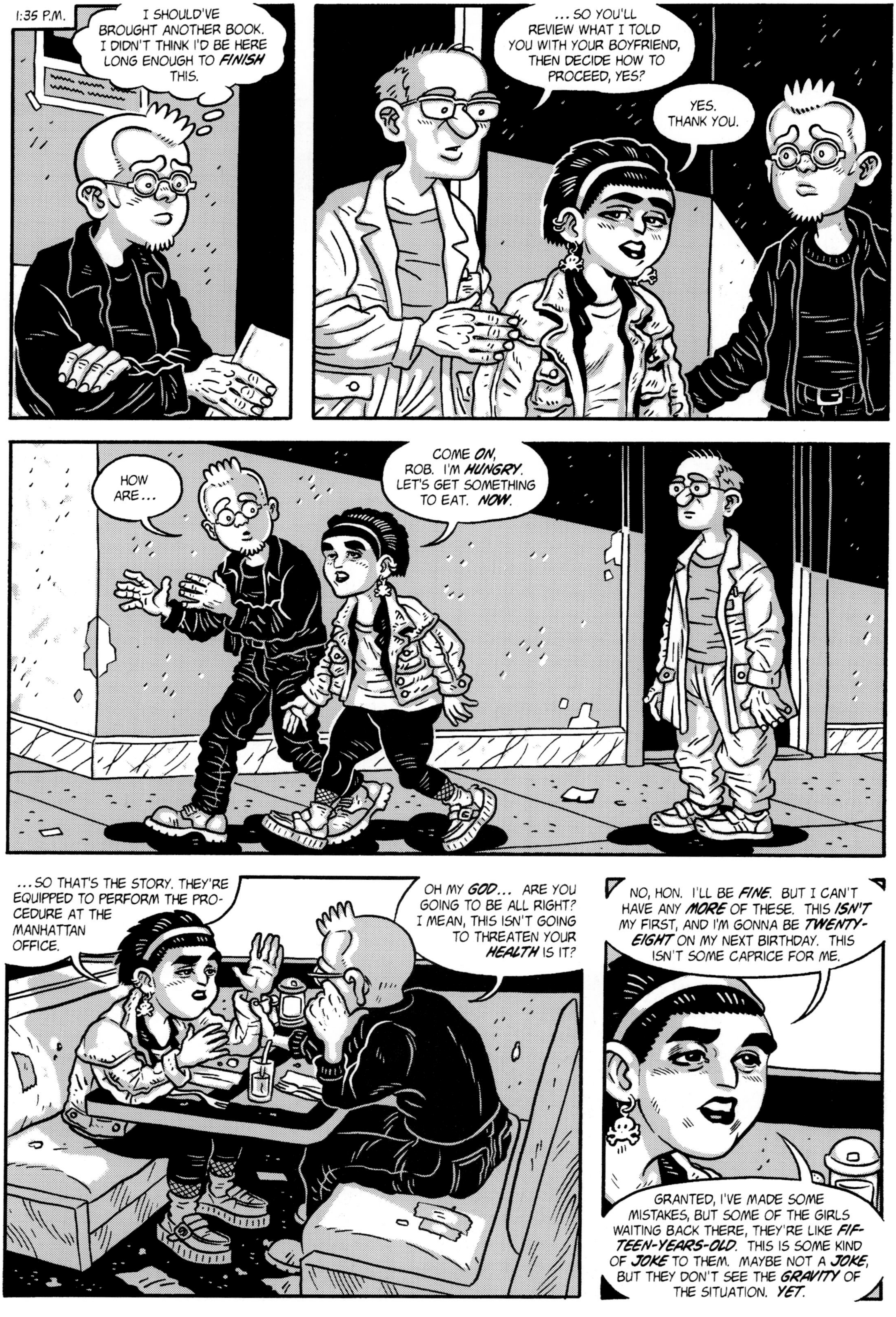
1:35 P.M.
I SHOULD'VE BROUGHT ANOTHER BOOK. I DIDN'T THINK I'D BE HERE LONG ENOUGH TO FINISH THIS.
... SO YOU'LL REVIEW WHAT I TOLD YOU WITH YOUR BOYFRIEND, THEN DECIDE HOW TO PROCEED, YES?
YES. THANK YOU.
HOW ARE...
COME ON, ROB. I'M HUNGRY. LET'S GET SOMETHING TO EAT. NOW.
...SO THAT'S THE STORY. THEY'RE EQUIPPED TO PERFORM THE PROCEDURE AT THE MANHATTAN OFFICE.
OH MY GOD... ARE YOU GOING TO BE ALL RIGHT? I MEAN, THIS ISN'T GOING TO THREATEN YOUR HEALTH IS IT?
NO, HON. I'LL BE FINE. BUT I CAN'T HAVE ANY MORE OF THESE. THIS ISN'T MY FIRST, AND I'M GONNA BE TWENTY-EIGHT ON MY NEXT BIRTHDAY. THIS ISN'T SOME CAPRICE FOR ME.
GRANTED, I'VE MADE SOME MISTAKES, BUT SOME OF THE GIRLS WAITING BACK THERE, THEY'RE LIKE FIFTEEN-YEARS-OLD. THIS IS SOME KIND OF JOKE TO THEM. MAYBE NOT A JOKE, BUT THEY DON'T SEE THE GRAVITY OF THE SITUATION. YET.

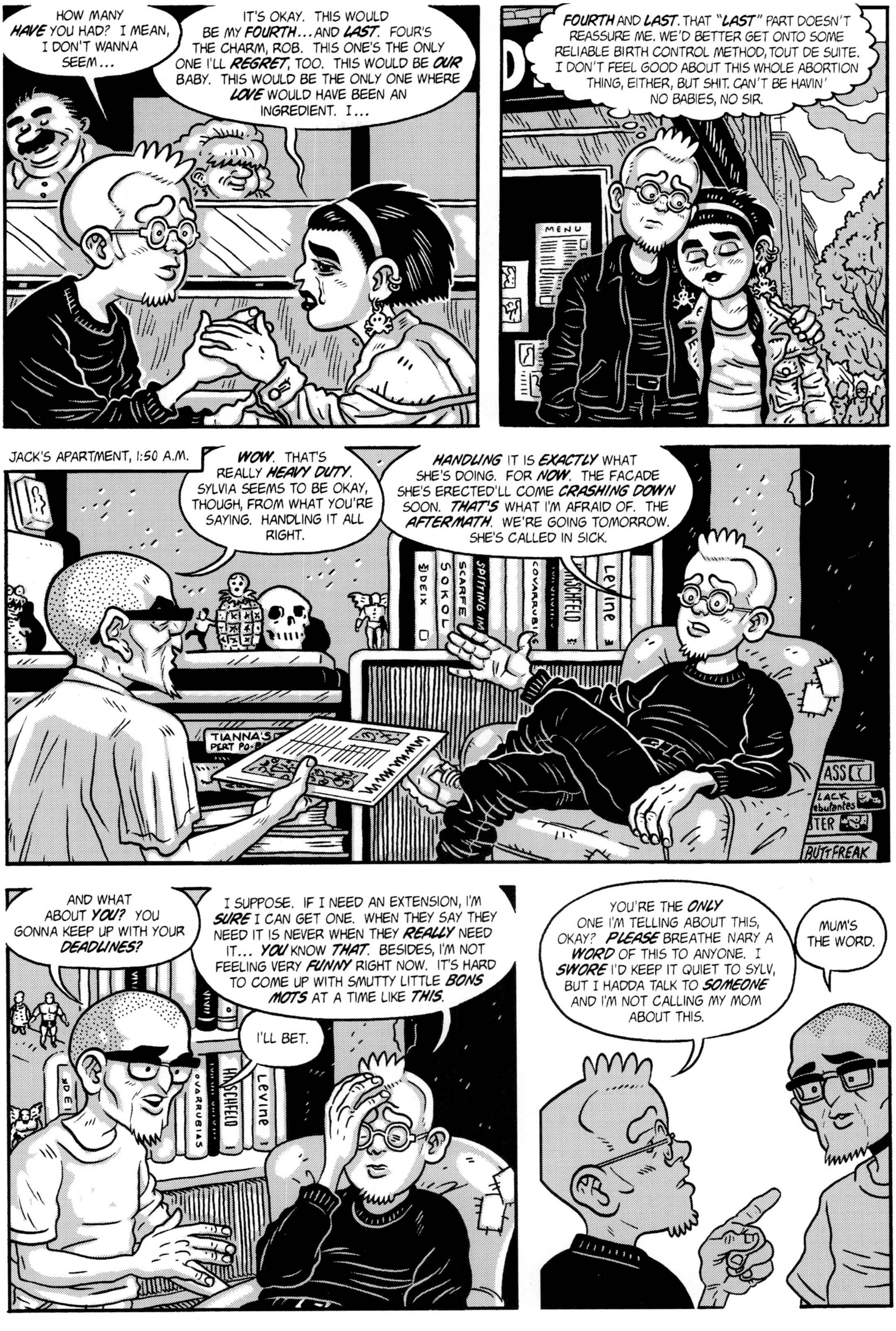
HOW MANY HAVE YOU HAD? I MEAN, I DON'T WANNA SEEM...
IT'S OKAY. THIS WOULD BE MY FOURTH... AND LAST. FOUR'S THE CHARM, ROB. THIS ONE'S THE ONLY ONE I'LL REGRET, TOO. THIS WOULD BE OUR BABY. THIS WOULD BE THE ONLY ONE WHERE LOVE WOULD HAVE BEEN AN INGREDIENT. I...
FOURTH AND LAST. THAT "LAST" PART DOESN'T REASSURE ME. WE'D BETTER GET ONTO SOME RELIABLE BIRTH CONTROL METHOD, TOUT DE SUITE. I DON'T FEEL GOOD ABOUT THIS WHOLE ABORTION THING, EITHER, BUT SHIT. CAN'T BE HAVIN' NO BABIES, NO SIR.
MENU
JACK'S APARTMENT, 1:50 A.M.
WOW. THAT'S REALLY HEAVY DUTY. SYLVIA SEEMS TO BE OKAY, THOUGH, FROM WHAT YOU'RE SAYING. HANDLING IT ALL RIGHT.
HANDLING IT IS EXACTLY WHAT SHE'S DOING. FOR NOW. THE FACADE SHE'S ERECTED'LL COME CRASHING DOWN SOON. THAT'S WHAT I'M AFRAID OF. THE AFTERMATH. WE'RE GOING TOMORROW. SHE'S CALLED IN SICK.
DEIX
SOKOL
SCARFE
COVARRUBIAS
Levine
BUTT FREAK
AND WHAT ABOUT YOU? YOU GONNA KEEP UP WITH YOUR DEADLINES?
I SUPPOSE. IF I NEED AN EXTENSION, I'M SURE I CAN GET ONE. WHEN THEY SAY THEY NEED IT IS NEVER WHEN THEY REALLY NEED IT... YOU KNOW THAT. BESIDES, I'M NOT FEELING VERY FUNNY RIGHT NOW. IT'S HARD TO COME UP WITH SMUTTY LITTLE BONS MOTS AT A TIME LIKE THIS.
I'LL BET.
YOU'RE THE ONLY ONE I'M TELLING ABOUT THIS, OKAY? PLEASE BREATHE NARY A WORD OF THIS TO ANYONE. I SWORE I'D KEEP IT QUIET TO SYLV, BUT I HADDA TALK TO SOMEONE AND I'M NOT CALLING MY MOM ABOUT THIS.
MUM'S THE WORD.

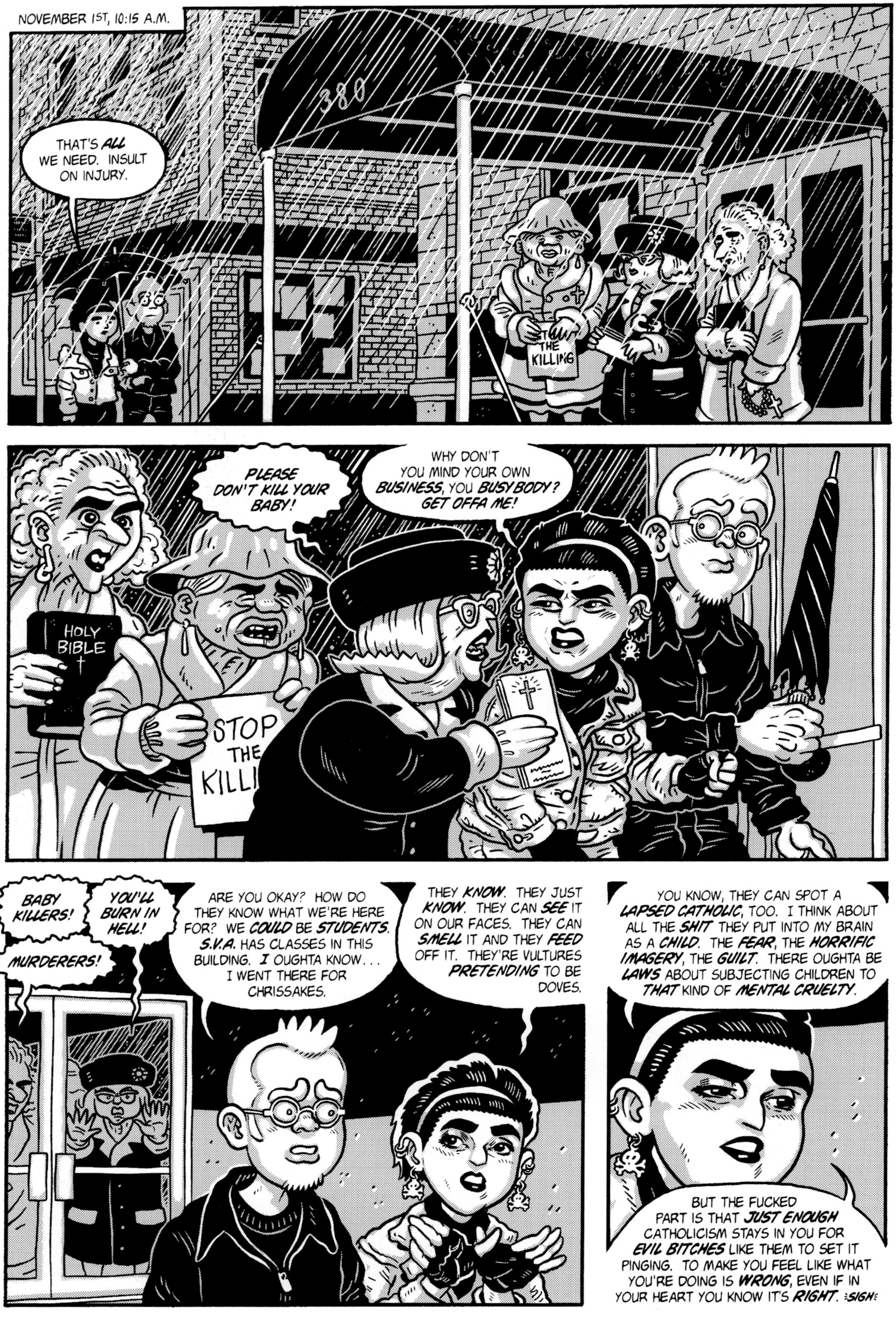
NOVEMBER 1ST, 10:15 A.M.
THAT'S ALL WE NEED. INSULT ON INJURY.
380
STOP THE KILLING
PLEASE DON'T KILL YOUR BABY!
WHY DON'T YOU MIND YOUR OWN BUSINESS, YOU BUSYBODY? GET OFFA ME!
HOLY BIBLE
STOP THE KILLI
BABY KILLERS!
YOU'LL BURN IN HELL!
MURDERERS!
ARE YOU OKAY? HOW DO THEY KNOW WHAT WE'RE HERE FOR? WE COULD BE STUDENTS. S.V.A. HAS CLASSES IN THIS BUILDING. I OUGHTA KNOW... I WENT THERE FOR CHRISSAKES.
THEY KNOW. THEY JUST KNOW. THEY CAN SEE IT ON OUR FACES. THEY CAN SMELL IT AND THEY FEED OFF IT. THEY'RE VULTURES PRETENDING TO BE DOVES.
YOU KNOW, THEY CAN SPOT A LAPSED CATHOLIC, TOO. I THINK ABOUT ALL THE SHIT THEY PUT INTO MY BRAIN AS A CHILD. THE FEAR, THE HORRIFIC IMAGERY, THE GUILT. THERE OUGHTA BE LAWS ABOUT SUBJECTING CHILDREN TO THAT KIND OF MENTAL CRUELTY.
BUT THE FUCKED PART IS THAT JUST ENOUGH CATHOLICISM STAYS IN YOU FOR EVIL BITCHES LIKE THEM TO SET IT PINGING. TO MAKE YOU FEEL LIKE WHAT YOU'RE DOING IS WRONG, EVEN IF IN YOUR HEART YOU KNOW IT'S RIGHT. SIGH

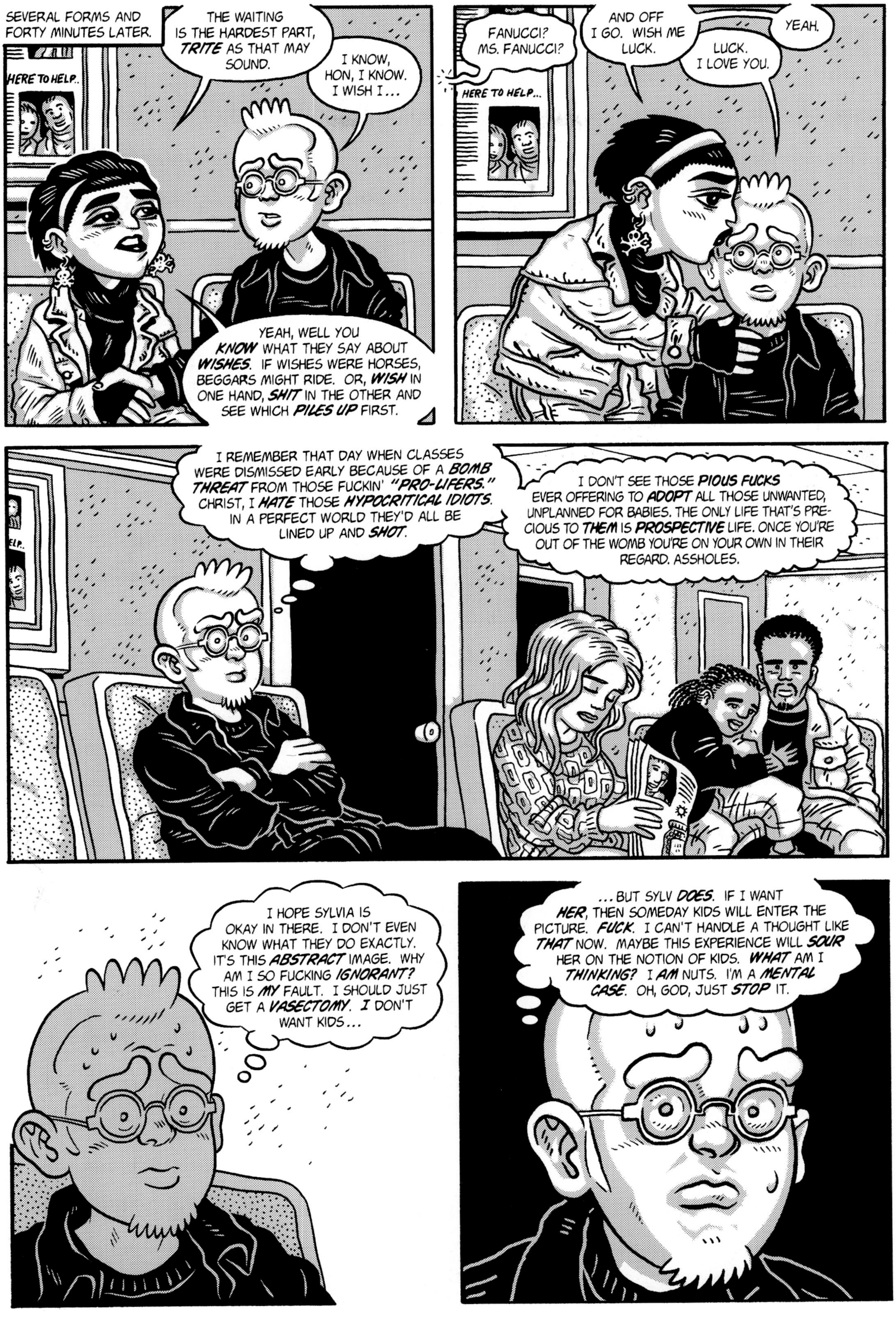
SEVERAL FORMS AND FORTY MINUTES LATER.
HERE TO HELP..
THE WAITING IS THE HARDEST PART, TRITE AS THAT MAY SOUND.
I KNOW, HON, I KNOW. I WISH I...
YEAH, WELL YOU KNOW WHAT THEY SAY ABOUT WISHES. IF WISHES WERE HORSES, BEGGARS MIGHT RIDE. OR, WISH IN ONE HAND, SHIT IN THE OTHER AND SEE WHICH PILES UP FIRST.
FANUCCI? MS. FANUCCI?
HERE TO HELP...
AND OFF I GO. WISH ME LUCK.
LUCK. I LOVE YOU.
YEAH.
I REMEMBER THAT DAY WHEN CLASSES WERE DISMISSED EARLY BECAUSE OF A BOMB THREAT FROM THOSE FUCKIN' "PRO-LIFERS." CHRIST, I HATE THOSE HYPOCRITICAL IDIOTS. IN A PERFECT WORLD THEY'D ALL BE LINED UP AND SHOT.
I DON'T SEE THOSE PIOUS FUCKS EVER OFFERING TO ADOPT ALL THOSE UNWANTED, UNPLANNED FOR BABIES. THE ONLY LIFE THAT'S PRECIOUS TO THEM IS PROSPECTIVE LIFE. ONCE YOU'RE OUT OF THE WOMB YOU'RE ON YOUR OWN IN THEIR REGARD. ASSHOLES.
I HOPE SYLVIA IS OKAY IN THERE. I DON'T EVEN KNOW WHAT THEY DO EXACTLY. IT'S THIS ABSTRACT IMAGE. WHY AM I SO FUCKING IGNORANT? THIS IS MY FAULT. I SHOULD JUST GET A VASECTOMY. I DON'T WANT KIDS...
...BUT SYLV DOES. IF I WANT HER, THEN SOMEDAY KIDS WILL ENTER THE PICTURE. FUCK. I CAN'T HANDLE A THOUGHT LIKE THAT NOW. MAYBE THIS EXPERIENCE WILL SOUR HER ON THE NOTION OF KIDS. WHAT AM I THINKING? I AM NUTS. I'M A MENTAL CASE. OH, GOD, JUST STOP IT.

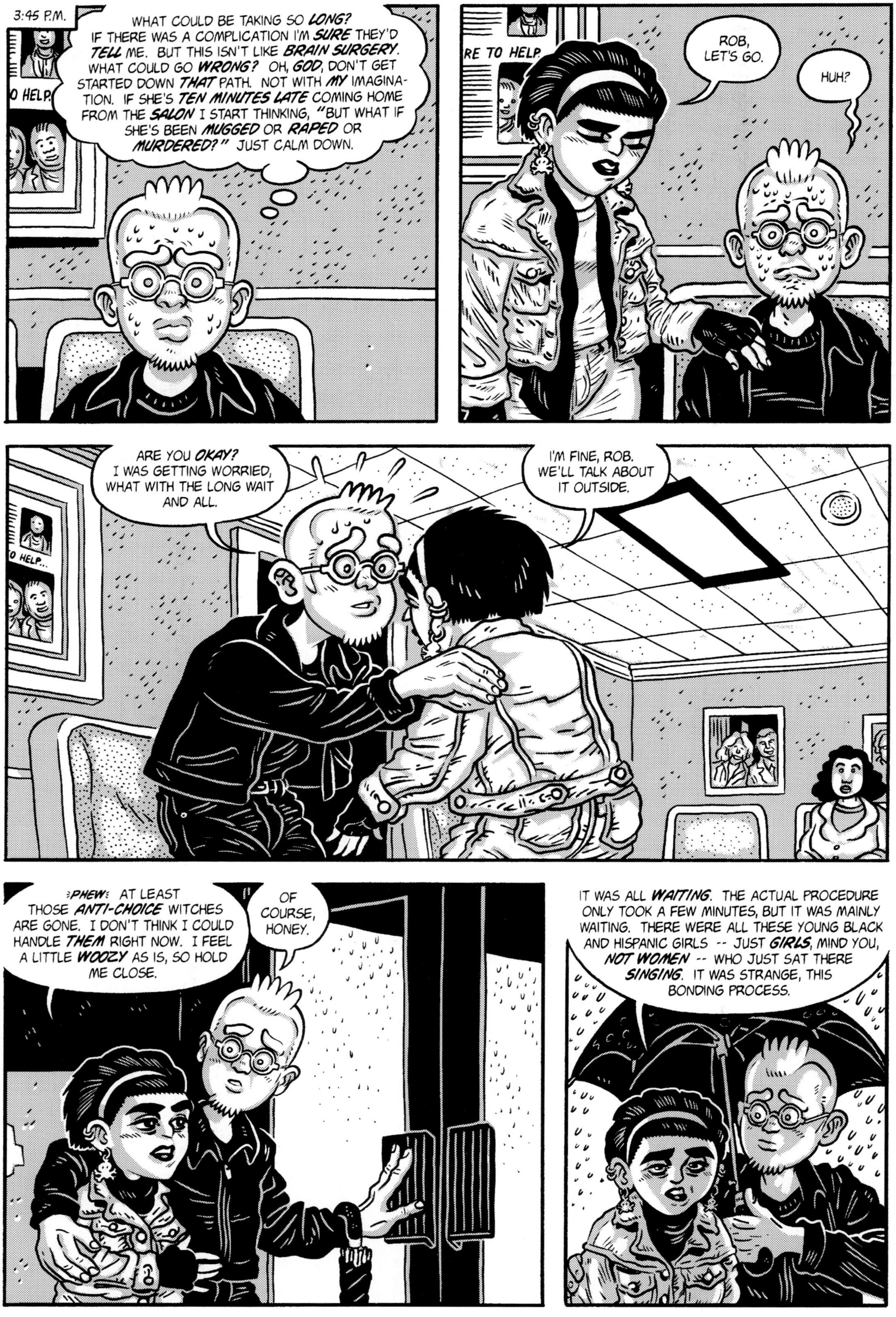
3:45 P.M.
WHAT COULD BE TAKING SO LONG? IF THERE WAS A COMPLICATION I'M SURE THEY'D TELL ME. BUT THIS ISN'T LIKE BRAIN SURGERY. WHAT COULD GO WRONG? OH, GOD, DON'T GET STARTED DOWN THAT PATH. NOT WITH MY IMAGINATION. IF SHE'S TEN MINUTES LATE COMING HOME FROM THE SALON I START THINKING, "BUT WHAT IF SHE'S BEEN MUGGED OR RAPED OR MURDERED?" JUST CALM DOWN.
ROB, LET'S GO.
HUH?
ARE YOU OKAY? I WAS GETTING WORRIED, WHAT WITH THE LONG WAIT AND ALL.
I'M FINE, ROB. WE'LL TALK ABOUT IT OUTSIDE.
PHEW AT LEAST THOSE ANTI-CHOICE WITCHES ARE GONE. I DON'T THINK I COULD HANDLE THEM RIGHT NOW. I FEEL A LITTLE WOOZY AS IS, SO HOLD ME CLOSE.
OF COURSE, HONEY.
IT WAS ALL WAITING. THE ACTUAL PROCEDURE ONLY TOOK A FEW MINUTES, BUT IT WAS MAINLY WAITING. THERE WERE ALL THESE YOUNG BLACK AND HISPANIC GIRLS -- JUST GIRLS, MIND YOU, NOT WOMEN -- WHO JUST SAT THERE SINGING. IT WAS STRANGE, THIS BONDING PROCESS.

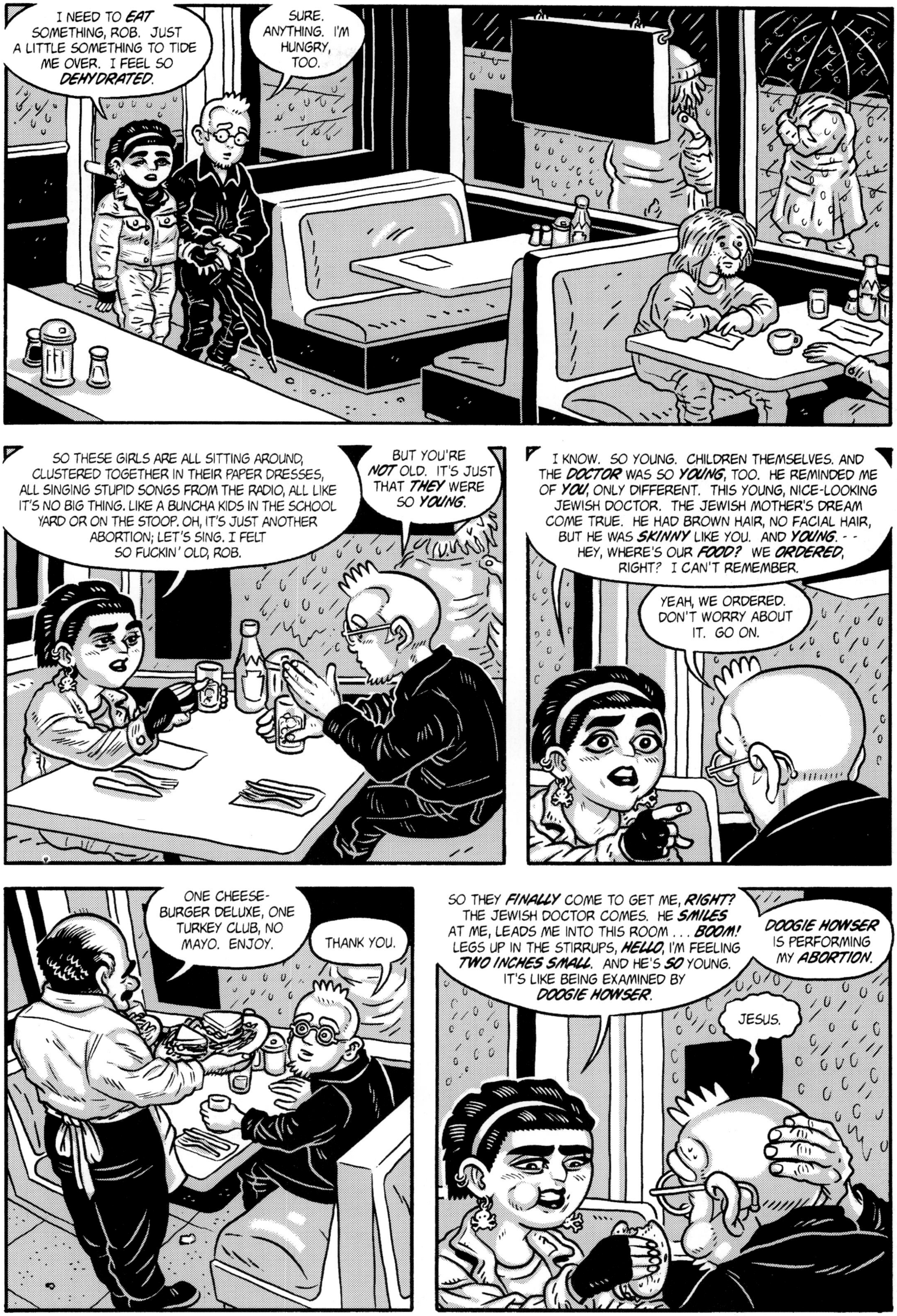
I NEED TO **EAT** SOMETHING, ROB. JUST A LITTLE SOMETHING TO TIDE ME OVER. I FEEL SO **DEHYDRATED**.
SURE. ANYTHING. I'M HUNGRY, TOO.
SO THESE GIRLS ARE ALL SITTING AROUND, CLUSTERED TOGETHER IN THEIR PAPER DRESSES, ALL SINGING STUPID SONGS FROM THE RADIO, ALL LIKE IT'S NO BIG THING. LIKE A BUNCHA KIDS IN THE SCHOOL YARD OR ON THE STOOP. OH, IT'S JUST ANOTHER ABORTION; LET'S SING. I FELT SO FUCKIN' OLD, ROB.
BUT YOU'RE **NOT** OLD. IT'S JUST THAT **THEY** WERE SO **YOUNG**.
I KNOW. SO YOUNG. CHILDREN THEMSELVES. AND THE **DOCTOR** WAS SO **YOUNG**, TOO. HE REMINDED ME OF **YOU**, ONLY DIFFERENT. THIS YOUNG, NICE-LOOKING JEWISH DOCTOR. THE JEWISH MOTHER'S DREAM COME TRUE. HE HAD BROWN HAIR, NO FACIAL HAIR, BUT HE WAS **SKINNY** LIKE YOU. AND **YOUNG**. - - HEY, WHERE'S OUR **FOOD?** WE **ORDERED**, RIGHT? I CAN'T REMEMBER.
YEAH, WE ORDERED. DON'T WORRY ABOUT IT. GO ON.
ONE CHEESE-BURGER DELUXE, ONE TURKEY CLUB, NO MAYO. ENJOY.
THANK YOU.
SO THEY **FINALLY** COME TO GET ME, **RIGHT?** THE JEWISH DOCTOR COMES. HE **SMILES** AT ME, LEADS ME INTO THIS ROOM . . . **BOOM!** LEGS UP IN THE STIRRUPS, **HELLO**, I'M FEELING **TWO INCHES SMALL**. AND HE'S **SO** YOUNG. IT'S LIKE BEING EXAMINED BY **DOOGIE HOWSER**.
DOOGIE HOWSER IS PERFORMING MY **ABORTION**.
JESUS.

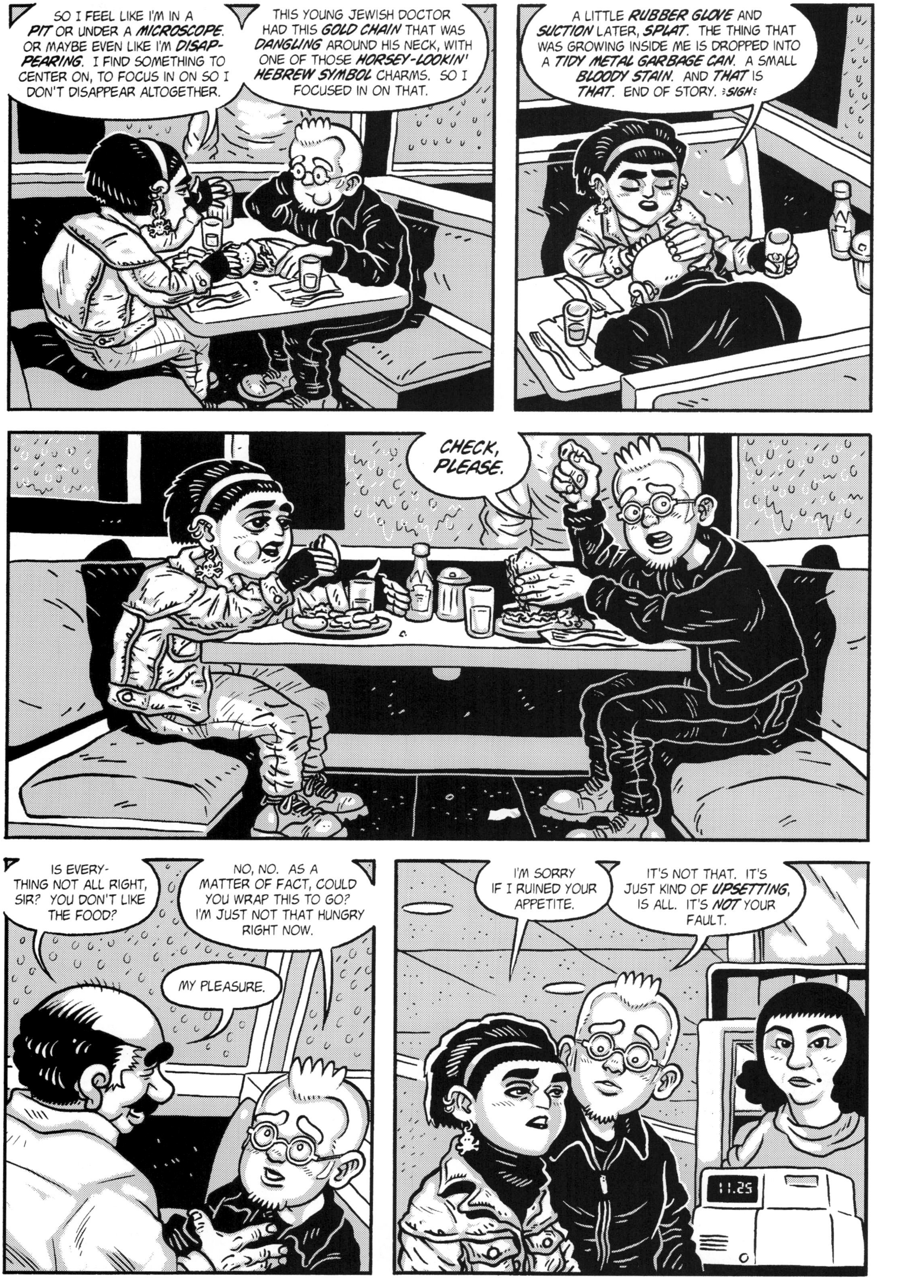
SO I FEEL LIKE I'M IN A PIT OR UNDER A MICROSCOPE. OR MAYBE EVEN LIKE I'M DISAP-PEARING. I FIND SOMETHING TO CENTER ON, TO FOCUS IN ON SO I DON'T DISAPPEAR ALTOGETHER.
THIS YOUNG JEWISH DOCTOR HAD THIS GOLD CHAIN THAT WAS DANGLING AROUND HIS NECK, WITH ONE OF THOSE HORSEY-LOOKIN' HEBREW SYMBOL CHARMS. SO I FOCUSED IN ON THAT.
A LITTLE RUBBER GLOVE AND SUCTION LATER, SPLAT. THE THING THAT WAS GROWING INSIDE ME IS DROPPED INTO A TIDY METAL GARBAGE CAN. A SMALL BLOODY STAIN. AND THAT IS THAT. END OF STORY. SIGH
CHECK, PLEASE.
IS EVERY-THING NOT ALL RIGHT, SIR? YOU DON'T LIKE THE FOOD?
NO, NO. AS A MATTER OF FACT, COULD YOU WRAP THIS TO GO? I'M JUST NOT THAT HUNGRY RIGHT NOW.
MY PLEASURE.
I'M SORRY IF I RUINED YOUR APPETITE.
IT'S NOT THAT. IT'S JUST KIND OF UPSETTING, IS ALL. IT'S NOT YOUR FAULT.
11:25

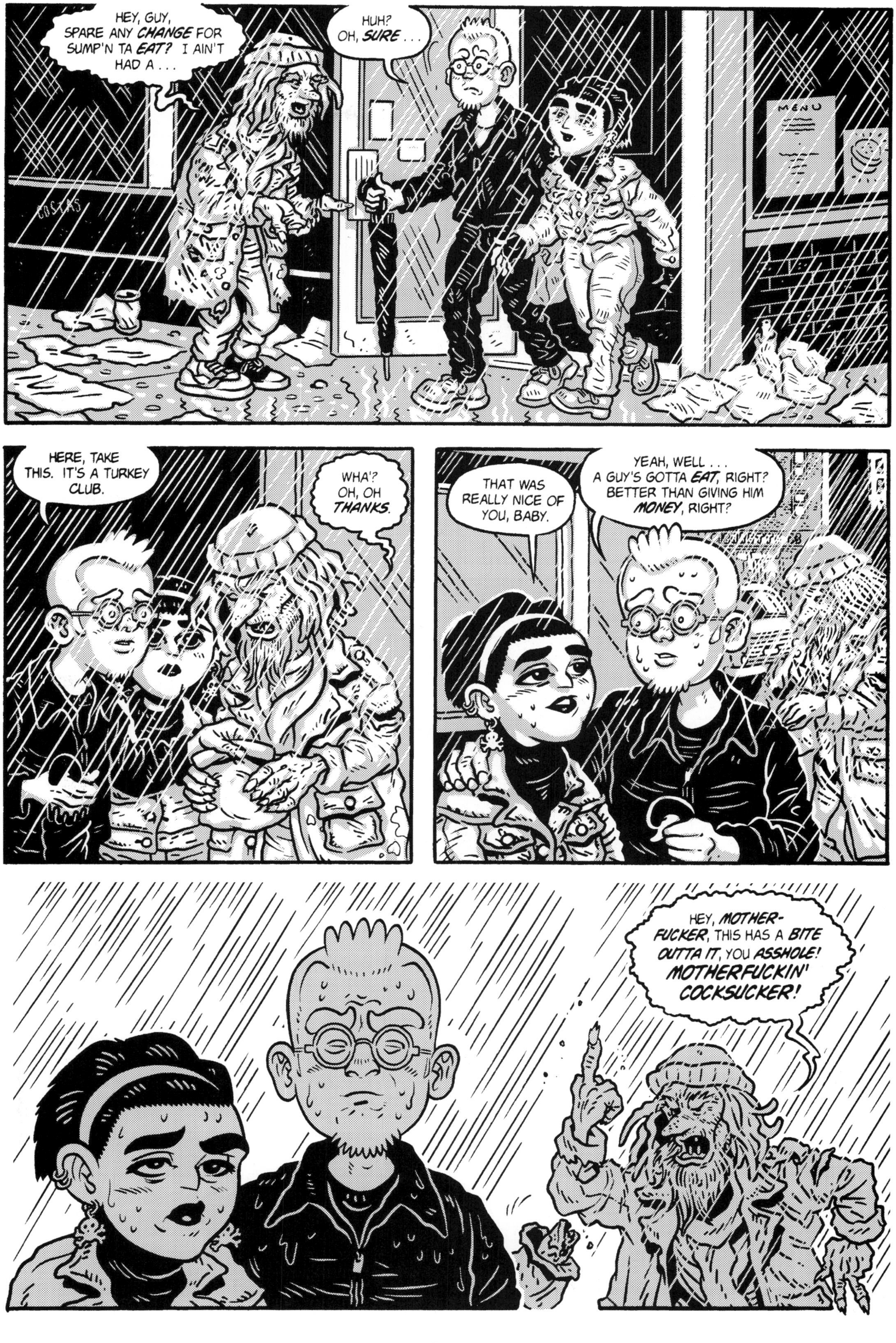

HEY, GUY, SPARE ANY CHANGE FOR SUMP'N TA EAT? I AIN'T HAD A . . .
HUH? OH, SURE . . .
HERE, TAKE THIS. IT'S A TURKEY CLUB.
WHA'? OH, OH THANKS.
THAT WAS REALLY NICE OF YOU, BABY.
YEAH, WELL . . . A GUY'S GOTTA EAT, RIGHT? BETTER THAN GIVING HIM MONEY, RIGHT?
HEY, MOTHER-FUCKER, THIS HAS A BITE OUTTA IT, YOU ASSHOLE! MOTHERFUCKIN' COCKSUCKER!

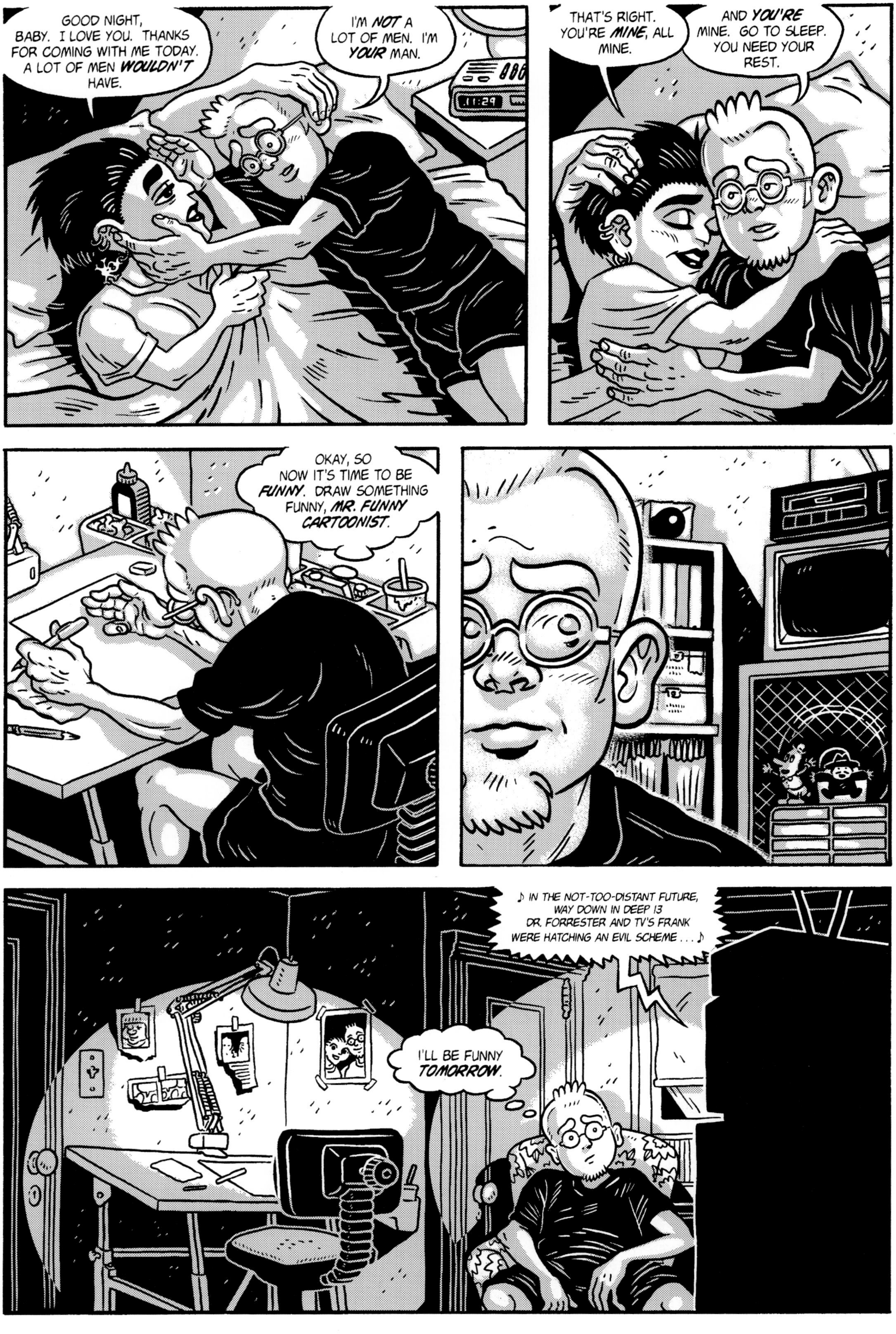
GOOD NIGHT, BABY. I LOVE YOU. THANKS FOR COMING WITH ME TODAY. A LOT OF MEN WOULDN'T HAVE.
I'M NOT A LOT OF MEN. I'M YOUR MAN.
11:29
THAT'S RIGHT. YOU'RE MINE, ALL MINE.
AND YOU'RE MINE. GO TO SLEEP. YOU NEED YOUR REST.
OKAY, SO NOW IT'S TIME TO BE FUNNY. DRAW SOMETHING FUNNY, MR. FUNNY CARTOONIST.
♪ IN THE NOT-TOO-DISTANT FUTURE, WAY DOWN IN DEEP 13 DR. FORRESTER AND TV'S FRANK WERE HATCHING AN EVIL SCHEME . . . ♪
I'LL BE FUNNY TOMORROW.

Chapter Four

CONVENTIONAL BEHAVIOR

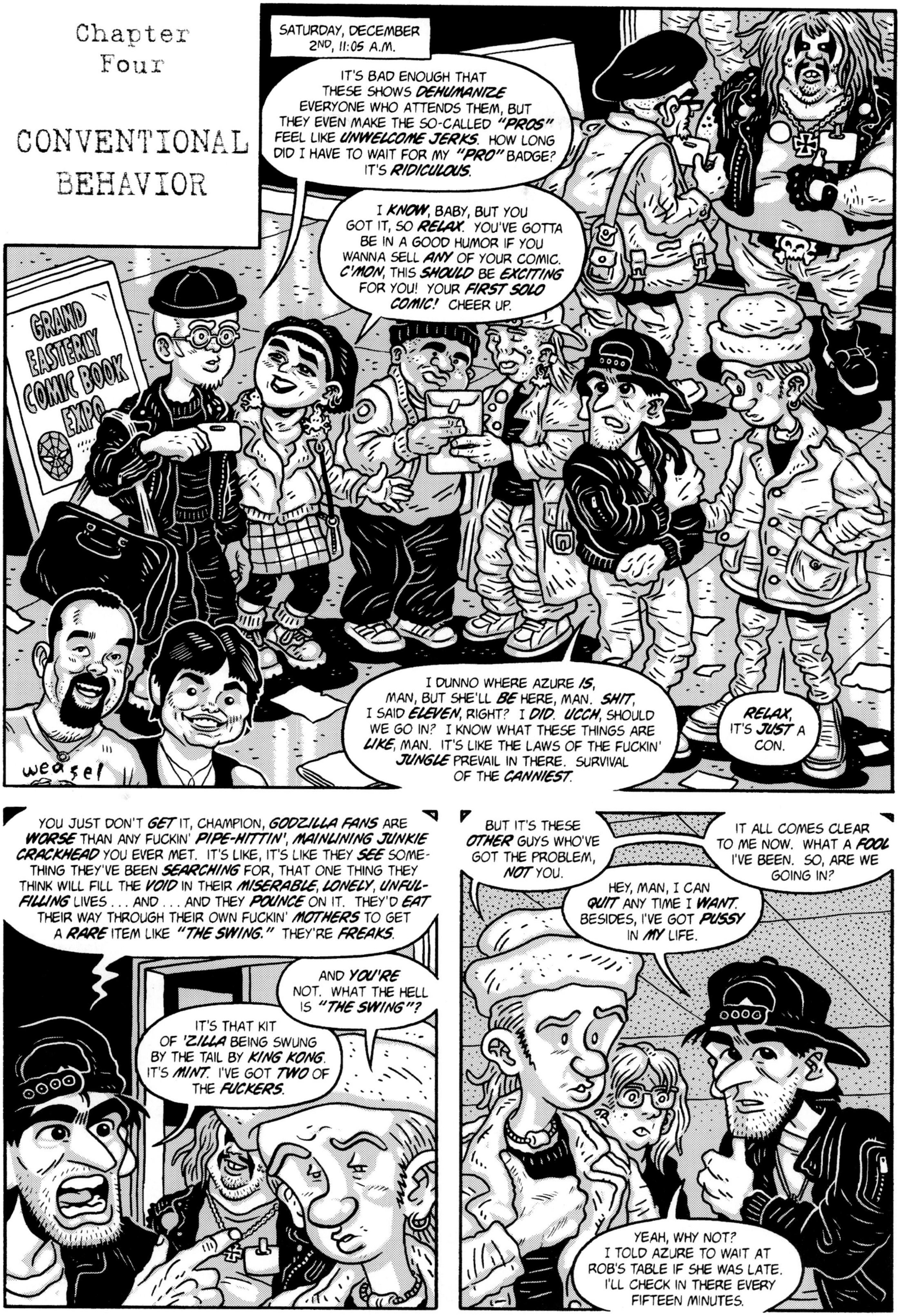

SATURDAY, DECEMBER 2ND, 11:05 A.M.
IT'S BAD ENOUGH THAT THESE SHOWS DEHUMANIZE EVERYONE WHO ATTENDS THEM, BUT THEY EVEN MAKE THE SO-CALLED "PROS" FEEL LIKE UNWELCOME JERKS. HOW LONG DID I HAVE TO WAIT FOR MY "PRO" BADGE? IT'S RIDICULOUS.
I KNOW, BABY, BUT YOU GOT IT, SO RELAX. YOU'VE GOTTA BE IN A GOOD HUMOR IF YOU WANNA SELL ANY OF YOUR COMIC. C'MON, THIS SHOULD BE EXCITING FOR YOU! YOUR FIRST SOLO COMIC! CHEER UP.
GRAND EASTERLY COMIC BOOK EXPO
I DUNNO WHERE AZURE IS, MAN, BUT SHE'LL BE HERE, MAN. SHIT, I SAID ELEVEN, RIGHT? I DID. UCCH, SHOULD WE GO IN? I KNOW WHAT THESE THINGS ARE LIKE, MAN. IT'S LIKE THE LAWS OF THE FUCKIN' JUNGLE PREVAIL IN THERE. SURVIVAL OF THE CANNIEST.
RELAX, IT'S JUST A CON.
weasel
YOU JUST DON'T GET IT, CHAMPION, GODZILLA FANS ARE WORSE THAN ANY FUCKIN' PIPE-HITTIN', MAINLINING JUNKIE CRACKHEAD YOU EVER MET. IT'S LIKE, IT'S LIKE THEY SEE SOMETHING THEY'VE BEEN SEARCHING FOR, THAT ONE THING THEY THINK WILL FILL THE VOID IN THEIR MISERABLE, LONELY, UNFULFILLING LIVES . . . AND . . . AND THEY POUNCE ON IT. THEY'D EAT THEIR WAY THROUGH THEIR OWN FUCKIN' MOTHERS TO GET A RARE ITEM LIKE "THE SWING." THEY'RE FREAKS.
AND YOU'RE NOT. WHAT THE HELL IS "THE SWING"?
IT'S THAT KIT OF 'ZILLA BEING SWUNG BY THE TAIL BY KING KONG. IT'S MINT. I'VE GOT TWO OF THE FUCKERS.
BUT IT'S THESE OTHER GUYS WHO'VE GOT THE PROBLEM, NOT YOU.
HEY, MAN, I CAN QUIT ANY TIME I WANT. BESIDES, I'VE GOT PUSSY IN MY LIFE.
IT ALL COMES CLEAR TO ME NOW. WHAT A FOOL I'VE BEEN. SO, ARE WE GOING IN?
YEAH, WHY NOT? I TOLD AZURE TO WAIT AT ROB'S TABLE IF SHE WAS LATE. I'LL CHECK IN THERE EVERY FIFTEEN MINUTES.

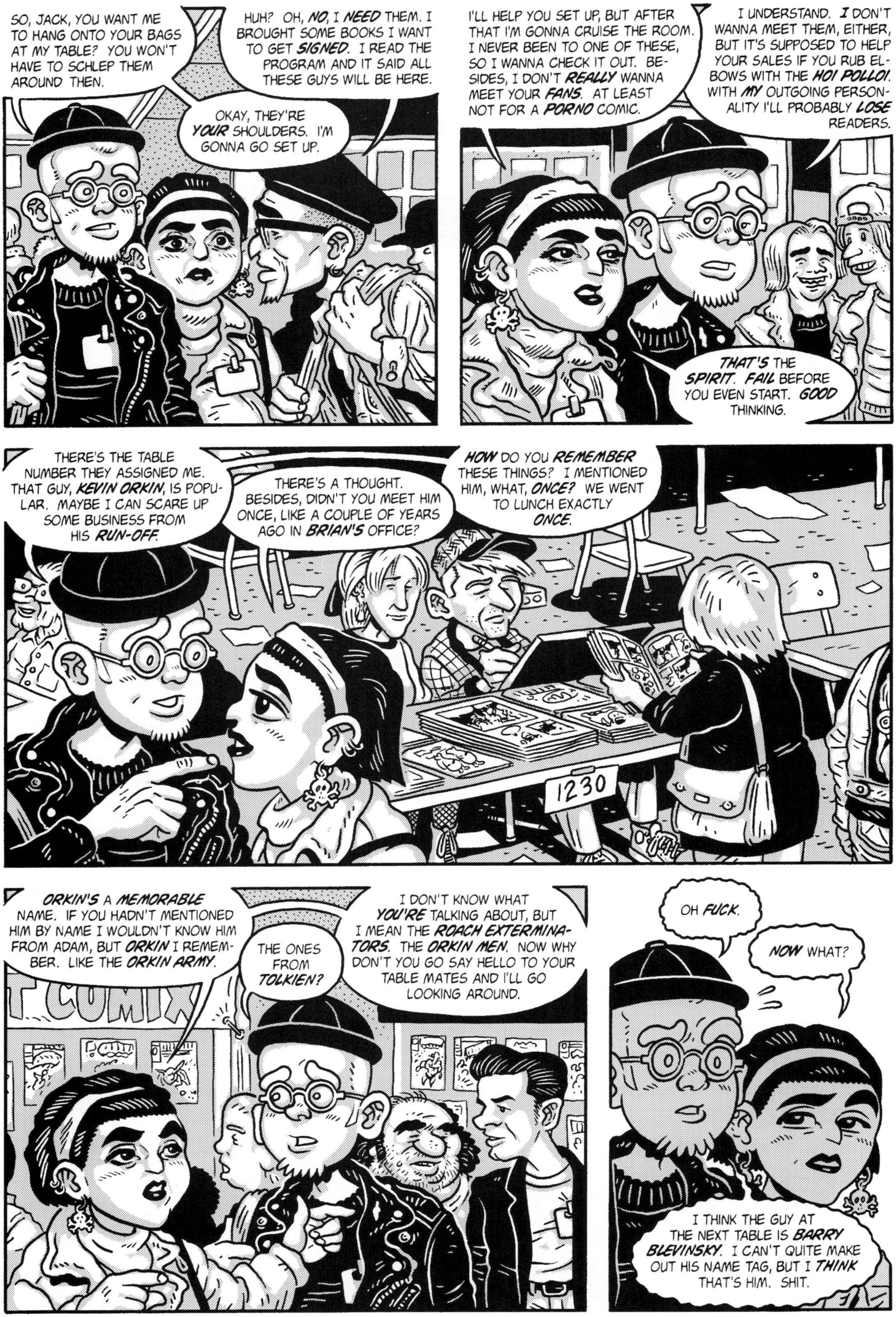
SO, JACK, YOU WANT ME TO HANG ONTO YOUR BAGS AT MY TABLE? YOU WON'T HAVE TO SCHLEP THEM AROUND THEN.
HUH? OH, NO, I NEED THEM. I BROUGHT SOME BOOKS I WANT TO GET SIGNED. I READ THE PROGRAM AND IT SAID ALL THESE GUYS WILL BE HERE.
OKAY, THEY'RE YOUR SHOULDERS. I'M GONNA GO SET UP.
I'LL HELP YOU SET UP, BUT AFTER THAT I'M GONNA CRUISE THE ROOM. I NEVER BEEN TO ONE OF THESE, SO I WANNA CHECK IT OUT. BESIDES, I DON'T REALLY WANNA MEET YOUR FANS. AT LEAST NOT FOR A PORNO COMIC.
I UNDERSTAND. I DON'T WANNA MEET THEM, EITHER, BUT IT'S SUPPOSED TO HELP YOUR SALES IF YOU RUB ELBOWS WITH THE HOI POLLOI. WITH MY OUTGOING PERSONALITY I'LL PROBABLY LOSE READERS.
THAT'S THE SPIRIT. FAIL BEFORE YOU EVEN START. GOOD THINKING.
THERE'S THE TABLE NUMBER THEY ASSIGNED ME. THAT GUY, KEVIN ORKIN, IS POPULAR. MAYBE I CAN SCARE UP SOME BUSINESS FROM HIS RUN-OFF.
THERE'S A THOUGHT. BESIDES, DIDN'T YOU MEET HIM ONCE, LIKE A COUPLE OF YEARS AGO IN BRIAN'S OFFICE?
HOW DO YOU REMEMBER THESE THINGS? I MENTIONED HIM, WHAT, ONCE? WE WENT TO LUNCH EXACTLY ONCE.
1230
ORKIN'S A MEMORABLE NAME. IF YOU HADN'T MENTIONED HIM BY NAME I WOULDN'T KNOW HIM FROM ADAM, BUT ORKIN I REMEMBER. LIKE THE ORKIN ARMY.
THE ONES FROM TOLKIEN?
I DON'T KNOW WHAT YOU'RE TALKING ABOUT, BUT I MEAN THE ROACH EXTERMINATORS. THE ORKIN MEN. NOW WHY DON'T YOU GO SAY HELLO TO YOUR TABLE MATES AND I'LL GO LOOKING AROUND.
COMIX
OH FUCK.
NOW WHAT?
I THINK THE GUY AT THE NEXT TABLE IS BARRY BLEVINSKY. I CAN'T QUITE MAKE OUT HIS NAME TAG, BUT I THINK THAT'S HIM. SHIT.

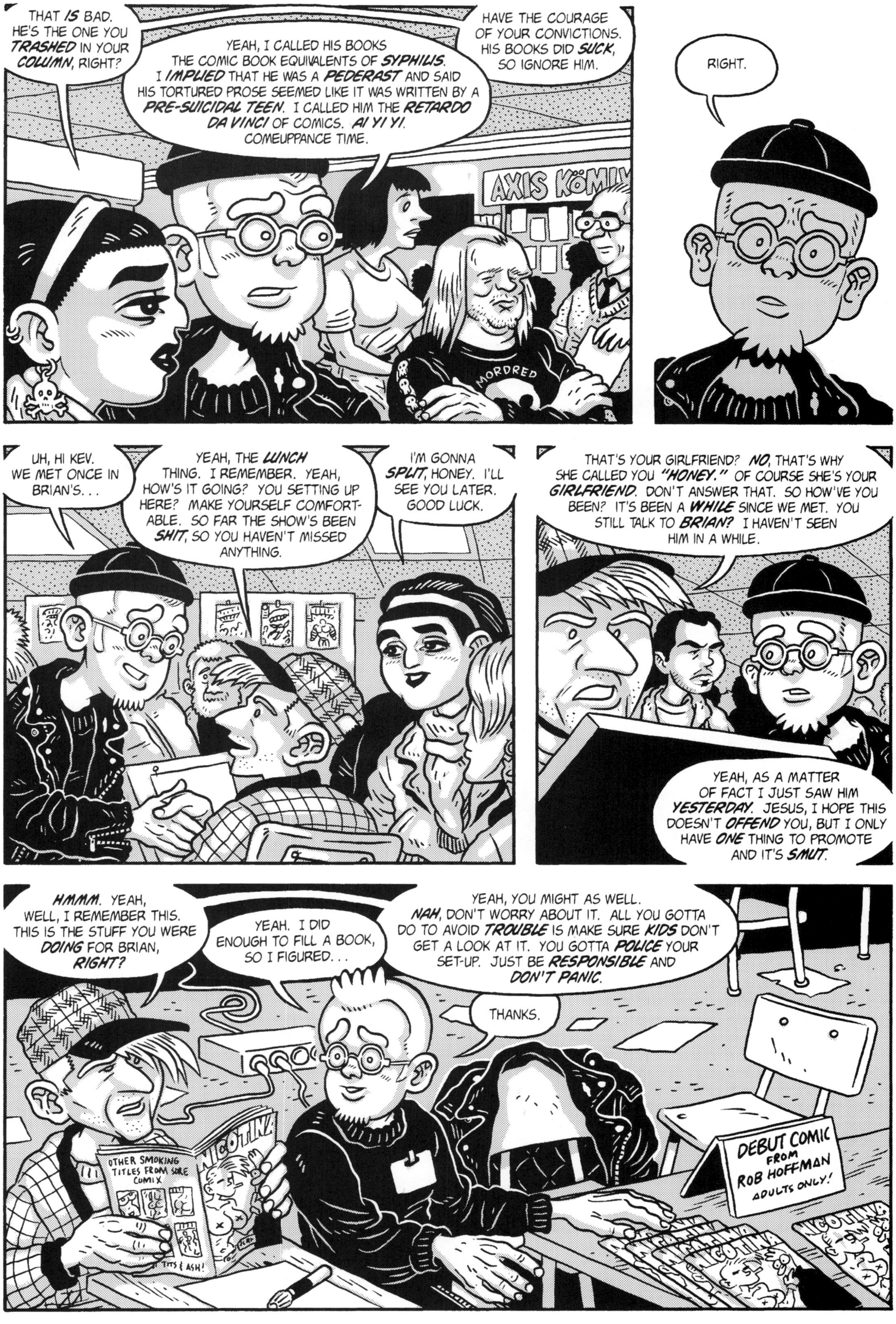

THAT IS BAD. HE'S THE ONE YOU TRASHED IN YOUR COLUMN, RIGHT?
YEAH, I CALLED HIS BOOKS THE COMIC BOOK EQUIVALENTS OF SYPHILIS. I IMPLIED THAT HE WAS A PEDERAST AND SAID HIS TORTURED PROSE SEEMED LIKE IT WAS WRITTEN BY A PRE-SUICIDAL TEEN. I CALLED HIM THE RETARDO DA VINCI OF COMICS. AI YI YI. COMEUPPANCE TIME.
HAVE THE COURAGE OF YOUR CONVICTIONS. HIS BOOKS DID SUCK, SO IGNORE HIM.
AXIS KÖMIX
MORDRED
RIGHT.
UH, HI KEV. WE MET ONCE IN BRIAN'S. . .
YEAH, THE LUNCH THING. I REMEMBER. YEAH, HOW'S IT GOING? YOU SETTING UP HERE? MAKE YOURSELF COMFORTABLE. SO FAR THE SHOW'S BEEN SHIT, SO YOU HAVEN'T MISSED ANYTHING.
I'M GONNA SPLIT, HONEY. I'LL SEE YOU LATER. GOOD LUCK.
THAT'S YOUR GIRLFRIEND? NO, THAT'S WHY SHE CALLED YOU "HONEY." OF COURSE SHE'S YOUR GIRLFRIEND. DON'T ANSWER THAT. SO HOW'VE YOU BEEN? IT'S BEEN A WHILE SINCE WE MET. YOU STILL TALK TO BRIAN? I HAVEN'T SEEN HIM IN A WHILE.
YEAH, AS A MATTER OF FACT I JUST SAW HIM YESTERDAY. JESUS, I HOPE THIS DOESN'T OFFEND YOU, BUT I ONLY HAVE ONE THING TO PROMOTE AND IT'S SMUT.
HMMM. YEAH, WELL, I REMEMBER THIS. THIS IS THE STUFF YOU WERE DOING FOR BRIAN, RIGHT?
YEAH. I DID ENOUGH TO FILL A BOOK, SO I FIGURED. . .
YEAH, YOU MIGHT AS WELL. NAH, DON'T WORRY ABOUT IT. ALL YOU GOTTA DO TO AVOID TROUBLE IS MAKE SURE KIDS DON'T GET A LOOK AT IT. YOU GOTTA POLICE YOUR SET-UP. JUST BE RESPONSIBLE AND DON'T PANIC.
THANKS.
OTHER SMOKING TITLES FROM SURE COMIX
NICOTINE
DEBUT COMIC FROM ROB HOFFMAN ADULTS ONLY!

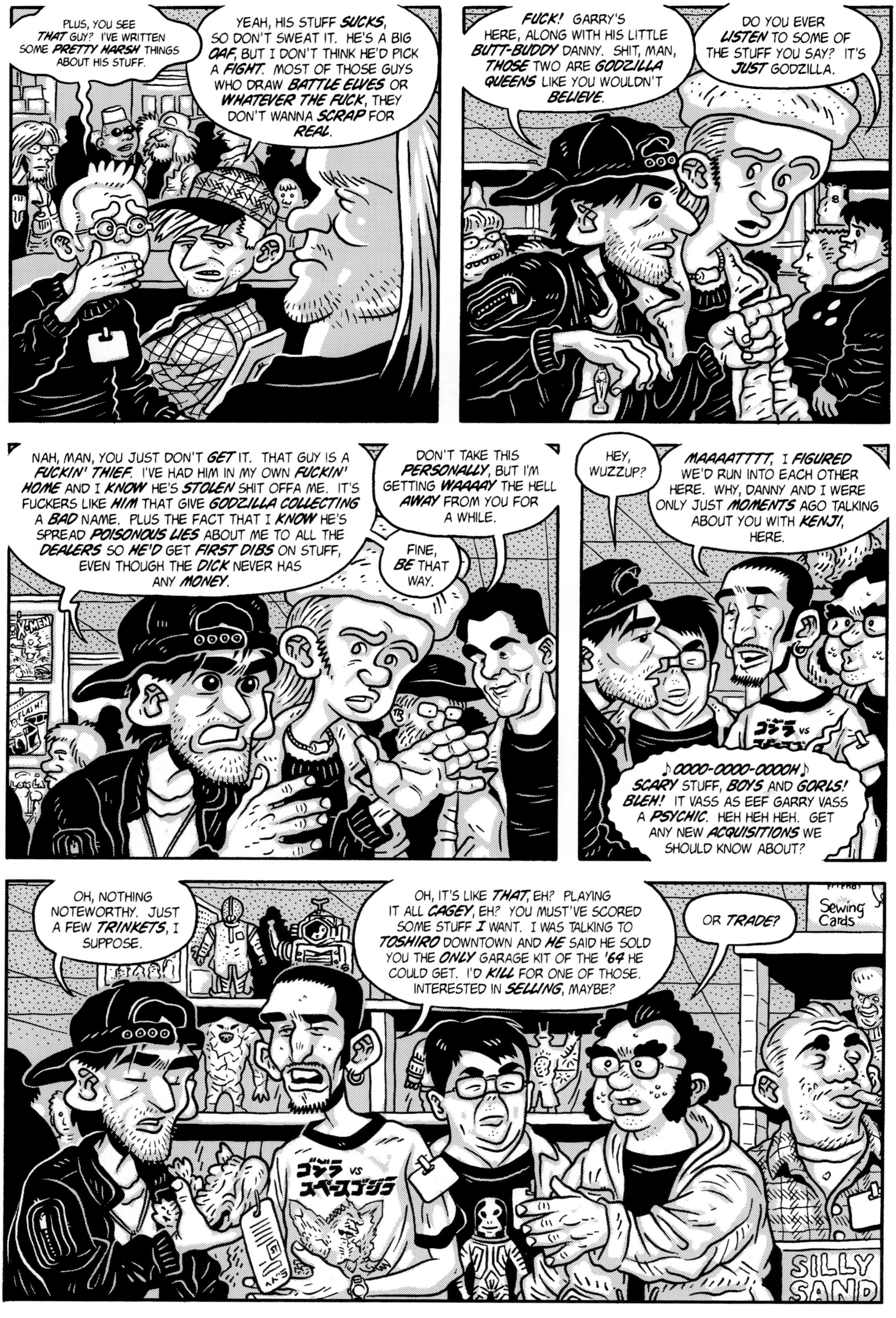
PLUS, YOU SEE THAT GUY? I'VE WRITTEN SOME PRETTY HARSH THINGS ABOUT HIS STUFF.
YEAH, HIS STUFF SUCKS, SO DON'T SWEAT IT. HE'S A BIG OAF, BUT I DON'T THINK HE'D PICK A FIGHT. MOST OF THOSE GUYS WHO DRAW BATTLE ELVES OR WHATEVER THE FUCK, THEY DON'T WANNA SCRAP FOR REAL.
FUCK! GARRY'S HERE, ALONG WITH HIS LITTLE BUTT-BUDDY DANNY. SHIT, MAN, THOSE TWO ARE GODZILLA QUEENS LIKE YOU WOULDN'T BELIEVE.
DO YOU EVER LISTEN TO SOME OF THE STUFF YOU SAY? IT'S JUST GODZILLA.
NAH, MAN, YOU JUST DON'T GET IT. THAT GUY IS A FUCKIN' THIEF. I'VE HAD HIM IN MY OWN FUCKIN' HOME AND I KNOW HE'S STOLEN SHIT OFFA ME. IT'S FUCKERS LIKE HIM THAT GIVE GODZILLA COLLECTING A BAD NAME. PLUS THE FACT THAT I KNOW HE'S SPREAD POISONOUS LIES ABOUT ME TO ALL THE DEALERS SO HE'D GET FIRST DIBS ON STUFF, EVEN THOUGH THE DICK NEVER HAS ANY MONEY.
DON'T TAKE THIS PERSONALLY, BUT I'M GETTING WAAAAY THE HELL AWAY FROM YOU FOR A WHILE.
FINE, BE THAT WAY.
X-MEN
FLASH!
HEY, WUZZUP?
MAAAATTTT, I FIGURED WE'D RUN INTO EACH OTHER HERE. WHY, DANNY AND I WERE ONLY JUST MOMENTS AGO TALKING ABOUT YOU WITH KENJI, HERE.
♪OOOO-OOOO-OOOOH♪ SCARY STUFF, BOYS AND GORLS! BLEH! IT VASS AS EEF GARRY VASS A PSYCHIC. HEH HEH HEH. GET ANY NEW ACQUISITIONS WE SHOULD KNOW ABOUT?
OH, NOTHING NOTEWORTHY. JUST A FEW TRINKETS, I SUPPOSE.
OH, IT'S LIKE THAT, EH? PLAYING IT ALL CAGEY, EH? YOU MUST'VE SCORED SOME STUFF I WANT. I WAS TALKING TO TOSHIRO DOWNTOWN AND HE SAID HE SOLD YOU THE ONLY GARAGE KIT OF THE '64 HE COULD GET. I'D KILL FOR ONE OF THOSE. INTERESTED IN SELLING, MAYBE?
OR TRADE?
Sewing Cards
ゴジラ vs スペースゴジラ
SILLY SAND

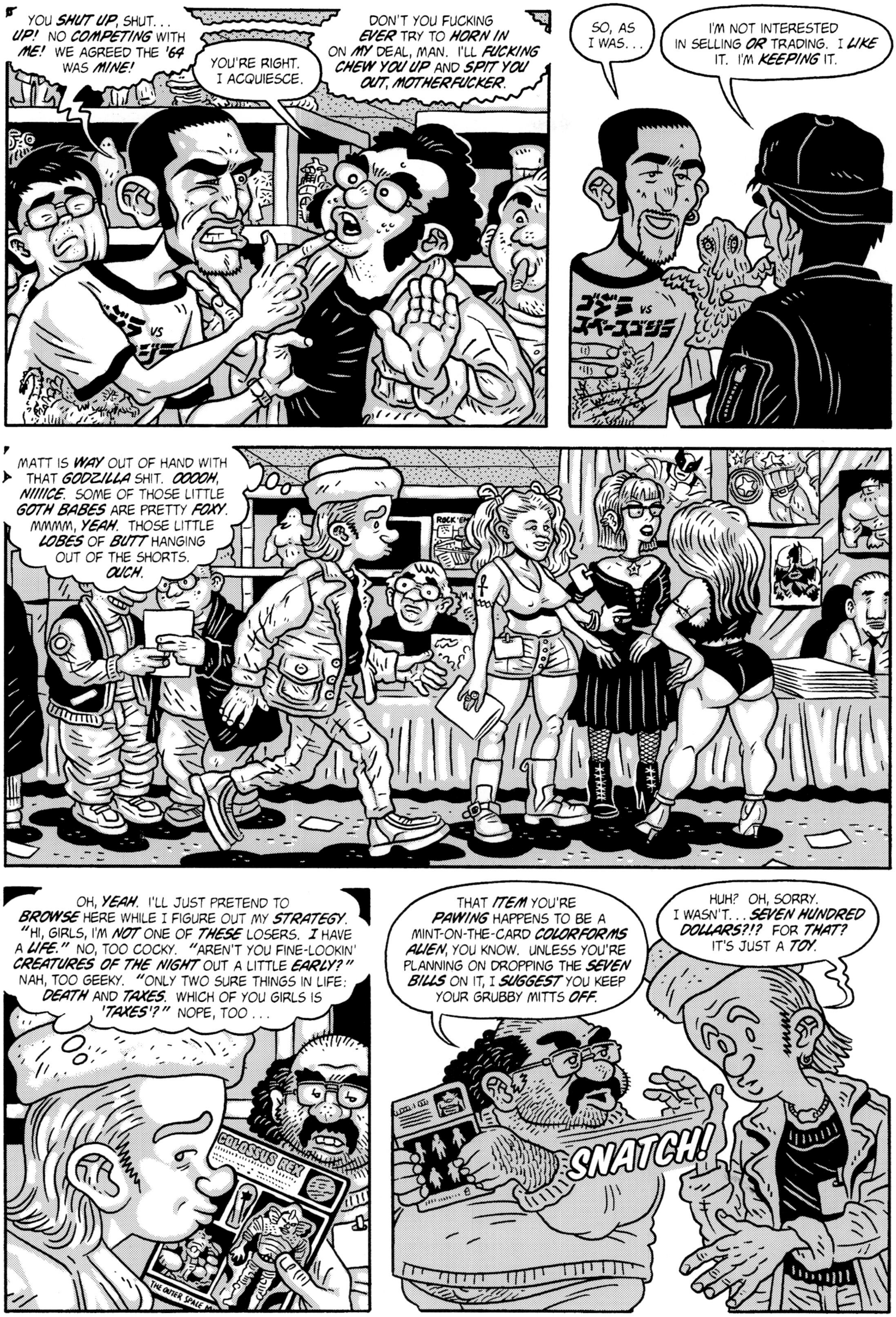
YOU SHUT UP, SHUT... UP! NO COMPETING WITH ME! WE AGREED THE '64 WAS MINE!
YOU'RE RIGHT. I ACQUIESCE.
DON'T YOU FUCKING EVER TRY TO HORN IN ON MY DEAL, MAN. I'LL FUCKING CHEW YOU UP AND SPIT YOU OUT, MOTHERFUCKER.
SO, AS I WAS...
I'M NOT INTERESTED IN SELLING OR TRADING. I LIKE IT. I'M KEEPING IT.
ゴジラ VS スペースゴジラ
MATT IS WAY OUT OF HAND WITH THAT GODZILLA SHIT. OOOOH, NIIIICE. SOME OF THOSE LITTLE GOTH BABES ARE PRETTY FOXY. MMMM, YEAH. THOSE LITTLE LOBES OF BUTT HANGING OUT OF THE SHORTS. OUCH.
OH, YEAH. I'LL JUST PRETEND TO BROWSE HERE WHILE I FIGURE OUT MY STRATEGY. "HI, GIRLS, I'M NOT ONE OF THESE LOSERS. I HAVE A LIFE." NO, TOO COCKY. "AREN'T YOU FINE-LOOKIN' CREATURES OF THE NIGHT OUT A LITTLE EARLY?" NAH, TOO GEEKY. "ONLY TWO SURE THINGS IN LIFE: DEATH AND TAXES. WHICH OF YOU GIRLS IS 'TAXES'?" NOPE, TOO...
COLOSSUS REX
THAT ITEM YOU'RE PAWING HAPPENS TO BE A MINT-ON-THE-CARD COLORFORMS ALIEN, YOU KNOW. UNLESS YOU'RE PLANNING ON DROPPING THE SEVEN BILLS ON IT, I SUGGEST YOU KEEP YOUR GRUBBY MITTS OFF.
HUH? OH, SORRY. I WASN'T... SEVEN HUNDRED DOLLARS?!? FOR THAT? IT'S JUST A TOY.
SNATCH!

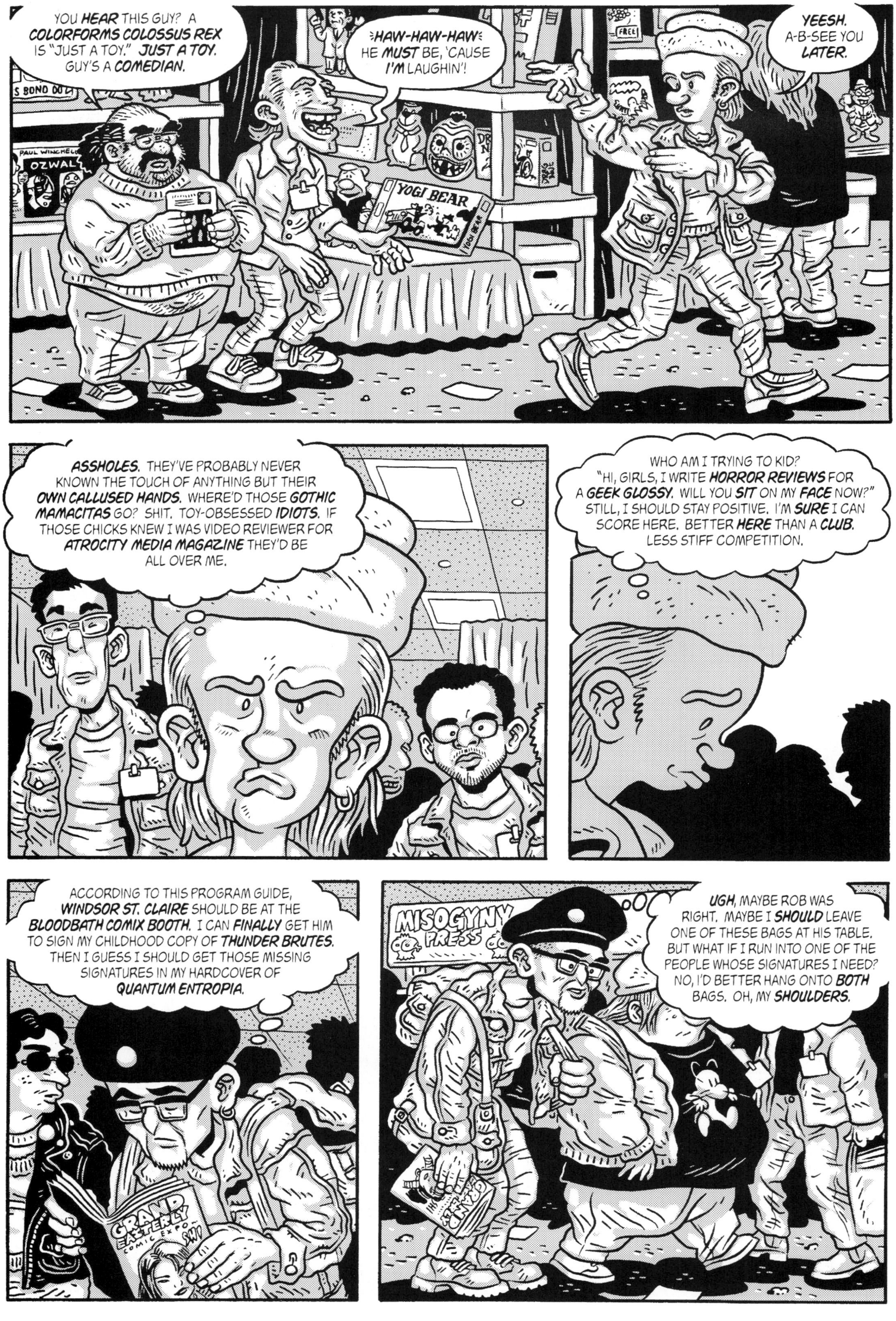
YOU HEAR THIS GUY? A COLORFORMS COLOSSUS REX IS "JUST A TOY." JUST A TOY. GUY'S A COMEDIAN.
HAW-HAW-HAW HE MUST BE, 'CAUSE I'M LAUGHIN'!
YEESH. A-B-SEE YOU LATER.
ASSHOLES. THEY'VE PROBABLY NEVER KNOWN THE TOUCH OF ANYTHING BUT THEIR OWN CALLUSED HANDS. WHERE'D THOSE GOTHIC MAMACITAS GO? SHIT. TOY-OBSESSED IDIOTS. IF THOSE CHICKS KNEW I WAS VIDEO REVIEWER FOR ATROCITY MEDIA MAGAZINE THEY'D BE ALL OVER ME.
WHO AM I TRYING TO KID? "HI, GIRLS, I WRITE HORROR REVIEWS FOR A GEEK GLOSSY. WILL YOU SIT ON MY FACE NOW?" STILL, I SHOULD STAY POSITIVE. I'M SURE I CAN SCORE HERE. BETTER HERE THAN A CLUB. LESS STIFF COMPETITION.
ACCORDING TO THIS PROGRAM GUIDE, WINDSOR ST. CLAIRE SHOULD BE AT THE BLOODBATH COMIX BOOTH. I CAN FINALLY GET HIM TO SIGN MY CHILDHOOD COPY OF THUNDER BRUTES. THEN I GUESS I SHOULD GET THOSE MISSING SIGNATURES IN MY HARDCOVER OF QUANTUM ENTROPIA.
GRAND EASTERLY COMIC EXPO
MISOGYNY PRESS
UGH, MAYBE ROB WAS RIGHT. MAYBE I SHOULD LEAVE ONE OF THESE BAGS AT HIS TABLE. BUT WHAT IF I RUN INTO ONE OF THE PEOPLE WHOSE SIGNATURES I NEED? NO, I'D BETTER HANG ONTO BOTH BAGS. OH, MY SHOULDERS.

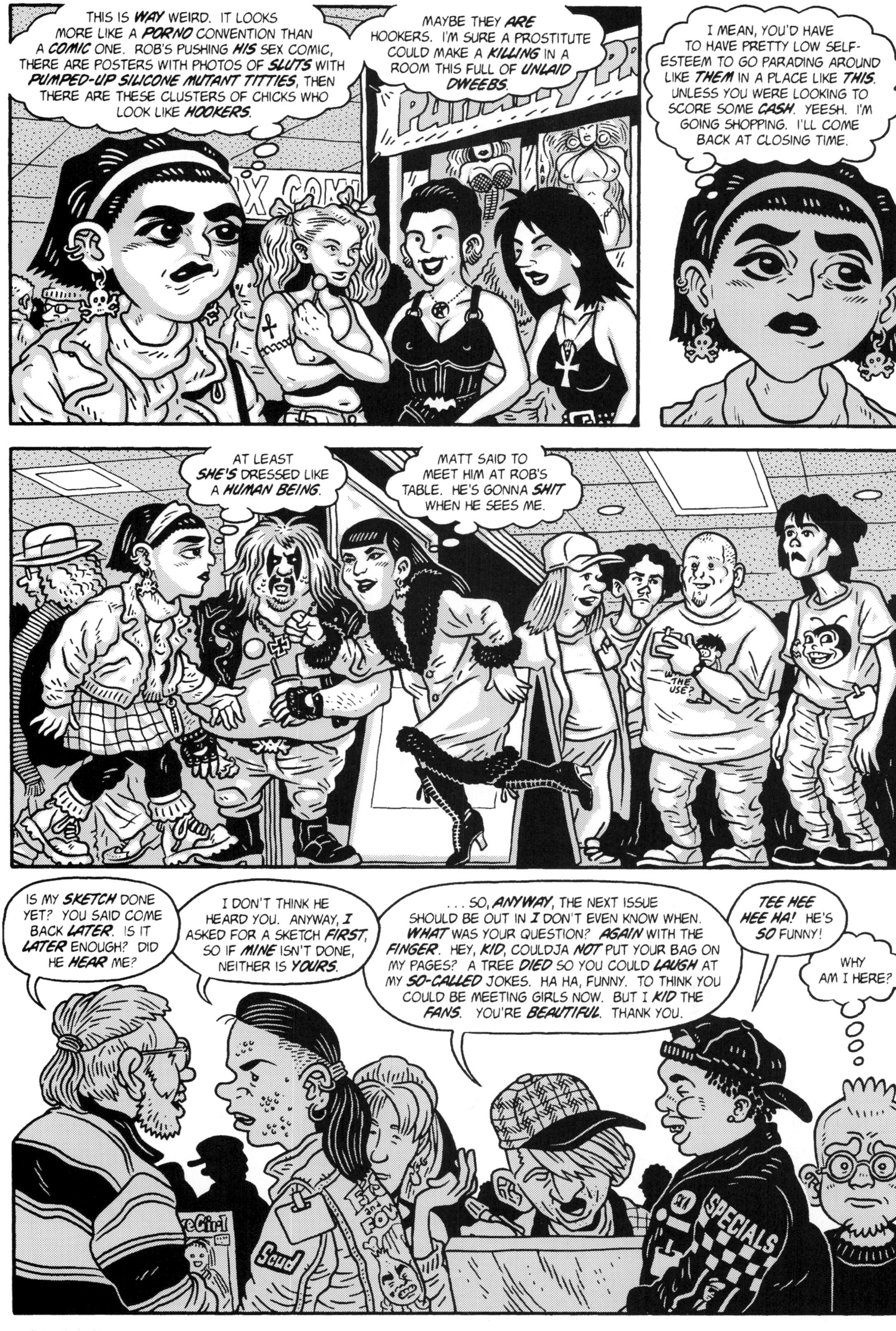
THIS IS WAY WEIRD. IT LOOKS MORE LIKE A PORNO CONVENTION THAN A COMIC ONE. ROB'S PUSHING HIS SEX COMIC, THERE ARE POSTERS WITH PHOTOS OF SLUTS WITH PUMPED-UP SILICONE MUTANT TITTIES, THEN THERE ARE THESE CLUSTERS OF CHICKS WHO LOOK LIKE HOOKERS.
MAYBE THEY ARE HOOKERS. I'M SURE A PROSTITUTE COULD MAKE A KILLING IN A ROOM THIS FULL OF UNLAID DWEEBS.
I MEAN, YOU'D HAVE TO HAVE PRETTY LOW SELF-ESTEEM TO GO PARADING AROUND LIKE THEM IN A PLACE LIKE THIS. UNLESS YOU WERE LOOKING TO SCORE SOME CASH. YEESH. I'M GOING SHOPPING. I'LL COME BACK AT CLOSING TIME.
AT LEAST SHE'S DRESSED LIKE A HUMAN BEING.
MATT SAID TO MEET HIM AT ROB'S TABLE. HE'S GONNA SHIT WHEN HE SEES ME.
IS MY SKETCH DONE YET? YOU SAID COME BACK LATER. IS IT LATER ENOUGH? DID HE HEAR ME?
I DON'T THINK HE HEARD YOU. ANYWAY, I ASKED FOR A SKETCH FIRST, SO IF MINE ISN'T DONE, NEITHER IS YOURS.
. . . SO, ANYWAY, THE NEXT ISSUE SHOULD BE OUT IN I DON'T EVEN KNOW WHEN. WHAT WAS YOUR QUESTION? AGAIN WITH THE FINGER. HEY, KID, COULDJA NOT PUT YOUR BAG ON MY PAGES? A TREE DIED SO YOU COULD LAUGH AT MY SO-CALLED JOKES. HA HA, FUNNY. TO THINK YOU COULD BE MEETING GIRLS NOW. BUT I KID THE FANS. YOU'RE BEAUTIFUL. THANK YOU.
TEE HEE HEE HA! HE'S SO FUNNY!
WHY AM I HERE?
SPECIALS

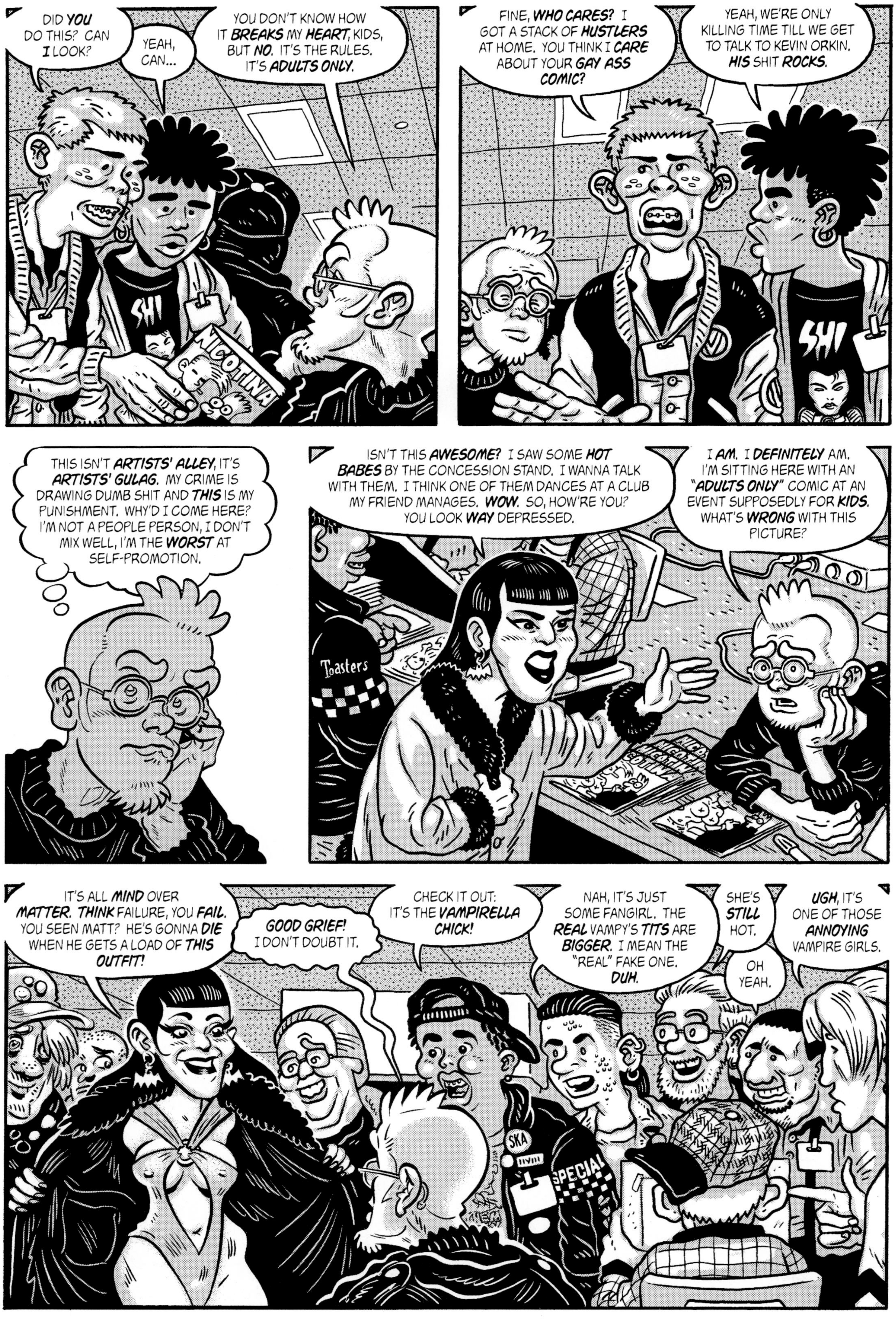

DID YOU DO THIS? CAN I LOOK?
YEAH, CAN...
YOU DON'T KNOW HOW IT BREAKS MY HEART, KIDS, BUT NO. IT'S THE RULES. IT'S ADULTS ONLY.
NICOTINA
FINE, WHO CARES? I GOT A STACK OF HUSTLERS AT HOME. YOU THINK I CARE ABOUT YOUR GAY ASS COMIC?
YEAH, WE'RE ONLY KILLING TIME TILL WE GET TO TALK TO KEVIN ORKIN. HIS SHIT ROCKS.
THIS ISN'T ARTISTS' ALLEY, IT'S ARTISTS' GULAG. MY CRIME IS DRAWING DUMB SHIT AND THIS IS MY PUNISHMENT. WHY'D I COME HERE? I'M NOT A PEOPLE PERSON, I DON'T MIX WELL, I'M THE WORST AT SELF-PROMOTION.
ISN'T THIS AWESOME? I SAW SOME HOT BABES BY THE CONCESSION STAND. I WANNA TALK WITH THEM. I THINK ONE OF THEM DANCES AT A CLUB MY FRIEND MANAGES. WOW. SO, HOW'RE YOU? YOU LOOK WAY DEPRESSED.
I AM. I DEFINITELY AM. I'M SITTING HERE WITH AN "ADULTS ONLY" COMIC AT AN EVENT SUPPOSEDLY FOR KIDS. WHAT'S WRONG WITH THIS PICTURE?
Toasters
IT'S ALL MIND OVER MATTER. THINK FAILURE, YOU FAIL. YOU SEEN MATT? HE'S GONNA DIE WHEN HE GETS A LOAD OF THIS OUTFIT!
GOOD GRIEF! I DON'T DOUBT IT.
CHECK IT OUT: IT'S THE VAMPIRELLA CHICK!
NAH, IT'S JUST SOME FANGIRL. THE REAL VAMPY'S TITS ARE BIGGER. I MEAN THE "REAL" FAKE ONE. DUH.
SHE'S STILL HOT.
OH YEAH.
UGH, IT'S ONE OF THOSE ANNOYING VAMPIRE GIRLS.
SKA
SPECIAL

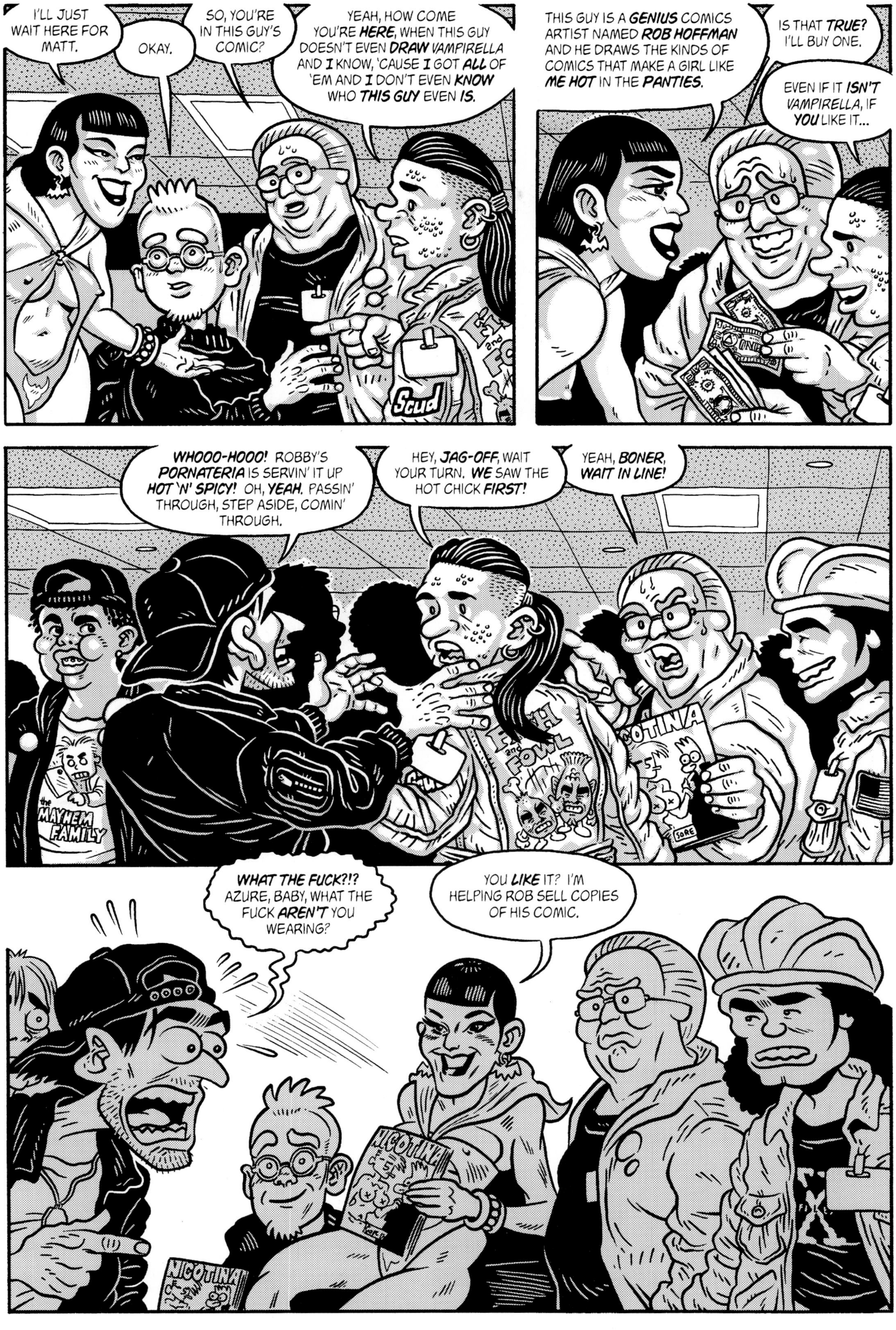
I'LL JUST WAIT HERE FOR MATT.
OKAY.
SO, YOU'RE IN THIS GUY'S COMIC?
YEAH, HOW COME YOU'RE HERE, WHEN THIS GUY DOESN'T EVEN DRAW VAMPIRELLA AND I KNOW, 'CAUSE I GOT ALL OF 'EM AND I DON'T EVEN KNOW WHO THIS GUY EVEN IS.
Scud
THIS GUY IS A GENIUS COMICS ARTIST NAMED ROB HOFFMAN AND HE DRAWS THE KINDS OF COMICS THAT MAKE A GIRL LIKE ME HOT IN THE PANTIES.
IS THAT TRUE? I'LL BUY ONE.
EVEN IF IT ISN'T VAMPIRELLA, IF YOU LIKE IT...
WHOOO-HOOO! ROBBY'S PORNATERIA IS SERVIN' IT UP HOT 'N' SPICY! OH, YEAH. PASSIN' THROUGH, STEP ASIDE, COMIN' THROUGH.
HEY, JAG-OFF, WAIT YOUR TURN. WE SAW THE HOT CHICK FIRST!
YEAH, BONER, WAIT IN LINE!
the MAYHEM FAMILY
WHAT THE FUCK?!? AZURE, BABY, WHAT THE FUCK AREN'T YOU WEARING?
YOU LIKE IT? I'M HELPING ROB SELL COPIES OF HIS COMIC.
NICOTINA

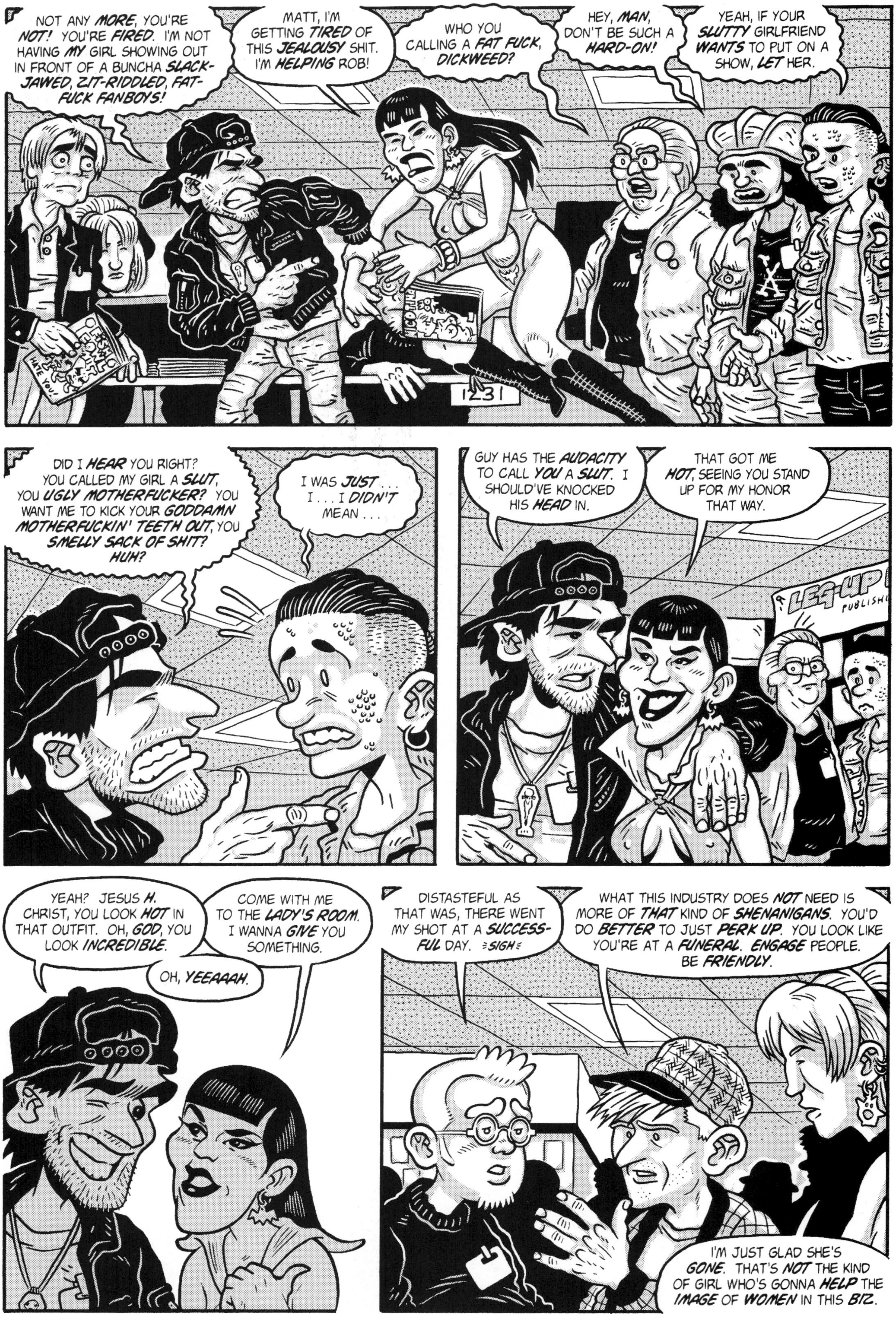
NOT ANY MORE, YOU'RE NOT! YOU'RE FIRED. I'M NOT HAVING MY GIRL SHOWING OUT IN FRONT OF A BUNCHA SLACK-JAWED, ZIT-RIDDLED, FAT-FUCK FANBOYS!
MATT, I'M GETTING TIRED OF THIS JEALOUSY SHIT. I'M HELPING ROB!
WHO YOU CALLING A FAT FUCK, DICKWEED?
HEY, MAN, DON'T BE SUCH A HARD-ON!
YEAH, IF YOUR SLUTTY GIRLFRIEND WANTS TO PUT ON A SHOW, LET HER.
1231
DID I HEAR YOU RIGHT? YOU CALLED MY GIRL A SLUT, YOU UGLY MOTHERFUCKER? YOU WANT ME TO KICK YOUR GODDAMN MOTHERFUCKIN' TEETH OUT, YOU SMELLY SACK OF SHIT? HUH?
I WAS JUST . . . I . . . I DIDN'T MEAN . . .
GUY HAS THE AUDACITY TO CALL YOU A SLUT. I SHOULD'VE KNOCKED HIS HEAD IN.
THAT GOT ME HOT, SEEING YOU STAND UP FOR MY HONOR THAT WAY.
LEG-UP
YEAH? JESUS H. CHRIST, YOU LOOK HOT IN THAT OUTFIT. OH, GOD, YOU LOOK INCREDIBLE.
COME WITH ME TO THE LADY'S ROOM. I WANNA GIVE YOU SOMETHING.
OH, YEEAAAH.
DISTASTEFUL AS THAT WAS, THERE WENT MY SHOT AT A SUCCESSFUL DAY. SIGH
WHAT THIS INDUSTRY DOES NOT NEED IS MORE OF THAT KIND OF SHENANIGANS. YOU'D DO BETTER TO JUST PERK UP. YOU LOOK LIKE YOU'RE AT A FUNERAL. ENGAGE PEOPLE. BE FRIENDLY.
I'M JUST GLAD SHE'S GONE. THAT'S NOT THE KIND OF GIRL WHO'S GONNA HELP THE IMAGE OF WOMEN IN THIS BIZ.

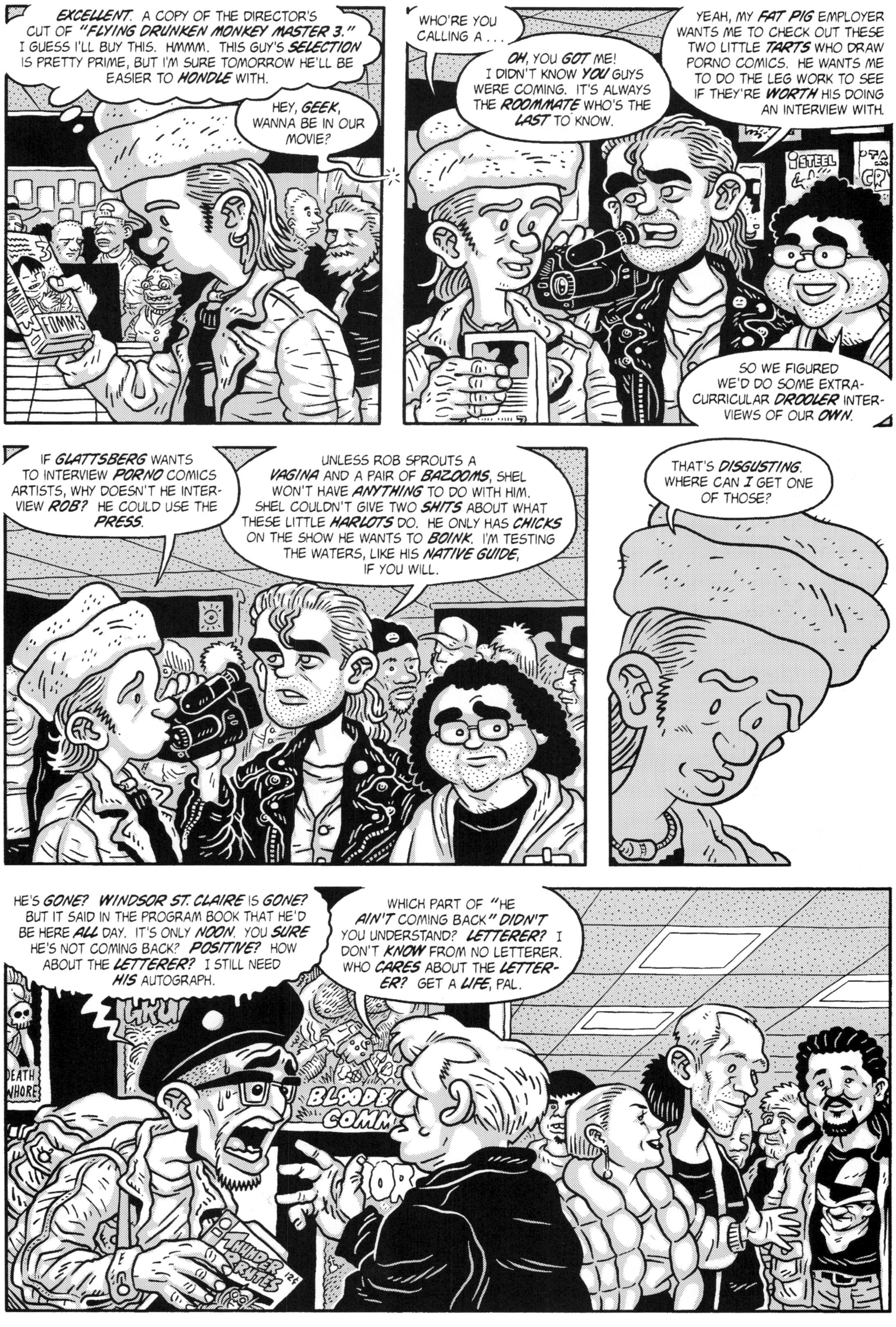

EXCELLENT. A COPY OF THE DIRECTOR'S CUT OF "FLYING DRUNKEN MONKEY MASTER 3." I GUESS I'LL BUY THIS. HMMM. THIS GUY'S SELECTION IS PRETTY PRIME, BUT I'M SURE TOMORROW HE'LL BE EASIER TO HONDLE WITH.
HEY, GEEK, WANNA BE IN OUR MOVIE?
FOMM3
WHO'RE YOU CALLING A . . .
OH, YOU GOT ME! I DIDN'T KNOW YOU GUYS WERE COMING. IT'S ALWAYS THE ROOMMATE WHO'S THE LAST TO KNOW.
YEAH, MY FAT PIG EMPLOYER WANTS ME TO CHECK OUT THESE TWO LITTLE TARTS WHO DRAW PORNO COMICS. HE WANTS ME TO DO THE LEG WORK TO SEE IF THEY'RE WORTH HIS DOING AN INTERVIEW WITH.
SO WE FIGURED WE'D DO SOME EXTRA-CURRICULAR DROOLER INTERVIEWS OF OUR OWN.
IF GLATTSBERG WANTS TO INTERVIEW PORNO COMICS ARTISTS, WHY DOESN'T HE INTERVIEW ROB? HE COULD USE THE PRESS.
UNLESS ROB SPROUTS A VAGINA AND A PAIR OF BAZOOMS, SHEL WON'T HAVE ANYTHING TO DO WITH HIM. SHEL COULDN'T GIVE TWO SHITS ABOUT WHAT THESE LITTLE HARLOTS DO. HE ONLY HAS CHICKS ON THE SHOW HE WANTS TO BOINK. I'M TESTING THE WATERS, LIKE HIS NATIVE GUIDE, IF YOU WILL.
THAT'S DISGUSTING. WHERE CAN I GET ONE OF THOSE?
HE'S GONE? WINDSOR ST. CLAIRE IS GONE? BUT IT SAID IN THE PROGRAM BOOK THAT HE'D BE HERE ALL DAY. IT'S ONLY NOON. YOU SURE HE'S NOT COMING BACK? POSITIVE? HOW ABOUT THE LETTERER? I STILL NEED HIS AUTOGRAPH.
WHICH PART OF "HE AIN'T COMING BACK" DIDN'T YOU UNDERSTAND? LETTERER? I DON'T KNOW FROM NO LETTERER. WHO CARES ABOUT THE LETTERER? GET A LIFE, PAL.
DEATH WHORE

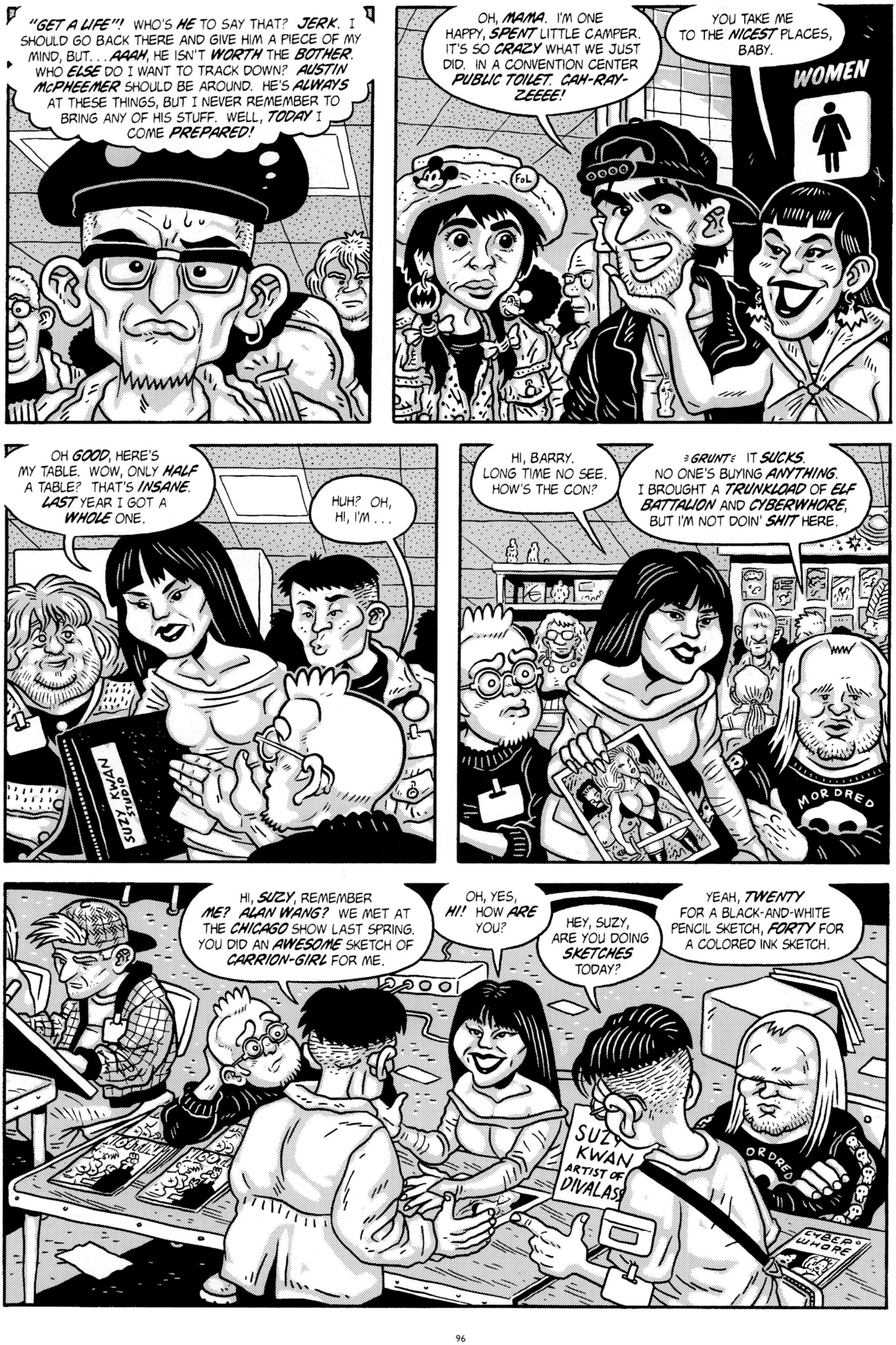

"GET A LIFE"! WHO'S HE TO SAY THAT? JERK. I SHOULD GO BACK THERE AND GIVE HIM A PIECE OF MY MIND, BUT. . . AAAH, HE ISN'T WORTH THE BOTHER. WHO ELSE DO I WANT TO TRACK DOWN? AUSTIN McPHEEMER SHOULD BE AROUND. HE'S ALWAYS AT THESE THINGS, BUT I NEVER REMEMBER TO BRING ANY OF HIS STUFF. WELL, TODAY I COME PREPARED!
OH, MAMA. I'M ONE HAPPY, SPENT LITTLE CAMPER. IT'S SO CRAZY WHAT WE JUST DID. IN A CONVENTION CENTER PUBLIC TOILET. CAH-RAY-ZEEEE!
YOU TAKE ME TO THE NICEST PLACES, BABY.
WOMEN
OH GOOD, HERE'S MY TABLE. WOW, ONLY HALF A TABLE? THAT'S INSANE. LAST YEAR I GOT A WHOLE ONE.
HUH? OH, HI, I'M . . .
SUZY KWAN STUDIO
HI, BARRY. LONG TIME NO SEE. HOW'S THE CON?
GRUNT IT SUCKS. NO ONE'S BUYING ANYTHING. I BROUGHT A TRUNKLOAD OF ELF BATTALION AND CYBERWHORE, BUT I'M NOT DOIN' SHIT HERE.
MORDRED
HI, SUZY, REMEMBER ME? ALAN WANG? WE MET AT THE CHICAGO SHOW LAST SPRING. YOU DID AN AWESOME SKETCH OF CARRION-GIRL FOR ME.
OH, YES, HI! HOW ARE YOU?
HEY, SUZY, ARE YOU DOING SKETCHES TODAY?
YEAH, TWENTY FOR A BLACK-AND-WHITE PENCIL SKETCH, FORTY FOR A COLORED INK SKETCH.
SUZY KWAN ARTIST OF DIVALASS
CYBER WHORE

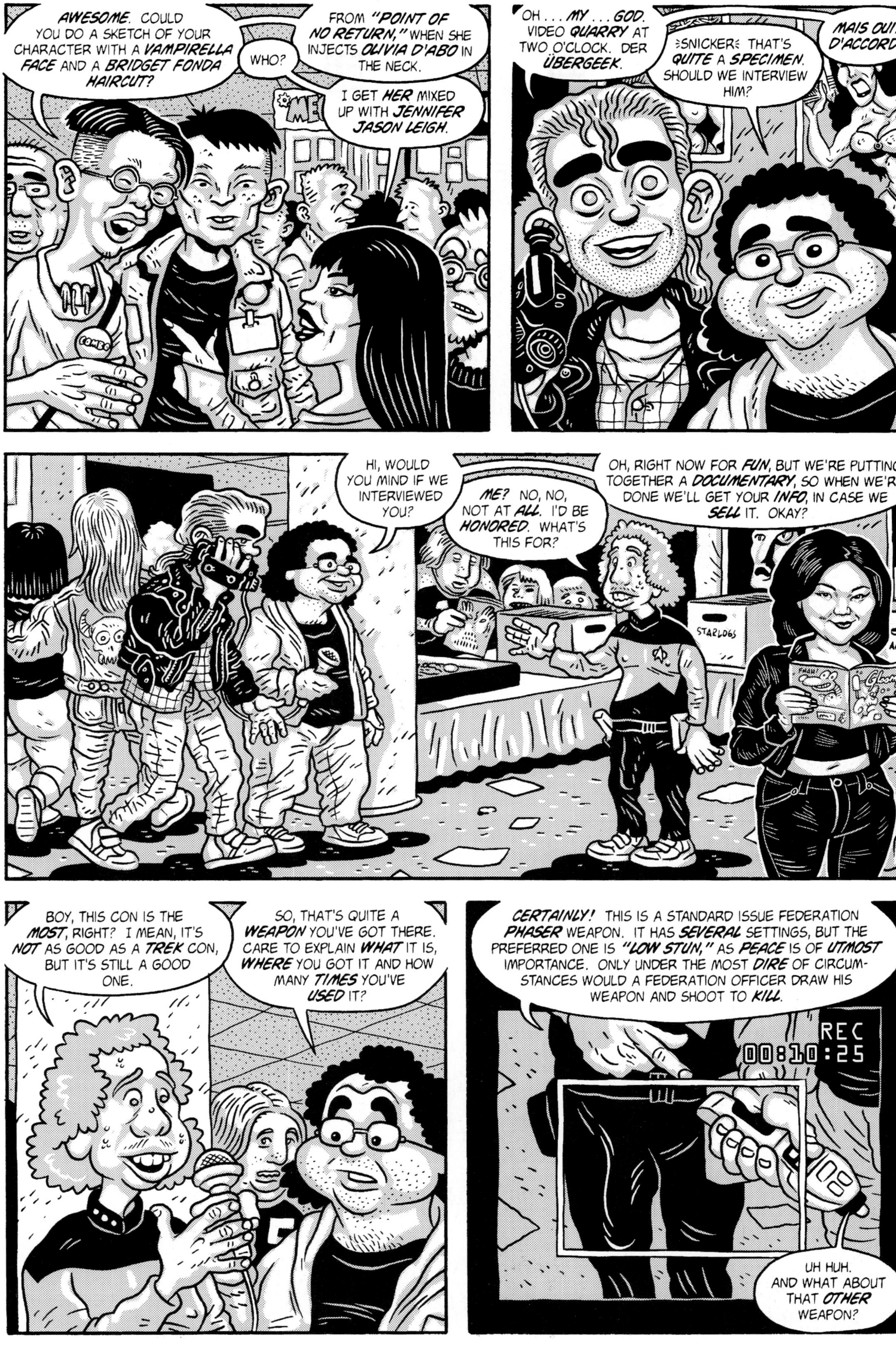
AWESOME. COULD YOU DO A SKETCH OF YOUR CHARACTER WITH A VAMPIRELLA FACE AND A BRIDGET FONDA HAIRCUT?
WHO?
FROM "POINT OF NO RETURN," WHEN SHE INJECTS OLIVIA D'ABO IN THE NECK.
I GET HER MIXED UP WITH JENNIFER JASON LEIGH.
OH . . . MY . . . GOD. VIDEO QUARRY AT TWO O'CLOCK. DER ÜBERGEEK.
≥SNICKER≤ THAT'S QUITE A SPECIMEN. SHOULD WE INTERVIEW HIM?
MAIS OUI! D'ACCORD!
HI, WOULD YOU MIND IF WE INTERVIEWED YOU?
ME? NO, NO, NOT AT ALL. I'D BE HONORED. WHAT'S THIS FOR?
OH, RIGHT NOW FOR FUN, BUT WE'RE PUTTING TOGETHER A DOCUMENTARY, SO WHEN WE'RE DONE WE'LL GET YOUR INFO, IN CASE WE SELL IT. OKAY?
STARLOGS
BOY, THIS CON IS THE MOST, RIGHT? I MEAN, IT'S NOT AS GOOD AS A TREK CON, BUT IT'S STILL A GOOD ONE.
SO, THAT'S QUITE A WEAPON YOU'VE GOT THERE. CARE TO EXPLAIN WHAT IT IS, WHERE YOU GOT IT AND HOW MANY TIMES YOU'VE USED IT?
CERTAINLY! THIS IS A STANDARD ISSUE FEDERATION PHASER WEAPON. IT HAS SEVERAL SETTINGS, BUT THE PREFERRED ONE IS "LOW STUN," AS PEACE IS OF UTMOST IMPORTANCE. ONLY UNDER THE MOST DIRE OF CIRCUMSTANCES WOULD A FEDERATION OFFICER DRAW HIS WEAPON AND SHOOT TO KILL.
REC
00:10:25
UH HUH. AND WHAT ABOUT THAT OTHER WEAPON?

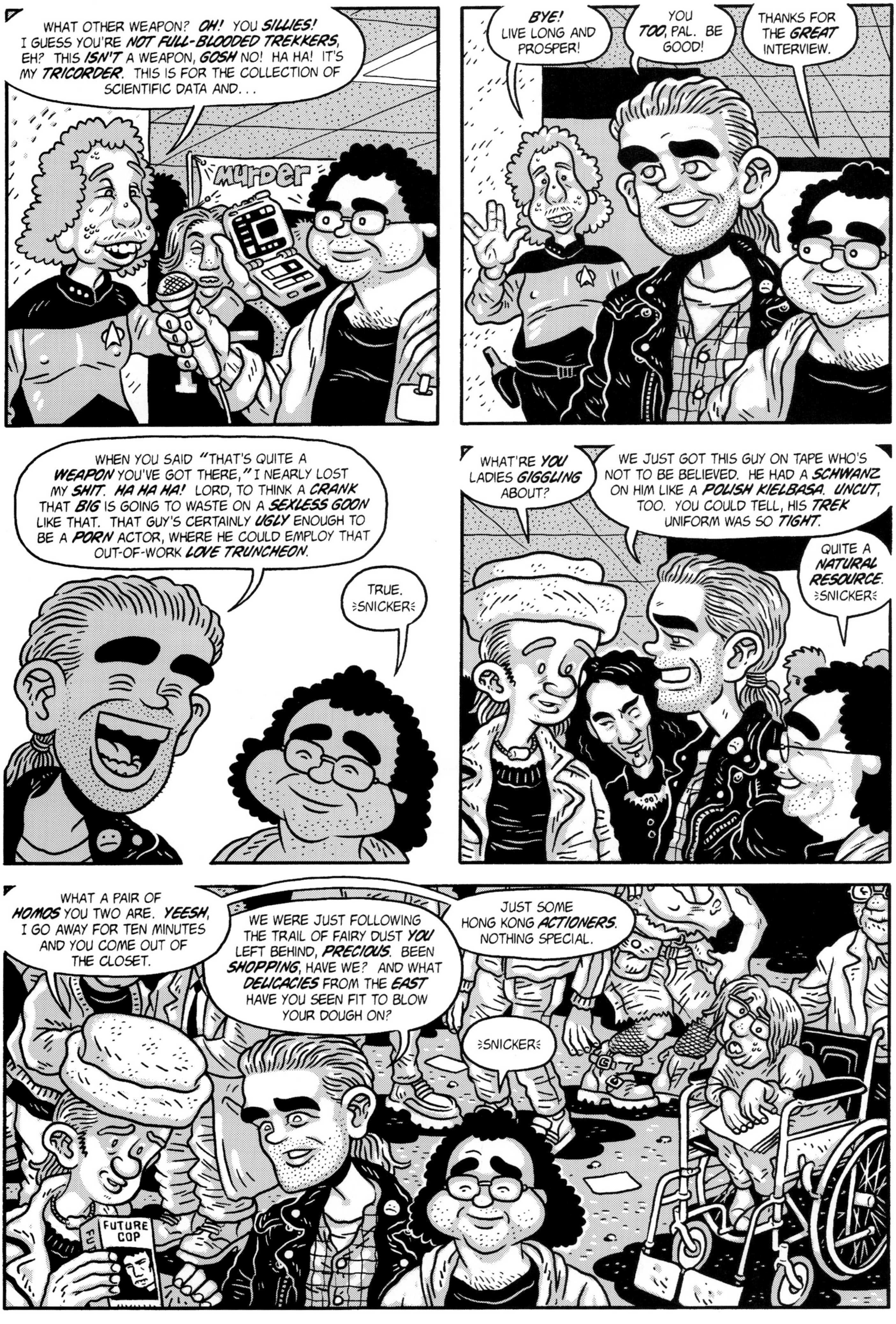
WHAT OTHER WEAPON? OH! YOU SILLIES! I GUESS YOU'RE NOT FULL-BLOODED TREKKERS, EH? THIS ISN'T A WEAPON, GOSH NO! HA HA! IT'S MY TRICORDER. THIS IS FOR THE COLLECTION OF SCIENTIFIC DATA AND...
MURDER
BYE! LIVE LONG AND PROSPER!
YOU TOO, PAL. BE GOOD!
THANKS FOR THE GREAT INTERVIEW.
WHEN YOU SAID "THAT'S QUITE A WEAPON YOU'VE GOT THERE," I NEARLY LOST MY SHIT. HA HA HA! LORD, TO THINK A CRANK THAT BIG IS GOING TO WASTE ON A SEXLESS GOON LIKE THAT. THAT GUY'S CERTAINLY UGLY ENOUGH TO BE A PORN ACTOR, WHERE HE COULD EMPLOY THAT OUT-OF-WORK LOVE TRUNCHEON.
TRUE. SNICKER
WHAT'RE YOU LADIES GIGGLING ABOUT?
WE JUST GOT THIS GUY ON TAPE WHO'S NOT TO BE BELIEVED. HE HAD A SCHWANZ ON HIM LIKE A POLISH KIELBASA. UNCUT, TOO. YOU COULD TELL, HIS TREK UNIFORM WAS SO TIGHT.
QUITE A NATURAL RESOURCE. SNICKER
WHAT A PAIR OF HOMOS YOU TWO ARE. YEESH, I GO AWAY FOR TEN MINUTES AND YOU COME OUT OF THE CLOSET.
WE WERE JUST FOLLOWING THE TRAIL OF FAIRY DUST YOU LEFT BEHIND, PRECIOUS. BEEN SHOPPING, HAVE WE? AND WHAT DELICACIES FROM THE EAST HAVE YOU SEEN FIT TO BLOW YOUR DOUGH ON?
JUST SOME HONG KONG ACTIONERS. NOTHING SPECIAL.
SNICKER
FUTURE COP

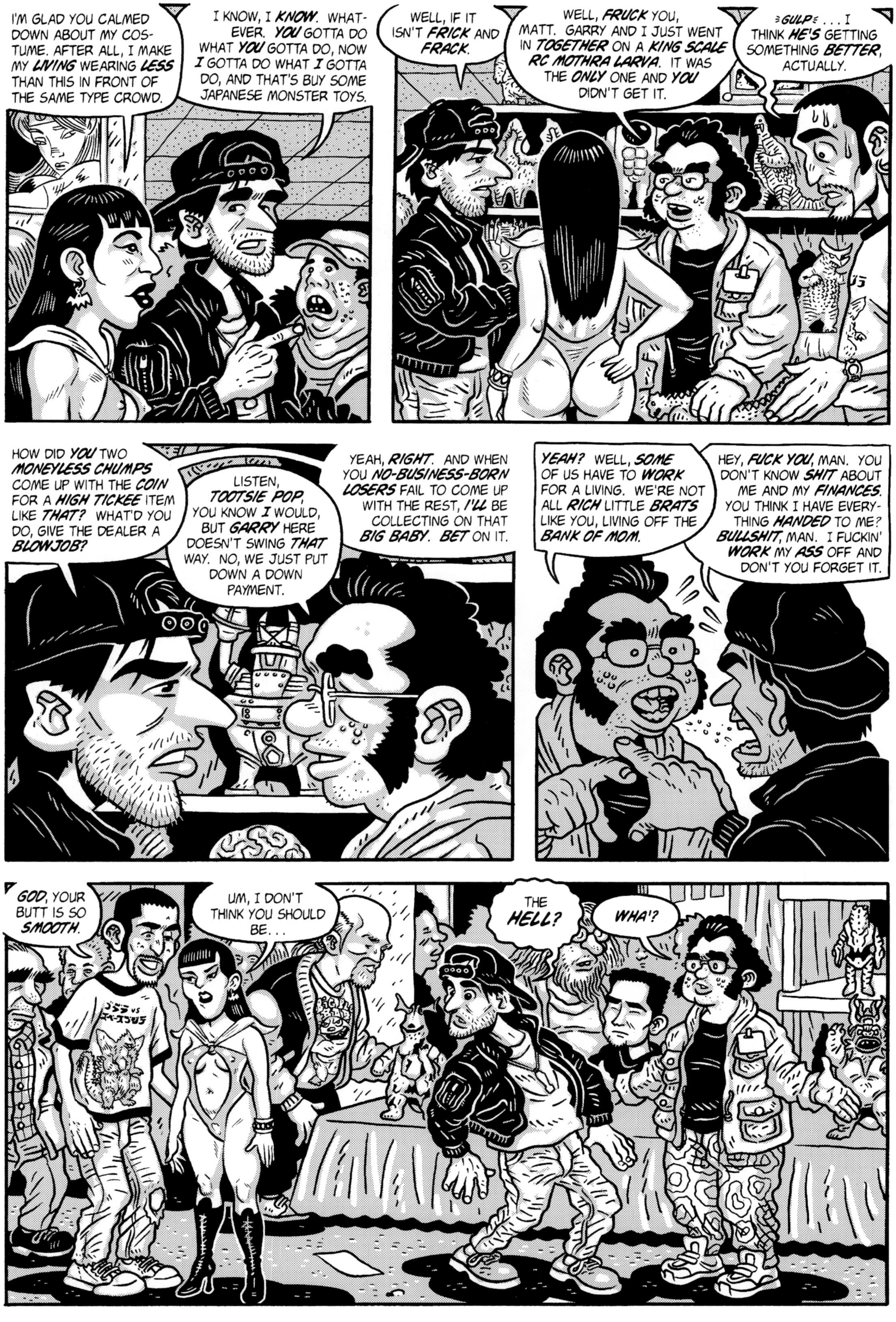
I'M GLAD YOU CALMED DOWN ABOUT MY COSTUME. AFTER ALL, I MAKE MY LIVING WEARING LESS THAN THIS IN FRONT OF THE SAME TYPE CROWD.
I KNOW, I KNOW. WHATEVER. YOU GOTTA DO WHAT YOU GOTTA DO, NOW I GOTTA DO WHAT I GOTTA DO, AND THAT'S BUY SOME JAPANESE MONSTER TOYS.
WELL, IF IT ISN'T FRICK AND FRACK.
WELL, FRUCK YOU, MATT. GARRY AND I JUST WENT IN TOGETHER ON A KING SCALE RC MOTHRA LARVA. IT WAS THE ONLY ONE AND YOU DIDN'T GET IT.
GULP . . . I THINK HE'S GETTING SOMETHING BETTER, ACTUALLY.
HOW DID YOU TWO MONEYLESS CHUMPS COME UP WITH THE COIN FOR A HIGH TICKEE ITEM LIKE THAT? WHAT'D YOU DO, GIVE THE DEALER A BLOWJOB?
LISTEN, TOOTSIE POP, YOU KNOW I WOULD, BUT GARRY HERE DOESN'T SWING THAT WAY. NO, WE JUST PUT DOWN A DOWN PAYMENT.
YEAH, RIGHT. AND WHEN YOU NO-BUSINESS-BORN LOSERS FAIL TO COME UP WITH THE REST, I'LL BE COLLECTING ON THAT BIG BABY. BET ON IT.
YEAH? WELL, SOME OF US HAVE TO WORK FOR A LIVING. WE'RE NOT ALL RICH LITTLE BRATS LIKE YOU, LIVING OFF THE BANK OF MOM.
HEY, FUCK YOU, MAN. YOU DON'T KNOW SHIT ABOUT ME AND MY FINANCES. YOU THINK I HAVE EVERYTHING HANDED TO ME? BULLSHIT, MAN. I FUCKIN' WORK MY ASS OFF AND DON'T YOU FORGET IT.
GOD, YOUR BUTT IS SO SMOOTH.
UM, I DON'T THINK YOU SHOULD BE. . .
THE HELL?
WHA'?

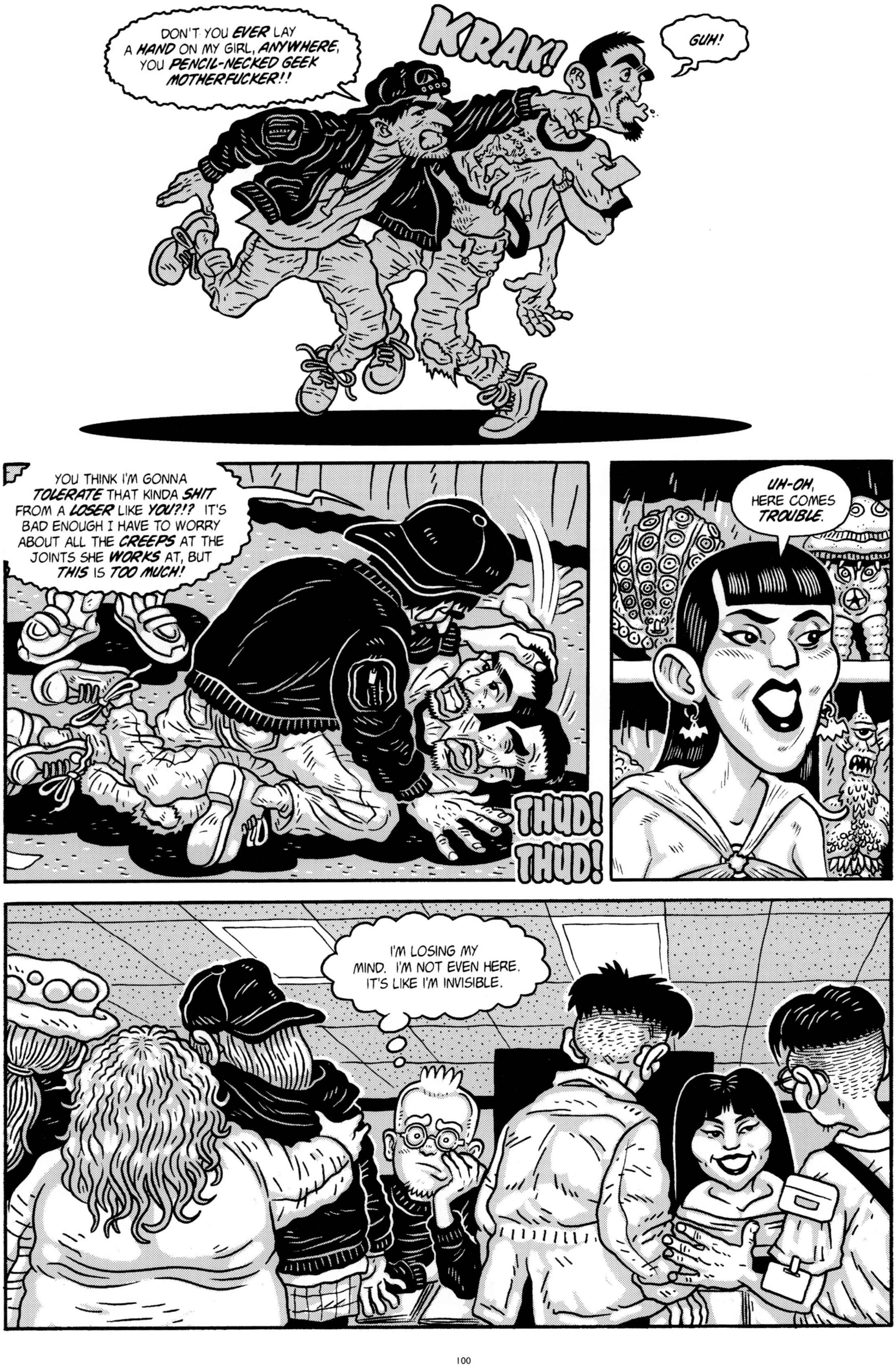
DON'T YOU EVER LAY A HAND ON MY GIRL, ANYWHERE, YOU PENCIL-NECKED GEEK MOTHERFUCKER!!
KRAK!
GUH!
YOU THINK I'M GONNA TOLERATE THAT KINDA SHIT FROM A LOSER LIKE YOU?!? IT'S BAD ENOUGH I HAVE TO WORRY ABOUT ALL THE CREEPS AT THE JOINTS SHE WORKS AT, BUT THIS IS TOO MUCH!
THUD! THUD!
UH-OH, HERE COMES TROUBLE.
I'M LOSING MY MIND. I'M NOT EVEN HERE. IT'S LIKE I'M INVISIBLE.

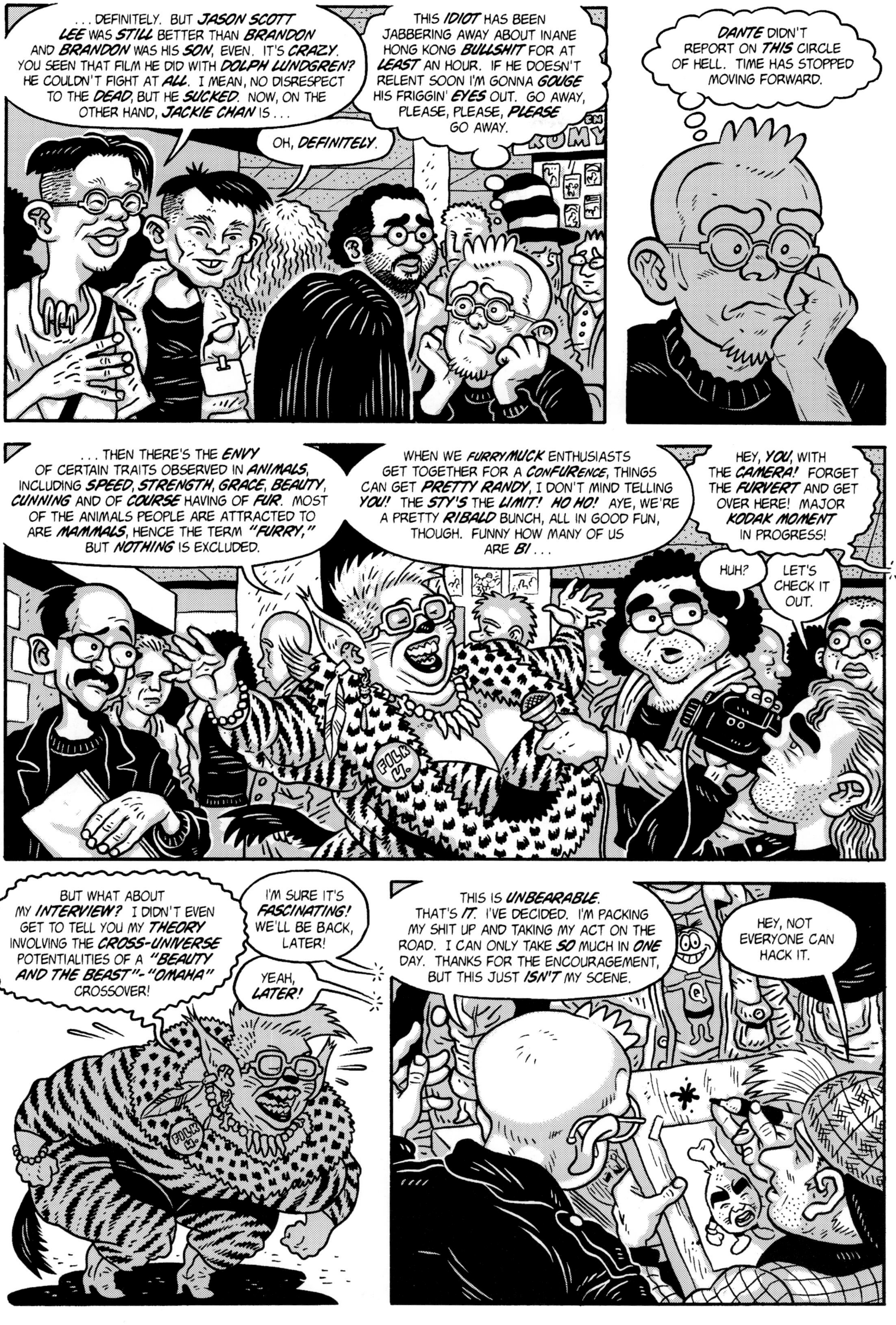

...DEFINITELY. BUT JASON SCOTT LEE WAS STILL BETTER THAN BRANDON AND BRANDON WAS HIS SON, EVEN. IT'S CRAZY. YOU SEEN THAT FILM HE DID WITH DOLPH LUNDGREN? HE COULDN'T FIGHT AT ALL. I MEAN, NO DISRESPECT TO THE DEAD, BUT HE SUCKED. NOW, ON THE OTHER HAND, JACKIE CHAN IS...
OH, DEFINITELY.
THIS IDIOT HAS BEEN JABBERING AWAY ABOUT INANE HONG KONG BULLSHIT FOR AT LEAST AN HOUR. IF HE DOESN'T RELENT SOON I'M GONNA GOUGE HIS FRIGGIN' EYES OUT. GO AWAY, PLEASE, PLEASE, PLEASE GO AWAY.
DANTE DIDN'T REPORT ON THIS CIRCLE OF HELL. TIME HAS STOPPED MOVING FORWARD.
...THEN THERE'S THE ENVY OF CERTAIN TRAITS OBSERVED IN ANIMALS, INCLUDING SPEED, STRENGTH, GRACE, BEAUTY, CUNNING AND OF COURSE HAVING OF FUR. MOST OF THE ANIMALS PEOPLE ARE ATTRACTED TO ARE MAMMALS, HENCE THE TERM "FURRY," BUT NOTHING IS EXCLUDED.
WHEN WE FURRYMUCK ENTHUSIASTS GET TOGETHER FOR A CONFURENCE, THINGS CAN GET PRETTY RANDY, I DON'T MIND TELLING YOU! THE STY'S THE LIMIT! HO HO! AYE, WE'RE A PRETTY RIBALD BUNCH, ALL IN GOOD FUN, THOUGH. FUNNY HOW MANY OF US ARE BI...
HEY, YOU, WITH THE CAMERA! FORGET THE FURVERT AND GET OVER HERE! MAJOR KODAK MOMENT IN PROGRESS!
HUH?
LET'S CHECK IT OUT.
FOLK U.
BUT WHAT ABOUT MY INTERVIEW? I DIDN'T EVEN GET TO TELL YOU MY THEORY INVOLVING THE CROSS-UNIVERSE POTENTIALITIES OF A "BEAUTY AND THE BEAST"-"OMAHA" CROSSOVER!
I'M SURE IT'S FASCINATING! WE'LL BE BACK, LATER!
YEAH, LATER!
THIS IS UNBEARABLE. THAT'S IT. I'VE DECIDED. I'M PACKING MY SHIT UP AND TAKING MY ACT ON THE ROAD. I CAN ONLY TAKE SO MUCH IN ONE DAY. THANKS FOR THE ENCOURAGEMENT, BUT THIS JUST ISN'T MY SCENE.
HEY, NOT EVERYONE CAN HACK IT.

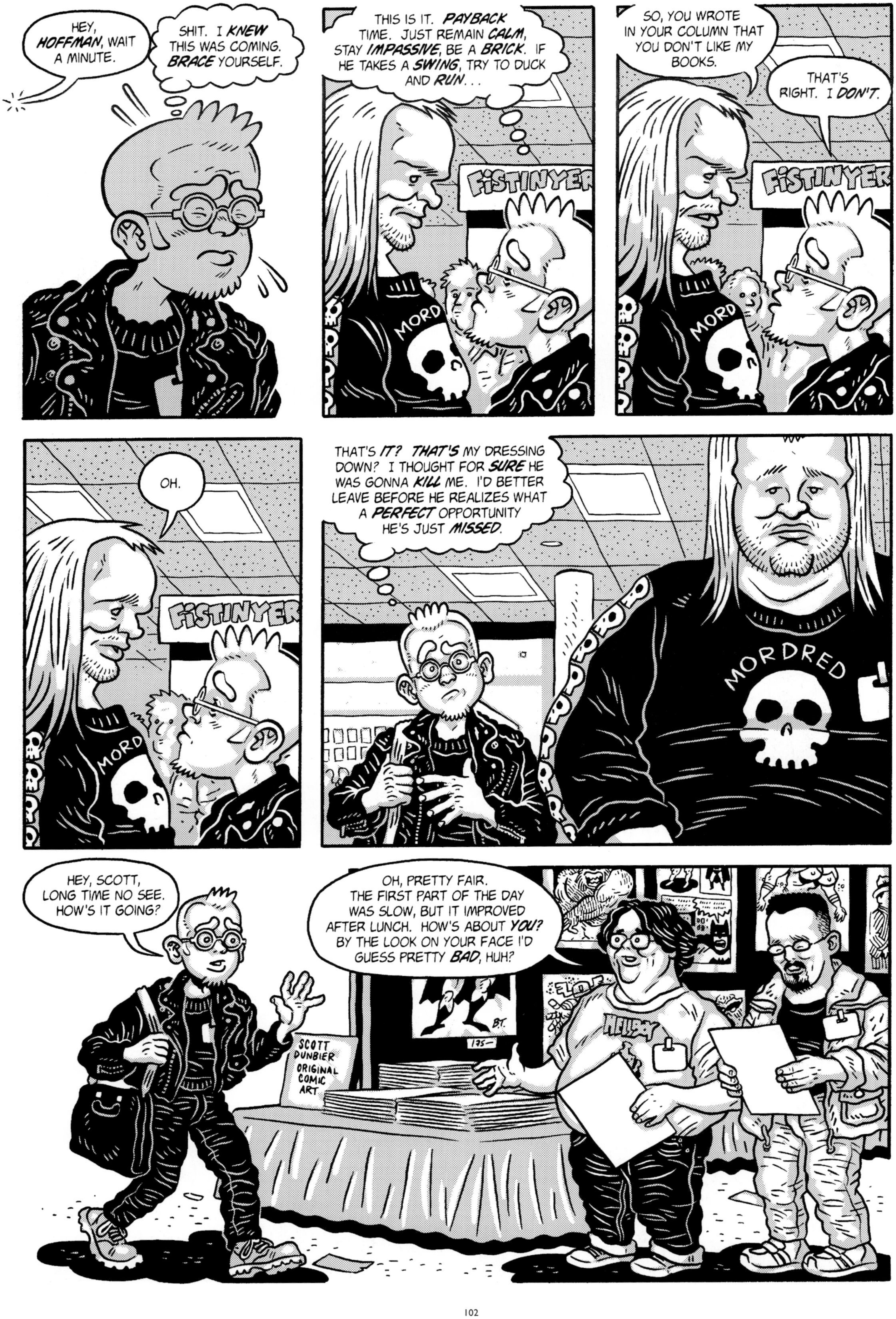
HEY, HOFFMAN, WAIT A MINUTE.
SHIT. I KNEW THIS WAS COMING. BRACE YOURSELF.
THIS IS IT. PAYBACK TIME. JUST REMAIN CALM, STAY IMPASSIVE, BE A BRICK. IF HE TAKES A SWING, TRY TO DUCK AND RUN. . .
FISTINYER
MORD
SO, YOU WROTE IN YOUR COLUMN THAT YOU DON'T LIKE MY BOOKS.
THAT'S RIGHT. I DON'T.
FISTINYER
MORD
OH.
FISTINYER
MORD
THAT'S IT? THAT'S MY DRESSING DOWN? I THOUGHT FOR SURE HE WAS GONNA KILL ME. I'D BETTER LEAVE BEFORE HE REALIZES WHAT A PERFECT OPPORTUNITY HE'S JUST MISSED.
MORDRED
HEY, SCOTT, LONG TIME NO SEE. HOW'S IT GOING?
OH, PRETTY FAIR. THE FIRST PART OF THE DAY WAS SLOW, BUT IT IMPROVED AFTER LUNCH. HOW'S ABOUT YOU? BY THE LOOK ON YOUR FACE I'D GUESS PRETTY BAD, HUH?
SCOTT DUNBIER ORIGINAL COMIC ART
175-
HELLBOY

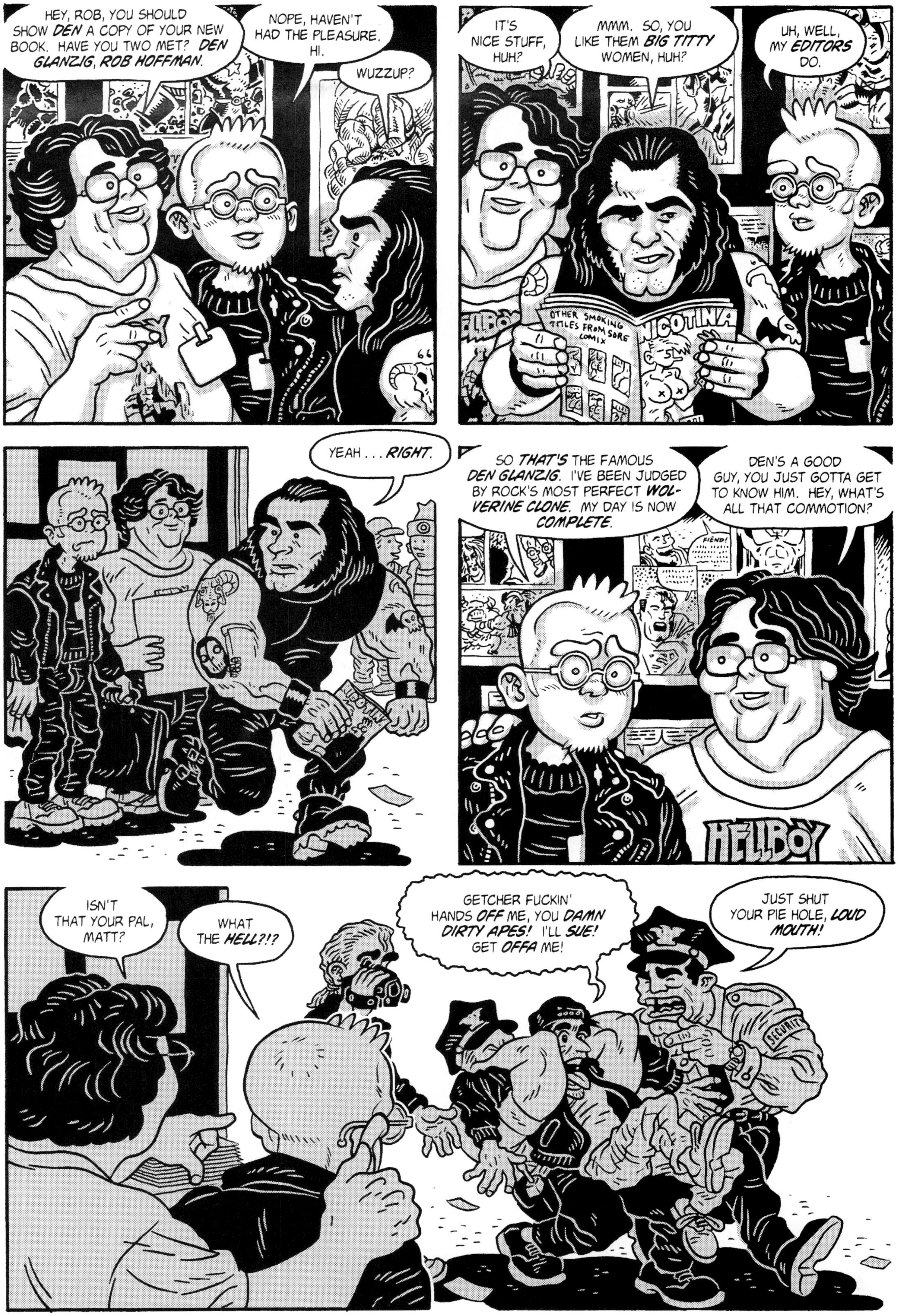
HEY, ROB, YOU SHOULD SHOW DEN A COPY OF YOUR NEW BOOK. HAVE YOU TWO MET? DEN GLANZIG, ROB HOFFMAN.
NOPE, HAVEN'T HAD THE PLEASURE. HI.
WUZZUP?
IT'S NICE STUFF, HUH?
MMM. SO, YOU LIKE THEM BIG TITTY WOMEN, HUH?
UH, WELL, MY EDITORS DO.
OTHER SMOKING TITLES FROM SORE COMIX
NICOTINA
HELLBOY
YEAH . . . RIGHT.
SO THAT'S THE FAMOUS DEN GLANZIG. I'VE BEEN JUDGED BY ROCK'S MOST PERFECT WOLVERINE CLONE. MY DAY IS NOW COMPLETE.
DEN'S A GOOD GUY, YOU JUST GOTTA GET TO KNOW HIM. HEY, WHAT'S ALL THAT COMMOTION?
FIEND!
HELLBOY
ISN'T THAT YOUR PAL, MATT?
WHAT THE HELL?!?
GETCHER FUCKIN' HANDS OFF ME, YOU DAMN DIRTY APES! I'LL SUE! GET OFFA ME!
JUST SHUT YOUR PIE HOLE, LOUD MOUTH!
SECURITY

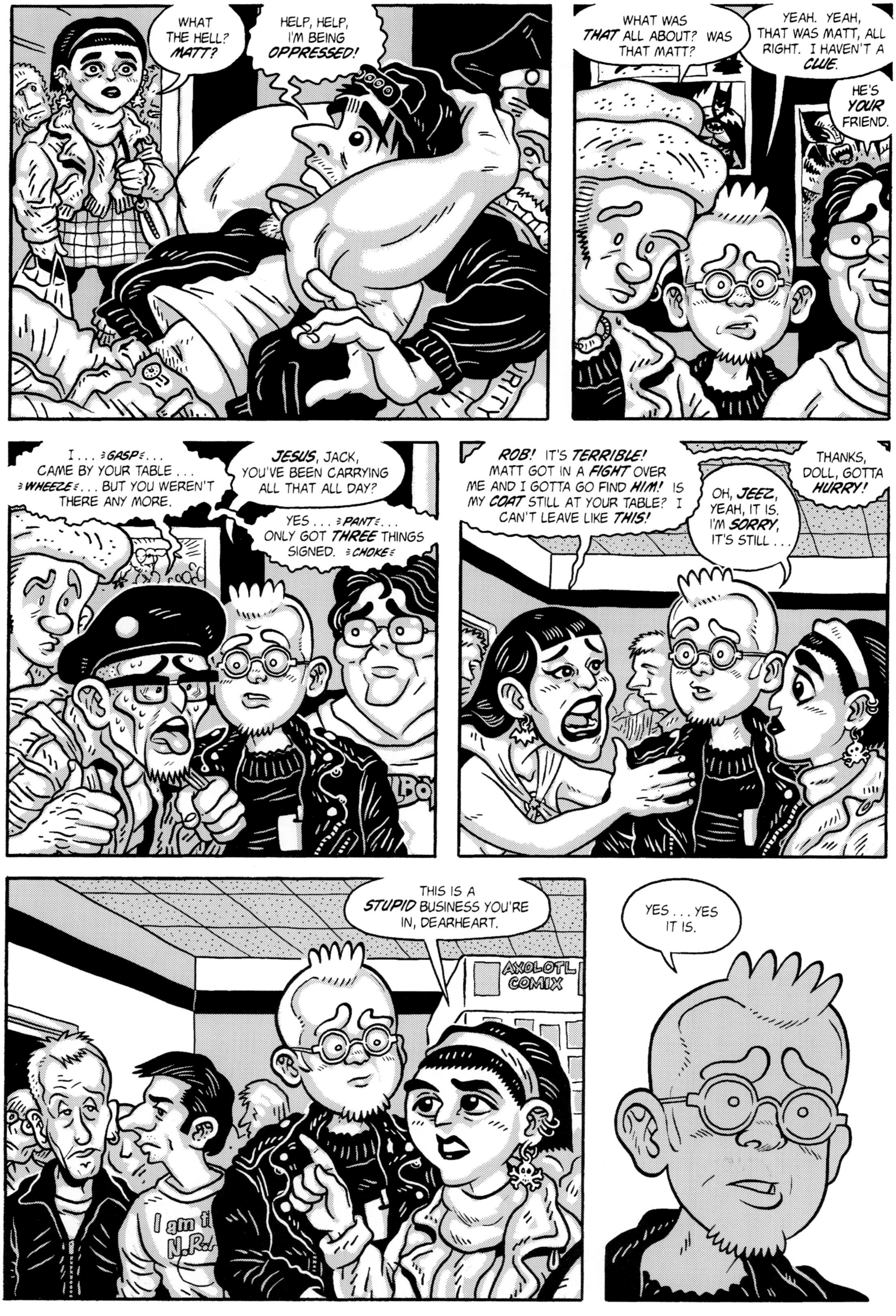
WHAT THE HELL? MATT?
HELP, HELP, I'M BEING OPPRESSED!
WHAT WAS THAT ALL ABOUT? WAS THAT MATT?
YEAH. YEAH, THAT WAS MATT, ALL RIGHT. I HAVEN'T A CLUE.
HE'S YOUR FRIEND.
I . . . GASP . . . CAME BY YOUR TABLE . . . WHEEZE . . . BUT YOU WEREN'T THERE ANY MORE.
JESUS, JACK, YOU'VE BEEN CARRYING ALL THAT ALL DAY?
YES . . . PANT . . . ONLY GOT THREE THINGS SIGNED. CHOKE
ROB! IT'S TERRIBLE! MATT GOT IN A FIGHT OVER ME AND I GOTTA GO FIND HIM! IS MY COAT STILL AT YOUR TABLE? I CAN'T LEAVE LIKE THIS!
OH, JEEZ, YEAH, IT IS. I'M SORRY, IT'S STILL . . .
THANKS, DOLL, GOTTA HURRY!
THIS IS A STUPID BUSINESS YOU'RE IN, DEARHEART.
AXOLOTL COMIX
YES . . . YES IT IS.

Chapter Five

BRUNCH ENGAGEMENT

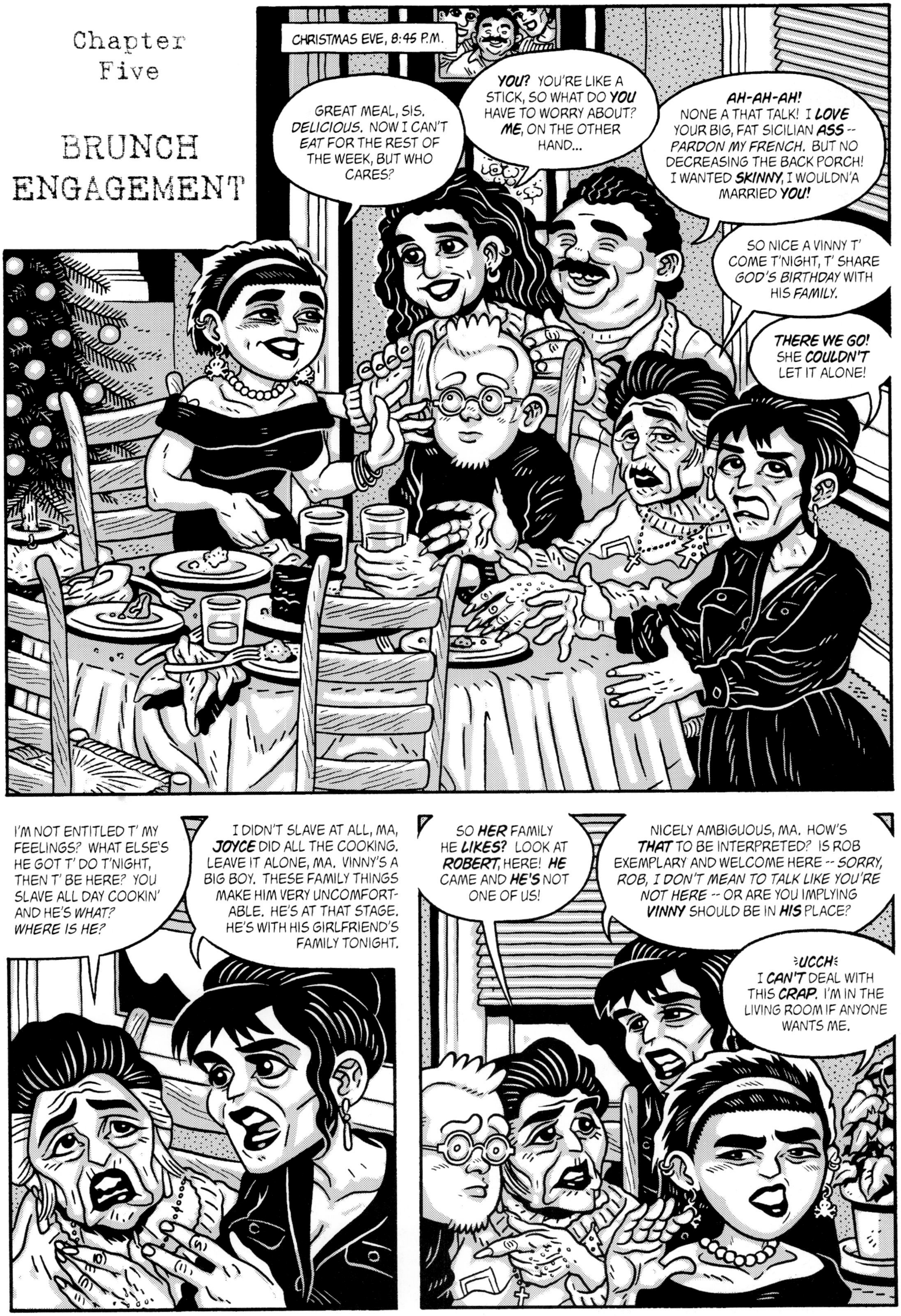
CHRISTMAS EVE, 8:45 P.M.
GREAT MEAL, SIS. *DELICIOUS.* NOW I CAN'T *EAT* FOR THE REST OF THE WEEK, BUT WHO CARES?
YOU? YOU'RE LIKE A STICK, SO WHAT DO ***YOU*** HAVE TO WORRY ABOUT? ***ME***, ON THE OTHER HAND...
AH-AH-AH! NONE A THAT TALK! I ***LOVE*** YOUR BIG, FAT SICILIAN ***ASS*** -- *PARDON MY FRENCH.* BUT NO DECREASING THE BACK PORCH! I WANTED ***SKINNY***, I WOULDN'A MARRIED ***YOU!***
SO NICE A VINNY T' COME T'NIGHT, T' SHARE *GOD'S BIRTHDAY* WITH HIS *FAMILY.*
THERE WE GO! SHE ***COULDN'T*** LET IT ALONE!
I'M NOT ENTITLED T' MY FEELINGS? WHAT ELSE'S HE GOT T' DO T'NIGHT, THEN T' BE HERE? YOU SLAVE ALL DAY COOKIN' AND HE'S *WHAT? WHERE IS HE?*
I DIDN'T SLAVE AT ALL, MA, ***JOYCE*** DID ALL THE COOKING. LEAVE IT ALONE, MA. VINNY'S A BIG BOY. THESE FAMILY THINGS MAKE HIM VERY UNCOMFORTABLE. HE'S AT THAT STAGE. HE'S WITH HIS GIRLFRIEND'S FAMILY TONIGHT.
SO ***HER*** FAMILY HE ***LIKES?*** LOOK AT ***ROBERT,*** HERE! ***HE*** CAME AND ***HE'S*** NOT ONE OF US!
NICELY AMBIGUOUS, MA. HOW'S ***THAT*** TO BE INTERPRETED? IS ROB EXEMPLARY AND WELCOME HERE -- *SORRY, ROB, I DON'T MEAN TO TALK LIKE YOU'RE NOT HERE* -- OR ARE YOU IMPLYING ***VINNY*** SHOULD BE IN ***HIS*** PLACE?
UCCH I ***CAN'T*** DEAL WITH THIS ***CRAP.*** I'M IN THE LIVING ROOM IF ANYONE WANTS ME.

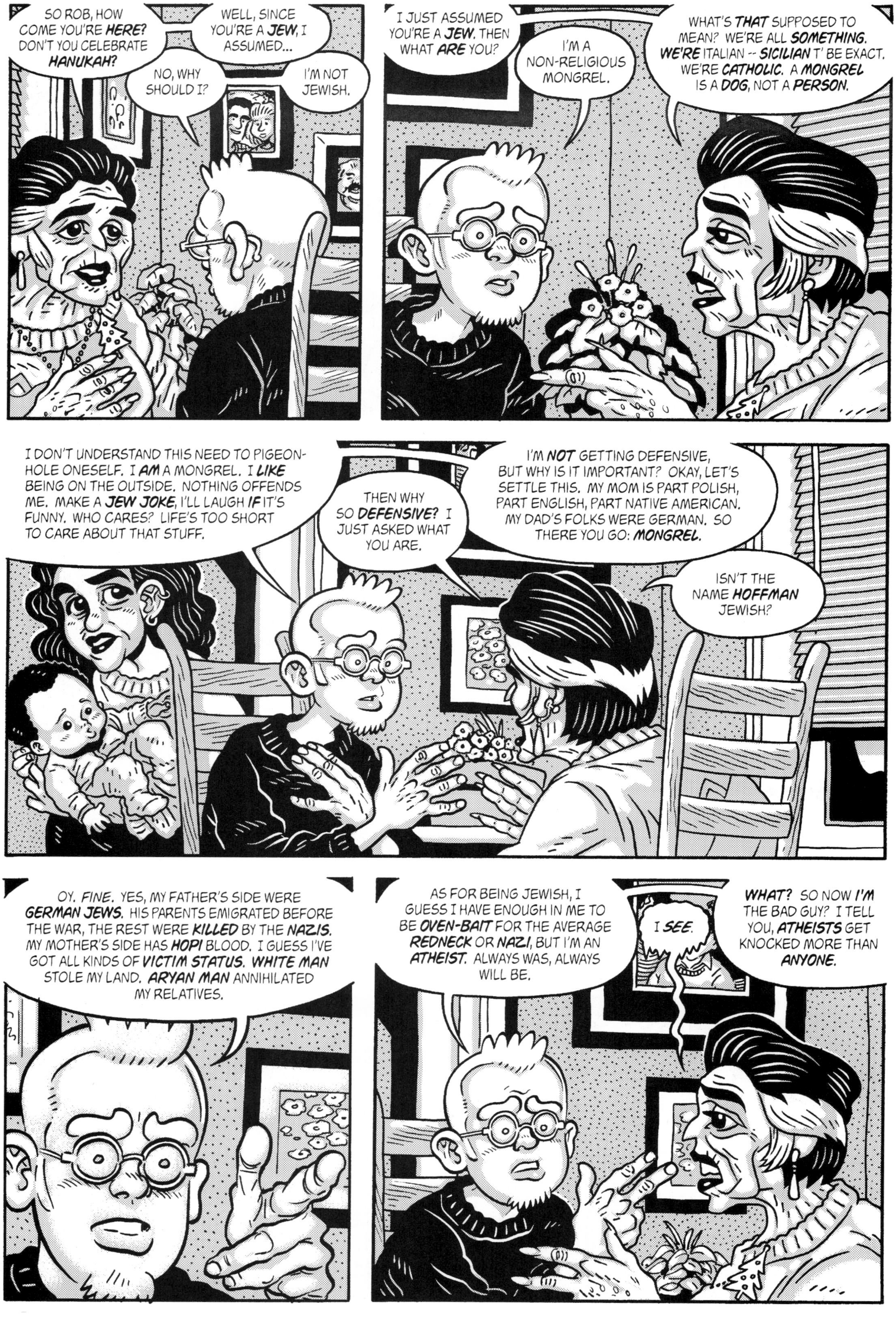

SO ROB, HOW COME YOU'RE HERE? DON'T YOU CELEBRATE HANUKAH?
NO, WHY SHOULD I?
WELL, SINCE YOU'RE A JEW, I ASSUMED...
I'M NOT JEWISH.
I JUST ASSUMED YOU'RE A JEW. THEN WHAT ARE YOU?
I'M A NON-RELIGIOUS MONGREL.
WHAT'S THAT SUPPOSED TO MEAN? WE'RE ALL SOMETHING. WE'RE ITALIAN -- SICILIAN T' BE EXACT. WE'RE CATHOLIC. A MONGREL IS A DOG, NOT A PERSON.
I DON'T UNDERSTAND THIS NEED TO PIGEON-HOLE ONESELF. I AM A MONGREL. I LIKE BEING ON THE OUTSIDE. NOTHING OFFENDS ME. MAKE A JEW JOKE, I'LL LAUGH IF IT'S FUNNY. WHO CARES? LIFE'S TOO SHORT TO CARE ABOUT THAT STUFF.
THEN WHY SO DEFENSIVE? I JUST ASKED WHAT YOU ARE.
I'M NOT GETTING DEFENSIVE, BUT WHY IS IT IMPORTANT? OKAY, LET'S SETTLE THIS. MY MOM IS PART POLISH, PART ENGLISH, PART NATIVE AMERICAN. MY DAD'S FOLKS WERE GERMAN. SO THERE YOU GO: MONGREL.
ISN'T THE NAME HOFFMAN JEWISH?
OY. FINE. YES, MY FATHER'S SIDE WERE GERMAN JEWS. HIS PARENTS EMIGRATED BEFORE THE WAR, THE REST WERE KILLED BY THE NAZIS. MY MOTHER'S SIDE HAS HOPI BLOOD. I GUESS I'VE GOT ALL KINDS OF VICTIM STATUS. WHITE MAN STOLE MY LAND. ARYAN MAN ANNIHILATED MY RELATIVES.
AS FOR BEING JEWISH, I GUESS I HAVE ENOUGH IN ME TO BE OVEN-BAIT FOR THE AVERAGE REDNECK OR NAZI, BUT I'M AN ATHEIST. ALWAYS WAS, ALWAYS WILL BE.
I SEE.
WHAT? SO NOW I'M THE BAD GUY? I TELL YOU, ATHEISTS GET KNOCKED MORE THAN ANYONE.

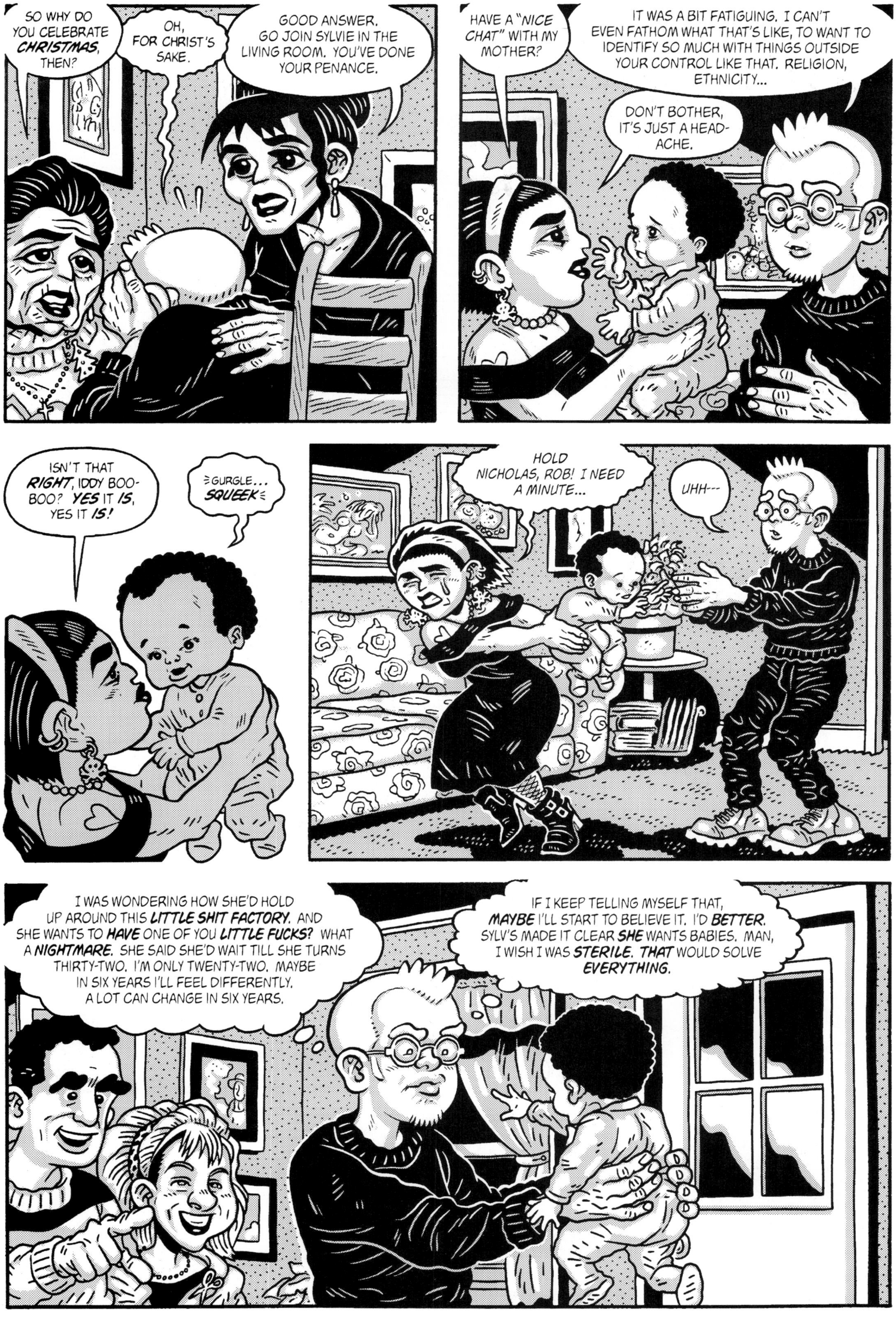

SO WHY DO YOU CELEBRATE CHRISTMAS, THEN?
OH, FOR CHRIST'S SAKE.
GOOD ANSWER. GO JOIN SYLVIE IN THE LIVING ROOM. YOU'VE DONE YOUR PENANCE.
HAVE A "NICE CHAT" WITH MY MOTHER?
IT WAS A BIT FATIGUING. I CAN'T EVEN FATHOM WHAT THAT'S LIKE, TO WANT TO IDENTIFY SO MUCH WITH THINGS OUTSIDE YOUR CONTROL LIKE THAT. RELIGION, ETHNICITY...
DON'T BOTHER, IT'S JUST A HEAD-ACHE.
ISN'T THAT RIGHT, IDDY BOO-BOO? YES IT IS, YES IT IS!
GURGLE... SQUEEK
HOLD NICHOLAS, ROB! I NEED A MINUTE...
UHH---
I WAS WONDERING HOW SHE'D HOLD UP AROUND THIS LITTLE SHIT FACTORY. AND SHE WANTS TO HAVE ONE OF YOU LITTLE FUCKS? WHAT A NIGHTMARE. SHE SAID SHE'D WAIT TILL SHE TURNS THIRTY-TWO. I'M ONLY TWENTY-TWO. MAYBE IN SIX YEARS I'LL FEEL DIFFERENTLY. A LOT CAN CHANGE IN SIX YEARS.
IF I KEEP TELLING MYSELF THAT, MAYBE I'LL START TO BELIEVE IT. I'D BETTER. SYLV'S MADE IT CLEAR SHE WANTS BABIES. MAN, I WISH I WAS STERILE. THAT WOULD SOLVE EVERYTHING.

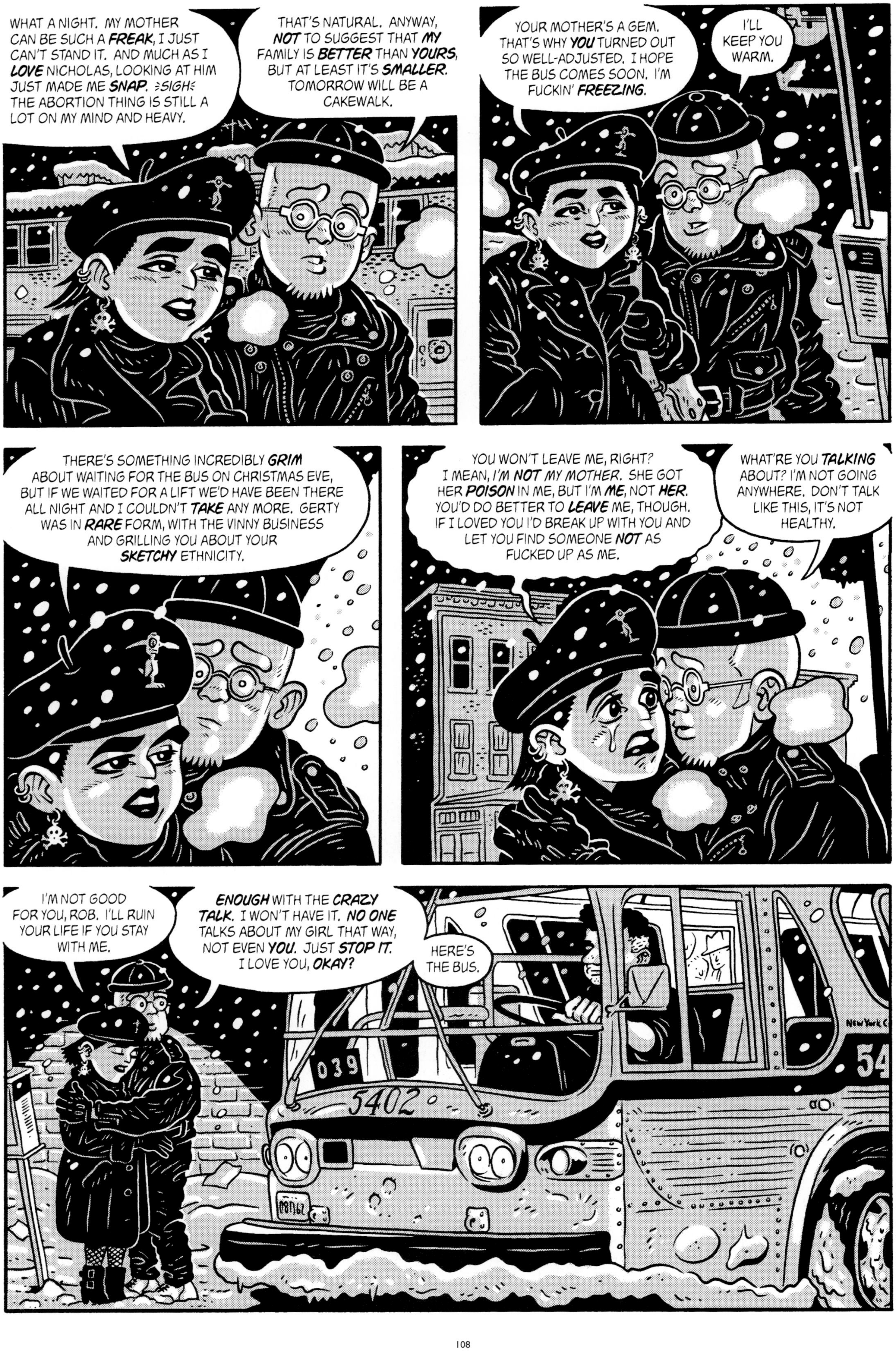
WHAT A NIGHT. MY MOTHER CAN BE SUCH A FREAK, I JUST CAN'T STAND IT. AND MUCH AS I LOVE NICHOLAS, LOOKING AT HIM JUST MADE ME SNAP. ≥SIGH≤ THE ABORTION THING IS STILL A LOT ON MY MIND AND HEAVY.
THAT'S NATURAL. ANYWAY, NOT TO SUGGEST THAT MY FAMILY IS BETTER THAN YOURS, BUT AT LEAST IT'S SMALLER. TOMORROW WILL BE A CAKEWALK.
YOUR MOTHER'S A GEM. THAT'S WHY YOU TURNED OUT SO WELL-ADJUSTED. I HOPE THE BUS COMES SOON. I'M FUCKIN' FREEZING.
I'LL KEEP YOU WARM.
THERE'S SOMETHING INCREDIBLY GRIM ABOUT WAITING FOR THE BUS ON CHRISTMAS EVE, BUT IF WE WAITED FOR A LIFT WE'D HAVE BEEN THERE ALL NIGHT AND I COULDN'T TAKE ANY MORE. GERTY WAS IN RARE FORM, WITH THE VINNY BUSINESS AND GRILLING YOU ABOUT YOUR SKETCHY ETHNICITY.
YOU WON'T LEAVE ME, RIGHT? I MEAN, I'M NOT MY MOTHER. SHE GOT HER POISON IN ME, BUT I'M ME, NOT HER. YOU'D DO BETTER TO LEAVE ME, THOUGH. IF I LOVED YOU I'D BREAK UP WITH YOU AND LET YOU FIND SOMEONE NOT AS FUCKED UP AS ME.
WHAT'RE YOU TALKING ABOUT? I'M NOT GOING ANYWHERE. DON'T TALK LIKE THIS, IT'S NOT HEALTHY.
I'M NOT GOOD FOR YOU, ROB. I'LL RUIN YOUR LIFE IF YOU STAY WITH ME.
ENOUGH WITH THE CRAZY TALK. I WON'T HAVE IT. NO ONE TALKS ABOUT MY GIRL THAT WAY, NOT EVEN YOU. JUST STOP IT. I LOVE YOU, OKAY?
HERE'S THE BUS.
039
5402

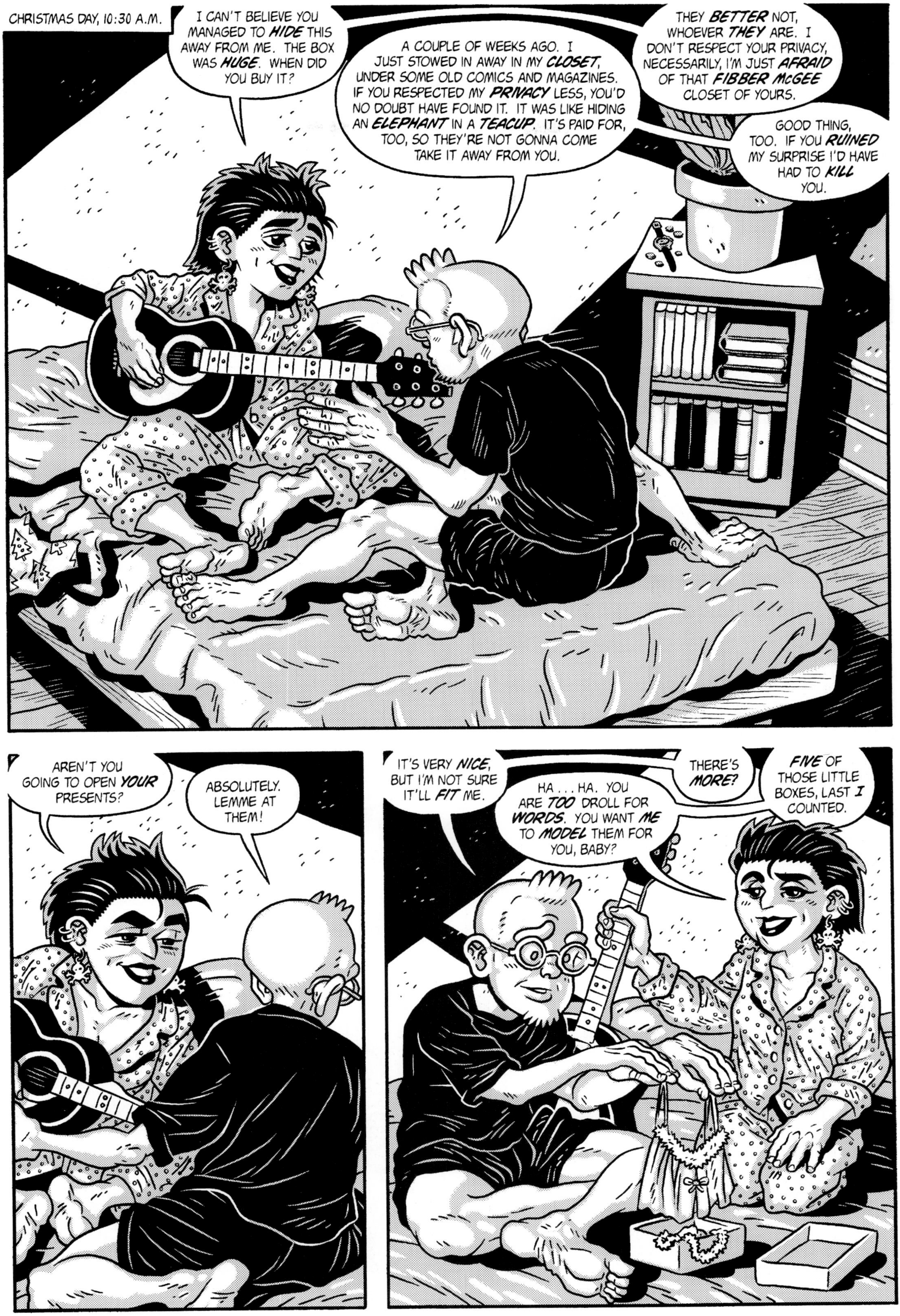
CHRISTMAS DAY, 10:30 A.M.
I CAN'T BELIEVE YOU MANAGED TO HIDE THIS AWAY FROM ME. THE BOX WAS HUGE. WHEN DID YOU BUY IT?
A COUPLE OF WEEKS AGO. I JUST STOWED IN AWAY IN MY CLOSET, UNDER SOME OLD COMICS AND MAGAZINES. IF YOU RESPECTED MY PRIVACY LESS, YOU'D NO DOUBT HAVE FOUND IT. IT WAS LIKE HIDING AN ELEPHANT IN A TEACUP. IT'S PAID FOR, TOO, SO THEY'RE NOT GONNA COME TAKE IT AWAY FROM YOU.
THEY BETTER NOT, WHOEVER THEY ARE. I DON'T RESPECT YOUR PRIVACY, NECESSARILY, I'M JUST AFRAID OF THAT FIBBER McGEE CLOSET OF YOURS.
GOOD THING, TOO. IF YOU RUINED MY SURPRISE I'D HAVE HAD TO KILL YOU.
AREN'T YOU GOING TO OPEN YOUR PRESENTS?
ABSOLUTELY. LEMME AT THEM!
IT'S VERY NICE, BUT I'M NOT SURE IT'LL FIT ME.
HA . . . HA. YOU ARE TOO DROLL FOR WORDS. YOU WANT ME TO MODEL THEM FOR YOU, BABY?
THERE'S MORE?
FIVE OF THOSE LITTLE BOXES, LAST I COUNTED.

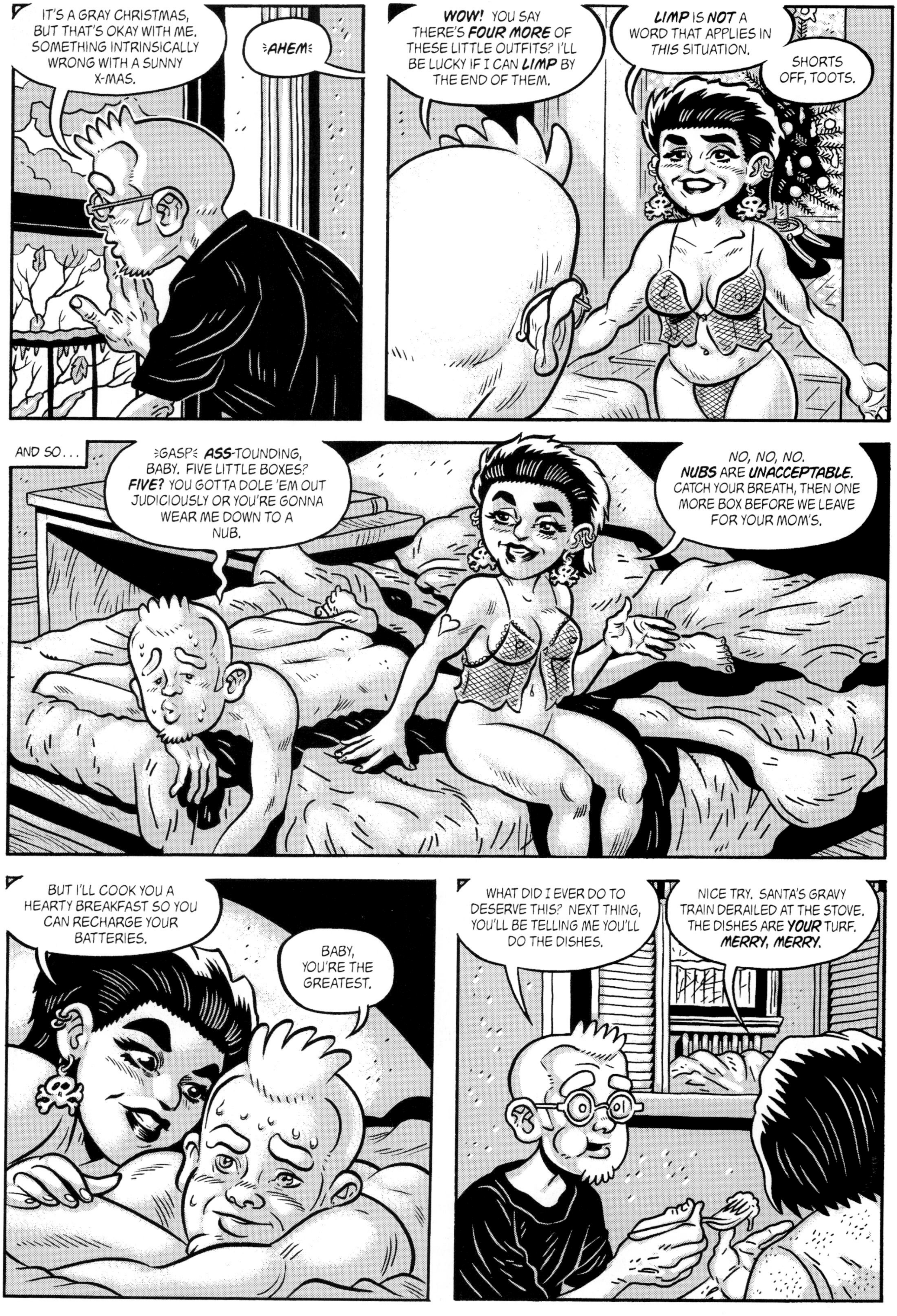
IT'S A GRAY CHRISTMAS, BUT THAT'S OKAY WITH ME. SOMETHING INTRINSICALLY WRONG WITH A SUNNY X-MAS.
AHEM
WOW! YOU SAY THERE'S FOUR MORE OF THESE LITTLE OUTFITS? I'LL BE LUCKY IF I CAN LIMP BY THE END OF THEM.
LIMP IS NOT A WORD THAT APPLIES IN THIS SITUATION.
SHORTS OFF, TOOTS.
AND SO...
GASP ASS-TOUNDING, BABY. FIVE LITTLE BOXES? FIVE? YOU GOTTA DOLE 'EM OUT JUDICIOUSLY OR YOU'RE GONNA WEAR ME DOWN TO A NUB.
NO, NO, NO. NUBS ARE UNACCEPTABLE. CATCH YOUR BREATH, THEN ONE MORE BOX BEFORE WE LEAVE FOR YOUR MOM'S.
BUT I'LL COOK YOU A HEARTY BREAKFAST SO YOU CAN RECHARGE YOUR BATTERIES.
BABY, YOU'RE THE GREATEST.
WHAT DID I EVER DO TO DESERVE THIS? NEXT THING, YOU'LL BE TELLING ME YOU'LL DO THE DISHES.
NICE TRY. SANTA'S GRAVY TRAIN DERAILED AT THE STOVE. THE DISHES ARE YOUR TURF. MERRY, MERRY.

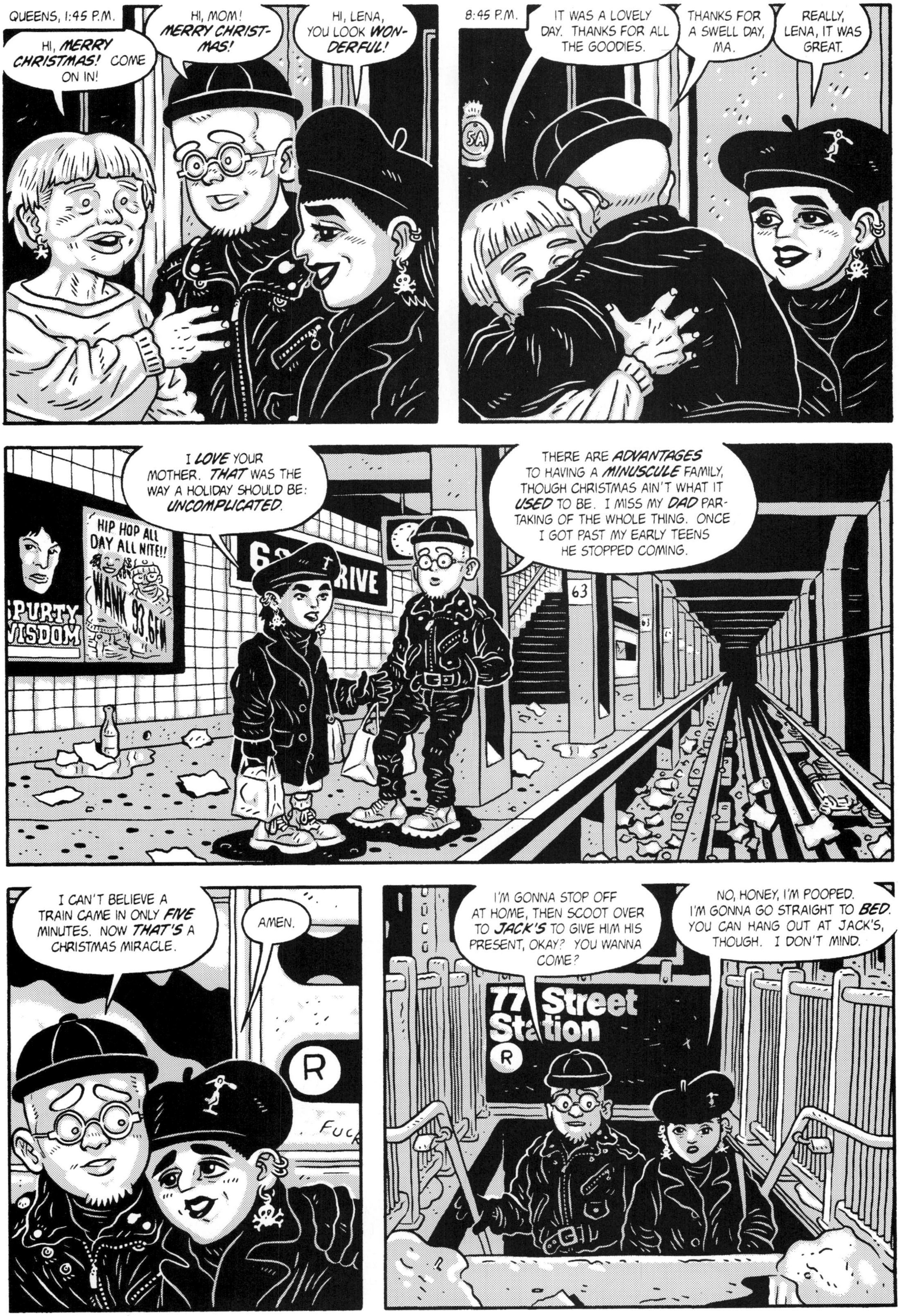

QUEENS, 1:45 P.M.
HI, MERRY CHRISTMAS! COME ON IN!
HI, MOM! MERRY CHRISTMAS!
HI, LENA, YOU LOOK WONDERFUL!
8:45 P.M.
IT WAS A LOVELY DAY. THANKS FOR ALL THE GOODIES.
THANKS FOR A SWELL DAY, MA.
REALLY, LENA, IT WAS GREAT.
HIP HOP ALL DAY ALL NITE!!
WANK 93.6FM
SPURTY WISDOM
I LOVE YOUR MOTHER. THAT WAS THE WAY A HOLIDAY SHOULD BE: UNCOMPLICATED.
THERE ARE ADVANTAGES TO HAVING A MINUSCULE FAMILY, THOUGH CHRISTMAS AIN'T WHAT IT USED TO BE. I MISS MY DAD PARTAKING OF THE WHOLE THING. ONCE I GOT PAST MY EARLY TEENS HE STOPPED COMING.
63
I CAN'T BELIEVE A TRAIN CAME IN ONLY FIVE MINUTES. NOW THAT'S A CHRISTMAS MIRACLE.
AMEN.
R
I'M GONNA STOP OFF AT HOME, THEN SCOOT OVER TO JACK'S TO GIVE HIM HIS PRESENT, OKAY? YOU WANNA COME?
NO, HONEY, I'M POOPED. I'M GONNA GO STRAIGHT TO BED. YOU CAN HANG OUT AT JACK'S, THOUGH. I DON'T MIND.
77 Street Station
R

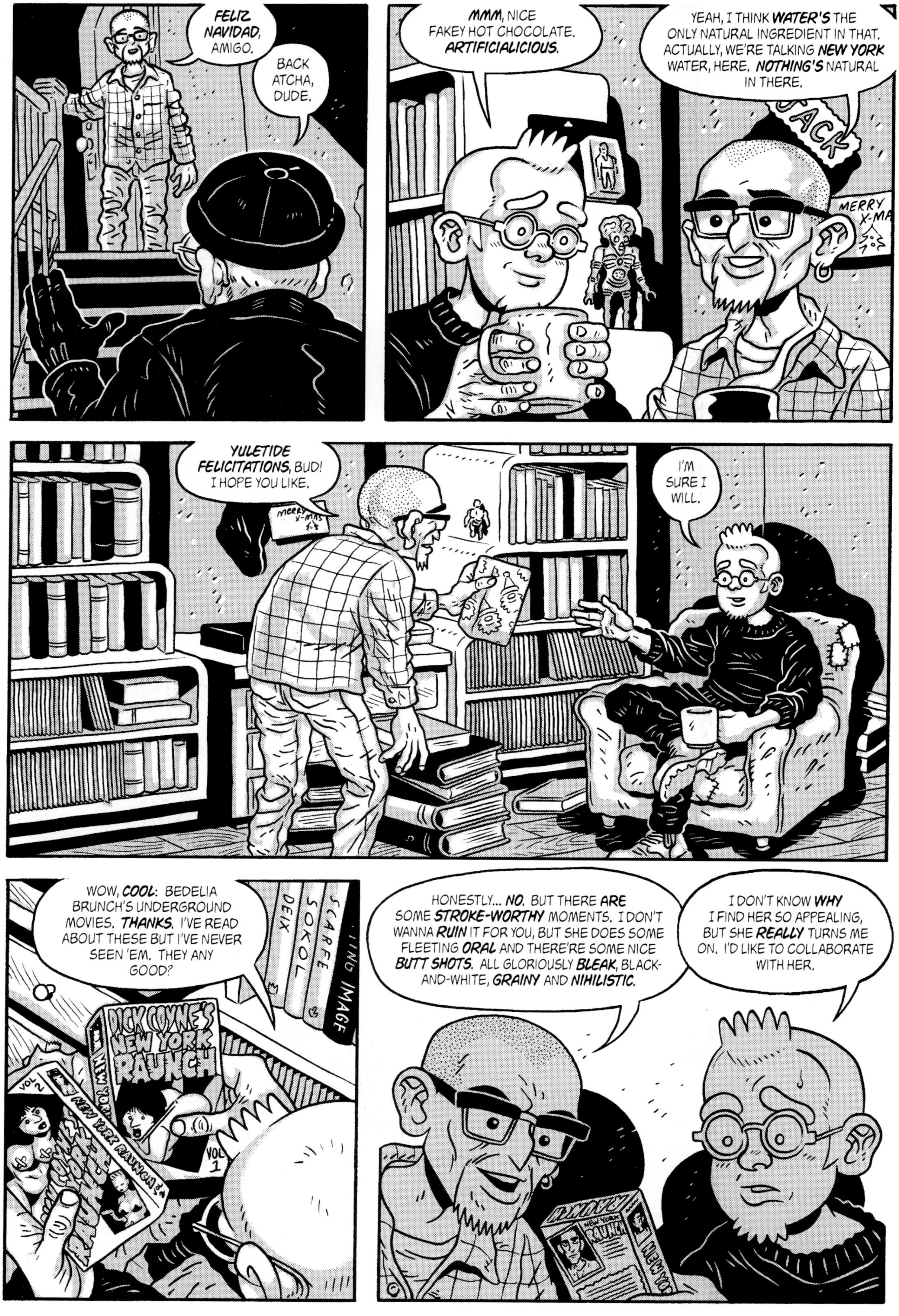
FELIZ NAVIDAD, AMIGO.
BACK ATCHA, DUDE.
MMM, NICE FAKEY HOT CHOCOLATE. ARTIFICIALICIOUS.
YEAH, I THINK WATER'S THE ONLY NATURAL INGREDIENT IN THAT. ACTUALLY, WE'RE TALKING NEW YORK WATER, HERE. NOTHING'S NATURAL IN THERE.
YULETIDE FELICITATIONS, BUD! I HOPE YOU LIKE.
I'M SURE I WILL.
WOW, COOL: BEDELIA BRUNCH'S UNDERGROUND MOVIES. THANKS. I'VE READ ABOUT THESE BUT I'VE NEVER SEEN 'EM. THEY ANY GOOD?
SCARFE
SOKOL
DEIX
IMAGE
DICK COYNE'S NEW YORK RAUNCH
VOL 1
VOL 2
HONESTLY... NO. BUT THERE ARE SOME STROKE-WORTHY MOMENTS. I DON'T WANNA RUIN IT FOR YOU, BUT SHE DOES SOME FLEETING ORAL AND THERE'RE SOME NICE BUTT SHOTS. ALL GLORIOUSLY BLEAK, BLACK-AND-WHITE, GRAINY AND NIHILISTIC.
I DON'T KNOW WHY I FIND HER SO APPEALING, BUT SHE REALLY TURNS ME ON. I'D LIKE TO COLLABORATE WITH HER.

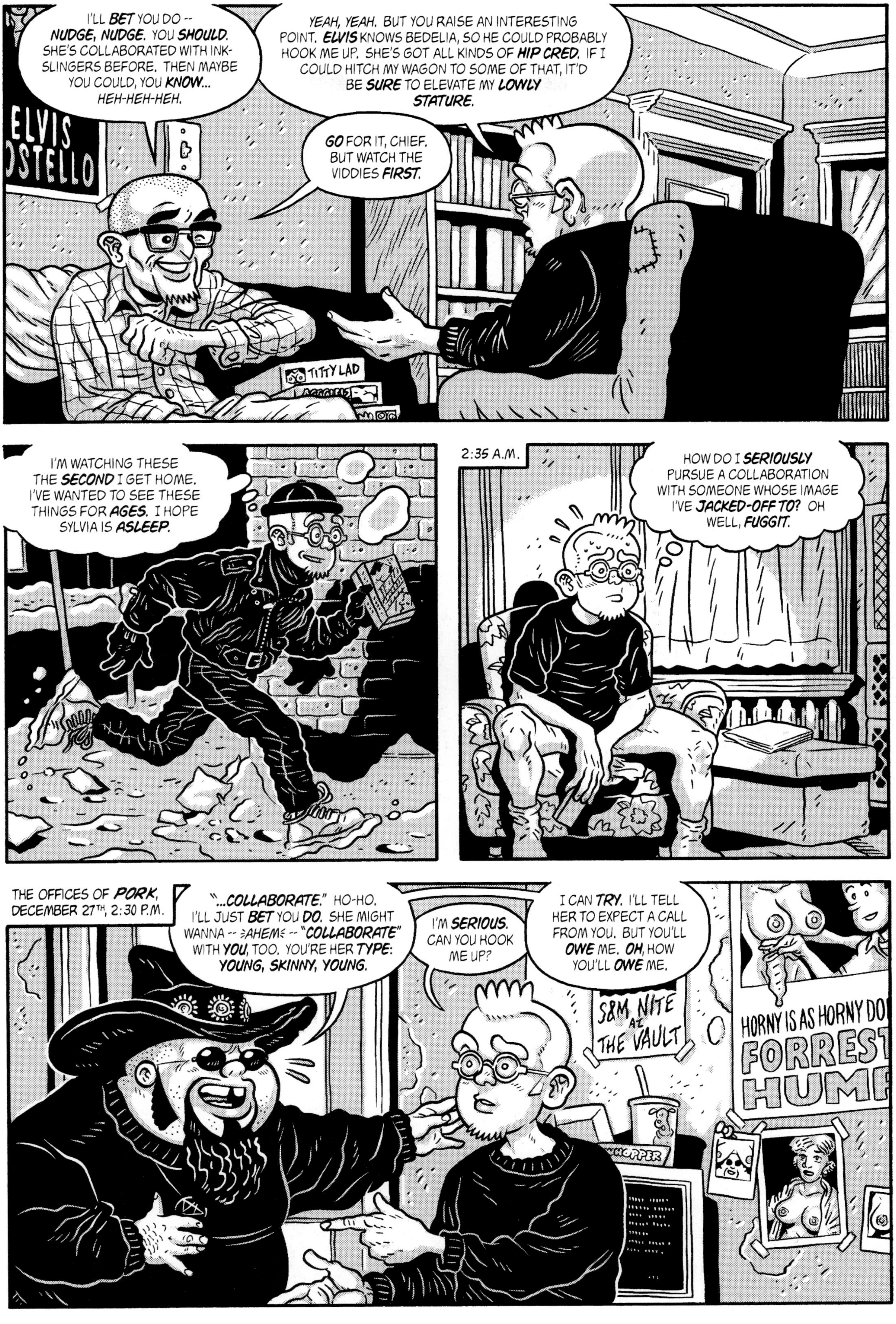
ELVIS COSTELLO
I'LL BET YOU DO -- NUDGE, NUDGE. YOU SHOULD. SHE'S COLLABORATED WITH INK-SLINGERS BEFORE. THEN MAYBE YOU COULD, YOU KNOW... HEH-HEH-HEH.
YEAH, YEAH. BUT YOU RAISE AN INTERESTING POINT. ELVIS KNOWS BEDELIA, SO HE COULD PROBABLY HOOK ME UP. SHE'S GOT ALL KINDS OF HIP CRED. IF I COULD HITCH MY WAGON TO SOME OF THAT, IT'D BE SURE TO ELEVATE MY LOWLY STATURE.
GO FOR IT, CHIEF. BUT WATCH THE VIDDIES FIRST.
TITTY LAD
I'M WATCHING THESE THE SECOND I GET HOME. I'VE WANTED TO SEE THESE THINGS FOR AGES. I HOPE SYLVIA IS ASLEEP.
2:35 A.M.
HOW DO I SERIOUSLY PURSUE A COLLABORATION WITH SOMEONE WHOSE IMAGE I'VE JACKED-OFF TO? OH WELL, FUGGIT.
THE OFFICES OF PORK, DECEMBER 27TH, 2:30 P.M.
"...COLLABORATE." HO-HO. I'LL JUST BET YOU DO. SHE MIGHT WANNA -- ≥AHEM≤ -- "COLLABORATE" WITH YOU, TOO. YOU'RE HER TYPE: YOUNG, SKINNY, YOUNG.
I'M SERIOUS. CAN YOU HOOK ME UP?
I CAN TRY. I'LL TELL HER TO EXPECT A CALL FROM YOU. BUT YOU'LL OWE ME. OH, HOW YOU'LL OWE ME.
S&M NITE AT THE VAULT
HORNY IS AS HORNY DO
FORREST HUMP

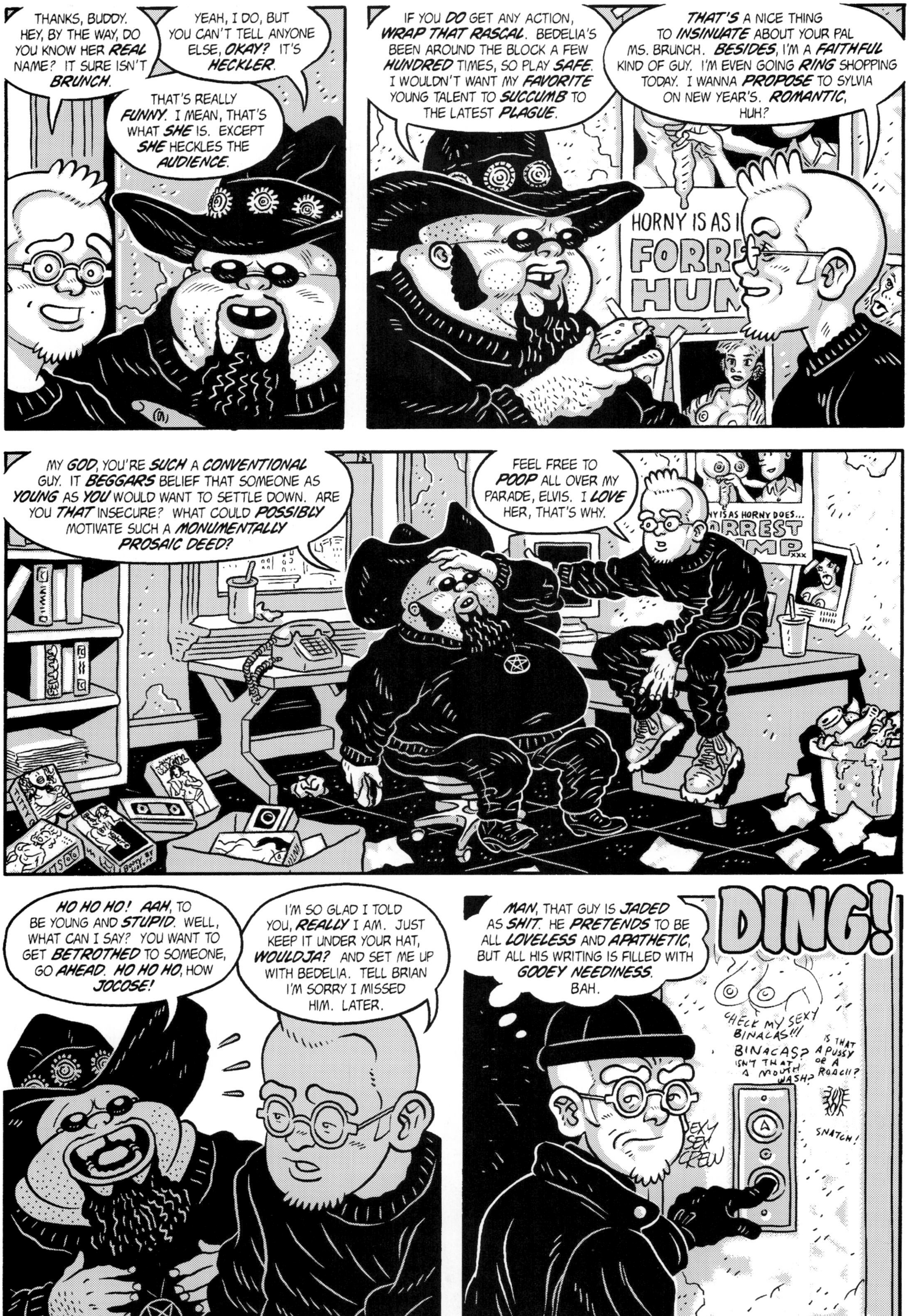

THANKS, BUDDY. HEY, BY THE WAY, DO YOU KNOW HER REAL NAME? IT SURE ISN'T BRUNCH.
YEAH, I DO, BUT YOU CAN'T TELL ANYONE ELSE, OKAY? IT'S HECKLER.
THAT'S REALLY FUNNY. I MEAN, THAT'S WHAT SHE IS. EXCEPT SHE HECKLES THE AUDIENCE.
IF YOU DO GET ANY ACTION, WRAP THAT RASCAL. BEDELIA'S BEEN AROUND THE BLOCK A FEW HUNDRED TIMES, SO PLAY SAFE. I WOULDN'T WANT MY FAVORITE YOUNG TALENT TO SUCCUMB TO THE LATEST PLAGUE.
THAT'S A NICE THING TO INSINUATE ABOUT YOUR PAL MS. BRUNCH. BESIDES, I'M A FAITHFUL KIND OF GUY. I'M EVEN GOING RING SHOPPING TODAY. I WANNA PROPOSE TO SYLVIA ON NEW YEAR'S. ROMANTIC, HUH?
HORNY IS AS I
FORR
HUM
MY GOD, YOU'RE SUCH A CONVENTIONAL GUY. IT BEGGARS BELIEF THAT SOMEONE AS YOUNG AS YOU WOULD WANT TO SETTLE DOWN. ARE YOU THAT INSECURE? WHAT COULD POSSIBLY MOTIVATE SUCH A MONUMENTALLY PROSAIC DEED?
FEEL FREE TO POOP ALL OVER MY PARADE, ELVIS. I LOVE HER, THAT'S WHY.
HO HO HO! AAH, TO BE YOUNG AND STUPID. WELL, WHAT CAN I SAY? YOU WANT TO GET BETROTHED TO SOMEONE, GO AHEAD. HO HO HO, HOW JOCOSE!
I'M SO GLAD I TOLD YOU, REALLY I AM. JUST KEEP IT UNDER YOUR HAT, WOULDJA? AND SET ME UP WITH BEDELIA. TELL BRIAN I'M SORRY I MISSED HIM. LATER.
MAN, THAT GUY IS JADED AS SHIT. HE PRETENDS TO BE ALL LOVELESS AND APATHETIC, BUT ALL HIS WRITING IS FILLED WITH GOOEY NEEDINESS. BAH.
DING!
CHECK MY SEXY BINACAS!!!
BINACAS? ISN'T THAT A MOUTH WASH?
IS THAT A PUSSY OR A ROACH?
SNATCH!
EXY SEX CREW

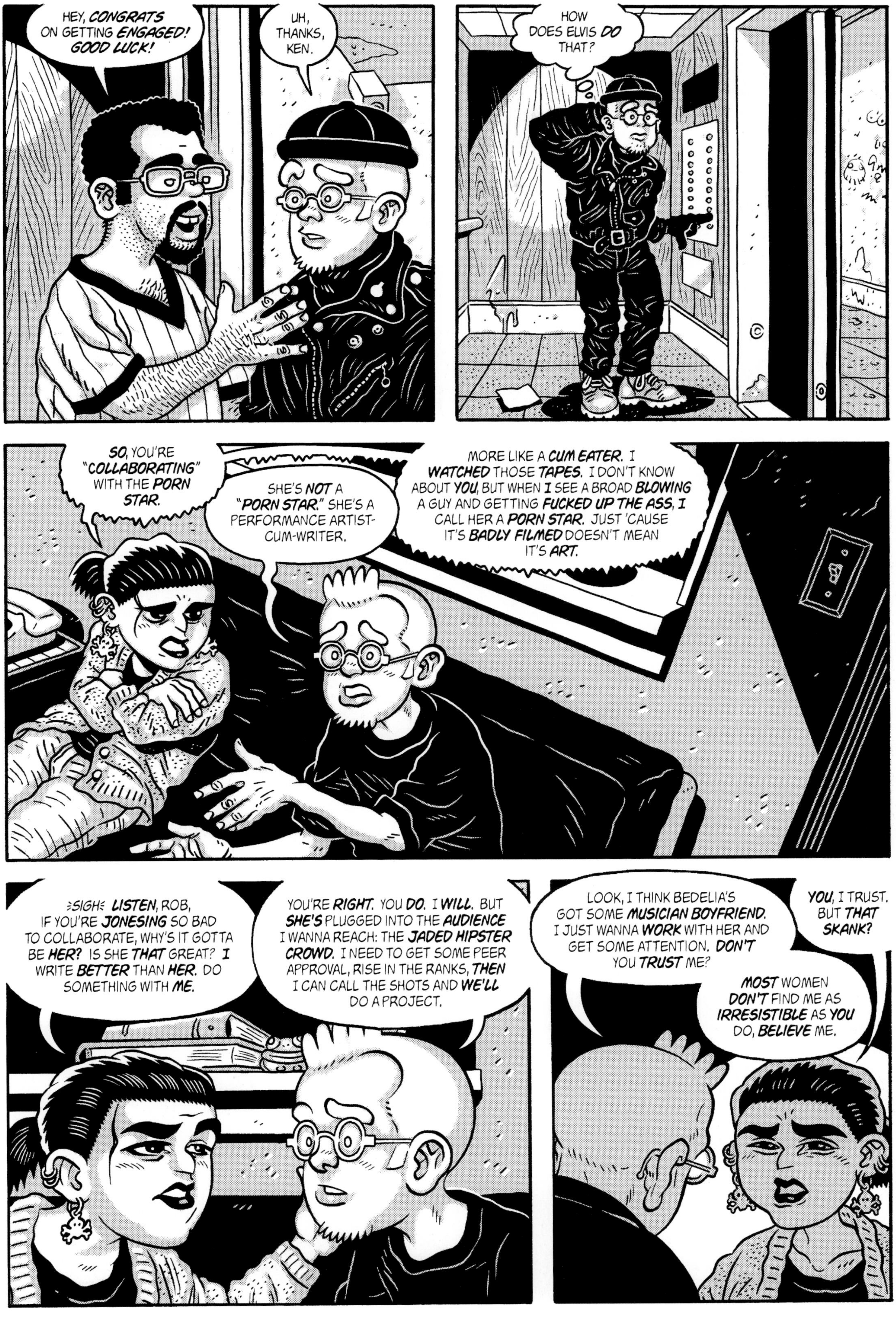

HEY, CONGRATS ON GETTING ENGAGED! GOOD LUCK!
UH, THANKS, KEN.
HOW DOES ELVIS DO THAT?
SO, YOU'RE "COLLABORATING" WITH THE PORN STAR.
SHE'S NOT A "PORN STAR." SHE'S A PERFORMANCE ARTIST-CUM-WRITER.
MORE LIKE A CUM EATER. I WATCHED THOSE TAPES. I DON'T KNOW ABOUT YOU, BUT WHEN I SEE A BROAD BLOWING A GUY AND GETTING FUCKED UP THE ASS, I CALL HER A PORN STAR. JUST 'CAUSE IT'S BADLY FILMED DOESN'T MEAN IT'S ART.
≥SIGH≤ LISTEN, ROB, IF YOU'RE JONESING SO BAD TO COLLABORATE, WHY'S IT GOTTA BE HER? IS SHE THAT GREAT? I WRITE BETTER THAN HER. DO SOMETHING WITH ME.
YOU'RE RIGHT. YOU DO. I WILL. BUT SHE'S PLUGGED INTO THE AUDIENCE I WANNA REACH: THE JADED HIPSTER CROWD. I NEED TO GET SOME PEER APPROVAL, RISE IN THE RANKS, THEN I CAN CALL THE SHOTS AND WE'LL DO A PROJECT.
LOOK, I THINK BEDELIA'S GOT SOME MUSICIAN BOYFRIEND. I JUST WANNA WORK WITH HER AND GET SOME ATTENTION. DON'T YOU TRUST ME?
YOU, I TRUST. BUT THAT SKANK?
MOST WOMEN DON'T FIND ME AS IRRESISTIBLE AS YOU DO, BELIEVE ME.

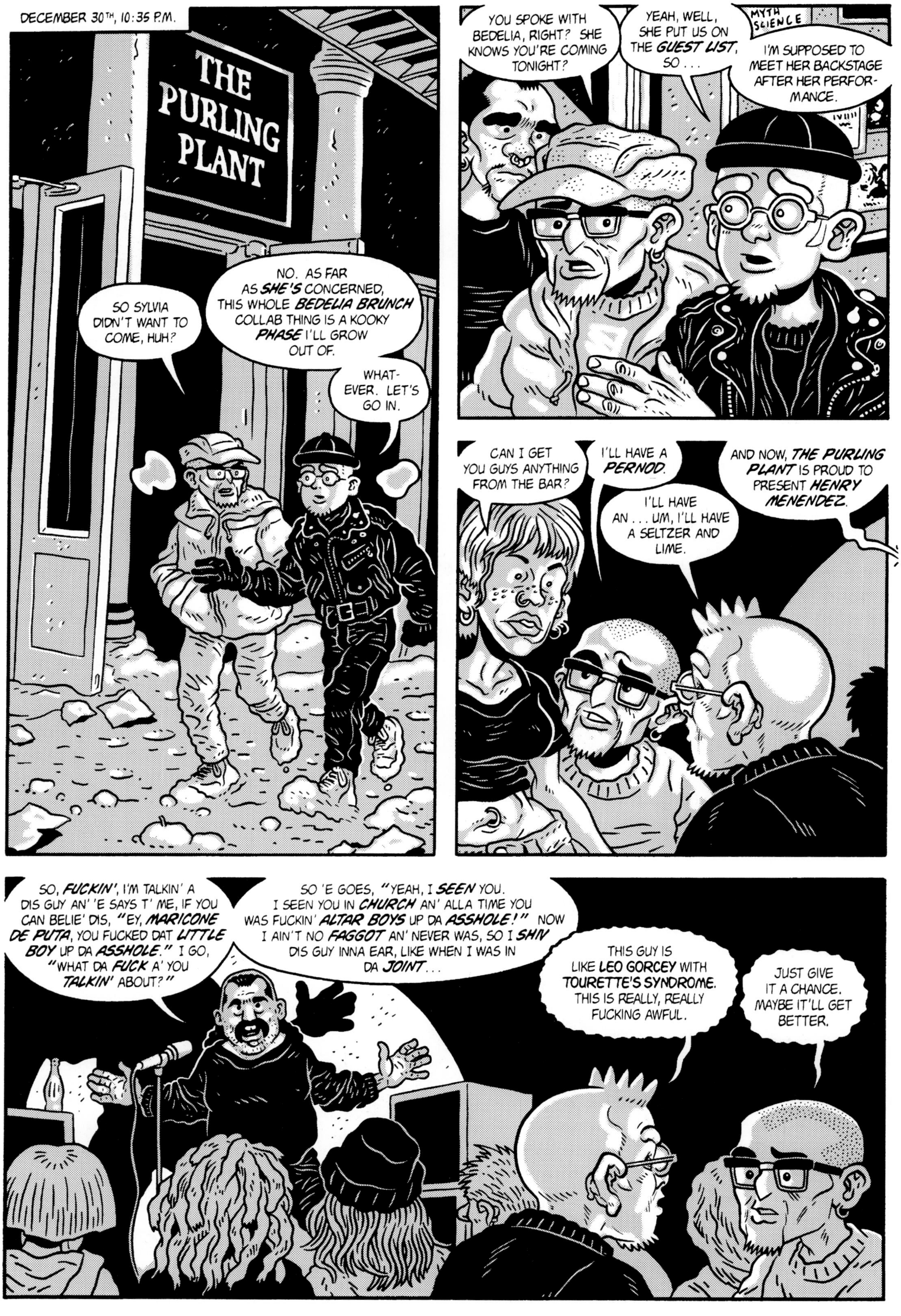
DECEMBER 30TH, 10:35 P.M.
THE PURLING PLANT
SO SYLVIA DIDN'T WANT TO COME, HUH?
NO. AS FAR AS SHE'S CONCERNED, THIS WHOLE BEDELIA BRUNCH COLLAB THING IS A KOOKY PHASE I'LL GROW OUT OF.
WHAT-EVER. LET'S GO IN.
YOU SPOKE WITH BEDELIA, RIGHT? SHE KNOWS YOU'RE COMING TONIGHT?
YEAH, WELL, SHE PUT US ON THE GUEST LIST, SO . . .
MYTH SCIENCE
I'M SUPPOSED TO MEET HER BACKSTAGE AFTER HER PERFOR-MANCE.
CAN I GET YOU GUYS ANYTHING FROM THE BAR?
I'LL HAVE A PERNOD.
I'LL HAVE AN . . . UM, I'LL HAVE A SELTZER AND LIME.
AND NOW, THE PURLING PLANT IS PROUD TO PRESENT HENRY MENENDEZ.
SO, FUCKIN', I'M TALKIN' A DIS GUY AN' 'E SAYS T' ME, IF YOU CAN BELIE' DIS, "EY, MARICONE DE PUTA, YOU FUCKED DAT LITTLE BOY UP DA ASSHOLE." I GO, "WHAT DA FUCK A' YOU TALKIN' ABOUT?"
SO 'E GOES, "YEAH, I SEEN YOU. I SEEN YOU IN CHURCH AN' ALLA TIME YOU WAS FUCKIN' ALTAR BOYS UP DA ASSHOLE!" NOW I AIN'T NO FAGGOT AN' NEVER WAS, SO I SHIV DIS GUY INNA EAR, LIKE WHEN I WAS IN DA JOINT . . .
THIS GUY IS LIKE LEO GORCEY WITH TOURETTE'S SYNDROME. THIS IS REALLY, REALLY FUCKING AWFUL.
JUST GIVE IT A CHANCE. MAYBE IT'LL GET BETTER.

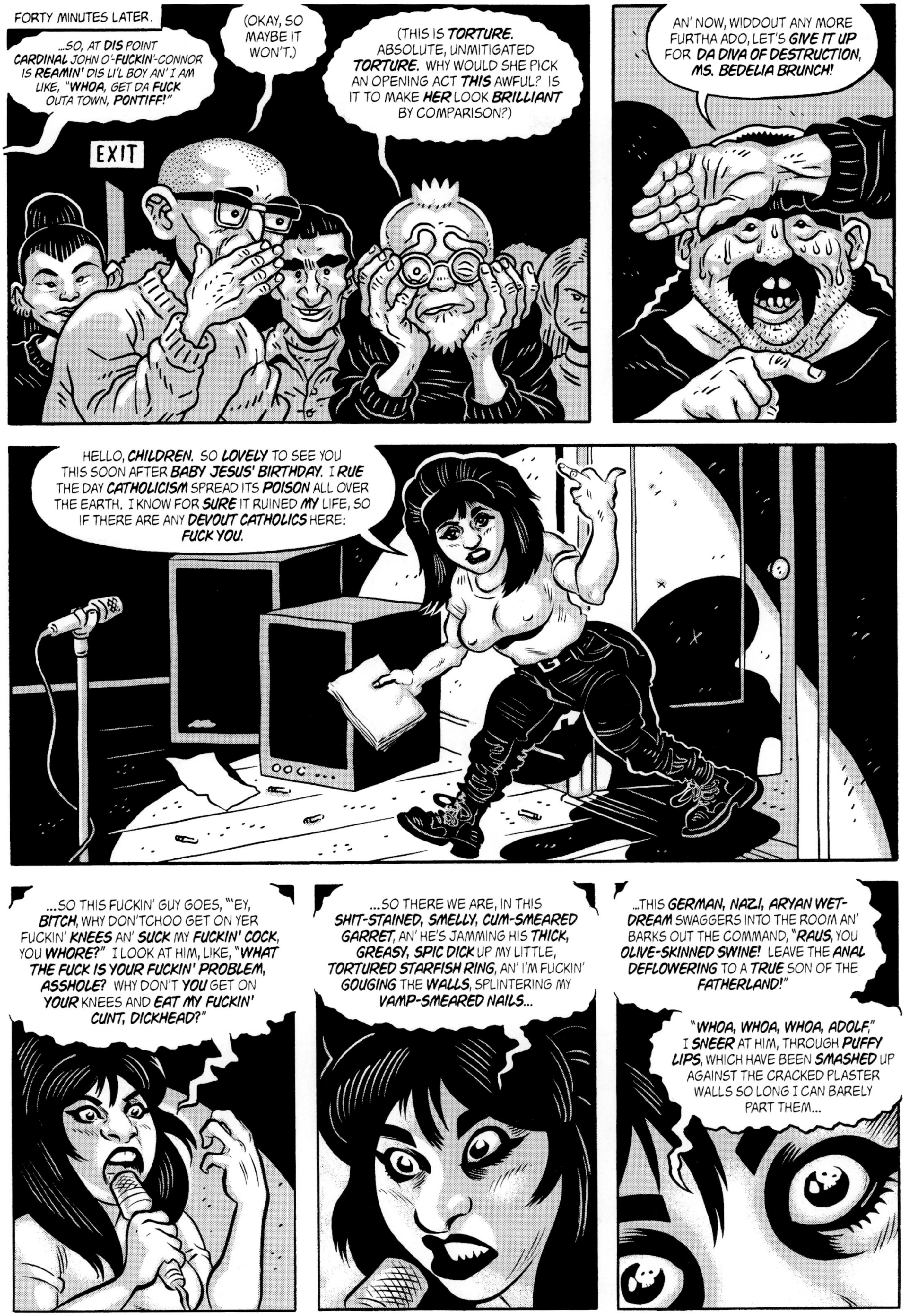
FORTY MINUTES LATER.
...SO, AT DIS POINT CARDINAL JOHN O'-FUCKIN'-CONNOR IS REAMIN' DIS LI'L BOY AN' I AM LIKE, "WHOA, GET DA FUCK OUTA TOWN, PONTIFF!"
(OKAY, SO MAYBE IT WON'T.)
(THIS IS TORTURE. ABSOLUTE, UNMITIGATED TORTURE. WHY WOULD SHE PICK AN OPENING ACT THIS AWFUL? IS IT TO MAKE HER LOOK BRILLIANT BY COMPARISON?)
EXIT
AN' NOW, WIDDOUT ANY MORE FURTHA ADO, LET'S GIVE IT UP FOR DA DIVA OF DESTRUCTION, MS. BEDELIA BRUNCH!
HELLO, CHILDREN. SO LOVELY TO SEE YOU THIS SOON AFTER BABY JESUS' BIRTHDAY. I RUE THE DAY CATHOLICISM SPREAD ITS POISON ALL OVER THE EARTH. I KNOW FOR SURE IT RUINED MY LIFE, SO IF THERE ARE ANY DEVOUT CATHOLICS HERE: FUCK YOU.
...SO THIS FUCKIN' GUY GOES, "'EY, BITCH, WHY DON'TCHOO GET ON YER FUCKIN' KNEES AN' SUCK MY FUCKIN' COCK, YOU WHORE?" I LOOK AT HIM, LIKE, "WHAT THE FUCK IS YOUR FUCKIN' PROBLEM, ASSHOLE? WHY DON'T YOU GET ON YOUR KNEES AND EAT MY FUCKIN' CUNT, DICKHEAD?"
...SO THERE WE ARE, IN THIS SHIT-STAINED, SMELLY, CUM-SMEARED GARRET, AN' HE'S JAMMING HIS THICK, GREASY, SPIC DICK UP MY LITTLE, TORTURED STARFISH RING, AN' I'M FUCKIN' GOUGING THE WALLS, SPLINTERING MY VAMP-SMEARED NAILS...
...THIS GERMAN, NAZI, ARYAN WET-DREAM SWAGGERS INTO THE ROOM AN' BARKS OUT THE COMMAND, "RAUS, YOU OLIVE-SKINNED SWINE! LEAVE THE ANAL DEFLOWERING TO A TRUE SON OF THE FATHERLAND!"
"WHOA, WHOA, WHOA, ADOLF," I SNEER AT HIM, THROUGH PUFFY LIPS, WHICH HAVE BEEN SMASHED UP AGAINST THE CRACKED PLASTER WALLS SO LONG I CAN BARELY PART THEM...

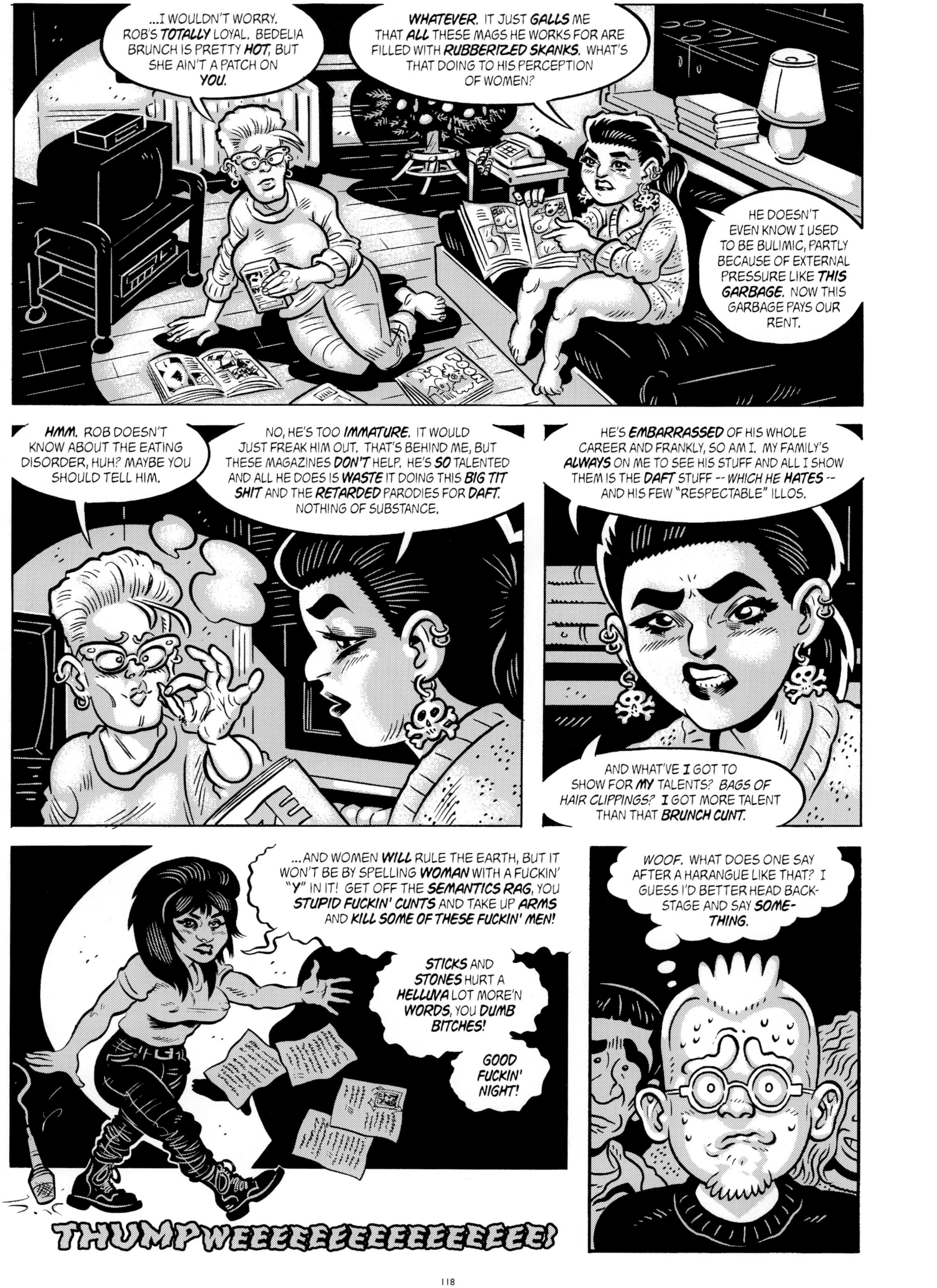
...I WOULDN'T WORRY. ROB'S TOTALLY LOYAL. BEDELIA BRUNCH IS PRETTY HOT, BUT SHE AIN'T A PATCH ON YOU.
WHATEVER. IT JUST GALLS ME THAT ALL THESE MAGS HE WORKS FOR ARE FILLED WITH RUBBERIZED SKANKS. WHAT'S THAT DOING TO HIS PERCEPTION OF WOMEN?
HE DOESN'T EVEN KNOW I USED TO BE BULIMIC, PARTLY BECAUSE OF EXTERNAL PRESSURE LIKE THIS GARBAGE. NOW THIS GARBAGE PAYS OUR RENT.
HMM. ROB DOESN'T KNOW ABOUT THE EATING DISORDER, HUH? MAYBE YOU SHOULD TELL HIM.
NO, HE'S TOO IMMATURE. IT WOULD JUST FREAK HIM OUT. THAT'S BEHIND ME, BUT THESE MAGAZINES DON'T HELP. HE'S SO TALENTED AND ALL HE DOES IS WASTE IT DOING THIS BIG TIT SHIT AND THE RETARDED PARODIES FOR DAFT. NOTHING OF SUBSTANCE.
HE'S EMBARRASSED OF HIS WHOLE CAREER AND FRANKLY, SO AM I. MY FAMILY'S ALWAYS ON ME TO SEE HIS STUFF AND ALL I SHOW THEM IS THE DAFT STUFF -- WHICH HE HATES -- AND HIS FEW "RESPECTABLE" ILLOS.
AND WHAT'VE I GOT TO SHOW FOR MY TALENTS? BAGS OF HAIR CLIPPINGS? I GOT MORE TALENT THAN THAT BRUNCH CUNT.
...AND WOMEN WILL RULE THE EARTH, BUT IT WON'T BE BY SPELLING WOMAN WITH A FUCKIN' "Y" IN IT! GET OFF THE SEMANTICS RAG, YOU STUPID FUCKIN' CUNTS AND TAKE UP ARMS AND KILL SOME OF THESE FUCKIN' MEN!
STICKS AND STONES HURT A HELLUVA LOT MORE'N WORDS, YOU DUMB BITCHES!
GOOD FUCKIN' NIGHT!
THUMPWEEEEEEEEEEEEEEEE!
WOOF. WHAT DOES ONE SAY AFTER A HARANGUE LIKE THAT? I GUESS I'D BETTER HEAD BACK-STAGE AND SAY SOME-THING.

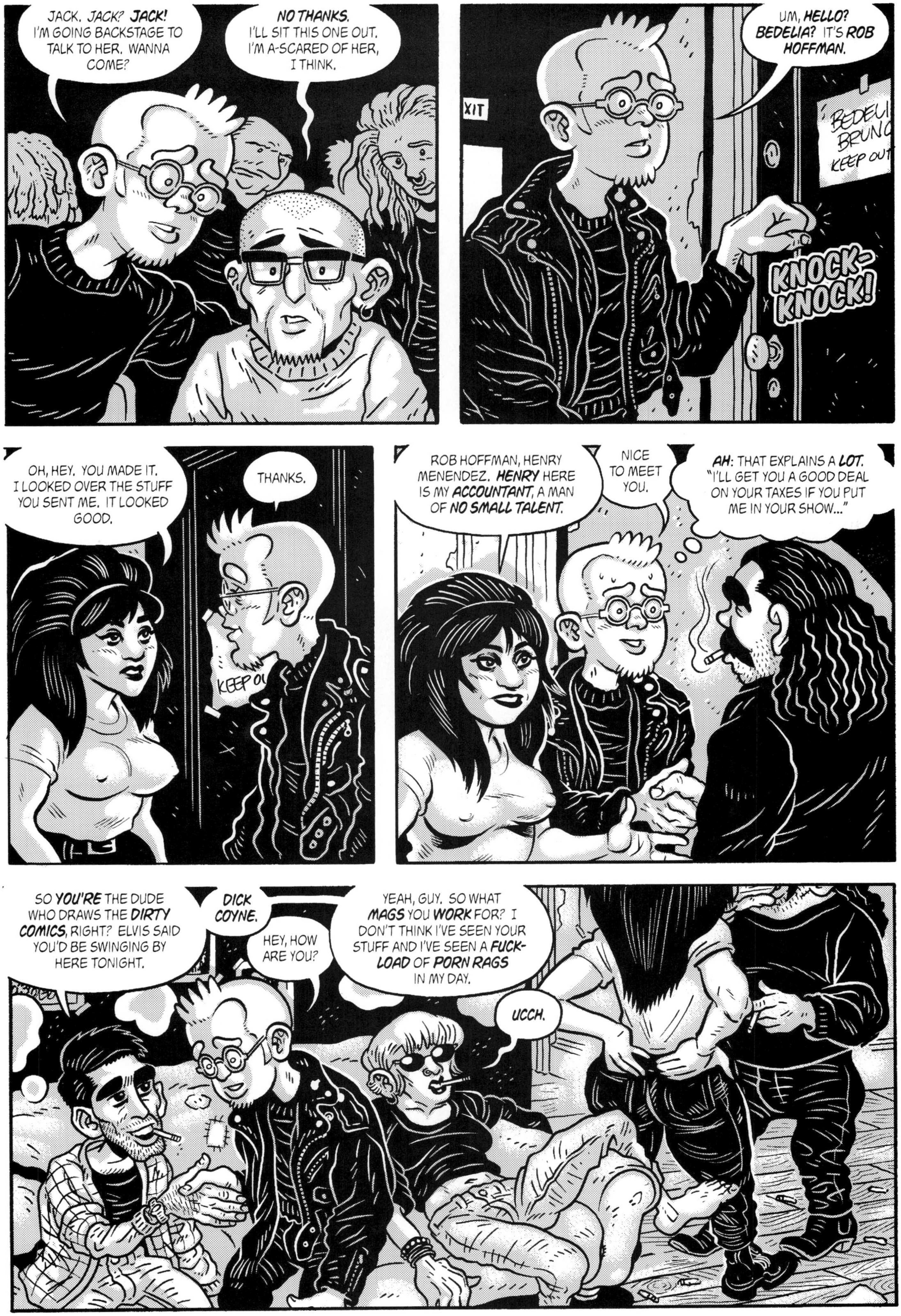
JACK. JACK? JACK! I'M GOING BACKSTAGE TO TALK TO HER. WANNA COME?
NO THANKS. I'LL SIT THIS ONE OUT. I'M A-SCARED OF HER, I THINK.
XIT
UM, HELLO? BEDELIA? IT'S ROB HOFFMAN.
KEEP OUT
KNOCK-KNOCK!
OH, HEY. YOU MADE IT. I LOOKED OVER THE STUFF YOU SENT ME. IT LOOKED GOOD.
THANKS.
ROB HOFFMAN, HENRY MENENDEZ. HENRY HERE IS MY ACCOUNTANT, A MAN OF NO SMALL TALENT.
NICE TO MEET YOU.
AH: THAT EXPLAINS A LOT. "I'LL GET YOU A GOOD DEAL ON YOUR TAXES IF YOU PUT ME IN YOUR SHOW..."
SO YOU'RE THE DUDE WHO DRAWS THE DIRTY COMICS, RIGHT? ELVIS SAID YOU'D BE SWINGING BY HERE TONIGHT.
DICK COYNE.
HEY, HOW ARE YOU?
YEAH, GUY. SO WHAT MAGS YOU WORK FOR? I DON'T THINK I'VE SEEN YOUR STUFF AND I'VE SEEN A FUCK-LOAD OF PORN RAGS IN MY DAY.
UCCH.

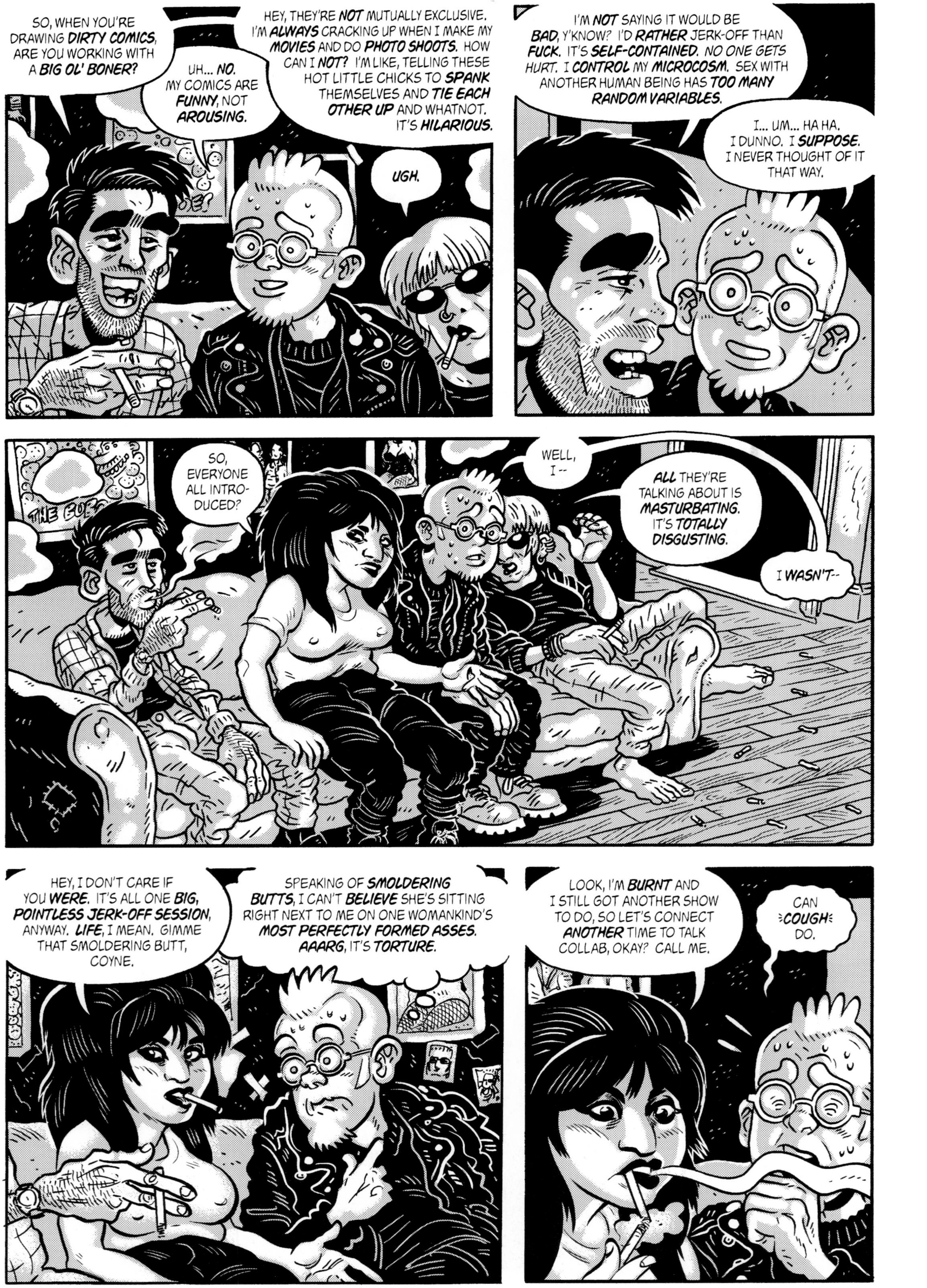
SO, WHEN YOU'RE DRAWING DIRTY COMICS, ARE YOU WORKING WITH A BIG OL' BONER?
UH... NO. MY COMICS ARE FUNNY, NOT AROUSING.
HEY, THEY'RE NOT MUTUALLY EXCLUSIVE. I'M ALWAYS CRACKING UP WHEN I MAKE MY MOVIES AND DO PHOTO SHOOTS. HOW CAN I NOT? I'M LIKE, TELLING THESE HOT LITTLE CHICKS TO SPANK THEMSELVES AND TIE EACH OTHER UP AND WHATNOT. IT'S HILARIOUS.
UGH.
I'M NOT SAYING IT WOULD BE BAD, Y'KNOW? I'D RATHER JERK-OFF THAN FUCK. IT'S SELF-CONTAINED. NO ONE GETS HURT. I CONTROL MY MICROCOSM. SEX WITH ANOTHER HUMAN BEING HAS TOO MANY RANDOM VARIABLES.
I... UM... HA HA. I DUNNO. I SUPPOSE. I NEVER THOUGHT OF IT THAT WAY.
SO, EVERYONE ALL INTRO-DUCED?
WELL, I--
ALL THEY'RE TALKING ABOUT IS MASTURBATING. IT'S TOTALLY DISGUSTING.
I WASN'T--
HEY, I DON'T CARE IF YOU WERE. IT'S ALL ONE BIG, POINTLESS JERK-OFF SESSION, ANYWAY. LIFE, I MEAN. GIMME THAT SMOLDERING BUTT, COYNE.
SPEAKING OF SMOLDERING BUTTS, I CAN'T BELIEVE SHE'S SITTING RIGHT NEXT TO ME ON ONE WOMANKIND'S MOST PERFECTLY FORMED ASSES. AAARG, IT'S TORTURE.
LOOK, I'M BURNT AND I STILL GOT ANOTHER SHOW TO DO, SO LET'S CONNECT ANOTHER TIME TO TALK COLLAB, OKAY? CALL ME.
CAN *COUGH* DO.

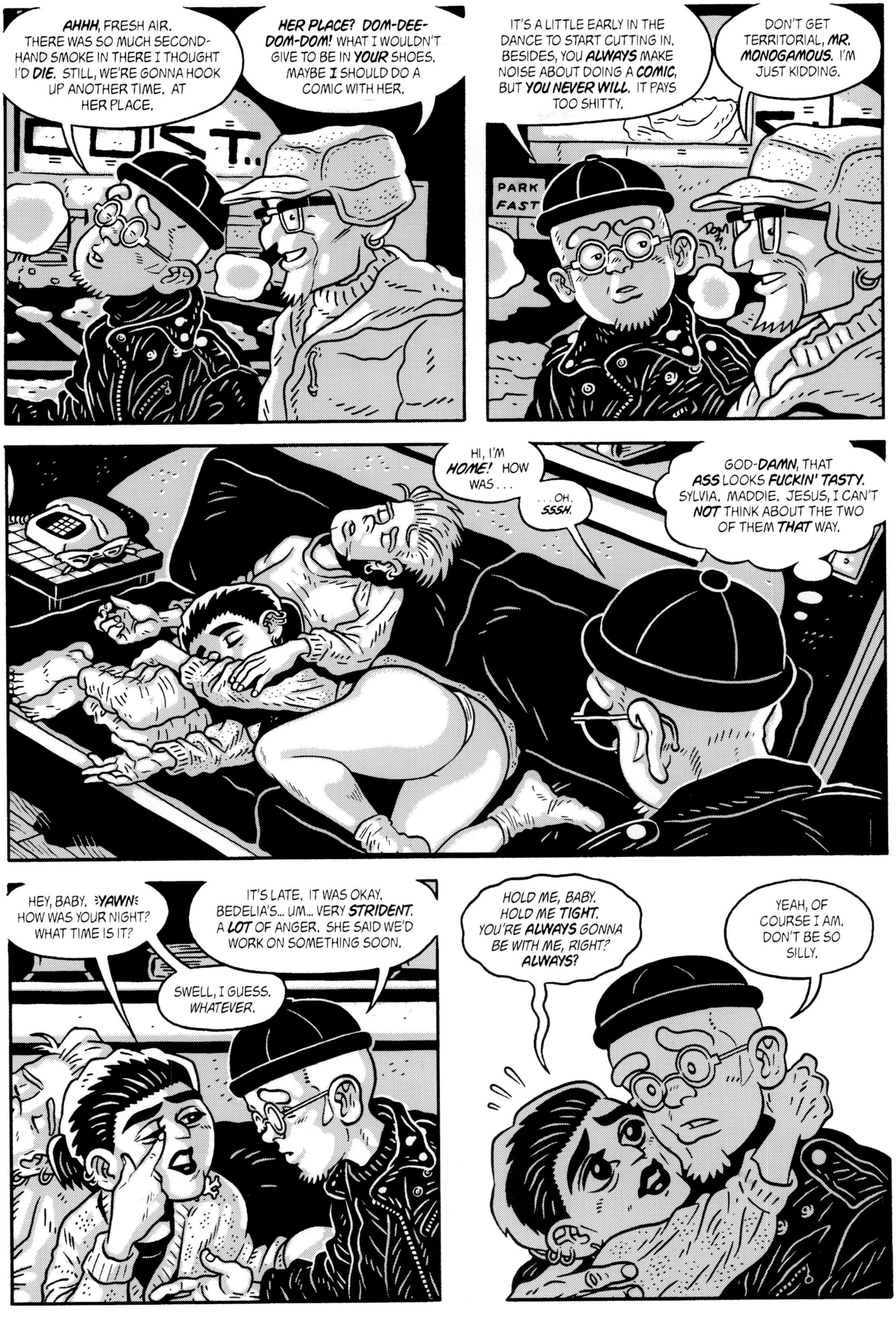
AHHH, FRESH AIR. THERE WAS SO MUCH SECOND-HAND SMOKE IN THERE I THOUGHT I'D DIE. STILL, WE'RE GONNA HOOK UP ANOTHER TIME. AT HER PLACE.
HER PLACE? DOM-DEE-DOM-DOM! WHAT I WOULDN'T GIVE TO BE IN YOUR SHOES. MAYBE I SHOULD DO A COMIC WITH HER.
IT'S A LITTLE EARLY IN THE DANCE TO START CUTTING IN. BESIDES, YOU ALWAYS MAKE NOISE ABOUT DOING A COMIC, BUT YOU NEVER WILL. IT PAYS TOO SHITTY.
DON'T GET TERRITORIAL, MR. MONOGAMOUS. I'M JUST KIDDING.
PARK FAST
HI, I'M HOME! HOW WAS . . .
. . .OH. SSSH.
GOD-DAMN, THAT ASS LOOKS FUCKIN' TASTY. SYLVIA. MADDIE. JESUS, I CAN'T NOT THINK ABOUT THE TWO OF THEM THAT WAY.
HEY, BABY. YAWN HOW WAS YOUR NIGHT? WHAT TIME IS IT?
IT'S LATE. IT WAS OKAY. BEDELIA'S... UM... VERY STRIDENT. A LOT OF ANGER. SHE SAID WE'D WORK ON SOMETHING SOON.
SWELL, I GUESS. WHATEVER.
HOLD ME, BABY. HOLD ME TIGHT. YOU'RE ALWAYS GONNA BE WITH ME, RIGHT? ALWAYS?
YEAH, OF COURSE I AM. DON'T BE SO SILLY.

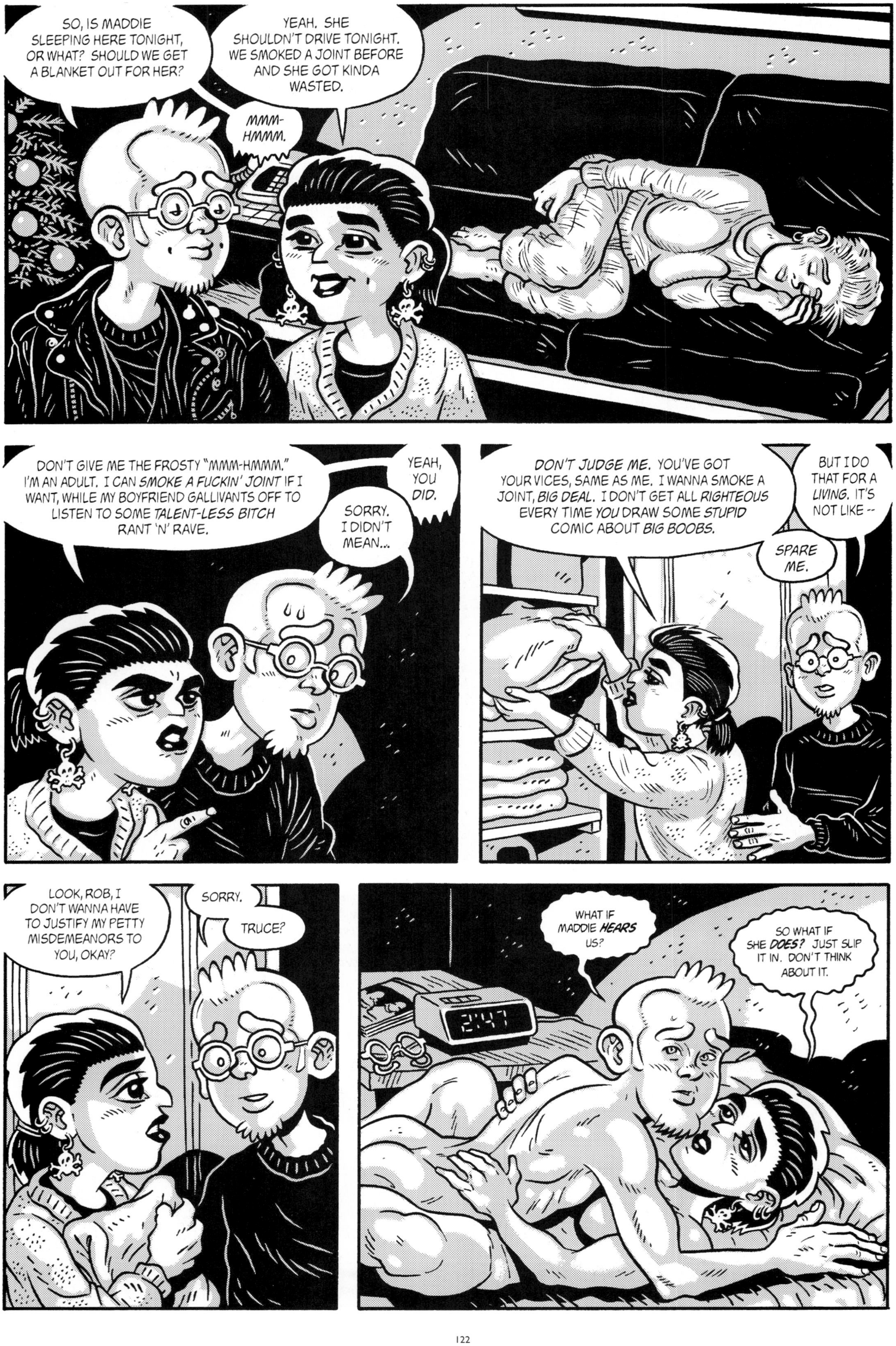
SO, IS MADDIE SLEEPING HERE TONIGHT, OR WHAT? SHOULD WE GET A BLANKET OUT FOR HER?
YEAH. SHE SHOULDN'T DRIVE TONIGHT. WE SMOKED A JOINT BEFORE AND SHE GOT KINDA WASTED.
MMM-HMMM.
DON'T GIVE ME THE FROSTY "MMM-HMMM." I'M AN ADULT. I CAN SMOKE A FUCKIN' JOINT IF I WANT, WHILE MY BOYFRIEND GALLIVANTS OFF TO LISTEN TO SOME TALENT-LESS BITCH RANT 'N' RAVE.
YEAH, YOU DID.
SORRY. I DIDN'T MEAN...
DON'T JUDGE ME. YOU'VE GOT YOUR VICES, SAME AS ME. I WANNA SMOKE A JOINT, BIG DEAL. I DON'T GET ALL RIGHTEOUS EVERY TIME YOU DRAW SOME STUPID COMIC ABOUT BIG BOOBS.
BUT I DO THAT FOR A LIVING. IT'S NOT LIKE --
SPARE ME.
LOOK, ROB, I DON'T WANNA HAVE TO JUSTIFY MY PETTY MISDEMEANORS TO YOU, OKAY?
SORRY.
TRUCE?
2:47
WHAT IF MADDIE HEARS US?
SO WHAT IF SHE DOES? JUST SLIP IT IN. DON'T THINK ABOUT IT.

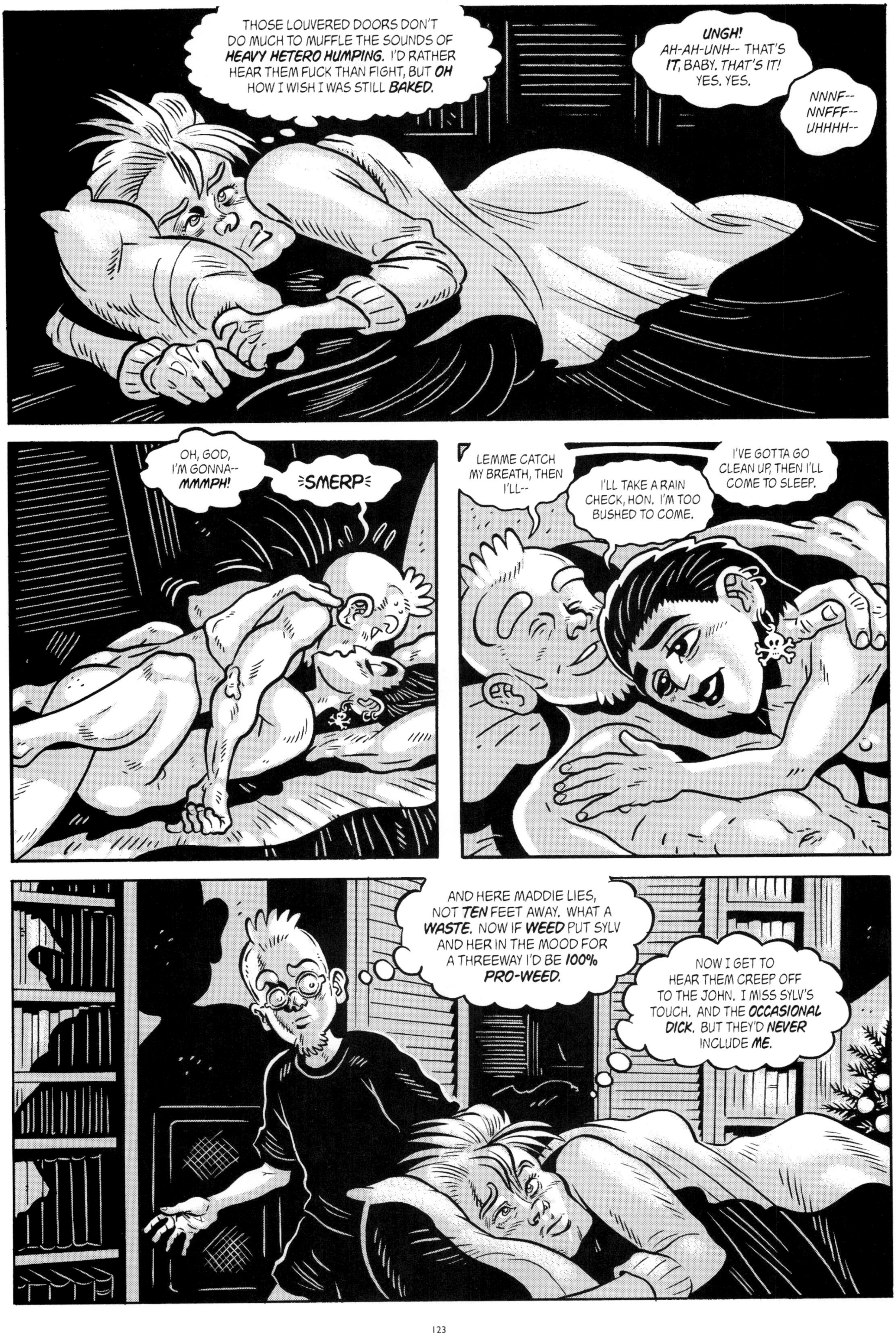

THOSE LOUVERED DOORS DON'T DO MUCH TO MUFFLE THE SOUNDS OF HEAVY HETERO HUMPING. I'D RATHER HEAR THEM FUCK THAN FIGHT, BUT OH HOW I WISH I WAS STILL BAKED.
UNGH! AH-AH-UNH-- THAT'S IT, BABY. THAT'S IT! YES. YES.
NNNF-- NNFFF-- UHHHH--
OH, GOD, I'M GONNA-- MMMPH!
SMERP
LEMME CATCH MY BREATH, THEN I'LL--
I'LL TAKE A RAIN CHECK, HON. I'M TOO BUSHED TO COME.
I'VE GOTTA GO CLEAN UP, THEN I'LL COME TO SLEEP.
AND HERE MADDIE LIES, NOT TEN FEET AWAY. WHAT A WASTE. NOW IF WEED PUT SYLV AND HER IN THE MOOD FOR A THREEWAY I'D BE 100% PRO-WEED.
NOW I GET TO HEAR THEM CREEP OFF TO THE JOHN. I MISS SYLV'S TOUCH. AND THE OCCASIONAL DICK. BUT THEY'D NEVER INCLUDE ME.

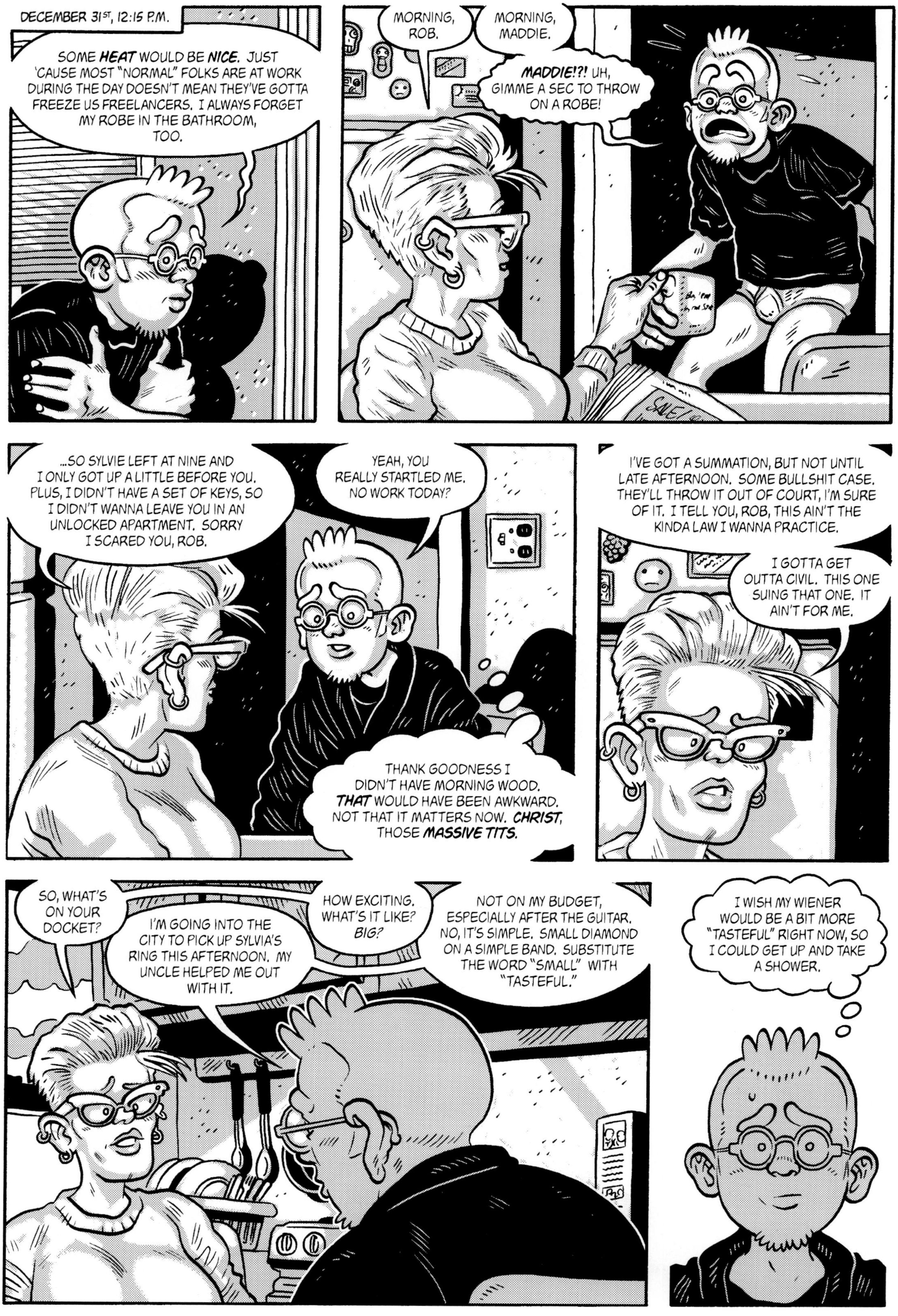
DECEMBER 31ST, 12:15 P.M.
SOME HEAT WOULD BE NICE. JUST 'CAUSE MOST "NORMAL" FOLKS ARE AT WORK DURING THE DAY DOESN'T MEAN THEY'VE GOTTA FREEZE US FREELANCERS. I ALWAYS FORGET MY ROBE IN THE BATHROOM, TOO.
MORNING, ROB.
MORNING, MADDIE.
MADDIE!?! UH, GIMME A SEC TO THROW ON A ROBE!
...SO SYLVIE LEFT AT NINE AND I ONLY GOT UP A LITTLE BEFORE YOU. PLUS, I DIDN'T HAVE A SET OF KEYS, SO I DIDN'T WANNA LEAVE YOU IN AN UNLOCKED APARTMENT. SORRY I SCARED YOU, ROB.
YEAH, YOU REALLY STARTLED ME. NO WORK TODAY?
THANK GOODNESS I DIDN'T HAVE MORNING WOOD. THAT WOULD HAVE BEEN AWKWARD. NOT THAT IT MATTERS NOW. CHRIST, THOSE MASSIVE TITS.
I'VE GOT A SUMMATION, BUT NOT UNTIL LATE AFTERNOON. SOME BULLSHIT CASE. THEY'LL THROW IT OUT OF COURT, I'M SURE OF IT. I TELL YOU, ROB, THIS AIN'T THE KINDA LAW I WANNA PRACTICE.
I GOTTA GET OUTTA CIVIL. THIS ONE SUING THAT ONE. IT AIN'T FOR ME.
SO, WHAT'S ON YOUR DOCKET?
I'M GOING INTO THE CITY TO PICK UP SYLVIA'S RING THIS AFTERNOON. MY UNCLE HELPED ME OUT WITH IT.
HOW EXCITING. WHAT'S IT LIKE? BIG?
NOT ON MY BUDGET, ESPECIALLY AFTER THE GUITAR. NO, IT'S SIMPLE. SMALL DIAMOND ON A SIMPLE BAND. SUBSTITUTE THE WORD "SMALL" WITH "TASTEFUL."
I WISH MY WIENER WOULD BE A BIT MORE "TASTEFUL" RIGHT NOW, SO I COULD GET UP AND TAKE A SHOWER.

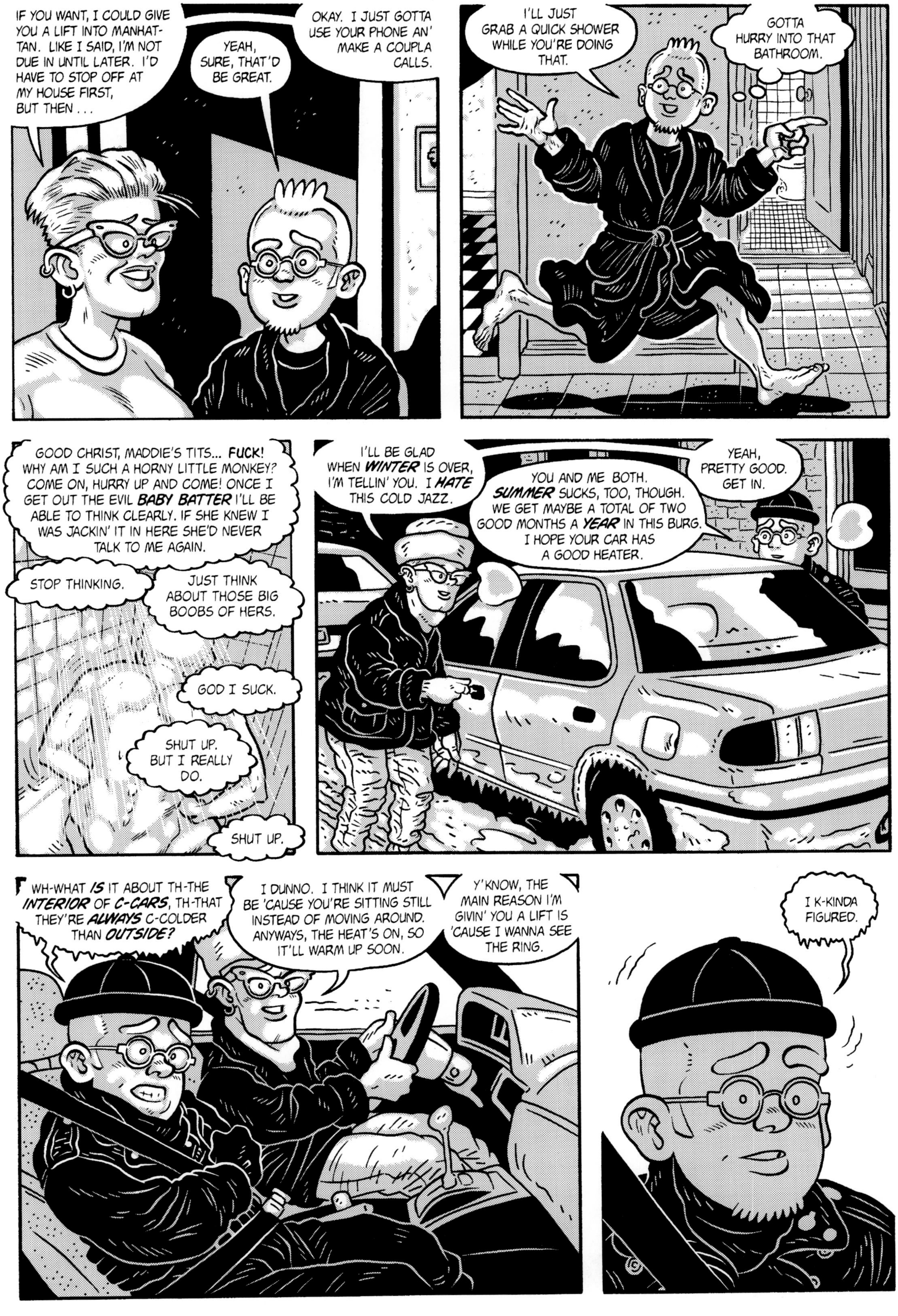
IF YOU WANT, I COULD GIVE YOU A LIFT INTO MANHATTAN. LIKE I SAID, I'M NOT DUE IN UNTIL LATER. I'D HAVE TO STOP OFF AT MY HOUSE FIRST, BUT THEN . . .
YEAH, SURE, THAT'D BE GREAT.
OKAY. I JUST GOTTA USE YOUR PHONE AN' MAKE A COUPLA CALLS.
I'LL JUST GRAB A QUICK SHOWER WHILE YOU'RE DOING THAT.
GOTTA HURRY INTO THAT BATHROOM.
GOOD CHRIST, MADDIE'S TITS... FUCK! WHY AM I SUCH A HORNY LITTLE MONKEY? COME ON, HURRY UP AND COME! ONCE I GET OUT THE EVIL BABY BATTER I'LL BE ABLE TO THINK CLEARLY. IF SHE KNEW I WAS JACKIN' IT IN HERE SHE'D NEVER TALK TO ME AGAIN.
STOP THINKING.
JUST THINK ABOUT THOSE BIG BOOBS OF HERS.
GOD I SUCK.
SHUT UP. BUT I REALLY DO.
SHUT UP.
I'LL BE GLAD WHEN WINTER IS OVER, I'M TELLIN' YOU. I HATE THIS COLD JAZZ.
YOU AND ME BOTH. SUMMER SUCKS, TOO, THOUGH. WE GET MAYBE A TOTAL OF TWO GOOD MONTHS A YEAR IN THIS BURG. I HOPE YOUR CAR HAS A GOOD HEATER.
YEAH, PRETTY GOOD. GET IN.
WH-WHAT IS IT ABOUT TH-THE INTERIOR OF C-CARS, TH-THAT THEY'RE ALWAYS C-COLDER THAN OUTSIDE?
I DUNNO. I THINK IT MUST BE 'CAUSE YOU'RE SITTING STILL INSTEAD OF MOVING AROUND. ANYWAYS, THE HEAT'S ON, SO IT'LL WARM UP SOON.
Y'KNOW, THE MAIN REASON I'M GIVIN' YOU A LIFT IS 'CAUSE I WANNA SEE THE RING.
I K-KINDA FIGURED.

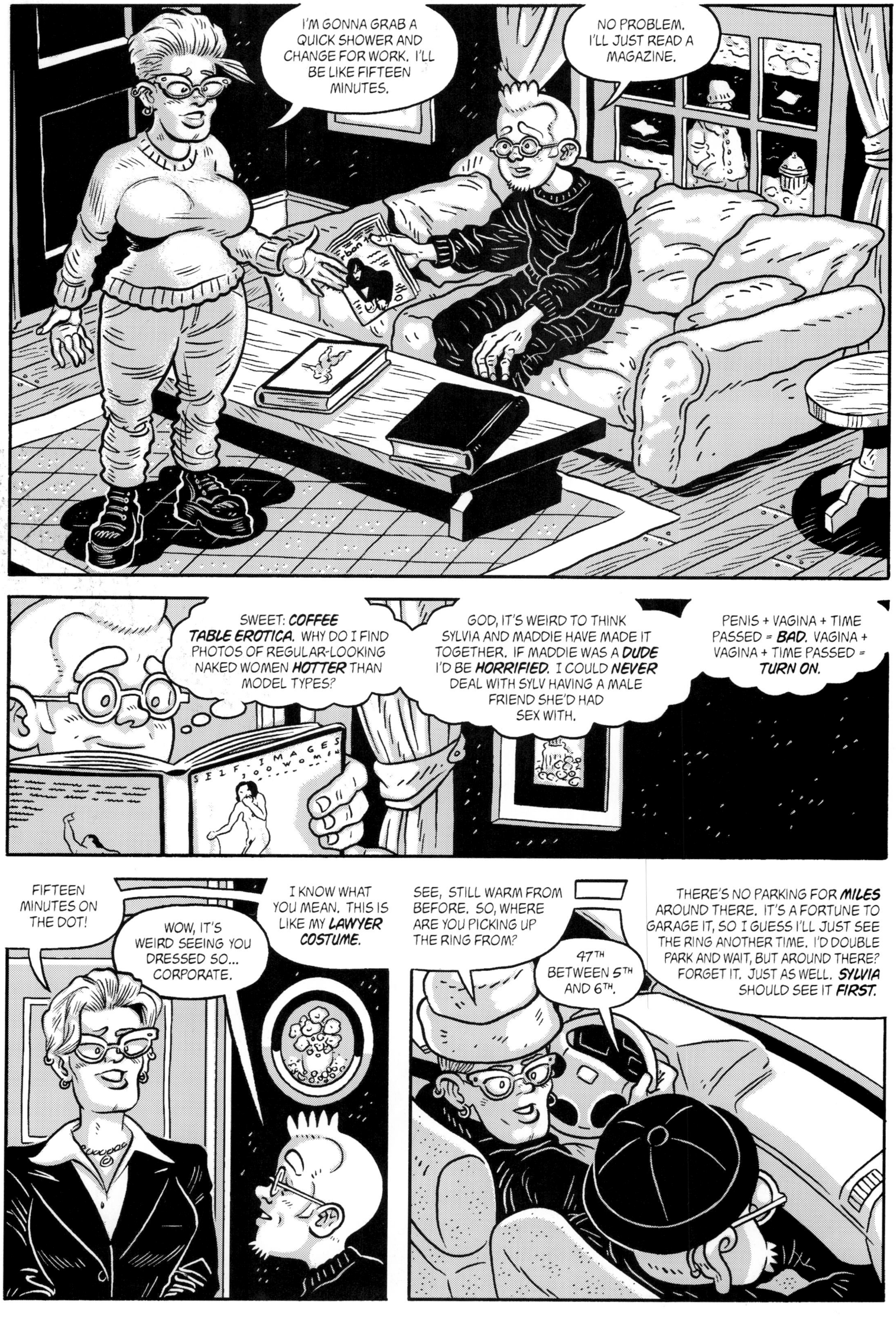
I'M GONNA GRAB A QUICK SHOWER AND CHANGE FOR WORK. I'LL BE LIKE FIFTEEN MINUTES.
NO PROBLEM. I'LL JUST READ A MAGAZINE.
SWEET: COFFEE TABLE EROTICA. WHY DO I FIND PHOTOS OF REGULAR-LOOKING NAKED WOMEN HOTTER THAN MODEL TYPES?
GOD, IT'S WEIRD TO THINK SYLVIA AND MADDIE HAVE MADE IT TOGETHER. IF MADDIE WAS A DUDE I'D BE HORRIFIED. I COULD NEVER DEAL WITH SYLV HAVING A MALE FRIEND SHE'D HAD SEX WITH.
PENIS + VAGINA + TIME PASSED = BAD. VAGINA + VAGINA + TIME PASSED = TURN ON.
FIFTEEN MINUTES ON THE DOT!
WOW, IT'S WEIRD SEEING YOU DRESSED SO... CORPORATE.
I KNOW WHAT YOU MEAN. THIS IS LIKE MY LAWYER COSTUME.
SEE, STILL WARM FROM BEFORE. SO, WHERE ARE YOU PICKING UP THE RING FROM?
47TH BETWEEN 5TH AND 6TH.
THERE'S NO PARKING FOR MILES AROUND THERE. IT'S A FORTUNE TO GARAGE IT, SO I GUESS I'LL JUST SEE THE RING ANOTHER TIME. I'D DOUBLE PARK AND WAIT, BUT AROUND THERE? FORGET IT. JUST AS WELL. SYLVIA SHOULD SEE IT FIRST.

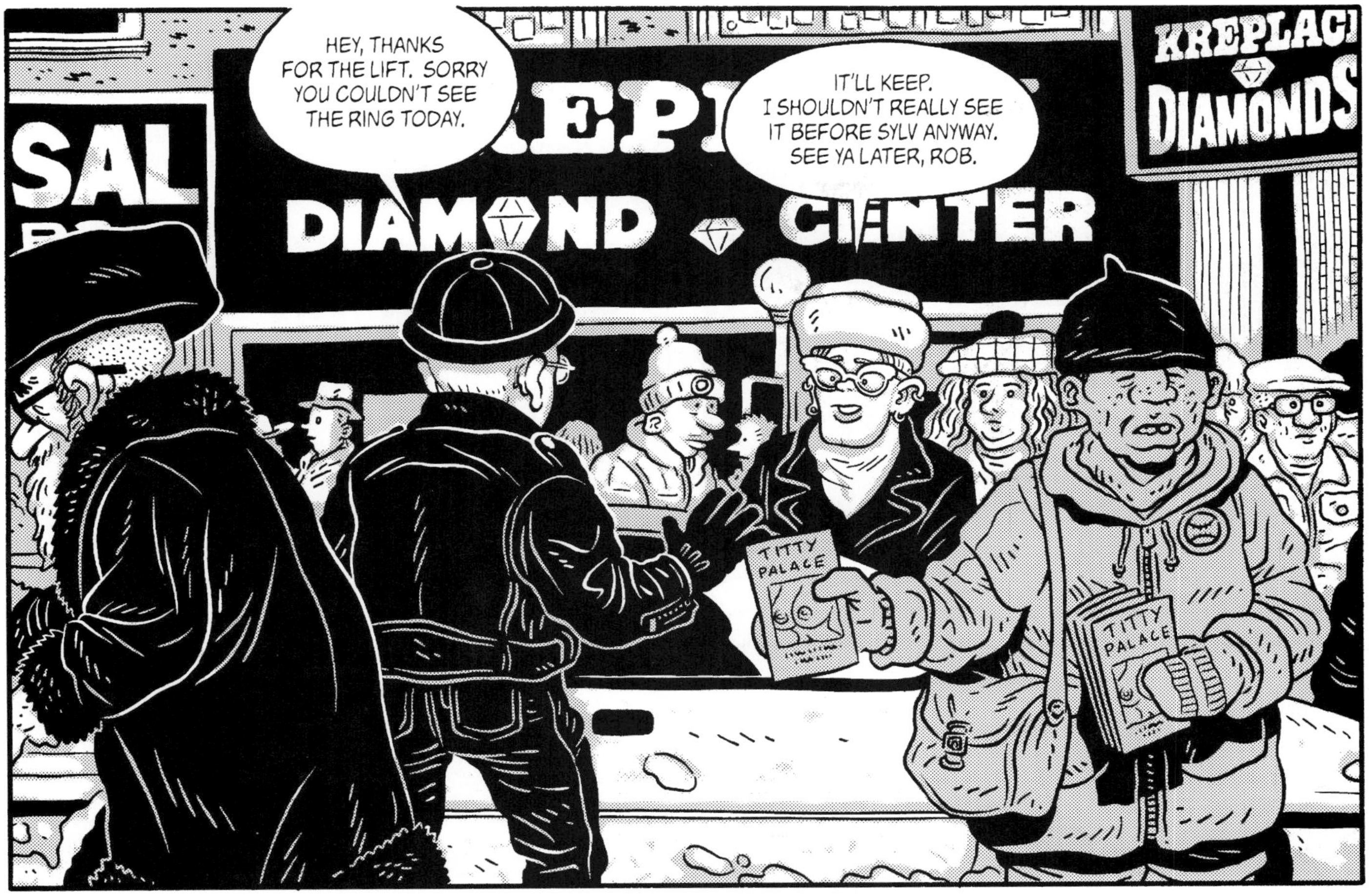
HEY, THANKS FOR THE LIFT. SORRY YOU COULDN'T SEE THE RING TODAY.
IT'LL KEEP. I SHOULDN'T REALLY SEE IT BEFORE SYLV ANYWAY. SEE YA LATER, ROB.
DIAMOND CENTER
KREPLACH DIAMONDS
SAL
TITTY PALACE

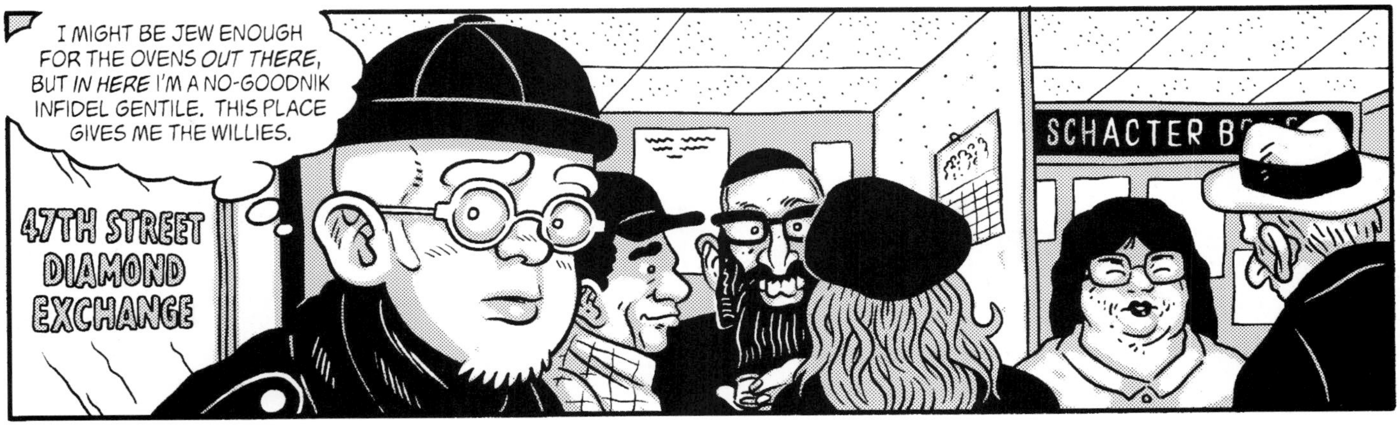
I MIGHT BE JEW ENOUGH FOR THE OVENS *OUT THERE*, BUT *IN HERE* I'M A NO-GOODNIK INFIDEL GENTILE. THIS PLACE GIVES ME THE WILLIES.
47TH STREET DIAMOND EXCHANGE
SCHACTER BR

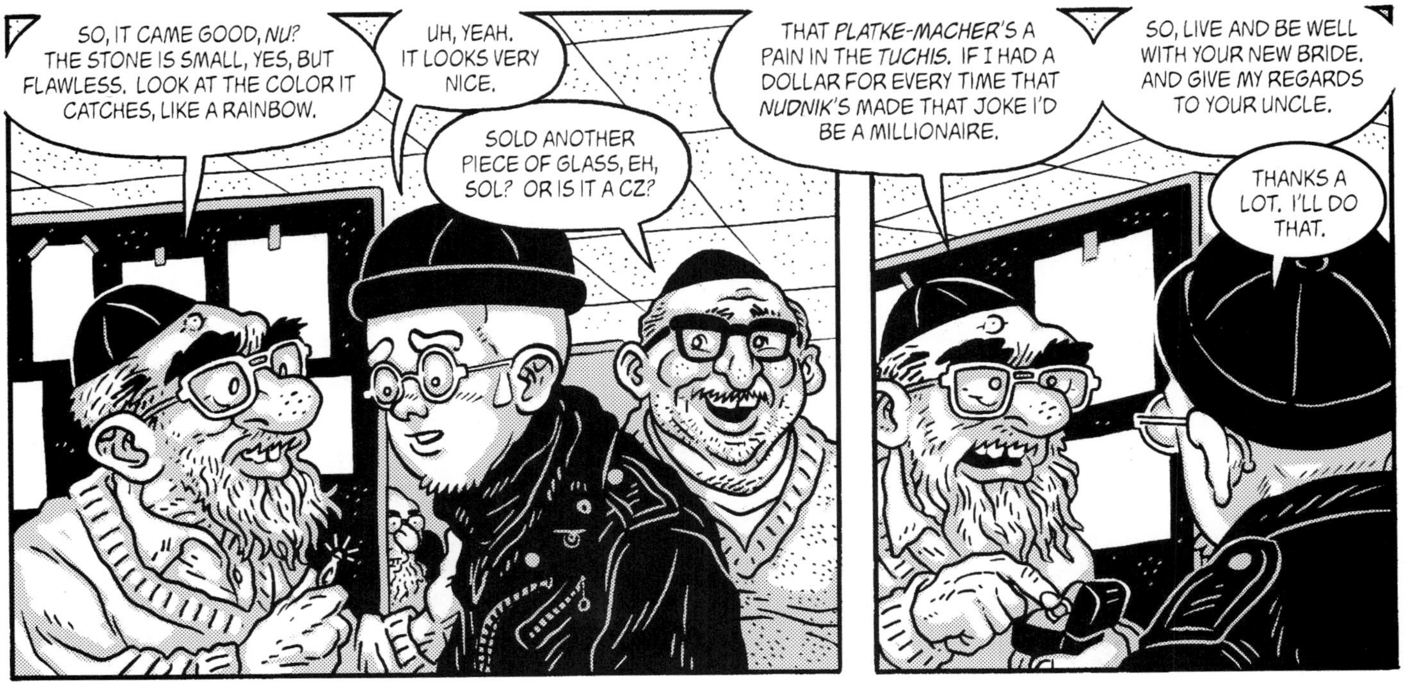
SO, IT CAME GOOD, *NU*? THE STONE IS SMALL, YES, BUT FLAWLESS. LOOK AT THE COLOR IT CATCHES, LIKE A RAINBOW.
UH, YEAH. IT LOOKS VERY NICE.
SOLD ANOTHER PIECE OF GLASS, EH, SOL? OR IS IT A CZ?
THAT *PLATKE-MACHER*'S A PAIN IN THE *TUCHIS*. IF I HAD A DOLLAR FOR EVERY TIME THAT *NUDNIK*'S MADE THAT JOKE I'D BE A MILLIONAIRE.
SO, LIVE AND BE WELL WITH YOUR NEW BRIDE. AND GIVE MY REGARDS TO YOUR UNCLE.
THANKS A LOT. I'LL DO THAT.

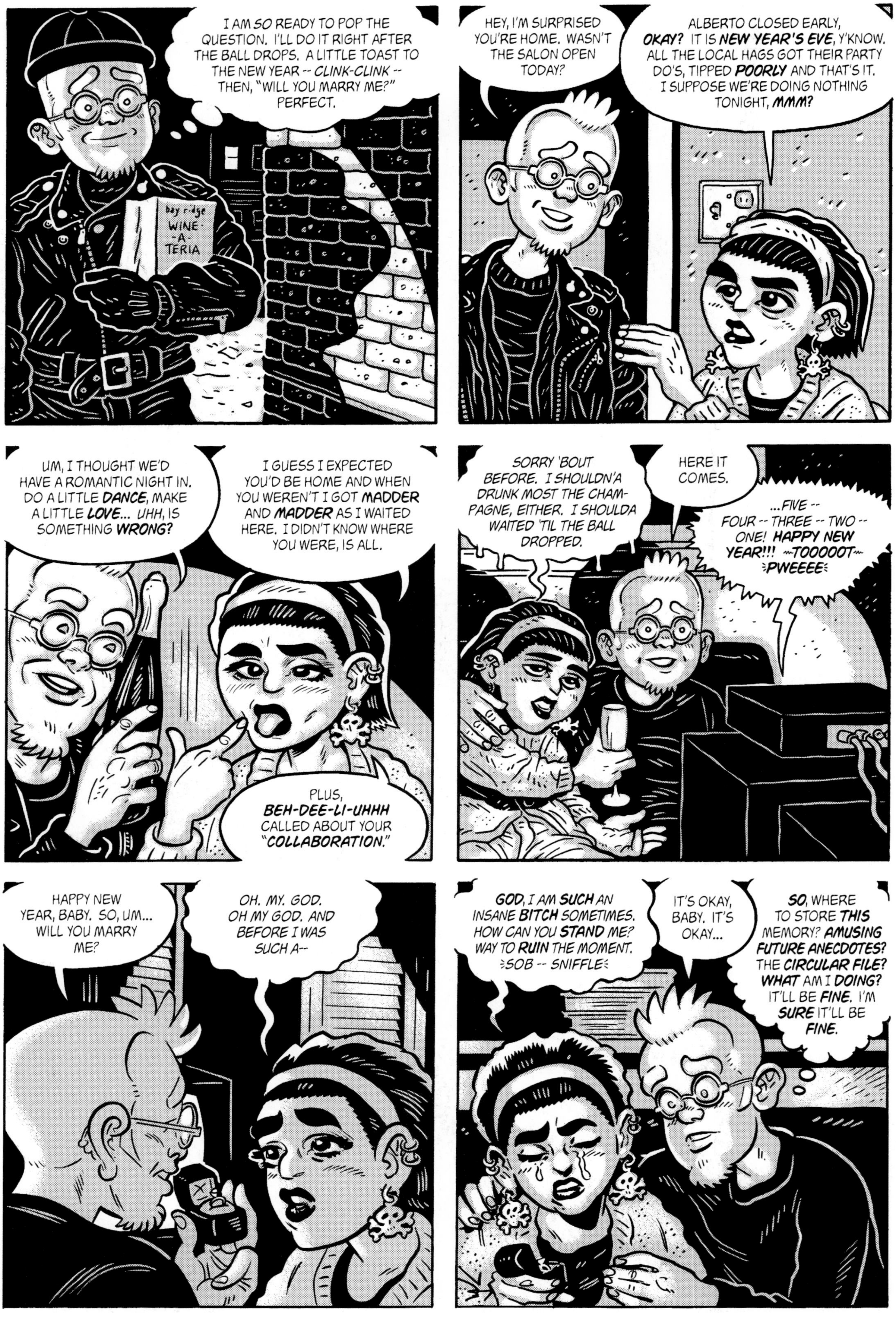
I AM SO READY TO POP THE QUESTION. I'LL DO IT RIGHT AFTER THE BALL DROPS. A LITTLE TOAST TO THE NEW YEAR -- CLINK-CLINK -- THEN, "WILL YOU MARRY ME?" PERFECT.
bay ridge WINE-A-TERIA
HEY, I'M SURPRISED YOU'RE HOME. WASN'T THE SALON OPEN TODAY?
ALBERTO CLOSED EARLY, OKAY? IT IS NEW YEAR'S EVE, Y'KNOW. ALL THE LOCAL HAGS GOT THEIR PARTY DO'S, TIPPED POORLY AND THAT'S IT. I SUPPOSE WE'RE DOING NOTHING TONIGHT, MMM?
UM, I THOUGHT WE'D HAVE A ROMANTIC NIGHT IN. DO A LITTLE DANCE, MAKE A LITTLE LOVE... UHH, IS SOMETHING WRONG?
I GUESS I EXPECTED YOU'D BE HOME AND WHEN YOU WEREN'T I GOT MADDER AND MADDER AS I WAITED HERE. I DIDN'T KNOW WHERE YOU WERE, IS ALL.
PLUS, BEH-DEE-LI-UHHH CALLED ABOUT YOUR "COLLABORATION."
SORRY 'BOUT BEFORE. I SHOULDN'A DRUNK MOST THE CHAMPAGNE, EITHER. I SHOULDA WAITED 'TIL THE BALL DROPPED.
HERE IT COMES.
...FIVE -- FOUR -- THREE -- TWO -- ONE! HAPPY NEW YEAR!!! TOOOOOT PWEEEE
HAPPY NEW YEAR, BABY. SO, UM... WILL YOU MARRY ME?
OH. MY. GOD. OH MY GOD. AND BEFORE I WAS SUCH A--
GOD, I AM SUCH AN INSANE BITCH SOMETIMES. HOW CAN YOU STAND ME? WAY TO RUIN THE MOMENT. SOB -- SNIFFLE
IT'S OKAY, BABY. IT'S OKAY...
SO, WHERE TO STORE THIS MEMORY? AMUSING FUTURE ANECDOTES? THE CIRCULAR FILE? WHAT AM I DOING? IT'LL BE FINE. I'M SURE IT'LL BE FINE.

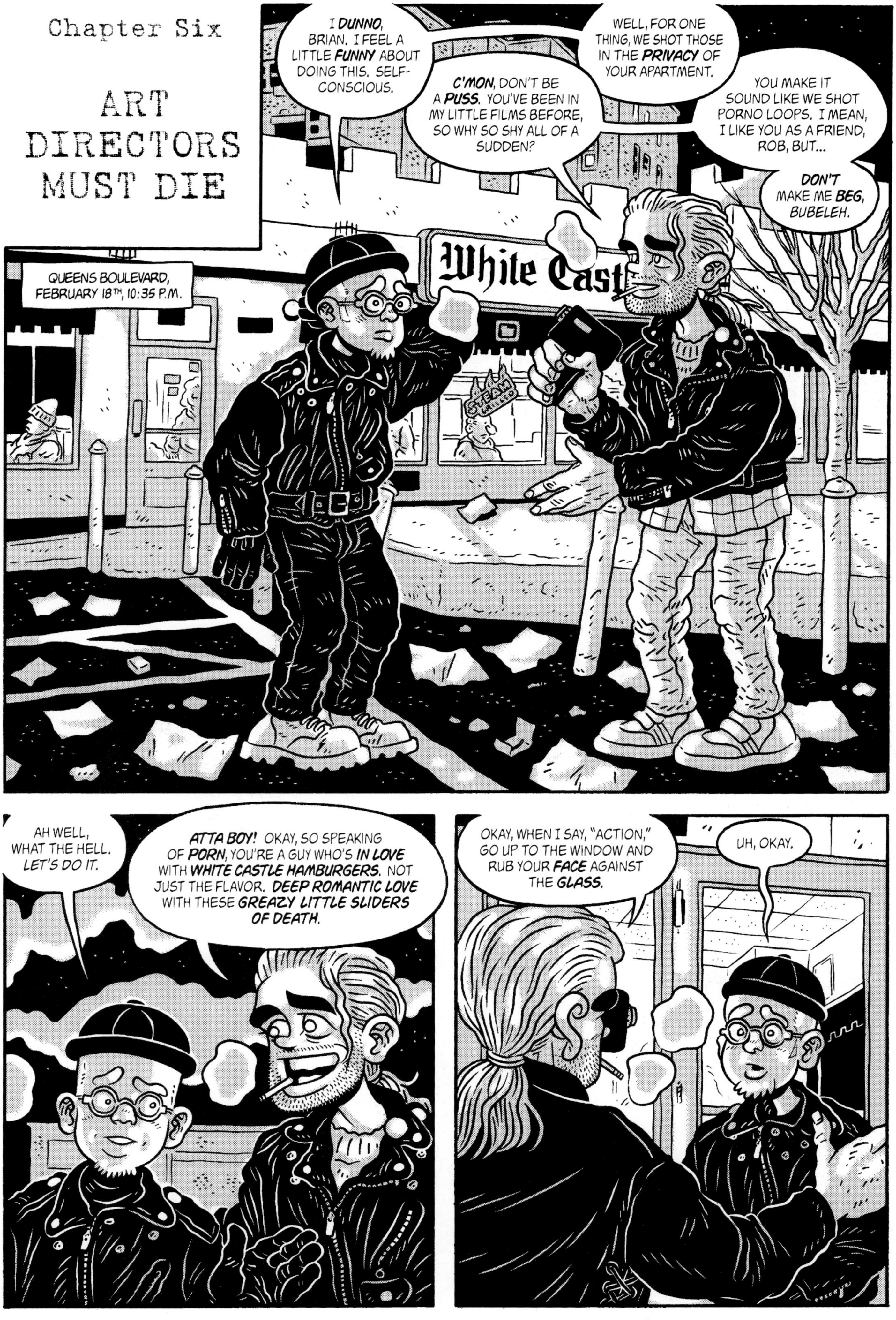
Chapter Six
ART DIRECTORS MUST DIE
QUEENS BOULEVARD, FEBRUARY 18TH, 10:35 P.M.
I DUNNO, BRIAN. I FEEL A LITTLE FUNNY ABOUT DOING THIS. SELF-CONSCIOUS.
C'MON, DON'T BE A PUSS. YOU'VE BEEN IN MY LITTLE FILMS BEFORE, SO WHY SO SHY ALL OF A SUDDEN?
WELL, FOR ONE THING, WE SHOT THOSE IN THE PRIVACY OF YOUR APARTMENT.
YOU MAKE IT SOUND LIKE WE SHOT PORNO LOOPS. I MEAN, I LIKE YOU AS A FRIEND, ROB, BUT...
DON'T MAKE ME BEG, BUBELEH.
White Cast
AH WELL, WHAT THE HELL. LET'S DO IT.
ATTA BOY! OKAY, SO SPEAKING OF PORN, YOU'RE A GUY WHO'S IN LOVE WITH WHITE CASTLE HAMBURGERS. NOT JUST THE FLAVOR. DEEP ROMANTIC LOVE WITH THESE GREAZY LITTLE SLIDERS OF DEATH.
OKAY, WHEN I SAY, "ACTION," GO UP TO THE WINDOW AND RUB YOUR FACE AGAINST THE GLASS.
UH, OKAY.

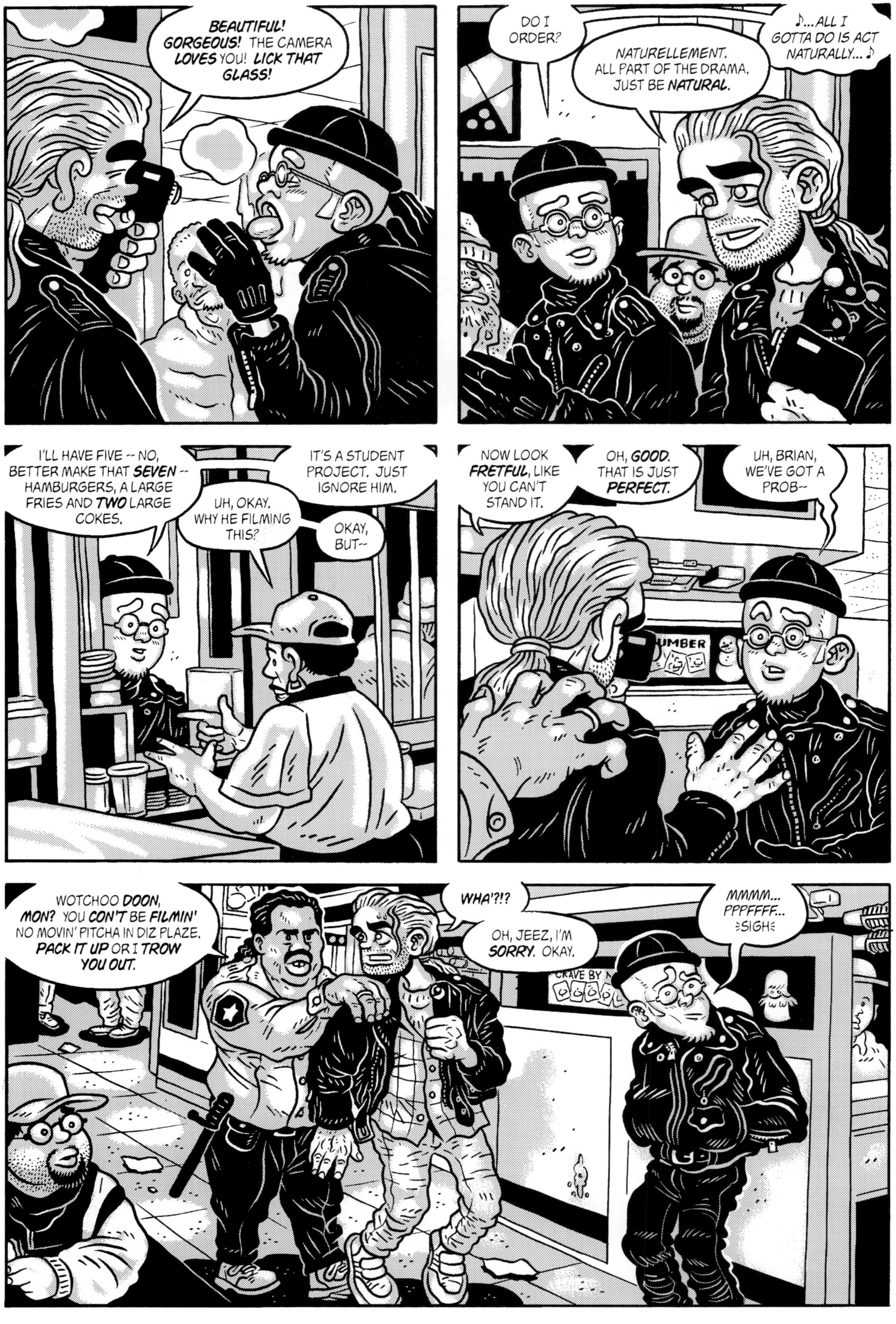
BEAUTIFUL! GORGEOUS! THE CAMERA LOVES YOU! LICK THAT GLASS!
DO I ORDER?
NATURELLEMENT. ALL PART OF THE DRAMA. JUST BE NATURAL.
♪...ALL I GOTTA DO IS ACT NATURALLY...♪
I'LL HAVE FIVE -- NO, BETTER MAKE THAT SEVEN -- HAMBURGERS, A LARGE FRIES AND TWO LARGE COKES.
UH, OKAY. WHY HE FILMING THIS?
IT'S A STUDENT PROJECT. JUST IGNORE HIM.
OKAY, BUT--
NOW LOOK FRETFUL, LIKE YOU CAN'T STAND IT.
OH, GOOD. THAT IS JUST PERFECT.
UH, BRIAN, WE'VE GOT A PROB--
WOTCHOO DOON, MON? YOU CON'T BE FILMIN' NO MOVIN' PITCHA IN DIZ PLAZE. PACK IT UP OR I TROW YOU OUT.
WHA'?!?
OH, JEEZ, I'M SORRY. OKAY.
MMMM... PPPFFFF.. ≷SIGH≶

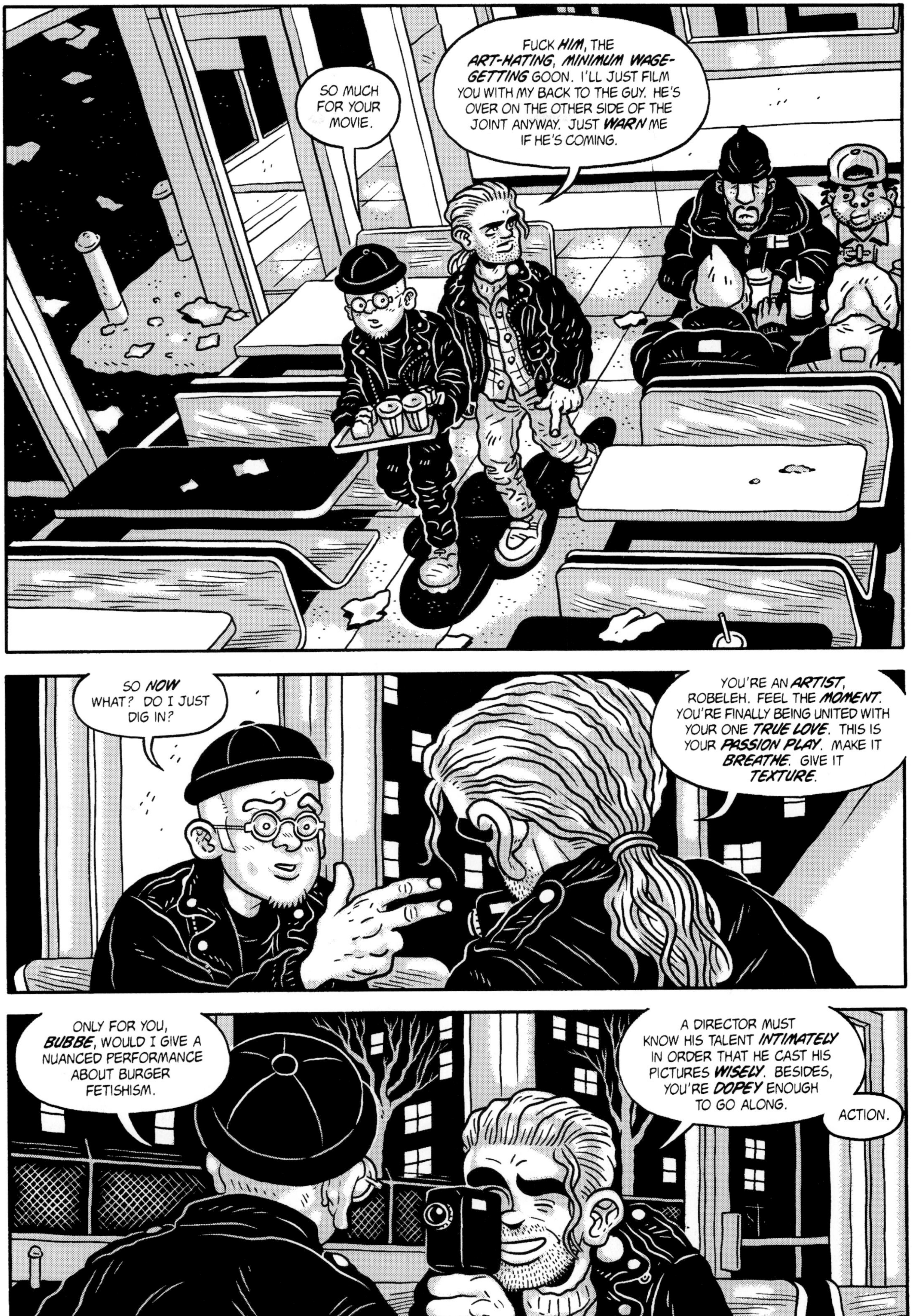
SO MUCH FOR YOUR MOVIE.
FUCK HIM, THE ART-HATING, MINIMUM WAGE-GETTING GOON. I'LL JUST FILM YOU WITH MY BACK TO THE GUY. HE'S OVER ON THE OTHER SIDE OF THE JOINT ANYWAY. JUST WARN ME IF HE'S COMING.
SO NOW WHAT? DO I JUST DIG IN?
YOU'RE AN ARTIST, ROBELEH. FEEL THE MOMENT. YOU'RE FINALLY BEING UNITED WITH YOUR ONE TRUE LOVE. THIS IS YOUR PASSION PLAY. MAKE IT BREATHE. GIVE IT TEXTURE.
ONLY FOR YOU, BUBBE, WOULD I GIVE A NUANCED PERFORMANCE ABOUT BURGER FETISHISM.
A DIRECTOR MUST KNOW HIS TALENT INTIMATELY IN ORDER THAT HE CAST HIS PICTURES WISELY. BESIDES, YOU'RE DOPEY ENOUGH TO GO ALONG.
ACTION.

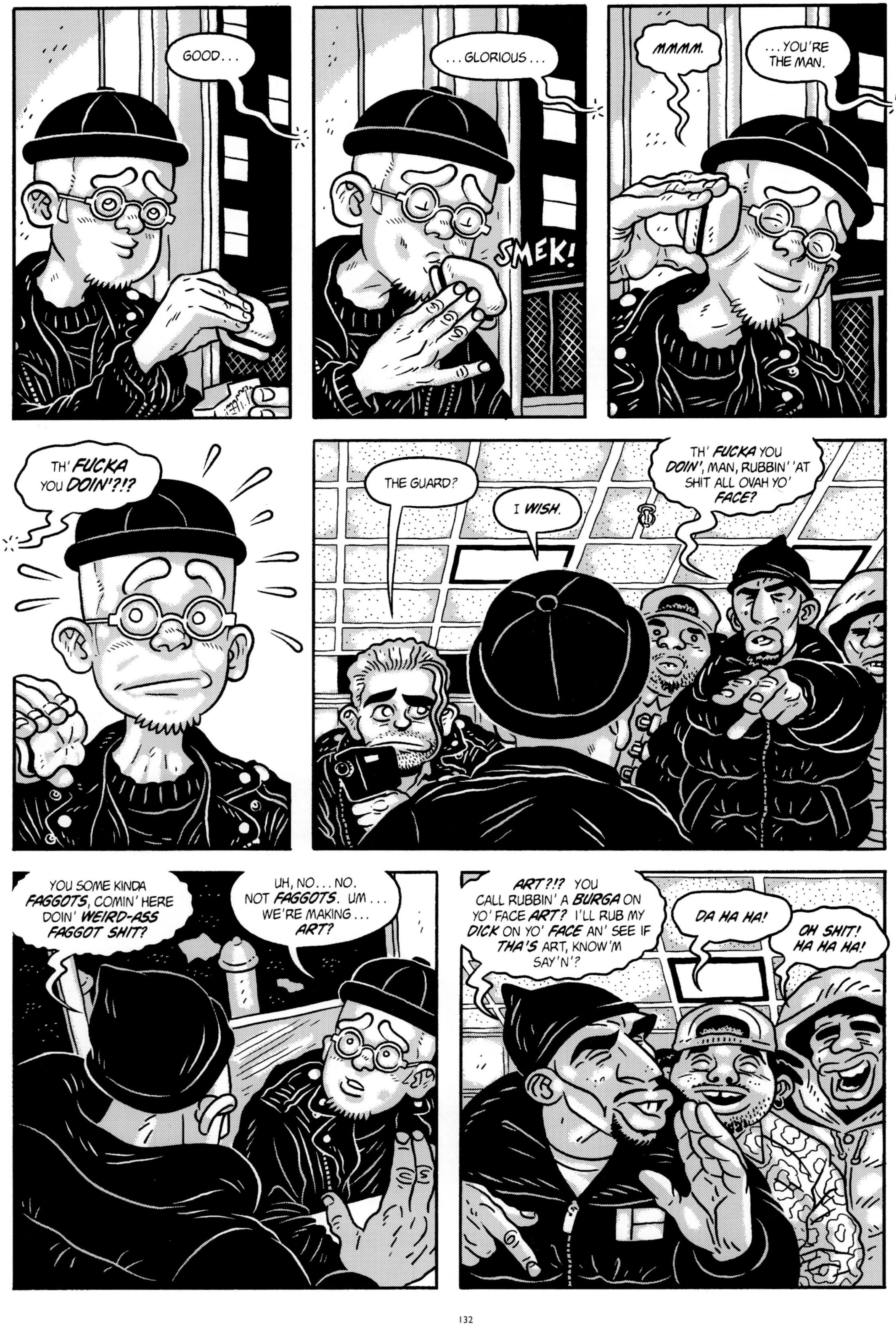
GOOD...
...GLORIOUS...
SMEK!
MMMM.
...YOU'RE THE MAN.
TH' FUCKA YOU DOIN'?!?
THE GUARD?
I WISH.
TH' FUCKA YOU DOIN', MAN, RUBBIN' 'AT SHIT ALL OVAH YO' FACE?
YOU SOME KINDA FAGGOTS, COMIN' HERE DOIN' WEIRD-ASS FAGGOT SHIT?
UH, NO... NO. NOT FAGGOTS. UM... WE'RE MAKING... ART?
ART?!? YOU CALL RUBBIN' A BURGA ON YO' FACE ART? I'LL RUB MY DICK ON YO' FACE AN' SEE IF THA'S ART, KNOW'M SAY'N'?
DA HA HA!
OH SHIT! HA HA HA!

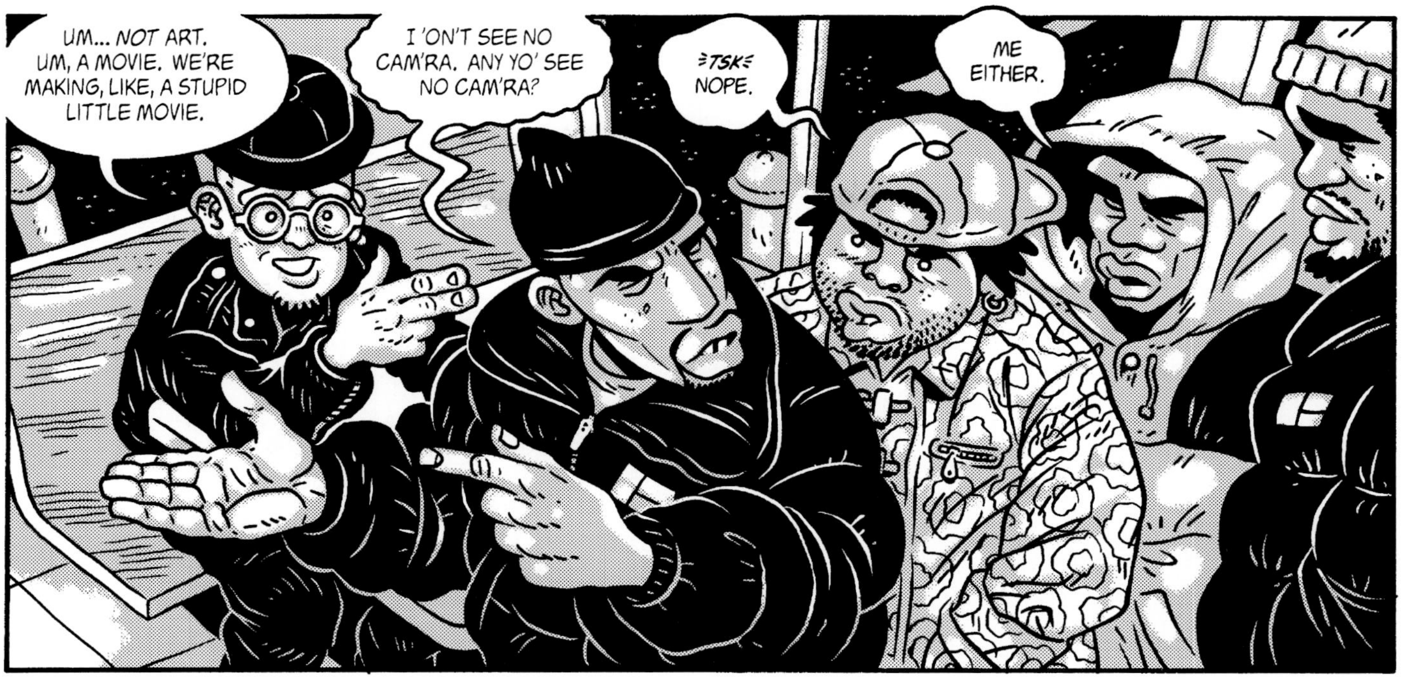
UM... *NOT* ART. UM, A MOVIE. WE'RE MAKING, LIKE, A STUPID LITTLE MOVIE.
I 'ON'T SEE NO CAM'RA. ANY YO' SEE NO CAM'RA?
TSK NOPE.
ME EITHER.

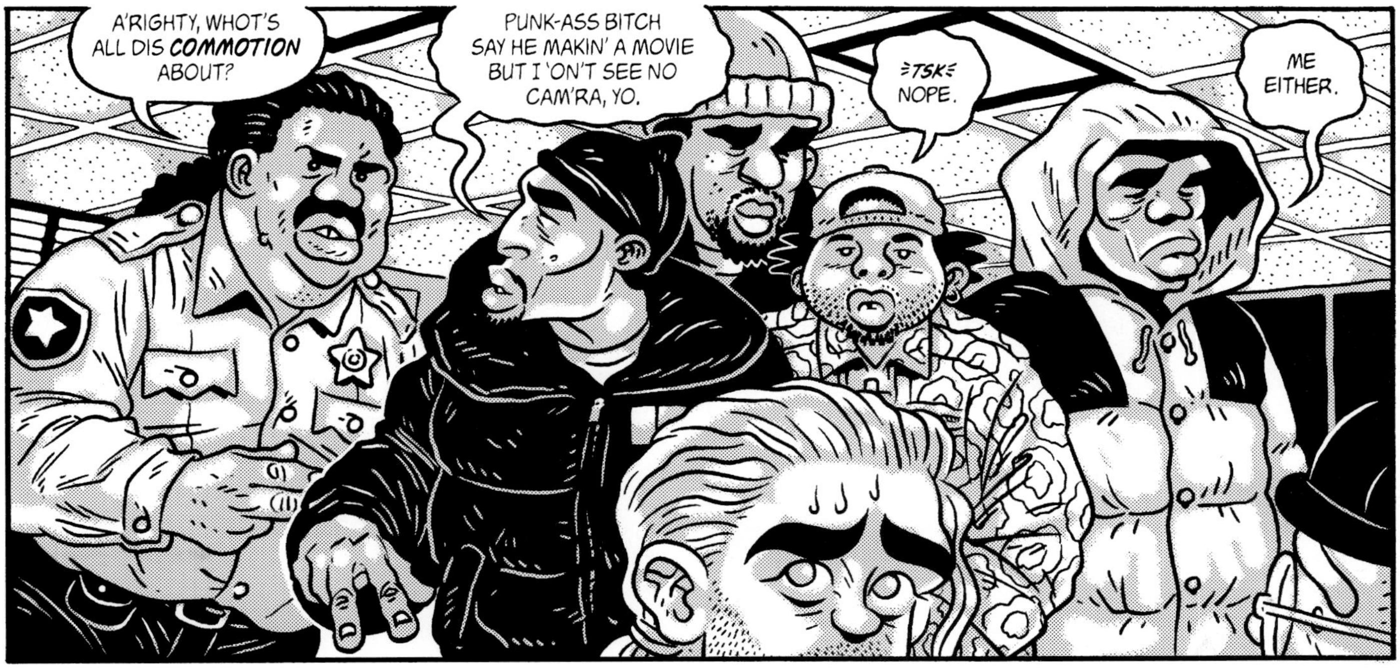
A'RIGHTY, WHOT'S ALL DIS ***COMMOTION*** ABOUT?
PUNK-ASS BITCH SAY HE MAKIN' A MOVIE BUT I 'ON'T SEE NO CAM'RA, YO.
TSK NOPE.
ME EITHER.

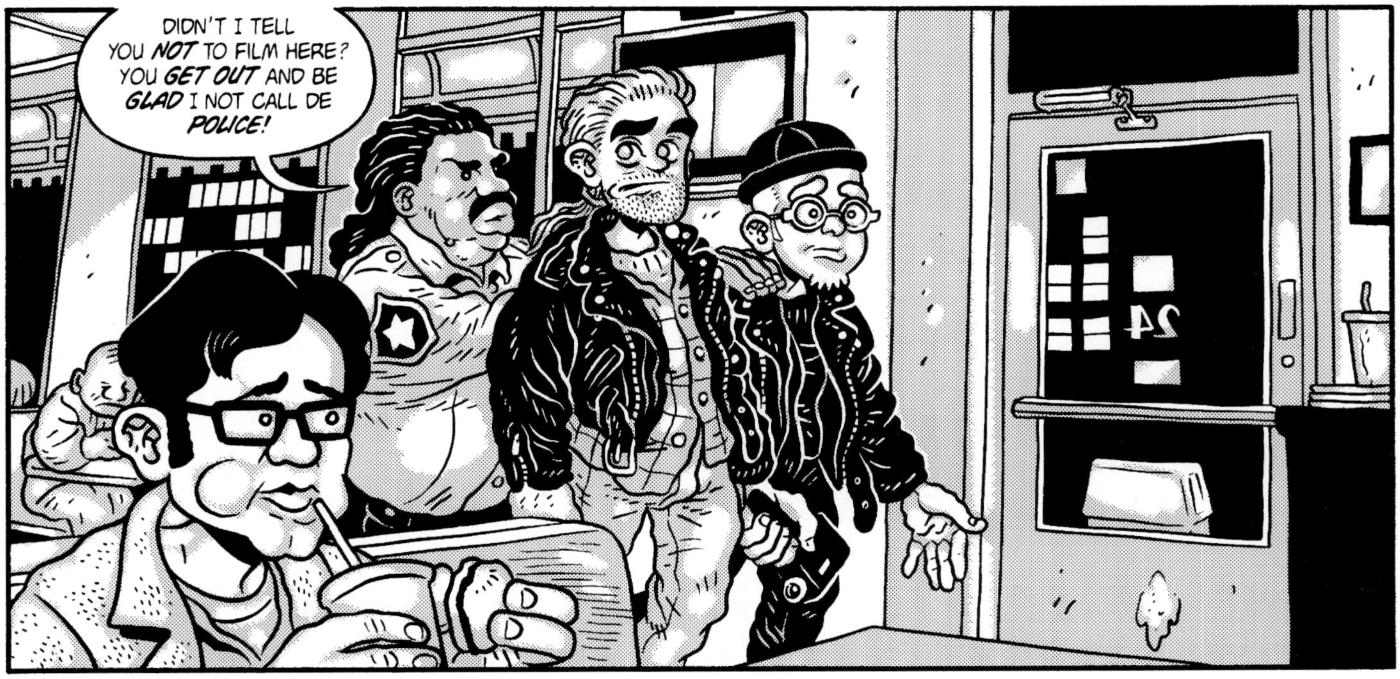
DIDN'T I TELL YOU ***NOT*** TO FILM HERE? YOU ***GET OUT*** AND BE ***GLAD*** I NOT CALL DE ***POLICE!***
24

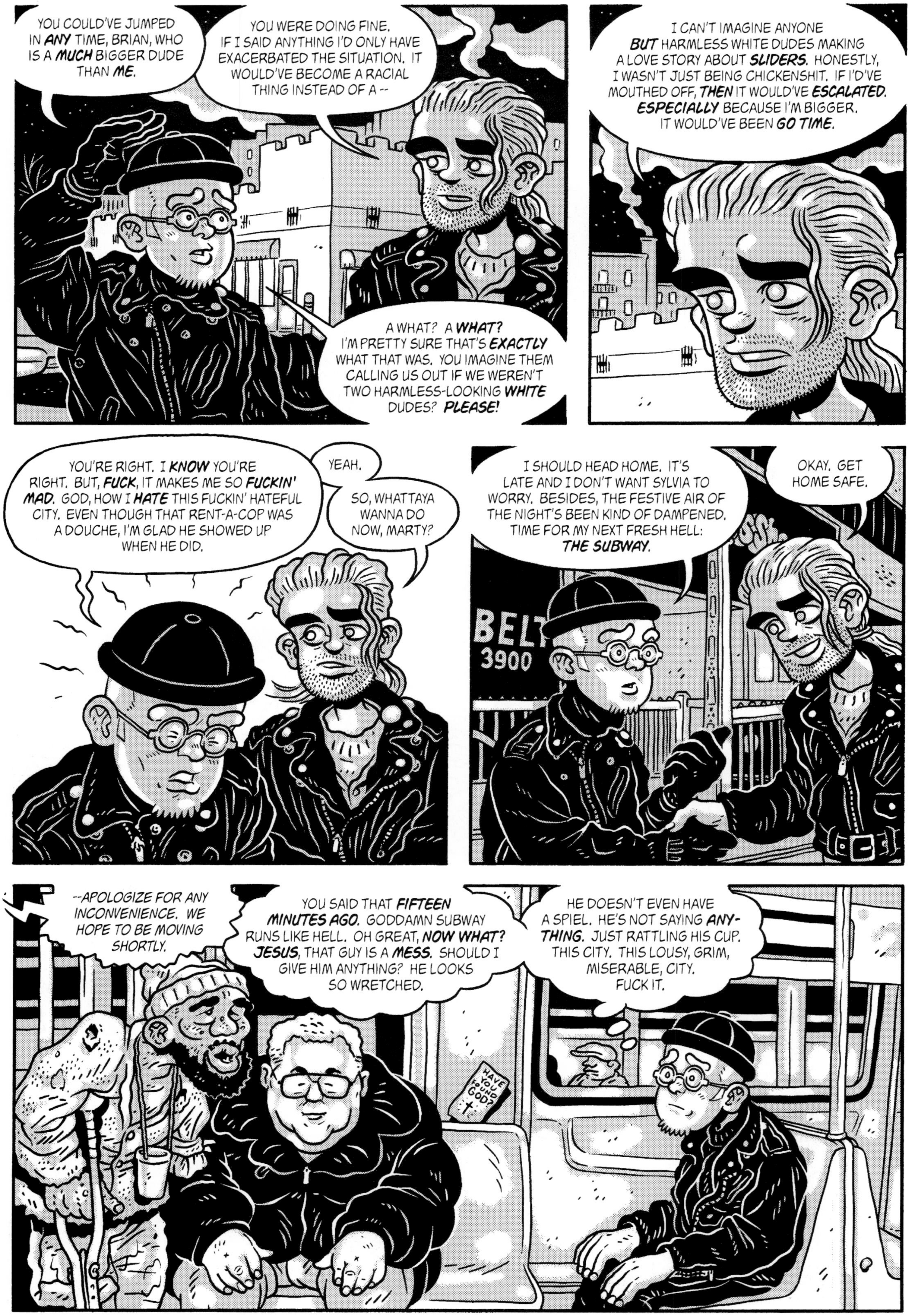
YOU COULD'VE JUMPED IN ANY TIME, BRIAN, WHO IS A MUCH BIGGER DUDE THAN ME.
YOU WERE DOING FINE. IF I SAID ANYTHING I'D ONLY HAVE EXACERBATED THE SITUATION. IT WOULD'VE BECOME A RACIAL THING INSTEAD OF A --
A WHAT? A WHAT? I'M PRETTY SURE THAT'S EXACTLY WHAT THAT WAS. YOU IMAGINE THEM CALLING US OUT IF WE WEREN'T TWO HARMLESS-LOOKING WHITE DUDES? PLEASE!
I CAN'T IMAGINE ANYONE BUT HARMLESS WHITE DUDES MAKING A LOVE STORY ABOUT SLIDERS. HONESTLY, I WASN'T JUST BEING CHICKENSHIT. IF I'D'VE MOUTHED OFF, THEN IT WOULD'VE ESCALATED. ESPECIALLY BECAUSE I'M BIGGER. IT WOULD'VE BEEN GO TIME.
YOU'RE RIGHT. I KNOW YOU'RE RIGHT. BUT, FUCK, IT MAKES ME SO FUCKIN' MAD. GOD, HOW I HATE THIS FUCKIN' HATEFUL CITY. EVEN THOUGH THAT RENT-A-COP WAS A DOUCHE, I'M GLAD HE SHOWED UP WHEN HE DID.
YEAH.
SO, WHATTAYA WANNA DO NOW, MARTY?
I SHOULD HEAD HOME. IT'S LATE AND I DON'T WANT SYLVIA TO WORRY. BESIDES, THE FESTIVE AIR OF THE NIGHT'S BEEN KIND OF DAMPENED. TIME FOR MY NEXT FRESH HELL: THE SUBWAY.
OKAY. GET HOME SAFE.
BELT
3900
--APOLOGIZE FOR ANY INCONVENIENCE. WE HOPE TO BE MOVING SHORTLY.
YOU SAID THAT FIFTEEN MINUTES AGO. GODDAMN SUBWAY RUNS LIKE HELL. OH GREAT, NOW WHAT? JESUS, THAT GUY IS A MESS. SHOULD I GIVE HIM ANYTHING? HE LOOKS SO WRETCHED.
HE DOESN'T EVEN HAVE A SPIEL. HE'S NOT SAYING ANY-THING. JUST RATTLING HIS CUP. THIS CITY. THIS LOUSY, GRIM, MISERABLE, CITY. FUCK IT.
HAVE YOU FOUND GOD?

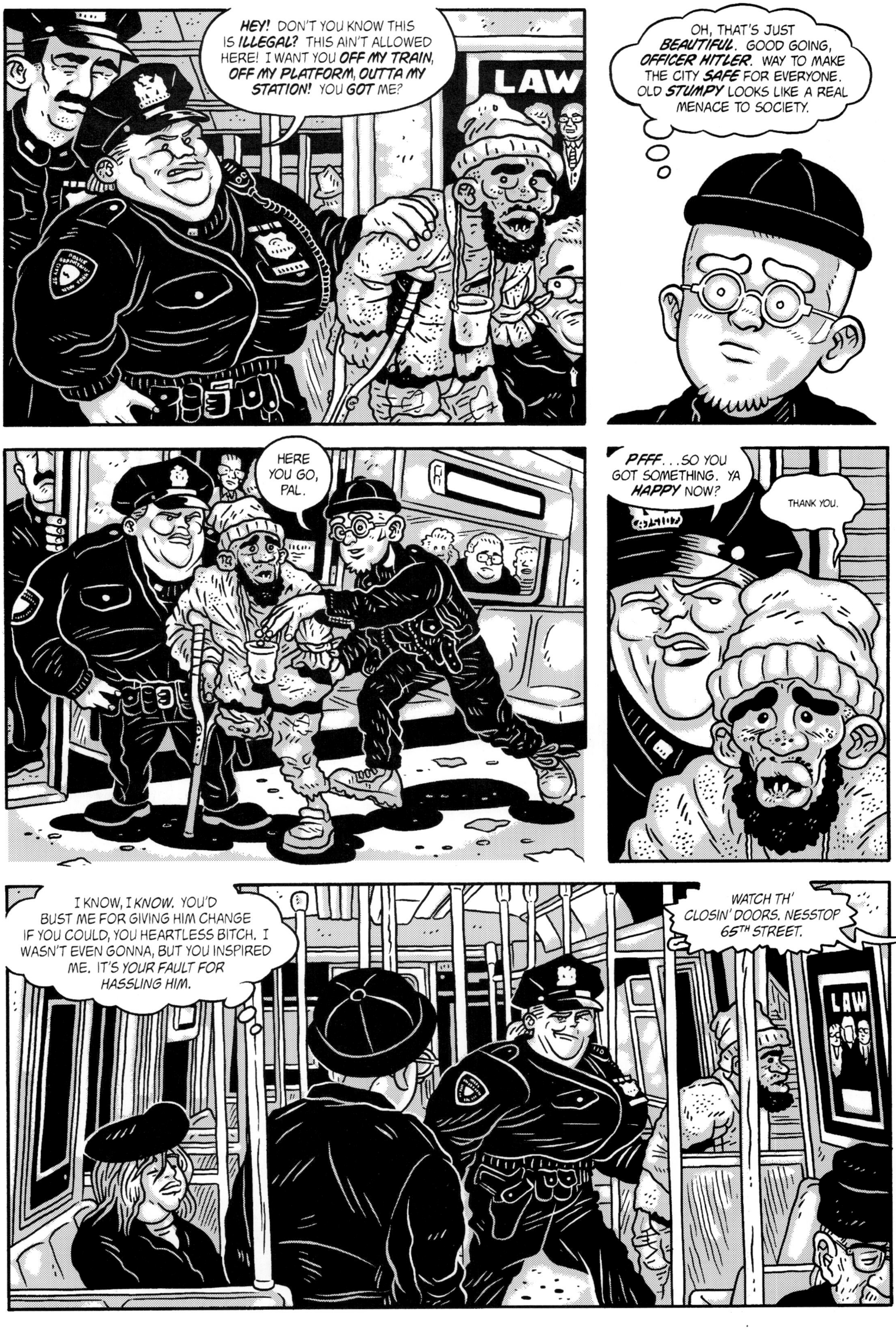
HEY! DON'T YOU KNOW THIS IS ILLEGAL? THIS AIN'T ALLOWED HERE! I WANT YOU OFF MY TRAIN, OFF MY PLATFORM, OUTTA MY STATION! YOU GOT ME?
LAW
OH, THAT'S JUST BEAUTIFUL. GOOD GOING, OFFICER HITLER. WAY TO MAKE THE CITY SAFE FOR EVERYONE. OLD STUMPY LOOKS LIKE A REAL MENACE TO SOCIETY.
HERE YOU GO, PAL.
PFFF...SO YOU GOT SOMETHING. YA HAPPY NOW?
THANK YOU.
I KNOW, I KNOW. YOU'D BUST ME FOR GIVING HIM CHANGE IF YOU COULD, YOU HEARTLESS BITCH. I WASN'T EVEN GONNA, BUT YOU INSPIRED ME. IT'S YOUR FAULT FOR HASSLING HIM.
WATCH TH' CLOSIN' DOORS. NESSTOP 65TH STREET.
LAW

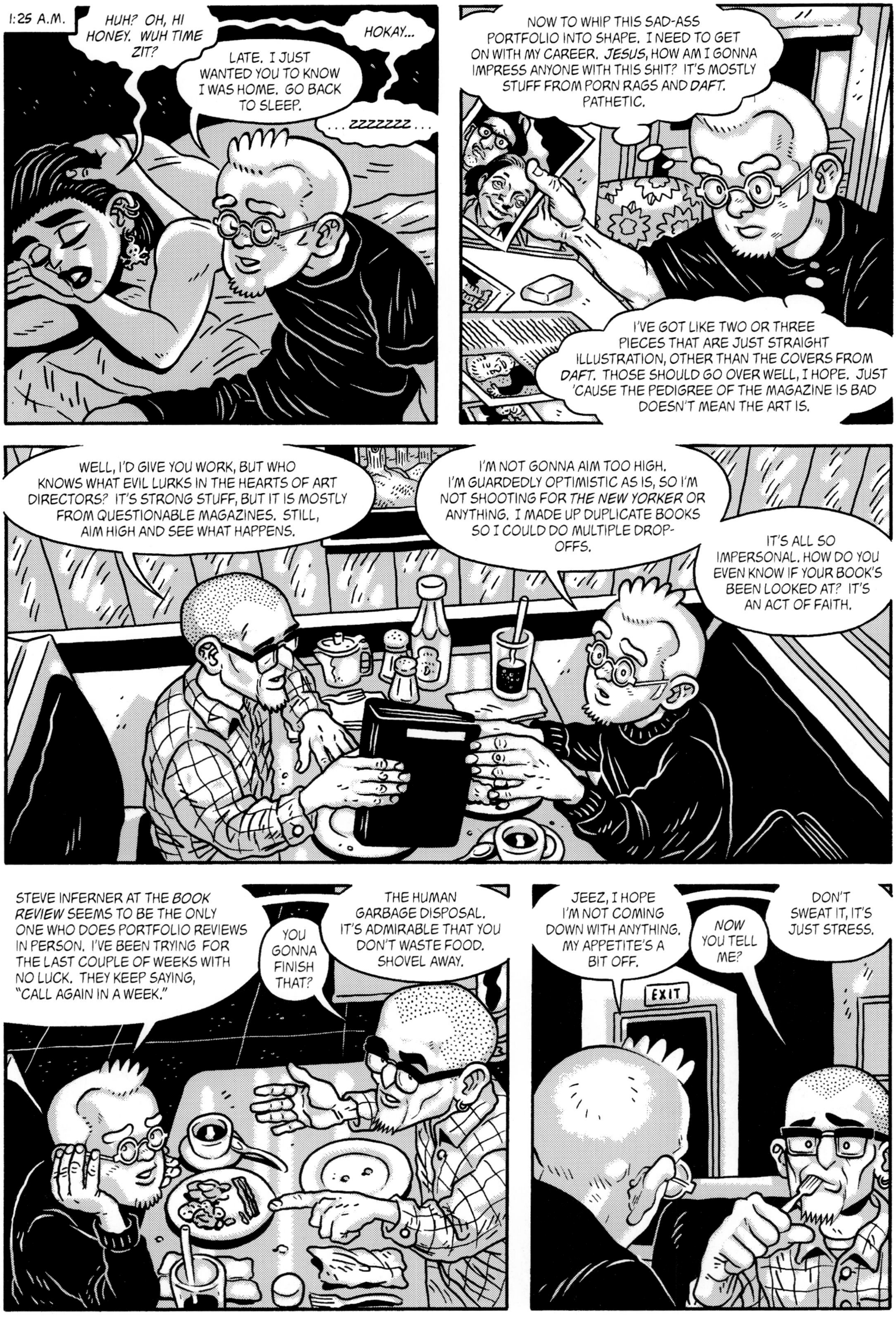
1:25 A.M.
HUH? OH, HI HONEY. WUH TIME ZIT?
LATE. I JUST WANTED YOU TO KNOW I WAS HOME. GO BACK TO SLEEP.
HOKAY...
. . . ZZZZZZZ . . .
NOW TO WHIP THIS SAD-ASS PORTFOLIO INTO SHAPE. I NEED TO GET ON WITH MY CAREER. JESUS, HOW AM I GONNA IMPRESS ANYONE WITH THIS SHIT? IT'S MOSTLY STUFF FROM PORN RAGS AND DAFT. PATHETIC.
I'VE GOT LIKE TWO OR THREE PIECES THAT ARE JUST STRAIGHT ILLUSTRATION, OTHER THAN THE COVERS FROM DAFT. THOSE SHOULD GO OVER WELL, I HOPE. JUST 'CAUSE THE PEDIGREE OF THE MAGAZINE IS BAD DOESN'T MEAN THE ART IS.
WELL, I'D GIVE YOU WORK, BUT WHO KNOWS WHAT EVIL LURKS IN THE HEARTS OF ART DIRECTORS? IT'S STRONG STUFF, BUT IT IS MOSTLY FROM QUESTIONABLE MAGAZINES. STILL, AIM HIGH AND SEE WHAT HAPPENS.
I'M NOT GONNA AIM TOO HIGH. I'M GUARDEDLY OPTIMISTIC AS IS, SO I'M NOT SHOOTING FOR THE NEW YORKER OR ANYTHING. I MADE UP DUPLICATE BOOKS SO I COULD DO MULTIPLE DROP-OFFS.
IT'S ALL SO IMPERSONAL. HOW DO YOU EVEN KNOW IF YOUR BOOK'S BEEN LOOKED AT? IT'S AN ACT OF FAITH.
STEVE INFERNER AT THE BOOK REVIEW SEEMS TO BE THE ONLY ONE WHO DOES PORTFOLIO REVIEWS IN PERSON. I'VE BEEN TRYING FOR THE LAST COUPLE OF WEEKS WITH NO LUCK. THEY KEEP SAYING, "CALL AGAIN IN A WEEK."
YOU GONNA FINISH THAT?
THE HUMAN GARBAGE DISPOSAL. IT'S ADMIRABLE THAT YOU DON'T WASTE FOOD. SHOVEL AWAY.
JEEZ, I HOPE I'M NOT COMING DOWN WITH ANYTHING. MY APPETITE'S A BIT OFF.
NOW YOU TELL ME?
DON'T SWEAT IT, IT'S JUST STRESS.
EXIT

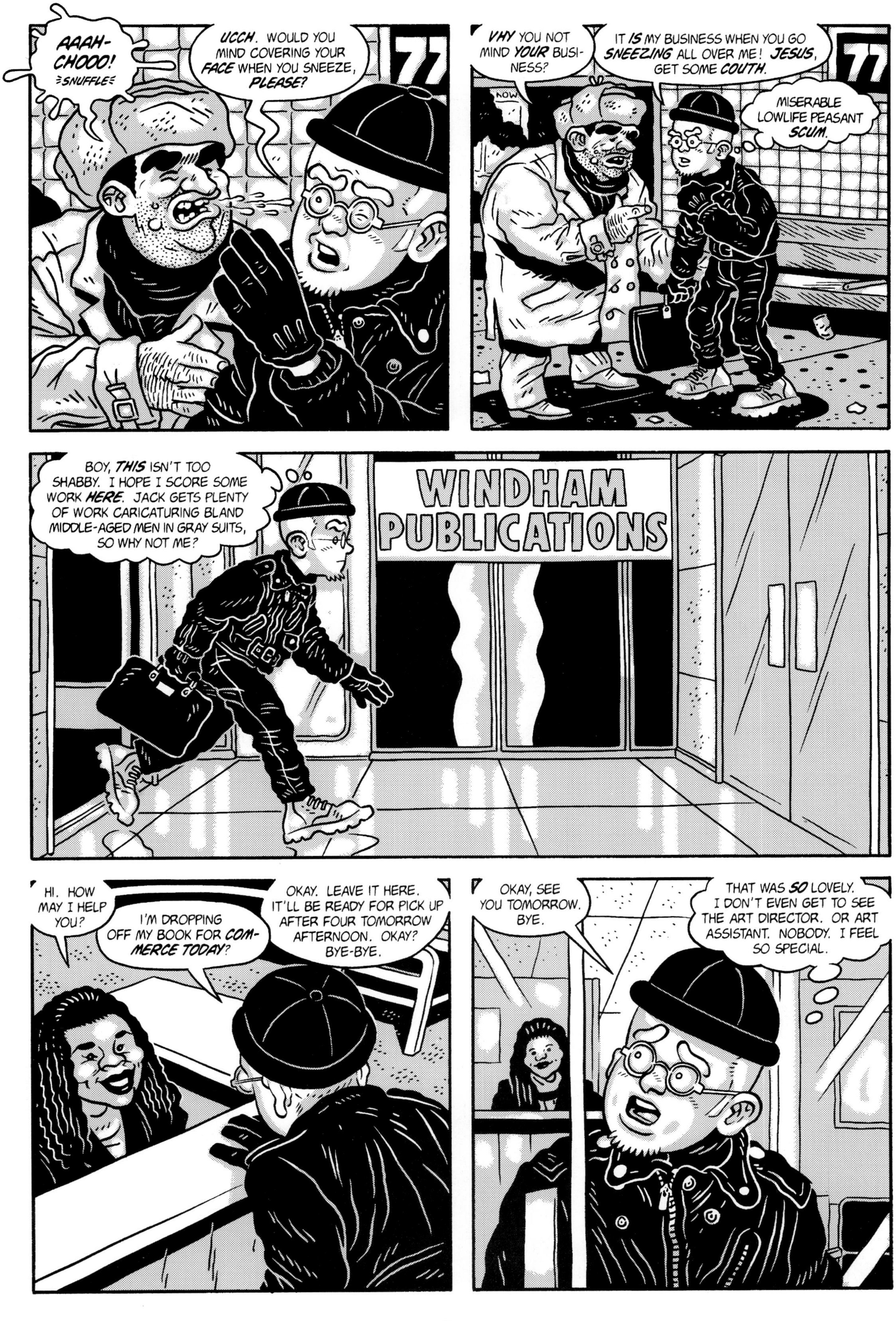
AAAH-CHOOO! SNUFFLE
UCCH. WOULD YOU MIND COVERING YOUR FACE WHEN YOU SNEEZE, PLEASE?
77
VHY YOU NOT MIND YOUR BUSINESS?
IT IS MY BUSINESS WHEN YOU GO SNEEZING ALL OVER ME! JESUS, GET SOME COUTH.
MISERABLE LOWLIFE PEASANT SCUM.
77
NOW
BOY, THIS ISN'T TOO SHABBY. I HOPE I SCORE SOME WORK HERE. JACK GETS PLENTY OF WORK CARICATURING BLAND MIDDLE-AGED MEN IN GRAY SUITS, SO WHY NOT ME?
WINDHAM PUBLICATIONS
HI. HOW MAY I HELP YOU?
I'M DROPPING OFF MY BOOK FOR COMMERCE TODAY?
OKAY. LEAVE IT HERE. IT'LL BE READY FOR PICK UP AFTER FOUR TOMORROW AFTERNOON. OKAY? BYE-BYE.
OKAY, SEE YOU TOMORROW. BYE.
THAT WAS SO LOVELY. I DON'T EVEN GET TO SEE THE ART DIRECTOR. OR ART ASSISTANT. NOBODY. I FEEL SO SPECIAL.

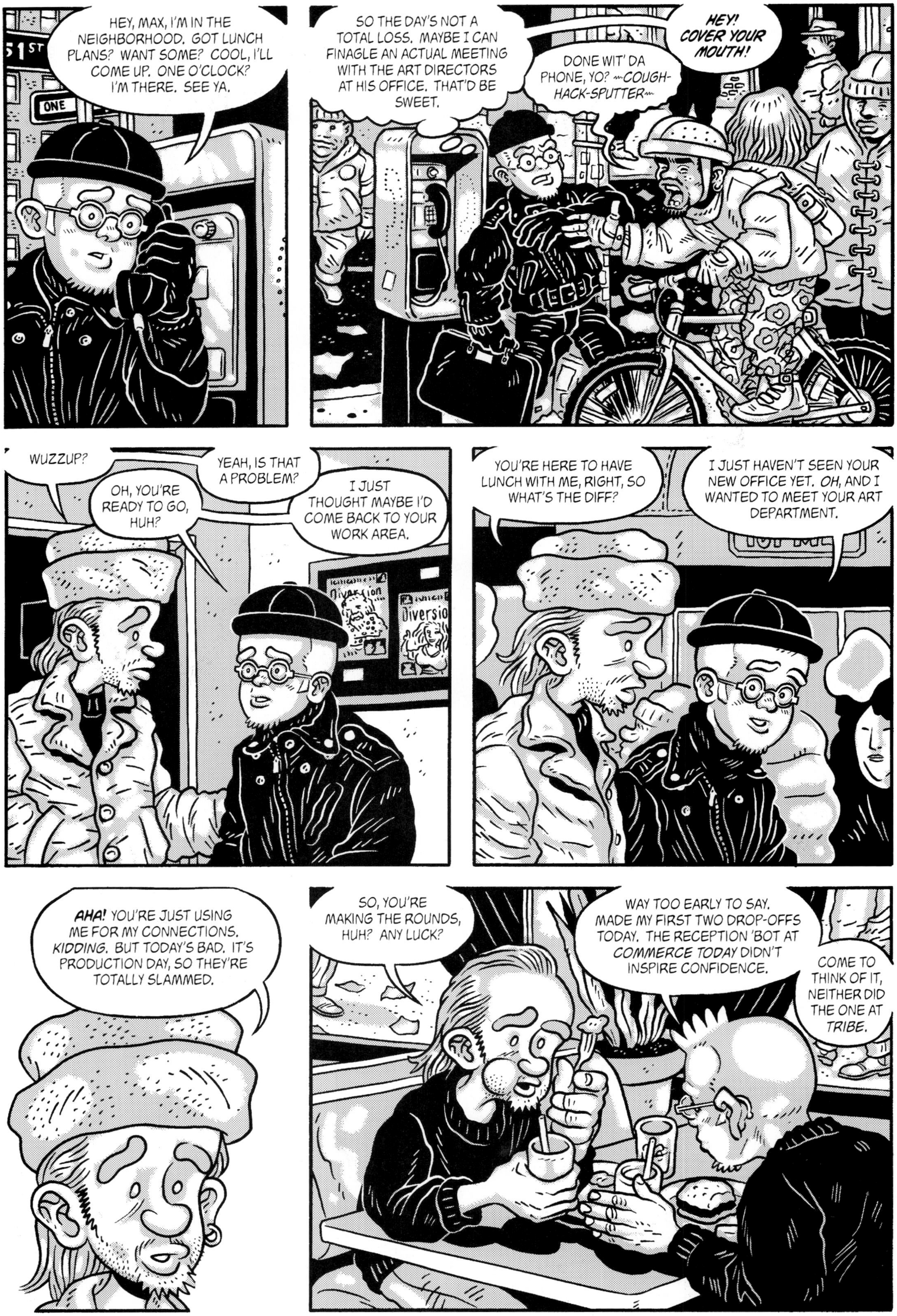
HEY, MAX, I'M IN THE NEIGHBORHOOD. GOT LUNCH PLANS? WANT SOME? COOL, I'LL COME UP. ONE O'CLOCK? I'M THERE. SEE YA.
51ST
ONE
SO THE DAY'S NOT A TOTAL LOSS. MAYBE I CAN FINAGLE AN ACTUAL MEETING WITH THE ART DIRECTORS AT HIS OFFICE. THAT'D BE SWEET.
DONE WIT' DA PHONE, YO? ~COUGH-HACK-SPUTTER~
HEY! COVER YOUR MOUTH!
WUZZUP?
OH, YOU'RE READY TO GO, HUH?
YEAH, IS THAT A PROBLEM?
I JUST THOUGHT MAYBE I'D COME BACK TO YOUR WORK AREA.
Diversion
YOU'RE HERE TO HAVE LUNCH WITH ME, RIGHT, SO WHAT'S THE DIFF?
I JUST HAVEN'T SEEN YOUR NEW OFFICE YET. OH, AND I WANTED TO MEET YOUR ART DEPARTMENT.
AHA! YOU'RE JUST USING ME FOR MY CONNECTIONS. KIDDING. BUT TODAY'S BAD. IT'S PRODUCTION DAY, SO THEY'RE TOTALLY SLAMMED.
SO, YOU'RE MAKING THE ROUNDS, HUH? ANY LUCK?
WAY TOO EARLY TO SAY. MADE MY FIRST TWO DROP-OFFS TODAY. THE RECEPTION 'BOT AT COMMERCE TODAY DIDN'T INSPIRE CONFIDENCE.
COME TO THINK OF IT, NEITHER DID THE ONE AT TRIBE.

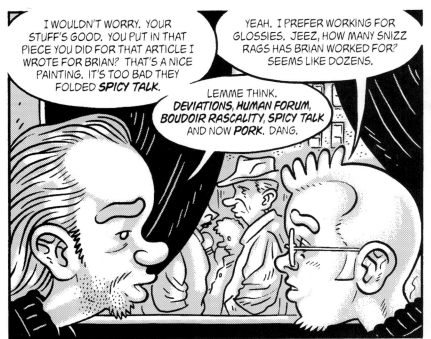

I WOULDN'T WORRY. YOUR STUFF'S GOOD. YOU PUT IN THAT PIECE YOU DID FOR THAT ARTICLE I WROTE FOR BRIAN? THAT'S A NICE PAINTING. IT'S TOO BAD THEY FOLDED *SPICY TALK*.

YEAH. I PREFER WORKING FOR GLOSSIES. JEEZ, HOW MANY SNIZZ RAGS HAS BRIAN WORKED FOR? SEEMS LIKE DOZENS.

LEMME THINK. *DEVIATIONS, HUMAN FORUM, BOUDOIR RASCALITY, SPICY TALK* AND NOW *PORK*. DANG.

WHOA: GOTTA JET! I'VE GOT A MEETING IN FIFTEEN MINUTES. HATE TO EAT A RUN, BUT...

NO SWEAT. SO, CAN YOU MAYBE MENTION ME TO YOUR ART DEPARTMENT?

MOS' DEF'.

THISH ISH ISH *KILLIN' ME'*. I *HATE* HAVIN' MY *JAW WIRED SHUT!* I MISH PUTTIN' SHOLID FOOD IN MY MOUF... *AMONGSH OTHER FINGSH*. ⸗GIGGLE⸗ I'M, LIKE, LOSHIN' *TONSH* OF WEIGHT. I'M TOO SHKINNY ALREADY!

YOU ARE *SOOOO CRAZY!* *TOO SKINNY?* GOD, YOU'RE LIKE SO *WHATEVER!* MAYBE I SHOULD GET *MY* JAW WIRED, TOO.

WE *ALL* SHOULD.

THERE'S A VACUOUS TRIO IF EVER I SAW ONE. STILL, I'D HATE TO HAVE MY JAW WIRED SHUT. I'D WITHER AWAY AND DIE OF MALNUTRITION. I SHOULDN'T BE SO JUDGMENTAL, BUT BOY THEY SOUND DUMB.

HERE WE ARE! GOODY, GOODY!

I'VE GOTTA HIT *MARILESE'S* APARTMENT BEFORE WE GO OUT TONIGHT.

PICKING UP A LITTLE *HMM-HMM-HMM?* ⸗SIMPER⸗

KNOW IT!

RUMBLE RUMBLE!

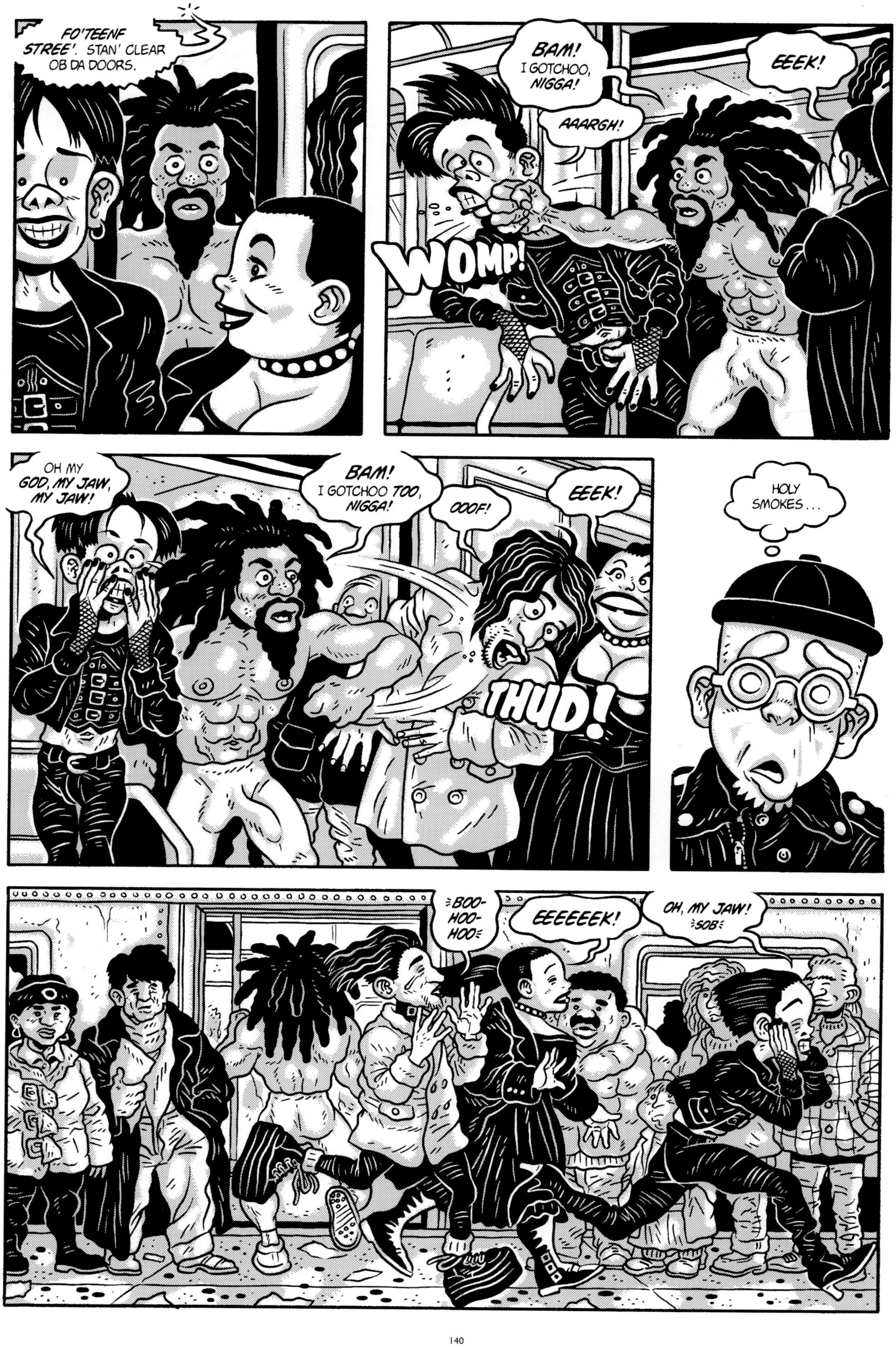
FO'TEENF STREE'. STAN' CLEAR OB DA DOORS.
BAM! I GOTCHOO, NIGGA!
AAARGH!
EEEK!
WOMP!
OH MY GOD, MY JAW, MY JAW!
BAM! I GOTCHOO TOO, NIGGA!
OOOF!
EEEK!
THUD!
HOLY SMOKES...
BOO-HOO-HOO
EEEEEEK!
OH, MY JAW!
SOB

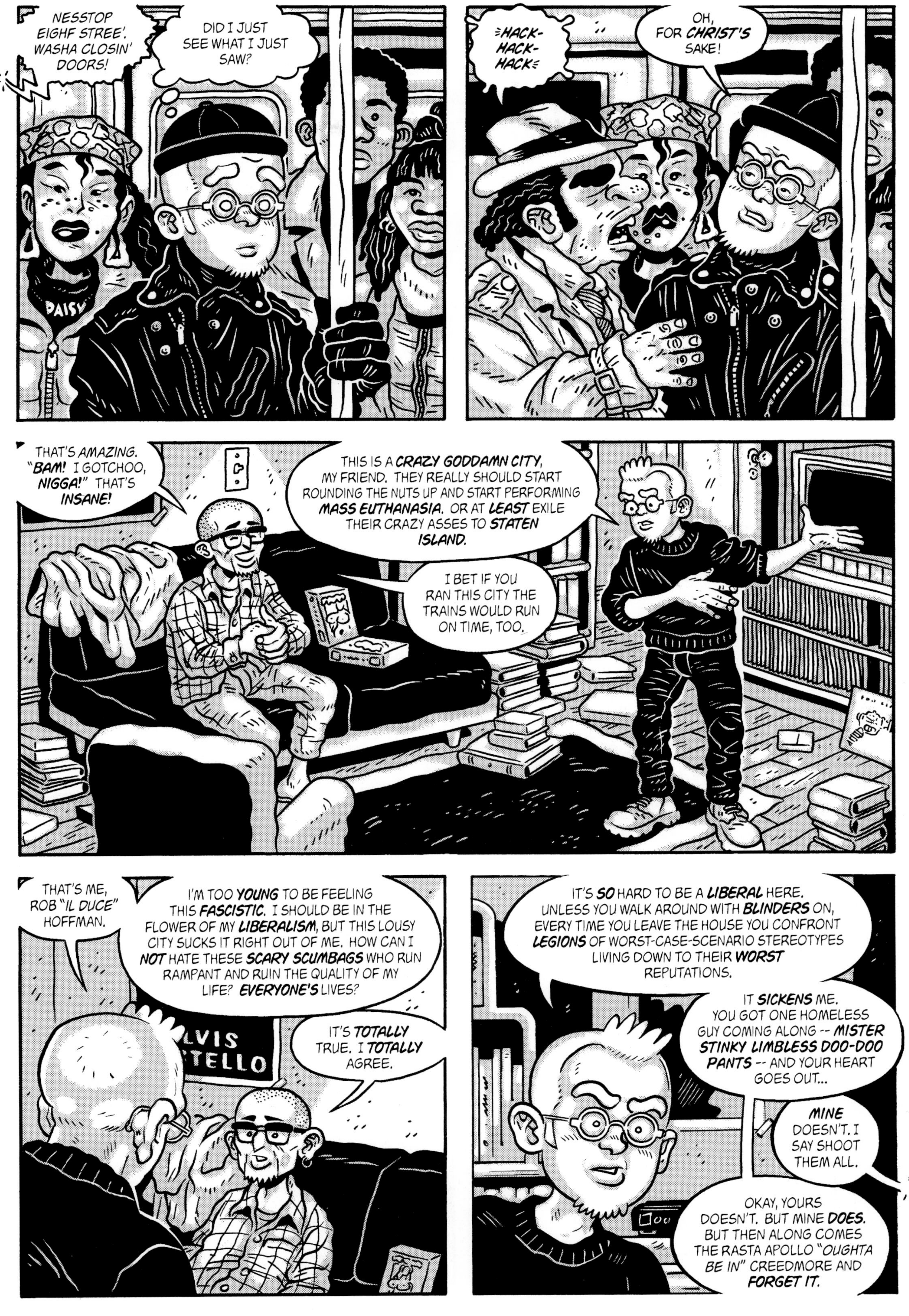

NESSTOP EIGHF STREE'. WASHA CLOSIN' DOORS!
DID I JUST SEE WHAT I JUST SAW?
≡HACK-HACK-HACK≡
OH, FOR CHRIST'S SAKE!
THAT'S AMAZING. "BAM! I GOTCHOO, NIGGA!" THAT'S INSANE!
THIS IS A CRAZY GODDAMN CITY, MY FRIEND. THEY REALLY SHOULD START ROUNDING THE NUTS UP AND START PERFORMING MASS EUTHANASIA. OR AT LEAST EXILE THEIR CRAZY ASSES TO STATEN ISLAND.
I BET IF YOU RAN THIS CITY THE TRAINS WOULD RUN ON TIME, TOO.
THAT'S ME, ROB "IL DUCE" HOFFMAN.
I'M TOO YOUNG TO BE FEELING THIS FASCISTIC. I SHOULD BE IN THE FLOWER OF MY LIBERALISM, BUT THIS LOUSY CITY SUCKS IT RIGHT OUT OF ME. HOW CAN I NOT HATE THESE SCARY SCUMBAGS WHO RUN RAMPANT AND RUIN THE QUALITY OF MY LIFE? EVERYONE'S LIVES?
IT'S TOTALLY TRUE. I TOTALLY AGREE.
IT'S SO HARD TO BE A LIBERAL HERE. UNLESS YOU WALK AROUND WITH BLINDERS ON, EVERY TIME YOU LEAVE THE HOUSE YOU CONFRONT LEGIONS OF WORST-CASE-SCENARIO STEREOTYPES LIVING DOWN TO THEIR WORST REPUTATIONS.
IT SICKENS ME. YOU GOT ONE HOMELESS GUY COMING ALONG -- MISTER STINKY LIMBLESS DOO-DOO PANTS -- AND YOUR HEART GOES OUT...
MINE DOESN'T. I SAY SHOOT THEM ALL.
OKAY, YOURS DOESN'T. BUT MINE DOES. BUT THEN ALONG COMES THE RASTA APOLLO "OUGHTA BE IN" CREEDMORE AND FORGET IT.

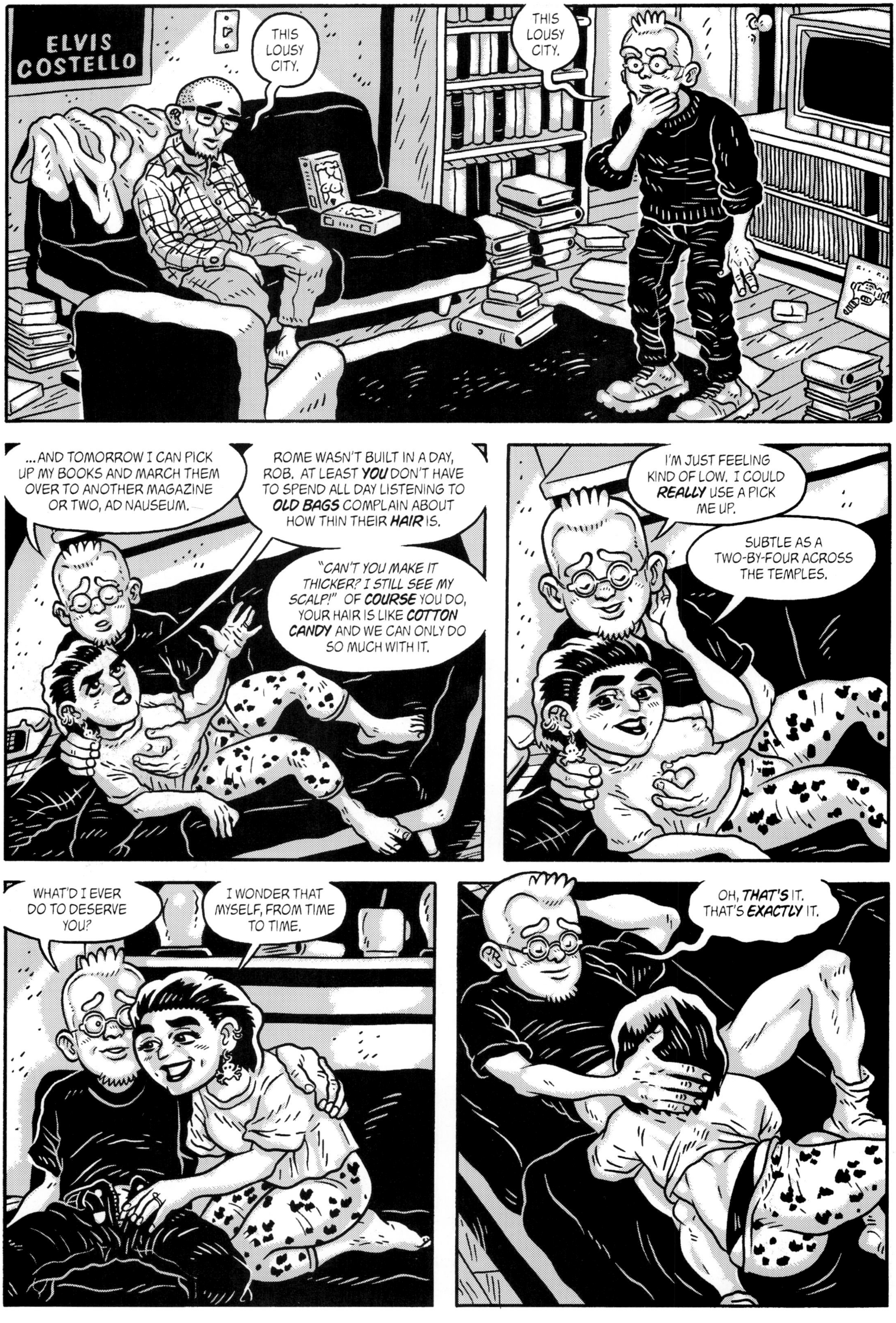

ELVIS COSTELLO
THIS LOUSY CITY.
THIS LOUSY CITY.
...AND TOMORROW I CAN PICK UP MY BOOKS AND MARCH THEM OVER TO ANOTHER MAGAZINE OR TWO, AD NAUSEUM.
ROME WASN'T BUILT IN A DAY, ROB. AT LEAST YOU DON'T HAVE TO SPEND ALL DAY LISTENING TO OLD BAGS COMPLAIN ABOUT HOW THIN THEIR HAIR IS.
"CAN'T YOU MAKE IT THICKER? I STILL SEE MY SCALP!" OF COURSE YOU DO, YOUR HAIR IS LIKE COTTON CANDY AND WE CAN ONLY DO SO MUCH WITH IT.
I'M JUST FEELING KIND OF LOW. I COULD REALLY USE A PICK ME UP.
SUBTLE AS A TWO-BY-FOUR ACROSS THE TEMPLES.
WHAT'D I EVER DO TO DESERVE YOU?
I WONDER THAT MYSELF, FROM TIME TO TIME.
OH, THAT'S IT. THAT'S EXACTLY IT.

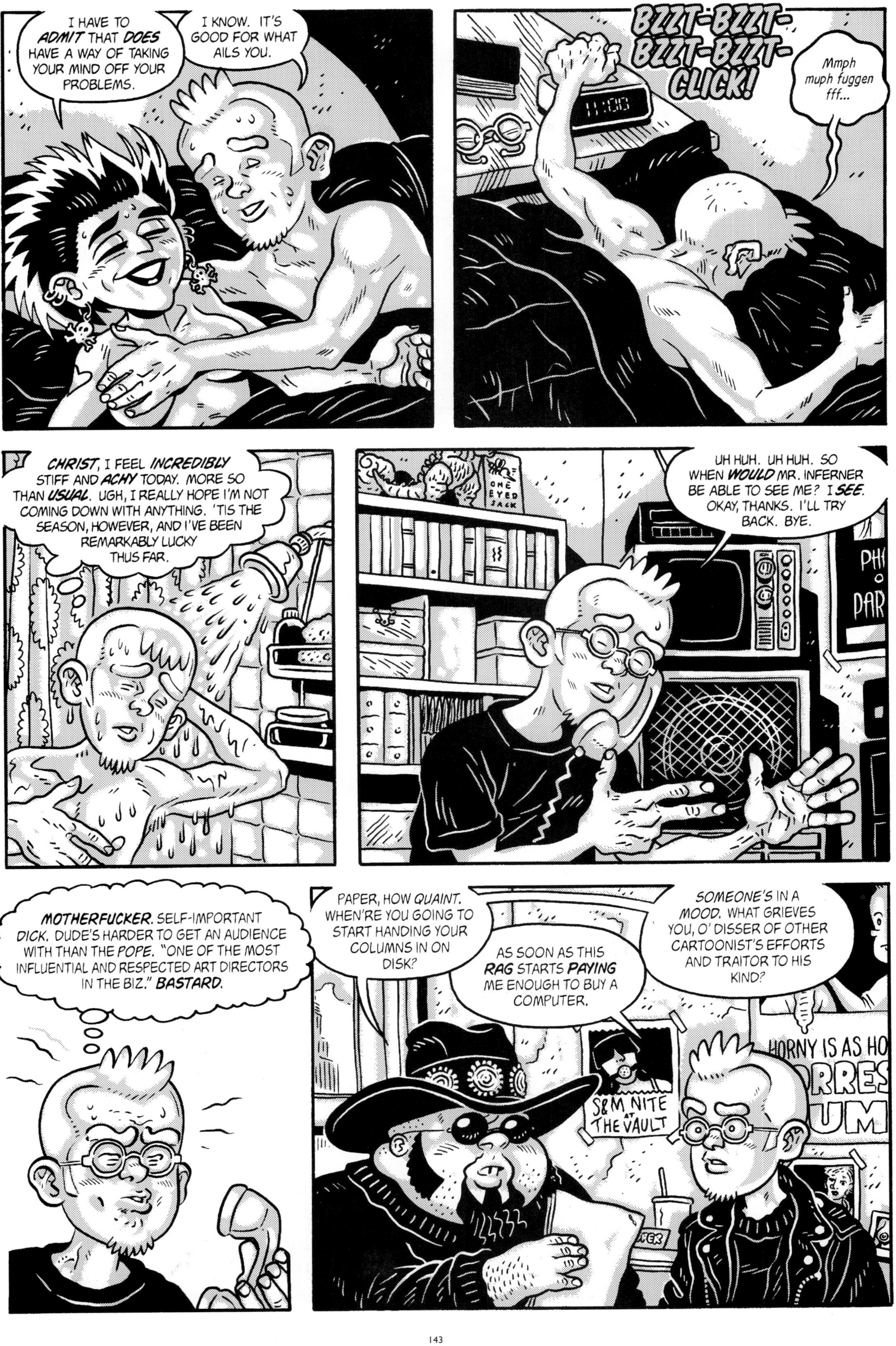
I HAVE TO ADMIT THAT DOES HAVE A WAY OF TAKING YOUR MIND OFF YOUR PROBLEMS.
I KNOW. IT'S GOOD FOR WHAT AILS YOU.
BZZT-BZZT-BZZT-BZZT-CLICK!
Mmph muph fuggen fff...
CHRIST, I FEEL INCREDIBLY STIFF AND ACHY TODAY. MORE SO THAN USUAL. UGH, I REALLY HOPE I'M NOT COMING DOWN WITH ANYTHING. 'TIS THE SEASON, HOWEVER, AND I'VE BEEN REMARKABLY LUCKY THUS FAR.
UH HUH. UH HUH. SO WHEN WOULD MR. INFERNER BE ABLE TO SEE ME? I SEE. OKAY, THANKS. I'LL TRY BACK. BYE.
MOTHERFUCKER. SELF-IMPORTANT DICK. DUDE'S HARDER TO GET AN AUDIENCE WITH THAN THE POPE. "ONE OF THE MOST INFLUENTIAL AND RESPECTED ART DIRECTORS IN THE BIZ." BASTARD.
PAPER, HOW QUAINT. WHEN'RE YOU GOING TO START HANDING YOUR COLUMNS IN ON DISK?
AS SOON AS THIS RAG STARTS PAYING ME ENOUGH TO BUY A COMPUTER.
SOMEONE'S IN A MOOD. WHAT GRIEVES YOU, O' DISSER OF OTHER CARTOONIST'S EFFORTS AND TRAITOR TO HIS KIND?
S&M NITE AT THE VAULT

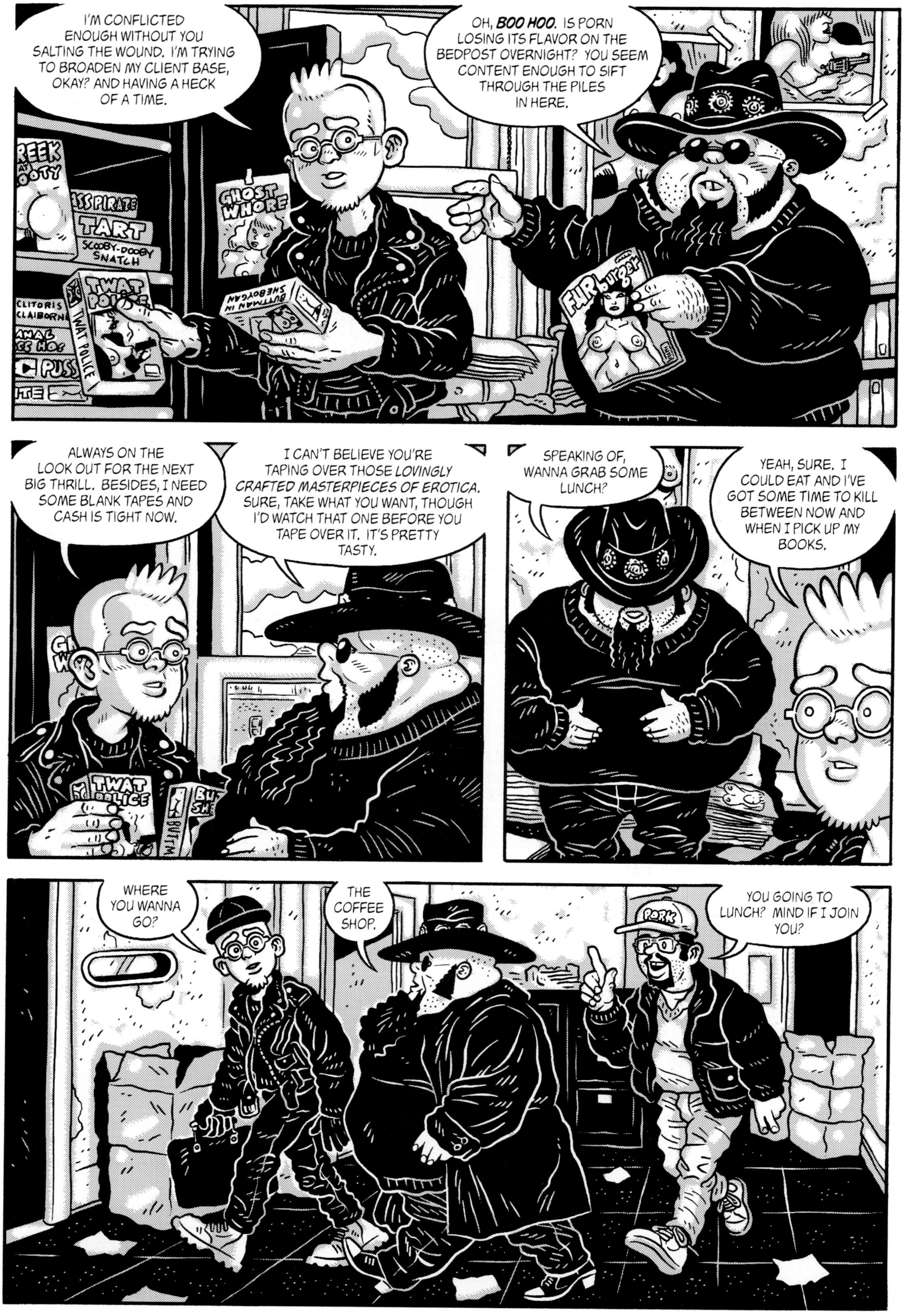
I'M CONFLICTED ENOUGH WITHOUT YOU SALTING THE WOUND. I'M TRYING TO BROADEN MY CLIENT BASE, OKAY? AND HAVING A HECK OF A TIME.
OH, **BOO HOO.** IS PORN LOSING ITS FLAVOR ON THE BEDPOST OVERNIGHT? YOU SEEM CONTENT ENOUGH TO SIFT THROUGH THE PILES IN HERE.
GHOST WHORE
TART
SCOOBY-DOOBY SNATCH
TWAT POLICE
BUTTMAN IN SHEBOYGAN
CLITORIS CLAIBORNE
FURburger
ALWAYS ON THE LOOK OUT FOR THE NEXT BIG THRILL. BESIDES, I NEED SOME BLANK TAPES AND CASH IS TIGHT NOW.
I CAN'T BELIEVE YOU'RE TAPING OVER THOSE *LOVINGLY CRAFTED MASTERPIECES OF EROTICA.* SURE, TAKE WHAT YOU WANT, THOUGH I'D WATCH THAT ONE BEFORE YOU TAPE OVER IT. IT'S PRETTY TASTY.
SPEAKING OF, WANNA GRAB SOME LUNCH?
YEAH, SURE. I COULD EAT AND I'VE GOT SOME TIME TO KILL BETWEEN NOW AND WHEN I PICK UP MY BOOKS.
WHERE YOU WANNA GO?
THE COFFEE SHOP.
YOU GOING TO LUNCH? MIND IF I JOIN YOU?
PORK

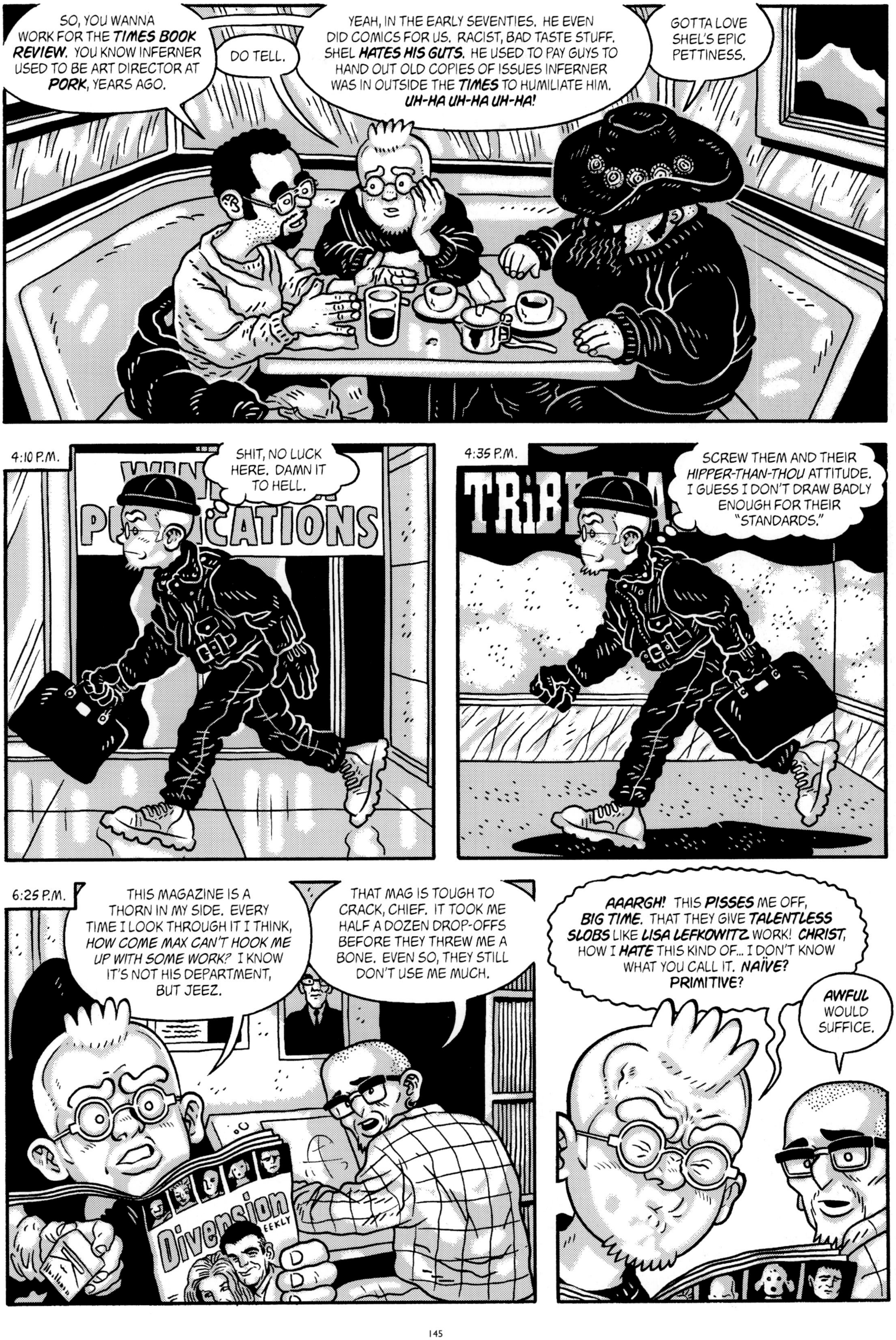

SO, YOU WANNA WORK FOR THE *TIMES BOOK REVIEW.* YOU KNOW INFERNER USED TO BE ART DIRECTOR AT *PORK*, YEARS AGO.
DO TELL.
YEAH, IN THE EARLY SEVENTIES. HE EVEN DID COMICS FOR US. RACIST, BAD TASTE STUFF. SHEL *HATES HIS GUTS.* HE USED TO PAY GUYS TO HAND OUT OLD COPIES OF ISSUES INFERNER WAS IN OUTSIDE THE *TIMES* TO HUMILIATE HIM. *UH-HA UH-HA UH-HA!*
GOTTA LOVE SHEL'S EPIC PETTINESS.
4:10 P.M.
PUBLICATIONS
SHIT, NO LUCK HERE. DAMN IT TO HELL.
4:35 P.M.
SCREW THEM AND THEIR *HIPPER-THAN-THOU* ATTITUDE. I GUESS I DON'T DRAW BADLY ENOUGH FOR THEIR "STANDARDS."
6:25 P.M.
THIS MAGAZINE IS A THORN IN MY SIDE. EVERY TIME I LOOK THROUGH IT I THINK, *HOW COME MAX CAN'T HOOK ME UP WITH SOME WORK?* I KNOW IT'S NOT HIS DEPARTMENT, BUT JEEZ.
THAT MAG IS TOUGH TO CRACK, CHIEF. IT TOOK ME HALF A DOZEN DROP-OFFS BEFORE THEY THREW ME A BONE. EVEN SO, THEY STILL DON'T USE ME MUCH.
AAARGH! THIS *PISSES* ME OFF, *BIG TIME.* THAT THEY GIVE *TALENTLESS SLOBS* LIKE *LISA LEFKOWITZ* WORK! *CHRIST*, HOW I *HATE* THIS KIND OF... I DON'T KNOW WHAT YOU CALL IT. *NAÏVE? PRIMITIVE?*
AWFUL WOULD SUFFICE.

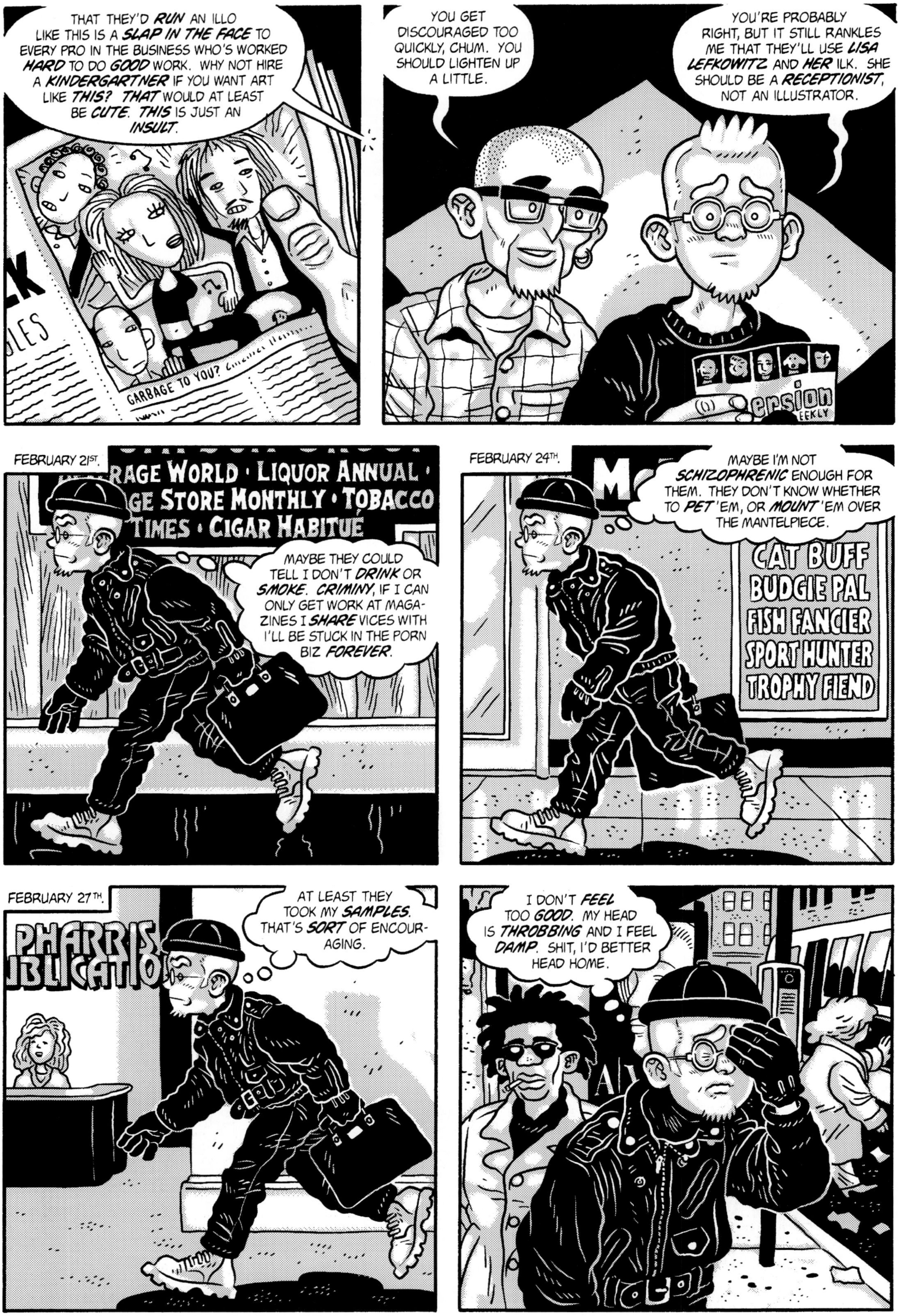
THAT THEY'D RUN AN ILLO LIKE THIS IS A SLAP IN THE FACE TO EVERY PRO IN THE BUSINESS WHO'S WORKED HARD TO DO GOOD WORK. WHY NOT HIRE A KINDERGARTNER IF YOU WANT ART LIKE THIS? THAT WOULD AT LEAST BE CUTE. THIS IS JUST AN INSULT.
GARBAGE TO YOU?
YOU GET DISCOURAGED TOO QUICKLY, CHUM. YOU SHOULD LIGHTEN UP A LITTLE.
YOU'RE PROBABLY RIGHT, BUT IT STILL RANKLES ME THAT THEY'LL USE LISA LEFKOWITZ AND HER ILK. SHE SHOULD BE A RECEPTIONIST, NOT AN ILLUSTRATOR.
FEBRUARY 21ST.
RAGE WORLD · LIQUOR ANNUAL · GE STORE MONTHLY · TOBACCO TIMES · CIGAR HABITUÉ
MAYBE THEY COULD TELL I DON'T DRINK OR SMOKE. CRIMINY, IF I CAN ONLY GET WORK AT MAGAZINES I SHARE VICES WITH I'LL BE STUCK IN THE PORN BIZ FOREVER.
FEBRUARY 24TH.
MAYBE I'M NOT SCHIZOPHRENIC ENOUGH FOR THEM. THEY DON'T KNOW WHETHER TO PET 'EM, OR MOUNT 'EM OVER THE MANTELPIECE.
CAT BUFF
BUDGIE PAL
FISH FANCIER
SPORT HUNTER
TROPHY FIEND
FEBRUARY 27TH.
PHARRIS
UBLICATIO
AT LEAST THEY TOOK MY SAMPLES. THAT'S SORT OF ENCOURAGING.
I DON'T FEEL TOO GOOD. MY HEAD IS THROBBING AND I FEEL DAMP. SHIT, I'D BETTER HEAD HOME.

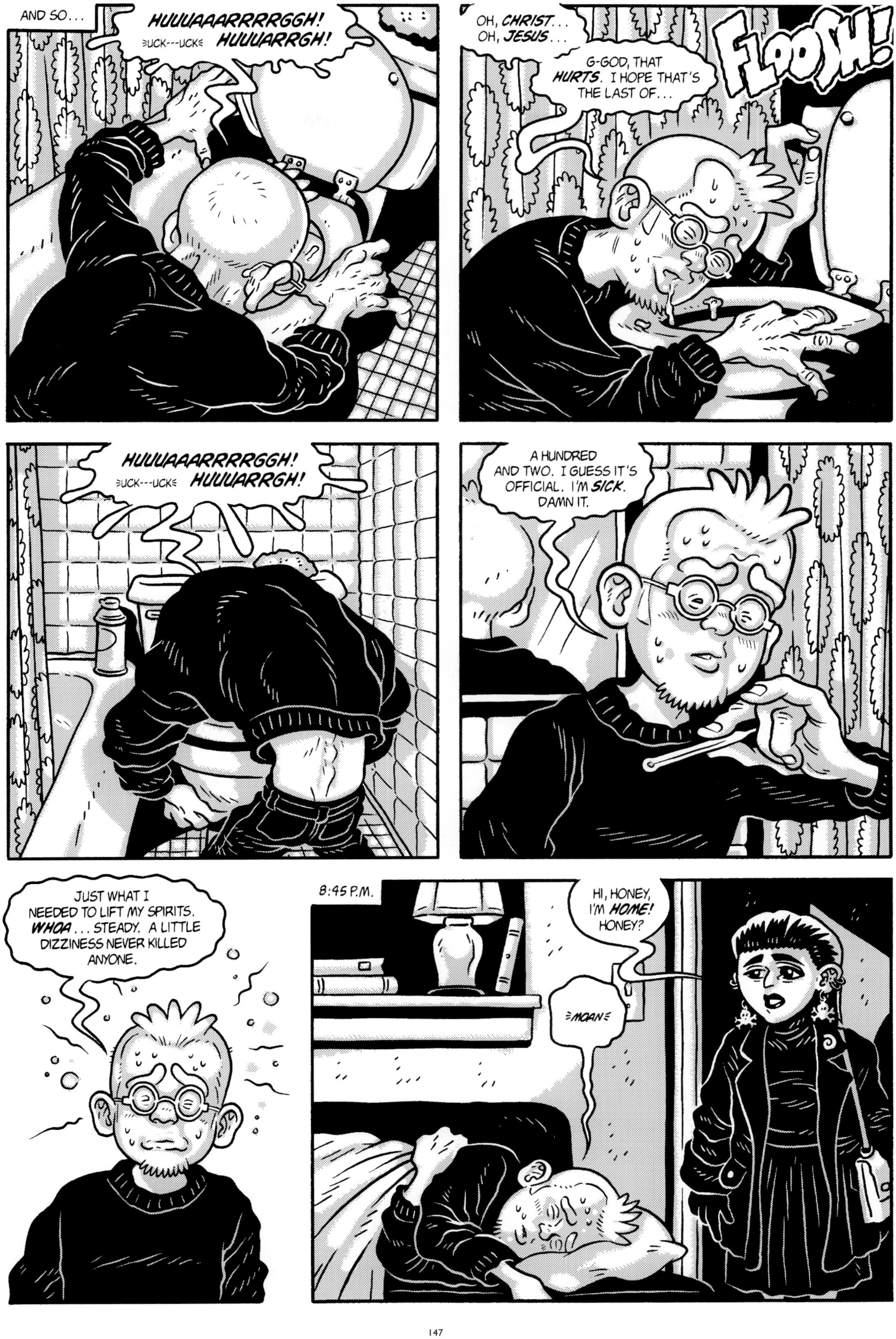
AND SO...
HUUUAAARRRRGGH! ⩶UCK---UCK⩶ HUUUARRGH!
OH, CHRIST... OH, JESUS...
G-GOD, THAT HURTS. I HOPE THAT'S THE LAST OF...
FLOOSH!
HUUUAAARRRRGGH! ⩶UCK---UCK⩶ HUUUARRGH!
A HUNDRED AND TWO. I GUESS IT'S OFFICIAL. I'M SICK. DAMN IT.
JUST WHAT I NEEDED TO LIFT MY SPIRITS. WHOA... STEADY. A LITTLE DIZZINESS NEVER KILLED ANYONE.
8:45 P.M.
HI, HONEY, I'M HOME! HONEY?
⩶MOAN⩶

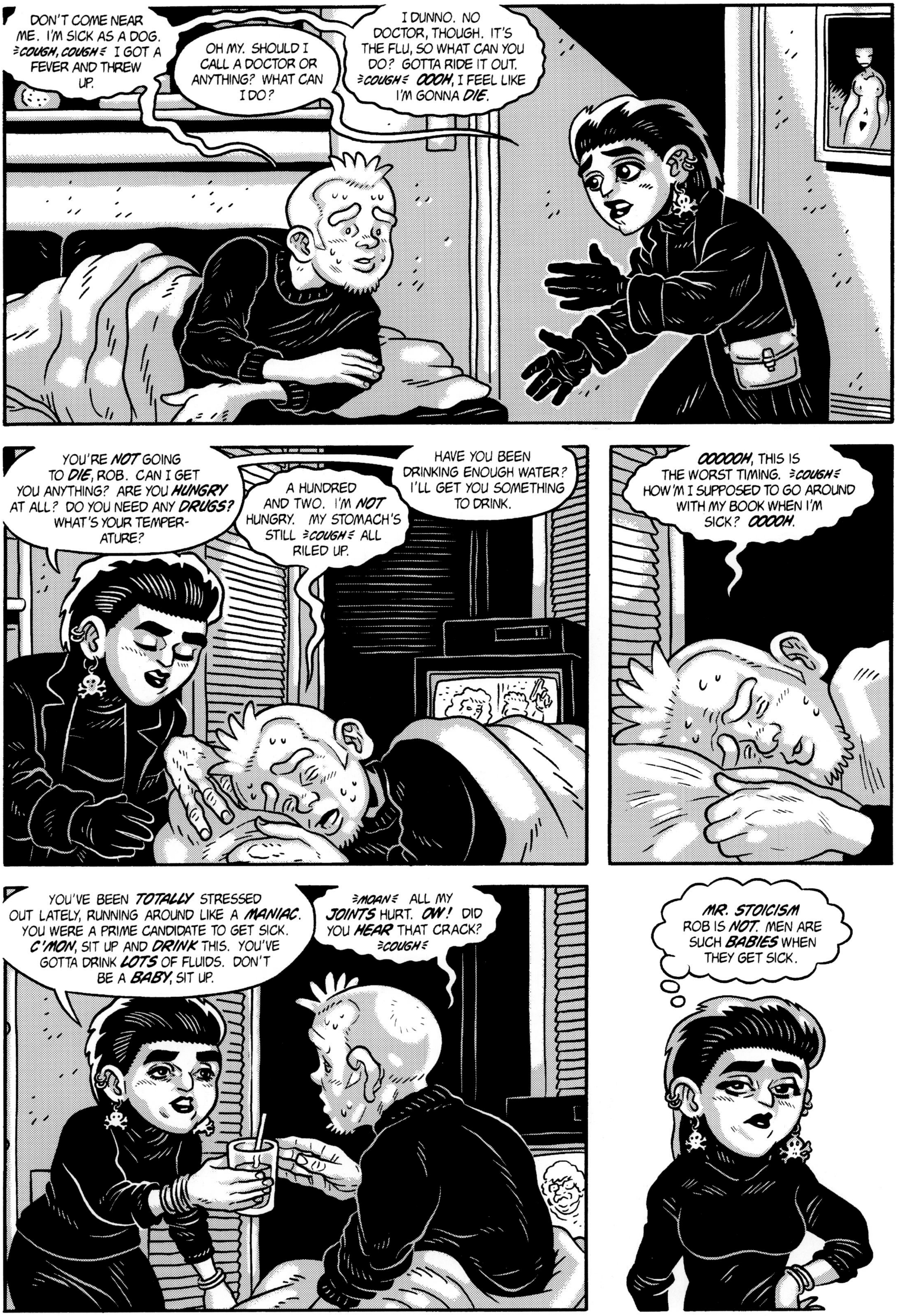
DON'T COME NEAR ME. I'M SICK AS A DOG. ≷COUGH, COUGH≶ I GOT A FEVER AND THREW UP.
OH MY. SHOULD I CALL A DOCTOR OR ANYTHING? WHAT CAN I DO?
I DUNNO. NO DOCTOR, THOUGH. IT'S THE FLU, SO WHAT CAN YOU DO? GOTTA RIDE IT OUT. ≷COUGH≶ OOOH, I FEEL LIKE I'M GONNA DIE.
YOU'RE NOT GOING TO DIE, ROB. CAN I GET YOU ANYTHING? ARE YOU HUNGRY AT ALL? DO YOU NEED ANY DRUGS? WHAT'S YOUR TEMPERATURE?
A HUNDRED AND TWO. I'M NOT HUNGRY. MY STOMACH'S STILL ≷COUGH≶ ALL RILED UP.
HAVE YOU BEEN DRINKING ENOUGH WATER? I'LL GET YOU SOMETHING TO DRINK.
OOOOOH, THIS IS THE WORST TIMING. ≷COUGH≶ HOW'M I SUPPOSED TO GO AROUND WITH MY BOOK WHEN I'M SICK? OOOOH.
YOU'VE BEEN TOTALLY STRESSED OUT LATELY, RUNNING AROUND LIKE A MANIAC. YOU WERE A PRIME CANDIDATE TO GET SICK. C'MON, SIT UP AND DRINK THIS. YOU'VE GOTTA DRINK LOTS OF FLUIDS. DON'T BE A BABY, SIT UP.
≷MOAN≶ ALL MY JOINTS HURT. OW! DID YOU HEAR THAT CRACK? ≷COUGH≶
MR. STOICISM ROB IS NOT. MEN ARE SUCH BABIES WHEN THEY GET SICK.

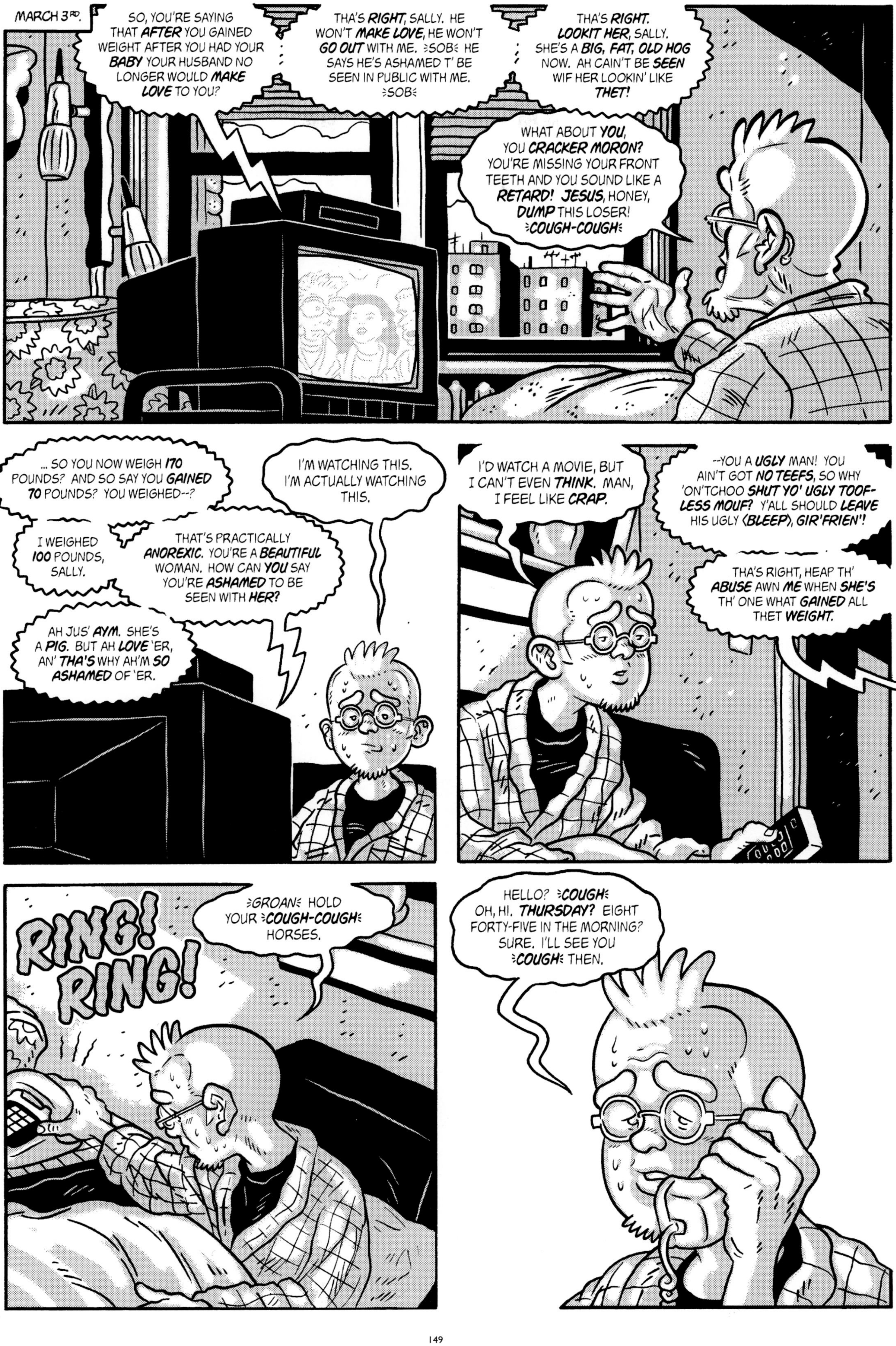
MARCH 3RD.
SO, YOU'RE SAYING THAT AFTER YOU GAINED WEIGHT AFTER YOU HAD YOUR BABY YOUR HUSBAND NO LONGER WOULD MAKE LOVE TO YOU?
THA'S RIGHT, SALLY. HE WON'T MAKE LOVE, HE WON'T GO OUT WITH ME. SOB HE SAYS HE'S ASHAMED T' BE SEEN IN PUBLIC WITH ME. SOB
THA'S RIGHT. LOOKIT HER, SALLY. SHE'S A BIG, FAT, OLD HOG NOW. AH CAIN'T BE SEEN WIF HER LOOKIN' LIKE THET!
WHAT ABOUT YOU, YOU CRACKER MORON? YOU'RE MISSING YOUR FRONT TEETH AND YOU SOUND LIKE A RETARD! JESUS, HONEY, DUMP THIS LOSER! COUGH-COUGH
... SO YOU NOW WEIGH 170 POUNDS? AND SO SAY YOU GAINED 70 POUNDS? YOU WEIGHED--?
I WEIGHED 100 POUNDS, SALLY.
THAT'S PRACTICALLY ANOREXIC. YOU'RE A BEAUTIFUL WOMAN. HOW CAN YOU SAY YOU'RE ASHAMED TO BE SEEN WITH HER?
AH JUS' AYM. SHE'S A PIG. BUT AH LOVE 'ER, AN' THA'S WHY AH'M SO ASHAMED OF 'ER.
I'M WATCHING THIS. I'M ACTUALLY WATCHING THIS.
I'D WATCH A MOVIE, BUT I CAN'T EVEN THINK. MAN, I FEEL LIKE CRAP.
--YOU A UGLY MAN! YOU AIN'T GOT NO TEEFS, SO WHY 'ON'TCHOO SHUT YO' UGLY TOOF-LESS MOUF? Y'ALL SHOULD LEAVE HIS UGLY (BLEEP), GIR'FRIEN'!
THA'S RIGHT, HEAP TH' ABUSE AWN ME WHEN SHE'S TH' ONE WHAT GAINED ALL THET WEIGHT.
RING! RING!
GROAN HOLD YOUR COUGH-COUGH HORSES.
HELLO? COUGH OH, HI. THURSDAY? EIGHT FORTY-FIVE IN THE MORNING? SURE. I'LL SEE YOU COUGH THEN.

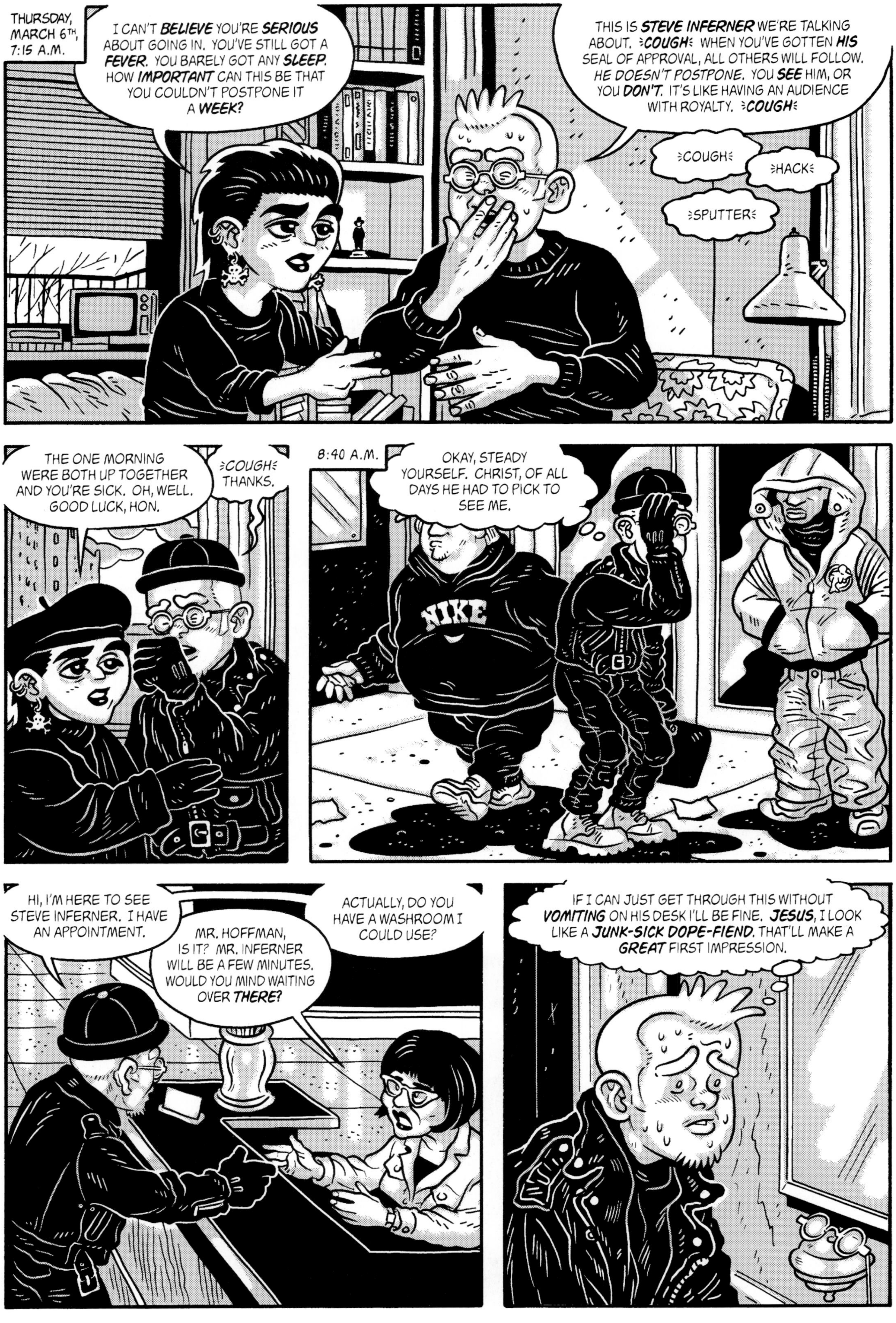
THURSDAY, MARCH 6TH, 7:15 A.M.
I CAN'T BELIEVE YOU'RE SERIOUS ABOUT GOING IN. YOU'VE STILL GOT A FEVER. YOU BARELY GOT ANY SLEEP. HOW IMPORTANT CAN THIS BE THAT YOU COULDN'T POSTPONE IT A WEEK?
THIS IS STEVE INFERNER WE'RE TALKING ABOUT. *COUGH* WHEN YOU'VE GOTTEN HIS SEAL OF APPROVAL, ALL OTHERS WILL FOLLOW. HE DOESN'T POSTPONE. YOU SEE HIM, OR YOU DON'T. IT'S LIKE HAVING AN AUDIENCE WITH ROYALTY. *COUGH*
COUGH
HACK
SPUTTER
THE ONE MORNING WERE BOTH UP TOGETHER AND YOU'RE SICK. OH, WELL. GOOD LUCK, HON.
COUGH THANKS.
8:40 A.M.
OKAY, STEADY YOURSELF. CHRIST, OF ALL DAYS HE HAD TO PICK TO SEE ME.
NIKE
HI, I'M HERE TO SEE STEVE INFERNER. I HAVE AN APPOINTMENT.
MR. HOFFMAN, IS IT? MR. INFERNER WILL BE A FEW MINUTES. WOULD YOU MIND WAITING OVER THERE?
ACTUALLY, DO YOU HAVE A WASHROOM I COULD USE?
IF I CAN JUST GET THROUGH THIS WITHOUT VOMITING ON HIS DESK I'LL BE FINE. JESUS, I LOOK LIKE A JUNK-SICK DOPE-FIEND. THAT'LL MAKE A GREAT FIRST IMPRESSION.

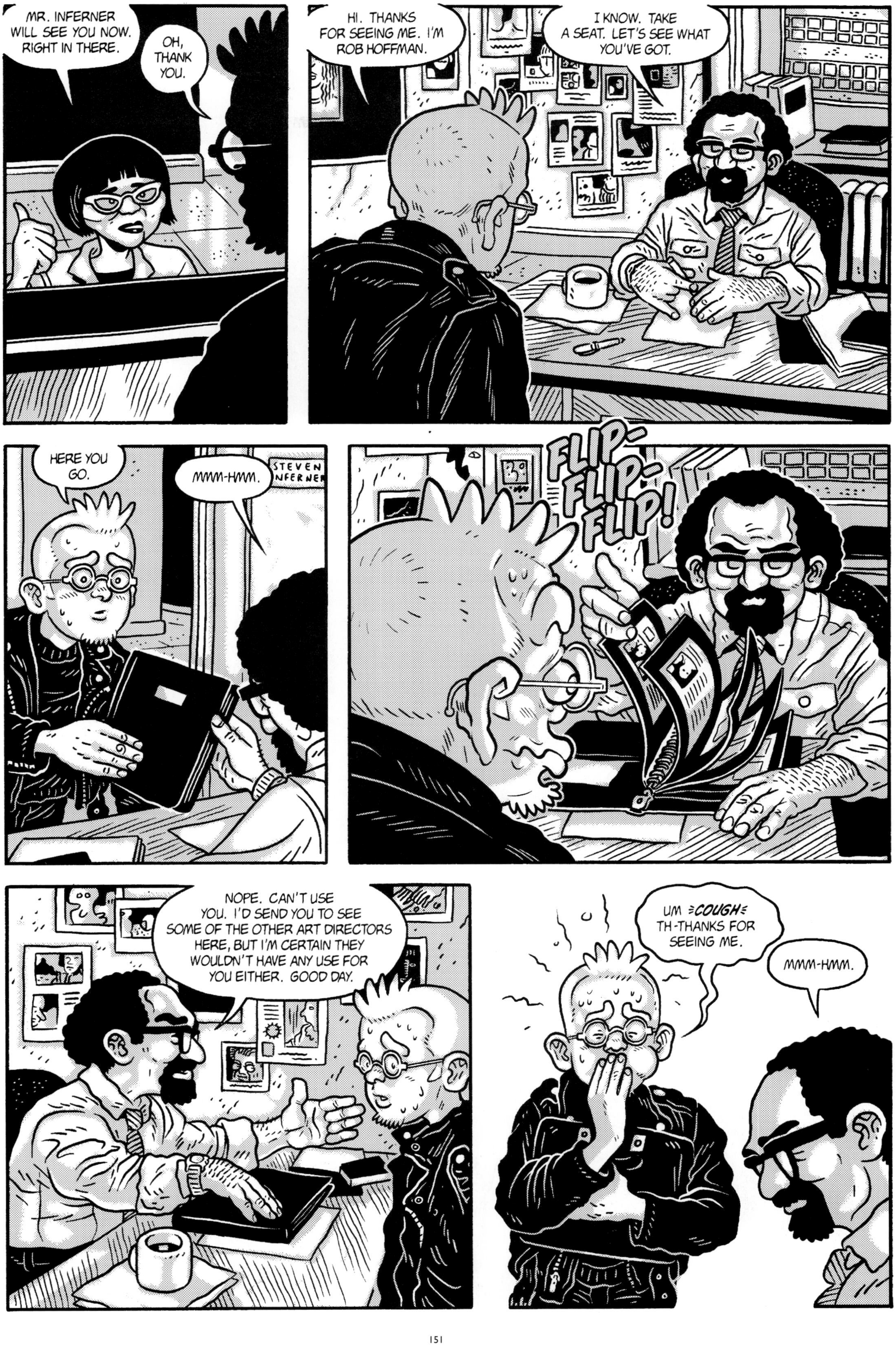
MR. INFERNER WILL SEE YOU NOW. RIGHT IN THERE.
OH, THANK YOU.
HI. THANKS FOR SEEING ME. I'M ROB HOFFMAN.
I KNOW. TAKE A SEAT. LET'S SEE WHAT YOU'VE GOT.
HERE YOU GO.
MMM-HMM.
STEVEN INFERNER
FLIP-FLIP-FLIP!
NOPE. CAN'T USE YOU. I'D SEND YOU TO SEE SOME OF THE OTHER ART DIRECTORS HERE, BUT I'M CERTAIN THEY WOULDN'T HAVE ANY USE FOR YOU EITHER. GOOD DAY.
UM COUGH TH-THANKS FOR SEEING ME.
MMM-HMM.

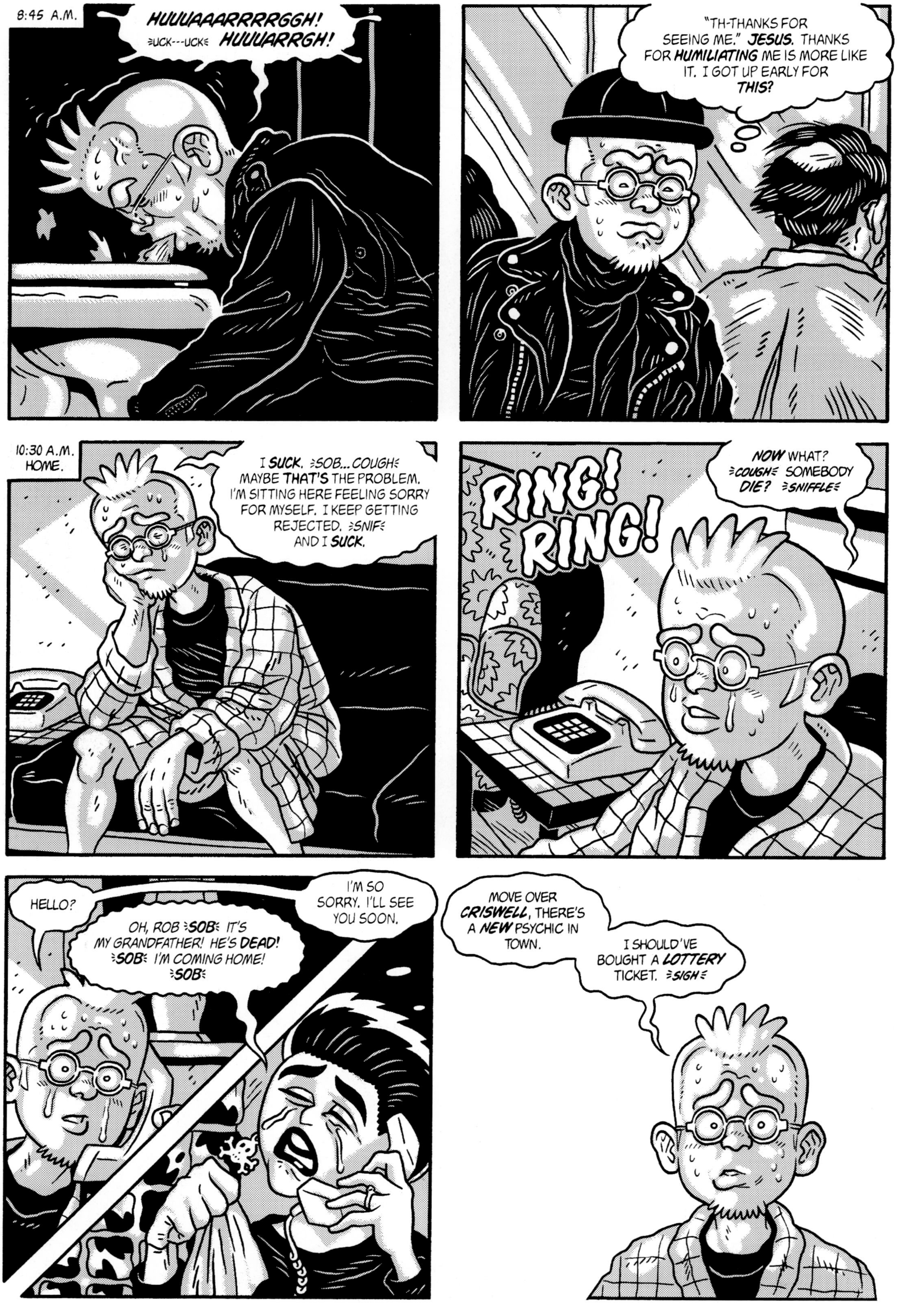
8:45 A.M.
HUUUAAARRRRGGH! ≥UCK---UCK≤ HUUUARRGH!
"TH-THANKS FOR SEEING ME." JESUS. THANKS FOR HUMILIATING ME IS MORE LIKE IT. I GOT UP EARLY FOR THIS?
10:30 A.M. HOME.
I SUCK. ≥SOB...COUGH≤ MAYBE THAT'S THE PROBLEM. I'M SITTING HERE FEELING SORRY FOR MYSELF. I KEEP GETTING REJECTED. ≥SNIF≤ AND I SUCK.
RING! RING!
NOW WHAT? ≥COUGH≤ SOMEBODY DIE? ≥SNIFFLE≤
HELLO?
OH, ROB ≥SOB≤ IT'S MY GRANDFATHER! HE'S DEAD! ≥SOB≤ I'M COMING HOME! ≥SOB≤
I'M SO SORRY. I'LL SEE YOU SOON.
MOVE OVER CRISWELL, THERE'S A NEW PSYCHIC IN TOWN.
I SHOULD'VE BOUGHT A LOTTERY TICKET. ≥SIGH≤

Chapter
Seven

BRIDGE WATCHING

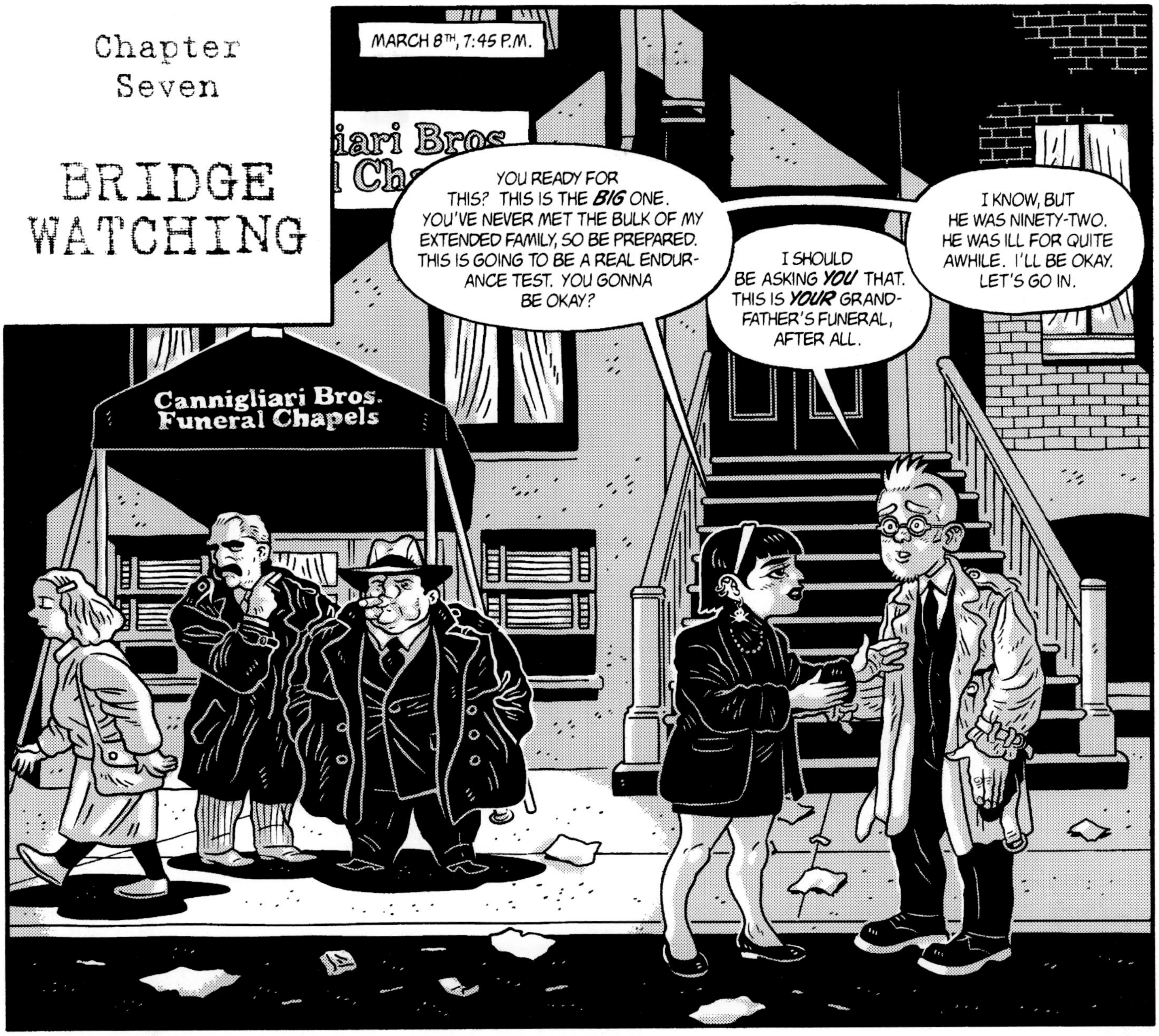
MARCH 8TH, 7:45 P.M.
Cannigliari Bros. Funeral Chapels
YOU READY FOR THIS? THIS IS THE BIG ONE. YOU'VE NEVER MET THE BULK OF MY EXTENDED FAMILY, SO BE PREPARED. THIS IS GOING TO BE A REAL ENDURANCE TEST. YOU GONNA BE OKAY?
I SHOULD BE ASKING YOU THAT. THIS IS YOUR GRANDFATHER'S FUNERAL, AFTER ALL.
I KNOW, BUT HE WAS NINETY-TWO. HE WAS ILL FOR QUITE AWHILE. I'LL BE OKAY. LET'S GO IN.

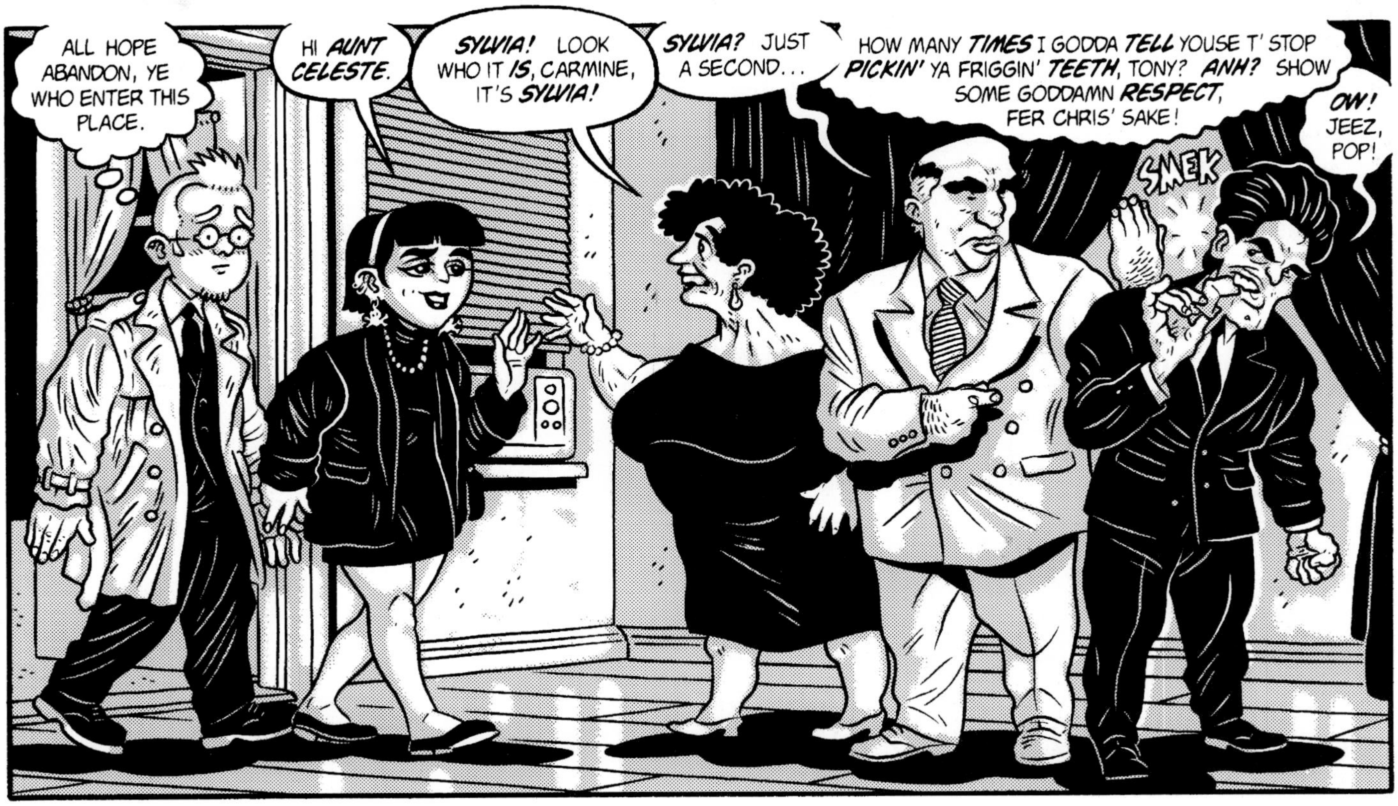
ALL HOPE ABANDON, YE WHO ENTER THIS PLACE.
HI AUNT CELESTE.
SYLVIA! LOOK WHO IT IS, CARMINE, IT'S SYLVIA!
SYLVIA? JUST A SECOND...
HOW MANY TIMES I GODDA TELL YOUSE T' STOP PICKIN' YA FRIGGIN' TEETH, TONY? ANH? SHOW SOME GODDAMN RESPECT, FER CHRIS' SAKE!
SMEK
OW! JEEZ, POP!

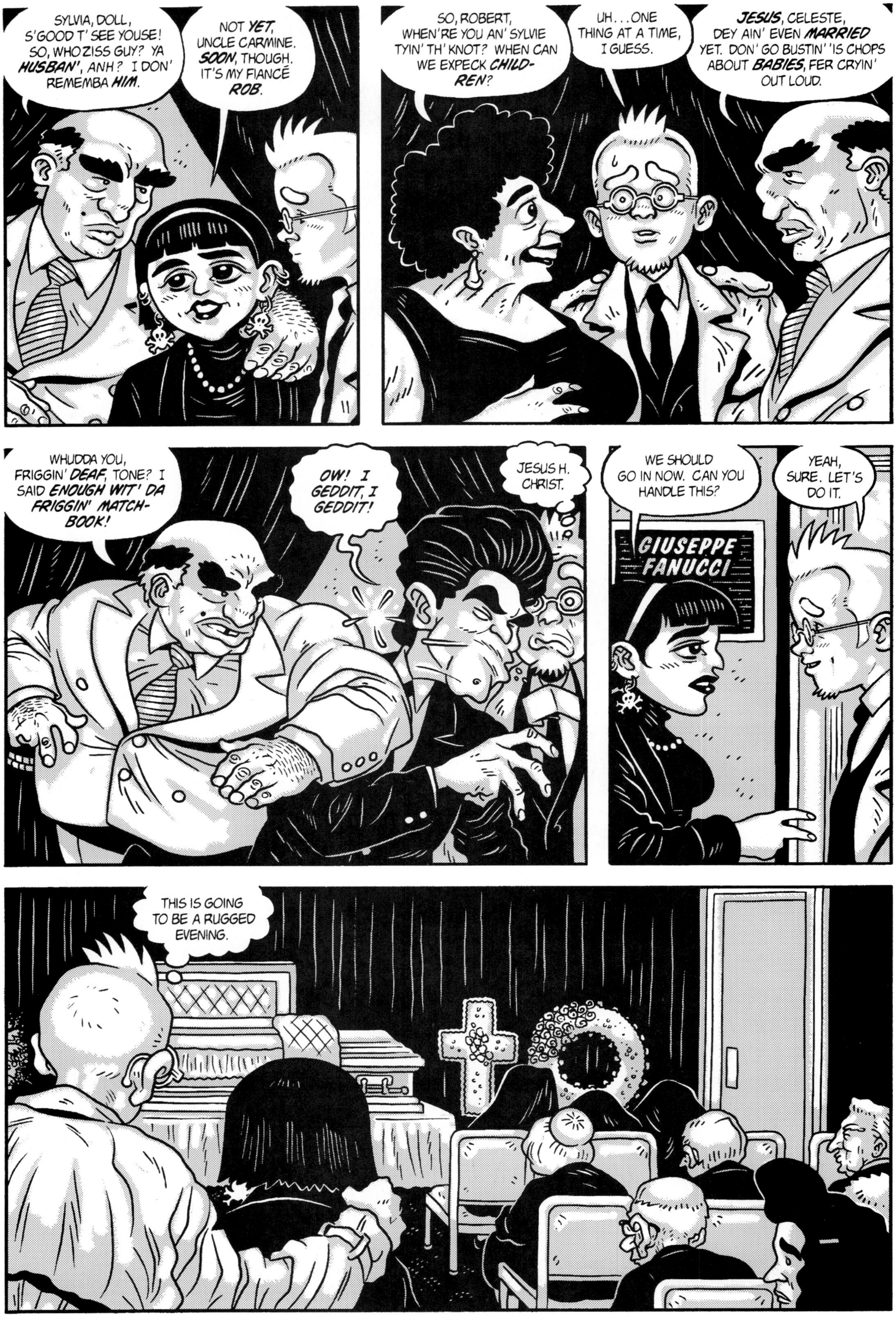
SYLVIA, DOLL, S'GOOD T' SEE YOUSE! SO, WHO ZISS GUY? YA HUSBAN', ANH? I DON' REMEMBA HIM.
NOT YET, UNCLE CARMINE. SOON, THOUGH. IT'S MY FIANCÉ ROB.
SO, ROBERT, WHEN'RE YOU AN' SYLVIE TYIN' TH' KNOT? WHEN CAN WE EXPECK CHILDREN?
UH...ONE THING AT A TIME, I GUESS.
JESUS, CELESTE, DEY AIN' EVEN MARRIED YET. DON' GO BUSTIN' 'IS CHOPS ABOUT BABIES, FER CRYIN' OUT LOUD.
WHUDDA YOU, FRIGGIN' DEAF, TONE? I SAID ENOUGH WIT' DA FRIGGIN' MATCH-BOOK!
OW! I GEDDIT, I GEDDIT!
JESUS H. CHRIST.
WE SHOULD GO IN NOW. CAN YOU HANDLE THIS?
GIUSEPPE FANUCCI
YEAH, SURE. LET'S DO IT.
THIS IS GOING TO BE A RUGGED EVENING.

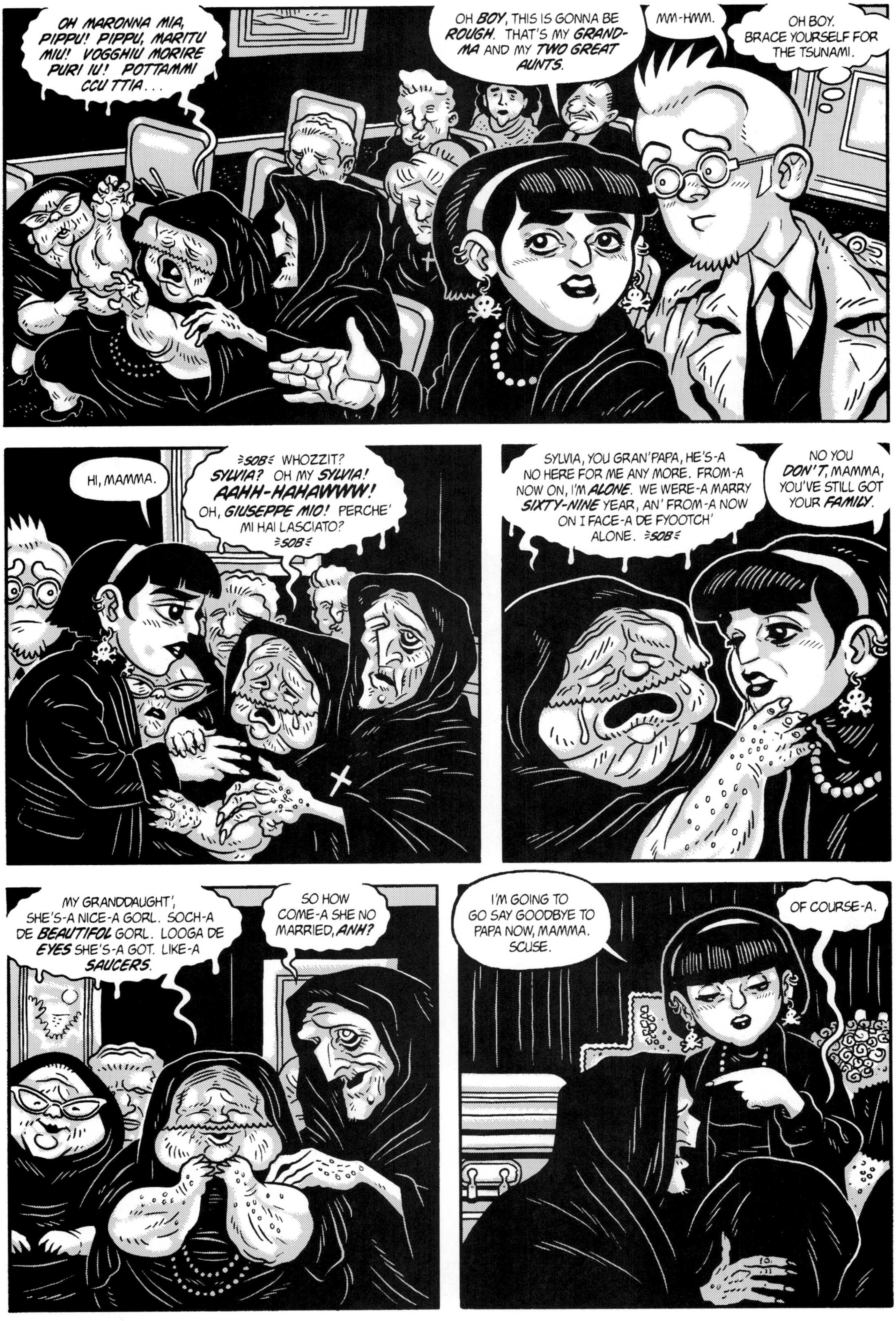
OH MARONNA MIA, PIPPU! PIPPU, MARITU MIU! VOGGHIU MORIRE PURI IU! POTTAMMI CCU TTIA...
OH BOY, THIS IS GONNA BE ROUGH. THAT'S MY GRANDMA AND MY TWO GREAT AUNTS.
MM-HMM.
OH BOY. BRACE YOURSELF FOR THE TSUNAMI.
HI, MAMMA.
SOB WHOZZIT? SYLVIA? OH MY SYLVIA! AAHH-HAHAWWW! OH, GIUSEPPE MIO! PERCHE' MI HAI LASCIATO? SOB
SYLVIA, YOU GRAN'PAPA, HE'S-A NO HERE FOR ME ANY MORE. FROM-A NOW ON, I'M ALONE. WE WERE-A MARRY SIXTY-NINE YEAR, AN' FROM-A NOW ON I FACE-A DE FYOOTCH' ALONE. SOB
NO YOU DON'T, MAMMA, YOU'VE STILL GOT YOUR FAMILY.
MY GRANDDAUGHT', SHE'S-A NICE-A GORL. SOCH-A DE BEAUTIFOL GORL. LOOGA DE EYES SHE'S-A GOT. LIKE-A SAUCERS.
SO HOW COME-A SHE NO MARRIED, ANH?
I'M GOING TO GO SAY GOODBYE TO PAPA NOW, MAMMA. SCUSE.
OF COURSE-A.

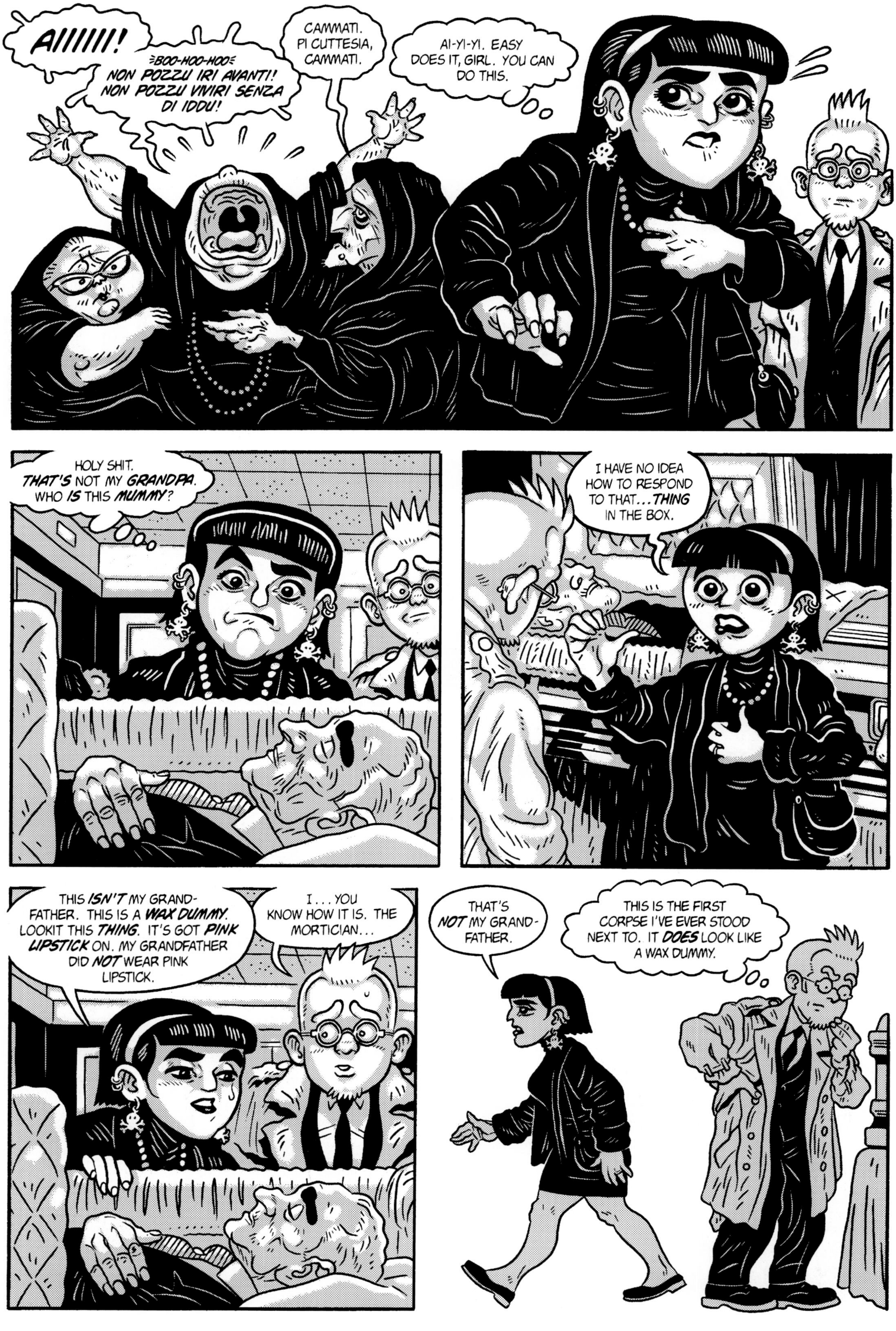
AIIIIII!
BOO-HOO-HOO
NON POZZU IRI AVANTI! NON POZZU VIVIRI SENZA DI IDDU!
CAMMATI. PI CUTTESIA, CAMMATI.
AI-YI-YI. EASY DOES IT, GIRL. YOU CAN DO THIS.
HOLY SHIT. THAT'S NOT MY GRANDPA. WHO IS THIS MUMMY?
I HAVE NO IDEA HOW TO RESPOND TO THAT...THING IN THE BOX.
THIS ISN'T MY GRAND-FATHER. THIS IS A WAX DUMMY. LOOKIT THIS THING. IT'S GOT PINK LIPSTICK ON. MY GRANDFATHER DID NOT WEAR PINK LIPSTICK.
I... YOU KNOW HOW IT IS. THE MORTICIAN...
THAT'S NOT MY GRAND-FATHER.
THIS IS THE FIRST CORPSE I'VE EVER STOOD NEXT TO. IT DOES LOOK LIKE A WAX DUMMY.

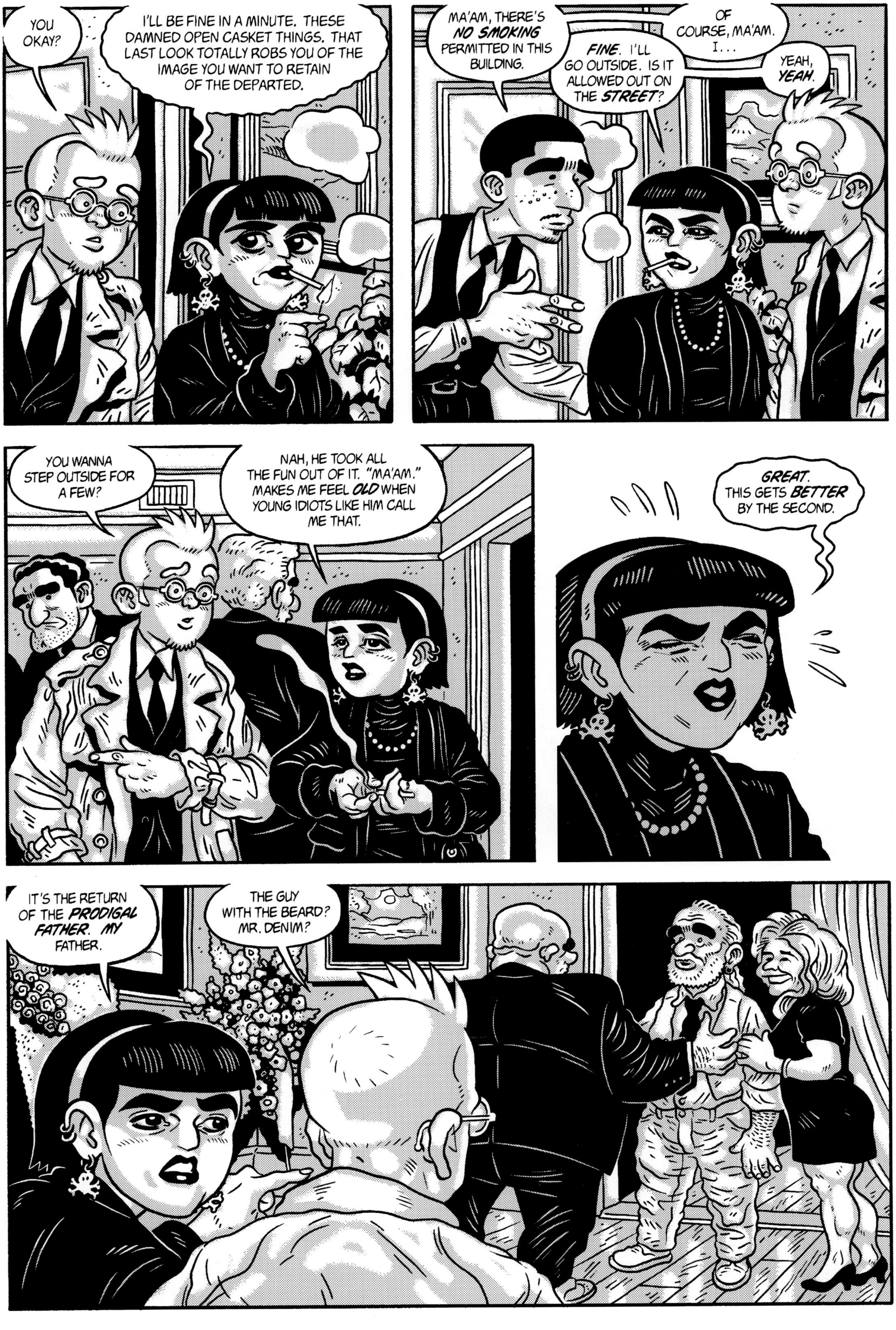
YOU OKAY?
I'LL BE FINE IN A MINUTE. THESE DAMNED OPEN CASKET THINGS. THAT LAST LOOK TOTALLY ROBS YOU OF THE IMAGE YOU WANT TO RETAIN OF THE DEPARTED.
MA'AM, THERE'S NO SMOKING PERMITTED IN THIS BUILDING.
FINE. I'LL GO OUTSIDE. IS IT ALLOWED OUT ON THE STREET?
OF COURSE, MA'AM. I...
YEAH, YEAH.
YOU WANNA STEP OUTSIDE FOR A FEW?
NAH, HE TOOK ALL THE FUN OUT OF IT. "MA'AM." MAKES ME FEEL OLD WHEN YOUNG IDIOTS LIKE HIM CALL ME THAT.
GREAT. THIS GETS BETTER BY THE SECOND.
IT'S THE RETURN OF THE PRODIGAL FATHER. MY FATHER.
THE GUY WITH THE BEARD? MR. DENIM?

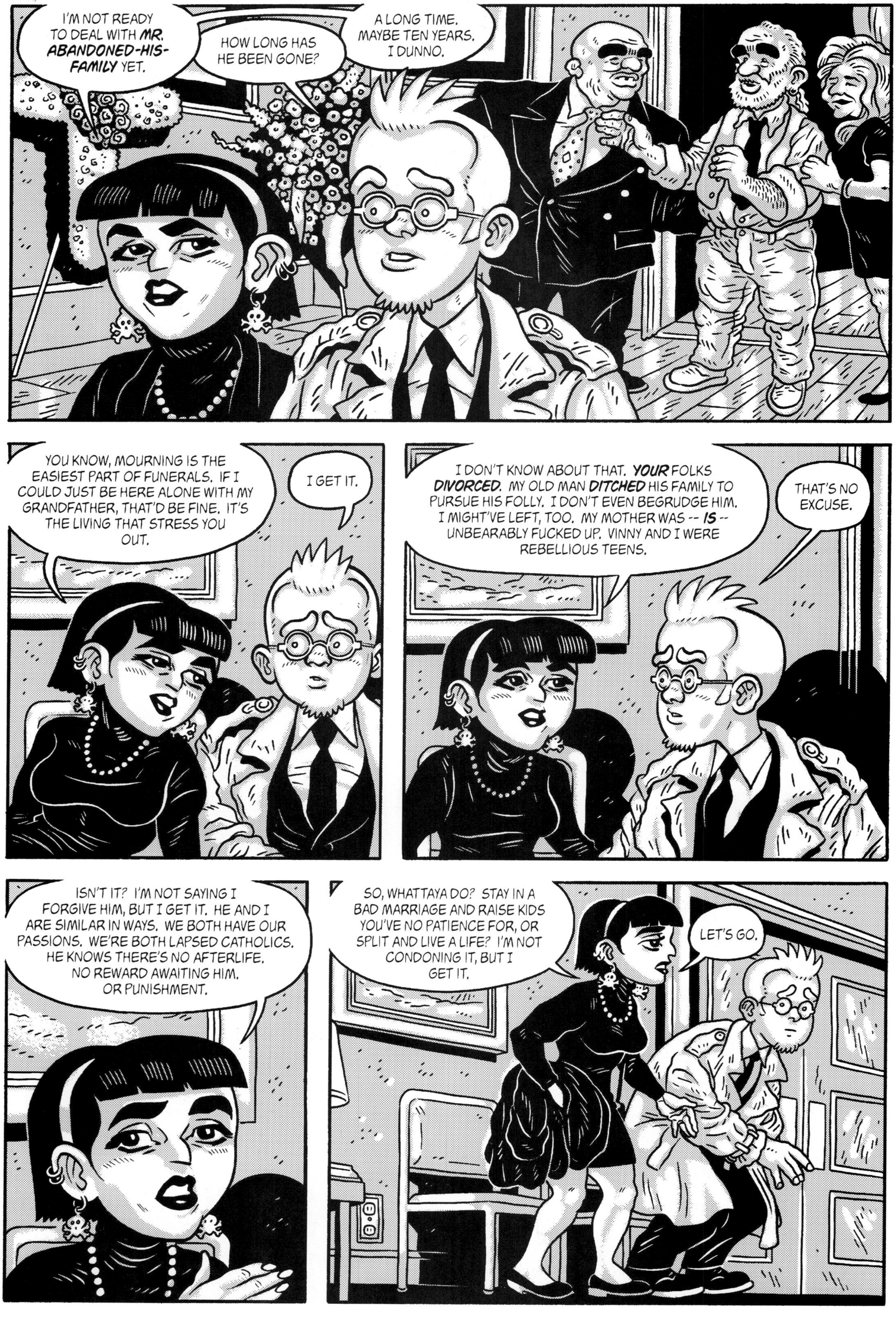

I'M NOT READY TO DEAL WITH MR. ABANDONED-HIS-FAMILY YET.
HOW LONG HAS HE BEEN GONE?
A LONG TIME. MAYBE TEN YEARS. I DUNNO.
YOU KNOW, MOURNING IS THE EASIEST PART OF FUNERALS. IF I COULD JUST BE HERE ALONE WITH MY GRANDFATHER, THAT'D BE FINE. IT'S THE LIVING THAT STRESS YOU OUT.
I GET IT.
I DON'T KNOW ABOUT THAT. YOUR FOLKS DIVORCED. MY OLD MAN DITCHED HIS FAMILY TO PURSUE HIS FOLLY. I DON'T EVEN BEGRUDGE HIM. I MIGHT'VE LEFT, TOO. MY MOTHER WAS -- IS -- UNBEARABLY FUCKED UP. VINNY AND I WERE REBELLIOUS TEENS.
THAT'S NO EXCUSE.
ISN'T IT? I'M NOT SAYING I FORGIVE HIM, BUT I GET IT. HE AND I ARE SIMILAR IN WAYS. WE BOTH HAVE OUR PASSIONS. WE'RE BOTH LAPSED CATHOLICS. HE KNOWS THERE'S NO AFTERLIFE. NO REWARD AWAITING HIM. OR PUNISHMENT.
SO, WHATTAYA DO? STAY IN A BAD MARRIAGE AND RAISE KIDS YOU'VE NO PATIENCE FOR, OR SPLIT AND LIVE A LIFE? I'M NOT CONDONING IT, BUT I GET IT.
LET'S GO.

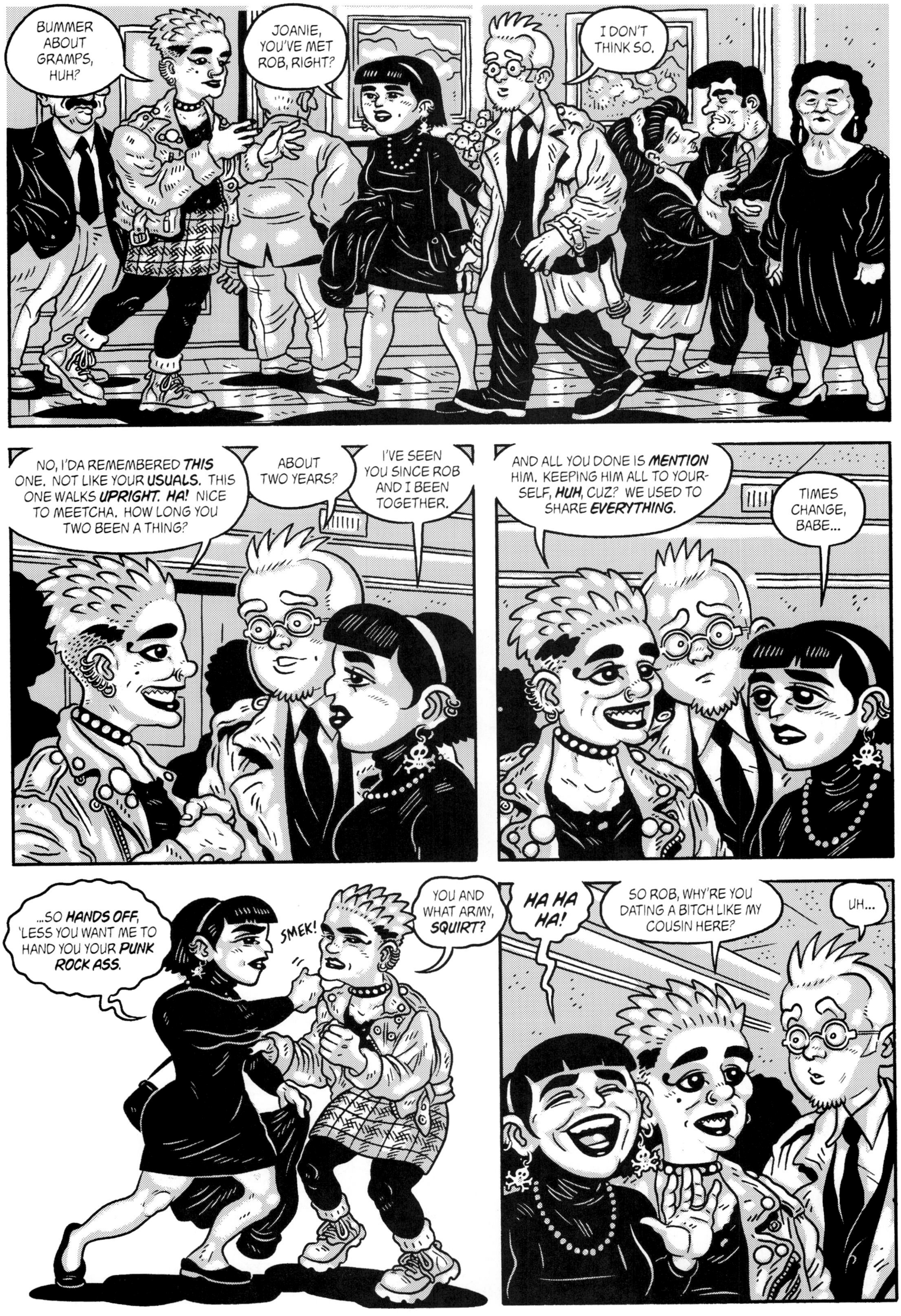

BUMMER ABOUT GRAMPS, HUH?
JOANIE, YOU'VE MET ROB, RIGHT?
I DON'T THINK SO.
NO, I'DA REMEMBERED **THIS** ONE. NOT LIKE YOUR **USUALS**. THIS ONE WALKS **UPRIGHT**. **HA!** NICE TO MEETCHA. HOW LONG YOU TWO BEEN A THING?
ABOUT TWO YEARS?
I'VE SEEN YOU SINCE ROB AND I BEEN TOGETHER.
AND ALL YOU DONE IS **MENTION** HIM. KEEPING HIM ALL TO YOURSELF, **HUH**, CUZ? WE USED TO SHARE **EVERYTHING**.
TIMES CHANGE, BABE...
...SO **HANDS OFF**, 'LESS YOU WANT ME TO HAND YOU YOUR **PUNK ROCK ASS**.
SMEK!
YOU AND WHAT ARMY, **SQUIRT**?
HA HA HA!
SO ROB, WHY'RE YOU DATING A BITCH LIKE MY COUSIN HERE?
UH...

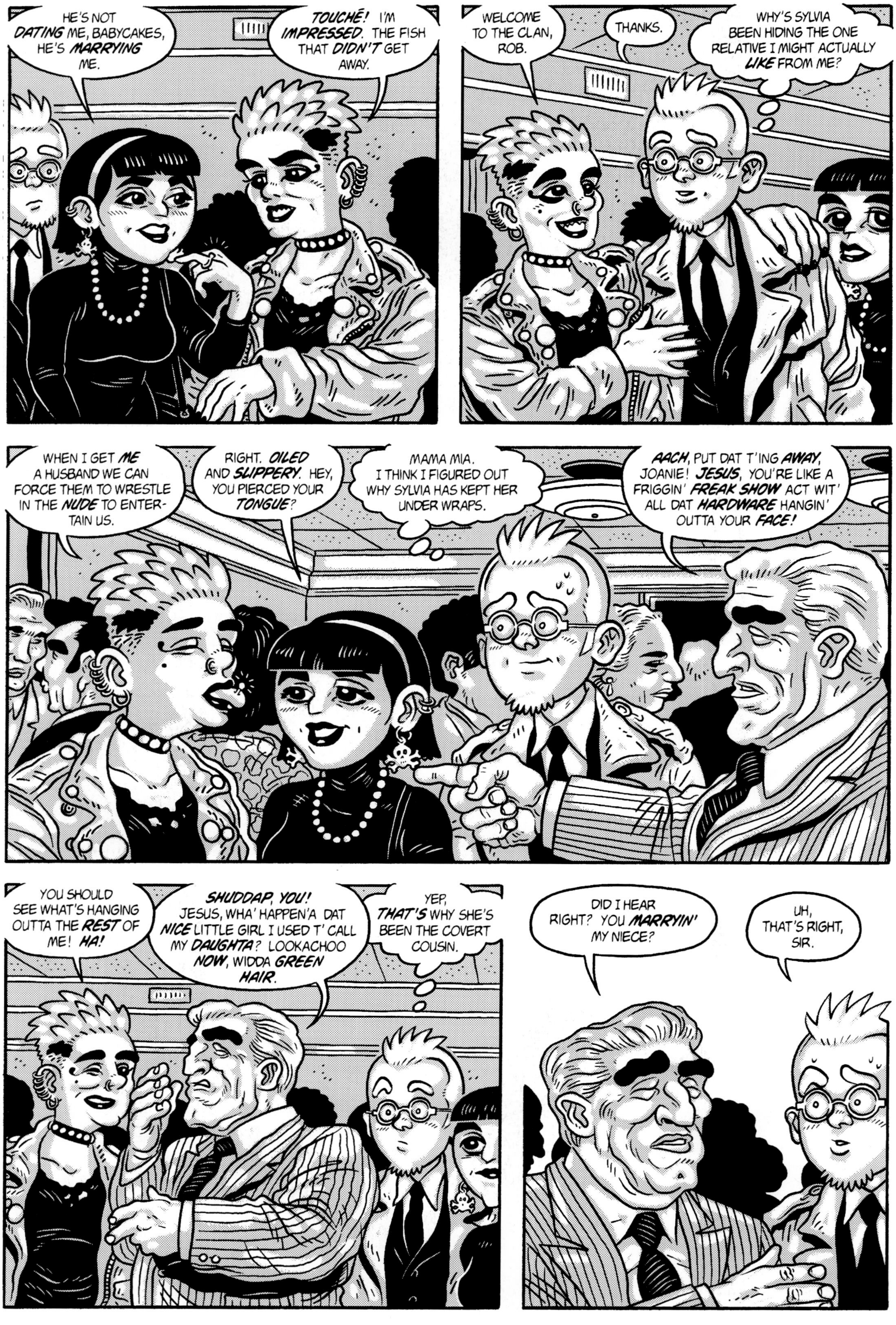
HE'S NOT DATING ME, BABYCAKES, HE'S MARRYING ME.
TOUCHÉ! I'M IMPRESSED. THE FISH THAT DIDN'T GET AWAY.
WELCOME TO THE CLAN, ROB.
THANKS.
WHY'S SYLVIA BEEN HIDING THE ONE RELATIVE I MIGHT ACTUALLY LIKE FROM ME?
WHEN I GET ME A HUSBAND WE CAN FORCE THEM TO WRESTLE IN THE NUDE TO ENTERTAIN US.
RIGHT. OILED AND SLIPPERY. HEY, YOU PIERCED YOUR TONGUE?
MAMA MIA. I THINK I FIGURED OUT WHY SYLVIA HAS KEPT HER UNDER WRAPS.
AACH, PUT DAT T'ING AWAY, JOANIE! JESUS, YOU'RE LIKE A FRIGGIN' FREAK SHOW ACT WIT' ALL DAT HARDWARE HANGIN' OUTTA YOUR FACE!
YOU SHOULD SEE WHAT'S HANGING OUTTA THE REST OF ME! HA!
SHUDDAP, YOU! JESUS, WHA' HAPPEN'A DAT NICE LITTLE GIRL I USED T' CALL MY DAUGHTA? LOOKACHOO NOW, WIDDA GREEN HAIR.
YEP, THAT'S WHY SHE'S BEEN THE COVERT COUSIN.
DID I HEAR RIGHT? YOU MARRYIN' MY NIECE?
UH, THAT'S RIGHT, SIR.

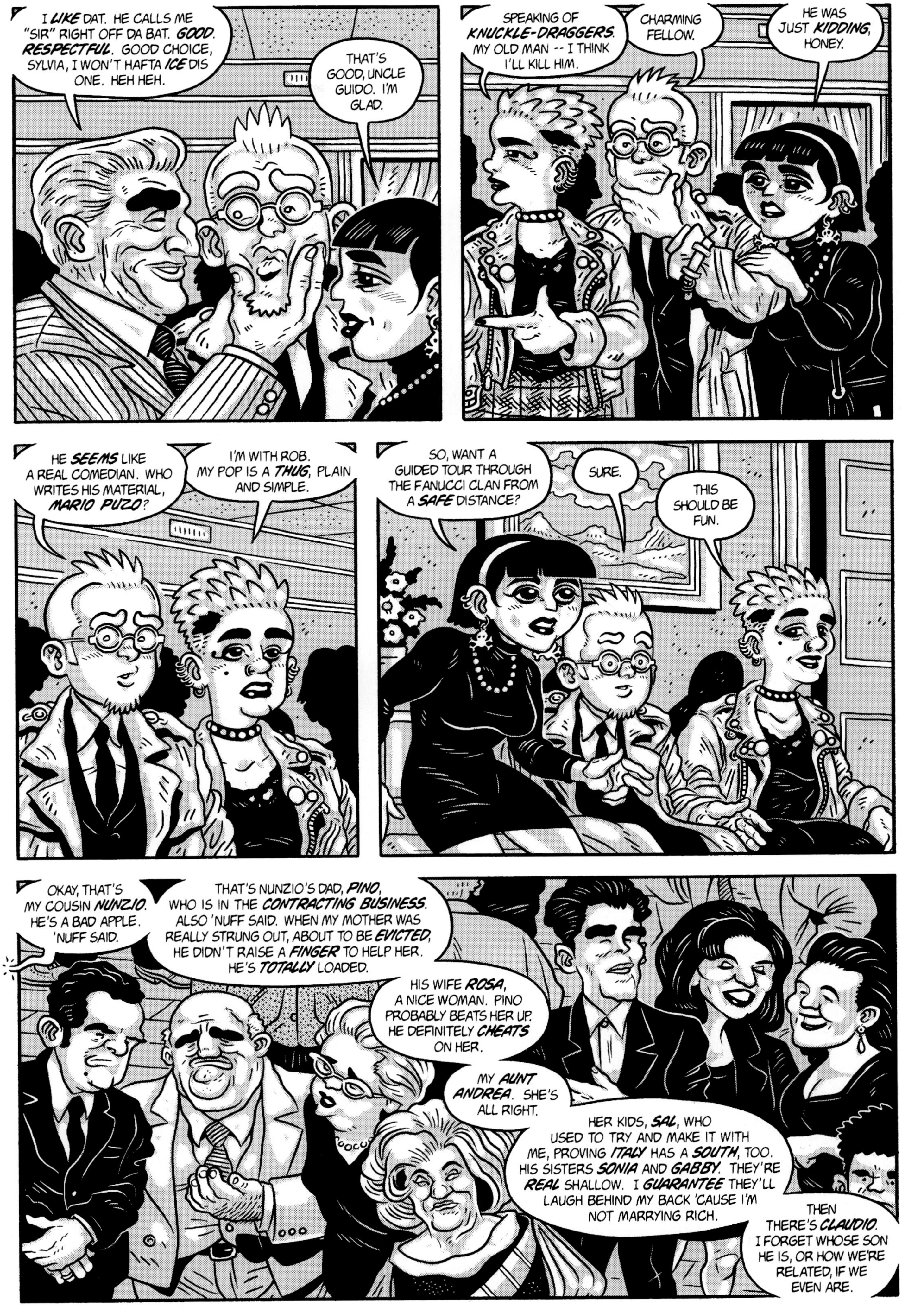
I LIKE DAT. HE CALLS ME "SIR" RIGHT OFF DA BAT. GOOD. RESPECTFUL. GOOD CHOICE, SYLVIA, I WON'T HAFTA ICE DIS ONE. HEH HEH.
THAT'S GOOD, UNCLE GUIDO. I'M GLAD.
SPEAKING OF KNUCKLE-DRAGGERS. MY OLD MAN -- I THINK I'LL KILL HIM.
CHARMING FELLOW.
HE WAS JUST KIDDING, HONEY.
HE SEEMS LIKE A REAL COMEDIAN. WHO WRITES HIS MATERIAL, MARIO PUZO?
I'M WITH ROB. MY POP IS A THUG, PLAIN AND SIMPLE.
SO, WANT A GUIDED TOUR THROUGH THE FANUCCI CLAN FROM A SAFE DISTANCE?
SURE.
THIS SHOULD BE FUN.
OKAY, THAT'S MY COUSIN NUNZIO. HE'S A BAD APPLE. 'NUFF SAID.
THAT'S NUNZIO'S DAD, PINO, WHO IS IN THE CONTRACTING BUSINESS. ALSO 'NUFF SAID. WHEN MY MOTHER WAS REALLY STRUNG OUT, ABOUT TO BE EVICTED, HE DIDN'T RAISE A FINGER TO HELP HER. HE'S TOTALLY LOADED.
HIS WIFE ROSA, A NICE WOMAN. PINO PROBABLY BEATS HER UP. HE DEFINITELY CHEATS ON HER.
MY AUNT ANDREA. SHE'S ALL RIGHT.
HER KIDS, SAL, WHO USED TO TRY AND MAKE IT WITH ME, PROVING ITALY HAS A SOUTH, TOO. HIS SISTERS SONIA AND GABBY. THEY'RE REAL SHALLOW. I GUARANTEE THEY'LL LAUGH BEHIND MY BACK 'CAUSE I'M NOT MARRYING RICH.
THEN THERE'S CLAUDIO. I FORGET WHOSE SON HE IS, OR HOW WE'RE RELATED, IF WE EVEN ARE.

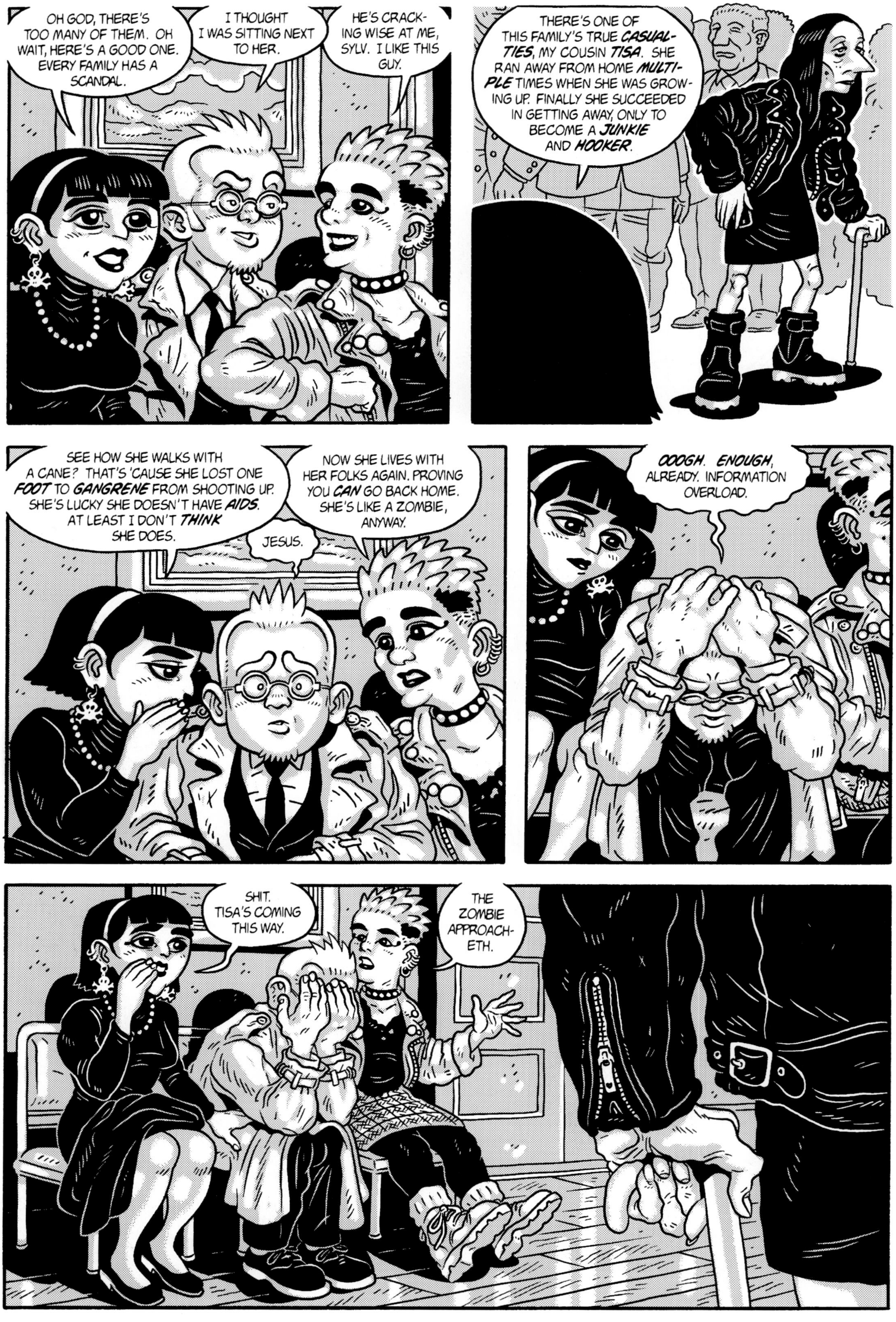
OH GOD, THERE'S TOO MANY OF THEM. OH WAIT, HERE'S A GOOD ONE. EVERY FAMILY HAS A SCANDAL.
I THOUGHT I WAS SITTING NEXT TO HER.
HE'S CRACKING WISE AT ME, SYLV. I LIKE THIS GUY.
THERE'S ONE OF THIS FAMILY'S TRUE CASUALTIES, MY COUSIN TISA. SHE RAN AWAY FROM HOME MULTIPLE TIMES WHEN SHE WAS GROWING UP. FINALLY SHE SUCCEEDED IN GETTING AWAY, ONLY TO BECOME A JUNKIE AND HOOKER.
SEE HOW SHE WALKS WITH A CANE? THAT'S 'CAUSE SHE LOST ONE FOOT TO GANGRENE FROM SHOOTING UP. SHE'S LUCKY SHE DOESN'T HAVE AIDS. AT LEAST I DON'T THINK SHE DOES.
JESUS.
NOW SHE LIVES WITH HER FOLKS AGAIN. PROVING YOU CAN GO BACK HOME. SHE'S LIKE A ZOMBIE, ANYWAY.
OOOGH. ENOUGH, ALREADY. INFORMATION OVERLOAD.
SHIT. TISA'S COMING THIS WAY.
THE ZOMBIE APPROACHETH.

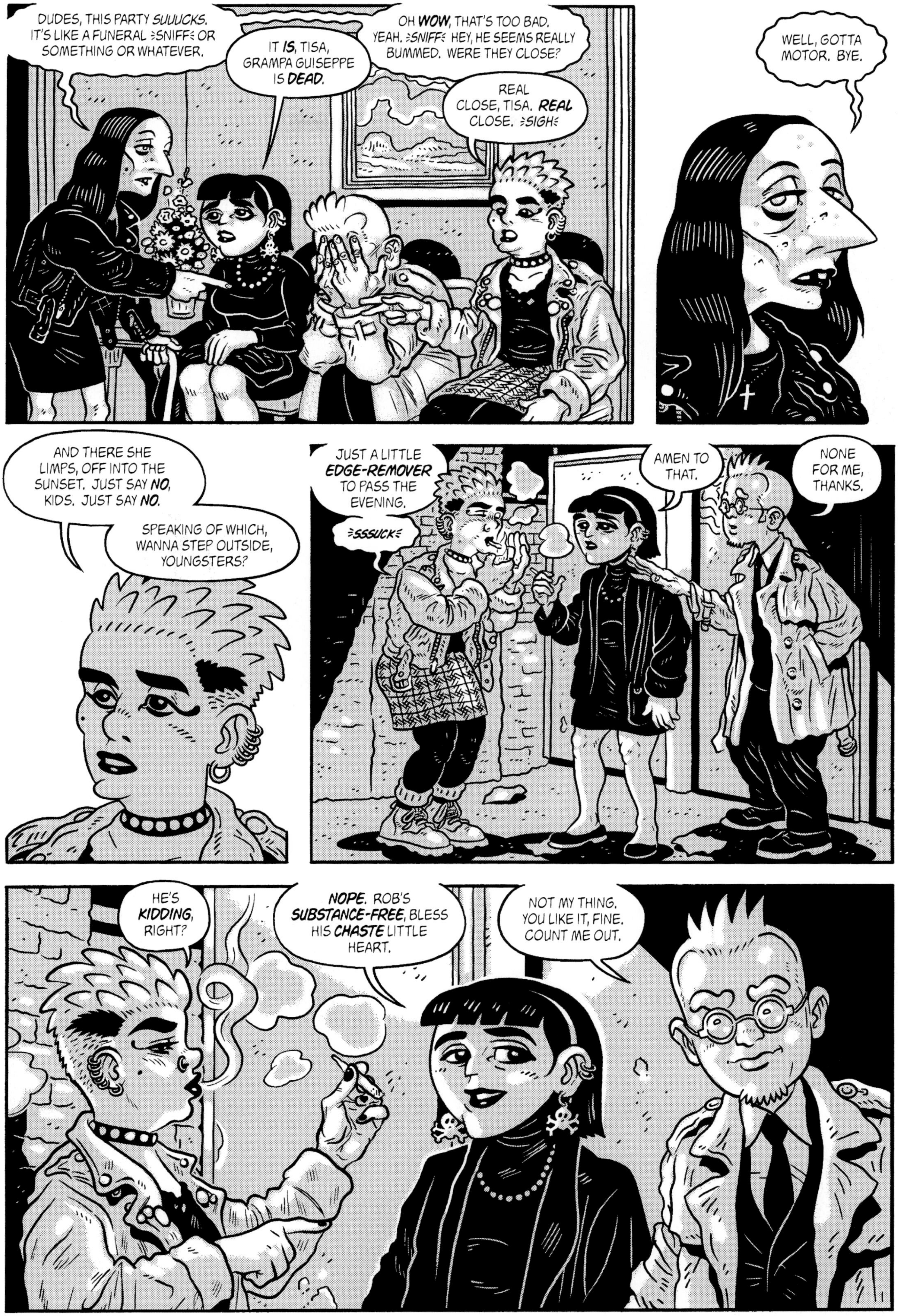
DUDES, THIS PARTY SUUUCKS. IT'S LIKE A FUNERAL ≷SNIFF≶ OR SOMETHING OR WHATEVER.
IT IS, TISA, GRAMPA GUISEPPE IS DEAD.
OH WOW, THAT'S TOO BAD. YEAH. ≷SNIFF≶ HEY, HE SEEMS REALLY BUMMED. WERE THEY CLOSE?
REAL CLOSE, TISA. REAL CLOSE. ≷SIGH≶
WELL, GOTTA MOTOR. BYE.
AND THERE SHE LIMPS, OFF INTO THE SUNSET. JUST SAY NO, KIDS. JUST SAY NO.
SPEAKING OF WHICH, WANNA STEP OUTSIDE, YOUNGSTERS?
JUST A LITTLE EDGE-REMOVER TO PASS THE EVENING.
≷SSSUCK≶
AMEN TO THAT.
NONE FOR ME, THANKS.
HE'S KIDDING, RIGHT?
NOPE. ROB'S SUBSTANCE-FREE, BLESS HIS CHASTE LITTLE HEART.
NOT MY THING. YOU LIKE IT, FINE. COUNT ME OUT.

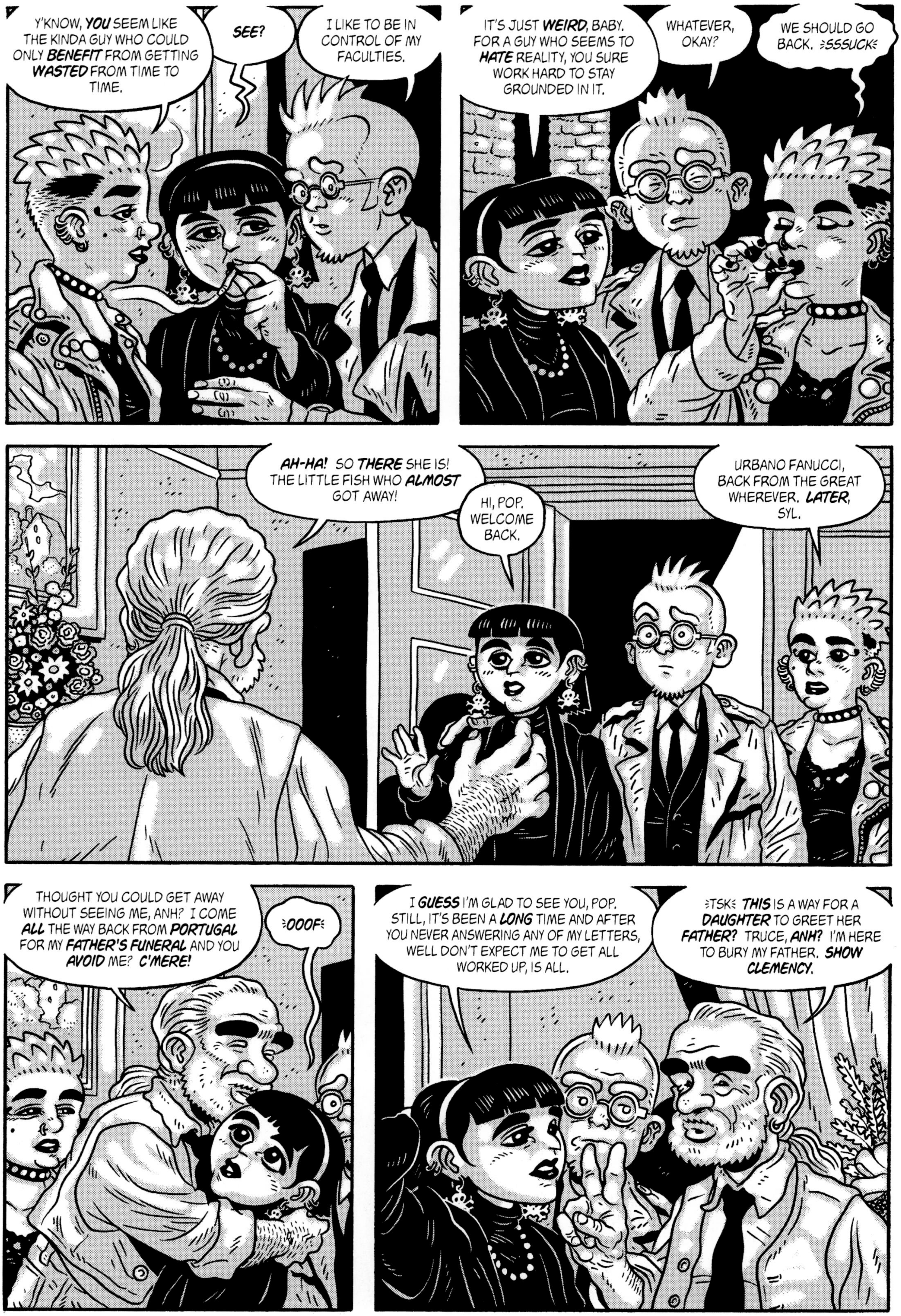
Y'KNOW, YOU SEEM LIKE THE KINDA GUY WHO COULD ONLY BENEFIT FROM GETTING WASTED FROM TIME TO TIME.
SEE?
I LIKE TO BE IN CONTROL OF MY FACULTIES.
IT'S JUST WEIRD, BABY. FOR A GUY WHO SEEMS TO HATE REALITY, YOU SURE WORK HARD TO STAY GROUNDED IN IT.
WHATEVER, OKAY?
WE SHOULD GO BACK. SSSUCK
AH-HA! SO THERE SHE IS! THE LITTLE FISH WHO ALMOST GOT AWAY!
HI, POP. WELCOME BACK.
URBANO FANUCCI, BACK FROM THE GREAT WHEREVER. LATER, SYL.
THOUGHT YOU COULD GET AWAY WITHOUT SEEING ME, ANH? I COME ALL THE WAY BACK FROM PORTUGAL FOR MY FATHER'S FUNERAL AND YOU AVOID ME? C'MERE!
OOOF
I GUESS I'M GLAD TO SEE YOU, POP. STILL, IT'S BEEN A LONG TIME AND AFTER YOU NEVER ANSWERING ANY OF MY LETTERS, WELL DON'T EXPECT ME TO GET ALL WORKED UP, IS ALL.
TSK THIS IS A WAY FOR A DAUGHTER TO GREET HER FATHER? TRUCE, ANH? I'M HERE TO BURY MY FATHER. SHOW CLEMENCY.

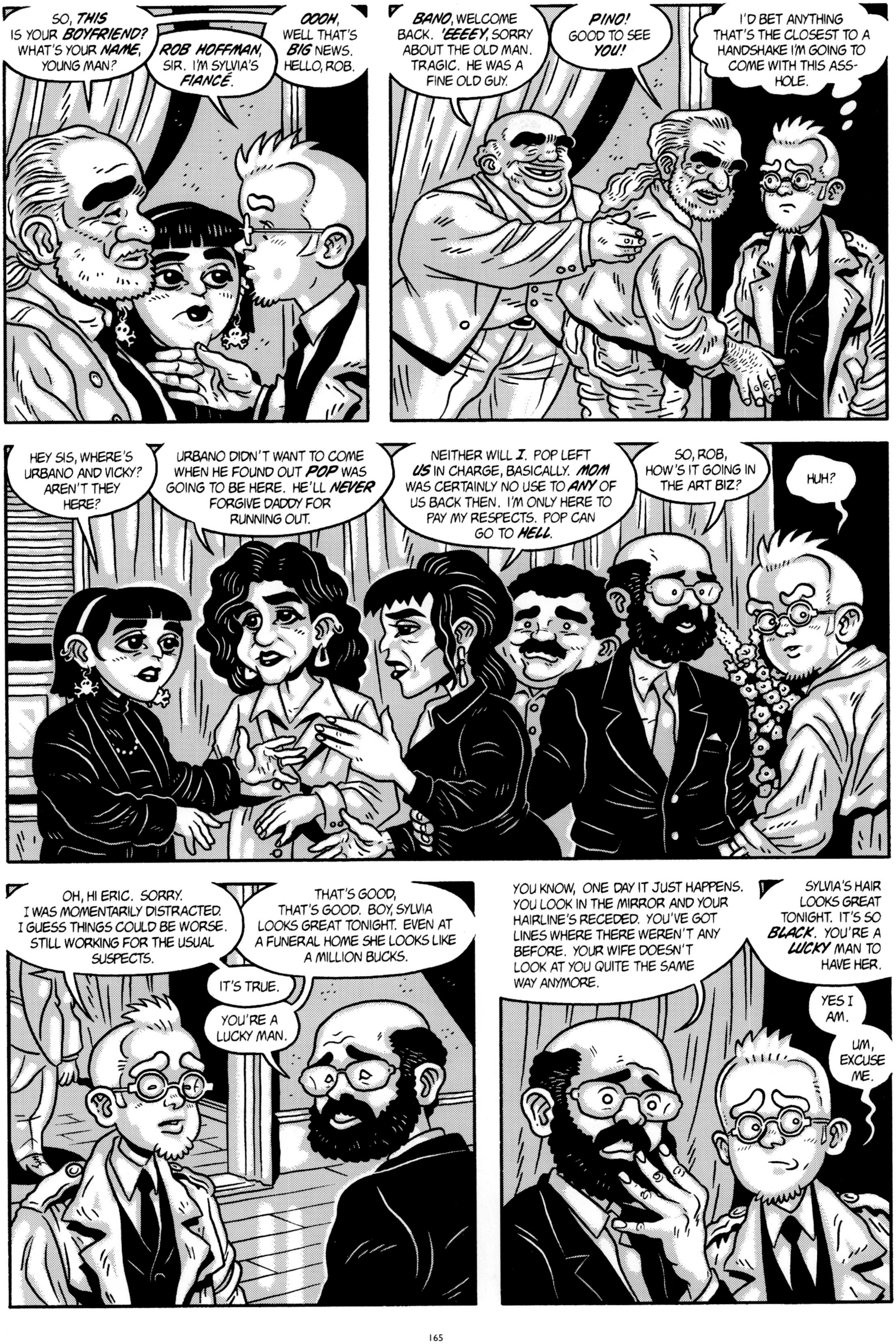

SO, THIS IS YOUR BOYFRIEND? WHAT'S YOUR NAME, YOUNG MAN?
ROB HOFFMAN, SIR. I'M SYLVIA'S FIANCÉ.
OOOH, WELL THAT'S BIG NEWS. HELLO, ROB.
BANO, WELCOME BACK. 'EEEEY, SORRY ABOUT THE OLD MAN. TRAGIC. HE WAS A FINE OLD GUY.
PINO! GOOD TO SEE YOU!
I'D BET ANYTHING THAT'S THE CLOSEST TO A HANDSHAKE I'M GOING TO COME WITH THIS ASS-HOLE.
HEY SIS, WHERE'S URBANO AND VICKY? AREN'T THEY HERE?
URBANO DIDN'T WANT TO COME WHEN HE FOUND OUT POP WAS GOING TO BE HERE. HE'LL NEVER FORGIVE DADDY FOR RUNNING OUT.
NEITHER WILL I. POP LEFT US IN CHARGE, BASICALLY. MOM WAS CERTAINLY NO USE TO ANY OF US BACK THEN. I'M ONLY HERE TO PAY MY RESPECTS. POP CAN GO TO HELL.
SO, ROB, HOW'S IT GOING IN THE ART BIZ?
HUH?
OH, HI ERIC. SORRY. I WAS MOMENTARILY DISTRACTED. I GUESS THINGS COULD BE WORSE. STILL WORKING FOR THE USUAL SUSPECTS.
THAT'S GOOD, THAT'S GOOD. BOY, SYLVIA LOOKS GREAT TONIGHT. EVEN AT A FUNERAL HOME SHE LOOKS LIKE A MILLION BUCKS.
IT'S TRUE.
YOU'RE A LUCKY MAN.
YOU KNOW, ONE DAY IT JUST HAPPENS. YOU LOOK IN THE MIRROR AND YOUR HAIRLINE'S RECEDED. YOU'VE GOT LINES WHERE THERE WEREN'T ANY BEFORE. YOUR WIFE DOESN'T LOOK AT YOU QUITE THE SAME WAY ANYMORE.
SYLVIA'S HAIR LOOKS GREAT TONIGHT. IT'S SO BLACK. YOU'RE A LUCKY MAN TO HAVE HER.
YES I AM.
UM, EXCUSE ME.

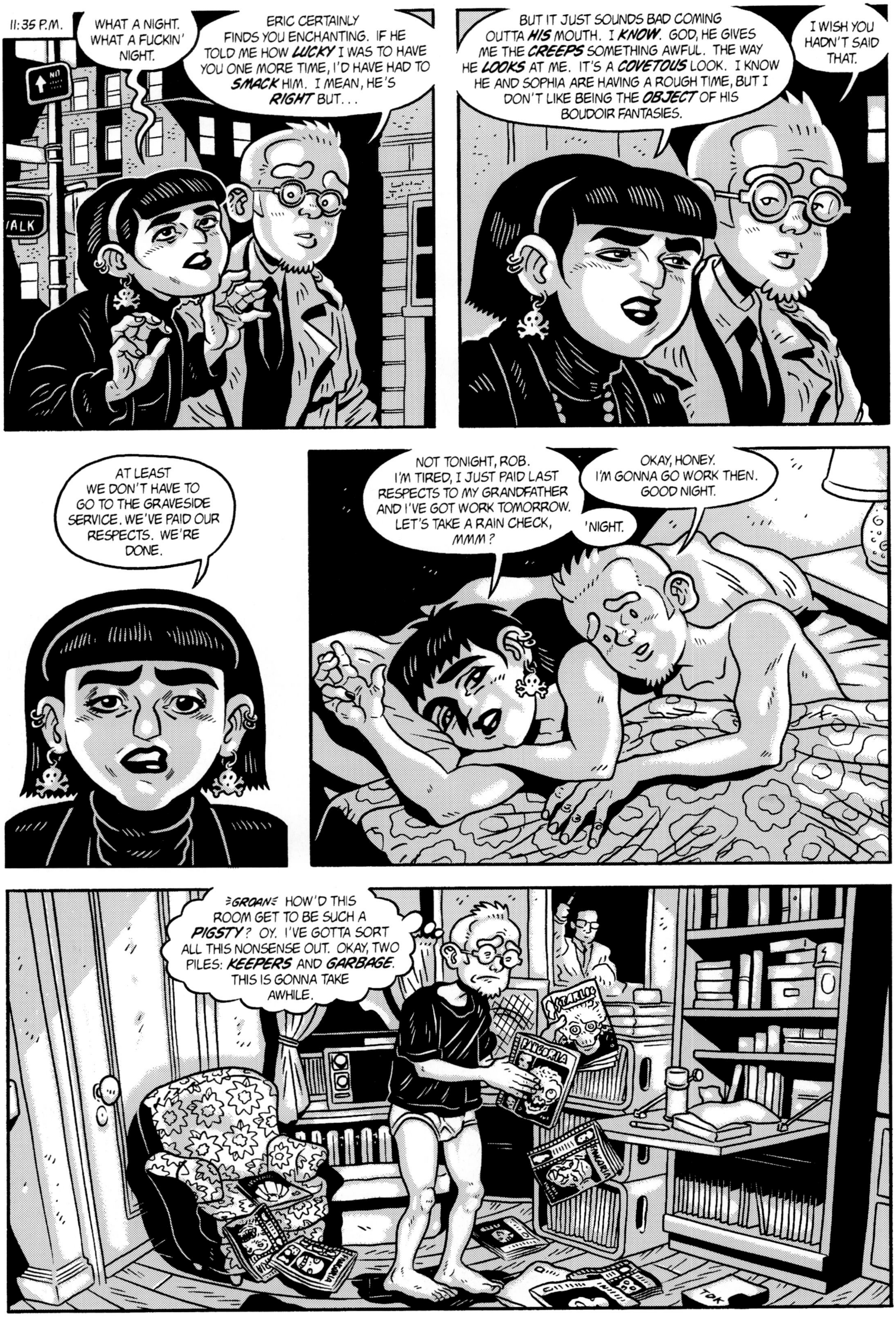
11:35 P.M.
WHAT A NIGHT. WHAT A FUCKIN' NIGHT.
ERIC CERTAINLY FINDS YOU ENCHANTING. IF HE TOLD ME HOW LUCKY I WAS TO HAVE YOU ONE MORE TIME, I'D HAVE HAD TO SMACK HIM. I MEAN, HE'S RIGHT BUT...
WALK
BUT IT JUST SOUNDS BAD COMING OUTTA HIS MOUTH. I KNOW. GOD, HE GIVES ME THE CREEPS SOMETHING AWFUL. THE WAY HE LOOKS AT ME. IT'S A COVETOUS LOOK. I KNOW HE AND SOPHIA ARE HAVING A ROUGH TIME, BUT I DON'T LIKE BEING THE OBJECT OF HIS BOUDOIR FANTASIES.
I WISH YOU HADN'T SAID THAT.
AT LEAST WE DON'T HAVE TO GO TO THE GRAVESIDE SERVICE. WE'VE PAID OUR RESPECTS. WE'RE DONE.
NOT TONIGHT, ROB. I'M TIRED, I JUST PAID LAST RESPECTS TO MY GRANDFATHER AND I'VE GOT WORK TOMORROW. LET'S TAKE A RAIN CHECK, MMM?
OKAY, HONEY. I'M GONNA GO WORK THEN. GOOD NIGHT.
'NIGHT.
GROAN HOW'D THIS ROOM GET TO BE SUCH A PIGSTY? OY. I'VE GOTTA SORT ALL THIS NONSENSE OUT. OKAY, TWO PILES: KEEPERS AND GARBAGE. THIS IS GONNA TAKE AWHILE.
STARLOG
FANGORIA
FANGORIA
TOK

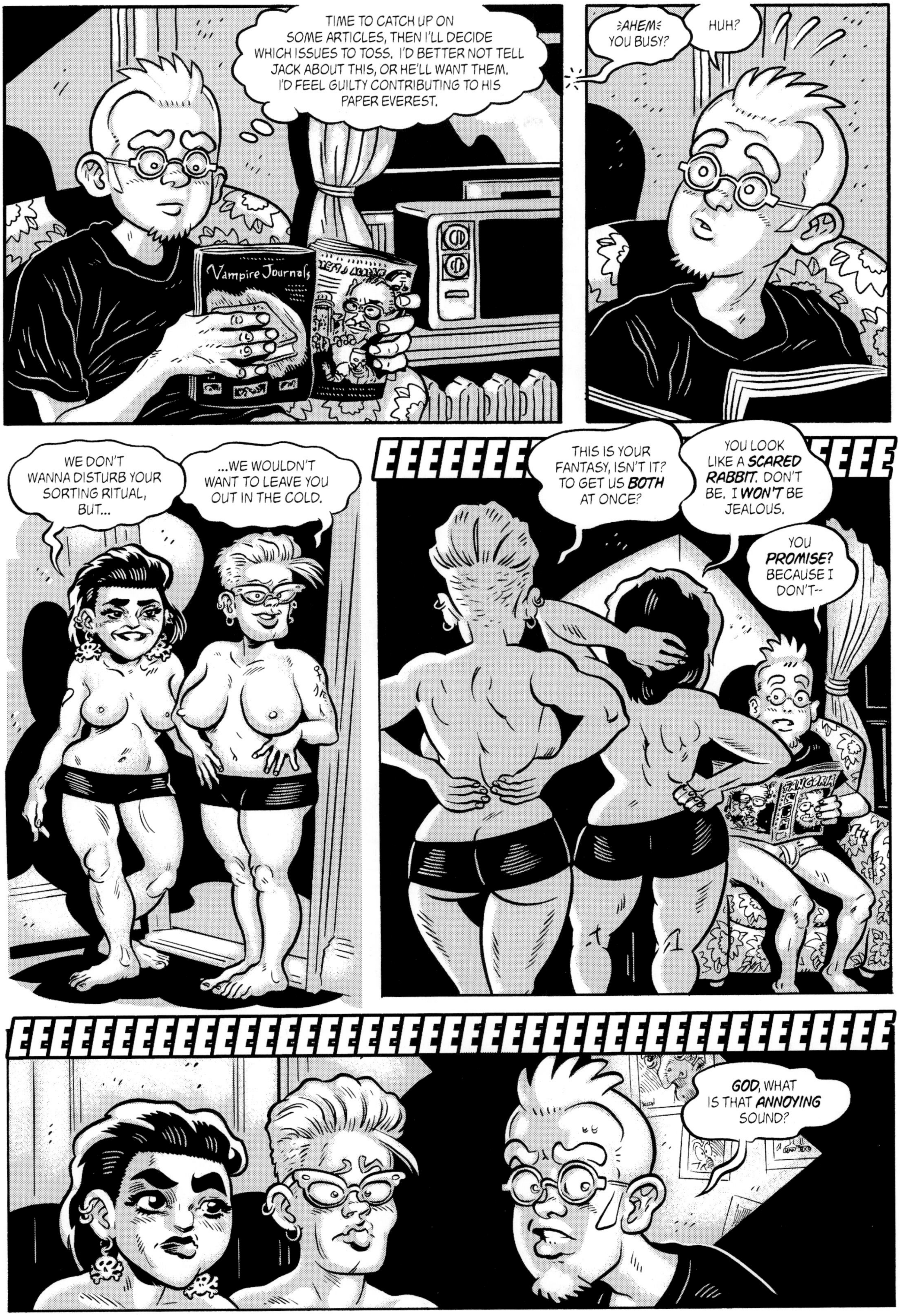
TIME TO CATCH UP ON SOME ARTICLES, THEN I'LL DECIDE WHICH ISSUES TO TOSS. I'D BETTER NOT TELL JACK ABOUT THIS, OR HE'LL WANT THEM. I'D FEEL GUILTY CONTRIBUTING TO HIS PAPER EVEREST.
Vampire Journals
AHEM YOU BUSY?
HUH?
WE DON'T WANNA DISTURB YOUR SORTING RITUAL, BUT...
...WE WOULDN'T WANT TO LEAVE YOU OUT IN THE COLD.
EEEEEEE
EEEE
THIS IS YOUR FANTASY, ISN'T IT? TO GET US **BOTH** AT ONCE?
YOU LOOK LIKE A **SCARED RABBIT**. DON'T BE. I **WON'T** BE JEALOUS.
YOU **PROMISE?** BECAUSE I DON'T--
EEEEEEEEEEEEEEEEEEEEEEEEEEEEEEEEEEEEEE
GOD, WHAT IS THAT **ANNOYING** SOUND?

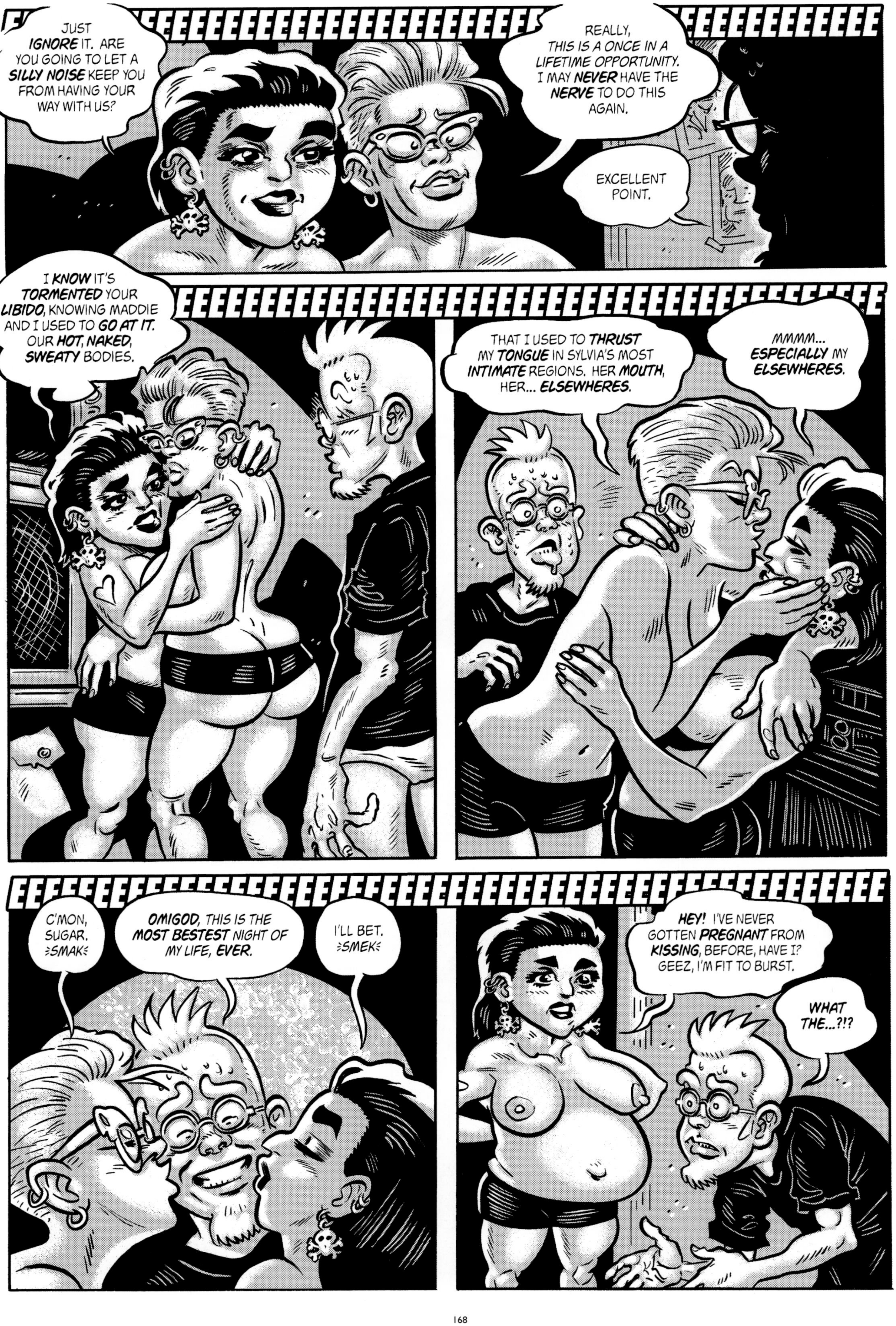

EEEEEEEEEEEEEEEEEEEEEEEEEEEEEEEEEEEEEEEE
JUST IGNORE IT. ARE YOU GOING TO LET A SILLY NOISE KEEP YOU FROM HAVING YOUR WAY WITH US?
REALLY, THIS IS A ONCE IN A LIFETIME OPPORTUNITY. I MAY NEVER HAVE THE NERVE TO DO THIS AGAIN.
EXCELLENT POINT.
EEEEEEEEEEEEEEEEEEEEEEEEEEEEEEEEEEEEEEEE
I KNOW IT'S TORMENTED YOUR LIBIDO, KNOWING MADDIE AND I USED TO GO AT IT. OUR HOT, NAKED, SWEATY BODIES.
THAT I USED TO THRUST MY TONGUE IN SYLVIA'S MOST INTIMATE REGIONS. HER MOUTH, HER... ELSEWHERES.
MMMM... ESPECIALLY MY ELSEWHERES.
EEEEEEEEEEEEEEEEEEEEEEEEEEEEEEEEEEEEEEEE
C'MON, SUGAR. SMAK
OMIGOD, THIS IS THE MOST BESTEST NIGHT OF MY LIFE, EVER.
I'LL BET. SMEK
HEY! I'VE NEVER GOTTEN PREGNANT FROM KISSING, BEFORE, HAVE I? GEEZ, I'M FIT TO BURST.
WHAT THE...?!?

EEEEEEEEEEEEEEEEEEEEEEEEEEEEEEEEEEEEEEEEEEEEEEEEEEEEEEEEEEEEEEEEEE

HUH, ME TOO. THAT'LL TEACH *ME* TO *STRAY* OFF THE *SAPPHIC RESERVATION.* UGH.

YOU CAN ALWAYS *ABORT* IT. HELL, ROB AND I *MURDERED* OUR FIRST PREGNANCY, BUT I'M *KEEPING* THIS ONE.

goo...

goo...

goo...

EEEEEEEEEEEEEEEEEEEEEEEEEEEEEEEEEEEEEEEEEEEEEEEEEEEEEEEEEEEEEEEEEE

MAYBE I *SHOULD* ABORT IT. I DON'T THINK ROB COULD *AFFORD* TO RAISE *TWO* KIDS.

WHAT IF I'M PREGGERS WITH *TWINS?*

ME, TOO.

ROB COULD *NEVER* AFFORD *THAT!*

EEEEEEEEEEEEEEEEEEEEEEEEEEEEEEEEEEEEEEEEEEEEEEEEEEEEEEEEEEEEEEE

HA! HA! HA! HA! HA! HA! HA! HA!

JESUS H. CHRIST, WHAT IS THAT FUCKING *HORRIBLE* SOUND?!?

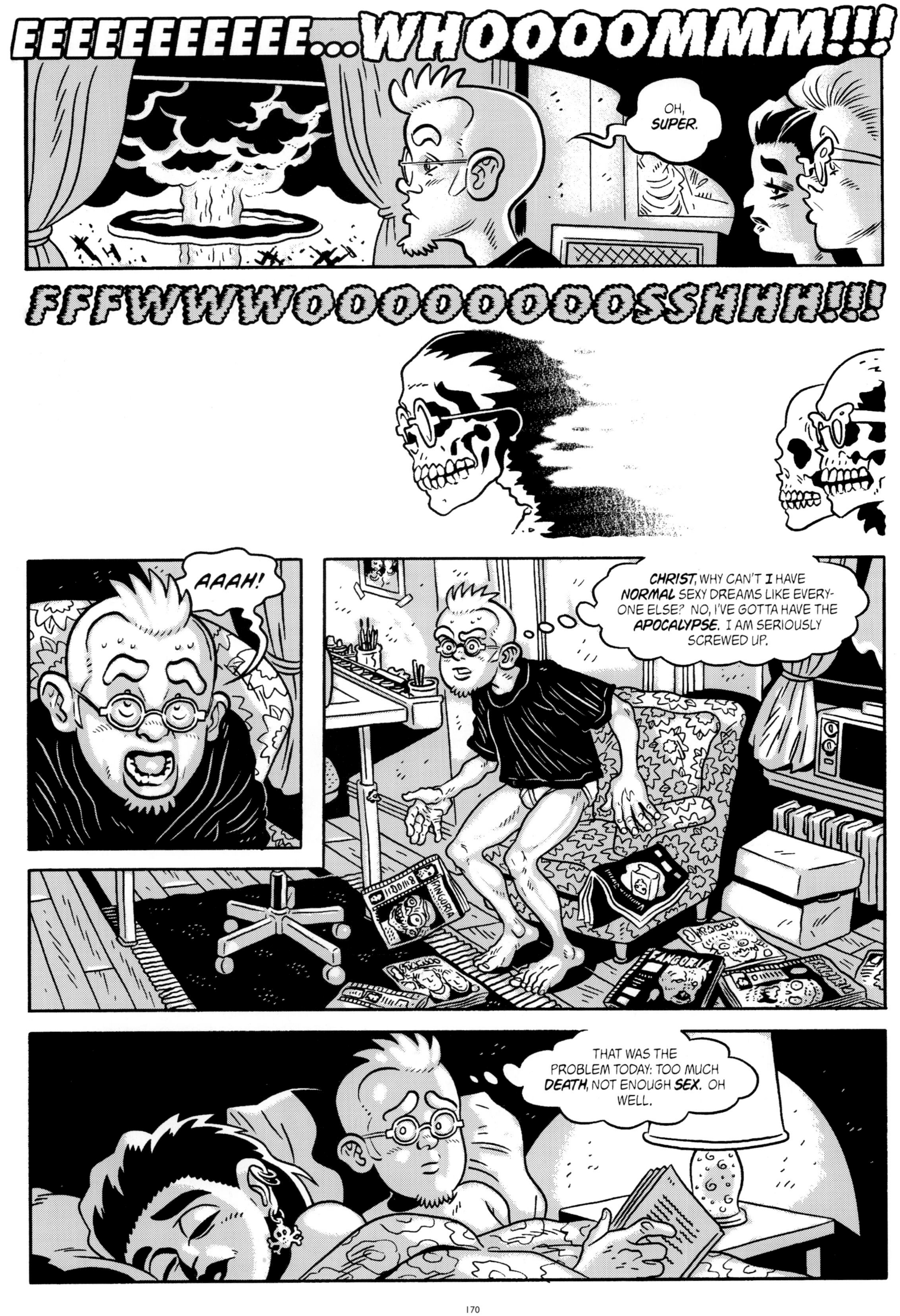

EEEEEEEEEEE...WHOOOOOMMMM!!!
OH, SUPER.
FFFWWWOOOOOOOOOSSHHH!!!
AAAH!
CHRIST, WHY CAN'T I HAVE NORMAL SEXY DREAMS LIKE EVERY-ONE ELSE? NO, I'VE GOTTA HAVE THE APOCALYPSE. I AM SERIOUSLY SCREWED UP.
FANGORIA
THAT WAS THE PROBLEM TODAY: TOO MUCH DEATH, NOT ENOUGH SEX. OH WELL.

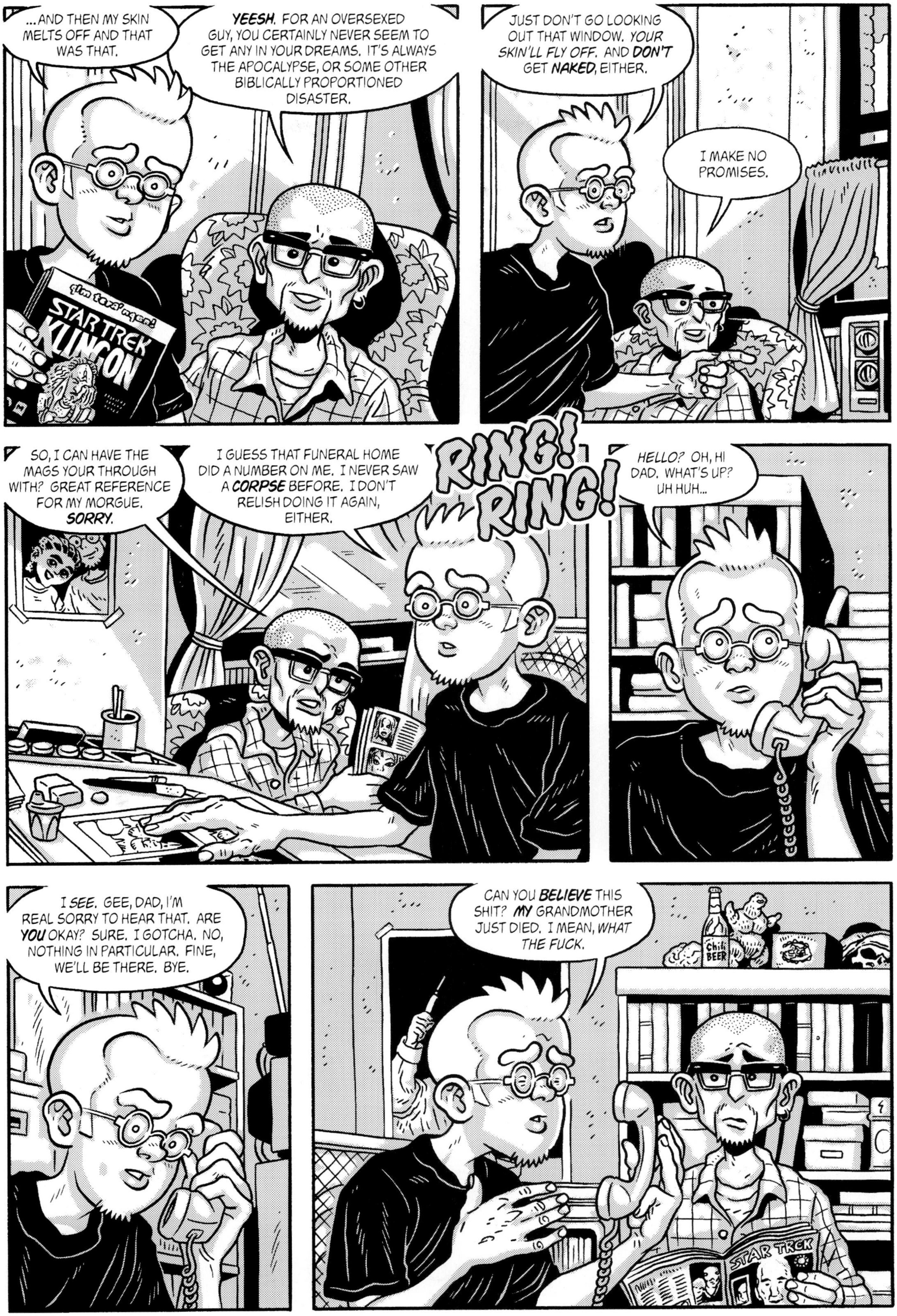
...AND THEN MY SKIN MELTS OFF AND THAT WAS THAT.
YEESH. FOR AN OVERSEXED GUY, YOU CERTAINLY NEVER SEEM TO GET ANY IN YOUR DREAMS. IT'S ALWAYS THE APOCALYPSE, OR SOME OTHER BIBLICALLY PROPORTIONED DISASTER.
STAR TREK KLINGON
JUST DON'T GO LOOKING OUT THAT WINDOW. YOUR SKIN'LL FLY OFF. AND DON'T GET NAKED, EITHER.
I MAKE NO PROMISES.
SO, I CAN HAVE THE MAGS YOUR THROUGH WITH? GREAT REFERENCE FOR MY MORGUE. SORRY.
I GUESS THAT FUNERAL HOME DID A NUMBER ON ME. I NEVER SAW A CORPSE BEFORE. I DON'T RELISH DOING IT AGAIN, EITHER.
RING! RING!
HELLO? OH, HI DAD. WHAT'S UP? UH HUH...
I SEE. GEE, DAD, I'M REAL SORRY TO HEAR THAT. ARE YOU OKAY? SURE. I GOTCHA. NO, NOTHING IN PARTICULAR. FINE, WE'LL BE THERE. BYE.
CAN YOU BELIEVE THIS SHIT? MY GRANDMOTHER JUST DIED. I MEAN, WHAT THE FUCK.
Chili BEER
STAR TREK

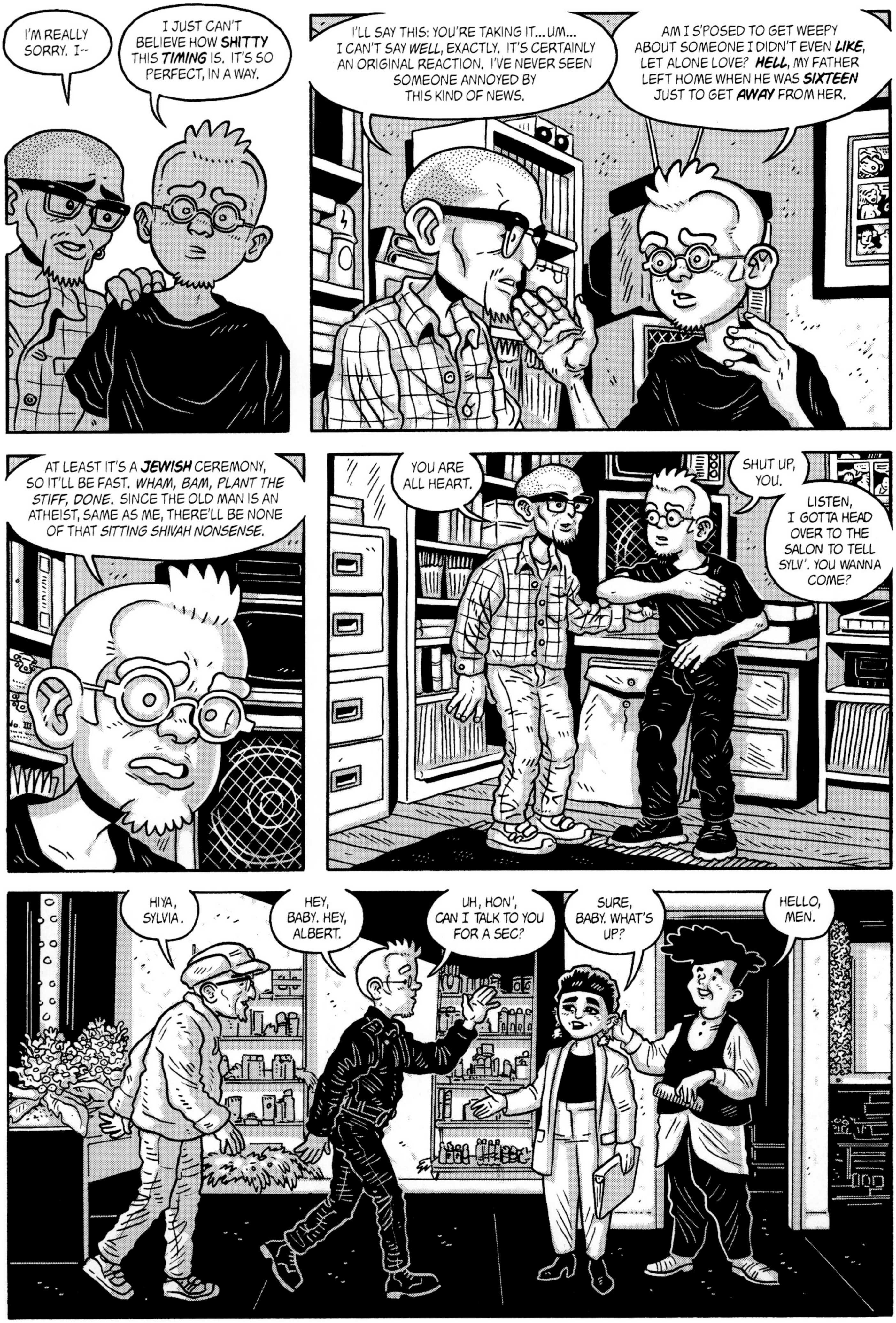

I'M REALLY SORRY. I--
I JUST CAN'T BELIEVE HOW **SHITTY** THIS ***TIMING*** IS. IT'S SO PERFECT, IN A WAY.
I'LL SAY THIS: YOU'RE TAKING IT... UM... I CAN'T SAY *WELL*, EXACTLY. IT'S CERTAINLY AN ORIGINAL REACTION. I'VE NEVER SEEN SOMEONE ANNOYED BY THIS KIND OF NEWS.
AM I S'POSED TO GET WEEPY ABOUT SOMEONE I DIDN'T EVEN ***LIKE***, LET ALONE LOVE? ***HELL***, MY FATHER LEFT HOME WHEN HE WAS ***SIXTEEN*** JUST TO GET ***AWAY*** FROM HER.
AT LEAST IT'S A ***JEWISH*** CEREMONY, SO IT'LL BE FAST. *WHAM, BAM, PLANT THE STIFF, DONE.* SINCE THE OLD MAN IS AN ATHEIST, SAME AS ME, THERE'LL BE NONE OF THAT *SITTING SHIVAH NONSENSE.*
YOU ARE ALL HEART.
SHUT UP, YOU.
LISTEN, I GOTTA HEAD OVER TO THE SALON TO TELL SYLV'. YOU WANNA COME?
HIYA, SYLVIA.
HEY, BABY. HEY, ALBERT.
UH, HON', CAN I TALK TO YOU FOR A SEC?
SURE, BABY. WHAT'S UP?
HELLO, MEN.

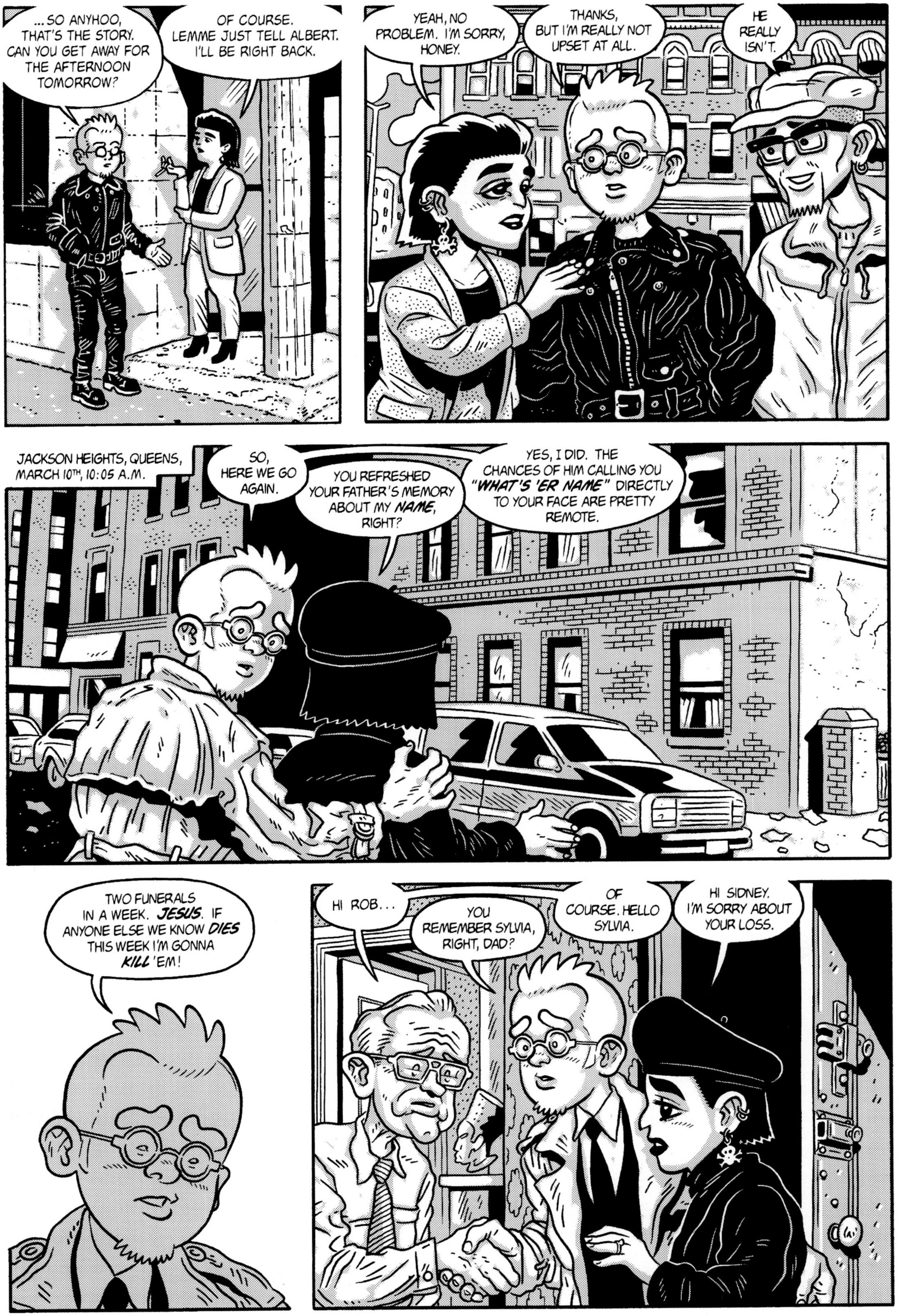
...SO ANYHOO, THAT'S THE STORY. CAN YOU GET AWAY FOR THE AFTERNOON TOMORROW?
OF COURSE. LEMME JUST TELL ALBERT. I'LL BE RIGHT BACK.
YEAH, NO PROBLEM. I'M SORRY, HONEY.
THANKS, BUT I'M REALLY NOT UPSET AT ALL.
HE REALLY ISN'T.
JACKSON HEIGHTS, QUEENS, MARCH 10TH, 10:05 A.M.
SO, HERE WE GO AGAIN.
YOU REFRESHED YOUR FATHER'S MEMORY ABOUT MY NAME, RIGHT?
YES, I DID. THE CHANCES OF HIM CALLING YOU "WHAT'S 'ER NAME" DIRECTLY TO YOUR FACE ARE PRETTY REMOTE.
TWO FUNERALS IN A WEEK. JESUS. IF ANYONE ELSE WE KNOW DIES THIS WEEK I'M GONNA KILL 'EM!
HI ROB...
YOU REMEMBER SYLVIA, RIGHT, DAD?
OF COURSE. HELLO SYLVIA.
HI SIDNEY. I'M SORRY ABOUT YOUR LOSS.

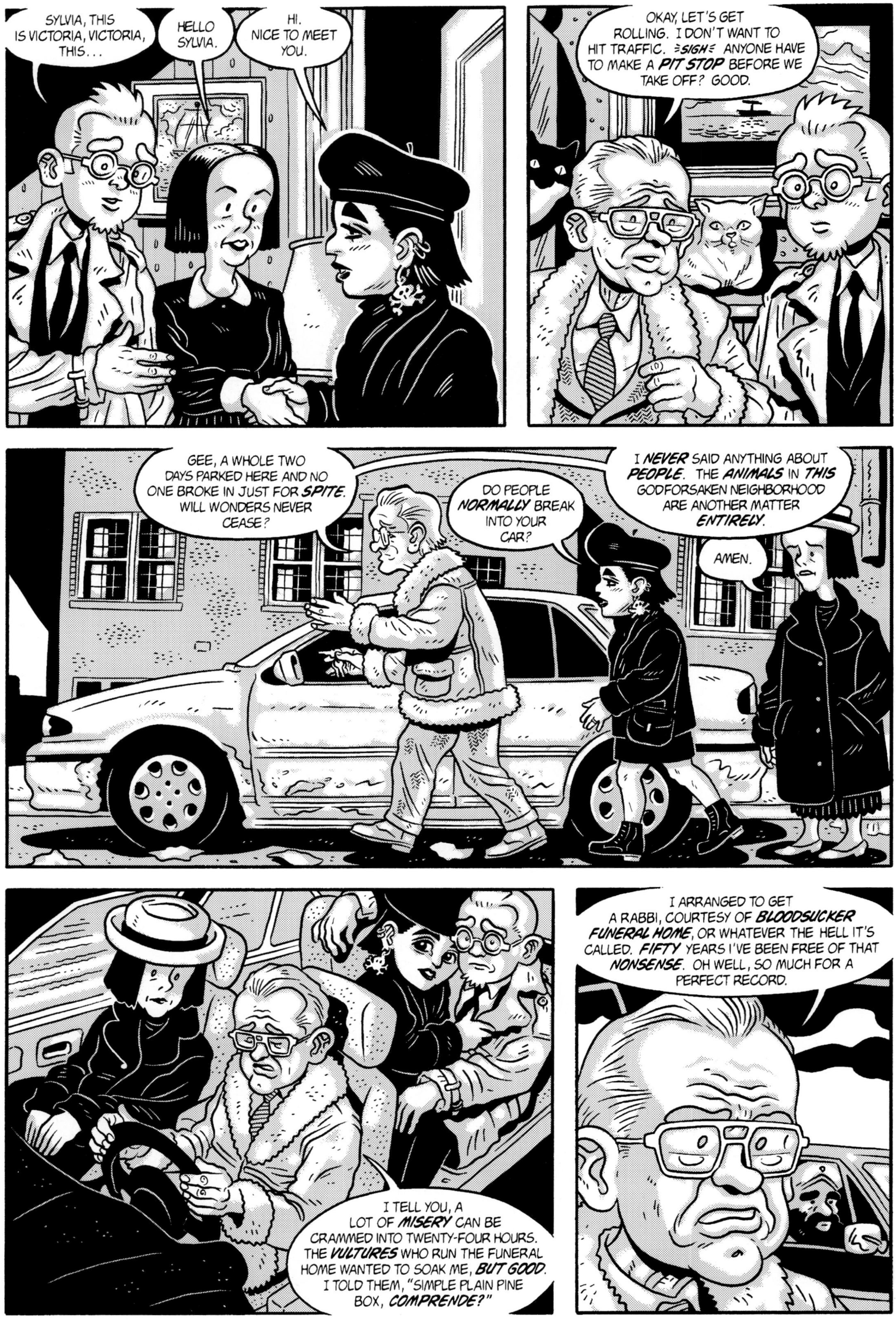
SYLVIA, THIS IS VICTORIA, VICTORIA, THIS. . .
HELLO SYLVIA.
HI. NICE TO MEET YOU.
OKAY, LET'S GET ROLLING. I DON'T WANT TO HIT TRAFFIC. ≷SIGH≶ ANYONE HAVE TO MAKE A PIT STOP BEFORE WE TAKE OFF? GOOD.
GEE, A WHOLE TWO DAYS PARKED HERE AND NO ONE BROKE IN JUST FOR SPITE. WILL WONDERS NEVER CEASE?
DO PEOPLE NORMALLY BREAK INTO YOUR CAR?
I NEVER SAID ANYTHING ABOUT PEOPLE. THE ANIMALS IN THIS GODFORSAKEN NEIGHBORHOOD ARE ANOTHER MATTER ENTIRELY.
AMEN.
I TELL YOU, A LOT OF MISERY CAN BE CRAMMED INTO TWENTY-FOUR HOURS. THE VULTURES WHO RUN THE FUNERAL HOME WANTED TO SOAK ME, BUT GOOD. I TOLD THEM, "SIMPLE PLAIN PINE BOX, COMPRENDE?"
I ARRANGED TO GET A RABBI, COURTESY OF BLOODSUCKER FUNERAL HOME, OR WHATEVER THE HELL IT'S CALLED. FIFTY YEARS I'VE BEEN FREE OF THAT NONSENSE. OH WELL, SO MUCH FOR A PERFECT RECORD.

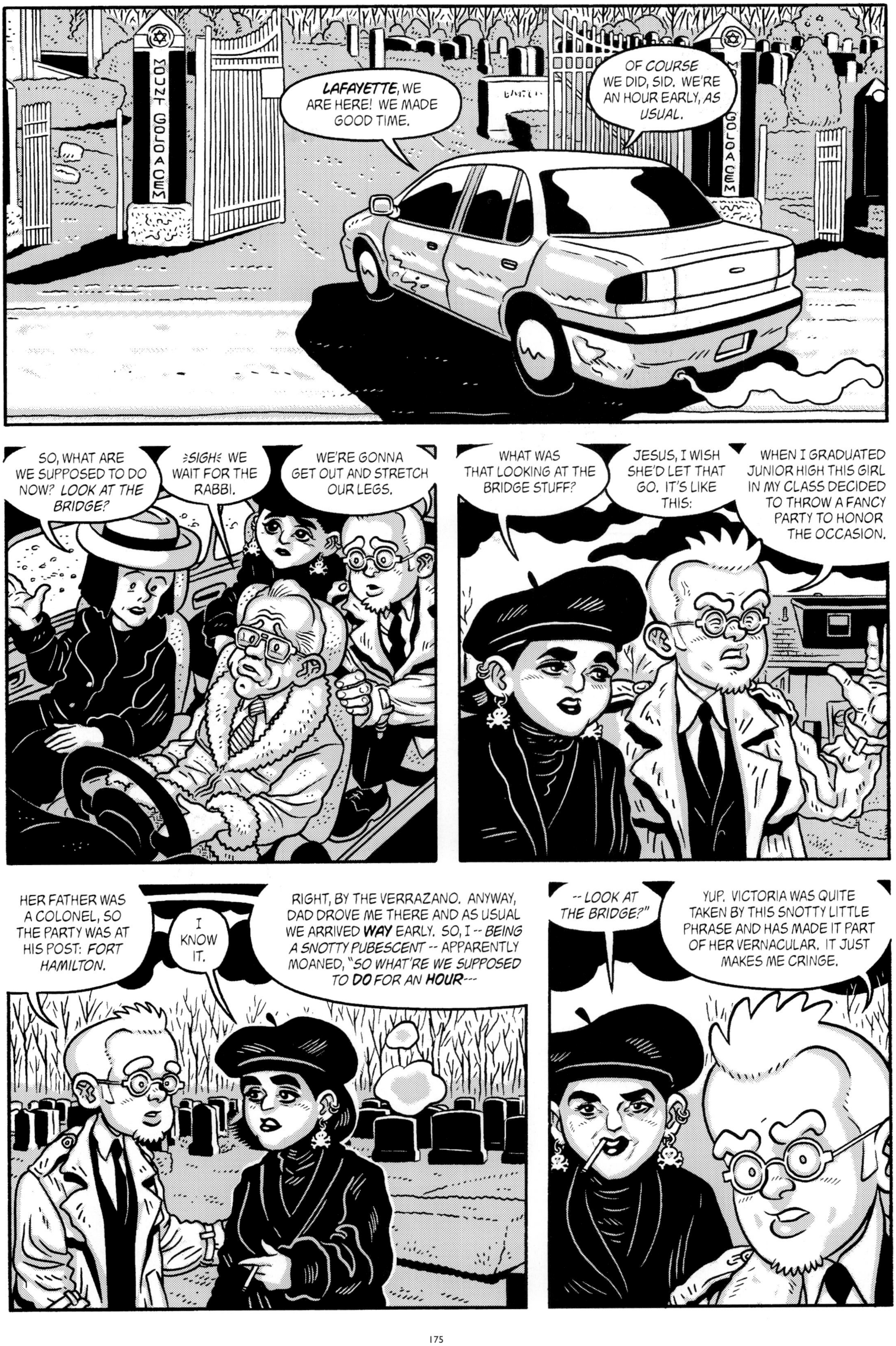
MOUNT GOLDA CEM
LAFAYETTE, WE ARE HERE! WE MADE GOOD TIME.
OF COURSE WE DID, SID. WE'RE AN HOUR EARLY, AS USUAL.
SO, WHAT ARE WE SUPPOSED TO DO NOW? LOOK AT THE BRIDGE?
SIGH WE WAIT FOR THE RABBI.
WE'RE GONNA GET OUT AND STRETCH OUR LEGS.
WHAT WAS THAT LOOKING AT THE BRIDGE STUFF?
JESUS, I WISH SHE'D LET THAT GO. IT'S LIKE THIS:
WHEN I GRADUATED JUNIOR HIGH THIS GIRL IN MY CLASS DECIDED TO THROW A FANCY PARTY TO HONOR THE OCCASION.
HER FATHER WAS A COLONEL, SO THE PARTY WAS AT HIS POST: FORT HAMILTON.
I KNOW IT.
RIGHT, BY THE VERRAZANO. ANYWAY, DAD DROVE ME THERE AND AS USUAL WE ARRIVED WAY EARLY. SO, I -- BEING A SNOTTY PUBESCENT -- APPARENTLY MOANED, "SO WHAT'RE WE SUPPOSED TO DO FOR AN HOUR---
-- LOOK AT THE BRIDGE?"
YUP. VICTORIA WAS QUITE TAKEN BY THIS SNOTTY LITTLE PHRASE AND HAS MADE IT PART OF HER VERNACULAR. IT JUST MAKES ME CRINGE.

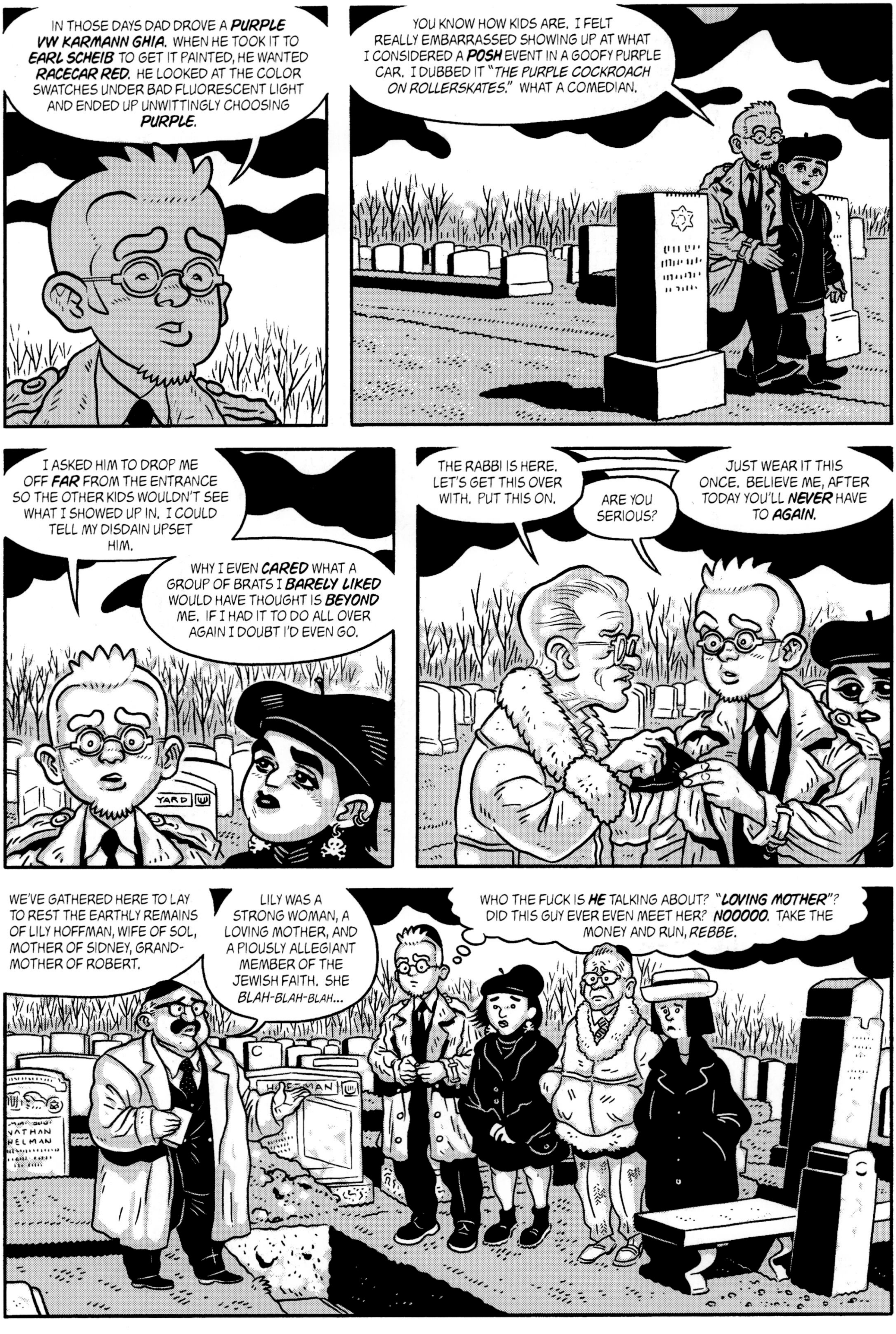
IN THOSE DAYS DAD DROVE A PURPLE VW KARMANN GHIA. WHEN HE TOOK IT TO EARL SCHEIB TO GET IT PAINTED, HE WANTED RACECAR RED. HE LOOKED AT THE COLOR SWATCHES UNDER BAD FLUORESCENT LIGHT AND ENDED UP UNWITTINGLY CHOOSING PURPLE.
YOU KNOW HOW KIDS ARE. I FELT REALLY EMBARRASSED SHOWING UP AT WHAT I CONSIDERED A POSH EVENT IN A GOOFY PURPLE CAR. I DUBBED IT "THE PURPLE COCKROACH ON ROLLERSKATES." WHAT A COMEDIAN.
I ASKED HIM TO DROP ME OFF FAR FROM THE ENTRANCE SO THE OTHER KIDS WOULDN'T SEE WHAT I SHOWED UP IN. I COULD TELL MY DISDAIN UPSET HIM.
WHY I EVEN CARED WHAT A GROUP OF BRATS I BARELY LIKED WOULD HAVE THOUGHT IS BEYOND ME. IF I HAD IT TO DO ALL OVER AGAIN I DOUBT I'D EVEN GO.
YARD
THE RABBI IS HERE. LET'S GET THIS OVER WITH. PUT THIS ON.
ARE YOU SERIOUS?
JUST WEAR IT THIS ONCE. BELIEVE ME, AFTER TODAY YOU'LL NEVER HAVE TO AGAIN.
WE'VE GATHERED HERE TO LAY TO REST THE EARTHLY REMAINS OF LILY HOFFMAN, WIFE OF SOL, MOTHER OF SIDNEY, GRAND-MOTHER OF ROBERT.
LILY WAS A STRONG WOMAN, A LOVING MOTHER, AND A PIOUSLY ALLEGIANT MEMBER OF THE JEWISH FAITH. SHE BLAH-BLAH-BLAH...
WHO THE FUCK IS HE TALKING ABOUT? "LOVING MOTHER"? DID THIS GUY EVER EVEN MEET HER? NOOOOO. TAKE THE MONEY AND RUN, REBBE.
NATHAN HELMAN
HOFFMAN

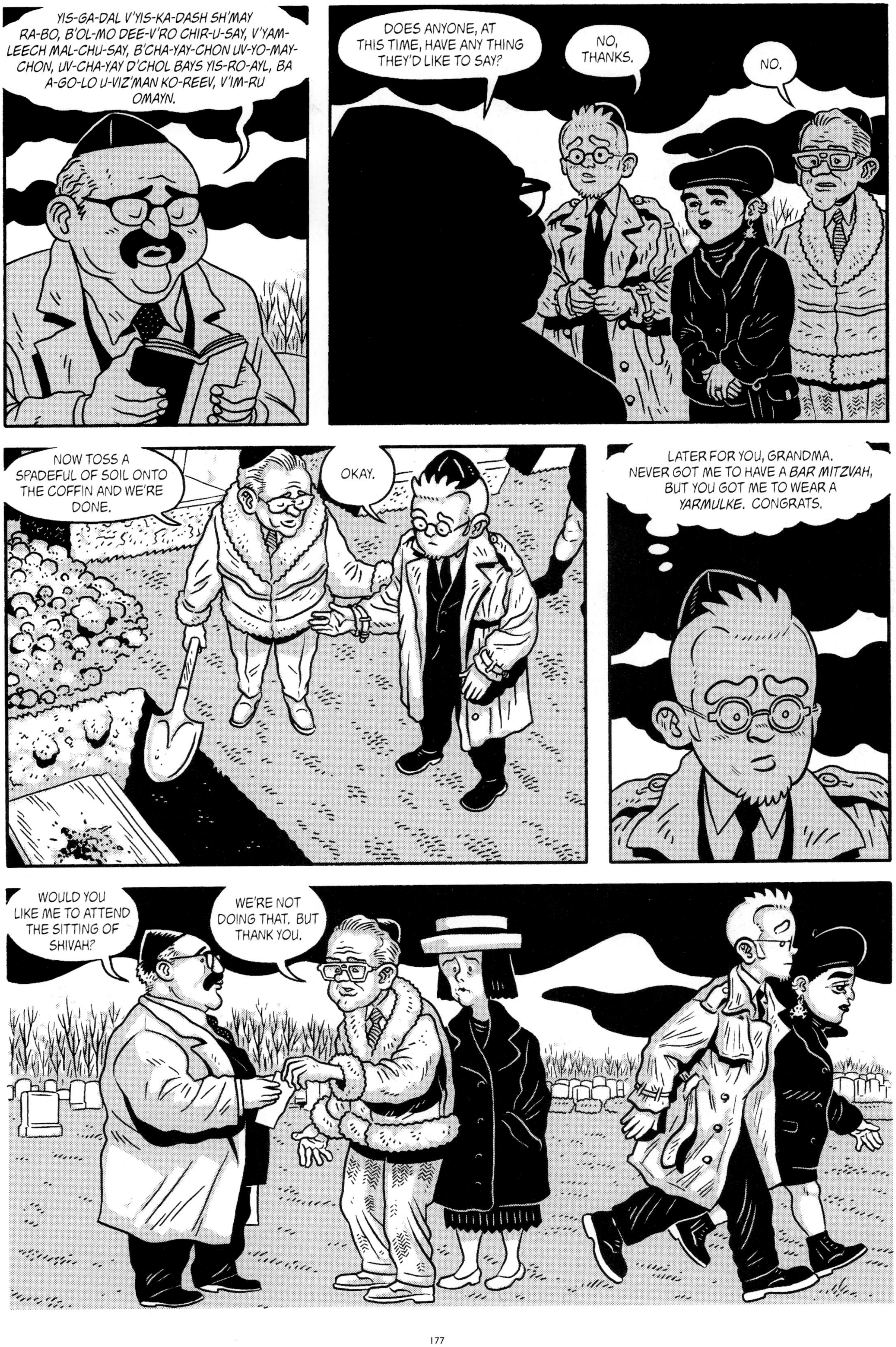
YIS-GA-DAL V'YIS-KA-DASH SH'MAY RA-BO, B'OL-MO DEE-V'RO CHIR-U-SAY, V'YAM-LEECH MAL-CHU-SAY, B'CHA-YAY-CHON UV-YO-MAY-CHON, UV-CHA-YAY D'CHOL BAYS YIS-RO-AYL, BA A-GO-LO U-VIZ'MAN KO-REEV, V'IM-RU OMAYN.
DOES ANYONE, AT THIS TIME, HAVE ANY THING THEY'D LIKE TO SAY?
NO, THANKS.
NO.
NOW TOSS A SPADEFUL OF SOIL ONTO THE COFFIN AND WE'RE DONE.
OKAY.
LATER FOR YOU, GRANDMA. NEVER GOT ME TO HAVE A *BAR MITZVAH*, BUT YOU GOT ME TO WEAR A *YARMULKE*. CONGRATS.
WOULD YOU LIKE ME TO ATTEND THE SITTING OF SHIVAH?
WE'RE NOT DOING THAT. BUT THANK YOU.

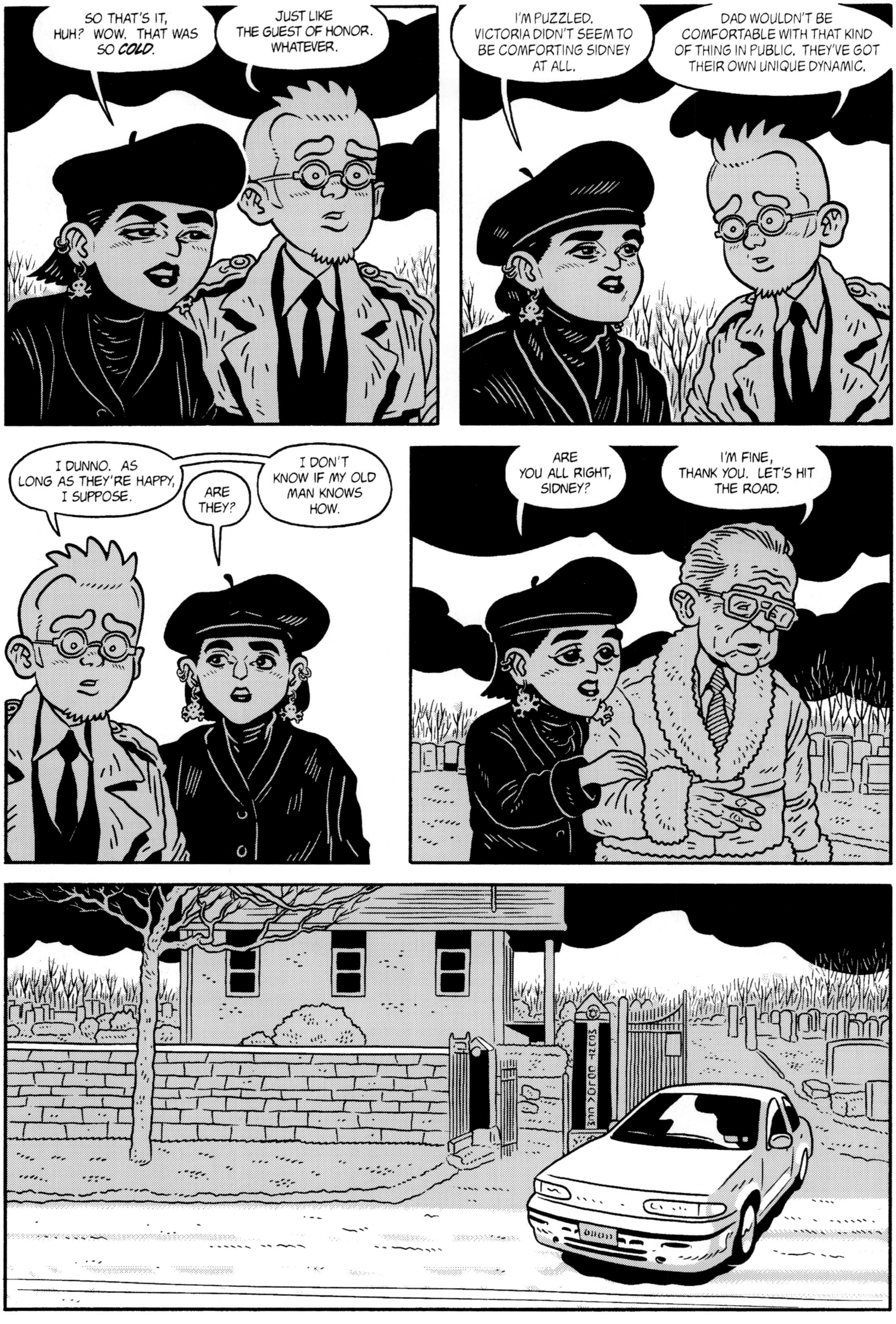
SO THAT'S IT, HUH? WOW. THAT WAS SO COLD.
JUST LIKE THE GUEST OF HONOR. WHATEVER.
I'M PUZZLED. VICTORIA DIDN'T SEEM TO BE COMFORTING SIDNEY AT ALL.
DAD WOULDN'T BE COMFORTABLE WITH THAT KIND OF THING IN PUBLIC. THEY'VE GOT THEIR OWN UNIQUE DYNAMIC.
I DUNNO. AS LONG AS THEY'RE HAPPY, I SUPPOSE.
ARE THEY?
I DON'T KNOW IF MY OLD MAN KNOWS HOW.
ARE YOU ALL RIGHT, SIDNEY?
I'M FINE, THANK YOU. LET'S HIT THE ROAD.

Chapter Eight

HOMO ERRATA

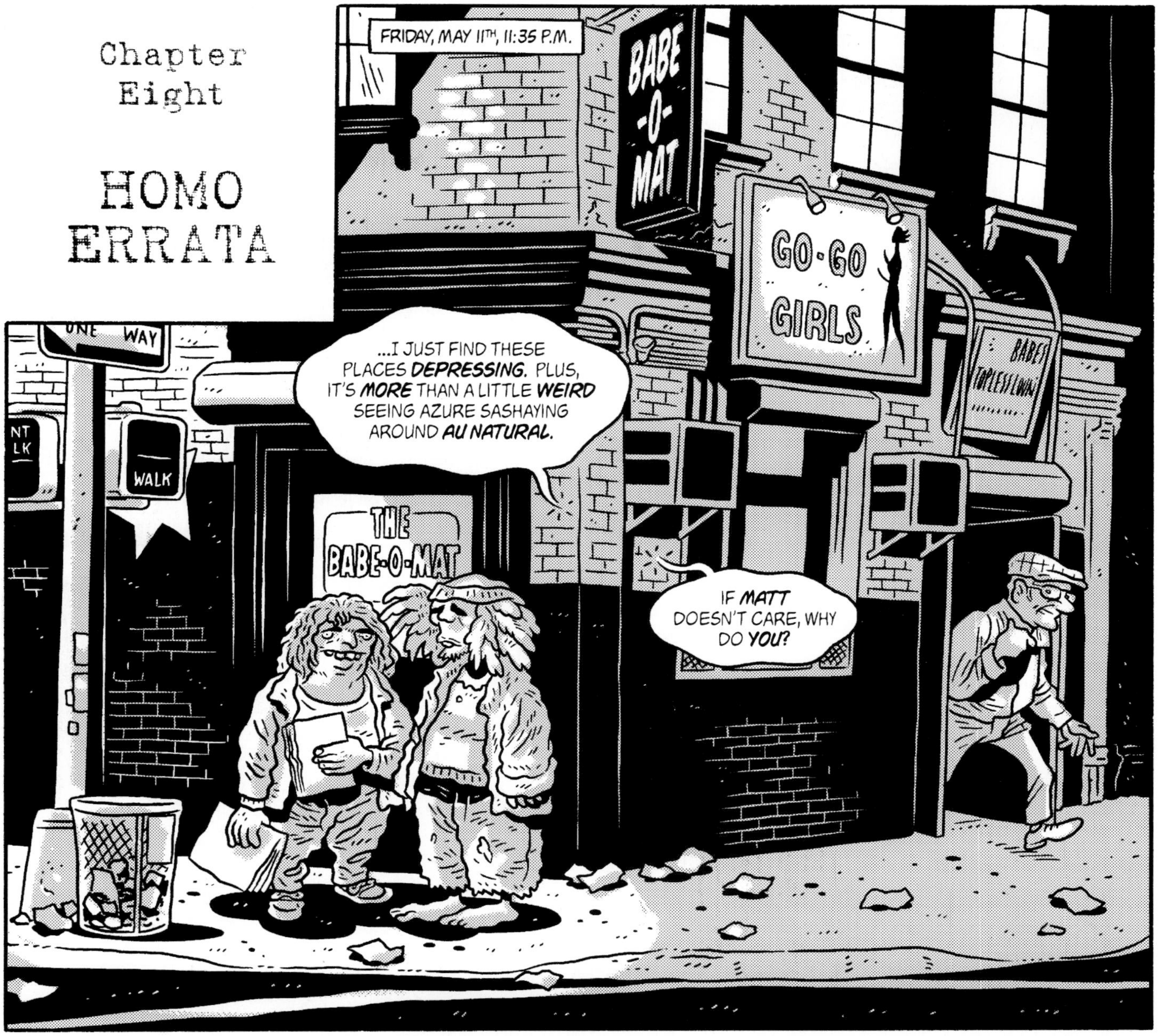

FRIDAY, MAY 11TH, 11:35 P.M.
BABE -O- MAT
GO-GO GIRLS
ONE WAY
WALK
THE BABE-O-MAT
...I JUST FIND THESE PLACES **DEPRESSING.** PLUS, IT'S **MORE** THAN A LITTLE **WEIRD** SEEING AZURE SASHAYING AROUND **AU NATURAL.**
IF **MATT** DOESN'T CARE, WHY DO **YOU?**

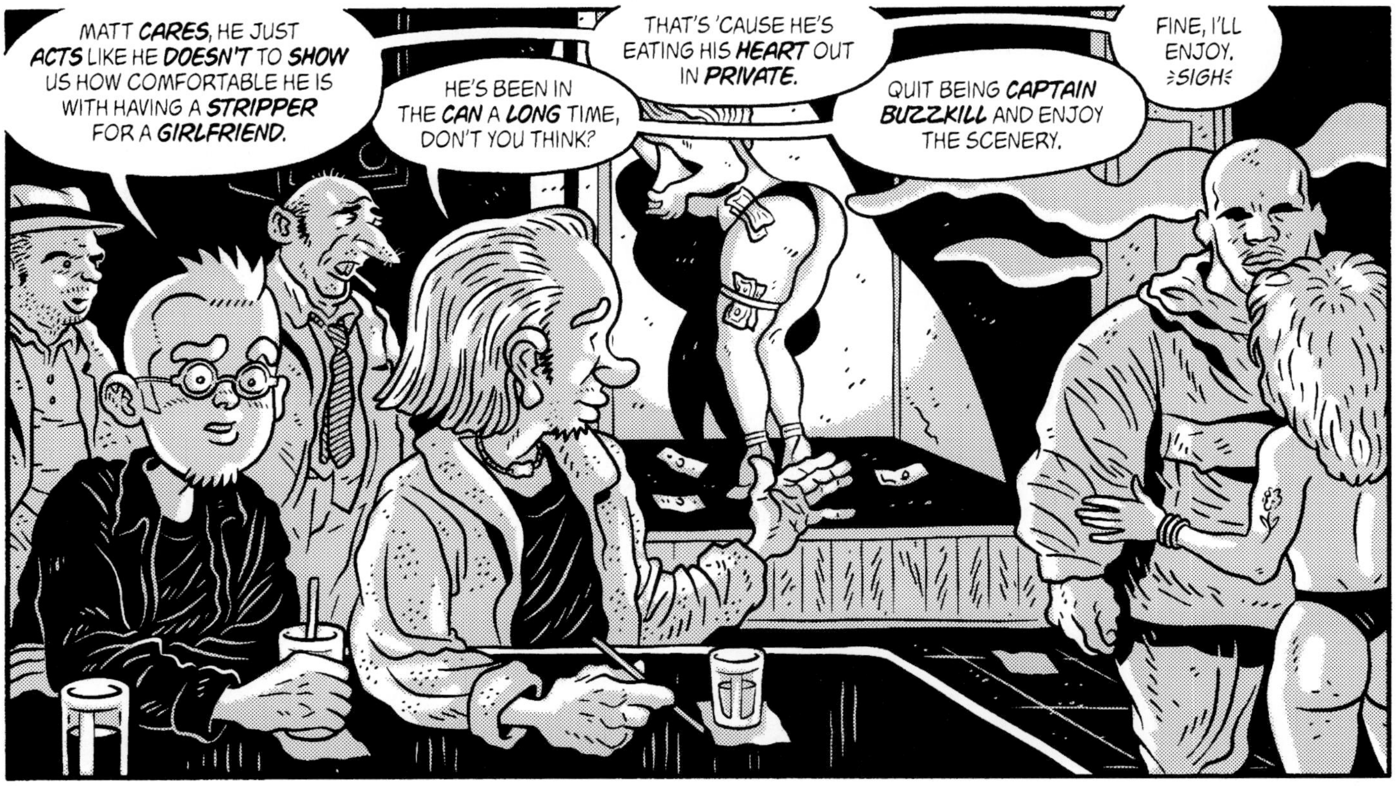

MATT **CARES**, HE JUST **ACTS** LIKE HE **DOESN'T** TO **SHOW** US HOW COMFORTABLE HE IS WITH HAVING A **STRIPPER** FOR A **GIRLFRIEND.**
HE'S BEEN IN THE **CAN** A **LONG** TIME, DON'T YOU THINK?
THAT'S 'CAUSE HE'S EATING HIS **HEART** OUT IN **PRIVATE.**
QUIT BEING **CAPTAIN BUZZKILL** AND ENJOY THE SCENERY.
FINE, I'LL ENJOY. ≶SIGH≶

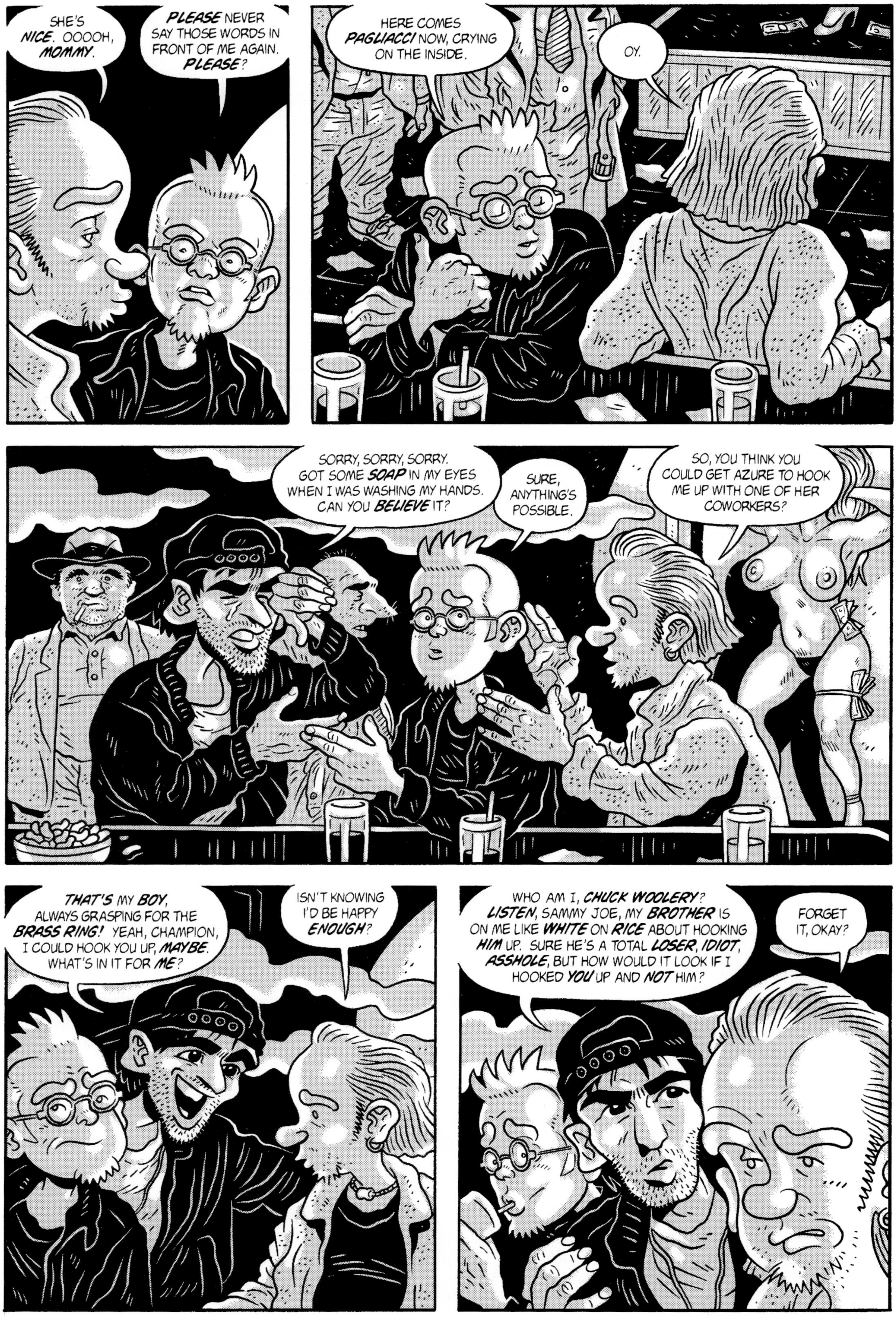

SHE'S NICE. OOOOH, MOMMY.
PLEASE NEVER SAY THOSE WORDS IN FRONT OF ME AGAIN. PLEASE?
HERE COMES PAGLIACCI NOW, CRYING ON THE INSIDE.
OY.
SORRY, SORRY, SORRY. GOT SOME SOAP IN MY EYES WHEN I WAS WASHING MY HANDS. CAN YOU BELIEVE IT?
SURE, ANYTHING'S POSSIBLE.
SO, YOU THINK YOU COULD GET AZURE TO HOOK ME UP WITH ONE OF HER COWORKERS?
THAT'S MY BOY, ALWAYS GRASPING FOR THE BRASS RING! YEAH, CHAMPION, I COULD HOOK YOU UP, MAYBE. WHAT'S IN IT FOR ME?
ISN'T KNOWING I'D BE HAPPY ENOUGH?
WHO AM I, CHUCK WOOLERY? LISTEN, SAMMY JOE, MY BROTHER IS ON ME LIKE WHITE ON RICE ABOUT HOOKING HIM UP. SURE HE'S A TOTAL LOSER, IDIOT, ASSHOLE, BUT HOW WOULD IT LOOK IF I HOOKED YOU UP AND NOT HIM?
FORGET IT, OKAY?

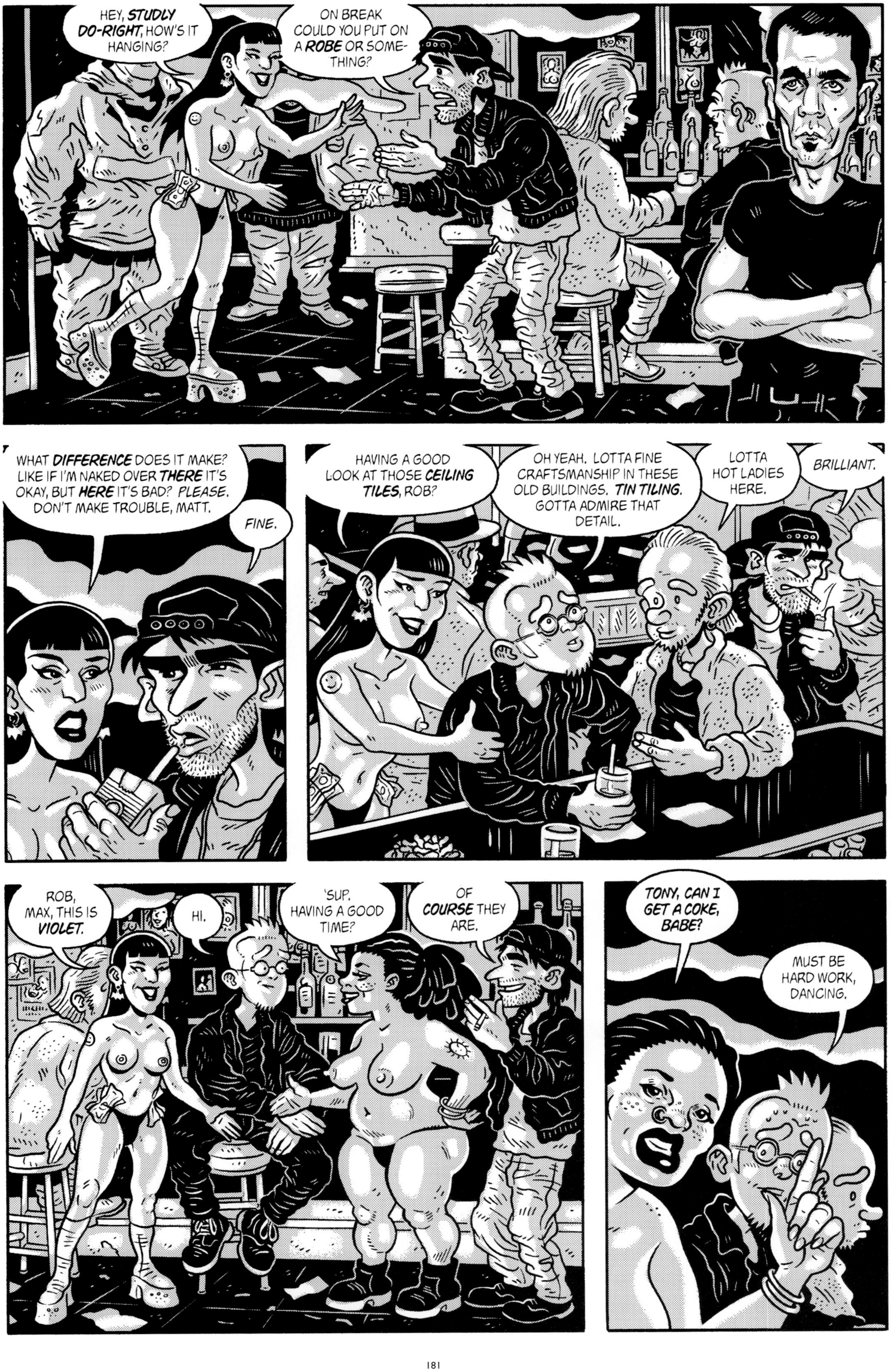

HEY, STUDLY DO-RIGHT, HOW'S IT HANGING?
ON BREAK COULD YOU PUT ON A ROBE OR SOMETHING?
WHAT DIFFERENCE DOES IT MAKE? LIKE IF I'M NAKED OVER THERE IT'S OKAY, BUT HERE IT'S BAD? PLEASE. DON'T MAKE TROUBLE, MATT.
FINE.
HAVING A GOOD LOOK AT THOSE CEILING TILES, ROB?
OH YEAH. LOTTA FINE CRAFTSMANSHIP IN THESE OLD BUILDINGS. TIN TILING. GOTTA ADMIRE THAT DETAIL.
LOTTA HOT LADIES HERE.
BRILLIANT.
ROB, MAX, THIS IS VIOLET.
HI.
'SUP. HAVING A GOOD TIME?
OF COURSE THEY ARE.
TONY, CAN I GET A COKE, BABE?
MUST BE HARD WORK, DANCING.

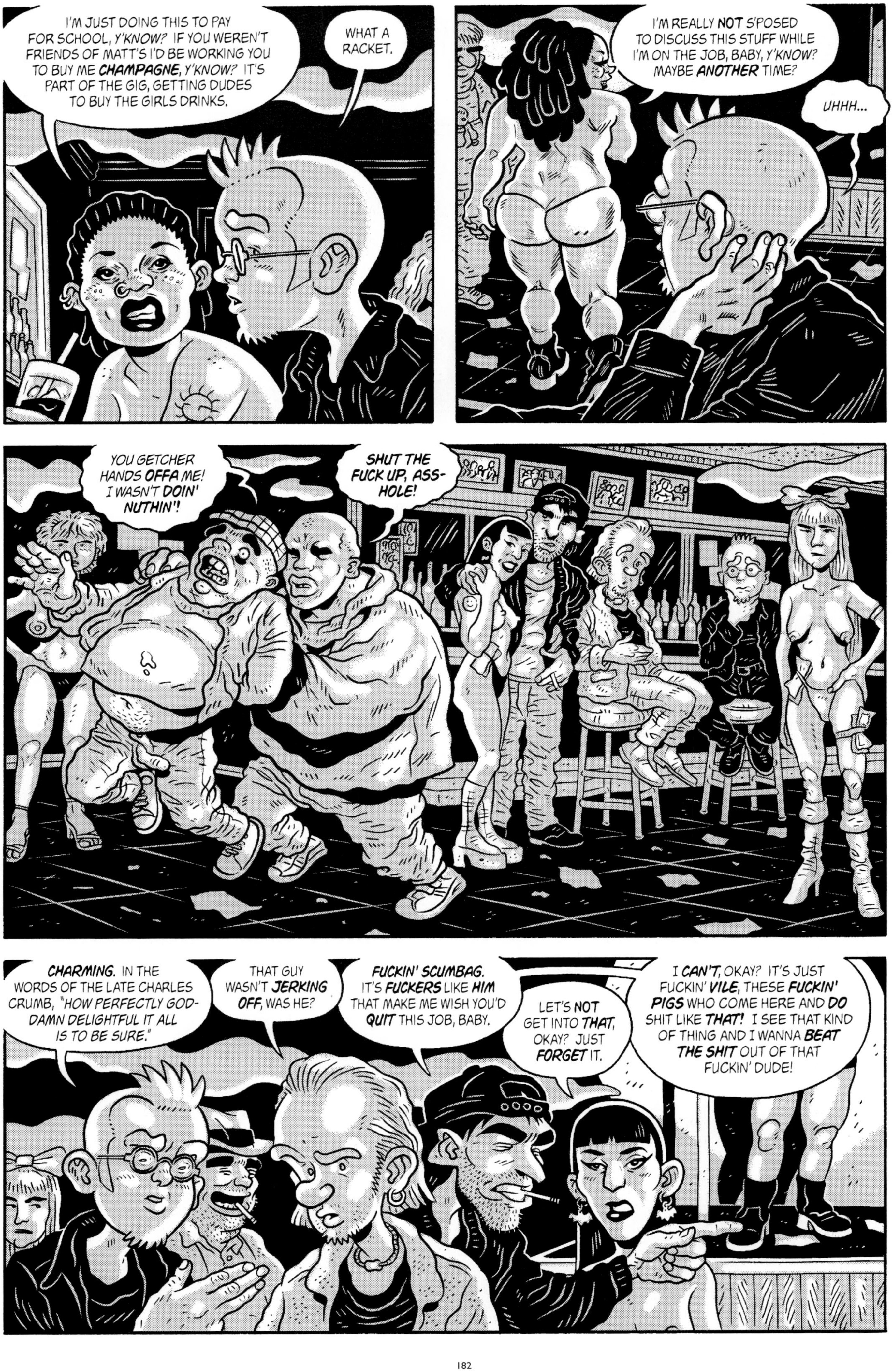
I'M JUST DOING THIS TO PAY FOR SCHOOL, Y'KNOW? IF YOU WEREN'T FRIENDS OF MATT'S I'D BE WORKING YOU TO BUY ME **CHAMPAGNE**, Y'KNOW? IT'S PART OF THE GIG, GETTING DUDES TO BUY THE GIRLS DRINKS.
WHAT A RACKET.
I'M REALLY **NOT** S'POSED TO DISCUSS THIS STUFF WHILE I'M ON THE JOB, BABY, Y'KNOW? MAYBE **ANOTHER** TIME?
UHHH...
YOU GETCHER HANDS **OFFA** ME! I WASN'T **DOIN'** NUTHIN'!
SHUT THE FUCK UP, ASS-HOLE!
CHARMING. IN THE WORDS OF THE LATE CHARLES CRUMB, "HOW PERFECTLY GOD-DAMN DELIGHTFUL IT ALL IS TO BE SURE."
THAT GUY WASN'T **JERKING OFF**, WAS HE?
FUCKIN' SCUMBAG. IT'S **FUCKERS** LIKE **HIM** THAT MAKE ME WISH YOU'D **QUIT** THIS JOB, BABY.
LET'S **NOT** GET INTO **THAT**, OKAY? JUST **FORGET** IT.
I **CAN'T**, OKAY? IT'S JUST FUCKIN' **VILE**, THESE **FUCKIN' PIGS** WHO COME HERE AND **DO** SHIT LIKE **THAT!** I SEE THAT KIND OF THING AND I WANNA **BEAT THE SHIT** OUT OF THAT FUCKIN' DUDE!

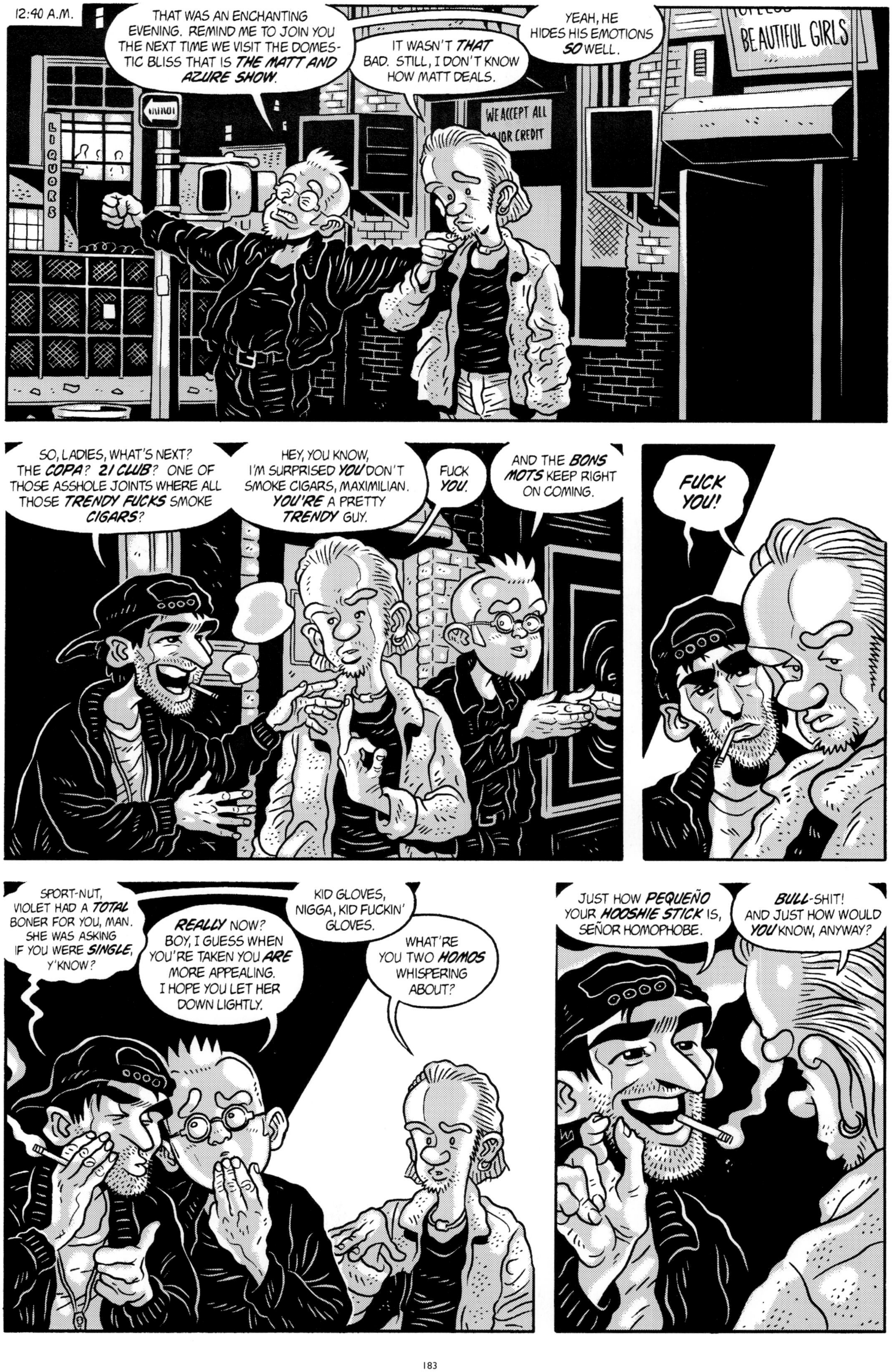
12:40 A.M.
THAT WAS AN ENCHANTING EVENING. REMIND ME TO JOIN YOU THE NEXT TIME WE VISIT THE DOMESTIC BLISS THAT IS THE MATT AND AZURE SHOW.
IT WASN'T THAT BAD. STILL, I DON'T KNOW HOW MATT DEALS.
YEAH, HE HIDES HIS EMOTIONS SO WELL.
BEAUTIFUL GIRLS
WE ACCEPT ALL
LIQUORS
SO, LADIES, WHAT'S NEXT? THE COPA? 21 CLUB? ONE OF THOSE ASSHOLE JOINTS WHERE ALL THOSE TRENDY FUCKS SMOKE CIGARS?
HEY, YOU KNOW, I'M SURPRISED YOU DON'T SMOKE CIGARS, MAXIMILIAN. YOU'RE A PRETTY TRENDY GUY.
FUCK YOU.
AND THE BONS MOTS KEEP RIGHT ON COMING.
FUCK YOU!
SPORT-NUT, VIOLET HAD A TOTAL BONER FOR YOU, MAN. SHE WAS ASKING IF YOU WERE SINGLE, Y'KNOW?
REALLY NOW? BOY, I GUESS WHEN YOU'RE TAKEN YOU ARE MORE APPEALING. I HOPE YOU LET HER DOWN LIGHTLY.
KID GLOVES, NIGGA, KID FUCKIN' GLOVES.
WHAT'RE YOU TWO HOMOS WHISPERING ABOUT?
JUST HOW PEQUEÑO YOUR HOOSHIE STICK IS, SEÑOR HOMOPHOBE.
BULL-SHIT! AND JUST HOW WOULD YOU KNOW, ANYWAY?

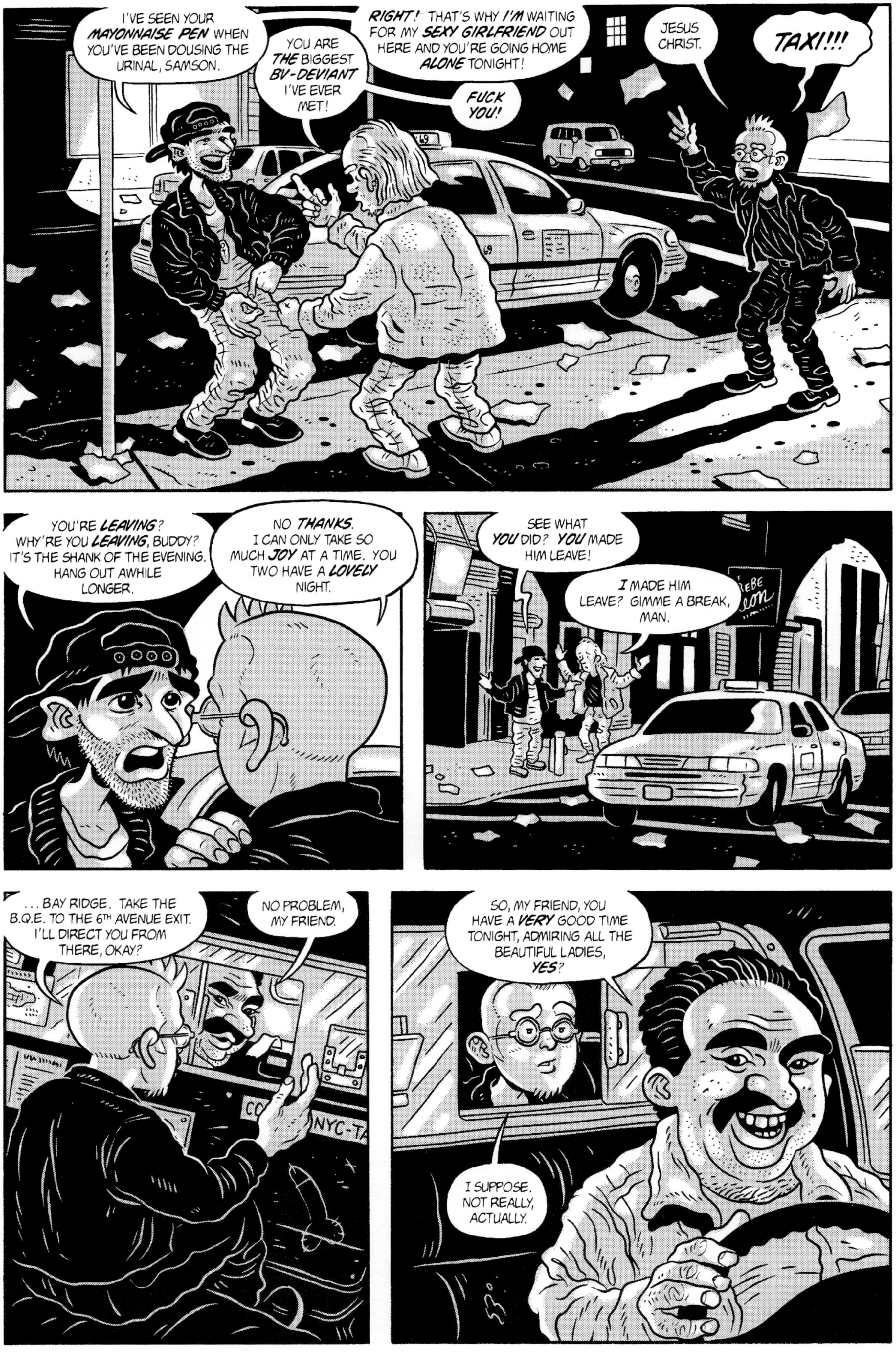

I'VE SEEN YOUR MAYONNAISE PEN WHEN YOU'VE BEEN DOUSING THE URINAL, SAMSON.
YOU ARE THE BIGGEST BV-DEVIANT I'VE EVER MET!
RIGHT! THAT'S WHY I'M WAITING FOR MY SEXY GIRLFRIEND OUT HERE AND YOU'RE GOING HOME ALONE TONIGHT!
FUCK YOU!
JESUS CHRIST.
TAXI!!!
YOU'RE LEAVING? WHY'RE YOU LEAVING, BUDDY? IT'S THE SHANK OF THE EVENING. HANG OUT AWHILE LONGER.
NO THANKS. I CAN ONLY TAKE SO MUCH JOY AT A TIME. YOU TWO HAVE A LOVELY NIGHT.
SEE WHAT YOU DID? YOU MADE HIM LEAVE!
I MADE HIM LEAVE? GIMME A BREAK, MAN.
... BAY RIDGE. TAKE THE B.Q.E. TO THE 6TH AVENUE EXIT. I'LL DIRECT YOU FROM THERE, OKAY?
NO PROBLEM, MY FRIEND.
SO, MY FRIEND, YOU HAVE A VERY GOOD TIME TONIGHT, ADMIRING ALL THE BEAUTIFUL LADIES, YES?
I SUPPOSE. NOT REALLY, ACTUALLY.

I UNDERSTAND. ZESE PLACE ARE **MESSY**, YES? FULL OF **UNPLEASANTNESS**, YES? TELL ME, MY FRIEND: **WHAT IS YOUR FAITH?**

I'D PREFER NOT TO GET INTO THAT, OKAY?

I SEE. IS **PERSONAL**, YES? BUT I TELL YOU, MY FRIEND, A GREAT REWARD AWAITS ME IN ZE **AFTERLIFE**. IT COULD FOR **YOU**.

IS **THAT SO?**

I ASSURE YOU IS **TRUE, IF** YOU ARE **GOOD MAN**. IN AFTERLIFE, YOU REWARDED WIZ A **PALACE**, YES? VERY **BIG PALACE** WIZ **MILLIONS ROOMS**, YES? AND A **MILLIONS GEMS** AND **FORTUNES** FOR YOU. IN EACH ROOM IS VERY BEAUTIFUL, CLEAN **VIRGIN** FOR YOU, YES?

ZESE GIRL ARE ZE **MOST BEAUTIFUL**, YES? LIKE TO MAKE **PLAYBOY MODEL** LOOK AS IF A **DOG**. ZESE GIRL ALL FOR YOU TO MAKE **SEX**. AND BEAUTIFUL, **CLEAN** SEX. NEVER WIZ ANY **MESSY CUM**. VERY **CLEAN**, YES?

"NEVER WITH ANY MESSY CUM." YEESH.

HUH?

MMMM. YOU SMELL REALLY **MANLY**. CIGARETTES AND... IS THAT **BOOZE** ON YOUR BREATH?

I HAD A COUPLE OF DRINKS TO HELP PASS THE TIME TONIGHT.

IT'S **SO** UNLIKE YOU. MMMM. CIGARETTES AND BOOZE. IT'S GETTING ME **HOT**.

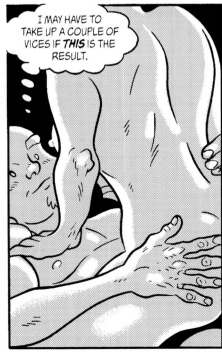

I MAY HAVE TO TAKE UP A COUPLE OF VICES IF **THIS** IS THE RESULT.

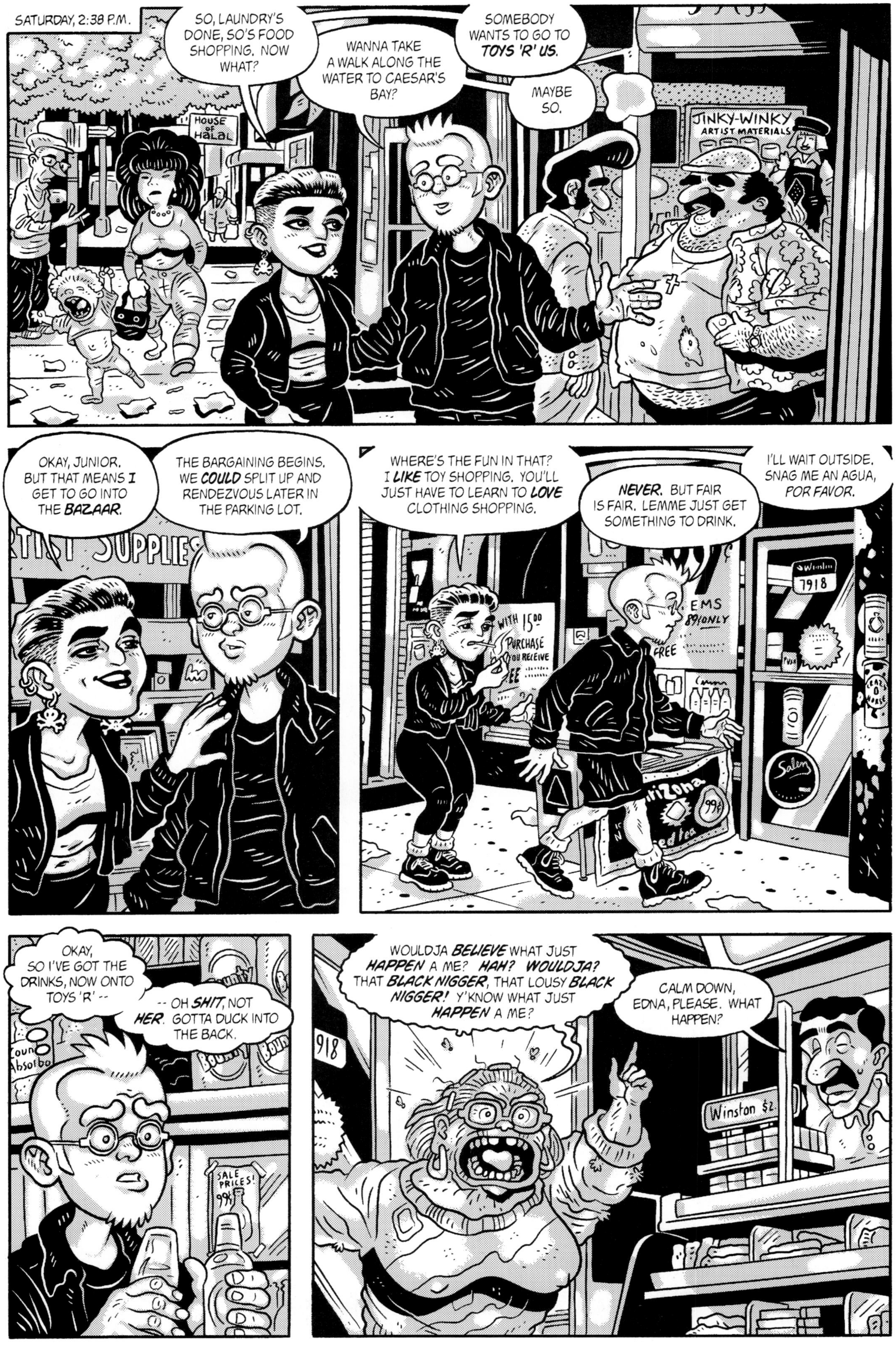
SATURDAY, 2:38 P.M.
SO, LAUNDRY'S DONE, SO'S FOOD SHOPPING. NOW WHAT?
WANNA TAKE A WALK ALONG THE WATER TO CAESAR'S BAY?
SOMEBODY WANTS TO GO TO **TOYS 'R' US**.
MAYBE SO.
HOUSE of HALAL
JINKY-WINKY
ARTIST MATERIALS
OKAY, JUNIOR. BUT THAT MEANS ***I*** GET TO GO INTO THE ***BAZAAR***.
THE BARGAINING BEGINS. WE ***COULD*** SPLIT UP AND RENDEZVOUS LATER IN THE PARKING LOT.
WHERE'S THE FUN IN THAT? I ***LIKE*** TOY SHOPPING. YOU'LL JUST HAVE TO LEARN TO ***LOVE*** CLOTHING SHOPPING.
NEVER. BUT FAIR IS FAIR. LEMME JUST GET SOMETHING TO DRINK.
I'LL WAIT OUTSIDE. SNAG ME AN AGUA, ***POR FAVOR***.
WITH 15.00 PURCHASE
7918
OKAY, SO I'VE GOT THE DRINKS, NOW ONTO TOYS 'R' --
-- OH ***SHIT***, NOT ***HER***. GOTTA DUCK INTO THE BACK.
SALE PRICES! 99¢
WOULDJA ***BELIEVE*** WHAT JUST ***HAPPEN*** A ME? ***HAH? WOULDJA?*** THAT ***BLACK NIGGER***, THAT LOUSY ***BLACK NIGGER!*** Y'KNOW WHAT JUST ***HAPPEN*** A ME?
CALM DOWN, EDNA, PLEASE. WHAT HAPPEN?
918
Winston $2.

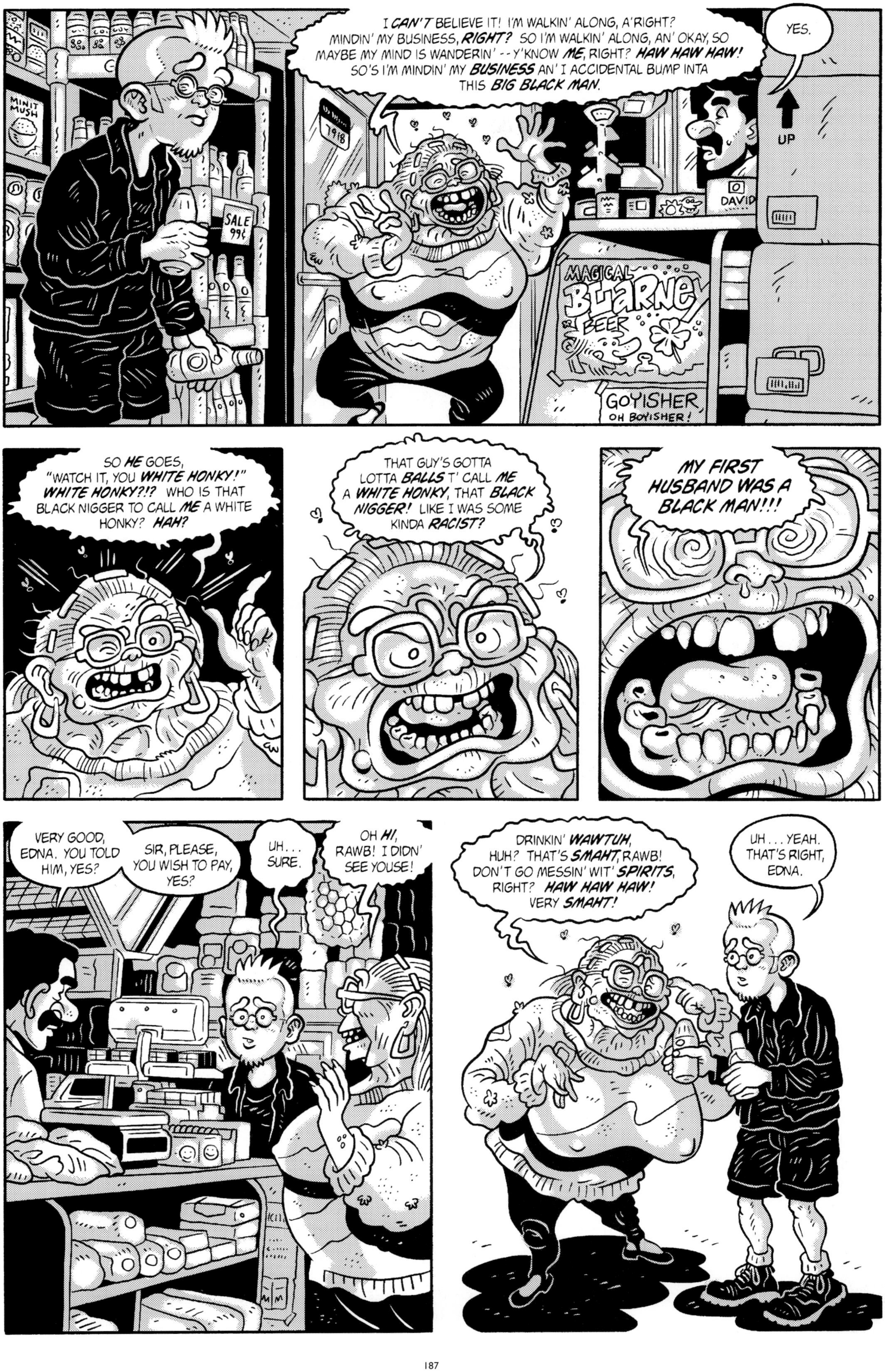
I CAN'T BELIEVE IT! I'M WALKIN' ALONG, A'RIGHT? MINDIN' MY BUSINESS, RIGHT? SO I'M WALKIN' ALONG, AN' OKAY, SO MAYBE MY MIND IS WANDERIN' --Y'KNOW ME, RIGHT? HAW HAW HAW! SO'S I'M MINDIN' MY BUSINESS AN' I ACCIDENTAL BUMP INTA THIS BIG BLACK MAN.
YES.
MINIT MUSH
SALE 99¢
1918
UP
DAVID
MAGICAL BLARNEY BEER
GOYISHER OH BOYISHER!
SO HE GOES, "WATCH IT, YOU WHITE HONKY!" WHITE HONKY?!? WHO IS THAT BLACK NIGGER TO CALL ME A WHITE HONKY? HAH?
THAT GUY'S GOTTA LOTTA BALLS T' CALL ME A WHITE HONKY, THAT BLACK NIGGER! LIKE I WAS SOME KINDA RACIST?
MY FIRST HUSBAND WAS A BLACK MAN!!!
VERY GOOD, EDNA. YOU TOLD HIM, YES?
SIR, PLEASE, YOU WISH TO PAY, YES?
UH... SURE.
OH HI, RAWB! I DIDN' SEE YOUSE!
DRINKIN' WAWTUH, HUH? THAT'S SMAHT, RAWB! DON'T GO MESSIN' WIT' SPIRITS, RIGHT? HAW HAW HAW! VERY SMAHT!
UH... YEAH. THAT'S RIGHT, EDNA.

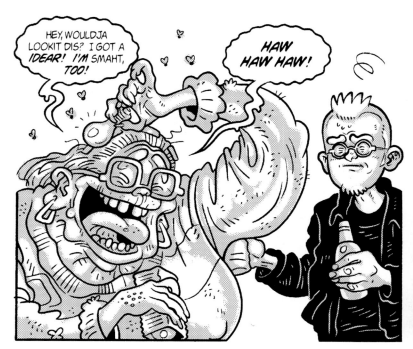

HEY, WOULDJA LOOKIT DIS? I GOT A *IDEAR!* I'M *SMAHT, TOO!*

HAW HAW HAW!

SHE'S MY SUPER. I DON'T REALLY *KNOW* HER.

VERY GOOD.

AI-YI-YI-YI-YIIII! WHAT A *NIGHTMARE.*

I SAW HER GO IN, BUT SHE DIDN'T SEE ME. THERE WAS NO TIME TO WARN YOU.

IT'S *SO* EMBARRASSING. I HATE THAT SHE TALKS TO ME LIKE WE'RE OLD BUDDIES. I DON'T WANT THE ASSOCIATION. AT LEAST IT'S OVER.

HAVE YOU SEEN THIS MAN?

HEEEEY, *RAAAAWB 'N' SYLVIAAAA!*

≥GROAN≤

HEY YOUSE GUYS! I FUHGOT T' SHOW YOUSE MY *NEW SWEATUH!* MY *SPRING FASHUNS!* I KNITTED IT *MYSELF,* AN' I'M *WEARIN'* IT! *PARIS,* LOOK OUT! HAW HAW HAW!

BEAUTIFUL, EDNA.

YEAH, UM... GREAT.

SEE YA!

ON SITE

10401

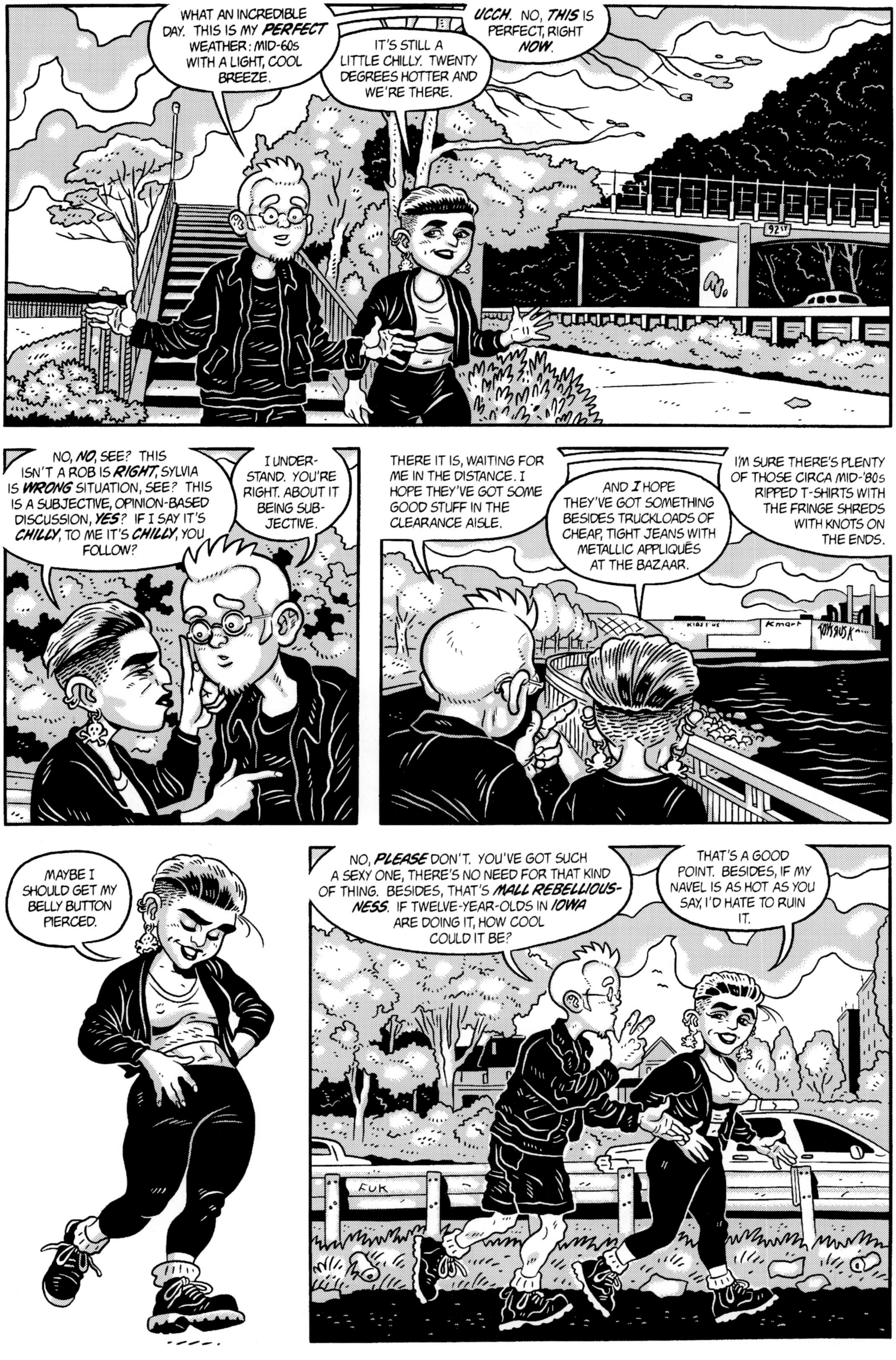
WHAT AN INCREDIBLE DAY. THIS IS MY PERFECT WEATHER: MID-60s WITH A LIGHT, COOL BREEZE.
IT'S STILL A LITTLE CHILLY. TWENTY DEGREES HOTTER AND WE'RE THERE.
UCCH. NO, THIS IS PERFECT, RIGHT NOW.
92 ST
NO, NO, SEE? THIS ISN'T A ROB IS RIGHT, SYLVIA IS WRONG SITUATION, SEE? THIS IS A SUBJECTIVE, OPINION-BASED DISCUSSION, YES? IF I SAY IT'S CHILLY, TO ME IT'S CHILLY, YOU FOLLOW?
I UNDER-STAND. YOU'RE RIGHT. ABOUT IT BEING SUB-JECTIVE.
THERE IT IS, WAITING FOR ME IN THE DISTANCE. I HOPE THEY'VE GOT SOME GOOD STUFF IN THE CLEARANCE AISLE.
AND I HOPE THEY'VE GOT SOMETHING BESIDES TRUCKLOADS OF CHEAP, TIGHT JEANS WITH METALLIC APPLIQUÉS AT THE BAZAAR.
I'M SURE THERE'S PLENTY OF THOSE CIRCA MID-'80s RIPPED T-SHIRTS WITH THE FRINGE SHREDS WITH KNOTS ON THE ENDS.
Kmart
MAYBE I SHOULD GET MY BELLY BUTTON PIERCED.
NO, PLEASE DON'T. YOU'VE GOT SUCH A SEXY ONE, THERE'S NO NEED FOR THAT KIND OF THING. BESIDES, THAT'S MALL REBELLIOUS-NESS. IF TWELVE-YEAR-OLDS IN IOWA ARE DOING IT, HOW COOL COULD IT BE?
THAT'S A GOOD POINT. BESIDES, IF MY NAVEL IS AS HOT AS YOU SAY, I'D HATE TO RUIN IT.
FUK

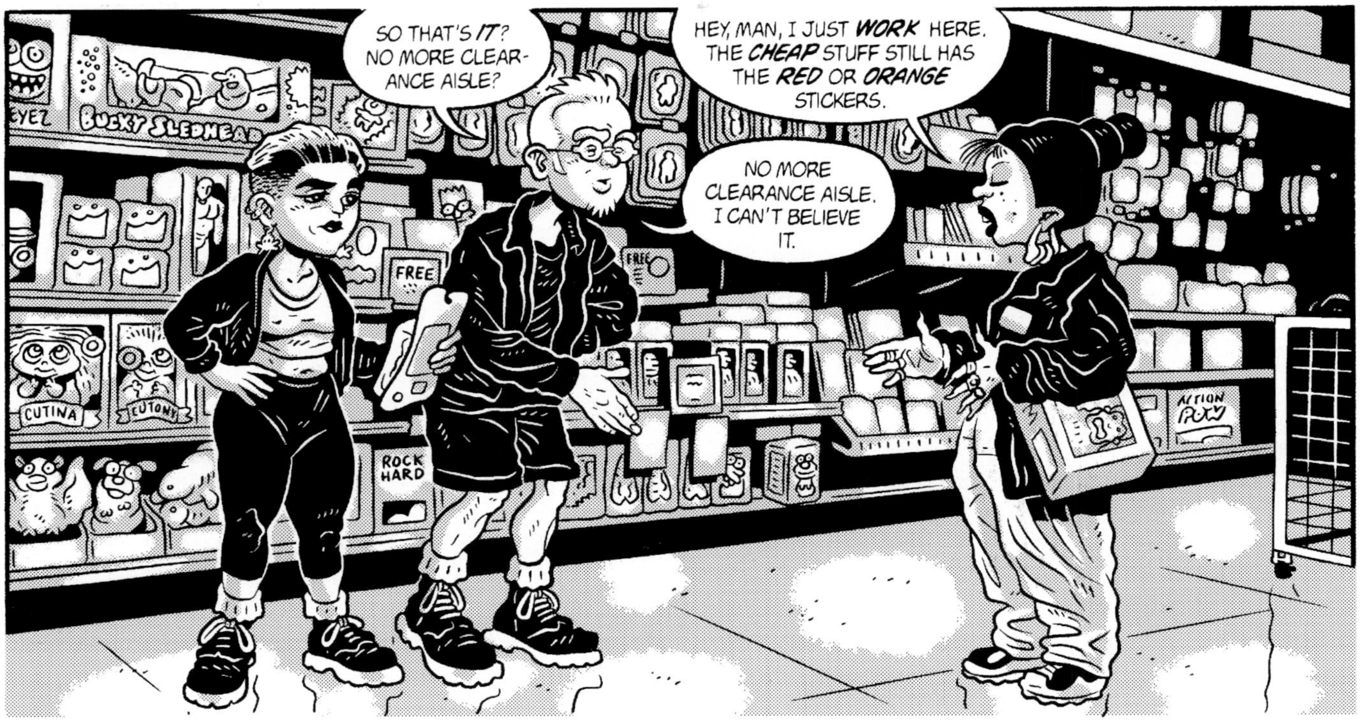
SO THAT'S IT? NO MORE CLEARANCE AISLE?
HEY, MAN, I JUST WORK HERE. THE CHEAP STUFF STILL HAS THE RED OR ORANGE STICKERS.
NO MORE CLEARANCE AISLE. I CAN'T BELIEVE IT.
EYEZ
BUCKY SLEDHEAD
FREE
CUTINA
CUTONY
ROCK HARD
ACTION PUTTY

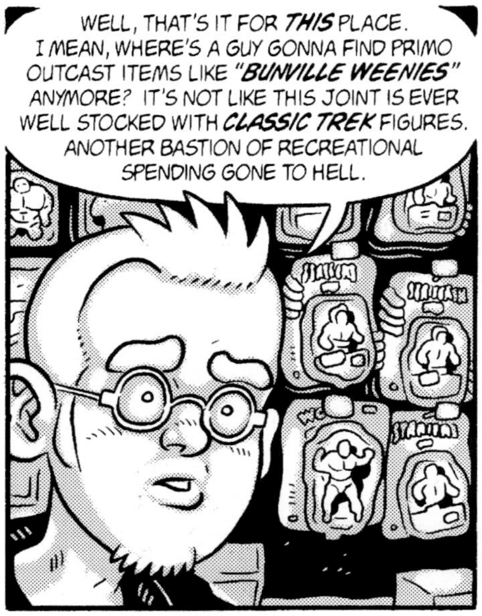
WELL, THAT'S IT FOR THIS PLACE. I MEAN, WHERE'S A GUY GONNA FIND PRIMO OUTCAST ITEMS LIKE "BUNVILLE WEENIES" ANYMORE? IT'S NOT LIKE THIS JOINT IS EVER WELL STOCKED WITH CLASSIC TREK FIGURES. ANOTHER BASTION OF RECREATIONAL SPENDING GONE TO HELL.

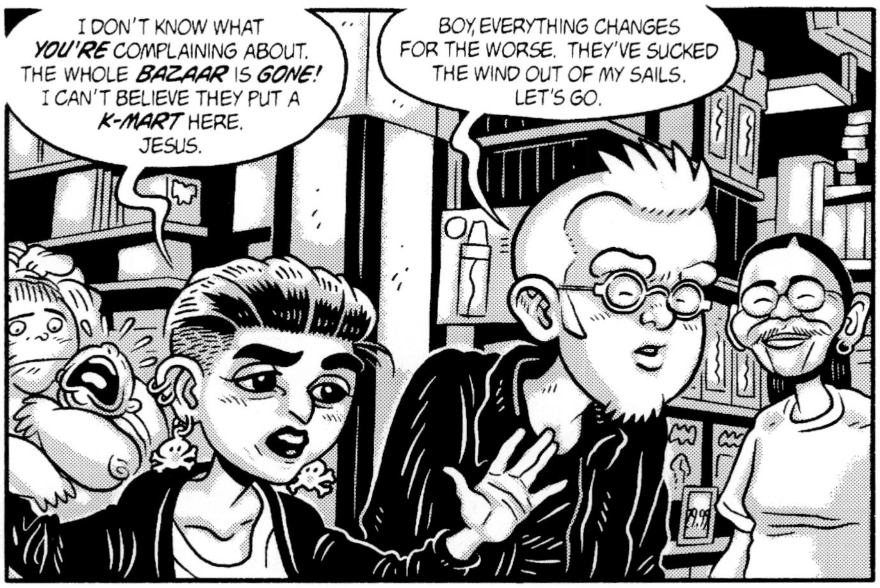
I DON'T KNOW WHAT YOU'RE COMPLAINING ABOUT. THE WHOLE BAZAAR IS GONE! I CAN'T BELIEVE THEY PUT A K-MART HERE. JESUS.
BOY, EVERYTHING CHANGES FOR THE WORSE. THEY'VE SUCKED THE WIND OUT OF MY SAILS. LET'S GO.

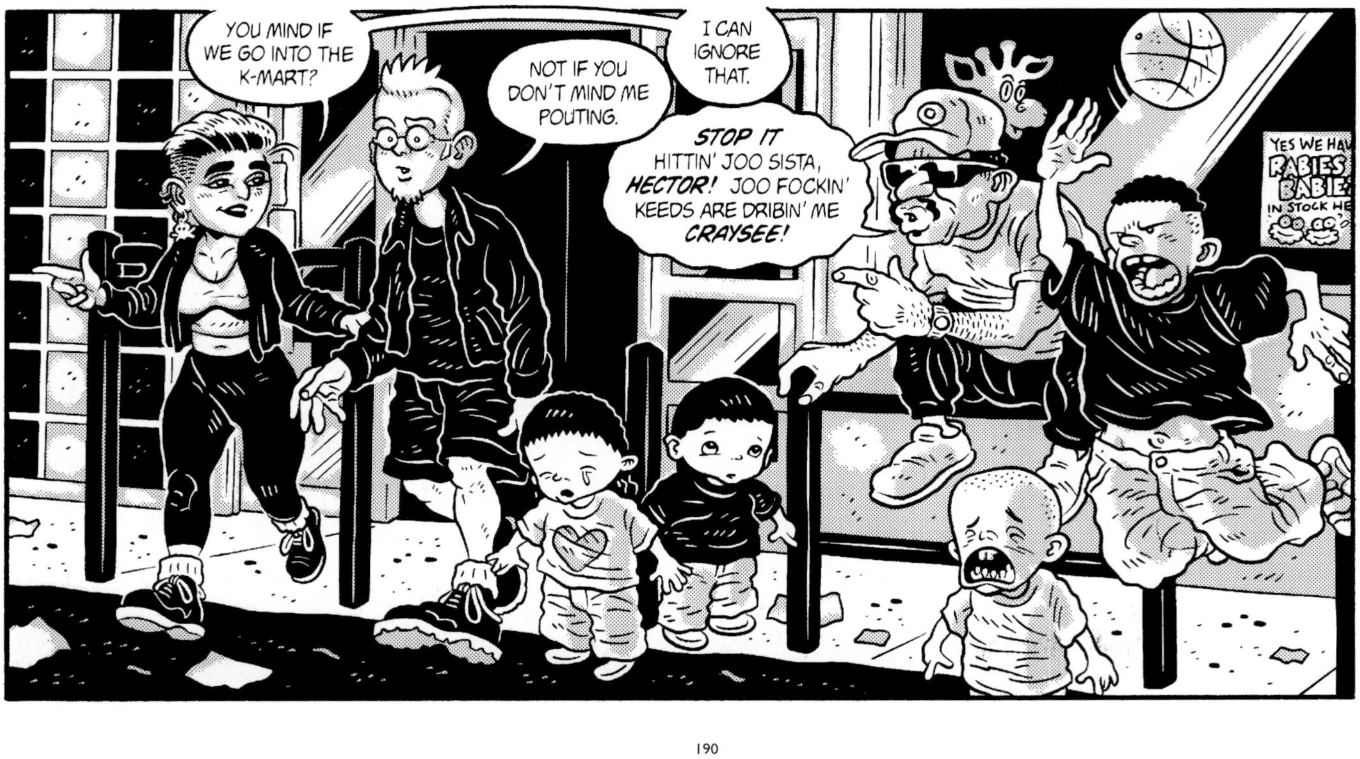
YOU MIND IF WE GO INTO THE K-MART?
NOT IF YOU DON'T MIND ME POUTING.
I CAN IGNORE THAT.
STOP IT HITTIN' JOO SISTA, HECTOR! JOO FOCKIN' KEEDS ARE DRIBIN' ME CRAYSEE!

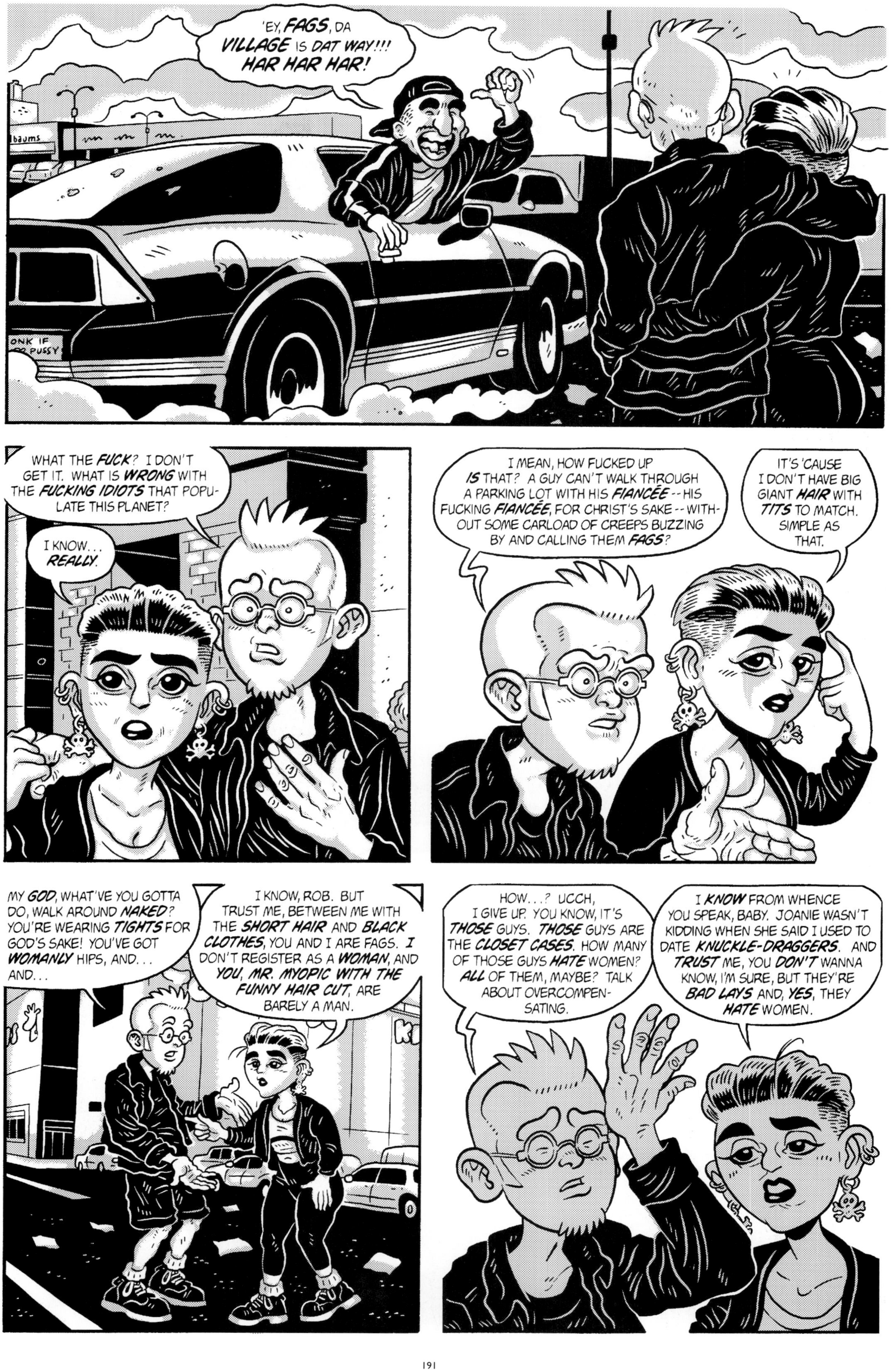
'EY, FAGS, DA VILLAGE IS DAT WAY!!! HAR HAR HAR!
WHAT THE FUCK? I DON'T GET IT. WHAT IS WRONG WITH THE FUCKING IDIOTS THAT POPULATE THIS PLANET?
I KNOW... REALLY.
I MEAN, HOW FUCKED UP IS THAT? A GUY CAN'T WALK THROUGH A PARKING LOT WITH HIS FIANCÉE--HIS FUCKING FIANCÉE, FOR CHRIST'S SAKE--WITHOUT SOME CARLOAD OF CREEPS BUZZING BY AND CALLING THEM FAGS?
IT'S 'CAUSE I DON'T HAVE BIG GIANT HAIR WITH TITS TO MATCH. SIMPLE AS THAT.
MY GOD, WHAT'VE YOU GOTTA DO, WALK AROUND NAKED? YOU'RE WEARING TIGHTS FOR GOD'S SAKE! YOU'VE GOT WOMANLY HIPS, AND... AND...
I KNOW, ROB. BUT TRUST ME, BETWEEN ME WITH THE SHORT HAIR AND BLACK CLOTHES, YOU AND I ARE FAGS. I DON'T REGISTER AS A WOMAN, AND YOU, MR. MYOPIC WITH THE FUNNY HAIR CUT, ARE BARELY A MAN.
HOW...? UCCH, I GIVE UP. YOU KNOW, IT'S THOSE GUYS. THOSE GUYS ARE THE CLOSET CASES. HOW MANY OF THOSE GUYS HATE WOMEN? ALL OF THEM, MAYBE? TALK ABOUT OVERCOMPENSATING.
I KNOW FROM WHENCE YOU SPEAK, BABY. JOANIE WASN'T KIDDING WHEN SHE SAID I USED TO DATE KNUCKLE-DRAGGERS. AND TRUST ME, YOU DON'T WANNA KNOW, I'M SURE, BUT THEY'RE BAD LAYS AND, YES, THEY HATE WOMEN.

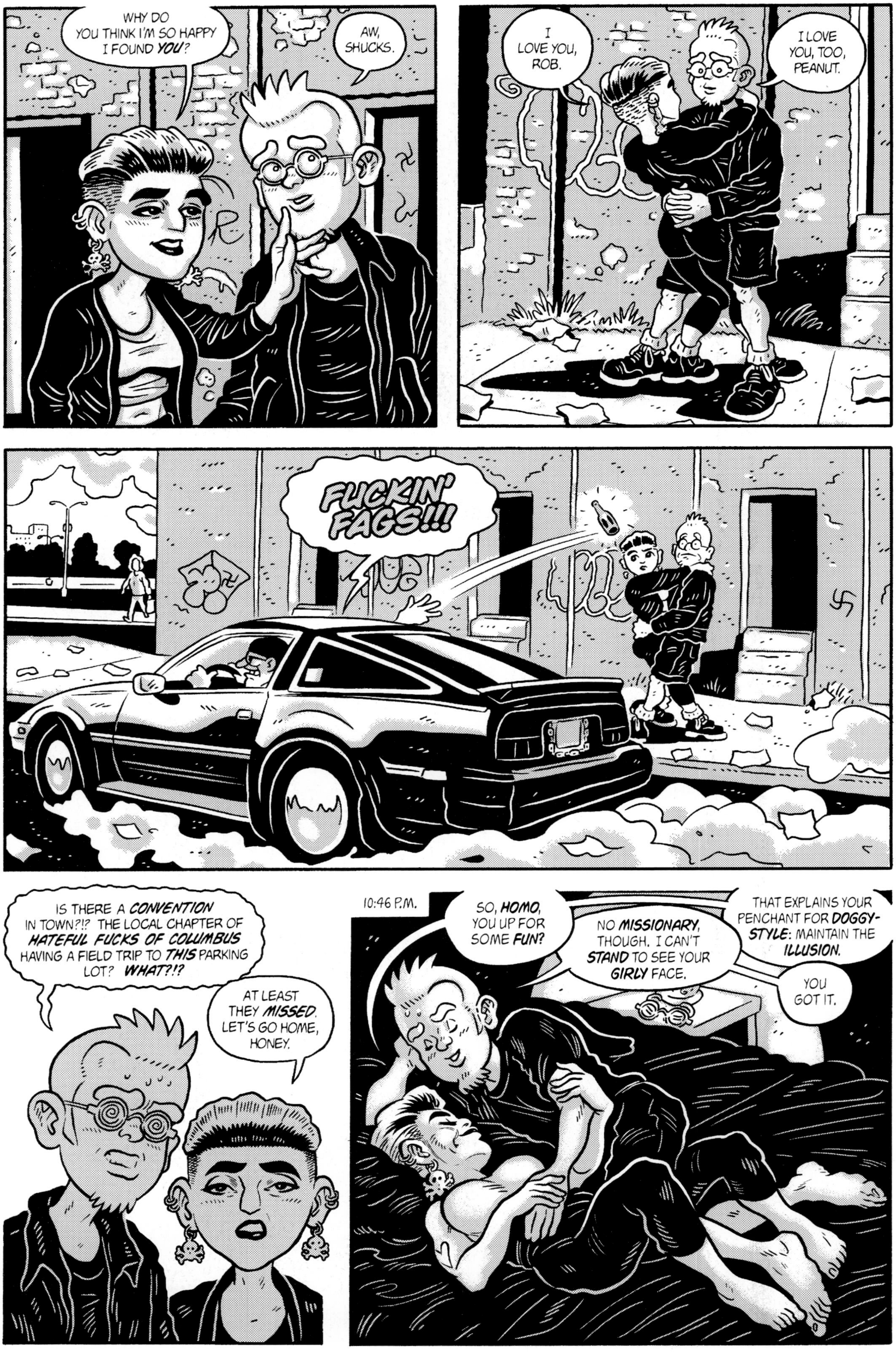

WHY DO YOU THINK I'M SO HAPPY I FOUND *YOU*?
AW, SHUCKS.
I LOVE YOU, ROB.
I LOVE YOU, TOO, PEANUT.
FUCKIN' FAGS!!!
IS THERE A *CONVENTION* IN TOWN?!? THE LOCAL CHAPTER OF *HATEFUL FUCKS OF COLUMBUS* HAVING A FIELD TRIP TO *THIS* PARKING LOT? *WHAT?!?*
AT LEAST THEY *MISSED*. LET'S GO HOME, HONEY.
10:46 P.M.
SO, *HOMO*, YOU UP FOR SOME *FUN*?
NO *MISSIONARY*, THOUGH. I CAN'T *STAND* TO SEE YOUR *GIRLY* FACE.
THAT EXPLAINS YOUR PENCHANT FOR *DOGGY-STYLE*: MAINTAIN THE *ILLUSION*.
YOU GOT IT.

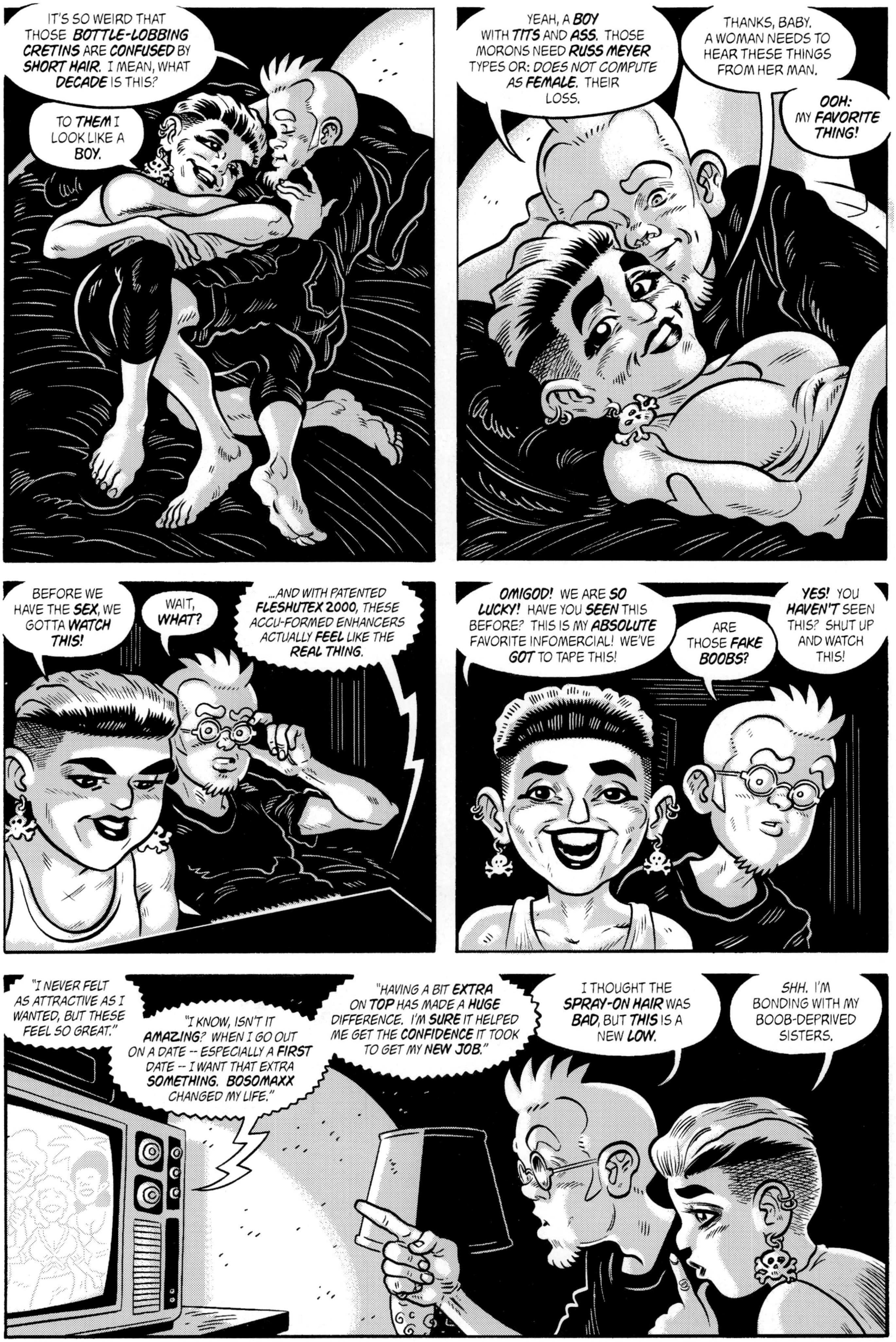
IT'S SO WEIRD THAT THOSE BOTTLE-LOBBING CRETINS ARE CONFUSED BY SHORT HAIR. I MEAN, WHAT DECADE IS THIS?
TO THEM I LOOK LIKE A BOY.
YEAH, A BOY WITH TITS AND ASS. THOSE MORONS NEED RUSS MEYER TYPES OR: DOES NOT COMPUTE AS FEMALE. THEIR LOSS.
THANKS, BABY. A WOMAN NEEDS TO HEAR THESE THINGS FROM HER MAN.
OOH: MY FAVORITE THING!
BEFORE WE HAVE THE SEX, WE GOTTA WATCH THIS!
WAIT, WHAT?
...AND WITH PATENTED FLESHUTEX 2000, THESE ACCU-FORMED ENHANCERS ACTUALLY FEEL LIKE THE REAL THING.
OMIGOD! WE ARE SO LUCKY! HAVE YOU SEEN THIS BEFORE? THIS IS MY ABSOLUTE FAVORITE INFOMERCIAL! WE'VE GOT TO TAPE THIS!
ARE THOSE FAKE BOOBS?
YES! YOU HAVEN'T SEEN THIS? SHUT UP AND WATCH THIS!
"I NEVER FELT AS ATTRACTIVE AS I WANTED, BUT THESE FEEL SO GREAT."
"I KNOW, ISN'T IT AMAZING? WHEN I GO OUT ON A DATE -- ESPECIALLY A FIRST DATE -- I WANT THAT EXTRA SOMETHING. BOSOMAXX CHANGED MY LIFE."
"HAVING A BIT EXTRA ON TOP HAS MADE A HUGE DIFFERENCE. I'M SURE IT HELPED ME GET THE CONFIDENCE IT TOOK TO GET MY NEW JOB."
I THOUGHT THE SPRAY-ON HAIR WAS BAD, BUT THIS IS A NEW LOW.
SHH. I'M BONDING WITH MY BOOB-DEPRIVED SISTERS.

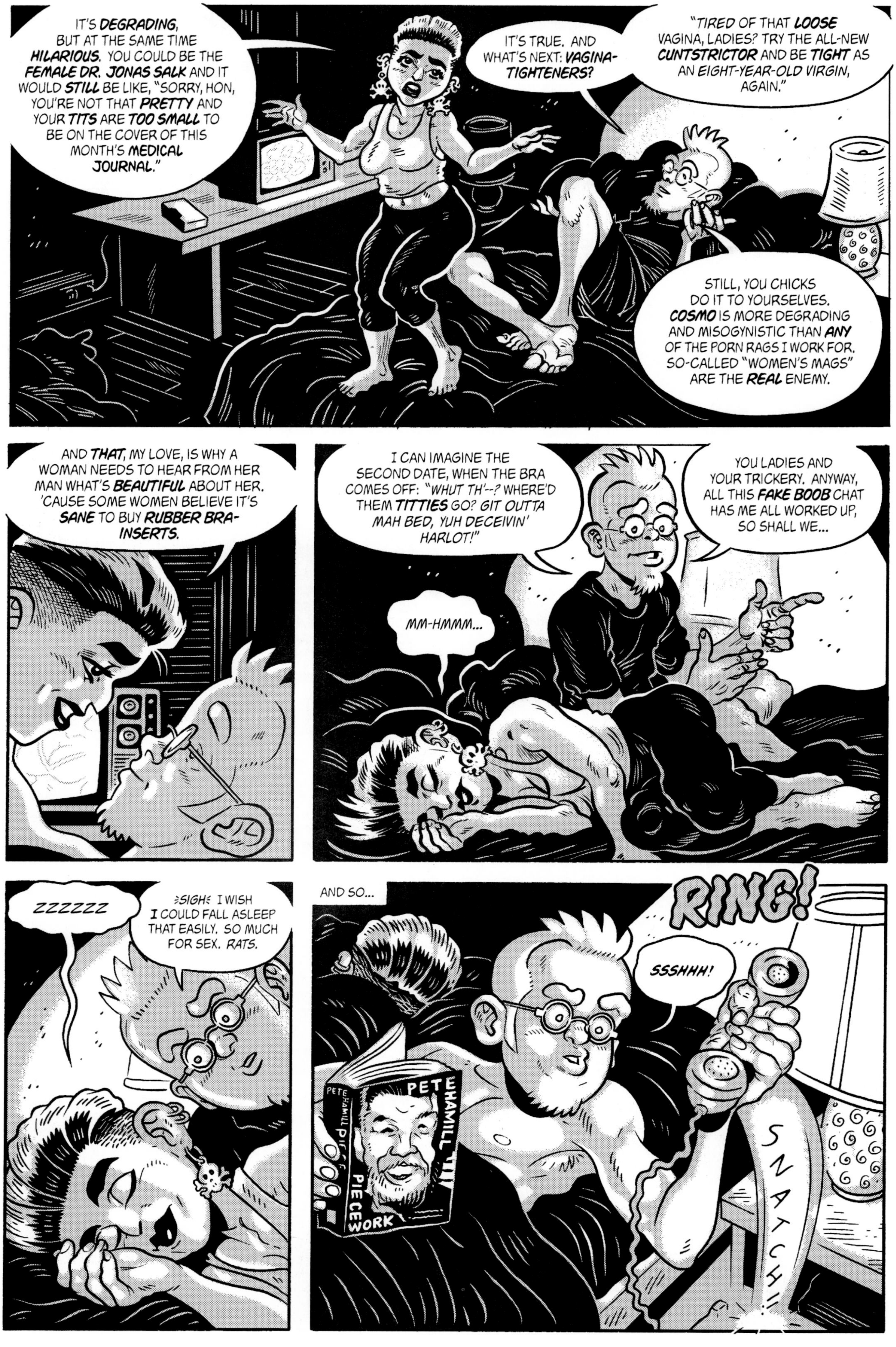
IT'S DEGRADING, BUT AT THE SAME TIME HILARIOUS. YOU COULD BE THE FEMALE DR. JONAS SALK AND IT WOULD STILL BE LIKE, "SORRY, HON, YOU'RE NOT THAT PRETTY AND YOUR TITS ARE TOO SMALL TO BE ON THE COVER OF THIS MONTH'S MEDICAL JOURNAL."
IT'S TRUE. AND WHAT'S NEXT: VAGINA-TIGHTENERS?
"TIRED OF THAT LOOSE VAGINA, LADIES? TRY THE ALL-NEW CUNTSTRICTOR AND BE TIGHT AS AN EIGHT-YEAR-OLD VIRGIN, AGAIN."
STILL, YOU CHICKS DO IT TO YOURSELVES. COSMO IS MORE DEGRADING AND MISOGYNISTIC THAN ANY OF THE PORN RAGS I WORK FOR. SO-CALLED "WOMEN'S MAGS" ARE THE REAL ENEMY.
AND THAT, MY LOVE, IS WHY A WOMAN NEEDS TO HEAR FROM HER MAN WHAT'S BEAUTIFUL ABOUT HER. 'CAUSE SOME WOMEN BELIEVE IT'S SANE TO BUY RUBBER BRA-INSERTS.
I CAN IMAGINE THE SECOND DATE, WHEN THE BRA COMES OFF: "WHUT TH'--? WHERE'D THEM TITTIES GO? GIT OUTTA MAH BED, YUH DECEIVIN' HARLOT!"
YOU LADIES AND YOUR TRICKERY. ANYWAY, ALL THIS FAKE BOOB CHAT HAS ME ALL WORKED UP, SO SHALL WE...
MM-HMMM...
ZZZZZZ
SIGH I WISH I COULD FALL ASLEEP THAT EASILY. SO MUCH FOR SEX. RATS.
AND SO...
RING!
SSSHHH!
PETE HAMILL PIECEWORK
SNATCH!

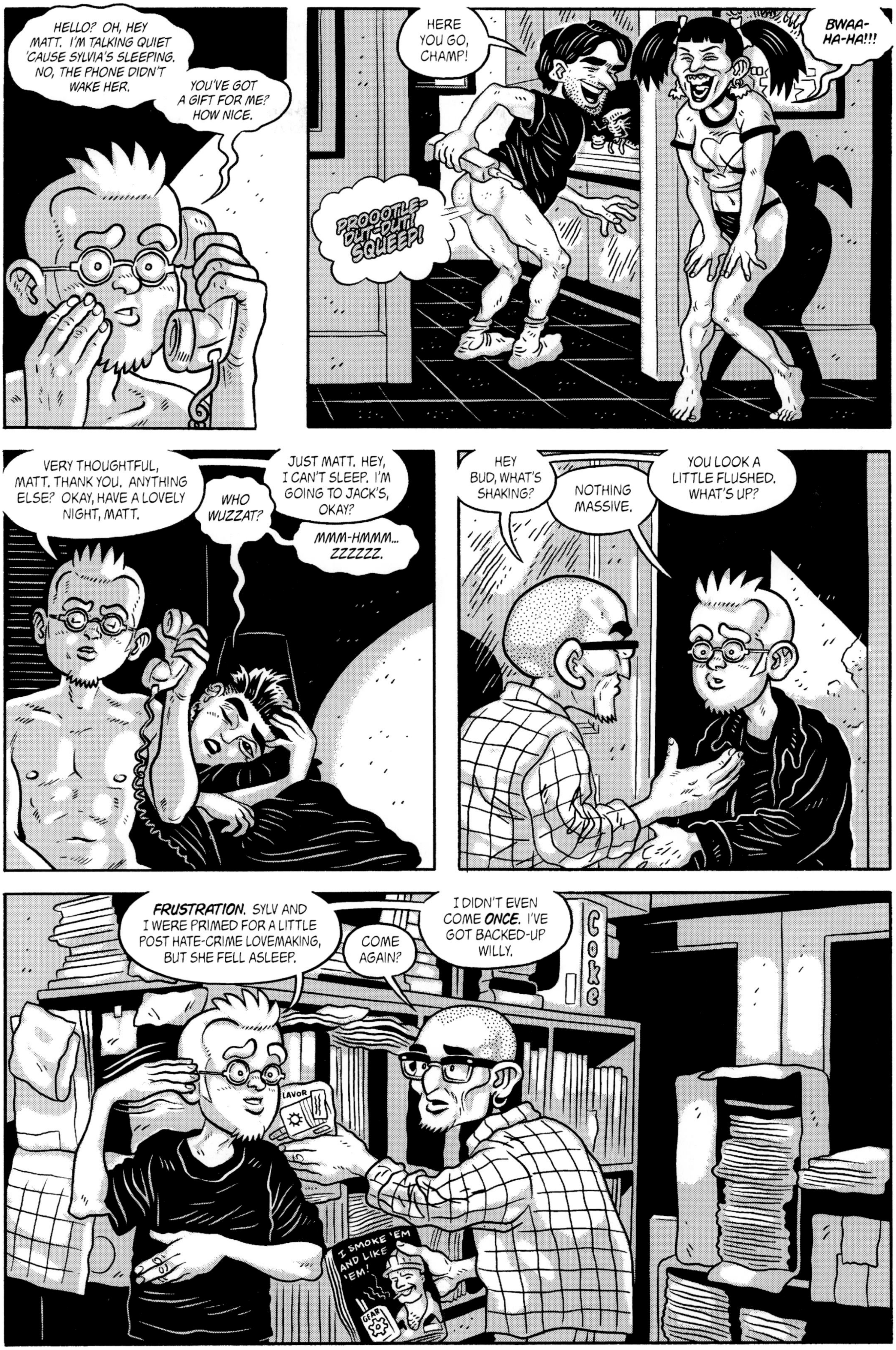
HELLO? OH, HEY MATT. I'M TALKING QUIET 'CAUSE SYLVIA'S SLEEPING. NO, THE PHONE DIDN'T WAKE HER.
YOU'VE GOT A GIFT FOR ME? HOW NICE.
HERE YOU GO, CHAMP!
BWAA-HA-HA!!!
PROOOTLE-DUT-DUT! SQUEEP!
VERY THOUGHTFUL, MATT. THANK YOU. ANYTHING ELSE? OKAY, HAVE A LOVELY NIGHT, MATT.
WHO WUZZAT?
JUST MATT. HEY, I CAN'T SLEEP. I'M GOING TO JACK'S, OKAY?
MMM-HMMM... ZZZZZZ.
HEY BUD, WHAT'S SHAKING?
NOTHING MASSIVE.
YOU LOOK A LITTLE FLUSHED. WHAT'S UP?
FRUSTRATION. SYLV AND I WERE PRIMED FOR A LITTLE POST HATE-CRIME LOVEMAKING, BUT SHE FELL ASLEEP.
COME AGAIN?
I DIDN'T EVEN COME ONCE. I'VE GOT BACKED-UP WILLY.
COKE
I SMOKE 'EM AND LIKE 'EM!

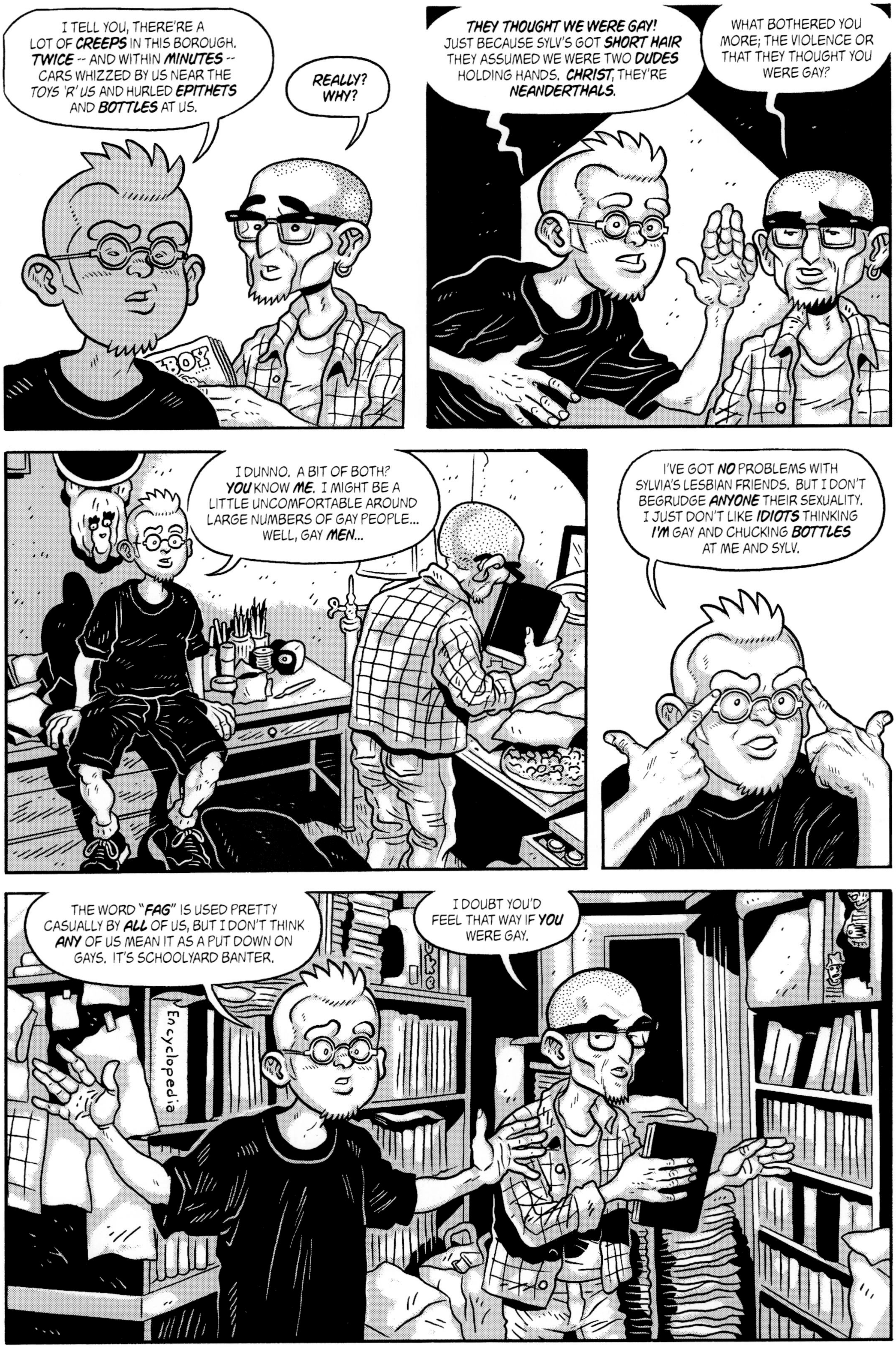

I TELL YOU, THERE'RE A LOT OF CREEPS IN THIS BOROUGH. TWICE -- AND WITHIN MINUTES -- CARS WHIZZED BY US NEAR THE TOYS 'R' US AND HURLED EPITHETS AND BOTTLES AT US.
REALLY? WHY?
THEY THOUGHT WE WERE GAY! JUST BECAUSE SYLV'S GOT SHORT HAIR THEY ASSUMED WE WERE TWO DUDES HOLDING HANDS. CHRIST, THEY'RE NEANDERTHALS.
WHAT BOTHERED YOU MORE; THE VIOLENCE OR THAT THEY THOUGHT YOU WERE GAY?
I DUNNO. A BIT OF BOTH? YOU KNOW ME. I MIGHT BE A LITTLE UNCOMFORTABLE AROUND LARGE NUMBERS OF GAY PEOPLE... WELL, GAY MEN...
I'VE GOT NO PROBLEMS WITH SYLVIA'S LESBIAN FRIENDS. BUT I DON'T BEGRUDGE ANYONE THEIR SEXUALITY. I JUST DON'T LIKE IDIOTS THINKING I'M GAY AND CHUCKING BOTTLES AT ME AND SYLV.
THE WORD "FAG" IS USED PRETTY CASUALLY BY ALL OF US, BUT I DON'T THINK ANY OF US MEAN IT AS A PUT DOWN ON GAYS. IT'S SCHOOLYARD BANTER.
I DOUBT YOU'D FEEL THAT WAY IF YOU WERE GAY.
Encyclopedia

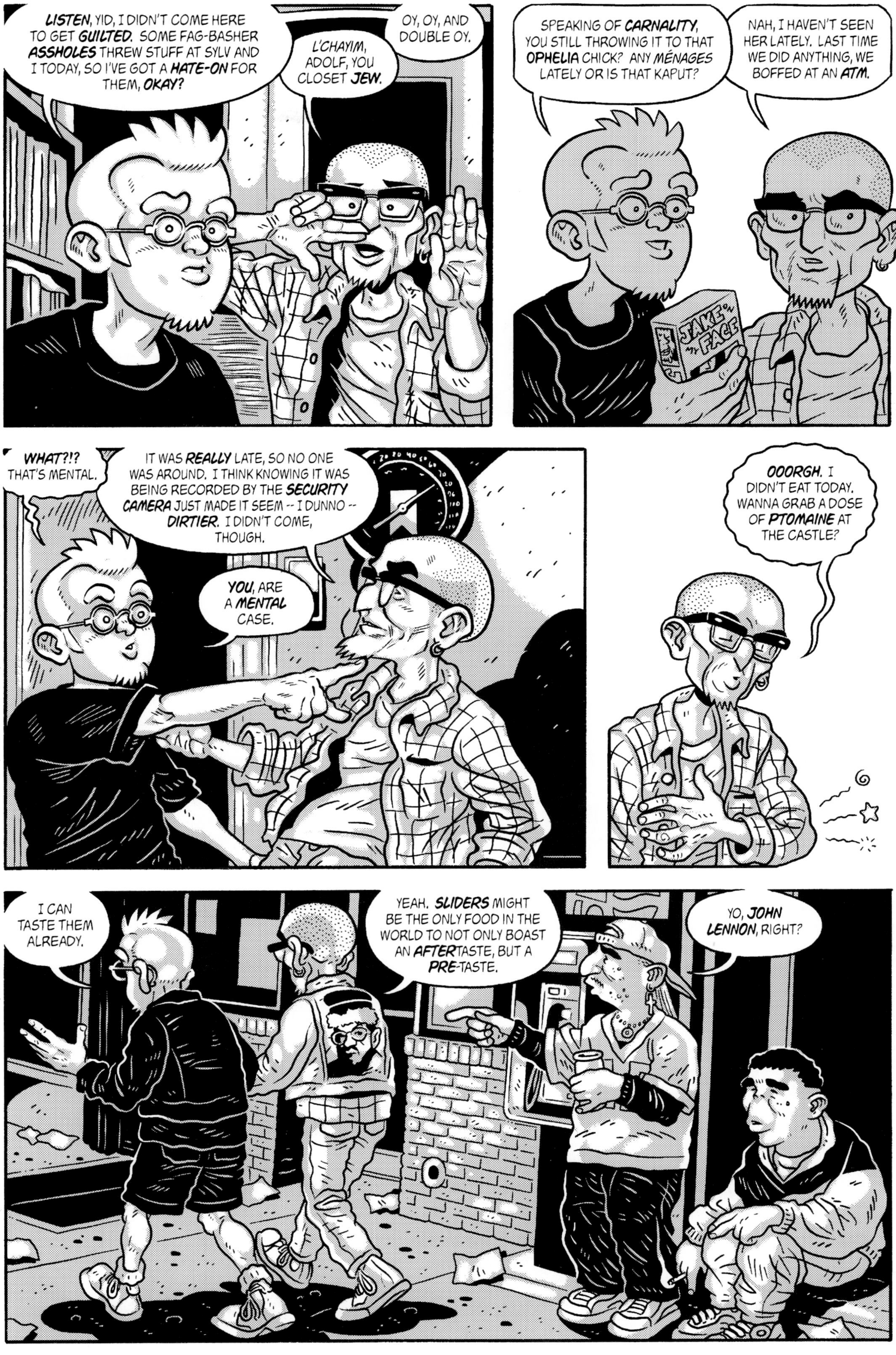

LISTEN, YID, I DIDN'T COME HERE TO GET GUILTED. SOME FAG-BASHER ASSHOLES THREW STUFF AT SYLV AND I TODAY, SO I'VE GOT A HATE-ON FOR THEM, OKAY?
L'CHAYIM, ADOLF, YOU CLOSET JEW.
OY, OY, AND DOUBLE OY.
SPEAKING OF CARNALITY, YOU STILL THROWING IT TO THAT OPHELIA CHICK? ANY MÉNAGES LATELY OR IS THAT KAPUT?
NAH, I HAVEN'T SEEN HER LATELY. LAST TIME WE DID ANYTHING, WE BOFFED AT AN ATM.
JAKE ON MY FACE
WHAT?!? THAT'S MENTAL.
IT WAS REALLY LATE, SO NO ONE WAS AROUND. I THINK KNOWING IT WAS BEING RECORDED BY THE SECURITY CAMERA JUST MADE IT SEEM -- I DUNNO -- DIRTIER. I DIDN'T COME, THOUGH.
YOU, ARE A MENTAL CASE.
OOORGH. I DIDN'T EAT TODAY. WANNA GRAB A DOSE OF PTOMAINE AT THE CASTLE?
I CAN TASTE THEM ALREADY.
YEAH. SLIDERS MIGHT BE THE ONLY FOOD IN THE WORLD TO NOT ONLY BOAST AN AFTERTASTE, BUT A PRE-TASTE.
YO, JOHN LENNON, RIGHT?

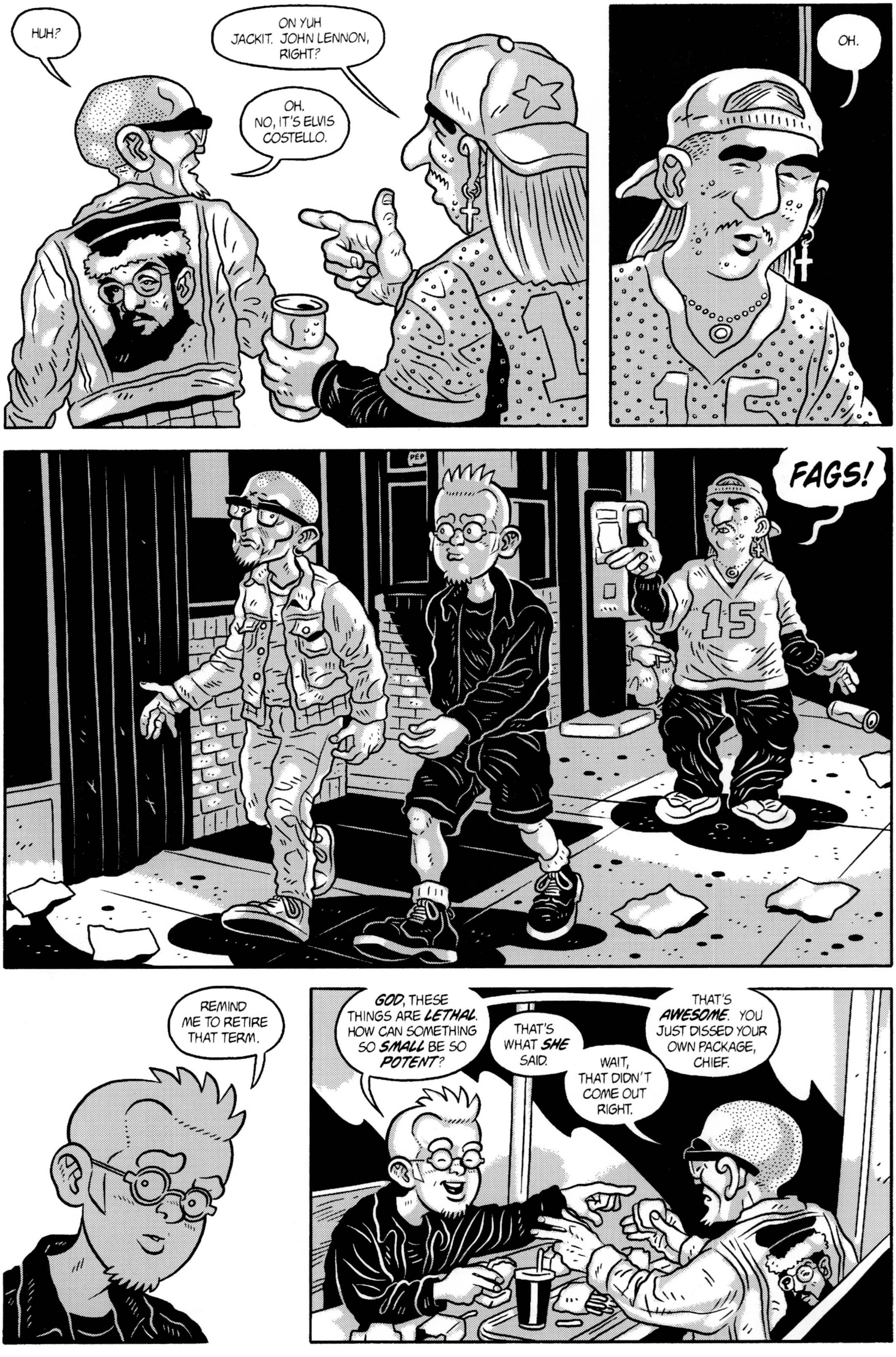
HUH?
ON YUH JACKIT. JOHN LENNON, RIGHT?
OH. NO, IT'S ELVIS COSTELLO.
OH.
FAGS!
REMIND ME TO RETIRE THAT TERM.
GOD, THESE THINGS ARE LETHAL. HOW CAN SOMETHING SO SMALL BE SO POTENT?
THAT'S WHAT SHE SAID.
WAIT, THAT DIDN'T COME OUT RIGHT.
THAT'S AWESOME. YOU JUST DISSED YOUR OWN PACKAGE, CHIEF.

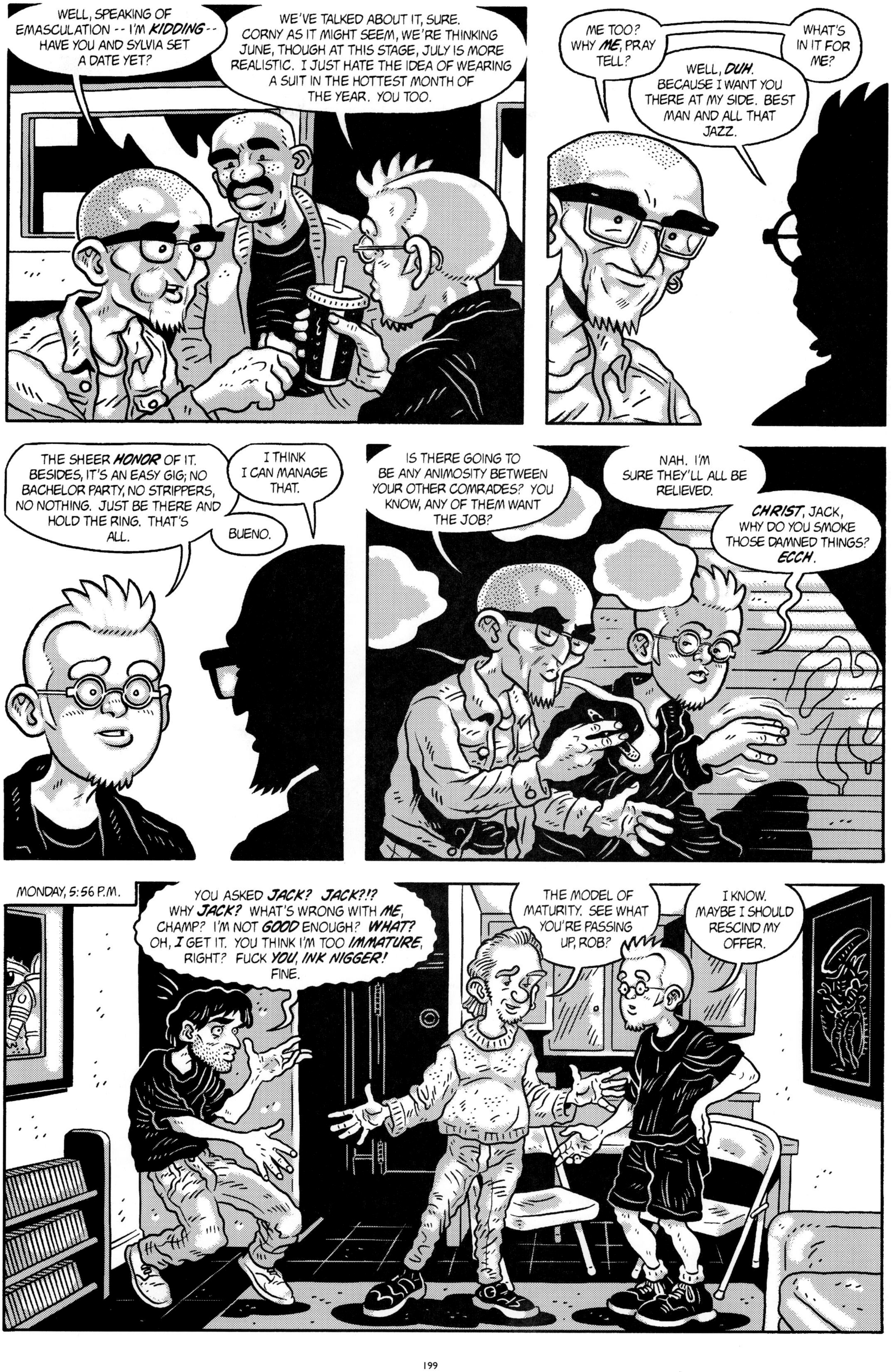
WELL, SPEAKING OF EMASCULATION -- I'M KIDDING -- HAVE YOU AND SYLVIA SET A DATE YET?
WE'VE TALKED ABOUT IT, SURE. CORNY AS IT MIGHT SEEM, WE'RE THINKING JUNE, THOUGH AT THIS STAGE, JULY IS MORE REALISTIC. I JUST HATE THE IDEA OF WEARING A SUIT IN THE HOTTEST MONTH OF THE YEAR. YOU TOO.
ME TOO? WHY ME, PRAY TELL?
WHAT'S IN IT FOR ME?
WELL, DUH. BECAUSE I WANT YOU THERE AT MY SIDE. BEST MAN AND ALL THAT JAZZ.
THE SHEER HONOR OF IT. BESIDES, IT'S AN EASY GIG; NO BACHELOR PARTY, NO STRIPPERS, NO NOTHING. JUST BE THERE AND HOLD THE RING. THAT'S ALL.
I THINK I CAN MANAGE THAT.
BUENO.
IS THERE GOING TO BE ANY ANIMOSITY BETWEEN YOUR OTHER COMRADES? YOU KNOW, ANY OF THEM WANT THE JOB?
NAH. I'M SURE THEY'LL ALL BE RELIEVED.
CHRIST, JACK, WHY DO YOU SMOKE THOSE DAMNED THINGS? ECCH.
MONDAY, 5:56 P.M.
YOU ASKED JACK? JACK?!? WHY JACK? WHAT'S WRONG WITH ME, CHAMP? I'M NOT GOOD ENOUGH? WHAT? OH, I GET IT. YOU THINK I'M TOO IMMATURE, RIGHT? FUCK YOU, INK NIGGER! FINE.
THE MODEL OF MATURITY. SEE WHAT YOU'RE PASSING UP, ROB?
I KNOW. MAYBE I SHOULD RESCIND MY OFFER.

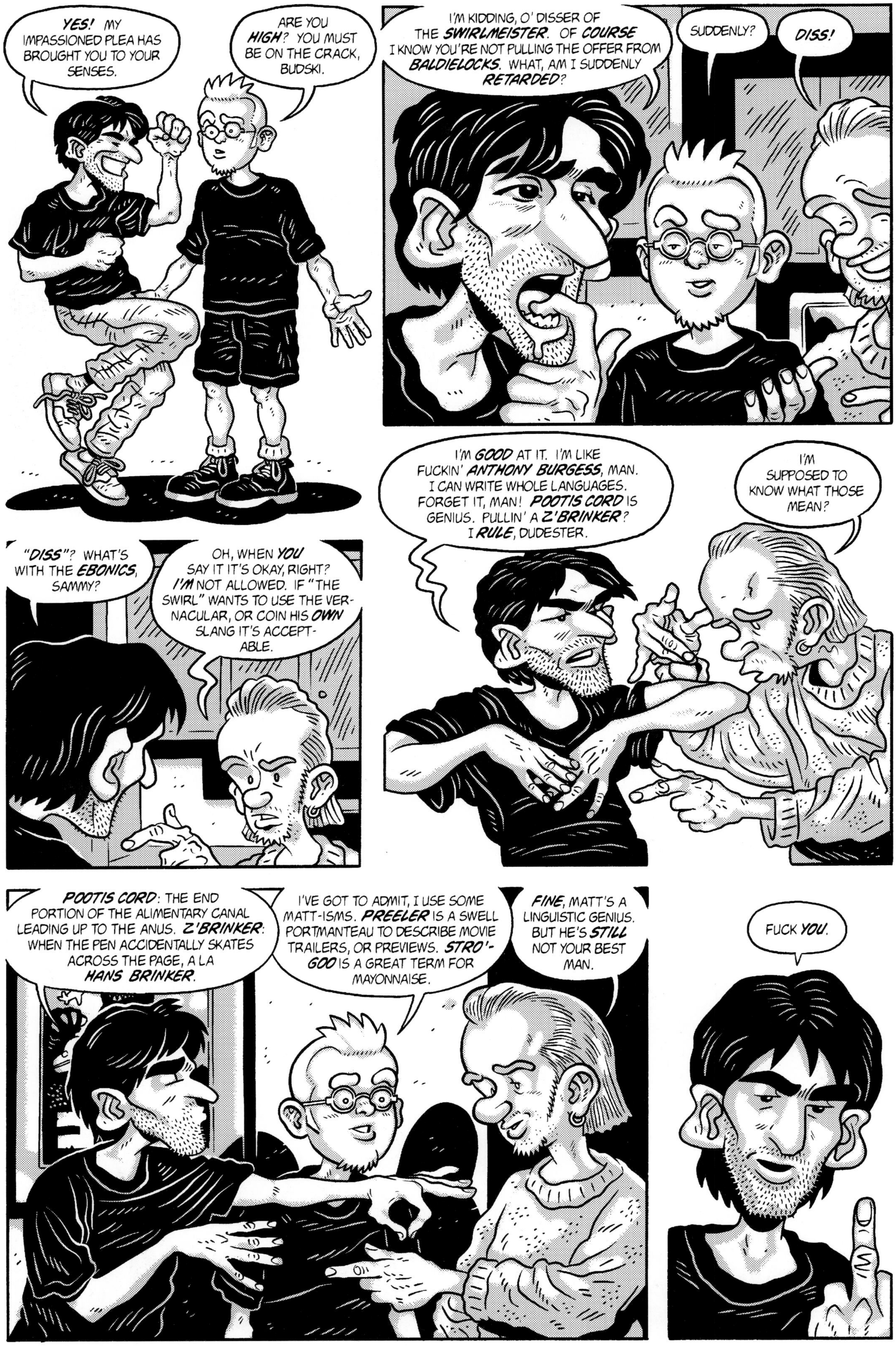
YES! MY IMPASSIONED PLEA HAS BROUGHT YOU TO YOUR SENSES.
ARE YOU HIGH? YOU MUST BE ON THE CRACK, BUDSKI.
I'M KIDDING, O' DISSER OF THE SWIRLMEISTER. OF COURSE I KNOW YOU'RE NOT PULLING THE OFFER FROM BALDIELOCKS. WHAT, AM I SUDDENLY RETARDED?
SUDDENLY?
DISS!
"DISS"? WHAT'S WITH THE EBONICS, SAMMY?
OH, WHEN YOU SAY IT IT'S OKAY, RIGHT? I'M NOT ALLOWED. IF "THE SWIRL" WANTS TO USE THE VERNACULAR, OR COIN HIS OWN SLANG IT'S ACCEPTABLE.
I'M GOOD AT IT. I'M LIKE FUCKIN' ANTHONY BURGESS, MAN. I CAN WRITE WHOLE LANGUAGES. FORGET IT, MAN! POOTIS CORD IS GENIUS. PULLIN' A Z'BRINKER? I RULE, DUDESTER.
I'M SUPPOSED TO KNOW WHAT THOSE MEAN?
POOTIS CORD: THE END PORTION OF THE ALIMENTARY CANAL LEADING UP TO THE ANUS. Z'BRINKER: WHEN THE PEN ACCIDENTALLY SKATES ACROSS THE PAGE, A LA HANS BRINKER.
I'VE GOT TO ADMIT, I USE SOME MATT-ISMS. PREELER IS A SWELL PORTMANTEAU TO DESCRIBE MOVIE TRAILERS, OR PREVIEWS. STRO'-GOO IS A GREAT TERM FOR MAYONNAISE.
FINE, MATT'S A LINGUISTIC GENIUS. BUT HE'S STILL NOT YOUR BEST MAN.
FUCK YOU.

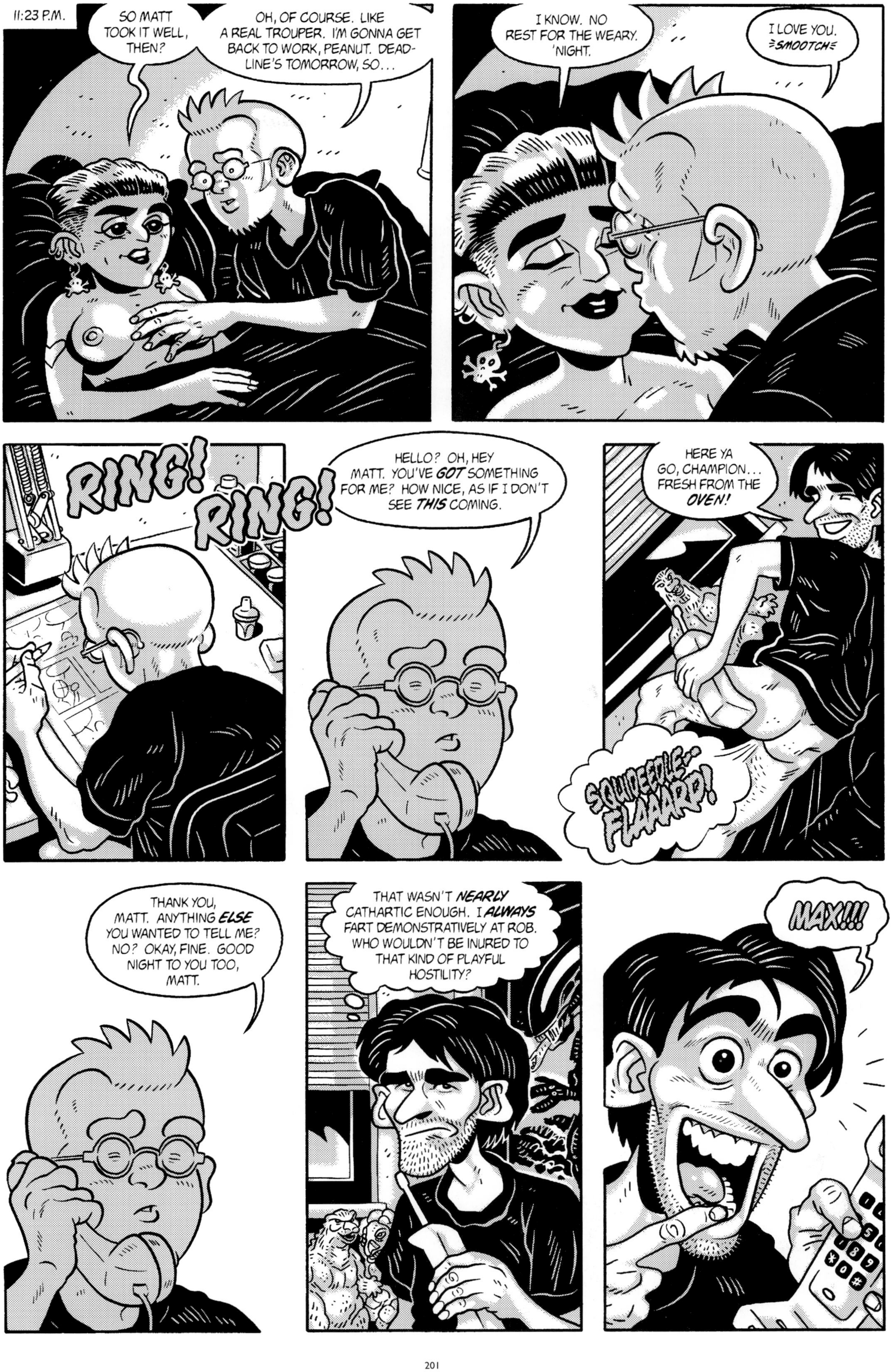

11:23 P.M.
SO MATT TOOK IT WELL, THEN?
OH, OF COURSE. LIKE A REAL TROUPER. I'M GONNA GET BACK TO WORK, PEANUT. DEAD-LINE'S TOMORROW, SO...
I KNOW. NO REST FOR THE WEARY. 'NIGHT.
I LOVE YOU. SMOOTCH
RING! RING!
HELLO? OH, HEY MATT. YOU'VE GOT SOMETHING FOR ME? HOW NICE, AS IF I DON'T SEE THIS COMING.
HERE YA GO, CHAMPION... FRESH FROM THE OVEN!
SQUIDEEDLE-- FLAAARP!
THANK YOU, MATT. ANYTHING ELSE YOU WANTED TO TELL ME? NO? OKAY, FINE. GOOD NIGHT TO YOU TOO, MATT.
THAT WASN'T NEARLY CATHARTIC ENOUGH. I ALWAYS FART DEMONSTRATIVELY AT ROB. WHO WOULDN'T BE INURED TO THAT KIND OF PLAYFUL HOSTILITY?
MAX!!!

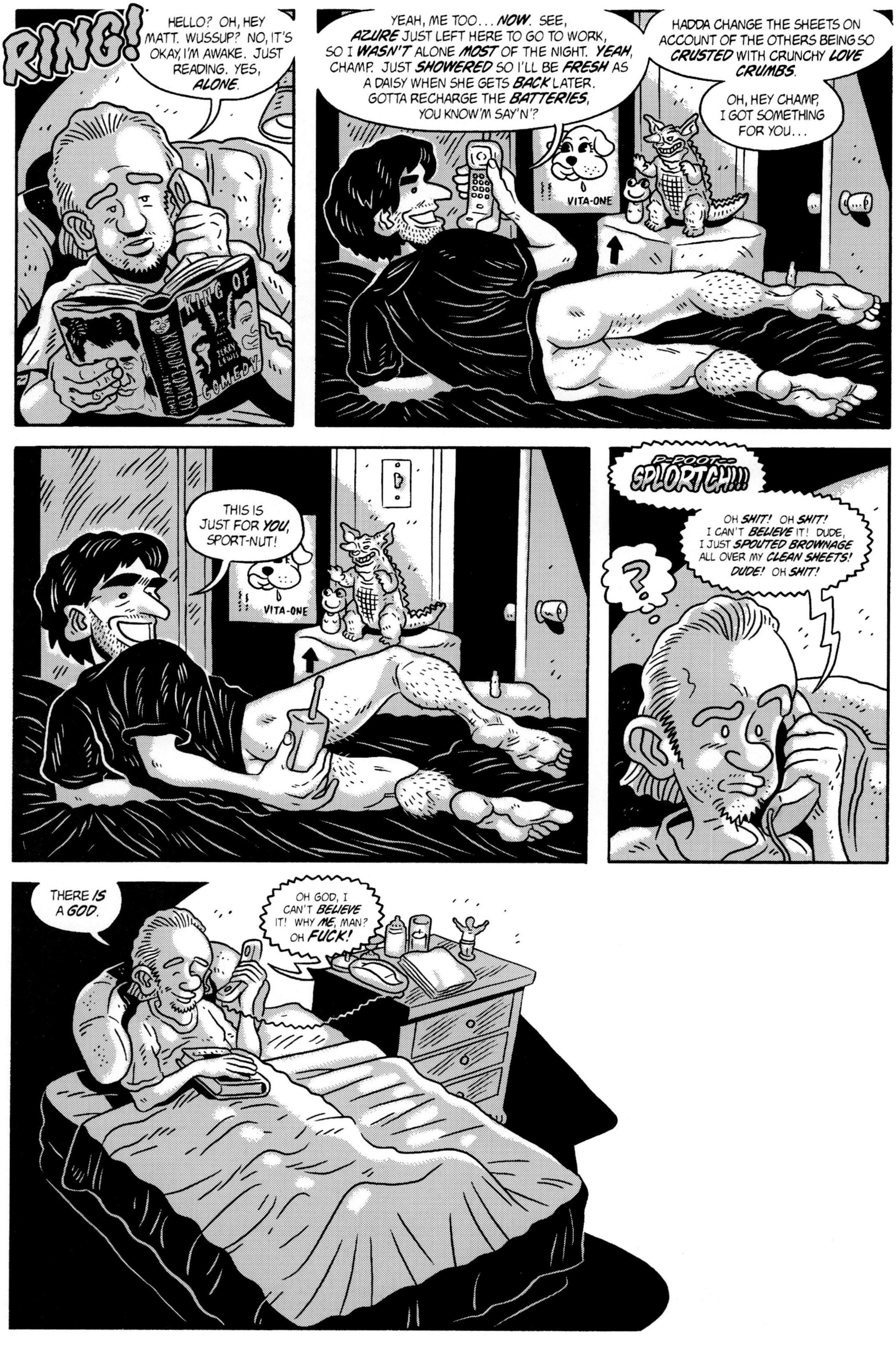
RING!
HELLO? OH, HEY MATT. WUSSUP? NO, IT'S OKAY, I'M AWAKE. JUST READING. YES, ALONE.
KING OF COMEDY
YEAH, ME TOO... NOW. SEE, AZURE JUST LEFT HERE TO GO TO WORK, SO I WASN'T ALONE MOST OF THE NIGHT. YEAH, CHAMP. JUST SHOWERED SO I'LL BE FRESH AS A DAISY WHEN SHE GETS BACK LATER. GOTTA RECHARGE THE BATTERIES, YOU KNOW'M SAY'N'?
VITA-ONE
HADDA CHANGE THE SHEETS ON ACCOUNT OF THE OTHERS BEING SO CRUSTED WITH CRUNCHY LOVE CRUMBS.
OH, HEY CHAMP, I GOT SOMETHING FOR YOU...
THIS IS JUST FOR YOU, SPORT-NUT!
VITA-ONE
P-POOT-- SPLORTCH!!!
OH SHIT! OH SHIT! I CAN'T BELIEVE IT! DUDE, I JUST SPOUTED BROWNAGE ALL OVER MY CLEAN SHEETS! DUDE! OH SHIT!
?
THERE IS A GOD.
OH GOD, I CAN'T BELIEVE IT! WHY ME, MAN? OH FUCK!

Chapter Nine

ECCH LIBRIS

THURSDAY, JUNE 2ND, 8:45 P.M.

AND HOW MANY BOOKS DID YOU BRING *THIS* TIME?

I DUNNO...ABOUT **25**, GIVE OR TAKE. UNCORRECTED PROOFS AND SOME FOREIGN EDITIONS, MOSTLY.

IT'S TIMES LIKE THIS I REGRET HAVING INTRODUCED YOU TO AMIS' WORK.

I'VE BROUGHT MORE THAN THIS BE-FORE. IT DIDN'T SEEM TO BOTHER HIM.

THAT'S BECAUSE HE'S TOO GRACIOUS TO SAY, "GET THE HELL OUTTA HERE, NUTJOB!" LOOK, I'M GONNA GO TO THE ART SECTION WHILE YOU GET YOUR STUFF SIGNED.

FINE.

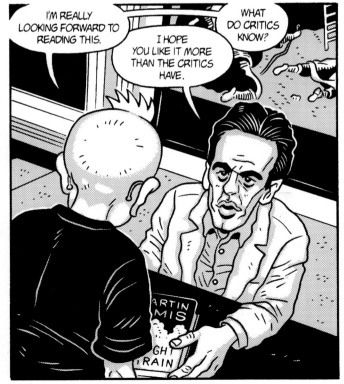

I'M REALLY LOOKING FORWARD TO READING THIS.

I HOPE YOU LIKE IT MORE THAN THE CRITICS HAVE.

WHAT DO CRITICS KNOW?

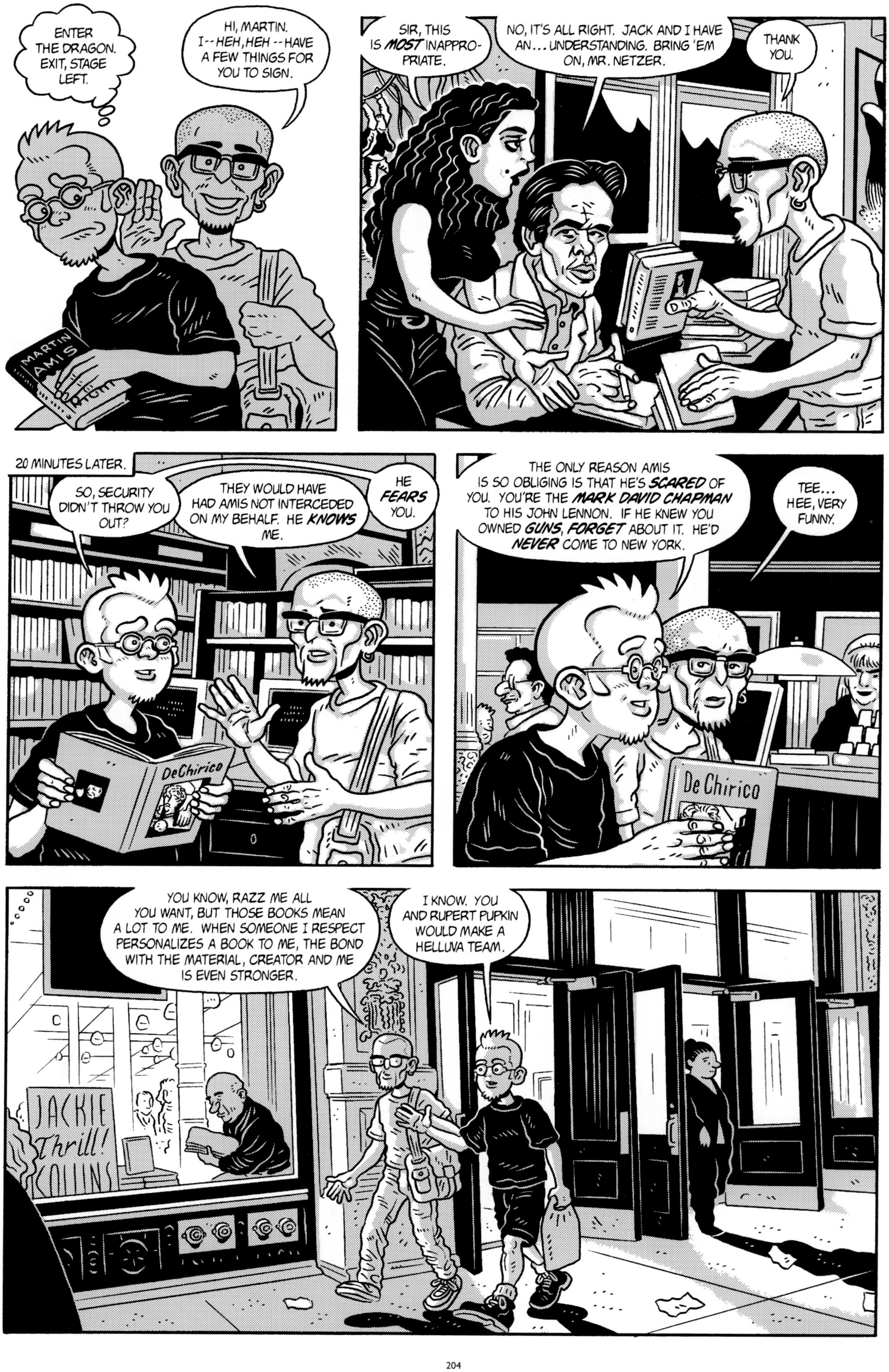
ENTER THE DRAGON. EXIT, STAGE LEFT.
HI, MARTIN. I--HEH, HEH--HAVE A FEW THINGS FOR YOU TO SIGN.
MARTIN AMIS
SIR, THIS IS MOST INAPPROPRIATE.
NO, IT'S ALL RIGHT. JACK AND I HAVE AN... UNDERSTANDING. BRING 'EM ON, MR. NETZER.
THANK YOU.
20 MINUTES LATER.
SO, SECURITY DIDN'T THROW YOU OUT?
THEY WOULD HAVE HAD AMIS NOT INTERCEDED ON MY BEHALF. HE KNOWS ME.
HE FEARS YOU.
DeChirico
THE ONLY REASON AMIS IS SO OBLIGING IS THAT HE'S SCARED OF YOU. YOU'RE THE MARK DAVID CHAPMAN TO HIS JOHN LENNON. IF HE KNEW YOU OWNED GUNS, FORGET ABOUT IT. HE'D NEVER COME TO NEW YORK.
TEE... HEE, VERY FUNNY.
De Chirico
YOU KNOW, RAZZ ME ALL YOU WANT, BUT THOSE BOOKS MEAN A LOT TO ME. WHEN SOMEONE I RESPECT PERSONALIZES A BOOK TO ME, THE BOND WITH THE MATERIAL, CREATOR AND ME IS EVEN STRONGER.
I KNOW. YOU AND RUPERT PUPKIN WOULD MAKE A HELLUVA TEAM.
JACKIE Thrill! COLLINS

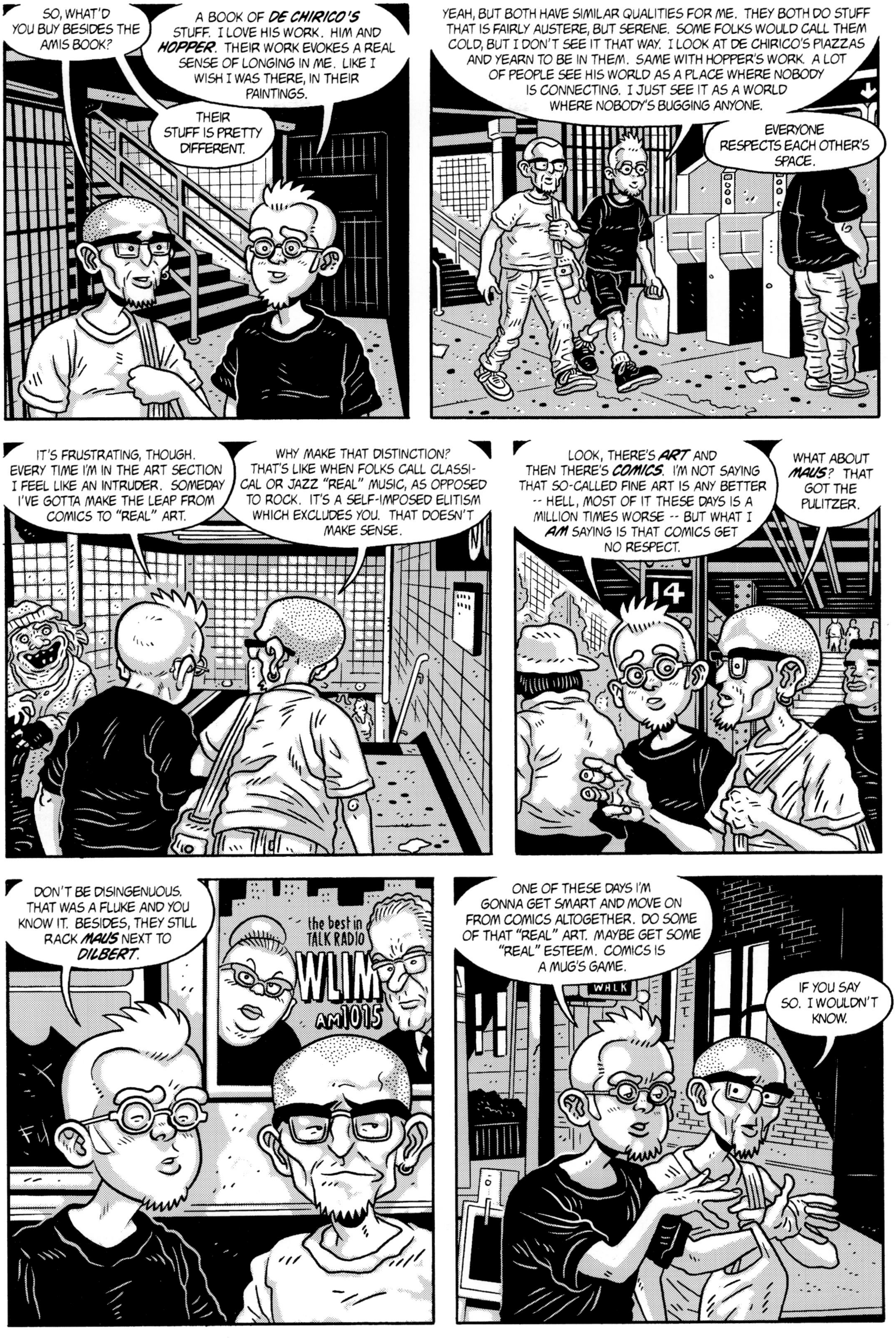
SO, WHAT'D YOU BUY BESIDES THE AMIS BOOK?
A BOOK OF DE CHIRICO'S STUFF. I LOVE HIS WORK. HIM AND HOPPER. THEIR WORK EVOKES A REAL SENSE OF LONGING IN ME. LIKE I WISH I WAS THERE, IN THEIR PAINTINGS.
THEIR STUFF IS PRETTY DIFFERENT.
YEAH, BUT BOTH HAVE SIMILAR QUALITIES FOR ME. THEY BOTH DO STUFF THAT IS FAIRLY AUSTERE, BUT SERENE. SOME FOLKS WOULD CALL THEM COLD, BUT I DON'T SEE IT THAT WAY. I LOOK AT DE CHIRICO'S PIAZZAS AND YEARN TO BE IN THEM. SAME WITH HOPPER'S WORK. A LOT OF PEOPLE SEE HIS WORLD AS A PLACE WHERE NOBODY IS CONNECTING. I JUST SEE IT AS A WORLD WHERE NOBODY'S BUGGING ANYONE.
EVERYONE RESPECTS EACH OTHER'S SPACE.
IT'S FRUSTRATING, THOUGH. EVERY TIME I'M IN THE ART SECTION I FEEL LIKE AN INTRUDER. SOMEDAY I'VE GOTTA MAKE THE LEAP FROM COMICS TO "REAL" ART.
WHY MAKE THAT DISTINCTION? THAT'S LIKE WHEN FOLKS CALL CLASSI-CAL OR JAZZ "REAL" MUSIC, AS OPPOSED TO ROCK. IT'S A SELF-IMPOSED ELITISM WHICH EXCLUDES YOU. THAT DOESN'T MAKE SENSE.
LOOK, THERE'S ART AND THEN THERE'S COMICS. I'M NOT SAYING THAT SO-CALLED FINE ART IS ANY BETTER -- HELL, MOST OF IT THESE DAYS IS A MILLION TIMES WORSE -- BUT WHAT I AM SAYING IS THAT COMICS GET NO RESPECT.
WHAT ABOUT MAUS? THAT GOT THE PULITZER.
14
DON'T BE DISINGENUOUS. THAT WAS A FLUKE AND YOU KNOW IT. BESIDES, THEY STILL RACK MAUS NEXT TO DILBERT.
the best in TALK RADIO
WLIM
AM1015
ONE OF THESE DAYS I'M GONNA GET SMART AND MOVE ON FROM COMICS ALTOGETHER. DO SOME OF THAT "REAL" ART. MAYBE GET SOME "REAL" ESTEEM. COMICS IS A MUG'S GAME.
WALK
IF YOU SAY SO. I WOULDN'T KNOW.

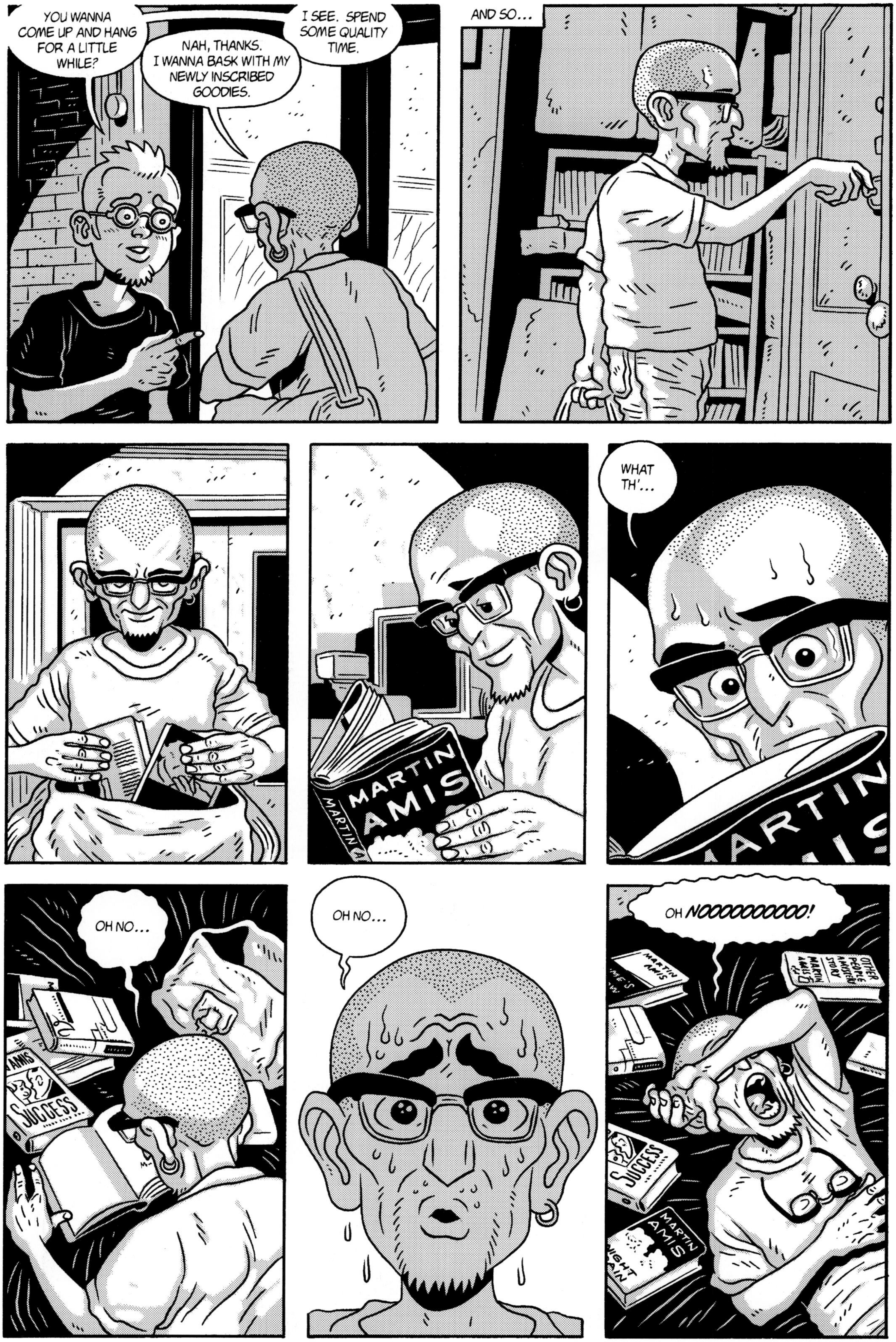
YOU WANNA COME UP AND HANG FOR A LITTLE WHILE?
NAH, THANKS. I WANNA BASK WITH MY NEWLY INSCRIBED GOODIES.
I SEE. SPEND SOME QUALITY TIME.
AND SO...
MARTIN AMIS
MARTIN AMIS
WHAT TH'...
MARTIN AMIS
OH NO...
SUCCESS
AMIS
OH NO...
OH NOOOOOOOOOO!
MARTIN AMIS
OTHER PEOPLE A MYSTERY STORY MARTIN AMIS
SUCCESS
MARTIN AMIS NIGHT TRAIN

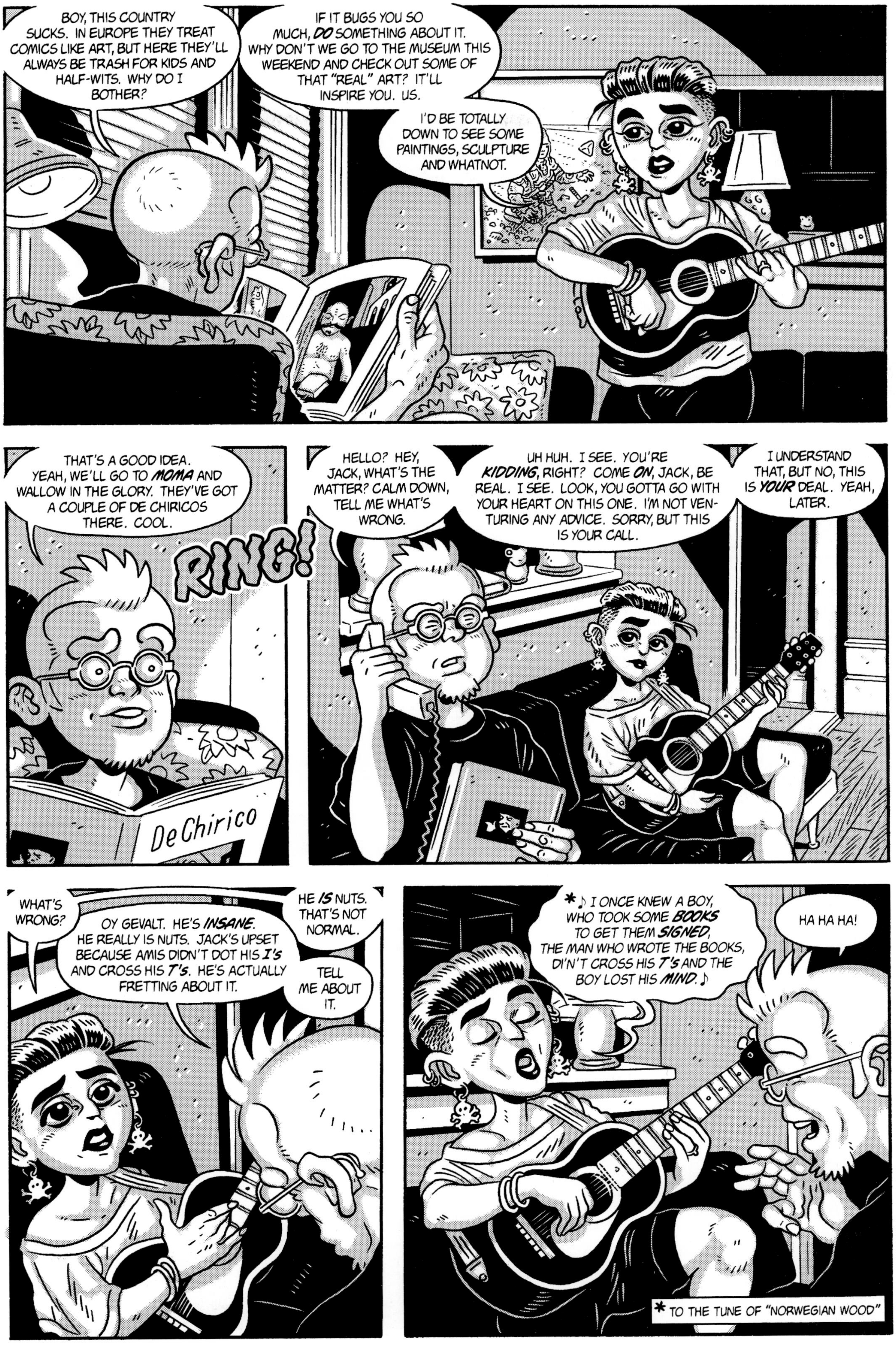

BOY, THIS COUNTRY SUCKS. IN EUROPE THEY TREAT COMICS LIKE ART, BUT HERE THEY'LL ALWAYS BE TRASH FOR KIDS AND HALF-WITS. WHY DO I BOTHER?
IF IT BUGS YOU SO MUCH, DO SOMETHING ABOUT IT. WHY DON'T WE GO TO THE MUSEUM THIS WEEKEND AND CHECK OUT SOME OF THAT "REAL" ART? IT'LL INSPIRE YOU. US.
I'D BE TOTALLY DOWN TO SEE SOME PAINTINGS, SCULPTURE AND WHATNOT.
THAT'S A GOOD IDEA. YEAH, WE'LL GO TO MOMA AND WALLOW IN THE GLORY. THEY'VE GOT A COUPLE OF DE CHIRICOS THERE. COOL.
RING!
De Chirico
HELLO? HEY, JACK, WHAT'S THE MATTER? CALM DOWN, TELL ME WHAT'S WRONG.
UH HUH. I SEE. YOU'RE KIDDING, RIGHT? COME ON, JACK, BE REAL. I SEE. LOOK, YOU GOTTA GO WITH YOUR HEART ON THIS ONE. I'M NOT VENTURING ANY ADVICE. SORRY, BUT THIS IS YOUR CALL.
I UNDERSTAND THAT, BUT NO, THIS IS YOUR DEAL. YEAH, LATER.
WHAT'S WRONG?
OY GEVALT. HE'S INSANE. HE REALLY IS NUTS. JACK'S UPSET BECAUSE AMIS DIDN'T DOT HIS I's AND CROSS HIS T's. HE'S ACTUALLY FRETTING ABOUT IT.
HE IS NUTS. THAT'S NOT NORMAL.
TELL ME ABOUT IT.
*♪ I ONCE KNEW A BOY, WHO TOOK SOME BOOKS TO GET THEM SIGNED, THE MAN WHO WROTE THE BOOKS, DI'N'T CROSS HIS T's AND THE BOY LOST HIS MIND.♪
HA HA HA!
* TO THE TUNE OF "NORWEGIAN WOOD"

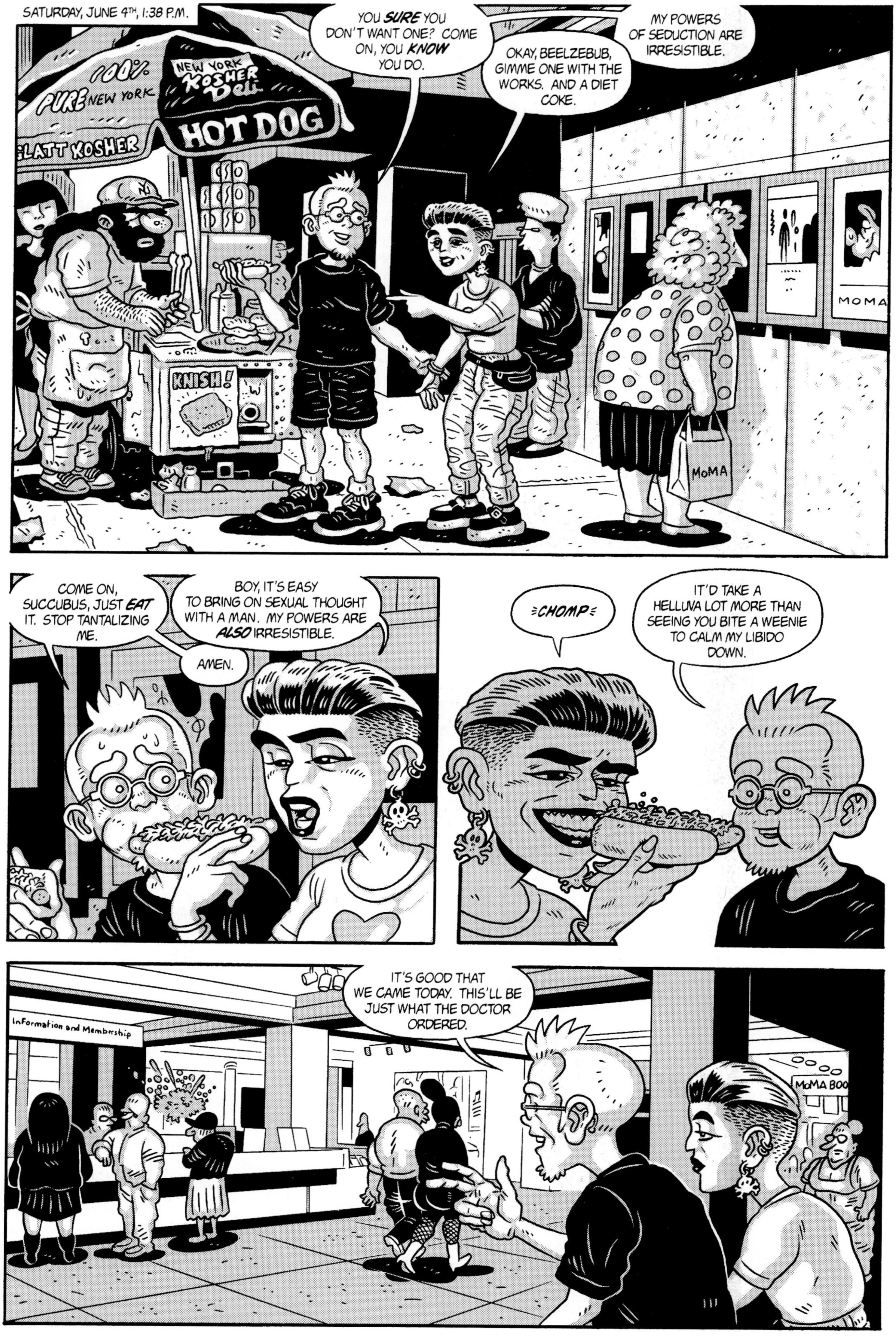

SATURDAY, JUNE 4TH, 1:38 P.M.
YOU SURE YOU DON'T WANT ONE? COME ON, YOU KNOW YOU DO.
OKAY, BEELZEBUB, GIMME ONE WITH THE WORKS. AND A DIET COKE.
MY POWERS OF SEDUCTION ARE IRRESISTIBLE.
100% PURE NEW YORK
NEW YORK KOSHER DELI
HOT DOG
GLATT KOSHER
KNISH!
MOMA
MoMA
COME ON, SUCCUBUS, JUST EAT IT. STOP TANTALIZING ME.
BOY, IT'S EASY TO BRING ON SEXUAL THOUGHT WITH A MAN. MY POWERS ARE ALSO IRRESISTIBLE.
AMEN.
CHOMP
IT'D TAKE A HELLUVA LOT MORE THAN SEEING YOU BITE A WEENIE TO CALM MY LIBIDO DOWN.
IT'S GOOD THAT WE CAME TODAY. THIS'LL BE JUST WHAT THE DOCTOR ORDERED.
Information and Membership
MoMA BOO

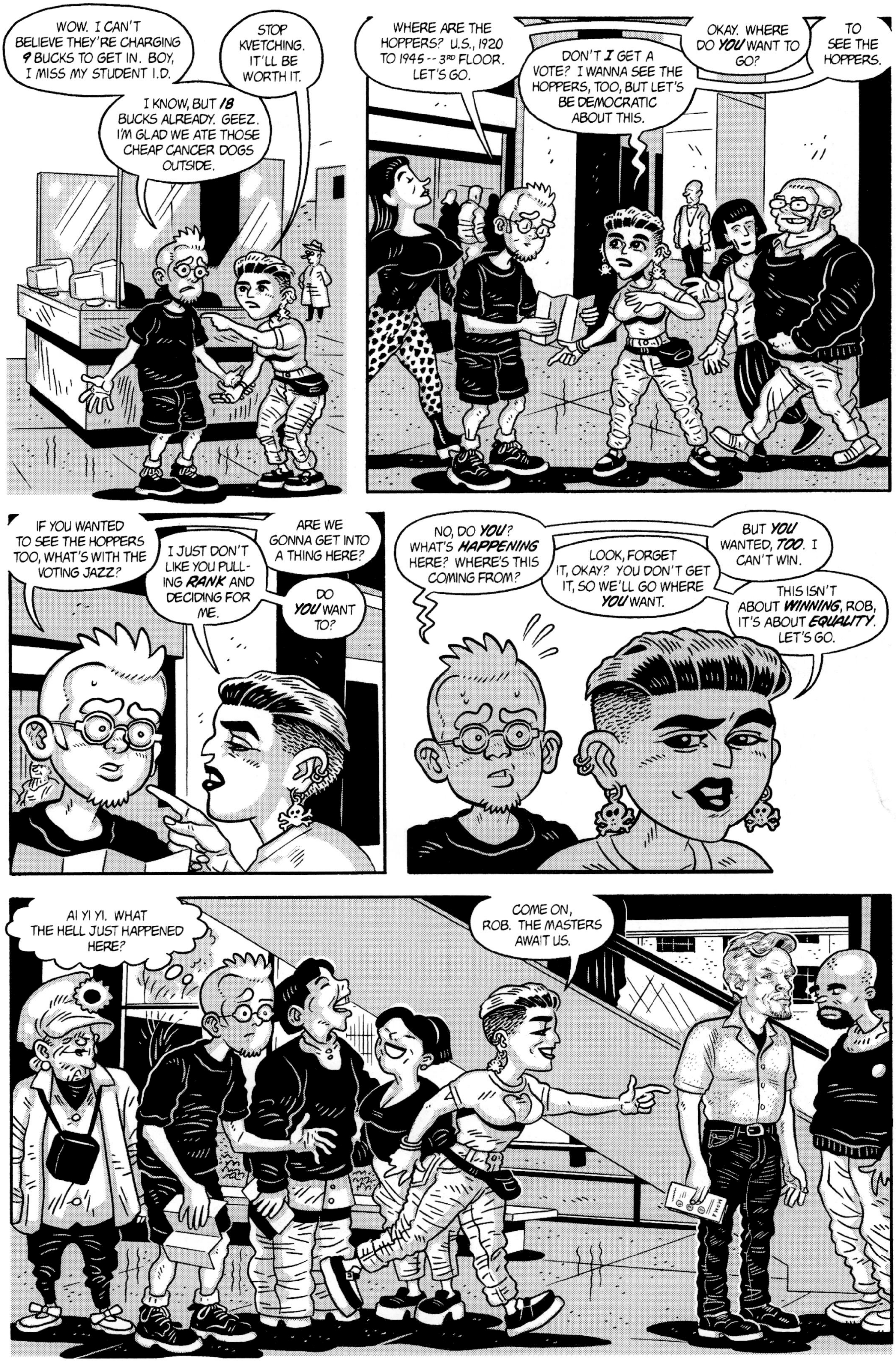
WOW. I CAN'T BELIEVE THEY'RE CHARGING 9 BUCKS TO GET IN. BOY, I MISS MY STUDENT I.D.
STOP KVETCHING. IT'LL BE WORTH IT.
I KNOW, BUT 18 BUCKS ALREADY. GEEZ. I'M GLAD WE ATE THOSE CHEAP CANCER DOGS OUTSIDE.
WHERE ARE THE HOPPERS? U.S., 1920 TO 1945 -- 3RD FLOOR. LET'S GO.
DON'T I GET A VOTE? I WANNA SEE THE HOPPERS, TOO, BUT LET'S BE DEMOCRATIC ABOUT THIS.
OKAY. WHERE DO YOU WANT TO GO?
TO SEE THE HOPPERS.
IF YOU WANTED TO SEE THE HOPPERS TOO, WHAT'S WITH THE VOTING JAZZ?
I JUST DON'T LIKE YOU PULL-ING RANK AND DECIDING FOR ME.
ARE WE GONNA GET INTO A THING HERE?
DO YOU WANT TO?
NO, DO YOU? WHAT'S HAPPENING HERE? WHERE'S THIS COMING FROM?
LOOK, FORGET IT, OKAY? YOU DON'T GET IT, SO WE'LL GO WHERE YOU WANT.
BUT YOU WANTED, TOO. I CAN'T WIN.
THIS ISN'T ABOUT WINNING, ROB, IT'S ABOUT EQUALITY. LET'S GO.
AI YI YI. WHAT THE HELL JUST HAPPENED HERE?
COME ON, ROB. THE MASTERS AWAIT US.

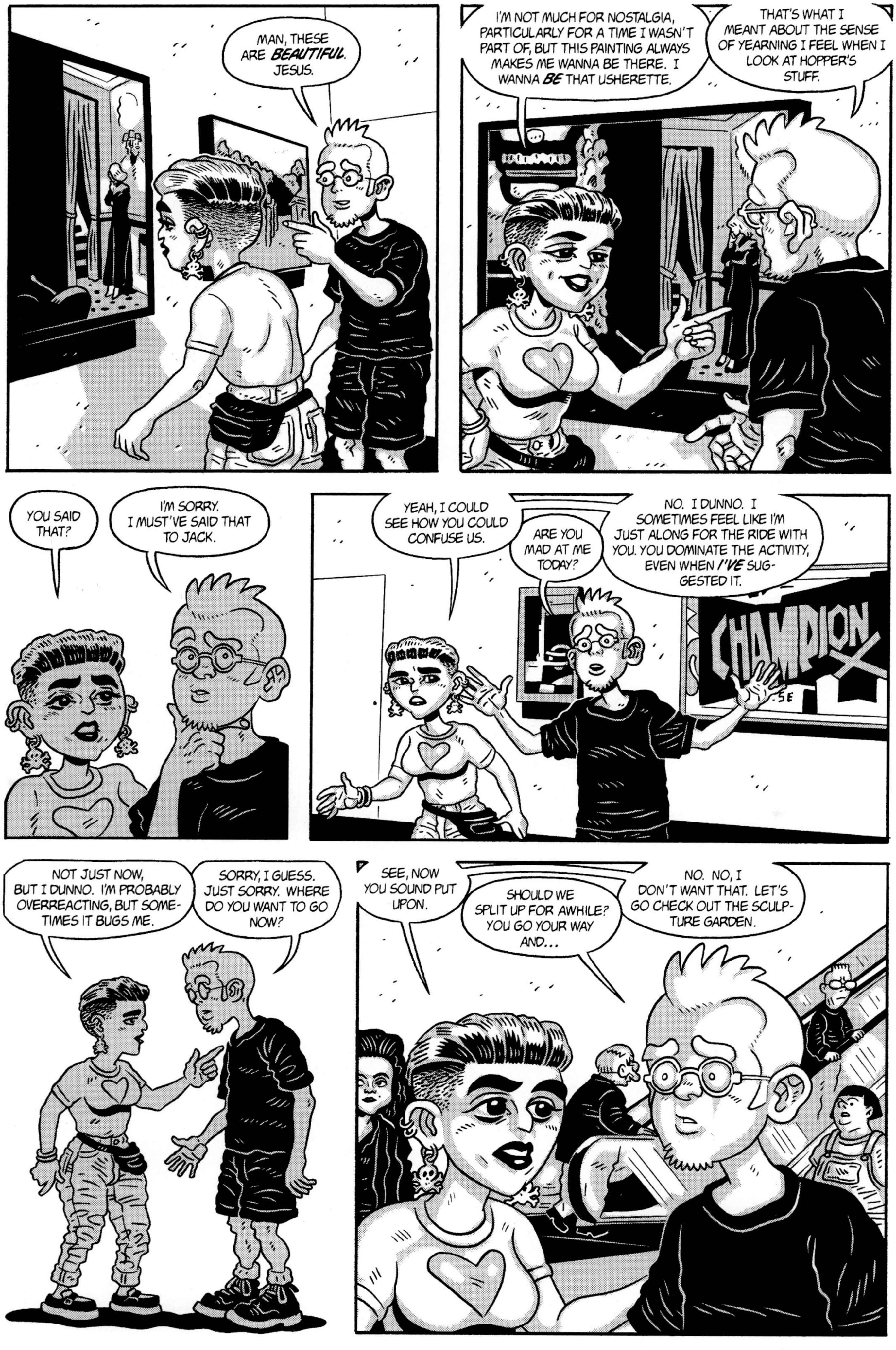
MAN, THESE ARE BEAUTIFUL. JESUS.
I'M NOT MUCH FOR NOSTALGIA, PARTICULARLY FOR A TIME I WASN'T PART OF, BUT THIS PAINTING ALWAYS MAKES ME WANNA BE THERE. I WANNA BE THAT USHERETTE.
THAT'S WHAT I MEANT ABOUT THE SENSE OF YEARNING I FEEL WHEN I LOOK AT HOPPER'S STUFF.
YOU SAID THAT?
I'M SORRY. I MUST'VE SAID THAT TO JACK.
YEAH, I COULD SEE HOW YOU COULD CONFUSE US.
ARE YOU MAD AT ME TODAY?
NO. I DUNNO. I SOMETIMES FEEL LIKE I'M JUST ALONG FOR THE RIDE WITH YOU. YOU DOMINATE THE ACTIVITY, EVEN WHEN I'VE SUGGESTED IT.
CHAMPION
NOT JUST NOW, BUT I DUNNO. I'M PROBABLY OVERREACTING, BUT SOMETIMES IT BUGS ME.
SORRY, I GUESS. JUST SORRY. WHERE DO YOU WANT TO GO NOW?
SEE, NOW YOU SOUND PUT UPON.
SHOULD WE SPLIT UP FOR AWHILE? YOU GO YOUR WAY AND...
NO. NO, I DON'T WANT THAT. LET'S GO CHECK OUT THE SCULPTURE GARDEN.

I FEEL MORE RELAXED NOW. I'M NOT TAKING BACK WHAT I SAID ABOUT YOU, BUT I'M SORRY I'VE BEEN KINDA DIFFICULT TODAY.

YOU'RE RIGHT. I'LL TRY TO BE LESS DOMINEERING.

THERE'S A LOT MORE TO SEE. WANNA GO BACK IN?

IT'S SO NICE OUT HERE. I JUST WANNA MELLOW FOR A FEW.

THIS IS BEAUTIFUL. IT KIND OF BUMS ME OUT, THOUGH. MAKES ME THINK OF MY FATHER. HE USED TO DO STUFF LIKE THIS. PROBABLY STILL DOES, NOT THAT I'D KNOW.

HMM.

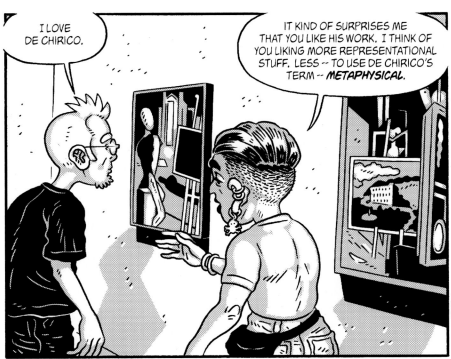

I LOVE DE CHIRICO.

IT KIND OF SURPRISES ME THAT YOU LIKE HIS WORK. I THINK OF YOU LIKING MORE REPRESENTATIONAL STUFF. LESS -- TO USE DE CHIRICO'S TERM -- *METAPHYSICAL*.

JEEZ, GIMME *SOME* CREDIT FOR BEING ABLE TO EMBRACE *MORE* THAN *ONE* KIND OF THING.

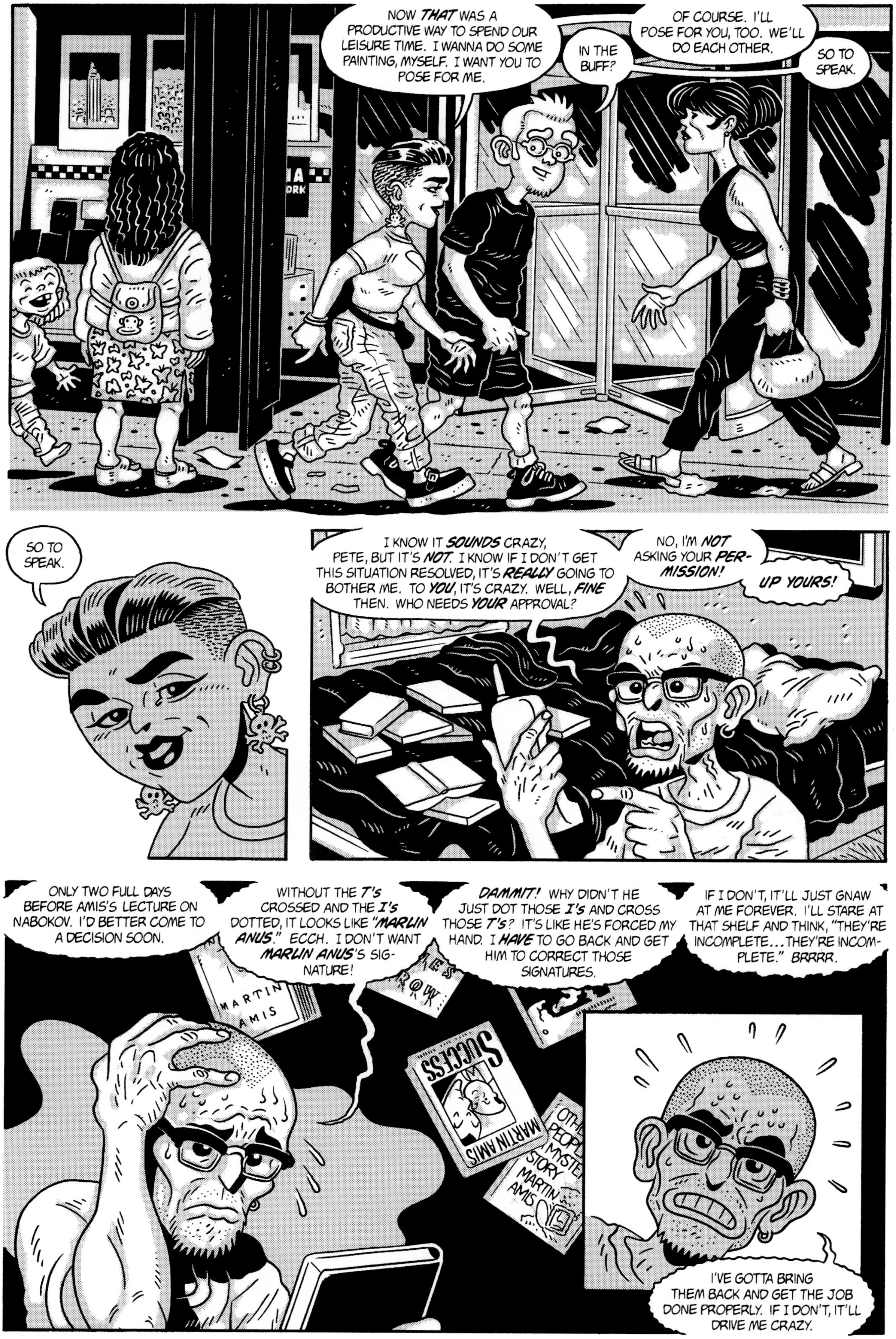

NOW THAT WAS A PRODUCTIVE WAY TO SPEND OUR LEISURE TIME. I WANNA DO SOME PAINTING, MYSELF. I WANT YOU TO POSE FOR ME.
IN THE BUFF?
OF COURSE. I'LL POSE FOR YOU, TOO. WE'LL DO EACH OTHER.
SO TO SPEAK.
SO TO SPEAK.
I KNOW IT SOUNDS CRAZY, PETE, BUT IT'S NOT. I KNOW IF I DON'T GET THIS SITUATION RESOLVED, IT'S REALLY GOING TO BOTHER ME. TO YOU, IT'S CRAZY. WELL, FINE THEN. WHO NEEDS YOUR APPROVAL?
NO, I'M NOT ASKING YOUR PERMISSION!
UP YOURS!
ONLY TWO FULL DAYS BEFORE AMIS'S LECTURE ON NABOKOV. I'D BETTER COME TO A DECISION SOON.
WITHOUT THE T's CROSSED AND THE I's DOTTED, IT LOOKS LIKE "MARLIN ANUS." ECCH. I DON'T WANT MARLIN ANUS'S SIGNATURE!
DAMMIT! WHY DIDN'T HE JUST DOT THOSE I's AND CROSS THOSE T's? IT'S LIKE HE'S FORCED MY HAND. I HAVE TO GO BACK AND GET HIM TO CORRECT THOSE SIGNATURES.
IF I DON'T, IT'LL JUST GNAW AT ME FOREVER. I'LL STARE AT THAT SHELF AND THINK, "THEY'RE INCOMPLETE... THEY'RE INCOMPLETE." BRRRR.
MARTIN AMIS
SUCCESS
MARTIN AMIS
OTHER PEOPLE MYSTERY STORY MARTIN AMIS
I'VE GOTTA BRING THEM BACK AND GET THE JOB DONE PROPERLY. IF I DON'T, IT'LL DRIVE ME CRAZY.

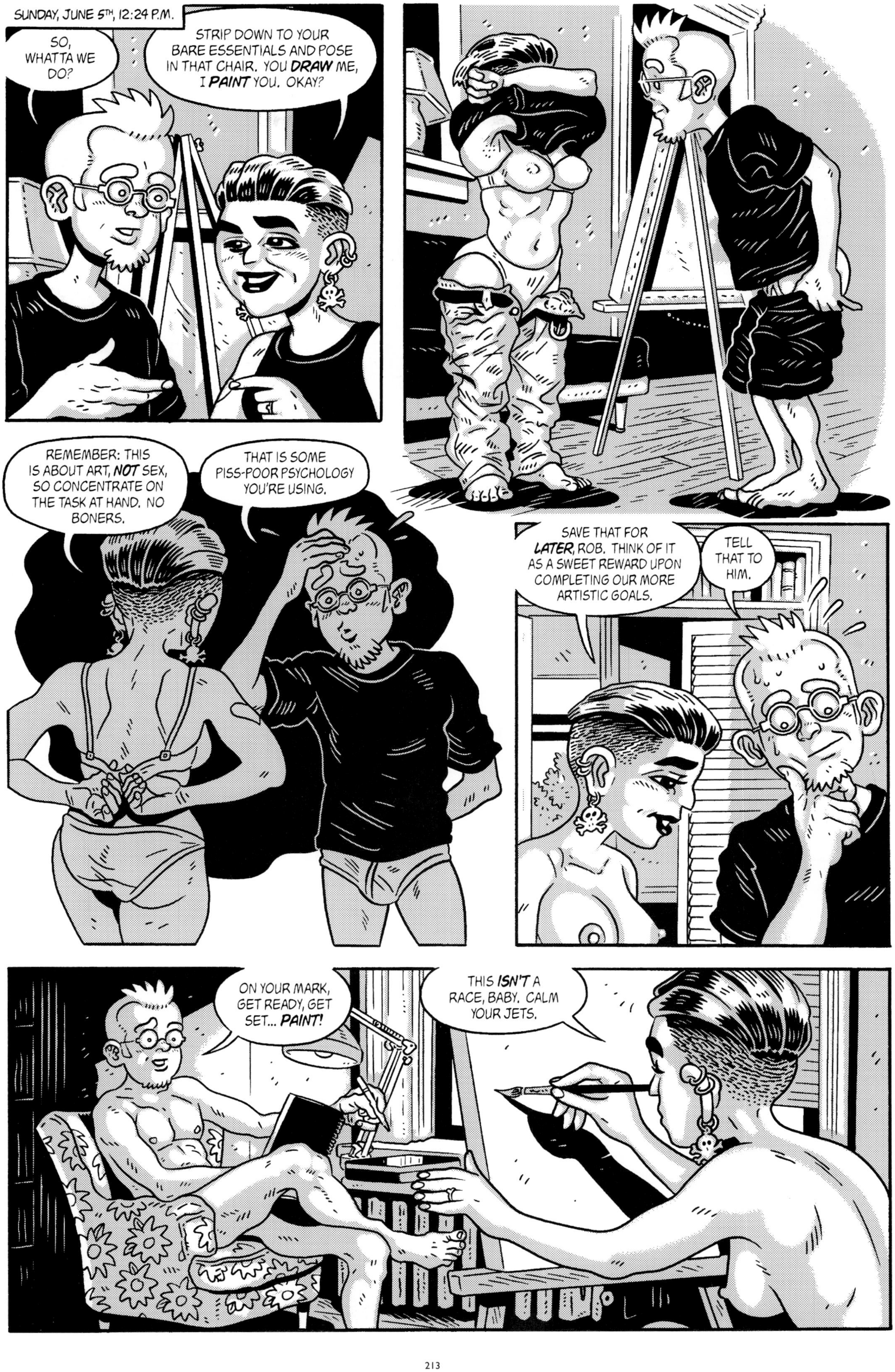
SUNDAY, JUNE 5TH, 12:24 P.M.
SO, WHATTA WE DO?
STRIP DOWN TO YOUR BARE ESSENTIALS AND POSE IN THAT CHAIR. YOU DRAW ME, I PAINT YOU. OKAY?
REMEMBER: THIS IS ABOUT ART, NOT SEX, SO CONCENTRATE ON THE TASK AT HAND. NO BONERS.
THAT IS SOME PISS-POOR PSYCHOLOGY YOU'RE USING.
SAVE THAT FOR LATER, ROB. THINK OF IT AS A SWEET REWARD UPON COMPLETING OUR MORE ARTISTIC GOALS.
TELL THAT TO HIM.
ON YOUR MARK, GET READY, GET SET... PAINT!
THIS ISN'T A RACE, BABY. CALM YOUR JETS.

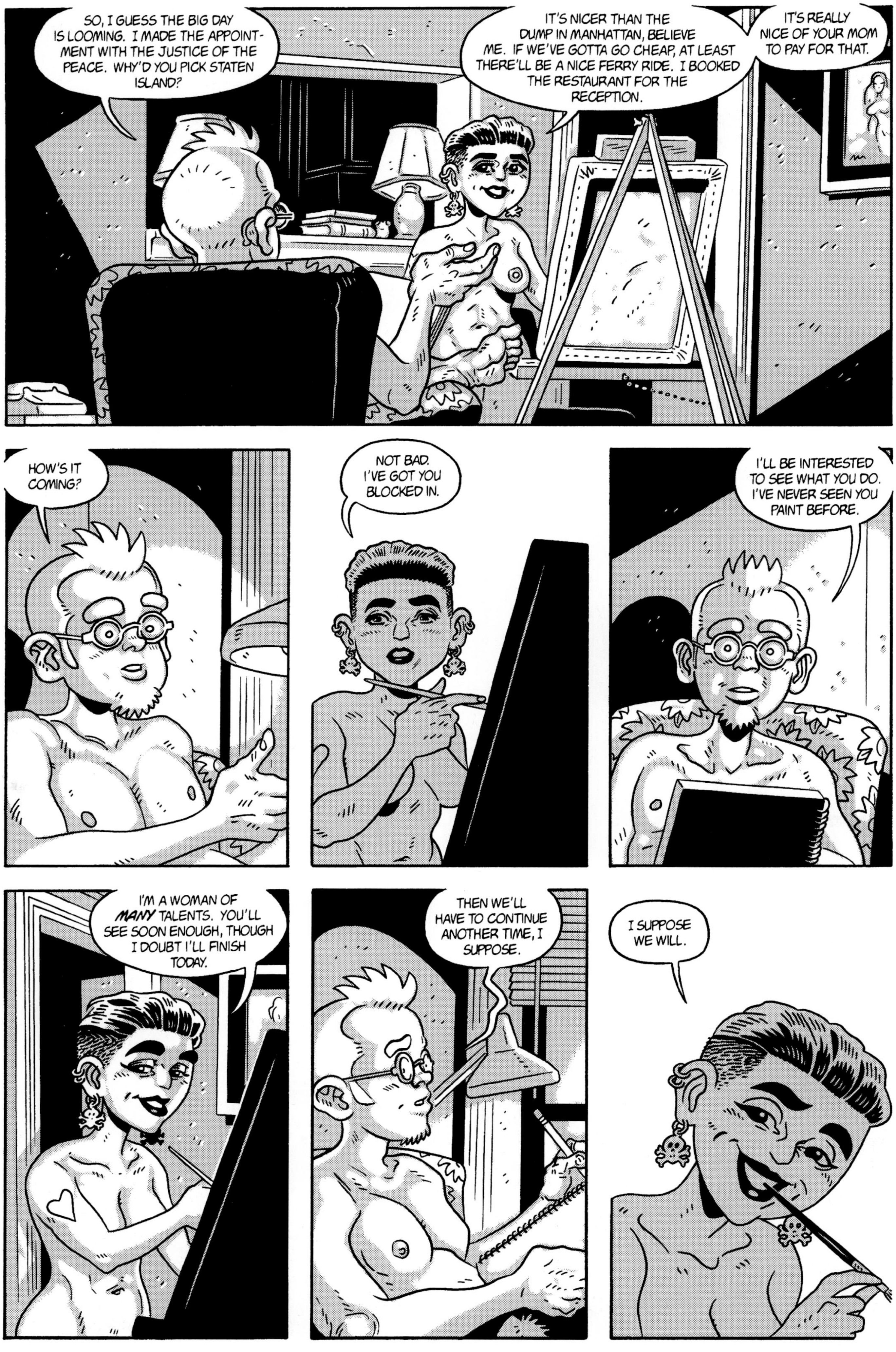
SO, I GUESS THE BIG DAY IS LOOMING. I MADE THE APPOINTMENT WITH THE JUSTICE OF THE PEACE. WHY'D YOU PICK STATEN ISLAND?
IT'S NICER THAN THE DUMP IN MANHATTAN, BELIEVE ME. IF WE'VE GOTTA GO CHEAP, AT LEAST THERE'LL BE A NICE FERRY RIDE. I BOOKED THE RESTAURANT FOR THE RECEPTION.
IT'S REALLY NICE OF YOUR MOM TO PAY FOR THAT.
HOW'S IT COMING?
NOT BAD. I'VE GOT YOU BLOCKED IN.
I'LL BE INTERESTED TO SEE WHAT YOU DO. I'VE NEVER SEEN YOU PAINT BEFORE.
I'M A WOMAN OF MANY TALENTS. YOU'LL SEE SOON ENOUGH, THOUGH I DOUBT I'LL FINISH TODAY.
THEN WE'LL HAVE TO CONTINUE ANOTHER TIME, I SUPPOSE.
I SUPPOSE WE WILL.

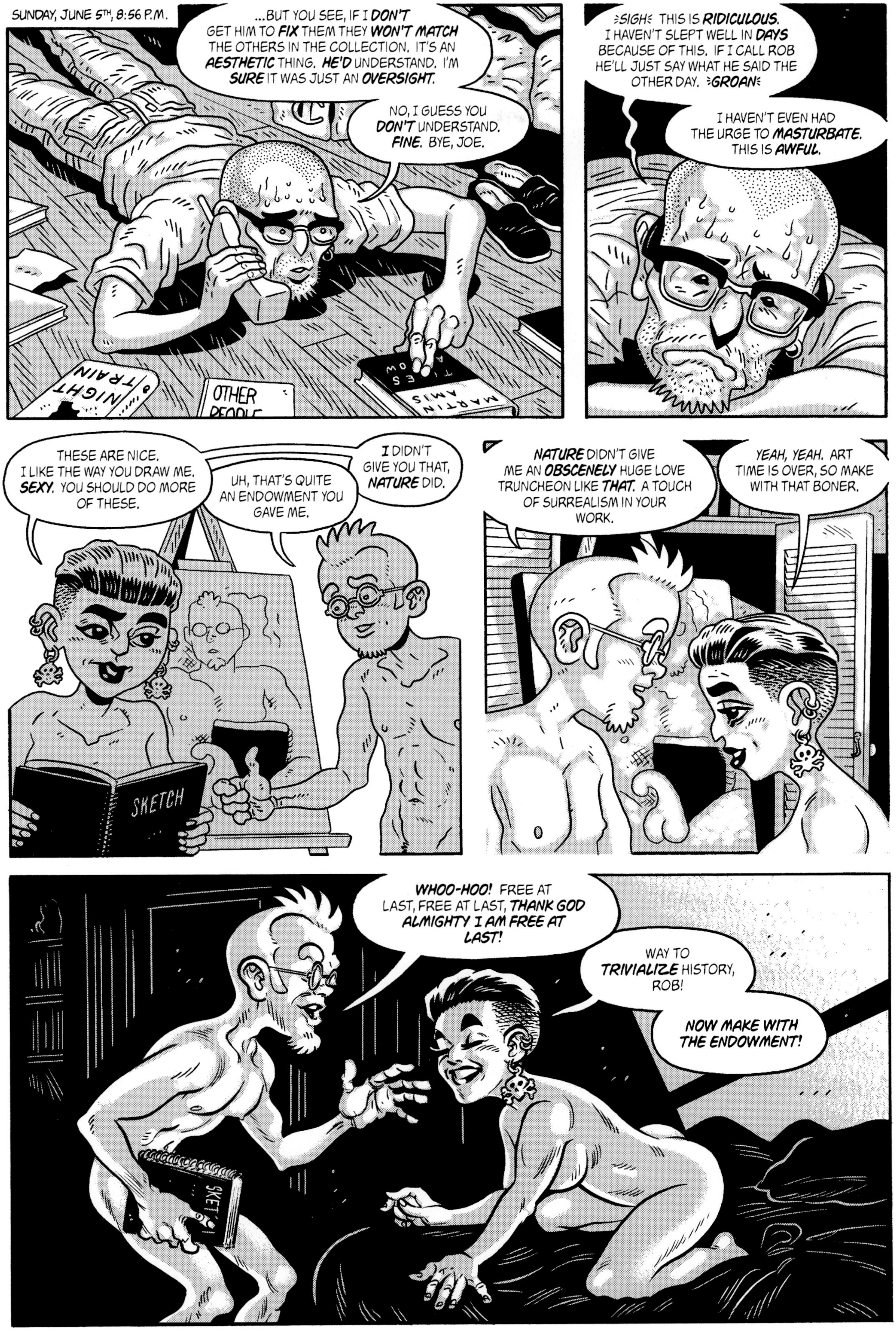

SUNDAY, JUNE 5TH, 8:56 P.M.
...BUT YOU SEE, IF I DON'T GET HIM TO FIX THEM THEY WON'T MATCH THE OTHERS IN THE COLLECTION. IT'S AN AESTHETIC THING. HE'D UNDERSTAND. I'M SURE IT WAS JUST AN OVERSIGHT.
NO, I GUESS YOU DON'T UNDERSTAND. FINE. BYE, JOE.
NIGHT TRAIN
OTHER PEOPLE
MARTIN AMIS
≷SIGH≶ THIS IS RIDICULOUS. I HAVEN'T SLEPT WELL IN DAYS BECAUSE OF THIS. IF I CALL ROB HE'LL JUST SAY WHAT HE SAID THE OTHER DAY. ≷GROAN≶
I HAVEN'T EVEN HAD THE URGE TO MASTURBATE. THIS IS AWFUL.
THESE ARE NICE. I LIKE THE WAY YOU DRAW ME. SEXY. YOU SHOULD DO MORE OF THESE.
UH, THAT'S QUITE AN ENDOWMENT YOU GAVE ME.
I DIDN'T GIVE YOU THAT, NATURE DID.
SKETCH
NATURE DIDN'T GIVE ME AN OBSCENELY HUGE LOVE TRUNCHEON LIKE THAT. A TOUCH OF SURREALISM IN YOUR WORK.
YEAH, YEAH. ART TIME IS OVER, SO MAKE WITH THAT BONER.
WHOO-HOO! FREE AT LAST, FREE AT LAST, THANK GOD ALMIGHTY I AM FREE AT LAST!
WAY TO TRIVIALIZE HISTORY, ROB!
NOW MAKE WITH THE ENDOWMENT!
SKET

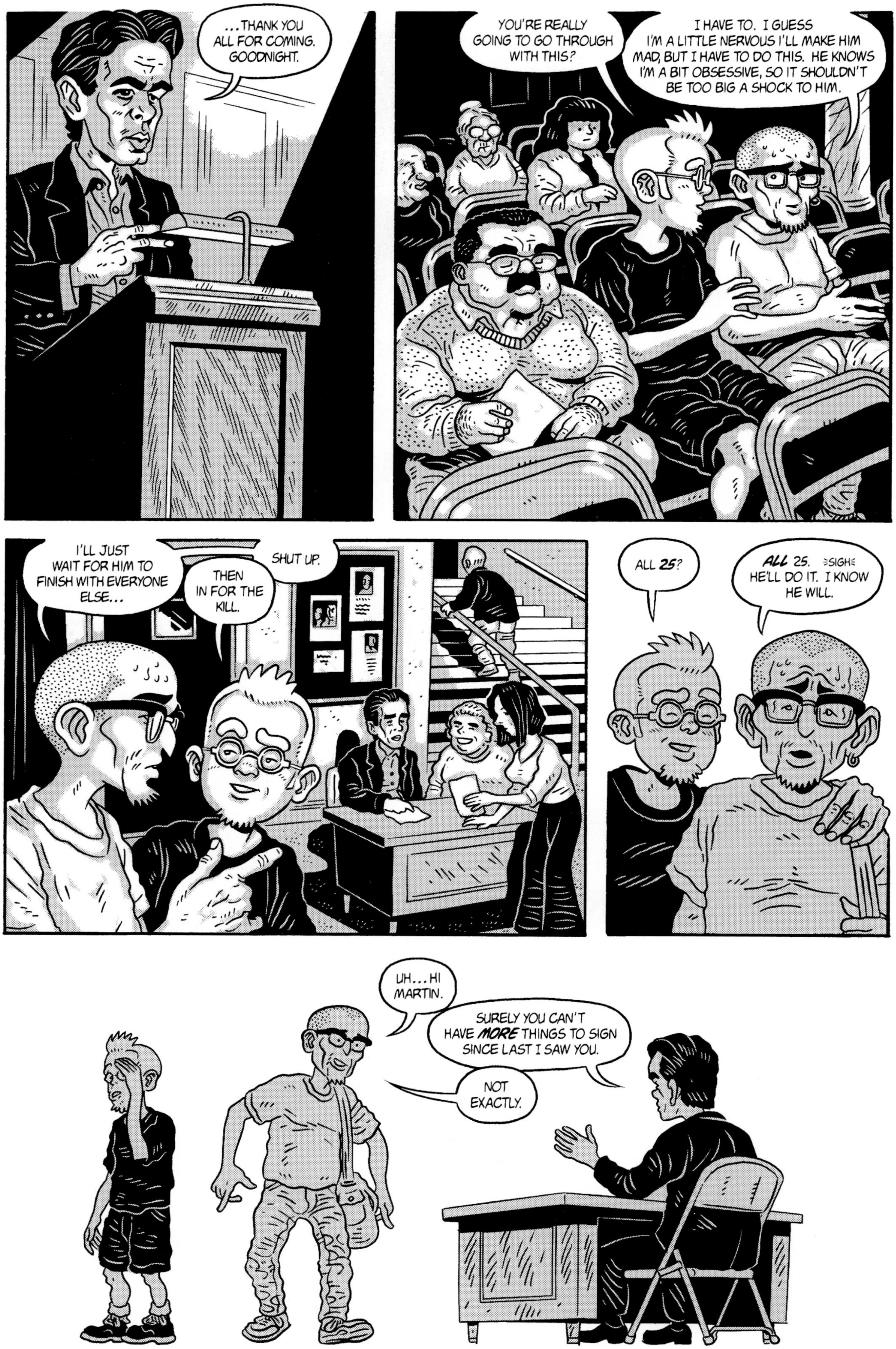
...THANK YOU ALL FOR COMING. GOODNIGHT.
YOU'RE REALLY GOING TO GO THROUGH WITH THIS?
I HAVE TO. I GUESS I'M A LITTLE NERVOUS I'LL MAKE HIM MAD, BUT I HAVE TO DO THIS. HE KNOWS I'M A BIT OBSESSIVE, SO IT SHOULDN'T BE TOO BIG A SHOCK TO HIM.
I'LL JUST WAIT FOR HIM TO FINISH WITH EVERYONE ELSE...
THEN IN FOR THE KILL.
SHUT UP.
ALL 25?
ALL 25. ⩾SIGH⩽ HE'LL DO IT. I KNOW HE WILL.
UH...HI MARTIN.
SURELY YOU CAN'T HAVE MORE THINGS TO SIGN SINCE LAST I SAW YOU.
NOT EXACTLY.

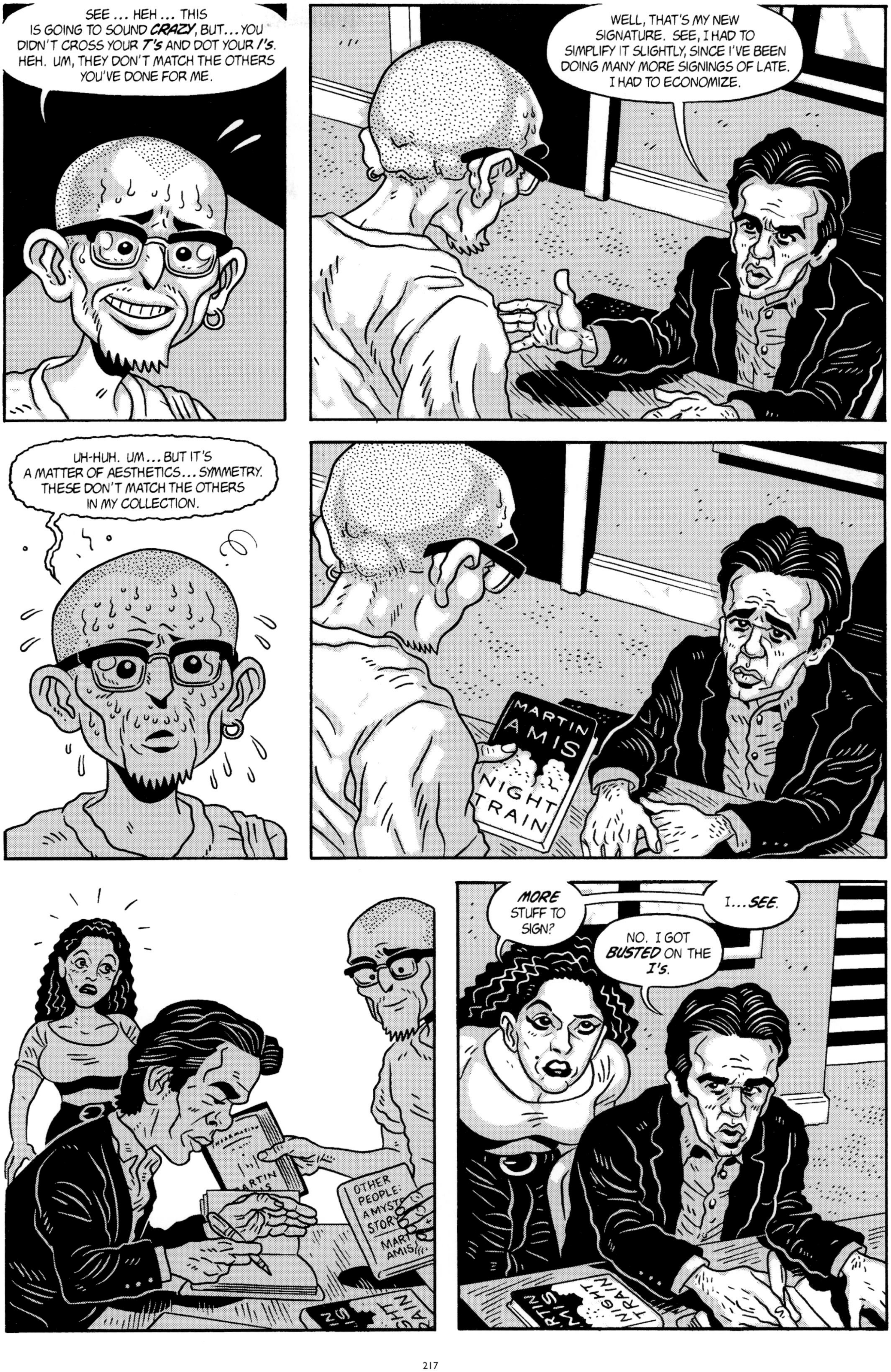
SEE ... HEH ... THIS IS GOING TO SOUND CRAZY, BUT... YOU DIDN'T CROSS YOUR T's AND DOT YOUR I's. HEH. UM, THEY DON'T MATCH THE OTHERS YOU'VE DONE FOR ME.
WELL, THAT'S MY NEW SIGNATURE. SEE, I HAD TO SIMPLIFY IT SLIGHTLY, SINCE I'VE BEEN DOING MANY MORE SIGNINGS OF LATE. I HAD TO ECONOMIZE.
UH-HUH. UM... BUT IT'S A MATTER OF AESTHETICS... SYMMETRY. THESE DON'T MATCH THE OTHERS IN MY COLLECTION.
MARTIN AMIS
NIGHT TRAIN
MORE STUFF TO SIGN?
I... SEE.
NO. I GOT BUSTED ON THE I's.

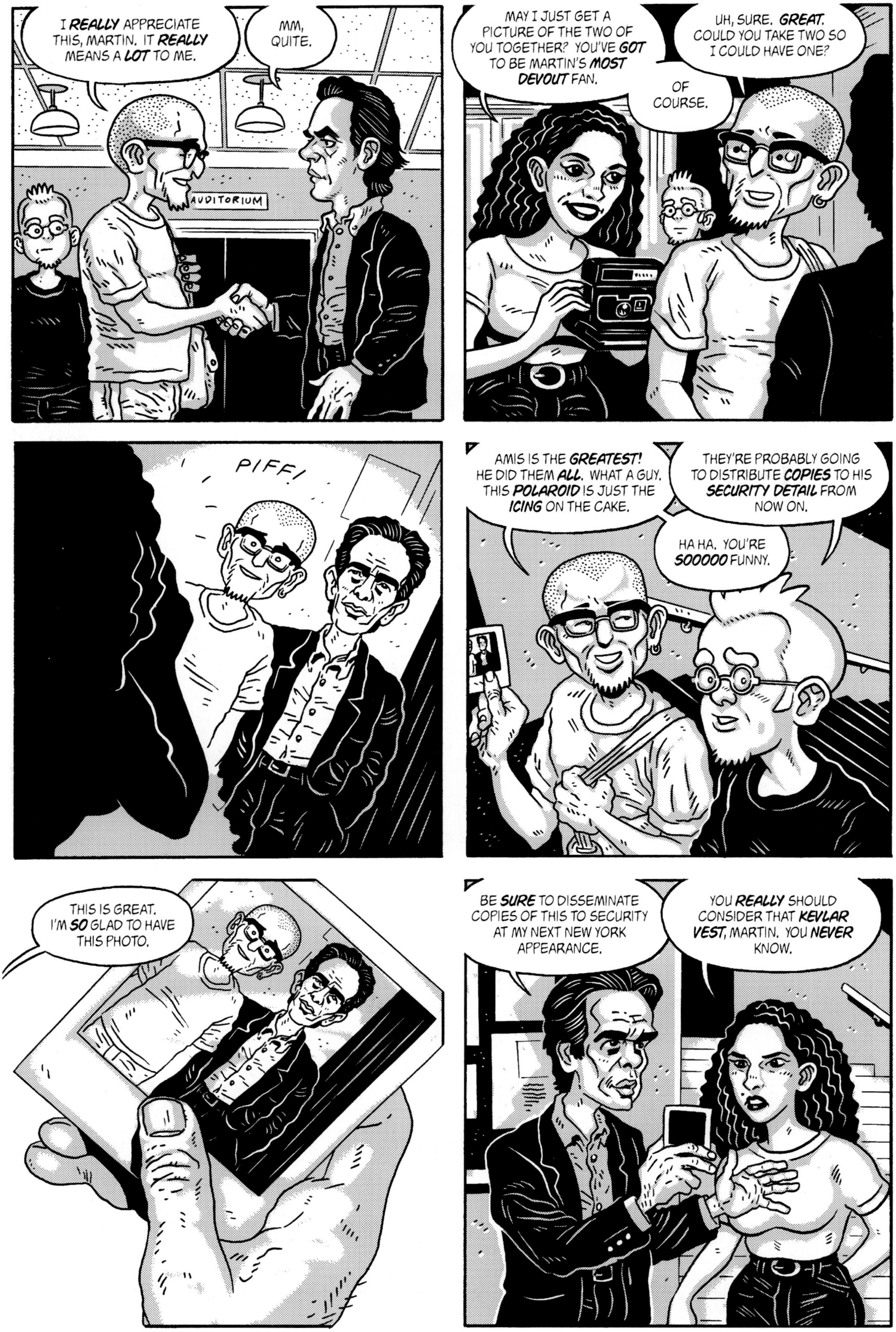
I REALLY APPRECIATE THIS, MARTIN. IT REALLY MEANS A LOT TO ME.
MM, QUITE.
AUDITORIUM
MAY I JUST GET A PICTURE OF THE TWO OF YOU TOGETHER? YOU'VE GOT TO BE MARTIN'S MOST DEVOUT FAN.
UH, SURE. GREAT. COULD YOU TAKE TWO SO I COULD HAVE ONE?
OF COURSE.
PIFF!
AMIS IS THE GREATEST! HE DID THEM ALL. WHAT A GUY. THIS POLAROID IS JUST THE ICING ON THE CAKE.
THEY'RE PROBABLY GOING TO DISTRIBUTE COPIES TO HIS SECURITY DETAIL FROM NOW ON.
HA HA. YOU'RE SOOOOO FUNNY.
THIS IS GREAT. I'M SO GLAD TO HAVE THIS PHOTO.
BE SURE TO DISSEMINATE COPIES OF THIS TO SECURITY AT MY NEXT NEW YORK APPEARANCE.
YOU REALLY SHOULD CONSIDER THAT KEVLAR VEST, MARTIN. YOU NEVER KNOW.

Chapter Ten

WEDLOCKED & LOADED

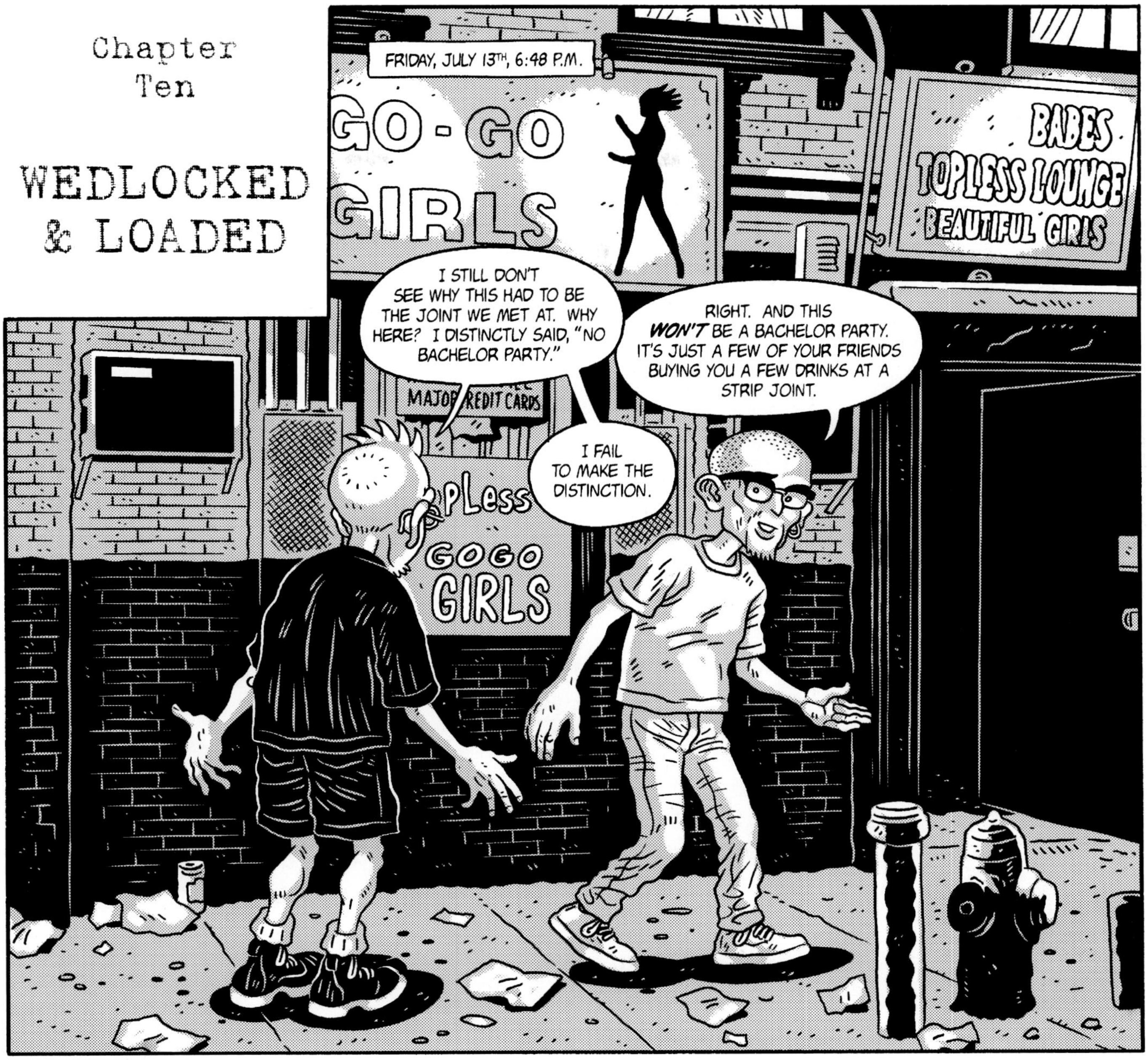

FRIDAY, JULY 13TH, 6:48 P.M.
GO-GO GIRLS
BABES TOPLESS LOUNGE BEAUTIFUL GIRLS
I STILL DON'T SEE WHY THIS HAD TO BE THE JOINT WE MET AT. WHY HERE? I DISTINCTLY SAID, "NO BACHELOR PARTY."
RIGHT. AND THIS *WON'T* BE A BACHELOR PARTY. IT'S JUST A FEW OF YOUR FRIENDS BUYING YOU A FEW DRINKS AT A STRIP JOINT.
I FAIL TO MAKE THE DISTINCTION.
MAJOR CREDIT CARDS
TOPLESS GOGO GIRLS

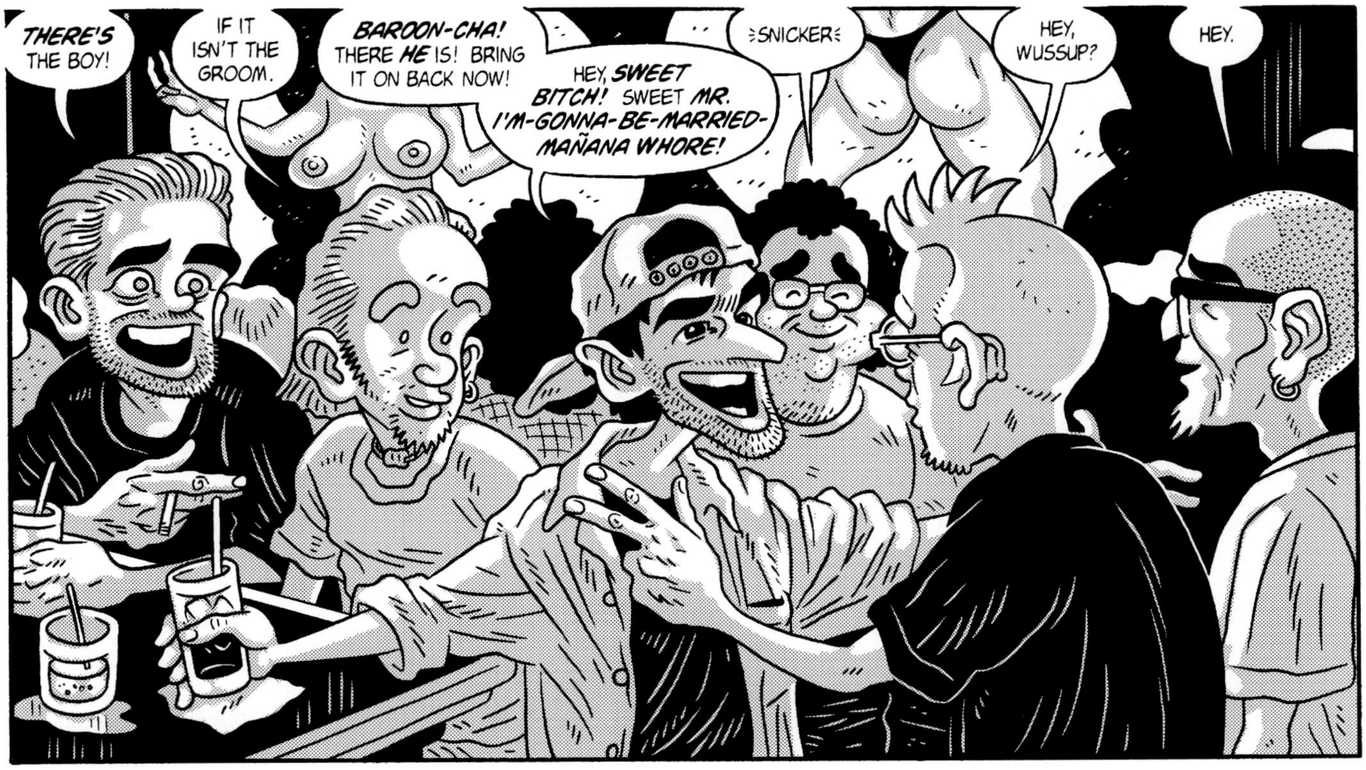

THERE'S THE BOY!
IF IT ISN'T THE GROOM.
BAROON-CHA! THERE *HE* IS! BRING IT ON BACK NOW!
HEY, *SWEET BITCH!* SWEET *MR. I'M-GONNA-BE-MARRIED-MAÑANA WHORE!*
SNICKER
HEY, WUSSUP?
HEY.

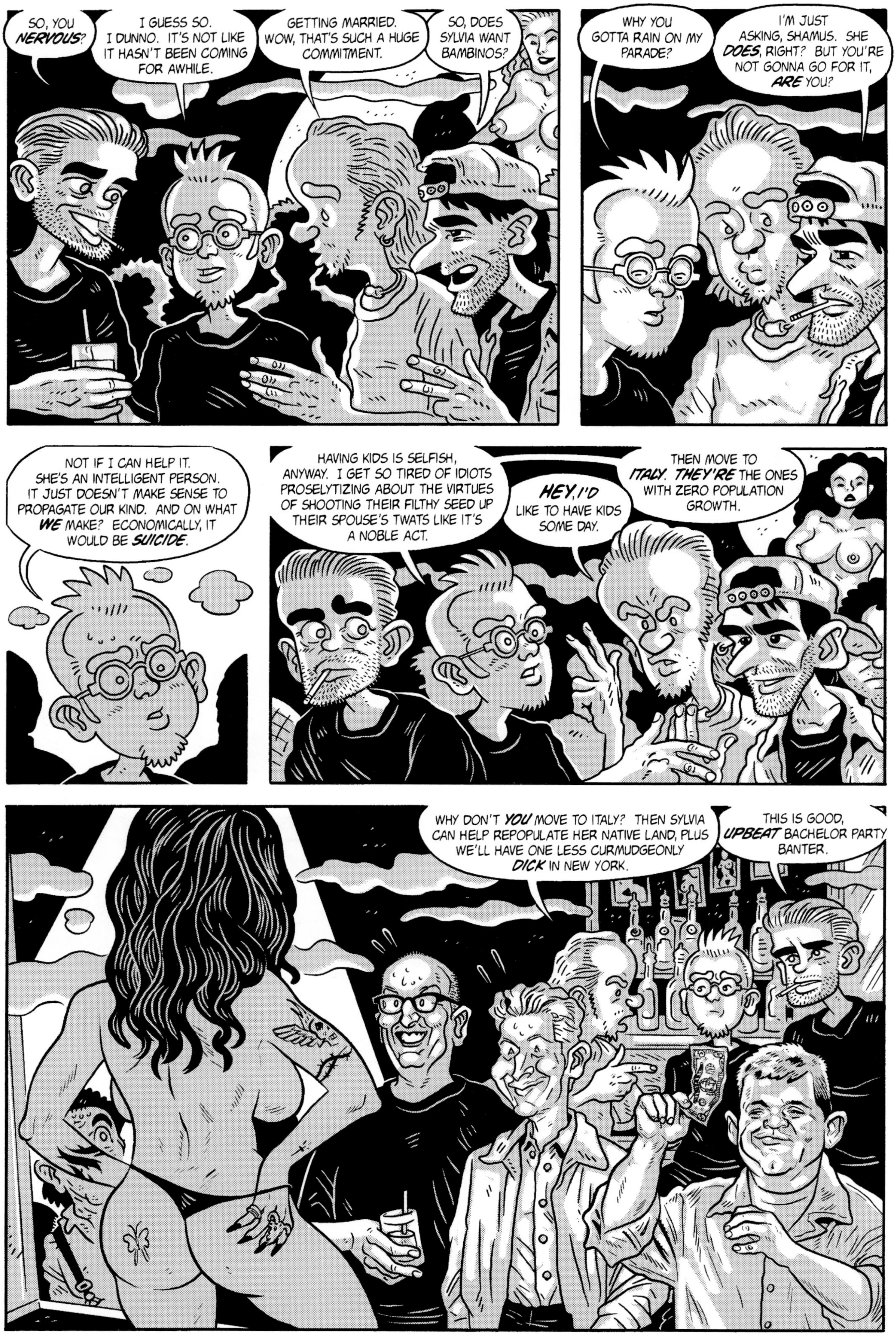
SO, YOU NERVOUS?
I GUESS SO. I DUNNO. IT'S NOT LIKE IT HASN'T BEEN COMING FOR AWHILE.
GETTING MARRIED. WOW, THAT'S SUCH A HUGE COMMITMENT.
SO, DOES SYLVIA WANT BAMBINOS?
WHY YOU GOTTA RAIN ON MY PARADE?
I'M JUST ASKING, SHAMUS. SHE DOES, RIGHT? BUT YOU'RE NOT GONNA GO FOR IT, ARE YOU?
NOT IF I CAN HELP IT. SHE'S AN INTELLIGENT PERSON. IT JUST DOESN'T MAKE SENSE TO PROPAGATE OUR KIND. AND ON WHAT WE MAKE? ECONOMICALLY, IT WOULD BE SUICIDE.
HAVING KIDS IS SELFISH, ANYWAY. I GET SO TIRED OF IDIOTS PROSELYTIZING ABOUT THE VIRTUES OF SHOOTING THEIR FILTHY SEED UP THEIR SPOUSE'S TWATS LIKE IT'S A NOBLE ACT.
HEY, I'D LIKE TO HAVE KIDS SOME DAY.
THEN MOVE TO ITALY. THEY'RE THE ONES WITH ZERO POPULATION GROWTH.
WHY DON'T YOU MOVE TO ITALY? THEN SYLVIA CAN HELP REPOPULATE HER NATIVE LAND, PLUS WE'LL HAVE ONE LESS CURMUDGEONLY DICK IN NEW YORK.
THIS IS GOOD, UPBEAT BACHELOR PARTY BANTER.

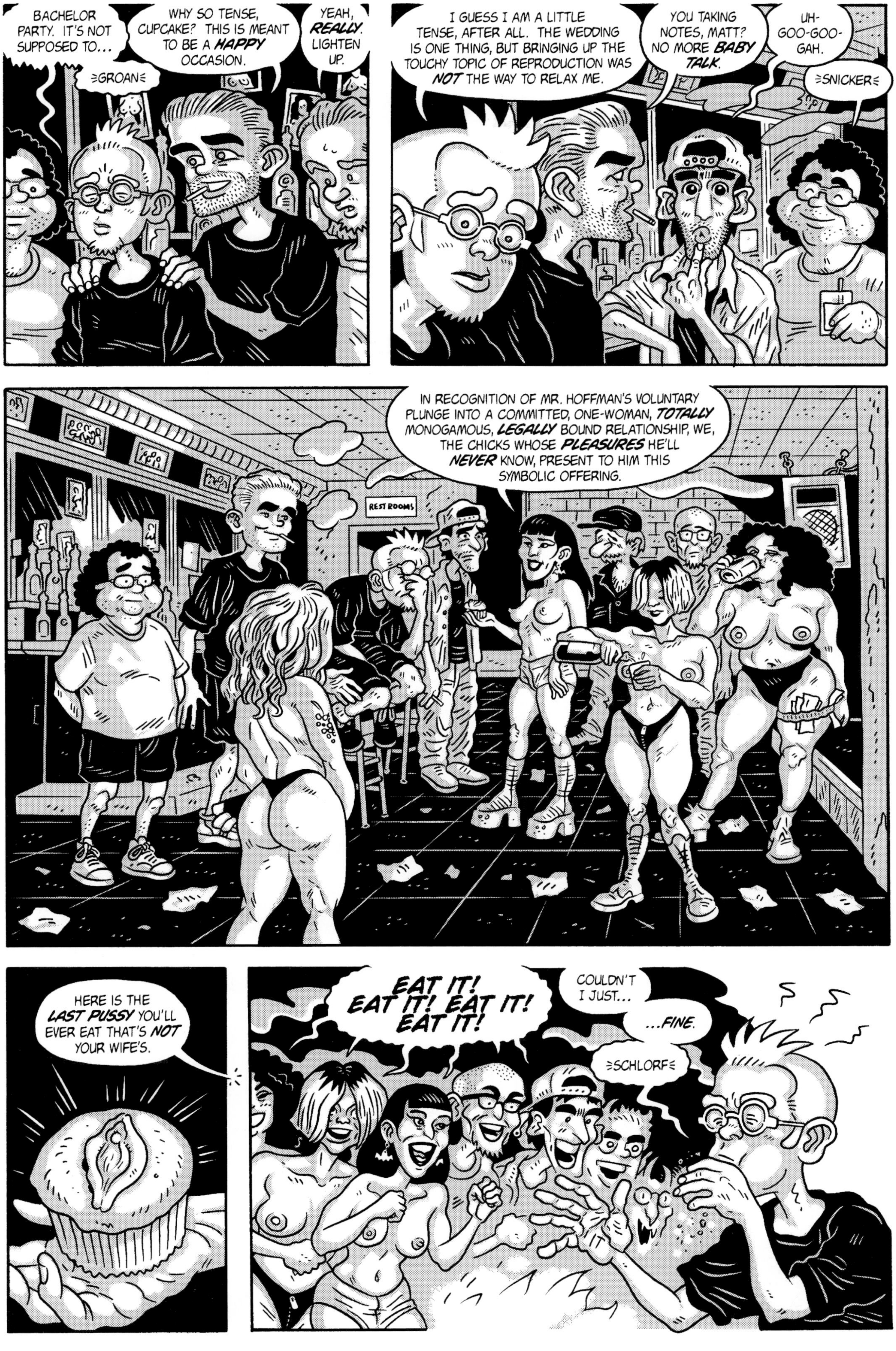
BACHELOR PARTY. IT'S NOT SUPPOSED TO...
≡GROAN≡
WHY SO TENSE, CUPCAKE? THIS IS MEANT TO BE A HAPPY OCCASION.
YEAH, REALLY. LIGHTEN UP.
I GUESS I AM A LITTLE TENSE, AFTER ALL. THE WEDDING IS ONE THING, BUT BRINGING UP THE TOUCHY TOPIC OF REPRODUCTION WAS NOT THE WAY TO RELAX ME.
YOU TAKING NOTES, MATT? NO MORE BABY TALK.
UH-GOO-GOO-GAH.
≡SNICKER≡
IN RECOGNITION OF MR. HOFFMAN'S VOLUNTARY PLUNGE INTO A COMMITTED, ONE-WOMAN, TOTALLY MONOGAMOUS, LEGALLY BOUND RELATIONSHIP, WE, THE CHICKS WHOSE PLEASURES HE'LL NEVER KNOW, PRESENT TO HIM THIS SYMBOLIC OFFERING.
RESTROOMS
HERE IS THE LAST PUSSY YOU'LL EVER EAT THAT'S NOT YOUR WIFE'S.
EAT IT! EAT IT! EAT IT! EAT IT!
COULDN'T I JUST...
...FINE.
≡SCHLORF≡

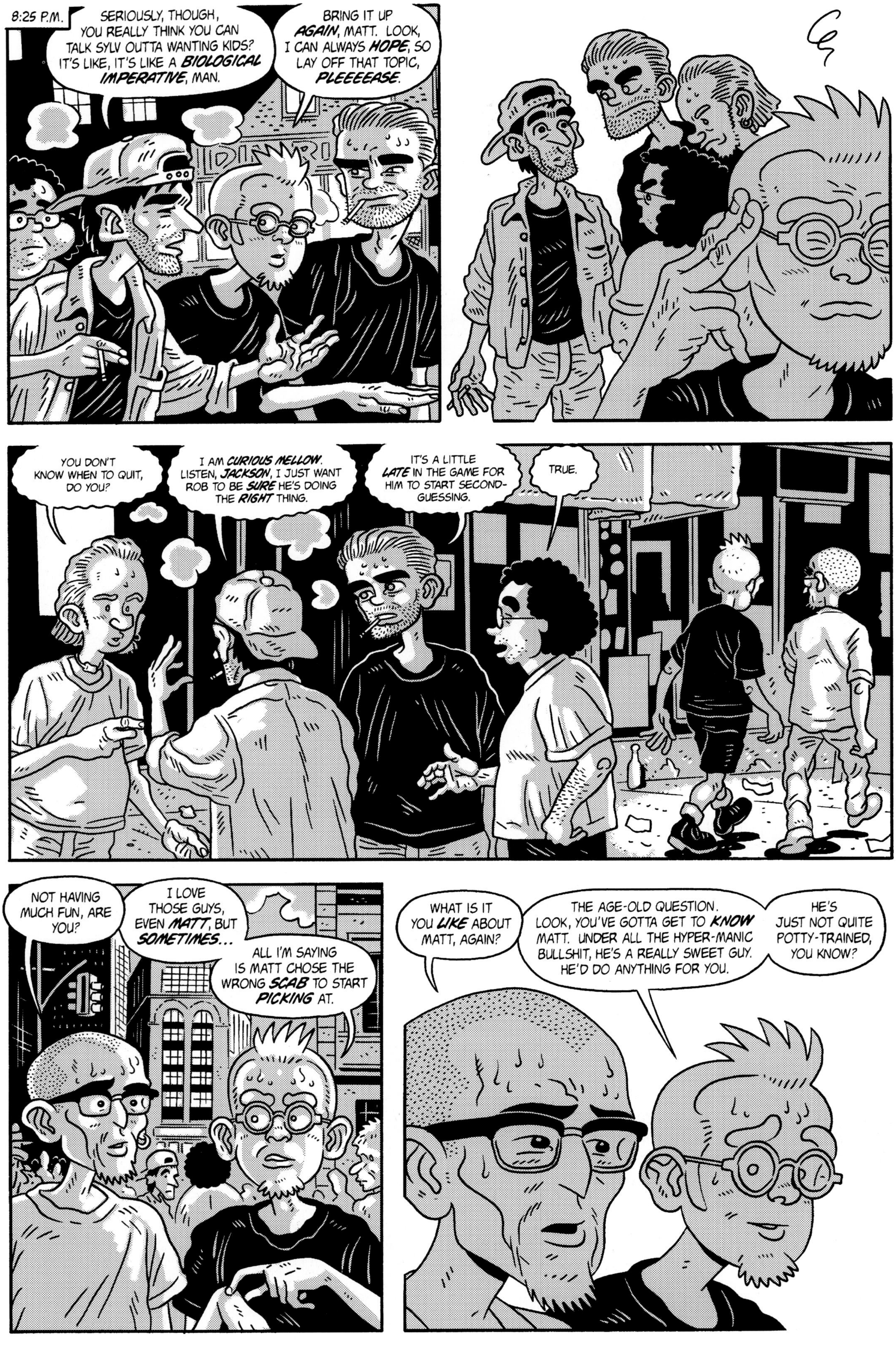
8:25 P.M.
SERIOUSLY, THOUGH, YOU REALLY THINK YOU CAN TALK SYLV OUTTA WANTING KIDS? IT'S LIKE, IT'S LIKE A *BIOLOGICAL IMPERATIVE*, MAN.
BRING IT UP *AGAIN*, MATT. LOOK, I CAN ALWAYS *HOPE*, SO LAY OFF THAT TOPIC, *PLEEEEASE*.
YOU DON'T KNOW WHEN TO QUIT, DO YOU?
I AM *CURIOUS MELLOW*. LISTEN, *JACKSON*, I JUST WANT ROB TO BE *SURE* HE'S DOING THE *RIGHT* THING.
IT'S A LITTLE *LATE* IN THE GAME FOR HIM TO START SECOND-GUESSING.
TRUE.
NOT HAVING MUCH FUN, ARE YOU?
I LOVE THOSE GUYS, EVEN *MATT*, BUT *SOMETIMES...*
ALL I'M SAYING IS MATT CHOSE THE WRONG *SCAB* TO START *PICKING* AT.
WHAT IS IT YOU *LIKE* ABOUT MATT, AGAIN?
THE AGE-OLD QUESTION. LOOK, YOU'VE GOTTA GET TO *KNOW* MATT. UNDER ALL THE HYPER-MANIC BULLSHIT, HE'S A REALLY SWEET GUY. HE'D DO ANYTHING FOR YOU.
HE'S JUST NOT QUITE POTTY-TRAINED, YOU KNOW?

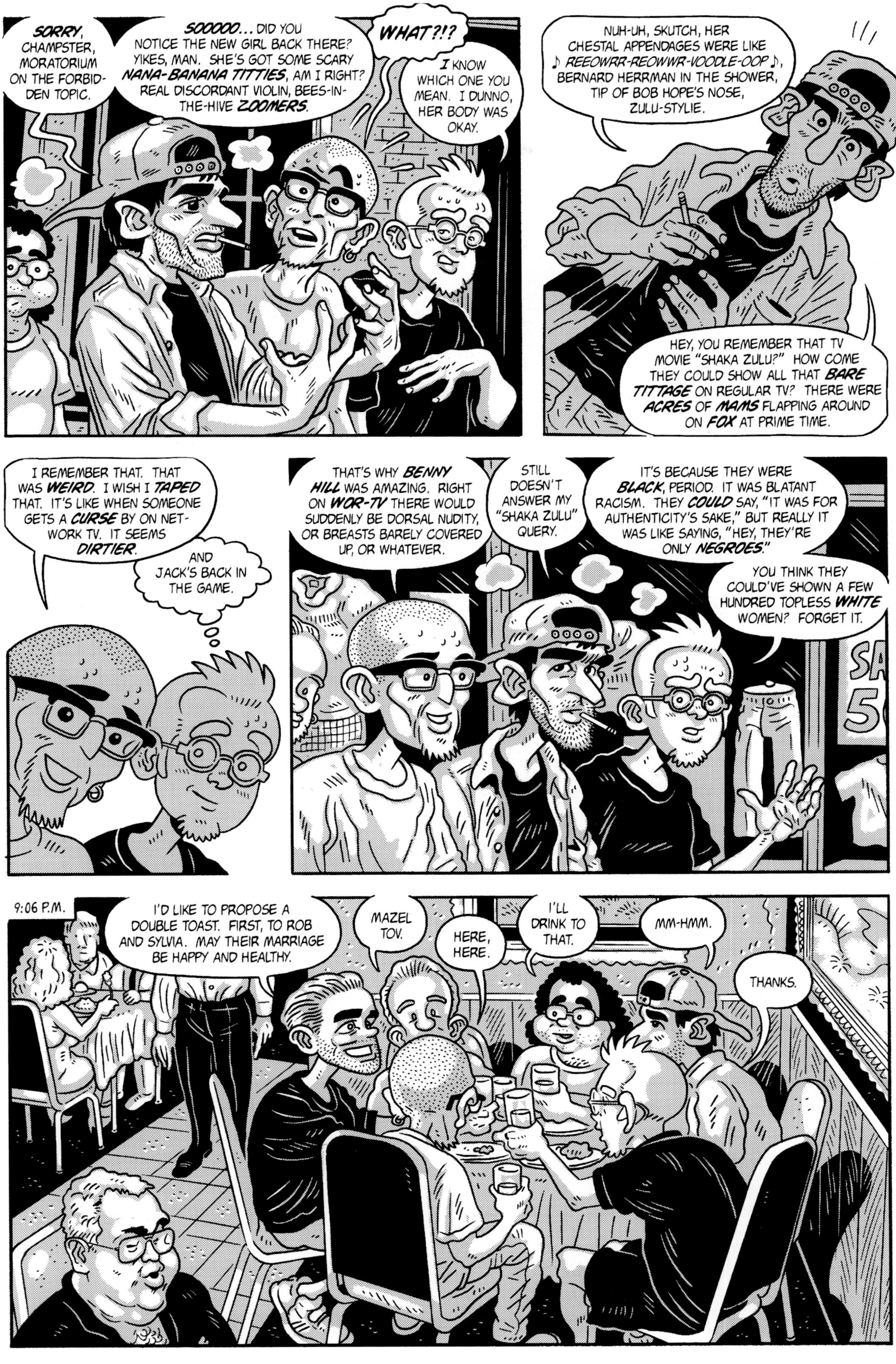
SORRY, CHAMPSTER, MORATORIUM ON THE FORBIDDEN TOPIC.
SOOOOO... DID YOU NOTICE THE NEW GIRL BACK THERE? YIKES, MAN. SHE'S GOT SOME SCARY NANA-BANANA TITTIES, AM I RIGHT? REAL DISCORDANT VIOLIN, BEES-IN-THE-HIVE ZOOMERS.
WHAT?!?
I KNOW WHICH ONE YOU MEAN. I DUNNO, HER BODY WAS OKAY.
NUH-UH, SKUTCH, HER CHESTAL APPENDAGES WERE LIKE ♪ REEOWRR-REOWWR-VOODLE-OOP ♪, BERNARD HERRMAN IN THE SHOWER, TIP OF BOB HOPE'S NOSE, ZULU-STYLIE.
HEY, YOU REMEMBER THAT TV MOVIE "SHAKA ZULU?" HOW COME THEY COULD SHOW ALL THAT BARE TITTAGE ON REGULAR TV? THERE WERE ACRES OF MAMS FLAPPING AROUND ON FOX AT PRIME TIME.
I REMEMBER THAT. THAT WAS WEIRD. I WISH I TAPED THAT. IT'S LIKE WHEN SOMEONE GETS A CURSE BY ON NETWORK TV. IT SEEMS DIRTIER.
AND JACK'S BACK IN THE GAME.
THAT'S WHY BENNY HILL WAS AMAZING. RIGHT ON WOR-TV THERE WOULD SUDDENLY BE DORSAL NUDITY, OR BREASTS BARELY COVERED UP, OR WHATEVER.
STILL DOESN'T ANSWER MY "SHAKA ZULU" QUERY.
IT'S BECAUSE THEY WERE BLACK, PERIOD. IT WAS BLATANT RACISM. THEY COULD SAY, "IT WAS FOR AUTHENTICITY'S SAKE," BUT REALLY IT WAS LIKE SAYING, "HEY, THEY'RE ONLY NEGROES."
YOU THINK THEY COULD'VE SHOWN A FEW HUNDRED TOPLESS WHITE WOMEN? FORGET IT.
9:06 P.M.
I'D LIKE TO PROPOSE A DOUBLE TOAST. FIRST, TO ROB AND SYLVIA. MAY THEIR MARRIAGE BE HAPPY AND HEALTHY.
MAZEL TOV.
HERE, HERE.
I'LL DRINK TO THAT.
MM-HMM.
THANKS.

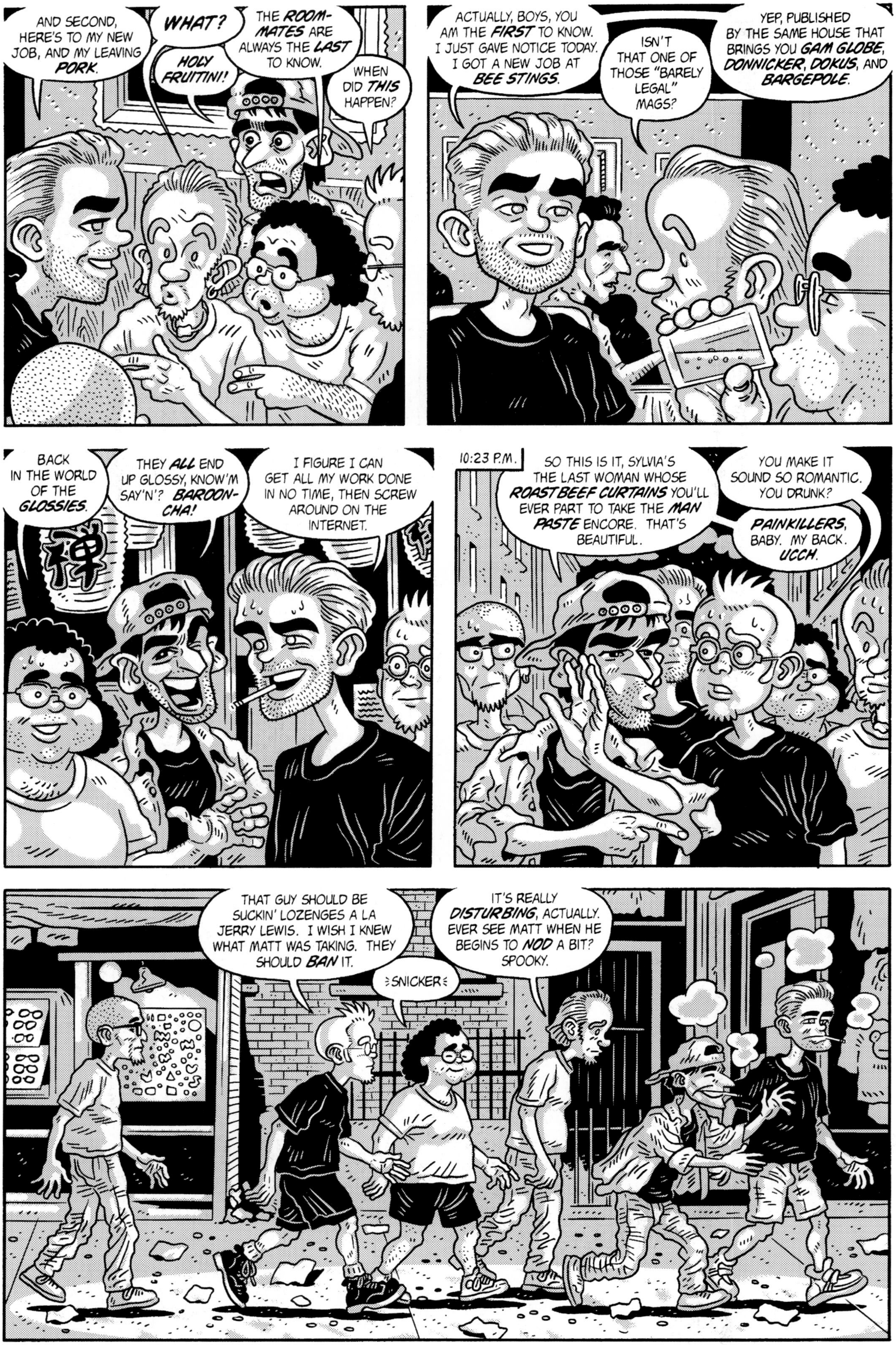
AND SECOND, HERE'S TO MY NEW JOB, AND MY LEAVING PORK.
WHAT?
HOLY FRUITINI!
THE ROOMMATES ARE ALWAYS THE LAST TO KNOW.
WHEN DID THIS HAPPEN?
ACTUALLY, BOYS, YOU AM THE FIRST TO KNOW. I JUST GAVE NOTICE TODAY. I GOT A NEW JOB AT BEE STINGS.
ISN'T THAT ONE OF THOSE "BARELY LEGAL" MAGS?
YEP, PUBLISHED BY THE SAME HOUSE THAT BRINGS YOU GAM GLOBE, DONNICKER, DOKUS, AND BARGEPOLE.
BACK IN THE WORLD OF THE GLOSSIES.
THEY ALL END UP GLOSSY, KNOW'M SAY'N'? BAROONCHA!
I FIGURE I CAN GET ALL MY WORK DONE IN NO TIME, THEN SCREW AROUND ON THE INTERNET.
10:23 P.M.
SO THIS IS IT, SYLVIA'S THE LAST WOMAN WHOSE ROASTBEEF CURTAINS YOU'LL EVER PART TO TAKE THE MAN PASTE ENCORE. THAT'S BEAUTIFUL.
YOU MAKE IT SOUND SO ROMANTIC. YOU DRUNK?
PAINKILLERS, BABY. MY BACK. UCCH.
THAT GUY SHOULD BE SUCKIN' LOZENGES A LA JERRY LEWIS. I WISH I KNEW WHAT MATT WAS TAKING. THEY SHOULD BAN IT.
SNICKER
IT'S REALLY DISTURBING, ACTUALLY. EVER SEE MATT WHEN HE BEGINS TO NOD A BIT? SPOOKY.

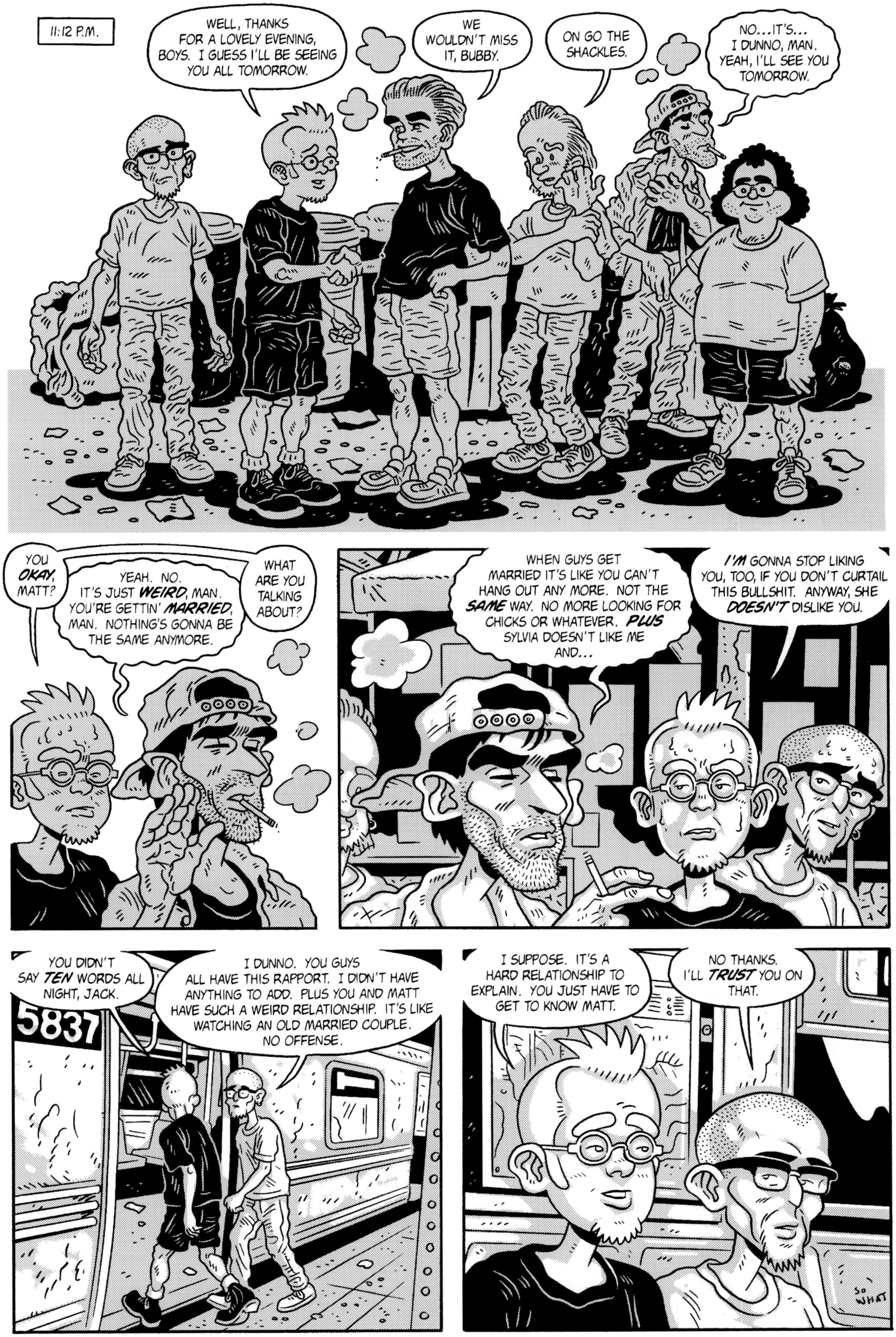
11:12 P.M.
WELL, THANKS FOR A LOVELY EVENING, BOYS. I GUESS I'LL BE SEEING YOU ALL TOMORROW.
WE WOULDN'T MISS IT, BUBBY.
ON GO THE SHACKLES.
NO...IT'S... I DUNNO, MAN. YEAH, I'LL SEE YOU TOMORROW.
YOU OKAY, MATT?
YEAH. NO. IT'S JUST WEIRD, MAN. YOU'RE GETTIN' MARRIED, MAN. NOTHING'S GONNA BE THE SAME ANYMORE.
WHAT ARE YOU TALKING ABOUT?
WHEN GUYS GET MARRIED IT'S LIKE YOU CAN'T HANG OUT ANY MORE. NOT THE SAME WAY. NO MORE LOOKING FOR CHICKS OR WHATEVER. PLUS SYLVIA DOESN'T LIKE ME AND...
I'M GONNA STOP LIKING YOU, TOO, IF YOU DON'T CURTAIL THIS BULLSHIT. ANYWAY, SHE DOESN'T DISLIKE YOU.
YOU DIDN'T SAY TEN WORDS ALL NIGHT, JACK.
5837
I DUNNO. YOU GUYS ALL HAVE THIS RAPPORT. I DIDN'T HAVE ANYTHING TO ADD. PLUS YOU AND MATT HAVE SUCH A WEIRD RELATIONSHIP. IT'S LIKE WATCHING AN OLD MARRIED COUPLE. NO OFFENSE.
I SUPPOSE. IT'S A HARD RELATIONSHIP TO EXPLAIN. YOU JUST HAVE TO GET TO KNOW MATT.
NO THANKS. I'LL TRUST YOU ON THAT.
SO WHAT

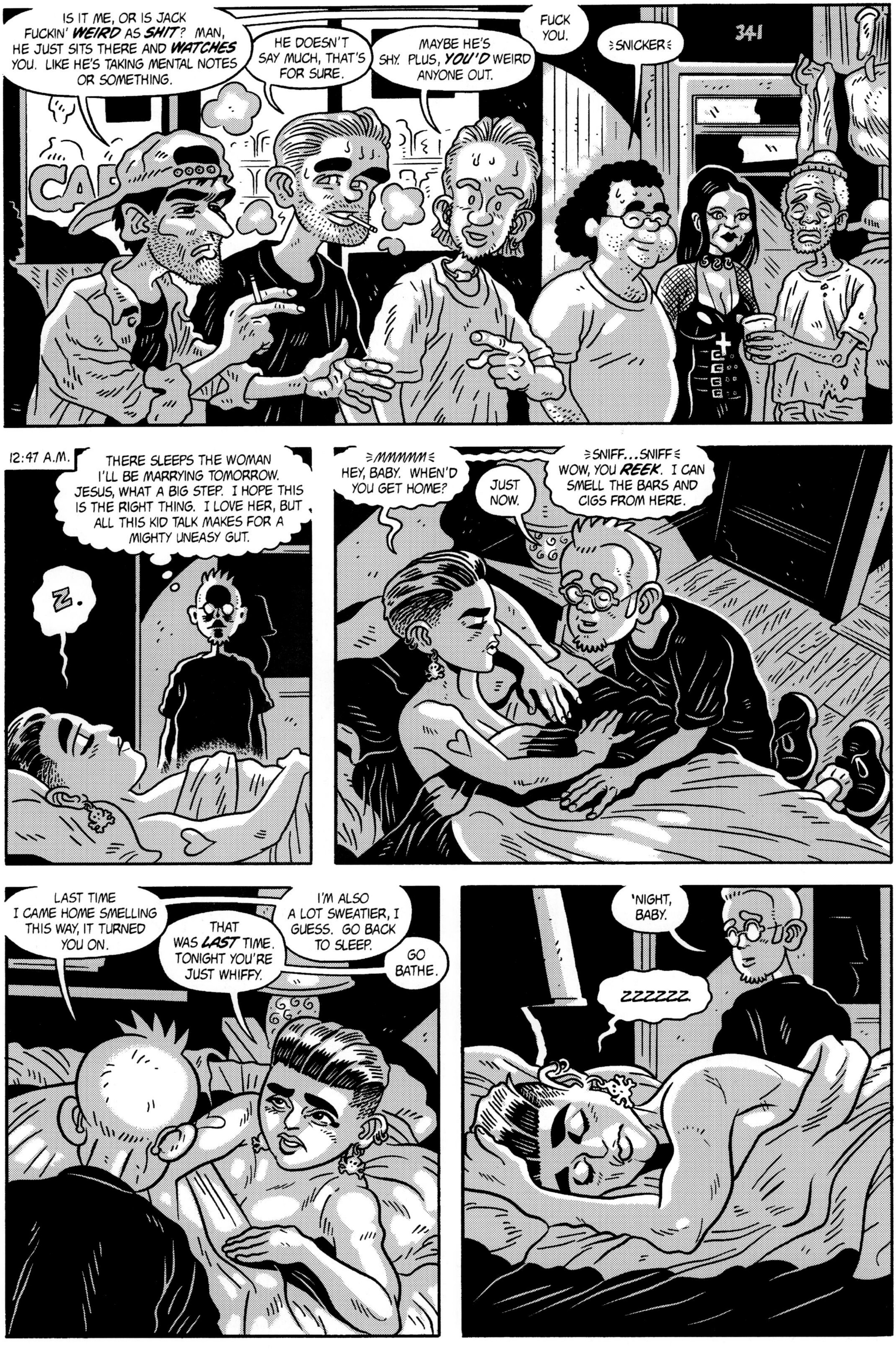
IS IT ME, OR IS JACK FUCKIN' WEIRD AS SHIT? MAN, HE JUST SITS THERE AND WATCHES YOU. LIKE HE'S TAKING MENTAL NOTES OR SOMETHING.
HE DOESN'T SAY MUCH, THAT'S FOR SURE.
MAYBE HE'S SHY. PLUS, YOU'D WEIRD ANYONE OUT.
FUCK YOU.
SNICKER
341
12:47 A.M.
THERE SLEEPS THE WOMAN I'LL BE MARRYING TOMORROW. JESUS, WHAT A BIG STEP. I HOPE THIS IS THE RIGHT THING. I LOVE HER, BUT ALL THIS KID TALK MAKES FOR A MIGHTY UNEASY GUT.
Z.
MMMMM
HEY, BABY. WHEN'D YOU GET HOME?
JUST NOW.
SNIFF...SNIFF
WOW, YOU REEK. I CAN SMELL THE BARS AND CIGS FROM HERE.
LAST TIME I CAME HOME SMELLING THIS WAY, IT TURNED YOU ON.
THAT WAS LAST TIME. TONIGHT YOU'RE JUST WHIFFY.
I'M ALSO A LOT SWEATIER, I GUESS. GO BACK TO SLEEP.
GO BATHE.
'NIGHT, BABY.
ZZZZZZ.

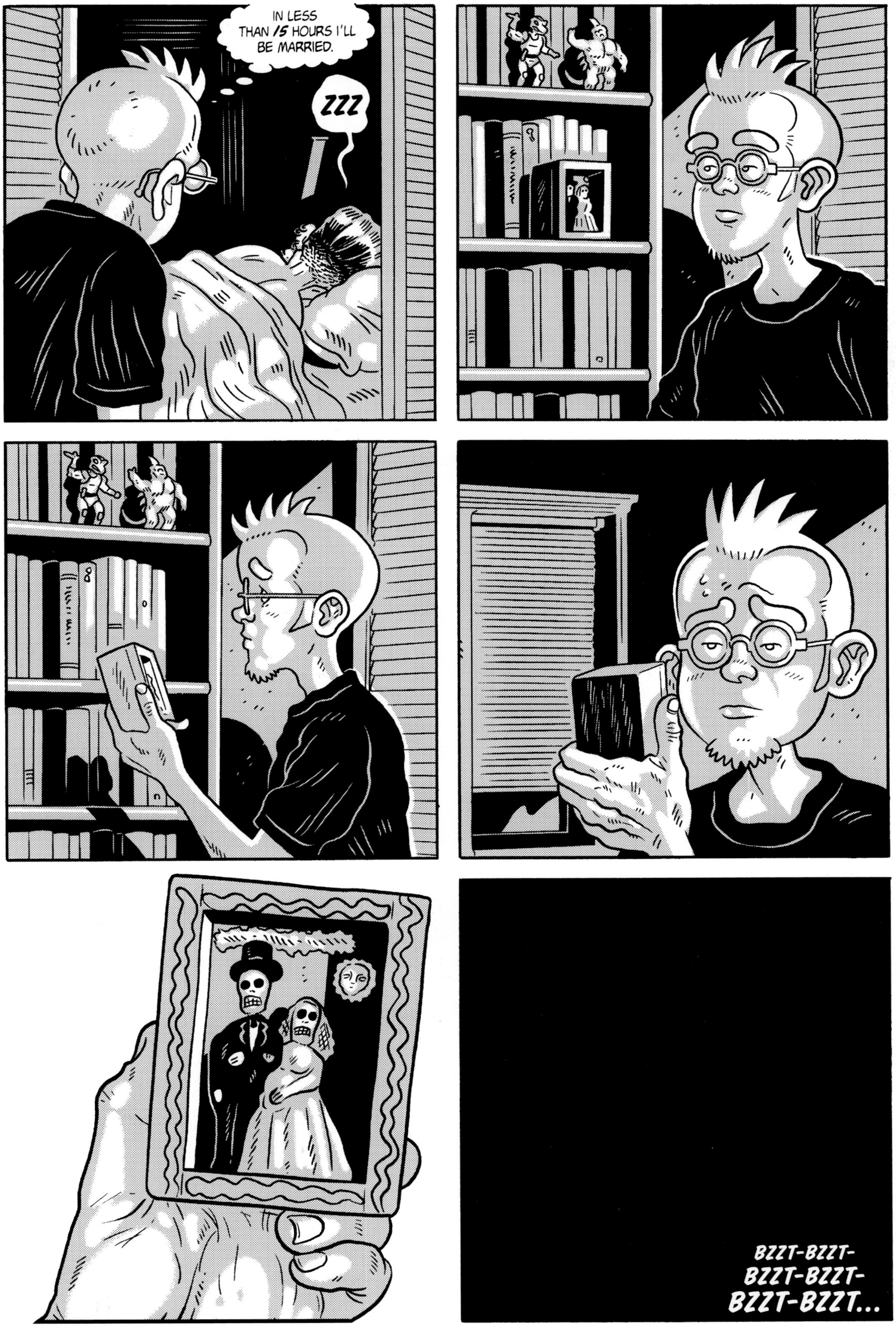
IN LESS THAN 15 HOURS I'LL BE MARRIED.
ZZZ
BZZT-BZZT-
BZZT-BZZT-
BZZT-BZZT...

...BZZT-BZZT-BZZT~~CLICK

≤MOAN≥ WHUZZA...? OH. IT'S THE BIG DAY.

SYLV'? SYLVIA, HONEY?

OH YEAH...

WAKE UP, HOFFMAN. WAKE UP. IT'S THE BIG ONE.

FUCK YEAH, IT'S THE BIG ONE ALRIGHT. JESUS. FUCKING MATT PUT THE **BABY DEMONS** IN MY HEAD ALL NIGHT. WHAT'D I GET, MAYBE THREE HOURS SLEEP? MORE FUCKING BABY NIGHTMARES.

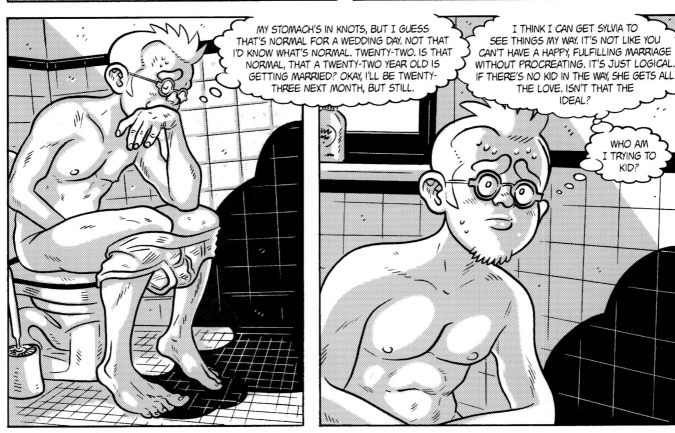

MY STOMACH'S IN KNOTS, BUT I GUESS THAT'S NORMAL FOR A WEDDING DAY. NOT THAT I'D KNOW WHAT'S NORMAL. TWENTY-TWO. IS THAT NORMAL, THAT A TWENTY-TWO YEAR OLD IS GETTING MARRIED? OKAY, I'LL BE TWENTY-THREE NEXT MONTH, BUT STILL.

I THINK I CAN GET SYLVIA TO SEE THINGS MY WAY. IT'S NOT LIKE YOU CAN'T HAVE A HAPPY, FULFILLING MARRIAGE WITHOUT PROCREATING. IT'S JUST LOGICAL. IF THERE'S NO KID IN THE WAY, SHE GETS ALL THE LOVE. ISN'T THAT THE IDEAL?

WHO AM I TRYING TO KID?

WELL, IT'S NOT LIKE MARRIAGE IS THE MOST **PERMANENT** INSTITUTION ANY MORE.

SHUT UP. WHAT THE FUCK IS **WRONG** WITH ME? I SHOULD BE THINKING HOW **GREAT** EVERYTHING IS GOING TO BE. I'M MARRYING THE GIRL OF MY DREAMS. EXCEPT FOR THE BABY PART.

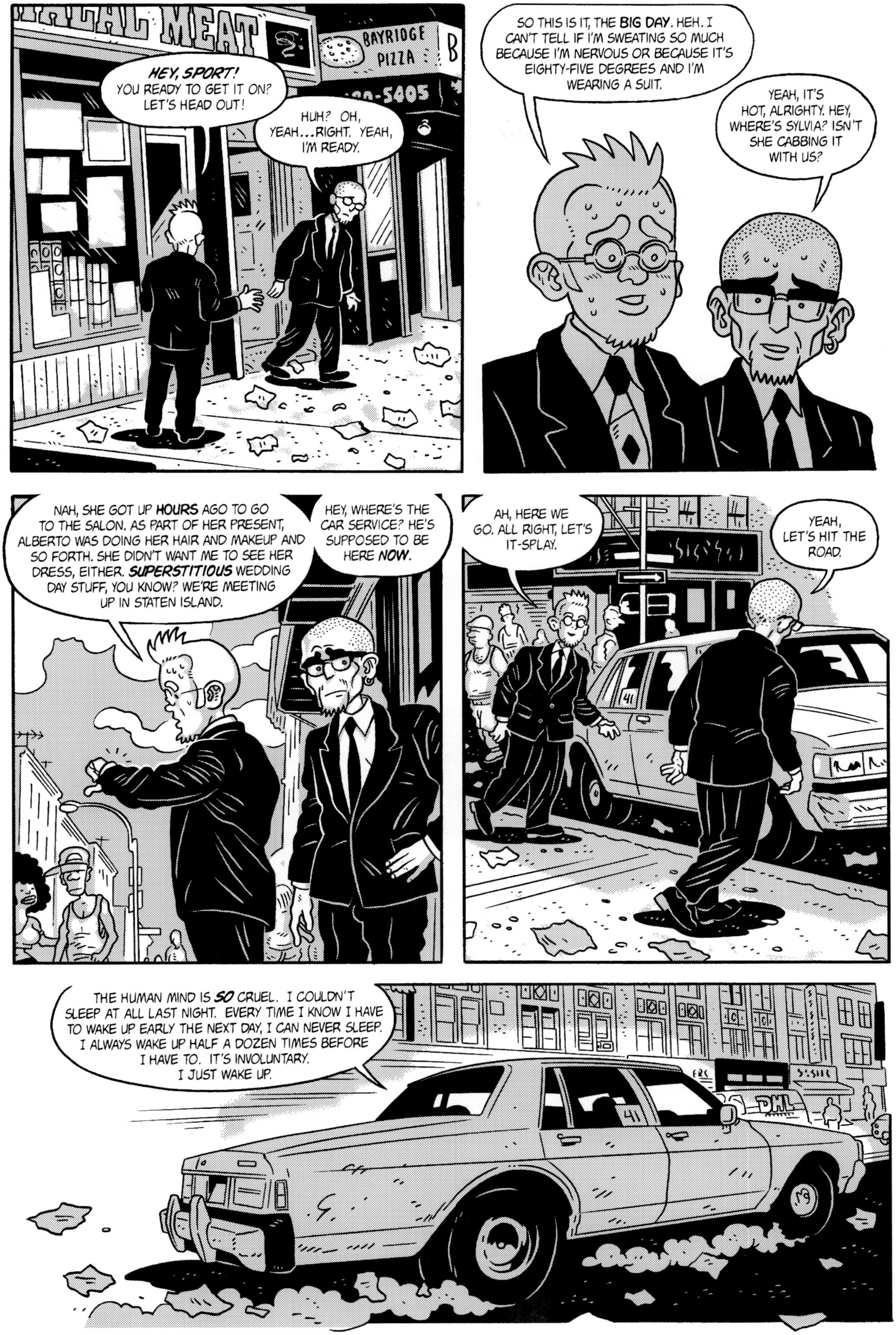
HALAL MEAT
BAYRIDGE PIZZA
HEY, SPORT! YOU READY TO GET IT ON? LET'S HEAD OUT!
HUH? OH, YEAH... RIGHT. YEAH, I'M READY.
SO THIS IS IT, THE BIG DAY. HEH. I CAN'T TELL IF I'M SWEATING SO MUCH BECAUSE I'M NERVOUS OR BECAUSE IT'S EIGHTY-FIVE DEGREES AND I'M WEARING A SUIT.
YEAH, IT'S HOT, ALRIGHTY. HEY, WHERE'S SYLVIA? ISN'T SHE CABBING IT WITH US?
NAH, SHE GOT UP HOURS AGO TO GO TO THE SALON. AS PART OF HER PRESENT, ALBERTO WAS DOING HER HAIR AND MAKEUP AND SO FORTH. SHE DIDN'T WANT ME TO SEE HER DRESS, EITHER. SUPERSTITIOUS WEDDING DAY STUFF, YOU KNOW? WE'RE MEETING UP IN STATEN ISLAND.
HEY, WHERE'S THE CAR SERVICE? HE'S SUPPOSED TO BE HERE NOW.
AH, HERE WE GO. ALL RIGHT, LET'S IT-SPLAY.
YEAH, LET'S HIT THE ROAD.
THE HUMAN MIND IS SO CRUEL. I COULDN'T SLEEP AT ALL LAST NIGHT. EVERY TIME I KNOW I HAVE TO WAKE UP EARLY THE NEXT DAY, I CAN NEVER SLEEP. I ALWAYS WAKE UP HALF A DOZEN TIMES BEFORE I HAVE TO. IT'S INVOLUNTARY. I JUST WAKE UP.
DHL

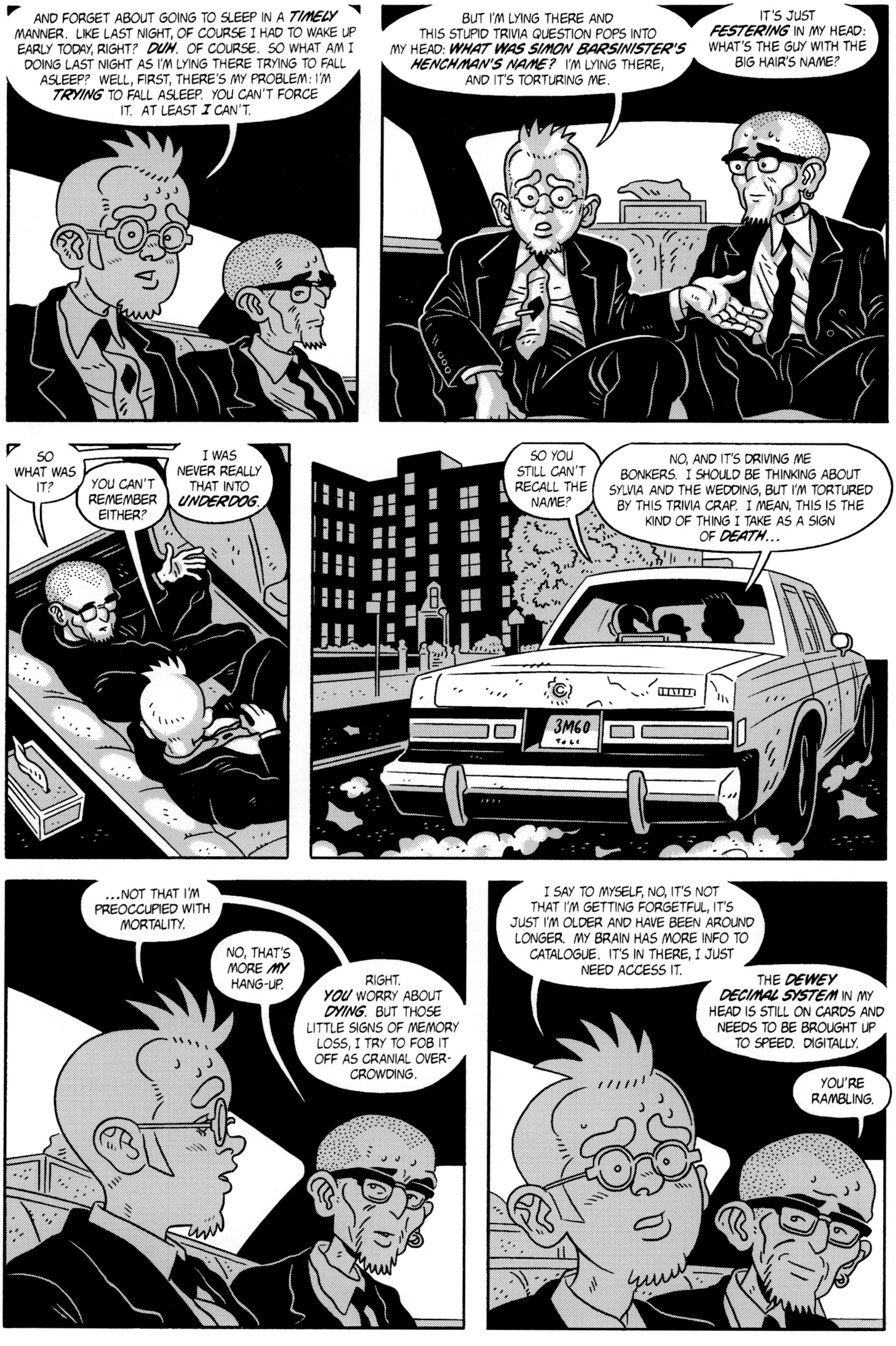
AND FORGET ABOUT GOING TO SLEEP IN A TIMELY MANNER. LIKE LAST NIGHT, OF COURSE I HAD TO WAKE UP EARLY TODAY, RIGHT? DUH. OF COURSE. SO WHAT AM I DOING LAST NIGHT AS I'M LYING THERE TRYING TO FALL ASLEEP? WELL, FIRST, THERE'S MY PROBLEM: I'M TRYING TO FALL ASLEEP. YOU CAN'T FORCE IT. AT LEAST I CAN'T.
BUT I'M LYING THERE AND THIS STUPID TRIVIA QUESTION POPS INTO MY HEAD: WHAT WAS SIMON BARSINISTER'S HENCHMAN'S NAME? I'M LYING THERE, AND IT'S TORTURING ME.
IT'S JUST FESTERING IN MY HEAD: WHAT'S THE GUY WITH THE BIG HAIR'S NAME?
SO WHAT WAS IT?
YOU CAN'T REMEMBER EITHER?
I WAS NEVER REALLY THAT INTO UNDERDOG.
SO YOU STILL CAN'T RECALL THE NAME?
NO, AND IT'S DRIVING ME BONKERS. I SHOULD BE THINKING ABOUT SYLVIA AND THE WEDDING, BUT I'M TORTURED BY THIS TRIVIA CRAP. I MEAN, THIS IS THE KIND OF THING I TAKE AS A SIGN OF DEATH...
3M60
...NOT THAT I'M PREOCCUPIED WITH MORTALITY.
NO, THAT'S MORE MY HANG-UP.
RIGHT. YOU WORRY ABOUT DYING. BUT THOSE LITTLE SIGNS OF MEMORY LOSS, I TRY TO FOB IT OFF AS CRANIAL OVER-CROWDING.
I SAY TO MYSELF, NO, IT'S NOT THAT I'M GETTING FORGETFUL, IT'S JUST I'M OLDER AND HAVE BEEN AROUND LONGER. MY BRAIN HAS MORE INFO TO CATALOGUE. IT'S IN THERE, I JUST NEED ACCESS IT.
THE DEWEY DECIMAL SYSTEM IN MY HEAD IS STILL ON CARDS AND NEEDS TO BE BROUGHT UP TO SPEED. DIGITALLY.
YOU'RE RAMBLING.

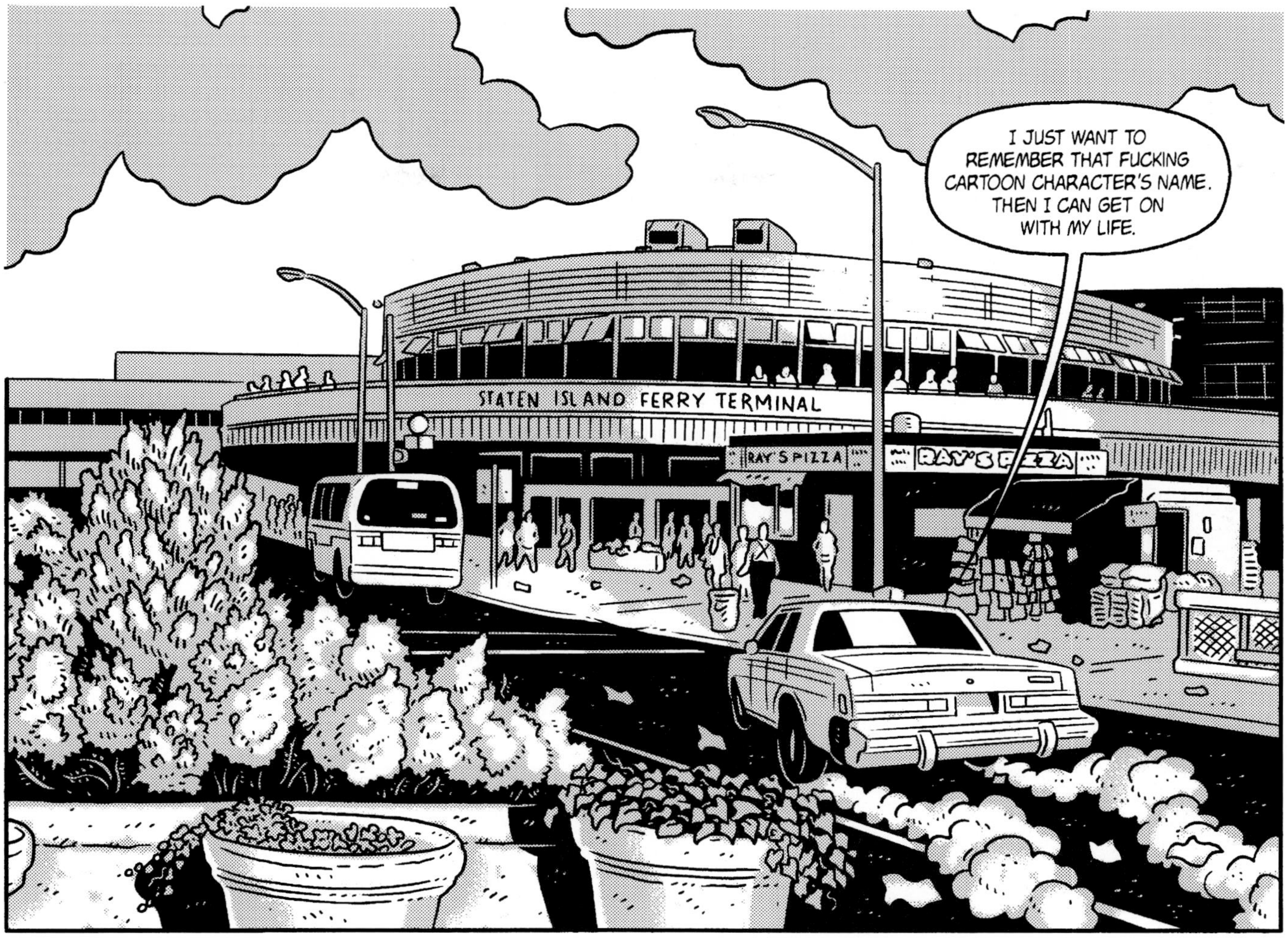
STATEN ISLAND FERRY TERMINAL
RAY'S PIZZA
I JUST WANT TO REMEMBER THAT FUCKING CARTOON CHARACTER'S NAME. THEN I CAN GET ON WITH MY LIFE.

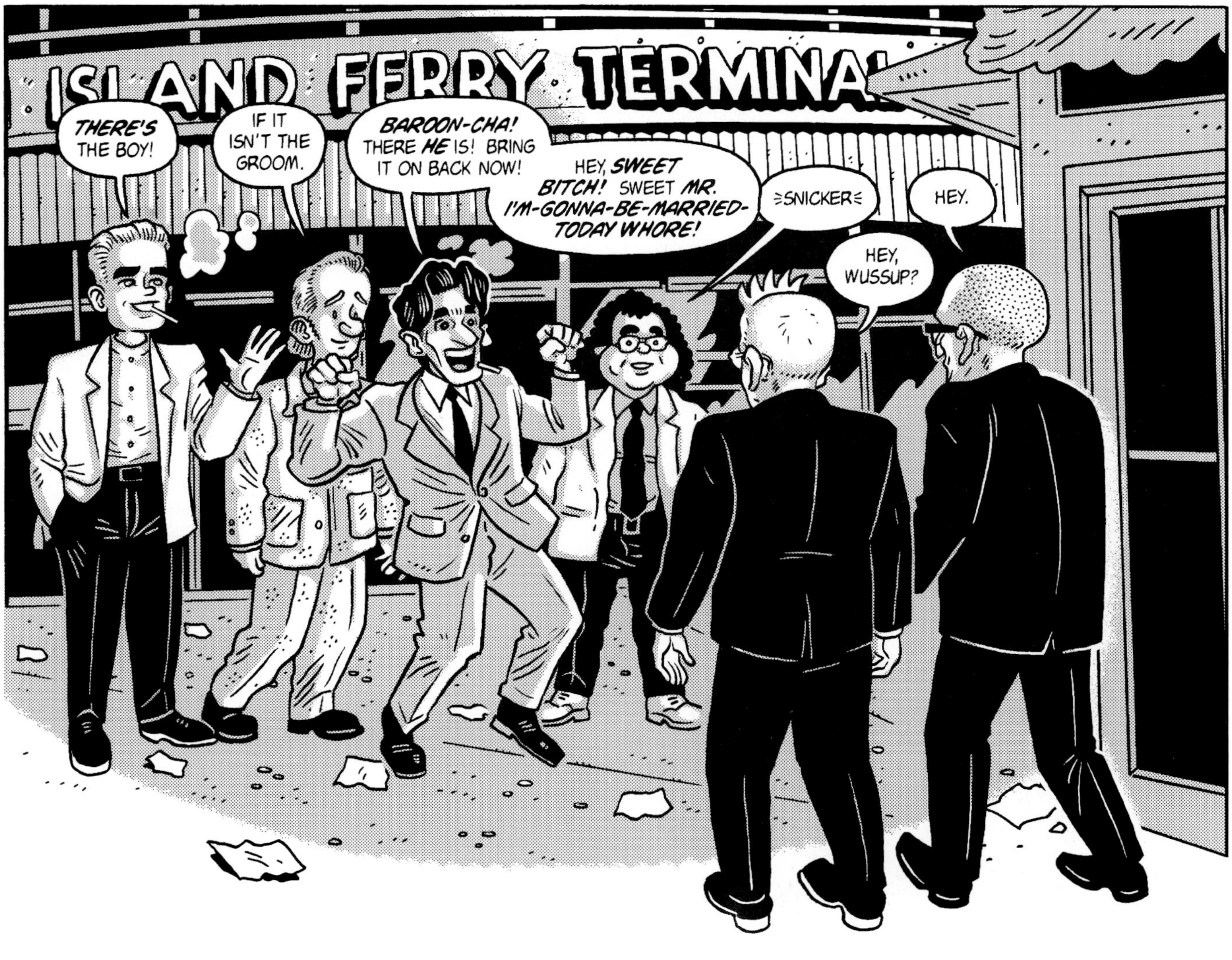
ISLAND FERRY TERMINA
THERE'S THE BOY!
IF IT ISN'T THE GROOM.
BAROON-CHA! THERE HE IS! BRING IT ON BACK NOW!
HEY, SWEET BITCH! SWEET MR. I'M-GONNA-BE-MARRIED-TODAY WHORE!
SNICKER
HEY.
HEY, WUSSUP?

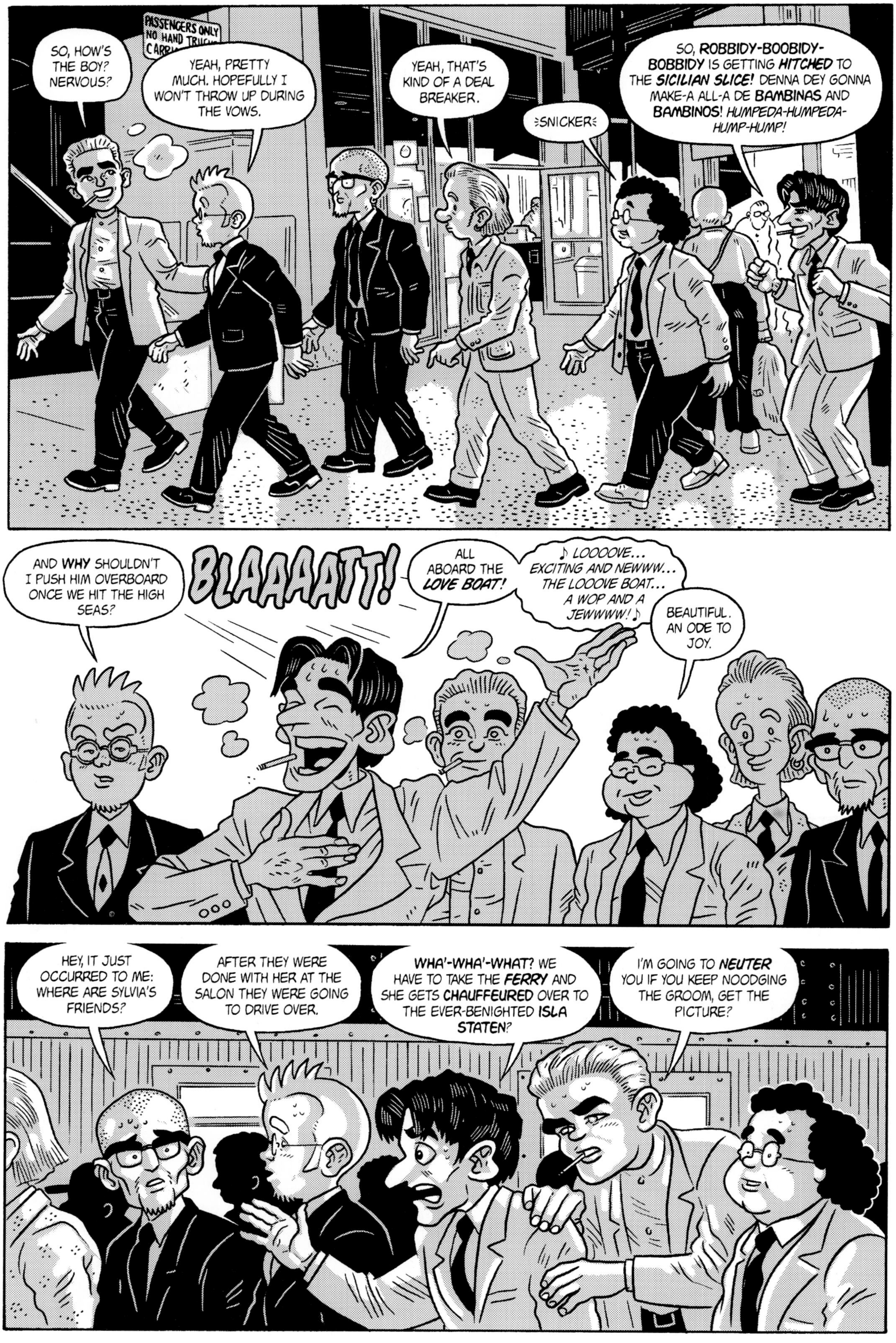
PASSENGERS ONLY
NO HAND TRUCK
SO, HOW'S THE BOY? NERVOUS?
YEAH, PRETTY MUCH. HOPEFULLY I WON'T THROW UP DURING THE VOWS.
YEAH, THAT'S KIND OF A DEAL BREAKER.
SNICKER
SO, ROBBIDY-BOOBIDY-BOBBIDY IS GETTING HITCHED TO THE SICILIAN SLICE! DENNA DEY GONNA MAKE-A ALL-A DE BAMBINAS AND BAMBINOS! HUMPEDA-HUMPEDA-HUMP-HUMP!
AND WHY SHOULDN'T I PUSH HIM OVERBOARD ONCE WE HIT THE HIGH SEAS?
BLAAAATT!
ALL ABOARD THE LOVE BOAT!
♪ LOOOOVE... EXCITING AND NEWWW... THE LOOOVE BOAT... A WOP AND A JEWWWW! ♪
BEAUTIFUL. AN ODE TO JOY.
HEY, IT JUST OCCURRED TO ME: WHERE ARE SYLVIA'S FRIENDS?
AFTER THEY WERE DONE WITH HER AT THE SALON THEY WERE GOING TO DRIVE OVER.
WHA'-WHA'-WHAT? WE HAVE TO TAKE THE FERRY AND SHE GETS CHAUFFEURED OVER TO THE EVER-BENIGHTED ISLA STATEN?
I'M GOING TO NEUTER YOU IF YOU KEEP NOODGING THE GROOM, GET THE PICTURE?

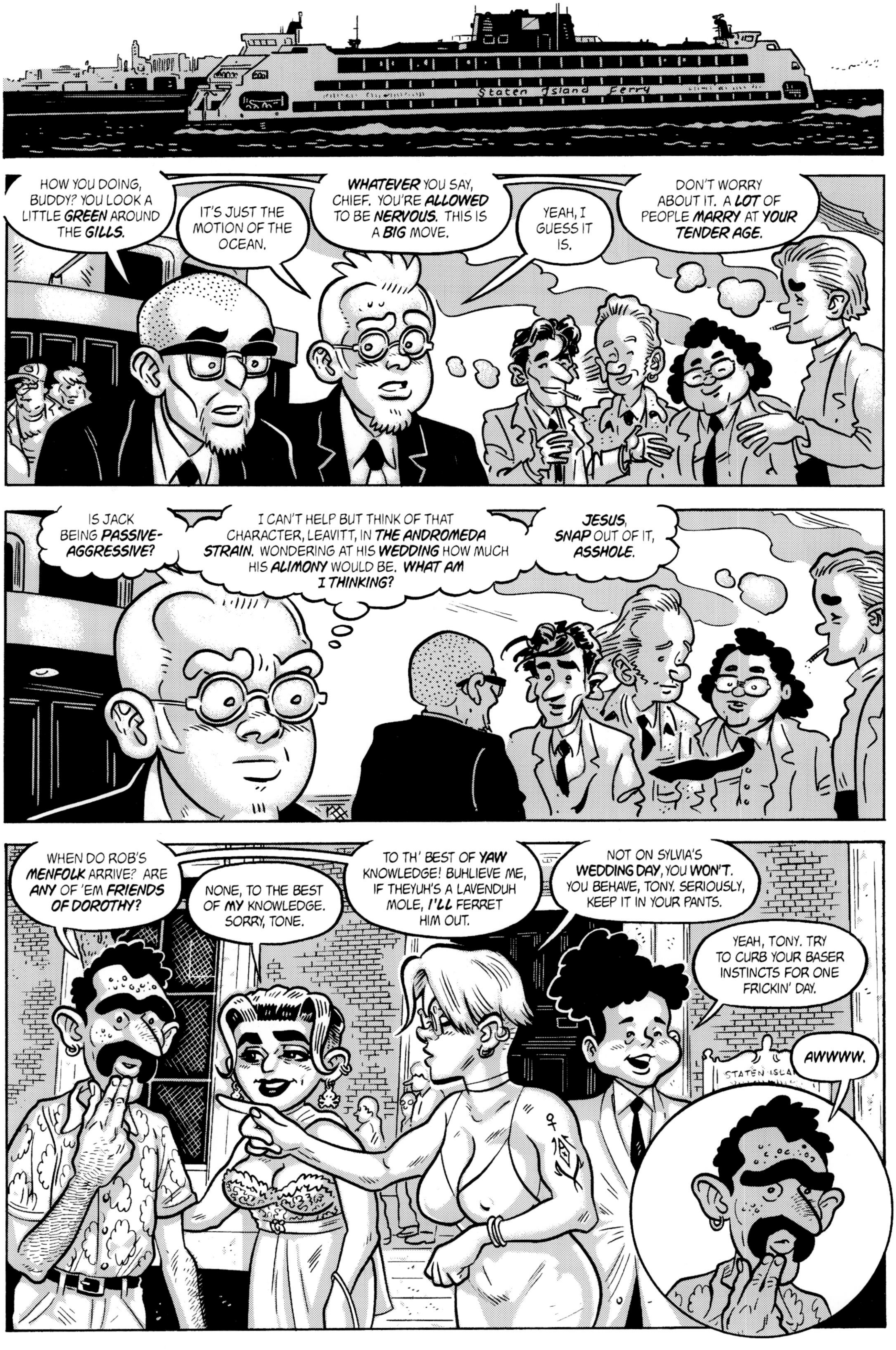
Staten Island Ferry
HOW YOU DOING, BUDDY? YOU LOOK A LITTLE GREEN AROUND THE GILLS.
IT'S JUST THE MOTION OF THE OCEAN.
WHATEVER YOU SAY, CHIEF. YOU'RE ALLOWED TO BE NERVOUS. THIS IS A BIG MOVE.
YEAH, I GUESS IT IS.
DON'T WORRY ABOUT IT. A LOT OF PEOPLE MARRY AT YOUR TENDER AGE.
IS JACK BEING PASSIVE-AGGRESSIVE?
I CAN'T HELP BUT THINK OF THAT CHARACTER, LEAVITT, IN THE ANDROMEDA STRAIN. WONDERING AT HIS WEDDING HOW MUCH HIS ALIMONY WOULD BE. WHAT AM I THINKING?
JESUS, SNAP OUT OF IT, ASSHOLE.
WHEN DO ROB'S MENFOLK ARRIVE? ARE ANY OF 'EM FRIENDS OF DOROTHY?
NONE, TO THE BEST OF MY KNOWLEDGE. SORRY, TONE.
TO TH' BEST OF YAW KNOWLEDGE! BUHLIEVE ME, IF THEYUH'S A LAVENDUH MOLE, I'LL FERRET HIM OUT.
NOT ON SYLVIA'S WEDDING DAY, YOU WON'T. YOU BEHAVE, TONY. SERIOUSLY, KEEP IT IN YOUR PANTS.
YEAH, TONY. TRY TO CURB YOUR BASER INSTINCTS FOR ONE FRICKIN' DAY.
AWWWW.

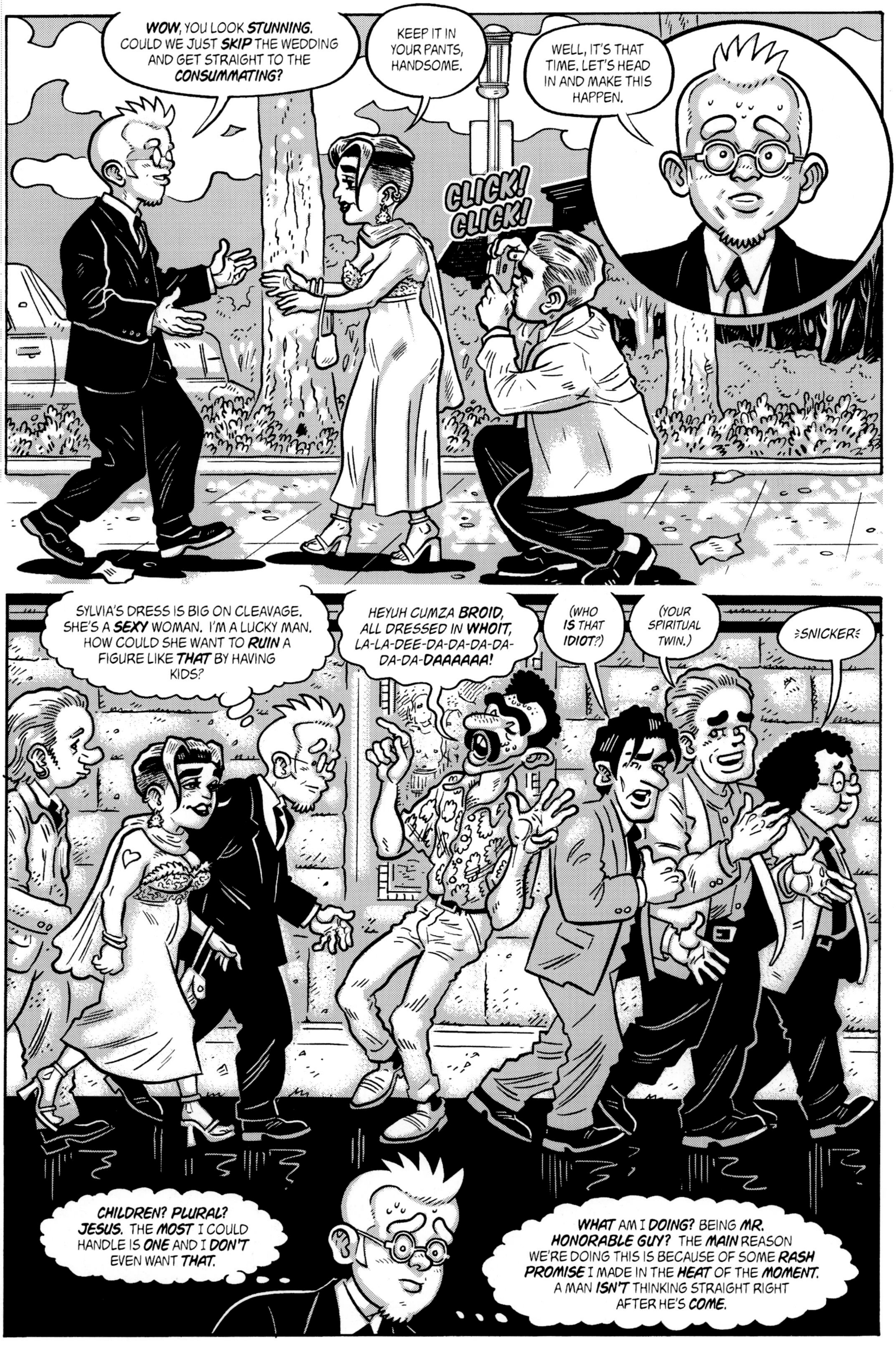
WOW, YOU LOOK STUNNING. COULD WE JUST SKIP THE WEDDING AND GET STRAIGHT TO THE CONSUMMATING?
KEEP IT IN YOUR PANTS, HANDSOME.
CLICK! CLICK!
WELL, IT'S THAT TIME. LET'S HEAD IN AND MAKE THIS HAPPEN.
SYLVIA'S DRESS IS BIG ON CLEAVAGE. SHE'S A SEXY WOMAN. I'M A LUCKY MAN. HOW COULD SHE WANT TO RUIN A FIGURE LIKE THAT BY HAVING KIDS?
HEYUH CUMZA BROID, ALL DRESSED IN WHOIT, LA-LA-DEE-DA-DA-DA-DA-DA-DA-DAAAAAA!
(WHO IS THAT IDIOT?)
(YOUR SPIRITUAL TWIN.)
SNICKER
CHILDREN? PLURAL? JESUS. THE MOST I COULD HANDLE IS ONE AND I DON'T EVEN WANT THAT.
WHAT AM I DOING? BEING MR. HONORABLE GUY? THE MAIN REASON WE'RE DOING THIS IS BECAUSE OF SOME RASH PROMISE I MADE IN THE HEAT OF THE MOMENT. A MAN ISN'T THINKING STRAIGHT RIGHT AFTER HE'S COME.

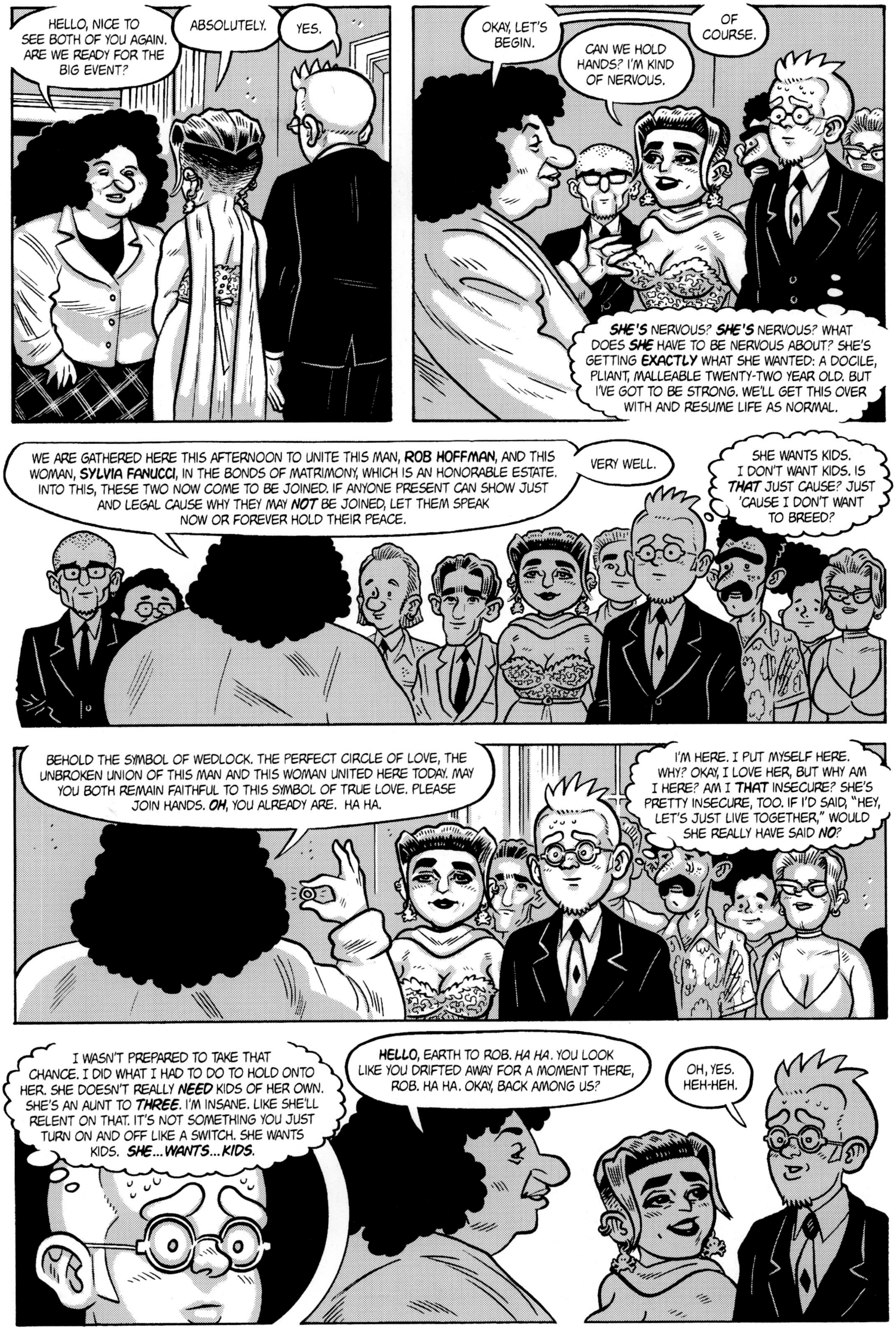
HELLO, NICE TO SEE BOTH OF YOU AGAIN. ARE WE READY FOR THE BIG EVENT?
ABSOLUTELY.
YES.
OKAY, LET'S BEGIN.
CAN WE HOLD HANDS? I'M KIND OF NERVOUS.
OF COURSE.
SHE'S NERVOUS? SHE'S NERVOUS? WHAT DOES SHE HAVE TO BE NERVOUS ABOUT? SHE'S GETTING EXACTLY WHAT SHE WANTED: A DOCILE, PLIANT, MALLEABLE TWENTY-TWO YEAR OLD. BUT I'VE GOT TO BE STRONG. WE'LL GET THIS OVER WITH AND RESUME LIFE AS NORMAL.
WE ARE GATHERED HERE THIS AFTERNOON TO UNITE THIS MAN, ROB HOFFMAN, AND THIS WOMAN, SYLVIA FANUCCI, IN THE BONDS OF MATRIMONY, WHICH IS AN HONORABLE ESTATE. INTO THIS, THESE TWO NOW COME TO BE JOINED. IF ANYONE PRESENT CAN SHOW JUST AND LEGAL CAUSE WHY THEY MAY NOT BE JOINED, LET THEM SPEAK NOW OR FOREVER HOLD THEIR PEACE.
VERY WELL.
SHE WANTS KIDS. I DON'T WANT KIDS. IS THAT JUST CAUSE? JUST 'CAUSE I DON'T WANT TO BREED?
BEHOLD THE SYMBOL OF WEDLOCK. THE PERFECT CIRCLE OF LOVE, THE UNBROKEN UNION OF THIS MAN AND THIS WOMAN UNITED HERE TODAY. MAY YOU BOTH REMAIN FAITHFUL TO THIS SYMBOL OF TRUE LOVE. PLEASE JOIN HANDS. OH, YOU ALREADY ARE. HA HA.
I'M HERE. I PUT MYSELF HERE. WHY? OKAY, I LOVE HER, BUT WHY AM I HERE? AM I THAT INSECURE? SHE'S PRETTY INSECURE, TOO. IF I'D SAID, "HEY, LET'S JUST LIVE TOGETHER," WOULD SHE REALLY HAVE SAID NO?
I WASN'T PREPARED TO TAKE THAT CHANCE. I DID WHAT I HAD TO DO TO HOLD ONTO HER. SHE DOESN'T REALLY NEED KIDS OF HER OWN. SHE'S AN AUNT TO THREE. I'M INSANE. LIKE SHE'LL RELENT ON THAT. IT'S NOT SOMETHING YOU JUST TURN ON AND OFF LIKE A SWITCH. SHE WANTS KIDS. SHE...WANTS...KIDS.
HELLO, EARTH TO ROB. HA HA. YOU LOOK LIKE YOU DRIFTED AWAY FOR A MOMENT THERE, ROB. HA HA. OKAY, BACK AMONG US?
OH, YES. HEH-HEH.

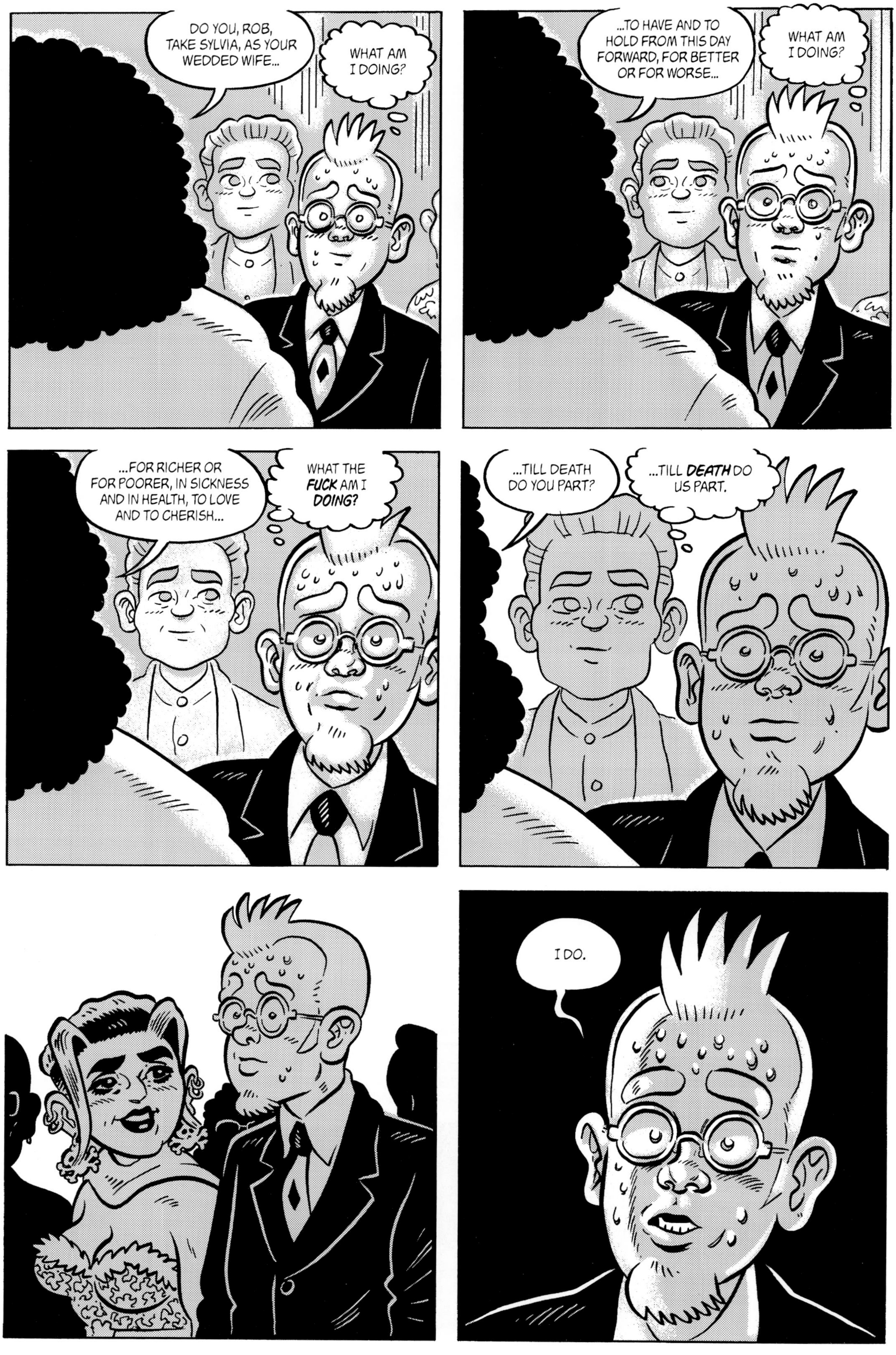
DO YOU, ROB, TAKE SYLVIA, AS YOUR WEDDED WIFE...
WHAT AM I DOING?
...TO HAVE AND TO HOLD FROM THIS DAY FORWARD, FOR BETTER OR FOR WORSE...
WHAT AM I DOING?
...FOR RICHER OR FOR POORER, IN SICKNESS AND IN HEALTH, TO LOVE AND TO CHERISH...
WHAT THE FUCK AM I DOING?
...TILL DEATH DO YOU PART?
...TILL DEATH DO US PART.
I DO.

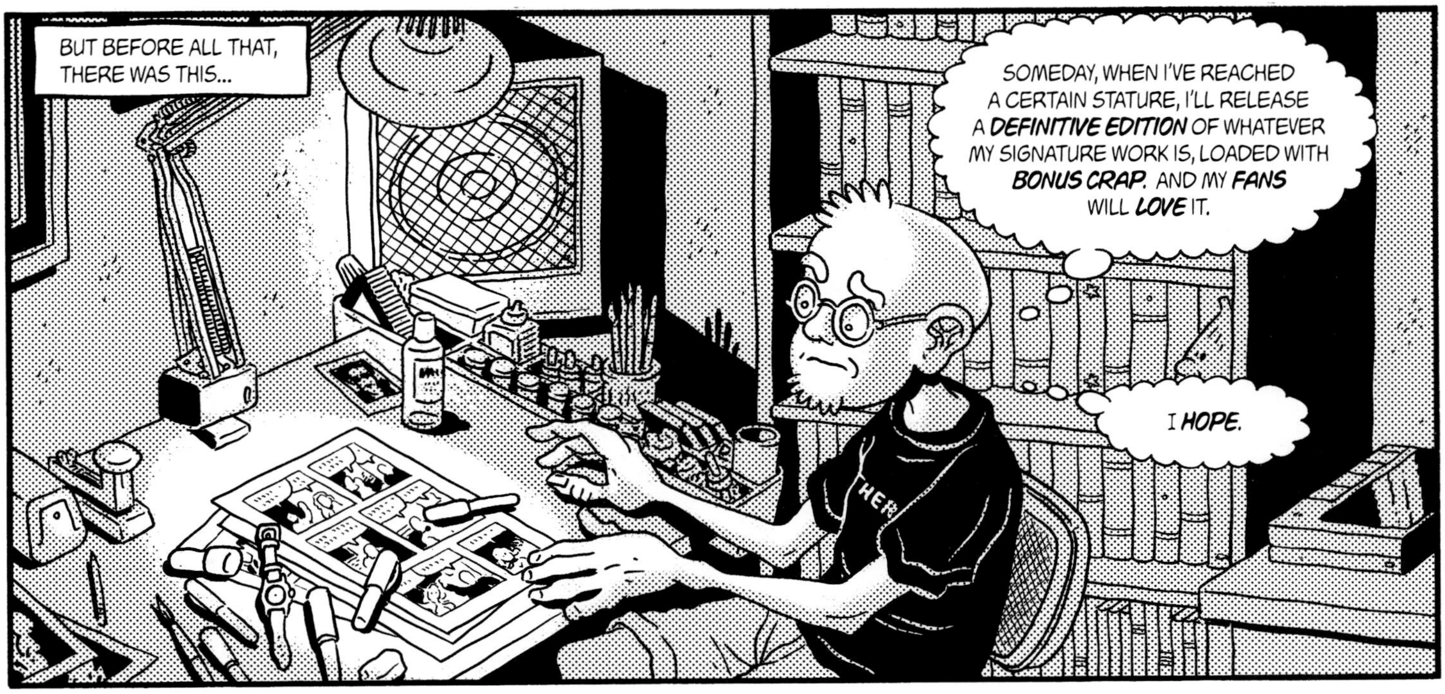
BUT BEFORE ALL THAT, THERE WAS THIS...
SOMEDAY, WHEN I'VE REACHED A CERTAIN STATURE, I'LL RELEASE A **DEFINITIVE EDITION** OF WHATEVER MY SIGNATURE WORK IS, LOADED WITH **BONUS CRAP.** AND MY **FANS** WILL **LOVE** IT.
I **HOPE.**

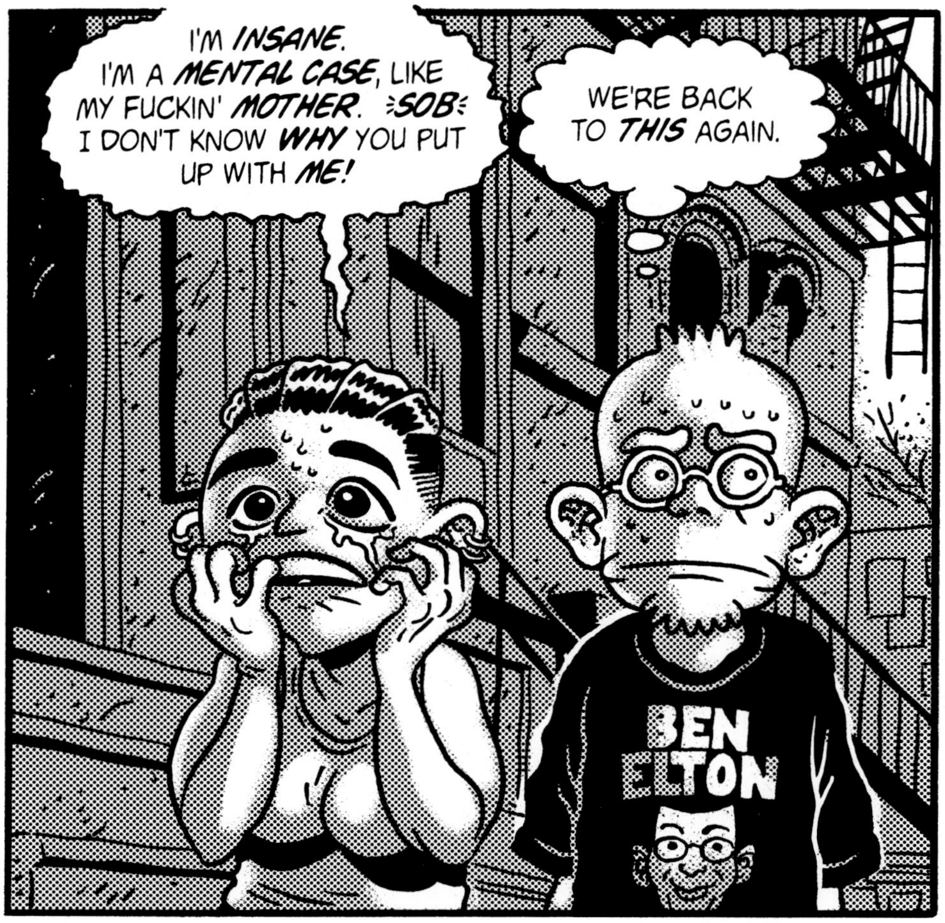
I'M *INSANE.* I'M A *MENTAL CASE*, LIKE MY FUCKIN' *MOTHER.* *SOB* I DON'T KNOW *WHY* YOU PUT UP WITH *ME!*
WE'RE BACK TO *THIS* AGAIN.
BEN ELTON

MINIMUM WAGE
BOOK ONE
(The "Pilot" Episode)

As noted in my intro to this collection, the first appearance of Rob, Sylvia and the gang, was the self-contained (yet open-ended) "pilot," a 72-page book done in large measure as a palliative to purge my system of my previous effort, *White Like She*, which was an experiment I now consider largely a failure (mainly in terms of the art). It was heavily photo referenced and very technical. It was also a drag to do. I wanted to go loose, cartoony and tell a more personal kind of story. I did and this was the result.

MINIMUM WAGE
ISSUE #1
(The "Lost" Episode)

The first serial issue was about Rob and Sylvia looking for a place of their own, much to Jack's barely stifled chagrin. It also really explored the lifestyle (and undesirability) of the freelancer and off-the-books worker. As you read these you'll see how I condensed portions of both sections into what became *Beg the Question*. I've gotten a lot of compliments over the years about the verisimilitude of this chapter in particular, which makes me happy. And a little depressed, because freelancers are still pretty danged undesirable as tenants.

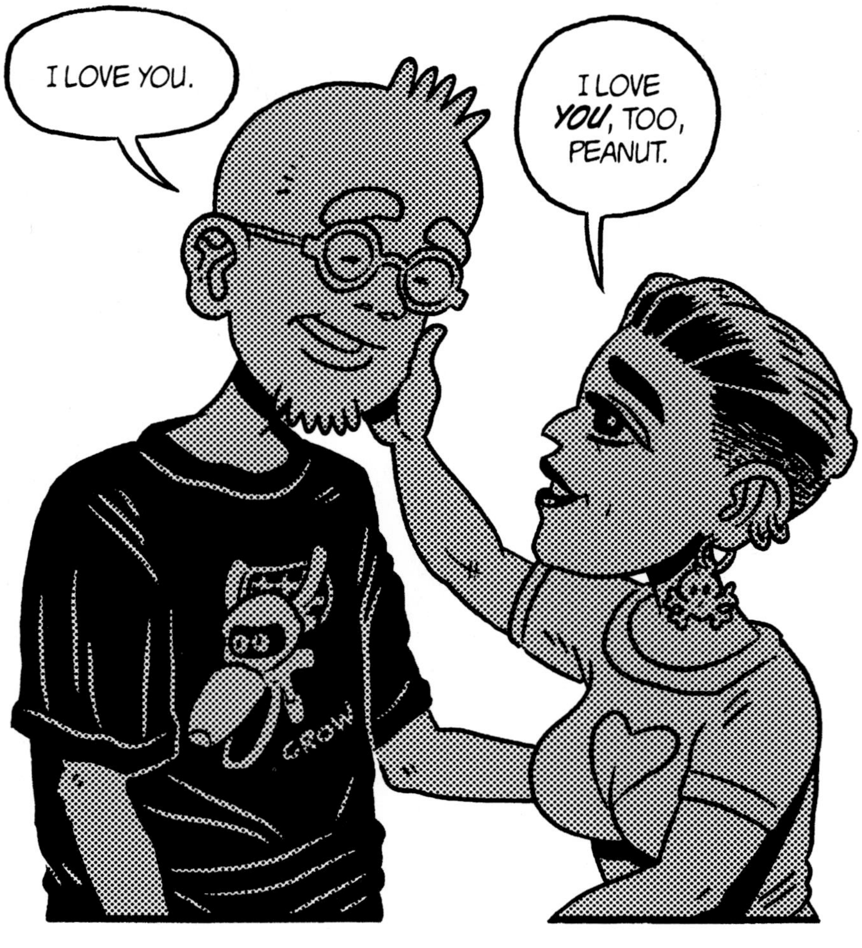
I LOVE YOU.
I LOVE *YOU*, TOO, PEANUT.
GROW

MINIMUM WAGE
BOOK ONE

BY BOB FINGERMAN

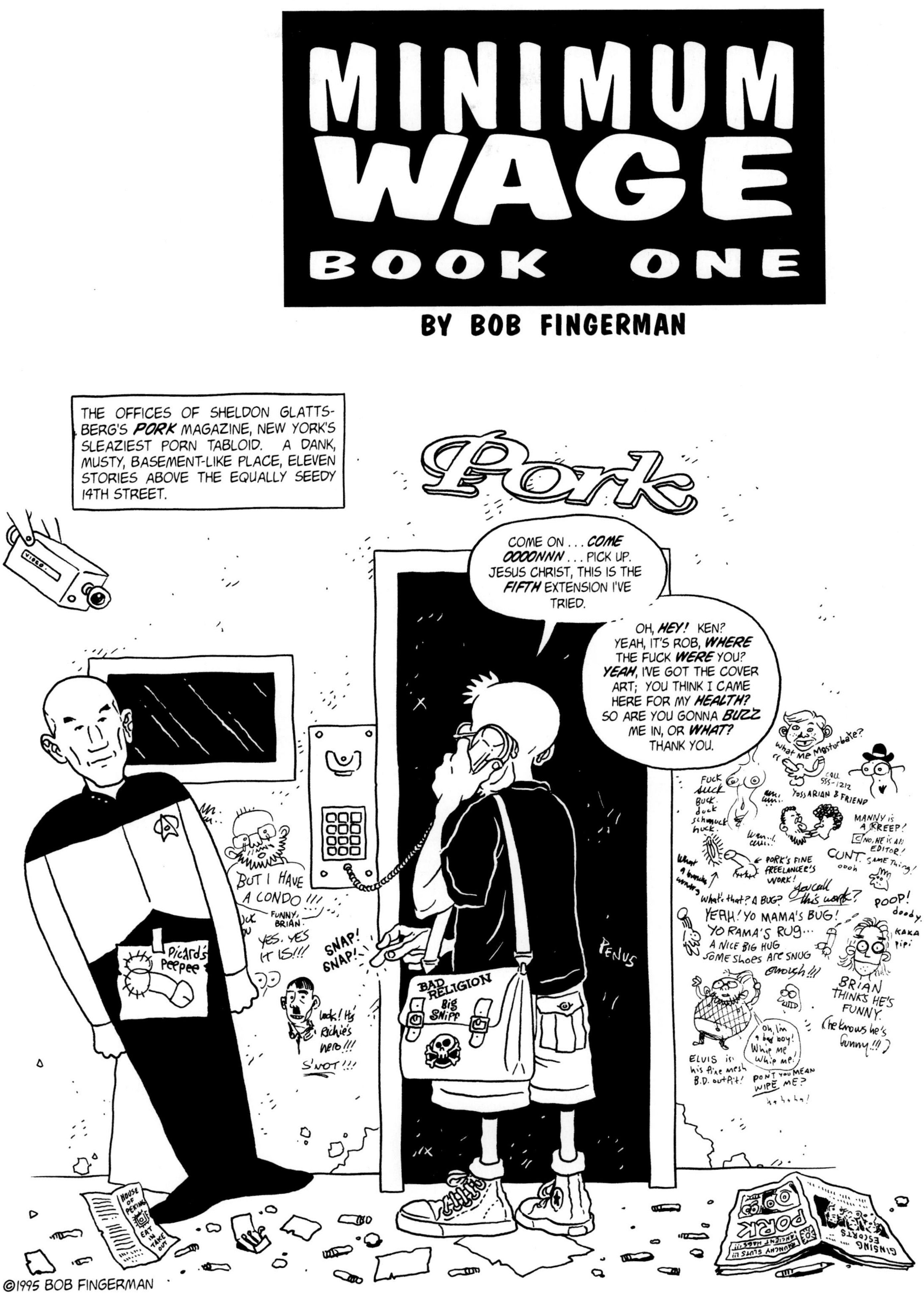
THE OFFICES OF SHELDON GLATTSBERG'S PORK MAGAZINE, NEW YORK'S SLEAZIEST PORN TABLOID. A DANK, MUSTY, BASEMENT-LIKE PLACE, ELEVEN STORIES ABOVE THE EQUALLY SEEDY 14TH STREET.
Pork
COME ON . . . COME OOOONNN . . . PICK UP. JESUS CHRIST, THIS IS THE FIFTH EXTENSION I'VE TRIED.
OH, HEY! KEN? YEAH, IT'S ROB, WHERE THE FUCK WERE YOU? YEAH, I'VE GOT THE COVER ART; YOU THINK I CAME HERE FOR MY HEALTH? SO ARE YOU GONNA BUZZ ME IN, OR WHAT? THANK YOU.
BUT I HAVE A CONDO!!!
FUNNY, BRIAN.
YES. YES IT IS!!!
SNAP! SNAP!
Picard's peepee
S'NOT!!!
PENUS
BAD RELIGION
Big SNIPP
What me Masturbate?
YOSSARIAN & FRIEND
MANNY IS A KREEP!
NO, HE IS AN EDITOR!
CUNT.
SAME Thing!
PORK'S FINE FREELANCER'S WORK!
What's that? A BUG?
you call this work?
POOP!
doody.
YEAH! YO MAMA'S BUG!
YO RAMA'S RUG...
A NICE BIG HUG
SOME Shoes Are SNUG
enough!!!
KAKA
pipi
BRIAN THINKS HE'S FUNNY.
(he knows he's funny!!!)
Oh, I'm a bad boy! Whip me. Whip me!
ELVIS is his fine mesh B.D. outfit!
DON'T YOU MEAN WIPE ME?
HOUSE OF PEKING
PORK

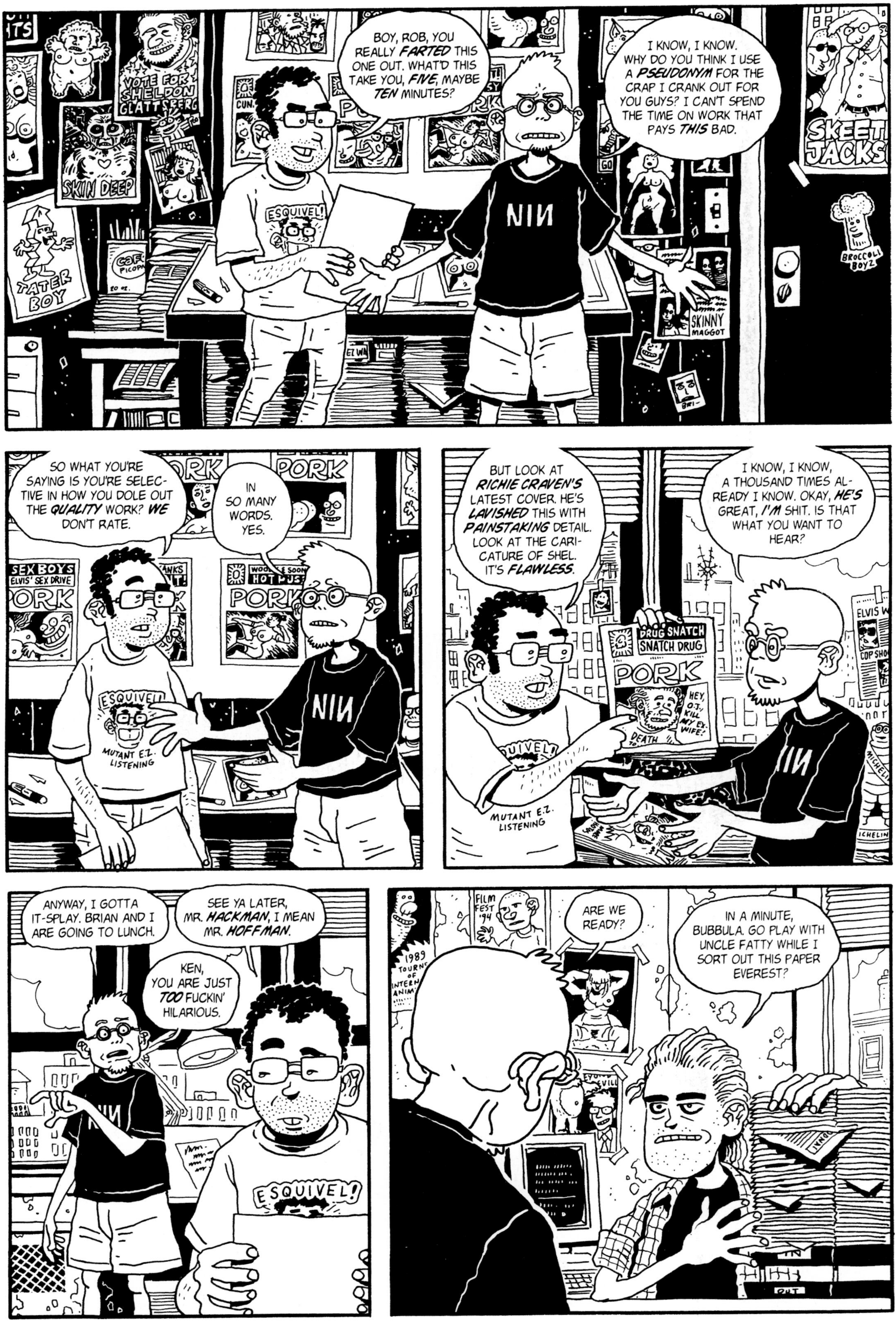
BOY, ROB, YOU REALLY FARTED THIS ONE OUT. WHAT'D THIS TAKE YOU, FIVE, MAYBE TEN MINUTES?
I KNOW, I KNOW. WHY DO YOU THINK I USE A PSEUDONYM FOR THE CRAP I CRANK OUT FOR YOU GUYS? I CAN'T SPEND THE TIME ON WORK THAT PAYS THIS BAD.
VOTE FOR SHELDON GLATTSBERG
SKIN DEEP
TATER BOY
SKEET JACKS
BROCCOLI BOYZ
SKINNY MAGGOT
NIN
ESQUIVEL!
SO WHAT YOU'RE SAYING IS YOU'RE SELECTIVE IN HOW YOU DOLE OUT THE QUALITY WORK? WE DON'T RATE.
IN SO MANY WORDS. YES.
SEX BOYS
ELVIS' SEX DRIVE
PORK
MUTANT E.Z. LISTENING
BUT LOOK AT RICHIE CRAVEN'S LATEST COVER. HE'S LAVISHED THIS WITH PAINSTAKING DETAIL. LOOK AT THE CARICATURE OF SHEL. IT'S FLAWLESS.
I KNOW, I KNOW, A THOUSAND TIMES ALREADY I KNOW. OKAY, HE'S GREAT, I'M SHIT. IS THAT WHAT YOU WANT TO HEAR?
DRUG SNATCH
SNATCH DRUG
PORK
HEY, O.J. KILL MY EX-WIFE!
ANYWAY, I GOTTA IT-SPLAY. BRIAN AND I ARE GOING TO LUNCH.
SEE YA LATER, MR. HACKMAN, I MEAN MR. HOFFMAN.
KEN, YOU ARE JUST TOO FUCKIN' HILARIOUS.
FILM FEST '94
ARE WE READY?
IN A MINUTE, BUBBULA. GO PLAY WITH UNCLE FATTY WHILE I SORT OUT THIS PAPER EVEREST?

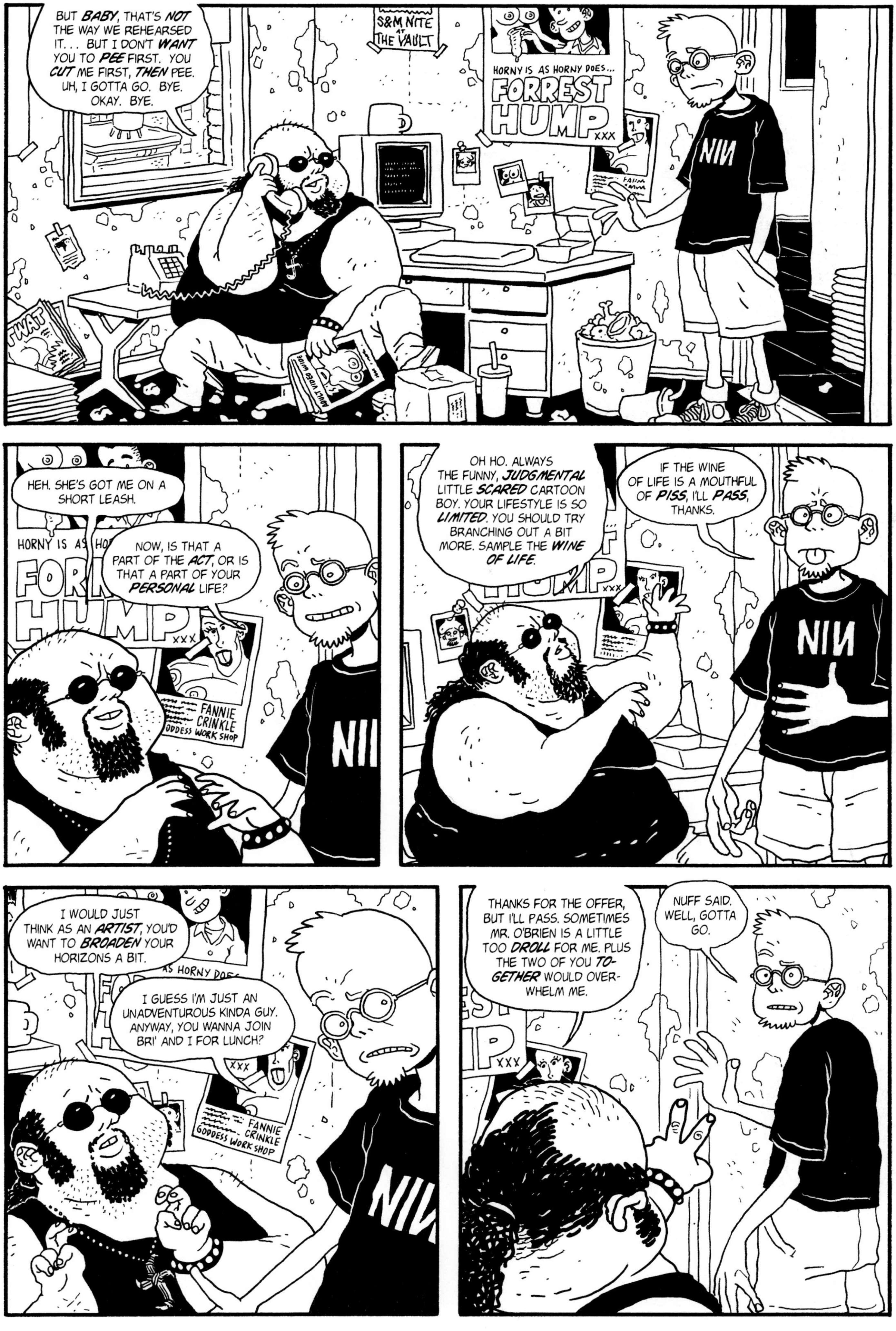

BUT BABY, THAT'S NOT THE WAY WE REHEARSED IT... BUT I DON'T WANT YOU TO PEE FIRST. YOU CUT ME FIRST, THEN PEE. UH, I GOTTA GO. BYE. OKAY. BYE.
S&M NITE AT THE VAULT
HORNY IS AS HORNY DOES... FORREST HUMP XXX
NIN
HEH. SHE'S GOT ME ON A SHORT LEASH.
NOW, IS THAT A PART OF THE ACT, OR IS THAT A PART OF YOUR PERSONAL LIFE?
FANNIE CRINKLE GODDESS WORK SHOP
OH HO. ALWAYS THE FUNNY, JUDGMENTAL LITTLE SCARED CARTOON BOY. YOUR LIFESTYLE IS SO LIMITED. YOU SHOULD TRY BRANCHING OUT A BIT MORE. SAMPLE THE WINE OF LIFE.
IF THE WINE OF LIFE IS A MOUTHFUL OF PISS, I'LL PASS, THANKS.
I WOULD JUST THINK AS AN ARTIST, YOU'D WANT TO BROADEN YOUR HORIZONS A BIT.
I GUESS I'M JUST AN UNADVENTUROUS KINDA GUY. ANYWAY, YOU WANNA JOIN BRI' AND I FOR LUNCH?
THANKS FOR THE OFFER, BUT I'LL PASS. SOMETIMES MR. O'BRIEN IS A LITTLE TOO DROLL FOR ME. PLUS THE TWO OF YOU TO-GETHER WOULD OVER-WHELM ME.
NUFF SAID. WELL, GOTTA GO.

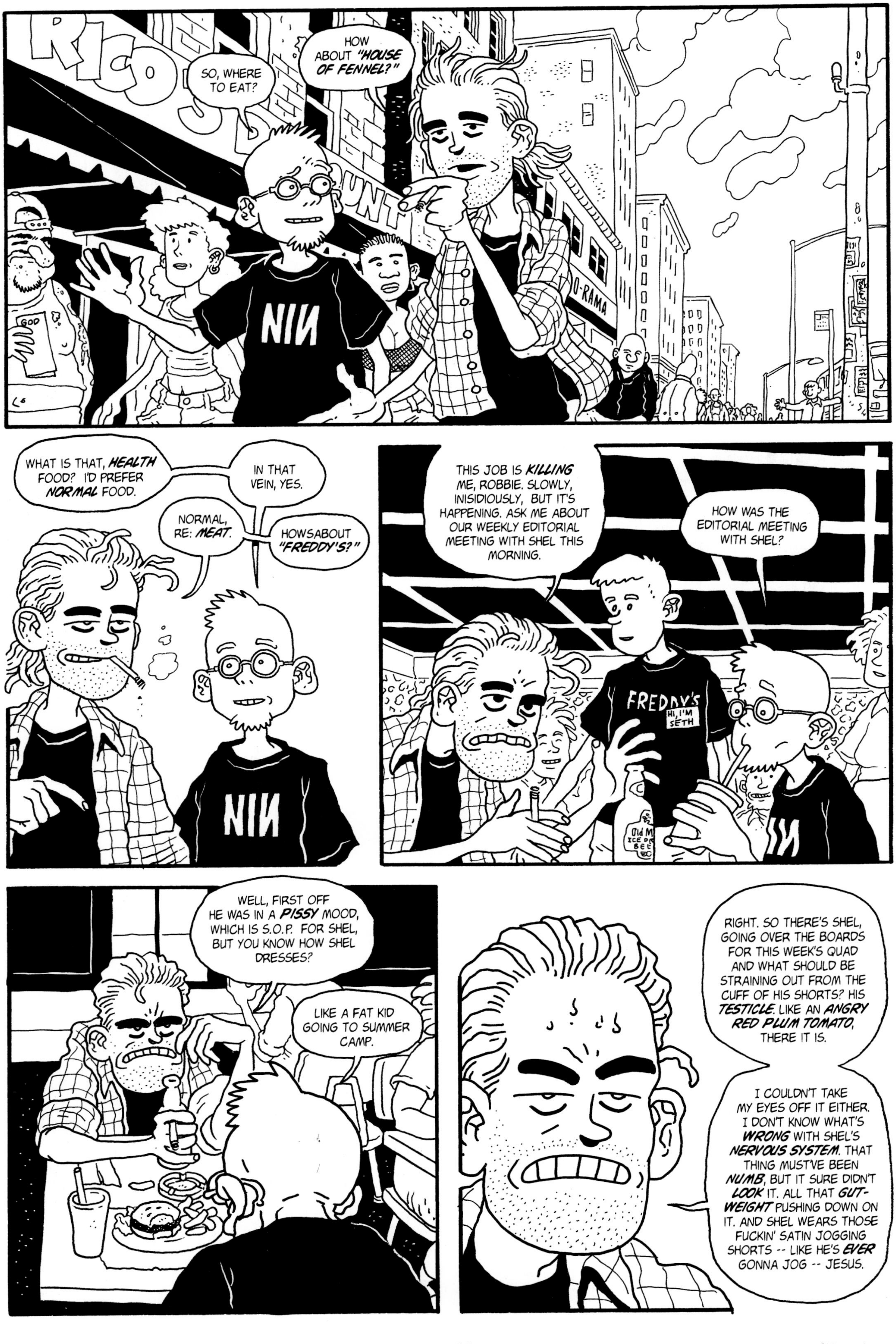
SO, WHERE TO EAT?
HOW ABOUT "HOUSE OF FENNEL?"
WHAT IS THAT, HEALTH FOOD? I'D PREFER NORMAL FOOD.
IN THAT VEIN, YES.
NORMAL, RE: MEAT.
HOWSABOUT "FREDDY'S?"
THIS JOB IS KILLING ME, ROBBIE. SLOWLY, INISIDIOUSLY, BUT IT'S HAPPENING. ASK ME ABOUT OUR WEEKLY EDITORIAL MEETING WITH SHEL THIS MORNING.
HOW WAS THE EDITORIAL MEETING WITH SHEL?
FREDDY'S
HI, I'M SETH
WELL, FIRST OFF HE WAS IN A PISSY MOOD, WHICH IS S.O.P. FOR SHEL, BUT YOU KNOW HOW SHEL DRESSES?
LIKE A FAT KID GOING TO SUMMER CAMP.
RIGHT. SO THERE'S SHEL, GOING OVER THE BOARDS FOR THIS WEEK'S QUAD AND WHAT SHOULD BE STRAINING OUT FROM THE CUFF OF HIS SHORTS? HIS TESTICLE. LIKE AN ANGRY RED PLUM TOMATO, THERE IT IS.
I COULDN'T TAKE MY EYES OFF IT EITHER. I DON'T KNOW WHAT'S WRONG WITH SHEL'S NERVOUS SYSTEM. THAT THING MUST'VE BEEN NUMB, BUT IT SURE DIDN'T LOOK IT. ALL THAT GUT-WEIGHT PUSHING DOWN ON IT. AND SHEL WEARS THOSE FUCKIN' SATIN JOGGING SHORTS -- LIKE HE'S EVER GONNA JOG -- JESUS.

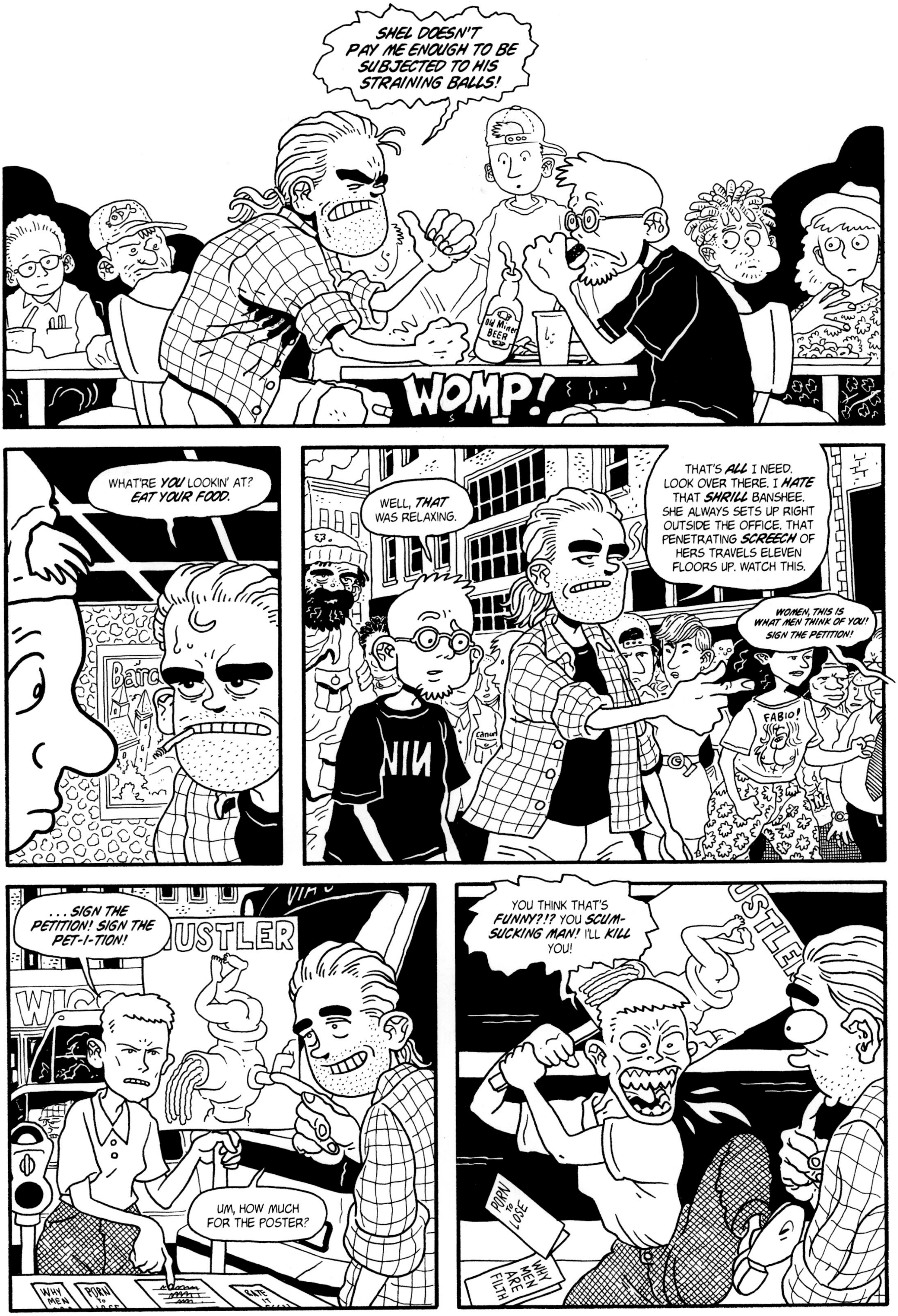
SHEL DOESN'T PAY ME ENOUGH TO BE SUBJECTED TO HIS STRAINING BALLS!
Old Miner BEER
WOMP!
WHAT'RE YOU LOOKIN' AT? EAT YOUR FOOD.
WELL, THAT WAS RELAXING.
THAT'S ALL I NEED. LOOK OVER THERE. I HATE THAT SHRILL BANSHEE. SHE ALWAYS SETS UP RIGHT OUTSIDE THE OFFICE. THAT PENETRATING SCREECH OF HERS TRAVELS ELEVEN FLOORS UP. WATCH THIS.
WOMEN, THIS IS WHAT MEN THINK OF YOU! SIGN THE PETITION!
NIN
FABIO!
...SIGN THE PETITION! SIGN THE PET-I-TION!
USTLER
UM, HOW MUCH FOR THE POSTER?
YOU THINK THAT'S FUNNY?!? YOU SCUM-SUCKING MAN! I'LL KILL YOU!
PORN TO LOSE
WHY MEN ARE FILTH

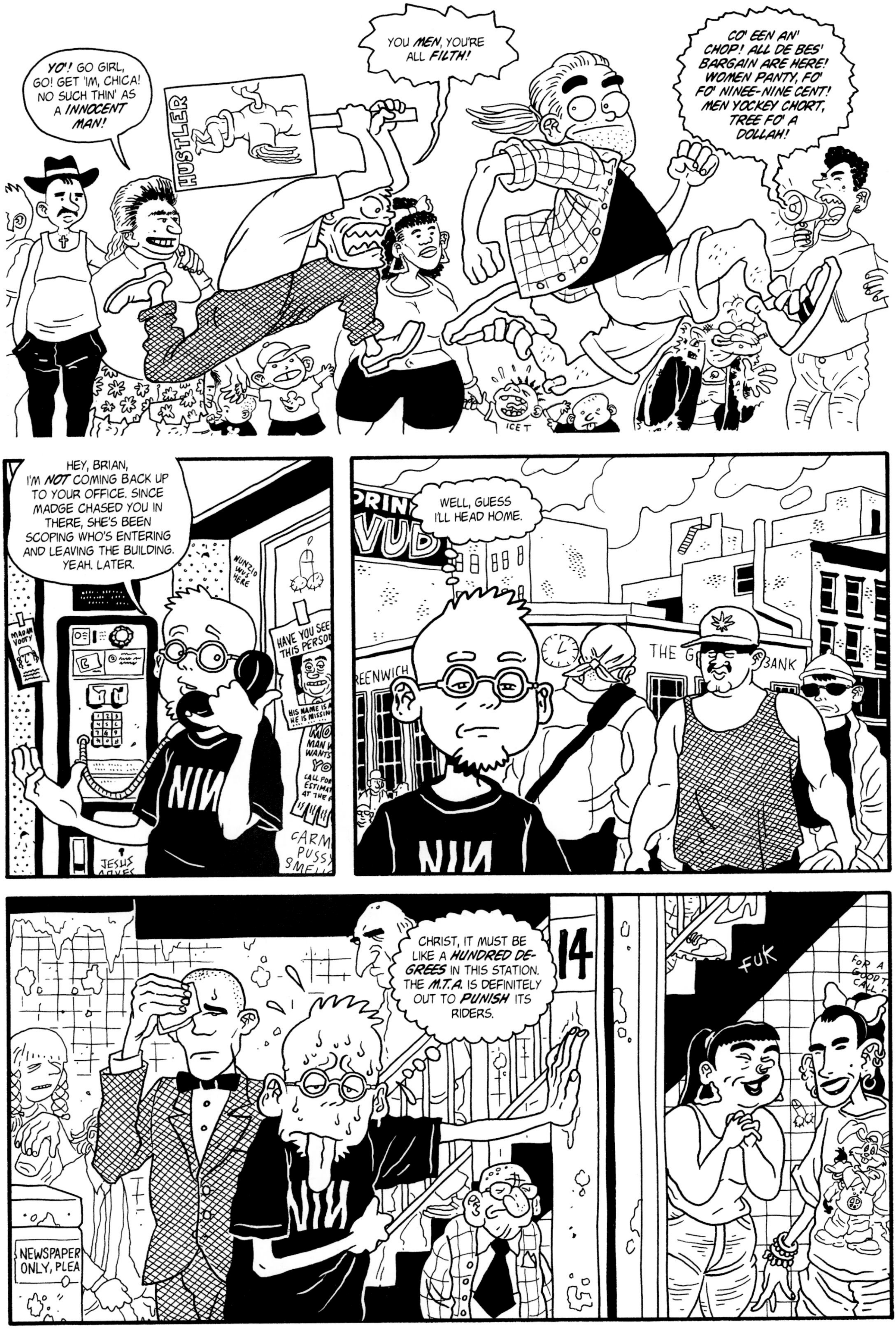

YO'! GO GIRL, GO! GET 'IM, CHICA! NO SUCH THIN' AS A INNOCENT MAN!
HUSTLER
YOU MEN, YOU'RE ALL FILTH!
CO' EEN AN' CHOP! ALL DE BES' BARGAIN ARE HERE! WOMEN PANTY, FO' FO' NINEE-NINE CENT! MEN YOCKEY CHORT, TREE FO' A DOLLAH!
ICE T
HEY, BRIAN, I'M NOT COMING BACK UP TO YOUR OFFICE. SINCE MADGE CHASED YOU IN THERE, SHE'S BEEN SCOPING WHO'S ENTERING AND LEAVING THE BUILDING. YEAH. LATER.
NUNZIO WUS HERE
MADAM VOOTY
HAVE YOU SEEN THIS PERSON
NIN
WELL, GUESS I'LL HEAD HOME.
NIN
CHRIST, IT MUST BE LIKE A HUNDRED DEGREES IN THIS STATION. THE M.T.A. IS DEFINITELY OUT TO PUNISH ITS RIDERS.
14
FUK
NEWSPAPER ONLY, PLEA

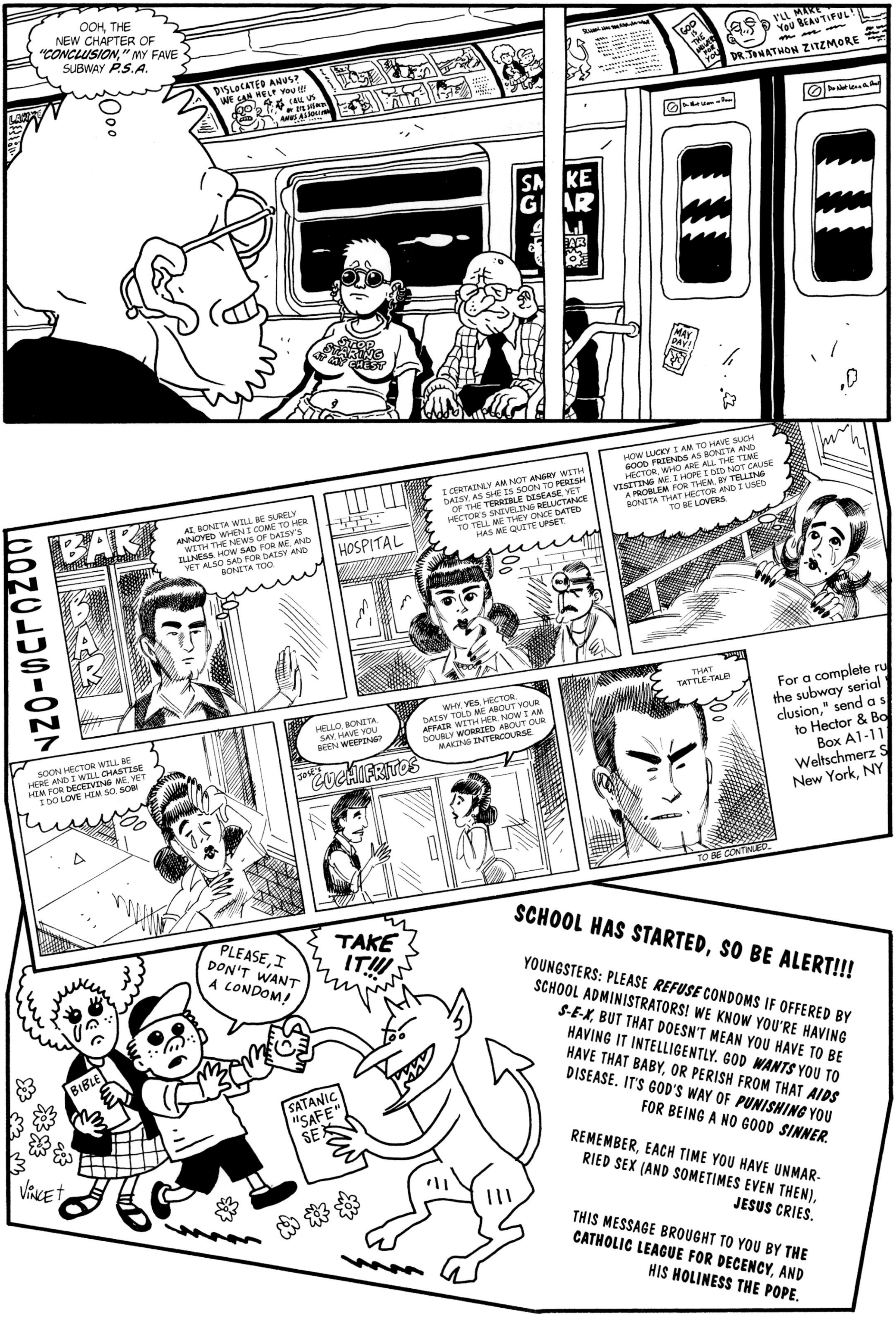

OOH, THE NEW CHAPTER OF "CONCLUSION," MY FAVE SUBWAY P.S.A.
DISLOCATED ANUS? WE CAN HELP YOU!!! CALL US
GOD IS THE ANSWER FOR YOU
I'LL MAKE YOU BEAUTIFUL!
DR. JONATHON ZITZMORE
STOP STARING AT MY CHEST
MAY DAY!
CONCLUSION 7
BAR
BAR
AI, BONITA WILL BE SURELY ANNOYED WHEN I COME TO HER WITH THE NEWS OF DAISY'S ILLNESS. HOW SAD FOR ME, AND YET ALSO SAD FOR DAISY AND BONITA TOO.
HOSPITAL
I CERTAINLY AM NOT ANGRY WITH DAISY, AS SHE IS SOON TO PERISH OF THE TERRIBLE DISEASE, YET HECTOR'S SNIVELING RELUCTANCE TO TELL ME THEY ONCE DATED HAS ME QUITE UPSET.
HOW LUCKY I AM TO HAVE SUCH GOOD FRIENDS AS BONITA AND HECTOR, WHO ARE ALL THE TIME VISITING ME. I HOPE I DID NOT CAUSE A PROBLEM FOR THEM, BY TELLING BONITA THAT HECTOR AND I USED TO BE LOVERS.
SOON HECTOR WILL BE HERE AND I WILL CHASTISE HIM FOR DECEIVING ME, YET I DO LOVE HIM SO. SOB!
HELLO, BONITA. SAY, HAVE YOU BEEN WEEPING?
WHY, YES, HECTOR. DAISY TOLD ME ABOUT YOUR AFFAIR WITH HER. NOW I AM DOUBLY WORRIED ABOUT OUR MAKING INTERCOURSE.
JOSE'S CUCHIFRITOS
THAT TATTLE-TALE!
TO BE CONTINUED...
For a complete ru
the subway serial
clusion," send a s
to Hector & Bo
Box A1-11
Weltschmerz S
New York, NY
PLEASE, I DON'T WANT A CONDOM!
TAKE IT!!!
BIBLE
SATANIC "SAFE" SEX
VINCENT
SCHOOL HAS STARTED, SO BE ALERT!!!
YOUNGSTERS: PLEASE REFUSE CONDOMS IF OFFERED BY SCHOOL ADMINISTRATORS! WE KNOW YOU'RE HAVING S-E-X, BUT THAT DOESN'T MEAN YOU HAVE TO BE HAVING IT INTELLIGENTLY. GOD WANTS YOU TO HAVE THAT BABY, OR PERISH FROM THAT AIDS DISEASE. IT'S GOD'S WAY OF PUNISHING YOU FOR BEING A NO GOOD SINNER.
REMEMBER, EACH TIME YOU HAVE UNMARRIED SEX (AND SOMETIMES EVEN THEN), JESUS CRIES.
THIS MESSAGE BROUGHT TO YOU BY THE CATHOLIC LEAGUE FOR DECENCY, AND HIS HOLINESS THE POPE.

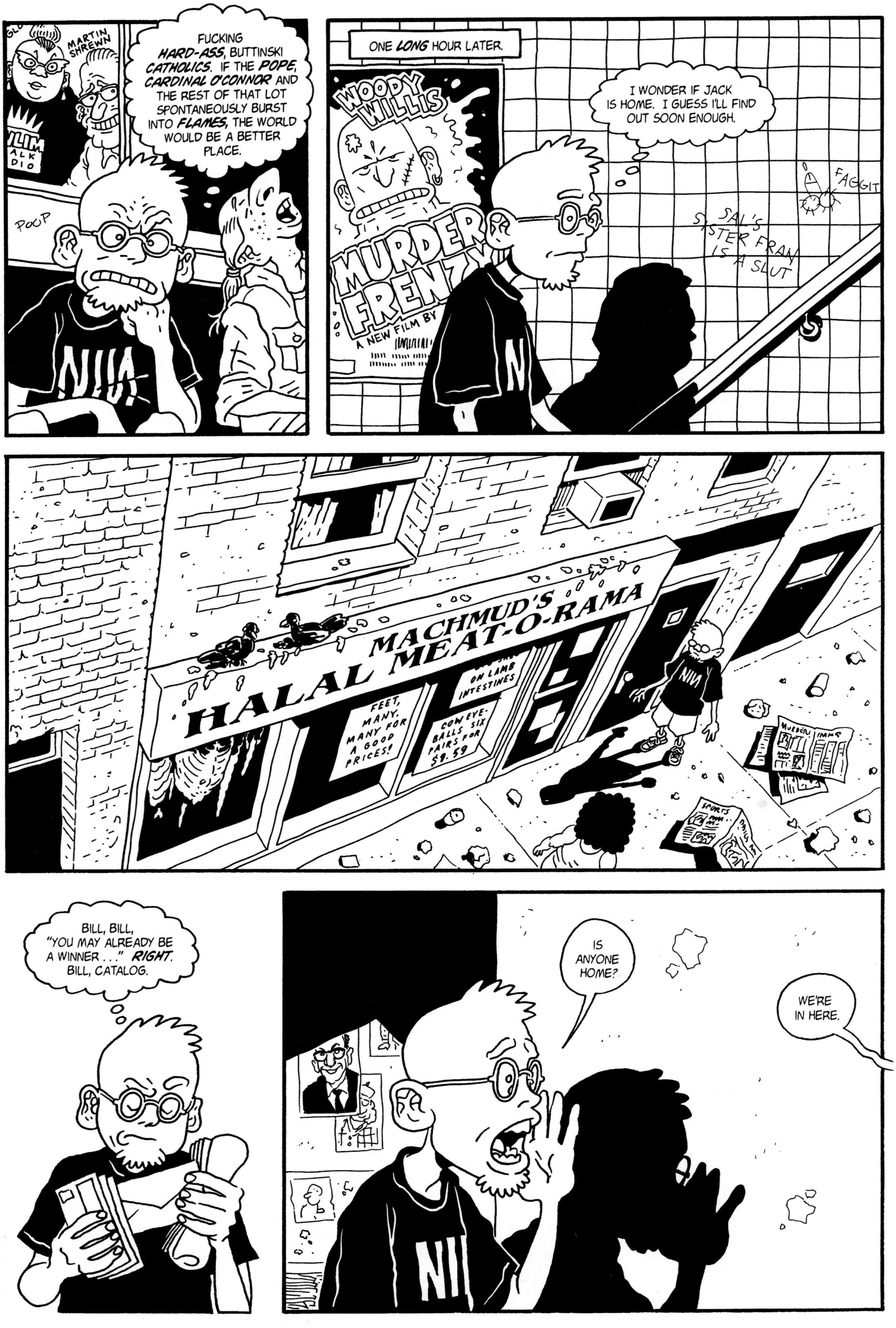
FUCKING HARD-ASS, BUTTINSKI CATHOLICS. IF THE POPE, CARDINAL O'CONNOR AND THE REST OF THAT LOT SPONTANEOUSLY BURST INTO FLAMES, THE WORLD WOULD BE A BETTER PLACE.
MARTIN SHREWN
POOP
ONE LONG HOUR LATER.
WOODY WILLIS
MURDER FRENZY
A NEW FILM BY
I WONDER IF JACK IS HOME. I GUESS I'LL FIND OUT SOON ENOUGH.
FAGGIT
SAL'S SISTER FRAN IS A SLUT
MACHMUD'S HALAL MEAT-O-RAMA
ON LAMB INTESTINES
FEET, MANY, MANY FOR A GOOD PRICES!
COW EYE-BALLS SIX PAIRS FOR $9.59
SPORTS
BILL, BILL, "YOU MAY ALREADY BE A WINNER..." RIGHT. BILL, CATALOG.
IS ANYONE HOME?
WE'RE IN HERE.

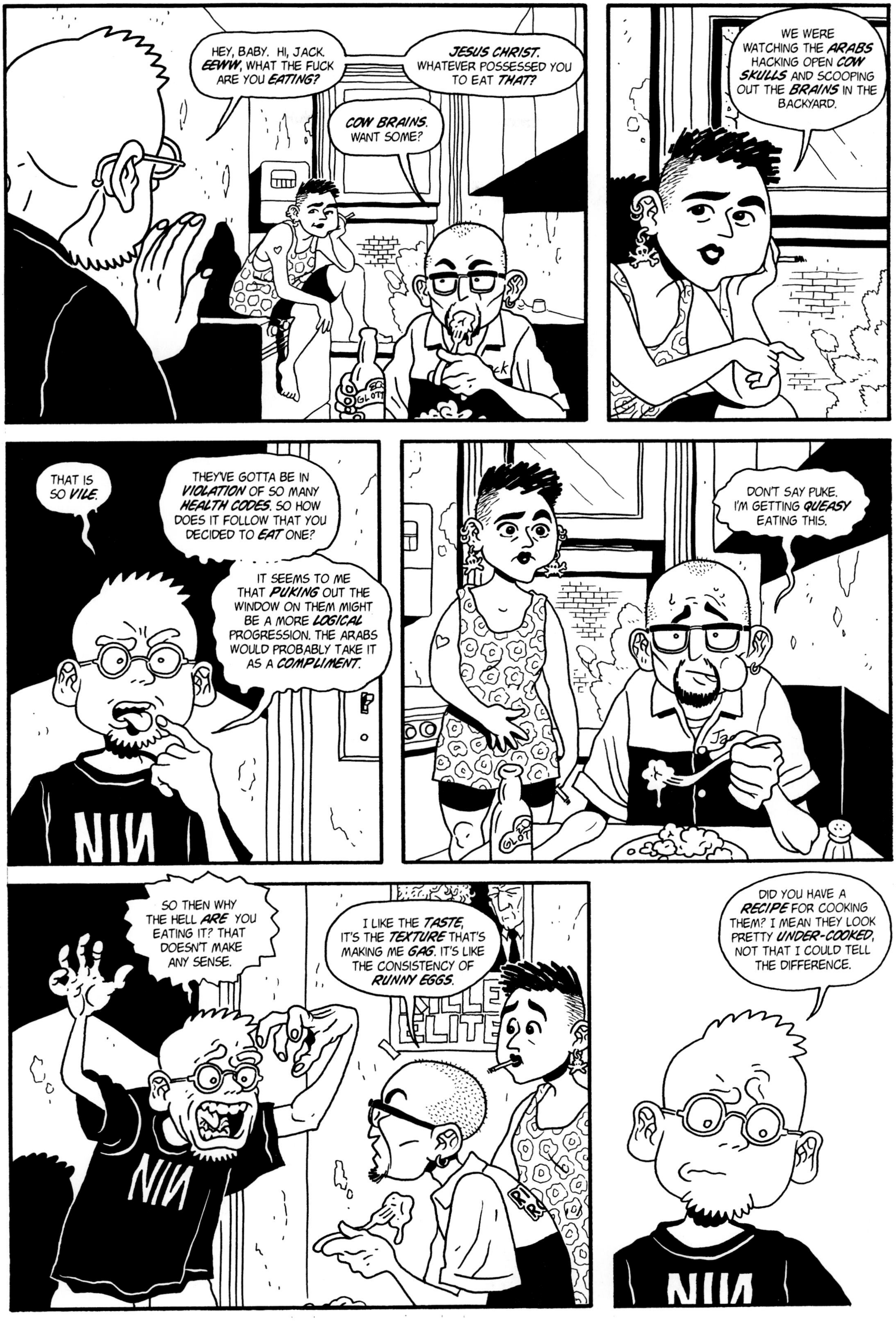

HEY, BABY. HI, JACK. EEWW, WHAT THE FUCK ARE YOU EATING?
JESUS CHRIST. WHATEVER POSSESSED YOU TO EAT THAT?
COW BRAINS. WANT SOME?
WE WERE WATCHING THE ARABS HACKING OPEN COW SKULLS AND SCOOPING OUT THE BRAINS IN THE BACKYARD.
THAT IS SO VILE.
THEY'VE GOTTA BE IN VIOLATION OF SO MANY HEALTH CODES. SO HOW DOES IT FOLLOW THAT YOU DECIDED TO EAT ONE?
IT SEEMS TO ME THAT PUKING OUT THE WINDOW ON THEM MIGHT BE A MORE LOGICAL PROGRESSION. THE ARABS WOULD PROBABLY TAKE IT AS A COMPLIMENT.
NIN
DON'T SAY PUKE. I'M GETTING QUEASY EATING THIS.
SO THEN WHY THE HELL ARE YOU EATING IT? THAT DOESN'T MAKE ANY SENSE.
I LIKE THE TASTE, IT'S THE TEXTURE THAT'S MAKING ME GAG. IT'S LIKE THE CONSISTENCY OF RUNNY EGGS.
NIN
DID YOU HAVE A RECIPE FOR COOKING THEM? I MEAN THEY LOOK PRETTY UNDER-COOKED, NOT THAT I COULD TELL THE DIFFERENCE.
NIN

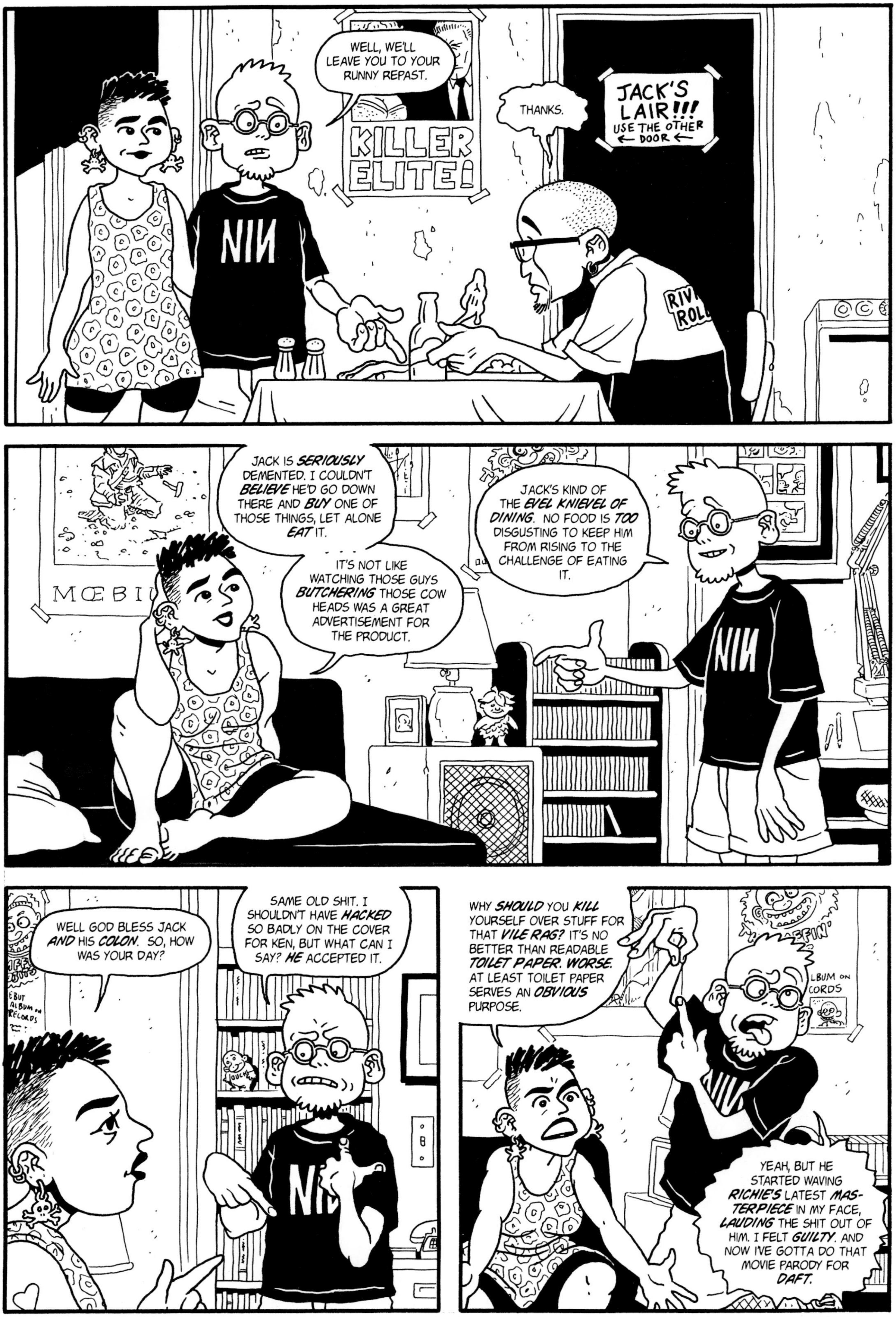
KILLER ELITE!
WELL, WE'LL LEAVE YOU TO YOUR RUNNY REPAST.
JACK'S LAIR!!! USE THE OTHER DOOR
THANKS.
MŒBIU
JACK IS SERIOUSLY DEMENTED. I COULDN'T BELIEVE HE'D GO DOWN THERE AND BUY ONE OF THOSE THINGS, LET ALONE EAT IT.
IT'S NOT LIKE WATCHING THOSE GUYS BUTCHERING THOSE COW HEADS WAS A GREAT ADVERTISEMENT FOR THE PRODUCT.
JACK'S KIND OF THE EVEL KNIEVEL OF DINING. NO FOOD IS TOO DISGUSTING TO KEEP HIM FROM RISING TO THE CHALLENGE OF EATING IT.
WELL GOD BLESS JACK AND HIS COLON. SO, HOW WAS YOUR DAY?
SAME OLD SHIT. I SHOULDN'T HAVE HACKED SO BADLY ON THE COVER FOR KEN, BUT WHAT CAN I SAY? HE ACCEPTED IT.
WHY SHOULD YOU KILL YOURSELF OVER STUFF FOR THAT VILE RAG? IT'S NO BETTER THAN READABLE TOILET PAPER. WORSE. AT LEAST TOILET PAPER SERVES AN OBVIOUS PURPOSE.
YEAH, BUT HE STARTED WAVING RICHIE'S LATEST MASTERPIECE IN MY FACE, LAUDING THE SHIT OUT OF HIM. I FELT GUILTY. AND NOW I'VE GOTTA DO THAT MOVIE PARODY FOR DAFT.

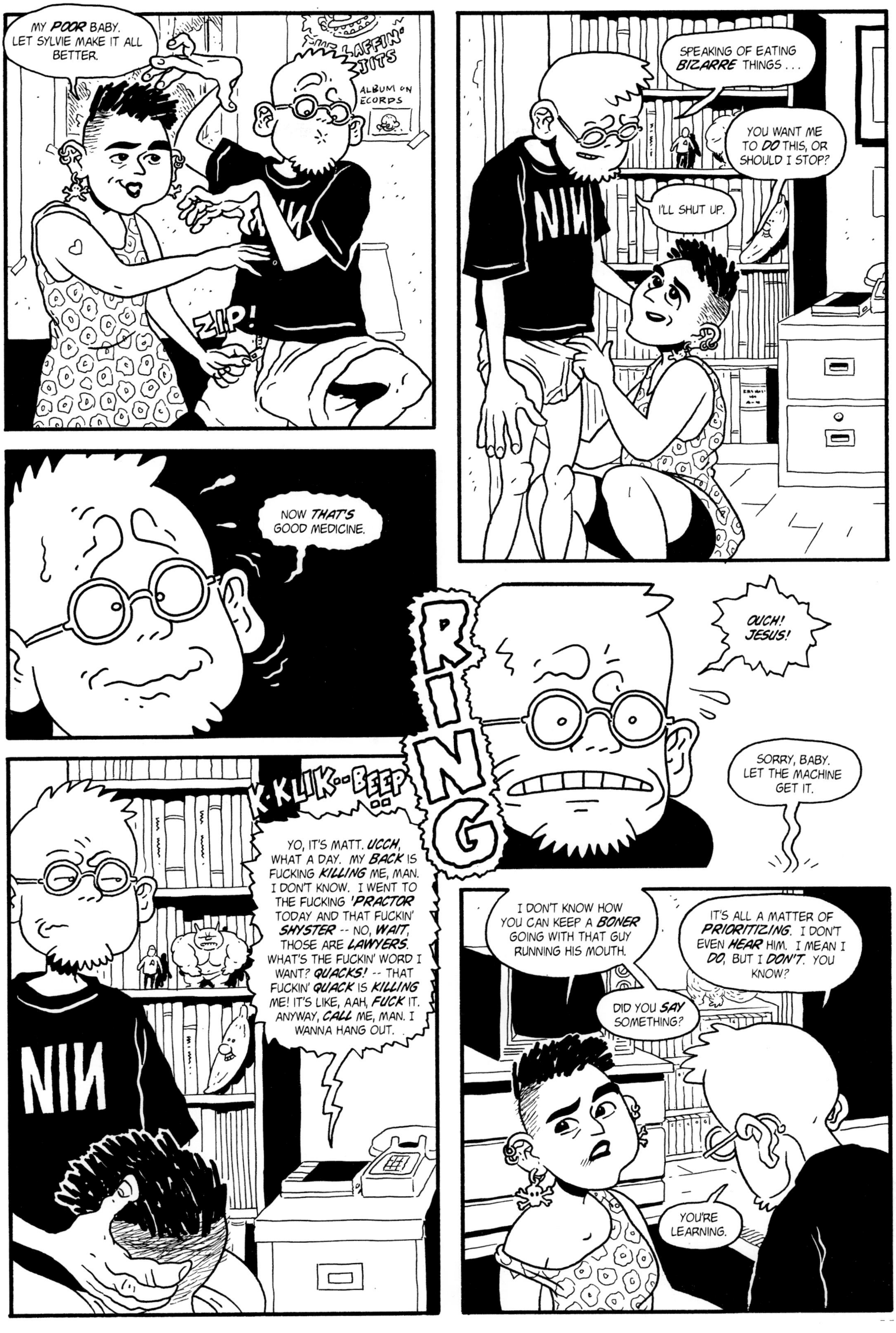

MY POOR BABY. LET SYLVIE MAKE IT ALL BETTER.
THE LAFFIN' JITS
ALBUM ON ECORDS
ZIP!
SPEAKING OF EATING BIZARRE THINGS . . .
YOU WANT ME TO DO THIS, OR SHOULD I STOP?
I'LL SHUT UP.
NOW THAT'S GOOD MEDICINE.
RING
OUCH! JESUS!
SORRY, BABY. LET THE MACHINE GET IT.
K-KLIK--BEEEP
YO, IT'S MATT. UCCH, WHAT A DAY. MY BACK IS FUCKING KILLING ME, MAN. I DON'T KNOW. I WENT TO THE FUCKING 'PRACTOR TODAY AND THAT FUCKIN' SHYSTER -- NO, WAIT, THOSE ARE LAWYERS. WHAT'S THE FUCKIN' WORD I WANT? QUACKS! -- THAT FUCKIN' QUACK IS KILLING ME! IT'S LIKE, AAH, FUCK IT. ANYWAY, CALL ME, MAN. I WANNA HANG OUT.
I DON'T KNOW HOW YOU CAN KEEP A BONER GOING WITH THAT GUY RUNNING HIS MOUTH.
IT'S ALL A MATTER OF PRIORITIZING. I DON'T EVEN HEAR HIM. I MEAN I DO, BUT I DON'T. YOU KNOW?
DID YOU SAY SOMETHING?
YOU'RE LEARNING.

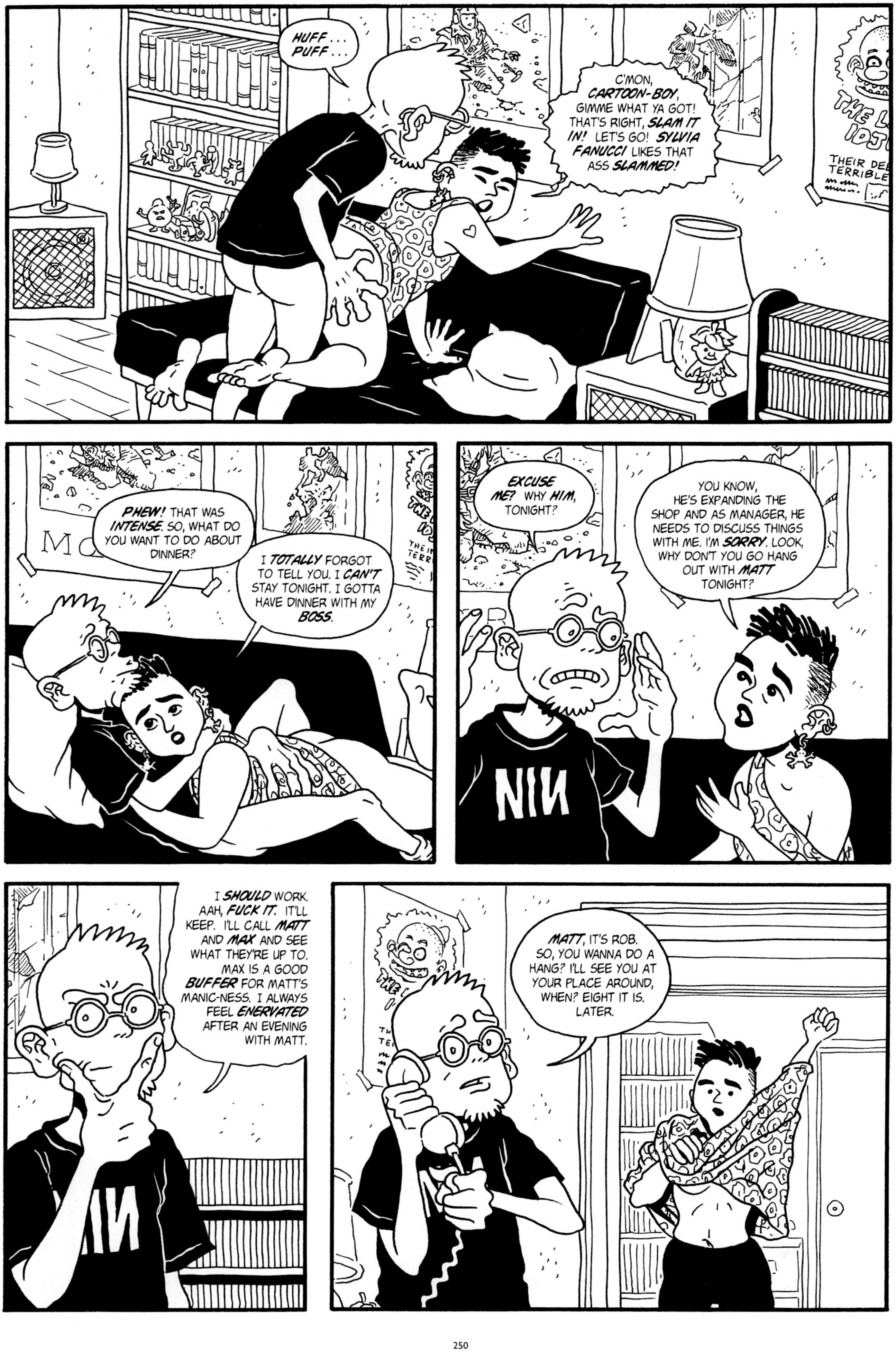
HUFF... PUFF...
C'MON, CARTOON-BOY, GIMME WHAT YA GOT! THAT'S RIGHT, SLAM IT IN! LET'S GO! SYLVIA FANUCCI LIKES THAT ASS SLAMMED!
PHEW! THAT WAS INTENSE. SO, WHAT DO YOU WANT TO DO ABOUT DINNER?
I TOTALLY FORGOT TO TELL YOU. I CAN'T STAY TONIGHT. I GOTTA HAVE DINNER WITH MY BOSS.
EXCUSE ME? WHY HIM, TONIGHT?
YOU KNOW, HE'S EXPANDING THE SHOP AND AS MANAGER, HE NEEDS TO DISCUSS THINGS WITH ME. I'M SORRY. LOOK, WHY DON'T YOU GO HANG OUT WITH MATT TONIGHT?
I SHOULD WORK. AAH, FUCK IT. IT'LL KEEP. I'LL CALL MATT AND MAX AND SEE WHAT THEY'RE UP TO. MAX IS A GOOD BUFFER FOR MATT'S MANIC-NESS. I ALWAYS FEEL ENERVATED AFTER AN EVENING WITH MATT.
MATT, IT'S ROB. SO, YOU WANNA DO A HANG? I'LL SEE YOU AT YOUR PLACE AROUND, WHEN? EIGHT IT IS. LATER.

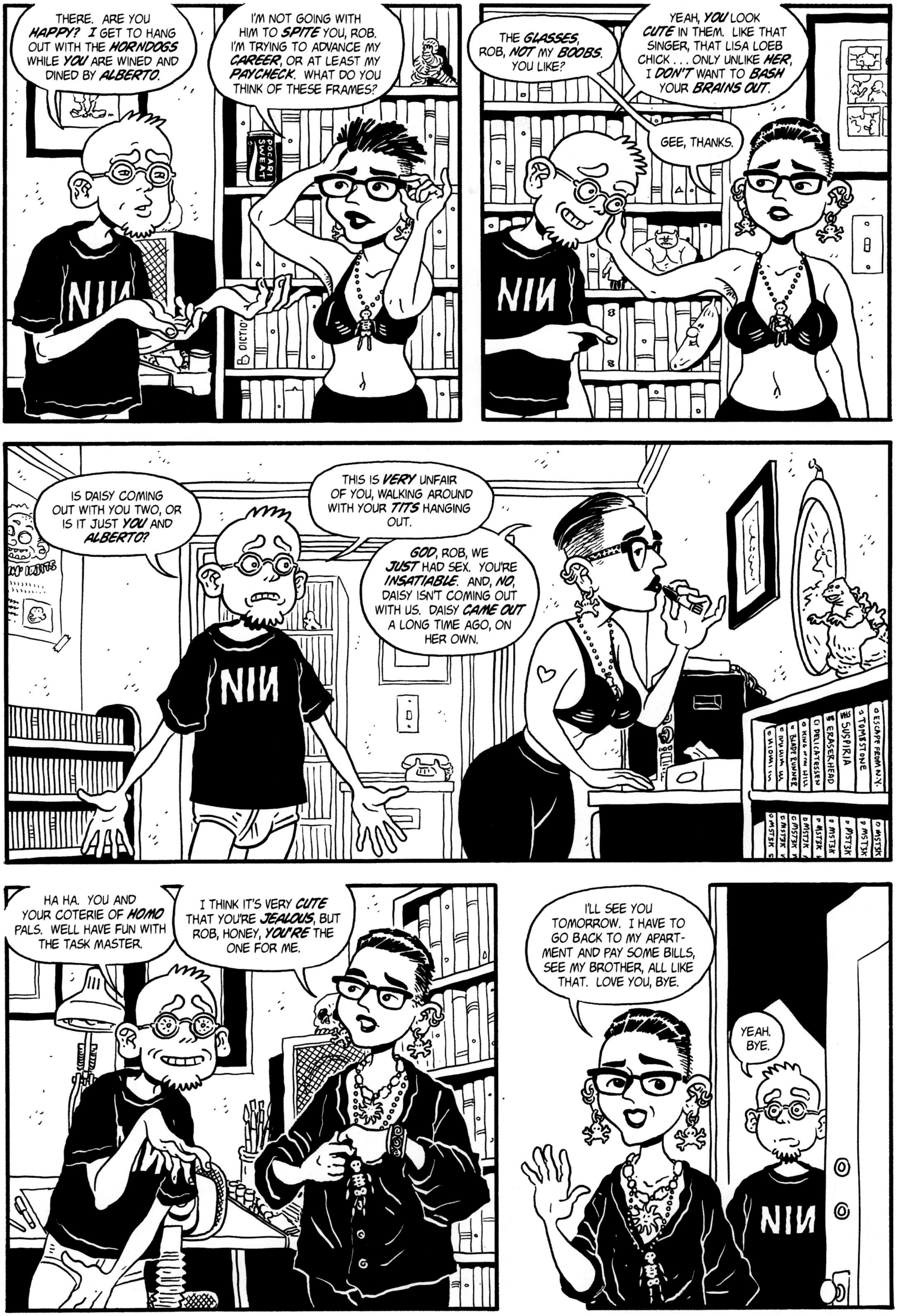
THERE. ARE YOU HAPPY? I GET TO HANG OUT WITH THE HORNDOGS WHILE YOU ARE WINED AND DINED BY ALBERTO.
I'M NOT GOING WITH HIM TO SPITE YOU, ROB. I'M TRYING TO ADVANCE MY CAREER, OR AT LEAST MY PAYCHECK. WHAT DO YOU THINK OF THESE FRAMES?
POCARI SWEAT
THE GLASSES, ROB, NOT MY BOOBS. YOU LIKE?
YEAH, YOU LOOK CUTE IN THEM. LIKE THAT SINGER, THAT LISA LOEB CHICK . . . ONLY UNLIKE HER, I DON'T WANT TO BASH YOUR BRAINS OUT.
GEE, THANKS.
IS DAISY COMING OUT WITH YOU TWO, OR IS IT JUST YOU AND ALBERTO?
THIS IS VERY UNFAIR OF YOU, WALKING AROUND WITH YOUR TITS HANGING OUT.
GOD, ROB, WE JUST HAD SEX. YOU'RE INSATIABLE. AND, NO, DAISY ISN'T COMING OUT WITH US. DAISY CAME OUT A LONG TIME AGO, ON HER OWN.
ESCAPE FROM N.Y.
TOMBSTONE
SUSPIRIA
ERASERHEAD
DELICATESSEN
BLADE RUNNER
HA HA. YOU AND YOUR COTERIE OF HOMO PALS. WELL HAVE FUN WITH THE TASK MASTER.
I THINK IT'S VERY CUTE THAT YOU'RE JEALOUS, BUT ROB, HONEY, YOU'RE THE ONE FOR ME.
I'LL SEE YOU TOMORROW. I HAVE TO GO BACK TO MY APARTMENT AND PAY SOME BILLS, SEE MY BROTHER, ALL LIKE THAT. LOVE YOU, BYE.
YEAH. BYE.

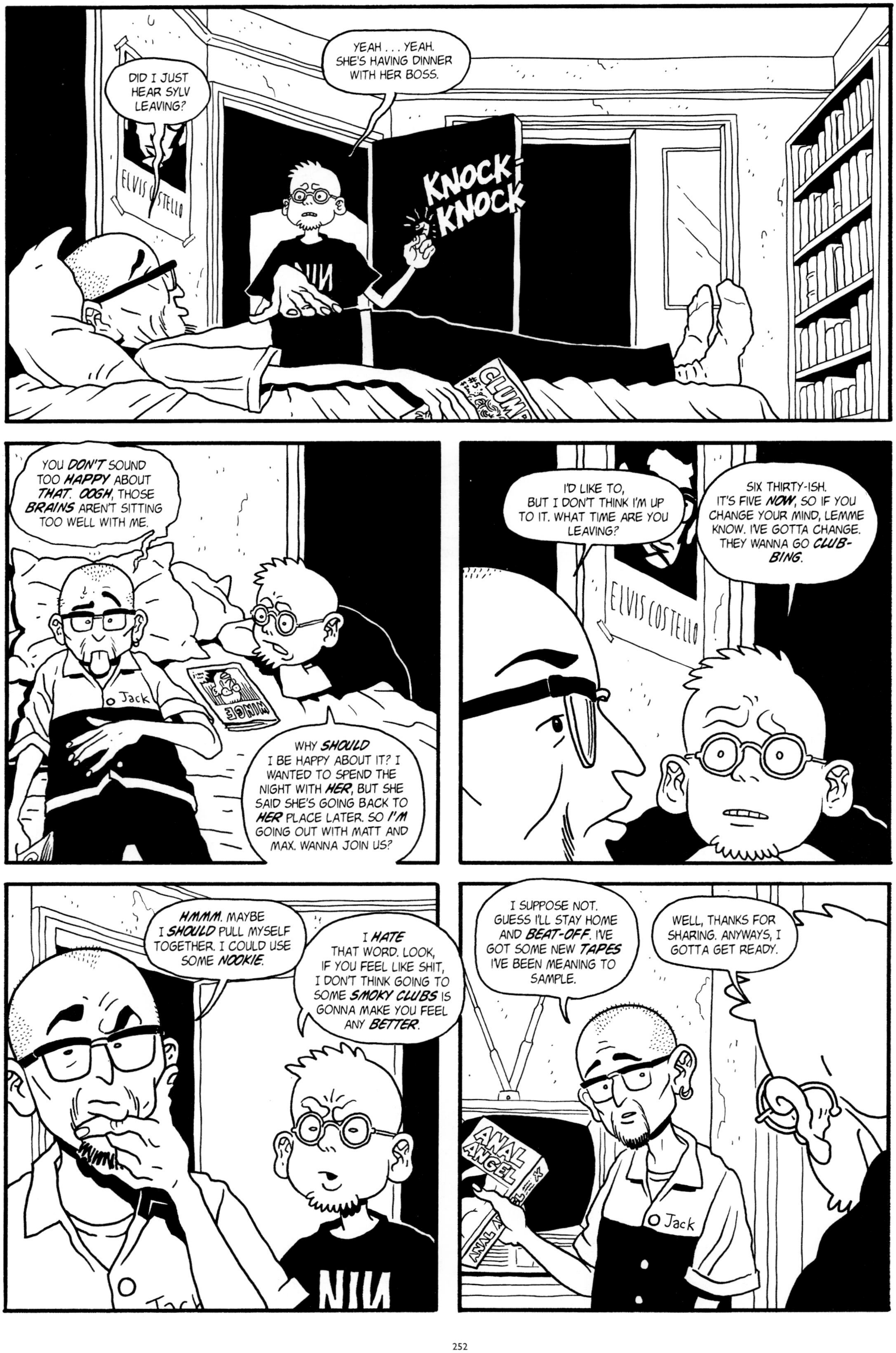
DID I JUST HEAR SYLV LEAVING?
YEAH . . . YEAH. SHE'S HAVING DINNER WITH HER BOSS.
KNOCK KNOCK
ELVIS COSTELLO
CLUMP #5
YOU DON'T SOUND TOO HAPPY ABOUT THAT. OOGH, THOSE BRAINS AREN'T SITTING TOO WELL WITH ME.
WHY SHOULD I BE HAPPY ABOUT IT? I WANTED TO SPEND THE NIGHT WITH HER, BUT SHE SAID SHE'S GOING BACK TO HER PLACE LATER. SO I'M GOING OUT WITH MATT AND MAX. WANNA JOIN US?
Jack
BINGE
I'D LIKE TO, BUT I DON'T THINK I'M UP TO IT. WHAT TIME ARE YOU LEAVING?
SIX THIRTY-ISH. IT'S FIVE NOW, SO IF YOU CHANGE YOUR MIND, LEMME KNOW. I'VE GOTTA CHANGE. THEY WANNA GO CLUB-BING.
ELVIS COSTELLO
HMMM. MAYBE I SHOULD PULL MYSELF TOGETHER. I COULD USE SOME NOOKIE.
I HATE THAT WORD. LOOK, IF YOU FEEL LIKE SHIT, I DON'T THINK GOING TO SOME SMOKY CLUBS IS GONNA MAKE YOU FEEL ANY BETTER.
I SUPPOSE NOT. GUESS I'LL STAY HOME AND BEAT-OFF. I'VE GOT SOME NEW TAPES I'VE BEEN MEANING TO SAMPLE.
WELL, THANKS FOR SHARING. ANYWAYS, I GOTTA GET READY.
ANAL ANGEL
Jack

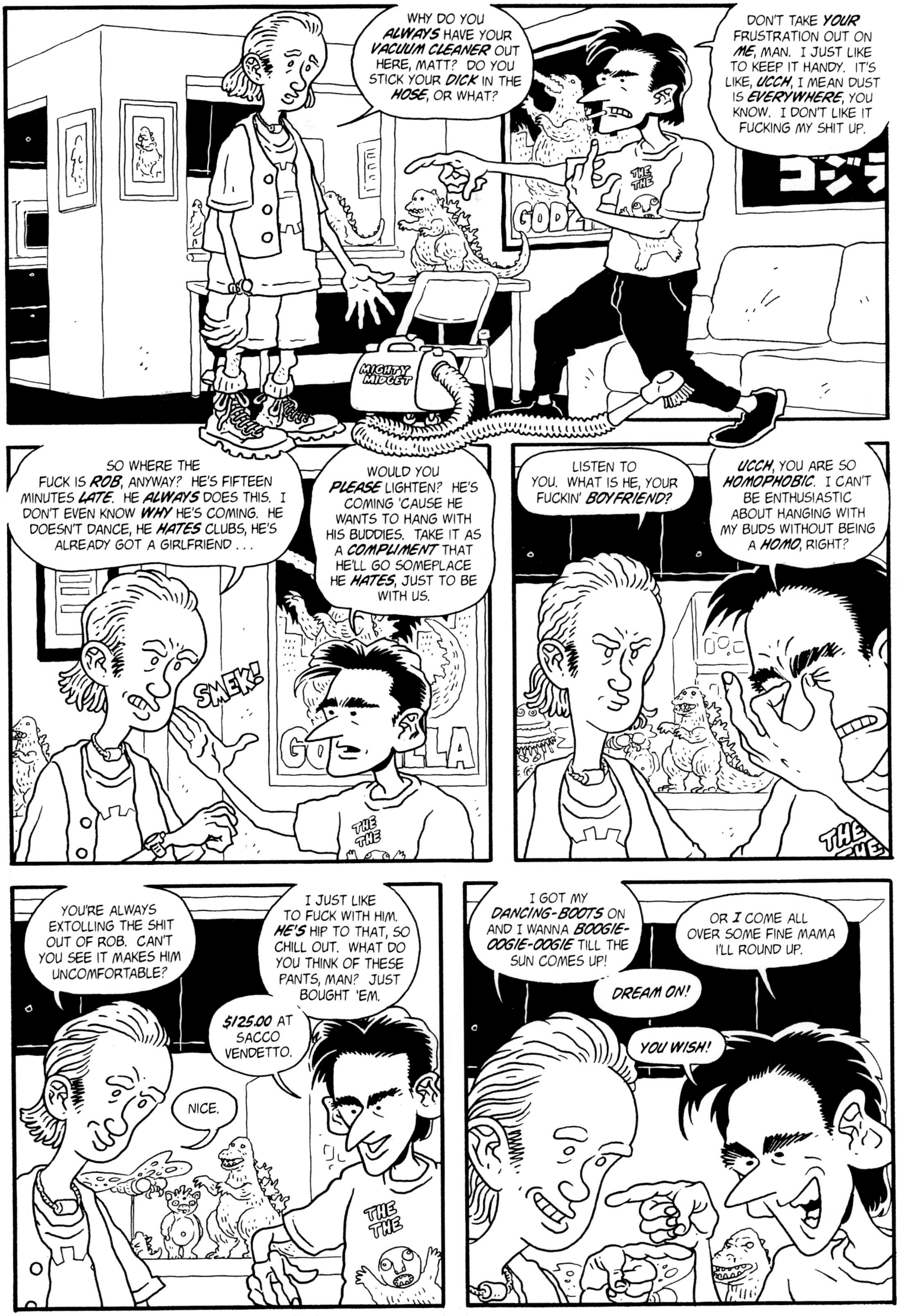
WHY DO YOU ALWAYS HAVE YOUR VACUUM CLEANER OUT HERE, MATT? DO YOU STICK YOUR DICK IN THE HOSE, OR WHAT?
DON'T TAKE YOUR FRUSTRATION OUT ON ME, MAN. I JUST LIKE TO KEEP IT HANDY. IT'S LIKE, UCCH, I MEAN DUST IS EVERYWHERE, YOU KNOW. I DON'T LIKE IT FUCKING MY SHIT UP.
THE THE
GODZ
MIGHTY MIDGET
SO WHERE THE FUCK IS ROB, ANYWAY? HE'S FIFTEEN MINUTES LATE. HE ALWAYS DOES THIS. I DON'T EVEN KNOW WHY HE'S COMING. HE DOESN'T DANCE, HE HATES CLUBS, HE'S ALREADY GOT A GIRLFRIEND . . .
WOULD YOU PLEASE LIGHTEN? HE'S COMING 'CAUSE HE WANTS TO HANG WITH HIS BUDDIES. TAKE IT AS A COMPLIMENT THAT HE'LL GO SOMEPLACE HE HATES, JUST TO BE WITH US.
SMEK!
LISTEN TO YOU. WHAT IS HE, YOUR FUCKIN' BOYFRIEND?
UCCH, YOU ARE SO HOMOPHOBIC. I CAN'T BE ENTHUSIASTIC ABOUT HANGING WITH MY BUDS WITHOUT BEING A HOMO, RIGHT?
YOU'RE ALWAYS EXTOLLING THE SHIT OUT OF ROB. CAN'T YOU SEE IT MAKES HIM UNCOMFORTABLE?
I JUST LIKE TO FUCK WITH HIM. HE'S HIP TO THAT, SO CHILL OUT. WHAT DO YOU THINK OF THESE PANTS, MAN? JUST BOUGHT 'EM.
$125.00 AT SACCO VENDETTO.
NICE.
I GOT MY DANCING-BOOTS ON AND I WANNA BOOGIE-OOGIE-OOGIE TILL THE SUN COMES UP!
OR I COME ALL OVER SOME FINE MAMA I'LL ROUND UP.
DREAM ON!
YOU WISH!

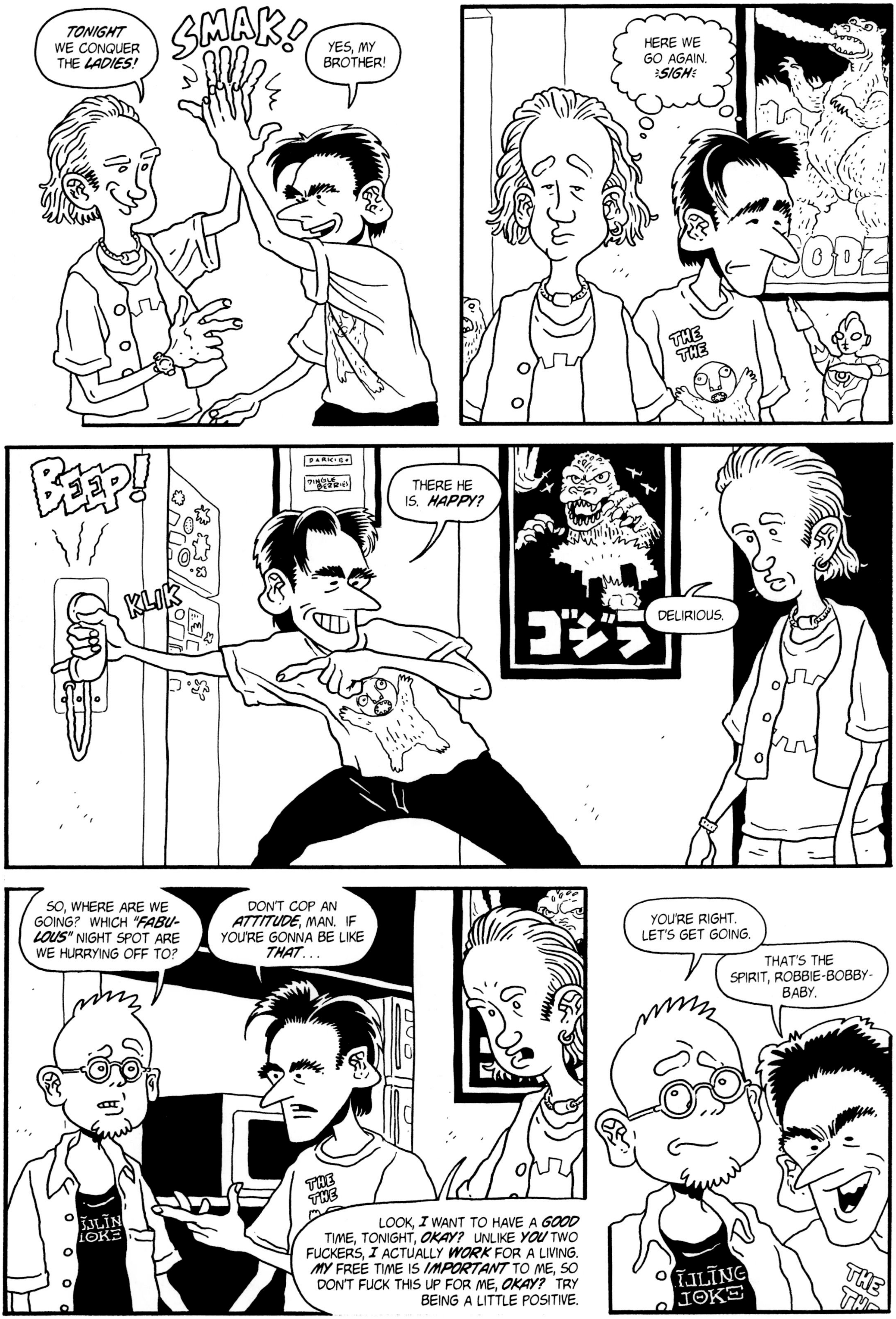
TONIGHT WE CONQUER THE LADIES!
SMAK!
YES, MY BROTHER!
HERE WE GO AGAIN. SIGH
GODZ
THE THE
BEEP!
DARKIES
DINGLE BERRIES
KLIK
THERE HE IS. HAPPY?
ゴジラ
DELIRIOUS.
SO, WHERE ARE WE GOING? WHICH "FABU-LOUS" NIGHT SPOT ARE WE HURRYING OFF TO?
DON'T COP AN ATTITUDE, MAN. IF YOU'RE GONNA BE LIKE THAT...
THE THE
LOOK, I WANT TO HAVE A GOOD TIME, TONIGHT, OKAY? UNLIKE YOU TWO FUCKERS, I ACTUALLY WORK FOR A LIVING. MY FREE TIME IS IMPORTANT TO ME, SO DON'T FUCK THIS UP FOR ME, OKAY? TRY BEING A LITTLE POSITIVE.
YOU'RE RIGHT. LET'S GET GOING.
THAT'S THE SPIRIT, ROBBIE-BOBBY-BABY.

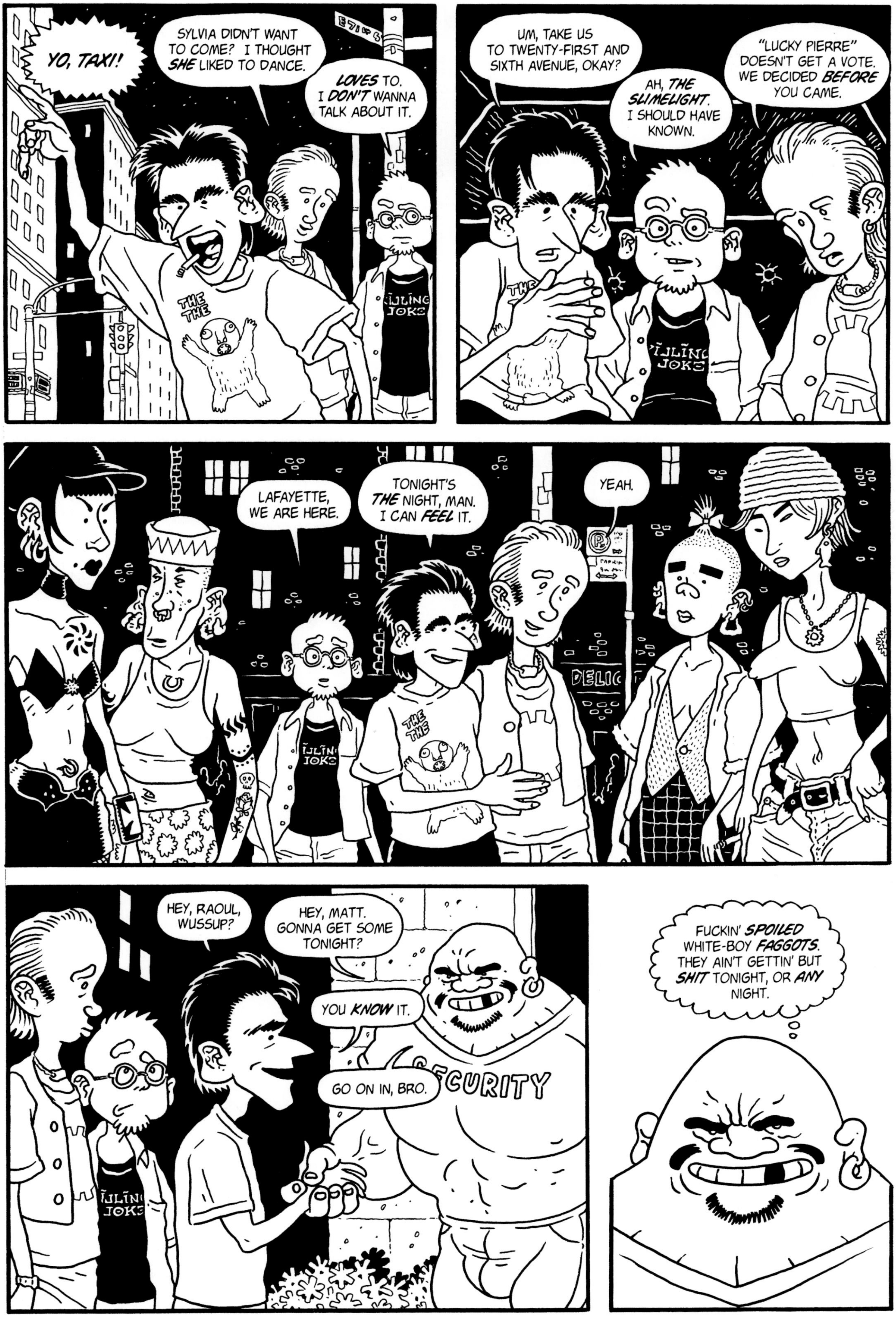
YO, TAXI!
SYLVIA DIDN'T WANT TO COME? I THOUGHT SHE LIKED TO DANCE.
LOVES TO. I DON'T WANNA TALK ABOUT IT.
UM, TAKE US TO TWENTY-FIRST AND SIXTH AVENUE, OKAY?
AH, THE SLIMELIGHT. I SHOULD HAVE KNOWN.
"LUCKY PIERRE" DOESN'T GET A VOTE. WE DECIDED BEFORE YOU CAME.
LAFAYETTE, WE ARE HERE.
TONIGHT'S THE NIGHT, MAN. I CAN FEEL IT.
YEAH.
HEY, RAOUL, WUSSUP?
HEY, MATT. GONNA GET SOME TONIGHT?
YOU KNOW IT.
GO ON IN, BRO.
SECURITY
FUCKIN' SPOILED WHITE-BOY FAGGOTS. THEY AIN'T GETTIN' BUT SHIT TONIGHT, OR ANY NIGHT.

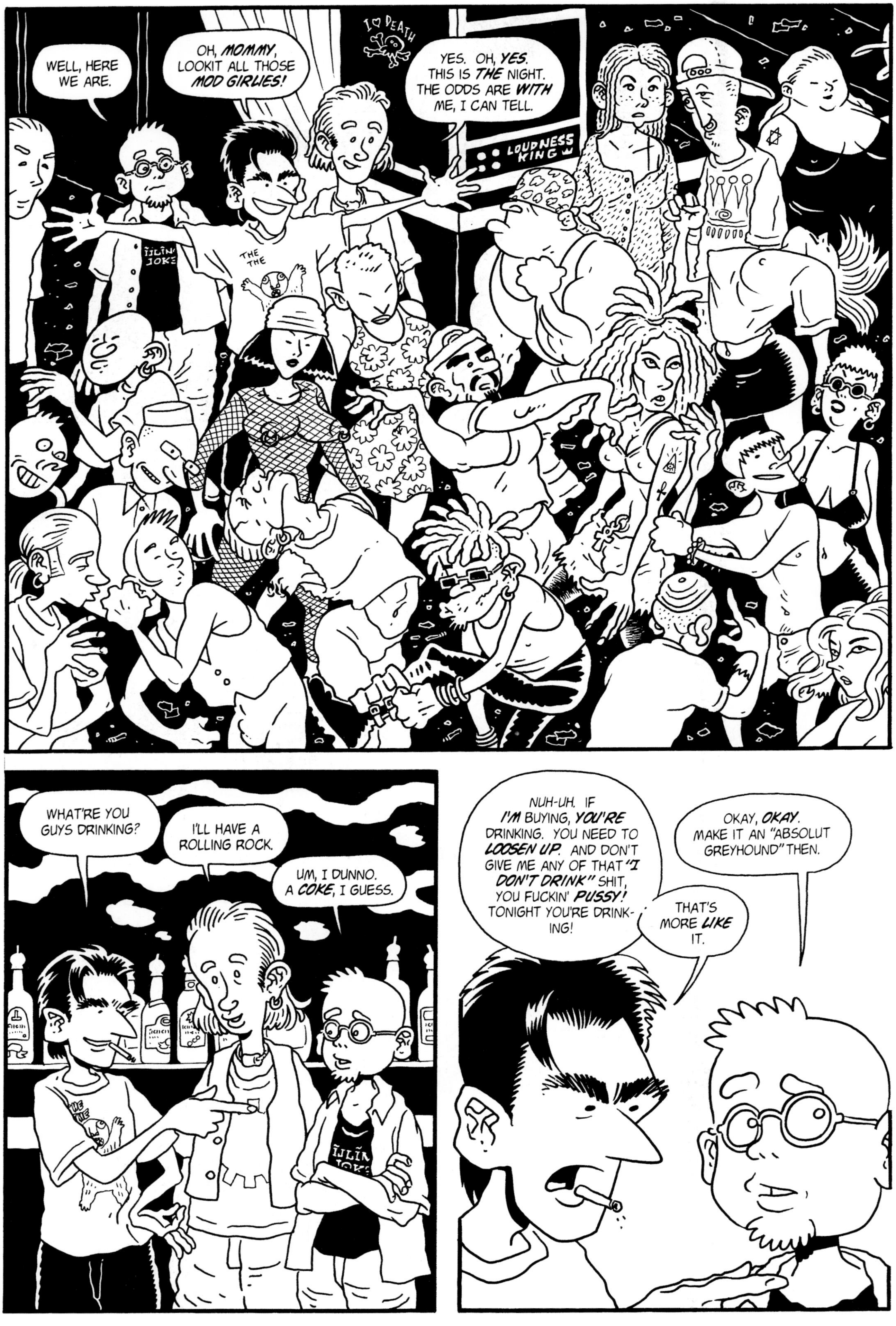
WELL, HERE WE ARE.
OH, MOMMY, LOOKIT ALL THOSE MOD GIRLIES!
I ♡ DEATH
YES. OH, YES. THIS IS THE NIGHT. THE ODDS ARE WITH ME, I CAN TELL.
LOUDNESS KING
WHAT'RE YOU GUYS DRINKING?
I'LL HAVE A ROLLING ROCK.
UM, I DUNNO. A COKE, I GUESS.
NUH-UH. IF I'M BUYING, YOU'RE DRINKING. YOU NEED TO LOOSEN UP. AND DON'T GIVE ME ANY OF THAT "I DON'T DRINK" SHIT, YOU FUCKIN' PUSSY! TONIGHT YOU'RE DRINK-ING!
OKAY, OKAY. MAKE IT AN "ABSOLUT GREYHOUND" THEN.
THAT'S MORE LIKE IT.

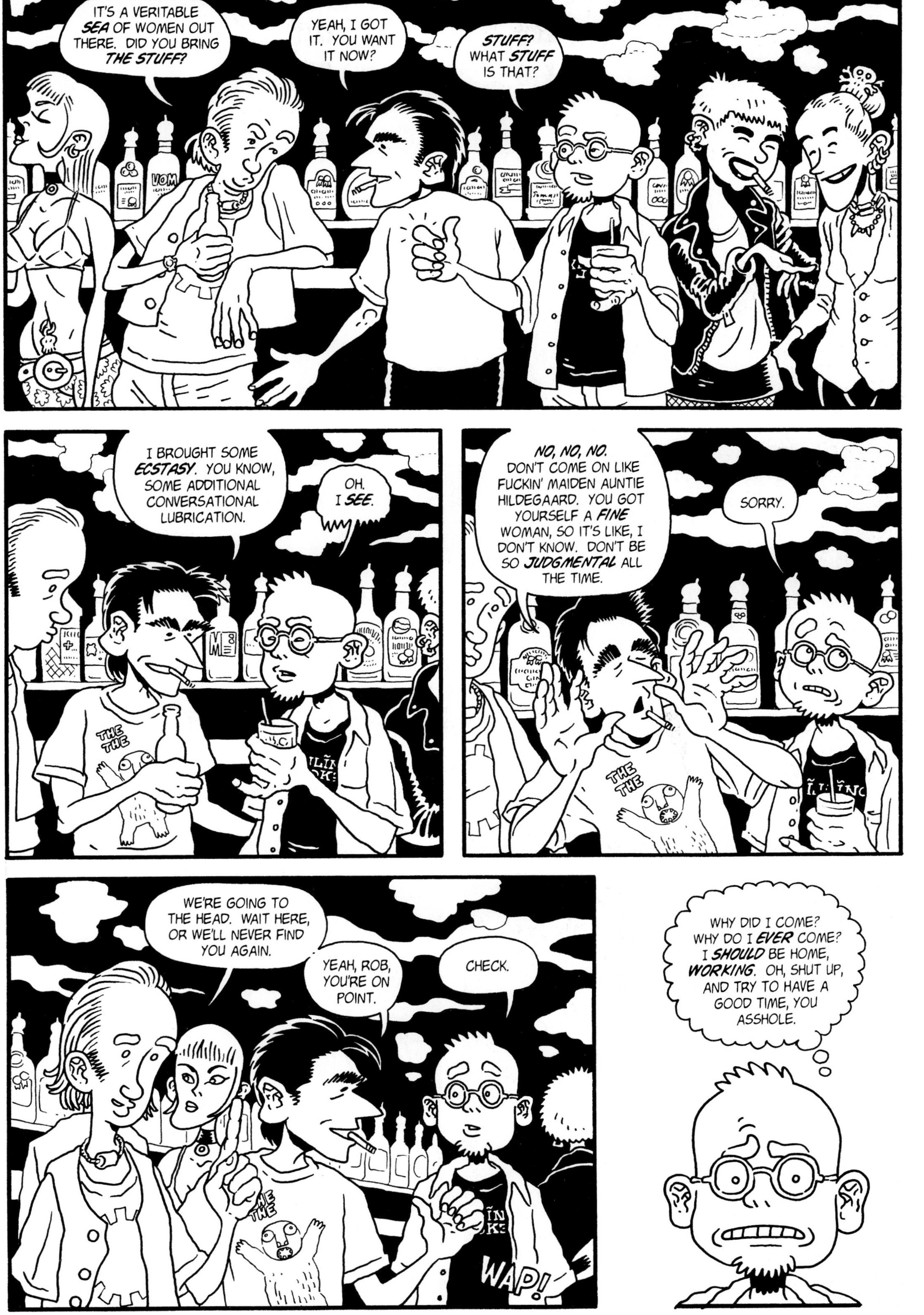
IT'S A VERITABLE SEA OF WOMEN OUT THERE. DID YOU BRING THE STUFF?
YEAH, I GOT IT. YOU WANT IT NOW?
STUFF? WHAT STUFF IS THAT?
I BROUGHT SOME ECSTASY. YOU KNOW, SOME ADDITIONAL CONVERSATIONAL LUBRICATION.
OH. I SEE.
THE THE
NO, NO, NO. DON'T COME ON LIKE FUCKIN' MAIDEN AUNTIE HILDEGAARD. YOU GOT YOURSELF A FINE WOMAN, SO IT'S LIKE, I DON'T KNOW. DON'T BE SO JUDGMENTAL ALL THE TIME.
SORRY.
WE'RE GOING TO THE HEAD. WAIT HERE, OR WE'LL NEVER FIND YOU AGAIN.
YEAH, ROB, YOU'RE ON POINT.
CHECK.
WAP!
WHY DID I COME? WHY DO I EVER COME? I SHOULD BE HOME, WORKING. OH, SHUT UP, AND TRY TO HAVE A GOOD TIME, YOU ASSHOLE.

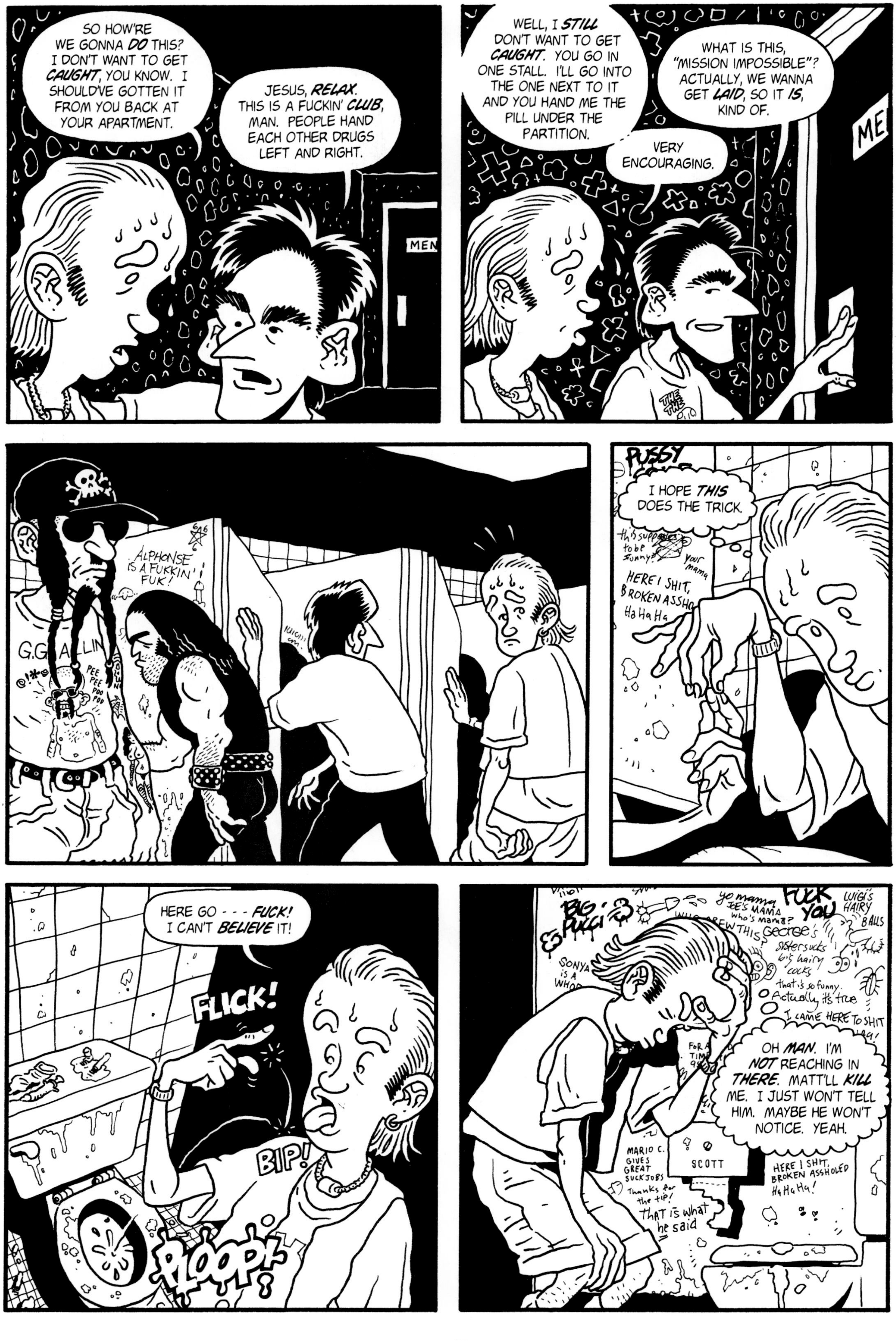
SO HOW'RE WE GONNA DO THIS? I DON'T WANT TO GET CAUGHT, YOU KNOW. I SHOULD'VE GOTTEN IT FROM YOU BACK AT YOUR APARTMENT.
JESUS, RELAX. THIS IS A FUCKIN' CLUB, MAN. PEOPLE HAND EACH OTHER DRUGS LEFT AND RIGHT.
MEN
WELL, I STILL DON'T WANT TO GET CAUGHT. YOU GO IN ONE STALL. I'LL GO INTO THE ONE NEXT TO IT AND YOU HAND ME THE PILL UNDER THE PARTITION.
WHAT IS THIS, "MISSION IMPOSSIBLE"? ACTUALLY, WE WANNA GET LAID, SO IT IS, KIND OF.
VERY ENCOURAGING.
ME
ALPHONSE IS A FUKKIN' FUK!
G.G. ALLIN
PEE PEE POO POO
PUSSY
I HOPE THIS DOES THE TRICK.
your mama
HERE I SHIT, BROKEN ASSHO
Ha Ha Ha
HERE GO - - - FUCK! I CAN'T BELIEVE IT!
FLICK!
BIP!
PLOOP!
BIG PULCI
yo mama
JOE'S MAMA
who's mama?
FUCK YOU
LUIGI'S HAIRY BALLS
SONYA IS A WHOR
that's so funny.
Actually, it's true
I CAME HERE TO SHIT
OH MAN. I'M NOT REACHING IN THERE. MATT'LL KILL ME. I JUST WON'T TELL HIM. MAYBE HE WON'T NOTICE. YEAH.
MARIO C. GIVES GREAT SUCKJOBS
Thanks for the tip!
THAT is what he said
SCOTT
HERE I SHIT, BROKEN ASSHOLED Ha Ha Ha!

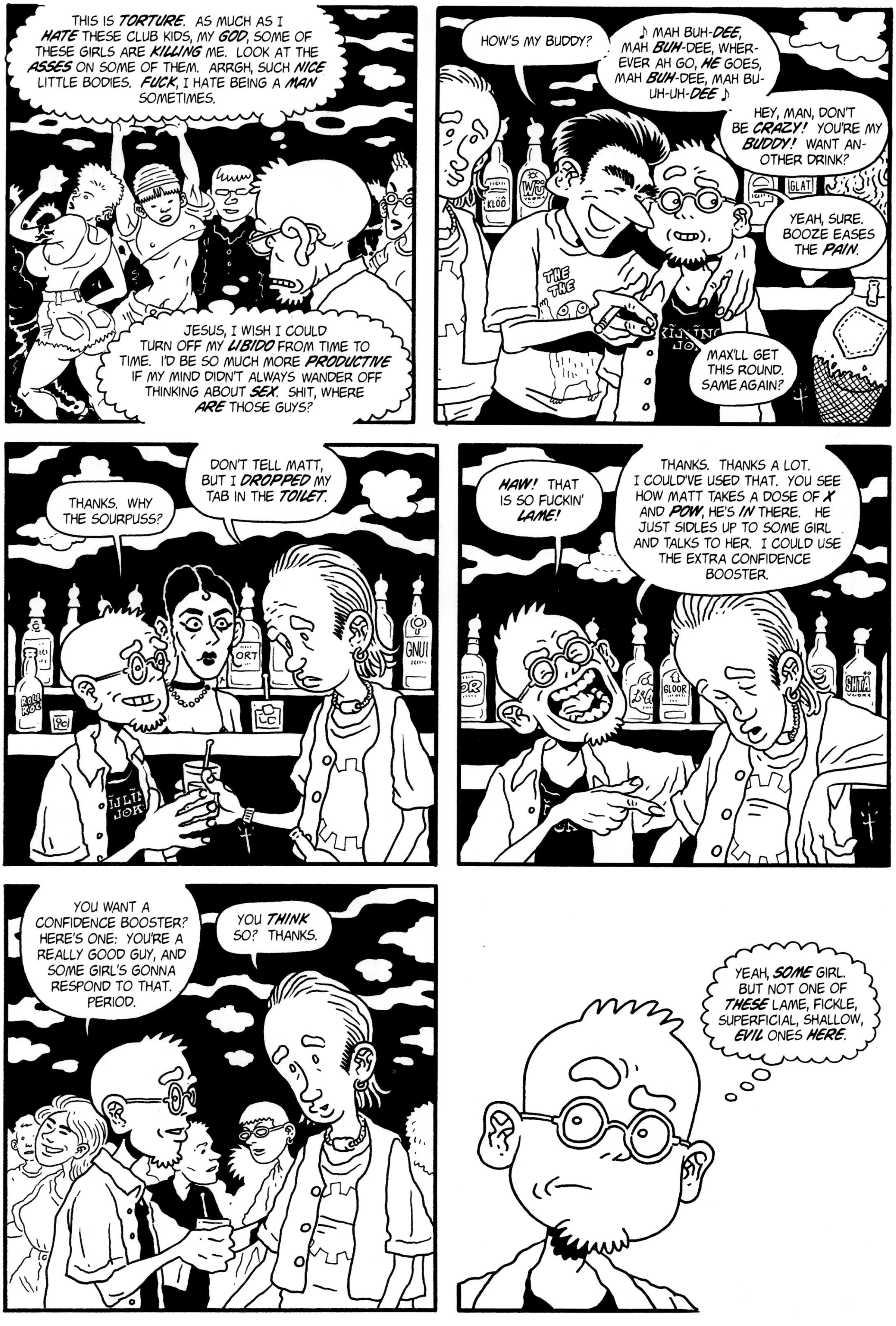

THIS IS TORTURE. AS MUCH AS I HATE THESE CLUB KIDS, MY GOD, SOME OF THESE GIRLS ARE KILLING ME. LOOK AT THE ASSES ON SOME OF THEM. ARRGH, SUCH NICE LITTLE BODIES. FUCK, I HATE BEING A MAN SOMETIMES.
JESUS, I WISH I COULD TURN OFF MY LIBIDO FROM TIME TO TIME. I'D BE SO MUCH MORE PRODUCTIVE IF MY MIND DIDN'T ALWAYS WANDER OFF THINKING ABOUT SEX. SHIT, WHERE ARE THOSE GUYS?
HOW'S MY BUDDY?
♪ MAH BUH-DEE, MAH BUH-DEE, WHEREVER AH GO, HE GOES, MAH BUH-DEE, MAH BUUH-UH-DEE ♪
HEY, MAN, DON'T BE CRAZY! YOU'RE MY BUDDY! WANT ANOTHER DRINK?
YEAH, SURE. BOOZE EASES THE PAIN.
MAX'LL GET THIS ROUND. SAME AGAIN?
THANKS. WHY THE SOURPUSS?
DON'T TELL MATT, BUT I DROPPED MY TAB IN THE TOILET.
HAW! THAT IS SO FUCKIN' LAME!
THANKS. THANKS A LOT. I COULD'VE USED THAT. YOU SEE HOW MATT TAKES A DOSE OF X AND POW, HE'S IN THERE. HE JUST SIDLES UP TO SOME GIRL AND TALKS TO HER. I COULD USE THE EXTRA CONFIDENCE BOOSTER.
YOU WANT A CONFIDENCE BOOSTER? HERE'S ONE: YOU'RE A REALLY GOOD GUY, AND SOME GIRL'S GONNA RESPOND TO THAT. PERIOD.
YOU THINK SO? THANKS.
YEAH, SOME GIRL. BUT NOT ONE OF THESE LAME, FICKLE, SUPERFICIAL, SHALLOW, EVIL ONES HERE.

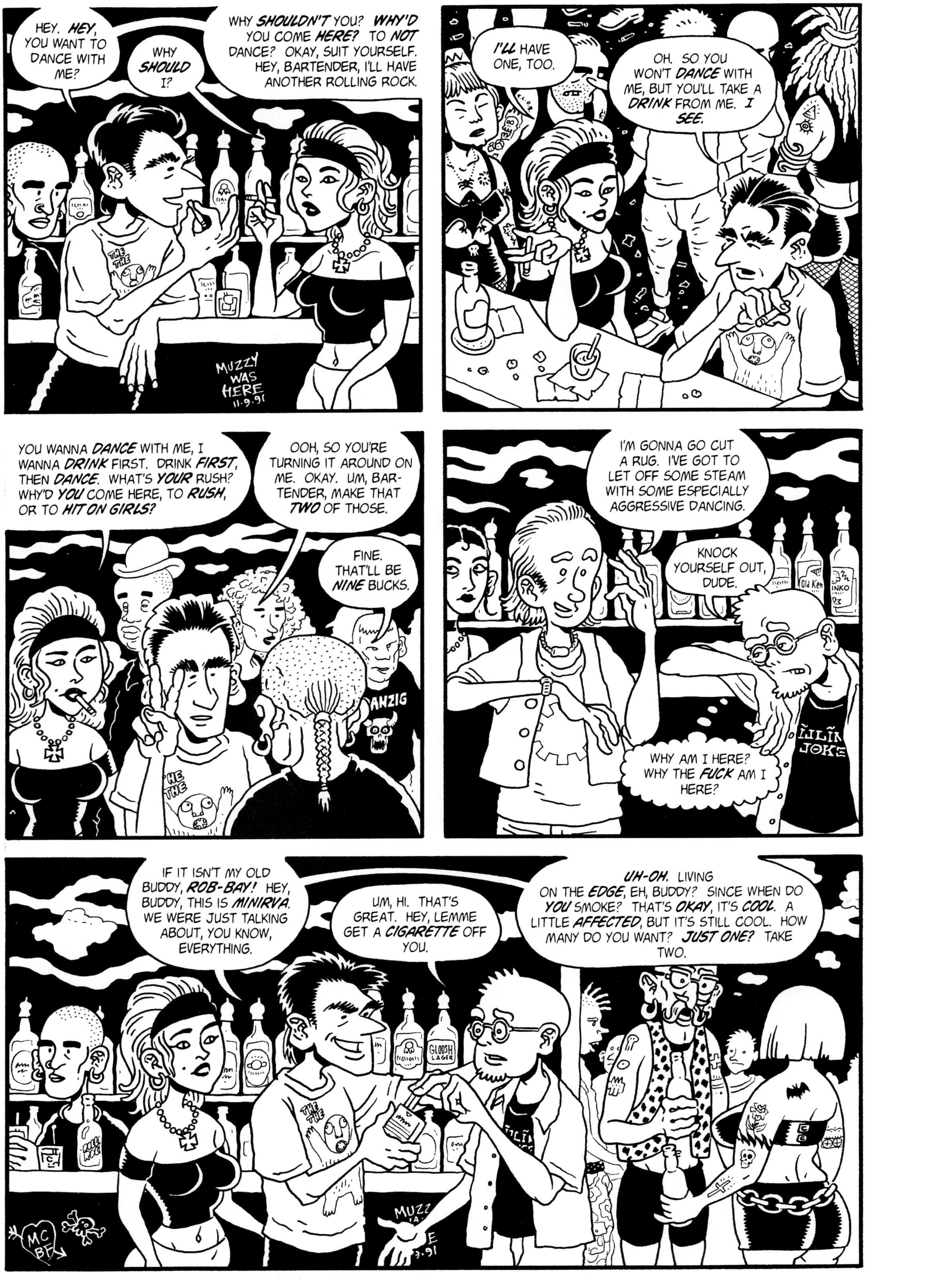
HEY. HEY, YOU WANT TO DANCE WITH ME?
WHY SHOULD I?
WHY SHOULDN'T YOU? WHY'D YOU COME HERE? TO NOT DANCE? OKAY, SUIT YOURSELF. HEY, BARTENDER, I'LL HAVE ANOTHER ROLLING ROCK.
THE THE
MUZZY WAS HERE 11.9.91
I'LL HAVE ONE, TOO.
OH. SO YOU WON'T DANCE WITH ME, BUT YOU'LL TAKE A DRINK FROM ME. I SEE.
YOU WANNA DANCE WITH ME, I WANNA DRINK FIRST. DRINK FIRST, THEN DANCE. WHAT'S YOUR RUSH? WHY'D YOU COME HERE, TO RUSH, OR TO HIT ON GIRLS?
OOH, SO YOU'RE TURNING IT AROUND ON ME. OKAY. UM, BARTENDER, MAKE THAT TWO OF THOSE.
FINE. THAT'LL BE NINE BUCKS.
ANZIG
I'M GONNA GO CUT A RUG. I'VE GOT TO LET OFF SOME STEAM WITH SOME ESPECIALLY AGGRESSIVE DANCING.
KNOCK YOURSELF OUT, DUDE.
WHY AM I HERE? WHY THE FUCK AM I HERE?
IF IT ISN'T MY OLD BUDDY, ROB-BAY! HEY, BUDDY, THIS IS MINIRVA. WE WERE JUST TALKING ABOUT, YOU KNOW, EVERYTHING.
UM, HI. THAT'S GREAT. HEY, LEMME GET A CIGARETTE OFF YOU.
UH-OH. LIVING ON THE EDGE, EH, BUDDY? SINCE WHEN DO YOU SMOKE? THAT'S OKAY, IT'S COOL. A LITTLE AFFECTED, BUT IT'S STILL COOL. HOW MANY DO YOU WANT? JUST ONE? TAKE TWO.
GLOOSH LAGER
MC BF

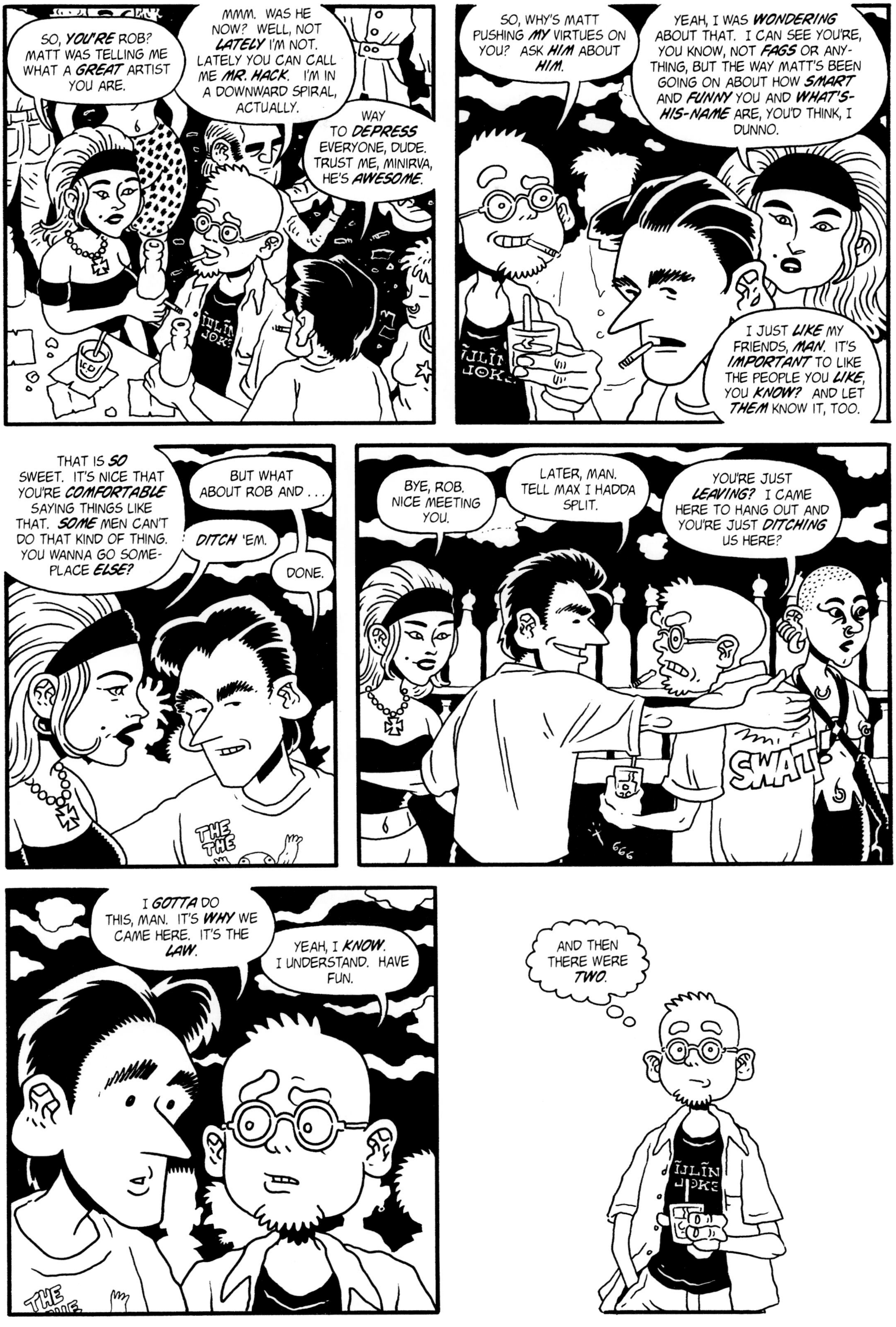
SO, YOU'RE ROB? MATT WAS TELLING ME WHAT A GREAT ARTIST YOU ARE.
MMM. WAS HE NOW? WELL, NOT LATELY I'M NOT. LATELY YOU CAN CALL ME MR. HACK. I'M IN A DOWNWARD SPIRAL, ACTUALLY.
WAY TO DEPRESS EVERYONE, DUDE. TRUST ME, MINIRVA, HE'S AWESOME.
SO, WHY'S MATT PUSHING MY VIRTUES ON YOU? ASK HIM ABOUT HIM.
YEAH, I WAS WONDERING ABOUT THAT. I CAN SEE YOU'RE, YOU KNOW, NOT FAGS OR ANY-THING, BUT THE WAY MATT'S BEEN GOING ON ABOUT HOW SMART AND FUNNY YOU AND WHAT'S-HIS-NAME ARE, YOU'D THINK, I DUNNO.
I JUST LIKE MY FRIENDS, MAN. IT'S IMPORTANT TO LIKE THE PEOPLE YOU LIKE, YOU KNOW? AND LET THEM KNOW IT, TOO.
THAT IS SO SWEET. IT'S NICE THAT YOU'RE COMFORTABLE SAYING THINGS LIKE THAT. SOME MEN CAN'T DO THAT KIND OF THING. YOU WANNA GO SOME-PLACE ELSE?
BUT WHAT ABOUT ROB AND . . .
DITCH 'EM.
DONE.
THE THE
BYE, ROB. NICE MEETING YOU.
LATER, MAN. TELL MAX I HADDA SPLIT.
YOU'RE JUST LEAVING? I CAME HERE TO HANG OUT AND YOU'RE JUST DITCHING US HERE?
SWAT
666
I GOTTA DO THIS, MAN. IT'S WHY WE CAME HERE. IT'S THE LAW.
YEAH, I KNOW. I UNDERSTAND. HAVE FUN.
AND THEN THERE WERE TWO.

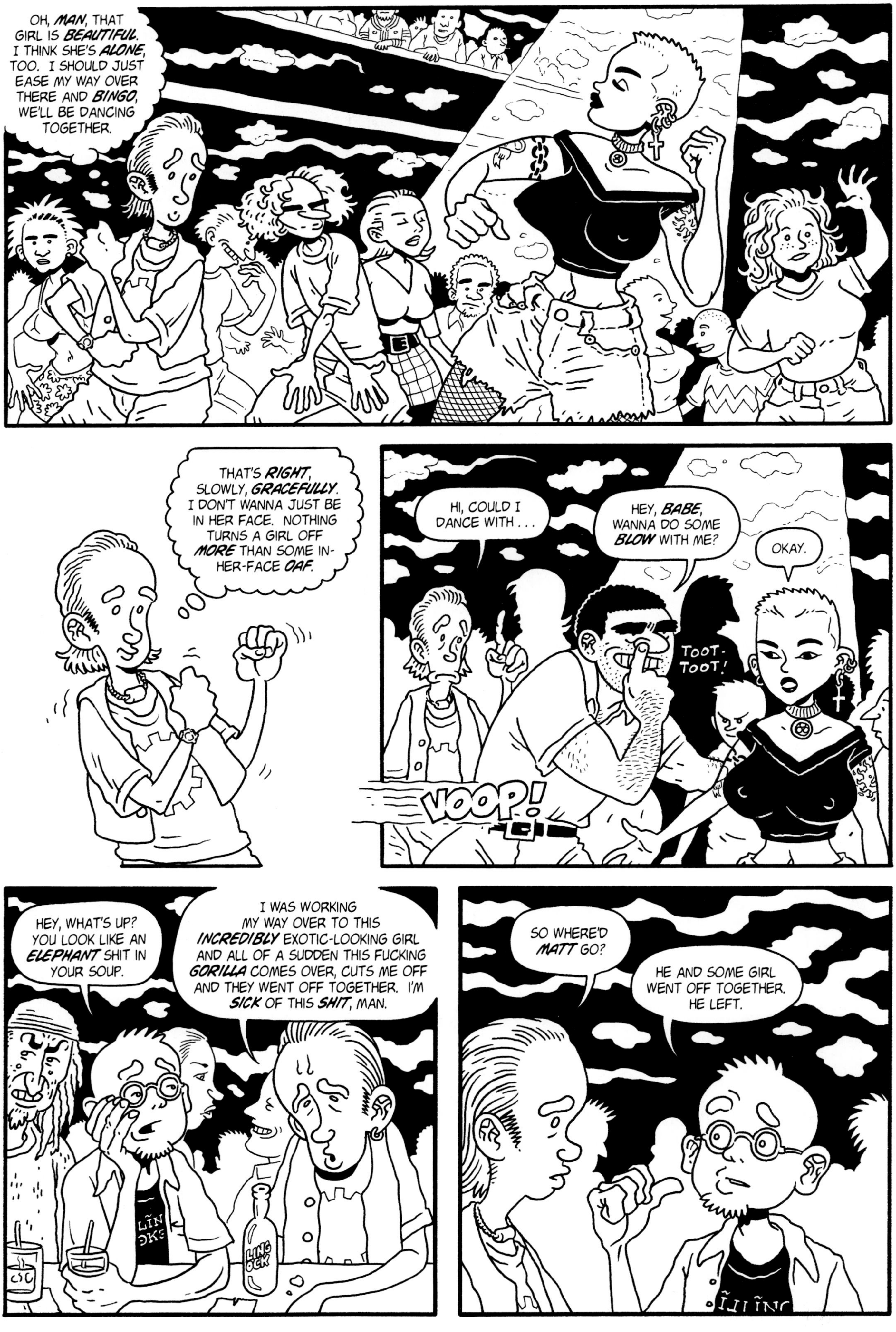

OH, MAN, THAT GIRL IS BEAUTIFUL. I THINK SHE'S ALONE, TOO. I SHOULD JUST EASE MY WAY OVER THERE AND BINGO, WE'LL BE DANCING TOGETHER.
THAT'S RIGHT, SLOWLY, GRACEFULLY. I DON'T WANNA JUST BE IN HER FACE. NOTHING TURNS A GIRL OFF MORE THAN SOME IN-HER-FACE OAF.
HI, COULD I DANCE WITH . . .
HEY, BABE, WANNA DO SOME BLOW WITH ME?
OKAY.
TOOT-TOOT!
VOOP!
HEY, WHAT'S UP? YOU LOOK LIKE AN ELEPHANT SHIT IN YOUR SOUP.
I WAS WORKING MY WAY OVER TO THIS INCREDIBLY EXOTIC-LOOKING GIRL AND ALL OF A SUDDEN THIS FUCKING GORILLA COMES OVER, CUTS ME OFF AND THEY WENT OFF TOGETHER. I'M SICK OF THIS SHIT, MAN.
SO WHERE'D MATT GO?
HE AND SOME GIRL WENT OFF TOGETHER. HE LEFT.

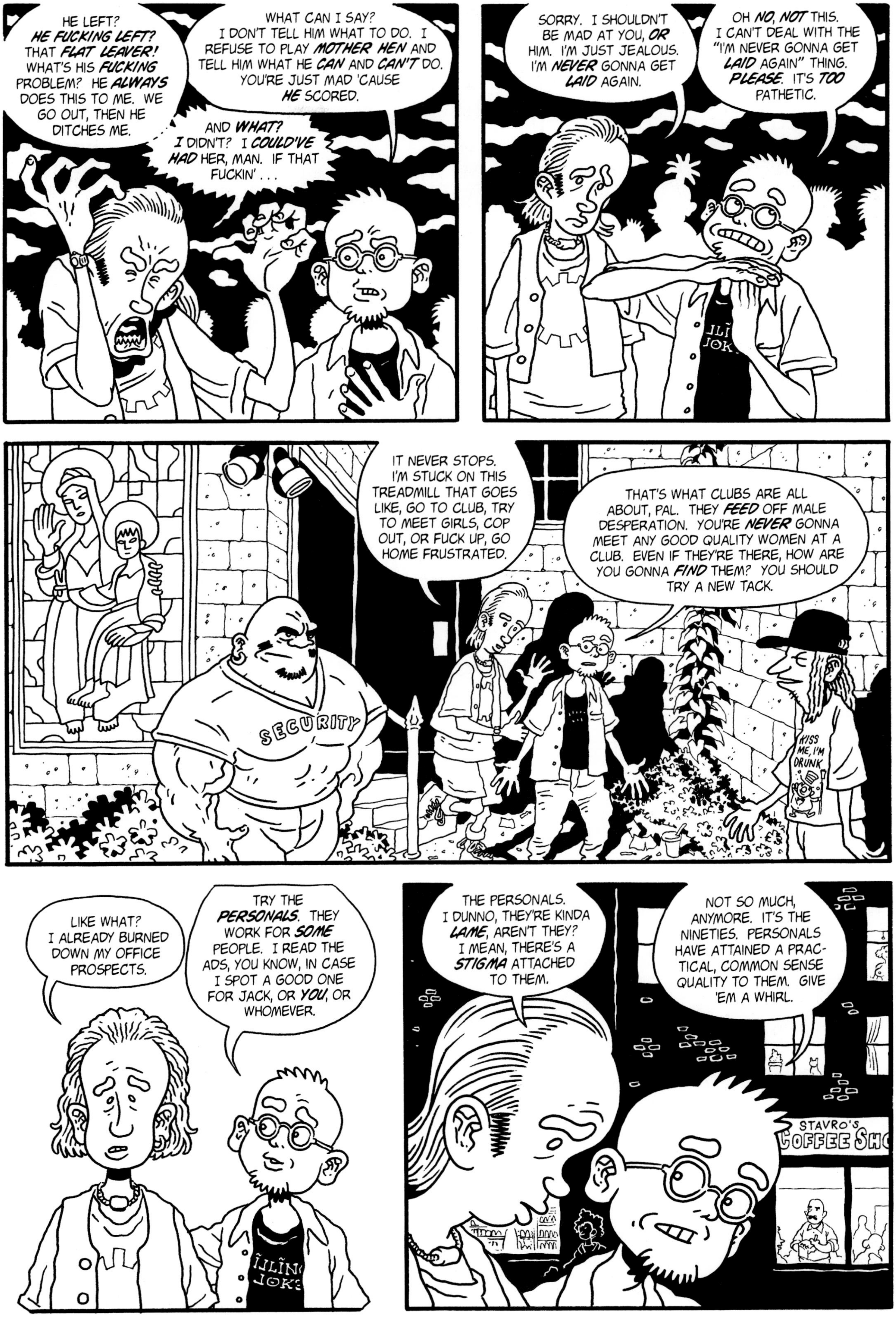

HE LEFT? HE FUCKING LEFT? THAT FLAT LEAVER! WHAT'S HIS FUCKING PROBLEM? HE ALWAYS DOES THIS TO ME. WE GO OUT, THEN HE DITCHES ME.
WHAT CAN I SAY? I DON'T TELL HIM WHAT TO DO. I REFUSE TO PLAY MOTHER HEN AND TELL HIM WHAT HE CAN AND CAN'T DO. YOU'RE JUST MAD 'CAUSE HE SCORED.
AND WHAT? I DIDN'T? I COULD'VE HAD HER, MAN. IF THAT FUCKIN'. . .
SORRY. I SHOULDN'T BE MAD AT YOU, OR HIM. I'M JUST JEALOUS. I'M NEVER GONNA GET LAID AGAIN.
OH NO, NOT THIS. I CAN'T DEAL WITH THE "I'M NEVER GONNA GET LAID AGAIN" THING. PLEASE. IT'S TOO PATHETIC.
IT NEVER STOPS. I'M STUCK ON THIS TREADMILL THAT GOES LIKE, GO TO CLUB, TRY TO MEET GIRLS, COP OUT, OR FUCK UP, GO HOME FRUSTRATED.
THAT'S WHAT CLUBS ARE ALL ABOUT, PAL. THEY FEED OFF MALE DESPERATION. YOU'RE NEVER GONNA MEET ANY GOOD QUALITY WOMEN AT A CLUB. EVEN IF THEY'RE THERE, HOW ARE YOU GONNA FIND THEM? YOU SHOULD TRY A NEW TACK.
SECURITY
KISS ME, I'M DRUNK
LIKE WHAT? I ALREADY BURNED DOWN MY OFFICE PROSPECTS.
TRY THE PERSONALS. THEY WORK FOR SOME PEOPLE. I READ THE ADS, YOU KNOW, IN CASE I SPOT A GOOD ONE FOR JACK, OR YOU, OR WHOMEVER.
THE PERSONALS. I DUNNO, THEY'RE KINDA LAME, AREN'T THEY? I MEAN, THERE'S A STIGMA ATTACHED TO THEM.
NOT SO MUCH, ANYMORE. IT'S THE NINETIES. PERSONALS HAVE ATTAINED A PRACTICAL, COMMON SENSE QUALITY TO THEM. GIVE 'EM A WHIRL.
STAVRO'S COFFEE SHO

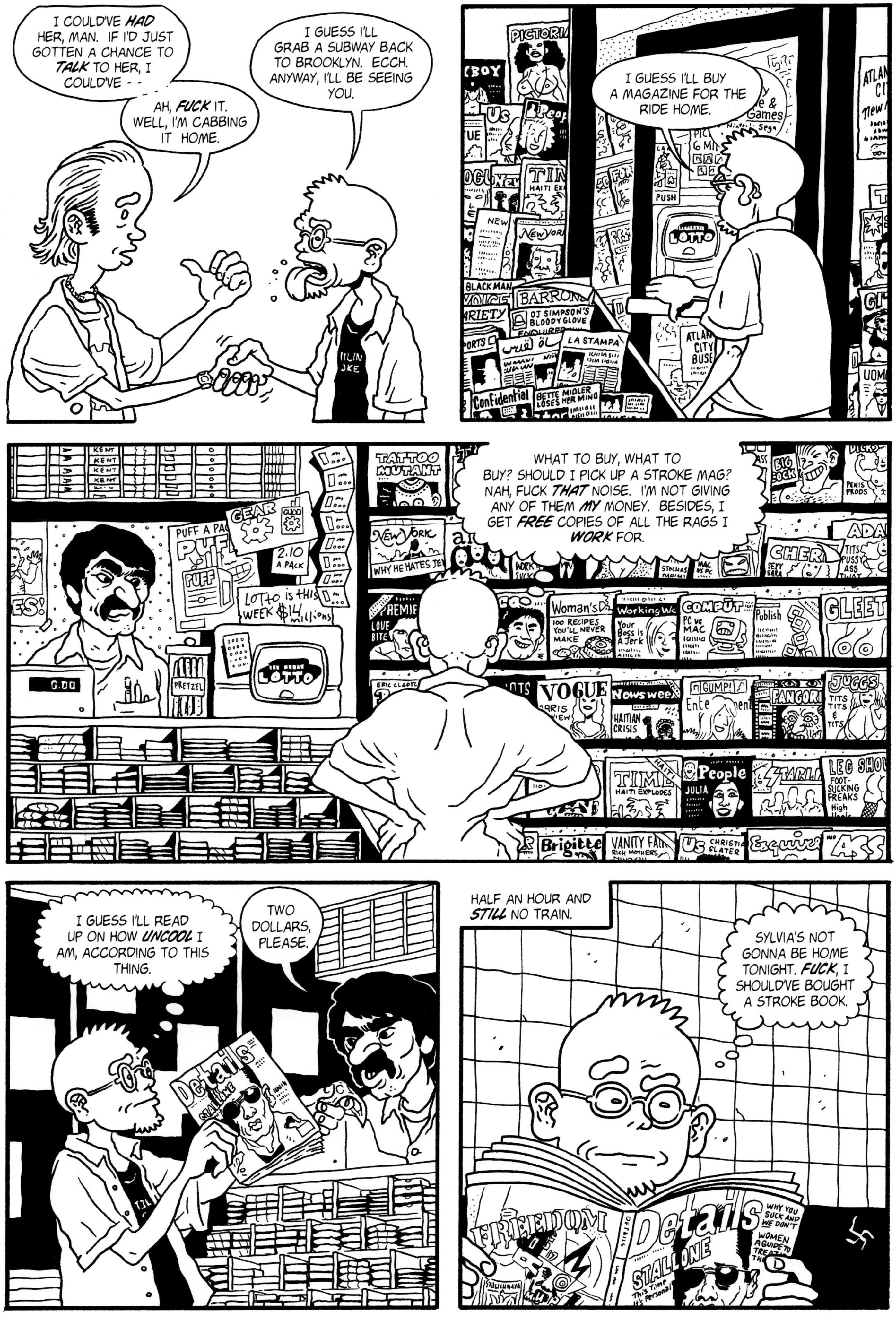

I COULD'VE HAD HER, MAN. IF I'D JUST GOTTEN A CHANCE TO TALK TO HER, I COULD'VE - - -
AH, FUCK IT. WELL, I'M CABBING IT HOME.
I GUESS I'LL GRAB A SUBWAY BACK TO BROOKLYN. ECCH. ANYWAY, I'LL BE SEEING YOU.
I GUESS I'LL BUY A MAGAZINE FOR THE RIDE HOME.
WHAT TO BUY, WHAT TO BUY? SHOULD I PICK UP A STROKE MAG? NAH, FUCK THAT NOISE. I'M NOT GIVING ANY OF THEM MY MONEY. BESIDES, I GET FREE COPIES OF ALL THE RAGS I WORK FOR.
I GUESS I'LL READ UP ON HOW UNCOOL I AM, ACCORDING TO THIS THING.
TWO DOLLARS, PLEASE.
HALF AN HOUR AND STILL NO TRAIN.
SYLVIA'S NOT GONNA BE HOME TONIGHT. FUCK, I SHOULD'VE BOUGHT A STROKE BOOK.

THREE FORTY-FIVE IN THE FUCKIN' MORNING. WHAT A *COLOSSAL* WASTE OF TIME. I CAN'T BELIEVE I WENT OUT TO A FUCKIN' *CLUB* INSTEAD OF *WORKING* ON THAT CHEESY MOVIE PARODY FOR THAT PIECE OF SHIT, RETARDED KIDDIE *"HUMOR"* MAG. JESUS H. FUCKING CHRIST, GODAMMIT.

KLIK-KLAK

I'D BETTER EAT SOMETHING BEFORE I TURN IN.

JINGLE!

~GURGLE ~OORP

THINGS WE NEED: MILK TV DINNERS WAFFLES O.J.

OH *BABY* . . . OOOH, *YES*, I LIKE THAT.

UNGH, UNGH, UNGH.

GWISH-GWISH!

JESUS, JACK, GOT THE *VOLUME* UP *LOUD* ENOUGH ON THAT PORNO TAPE?

KILLER ELITE

KLIK!

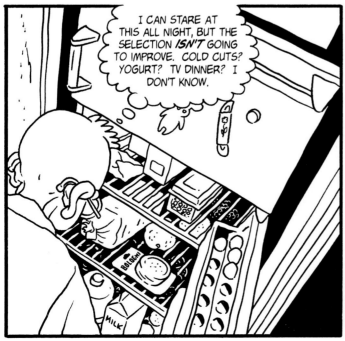

I CAN STARE AT THIS ALL NIGHT, BUT THE SELECTION *ISN'T* GOING TO IMPROVE. COLD CUTS? YOGURT? TV DINNER? I DON'T KNOW.

MILK

I JUST GOTTA TAKE A WHIZ. I'LL BE BACK IN A MINUTE.

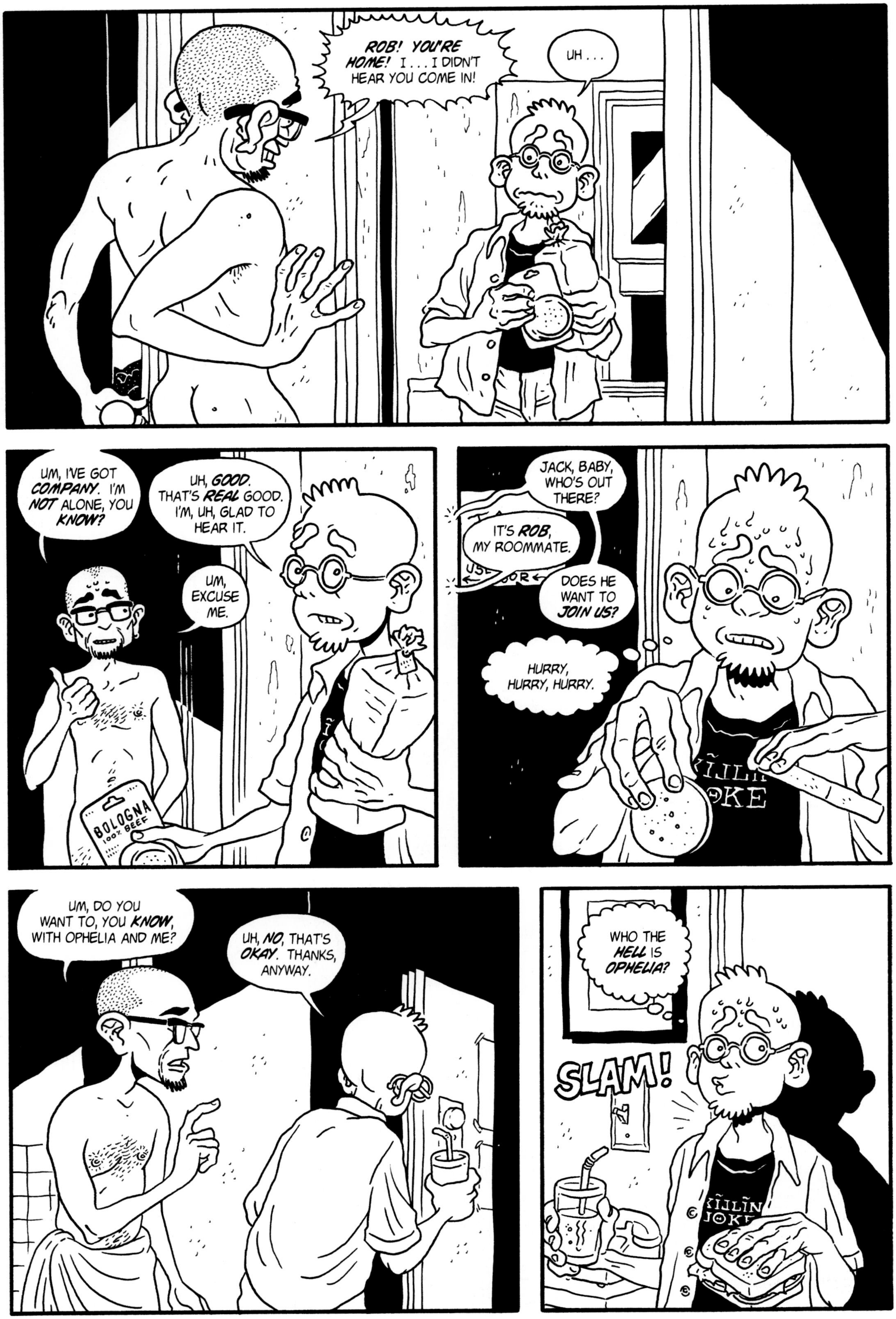
ROB! YOU'RE HOME! I . . . I DIDN'T HEAR YOU COME IN!
UH . . .
UM, I'VE GOT COMPANY. I'M NOT ALONE, YOU KNOW?
UH, GOOD. THAT'S REAL GOOD. I'M, UH, GLAD TO HEAR IT.
UM, EXCUSE ME.
BOLOGNA 100% BEEF
JACK, BABY, WHO'S OUT THERE?
IT'S ROB, MY ROOMMATE.
DOES HE WANT TO JOIN US?
HURRY, HURRY, HURRY.
UM, DO YOU WANT TO, YOU KNOW, WITH OPHELIA AND ME?
UH, NO, THAT'S OKAY. THANKS, ANYWAY.
WHO THE HELL IS OPHELIA?
SLAM!

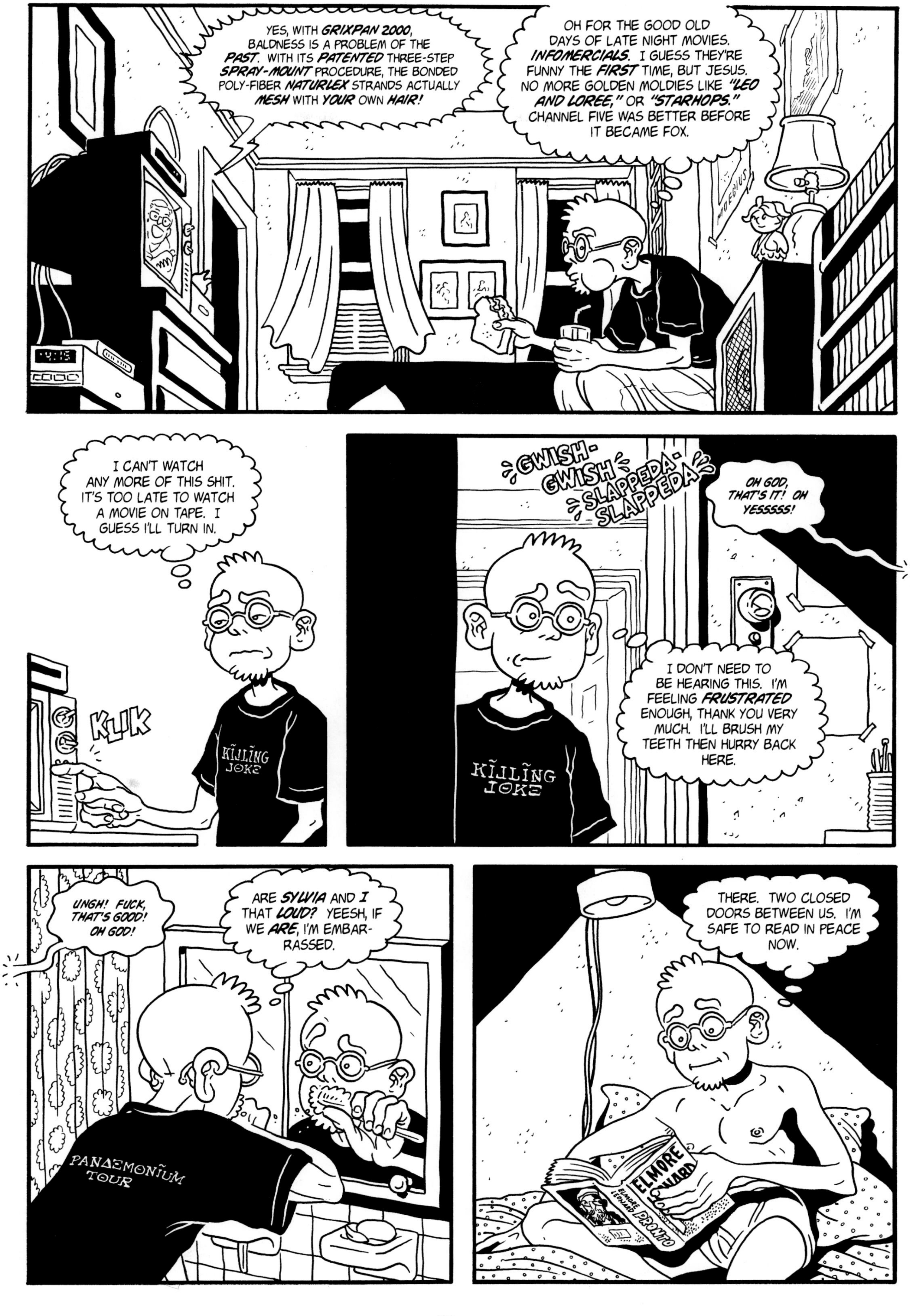
YES, WITH GRIXPAN 2000, BALDNESS IS A PROBLEM OF THE PAST. WITH ITS PATENTED THREE-STEP SPRAY-MOUNT PROCEDURE, THE BONDED POLY-FIBER NATURLEX STRANDS ACTUALLY MESH WITH YOUR OWN HAIR!
OH FOR THE GOOD OLD DAYS OF LATE NIGHT MOVIES. INFOMERCIALS. I GUESS THEY'RE FUNNY THE FIRST TIME, BUT JESUS. NO MORE GOLDEN MOLDIES LIKE "LEO AND LOREE," OR "STARHOPS." CHANNEL FIVE WAS BETTER BEFORE IT BECAME FOX.
MOEBIUS
I CAN'T WATCH ANY MORE OF THIS SHIT. IT'S TOO LATE TO WATCH A MOVIE ON TAPE. I GUESS I'LL TURN IN.
KLIK
KILLING JOKE
GWISH-GWISH SLAPPEDA-SLAPPEDA
OH GOD, THAT'S IT! OH YESSSSS!
I DON'T NEED TO BE HEARING THIS. I'M FEELING FRUSTRATED ENOUGH, THANK YOU VERY MUCH. I'LL BRUSH MY TEETH THEN HURRY BACK HERE.
KILLING JOKE
UNGH! FUCK, THAT'S GOOD! OH GOD!
ARE SYLVIA AND I THAT LOUD? YEESH, IF WE ARE, I'M EMBARRASSED.
PANDEMONIUM TOUR
THERE. TWO CLOSED DOORS BETWEEN US. I'M SAFE TO READ IN PEACE NOW.
ELMORE LEONARD
ELMORE LEONARD PRONTO

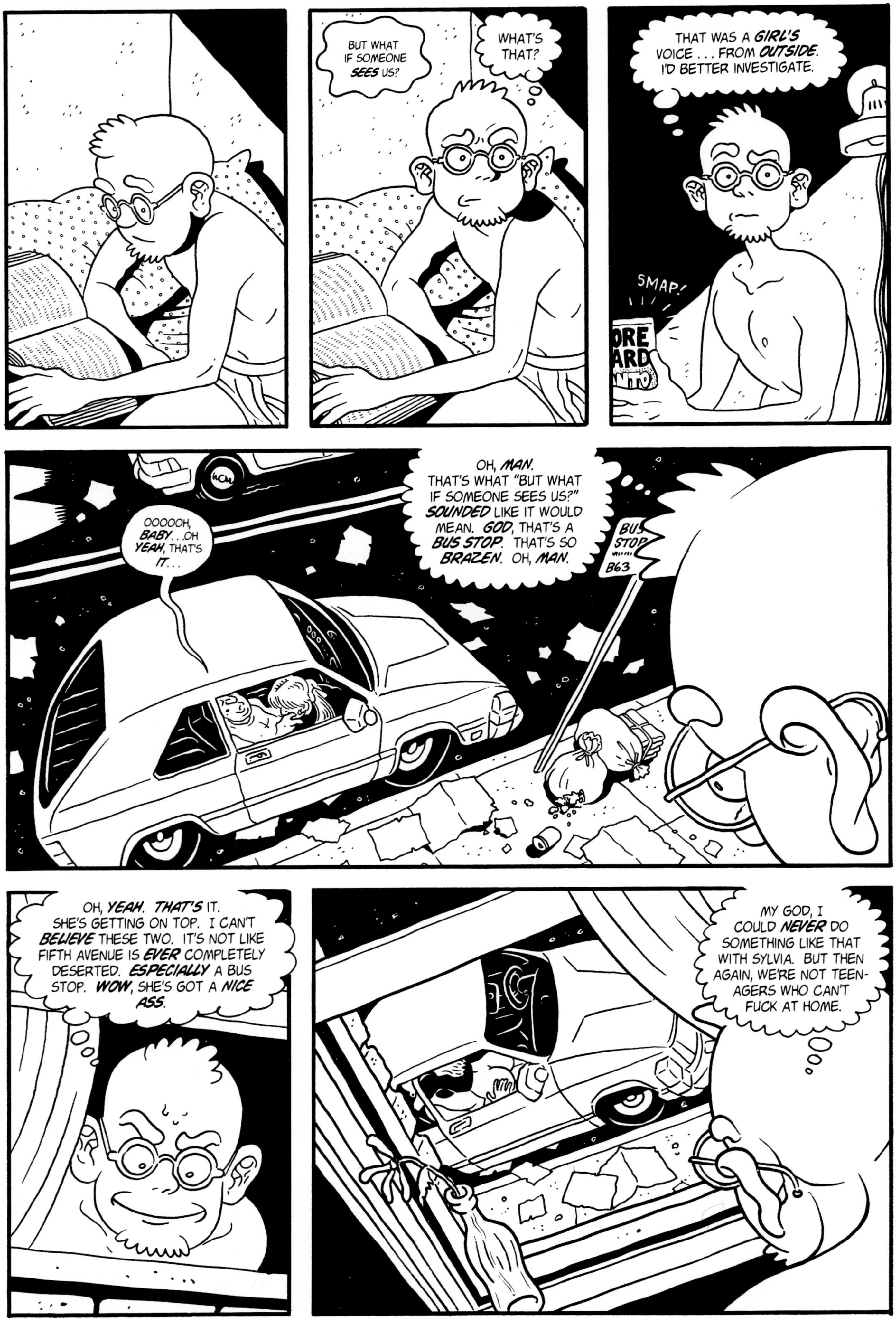
BUT WHAT IF SOMEONE SEES US?
WHAT'S THAT?
THAT WAS A GIRL'S VOICE . . . FROM OUTSIDE. I'D BETTER INVESTIGATE.
SMAP!
OOOOOH, BABY...OH YEAH, THAT'S IT...
OH, MAN. THAT'S WHAT "BUT WHAT IF SOMEONE SEES US?" SOUNDED LIKE IT WOULD MEAN. GOD, THAT'S A BUS STOP. THAT'S SO BRAZEN. OH, MAN.
BUS STOP
B63
OH, YEAH. THAT'S IT. SHE'S GETTING ON TOP. I CAN'T BELIEVE THESE TWO. IT'S NOT LIKE FIFTH AVENUE IS EVER COMPLETELY DESERTED. ESPECIALLY A BUS STOP. WOW, SHE'S GOT A NICE ASS.
MY GOD, I COULD NEVER DO SOMETHING LIKE THAT WITH SYLVIA. BUT THEN AGAIN, WE'RE NOT TEEN-AGERS WHO CAN'T FUCK AT HOME.

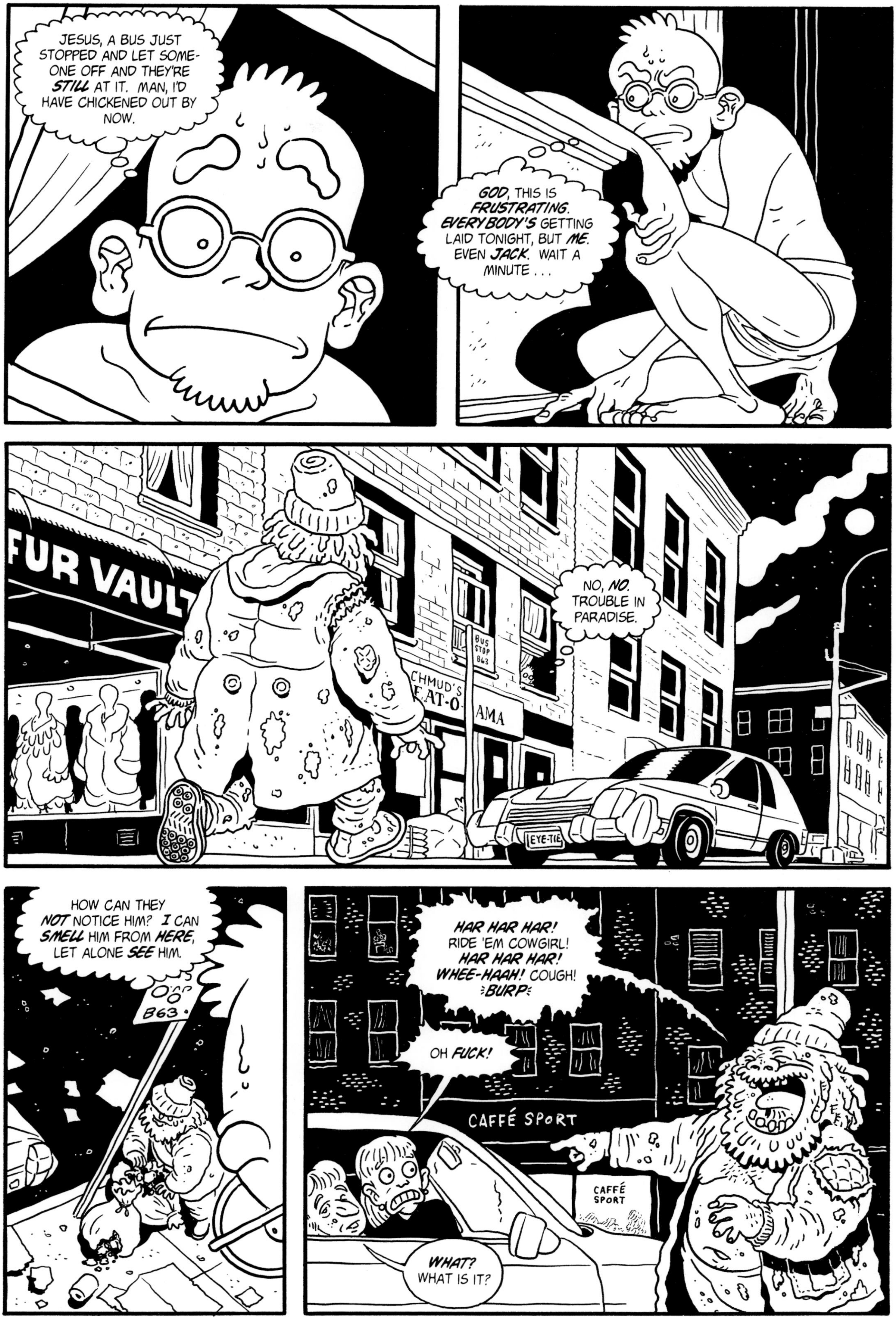
JESUS, A BUS JUST STOPPED AND LET SOME-ONE OFF AND THEY'RE STILL AT IT. MAN, I'D HAVE CHICKENED OUT BY NOW.
GOD, THIS IS FRUSTRATING. EVERYBODY'S GETTING LAID TONIGHT, BUT ME. EVEN JACK. WAIT A MINUTE . . .
FUR VAULT
BUS STOP B63
CHMUD'S EAT-O-AMA
NO, NO. TROUBLE IN PARADISE.
EYE-TIE
HOW CAN THEY NOT NOTICE HIM? I CAN SMELL HIM FROM HERE, LET ALONE SEE HIM.
B63
HAR HAR HAR! RIDE 'EM COWGIRL! HAR HAR HAR! WHEE-HAAH! COUGH! BURP
OH FUCK!
CAFFÉ SPORT
CAFFÉ SPORT
WHAT? WHAT IS IT?

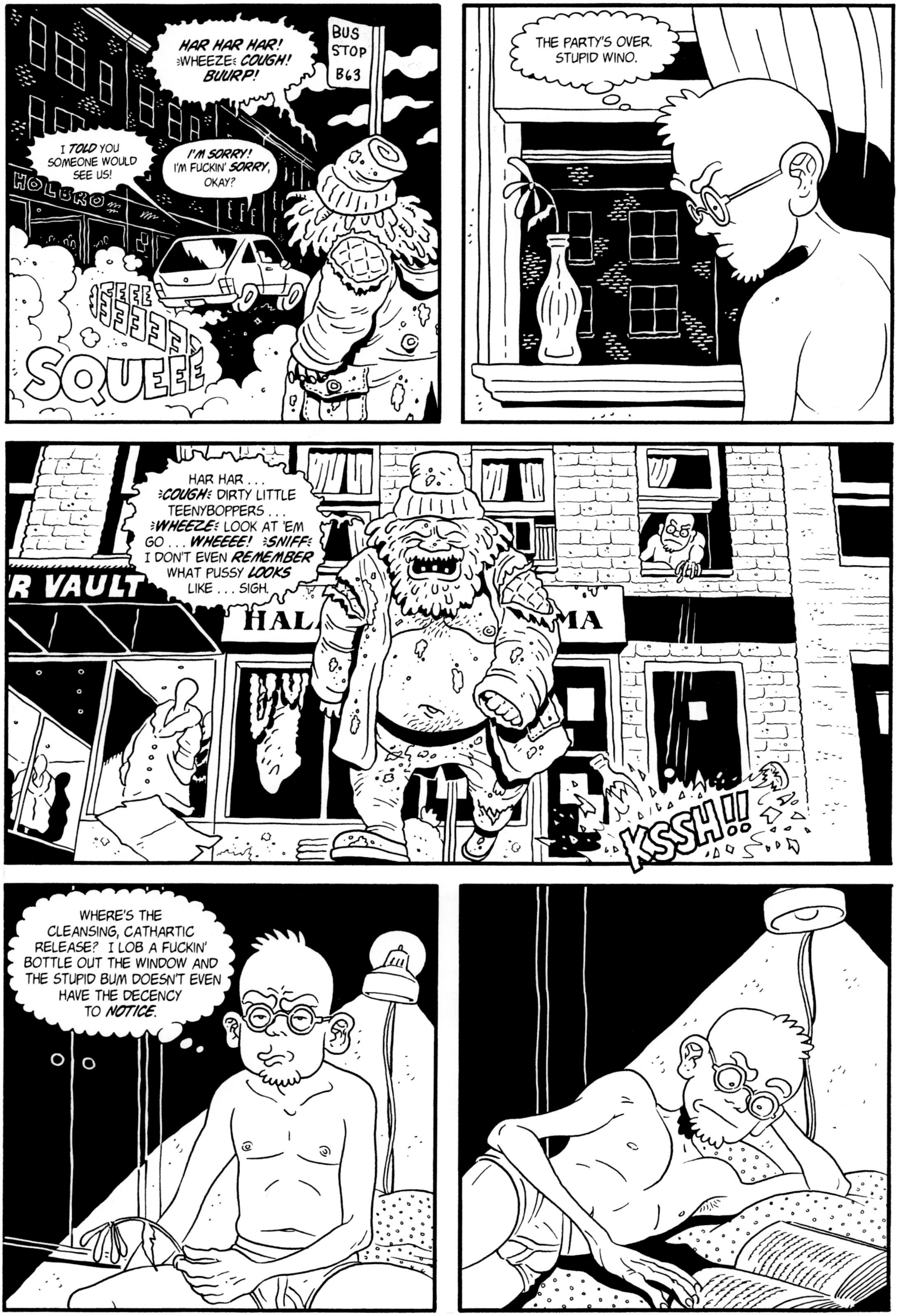

HAR HAR HAR! ≥WHEEZE≤ COUGH! BUURP!
BUS STOP B63
I TOLD YOU SOMEONE WOULD SEE US!
I'M SORRY! I'M FUCKIN' SORRY, OKAY?
HOLBRO
EEEE EEEEEE
SQUEEE
THE PARTY'S OVER. STUPID WINO.
HAR HAR . . . ≥COUGH≤ DIRTY LITTLE TEENYBOPPERS . . . ≥WHEEZE≤ LOOK AT 'EM GO . . . WHEEEE! ≥SNIFF≤ I DON'T EVEN REMEMBER WHAT PUSSY LOOKS LIKE . . . SIGH.
R VAULT
HAL
MA
KSSH!!
WHERE'S THE CLEANSING, CATHARTIC RELEASE? I LOB A FUCKIN' BOTTLE OUT THE WINDOW AND THE STUPID BUM DOESN'T EVEN HAVE THE DECENCY TO NOTICE.

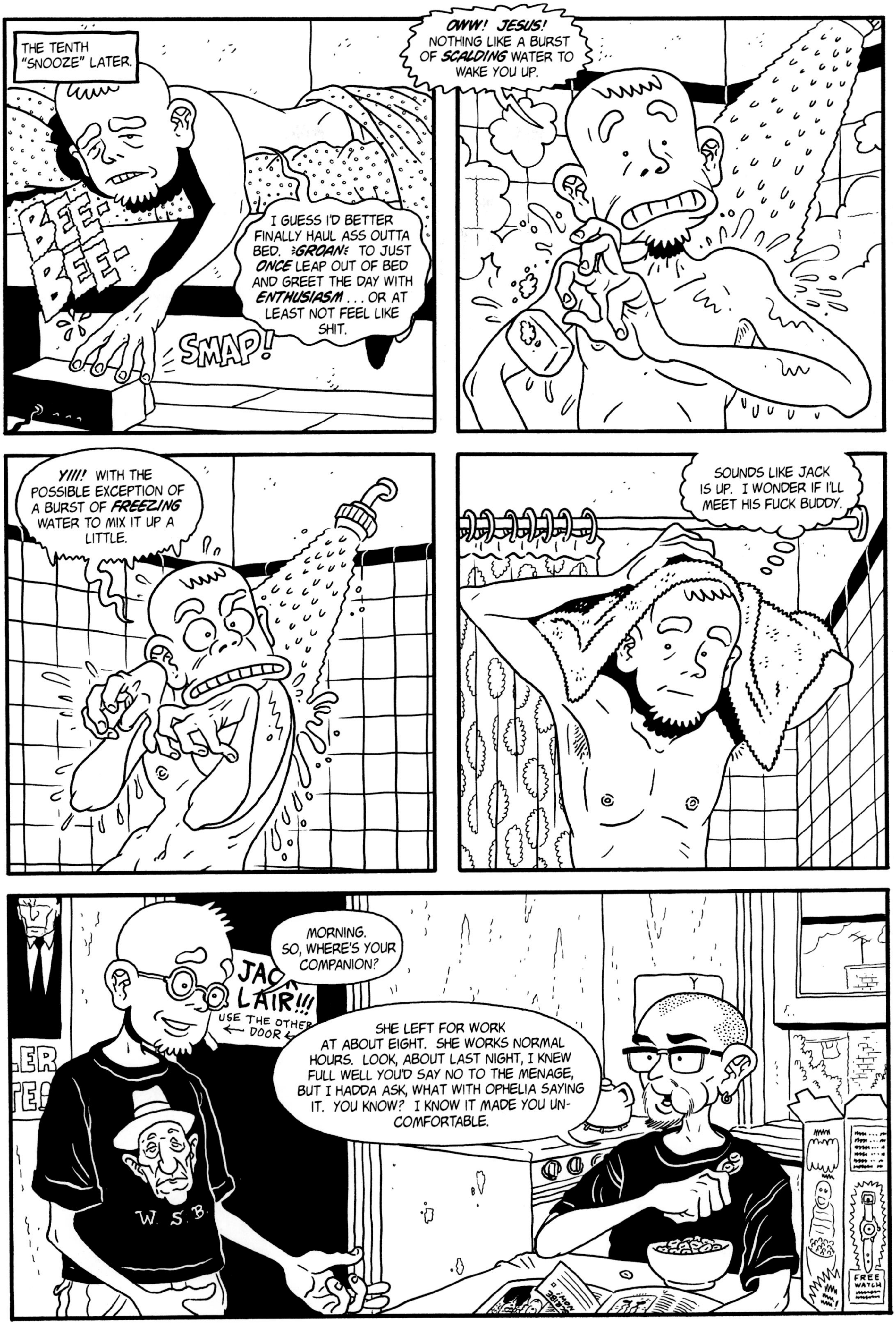
THE TENTH "SNOOZE" LATER.
BEE-BEE-
I GUESS I'D BETTER FINALLY HAUL ASS OUTTA BED. GROAN TO JUST ONCE LEAP OUT OF BED AND GREET THE DAY WITH ENTHUSIASM . . . OR AT LEAST NOT FEEL LIKE SHIT.
SMAP!
OWW! JESUS! NOTHING LIKE A BURST OF SCALDING WATER TO WAKE YOU UP.
YIII! WITH THE POSSIBLE EXCEPTION OF A BURST OF FREEZING WATER TO MIX IT UP A LITTLE.
SOUNDS LIKE JACK IS UP. I WONDER IF I'LL MEET HIS FUCK BUDDY.
MORNING. SO, WHERE'S YOUR COMPANION?
LAIR!!!
USE THE OTHER DOOR
SHE LEFT FOR WORK AT ABOUT EIGHT. SHE WORKS NORMAL HOURS. LOOK, ABOUT LAST NIGHT, I KNEW FULL WELL YOU'D SAY NO TO THE MENAGE, BUT I HADDA ASK, WHAT WITH OPHELIA SAYING IT. YOU KNOW? I KNOW IT MADE YOU UN-COMFORTABLE.
W. S. B.
FREE WATCH

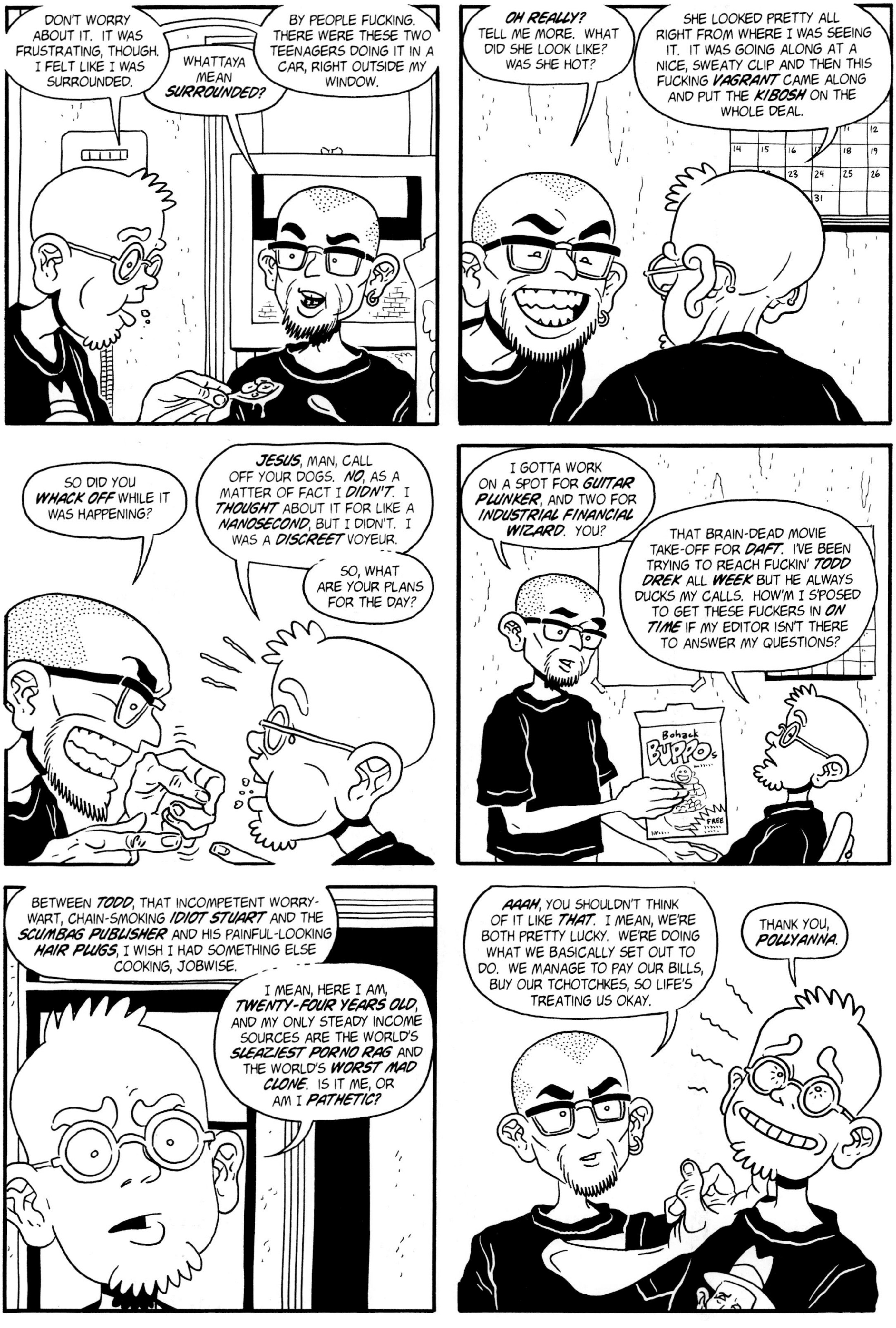
DON'T WORRY ABOUT IT. IT WAS FRUSTRATING, THOUGH. I FELT LIKE I WAS SURROUNDED.
WHATTAYA MEAN SURROUNDED?
BY PEOPLE FUCKING. THERE WERE THESE TWO TEENAGERS DOING IT IN A CAR, RIGHT OUTSIDE MY WINDOW.
OH REALLY? TELL ME MORE. WHAT DID SHE LOOK LIKE? WAS SHE HOT?
SHE LOOKED PRETTY ALL RIGHT FROM WHERE I WAS SEEING IT. IT WAS GOING ALONG AT A NICE, SWEATY CLIP AND THEN THIS FUCKING VAGRANT CAME ALONG AND PUT THE KIBOSH ON THE WHOLE DEAL.
SO DID YOU WHACK OFF WHILE IT WAS HAPPENING?
JESUS, MAN, CALL OFF YOUR DOGS. NO, AS A MATTER OF FACT I DIDN'T. I THOUGHT ABOUT IT FOR LIKE A NANOSECOND, BUT I DIDN'T. I WAS A DISCREET VOYEUR.
SO, WHAT ARE YOUR PLANS FOR THE DAY?
I GOTTA WORK ON A SPOT FOR GUITAR PLUNKER, AND TWO FOR INDUSTRIAL FINANCIAL WIZARD. YOU?
THAT BRAIN-DEAD MOVIE TAKE-OFF FOR DAFT. I'VE BEEN TRYING TO REACH FUCKIN' TODD DREK ALL WEEK BUT HE ALWAYS DUCKS MY CALLS. HOW'M I S'POSED TO GET THESE FUCKERS IN ON TIME IF MY EDITOR ISN'T THERE TO ANSWER MY QUESTIONS?
Bohack BUPPOs
FREE
BETWEEN TODD, THAT INCOMPETENT WORRY-WART, CHAIN-SMOKING IDIOT STUART AND THE SCUMBAG PUBLISHER AND HIS PAINFUL-LOOKING HAIR PLUGS, I WISH I HAD SOMETHING ELSE COOKING, JOBWISE.
I MEAN, HERE I AM, TWENTY-FOUR YEARS OLD, AND MY ONLY STEADY INCOME SOURCES ARE THE WORLD'S SLEAZIEST PORNO RAG AND THE WORLD'S WORST MAD CLONE. IS IT ME, OR AM I PATHETIC?
AAAH, YOU SHOULDN'T THINK OF IT LIKE THAT. I MEAN, WE'RE BOTH PRETTY LUCKY. WE'RE DOING WHAT WE BASICALLY SET OUT TO DO. WE MANAGE TO PAY OUR BILLS, BUY OUR TCHOTCHKES, SO LIFE'S TREATING US OKAY.
THANK YOU, POLLYANNA.

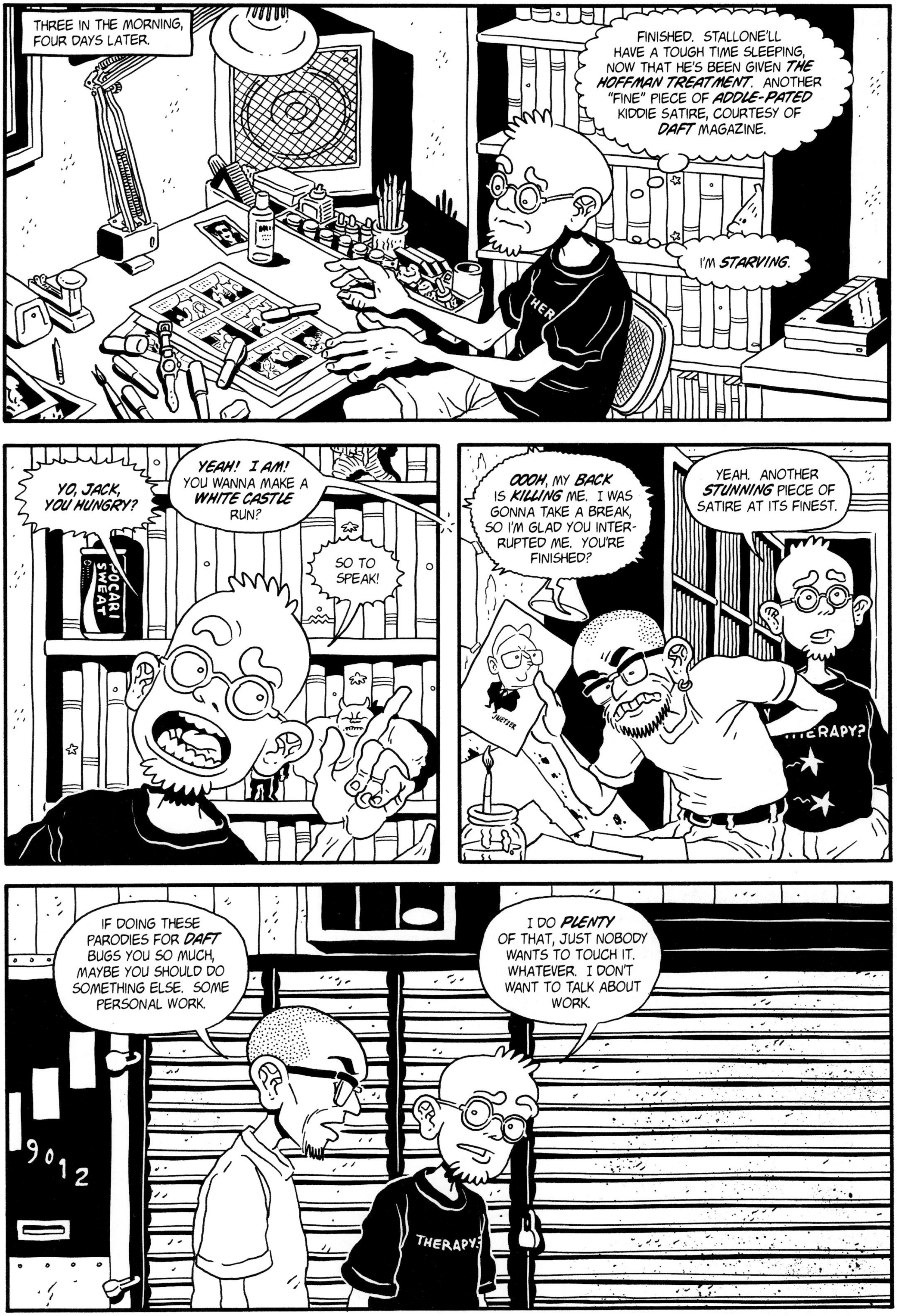
THREE IN THE MORNING, FOUR DAYS LATER.
FINISHED. STALLONE'LL HAVE A TOUGH TIME SLEEPING, NOW THAT HE'S BEEN GIVEN THE HOFFMAN TREATMENT. ANOTHER "FINE" PIECE OF ADDLE-PATED KIDDIE SATIRE, COURTESY OF DAFT MAGAZINE.
I'M STARVING.
YO, JACK, YOU HUNGRY?
YEAH! I AM! YOU WANNA MAKE A WHITE CASTLE RUN?
SO TO SPEAK!
POCARI SWEAT
OOOH, MY BACK IS KILLING ME. I WAS GONNA TAKE A BREAK, SO I'M GLAD YOU INTERRUPTED ME. YOU'RE FINISHED?
YEAH. ANOTHER STUNNING PIECE OF SATIRE AT ITS FINEST.
IF DOING THESE PARODIES FOR DAFT BUGS YOU SO MUCH, MAYBE YOU SHOULD DO SOMETHING ELSE. SOME PERSONAL WORK.
I DO PLENTY OF THAT, JUST NOBODY WANTS TO TOUCH IT. WHATEVER. I DON'T WANT TO TALK ABOUT WORK.
9012
THERAPY?

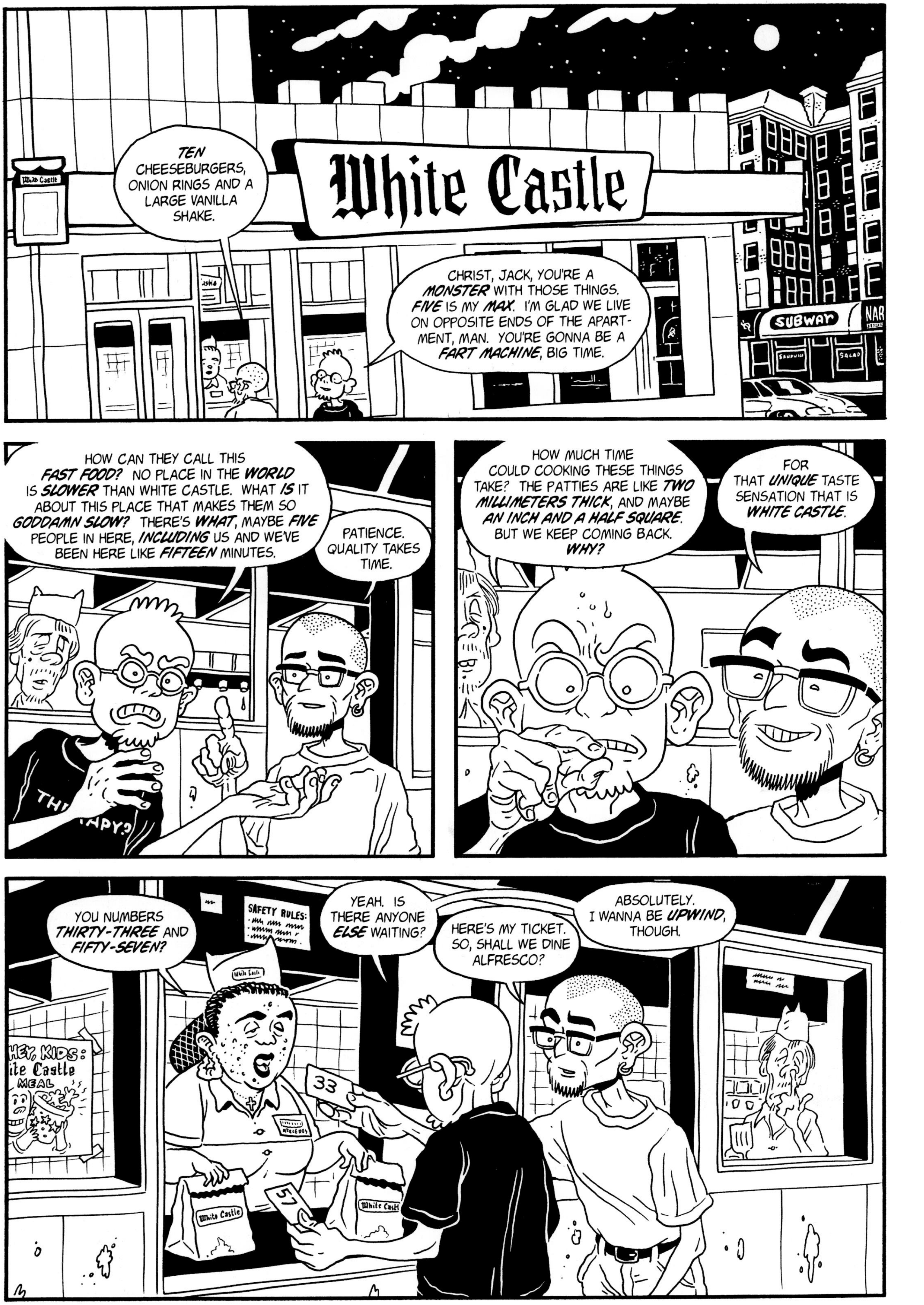
White Castle
TEN CHEESEBURGERS, ONION RINGS AND A LARGE VANILLA SHAKE.
CHRIST, JACK, YOU'RE A MONSTER WITH THOSE THINGS. FIVE IS MY MAX. I'M GLAD WE LIVE ON OPPOSITE ENDS OF THE APARTMENT, MAN. YOU'RE GONNA BE A FART MACHINE, BIG TIME.
SUBWAY
HOW CAN THEY CALL THIS FAST FOOD? NO PLACE IN THE WORLD IS SLOWER THAN WHITE CASTLE. WHAT IS IT ABOUT THIS PLACE THAT MAKES THEM SO GODDAMN SLOW? THERE'S WHAT, MAYBE FIVE PEOPLE IN HERE, INCLUDING US AND WE'VE BEEN HERE LIKE FIFTEEN MINUTES.
PATIENCE. QUALITY TAKES TIME.
HOW MUCH TIME COULD COOKING THESE THINGS TAKE? THE PATTIES ARE LIKE TWO MILLIMETERS THICK, AND MAYBE AN INCH AND A HALF SQUARE. BUT WE KEEP COMING BACK. WHY?
FOR THAT UNIQUE TASTE SENSATION THAT IS WHITE CASTLE.
YOU NUMBERS THIRTY-THREE AND FIFTY-SEVEN?
SAFETY RULES:
YEAH. IS THERE ANYONE ELSE WAITING?
HERE'S MY TICKET. SO, SHALL WE DINE ALFRESCO?
ABSOLUTELY. I WANNA BE UPWIND, THOUGH.
HEY, KIDS: ite Castle MEAL
33
57
White Castle

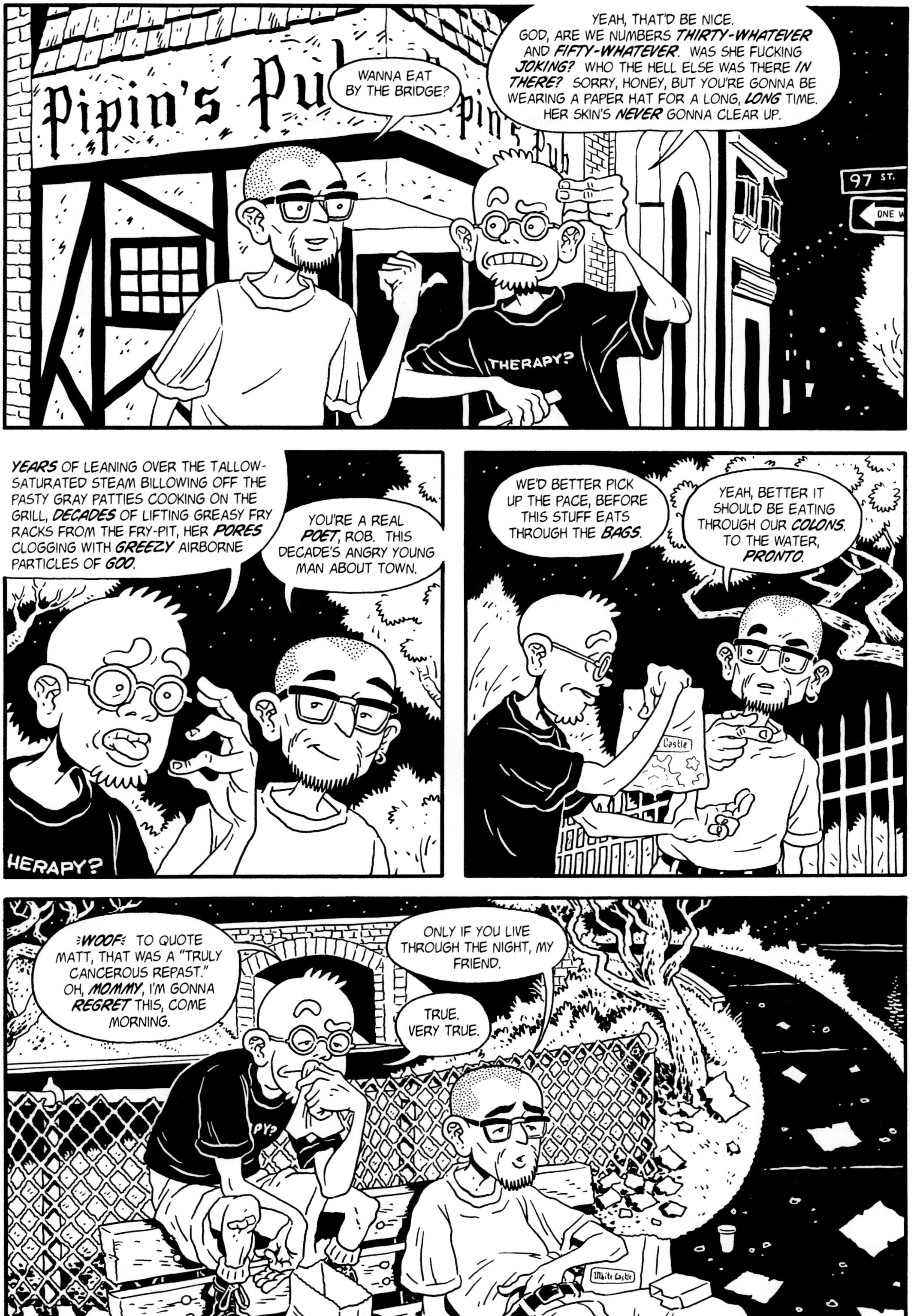
Pipin's Pub
WANNA EAT BY THE BRIDGE?
YEAH, THAT'D BE NICE. GOD, ARE WE NUMBERS THIRTY-WHATEVER AND FIFTY-WHATEVER. WAS SHE FUCKING JOKING? WHO THE HELL ELSE WAS THERE IN THERE? SORRY, HONEY, BUT YOU'RE GONNA BE WEARING A PAPER HAT FOR A LONG, LONG TIME. HER SKIN'S NEVER GONNA CLEAR UP.
97 ST.
ONE W
THERAPY?
YEARS OF LEANING OVER THE TALLOW-SATURATED STEAM BILLOWING OFF THE PASTY GRAY PATTIES COOKING ON THE GRILL, DECADES OF LIFTING GREASY FRY RACKS FROM THE FRY-PIT, HER PORES CLOGGING WITH GREEZY AIRBORNE PARTICLES OF GOO.
YOU'RE A REAL POET, ROB. THIS DECADE'S ANGRY YOUNG MAN ABOUT TOWN.
HERAPY?
WE'D BETTER PICK UP THE PACE, BEFORE THIS STUFF EATS THROUGH THE BAGS.
YEAH, BETTER IT SHOULD BE EATING THROUGH OUR COLONS. TO THE WATER, PRONTO.
Castle
WOOF. TO QUOTE MATT, THAT WAS A "TRULY CANCEROUS REPAST." OH, MOMMY, I'M GONNA REGRET THIS, COME MORNING.
ONLY IF YOU LIVE THROUGH THE NIGHT, MY FRIEND.
TRUE. VERY TRUE.
White Castle

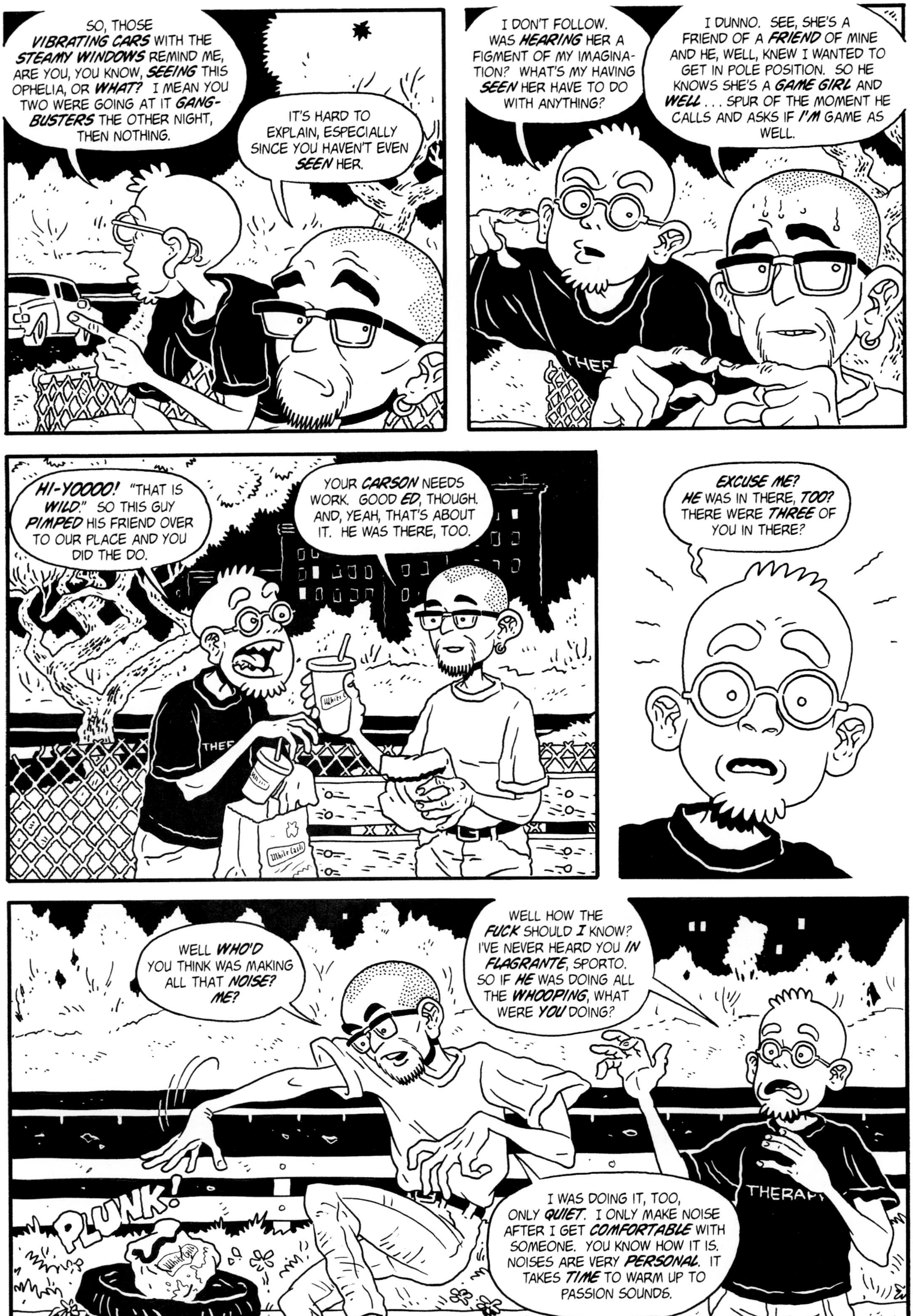
SO, THOSE VIBRATING CARS WITH THE STEAMY WINDOWS REMIND ME, ARE YOU, YOU KNOW, SEEING THIS OPHELIA, OR WHAT? I MEAN YOU TWO WERE GOING AT IT GANGBUSTERS THE OTHER NIGHT, THEN NOTHING.
IT'S HARD TO EXPLAIN, ESPECIALLY SINCE YOU HAVEN'T EVEN SEEN HER.
I DON'T FOLLOW. WAS HEARING HER A FIGMENT OF MY IMAGINATION? WHAT'S MY HAVING SEEN HER HAVE TO DO WITH ANYTHING?
I DUNNO. SEE, SHE'S A FRIEND OF A FRIEND OF MINE AND HE, WELL, KNEW I WANTED TO GET IN POLE POSITION. SO HE KNOWS SHE'S A GAME GIRL AND WELL . . . SPUR OF THE MOMENT HE CALLS AND ASKS IF I'M GAME AS WELL.
HI-YOOOO! "THAT IS WILD." SO THIS GUY PIMPED HIS FRIEND OVER TO OUR PLACE AND YOU DID THE DO.
YOUR CARSON NEEDS WORK. GOOD ED, THOUGH. AND, YEAH, THAT'S ABOUT IT. HE WAS THERE, TOO.
EXCUSE ME? HE WAS IN THERE, TOO? THERE WERE THREE OF YOU IN THERE?
WELL WHO'D YOU THINK WAS MAKING ALL THAT NOISE? ME?
WELL HOW THE FUCK SHOULD I KNOW? I'VE NEVER HEARD YOU IN FLAGRANTE, SPORTO. SO IF HE WAS DOING ALL THE WHOOPING, WHAT WERE YOU DOING?
PLUNK!
I WAS DOING IT, TOO, ONLY QUIET. I ONLY MAKE NOISE AFTER I GET COMFORTABLE WITH SOMEONE. YOU KNOW HOW IT IS. NOISES ARE VERY PERSONAL. IT TAKES TIME TO WARM UP TO PASSION SOUNDS.

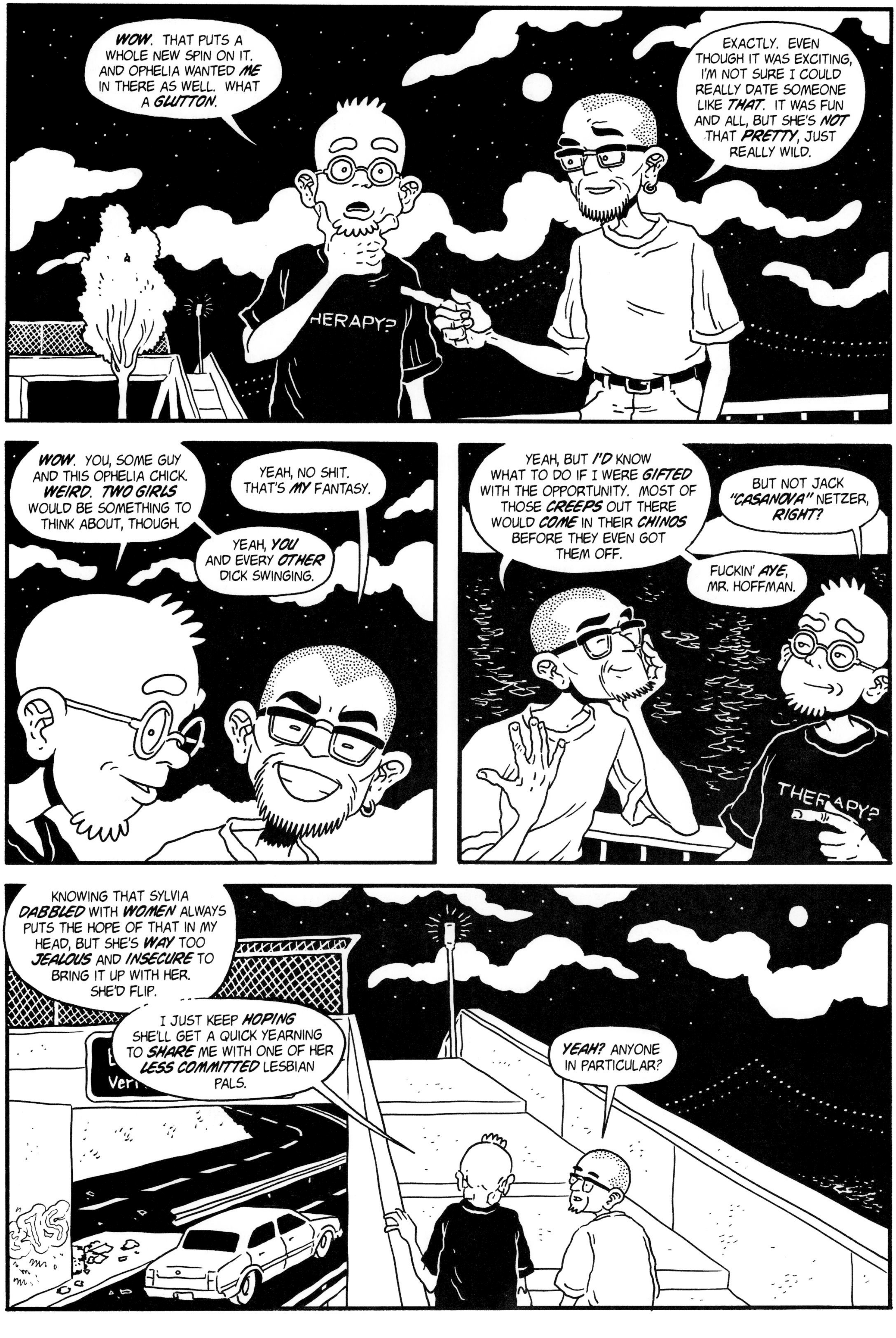
WOW. THAT PUTS A WHOLE NEW SPIN ON IT. AND OPHELIA WANTED ME IN THERE AS WELL. WHAT A GLUTTON.
EXACTLY. EVEN THOUGH IT WAS EXCITING, I'M NOT SURE I COULD REALLY DATE SOMEONE LIKE THAT. IT WAS FUN AND ALL, BUT SHE'S NOT THAT PRETTY, JUST REALLY WILD.
HERAPY?
WOW. YOU, SOME GUY AND THIS OPHELIA CHICK. WEIRD. TWO GIRLS WOULD BE SOMETHING TO THINK ABOUT, THOUGH.
YEAH, NO SHIT. THAT'S MY FANTASY.
YEAH, YOU AND EVERY OTHER DICK SWINGING.
YEAH, BUT I'D KNOW WHAT TO DO IF I WERE GIFTED WITH THE OPPORTUNITY. MOST OF THOSE CREEPS OUT THERE WOULD COME IN THEIR CHINOS BEFORE THEY EVEN GOT THEM OFF.
BUT NOT JACK "CASANOVA" NETZER, RIGHT?
FUCKIN' AYE, MR. HOFFMAN.
THERAPY?
KNOWING THAT SYLVIA DABBLED WITH WOMEN ALWAYS PUTS THE HOPE OF THAT IN MY HEAD, BUT SHE'S WAY TOO JEALOUS AND INSECURE TO BRING IT UP WITH HER. SHE'D FLIP.
I JUST KEEP HOPING SHE'LL GET A QUICK YEARNING TO SHARE ME WITH ONE OF HER LESS COMMITTED LESBIAN PALS.
YEAH? ANYONE IN PARTICULAR?

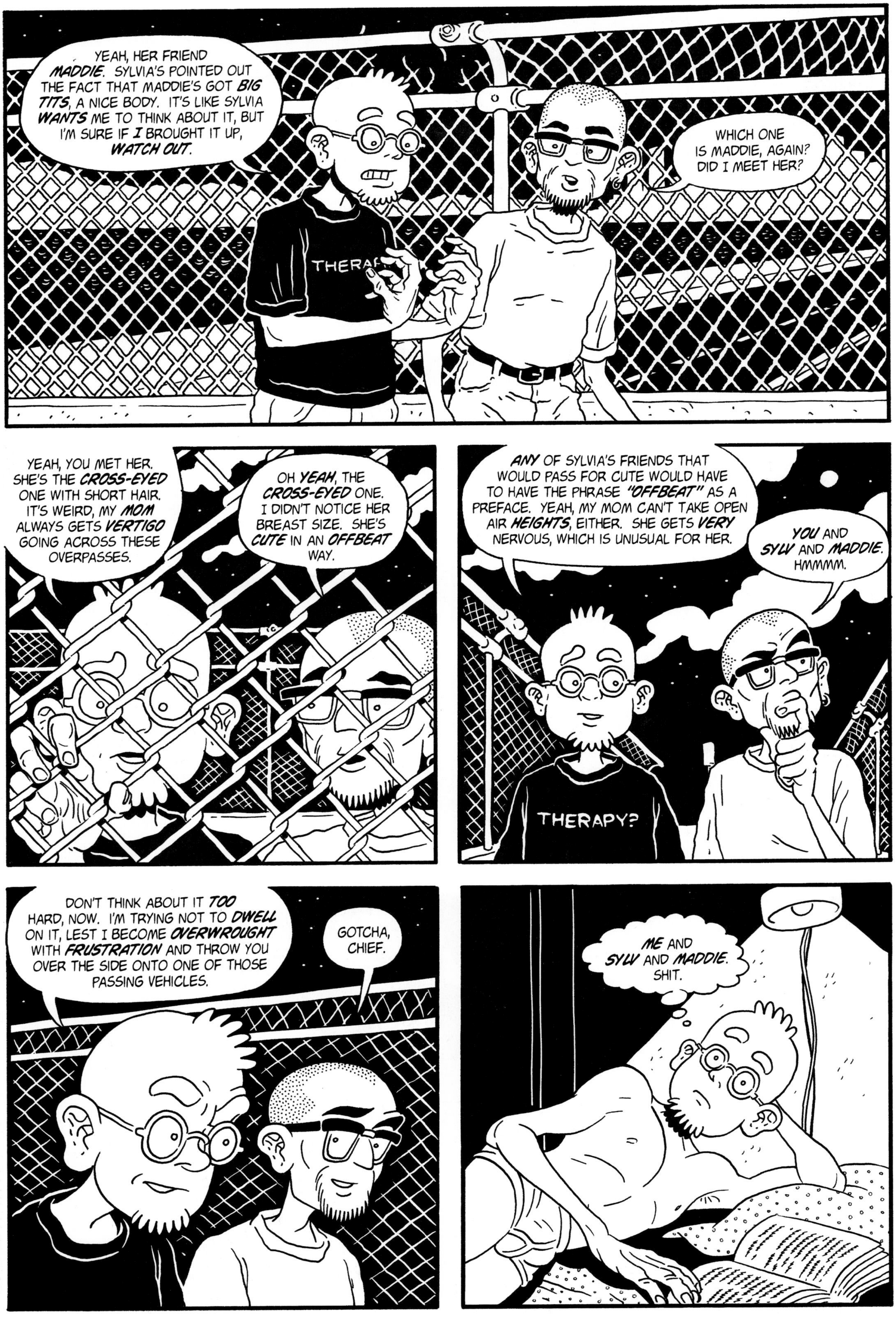
YEAH, HER FRIEND MADDIE. SYLVIA'S POINTED OUT THE FACT THAT MADDIE'S GOT BIG TITS, A NICE BODY. IT'S LIKE SYLVIA WANTS ME TO THINK ABOUT IT, BUT I'M SURE IF I BROUGHT IT UP, WATCH OUT.
WHICH ONE IS MADDIE, AGAIN? DID I MEET HER?
THERAP
YEAH, YOU MET HER. SHE'S THE CROSS-EYED ONE WITH SHORT HAIR. IT'S WEIRD, MY MOM ALWAYS GETS VERTIGO GOING ACROSS THESE OVERPASSES.
OH YEAH, THE CROSS-EYED ONE. I DIDN'T NOTICE HER BREAST SIZE. SHE'S CUTE IN AN OFFBEAT WAY.
ANY OF SYLVIA'S FRIENDS THAT WOULD PASS FOR CUTE WOULD HAVE TO HAVE THE PHRASE "OFFBEAT" AS A PREFACE. YEAH, MY MOM CAN'T TAKE OPEN AIR HEIGHTS, EITHER. SHE GETS VERY NERVOUS, WHICH IS UNUSUAL FOR HER.
YOU AND SYLV AND MADDIE. HMMMM.
THERAPY?
DON'T THINK ABOUT IT TOO HARD, NOW. I'M TRYING NOT TO DWELL ON IT, LEST I BECOME OVERWROUGHT WITH FRUSTRATION AND THROW YOU OVER THE SIDE ONTO ONE OF THOSE PASSING VEHICLES.
GOTCHA, CHIEF.
ME AND SYLV AND MADDIE. SHIT.

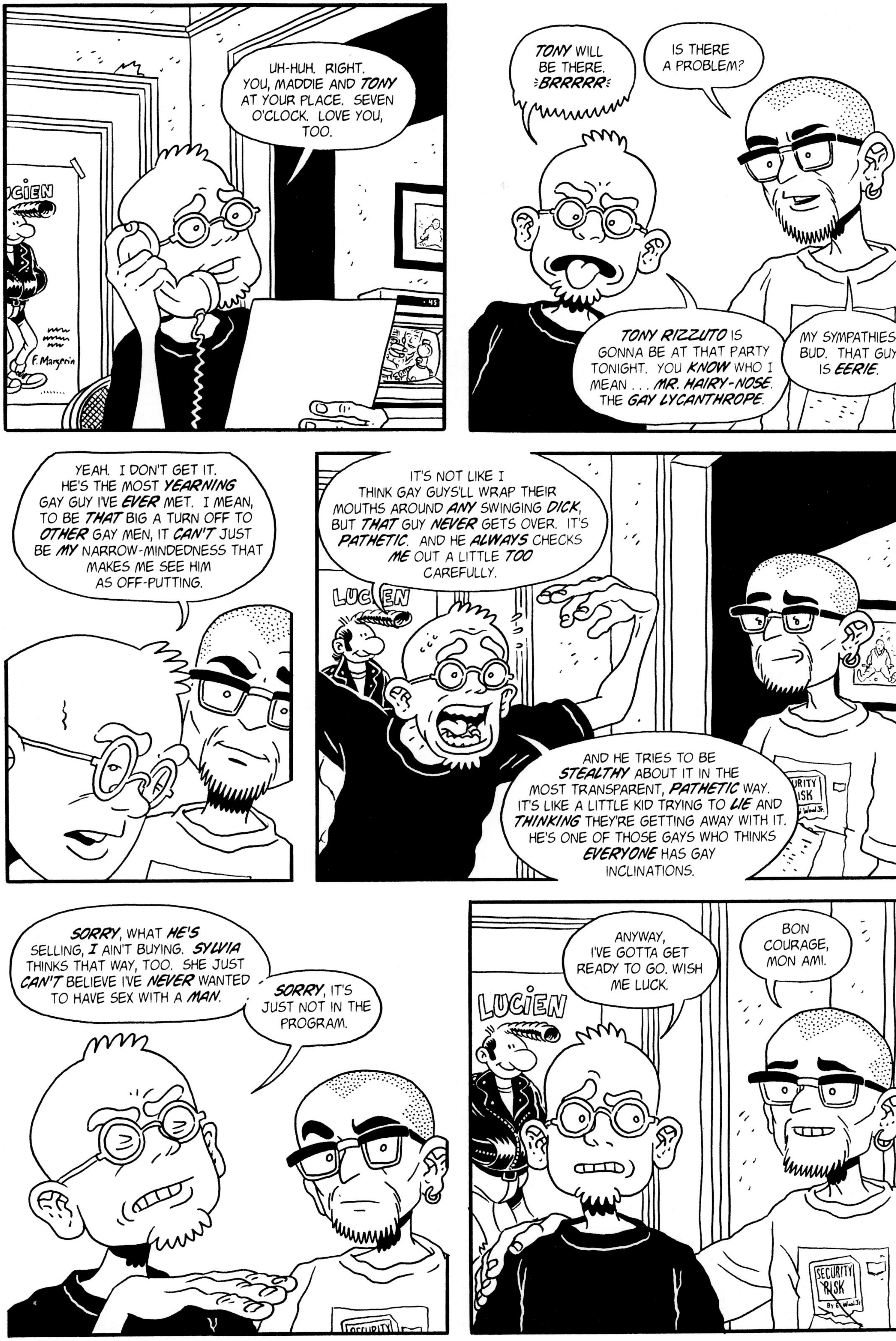
UH-HUH. RIGHT. YOU, MADDIE AND TONY AT YOUR PLACE. SEVEN O'CLOCK. LOVE YOU, TOO.
LUCIEN
F. Margerin
TONY WILL BE THERE. BRRRRR
IS THERE A PROBLEM?
TONY RIZZUTO IS GONNA BE AT THAT PARTY TONIGHT. YOU KNOW WHO I MEAN . . . MR. HAIRY-NOSE. THE GAY LYCANTHROPE.
MY SYMPATHIES, BUD. THAT GUY IS EERIE.
YEAH. I DON'T GET IT. HE'S THE MOST YEARNING GAY GUY I'VE EVER MET. I MEAN, TO BE THAT BIG A TURN OFF TO OTHER GAY MEN, IT CAN'T JUST BE MY NARROW-MINDEDNESS THAT MAKES ME SEE HIM AS OFF-PUTTING.
IT'S NOT LIKE I THINK GAY GUYS'LL WRAP THEIR MOUTHS AROUND ANY SWINGING DICK, BUT THAT GUY NEVER GETS OVER. IT'S PATHETIC. AND HE ALWAYS CHECKS ME OUT A LITTLE TOO CAREFULLY.
AND HE TRIES TO BE STEALTHY ABOUT IT IN THE MOST TRANSPARENT, PATHETIC WAY. IT'S LIKE A LITTLE KID TRYING TO LIE AND THINKING THEY'RE GETTING AWAY WITH IT. HE'S ONE OF THOSE GAYS WHO THINKS EVERYONE HAS GAY INCLINATIONS.
SORRY, WHAT HE'S SELLING, I AIN'T BUYING. SYLVIA THINKS THAT WAY, TOO. SHE JUST CAN'T BELIEVE I'VE NEVER WANTED TO HAVE SEX WITH A MAN.
SORRY, IT'S JUST NOT IN THE PROGRAM.
ANYWAY, I'VE GOTTA GET READY TO GO. WISH ME LUCK.
BON COURAGE, MON AMI.
LUCIEN
SECURITY RISK

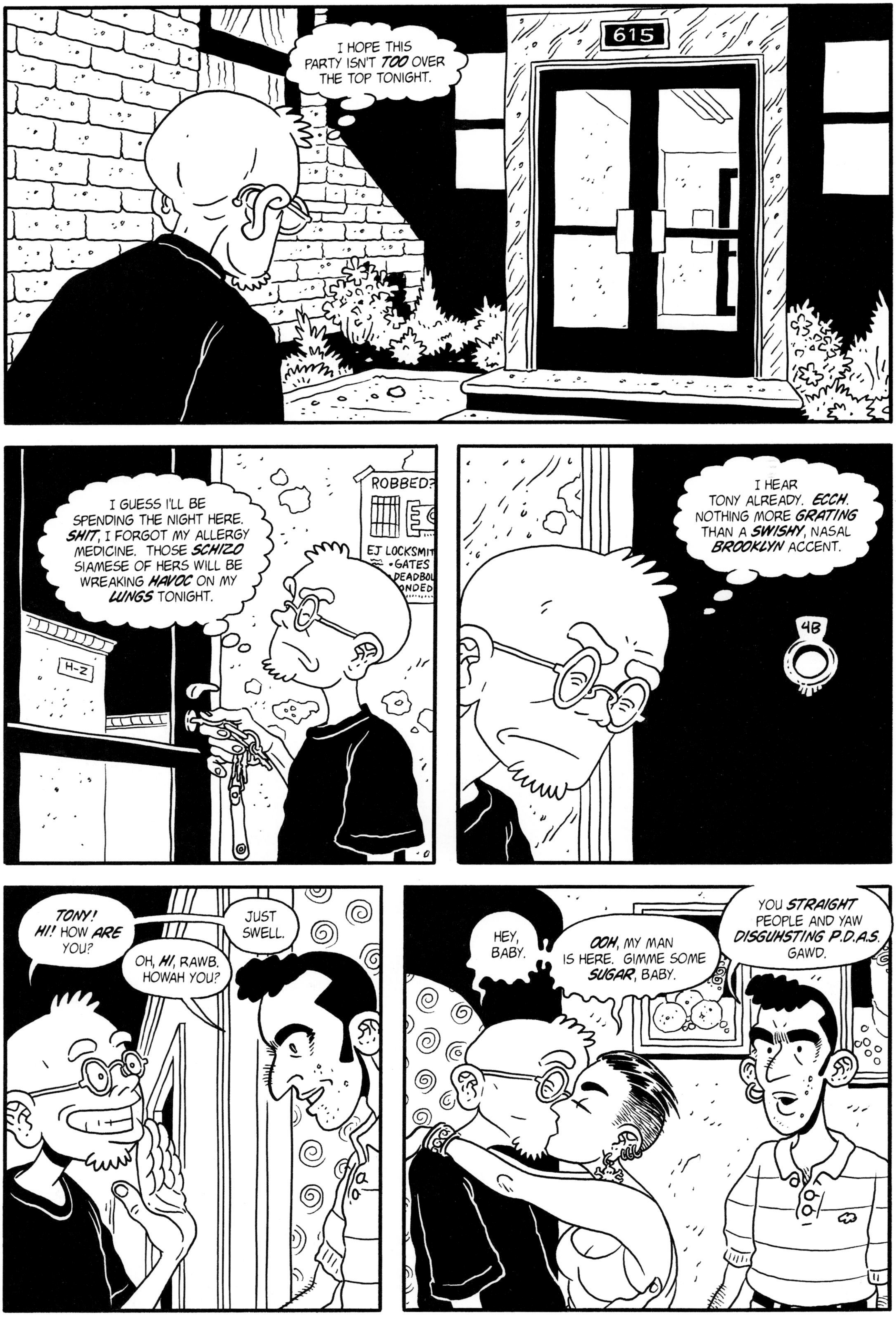

615
I HOPE THIS PARTY ISN'T TOO OVER THE TOP TONIGHT.
I GUESS I'LL BE SPENDING THE NIGHT HERE. SHIT, I FORGOT MY ALLERGY MEDICINE. THOSE SCHIZO SIAMESE OF HERS WILL BE WREAKING HAVOC ON MY LUNGS TONIGHT.
ROBBED?
EJ LOCKSMIT
•GATES
DEADBOL
ONDED
H-Z
I HEAR TONY ALREADY. ECCH. NOTHING MORE GRATING THAN A SWISHY, NASAL BROOKLYN ACCENT.
4B
TONY! HI! HOW ARE YOU?
OH, HI, RAWB. HOWAH YOU?
JUST SWELL.
HEY, BABY.
OOH, MY MAN IS HERE. GIMME SOME SUGAR, BABY.
YOU STRAIGHT PEOPLE AND YAW DISGUHSTING P.D.A.S. GAWD.

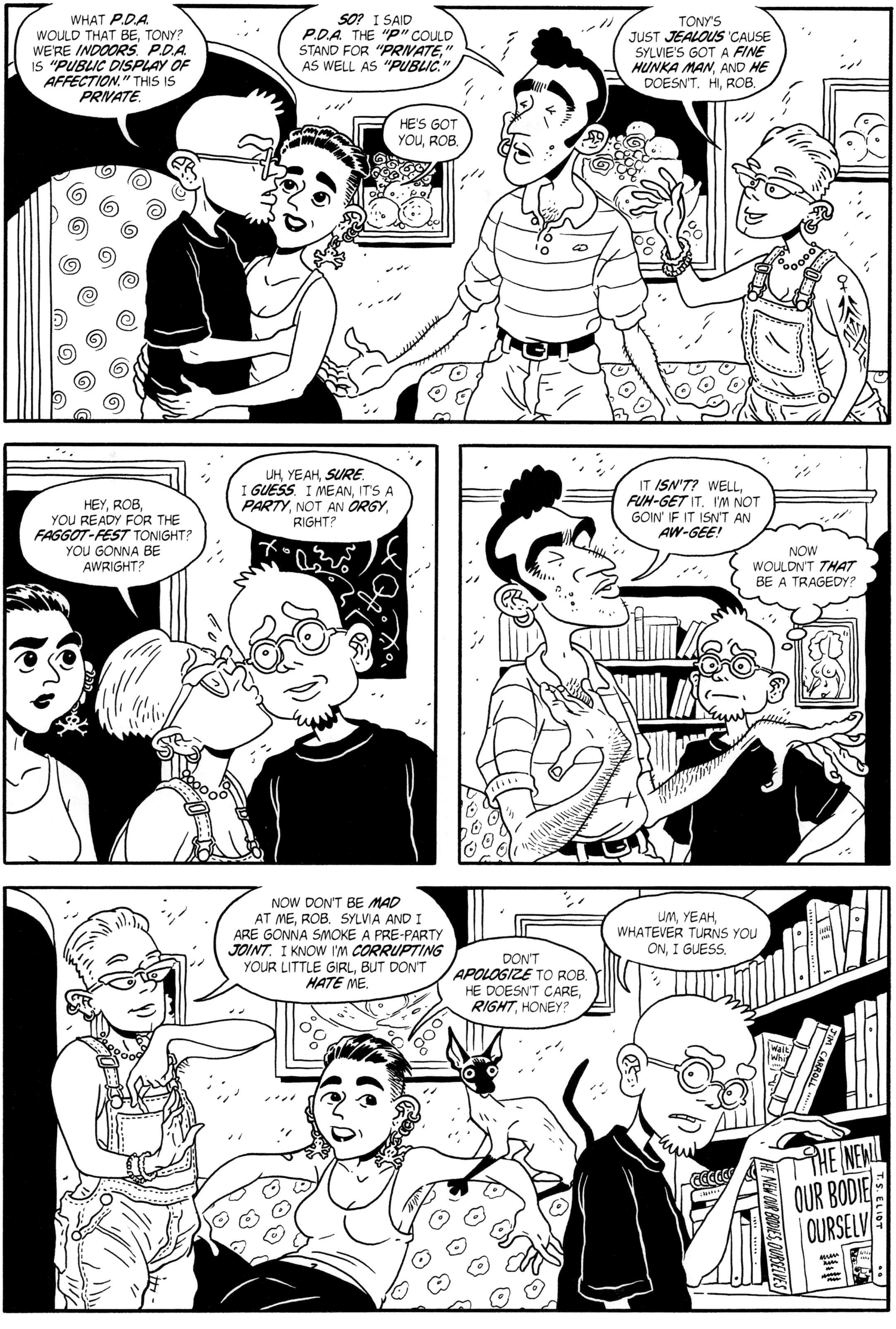
WHAT P.D.A. WOULD THAT BE, TONY? WE'RE INDOORS. P.D.A. IS "PUBLIC DISPLAY OF AFFECTION." THIS IS PRIVATE.
SO? I SAID P.D.A. THE "P" COULD STAND FOR "PRIVATE," AS WELL AS "PUBLIC."
HE'S GOT YOU, ROB.
TONY'S JUST JEALOUS 'CAUSE SYLVIE'S GOT A FINE HUNKA MAN, AND HE DOESN'T. HI, ROB.
HEY, ROB, YOU READY FOR THE FAGGOT-FEST TONIGHT? YOU GONNA BE AWRIGHT?
UH, YEAH, SURE. I GUESS. I MEAN, IT'S A PARTY, NOT AN ORGY, RIGHT?
IT ISN'T? WELL, FUH-GET IT. I'M NOT GOIN' IF IT ISN'T AN AW-GEE!
NOW WOULDN'T THAT BE A TRAGEDY?
NOW DON'T BE MAD AT ME, ROB. SYLVIA AND I ARE GONNA SMOKE A PRE-PARTY JOINT. I KNOW I'M CORRUPTING YOUR LITTLE GIRL, BUT DON'T HATE ME.
DON'T APOLOGIZE TO ROB. HE DOESN'T CARE, RIGHT, HONEY?
UM, YEAH, WHATEVER TURNS YOU ON, I GUESS.
JIM CARROLL
THE NEW OUR BODIE OURSELV
THE NEW OUR BODIES OURSELVES
T.S. ELIOT

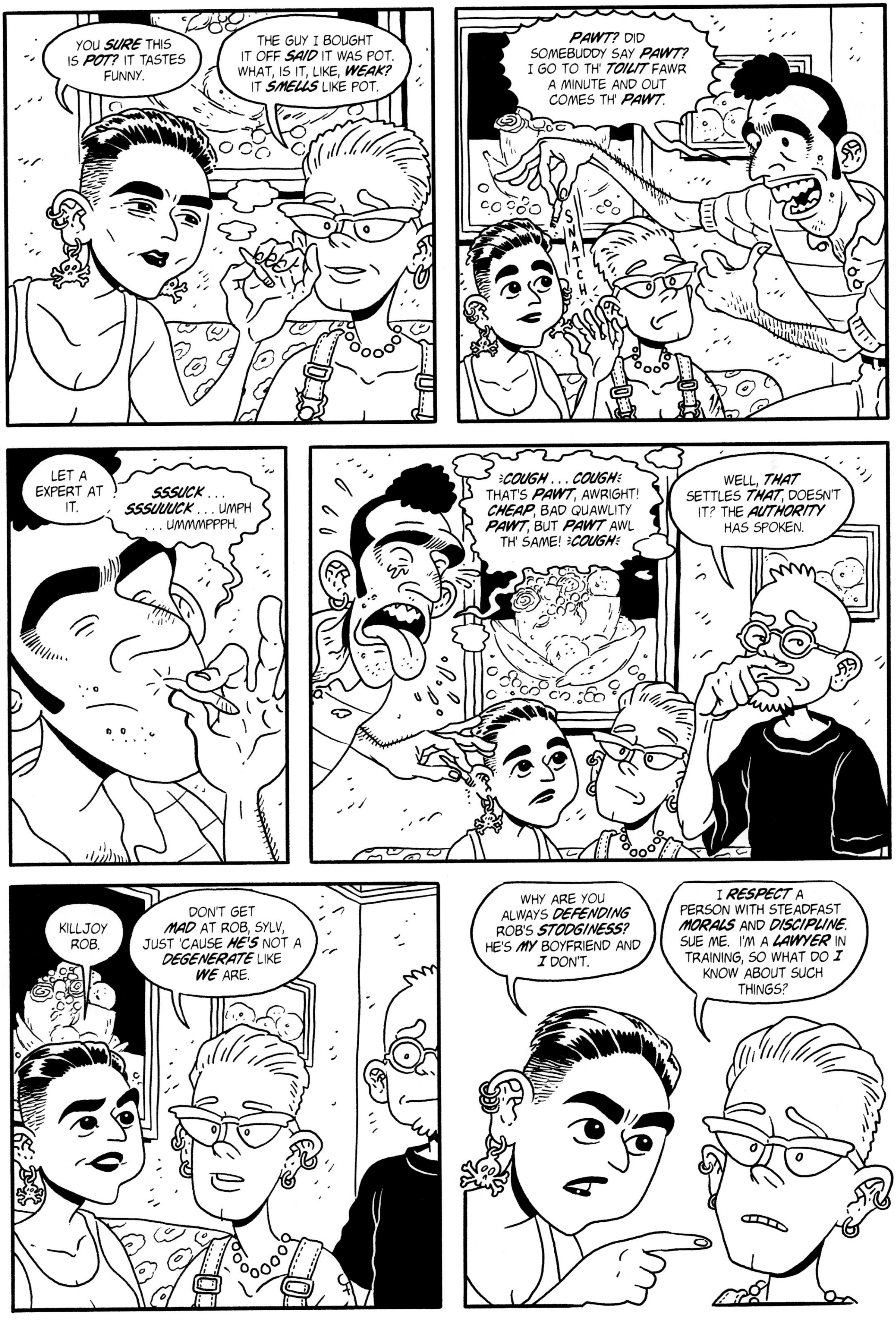

YOU SURE THIS IS POT? IT TASTES FUNNY.
THE GUY I BOUGHT IT OFF SAID IT WAS POT. WHAT, IS IT, LIKE, WEAK? IT SMELLS LIKE POT.
PAWT? DID SOMEBUDDY SAY PAWT? I GO TO TH' TOILIT FAWR A MINUTE AND OUT COMES TH' PAWT.
SNATCH
LET A EXPERT AT IT.
SSSUCK . . . SSSUUUCK . . . UMPH . . . UMMMPPPH.
COUGH . . . COUGH THAT'S PAWT, AWRIGHT! CHEAP, BAD QUAWLITY PAWT, BUT PAWT AWL TH' SAME! COUGH
WELL, THAT SETTLES THAT, DOESN'T IT? THE AUTHORITY HAS SPOKEN.
KILLJOY ROB.
DON'T GET MAD AT ROB, SYLV, JUST 'CAUSE HE'S NOT A DEGENERATE LIKE WE ARE.
WHY ARE YOU ALWAYS DEFENDING ROB'S STODGINESS? HE'S MY BOYFRIEND AND I DON'T.
I RESPECT A PERSON WITH STEADFAST MORALS AND DISCIPLINE. SUE ME. I'M A LAWYER IN TRAINING, SO WHAT DO I KNOW ABOUT SUCH THINGS?

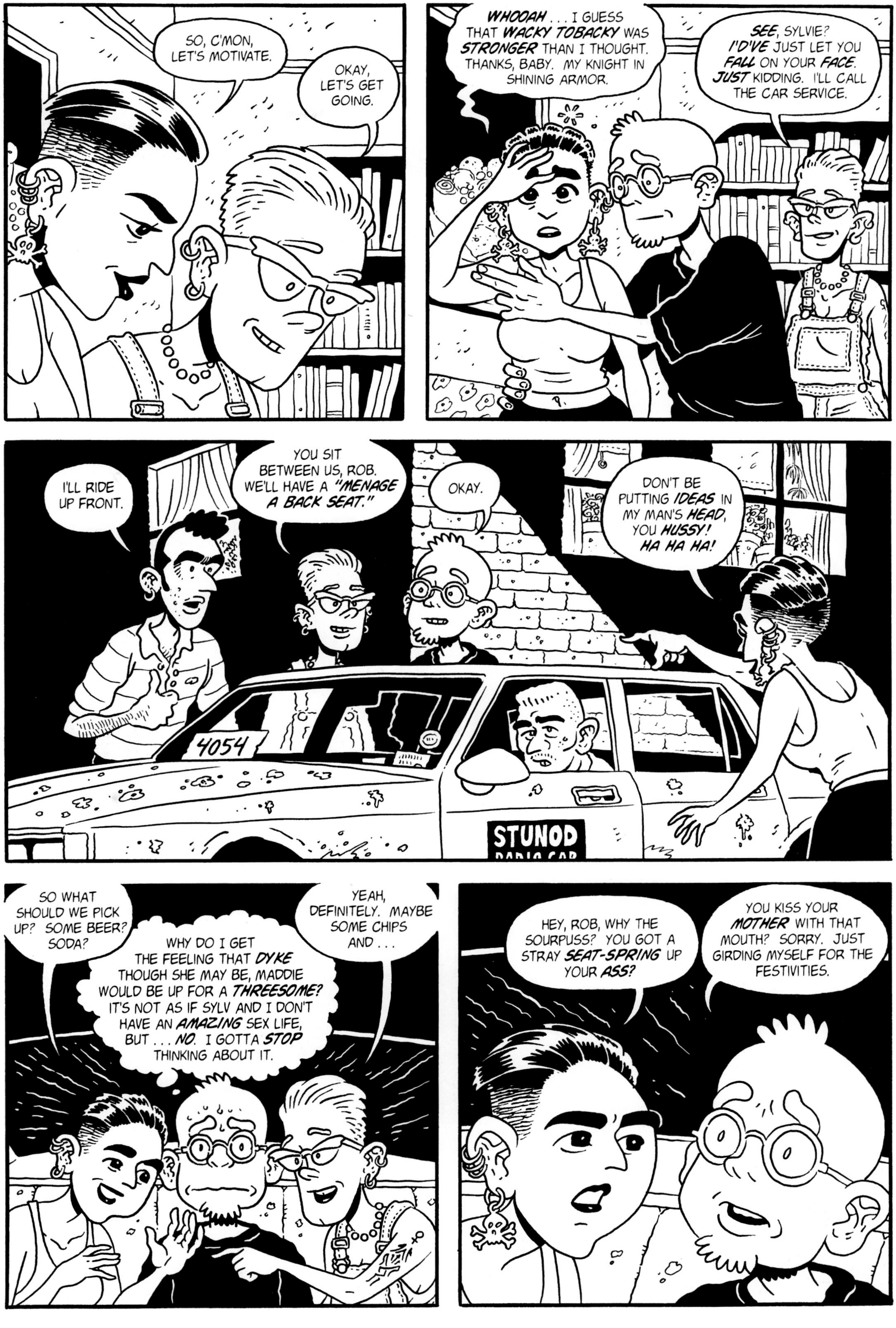
SO, C'MON, LET'S MOTIVATE.
OKAY, LET'S GET GOING.
WHOOAH . . . I GUESS THAT WACKY TOBACKY WAS STRONGER THAN I THOUGHT. THANKS, BABY. MY KNIGHT IN SHINING ARMOR.
SEE, SYLVIE? I'D'VE JUST LET YOU FALL ON YOUR FACE. JUST KIDDING. I'LL CALL THE CAR SERVICE.
I'LL RIDE UP FRONT.
YOU SIT BETWEEN US, ROB. WE'LL HAVE A "MENAGE A BACK SEAT."
OKAY.
DON'T BE PUTTING IDEAS IN MY MAN'S HEAD, YOU HUSSY! HA HA HA!
4054
STUNOD
SO WHAT SHOULD WE PICK UP? SOME BEER? SODA?
WHY DO I GET THE FEELING THAT DYKE THOUGH SHE MAY BE, MADDIE WOULD BE UP FOR A THREESOME? IT'S NOT AS IF SYLV AND I DON'T HAVE AN AMAZING SEX LIFE, BUT . . . NO. I GOTTA STOP THINKING ABOUT IT.
YEAH, DEFINITELY. MAYBE SOME CHIPS AND . . .
HEY, ROB, WHY THE SOURPUSS? YOU GOT A STRAY SEAT-SPRING UP YOUR ASS?
YOU KISS YOUR MOTHER WITH THAT MOUTH? SORRY. JUST GIRDING MYSELF FOR THE FESTIVITIES.

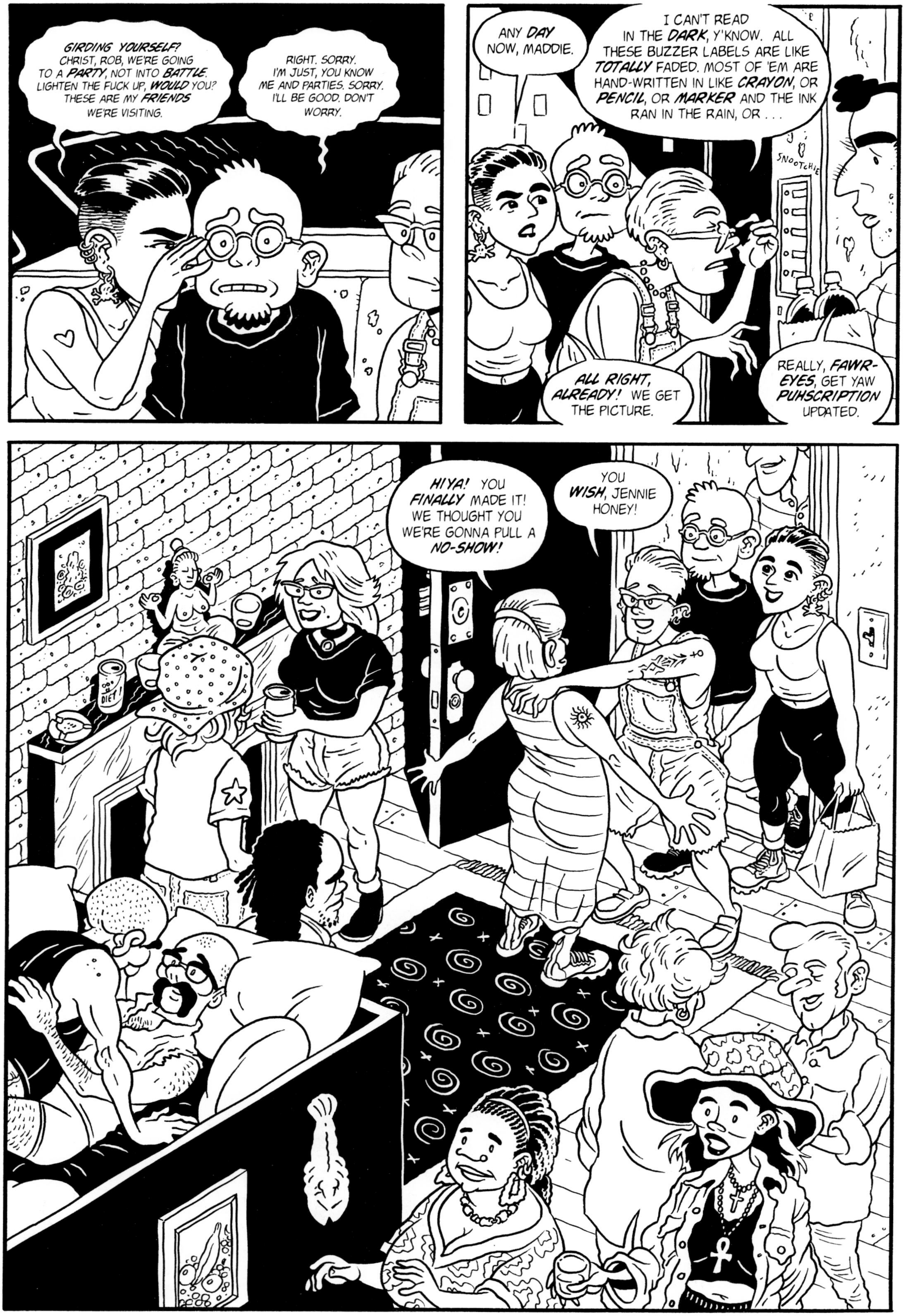
GIRDING YOURSELF? CHRIST, ROB, WE'RE GOING TO A PARTY, NOT INTO BATTLE. LIGHTEN THE FUCK UP, WOULD YOU? THESE ARE MY FRIENDS WE'RE VISITING.
RIGHT. SORRY. I'M JUST, YOU KNOW ME AND PARTIES. SORRY. I'LL BE GOOD. DON'T WORRY.
ANY DAY NOW, MADDIE.
I CAN'T READ IN THE DARK, Y'KNOW. ALL THESE BUZZER LABELS ARE LIKE TOTALLY FADED. MOST OF 'EM ARE HAND-WRITTEN IN LIKE CRAYON, OR PENCIL, OR MARKER AND THE INK RAN IN THE RAIN, OR . . .
SNOOTCHIE
ALL RIGHT, ALREADY! WE GET THE PICTURE.
REALLY, FAWR-EYES, GET YAW PUHSCRIPTION UPDATED.
HIYA! YOU FINALLY MADE IT! WE THOUGHT YOU WE'RE GONNA PULL A NO-SHOW!
YOU WISH, JENNIE HONEY!
DIET

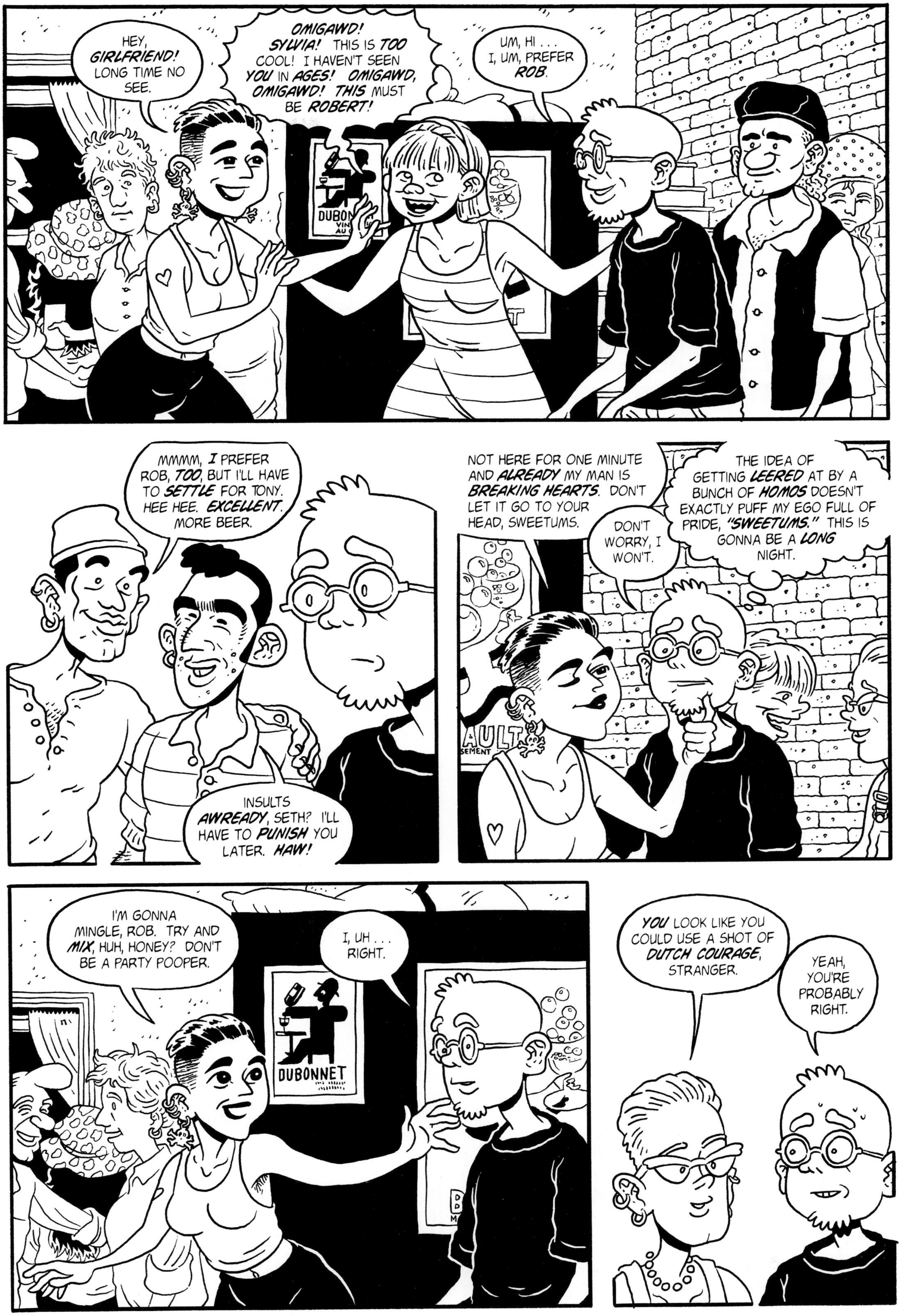
HEY, GIRLFRIEND! LONG TIME NO SEE.
OMIGAWD! SYLVIA! THIS IS TOO COOL! I HAVEN'T SEEN YOU IN AGES! OMIGAWD, OMIGAWD! THIS MUST BE ROBERT!
UM, HI . . . I, UM, PREFER ROB.
DUBONNET
MMMM, I PREFER ROB, TOO, BUT I'LL HAVE TO SETTLE FOR TONY. HEE HEE. EXCELLENT. MORE BEER.
INSULTS AWREADY, SETH? I'LL HAVE TO PUNISH YOU LATER. HAW!
NOT HERE FOR ONE MINUTE AND ALREADY MY MAN IS BREAKING HEARTS. DON'T LET IT GO TO YOUR HEAD, SWEETUMS.
DON'T WORRY, I WON'T.
THE IDEA OF GETTING LEERED AT BY A BUNCH OF HOMOS DOESN'T EXACTLY PUFF MY EGO FULL OF PRIDE, "SWEETUMS." THIS IS GONNA BE A LONG NIGHT.
I'M GONNA MINGLE, ROB. TRY AND MIX, HUH, HONEY? DON'T BE A PARTY POOPER.
I, UH . . . RIGHT.
DUBONNET
YOU LOOK LIKE YOU COULD USE A SHOT OF DUTCH COURAGE, STRANGER.
YEAH, YOU'RE PROBABLY RIGHT.

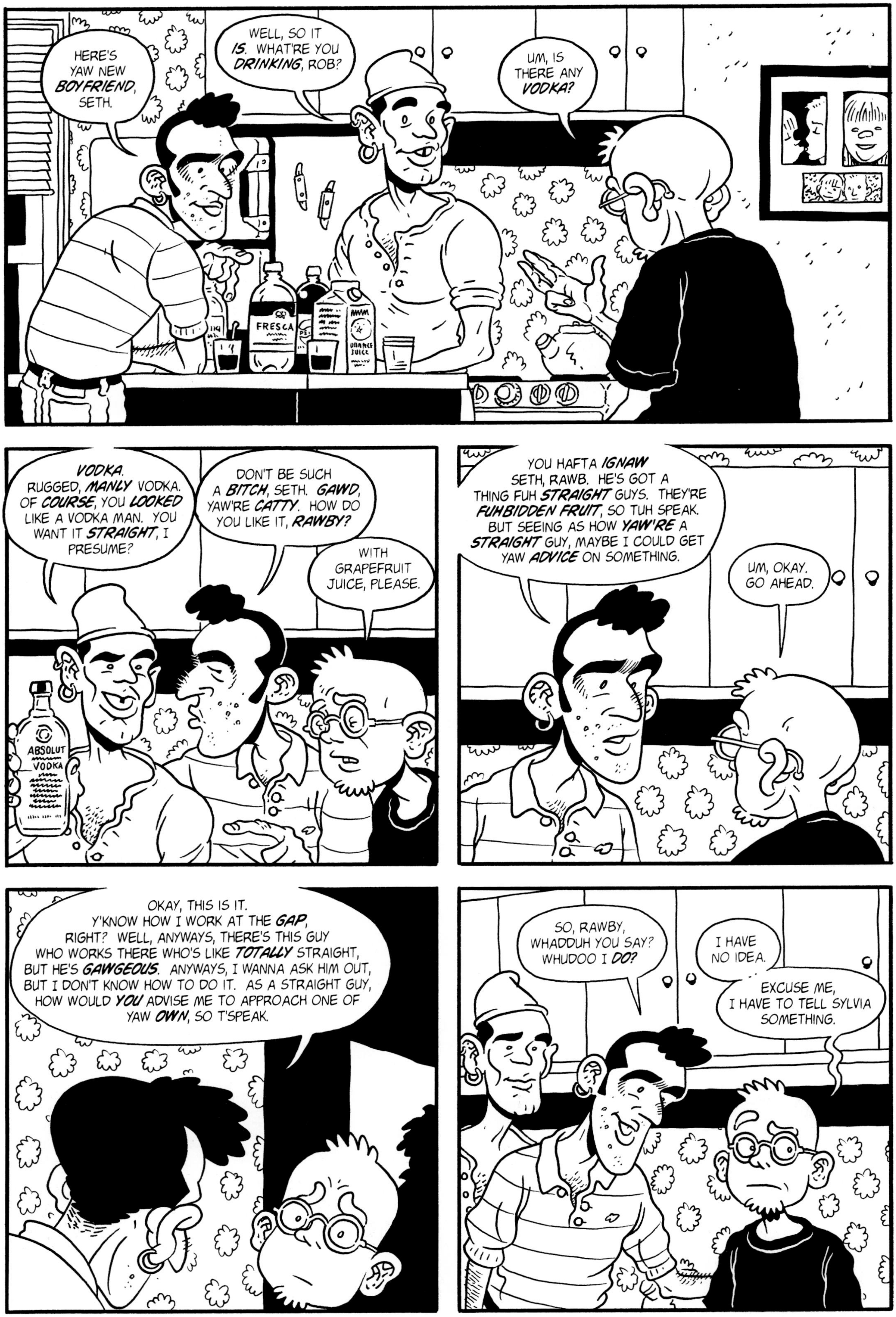
HERE'S YAW NEW BOYFRIEND, SETH.
WELL, SO IT IS. WHAT'RE YOU DRINKING, ROB?
UM, IS THERE ANY VODKA?
FRESCA
ORANGE JUICE
VODKA. RUGGED, MANLY VODKA. OF COURSE, YOU LOOKED LIKE A VODKA MAN. YOU WANT IT STRAIGHT, I PRESUME?
DON'T BE SUCH A BITCH, SETH. GAWD, YAW'RE CATTY. HOW DO YOU LIKE IT, RAWBY?
WITH GRAPEFRUIT JUICE, PLEASE.
ABSOLUT VODKA
YOU HAFTA IGNAW SETH, RAWB. HE'S GOT A THING FUH STRAIGHT GUYS. THEY'RE FUHBIDDEN FRUIT, SO TUH SPEAK. BUT SEEING AS HOW YAW'RE A STRAIGHT GUY, MAYBE I COULD GET YAW ADVICE ON SOMETHING.
UM, OKAY. GO AHEAD.
OKAY, THIS IS IT. Y'KNOW HOW I WORK AT THE GAP, RIGHT? WELL, ANYWAYS, THERE'S THIS GUY WHO WORKS THERE WHO'S LIKE TOTALLY STRAIGHT, BUT HE'S GAWGEOUS. ANYWAYS, I WANNA ASK HIM OUT, BUT I DON'T KNOW HOW TO DO IT. AS A STRAIGHT GUY, HOW WOULD YOU ADVISE ME TO APPROACH ONE OF YAW OWN, SO T'SPEAK.
SO, RAWBY, WHADDUH YOU SAY? WHUDOO I DO?
I HAVE NO IDEA.
EXCUSE ME, I HAVE TO TELL SYLVIA SOMETHING.

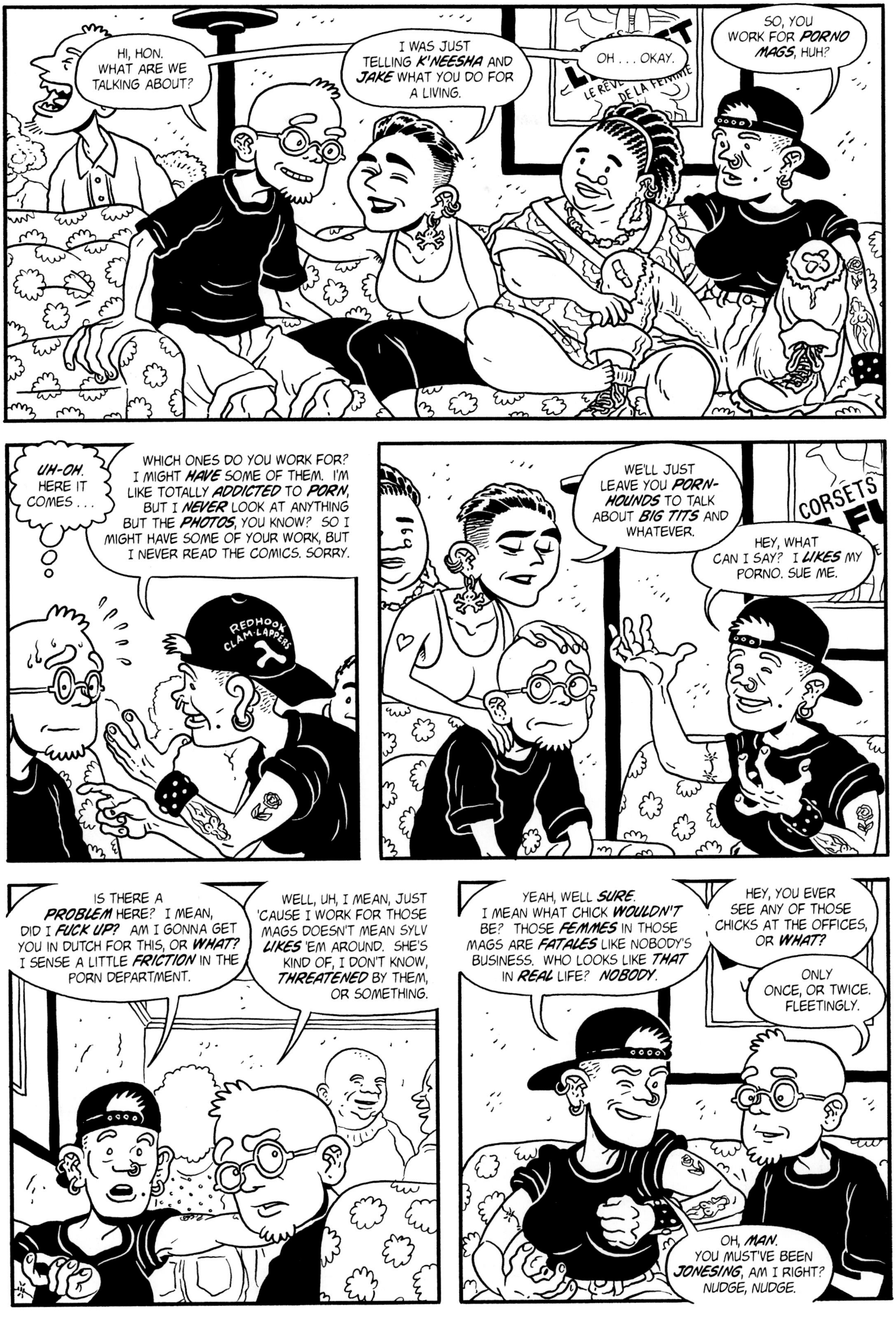
HI, HON. WHAT ARE WE TALKING ABOUT?
I WAS JUST TELLING K'NEESHA AND JAKE WHAT YOU DO FOR A LIVING.
OH . . . OKAY.
SO, YOU WORK FOR PORNO MAGS, HUH?
LE RÊVE DE LA FEMME
UH-OH. HERE IT COMES . . .
WHICH ONES DO YOU WORK FOR? I MIGHT HAVE SOME OF THEM. I'M LIKE TOTALLY ADDICTED TO PORN, BUT I NEVER LOOK AT ANYTHING BUT THE PHOTOS, YOU KNOW? SO I MIGHT HAVE SOME OF YOUR WORK, BUT I NEVER READ THE COMICS. SORRY.
REDHOOK CLAM-LAPPERS
WE'LL JUST LEAVE YOU PORN-HOUNDS TO TALK ABOUT BIG TITS AND WHATEVER.
CORSETS
HEY, WHAT CAN I SAY? I LIKES MY PORNO. SUE ME.
IS THERE A PROBLEM HERE? I MEAN, DID I FUCK UP? AM I GONNA GET YOU IN DUTCH FOR THIS, OR WHAT? I SENSE A LITTLE FRICTION IN THE PORN DEPARTMENT.
WELL, UH, I MEAN, JUST 'CAUSE I WORK FOR THOSE MAGS DOESN'T MEAN SYLV LIKES 'EM AROUND. SHE'S KIND OF, I DON'T KNOW, THREATENED BY THEM, OR SOMETHING.
YEAH, WELL SURE. I MEAN WHAT CHICK WOULDN'T BE? THOSE FEMMES IN THOSE MAGS ARE FATALES LIKE NOBODY'S BUSINESS. WHO LOOKS LIKE THAT IN REAL LIFE? NOBODY.
HEY, YOU EVER SEE ANY OF THOSE CHICKS AT THE OFFICES, OR WHAT?
ONLY ONCE, OR TWICE. FLEETINGLY.
OH, MAN. YOU MUST'VE BEEN JONESING, AM I RIGHT? NUDGE, NUDGE.

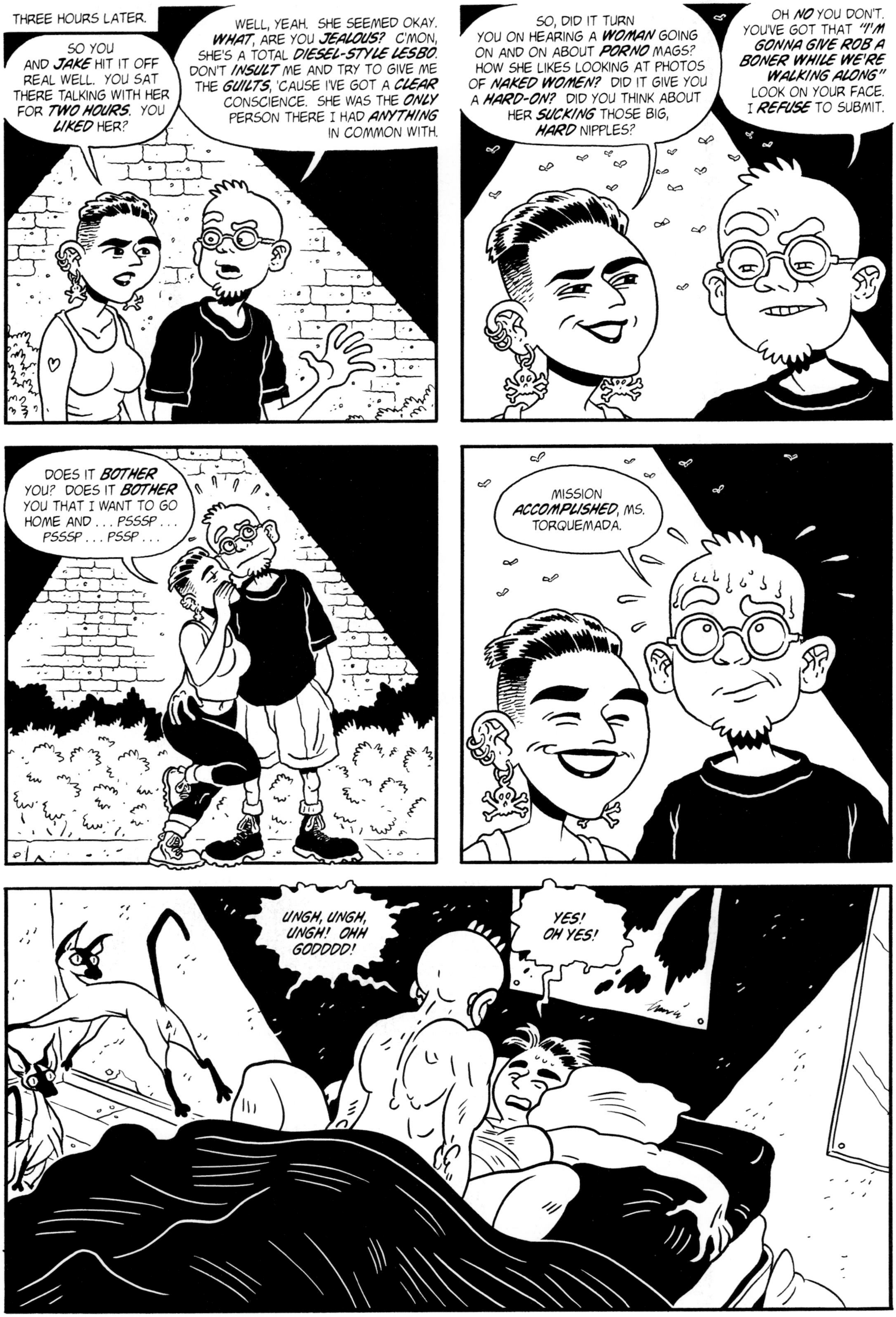
THREE HOURS LATER.
SO YOU AND JAKE HIT IT OFF REAL WELL. YOU SAT THERE TALKING WITH HER FOR TWO HOURS. YOU LIKED HER?
WELL, YEAH. SHE SEEMED OKAY. WHAT, ARE YOU JEALOUS? C'MON, SHE'S A TOTAL DIESEL-STYLE LESBO. DON'T INSULT ME AND TRY TO GIVE ME THE GUILTS, 'CAUSE I'VE GOT A CLEAR CONSCIENCE. SHE WAS THE ONLY PERSON THERE I HAD ANYTHING IN COMMON WITH.
SO, DID IT TURN YOU ON HEARING A WOMAN GOING ON AND ON ABOUT PORNO MAGS? HOW SHE LIKES LOOKING AT PHOTOS OF NAKED WOMEN? DID IT GIVE YOU A HARD-ON? DID YOU THINK ABOUT HER SUCKING THOSE BIG, HARD NIPPLES?
OH NO YOU DON'T. YOU'VE GOT THAT "I'M GONNA GIVE ROB A BONER WHILE WE'RE WALKING ALONG" LOOK ON YOUR FACE. I REFUSE TO SUBMIT.
DOES IT BOTHER YOU? DOES IT BOTHER YOU THAT I WANT TO GO HOME AND . . . PSSSP . . . PSSSP . . . PSSP . . .
MISSION ACCOMPLISHED, MS. TORQUEMADA.
UNGH, UNGH, UNGH! OHH GODDDD!
YES! OH YES!

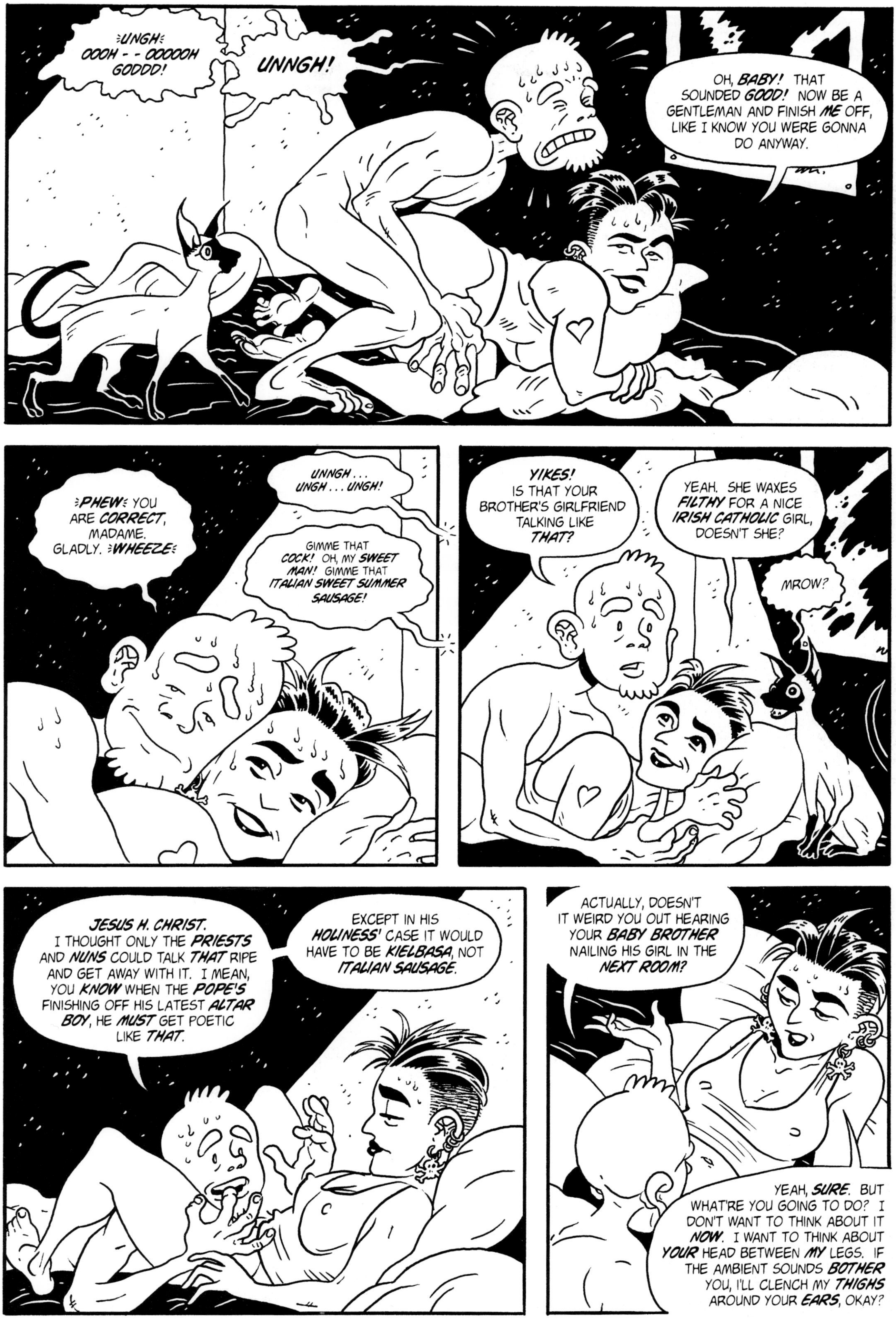

UNGH OOOH - - OOOOOH GODDD!
UNNGH!
OH, BABY! THAT SOUNDED GOOD! NOW BE A GENTLEMAN AND FINISH ME OFF, LIKE I KNOW YOU WERE GONNA DO ANYWAY.
PHEW YOU ARE CORRECT, MADAME. GLADLY. WHEEZE
UNNGH . . . UNGH . . . UNGH!
GIMME THAT COCK! OH, MY SWEET MAN! GIMME THAT ITALIAN SWEET SUMMER SAUSAGE!
YIKES! IS THAT YOUR BROTHER'S GIRLFRIEND TALKING LIKE THAT?
YEAH. SHE WAXES FILTHY FOR A NICE IRISH CATHOLIC GIRL, DOESN'T SHE?
MROW?
JESUS H. CHRIST. I THOUGHT ONLY THE PRIESTS AND NUNS COULD TALK THAT RIPE AND GET AWAY WITH IT. I MEAN, YOU KNOW WHEN THE POPE'S FINISHING OFF HIS LATEST ALTAR BOY, HE MUST GET POETIC LIKE THAT.
EXCEPT IN HIS HOLINESS' CASE IT WOULD HAVE TO BE KIELBASA, NOT ITALIAN SAUSAGE.
ACTUALLY, DOESN'T IT WEIRD YOU OUT HEARING YOUR BABY BROTHER NAILING HIS GIRL IN THE NEXT ROOM?
YEAH, SURE. BUT WHAT'RE YOU GOING TO DO? I DON'T WANT TO THINK ABOUT IT NOW. I WANT TO THINK ABOUT YOUR HEAD BETWEEN MY LEGS. IF THE AMBIENT SOUNDS BOTHER YOU, I'LL CLENCH MY THIGHS AROUND YOUR EARS, OKAY?

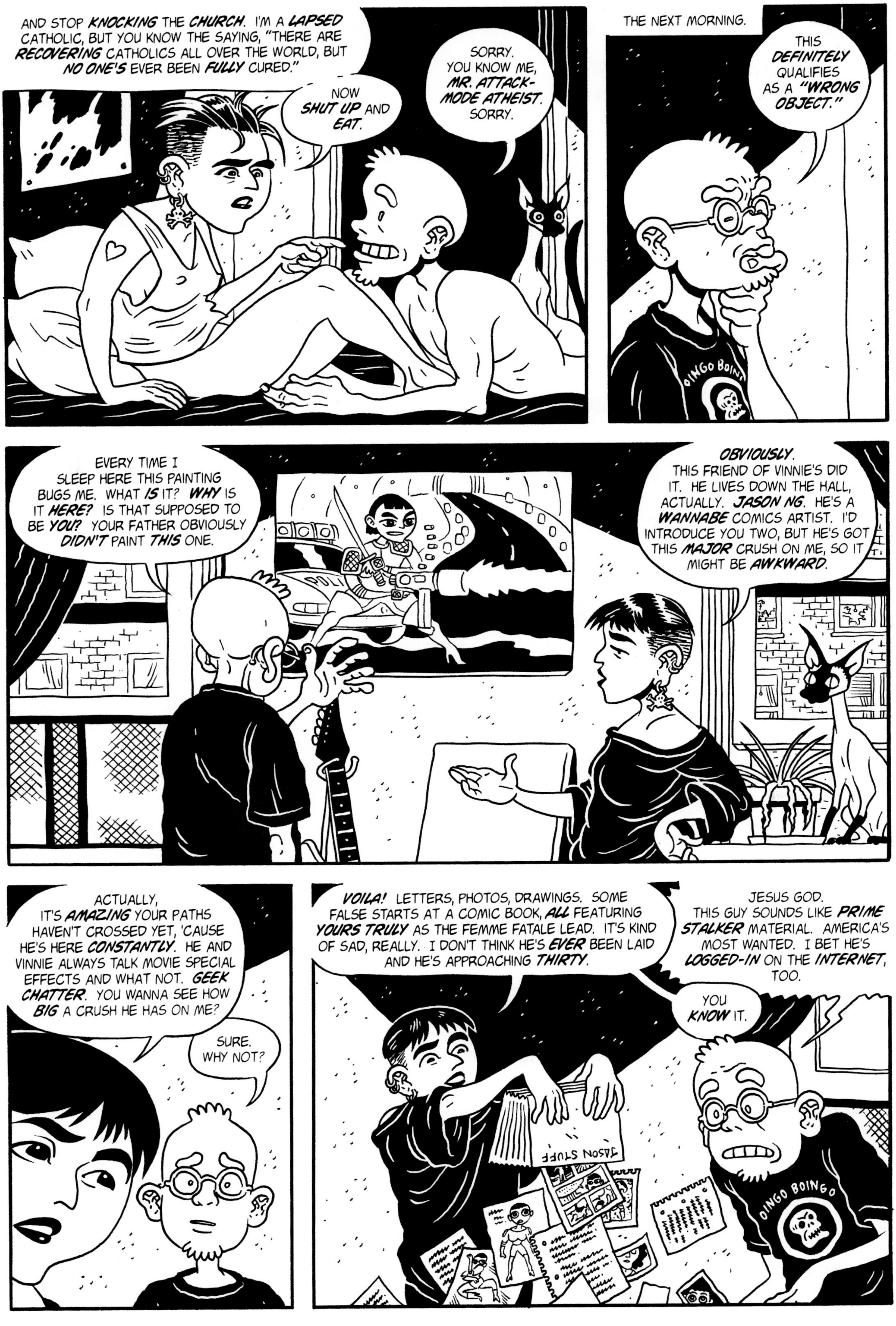

AND STOP KNOCKING THE CHURCH. I'M A LAPSED CATHOLIC, BUT YOU KNOW THE SAYING, "THERE ARE RECOVERING CATHOLICS ALL OVER THE WORLD, BUT NO ONE'S EVER BEEN FULLY CURED."
NOW SHUT UP AND EAT.
SORRY. YOU KNOW ME, MR. ATTACK-MODE ATHEIST. SORRY.
THE NEXT MORNING.
THIS DEFINITELY QUALIFIES AS A "WRONG OBJECT."
OINGO BOINGO
EVERY TIME I SLEEP HERE THIS PAINTING BUGS ME. WHAT IS IT? WHY IS IT HERE? IS THAT SUPPOSED TO BE YOU? YOUR FATHER OBVIOUSLY DIDN'T PAINT THIS ONE.
OBVIOUSLY. THIS FRIEND OF VINNIE'S DID IT. HE LIVES DOWN THE HALL, ACTUALLY. JASON NG. HE'S A WANNABE COMICS ARTIST. I'D INTRODUCE YOU TWO, BUT HE'S GOT THIS MAJOR CRUSH ON ME, SO IT MIGHT BE AWKWARD.
ACTUALLY, IT'S AMAZING YOUR PATHS HAVEN'T CROSSED YET, 'CAUSE HE'S HERE CONSTANTLY. HE AND VINNIE ALWAYS TALK MOVIE SPECIAL EFFECTS AND WHAT NOT. GEEK CHATTER. YOU WANNA SEE HOW BIG A CRUSH HE HAS ON ME?
SURE. WHY NOT?
VOILA! LETTERS, PHOTOS, DRAWINGS. SOME FALSE STARTS AT A COMIC BOOK, ALL FEATURING YOURS TRULY AS THE FEMME FATALE LEAD. IT'S KIND OF SAD, REALLY. I DON'T THINK HE'S EVER BEEN LAID AND HE'S APPROACHING THIRTY.
JESUS GOD. THIS GUY SOUNDS LIKE PRIME STALKER MATERIAL. AMERICA'S MOST WANTED. I BET HE'S LOGGED-IN ON THE INTERNET, TOO.
YOU KNOW IT.
JASON STUFF
OINGO BOINGO

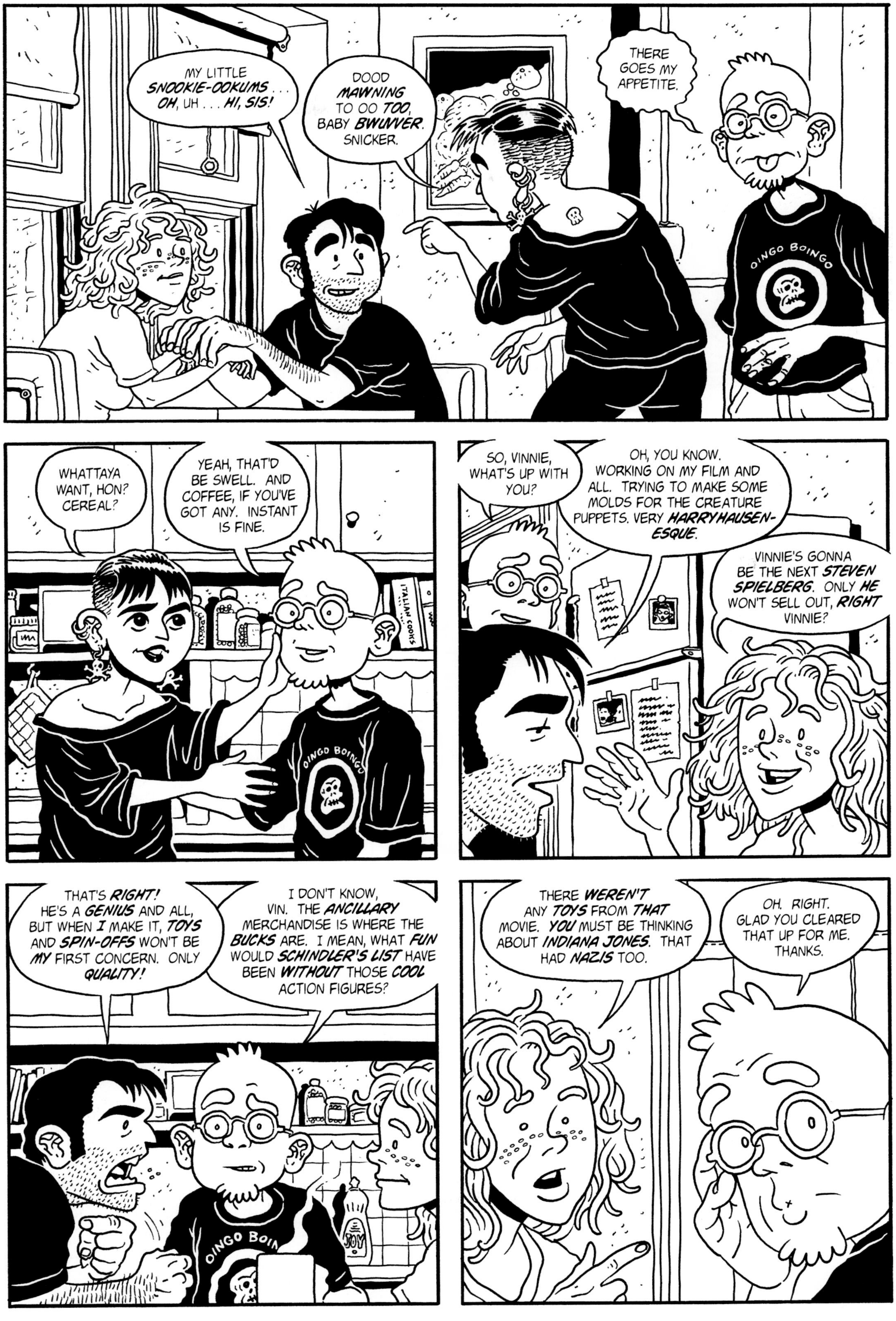
MY LITTLE SNOOKIE-OOKUMS . . . OH, UH . . . HI, SIS!
DOOD MAWNING TO OO TOO, BABY BWUVVER. SNICKER.
THERE GOES MY APPETITE.
WHATTAYA WANT, HON? CEREAL?
YEAH, THAT'D BE SWELL. AND COFFEE, IF YOU'VE GOT ANY. INSTANT IS FINE.
ITALIAN COOKS
OINGO BOINGO
SO, VINNIE, WHAT'S UP WITH YOU?
OH, YOU KNOW. WORKING ON MY FILM AND ALL. TRYING TO MAKE SOME MOLDS FOR THE CREATURE PUPPETS. VERY HARRYHAUSEN-ESQUE.
VINNIE'S GONNA BE THE NEXT STEVEN SPIELBERG. ONLY HE WON'T SELL OUT, RIGHT VINNIE?
THAT'S RIGHT! HE'S A GENIUS AND ALL, BUT WHEN I MAKE IT, TOYS AND SPIN-OFFS WON'T BE MY FIRST CONCERN. ONLY QUALITY!
I DON'T KNOW, VIN. THE ANCILLARY MERCHANDISE IS WHERE THE BUCKS ARE. I MEAN, WHAT FUN WOULD SCHINDLER'S LIST HAVE BEEN WITHOUT THOSE COOL ACTION FIGURES?
JOY
THERE WEREN'T ANY TOYS FROM THAT MOVIE. YOU MUST BE THINKING ABOUT INDIANA JONES. THAT HAD NAZIS TOO.
OH. RIGHT. GLAD YOU CLEARED THAT UP FOR ME. THANKS.

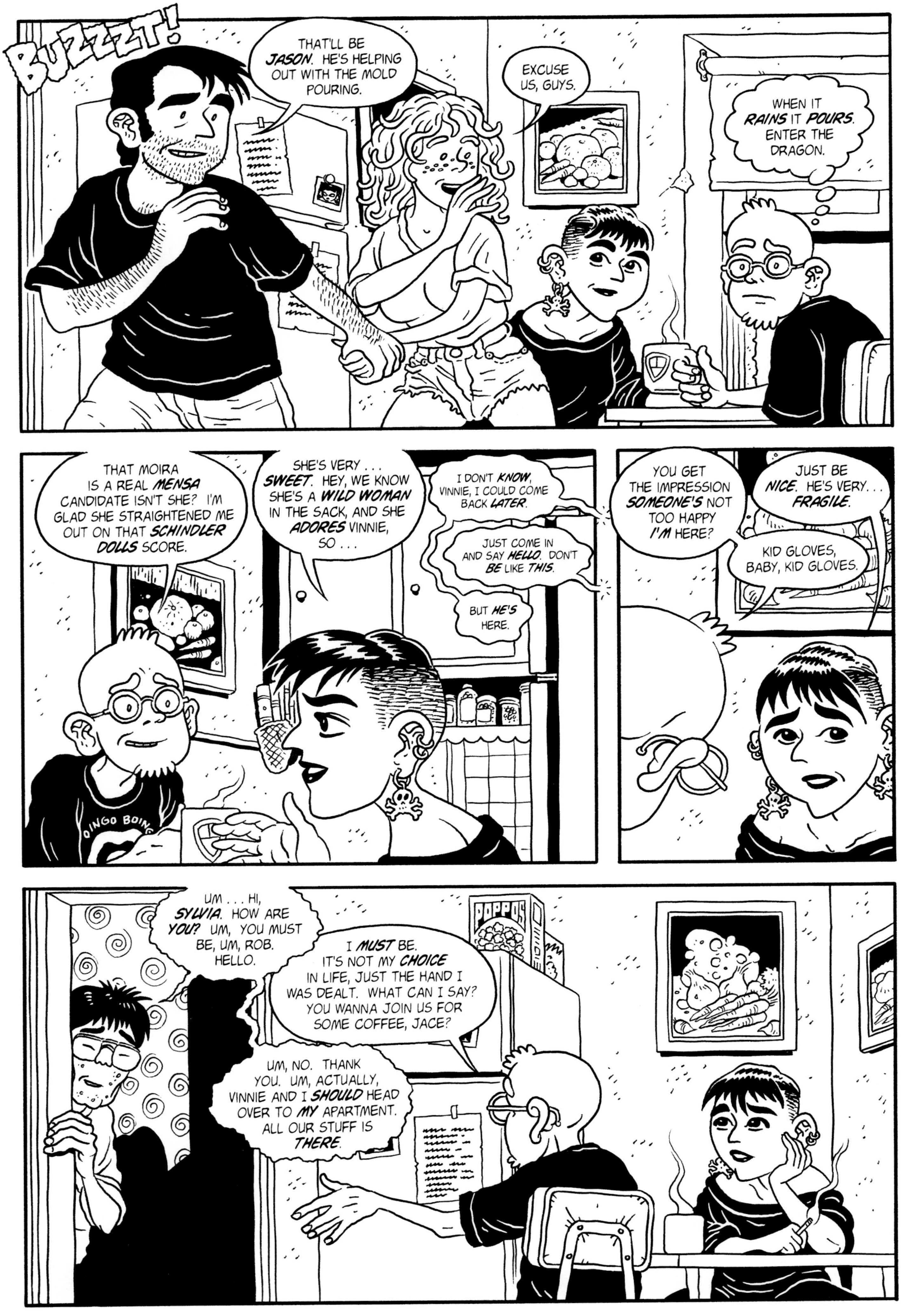
BUZZZT!
THAT'LL BE JASON. HE'S HELPING OUT WITH THE MOLD POURING.
EXCUSE US, GUYS.
WHEN IT RAINS IT POURS. ENTER THE DRAGON.
THAT MOIRA IS A REAL MENSA CANDIDATE ISN'T SHE? I'M GLAD SHE STRAIGHTENED ME OUT ON THAT SCHINDLER DOLLS SCORE.
SHE'S VERY . . . SWEET. HEY, WE KNOW SHE'S A WILD WOMAN IN THE SACK, AND SHE ADORES VINNIE, SO . . .
I DON'T KNOW, VINNIE, I COULD COME BACK LATER.
JUST COME IN AND SAY HELLO. DON'T BE LIKE THIS.
BUT HE'S HERE.
OINGO BOING
YOU GET THE IMPRESSION SOMEONE'S NOT TOO HAPPY I'M HERE?
JUST BE NICE. HE'S VERY... FRAGILE.
KID GLOVES, BABY, KID GLOVES.
UM . . . HI, SYLVIA. HOW ARE YOU? UM, YOU MUST BE, UM, ROB. HELLO.
I MUST BE. IT'S NOT MY CHOICE IN LIFE, JUST THE HAND I WAS DEALT. WHAT CAN I SAY? YOU WANNA JOIN US FOR SOME COFFEE, JACE?
UM, NO. THANK YOU. UM, ACTUALLY, VINNIE AND I SHOULD HEAD OVER TO MY APARTMENT. ALL OUR STUFF IS THERE.
POPPOS

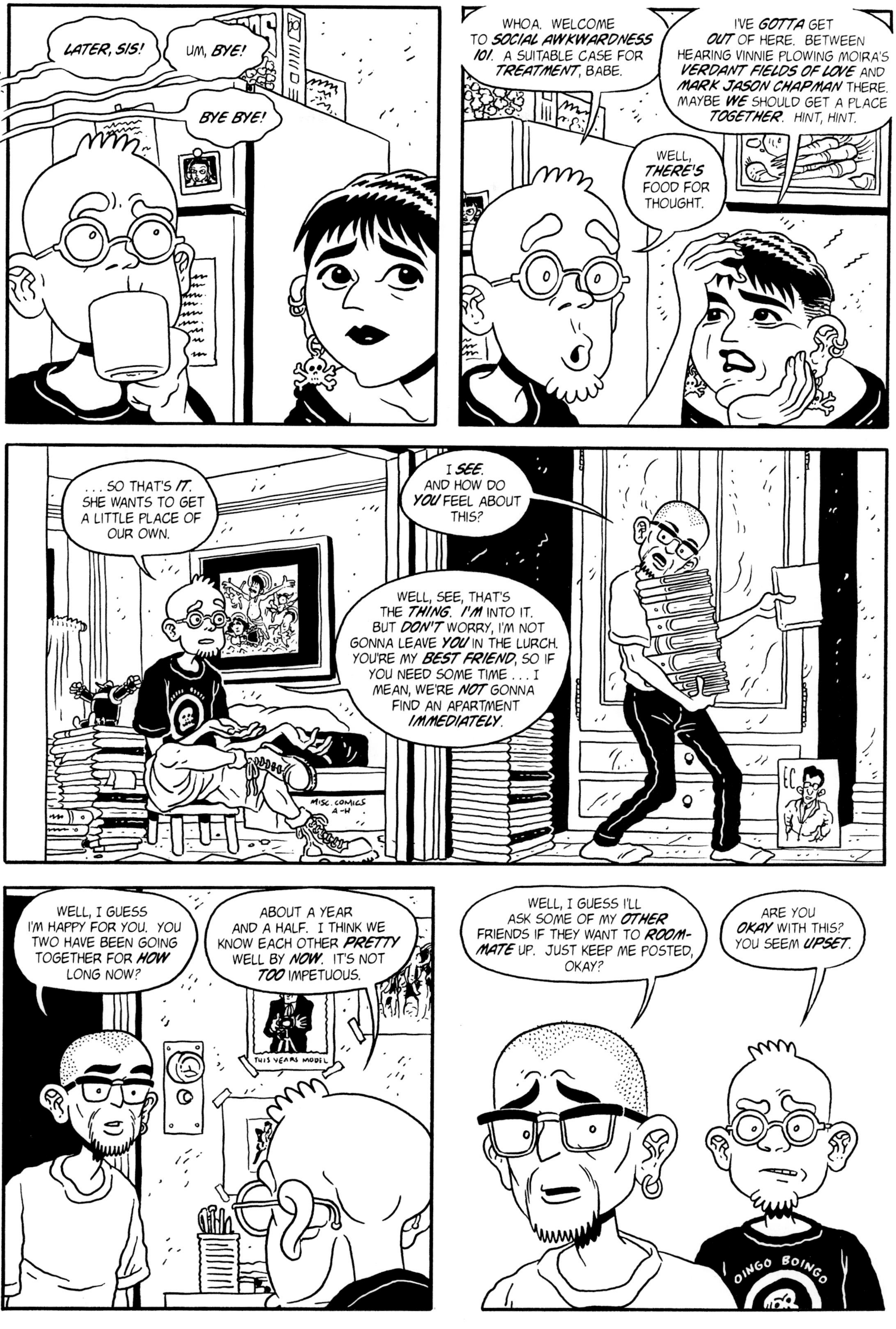
LATER, SIS!
UM, BYE!
BYE BYE!
WHOA. WELCOME TO SOCIAL AWKWARDNESS 101. A SUITABLE CASE FOR TREATMENT, BABE.
I'VE GOTTA GET OUT OF HERE. BETWEEN HEARING VINNIE PLOWING MOIRA'S VERDANT FIELDS OF LOVE AND MARK JASON CHAPMAN THERE. MAYBE WE SHOULD GET A PLACE TOGETHER. HINT, HINT.
WELL, THERE'S FOOD FOR THOUGHT.
. . . SO THAT'S IT. SHE WANTS TO GET A LITTLE PLACE OF OUR OWN.
I SEE. AND HOW DO YOU FEEL ABOUT THIS?
WELL, SEE, THAT'S THE THING. I'M INTO IT. BUT DON'T WORRY, I'M NOT GONNA LEAVE YOU IN THE LURCH. YOU'RE MY BEST FRIEND, SO IF YOU NEED SOME TIME . . . I MEAN, WE'RE NOT GONNA FIND AN APARTMENT IMMEDIATELY.
MISC. COMICS A-H
EC
WELL, I GUESS I'M HAPPY FOR YOU. YOU TWO HAVE BEEN GOING TOGETHER FOR HOW LONG NOW?
ABOUT A YEAR AND A HALF. I THINK WE KNOW EACH OTHER PRETTY WELL BY NOW. IT'S NOT TOO IMPETUOUS.
THIS YEARS MODEL
WELL, I GUESS I'LL ASK SOME OF MY OTHER FRIENDS IF THEY WANT TO ROOM-MATE UP. JUST KEEP ME POSTED, OKAY?
ARE YOU OKAY WITH THIS? YOU SEEM UPSET.
OINGO BOINGO

NO. NO, I'M *FINE*. YOU HAVE MY *BLESSING*. LIKE YOU SAID, IT'S NOT LIKE YOU'RE OUTTA HERE TOMORROW, *RIGHT?*

RIGHT. *DEFINITELY* NOT. IT'S CERTAINLY *UNLIKELY*. I MEAN, WHAT'RE THE ODDS, *RIGHT?* A GOOD APARTMENT IS HARD TO FIND.

MMM-HMMM.

UH-HA UH-HA UH-HA! OUR LITTLE ROBBY IS ALL *GROWED-UP*. THE *CO-HABITATION JAMMY!* SO, ARE YOU GONNA BE ALLOWED TO DRAW *PEENIES* AND *PUSSIES* FOR US, OR WILL THAT ANTISOCIAL BEHAVIOR BE *VERBOTEN?*

SO LONG AS I'VE GOT *BILLS* TO PAY, I'LL BE RENDERING UP THE *SPLAYED GENITALS DE JOUR.*

WELL *BULLY* FOR THAT. YOUR TALENTS WOULD BE *WASTED* IF YOU DENIED YOUR *PORN-DOGGISH* ENDOWMENTS. SO YOU'RE MOVING IN WITH SYLVIA, HUH?

AND SO BEGINS YOUR *SPIRAL* INTO *FEMALE SERVITUDE* AND AT-HOME *WORSHIP* AT THE *TEMPLE OF WOMANHOOD.*

BRAVO. THE SERMON FROM THE MOUNT, LADIES AND GENTLEMEN. THE RIGHT *REVEREND ELVIS SEWARD FOUCAULT III* PRESIDING AT THE PULPIT.

WELL IN *HONOR* OF YOUR FIRST STEP INTO *MANHOOD*, I INVITE YOU TO MY *PERFORMANCE* TONIGHT, FOR THE *HUNDREDTH* TIME. *DON'T* DISAPPOINT ME, ROB. YOU *MIGHT* FIND IT . . . *INSTRUCTIVE.*

ALL RIGHT, *ALL RIGHT*. I'LL COME TO *THIS* ONE. GIMME AN *EXTRA* PASS, THOUGH. I'LL ASK JACK TO JOIN ME.

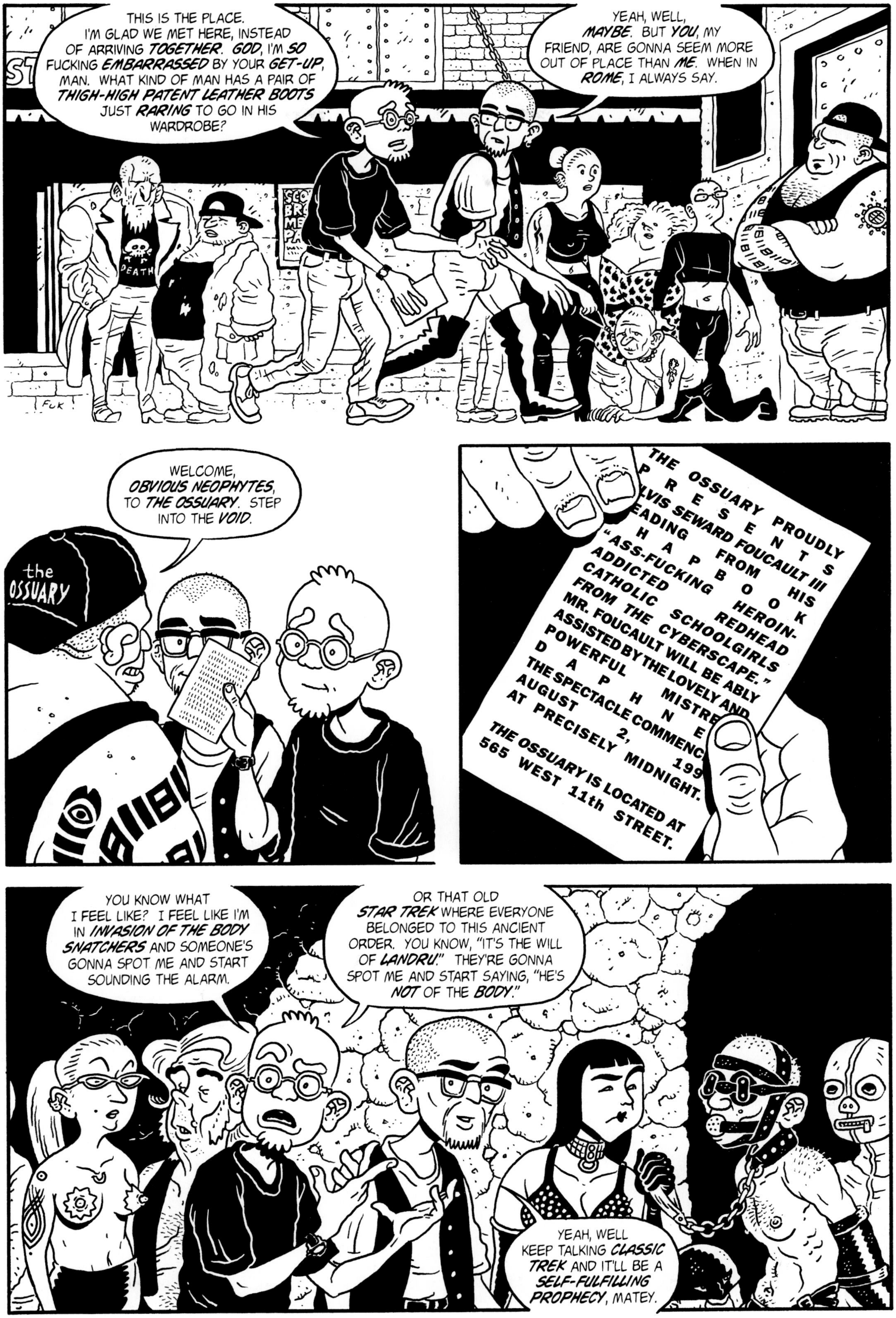
THIS IS THE PLACE. I'M GLAD WE MET HERE, INSTEAD OF ARRIVING TOGETHER. GOD, I'M SO FUCKING EMBARRASSED BY YOUR GET-UP, MAN. WHAT KIND OF MAN HAS A PAIR OF THIGH-HIGH PATENT LEATHER BOOTS JUST RARING TO GO IN HIS WARDROBE?
YEAH, WELL, MAYBE. BUT YOU, MY FRIEND, ARE GONNA SEEM MORE OUT OF PLACE THAN ME. WHEN IN ROME, I ALWAYS SAY.
DEATH
FUK
WELCOME, OBVIOUS NEOPHYTES, TO THE OSSUARY. STEP INTO THE VOID.
the OSSUARY
THE OSSUARY PROUDLY
P R E S E N T S
LVIS SEWARD FOUCAULT III
EADING FROM HIS
H A P B O O K
"ASS-FUCKING HEROIN-
ADDICTED REDHEAD
CATHOLIC SCHOOLGIRLS
FROM THE CYBERSCAPE."
MR. FOUCAULT WILL BE ABLY
ASSISTED BY THE LOVELY AND
POWERFUL MISTRE
D A P H N E
THE SPECTACLE COMMENC
AUGUST 2, 199
AT PRECISELY MIDNIGHT.
THE OSSUARY IS LOCATED AT
565 WEST 11th STREET.
YOU KNOW WHAT I FEEL LIKE? I FEEL LIKE I'M IN INVASION OF THE BODY SNATCHERS AND SOMEONE'S GONNA SPOT ME AND START SOUNDING THE ALARM.
OR THAT OLD STAR TREK WHERE EVERYONE BELONGED TO THIS ANCIENT ORDER. YOU KNOW, "IT'S THE WILL OF LANDRU." THEY'RE GONNA SPOT ME AND START SAYING, "HE'S NOT OF THE BODY."
YEAH, WELL KEEP TALKING CLASSIC TREK AND IT'LL BE A SELF-FULFILLING PROPHECY, MATEY.

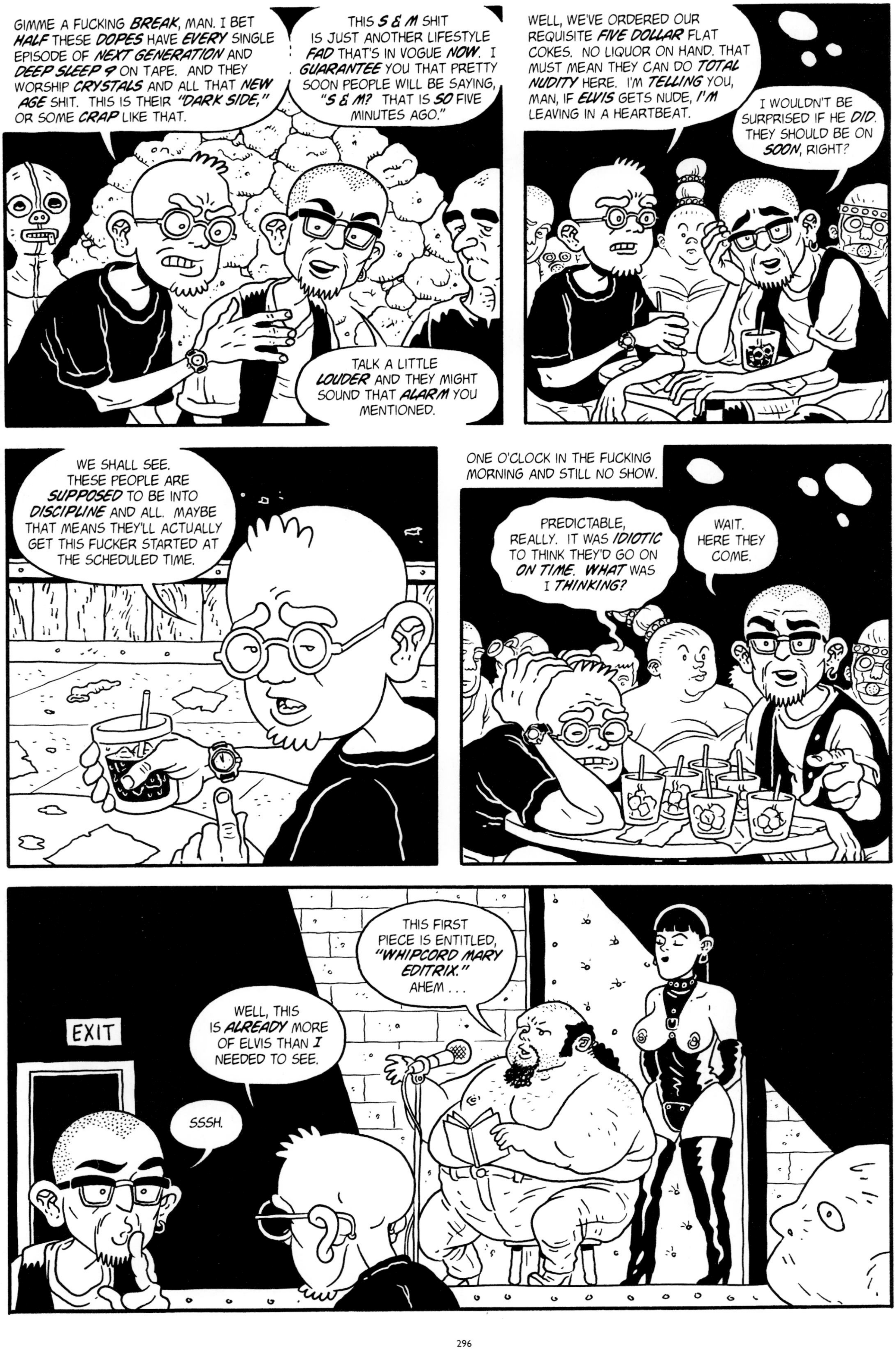
GIMME A FUCKING BREAK, MAN. I BET HALF THESE DOPES HAVE EVERY SINGLE EPISODE OF NEXT GENERATION AND DEEP SLEEP 9 ON TAPE. AND THEY WORSHIP CRYSTALS AND ALL THAT NEW AGE SHIT. THIS IS THEIR "DARK SIDE," OR SOME CRAP LIKE THAT.
THIS S & M SHIT IS JUST ANOTHER LIFESTYLE FAD THAT'S IN VOGUE NOW. I GUARANTEE YOU THAT PRETTY SOON PEOPLE WILL BE SAYING, "S & M? THAT IS SO FIVE MINUTES AGO."
TALK A LITTLE LOUDER AND THEY MIGHT SOUND THAT ALARM YOU MENTIONED.
WELL, WE'VE ORDERED OUR REQUISITE FIVE DOLLAR FLAT COKES. NO LIQUOR ON HAND. THAT MUST MEAN THEY CAN DO TOTAL NUDITY HERE. I'M TELLING YOU, MAN, IF ELVIS GETS NUDE, I'M LEAVING IN A HEARTBEAT.
I WOULDN'T BE SURPRISED IF HE DID. THEY SHOULD BE ON SOON, RIGHT?
WE SHALL SEE. THESE PEOPLE ARE SUPPOSED TO BE INTO DISCIPLINE AND ALL. MAYBE THAT MEANS THEY'LL ACTUALLY GET THIS FUCKER STARTED AT THE SCHEDULED TIME.
ONE O'CLOCK IN THE FUCKING MORNING AND STILL NO SHOW.
PREDICTABLE, REALLY. IT WAS IDIOTIC TO THINK THEY'D GO ON ON TIME. WHAT WAS I THINKING?
WAIT. HERE THEY COME.
EXIT
WELL, THIS IS ALREADY MORE OF ELVIS THAN I NEEDED TO SEE.
THIS FIRST PIECE IS ENTITLED, "WHIPCORD MARY EDITRIX." AHEM . . .
SSSH.

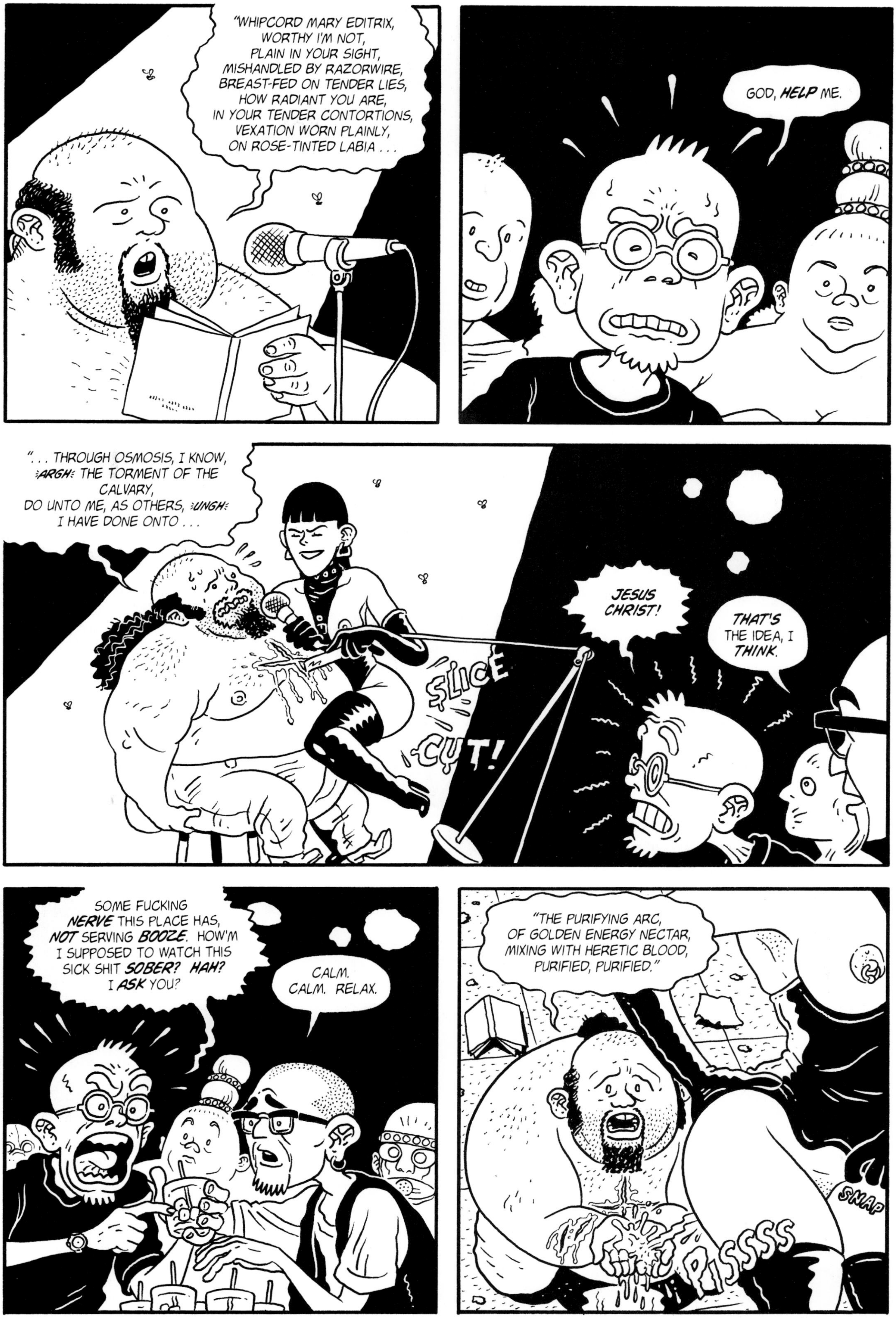
"WHIPCORD MARY EDITRIX, WORTHY I'M NOT, PLAIN IN YOUR SIGHT, MISHANDLED BY RAZORWIRE, BREAST-FED ON TENDER LIES, HOW RADIANT YOU ARE, IN YOUR TENDER CONTORTIONS, VEXATION WORN PLAINLY, ON ROSE-TINTED LABIA . . .
GOD, HELP ME.
". . . THROUGH OSMOSIS, I KNOW, ARGH THE TORMENT OF THE CALVARY, DO UNTO ME, AS OTHERS, UNGH I HAVE DONE ONTO . . .
SLICE
CUT!
JESUS CHRIST!
THAT'S THE IDEA, I THINK.
SOME FUCKING NERVE THIS PLACE HAS, NOT SERVING BOOZE. HOW'M I SUPPOSED TO WATCH THIS SICK SHIT SOBER? HAH? I ASK YOU?
CALM. CALM. RELAX.
"THE PURIFYING ARC, OF GOLDEN ENERGY NECTAR, MIXING WITH HERETIC BLOOD, PURIFIED, PURIFIED."
SNAP
PISSSSS

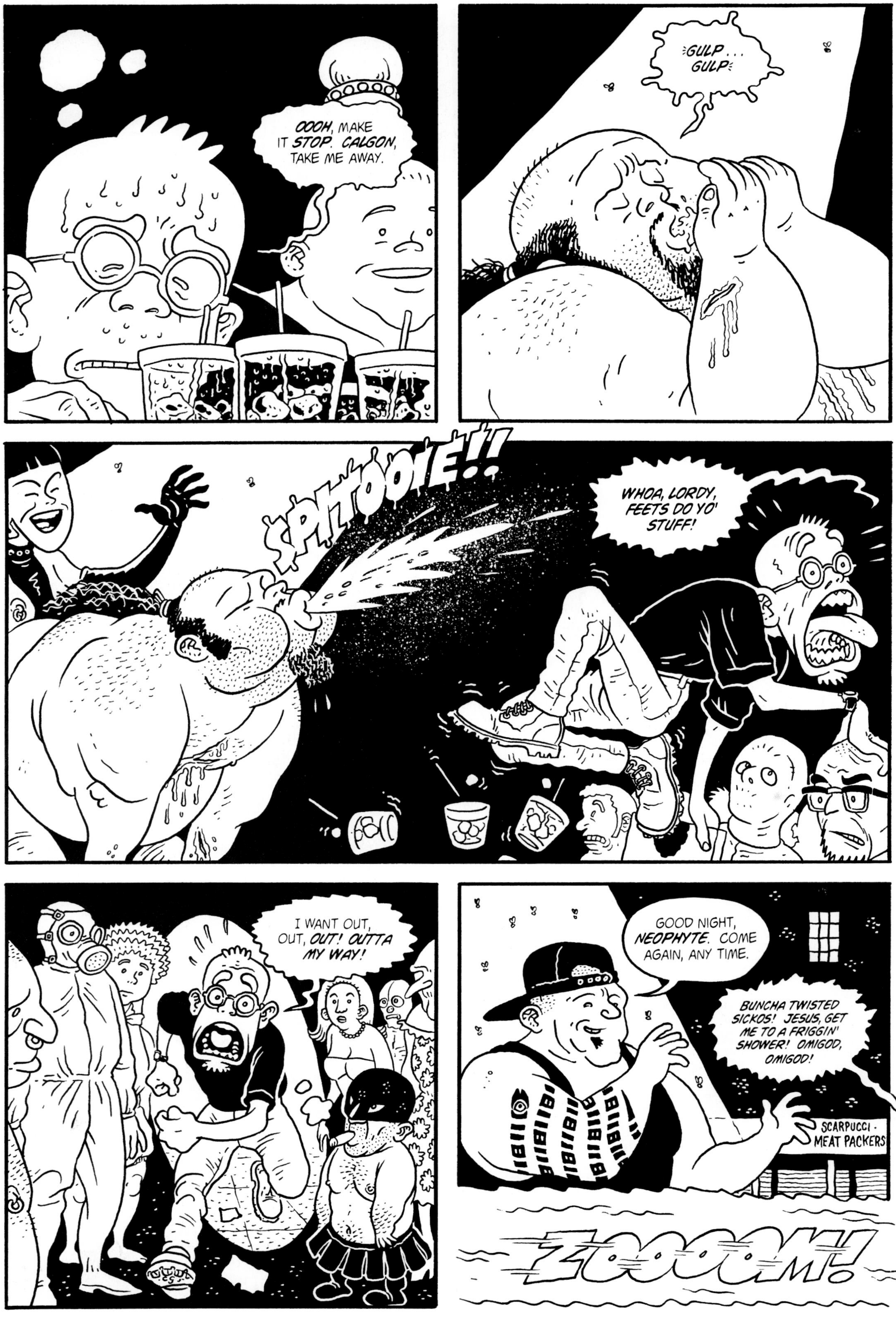
OOOH, MAKE IT STOP. CALGON, TAKE ME AWAY.
GULP... GULP
SPHTOOIE!!
WHOA, LORDY, FEETS DO YO' STUFF!
I WANT OUT, OUT, OUT! OUTTA MY WAY!
GOOD NIGHT, NEOPHYTE. COME AGAIN, ANY TIME.
BUNCHA TWISTED SICKOS! JESUS, GET ME TO A FRIGGIN' SHOWER! OMIGOD, OMIGOD!
SCARPUCCI - MEAT PACKERS
ZOOOOM!

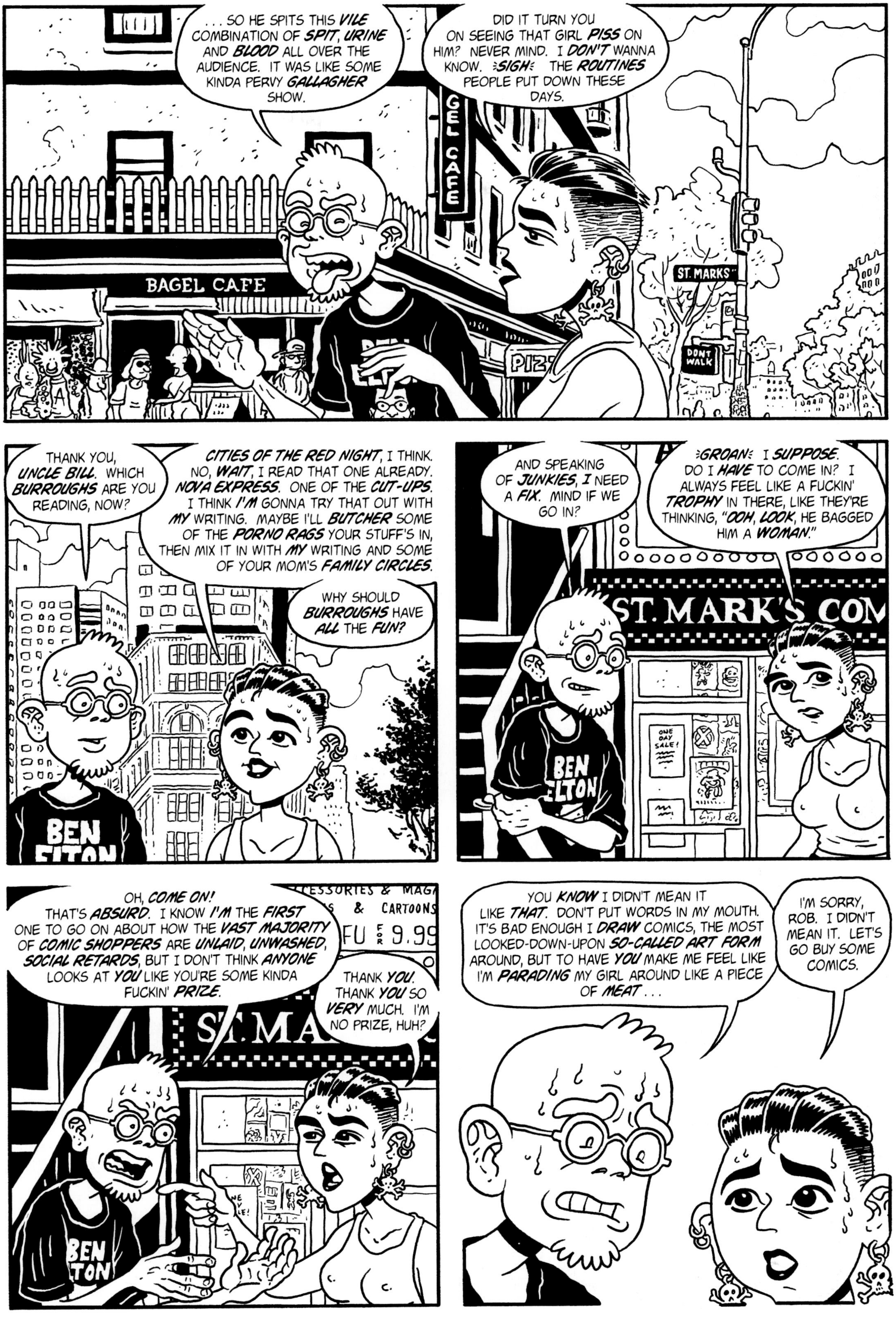

. . . SO HE SPITS THIS VILE COMBINATION OF SPIT, URINE AND BLOOD ALL OVER THE AUDIENCE. IT WAS LIKE SOME KINDA PERVY GALLAGHER SHOW.
DID IT TURN YOU ON SEEING THAT GIRL PISS ON HIM? NEVER MIND. I DON'T WANNA KNOW. SIGH THE ROUTINES PEOPLE PUT DOWN THESE DAYS.
BAGEL CAFE
ST. MARKS
DON'T WALK
THANK YOU, UNCLE BILL. WHICH BURROUGHS ARE YOU READING, NOW?
CITIES OF THE RED NIGHT, I THINK. NO, WAIT, I READ THAT ONE ALREADY. NOVA EXPRESS. ONE OF THE CUT-UPS. I THINK I'M GONNA TRY THAT OUT WITH MY WRITING. MAYBE I'LL BUTCHER SOME OF THE PORNO RAGS YOUR STUFF'S IN, THEN MIX IT IN WITH MY WRITING AND SOME OF YOUR MOM'S FAMILY CIRCLES.
WHY SHOULD BURROUGHS HAVE ALL THE FUN?
BEN
AND SPEAKING OF JUNKIES, I NEED A FIX. MIND IF WE GO IN?
GROAN I SUPPOSE. DO I HAVE TO COME IN? I ALWAYS FEEL LIKE A FUCKIN' TROPHY IN THERE, LIKE THEY'RE THINKING, "OOH, LOOK, HE BAGGED HIM A WOMAN."
ST. MARK'S COM
ONE DAY SALE!
BEN ELTON
OH, COME ON! THAT'S ABSURD. I KNOW I'M THE FIRST ONE TO GO ON ABOUT HOW THE VAST MAJORITY OF COMIC SHOPPERS ARE UNLAID, UNWASHED, SOCIAL RETARDS, BUT I DON'T THINK ANYONE LOOKS AT YOU LIKE YOU'RE SOME KINDA FUCKIN' PRIZE.
THANK YOU. THANK YOU SO VERY MUCH. I'M NO PRIZE, HUH?
CESSORIES & MAG
& CARTOONS
ST. MA
BEN LTON
YOU KNOW I DIDN'T MEAN IT LIKE THAT. DON'T PUT WORDS IN MY MOUTH. IT'S BAD ENOUGH I DRAW COMICS, THE MOST LOOKED-DOWN-UPON SO-CALLED ART FORM AROUND, BUT TO HAVE YOU MAKE ME FEEL LIKE I'M PARADING MY GIRL AROUND LIKE A PIECE OF MEAT . . .
I'M SORRY, ROB. I DIDN'T MEAN IT. LET'S GO BUY SOME COMICS.

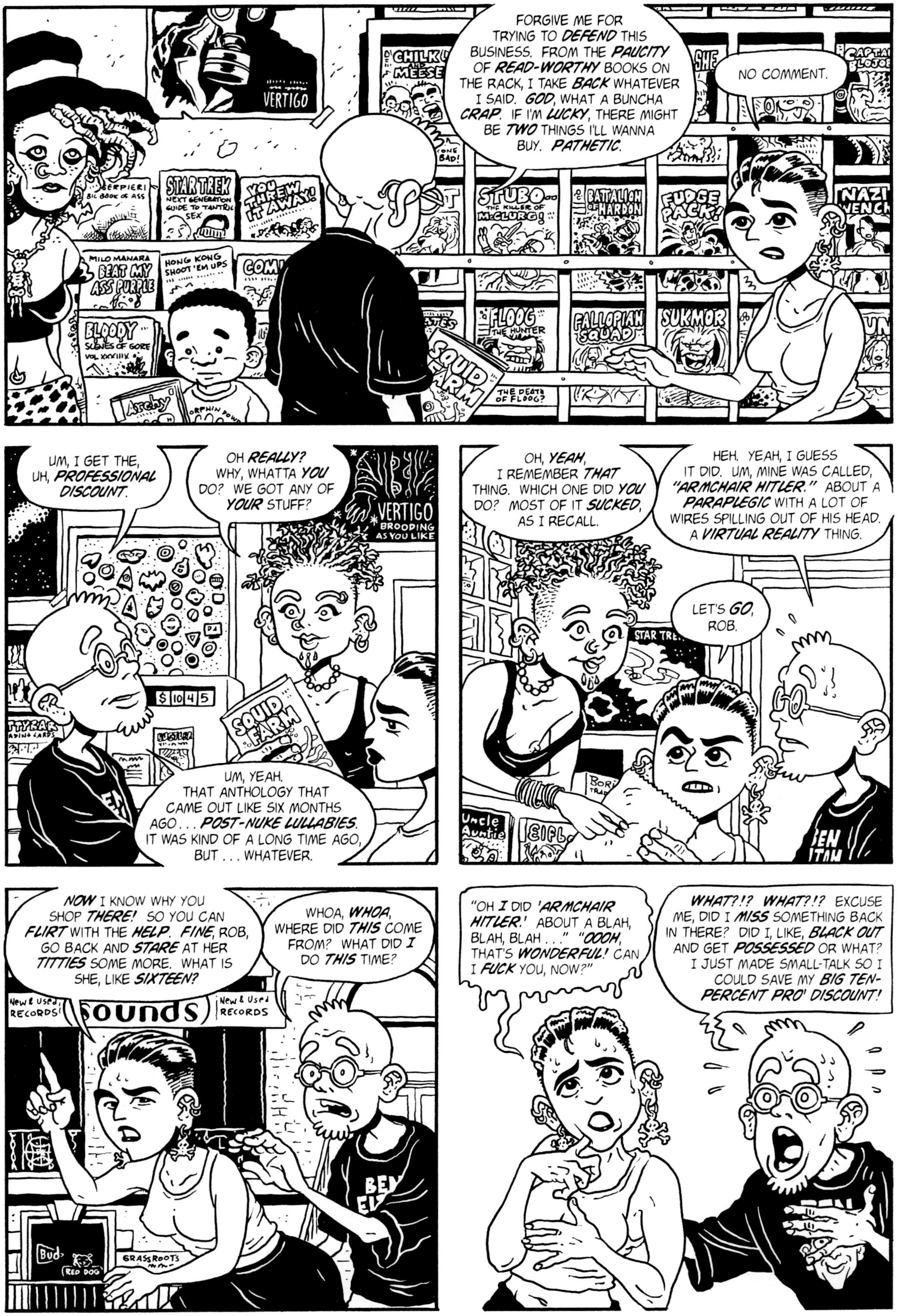
VERTIGO
FORGIVE ME FOR TRYING TO DEFEND THIS BUSINESS. FROM THE PAUCITY OF READ-WORTHY BOOKS ON THE RACK, I TAKE BACK WHATEVER I SAID. GOD, WHAT A BUNCHA CRAP. IF I'M LUCKY, THERE MIGHT BE TWO THINGS I'LL WANNA BUY. PATHETIC.
NO COMMENT.
CHILK AND MEESE
STAR TREK NEXT GENERATION GUIDE TO TANTRIC SEX
YOU THREW IT AWAY!
STUBO THE KILLER OF McCLURG!
BATTALION OF HARDON
FUDGE PACK!
MILO MANARA BEAT MY ASS PURPLE
HONG KONG SHOOT 'EM UPS
BLOODY SCENES OF GORE VOL XXXIIIX
FLOOG THE HUNTER
FALLOPIAN SQUAD
SUKMOR
SQUID FARM
THE DEATH OF FLOOG?
UM, I GET THE, UH, PROFESSIONAL DISCOUNT.
OH REALLY? WHY, WHATTA YOU DO? WE GOT ANY OF YOUR STUFF?
VERTIGO BROODING AS YOU LIKE
$1045
SQUID FARM
UM, YEAH. THAT ANTHOLOGY THAT CAME OUT LIKE SIX MONTHS AGO . . . POST-NUKE LULLABIES. IT WAS KIND OF A LONG TIME AGO, BUT . . . WHATEVER.
OH, YEAH, I REMEMBER THAT THING. WHICH ONE DID YOU DO? MOST OF IT SUCKED, AS I RECALL.
HEH. YEAH, I GUESS IT DID. UM, MINE WAS CALLED, "ARMCHAIR HITLER." ABOUT A PARAPLEGIC WITH A LOT OF WIRES SPILLING OUT OF HIS HEAD. A VIRTUAL REALITY THING.
LET'S GO, ROB.
STAR TREK
Uncle Auntie
NOW I KNOW WHY YOU SHOP THERE! SO YOU CAN FLIRT WITH THE HELP. FINE, ROB, GO BACK AND STARE AT HER TITTIES SOME MORE. WHAT IS SHE, LIKE SIXTEEN?
WHOA, WHOA, WHERE DID THIS COME FROM? WHAT DID I DO THIS TIME?
New & Used RECORDS
SOUNDS
New & Used RECORDS
Bud
RED DOG
GRASSROOTS
"OH I DID 'ARMCHAIR HITLER.' ABOUT A BLAH, BLAH, BLAH . . ." "OOOH, THAT'S WONDERFUL! CAN I FUCK YOU, NOW?"
WHAT?!? WHAT?!? EXCUSE ME, DID I MISS SOMETHING BACK IN THERE? DID I, LIKE, BLACK OUT AND GET POSSESSED OR WHAT? I JUST MADE SMALL-TALK SO I COULD SAVE MY BIG TEN-PERCENT PRO' DISCOUNT!

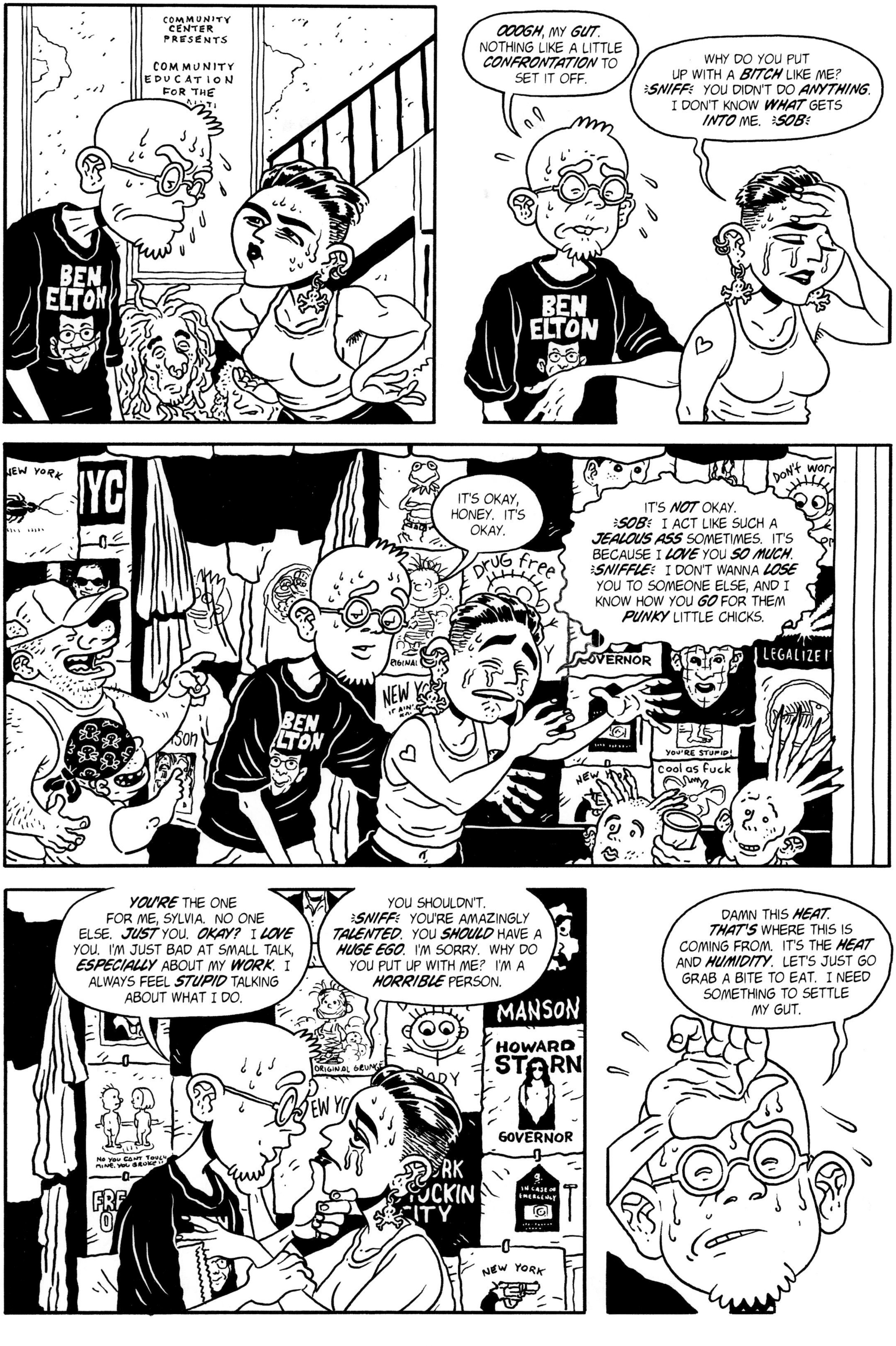

COMMUNITY CENTER PRESENTS
COMMUNITY EDUCATION FOR THE
BEN ELTON
OOOGH, MY GUT. NOTHING LIKE A LITTLE CONFRONTATION TO SET IT OFF.
WHY DO YOU PUT UP WITH A BITCH LIKE ME? ⸗SNIFF⸗ YOU DIDN'T DO ANYTHING. I DON'T KNOW WHAT GETS INTO ME. ⸗SOB⸗
BEN ELTON
NEW YORK
NYC
DON'T WORRY
IT'S OKAY, HONEY. IT'S OKAY.
IT'S NOT OKAY. ⸗SOB⸗ I ACT LIKE SUCH A JEALOUS ASS SOMETIMES. IT'S BECAUSE I LOVE YOU SO MUCH. ⸗SNIFFLE⸗ I DON'T WANNA LOSE YOU TO SOMEONE ELSE, AND I KNOW HOW YOU GO FOR THEM PUNKY LITTLE CHICKS.
DruG free
GOVERNOR
LEGALIZE IT
BEN ELTON
YOU'RE STUPID!
cool as fuck
YOU'RE THE ONE FOR ME, SYLVIA. NO ONE ELSE. JUST YOU. OKAY? I LOVE YOU. I'M JUST BAD AT SMALL TALK, ESPECIALLY ABOUT MY WORK. I ALWAYS FEEL STUPID TALKING ABOUT WHAT I DO.
YOU SHOULDN'T. ⸗SNIFF⸗ YOU'RE AMAZINGLY TALENTED. YOU SHOULD HAVE A HUGE EGO. I'M SORRY. WHY DO YOU PUT UP WITH ME? I'M A HORRIBLE PERSON.
MANSON
HOWARD STERN
GOVERNOR
ORIGINAL GRUNGE
IN CASE OF EMERGENCY
NEW YORK
DAMN THIS HEAT. THAT'S WHERE THIS IS COMING FROM. IT'S THE HEAT AND HUMIDITY. LET'S JUST GO GRAB A BITE TO EAT. I NEED SOMETHING TO SETTLE MY GUT.

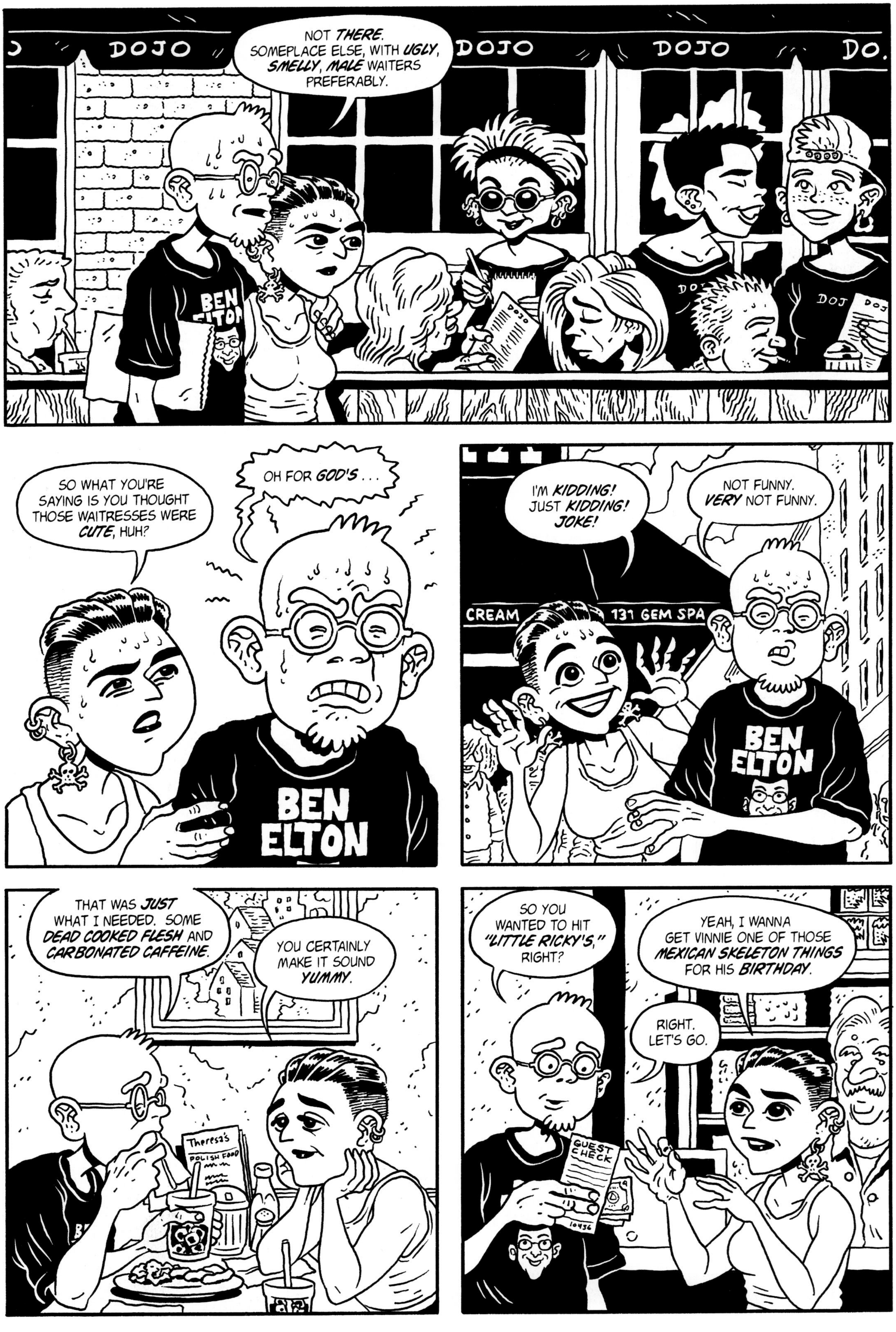

DOJO
NOT THERE. SOMEPLACE ELSE, WITH UGLY, SMELLY, MALE WAITERS PREFERABLY.
BEN ELTON
SO WHAT YOU'RE SAYING IS YOU THOUGHT THOSE WAITRESSES WERE CUTE, HUH?
OH FOR GOD'S . . .
BEN ELTON
I'M KIDDING! JUST KIDDING! JOKE!
NOT FUNNY. VERY NOT FUNNY.
CREAM
131 GEM SPA
BEN ELTON
THAT WAS JUST WHAT I NEEDED. SOME DEAD COOKED FLESH AND CARBONATED CAFFEINE.
YOU CERTAINLY MAKE IT SOUND YUMMY.
Theresa's
POLISH FOOD
SO YOU WANTED TO HIT "LITTLE RICKY'S," RIGHT?
YEAH, I WANNA GET VINNIE ONE OF THOSE MEXICAN SKELETON THINGS FOR HIS BIRTHDAY.
RIGHT. LET'S GO.
GUEST CHECK

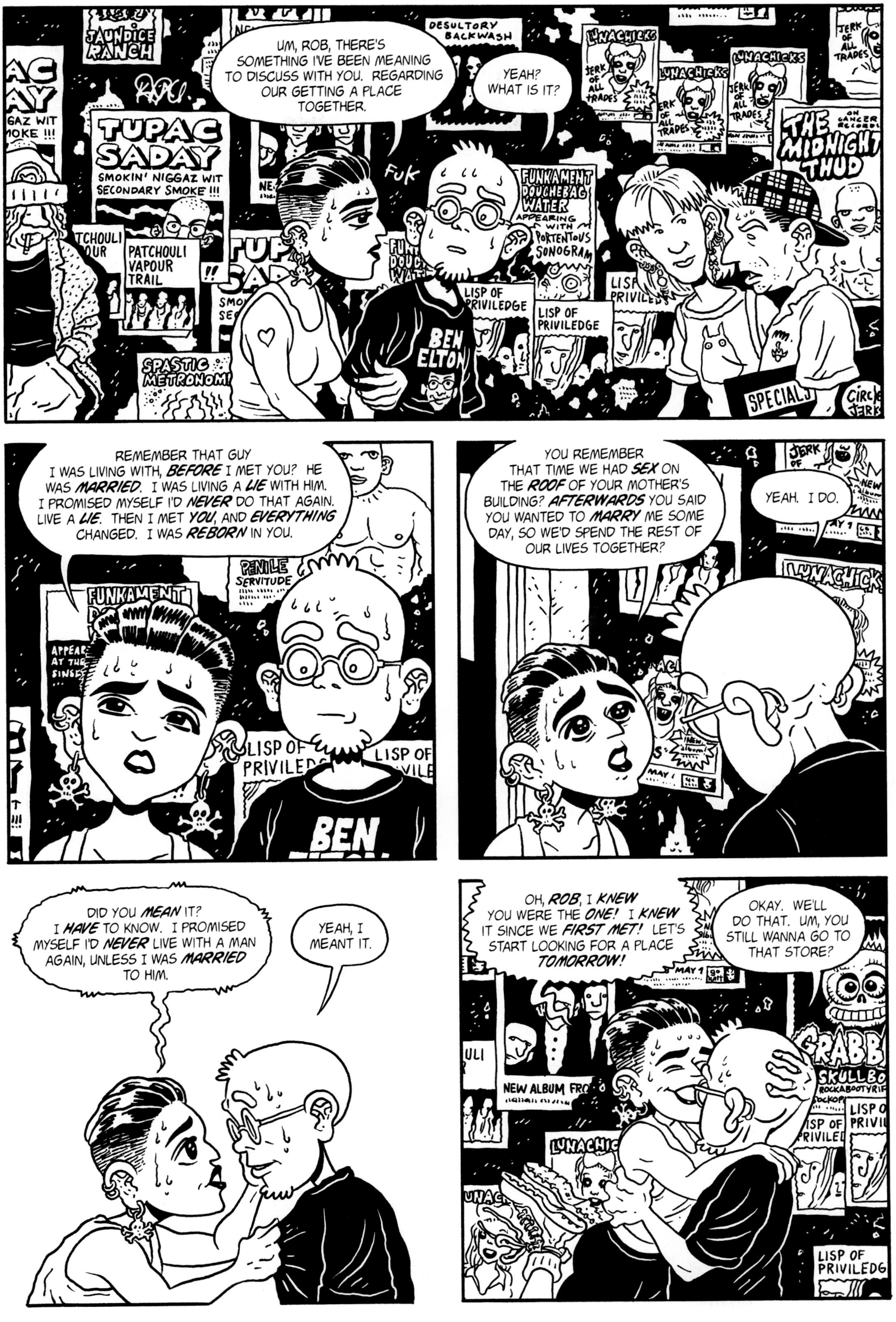
JAUNDICE RANCH
DESULTORY BACKWASH
LUNACHICKS
JERK OF ALL TRADES
UM, ROB, THERE'S SOMETHING I'VE BEEN MEANING TO DISCUSS WITH YOU. REGARDING OUR GETTING A PLACE TOGETHER.
YEAH? WHAT IS IT?
TUPAC SADAY
SMOKIN' NIGGAZ WIT SECONDARY SMOKE !!!
FUK
FUNKAMENT DOUCHEBAG WATER
APPEARING WITH PORTENTOUS SONOGRAM
THE MIDNIGHT THUD
PATCHOULI VAPOUR TRAIL
LISP OF PRIVILEDGE
BEN ELTON
SPASTIC METRONOME
SPECIALS
CIRCLE JERKS
REMEMBER THAT GUY I WAS LIVING WITH, BEFORE I MET YOU? HE WAS MARRIED. I WAS LIVING A LIE WITH HIM. I PROMISED MYSELF I'D NEVER DO THAT AGAIN. LIVE A LIE. THEN I MET YOU, AND EVERYTHING CHANGED. I WAS REBORN IN YOU.
PENILE SERVITUDE
YOU REMEMBER THAT TIME WE HAD SEX ON THE ROOF OF YOUR MOTHER'S BUILDING? AFTERWARDS YOU SAID YOU WANTED TO MARRY ME SOME DAY, SO WE'D SPEND THE REST OF OUR LIVES TOGETHER?
YEAH. I DO.
DID YOU MEAN IT? I HAVE TO KNOW. I PROMISED MYSELF I'D NEVER LIVE WITH A MAN AGAIN, UNLESS I WAS MARRIED TO HIM.
YEAH, I MEANT IT.
OH, ROB, I KNEW YOU WERE THE ONE! I KNEW IT SINCE WE FIRST MET! LET'S START LOOKING FOR A PLACE TOMORROW!
OKAY. WE'LL DO THAT. UM, YOU STILL WANNA GO TO THAT STORE?
NEW ALBUM FRO

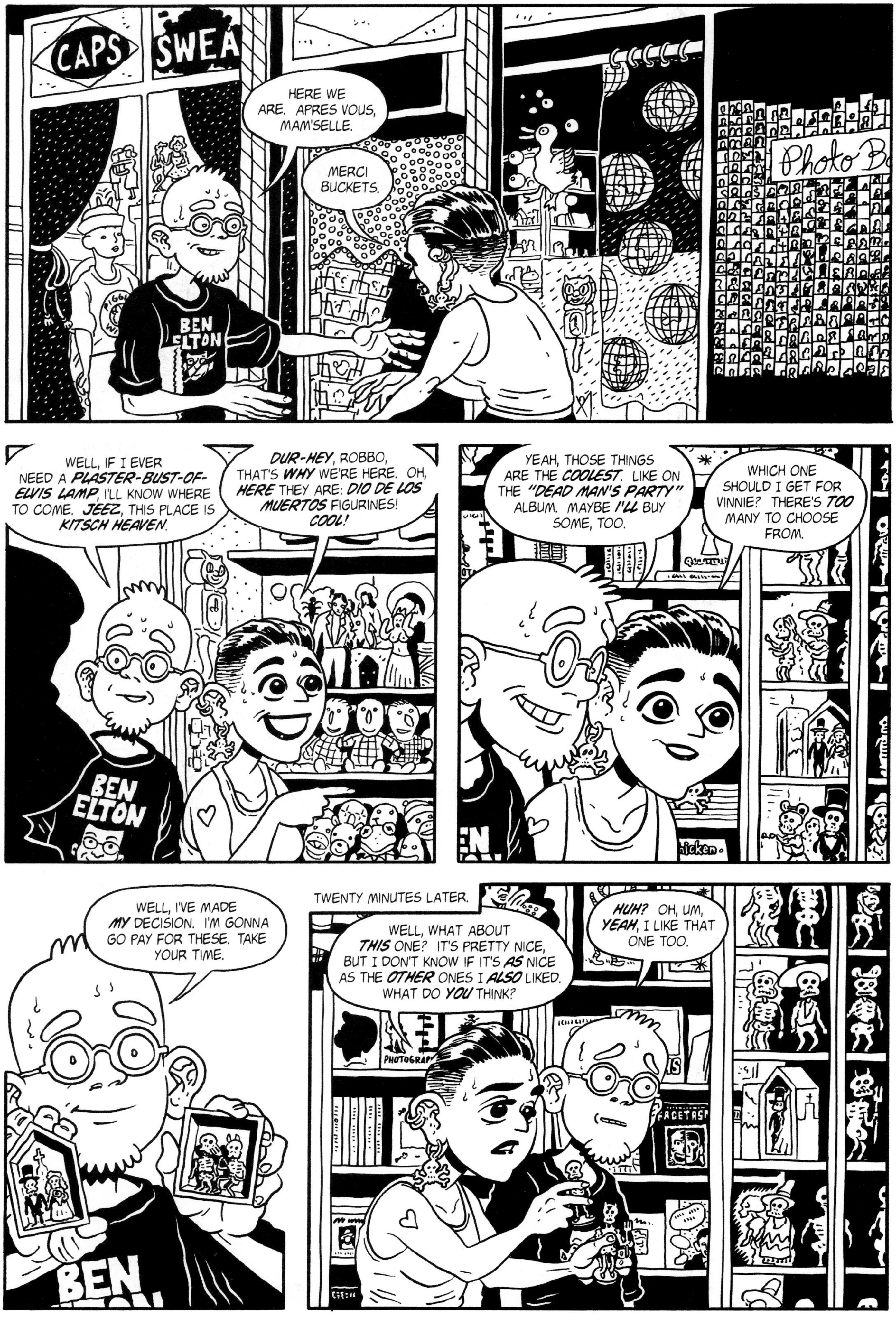
CAPS
SWEA
HERE WE ARE. APRES VOUS, MAM'SELLE.
MERCI BUCKETS.
BEN ELTON
Photo B
WELL, IF I EVER NEED A PLASTER-BUST-OF-ELVIS LAMP, I'LL KNOW WHERE TO COME. JEEZ, THIS PLACE IS KITSCH HEAVEN.
DUR-HEY, ROBBO, THAT'S WHY WE'RE HERE. OH, HERE THEY ARE: DIO DE LOS MUERTOS FIGURINES! COOL!
BEN ELTON
YEAH, THOSE THINGS ARE THE COOLEST. LIKE ON THE "DEAD MAN'S PARTY" ALBUM. MAYBE I'LL BUY SOME, TOO.
WHICH ONE SHOULD I GET FOR VINNIE? THERE'S TOO MANY TO CHOOSE FROM.
WELL, I'VE MADE MY DECISION. I'M GONNA GO PAY FOR THESE. TAKE YOUR TIME.
BEN
TWENTY MINUTES LATER.
WELL, WHAT ABOUT THIS ONE? IT'S PRETTY NICE, BUT I DON'T KNOW IF IT'S AS NICE AS THE OTHER ONES I ALSO LIKED. WHAT DO YOU THINK?
HUH? OH, UM, YEAH, I LIKE THAT ONE TOO.

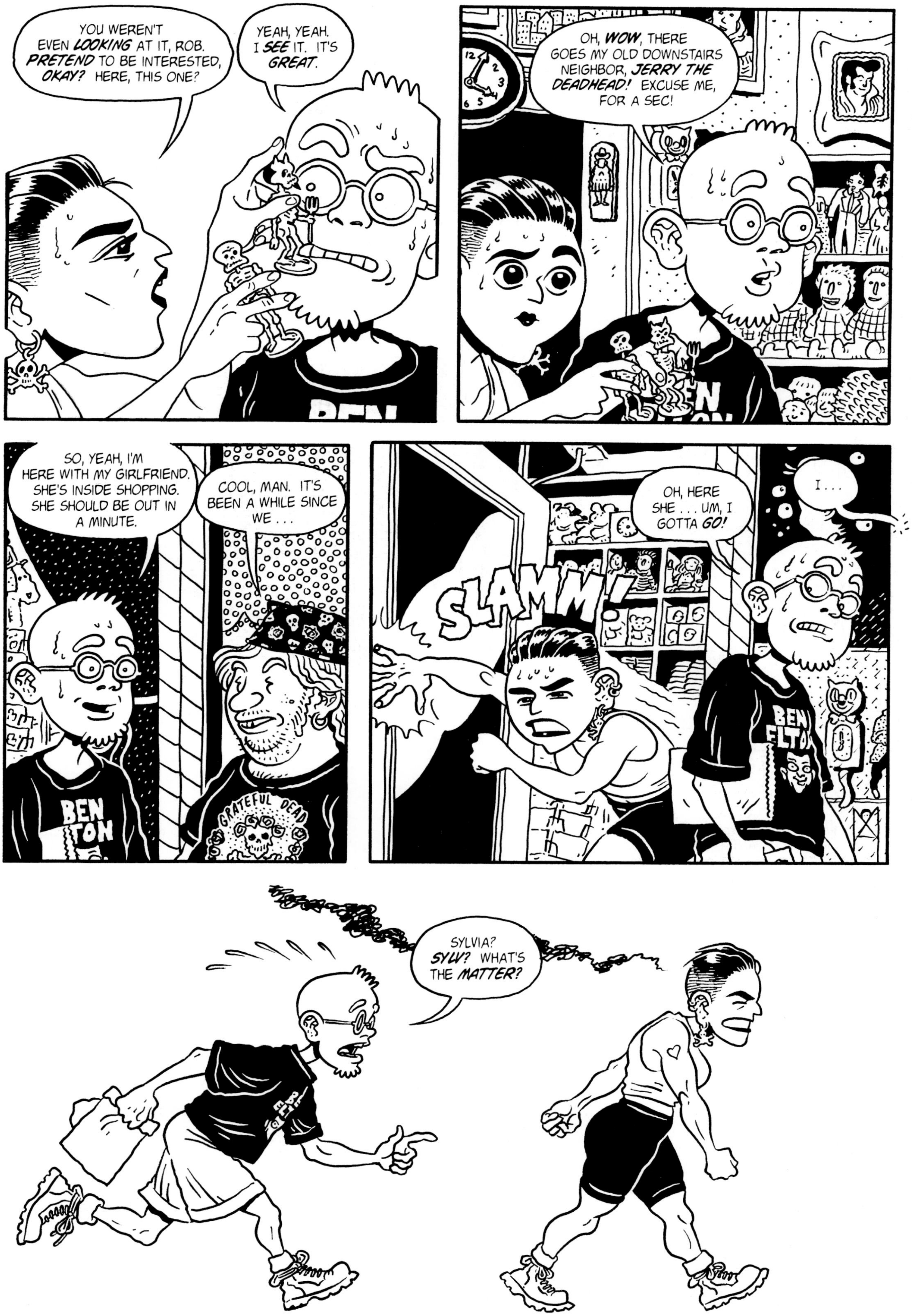
YOU WEREN'T EVEN LOOKING AT IT, ROB. PRETEND TO BE INTERESTED, OKAY? HERE, THIS ONE?
YEAH, YEAH. I SEE IT. IT'S GREAT.
OH, WOW, THERE GOES MY OLD DOWNSTAIRS NEIGHBOR, JERRY THE DEADHEAD! EXCUSE ME, FOR A SEC!
SO, YEAH, I'M HERE WITH MY GIRLFRIEND. SHE'S INSIDE SHOPPING. SHE SHOULD BE OUT IN A MINUTE.
COOL, MAN. IT'S BEEN A WHILE SINCE WE . . .
GRATEFUL DEAD
OH, HERE SHE . . . UM, I GOTTA GO!
I . . .
SLAMM!
SYLVIA? SYLV? WHAT'S THE MATTER?

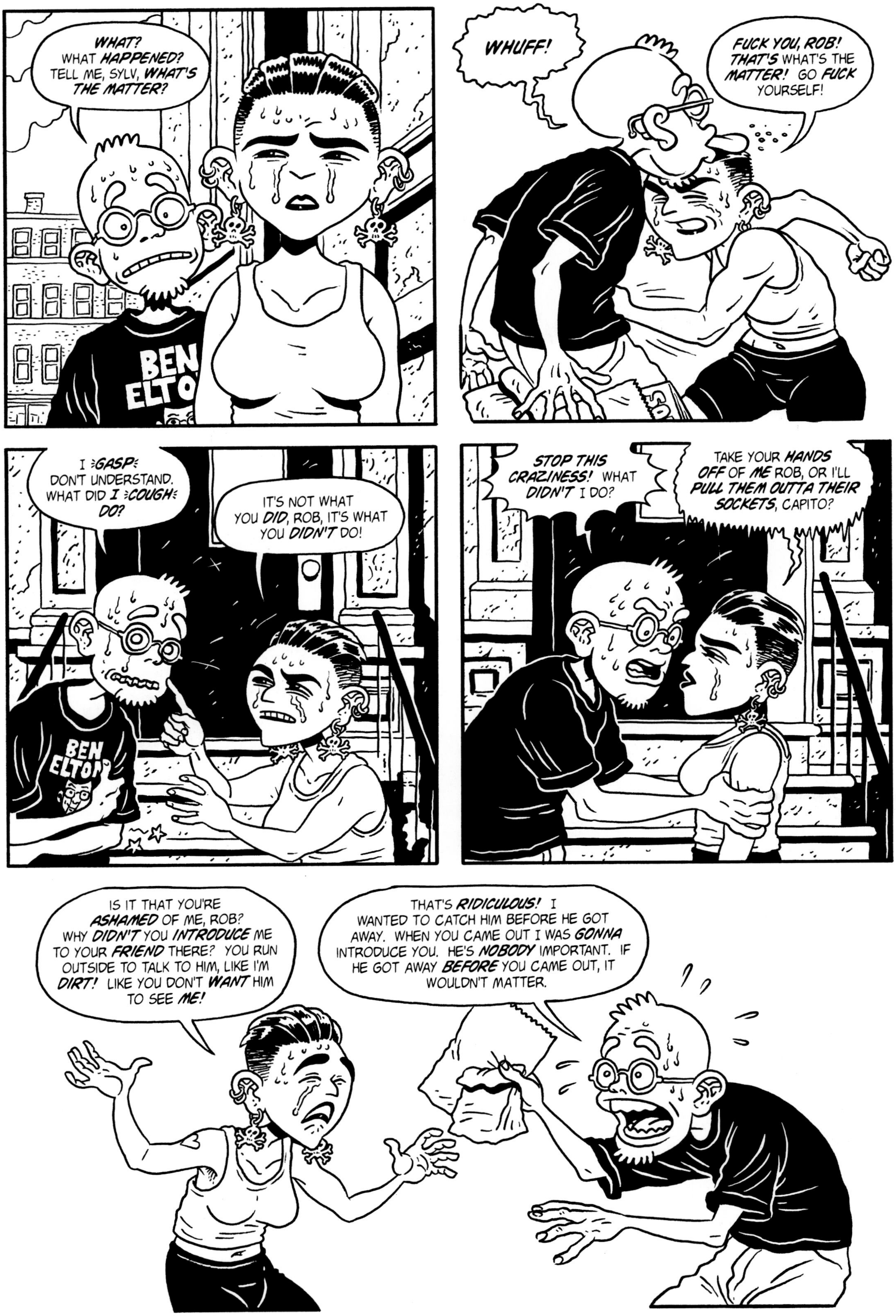
WHAT? WHAT HAPPENED? TELL ME, SYLV, WHAT'S THE MATTER?
BEN ELTON
WHUFF!
FUCK YOU, ROB! THAT'S WHAT'S THE MATTER! GO FUCK YOURSELF!
I GASP DON'T UNDERSTAND. WHAT DID I COUGH DO?
IT'S NOT WHAT YOU DID, ROB, IT'S WHAT YOU DIDN'T DO!
BEN ELTON
STOP THIS CRAZINESS! WHAT DIDN'T I DO?
TAKE YOUR HANDS OFF OF ME ROB, OR I'LL PULL THEM OUTTA THEIR SOCKETS, CAPITO?
IS IT THAT YOU'RE ASHAMED OF ME, ROB? WHY DIDN'T YOU INTRODUCE ME TO YOUR FRIEND THERE? YOU RUN OUTSIDE TO TALK TO HIM, LIKE I'M DIRT! LIKE YOU DON'T WANT HIM TO SEE ME!
THAT'S RIDICULOUS! I WANTED TO CATCH HIM BEFORE HE GOT AWAY. WHEN YOU CAME OUT I WAS GONNA INTRODUCE YOU. HE'S NOBODY IMPORTANT. IF HE GOT AWAY BEFORE YOU CAME OUT, IT WOULDN'T MATTER.

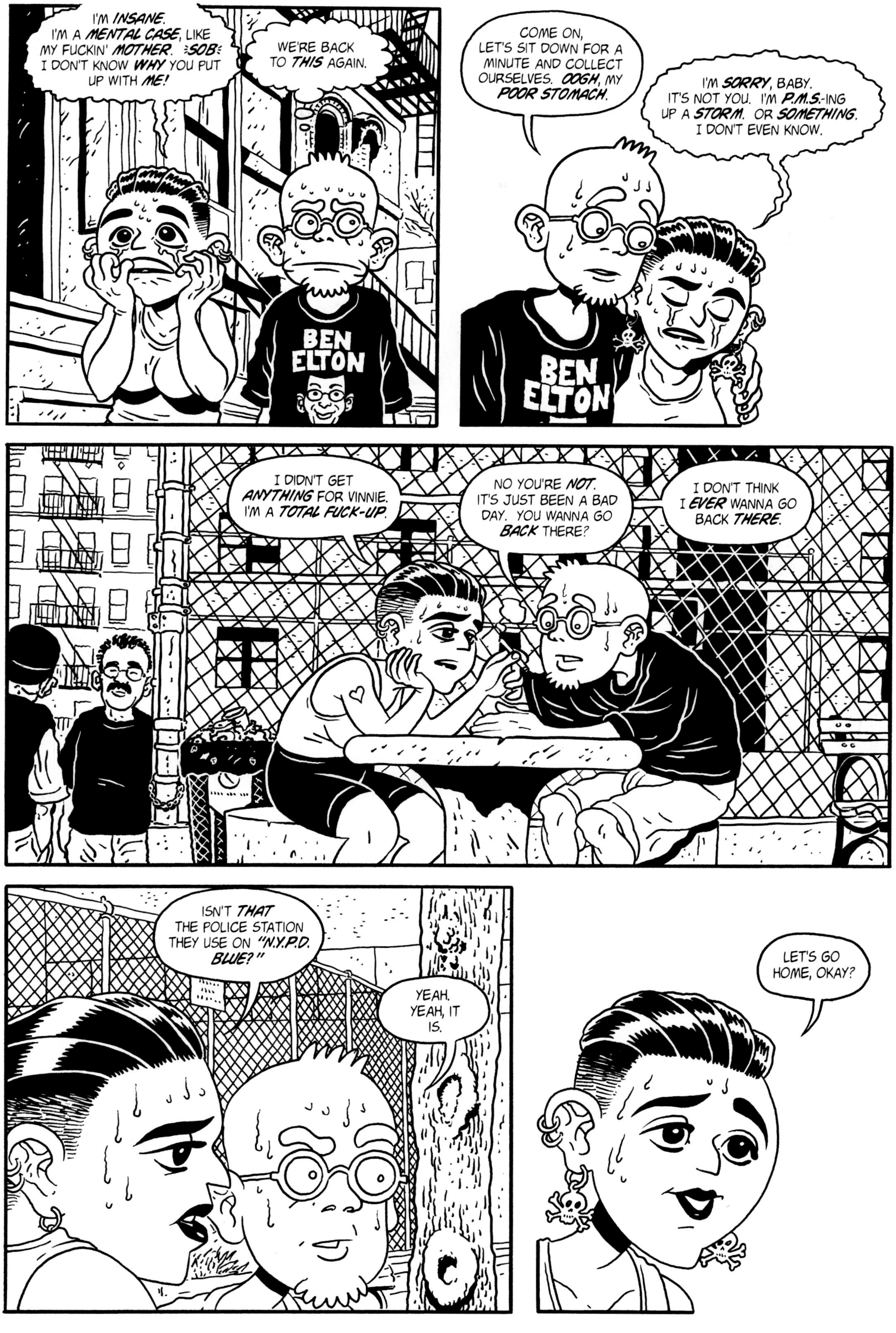

I'M INSANE. I'M A MENTAL CASE, LIKE MY FUCKIN' MOTHER. ~SOB~ I DON'T KNOW WHY YOU PUT UP WITH ME!
WE'RE BACK TO THIS AGAIN.
BEN ELTON
COME ON, LET'S SIT DOWN FOR A MINUTE AND COLLECT OURSELVES. OOGH, MY POOR STOMACH.
I'M SORRY, BABY. IT'S NOT YOU. I'M P.M.S.-ING UP A STORM. OR SOMETHING. I DON'T EVEN KNOW.
BEN ELTON
I DIDN'T GET ANYTHING FOR VINNIE. I'M A TOTAL FUCK-UP.
NO YOU'RE NOT. IT'S JUST BEEN A BAD DAY. YOU WANNA GO BACK THERE?
I DON'T THINK I EVER WANNA GO BACK THERE.
ISN'T THAT THE POLICE STATION THEY USE ON "N.Y.P.D. BLUE?"
YEAH. YEAH, IT IS.
LET'S GO HOME, OKAY?

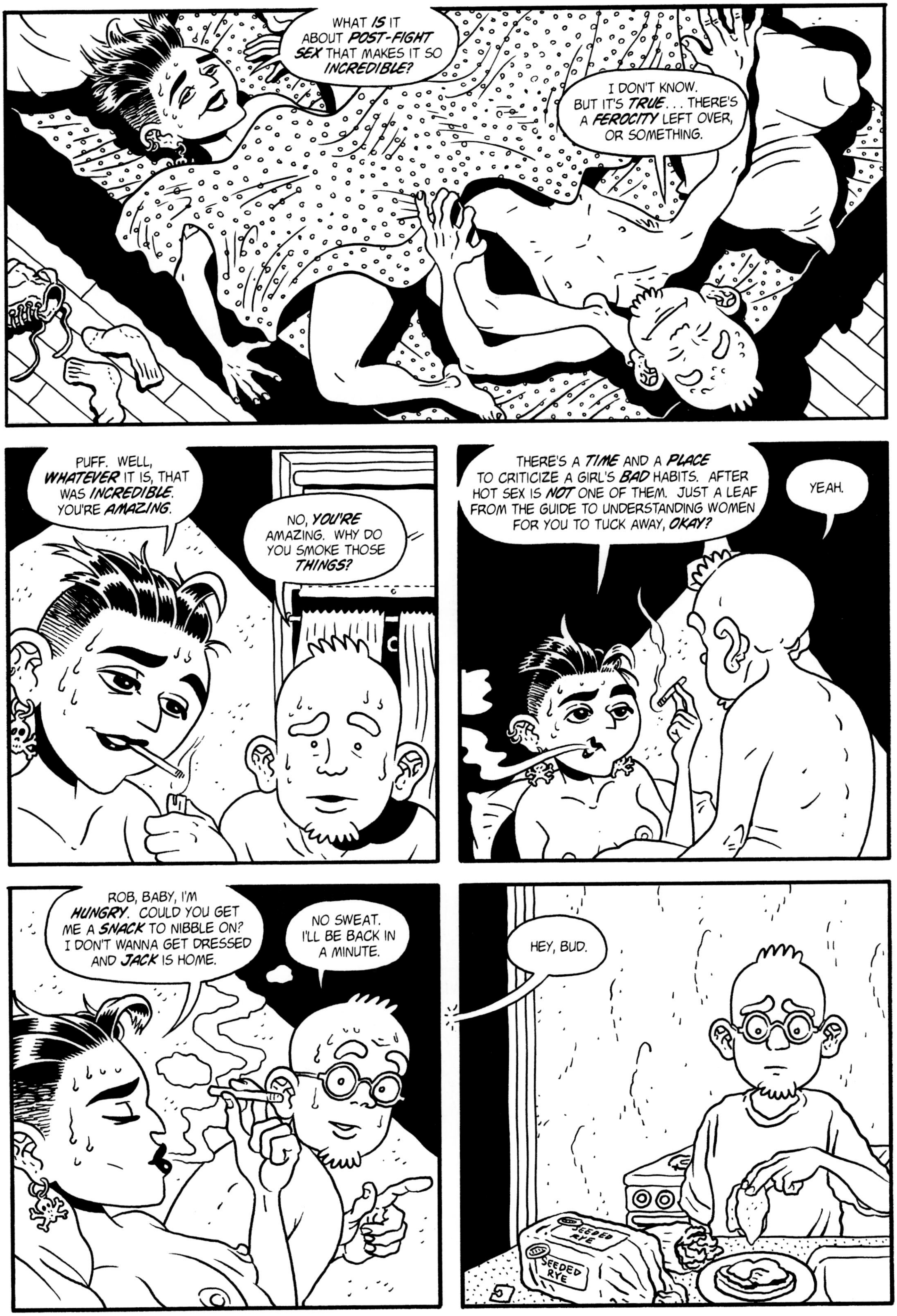
WHAT IS IT ABOUT POST-FIGHT SEX THAT MAKES IT SO INCREDIBLE?
I DON'T KNOW. BUT IT'S TRUE . . . THERE'S A FEROCITY LEFT OVER, OR SOMETHING.
PUFF. WELL, WHATEVER IT IS, THAT WAS INCREDIBLE. YOU'RE AMAZING.
NO, YOU'RE AMAZING. WHY DO YOU SMOKE THOSE THINGS?
THERE'S A TIME AND A PLACE TO CRITICIZE A GIRL'S BAD HABITS. AFTER HOT SEX IS NOT ONE OF THEM. JUST A LEAF FROM THE GUIDE TO UNDERSTANDING WOMEN FOR YOU TO TUCK AWAY, OKAY?
YEAH.
ROB, BABY, I'M HUNGRY. COULD YOU GET ME A SNACK TO NIBBLE ON? I DON'T WANNA GET DRESSED AND JACK IS HOME.
NO SWEAT. I'LL BE BACK IN A MINUTE.
HEY, BUD.
SEEDED RYE
SEEDED RYE

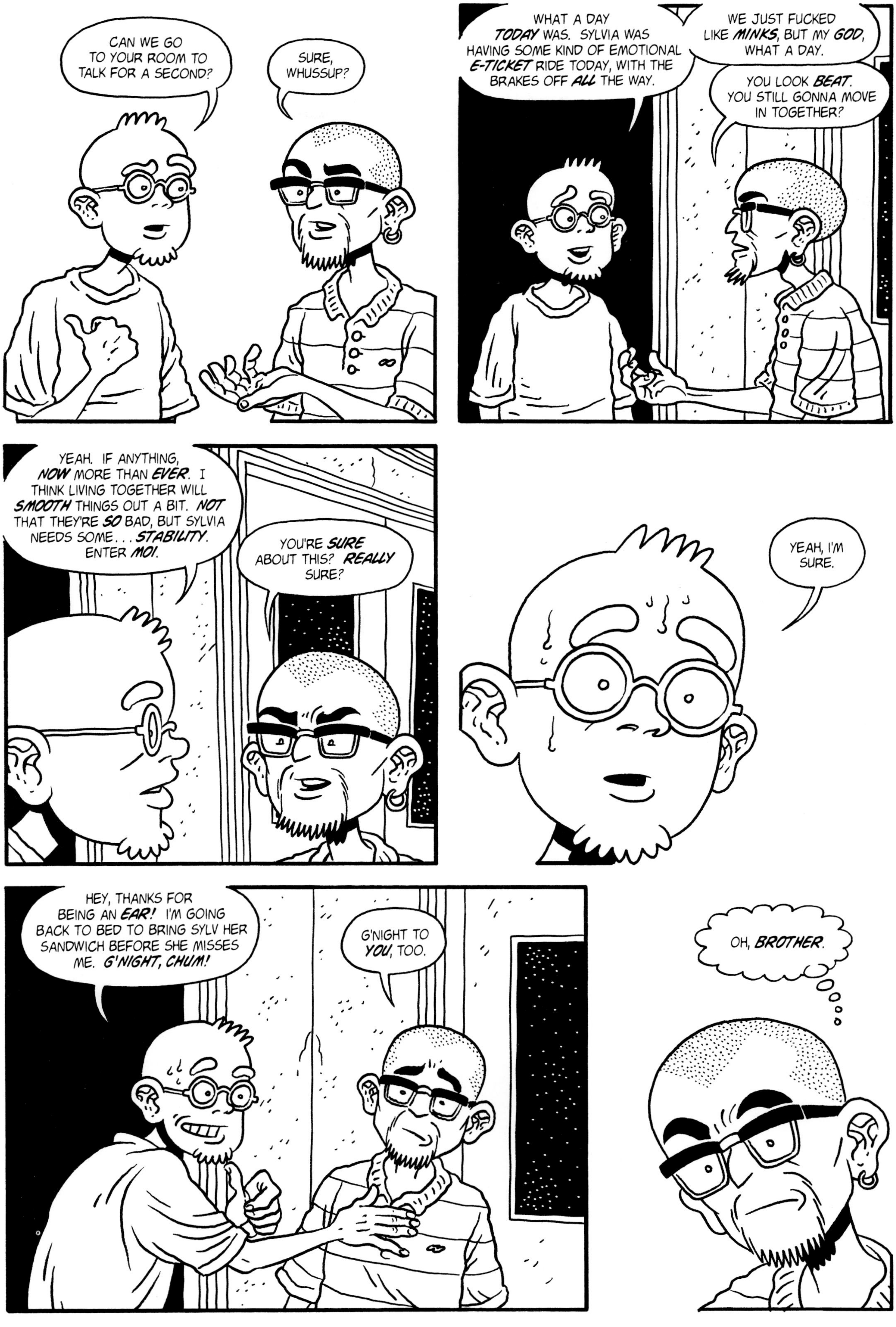
CAN WE GO TO YOUR ROOM TO TALK FOR A SECOND?
SURE, WHUSSUP?
WHAT A DAY TODAY WAS. SYLVIA WAS HAVING SOME KIND OF EMOTIONAL E-TICKET RIDE TODAY, WITH THE BRAKES OFF ALL THE WAY.
WE JUST FUCKED LIKE MINKS, BUT MY GOD, WHAT A DAY.
YOU LOOK BEAT. YOU STILL GONNA MOVE IN TOGETHER?
YEAH. IF ANYTHING, NOW MORE THAN EVER. I THINK LIVING TOGETHER WILL SMOOTH THINGS OUT A BIT. NOT THAT THEY'RE SO BAD, BUT SYLVIA NEEDS SOME... STABILITY. ENTER MOI.
YOU'RE SURE ABOUT THIS? REALLY SURE?
YEAH, I'M SURE.
HEY, THANKS FOR BEING AN EAR! I'M GOING BACK TO BED TO BRING SYLV HER SANDWICH BEFORE SHE MISSES ME. G'NIGHT, CHUM!
G'NIGHT TO YOU, TOO.
OH, BROTHER.

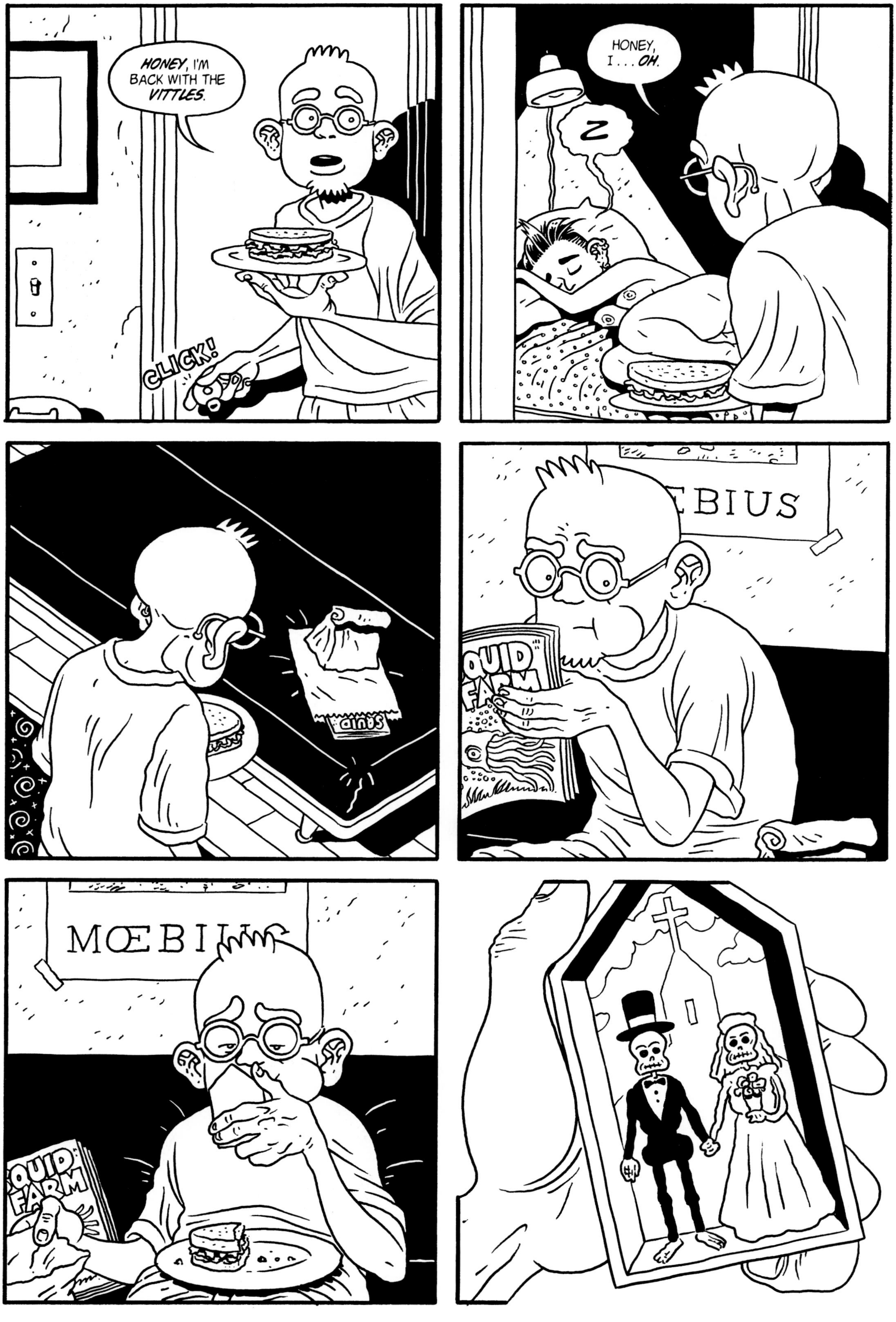
HONEY, I'M BACK WITH THE VITTLES.
CLICK!
HONEY, I... OH.
Z
SQUID
MŒBIUS
SQUID FARM
MŒBIU
SQUID FARM

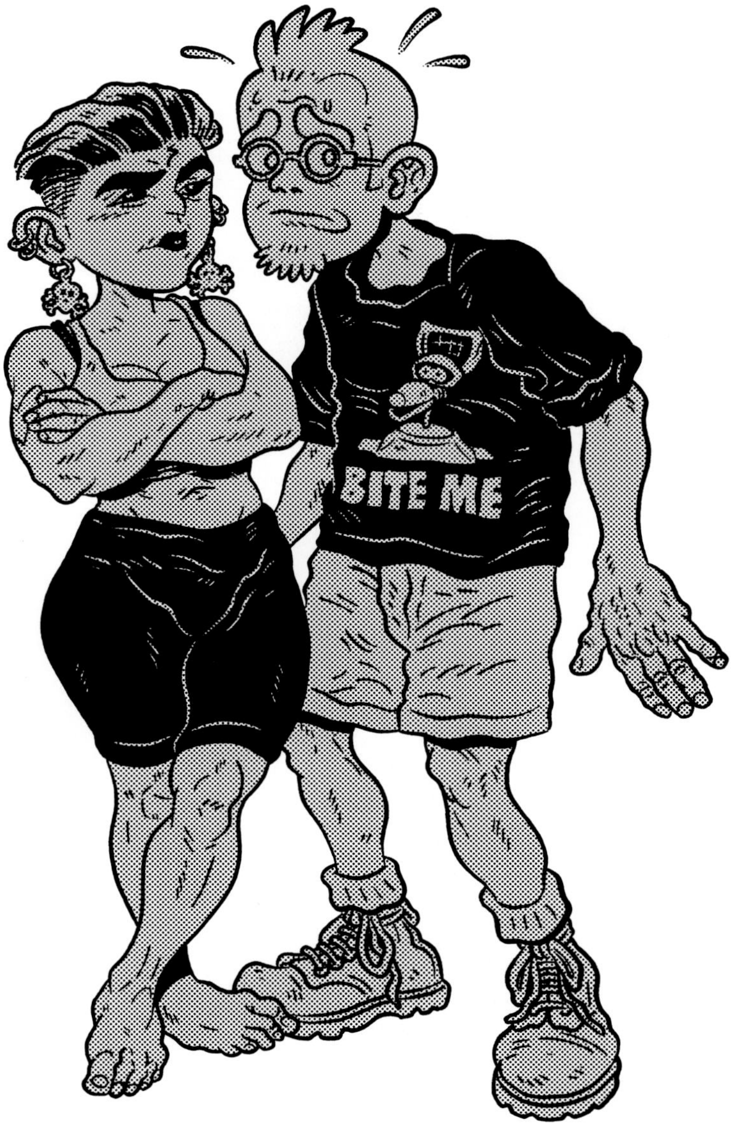
BITE ME

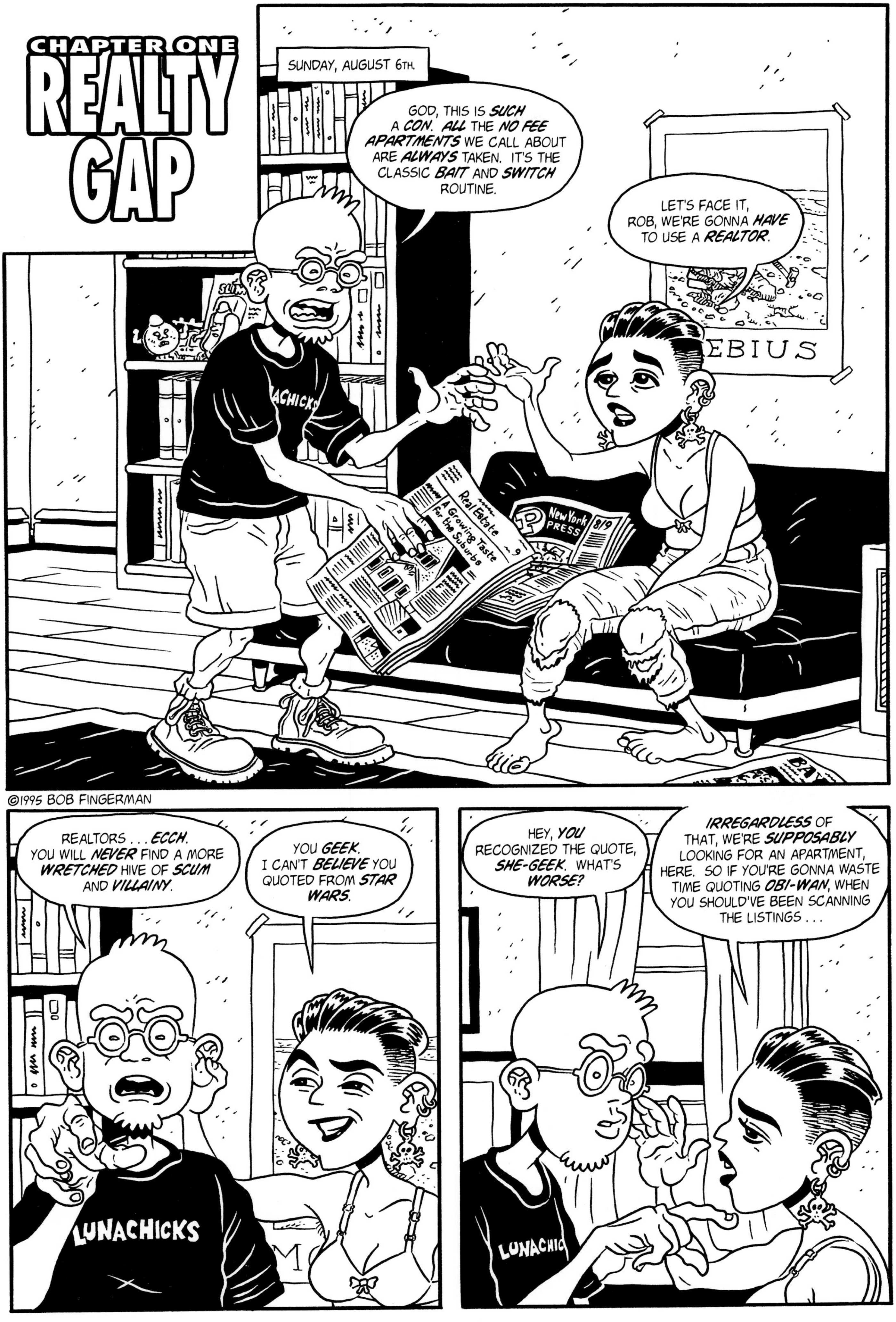
CHAPTER ONE
REALTY GAP
SUNDAY, AUGUST 6TH.
GOD, THIS IS SUCH A CON. ALL THE NO FEE APARTMENTS WE CALL ABOUT ARE ALWAYS TAKEN. IT'S THE CLASSIC BAIT AND SWITCH ROUTINE.
LET'S FACE IT, ROB, WE'RE GONNA HAVE TO USE A REALTOR.
EBIUS
Real Estate
A Growing Taste for the Suburbs
New York PRESS
8/9
©1995 BOB FINGERMAN
REALTORS . . . ECCH. YOU WILL NEVER FIND A MORE WRETCHED HIVE OF SCUM AND VILLAINY.
YOU GEEK. I CAN'T BELIEVE YOU QUOTED FROM STAR WARS.
LUNACHICKS
HEY, YOU RECOGNIZED THE QUOTE, SHE-GEEK. WHAT'S WORSE?
IRREGARDLESS OF THAT, WE'RE SUPPOSABLY LOOKING FOR AN APARTMENT, HERE. SO IF YOU'RE GONNA WASTE TIME QUOTING OBI-WAN, WHEN YOU SHOULD'VE BEEN SCANNING THE LISTINGS . . .
LUNACHIC

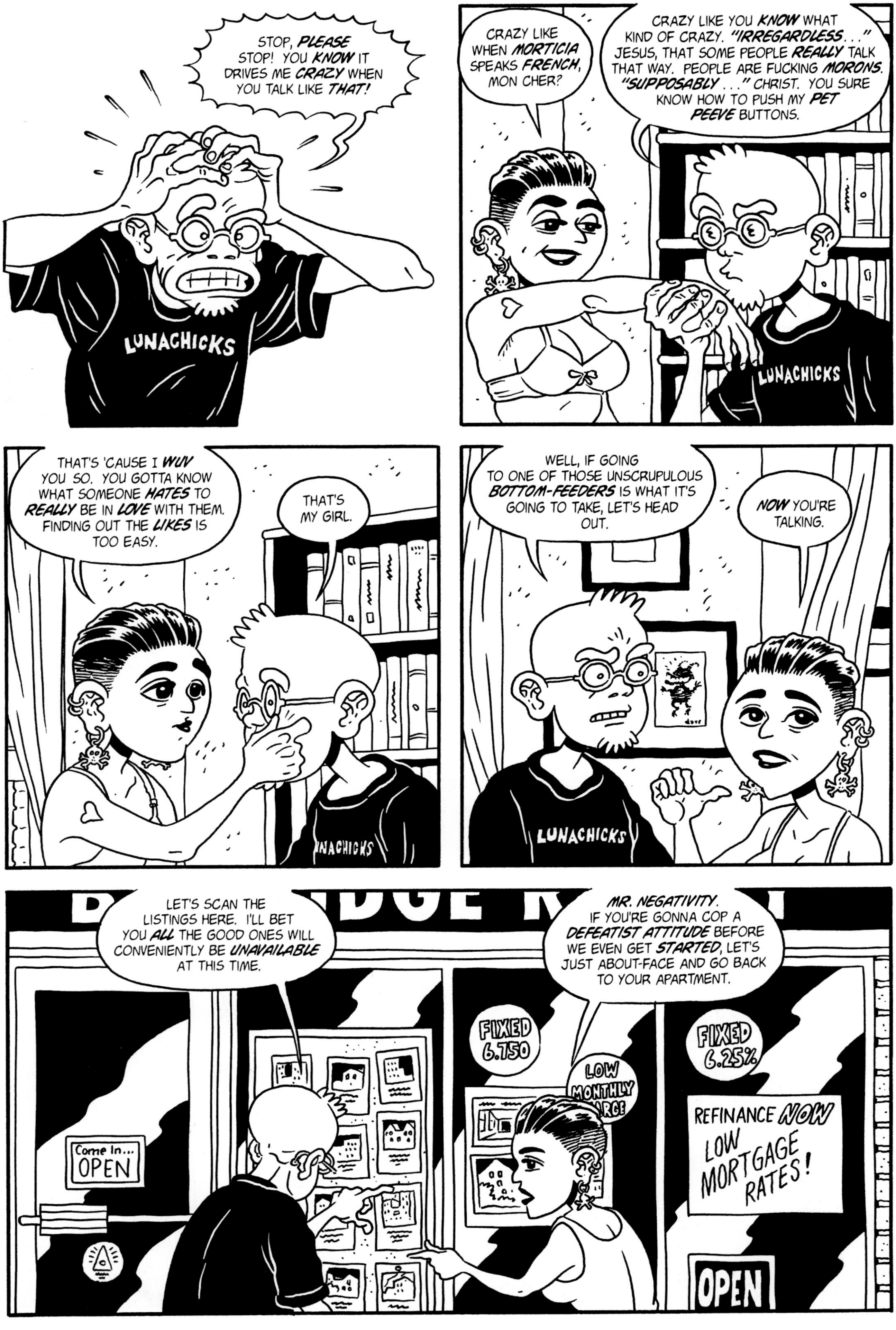
STOP, PLEASE STOP! YOU KNOW IT DRIVES ME CRAZY WHEN YOU TALK LIKE THAT!
LUNACHICKS
CRAZY LIKE WHEN MORTICIA SPEAKS FRENCH, MON CHER?
CRAZY LIKE YOU KNOW WHAT KIND OF CRAZY. "IRREGARDLESS..." JESUS, THAT SOME PEOPLE REALLY TALK THAT WAY. PEOPLE ARE FUCKING MORONS. "SUPPOSABLY..." CHRIST. YOU SURE KNOW HOW TO PUSH MY PET PEEVE BUTTONS.
LUNACHICKS
THAT'S 'CAUSE I WUV YOU SO. YOU GOTTA KNOW WHAT SOMEONE HATES TO REALLY BE IN LOVE WITH THEM. FINDING OUT THE LIKES IS TOO EASY.
THAT'S MY GIRL.
WELL, IF GOING TO ONE OF THOSE UNSCRUPULOUS BOTTOM-FEEDERS IS WHAT IT'S GOING TO TAKE, LET'S HEAD OUT.
NOW YOU'RE TALKING.
LUNACHICKS
LET'S SCAN THE LISTINGS HERE. I'LL BET YOU ALL THE GOOD ONES WILL CONVENIENTLY BE UNAVAILABLE AT THIS TIME.
MR. NEGATIVITY. IF YOU'RE GONNA COP A DEFEATIST ATTITUDE BEFORE WE EVEN GET STARTED, LET'S JUST ABOUT-FACE AND GO BACK TO YOUR APARTMENT.
FIXED 6.750
LOW MONTHLY
FIXED 6.25%
Come In... OPEN
REFINANCE NOW
LOW MORTGAGE RATES!
OPEN

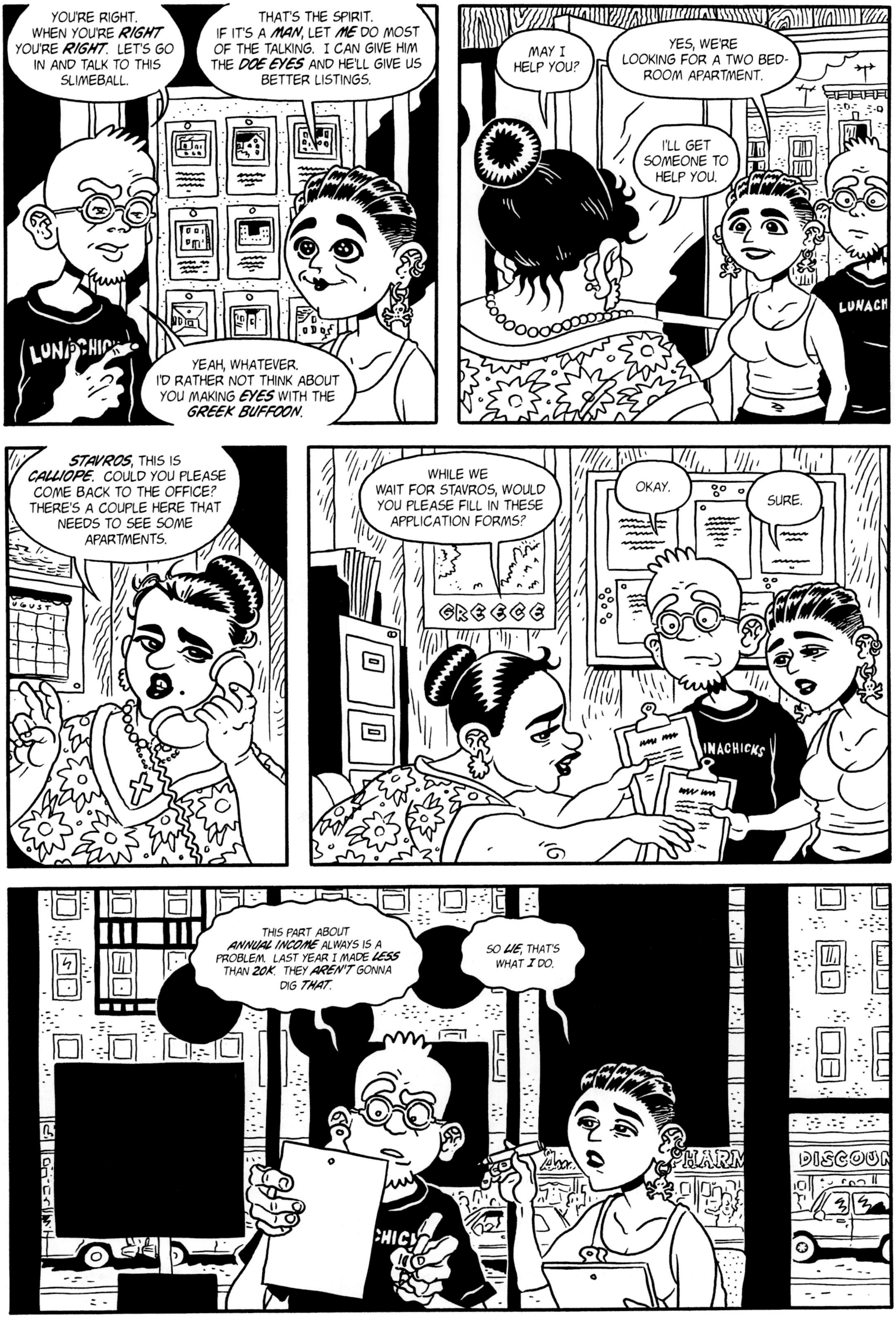
YOU'RE RIGHT. WHEN YOU'RE RIGHT YOU'RE RIGHT. LET'S GO IN AND TALK TO THIS SLIMEBALL.
THAT'S THE SPIRIT. IF IT'S A MAN, LET ME DO MOST OF THE TALKING. I CAN GIVE HIM THE DOE EYES AND HE'LL GIVE US BETTER LISTINGS.
YEAH, WHATEVER. I'D RATHER NOT THINK ABOUT YOU MAKING EYES WITH THE GREEK BUFFOON.
LUNACHICKS
MAY I HELP YOU?
YES, WE'RE LOOKING FOR A TWO BEDROOM APARTMENT.
I'LL GET SOMEONE TO HELP YOU.
STAVROS, THIS IS CALLIOPE. COULD YOU PLEASE COME BACK TO THE OFFICE? THERE'S A COUPLE HERE THAT NEEDS TO SEE SOME APARTMENTS.
WHILE WE WAIT FOR STAVROS, WOULD YOU PLEASE FILL IN THESE APPLICATION FORMS?
OKAY.
SURE.
GREECE
THIS PART ABOUT ANNUAL INCOME ALWAYS IS A PROBLEM. LAST YEAR I MADE LESS THAN 20K. THEY AREN'T GONNA DIG THAT.
SO LIE, THAT'S WHAT I DO.
DISCOUN

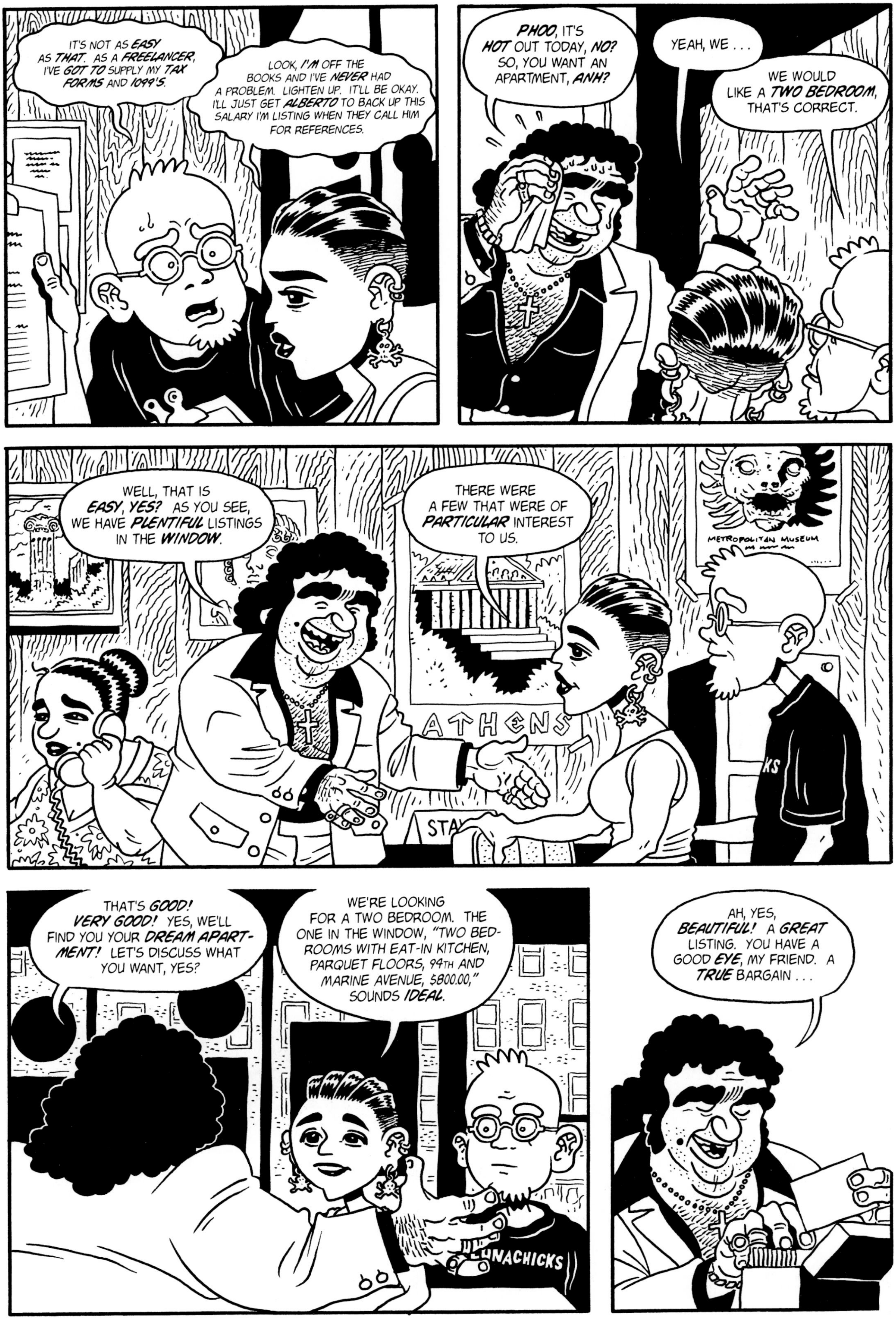
IT'S NOT AS EASY AS THAT. AS A FREELANCER, I'VE GOT TO SUPPLY MY TAX FORMS AND 1099'S.
LOOK, I'M OFF THE BOOKS AND I'VE NEVER HAD A PROBLEM. LIGHTEN UP. IT'LL BE OKAY. I'LL JUST GET ALBERTO TO BACK UP THIS SALARY I'M LISTING WHEN THEY CALL HIM FOR REFERENCES.
PHOO, IT'S HOT OUT TODAY, NO? SO, YOU WANT AN APARTMENT, ANH?
YEAH, WE . . .
WE WOULD LIKE A TWO BEDROOM, THAT'S CORRECT.
WELL, THAT IS EASY, YES? AS YOU SEE, WE HAVE PLENTIFUL LISTINGS IN THE WINDOW.
THERE WERE A FEW THAT WERE OF PARTICULAR INTEREST TO US.
METROPOLITAN MUSEUM
ATHENS
THAT'S GOOD! VERY GOOD! YES, WE'LL FIND YOU YOUR DREAM APARTMENT! LET'S DISCUSS WHAT YOU WANT, YES?
WE'RE LOOKING FOR A TWO BEDROOM. THE ONE IN THE WINDOW, "TWO BEDROOMS WITH EAT-IN KITCHEN, PARQUET FLOORS, 94TH AND MARINE AVENUE, $800.00," SOUNDS IDEAL.
NACHICKS
AH, YES, BEAUTIFUL! A GREAT LISTING. YOU HAVE A GOOD EYE, MY FRIEND. A TRUE BARGAIN . . .

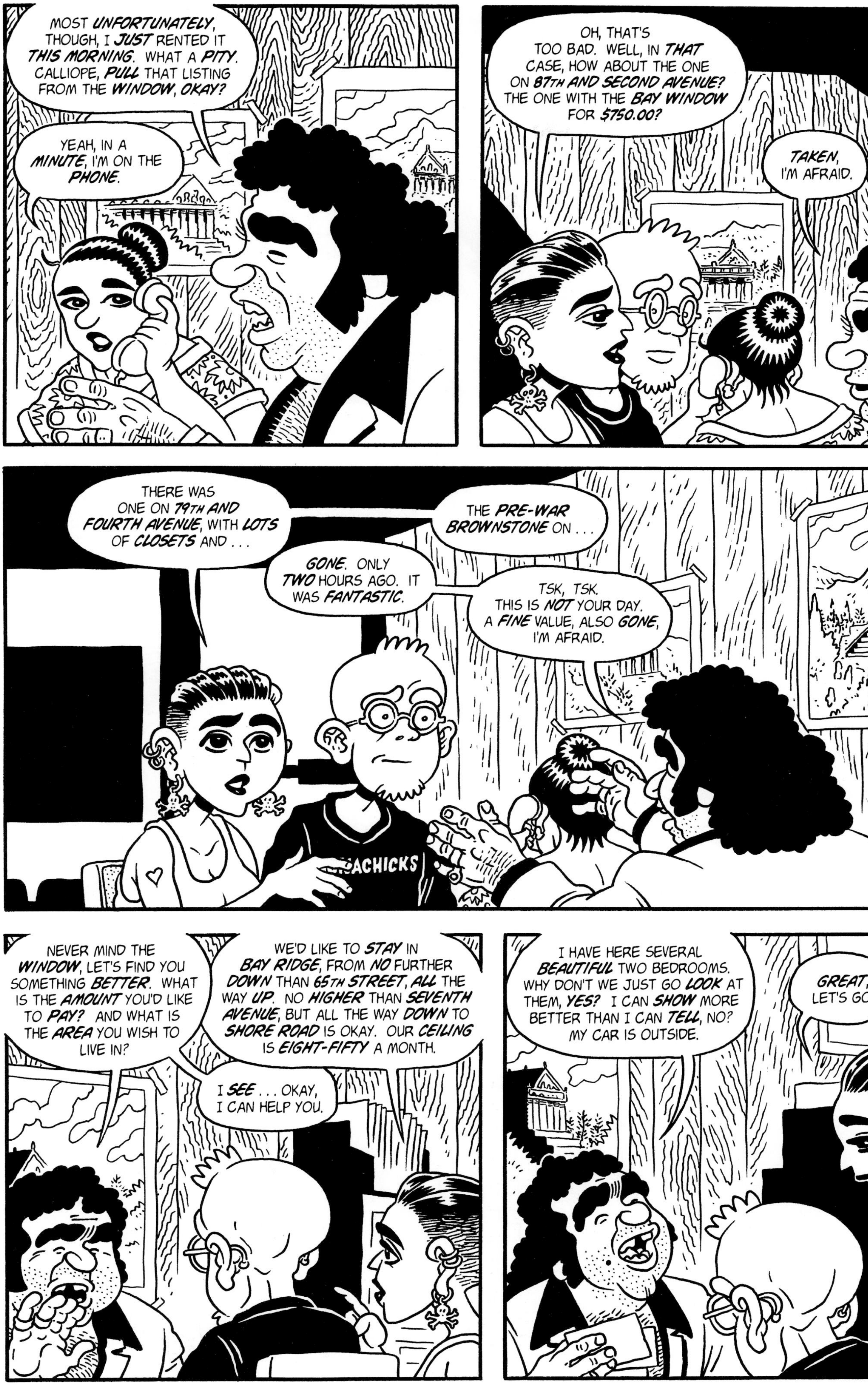
MOST UNFORTUNATELY, THOUGH, I JUST RENTED IT THIS MORNING. WHAT A PITY. CALLIOPE, PULL THAT LISTING FROM THE WINDOW, OKAY?
YEAH, IN A MINUTE, I'M ON THE PHONE.
OH, THAT'S TOO BAD. WELL, IN THAT CASE, HOW ABOUT THE ONE ON 87TH AND SECOND AVENUE? THE ONE WITH THE BAY WINDOW FOR $750.00?
TAKEN, I'M AFRAID.
THERE WAS ONE ON 79TH AND FOURTH AVENUE, WITH LOTS OF CLOSETS AND . . .
GONE. ONLY TWO HOURS AGO. IT WAS FANTASTIC.
THE PRE-WAR BROWNSTONE ON . . .
TSK, TSK. THIS IS NOT YOUR DAY. A FINE VALUE, ALSO GONE, I'M AFRAID.
NEVER MIND THE WINDOW, LET'S FIND YOU SOMETHING BETTER. WHAT IS THE AMOUNT YOU'D LIKE TO PAY? AND WHAT IS THE AREA YOU WISH TO LIVE IN?
WE'D LIKE TO STAY IN BAY RIDGE, FROM NO FURTHER DOWN THAN 65TH STREET, ALL THE WAY UP. NO HIGHER THAN SEVENTH AVENUE, BUT ALL THE WAY DOWN TO SHORE ROAD IS OKAY. OUR CEILING IS EIGHT-FIFTY A MONTH.
I SEE . . . OKAY, I CAN HELP YOU.
I HAVE HERE SEVERAL BEAUTIFUL TWO BEDROOMS. WHY DON'T WE JUST GO LOOK AT THEM, YES? I CAN SHOW MORE BETTER THAN I CAN TELL, NO? MY CAR IS OUTSIDE.
GREAT, LET'S GO.

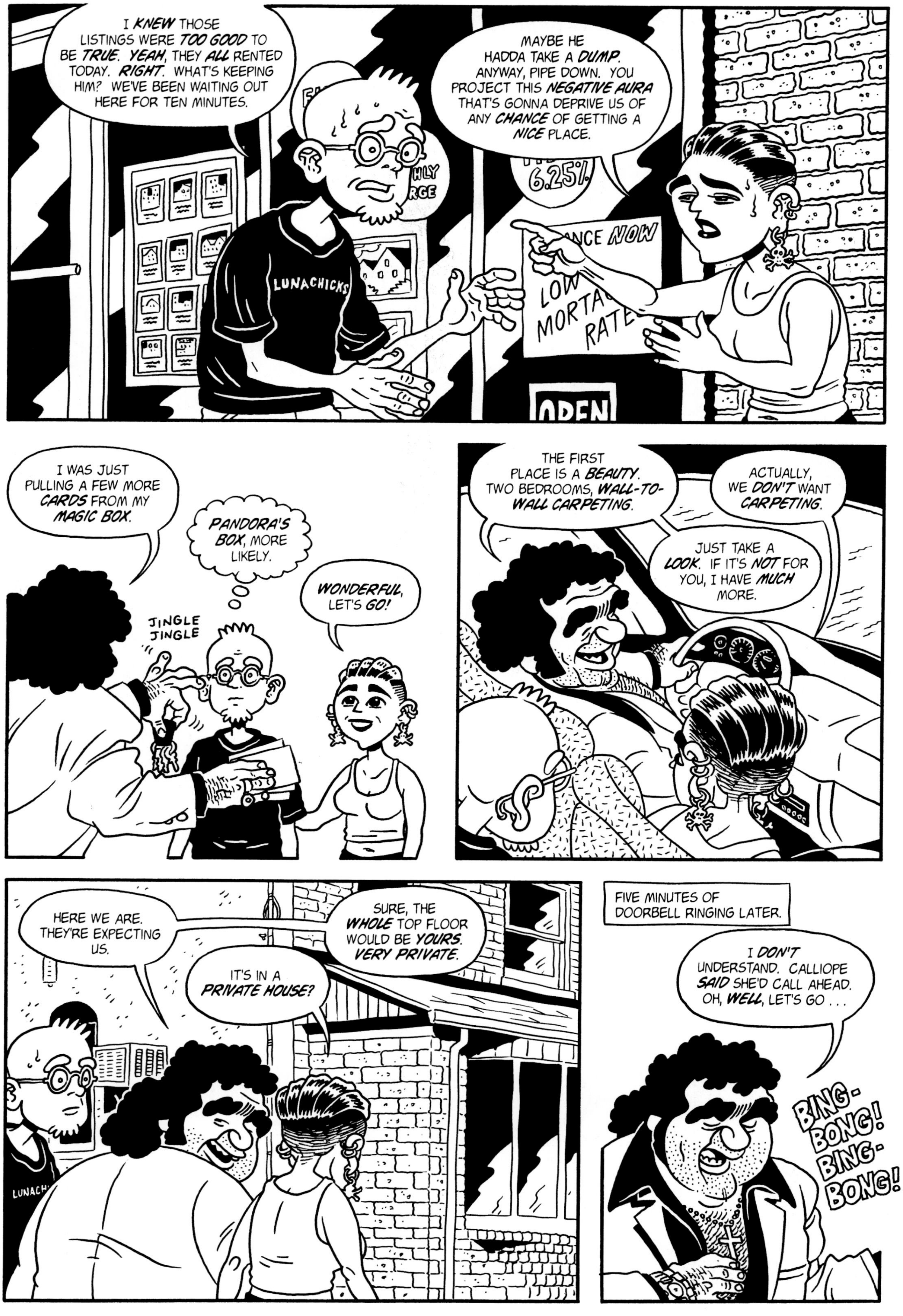

I KNEW THOSE LISTINGS WERE TOO GOOD TO BE TRUE. YEAH, THEY ALL RENTED TODAY. RIGHT. WHAT'S KEEPING HIM? WE'VE BEEN WAITING OUT HERE FOR TEN MINUTES.
MAYBE HE HADDA TAKE A DUMP. ANYWAY, PIPE DOWN. YOU PROJECT THIS NEGATIVE AURA THAT'S GONNA DEPRIVE US OF ANY CHANCE OF GETTING A NICE PLACE.
LUNACHICKS
6.25%
NOW
LOW MORTA RATE
OPEN
I WAS JUST PULLING A FEW MORE CARDS FROM MY MAGIC BOX.
PANDORA'S BOX, MORE LIKELY.
WONDERFUL, LET'S GO!
JINGLE JINGLE
THE FIRST PLACE IS A BEAUTY. TWO BEDROOMS, WALL-TO-WALL CARPETING.
ACTUALLY, WE DON'T WANT CARPETING.
JUST TAKE A LOOK. IF IT'S NOT FOR YOU, I HAVE MUCH MORE.
HERE WE ARE. THEY'RE EXPECTING US.
IT'S IN A PRIVATE HOUSE?
SURE, THE WHOLE TOP FLOOR WOULD BE YOURS. VERY PRIVATE.
LUNACH
FIVE MINUTES OF DOORBELL RINGING LATER.
I DON'T UNDERSTAND. CALLIOPE SAID SHE'D CALL AHEAD. OH, WELL, LET'S GO . . .
BING-BONG! BING-BONG!

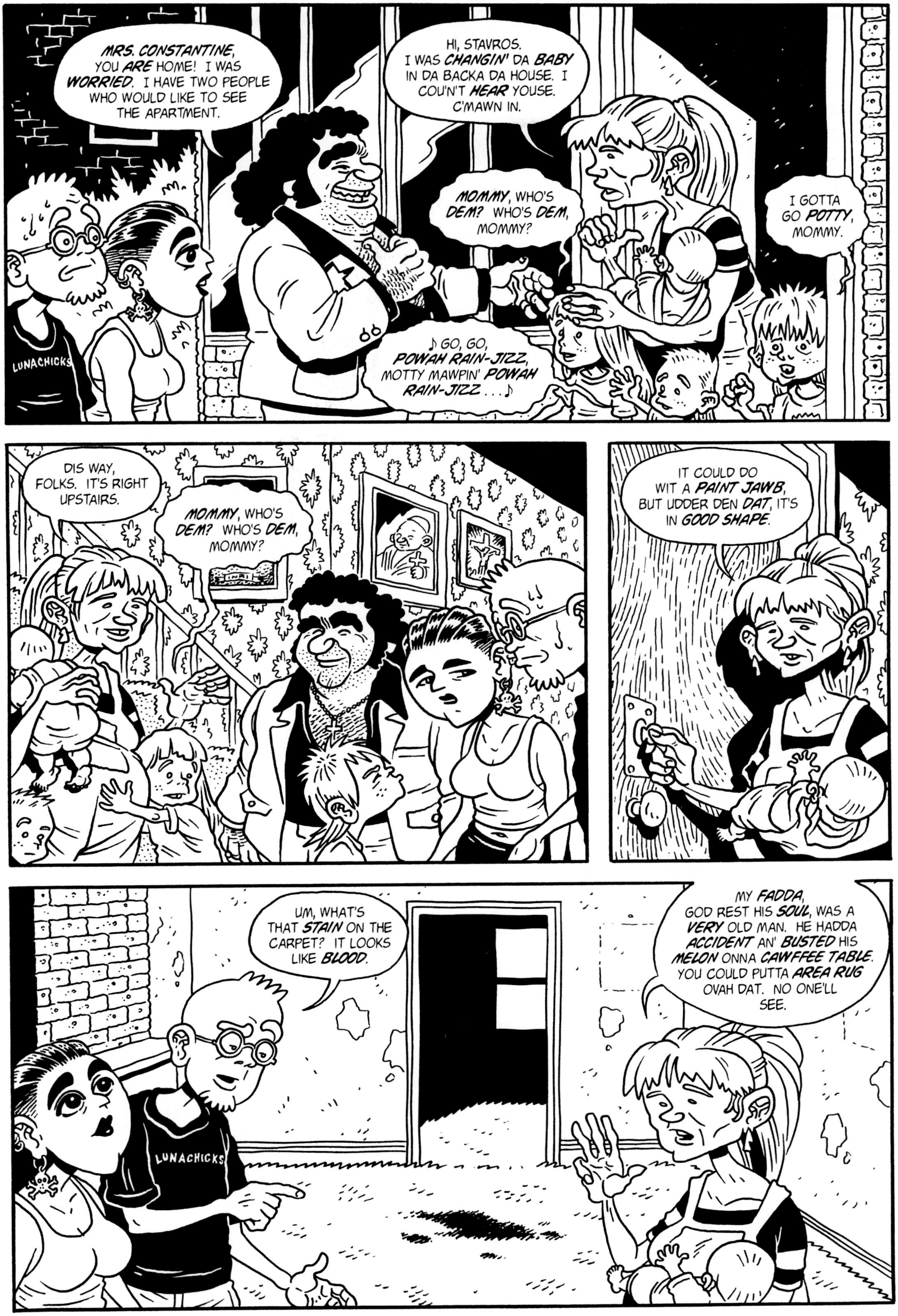
MRS. CONSTANTINE, YOU ARE HOME! I WAS WORRIED. I HAVE TWO PEOPLE WHO WOULD LIKE TO SEE THE APARTMENT.
HI, STAVROS. I WAS CHANGIN' DA BABY IN DA BACKA DA HOUSE. I COU'N'T HEAR YOUSE. C'MAWN IN.
MOMMY, WHO'S DEM? WHO'S DEM, MOMMY?
I GOTTA GO POTTY, MOMMY.
♪ GO, GO, POWAH RAIN-JIZZ, MOTTY MAWPIN' POWAH RAIN-JIZZ . . . ♪
LUNACHICKS
DIS WAY, FOLKS. IT'S RIGHT UPSTAIRS.
MOMMY, WHO'S DEM? WHO'S DEM, MOMMY?
IT COULD DO WIT A PAINT JAWB, BUT UDDER DEN DAT, IT'S IN GOOD SHAPE.
UM, WHAT'S THAT STAIN ON THE CARPET? IT LOOKS LIKE BLOOD.
MY FADDA, GOD REST HIS SOUL, WAS A VERY OLD MAN. HE HADDA ACCIDENT AN' BUSTED HIS MELON ONNA CAWFFEE TABLE. YOU COULD PUTTA AREA RUG OVAH DAT. NO ONE'LL SEE.
LUNACHICKS

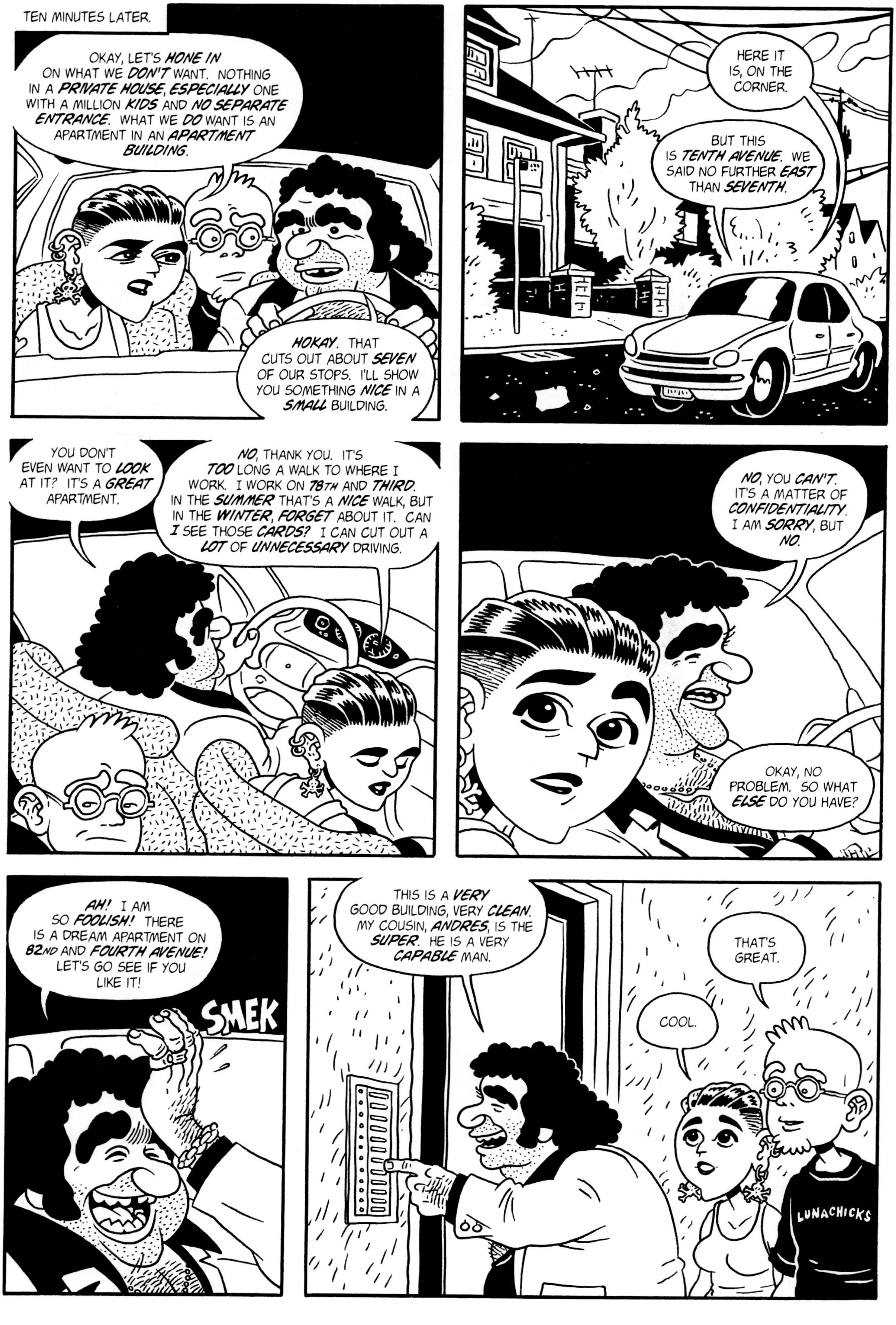
TEN MINUTES LATER.
OKAY, LET'S HONE IN ON WHAT WE DON'T WANT. NOTHING IN A PRIVATE HOUSE, ESPECIALLY ONE WITH A MILLION KIDS AND NO SEPARATE ENTRANCE. WHAT WE DO WANT IS AN APARTMENT IN AN APARTMENT BUILDING.
HOKAY. THAT CUTS OUT ABOUT SEVEN OF OUR STOPS. I'LL SHOW YOU SOMETHING NICE IN A SMALL BUILDING.
HERE IT IS, ON THE CORNER.
BUT THIS IS TENTH AVENUE. WE SAID NO FURTHER EAST THAN SEVENTH.
YOU DON'T EVEN WANT TO LOOK AT IT? IT'S A GREAT APARTMENT.
NO, THANK YOU. IT'S TOO LONG A WALK TO WHERE I WORK. I WORK ON 78TH AND THIRD. IN THE SUMMER THAT'S A NICE WALK, BUT IN THE WINTER, FORGET ABOUT IT. CAN I SEE THOSE CARDS? I CAN CUT OUT A LOT OF UNNECESSARY DRIVING.
NO, YOU CAN'T. IT'S A MATTER OF CONFIDENTIALITY. I AM SORRY, BUT NO.
OKAY, NO PROBLEM. SO WHAT ELSE DO YOU HAVE?
AH! I AM SO FOOLISH! THERE IS A DREAM APARTMENT ON 82ND AND FOURTH AVENUE! LET'S GO SEE IF YOU LIKE IT!
SMEK
THIS IS A VERY GOOD BUILDING, VERY CLEAN. MY COUSIN, ANDRES, IS THE SUPER. HE IS A VERY CAPABLE MAN.
THAT'S GREAT.
COOL.
LUNACHICKS

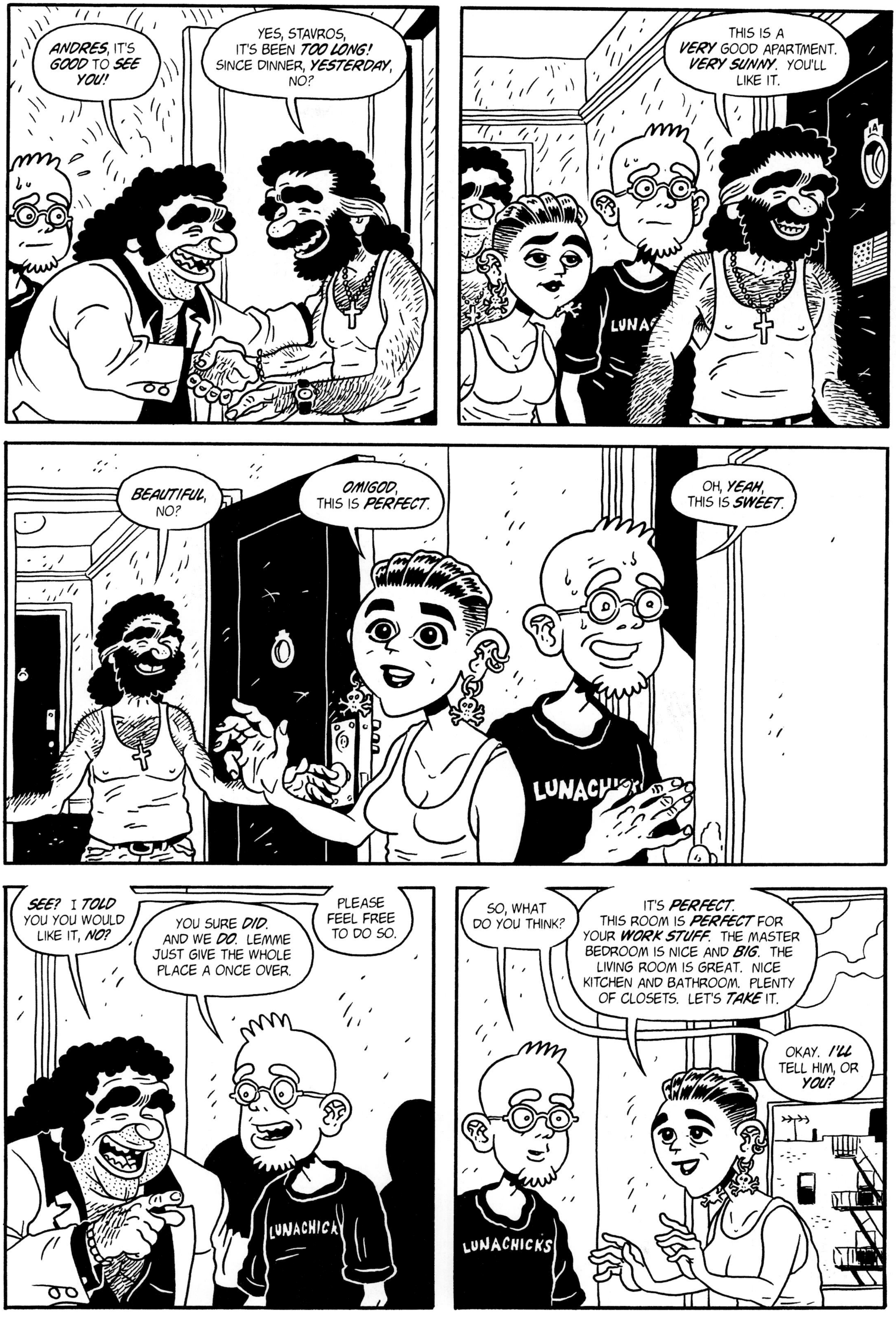
ANDRES, IT'S GOOD TO SEE YOU!
YES, STAVROS, IT'S BEEN TOO LONG! SINCE DINNER, YESTERDAY, NO?
THIS IS A VERY GOOD APARTMENT. VERY SUNNY. YOU'LL LIKE IT.
LUNA
BEAUTIFUL, NO?
OMIGOD, THIS IS PERFECT.
OH, YEAH, THIS IS SWEET.
LUNACHI
SEE? I TOLD YOU YOU WOULD LIKE IT, NO?
YOU SURE DID. AND WE DO. LEMME JUST GIVE THE WHOLE PLACE A ONCE OVER.
PLEASE FEEL FREE TO DO SO.
LUNACHICK
SO, WHAT DO YOU THINK?
IT'S PERFECT. THIS ROOM IS PERFECT FOR YOUR WORK STUFF. THE MASTER BEDROOM IS NICE AND BIG. THE LIVING ROOM IS GREAT. NICE KITCHEN AND BATHROOM. PLENTY OF CLOSETS. LET'S TAKE IT.
OKAY. I'LL TELL HIM, OR YOU?
LUNACHICKS

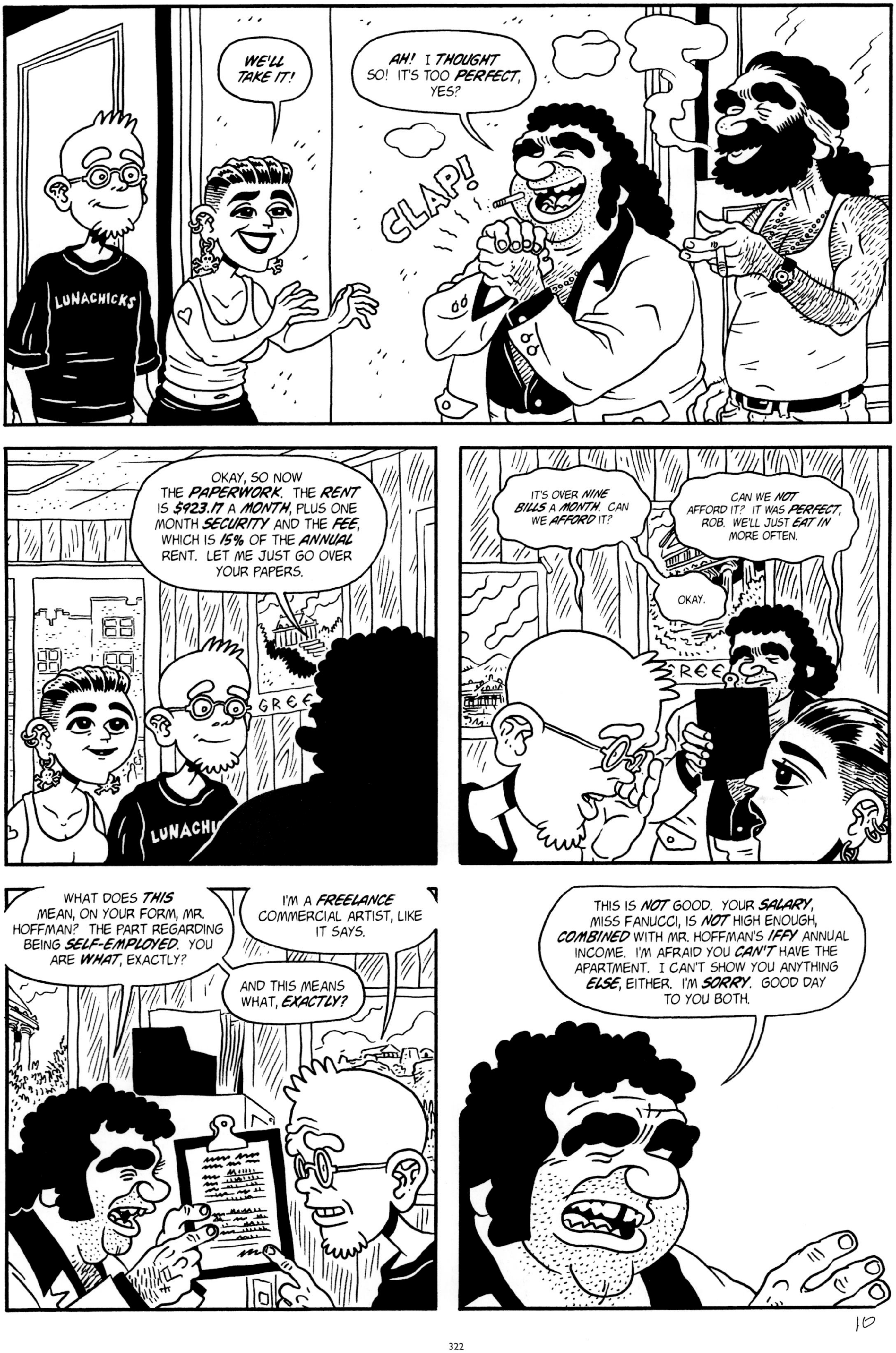
WE'LL TAKE IT!
AH! I THOUGHT SO! IT'S TOO PERFECT, YES?
CLAP!
LUNACHICKS
OKAY, SO NOW THE PAPERWORK. THE RENT IS $923.17 A MONTH, PLUS ONE MONTH SECURITY AND THE FEE, WHICH IS 15% OF THE ANNUAL RENT. LET ME JUST GO OVER YOUR PAPERS.
IT'S OVER NINE BILLS A MONTH. CAN WE AFFORD IT?
CAN WE NOT AFFORD IT? IT WAS PERFECT, ROB. WE'LL JUST EAT IN MORE OFTEN.
OKAY.
WHAT DOES THIS MEAN, ON YOUR FORM, MR. HOFFMAN? THE PART REGARDING BEING SELF-EMPLOYED. YOU ARE WHAT, EXACTLY?
I'M A FREELANCE COMMERCIAL ARTIST, LIKE IT SAYS.
AND THIS MEANS WHAT, EXACTLY?
THIS IS NOT GOOD. YOUR SALARY, MISS FANUCCI, IS NOT HIGH ENOUGH, COMBINED WITH MR. HOFFMAN'S IFFY ANNUAL INCOME. I'M AFRAID YOU CAN'T HAVE THE APARTMENT. I CAN'T SHOW YOU ANYTHING ELSE, EITHER. I'M SORRY. GOOD DAY TO YOU BOTH.
10

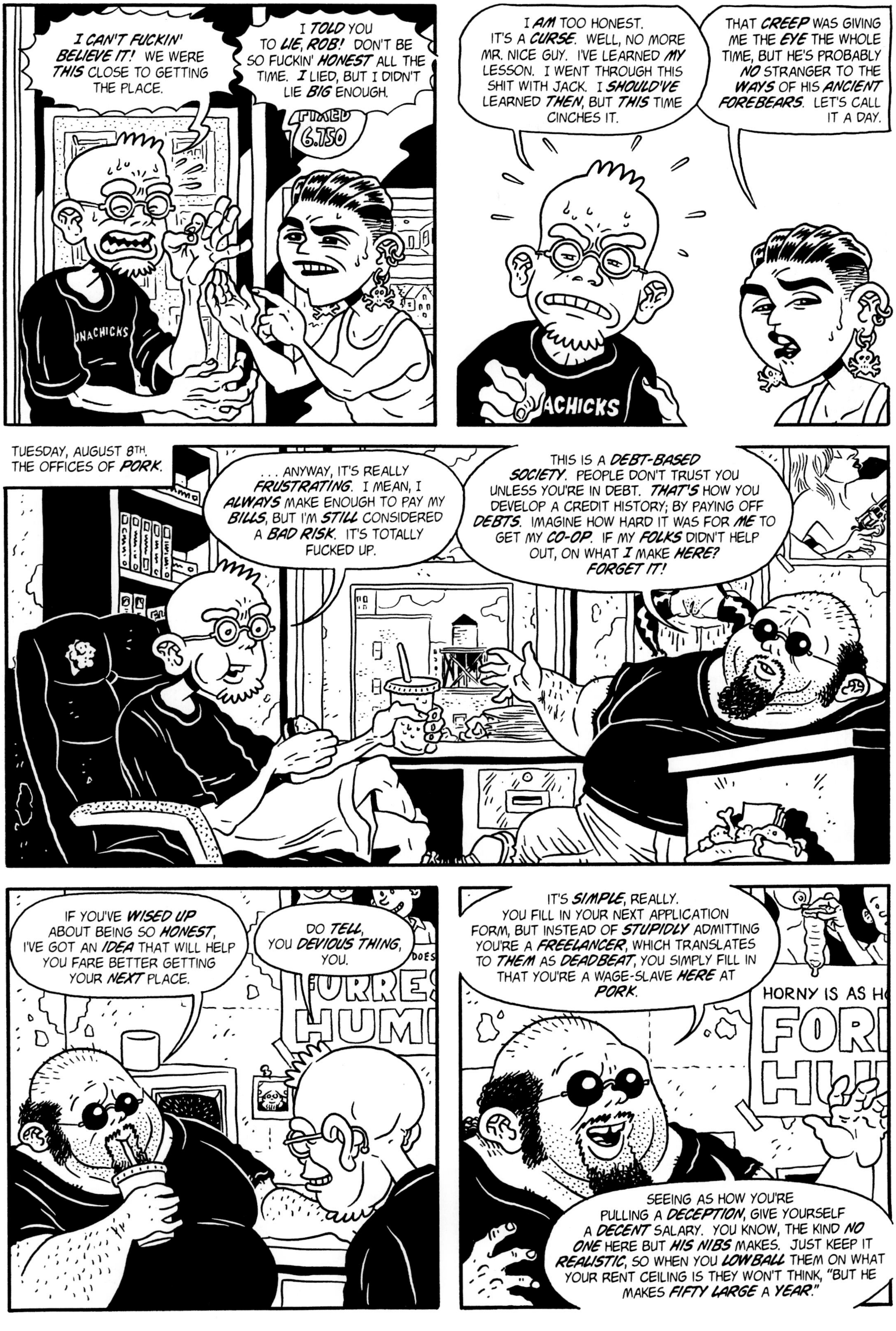
I CAN'T FUCKIN' BELIEVE IT! WE WERE THIS CLOSE TO GETTING THE PLACE.
I TOLD YOU TO LIE, ROB! DON'T BE SO FUCKIN' HONEST ALL THE TIME. I LIED, BUT I DIDN'T LIE BIG ENOUGH.
FIXED 6,750
UNACHICKS
I AM TOO HONEST. IT'S A CURSE. WELL, NO MORE MR. NICE GUY. I'VE LEARNED MY LESSON. I WENT THROUGH THIS SHIT WITH JACK. I SHOULD'VE LEARNED THEN, BUT THIS TIME CINCHES IT.
THAT CREEP WAS GIVING ME THE EYE THE WHOLE TIME, BUT HE'S PROBABLY NO STRANGER TO THE WAYS OF HIS ANCIENT FOREBEARS. LET'S CALL IT A DAY.
ACHICKS
TUESDAY, AUGUST 8TH. THE OFFICES OF PORK.
. . . ANYWAY, IT'S REALLY FRUSTRATING. I MEAN, I ALWAYS MAKE ENOUGH TO PAY MY BILLS, BUT I'M STILL CONSIDERED A BAD RISK. IT'S TOTALLY FUCKED UP.
THIS IS A DEBT-BASED SOCIETY. PEOPLE DON'T TRUST YOU UNLESS YOU'RE IN DEBT. THAT'S HOW YOU DEVELOP A CREDIT HISTORY; BY PAYING OFF DEBTS. IMAGINE HOW HARD IT WAS FOR ME TO GET MY CO-OP. IF MY FOLKS DIDN'T HELP OUT, ON WHAT I MAKE HERE? FORGET IT!
IF YOU'VE WISED UP ABOUT BEING SO HONEST, I'VE GOT AN IDEA THAT WILL HELP YOU FARE BETTER GETTING YOUR NEXT PLACE.
DO TELL, YOU DEVIOUS THING, YOU.
DOES
FORRES
HUM
IT'S SIMPLE, REALLY. YOU FILL IN YOUR NEXT APPLICATION FORM, BUT INSTEAD OF STUPIDLY ADMITTING YOU'RE A FREELANCER, WHICH TRANSLATES TO THEM AS DEADBEAT, YOU SIMPLY FILL IN THAT YOU'RE A WAGE-SLAVE HERE AT PORK.
HORNY IS AS H
FOR
HU
SEEING AS HOW YOU'RE PULLING A DECEPTION, GIVE YOURSELF A DECENT SALARY. YOU KNOW, THE KIND NO ONE HERE BUT HIS NIBS MAKES. JUST KEEP IT REALISTIC, SO WHEN YOU LOWBALL THEM ON WHAT YOUR RENT CEILING IS THEY WON'T THINK, "BUT HE MAKES FIFTY LARGE A YEAR."

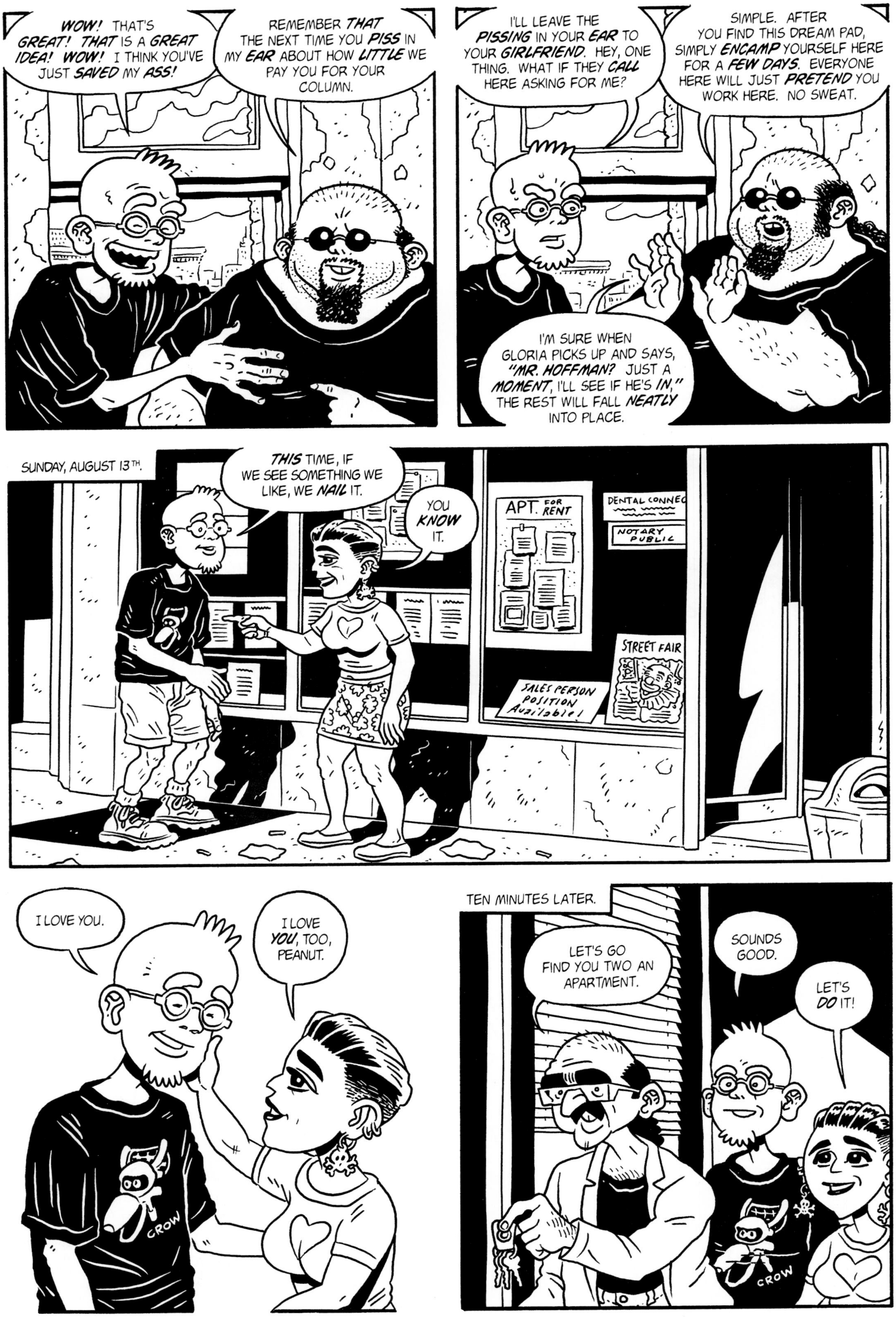
WOW! THAT'S GREAT! THAT IS A GREAT IDEA! WOW! I THINK YOU'VE JUST SAVED MY ASS!
REMEMBER THAT THE NEXT TIME YOU PISS IN MY EAR ABOUT HOW LITTLE WE PAY YOU FOR YOUR COLUMN.
I'LL LEAVE THE PISSING IN YOUR EAR TO YOUR GIRLFRIEND. HEY, ONE THING. WHAT IF THEY CALL HERE ASKING FOR ME?
SIMPLE. AFTER YOU FIND THIS DREAM PAD, SIMPLY ENCAMP YOURSELF HERE FOR A FEW DAYS. EVERYONE HERE WILL JUST PRETEND YOU WORK HERE. NO SWEAT.
I'M SURE WHEN GLORIA PICKS UP AND SAYS, "MR. HOFFMAN? JUST A MOMENT, I'LL SEE IF HE'S IN," THE REST WILL FALL NEATLY INTO PLACE.
SUNDAY, AUGUST 13TH.
THIS TIME, IF WE SEE SOMETHING WE LIKE, WE NAIL IT.
YOU KNOW IT.
APT. FOR RENT
NOTARY PUBLIC
STREET FAIR
SALES PERSON POSITION Available!
I LOVE YOU.
I LOVE YOU, TOO, PEANUT.
CROW
TEN MINUTES LATER.
LET'S GO FIND YOU TWO AN APARTMENT.
SOUNDS GOOD.
LET'S DO IT!
CROW

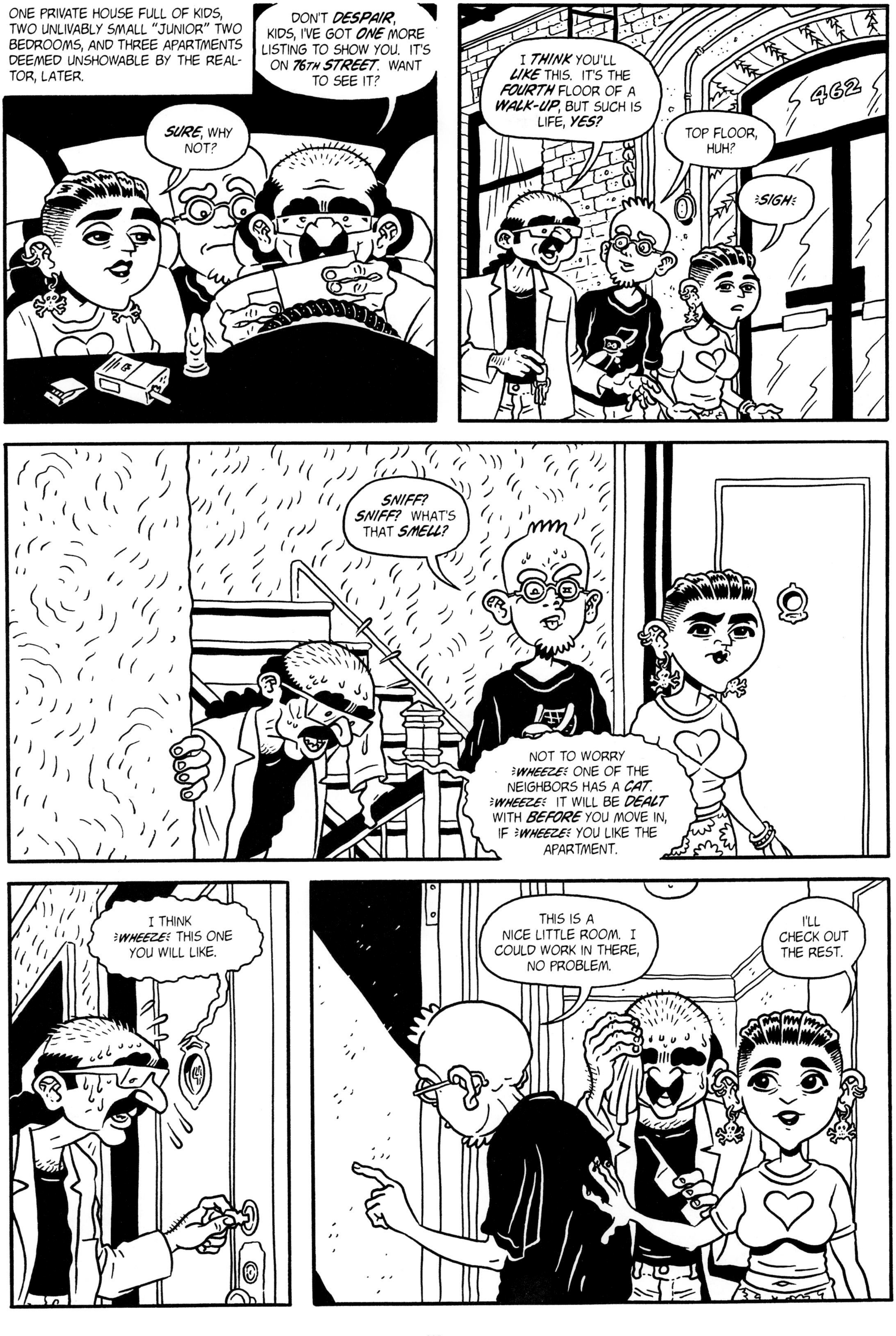

ONE PRIVATE HOUSE FULL OF KIDS, TWO UNLIVABLY SMALL "JUNIOR" TWO BEDROOMS, AND THREE APARTMENTS DEEMED UNSHOWABLE BY THE REALTOR, LATER.
DON'T DESPAIR, KIDS, I'VE GOT ONE MORE LISTING TO SHOW YOU. IT'S ON 76TH STREET. WANT TO SEE IT?
SURE, WHY NOT?
I THINK YOU'LL LIKE THIS. IT'S THE FOURTH FLOOR OF A WALK-UP, BUT SUCH IS LIFE, YES?
462
TOP FLOOR, HUH?
SIGH
SNIFF? SNIFF? WHAT'S THAT SMELL?
NOT TO WORRY WHEEZE ONE OF THE NEIGHBORS HAS A CAT. WHEEZE IT WILL BE DEALT WITH BEFORE YOU MOVE IN, IF WHEEZE YOU LIKE THE APARTMENT.
I THINK WHEEZE THIS ONE YOU WILL LIKE.
THIS IS A NICE LITTLE ROOM. I COULD WORK IN THERE, NO PROBLEM.
I'LL CHECK OUT THE REST.

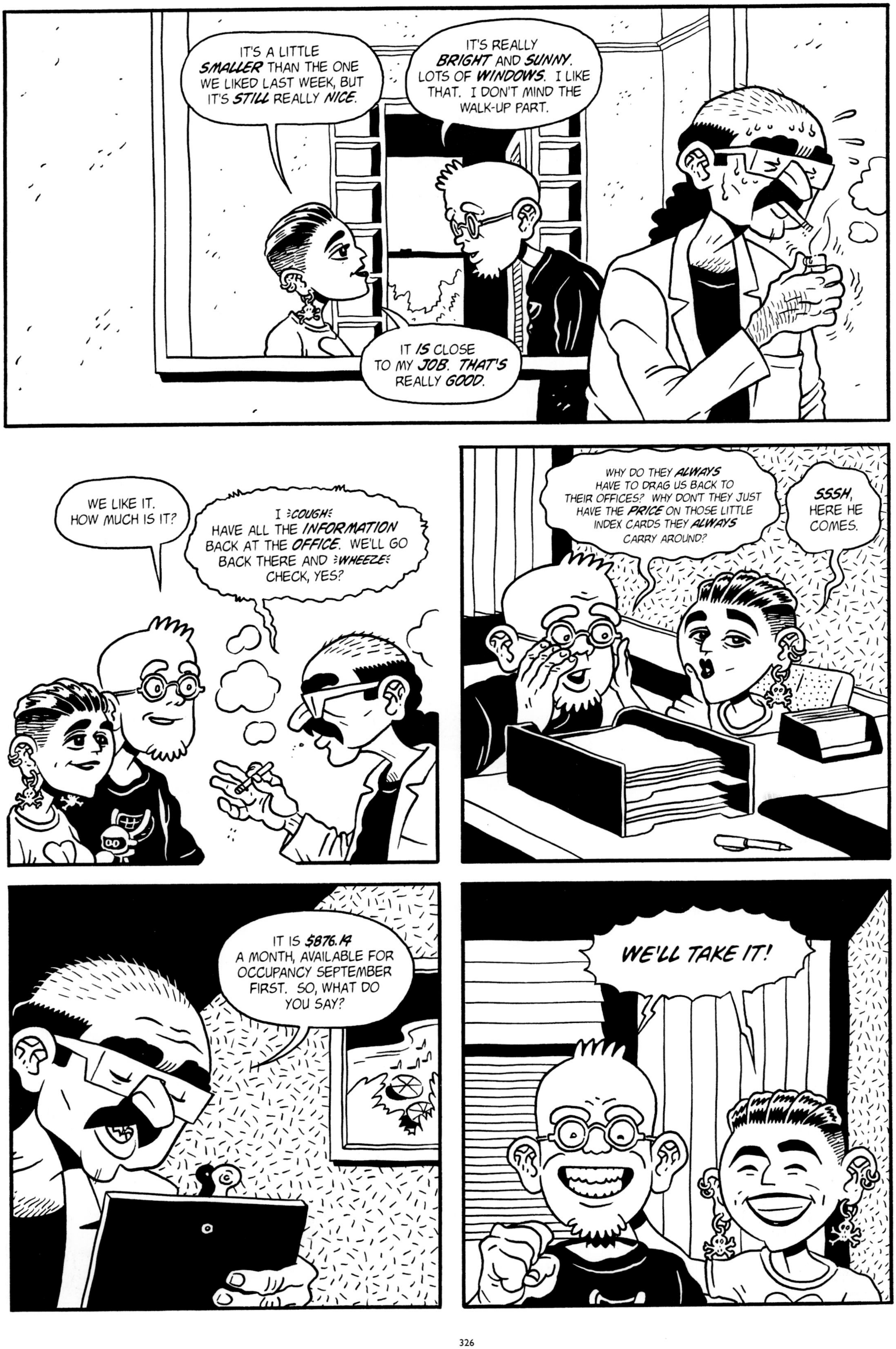
IT'S A LITTLE SMALLER THAN THE ONE WE LIKED LAST WEEK, BUT IT'S STILL REALLY NICE.
IT'S REALLY BRIGHT AND SUNNY. LOTS OF WINDOWS. I LIKE THAT. I DON'T MIND THE WALK-UP PART.
IT IS CLOSE TO MY JOB. THAT'S REALLY GOOD.
WE LIKE IT. HOW MUCH IS IT?
I COUGH HAVE ALL THE INFORMATION BACK AT THE OFFICE. WE'LL GO BACK THERE AND WHEEZE CHECK, YES?
WHY DO THEY ALWAYS HAVE TO DRAG US BACK TO THEIR OFFICES? WHY DON'T THEY JUST HAVE THE PRICE ON THOSE LITTLE INDEX CARDS THEY ALWAYS CARRY AROUND?
SSSH, HERE HE COMES.
IT IS $876.14 A MONTH, AVAILABLE FOR OCCUPANCY SEPTEMBER FIRST. SO, WHAT DO YOU SAY?
WE'LL TAKE IT!

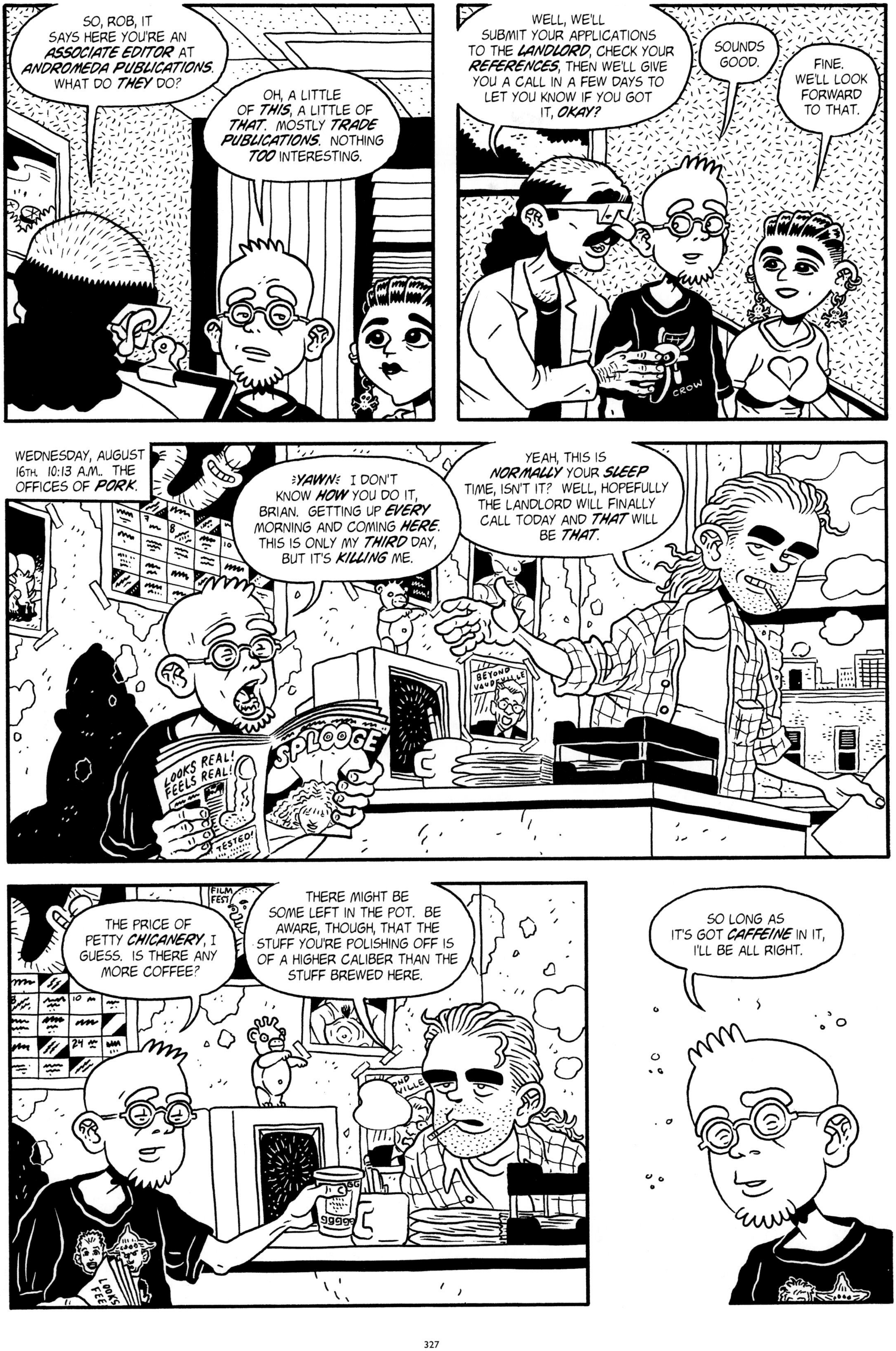
SO, ROB, IT SAYS HERE YOU'RE AN ASSOCIATE EDITOR AT ANDROMEDA PUBLICATIONS. WHAT DO THEY DO?
OH, A LITTLE OF THIS, A LITTLE OF THAT. MOSTLY TRADE PUBLICATIONS. NOTHING TOO INTERESTING.
WELL, WE'LL SUBMIT YOUR APPLICATIONS TO THE LANDLORD, CHECK YOUR REFERENCES, THEN WE'LL GIVE YOU A CALL IN A FEW DAYS TO LET YOU KNOW IF YOU GOT IT, OKAY?
SOUNDS GOOD.
FINE. WE'LL LOOK FORWARD TO THAT.
CROW
WEDNESDAY, AUGUST 16TH. 10:13 A.M.. THE OFFICES OF PORK.
YAWN I DON'T KNOW HOW YOU DO IT, BRIAN. GETTING UP EVERY MORNING AND COMING HERE. THIS IS ONLY MY THIRD DAY, BUT IT'S KILLING ME.
YEAH, THIS IS NORMALLY YOUR SLEEP TIME, ISN'T IT? WELL, HOPEFULLY THE LANDLORD WILL FINALLY CALL TODAY AND THAT WILL BE THAT.
BEYOND VAUDEVILLE
SPLOOGE
LOOKS REAL! FEELS REAL!
TESTED!
THE PRICE OF PETTY CHICANERY, I GUESS. IS THERE ANY MORE COFFEE?
THERE MIGHT BE SOME LEFT IN THE POT. BE AWARE, THOUGH, THAT THE STUFF YOU'RE POLISHING OFF IS OF A HIGHER CALIBER THAN THE STUFF BREWED HERE.
FILM FEST
SO LONG AS IT'S GOT CAFFEINE IN IT, I'LL BE ALL RIGHT.

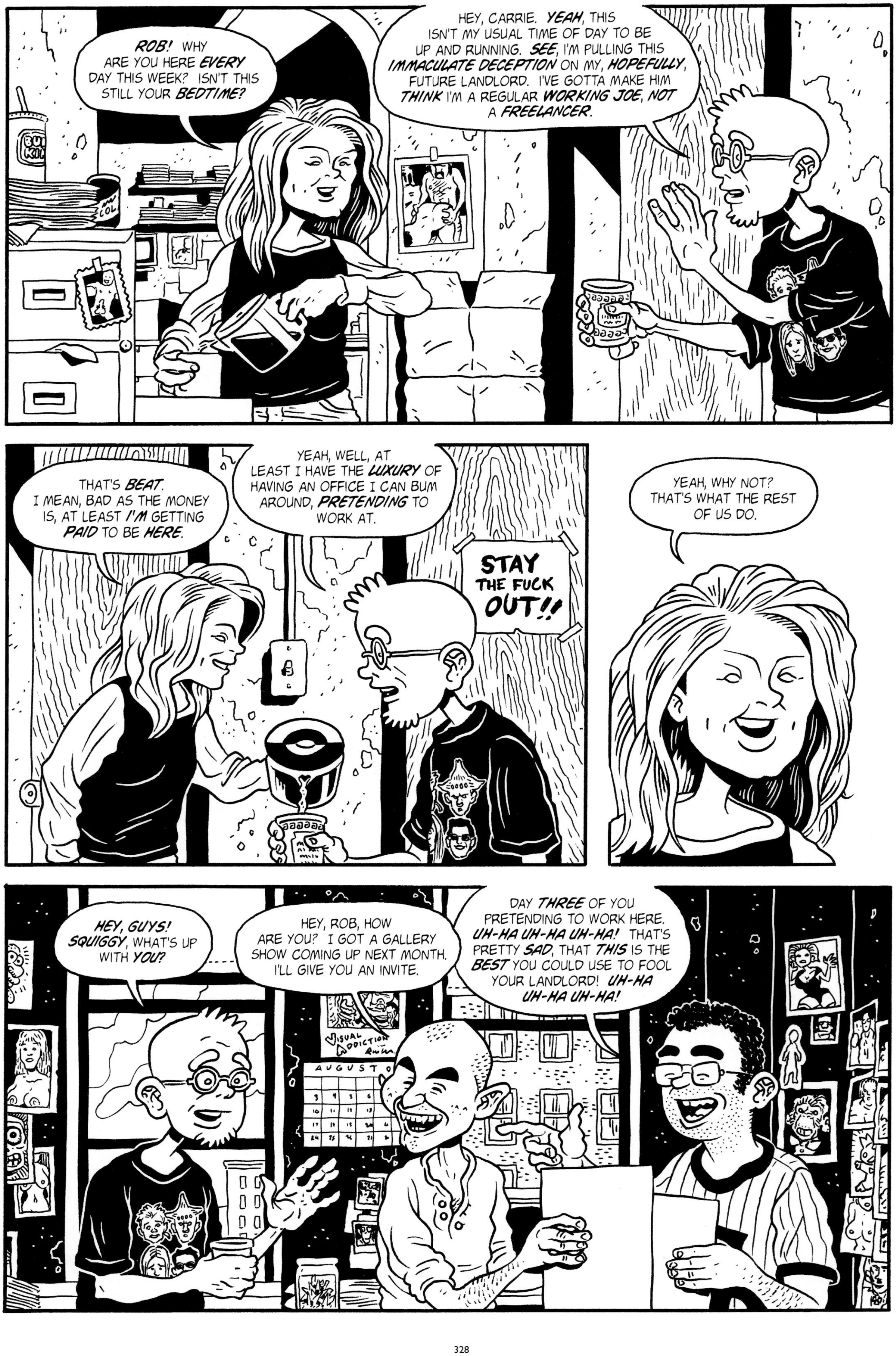
ROB! WHY ARE YOU HERE EVERY DAY THIS WEEK? ISN'T THIS STILL YOUR BEDTIME?
HEY, CARRIE. YEAH, THIS ISN'T MY USUAL TIME OF DAY TO BE UP AND RUNNING. SEE, I'M PULLING THIS IMMACULATE DECEPTION ON MY, HOPEFULLY, FUTURE LANDLORD. I'VE GOTTA MAKE HIM THINK I'M A REGULAR WORKING JOE, NOT A FREELANCER.
THAT'S BEAT. I MEAN, BAD AS THE MONEY IS, AT LEAST I'M GETTING PAID TO BE HERE.
YEAH, WELL, AT LEAST I HAVE THE LUXURY OF HAVING AN OFFICE I CAN BUM AROUND, PRETENDING TO WORK AT.
STAY THE FUCK OUT!!
YEAH, WHY NOT? THAT'S WHAT THE REST OF US DO.
HEY, GUYS! SQUIGGY, WHAT'S UP WITH YOU?
HEY, ROB, HOW ARE YOU? I GOT A GALLERY SHOW COMING UP NEXT MONTH. I'LL GIVE YOU AN INVITE.
DAY THREE OF YOU PRETENDING TO WORK HERE. UH-HA UH-HA UH-HA! THAT'S PRETTY SAD, THAT THIS IS THE BEST YOU COULD USE TO FOOL YOUR LANDLORD! UH-HA UH-HA UH-HA!
AUGUST

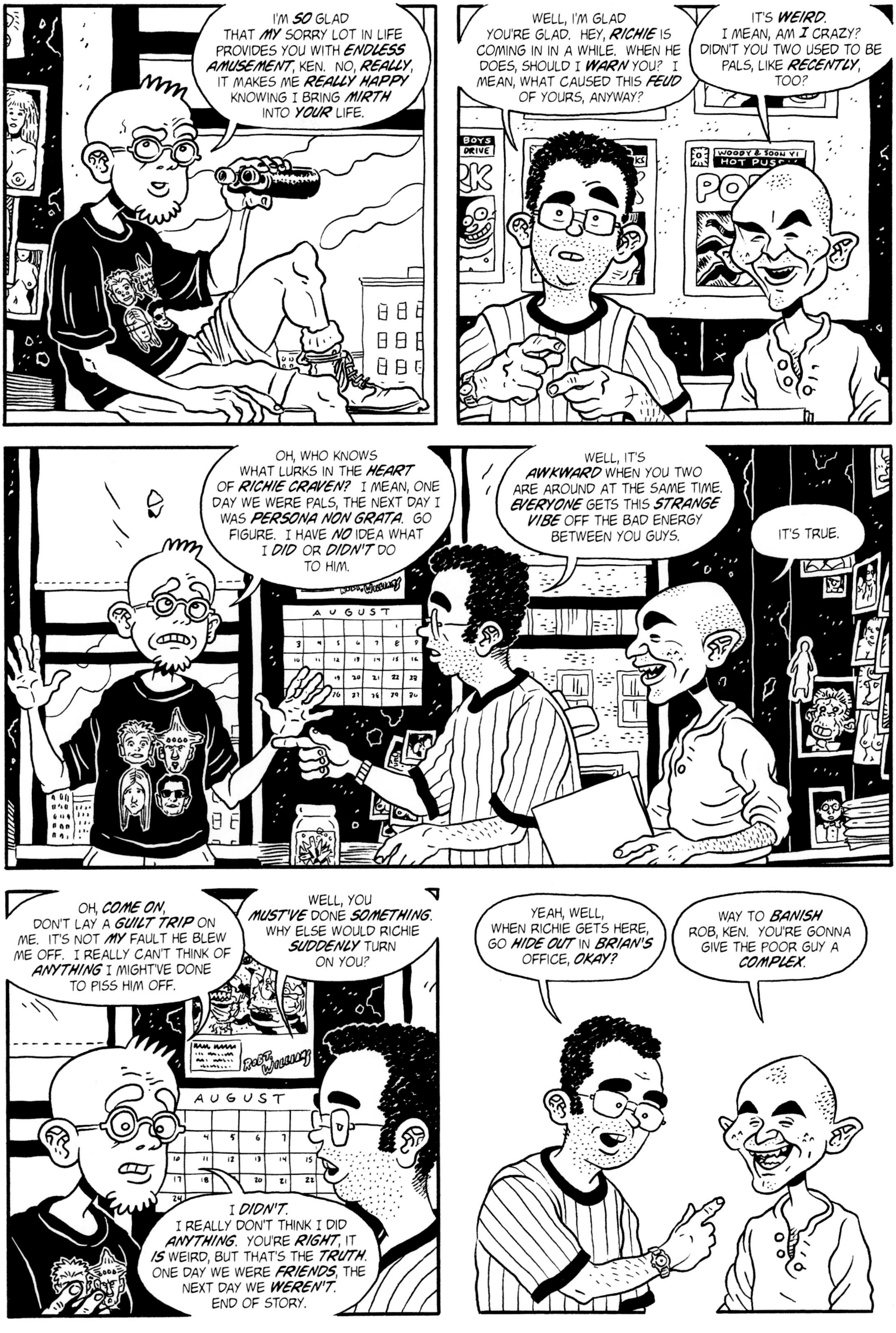
I'M SO GLAD THAT MY SORRY LOT IN LIFE PROVIDES YOU WITH ENDLESS AMUSEMENT, KEN. NO, REALLY, IT MAKES ME REALLY HAPPY KNOWING I BRING MIRTH INTO YOUR LIFE.
WELL, I'M GLAD YOU'RE GLAD. HEY, RICHIE IS COMING IN IN A WHILE. WHEN HE DOES, SHOULD I WARN YOU? I MEAN, WHAT CAUSED THIS FEUD OF YOURS, ANYWAY?
IT'S WEIRD. I MEAN, AM I CRAZY? DIDN'T YOU TWO USED TO BE PALS, LIKE RECENTLY, TOO?
WOODY & SOON YI
HOT PUSSY
OH, WHO KNOWS WHAT LURKS IN THE HEART OF RICHIE CRAVEN? I MEAN, ONE DAY WE WERE PALS, THE NEXT DAY I WAS PERSONA NON GRATA. GO FIGURE. I HAVE NO IDEA WHAT I DID OR DIDN'T DO TO HIM.
WELL, IT'S AWKWARD WHEN YOU TWO ARE AROUND AT THE SAME TIME. EVERYONE GETS THIS STRANGE VIBE OFF THE BAD ENERGY BETWEEN YOU GUYS.
IT'S TRUE.
AUGUST
OH, COME ON, DON'T LAY A GUILT TRIP ON ME. IT'S NOT MY FAULT HE BLEW ME OFF. I REALLY CAN'T THINK OF ANYTHING I MIGHT'VE DONE TO PISS HIM OFF.
WELL, YOU MUST'VE DONE SOMETHING. WHY ELSE WOULD RICHIE SUDDENLY TURN ON YOU?
ROBT. WILLIAMS
AUGUST
I DIDN'T. I REALLY DON'T THINK I DID ANYTHING. YOU'RE RIGHT, IT IS WEIRD, BUT THAT'S THE TRUTH. ONE DAY WE WERE FRIENDS, THE NEXT DAY WE WEREN'T. END OF STORY.
YEAH, WELL, WHEN RICHIE GETS HERE, GO HIDE OUT IN BRIAN'S OFFICE, OKAY?
WAY TO BANISH ROB, KEN. YOU'RE GONNA GIVE THE POOR GUY A COMPLEX.

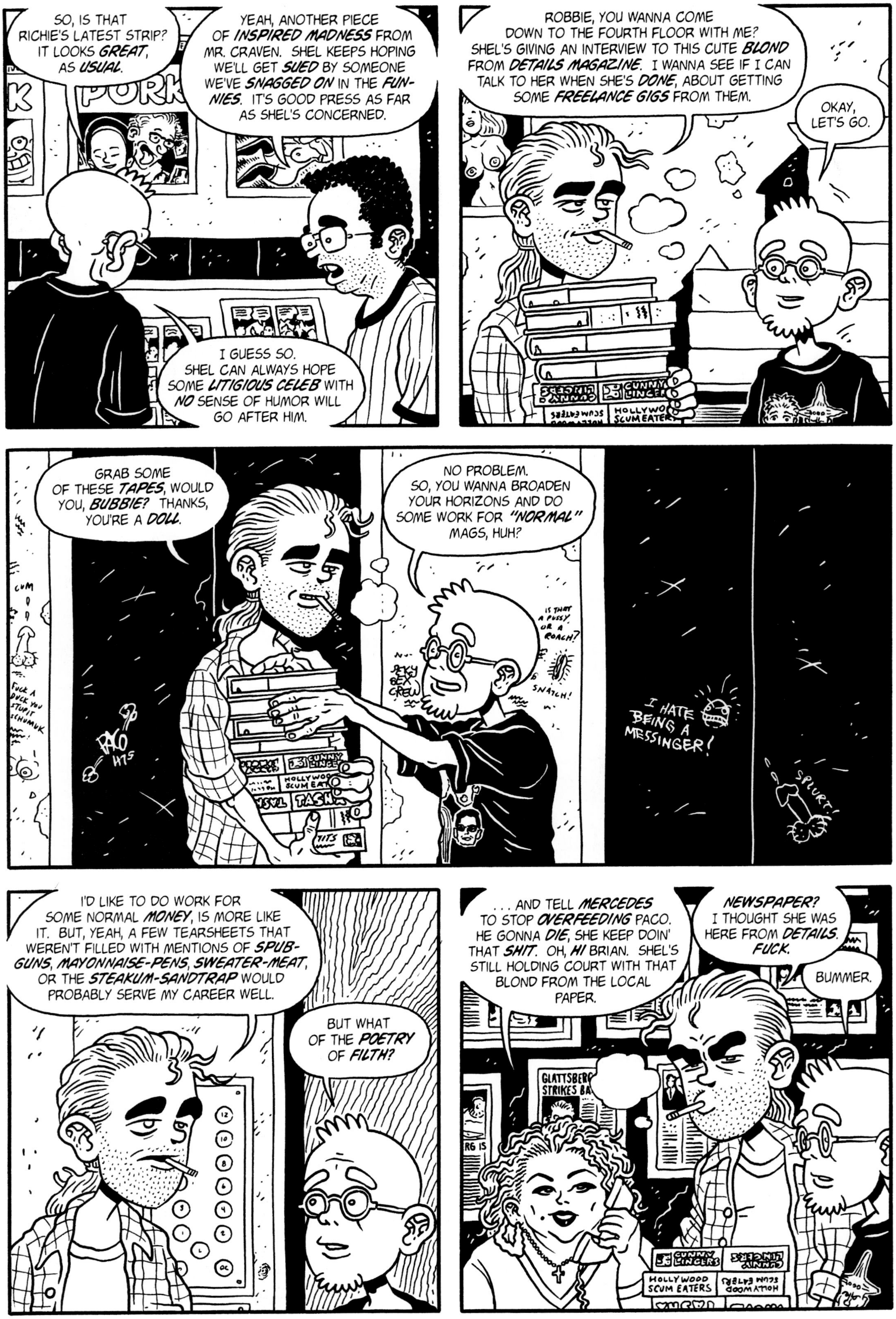
SO, IS THAT RICHIE'S LATEST STRIP? IT LOOKS GREAT, AS USUAL.
YEAH, ANOTHER PIECE OF INSPIRED MADNESS FROM MR. CRAVEN. SHEL KEEPS HOPING WE'LL GET SUED BY SOMEONE WE'VE SNAGGED ON IN THE FUNNIES. IT'S GOOD PRESS AS FAR AS SHEL'S CONCERNED.
I GUESS SO. SHEL CAN ALWAYS HOPE SOME LITIGIOUS CELEB WITH NO SENSE OF HUMOR WILL GO AFTER HIM.
ROBBIE, YOU WANNA COME DOWN TO THE FOURTH FLOOR WITH ME? SHEL'S GIVING AN INTERVIEW TO THIS CUTE BLOND FROM DETAILS MAGAZINE. I WANNA SEE IF I CAN TALK TO HER WHEN SHE'S DONE, ABOUT GETTING SOME FREELANCE GIGS FROM THEM.
OKAY, LET'S GO.
CUNNY LINGERS
HOLLYWOOD SCUM EATERS
GRAB SOME OF THESE TAPES, WOULD YOU, BUBBIE? THANKS, YOU'RE A DOLL.
NO PROBLEM. SO, YOU WANNA BROADEN YOUR HORIZONS AND DO SOME WORK FOR "NORMAL" MAGS, HUH?
IS THAT A PUSSY, OR A ROACH?
SNATCH!
SEXY SEX CREW
I HATE BEING A MESSINGER!
SPLURT!
FUCK A DUCK YOU STUPIT SCHMUCK
PACO
TITS
I'D LIKE TO DO WORK FOR SOME NORMAL MONEY, IS MORE LIKE IT. BUT, YEAH, A FEW TEARSHEETS THAT WEREN'T FILLED WITH MENTIONS OF SPUB-GUNS, MAYONNAISE-PENS, SWEATER-MEAT, OR THE STEAKUM-SANDTRAP WOULD PROBABLY SERVE MY CAREER WELL.
BUT WHAT OF THE POETRY OF FILTH?
. . . AND TELL MERCEDES TO STOP OVERFEEDING PACO. HE GONNA DIE, SHE KEEP DOIN' THAT SHIT. OH, HI BRIAN. SHEL'S STILL HOLDING COURT WITH THAT BLOND FROM THE LOCAL PAPER.
NEWSPAPER? I THOUGHT SHE WAS HERE FROM DETAILS. FUCK.
BUMMER.
GLATTSBERG STRIKES BA
CUNNY LINGERS
HOLLYWOOD SCUM EATERS

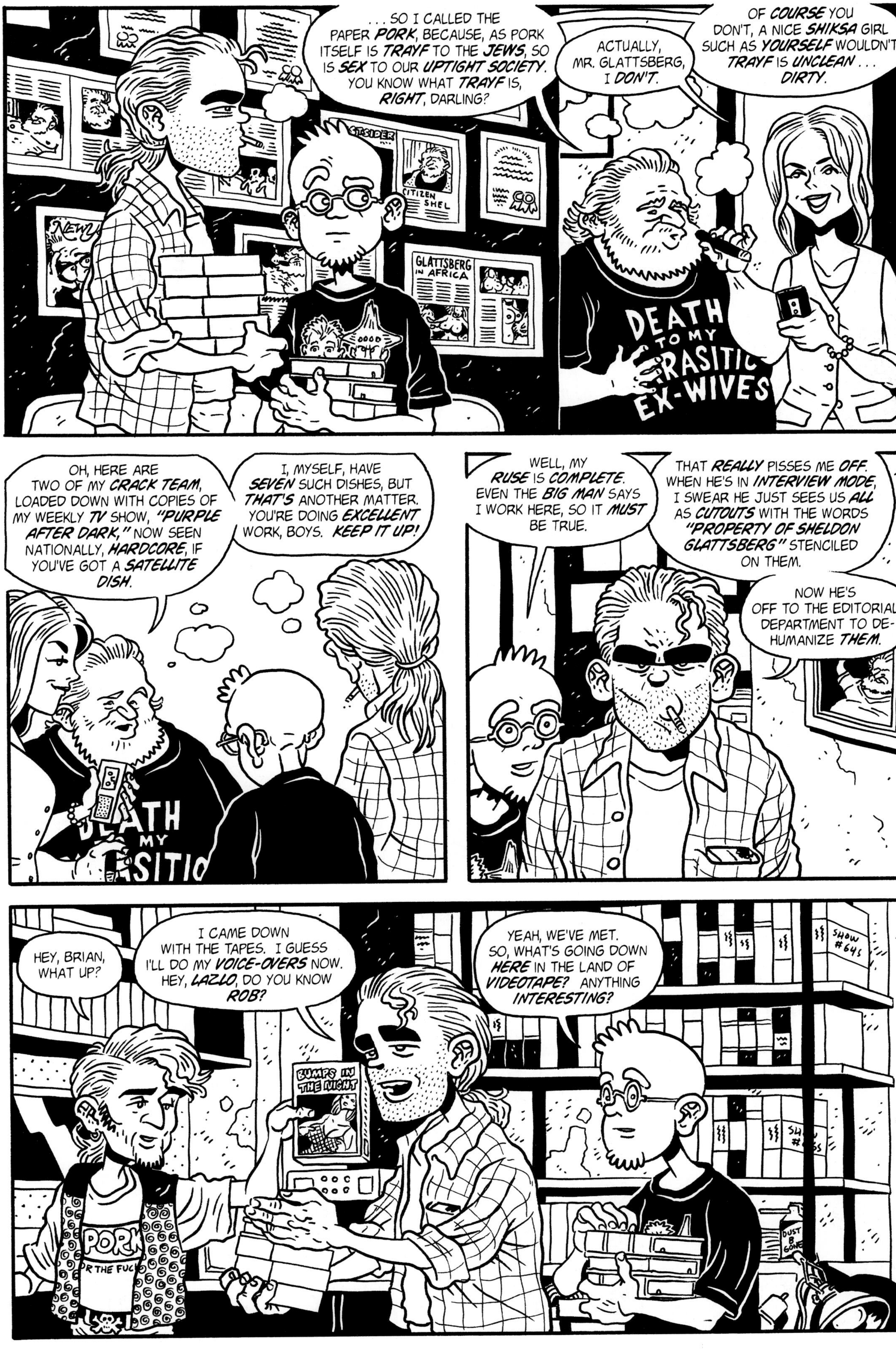

. . . SO I CALLED THE PAPER PORK, BECAUSE, AS PORK ITSELF IS TRAYF TO THE JEWS, SO IS SEX TO OUR UPTIGHT SOCIETY. YOU KNOW WHAT TRAYF IS, RIGHT, DARLING?
CITIZEN SHEL
GLATTSBERG IN AFRICA
ACTUALLY, MR. GLATTSBERG, I DON'T.
OF COURSE YOU DON'T, A NICE SHIKSA GIRL SUCH AS YOURSELF WOULDN'T. TRAYF IS UNCLEAN . . . DIRTY.
DEATH TO MY ARASITIC EX-WIVES
OH, HERE ARE TWO OF MY CRACK TEAM, LOADED DOWN WITH COPIES OF MY WEEKLY TV SHOW, "PURPLE AFTER DARK," NOW SEEN NATIONALLY, HARDCORE, IF YOU'VE GOT A SATELLITE DISH.
I, MYSELF, HAVE SEVEN SUCH DISHES, BUT THAT'S ANOTHER MATTER. YOU'RE DOING EXCELLENT WORK, BOYS. KEEP IT UP!
WELL, MY RUSE IS COMPLETE. EVEN THE BIG MAN SAYS I WORK HERE, SO IT MUST BE TRUE.
THAT REALLY PISSES ME OFF. WHEN HE'S IN INTERVIEW MODE, I SWEAR HE JUST SEES US ALL AS CUTOUTS WITH THE WORDS "PROPERTY OF SHELDON GLATTSBERG" STENCILED ON THEM.
NOW HE'S OFF TO THE EDITORIAL DEPARTMENT TO DE-HUMANIZE THEM.
HEY, BRIAN, WHAT UP?
I CAME DOWN WITH THE TAPES. I GUESS I'LL DO MY VOICE-OVERS NOW. HEY, LAZLO, DO YOU KNOW ROB?
YEAH, WE'VE MET. SO, WHAT'S GOING DOWN HERE IN THE LAND OF VIDEOTAPE? ANYTHING INTERESTING?
SHOW #645
BUMPS IN THE NIGHT
PORK
DUST B GONE

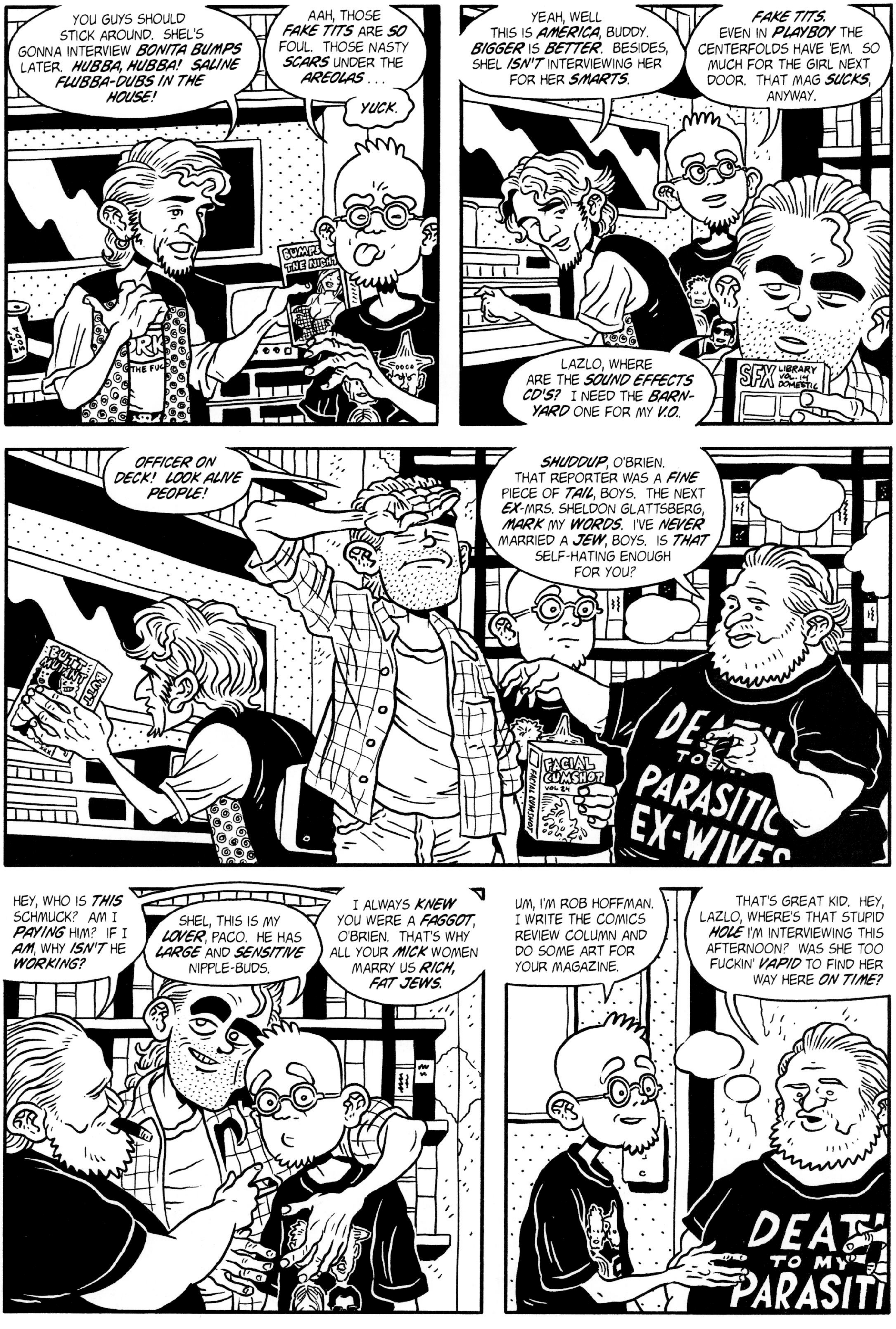

YOU GUYS SHOULD STICK AROUND. SHEL'S GONNA INTERVIEW BONITA BUMPS LATER. HUBBA, HUBBA! SALINE FLUBBA-DUBS IN THE HOUSE!
AAH, THOSE FAKE TITS ARE SO FOUL. THOSE NASTY SCARS UNDER THE AREOLAS . . .
YUCK.
BUMPS IN THE NIGHT
YEAH, WELL THIS IS AMERICA, BUDDY. BIGGER IS BETTER. BESIDES, SHEL ISN'T INTERVIEWING HER FOR HER SMARTS.
FAKE TITS. EVEN IN PLAYBOY THE CENTERFOLDS HAVE 'EM. SO MUCH FOR THE GIRL NEXT DOOR. THAT MAG SUCKS, ANYWAY.
LAZLO, WHERE ARE THE SOUND EFFECTS CD'S? I NEED THE BARNYARD ONE FOR MY V.O.
SFX LIBRARY VOL. 14 DOMESTIC
OFFICER ON DECK! LOOK ALIVE PEOPLE!
SHUDDUP, O'BRIEN. THAT REPORTER WAS A FINE PIECE OF TAIL, BOYS. THE NEXT EX-MRS. SHELDON GLATTSBERG, MARK MY WORDS. I'VE NEVER MARRIED A JEW, BOYS. IS THAT SELF-HATING ENOUGH FOR YOU?
BUTT MUTANT
FACIAL CUMSHOT VOL 24
PARASITIC EX-WIVES
HEY, WHO IS THIS SCHMUCK? AM I PAYING HIM? IF I AM, WHY ISN'T HE WORKING?
SHEL, THIS IS MY LOVER, PACO. HE HAS LARGE AND SENSITIVE NIPPLE-BUDS.
I ALWAYS KNEW YOU WERE A FAGGOT, O'BRIEN. THAT'S WHY ALL YOUR MICK WOMEN MARRY US RICH, FAT JEWS.
UM, I'M ROB HOFFMAN. I WRITE THE COMICS REVIEW COLUMN AND DO SOME ART FOR YOUR MAGAZINE.
THAT'S GREAT KID. HEY, LAZLO, WHERE'S THAT STUPID HOLE I'M INTERVIEWING THIS AFTERNOON? WAS SHE TOO FUCKIN' VAPID TO FIND HER WAY HERE ON TIME?
DEATH TO MY PARASITI

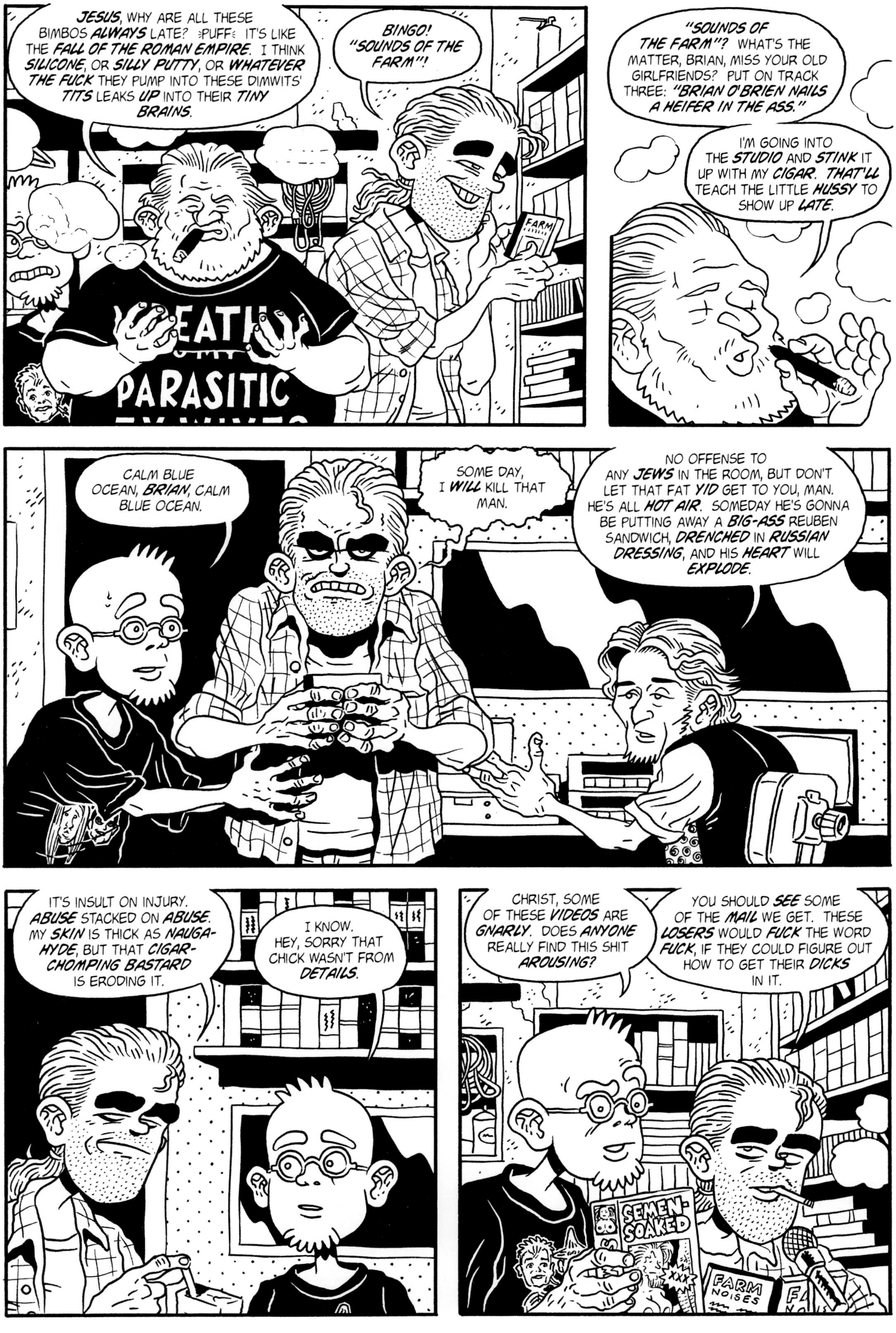
JESUS, WHY ARE ALL THESE BIMBOS ALWAYS LATE? ≥PUFF≤ IT'S LIKE THE FALL OF THE ROMAN EMPIRE. I THINK SILICONE, OR SILLY PUTTY, OR WHATEVER THE FUCK THEY PUMP INTO THESE DIMWITS' TITS LEAKS UP INTO THEIR TINY BRAINS.
BINGO! "SOUNDS OF THE FARM"!
PARASITIC
FARM
"SOUNDS OF THE FARM"? WHAT'S THE MATTER, BRIAN, MISS YOUR OLD GIRLFRIENDS? PUT ON TRACK THREE: "BRIAN O'BRIEN NAILS A HEIFER IN THE ASS."
I'M GOING INTO THE STUDIO AND STINK IT UP WITH MY CIGAR. THAT'LL TEACH THE LITTLE HUSSY TO SHOW UP LATE.
CALM BLUE OCEAN, BRIAN, CALM BLUE OCEAN.
SOME DAY, I WILL KILL THAT MAN.
NO OFFENSE TO ANY JEWS IN THE ROOM, BUT DON'T LET THAT FAT YID GET TO YOU, MAN. HE'S ALL HOT AIR. SOMEDAY HE'S GONNA BE PUTTING AWAY A BIG-ASS REUBEN SANDWICH, DRENCHED IN RUSSIAN DRESSING, AND HIS HEART WILL EXPLODE.
IT'S INSULT ON INJURY. ABUSE STACKED ON ABUSE. MY SKIN IS THICK AS NAUGA-HYDE, BUT THAT CIGAR-CHOMPING BASTARD IS ERODING IT.
I KNOW. HEY, SORRY THAT CHICK WASN'T FROM DETAILS.
CHRIST, SOME OF THESE VIDEOS ARE GNARLY. DOES ANYONE REALLY FIND THIS SHIT AROUSING?
YOU SHOULD SEE SOME OF THE MAIL WE GET. THESE LOSERS WOULD FUCK THE WORD FUCK, IF THEY COULD FIGURE OUT HOW TO GET THEIR DICKS IN IT.
SEMEN-SOAKED
XXX
FARM NOISES

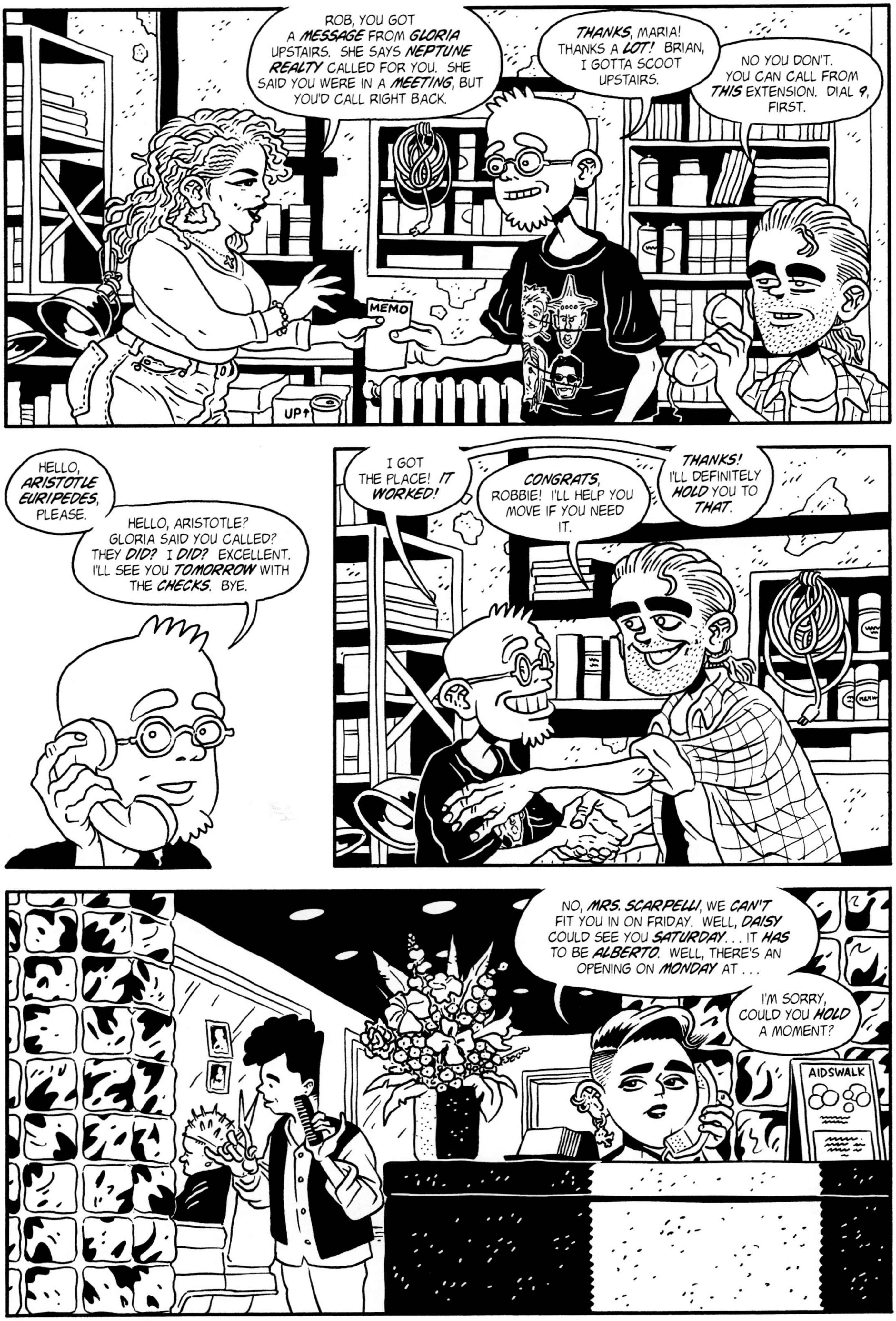
ROB, YOU GOT A MESSAGE FROM GLORIA UPSTAIRS. SHE SAYS NEPTUNE REALTY CALLED FOR YOU. SHE SAID YOU WERE IN A MEETING, BUT YOU'D CALL RIGHT BACK.
THANKS, MARIA! THANKS A LOT! BRIAN, I GOTTA SCOOT UPSTAIRS.
NO YOU DON'T. YOU CAN CALL FROM THIS EXTENSION. DIAL 9, FIRST.
MEMO
UP
HELLO, ARISTOTLE EURIPEDES, PLEASE.
HELLO, ARISTOTLE? GLORIA SAID YOU CALLED? THEY DID? I DID? EXCELLENT. I'LL SEE YOU TOMORROW WITH THE CHECKS. BYE.
I GOT THE PLACE! IT WORKED!
CONGRATS, ROBBIE! I'LL HELP YOU MOVE IF YOU NEED IT.
THANKS! I'LL DEFINITELY HOLD YOU TO THAT.
NO, MRS. SCARPELLI, WE CAN'T FIT YOU IN ON FRIDAY. WELL, DAISY COULD SEE YOU SATURDAY... IT HAS TO BE ALBERTO. WELL, THERE'S AN OPENING ON MONDAY AT...
I'M SORRY, COULD YOU HOLD A MOMENT?
AIDSWALK

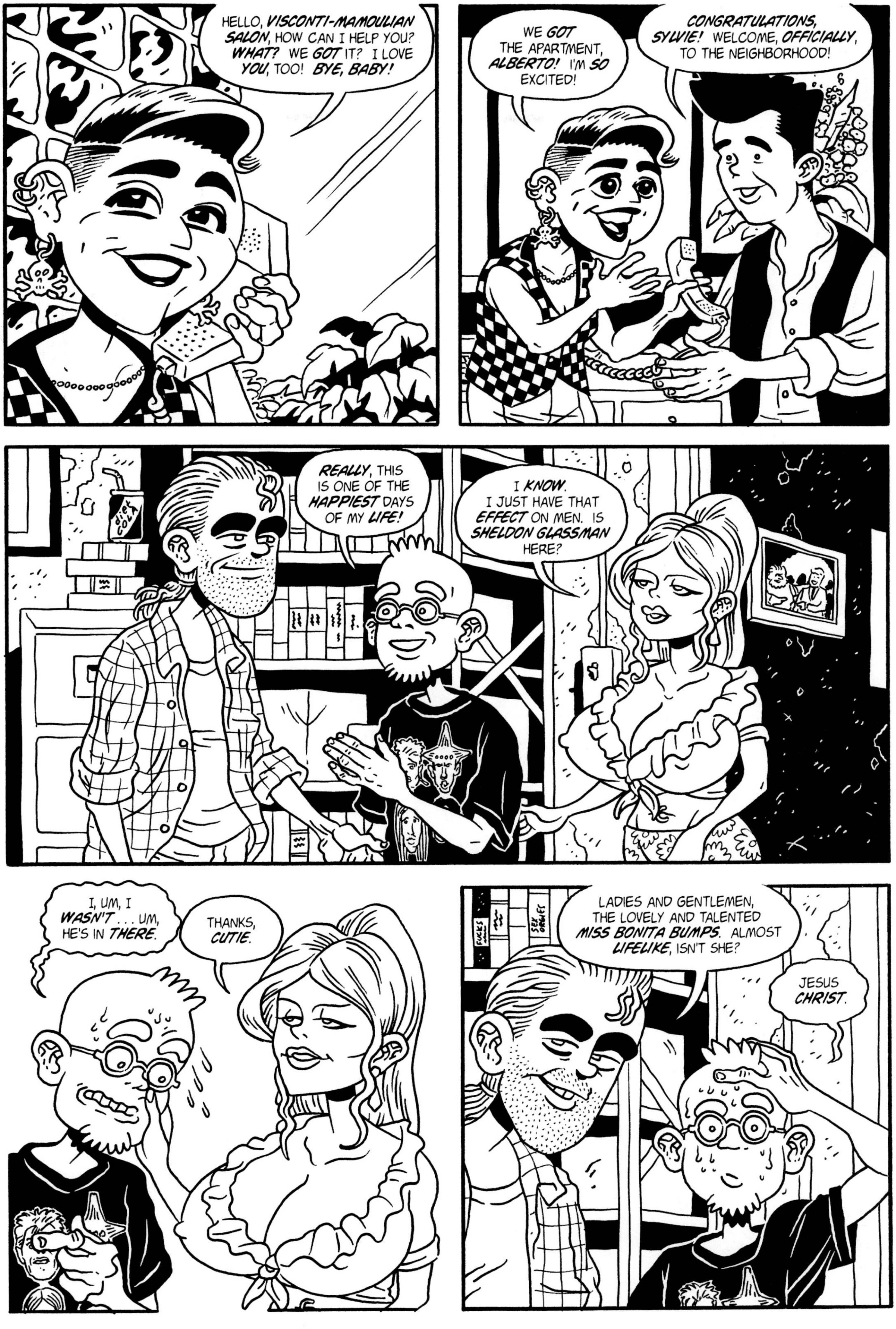
HELLO, VISCONTI-MAMOULIAN SALON, HOW CAN I HELP YOU? WHAT? WE GOT IT? I LOVE YOU, TOO! BYE, BABY!
WE GOT THE APARTMENT, ALBERTO! I'M SO EXCITED!
CONGRATULATIONS, SYLVIE! WELCOME, OFFICIALLY, TO THE NEIGHBORHOOD!
REALLY, THIS IS ONE OF THE HAPPIEST DAYS OF MY LIFE!
I KNOW. I JUST HAVE THAT EFFECT ON MEN. IS SHELDON GLASSMAN HERE?
I, UM, I WASN'T . . . UM, HE'S IN THERE.
THANKS, CUTIE.
LADIES AND GENTLEMEN, THE LOVELY AND TALENTED MISS BONITA BUMPS. ALMOST LIFELIKE, ISN'T SHE?
JESUS CHRIST.

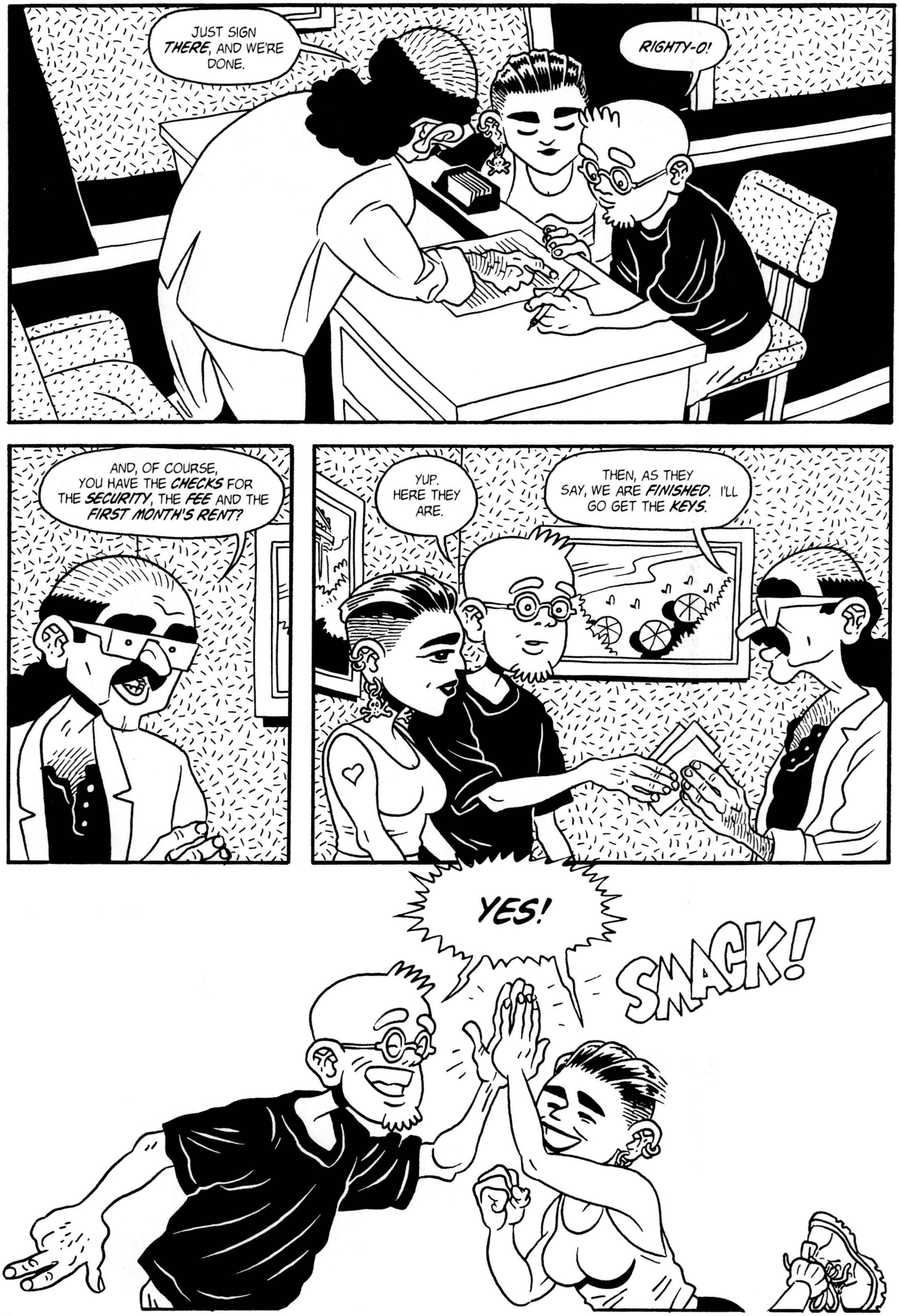
JUST SIGN THERE, AND WE'RE DONE.
RIGHTY-O!
AND, OF COURSE, YOU HAVE THE CHECKS FOR THE SECURITY, THE FEE AND THE FIRST MONTH'S RENT?
YUP. HERE THEY ARE.
THEN, AS THEY SAY, WE ARE FINISHED. I'LL GO GET THE KEYS.
YES!
SMACK!

BONUS SUPPLIMENTS

Featuring:
- **COVER GALLERY**
- **GUEST PINUP GALLERY**
- **SPOTS, SKETCHES & MISCELLANEA**
- **SCRIPT FOR THE "MISSING" ISSUE**

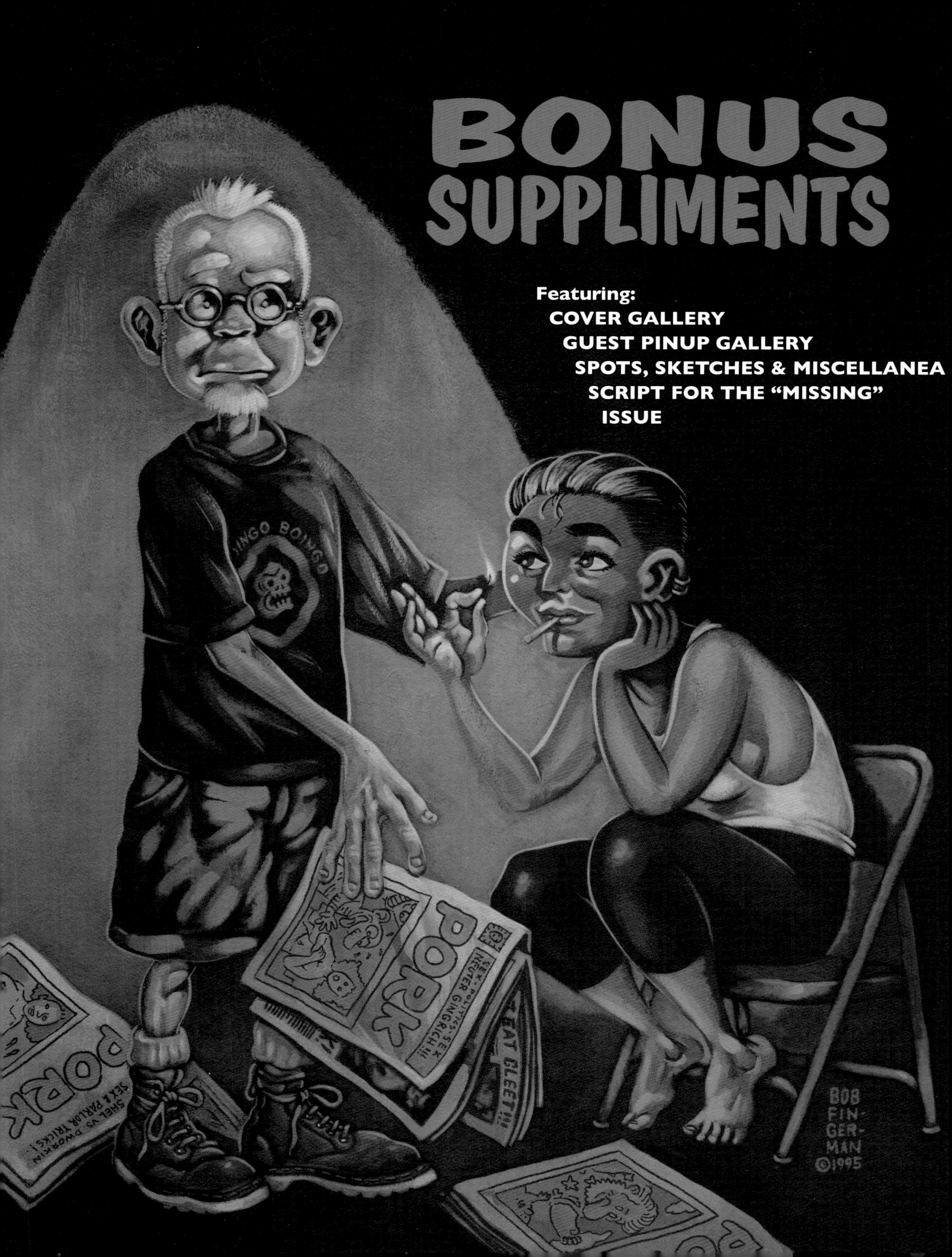
PORK
SEX·POLITICS·SEX NEUTER GINGRICH!!!
EAT GLEET!!!
PORK
SHEL VS. DWORKIN SEX & PARLOR TRICKS!
BOB FIN-GER-MAN ©1995

Previous page: *Minimum Wage Book One*. Left and Below: covers for issues 1, 2 and 3. (Acrylic)

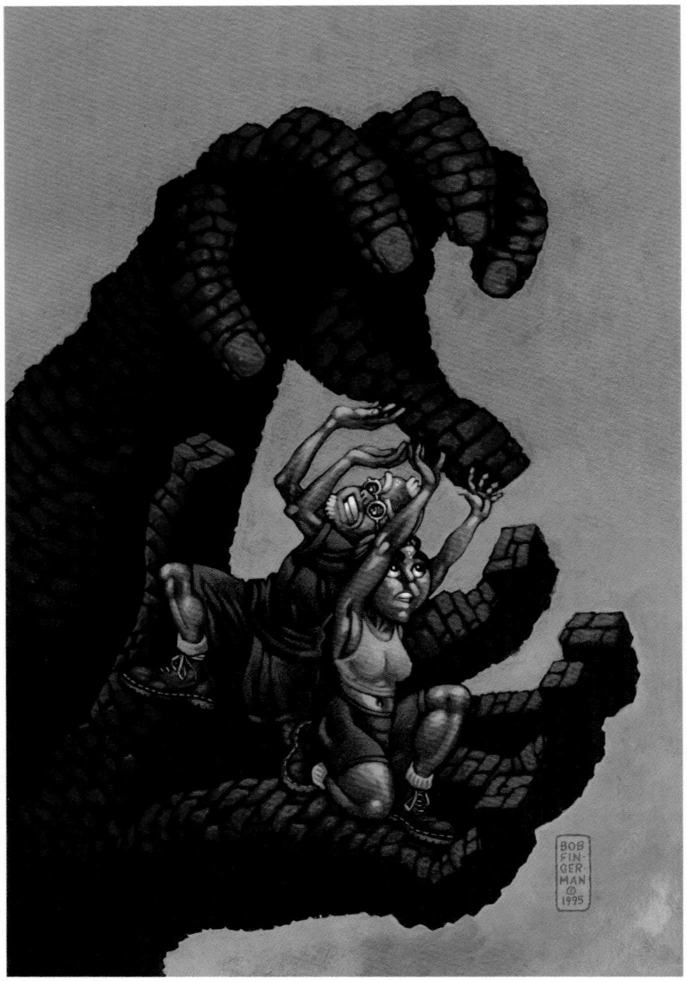
BOB FIN-GER-MAN © 1995

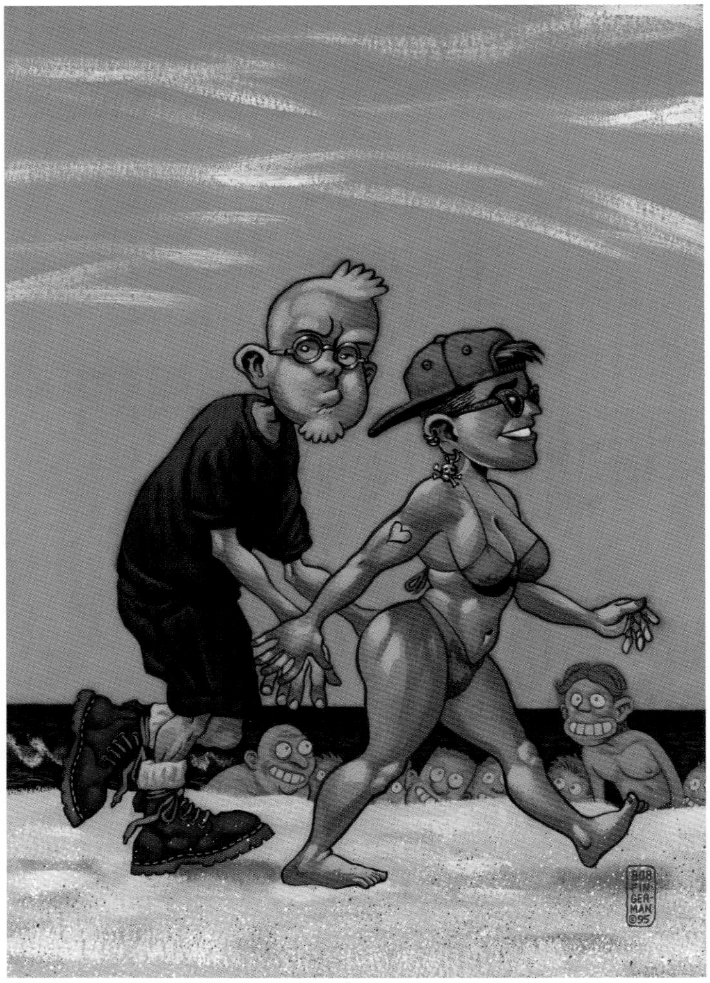
BOB FIN-GER-MAN ©95

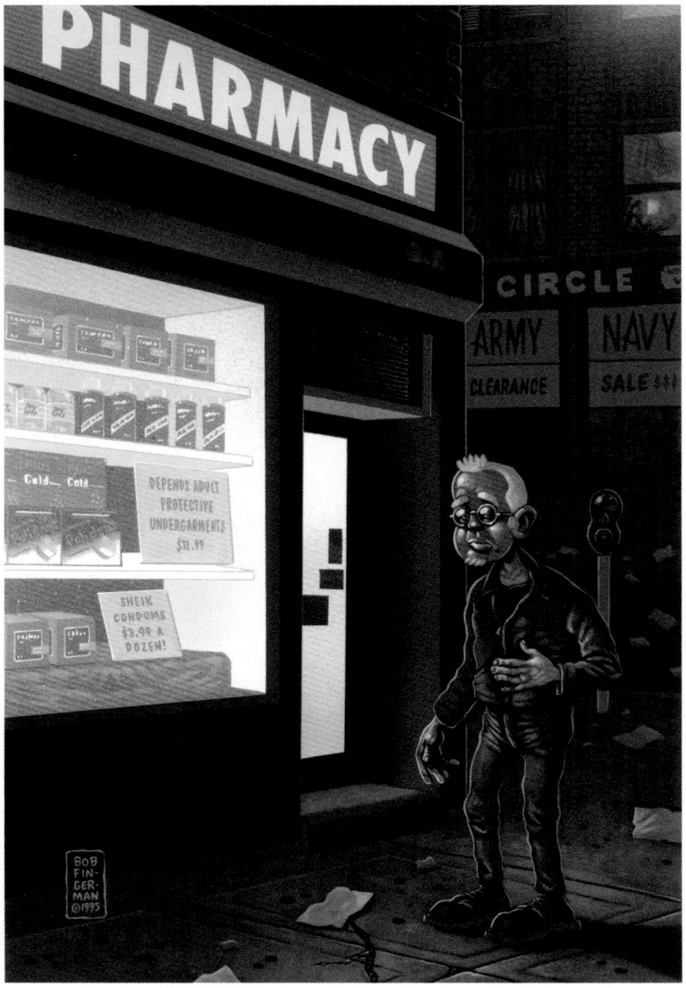
PHARMACY
CIRCLE
ARMY
NAVY
CLEARANCE
SALE
DEPENDS ADULT PROTECTIVE UNDERGARMENTS $12.99
SHEIK CONDOMS $3.99 A DOZEN!
BOB FIN-GER-MAN ©1995

My goal with the covers was to not always depict the literal, but sometimes go more with the flavor of the chapter than to illustrate the actual content. The first issue dealt with the soul-crushing endeavor of looking for an apartment when your finances are iffy. I was going for something comic-booky/pulpy. I also wanted to take advantage of full-color and do painted covers. This was in my pre-digital color days, back when I got actual brushes dirty.

For issue 2 I wanted to deal with Rob's insecurity regarding Sylvia's wantonness compared to his uptightness. So, where better to situate them than on a public beach?

Chapter 3 dealt with the unwanted pregnancy. Since this series was mostly centered on Rob's POV, I felt it better—and less melodramatic—to focus on his dreary task of procuring the home pregnancy tests. I was going for an homage to Edward Hopper. And failing.

For me, comic conventions have always been a mixed bag. I enjoy them more now than I used to, but for many years attending them was stress, stress and more stress. Comedian Patton Oswalt actually listed me as an item on his 2007 San Diego Comic Con scavenger hunt: "Bob Fingerman muttering he's going to kill himself." Joke's on anyone who looked; I wasn't there that year. *Ha!* Granted, the year prior he'd encountered me feeling mighty low—the book I'd traveled to promote having not arrived at the show—but his jest still landed pretty much on the nose. Not sure why the cover to the convention issue came out like a grayscale black velvet painting, but I think it works.

For Chapter 5, Sylvia's the one who feels threatened, in this case by Rob's fixation on working with underground diva Bedelia Brunch. Not all that happy with this one, frankly. Wasn't then. Still feel the same.

The cover for the "Art Directors Must Die" issue, however, is one of my favorites. I still like this one. The lava and background elements, in particular, still look good to me.

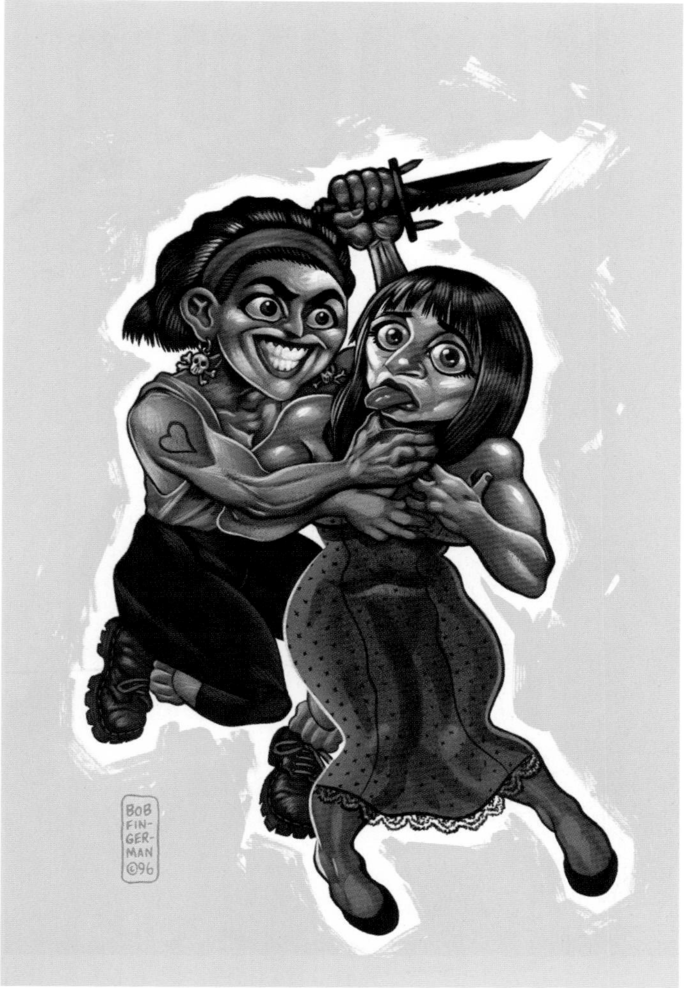
BOB
FIN-
GER-
MAN
©96

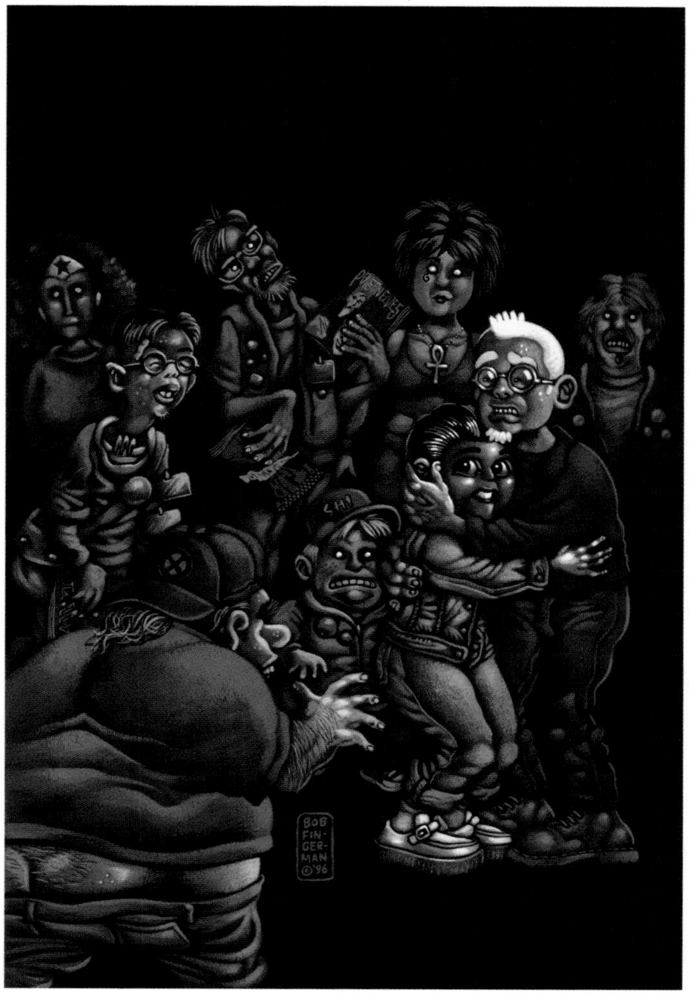
BOB
FIN-
GER-
MAN
©96

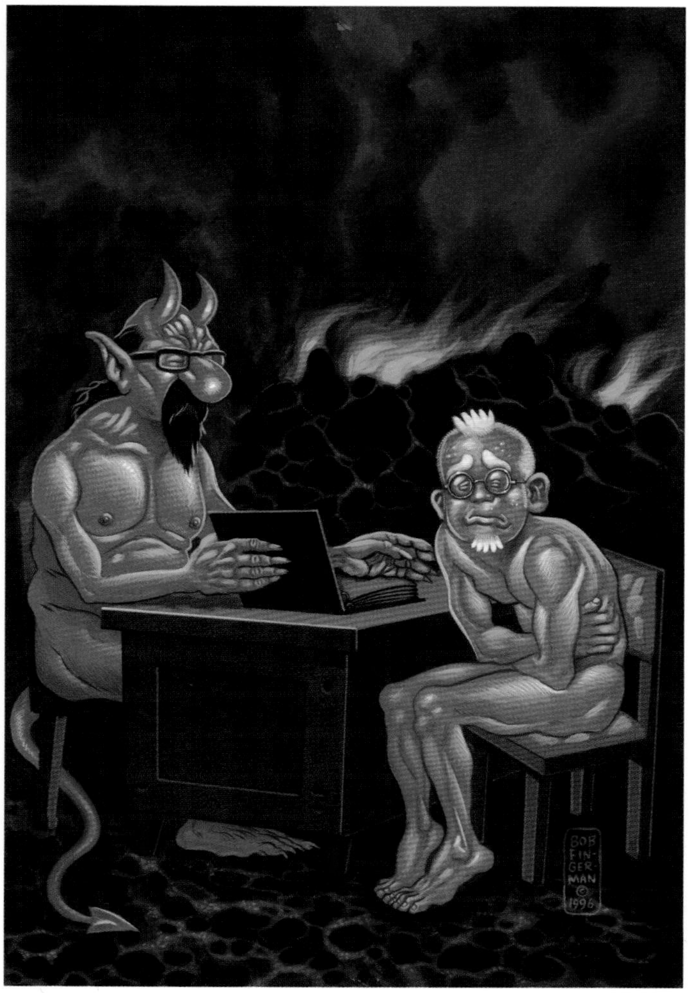
BOB
FIN-
GER-
MAN
©
1996

Above and Right: covers for issues 4, 5 and 6 (Acrylic)

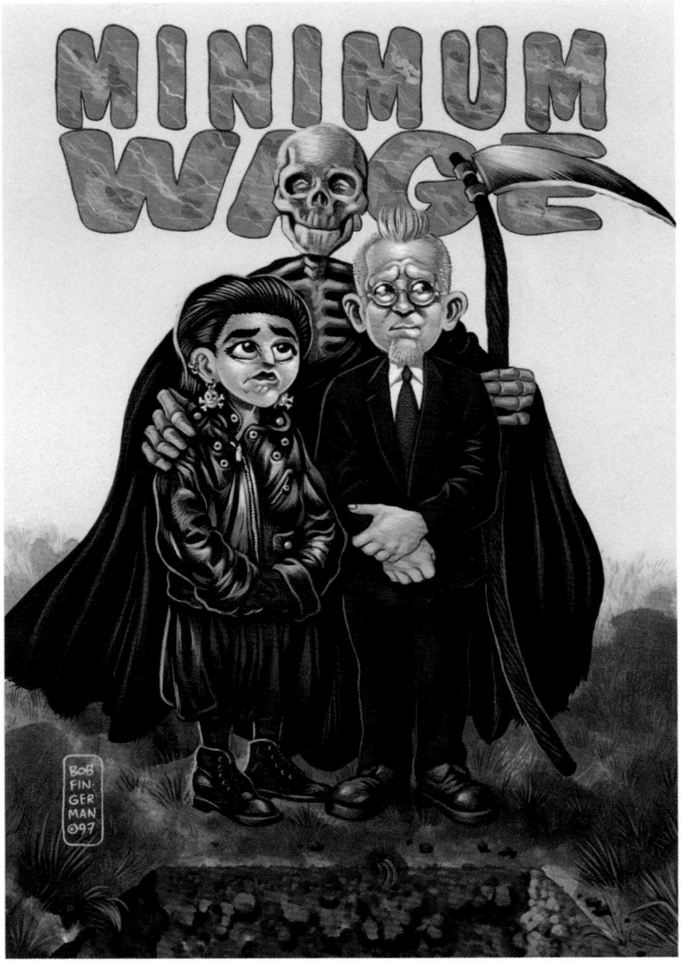
MINIMUM
WAGE
BOB FIN-GER-MAN ©97

Left and below: covers for issues 7, 10 and 8 (Acrylic & Digital).
Opposite: cover to issue 9 (Acrylic)

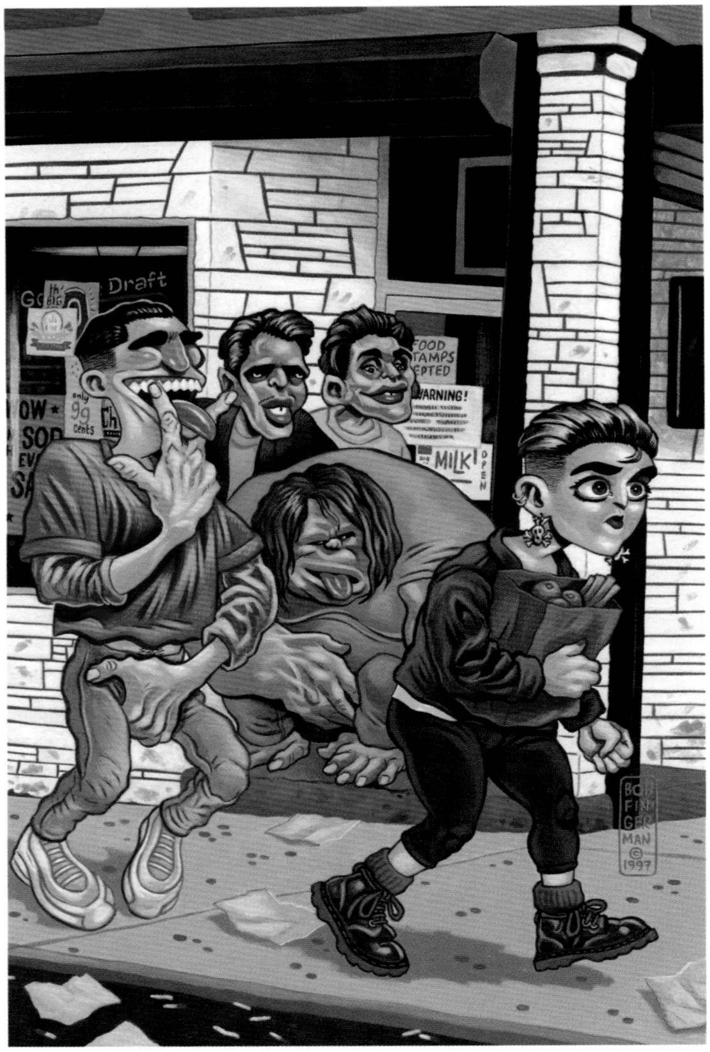
Draft
only 99 cents
WARNING!
MILK!
OPEN
BOB FIN-GER-MAN © 1997

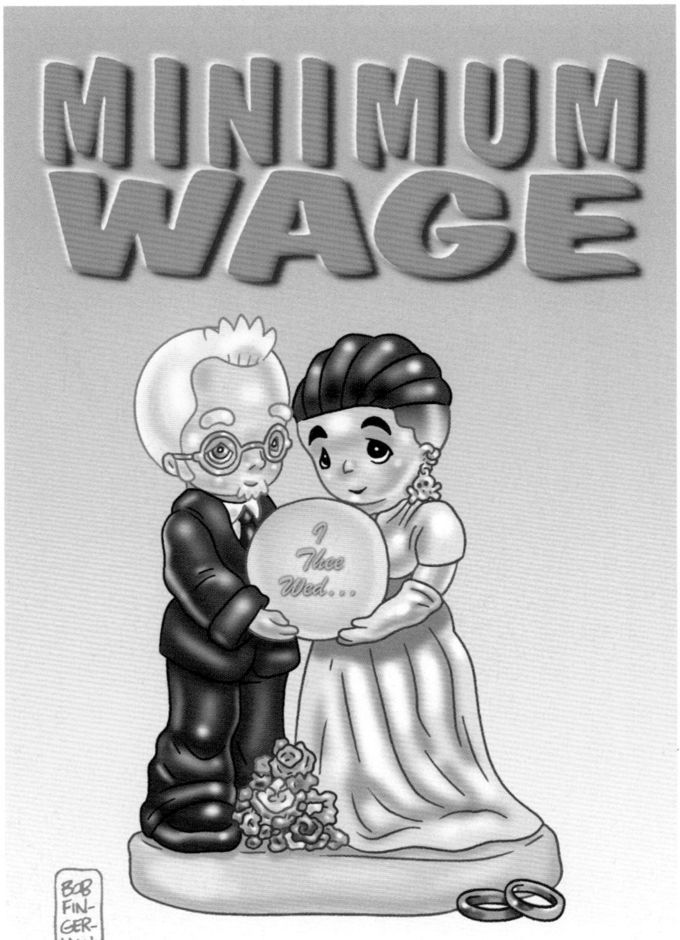
MINIMUM
WAGE
I Thee Wed...
BOB FIN-GER-MAN ©98

The funerals chapter is one of my favorites. The same cannot be said of its accompanying cover. The concept is a bit weak, though I do like the way Rob's shoes came out. So, not a total loss.

Chapter 8 featured Sylvia being mistaken for a dude by some knuckleheads, so I thought having her harassed as a genuine female on the cover created a balance. Actually, you know what? I'm full of crap. I don't really remember why this was the image I chose for that chapter. It was a long time ago. Sue me.

Issue 10's cover was an early foray into digital. The concept is cute, if intentionally a bit nauseating. It also, as it turned out, was the final one of *Minimum Wage*'s serial run. As you can read elsewhere in this book, there's a subsequent chapter, but I never drew it. *MW* never drew as big an audience as I needed to continue it. Maybe this volume will change that.

On the opposite page is the cover to the "Art" issue (*MW* #9). It's my favorite one, since it pays homage to two of my favorite modern artists, Giorgio de Chirico and Pablo Picasso. I think I pulled it off.

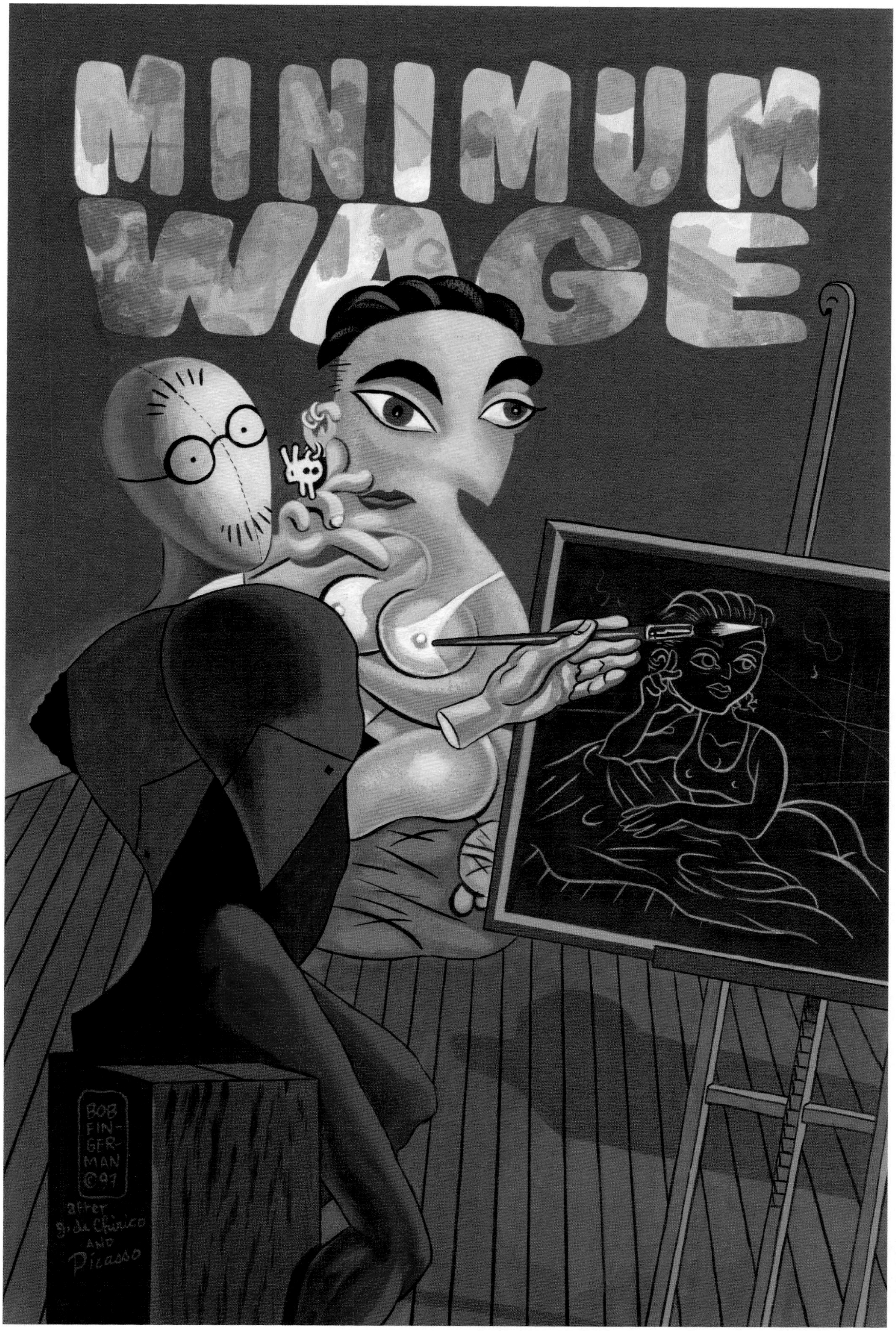
MINIMUM WAGE
BOB FIN-GER-MAN ©97
after G. de Chirico AND Picasso

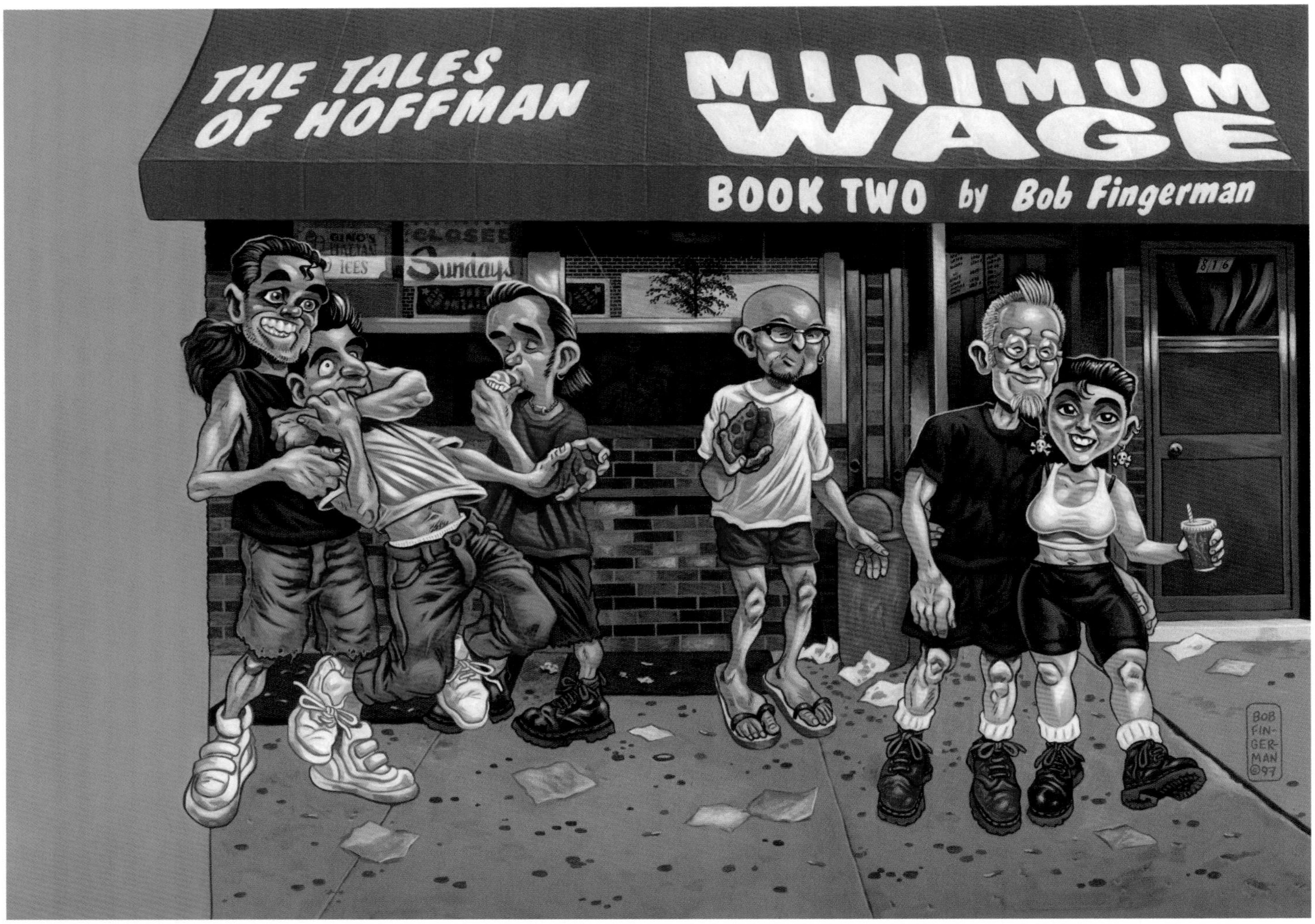
THE TALES OF HOFFMAN
MINIMUM WAGE
BOOK TWO by Bob Fingerman
CLOSED Sundays
BOB FIN-GER-MAN ©97

Above: *Minimum Wage Book Two* (Acrylic). Below and opposite: covers for Italian editions (Ink & Digital)

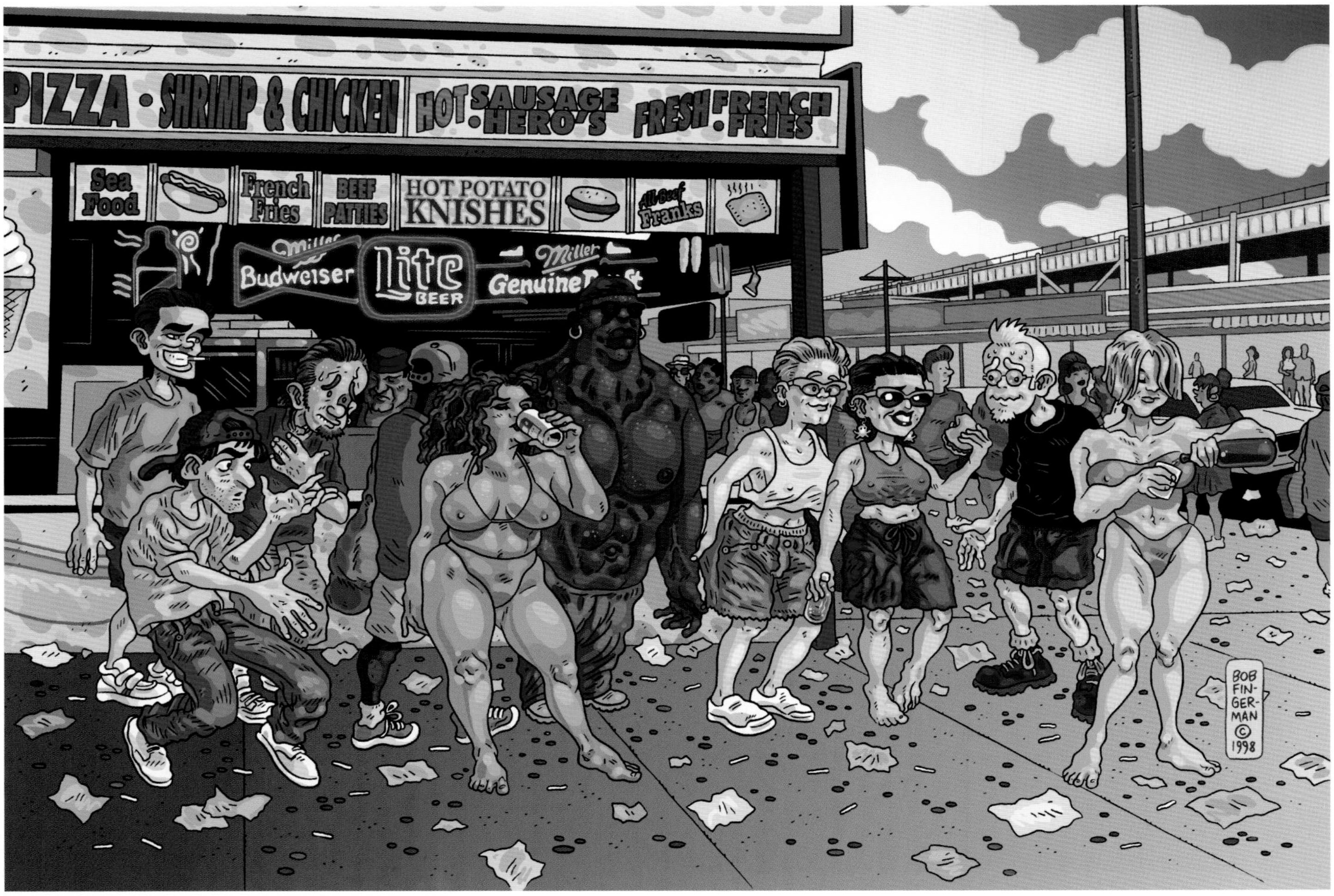
PIZZA · SHRIMP & CHICKEN
HOT SAUSAGE HERO'S
FRESH FRENCH FRIES
Sea Food
French Fries
BEEF PATTIES
HOT POTATO KNISHES
All-Beef Franks
Budweiser
Lite BEER
Miller
BOB FIN-GER-MAN © 1998

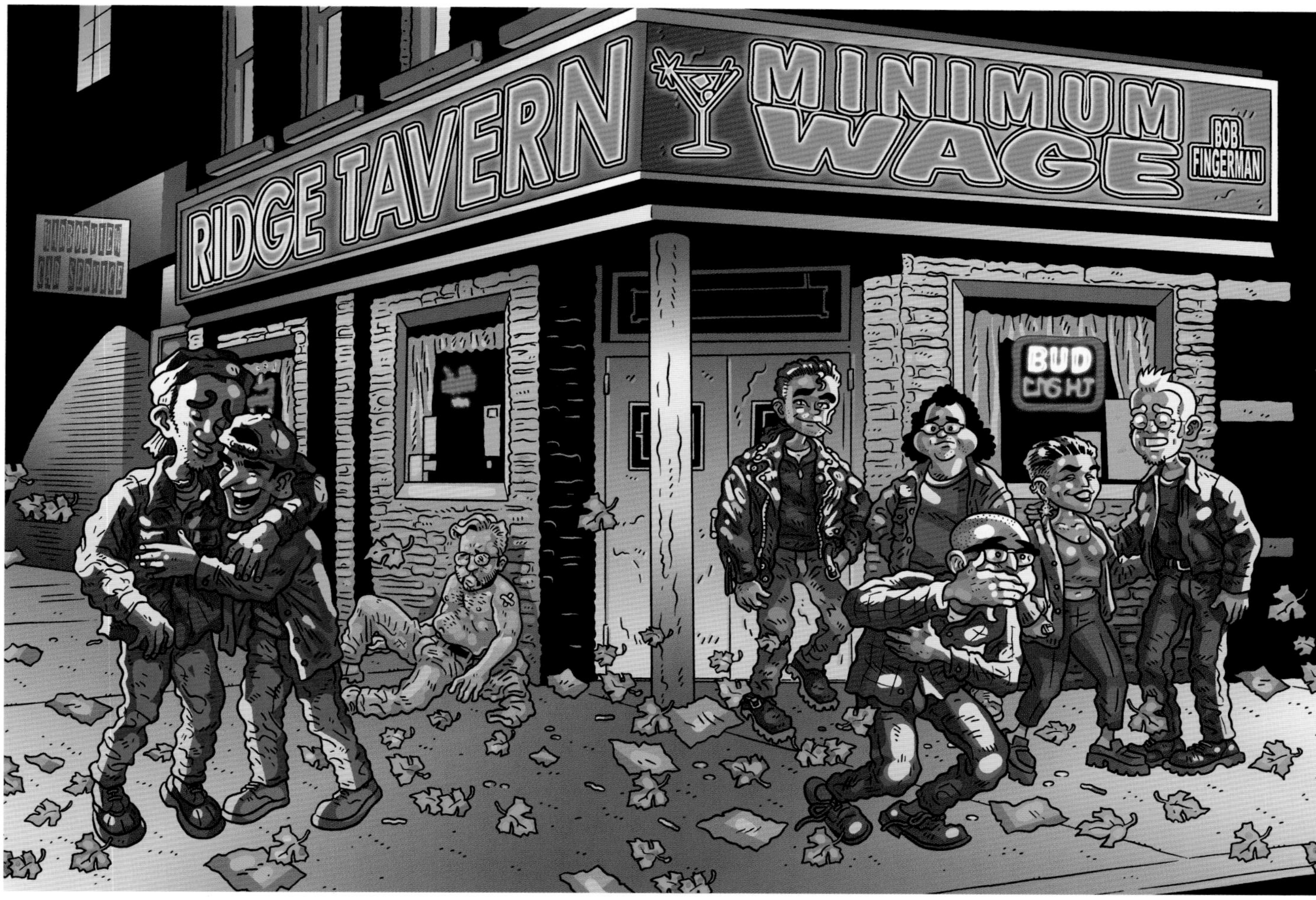
RIDGE TAVERN
MINIMUM WAGE
BOB FINGERMAN
BUD LIGHT

The Italian publisher, Magic Press, released three volumes, collecting *Minimum Wage Book One* and the subsequent 10 issues. The art inside was all the pre-rejiggered stuff, without the added gray tone.

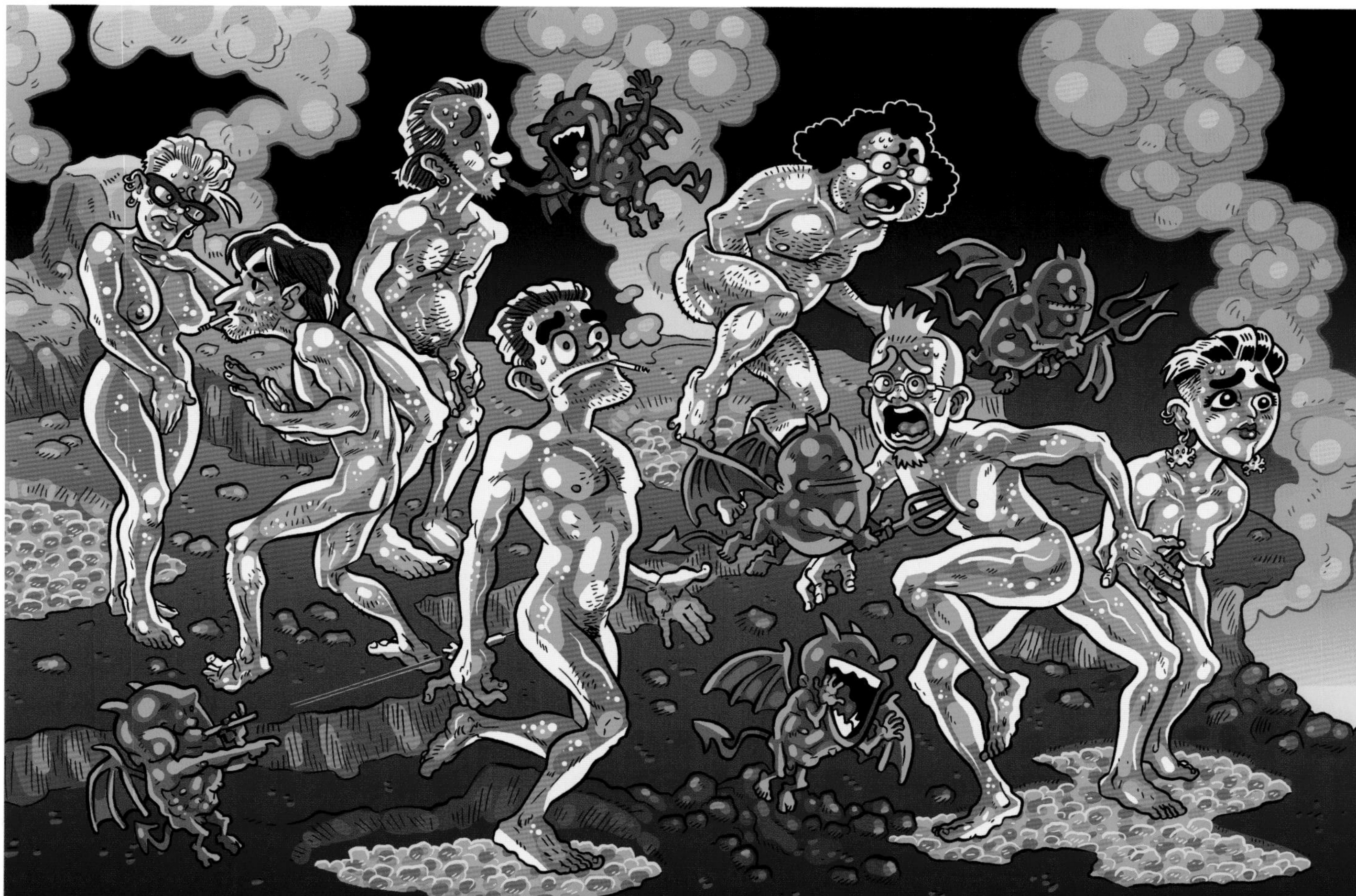

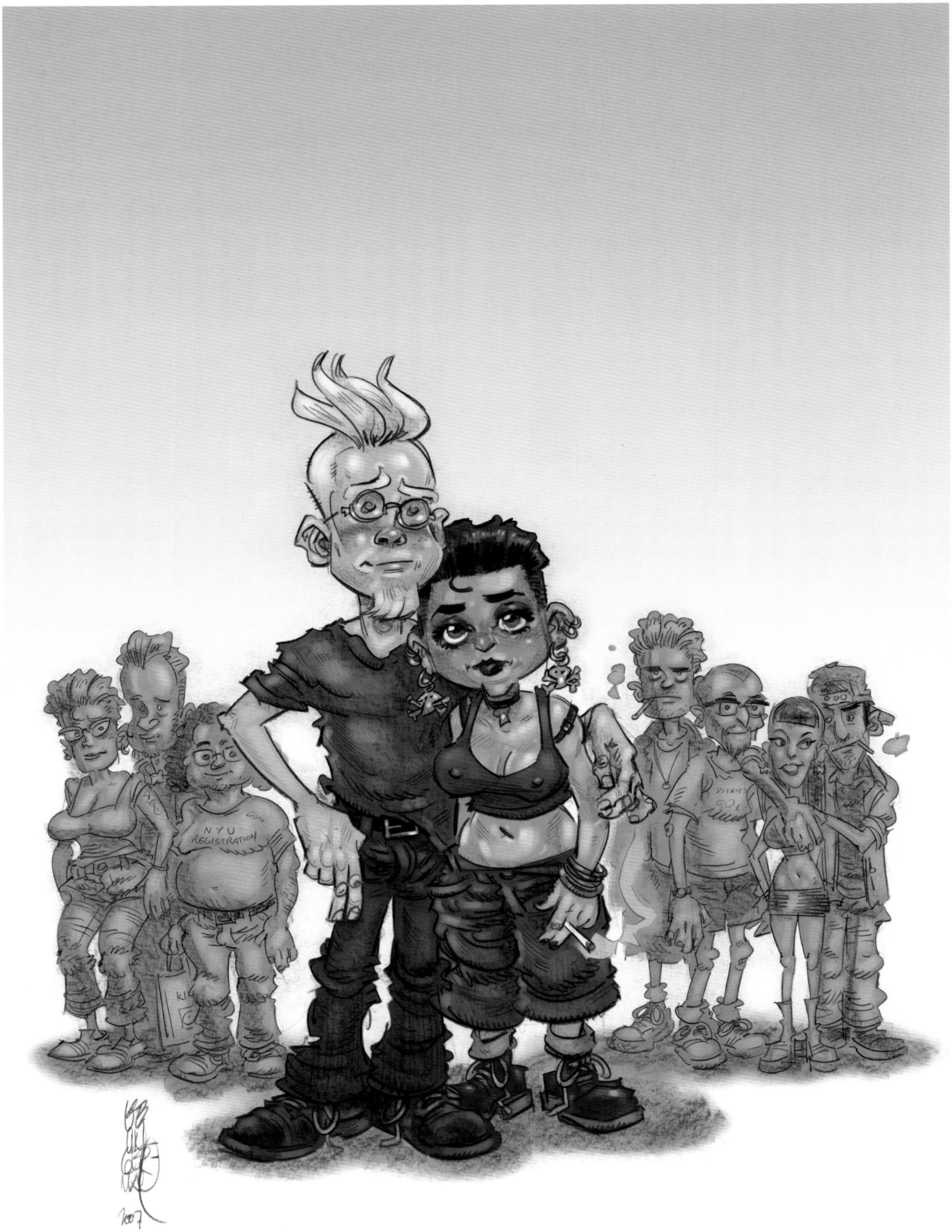
N Y U
REGISTRATION

Above: cover for the Spanish edition, *Salario Mínimo* (Dolmen). (Pencil & Digital)

GUEST GALLERY

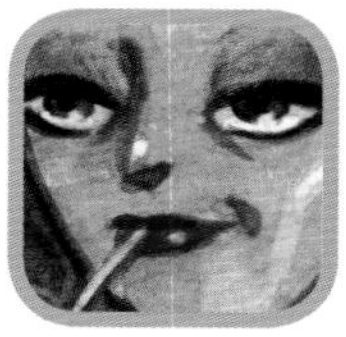
Dave Johnson
1996

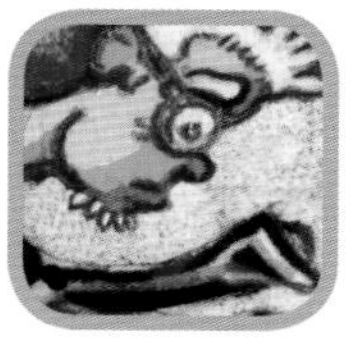
Peter Kuper
2012

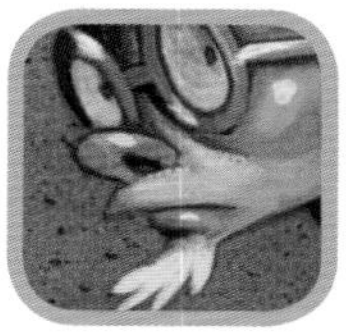
Glenn Barr
1997

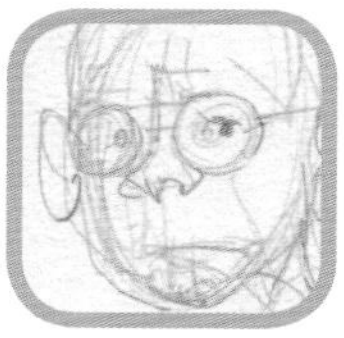
Kevin Nowlan
1996

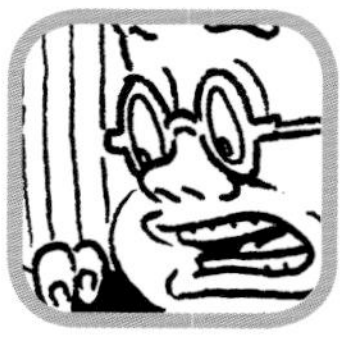
Patrick McEown
1995

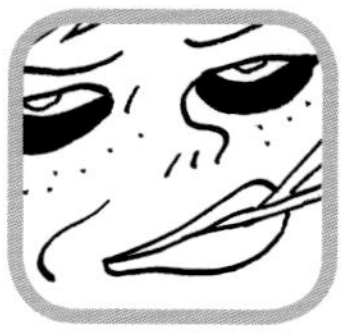
Gilbert Hernandez
2012

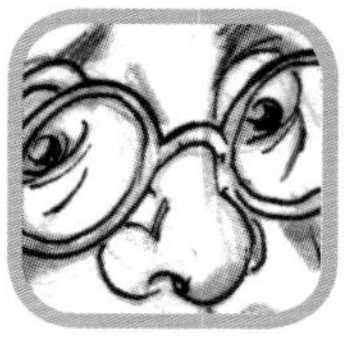
Glenn Fabry
2012

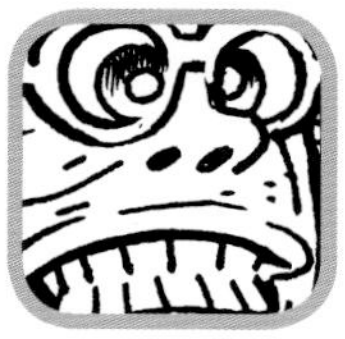
Bill Wray
1996

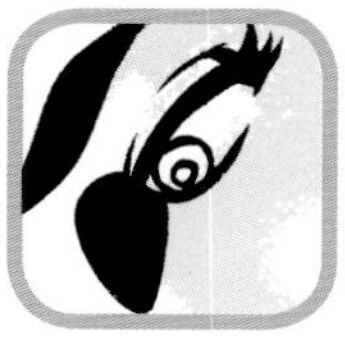
Dean Haspiel
2012

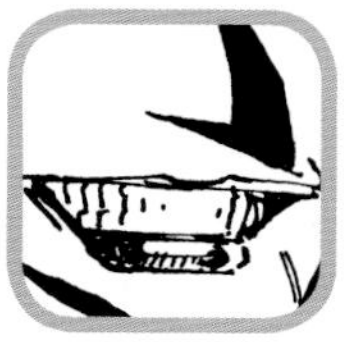
Ted McKeever
1997

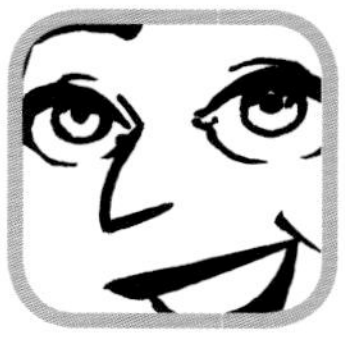
Dan Steffan
1998

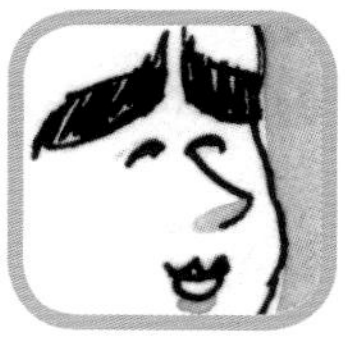
Joe Dator
2012

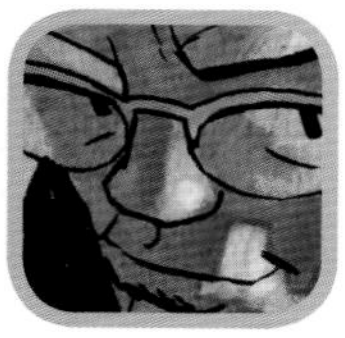
Dave Johnson
2012

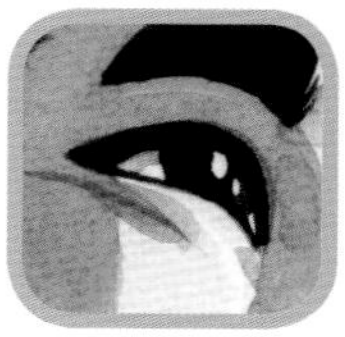
Jill Thompson
1997

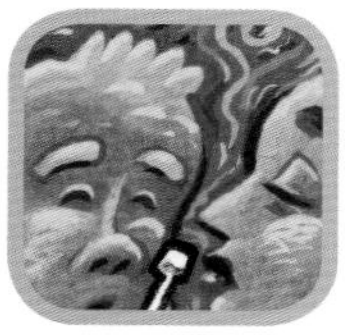
Dave Cooper
1995

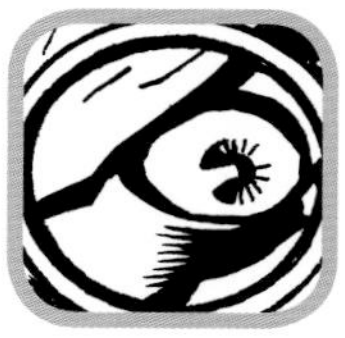
Kevin Nowlan
1996

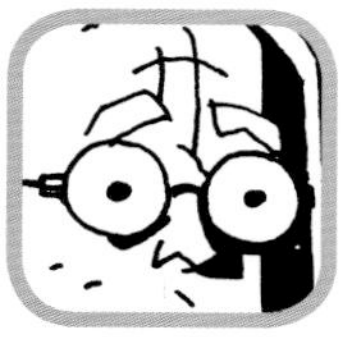
Mike Mignola
1996

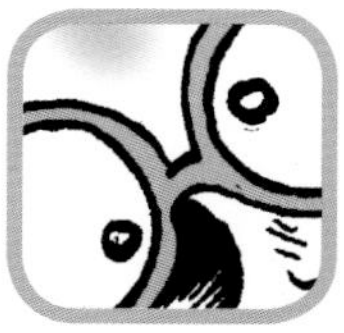
Peter Bagge
2012

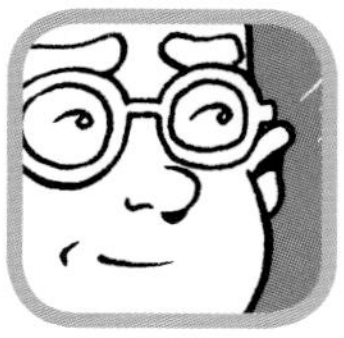
Roger Langridge
2012

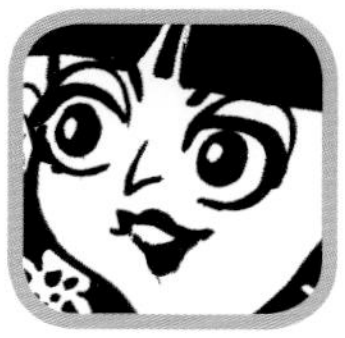
Hunt Emerson
2012

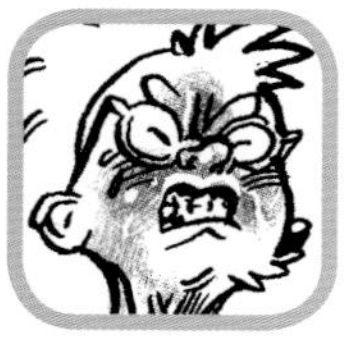
Joe Infurnari
2012

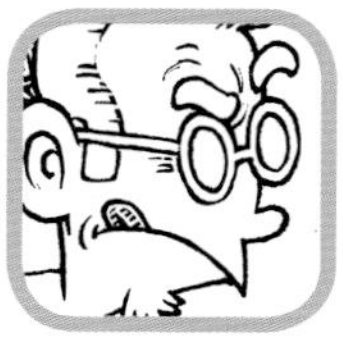
John Kerschbaum
2012

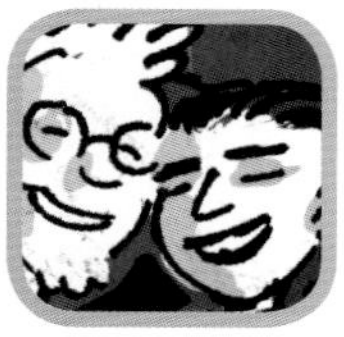
Guy Davis
2012

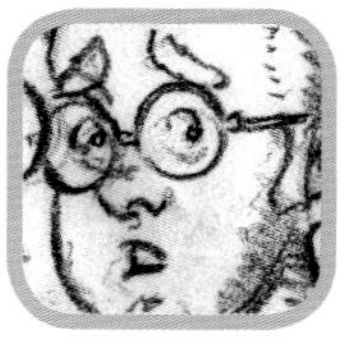
Jeff Wong
2012

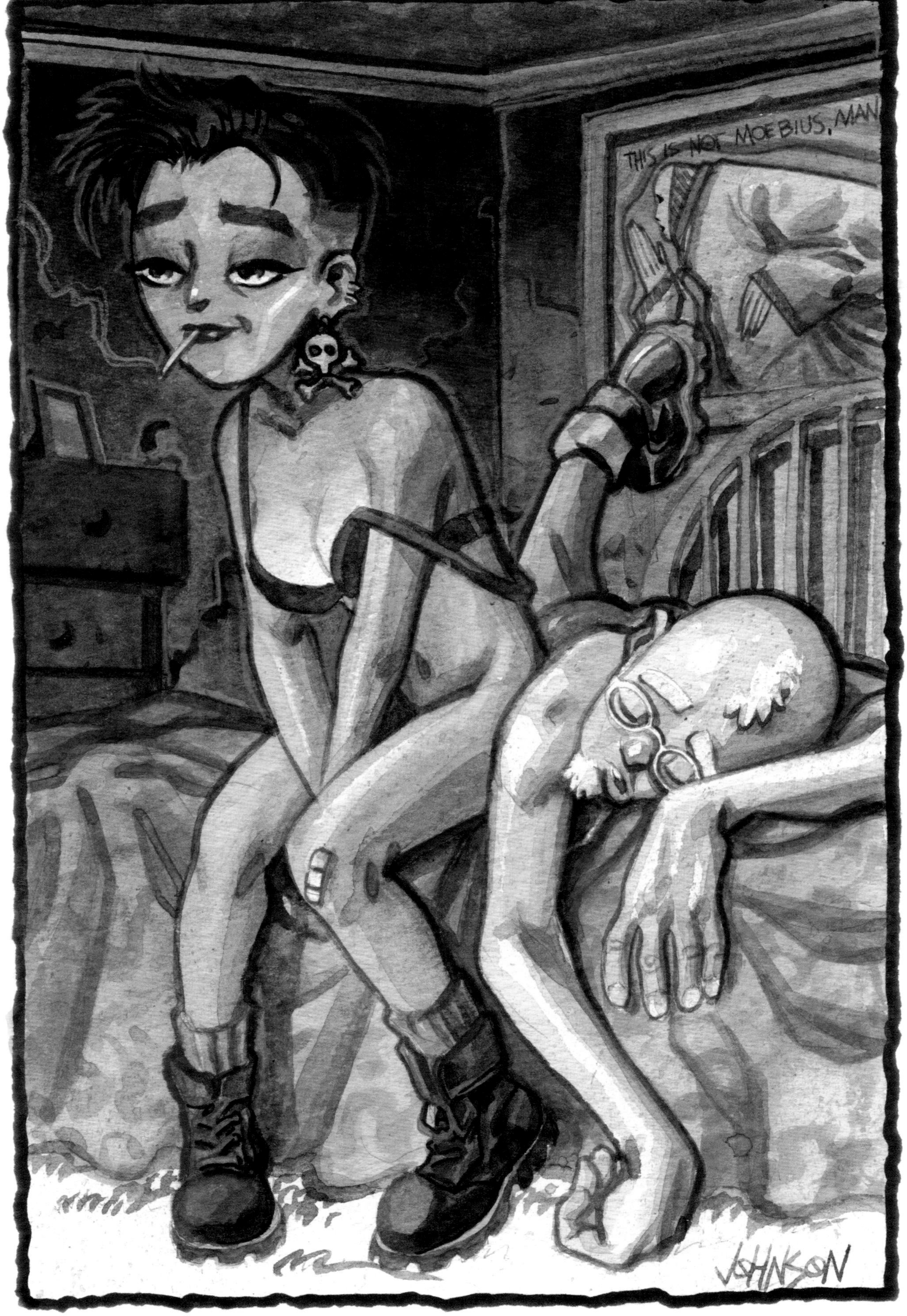
THIS IS NOT MOEBIUS, MAN
JOHNSON

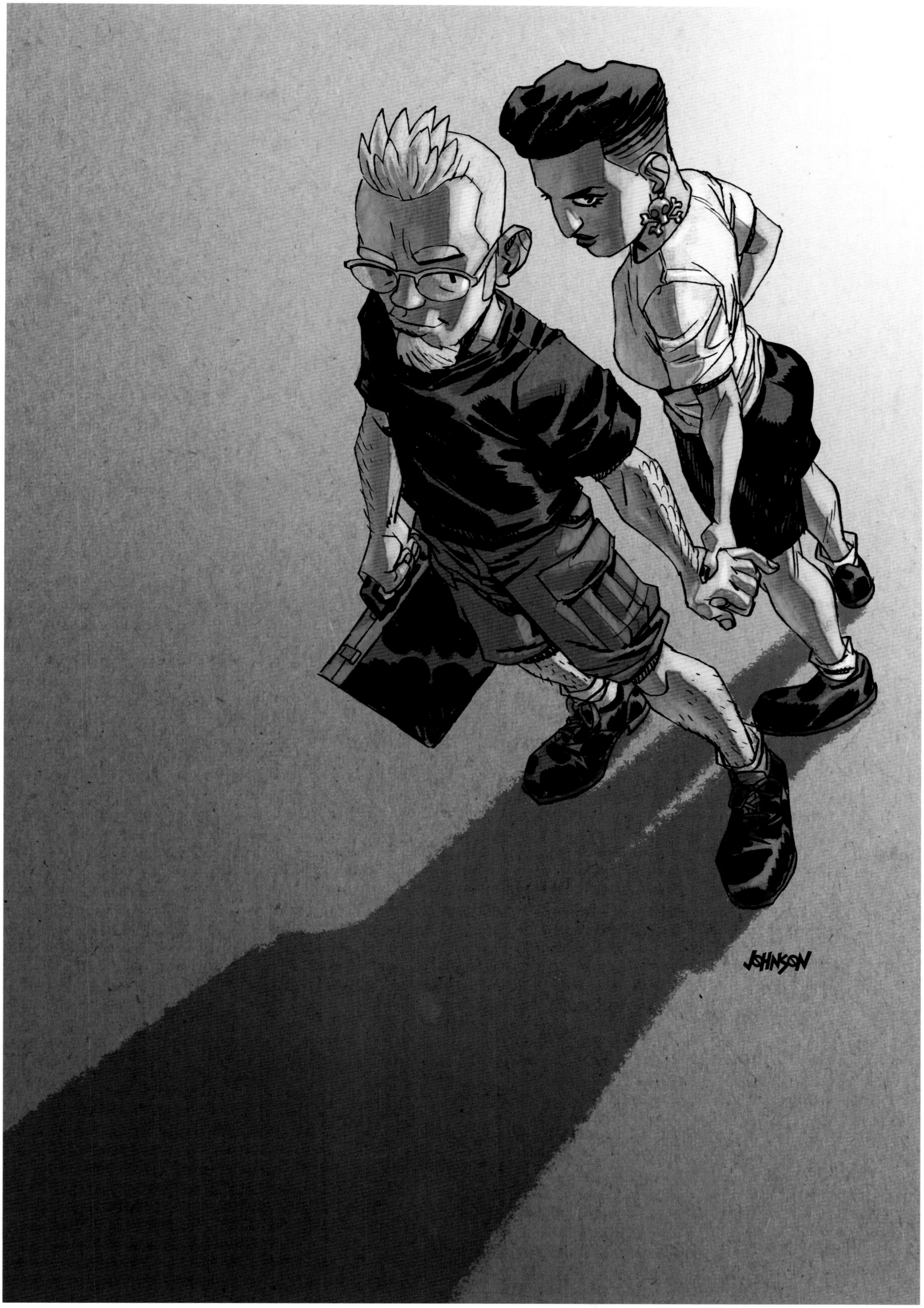
JOHNSON

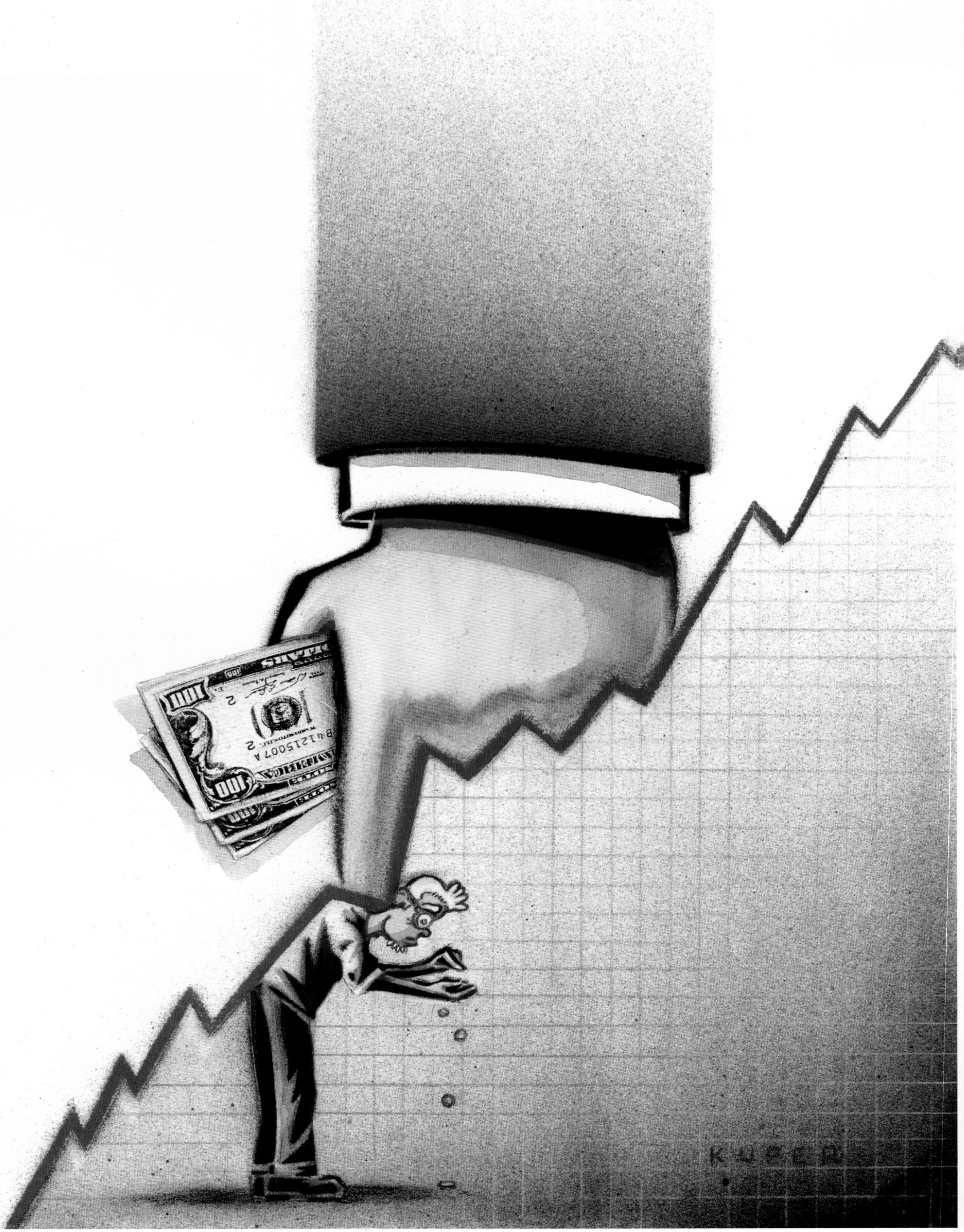
KUPER

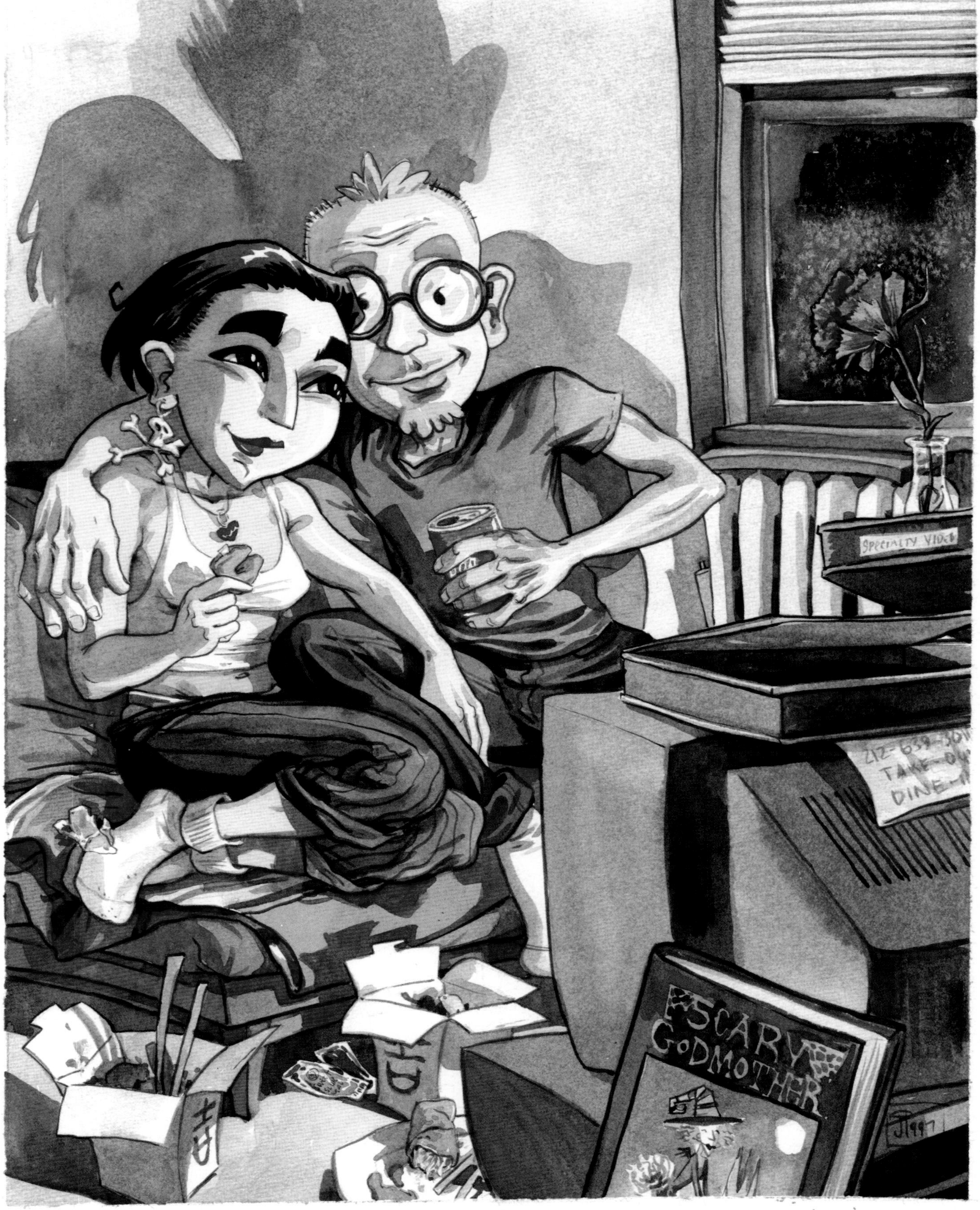
SPECIALTY VIDEO
SCARY GODMOTHER

TO BOB — I call this one "Royalty Check!"

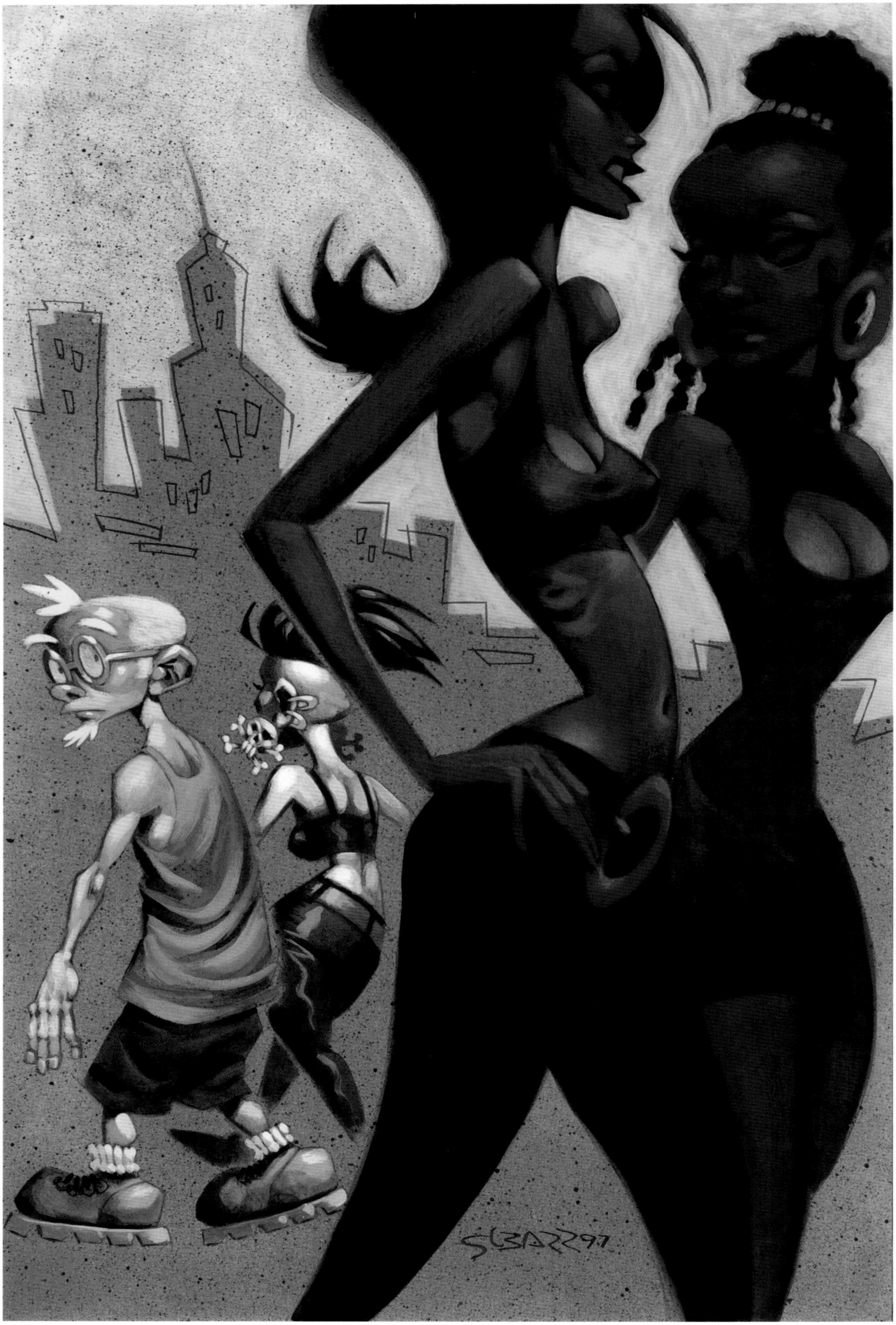

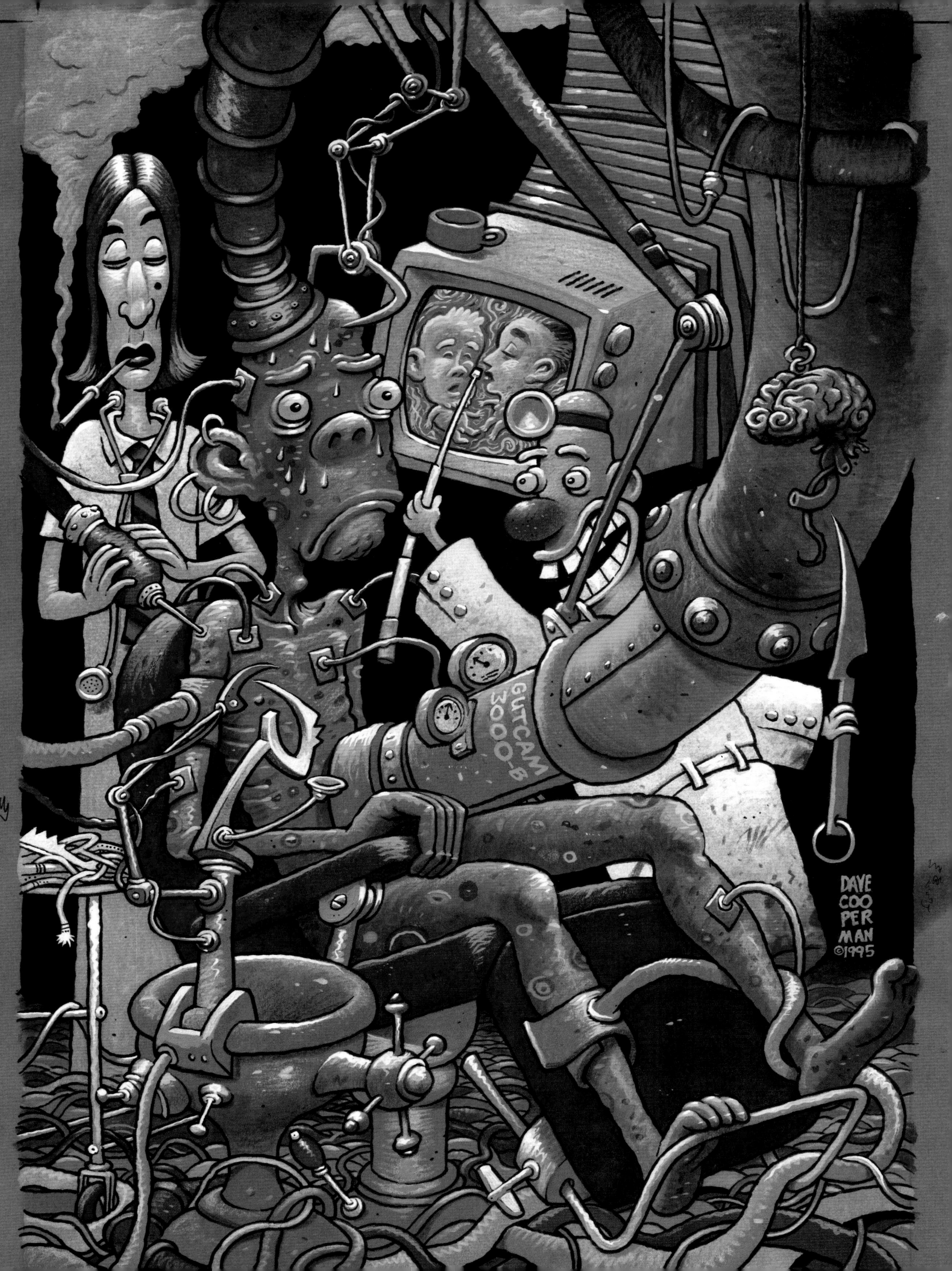
GUTCAM
3000-B
DAVE
COOPER
MAN
©1995

DC #2

M20,

C10, M20, Y100, K50

30, K60

50, M50, Y50, K60

6 C2

G C3
C40,

G C10, M
C30, M10, Y50

M40, Y2

Top left: Pencil on bond paper.
Right: Magic marker and colored pencil on photocopy.
Bottom left: Magic marker and pencil on photocopy.
Background: Tissue overlay with felt tip over colored copy.

NOWLAN

NOWLA

Not only was I fortunate enough to get a back cover from the illustrious Kevin Nowlan, but years later when he was going through his files he came across the original thumbnail sketches he did for his magnificent piece. He also included the hand-colored photocopy that was supplied to the separator (including the tissue overlay with all the color codes; the pre-digital days were labor intensive, that's for sure).

C70, M50, Y30, K40 — C70, M20, Y40

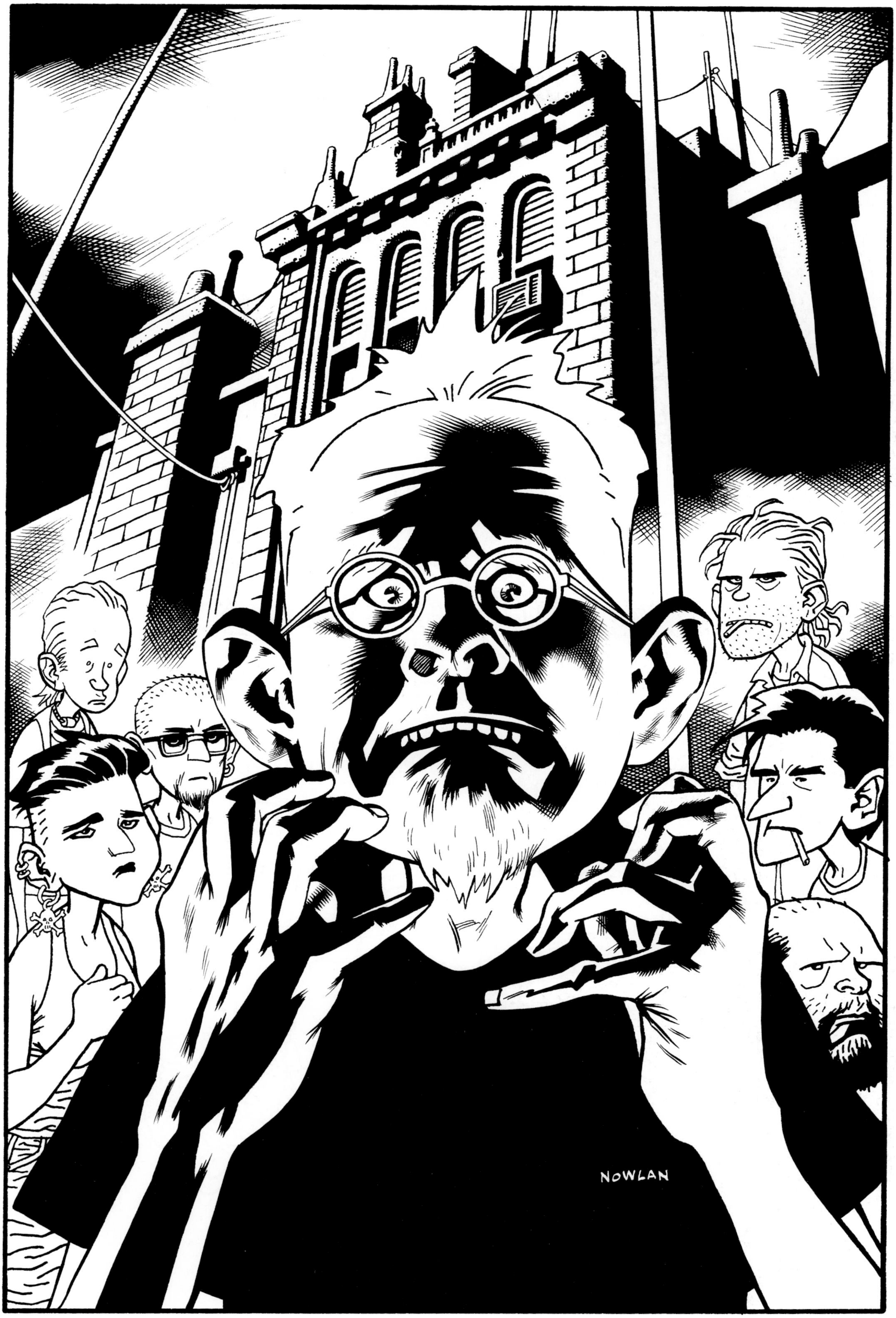
NOWLAN

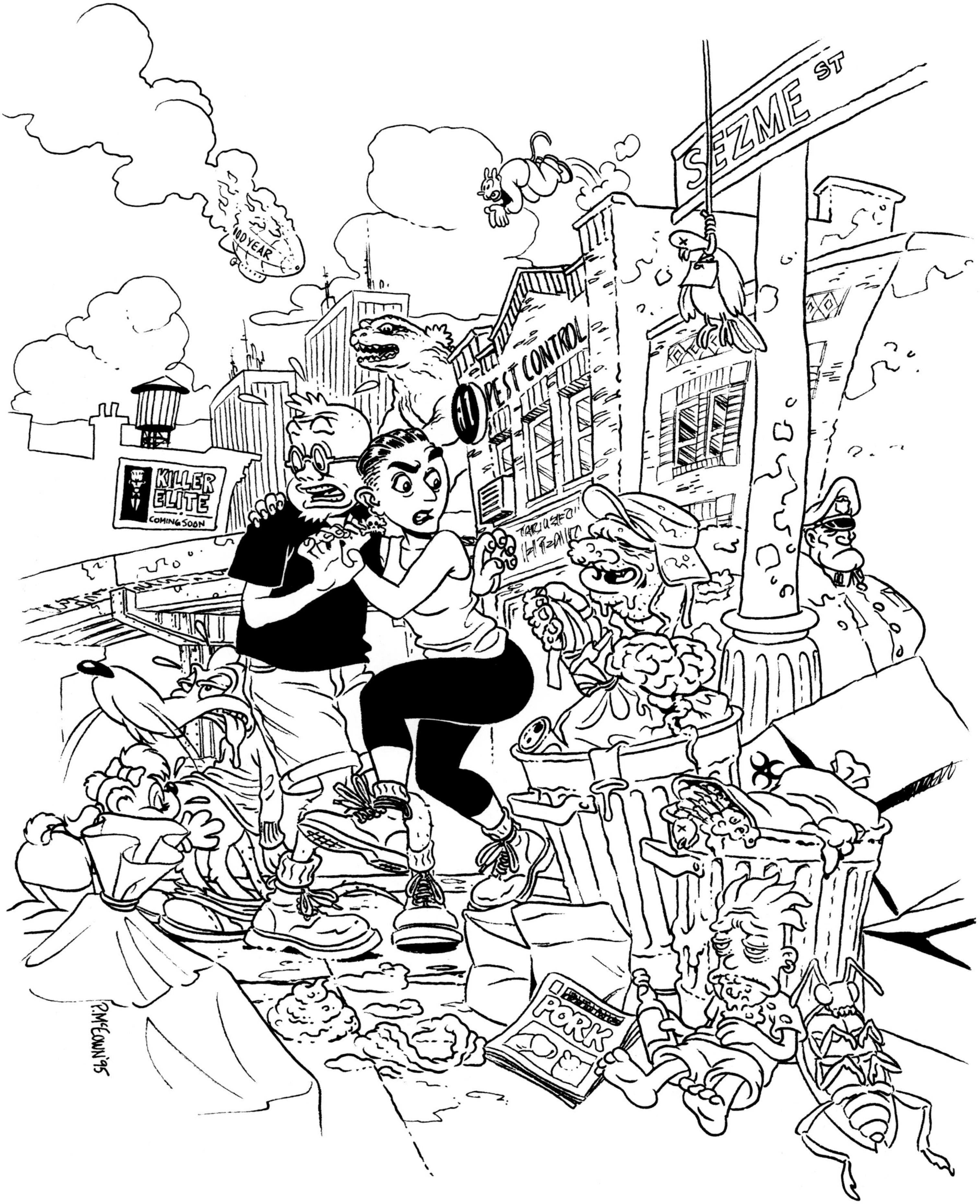
SEZME ST
PEST CONTROL
KILLER ELITE
COMING SOON
PORK

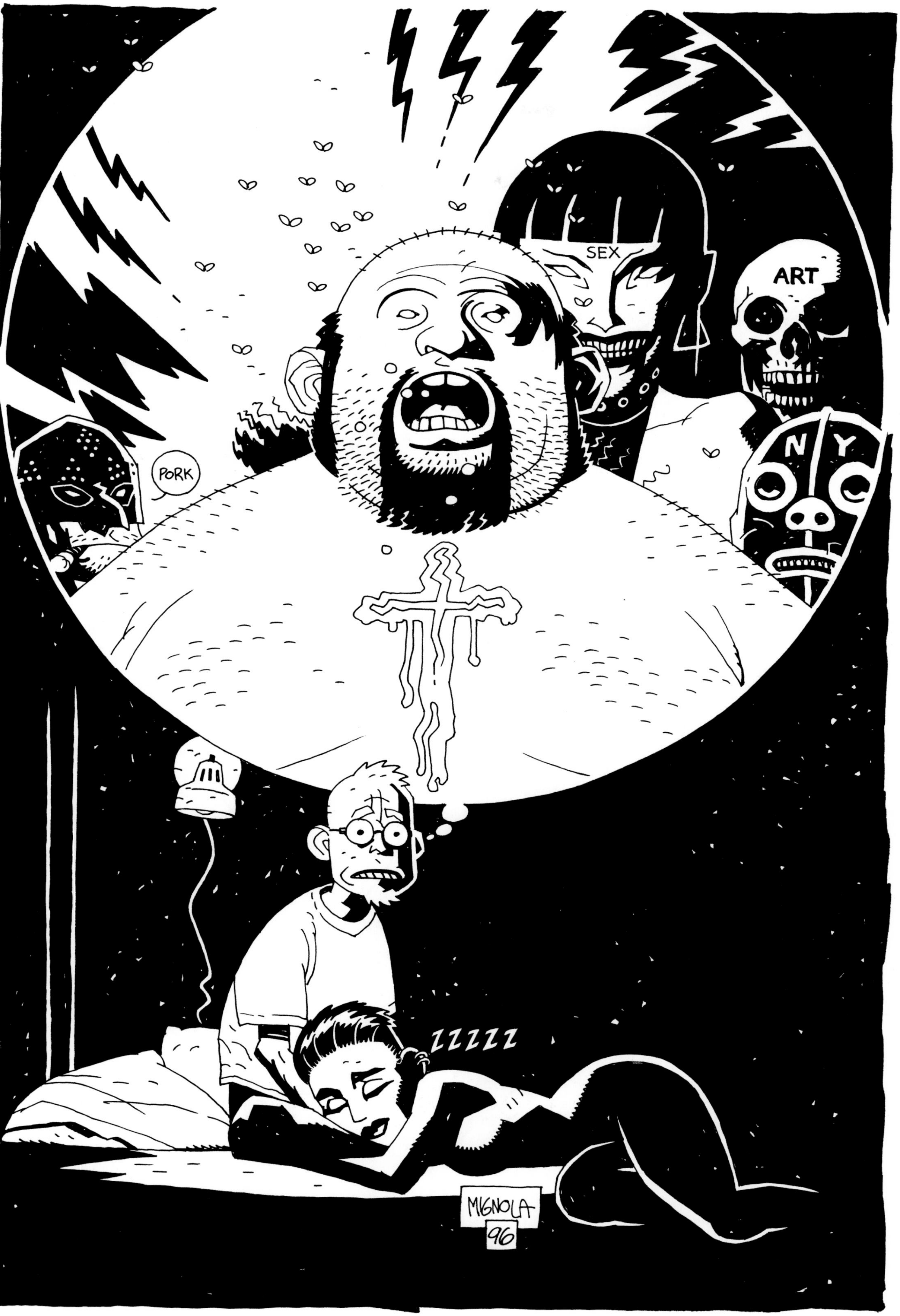
SEX
ART
PORK
N Y
ZZZZZ
MIGNOLA 96

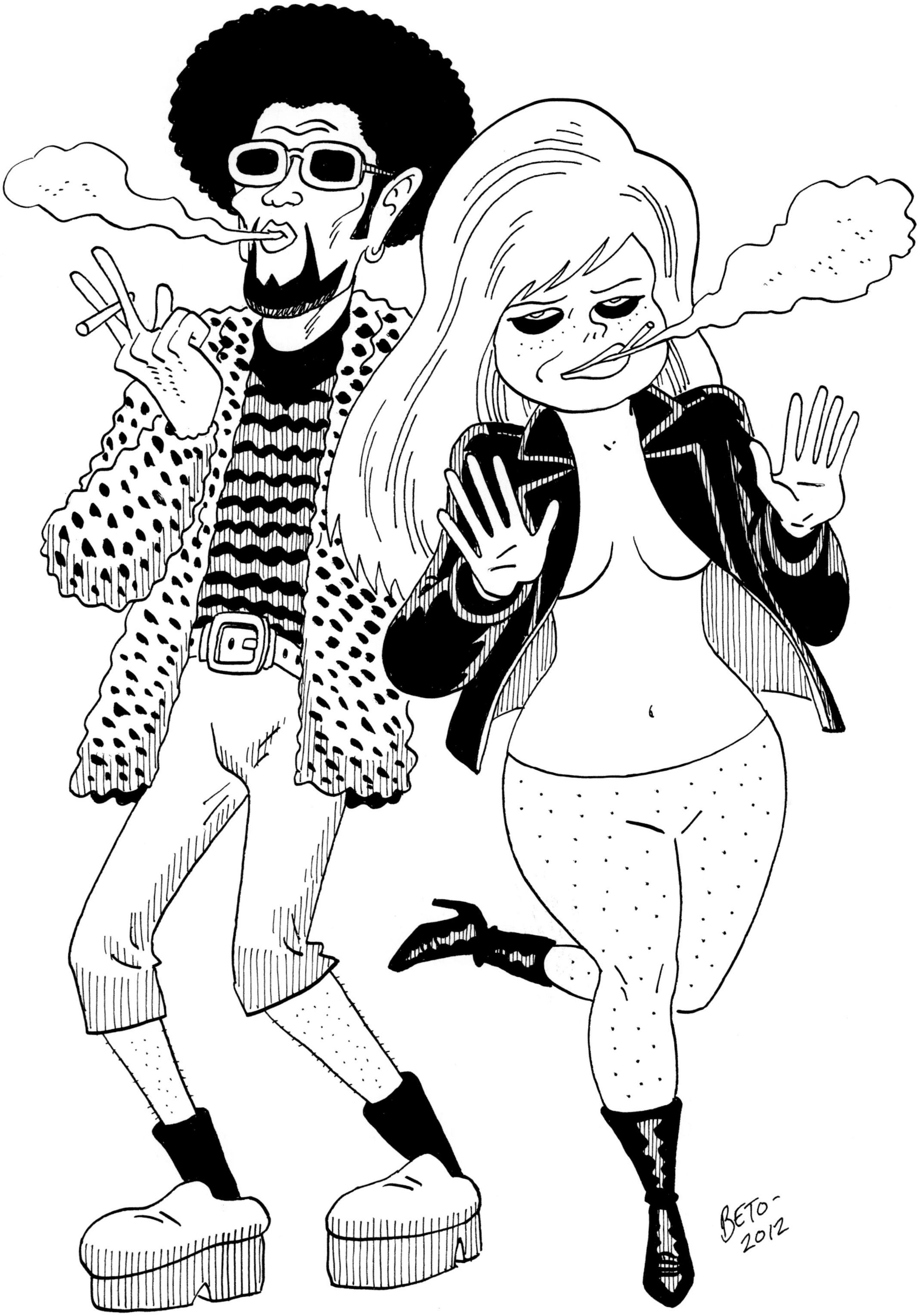
BETO-
2012

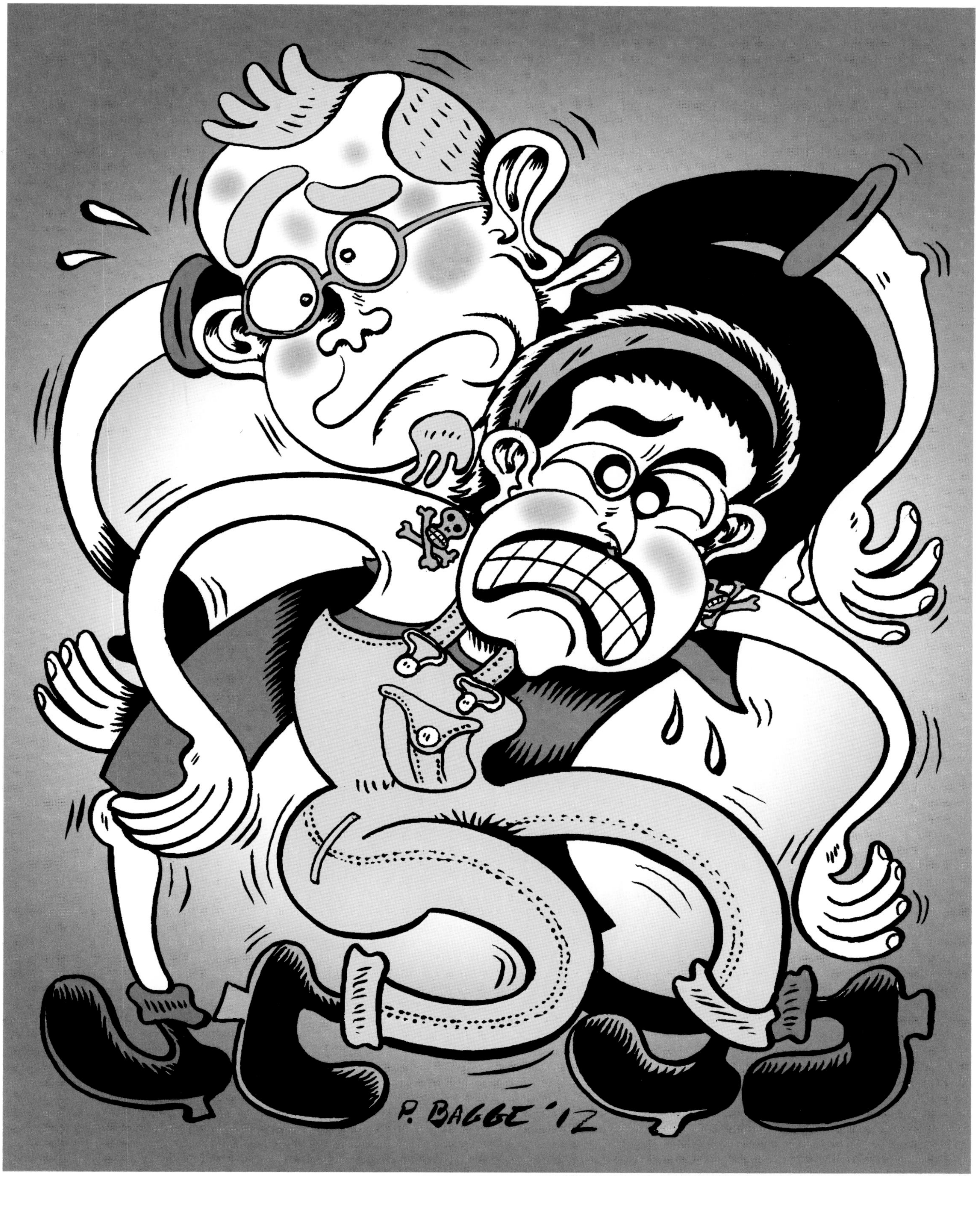
P. BAGGE '12

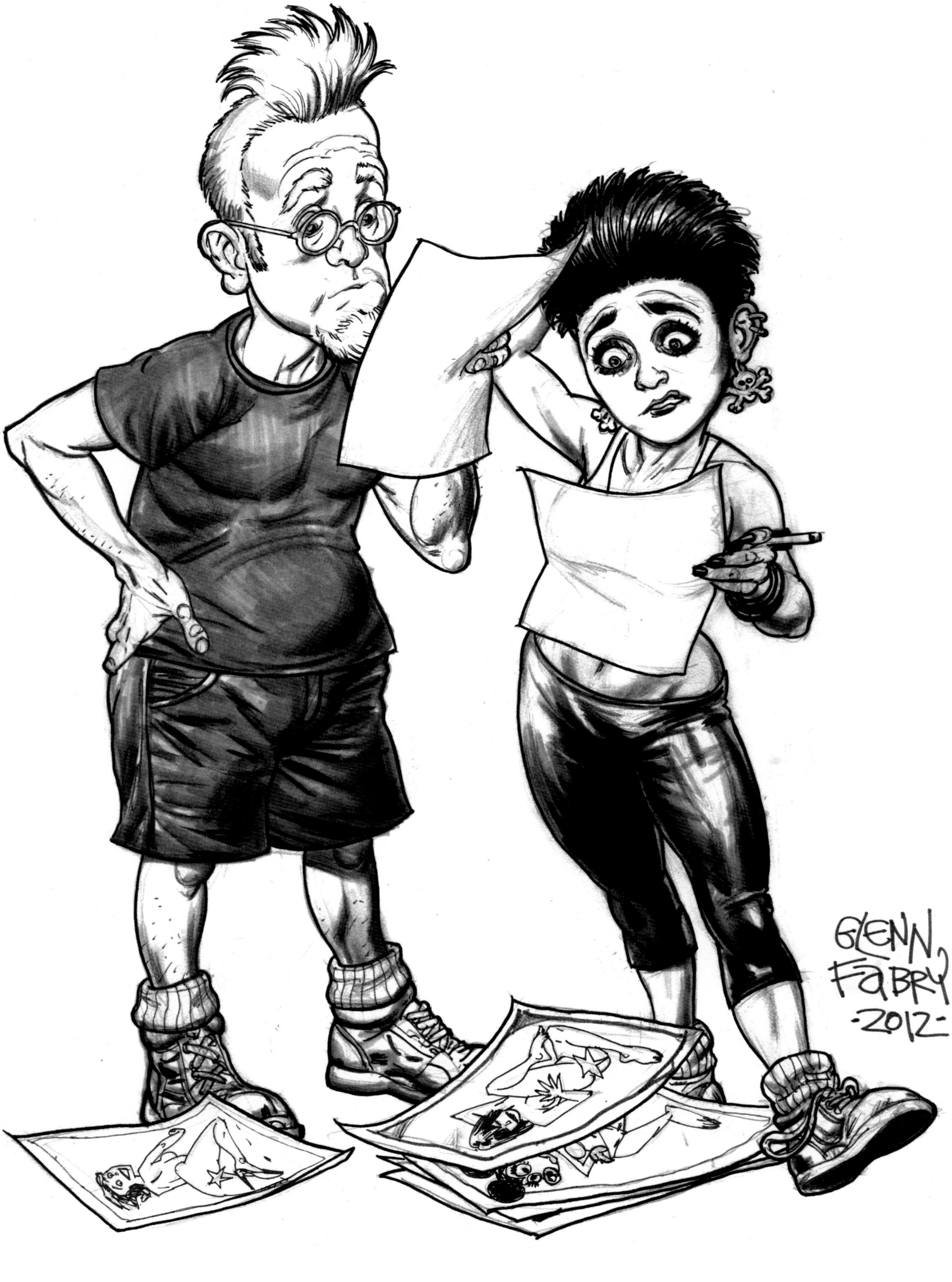
GLENN FABRY
-2012-

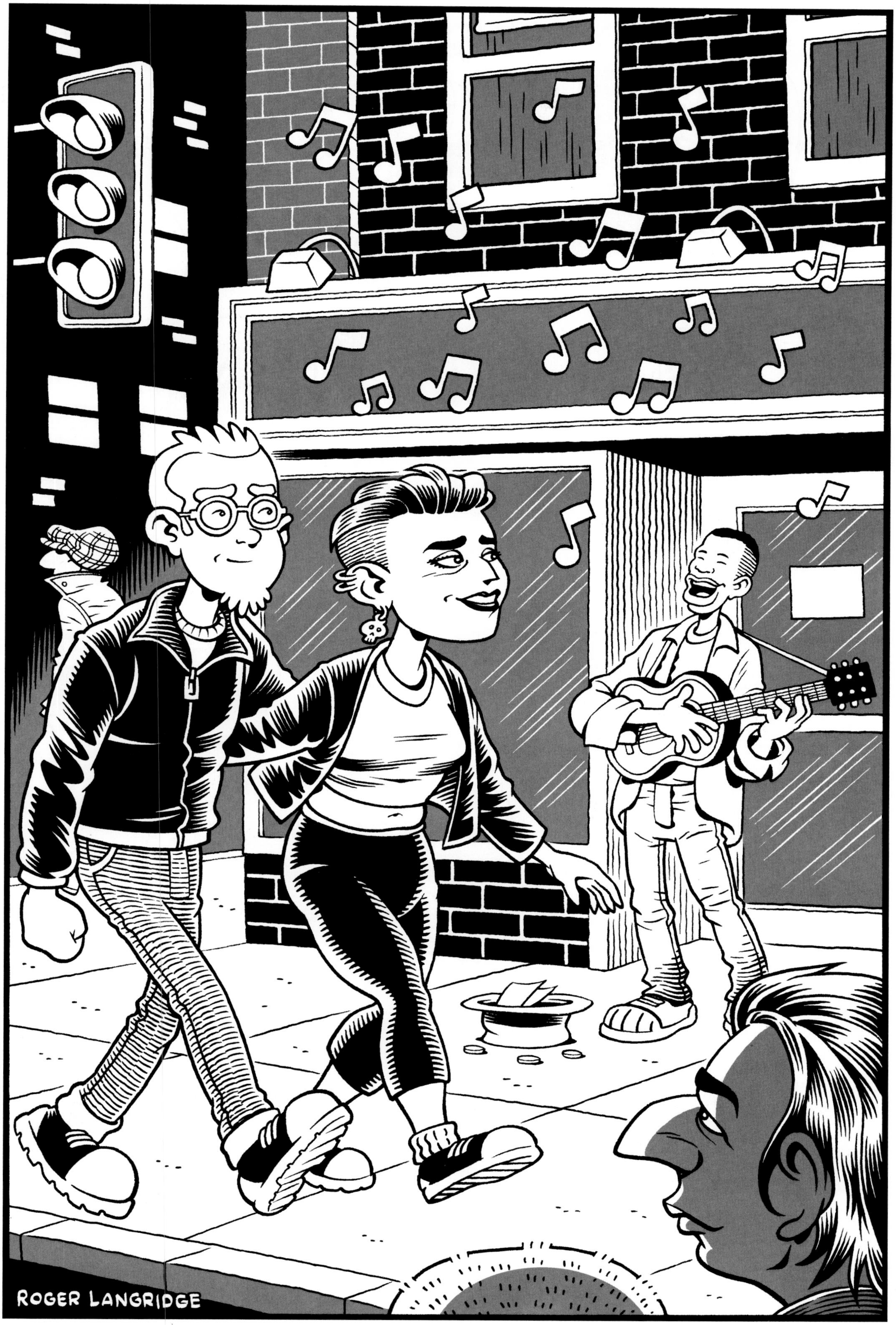
ROGER LANGRIDGE

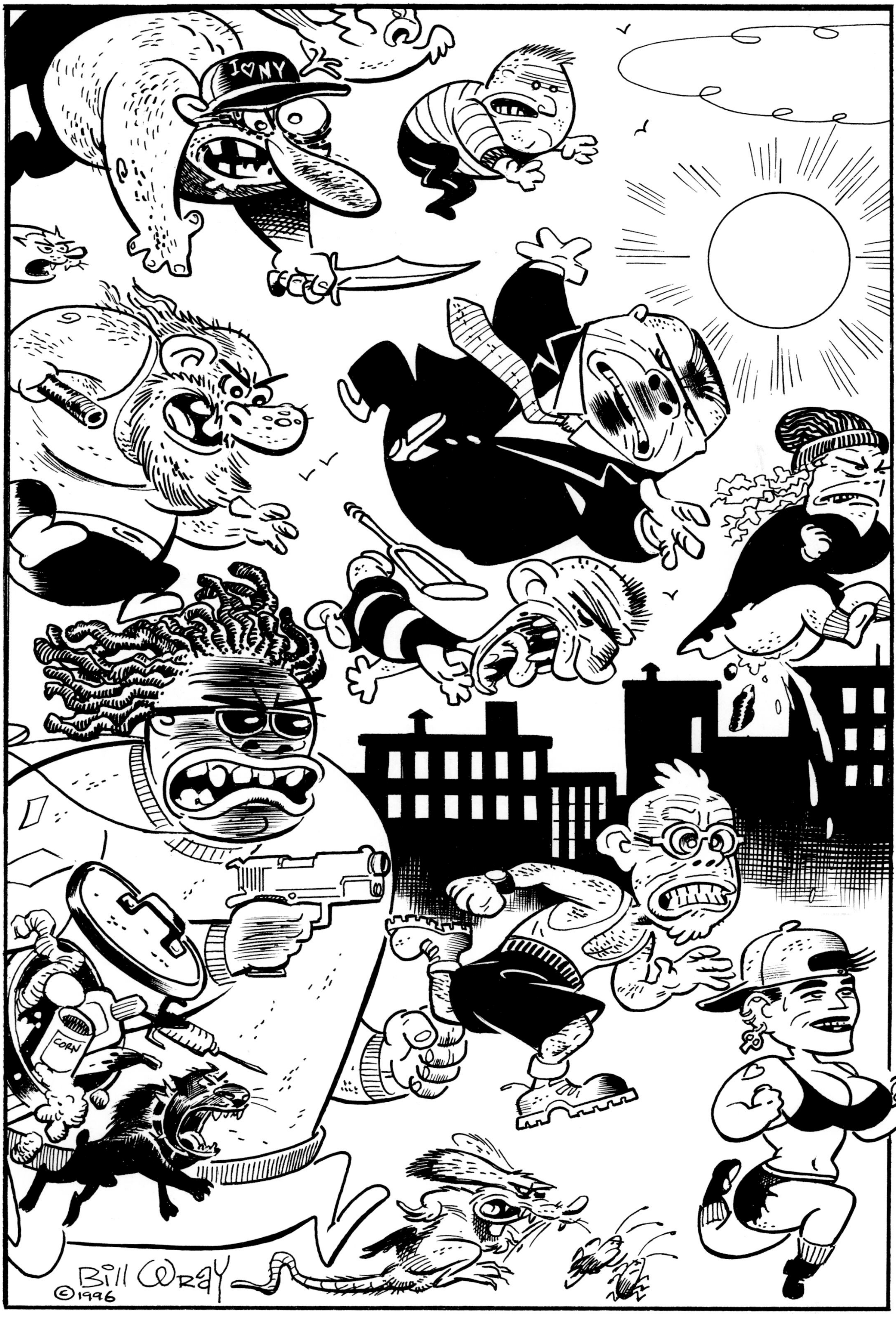

I ♥ NY
CORN
Bill Wray
©1996

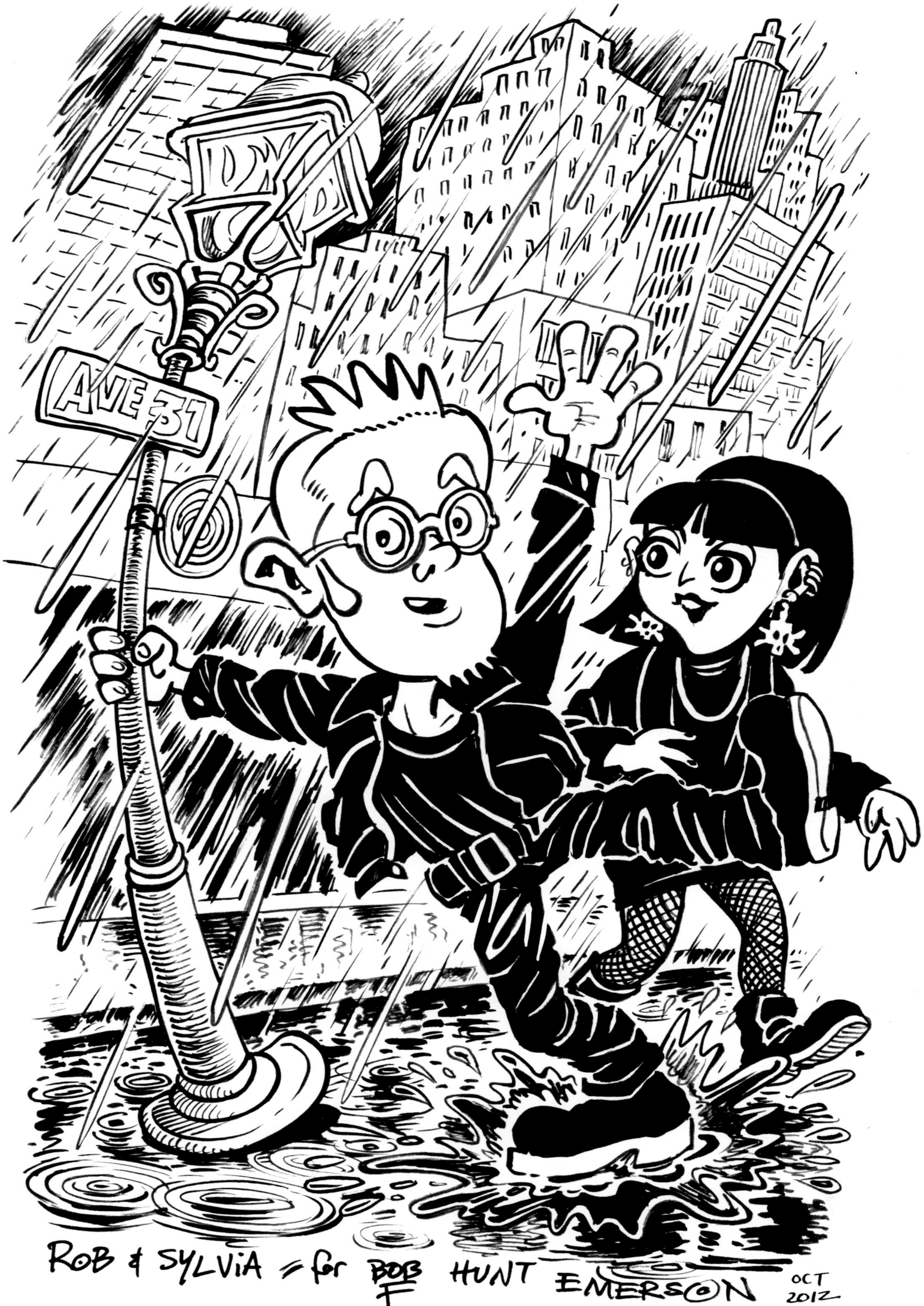
AVE 31
ROB & SYLVIA = for BOB F HUNT EMERSON
OCT 2012

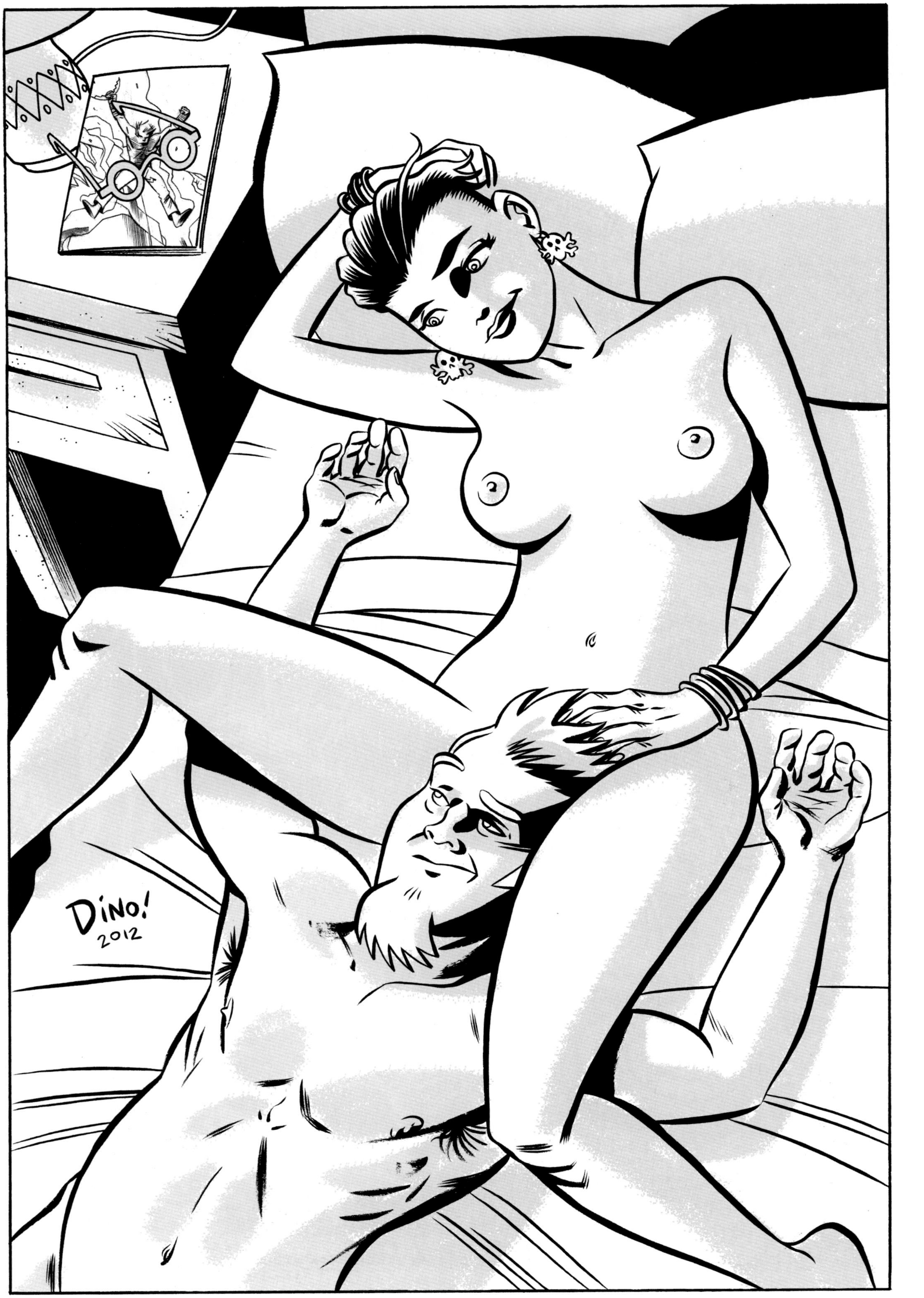
DiNO!
2012

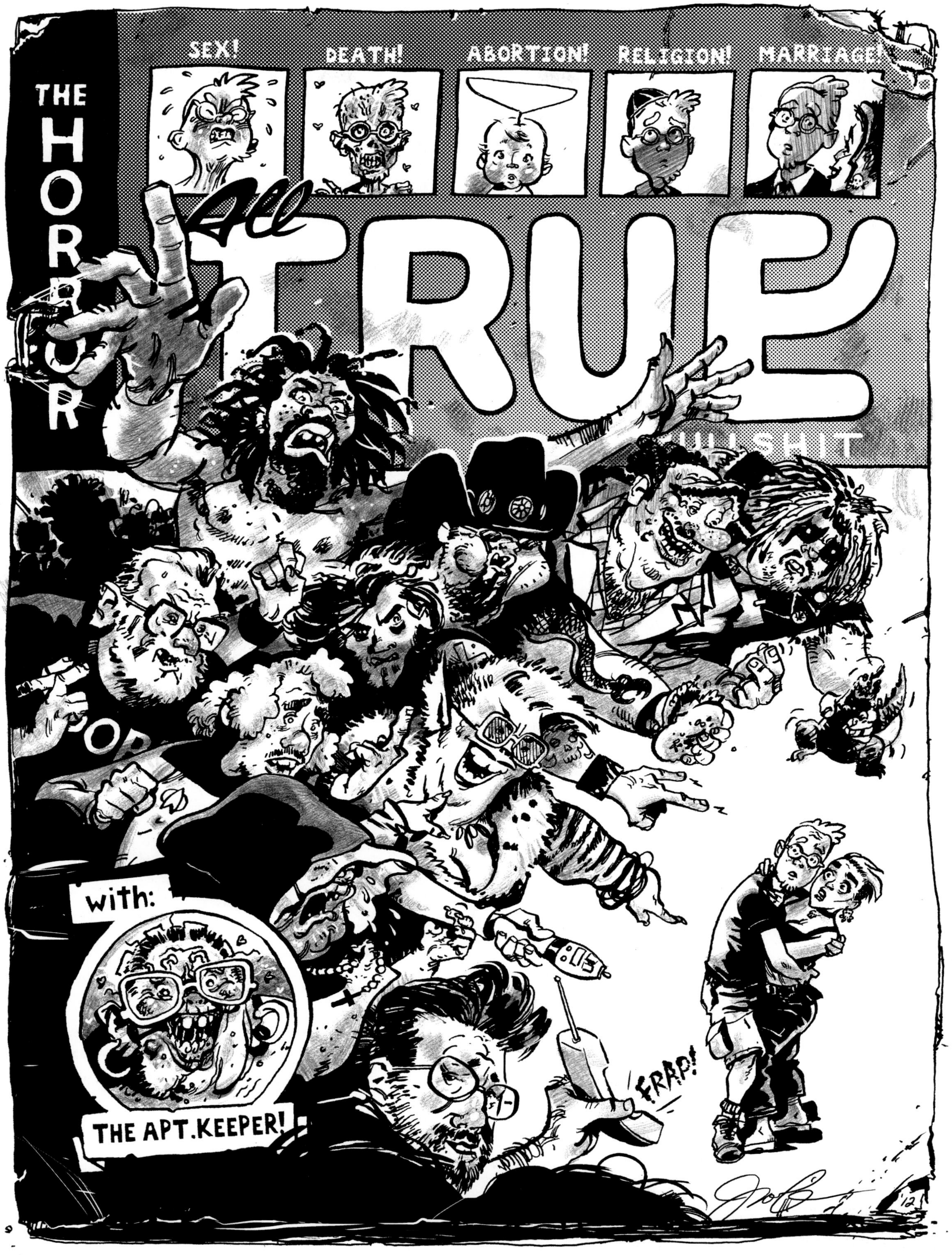

SEX!
DEATH!
ABORTION!
RELIGION!
MARRIAGE!
THE HORROR
All TRUE
with:
THE APT. KEEPER!
FRAP!

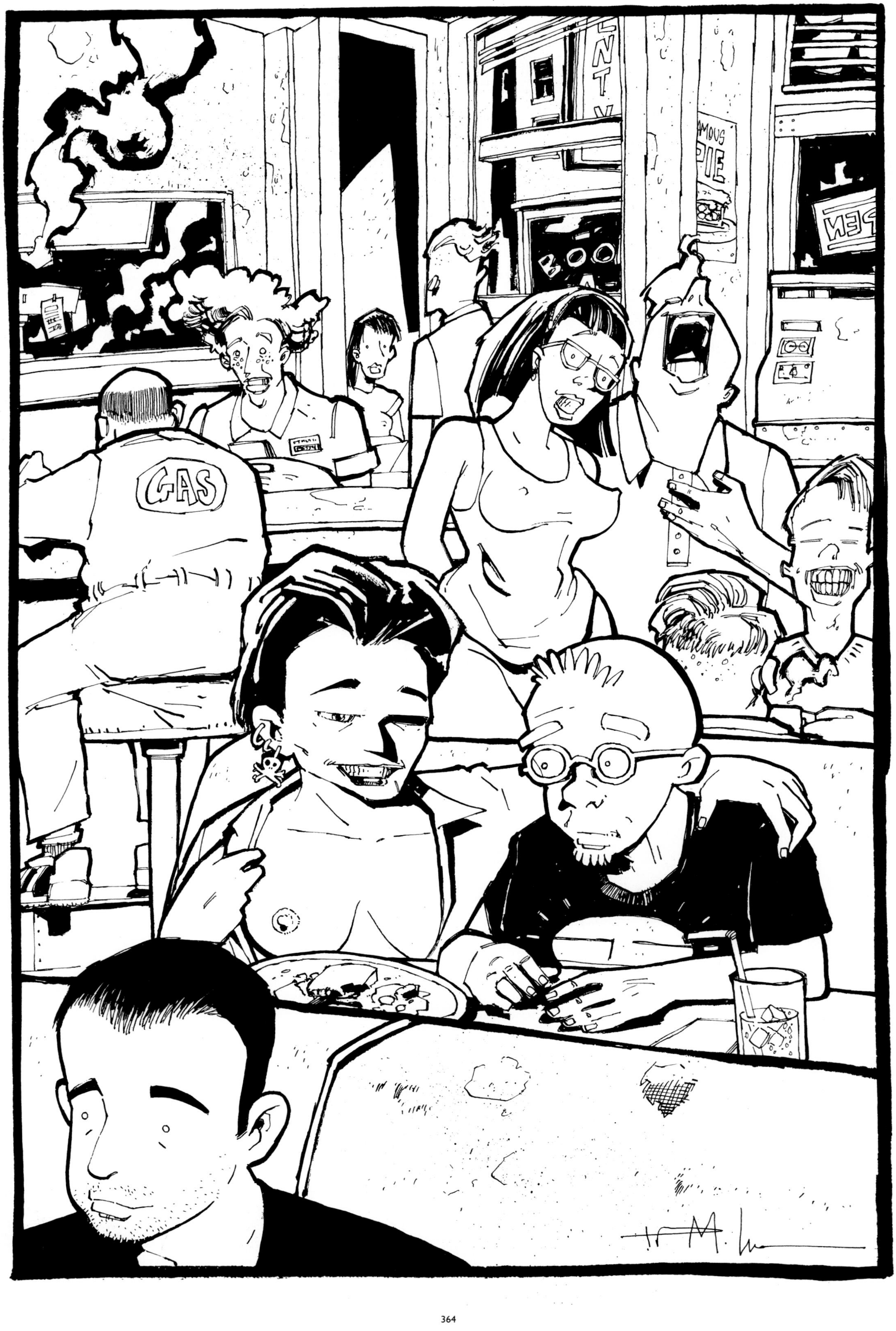
GAS
PIE

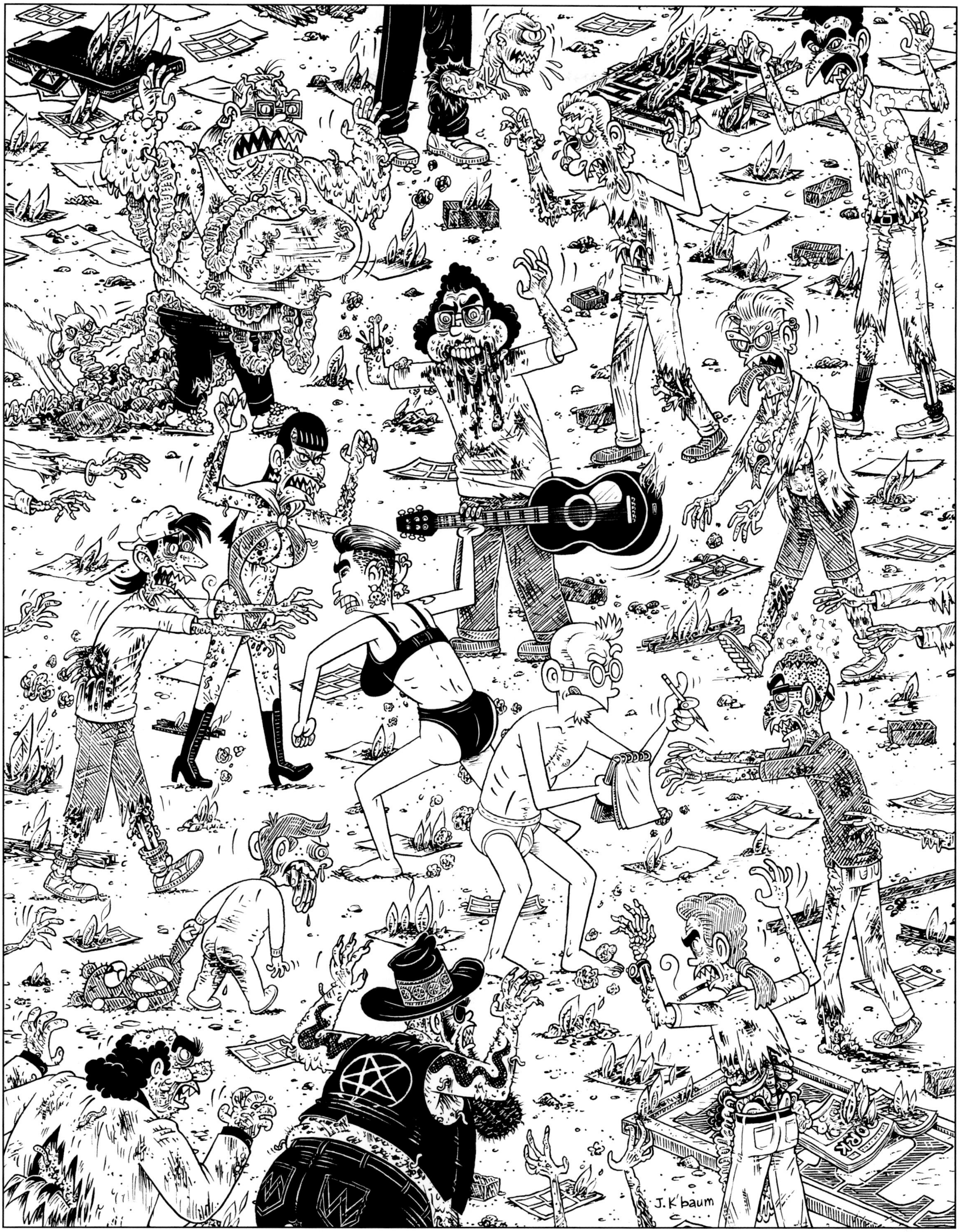
J. K'baum

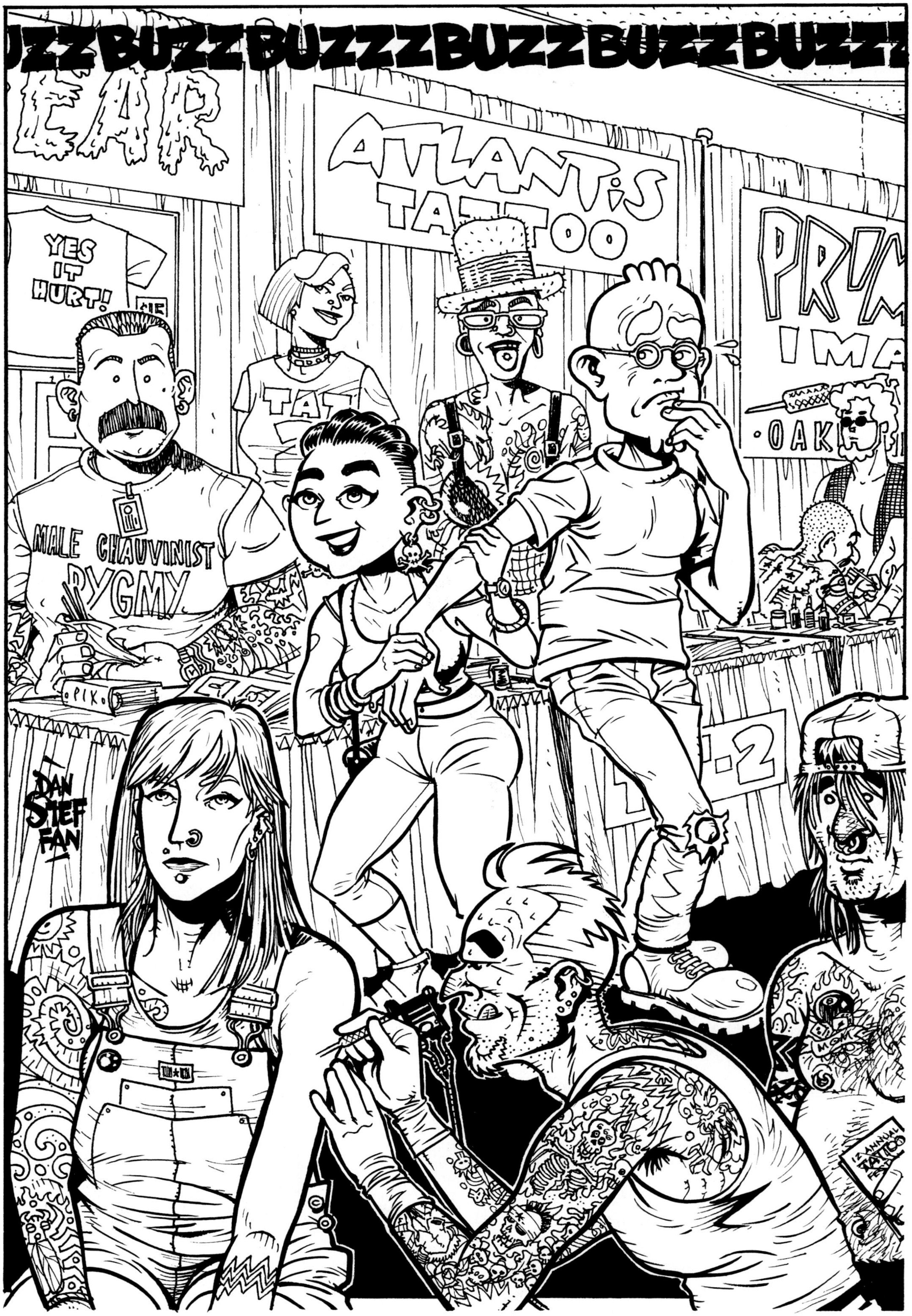

ZZBUZZBUZZZBUZZBUZZBUZZZ
EAR
ATLANTIS TATTOO
PRIM IMA
OAK
YES IT HURT!
TAT
MALE CHAUVINIST PYGMY
PIK
-2
DAN STEFFAN
MOM
TATTOO

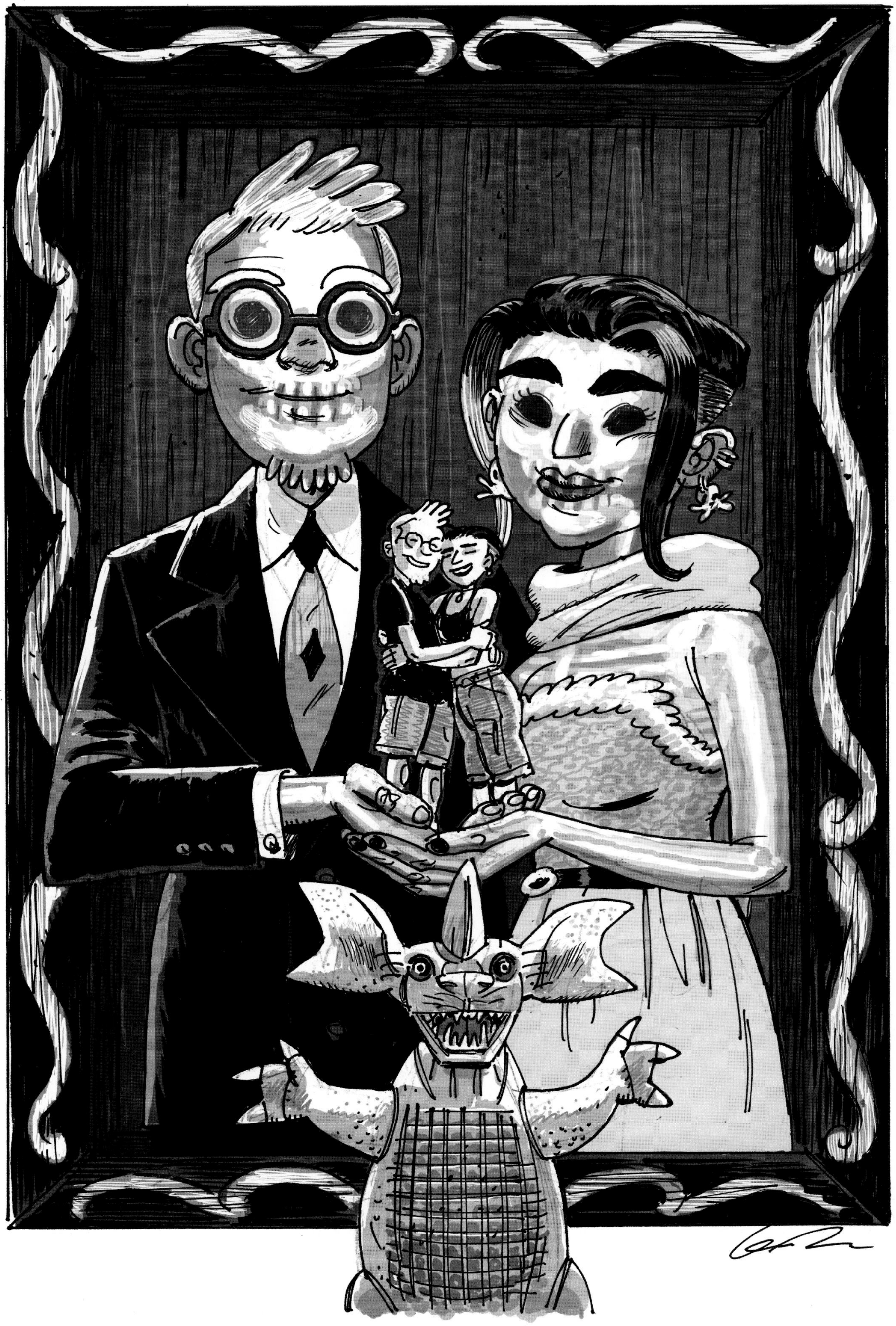

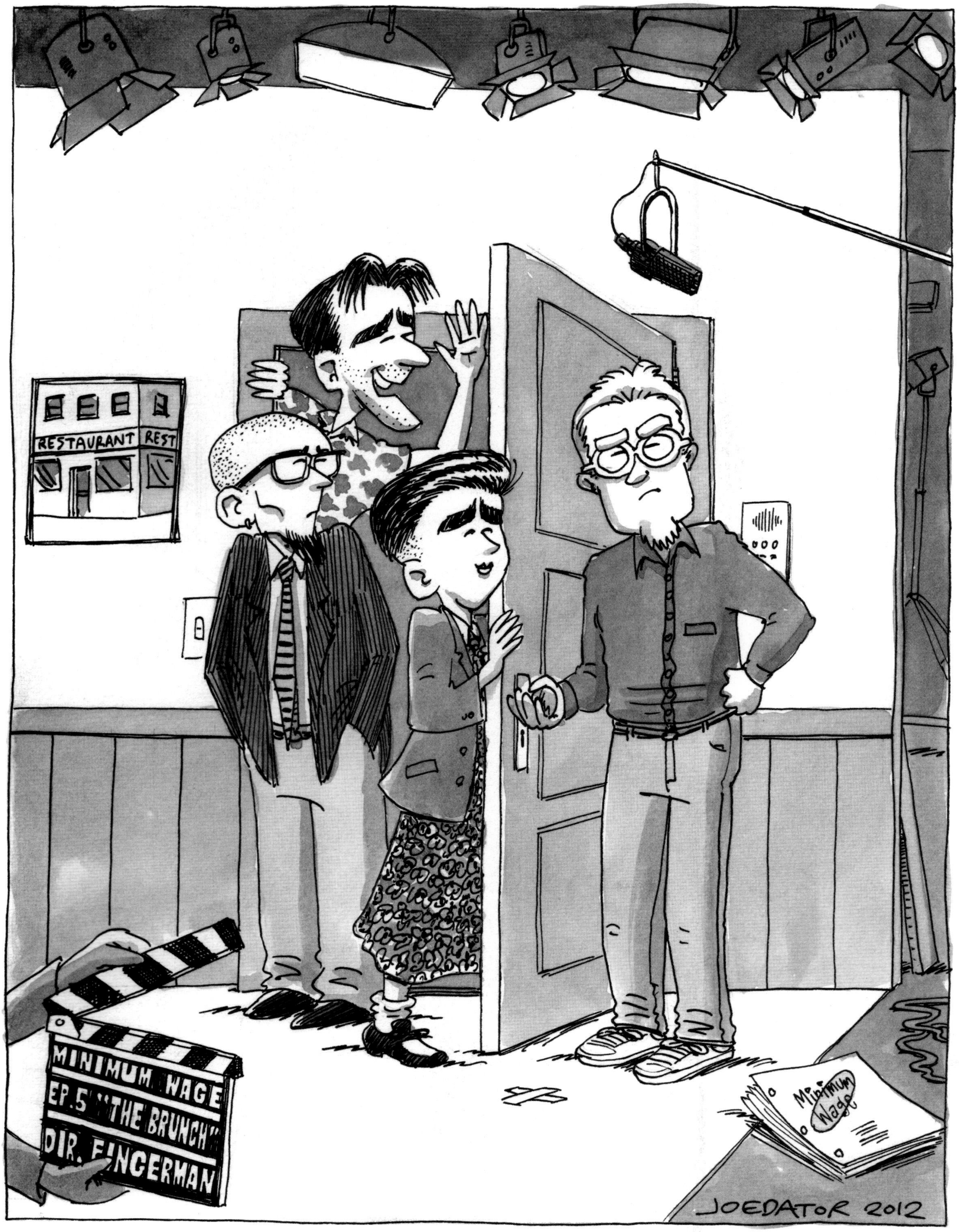
RESTAURANT
REST
MINIMUM WAGE
EP.5 "THE BRUNCH"
DIR. FINGERMAN
Minimum Wage
JOEDATOR 2012

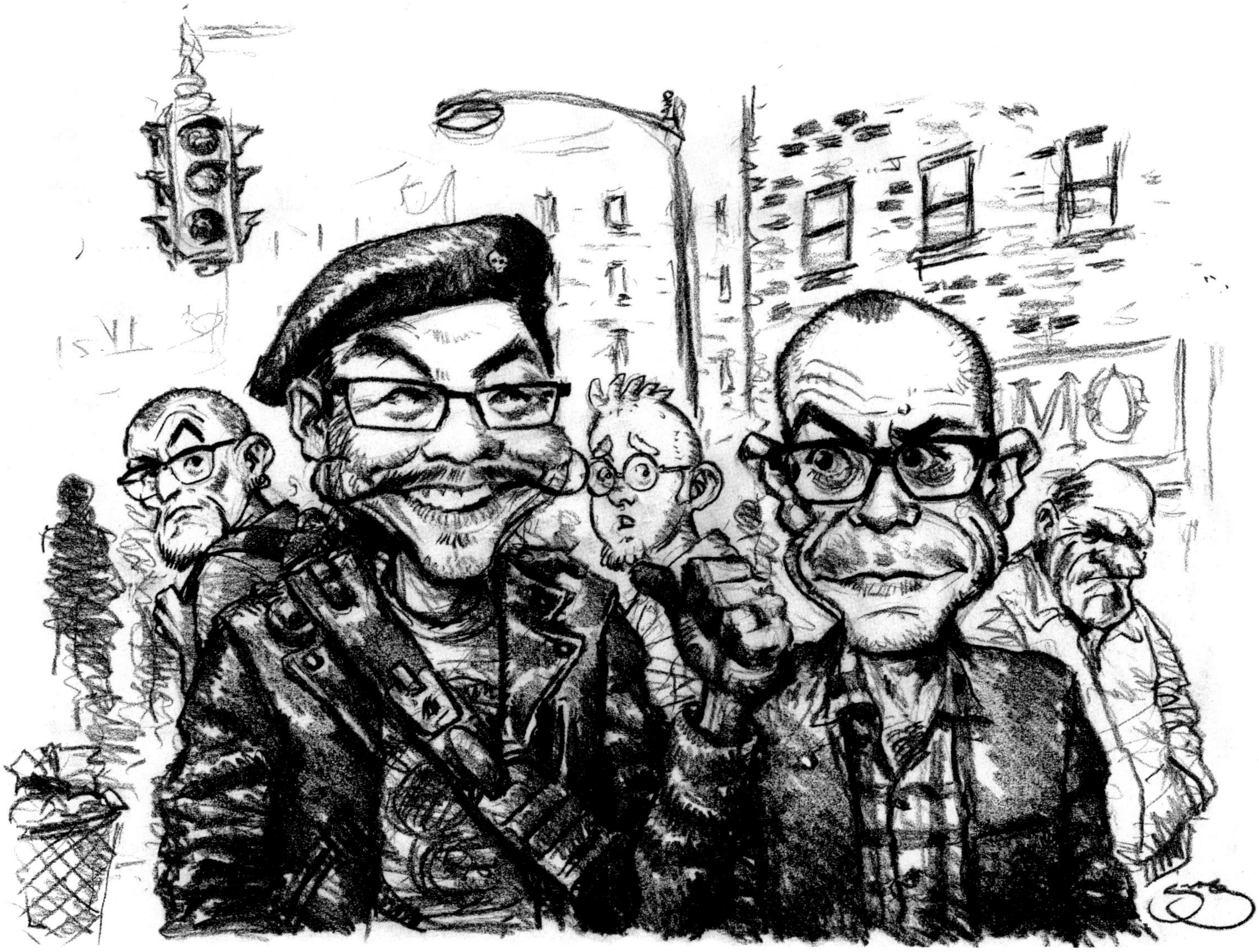
MO

This piece is especially special because it's by my dear friend, Jeff Wong. Jeff and I have been friends for almost thirty years and he is the only one in this gallery upon whom one of the principal cast is based. Okay, so Jeff's Chinese-American and Jack is Israeli-American. *Minimum Wage*, for all its honesty, is more a product of truthiness. It is, after all, a work of fiction. Anyway, I wanted to protect Jeff's privacy. But Jack, foibles and all, is Rob's bestie and I feel likewise about Jeff. And the one thing the two definitely share is their love of Martin Amis. And Elvis Costello. And, well, lots of things.

As noted in the short bio on the contributors page, Jeff and I were roommates. He's the only roommate I ever had (I don't include wives in that category, but if I did my total would be three). I've never wanted to work in a studio with other people, but I did always enjoy talking with Jeff as we toiled on assignments at our respective drafting tables, separated by a wall. As students, before being roommates, we ruined our necks cradling handsets of our mom's phones, talking as we worked into the wee hours. It was nice just talking room to room to while away the hours as I labored for *Cracked* and sundry other magazines (but mainly *Cracked*) and Jeff worked for his various clients.

Our late night runs to White Castle, as depicted on these pages, were a simple pleasure. I'd marvel as he could wolf down ten in a sitting and not get sick (I think five was my max). Though there was much I didn't like about living in Bay Ridge, what I did love about it was having my buddy so nearby. We still live in the same city, but boroughs apart. We don't see each other as often as we used to, or as much as we'd like, but the friendship endures and always will.

Here's to Jack. Here's to Jeff. Cheers.

Big thanks for all these wonderful interpretations of my characters by all these talented and generous people. I already love their work. You should, too. Here is some info about them. Check out their stuff if you haven't already.

Peter Bagge is a comic book writer and artist best known for the 1990s series *HATE*, featuring the misadventures of Buddy Bradley. His most recent work is a graphic novel for Dark Horse entitled *RESET*. www.peterbagge.com

Glenn Barr's surreal creatures, specters and tragic characters live in a seedy universe, drenched in the grit and haze of a post-apocalyptic urban dreamscape. His Detroit work has been labeled Pop Surrealism, Pop Pluralism, Lowbrow, Underground, Regional, Outsider, Ashcan or as he coins the phrase "B Culturalism". With a nod to old master painting, pulp art, and cartooning, Barr's paintings are mesmerizing in their narrative complexities and technical depth. www.glbarr.com

Dave Cooper used to be a cartoonist. Then he was a painter. Then he spent many years attempting to be a TV show creator. He's the father of two and lives in Canada. Please follow his antics here: davegraphicsyeah.wordpress.com

Joe Dator is a gregarious and debonair bon vivant whose cartoons appear regularly in *The New Yorker*. He can be seen gregariously and debonairily bon vivanting all over New York City. Bob is his good friend. And so is coffee. www.joedator.com

Guy Davis is a self taught illustrator best known for his work on *Sandman Mystery Theatre* and *B.P.R.D.*. Currently Guy provides concept artwork for film and video games while continuing his creator owned comic series, *The Marquis*. www.guydavisartworks.com/

Hunt Emerson has drawn comix since the mid 1970s, and has published around 30 books and comics, mainly with Knockabout Comics, London. His favorite pastime is sleeping and his favorite wine is wine. www.largecow.com

Glenn Fabry is an Eisner Award-winning British comics artist known for his detailed, realistic work in both ink and painted color. His latest is the horror *Lot 13*, written by Steve Niles. www.glennfabry.co.uk

Dean Haspiel, an Emmy award winner and Eisner Award nominee, created BILLY DOGMA, illustrated for HBO's *Bored To Death*, and has written and drawn many superhero and semi-autobiographical comix, including collaborations with Harvey Pekar, Jonathan Ames, Inverna Lockpez, and Jonathan Lethem. Dino also curates and creates for TripCity.net

Gilbert Hernandez is the co-creator of *Love & Rockets*, which began in 1982. He's mostly known for his Palomar series, about a mythical Latin American town, featuring the buxom firebrand Luba.

Joe "The Towering" Infurnari is a Canadian cartoonist living and working in Brooklyn, NY. Highfalutin Eisner nominations and pretty books with fancy pants publishers mean nothing to him! *NOTHING!* Now he's gone rogue with his latest "magnum o'pussy," *TIME FUCKER!* www.joeinfurnari.com and www.timefucker.com

Reverend Dave Johnson is an art monkey primarily known for his cover work on *100 Bullets*, *Punisher Max*, *Deadpool*, and *BPRD*. He also designed the original *Ben 10*, and has worked on the animated shows *Batman Beyond*, *Justice League* and *Justice League Unlimited* as a designer. His greatest achievement to date was being one of the founding fathers of the Drink and Draw Social Club. Bob *asked* him to do a new pinup, *that's* why there're two.

John Kerschbaum is a comedic genius. He'd be too modest to declare this of himself, but he's not writing this, Bob is (and referring to himself in third-person, which is awkward). His graphic novel, *Petey & Pussy*, is a sustained work of hilarity that made Bob (doing it again) laugh so hard he choked and wept. No lie. Buy it! And check out his *Cartoon Boy* series and more online. www.johnkerschbaum.com and www.fontanellepress.com

Peter Kuper is a cartoonist, illustrator and former busboy. He is co-founder of the political graphics magazine *World War 3 Illustrated* and has been *Mad* magazine's "Spy vs. Spy" artist/writer since 1997. He has produced a pile of books including *The System* and an adaptation of Franz Kafka's *The Metamorphosis*. www.peterkuper.com

Roger Langridge is an award-winning cartoonist best known for his work on the *Muppet Show* comic books and his own self-published series, *Fred the Clown*. You can find his work at www.hotelfred.com.

Patrick McEown lives and works in Montreal, QC, Canada. He got in on the ground floor with *Minimum Wage* and while he stepped out just a few stories above the mezzanine he has fond memories of his time on the way up. The ascent shows no sign of stopping any time soon, either, so he encourages the curious reader to get in when those doors open. If you're going to spend even just a brief time in a small compartment, you'd be hard pressed to find better company.

Ted McKeever has worked on various titles and characters for Marvel, DC and Vertigo, but is best known for his dark, twisted and gritty creator-own titles such as *Transit*, *Metropol* and *Eddy Current*. His most recent projects are the allegorically intense and personal *Meta 4*, and over-the-top roid-raging *Mondo*. Both of which are published by Image.

Mike Mignola is best known as the award-winning creator/writer/artist of *Hellboy*. He was also visual consultant to director Guillermo del Toro on both *Hellboy and Hellboy 2:The Golden Army* films. He also co-authored (with Christopher Golden) 2 novels *BALTIMORE, or, The Steadfast Tin Soldier and the Vampire* and *Joe Golem and the Drowning City*. Mignola lives in southern California with his wife, daughter, and cat. www.artofmikemignola.com

Kevin Nowlan has been called "one of the few artists who can be called 'artists's artist,'" a master of the various disciplines of comic production, from "design to draftsmanship to dramatics." He's worked for every major comic publisher on nearly every major title. And done so brilliantly. His work is awesome. And he'd never say this about himself because he's also inordinately modest. Bob wrote this. Because it's true! kevinnowlan.blogspot.com

Dan Steffan has contributed to both mainstream and underground publications for several decades. During the early 1980s, his work appeared frequently in *Heavy Metal*. He co-founded the science fiction magazine *Eye* in 1986, and he contributed extensively to science fiction fanzines. dansteffan.tumblr.com

Jill Thompson is the most well-known female comic book artist working in the comics industry today, having risen to the top of the male-dominated field garnering acclaim for her work on *Wonder Woman*, *Swamp Thing* and the award-wining title *Sandman*, with Neil Gaiman. In 1997 she launched her children's book series, *Scary Godmother*, which has become a huge hit with children and adults alike. www.jillthompsonart.com

Jeff Wong is a caricaturist, illustrator and graphic designer. He created the cover art for the 50th Anniversary issue of *Sports Illustrated* (a recreation, with sports figures, of the entire Sistine Chapel ceiling). He's also been Bob's friend since their days together at SVA and briefly had the dubious honor of being Bob's first and only roommate. He is the inspiration for the character Jack Netzer. Bob introduced him to Martin Amis's work and has never forgiven himself. www.jeffwong.com

Bill Wray is a veteran cartoonist making the transition into the world of fine art. He's worked for most of the major animation studios and comic book companies. A fourth collection of his paintings will be out in 2013. He is a longtime friend of the Fingermans and is proud to have many paintings in their amazing art collection. www.williamwray.com

SPOTS, SKETCHES AND MISCELLANEA

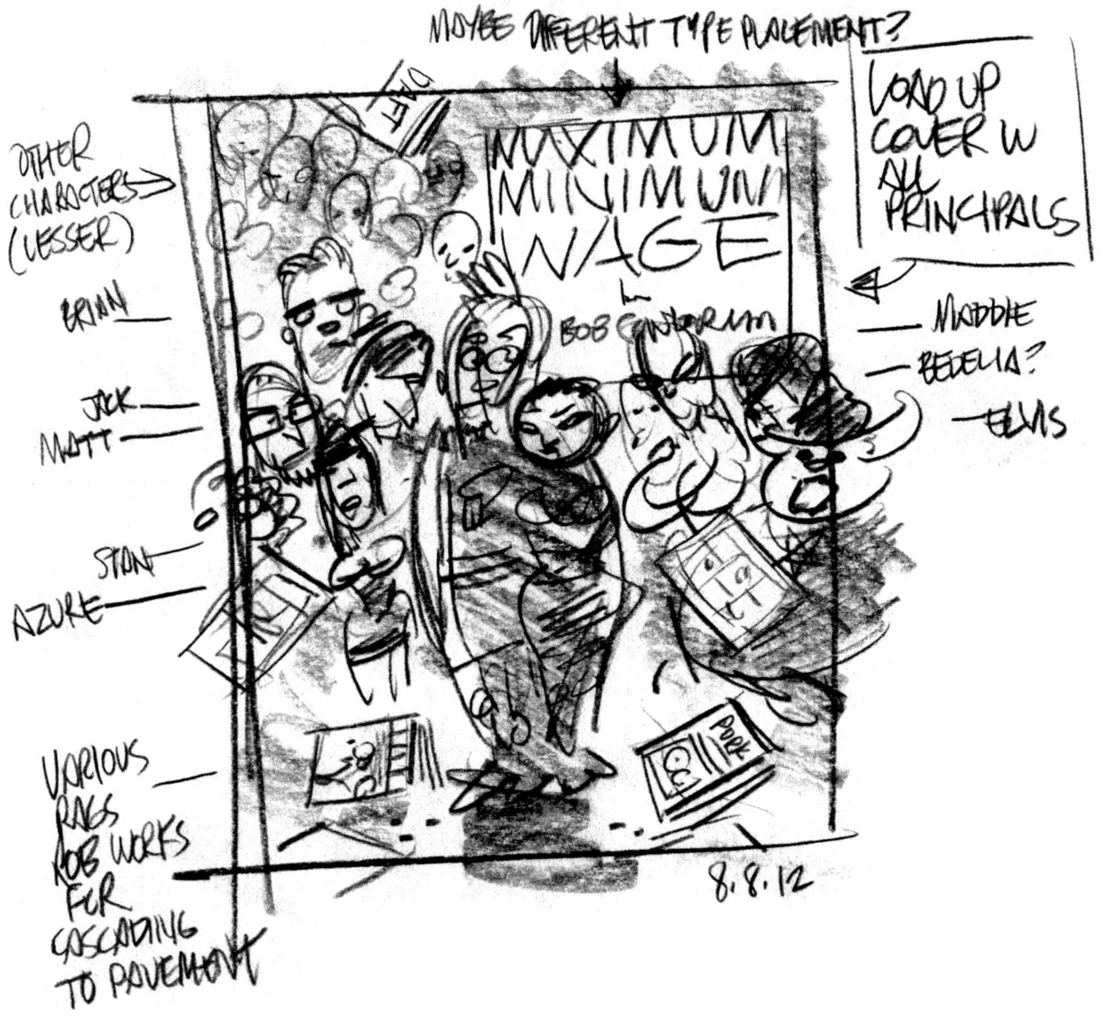
MAYBE DIFFERENT TYPE PLACEMENT?
LOAD UP COVER W ALL PRINCIPALS
OTHER CHARACTERS (LESSER)
MAXIMUM MINIMUM WAGE
BRIAN
JACK
MATT
STAN
AZURE
MADDIE
BEDELIA?
ELVIS
VARIOUS RAGS ROB WORKS FOR CASCADING TO PAVEMENT
8.8.12

The very first sketches of Rob and Sylvia. I had only the vaguest notion of what the project would be.

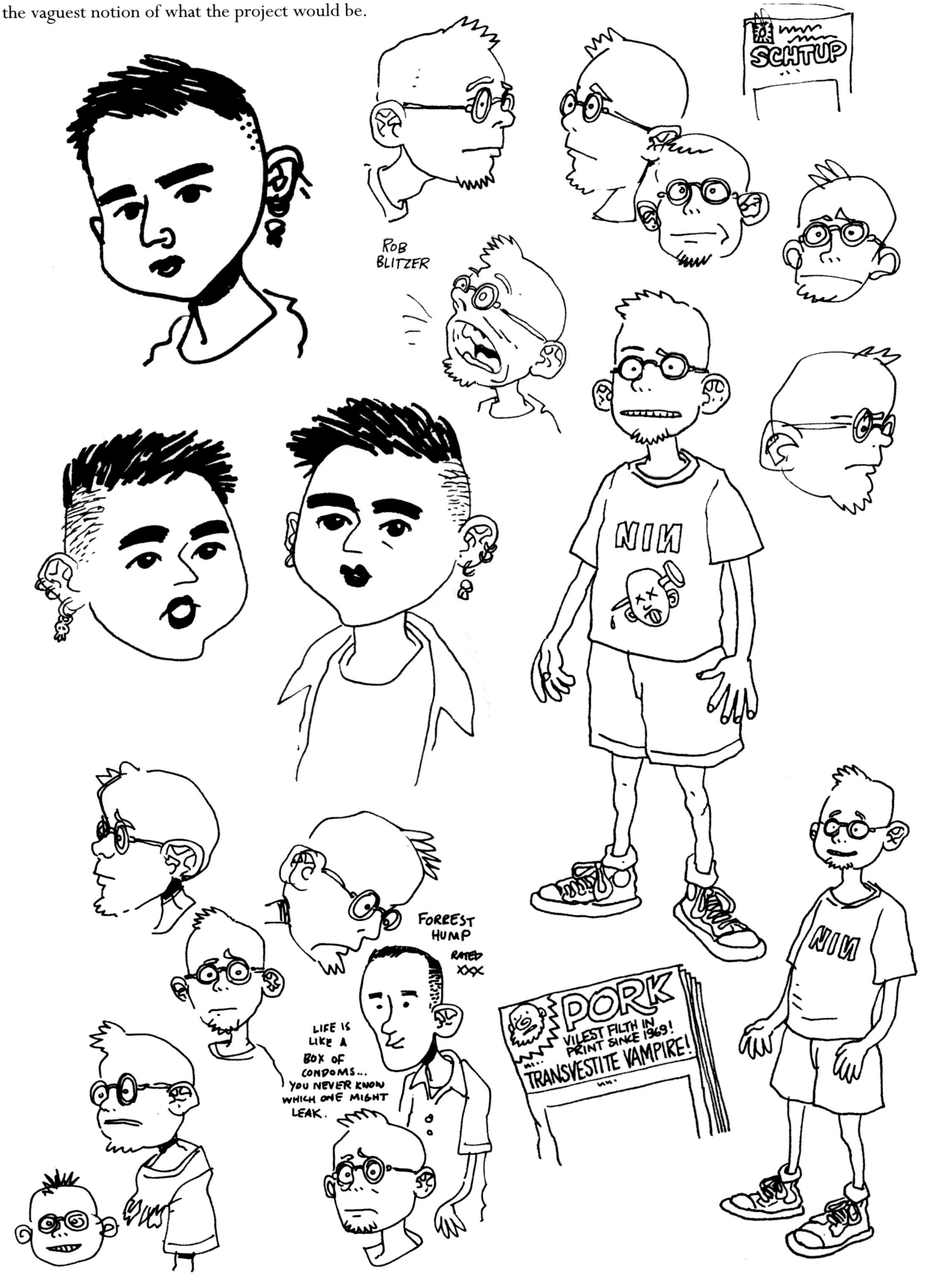
SCHTUP
ROB BLITZER
NIN
FORREST HUMP
RATED XXX
LIFE IS LIKE A BOX OF CONDOMS... YOU NEVER KNOW WHICH ONE MIGHT LEAK.
PORK
VILEST FILTH IN PRINT SINCE 1969!
TRANSVESTITE VAMPIRE!
NIN

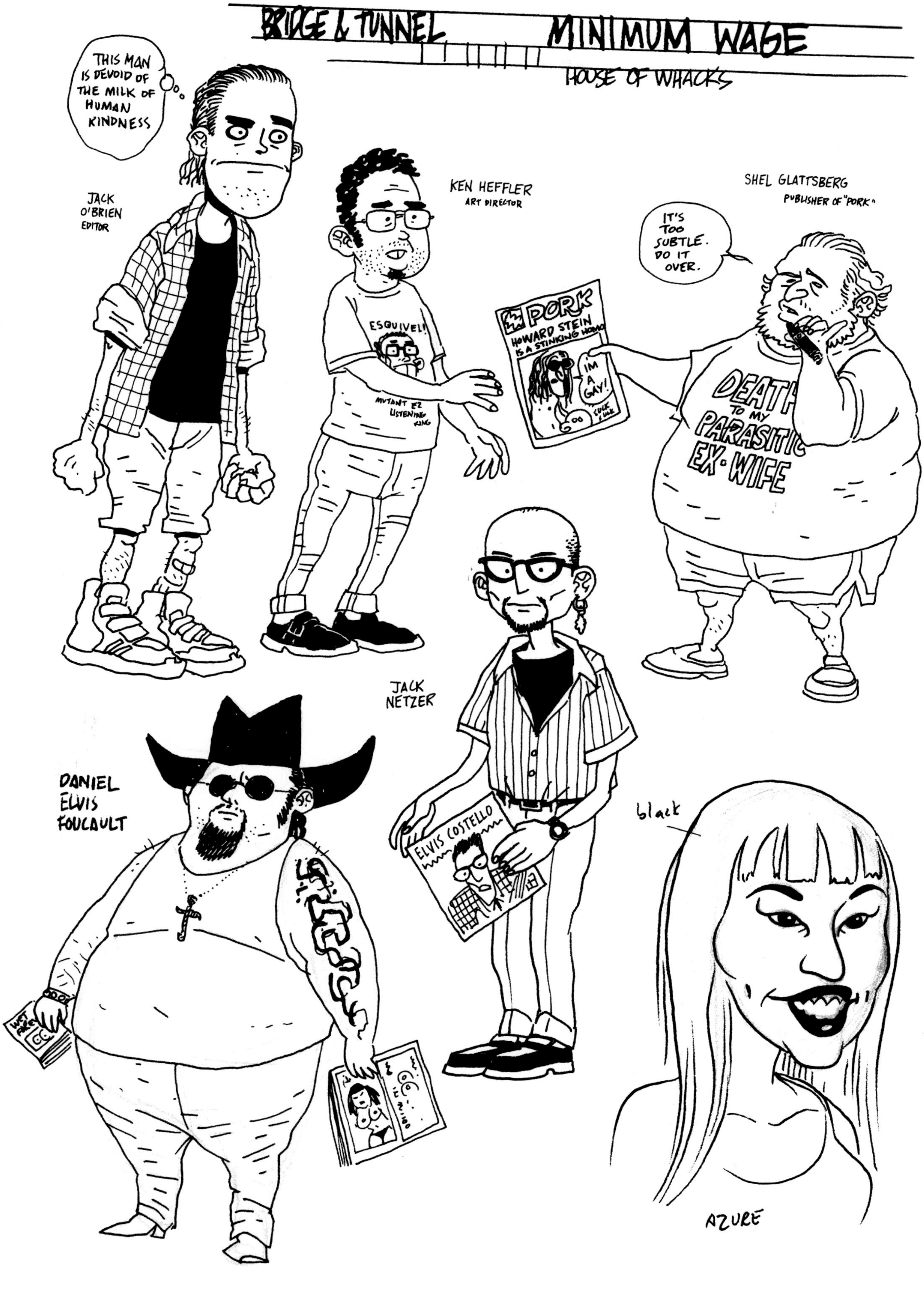

BRIDGE & TUNNEL
MINIMUM WAGE
HOUSE OF WHACKS
THIS MAN IS DEVOID OF THE MILK OF HUMAN KINDNESS
JACK O'BRIEN EDITOR
KEN HEFFLER ART DIRECTOR
ESQUIVEL!
MUTANT EZ LISTENING KING
SHEL GLATTSBERG PUBLISHER OF "PORK"
IT'S TOO SUBTLE. DO IT OVER.
PORK
HOWARD STEIN IS A STINKING HOMO
I'M A GAY!
DEATH TO MY PARASITIC EX-WIFE
JACK NETZER
ELVIS COSTELLO
DANIEL ELVIS FOUCAULT
black
AZURE

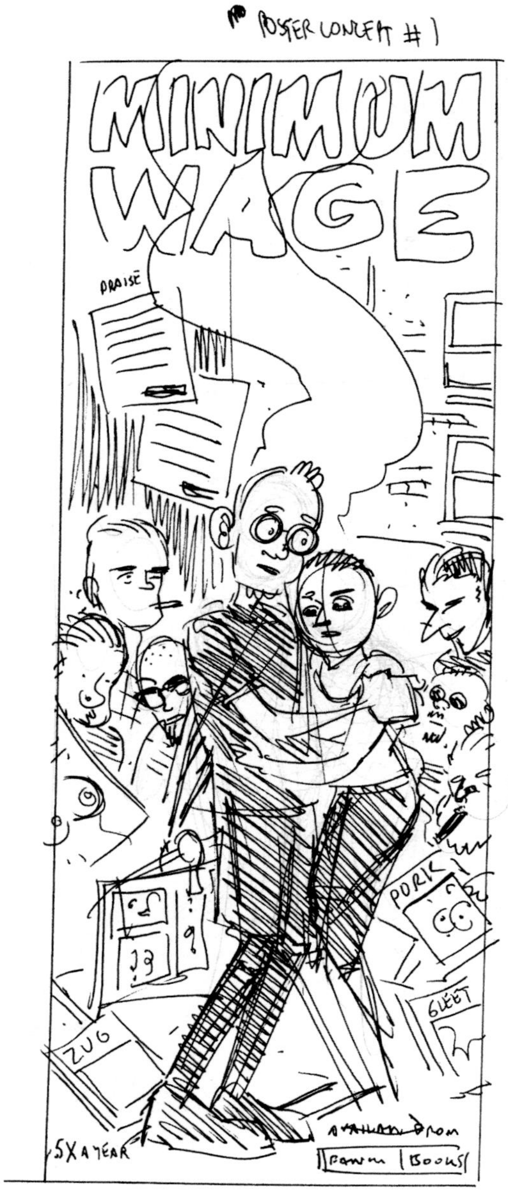
MINIMUM WAGE
5X A YEAR

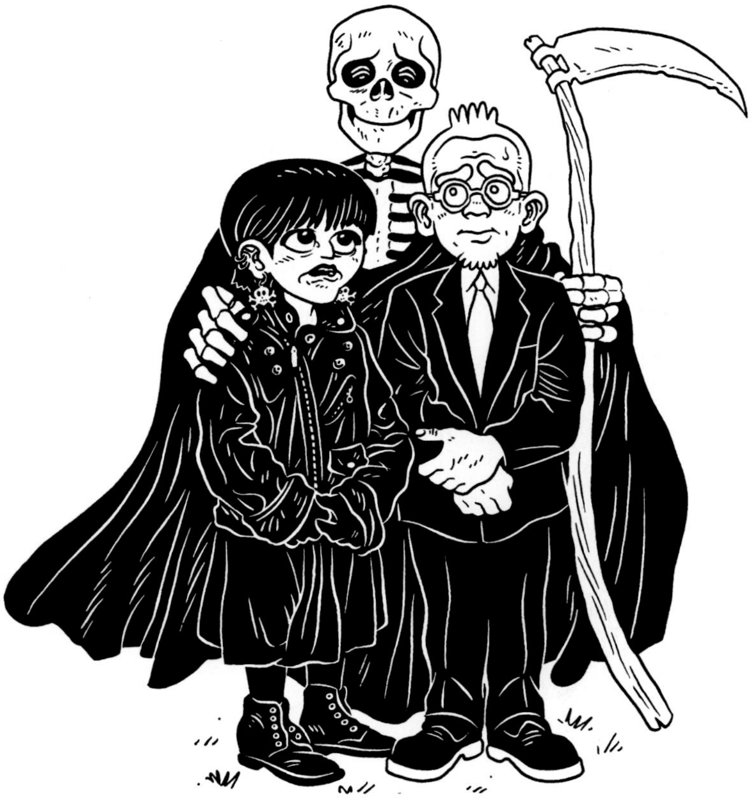

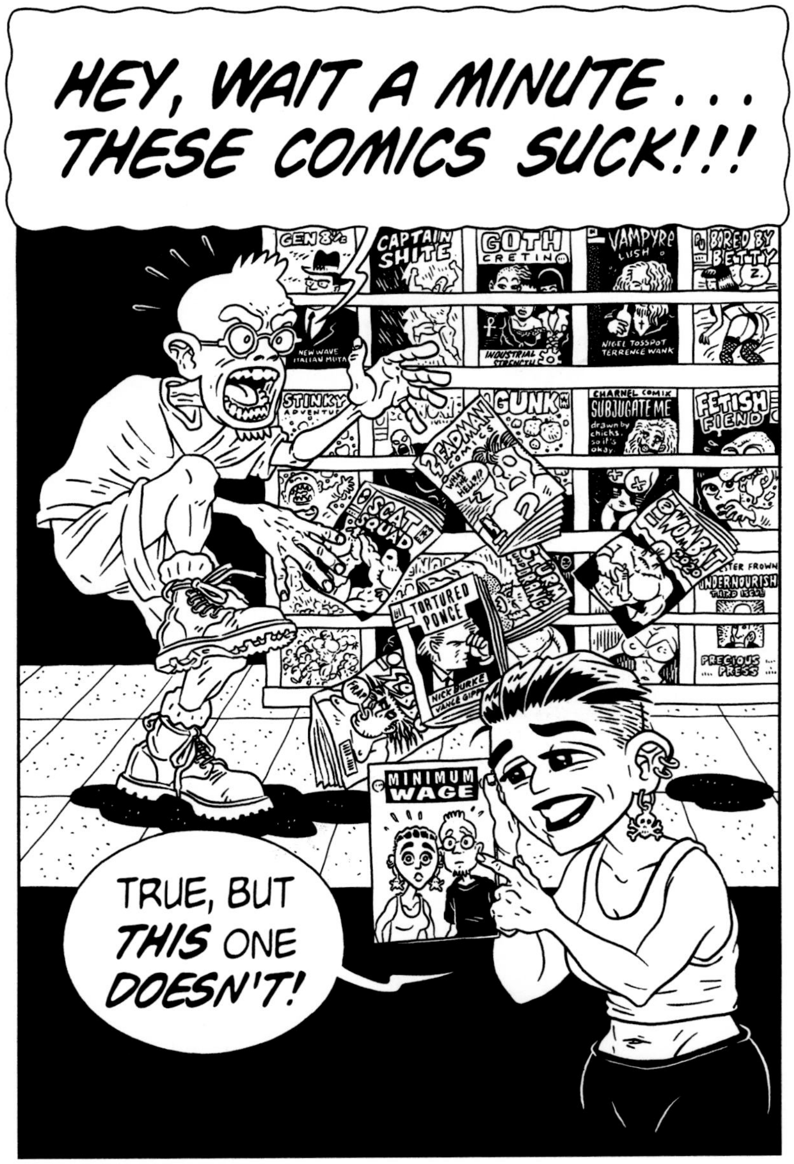
HEY, WAIT A MINUTE . . . THESE COMICS SUCK!!!
CAPTAIN SHITE
GOTH CRETIN
VAMPYRE LUSH
BORED BY BETTY
STINKY
GUNK
SUBJUGATE ME
FETISH FIEND
TORTURED PONCE
PRECIOUS PRESS
MINIMUM WAGE
TRUE, BUT THIS ONE DOESN'T!

In the realm of rare *Minimum Wage*-o-mabilia, the hand-pulled six-color silkscreen poster would rank pretty high. I don't think more than twenty of them were printed and shipped to select comics retailers. Above left is the sketch and bottom right is the line art.

I was toying with the cover for the funeral issue to be line art. Not sure why, Maybe I was running late. I really can't remember why, but in addition to the painted version I did this line version. So, I have two versions I'm not wild about.

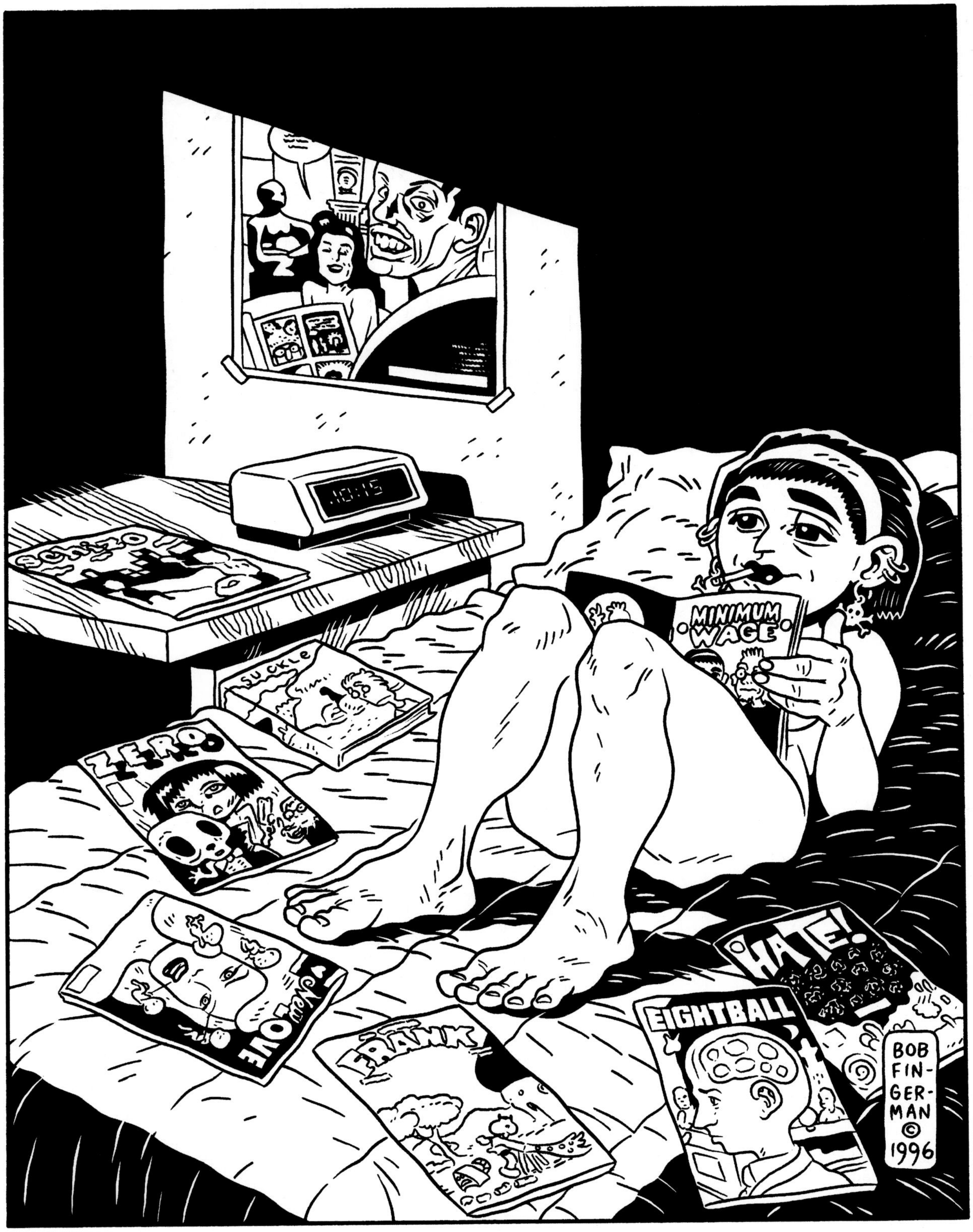
MINIMUM WAGE
ZERO
SUCKLE
NEW LOVE
FRANK
EIGHTBALL
HATE!
BOB FIN-GER-MAN © 1996

The ad that caught young Robert Kirkman's eye. It ran as a back cover on my two-issue Dark Horse micro-series (is that even a thing?), *Otis Goes Hollywood*.

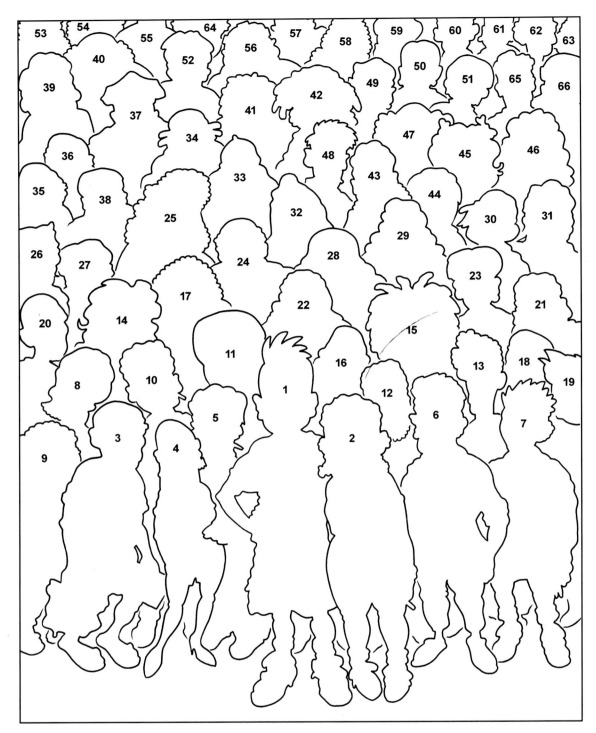

1)	Rob Hoffman	23)	Goth subway ninny	45)	Foxy comic con babe
2)	Sylvia Fanucci	24)	Uncle Carmine	46)	Joyce
3)	Jack Netzer	25)	Aunt Celeste	47)	"Colossus Rex" dealer
4)	Azure	26)	Hector	48)	Dick Coyne
5)	Matt Swirlberg	27)	Lena (Rob's mom)	49)	"Fags!" dude
6)	Maddie Odde	28)	Grandma Fanucci	50)	Josh
7)	Joanie	29)	White Castle Rent-a-Cop	51)	Cheryl
8)	Max	30)	Kevin Orkin	52)	Martin Amis
9)	Stan	31)	Gertrude (Sylvia's mom)	53)	Danny (Godzilla collector 2)
10)	Brian O'Brien	32)	Great Aunt	54)	Pro-life busybody 1
11)	Bedelia Brunch	33)	White Castle thug 1	55)	Pro-life busybody 2
12)	Ken	34)	White Castle thug 2	56)	Edna
13)	Tony	35)	Diamond merchant 1	57)	Henry Menendez
14)	Todd Drek	36)	Diamond merchant 2	58)	Hugely endowed Trekker
15)	"Bam! I gotchoo!" loony	37)	MTA Cop	59)	Suzy Kwan fanboy
16)	Ungrateful homeless dude	38)	Toy dealer at comic con	60)	"Stack of Hustlers" kid
17)	Steve Inferner	39)	Violet	61)	Zit-faced fanboy
18)	Ska-loving Comic Fan	40)	Stavros	62)	Planned Parenthood doctor
19)	Furry	41)	Creep outside titty bar 1	63)	Eric
20)	Garry (Godzilla collector 1)	42)	Creep outside titty bar 2	64)	Scott Dunbier
21)	Sheldon Glattsberg	43)	Sidney (Rob's dad)	65)	Todd Drek's buddy
22)	Goth subway diva	44)	Barry Blevinski	66)	Domino's delivery guy

Going through the archives for bonus material, I unearthed the script for what was to be the eleventh issue, which would have marked the beginning of the second arc of the story.

There are things I think still read well in this chapter, and some things I think are a tad too much like that old HBO series, *Dream On*. In fact, in one balloon I even had Rob think much the same. Rob is a serial fantasist, what can I say? And this script, never drawn, is a first draft.

It does resume the Bedelia Brunch thread. I can save us all a lot of time and speculation: Rob never would have cheated with her, even if given the opportunity. Like Jimmy Carter, Rob lusted in his heart many times. Unlike Carter, though, he didn't require God's hall pass for fantasizing. Advantage atheist.

On a personal note, this chapter is a bit tough to read because the person upon whom Elvis was based has since passed on. He was an editor first, a friend soon thereafter. Sadly, we drifted apart as he delved deeper into a dark, sordid, lifestyle and morphed from portly sci-fi nerd to metaphorically and literally tortured soul. His move to the West Coast severed our tie almost completely. The last time I saw him in person--which was at the San Diego Comic Con--he told me he'd been reading and enjoying *Minimum Wage*, which meant a lot to me. He found my portrayal of him droll and brutally fair. The somewhat fictionalized Elvis event (as most events in the comic were, to greater and lesser degrees embellished, altered, fabricated to suit the narrative) was one I was looking forward to depicting; a genuine slice of tabloid madness. Literally. It was written up in *The New York Post*.

I had also spoken, at some later point, with the personality upon whom Bedelia was based (if you can't figure out who that might have been, try harder). She seemed more bemused than amused, but so be it. Not everyone can give a full-throated benediction.

There was quite a bit more in the saga and perhaps someday I'll revisit it, but for now you can read this taste of what was to come.

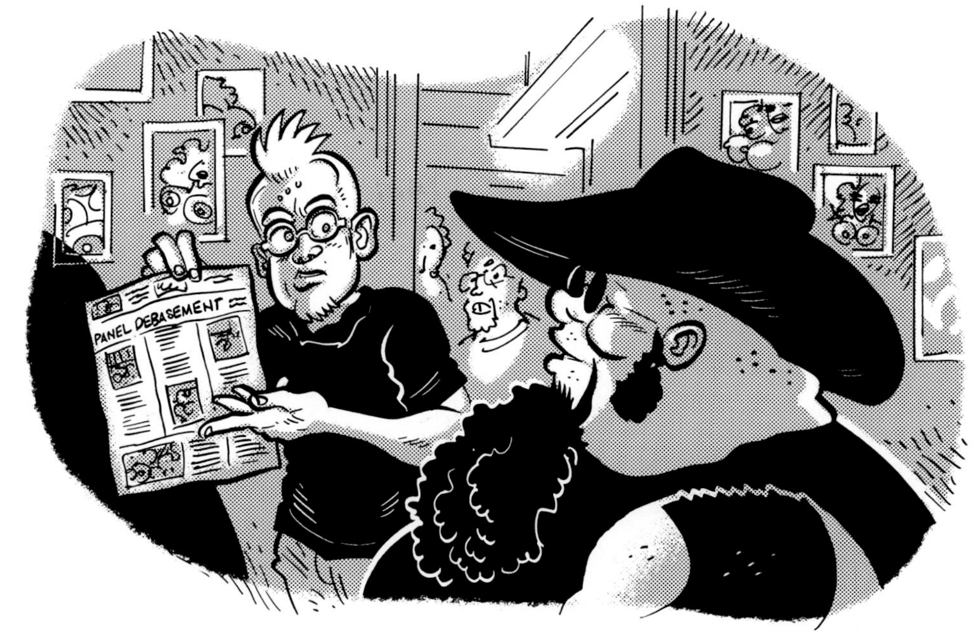
PANEL DEBASEMENT

(Issue 11)

1, 1

(Rob is holding the new copy of Pork, waving it angrily at Ken, the art director. Ken looks uncomfortable as Rob rants. Elvis is in the background, smirking.)

CAPTION: Wednesday, August 25th, 4:45 P.M.

ROB: This is perfect, just what I needed to leaven my spirits.

KEN: People get bad reviews. It happens.

ROB: Yeah, but who is this bitch to get uppity on my ass in my old column?

ELVIS: He can dish it out, but he can't take it. Oh, the irony is too much for me to bear. Chuckle.

1, 2

ROB: Yeah, yeah. Very amusing. I suppose it is a little karma coming back to me, but jeez. My own column.

ELVIS: The very same. See what happens when you leave the fold to go pursue your folly elsewhere?
A young turk comes in, takes your place and buries you.

1, 3

ROB: Buries? Who is she, Kruschev? She writes like she's from Kalinovka. It's off-topic for half the column, her syntax stinks and frankly, who cares who she hangs out with and that can't hold her liquor? Oh, and in between the scintillatingly self-absorbed tidbits she manages to shred my work. Kudos.

(2nd balloon): Fuck, this really is bothering me.

ELVIS: Really? You mask your feelings so elegantly one would hardly notice.

1, 4

ROB: In my own column. Jesus, Elvis, the least you could've done was retire the column title and give it a new one. Something like "On the Rag," or "The Vapid Twat."

2, 1

ELVIS: I wanted to retire your column title. I never liked it, but the head bwana insisted we keep it for continuity. He thinks it's clever. I always thought it was stupid.

ROB: You thought it was stupid because Brian came up with it.

ELVIS: Regardless, the bitter bee of irony has left its stinger in your tuchis.

2, 2

ROB: Ever the poet. I tell you, this place has gone to the dogs since Brian left. I wouldn't have gotten slammed in my old column if he was here to watch my back.

ELVIS: Stop being such a pussy, Rob. It's a bad review. The first of many to come. All "artistes" suffer the slings and arrows of fickle tastemakers. Plus the new crit is a cute little blonde.
ROB: So am I.

2, 3
(Small panel.)

ROB: Anyway, I guess now I'm regretting quitting my column. Sure the money sucked, but at least...

2, 4

ELVIS: At least you knew your work would never get bad ink here.

ROB: Right. Ah, what do I care? I do care. It's irrational. Why should I care?

2, 5

ELVIS: Could you go sulk somewhere else? I've got work to do. Go home, Rob. Go home and hate fuck your new wife. Fantasize that she's the chick who gave you the bad press. It'll make you fuck better.

2, 6

(Close-up of Rob.)

ROB: That's sick. I hope you're joking.

(2nd balloon): "Hate fuck"? Grief.

3, 1

(Rob at home. Sylvia is reading the Pork, looking disgusted.)

CAPTION: 6:52 P.M.

SYLVIA: So she's an asshole. You can't let it get to you. You wrote some harsh stuff in the past and now you're feeling the karmic sting.

ROB: Thanks for the wisdom. That's basically what Fatty said.

SYLVIA: Rob, people get bad reviews. If it was for something that had meaning to you I'd really get behind you, but it was a collection of porno strips.

3, 2

ROB: But they were my porno strips. Mine. Ah, what would you know about it?

SYLVIA: Excuse me?

3, 3

(Rob looks nervous.)

ROB: That came out surlier than I meant, but I mean, you've never put your work out for public consumption.

SYLVIA: I've got my nice little stash of rejection slips from poetry anthologies. What do you call that?

3, 4

ROB: Not the same thing. That's private. A bad review is a public humiliation.

SYLVIA: So that makes my rejections less important? At least you get your stuff out there. Now you act all baby-ish if you get a bad review?

(2nd balloon): It's a stupid porno comic reviewed in a disgusting porno rag that nobody but subhuman scum reads. What's the diff?

3, 5

ROB: So we go from weak consolation to outright hostility in about 60 seconds. Great. Thank you.
SYLVIA: No, thank you. Maybe you got a bad review because the comic sucks. Ever think of that?

4, 1

(Close up on Rob's disbelieving face.)

ROB: What?!?

(2nd balloon): Tell me I didn't hear what I just heard.

4, 2

(Sylvia up on her feet now, looking furious.)

SYLVIA: There's nothing wrong with your ears, baby, just your comics. They're superficial, exploitative shit about big-titted bimbos. That's some artistic legacy you're putting out there.

ROB: This conversation is over. I'm going out for a while to cool off before this gets even uglier.

4, 3

(Close on Sylvia.)

SYLVIA: Oh no you don't. You're not walking out on me while we're in this. I put up with all your sexist shit because you can justify it with a paycheck, but I'm sick of those strips. I'm embarrassed I can't show my family what you do.

4, 4

ROB: Your family? Sexist? They're harmless strips. I make sure I don't exploit anyone more than anyone else. Jesus, don't make me have to defend my only well-paying work.

(2nd balloon): Those big tits pay our rent.

4, 5

ROB: How long has this been festering away? It's like your whole spiel was prepared. Have you rehearsed this? The bad review was a sheer delight compared to this.

(2nd balloon): I'm going out for a while.

4, 6

(Real close on Sylvia's livid face.)

SYLVIA: You leave and I'll…I'll tear up those fuckin' porno pages!

(2nd balloon): I'll do it! Don't test me!

5, 1

(Wide panel of Rob midway towards the door, his back to Sylvia who stands there panting.)

ROB: Have you lost your fucking mind? You threatening to destroy my originals?

SYLVIA: Only if you walk out that door.

5, 2

(Rob with Jack. They are in a local bar. Rob looks shaken. Jack looks baffled.)

CAPTION: 12:39 A.M.

JACK: That's pretty fucked up.

ROB: Yeah, tell me about it. My staying only prolonged the argument for another hour. What did that achieve? Okay, so now I really, really, really know how much Sylvia dislikes my porno strips.

(2nd balloon): Hooray for me. I'm a winner.

5, 3

(Same basic scene.)

JACK: If you don't mind my asking, has she ever threatened you like this before?

ROB: Ummmm…

JACK: You have to think about it?

5, 4

(Close on Rob.)

ROB: Sort of. We've had scraps before. Sometimes she gets very…passionate about things. It gets very heated. She knows what buttons to push to get me to stay.

(2nd balloon): Personally, I think walking away and clearing your head is a better alternative to screaming, but she's Italian. What can you do?

5, 5

(Same basic two shot.)

JACK: Whatever, dude.
ROB: Yeah. Whatever, indeed.

6, 1

(Same basic scene.)

JACK: So, to change the topic, any action on the Bedelia collab?

ROB: Ai. From one tempestuous chick to another. Actually, I just spoke to her the other day. We're having a story meeting at her place soon.
JACK: No kidding. Well, well.

6, 2

(Same basic scene.)

ROB: Yeah. Well, well. It's kinda fucked up, though. I mean I take her calls like it's a clandestine thing we're doing, instead of a legitimate collaboration.

JACK: Legitimate.

6, 3

(Same basic scene.)

JACK: So what you're telling me is that if the opportunity to nail Bedelia presented itself you'd demur.

ROB: Of course.

6, 4

(Same basic scene, only Jack eyes Rob suspiciously.)

JACK: Of course.

6, 5

(Same exact scene.)

SILENCE.

6, 6

(Same exact scene.)

ROB: Shut up.

7, 1

(Rob entering the living room. Sylvia is reading a book. She looks disgruntled.)

CAPTION: 2:08 A.M.

SYLVIA: The whore called. She said she'd be up if you wanted to ring her back tonight.

ROB: Whatever happened to "hello?"

7, 2

(CU on Sylvia's heavy-lidded stony puss.)

SYLVIA: Sorry. Hello, Rob. The whore called and she…

7, 3

(Rob walking into his studio looking like he wants to strangle Sylvia.)

ROB: Yeah, yeah, I got the message.

(2nd balloon, small letters): Jesus, I don't need to come home to that kind of fuckin' attitude.

7, 4

(Rob on the phone.)

ROB: Hi, Bedelia, it's Rob. Am I calling too late? Cool. Uh huh. I see. Yeah, no that'd be fine. I can be there. Cool. See you then. Bye.

7, 5

(Sylvia stands in the doorway to Rob's studio giving him the evil eye.)

SYLVIA: So, make your fuck date? You gonna

knock boots with…

ROB: Okay, that's enough. Honestly, I don't know why you're reacting like this. We just got married for crying out loud. Isn't that enough to show my fealty to you?

SYLVIA: "Fealty?" Don't get fancy with me.

8, 1

(Rob gets up from his drafting chair. Sylvia still in the doorway, REVERSE ANGLE.)

ROB: Listen, this is silly. Truce, please. I don't wanna start up again with the human piñata routine again. I love you, I'm loyal to you, I only want to work in partnership with Bedelia to garner a little more attention to my work.

SYLVIA: That's all?

ROB: That's it. Period.

8, 2

(Sylvia embraces Rob, her head buried in his chest.)

SYLVIA: I'm sorry, baby. I know I can drive you crazy, but I love you so much.

ROB: It's okay, honey. It's okay.

8, 3

(She starts walking away from Rob towards the bedroom.)

SYLVIA: I'm exhausted. It's way past my bedtime, plus all this emotion wears me out. Come tuck me in?

ROB: Yeah, of course.

8, 4

(Rob tucking her in. Her eyes are barely open but she still manages to get one last shot in that causes Rob to slap a disbelieving hand over his eyes.)

ROB: Good night, honey. Sleep tight.

SYLVIA: I will. <yawn> So, you're seeing her when?

ROB: Oy. Go to sleep, please.

8, 5

(Rob holding open a porno magazine spread of Bedelia, looking at the pictures of her naked.)

CAPTION: 2:30 A.M.

ROB (thinking): Jesus, that ass. If Sylvia ever saw this mag she'd never let me join forces with Bedelia. God, that shapely Italo-Teutonic ass. Fuck.

(2nd thought balloon): If I'm going to be able to focus on work mañana I'd better purge.

9, 1

(Large establishing panel of a factory building in a desolate part of Queens.)

CAPTION: Long Island City. Thursday, August 26th, 1:27 P.M.

ROB (thinking): Leave it to Bedelia to live in the one ungentrified factory building in New York.

(2nd thought balloon): No buzzer, either. She told me to call from the station and she'd be down by one-thirty.

9, 2

(Rob seated on a small flight of cracked concrete steps, a closed metal door behind him.)

CAPTION: 1:45 P.M.

ROB (thinking): I wonder if I should try to find a phone and call again.

9, 3

(A burly MIDDLE-AGED BLACK GUY in coveralls steps out the door, Rob looking expectant and disappointed.)

SFX: Clank!

ROB: Bedelia?

GUY: I look like a Buhdelia t'you? I think you need new glasses, son.

ROB: Oh, sorry.

10, 1

(The guy stops to talk with Rob for a minute, a pleasant, jovial type.)

GUY: Y'all stop by t' gets a li'l nookie offa that sweet peach while her man away? Damn, son, she eat a stick-bug like you alive. Huh-huh-huh! Yes, indeed.

ROB: Heh. I suppose.

10, 2

(Same scene.)

GUY: I see the crazy types goes in 'n' out from her house -- got-dayum! With the tattoos and what-has-you. Shee-it, boy. Least you look almos' normal.

(2nd balloon): Gotta say fo' a white girl she got booty t' spare. She think I'm too ol' t' notice? I ain' dead. She got the rump an' I got th' eyes fo' it. Huh-huh-huh!
10, 3

(Wide larger panel. Bedelia has emerged from the doorway. The guy looks a little abashed, bowing his head in a slightly anachronistically deferential manner.)

BEDELIA: Hey, Hoffman. Let's go upstairs.

ROB: Oh, hey Bedelia. Sure.

GUY: Aftanoon, ma'am.

10, 4

(Rob looks back over his shoulder at the guy who is doing the "pussy-eating" finger/tongue gesture with one hand and the "okay" sign with the other.)

10, 5

(Interior. Stairwell. A sign reads Schrecklicher Geruch Plastics.)

BEDELIA: So, you found the place. That puts

you in an elite minority. Speaking of minorities, what's that pervy old bastard have to say for himself, as if I didn't know.

ROB: I, uh…he was just saying…you know. I guess you know his shtick, yeah?

11, 1

(They are still on the steps. Rob makes a face.)

BEDELIA: Yeah, "Ah knows abouts it." He comes on gangbusters with the phony Stepin Fetchit routine. Ridiculous.

ROB: What's that godawful stench?

11, 2

(Outside a heavy metal door with myriad locks.)

BEDELIA: It's a plastics manufacturer. I don't know what they make. Could be Lucite picture frames, could be dildos. I wouldn't know.

11, 3

(Establishing shot of Bedelia's loft. Spacious with a big black X-shaped crucifix by one wall.)

BEDELIA: Be it ever so humble. Wanna drink? I have carbonated water and orange juice.

ROB: Could I have a splash of both?

BEDELIA: Seltzer and OJ, what a concept.

11, 4

(She returns to the room carrying two glasses. Her nipples are now erect, presumably from the cold of the open freezer. Rob tries not to look.)

BEDELIA: Okay, so let's get down to brass tacks. What'd you have in mind?

ROB: Uh, well that crack babies thing sounded like a possibility.

ROB (thinking): Oh fuck me, look at those nipples. Is she even wearing a bra? Shut up, shut up. Stay frosty, focus on the mission.

12, 1

(WIDER CLOSED PANEL. Bedelia sits on a big vintage couch in a sexy pose. Rob thumbs through a book she has on her coffee table.)

BEDELIA: Oh yeah, the legion of crack teens with no emotions who rove the city like wolves.

ROB: Uh, yeah. That sounded promising.

ROB (thinking): Could you sit in a more provocative pose, Bedelia? Oy, the Temptation of St. Rob.

12, 2

(NARROW OPEN PANEL. Bedelia removes her top to reveal her bare breasts. Rob just stares, dumbfounded.)

BEDELIA: Christ, it's fucking hot in here. I've gotta get the damned AC fixed.

ROB (thinking): No.

12, 3

(NARROW OPEN PANEL. Bedelia stepping out of her tights, revealing a gloriously round ass.)

BEDELIA: Okay, junior, the broken AC is a ruse. I gotta be plain with you: I fuck all my potential collaborators to make sure they're worthy of my time and talent.

(2nd balloon): If you're a bad lay, project's canceled.

ROB: Buh-buh-but I'm muh-muh-married.

12, 4

(SAME PANEL AS THE FIRST. Bedelia is still fully clothed.)

BEDELIA: --and that crack thing could work out. I'll get my story notes out. Hang on for a sec and just don't stray from the path.

ROB: Oh, okay. I'll just sit right here.

12, 5

(Rob staring down at his betraying groin. He has a

boner pushing up from inside his shorts.)

ROB (thinking): Oh shut up, you. Down, you idiot. She's not interested in your credentials, so put your résumé away. Come on, idiot, stop it.

(2nd thought balloon): Think of gross things. That dead dog by the train tracks with the black oozing wound filled with maggots. Rotting cantaloupes. That clump of hair that you sucked up a straw at that diner. Ucch.

(3rd thought balloon): Plus, now I'm double mad at myself for slipping into Dream On territory. Weak.

13, 1

(Rob walking back to the subway.)

ROB (thinking): Maybe Sylvia is right about this whole Bedelia thing. Maybe I shouldn't work with her. Not that anything would ever happen but why tempt fate and jeopardize my marriage?

13, 2

(Still walking.)
ROB (thinking): If it makes Sylv this unhappy and gets me this worked up with Bedelia just being normal. Why can't I just switch off my libido from time to time? I rubberneck even passably decent looking girls.

13, 3

(Still walking, only a moderately cute Latina passes by.)

ROB (thinking): See? She was cute and I had to look. It's not like I want to, but my eyes and dick rule the roost. I hate summer. Hate it.

(2nd balloon): It's better in the winter when they're all bundled up.

13, 4

(Rob on the subway platform. More cute girls.)

ROB (thinking): Great, more hotties.
Enough already.
HOTTIE 1: …an' I'm all like, "Listen, nigga, don' be getting' all up in my muthafuckin' shit, yo," you know'm sayin'? An he be all like, "Day-um, don' be gettin' all loud an' shit!"

HOTTIE 2: Mira: you don' even shou'n' be talkin' wi' him, yo. That fuckin' nigga is fuckin' fucked up.

13, 5

(Rob looks appalled by their chatter.)

ROB (thinking): On the other hand, when most of these dummies open their stupid pie-holes it's the equivalent of a lapful of ice water.

HOTTIE 1: I know, yo, it's my bad, but he so fuckin' fly, yo!

HOTTIE 2: True. I'm feelin' you. But fo' serious, yo, tha' muthafuckin' nigga shou'n' be all up in yo muthafuckin' shit. Fo' real!

13, 6

(Close inset of Rob's face looking heavenward.)
ROB (thinking): Praise be the cleansing waters of stupid, that they purgeth my sinful, wayward, thoughts.

14, 1

(Large establishing interior of Elvis's apartment. It is filled with pop culture ephemera and Italian gialli posters. Elvis is on his feet, walking toward the kitchen.)

CAPTION: Saturday, August 28th, 3:30 P.M.

SFX: …Woo-weeee-woo-wo-chugga-chugga-wooo-weee-woooh…

ELVIS: Heh-heh-heh, I'll just bet you did. Poor little guy sitting there with a notebook in his lap to hide his shameful purple-helmeted betrayer.

ROB (annoyed): Why do I tell you these things?

14, 2

(Close on Elvis' chuckling visage.)

ELVIS: Because I was your hookup and you owe me the small satisfaction of at least telling me about your humiliations in the estimable Ms. Brunch's presence.

(2nd balloon): Want another Diet Coke?

ROB OOP: Sure, thanks.

(2nd balloon): Hey, can I turn the music down? I can barely hear myself regret telling you things.

14, 3

(Elvis returning with two cans of Diet Coke from his kitchen area, taking a seat. Rob thumbs through a book of Italian Zombie flicks.)

ELVIS: I prefer the tunes loud. Acid Reflux didn't record this to be played at old lady decibel level.

(2nd balloon): So now your new bride is steamed at you. It's all too tawdry, yet banal. Ho-ho.

15, 1

(Same scene only Elvis' girlfriend has entered the apartment. Elvis doesn't hear because the music is too loud.)

ELVIS: Listen, junior, take some advice from an old warhorse: if you dabble, dabble smart and just don't get caught.

ROB: I don't want to dabble.

ELVIS: We all want to dabble.

15, 2

(The girlfriend is looking at Elvis as he speaks. Rob has his nose buried in the book.)

ROB: Have you ever?

ELVIS: Of course. Listen, a man in the porn trade can't walk the straight and narrow path of the typical civilian.

(2nd balloon): Sometimes a man's got to walk the Doberman, you know?

GIRLFRIEND: You fucking asshole!

15, 3

(She has produced a scary knife from her bag and

gestures threateningly at Elvis, who has stumbled half to his feet.)

ELVIS: Baby! I didn't know you were there! I mean I didn't hear you come in!

GIRLFRIEND: So you strayed, huh? You cheated, huh? You think you can get away with that shit with me?

ELVIS: But, but, but…

15, 4

(She lunges at the ungraceful Elvis. Rob looks on in horror.)

GIRLFRIEND: But me no buts, fat man!

ELVIS: This isn't what it--

(2nd balloon): We were just talking. It's guy talk, baby. It doesn't mean--

15, 5

(She stabs Elvis in one of his upward turned protesting wrists. Blood splashes out.)

GIRLFRIEND: Fuck you!

ELVIS: Owwwwww!

16, 1

(Elvis clutching his bleeding wrist. The girlfriend now looks a little unsure of what she did.)

ELVIS: You stabbed me. Oh, baby, I'm bleeding.

GIRLFRIEND: Oh, Cheeksie-Puppet, I didn't mean-- I mean I did mean to, but… I…

ROB (thinking): How fucked up is this? An unrehearsed bloodletting.

16, 2

(Exterior establishing shot of a hospital emergency room.)

ELVIS (from inside): If you even breathe a word of this to Brian I will fucking end you, Rob.

ROB (from inside): Rest assured, Elvis: your sordid private life shall remain private.

16, 3

(A nurse comes in and calls to Elvis, who looks imploringly at Rob.)

NURSE: Mr. Foucault, the doctor will see you now.

ELVIS: Would you come with? I hate being alone with doctors.

ROB: (sigh) I've come this far with you.

16, 4

(Elvis is now shirtless on an examining table. There is a big cross-shaped scar on his chest. The doctor enters holding a clipboard.)

ELVIS: It's my wrist that was cut. I don't know why they need to see me with my shirt off.

ROB: I don't know why I need to see you with your shirt off.

ELVIS: Ha ha. Very comforting.

DOCTOR: So, Mr. Foucault, I see here that--

(2nd balloon): Oh my.

17, 1

(The doctor looking at Elvis' chest.)
DOCTOR: That's quite a scar you've got on your chest, Mr. Foucault. Have you ever had open-heart surgery?

ELVIS: No.

17, 2

(Same basic panel, only the doctor is now silently looking directly at Elvis' face.)

SILENCE.

17, 3

(Same basic panel, only the doctor is now silently looking directly at Elvis' face.)

DOCTOR: I see.

(2nd balloon): Okay, let's have a look at that wrist, shall we?

17, 4

(Exterior of the hospital. Rob and Elvis leaving. Elvis' wrist is bandaged.)

ROB: That was priceless. When the doctor asked about the open-heart surgery I nearly lost it.

ELVIS: Not a word, Hoffman. Not a fucking syllable.

17, 5

(The two walking along.)

ROB: You've got my promise, big guy. But seriously, that was classic. Thanks for the very special episode.

ELVIS: You're welcome. I'm just glad she missed the arteries.

18, 1

(Brian's office at Bee Stings Magazine. Brian has a copy of The New York Post.)

CAPTION: Monday, August 30th, 1:05 P.M.
BRIAN: ...and you saw this transpire right before your very eyes. I am so fucking jealous.

ROB: I'd feel worse about telling you if his girl-friend hadn't turned herself in to the cops in a fit of remorse while we were at the hospital.

18, 2

(Brian, grinning, holds open the story in the Post. Headline: PORTLY PORK PORNSTER PERFO-RATED BY PETULENT PARAMOUR.)

BRIAN: And the Post was there to get the story. Sweet. Shel must be going apeshit. I wonder if Fatty even showed up for work today.

18, 3

(Interior of the Pork offices where Shel, holding the same issue of the Post, tears Elvis a new one in front of the bemused staff.)

CAPTION: Across town at that very moment...

SHEL: ...and this is just the kind of cockamamie publicity I fucking need my jackoff senior editors generating. You pathetic fat fucking bastard. I'm going to run this story every week on the show about how my fat fuck -- even fatter than my fat fucking Jew ass -- my fat fuck senior editor who is a sick, twisted, pretentious pseudo-poet-intellec-tual performance artist got butchered in his own home for being a schmucky numbskull dimwit! If

you think I'm ever going to let you forget this--

18, 4

(Back to Brian and Rob.)

BRIAN: Let's get some lunch. You hungry?

ROB: I could eat.

19, 1

(Sylvia and Maddie on the roof sunbathing, both topless.)

CAPTION: Also at that same moment, back at the ranch...

SYLVIA: I think I really overreacted. Rob just wants to further his career. I just wish he'd find some more worthy coattails.

MADDIE: I can dig. But Rob is true blue.

19, 2

(Maddie sits up looking at Sylvia's back.)

MADDIE: Your back is looking a little dry, Sylv. More lotion?

SYLVIA: Yeah, thanks. Brown good, burn bad.

19, 3

(Maddie squirting some suntan lotion into her palm.)

MADDIE: I don't know why you worry so much. You've totally got it going on.

SYLVIA: Thanks. So do you.

19, 4

(Maddie rubbing the lotion on.)

MADDIE: Noooo. Not me. I'm too flabby. I need to go to the gym and tighten up.

SYLVIA: Nuh-uh. You look good. Supple.

19, 5

(Sylvia sits up and Maddie mechanically starts rubbing lotion on Sylvia's breasts.)

MADDIE: No, I'm too pasty and out of shape. My friend Margie the cop keeps telling me I should jog with her but no sports bras are--

(2nd balloon): Oops. I am so sorry. I just kept go-ing instinctively. I didn't mean nothing.

SYLVIA: It's okay. It feels good.

20, 1

(Rob and Brian eating lunch.)

ROB: So how is it working back in the glossies?

BRIAN: It's pretty decent for a completely inde-cent outfit. The whole barely legal angle is a trifle creepy, but I only work about two hours a day.

20, 2

(Same basic.)
BRIAN: The rest of the time I've been learning HTML and web stuff.

ROB: I've gotta get on the computer jammy. I'm so behind the times.

20, 3

(Same scene.)

BRIAN: You wanna go Mac or PC?

ROB: Aren't Macs more user-friendly?

BRIAN: Depends. PCs can do pretty much eve-rything Macs used to be exclusively good at, plus there are way more games for PC.

20, 4

(Same.)

BRIAN: The price differential is huge, though. If you go PC you can get a really sweet recondi-tioned one at J & R for under five.

ROB: Hundred or thousand?

BRIAN: Hundred. Jesus, you really are out of the loop.

ROB: I was raised by a Luddite.

20, 5

(Exterior of J&R Computer World. Rob and Brian are loading a large box into the trunk of a taxi.)

TEXT: Half an hour later.
BRIAN: I've got to admire your impetuosity.

ROB: Thanks. I feel like <grunt> this is a positive step in the <oof> right direction.

21, 1

(Rob shaking hands with Brian.)

ROB: Hey, thanks for coming down here with me. I appreciate your talking me through this.

BRIAN: No prob. And I'll get you copies of all that software. I can burn CDs of Photoshop, Quark, Illustrator, whatever. It's theft, but you're poor.

ROB: Poorer than I was half an hour ago, anyway.

21, 2

(Rob in the cab, Brian not.)

ROB: You sure you don't want a ride back to work?

BRIAN: I'd rather walk. Go home and play with your new toy.

21, 4

(Interior of the cab, Rob happy.)

ROB (thinking): I have a new toy. An expensive, if reasonably priced, totally tax-deductible, new toy.

21, 5

(Rob looking less certain.)

ROB (thinking): A new toy that I have absolutely no idea how to use, but important for me to learn before I totally fall behind the curve. I shoulda bought a Mac. Couldn't afford it.

21, 6

(Rob smiling again, but sweating profusely.)

ROB (thinking): Fucking buyer's remorse. I hope Sylvia doesn't get mad at me for spending so much on this new toy.

22, 1

(Overhead shot of Sylvia and Maddie both nude in bed.)

SYLVIA: We shouldn't have let this happen.

MADDIE: Probably not.

22, 2

(Closer on both.)

SYLVIA: Same sex or not, this was a major no-no. I transgressed here, big time.

MADDIE: It's hard to fight temptation all the time.

22, 3

(Close on Sylvia's guilty face.)

SYLVIA: That doesn't make it right. Rob would die if he knew this happened.

22, 4

(Close on Maddie.)

MADDIE: So don't tell him. Ever. It'll be our secret. It wasn't like we planned it or anything; it just happened. It was you and me before it was you and him.

(2nd balloon): We backslid is all. It happens.

22, 5

(Both in shot.)

SYLVIA: Not to me it doesn't. I love you, Maddie, but this was a one-shot relapse. I can't go back there. Ever. I'm happily married now. Understand?
MADDIE: Understood.

23, 1

(Both are off the bed, dressing.)

MADDIE: Rob is lucky to have you, Sylvie.

SYLVIA: Yeah, right.

23, 2

(Still dressing.)

MADDIE: Ummmm, maybe someday we could both make it up to him. You know?

23, 3

(Close on Sylvia's stern face.)

SYLVIA: No way, Maddie. Rob is way too straitlaced for that kind of thing. Besides, we've got nothing to make up to him because nothing happened here, capite?

23, 4

(Close on Maddie's face.)

MADDIE: Yeah, capisco. È il nostro segreto.

23, 5

(They embrace.)

SYLVIA: Grazie, amica anziano.

MADDIE: È niente.

24, 1

(Exterior of the hall landing. Rob is hefting the heavy box as Maddie exits the apartment, almost bashing into Rob.)

CAPTION: 4:12 P.M.

MADDIE: Bye, baby, see you soo--

(2nd balloon): Oops! Sorry. 'Scuse me!

ROB: <gasp> No <wheeze> problem.

24, 2

(Maddie stops for a second and realizes it's Rob, her eyes widening.)

MADDIE: Rob! I didn't know it was you! Sorry!

(2nd balloon): Need a hand?

ROB: <pant> No, really, I've <puff> got it under control. Just maybe <gasp> get the front door?

24, 3

(Rob deposits the large box on the floor in the hall. Sylvia looks incredulously at the box.)

ROB: Ooooooh. Ouch. Oh to have an elevator. Thanks, Maddie.

MADDIE: No prob, Rob. Gotta split. By-eee!

ROB (2nd balloon): Now don't be mad, honey, but I was bad today. I bought a computer. I know it's expen—

24, 4

(Sylvia hugs Rob hard, taking him by surprise.)

SYLVIA: No, no, no, baby, you weren't bad at all. It's fine. Great.

ROB: Really? I thought you might be mad.

SYLVIA: Not at all. I love you. I love you, I love you, I love you a thousand million times.

24, 5

(Close on Rob.)

ROB (thinking): If I'd known she'd react like this I might've sprung for the printer, too.

MWEEP-MWAH

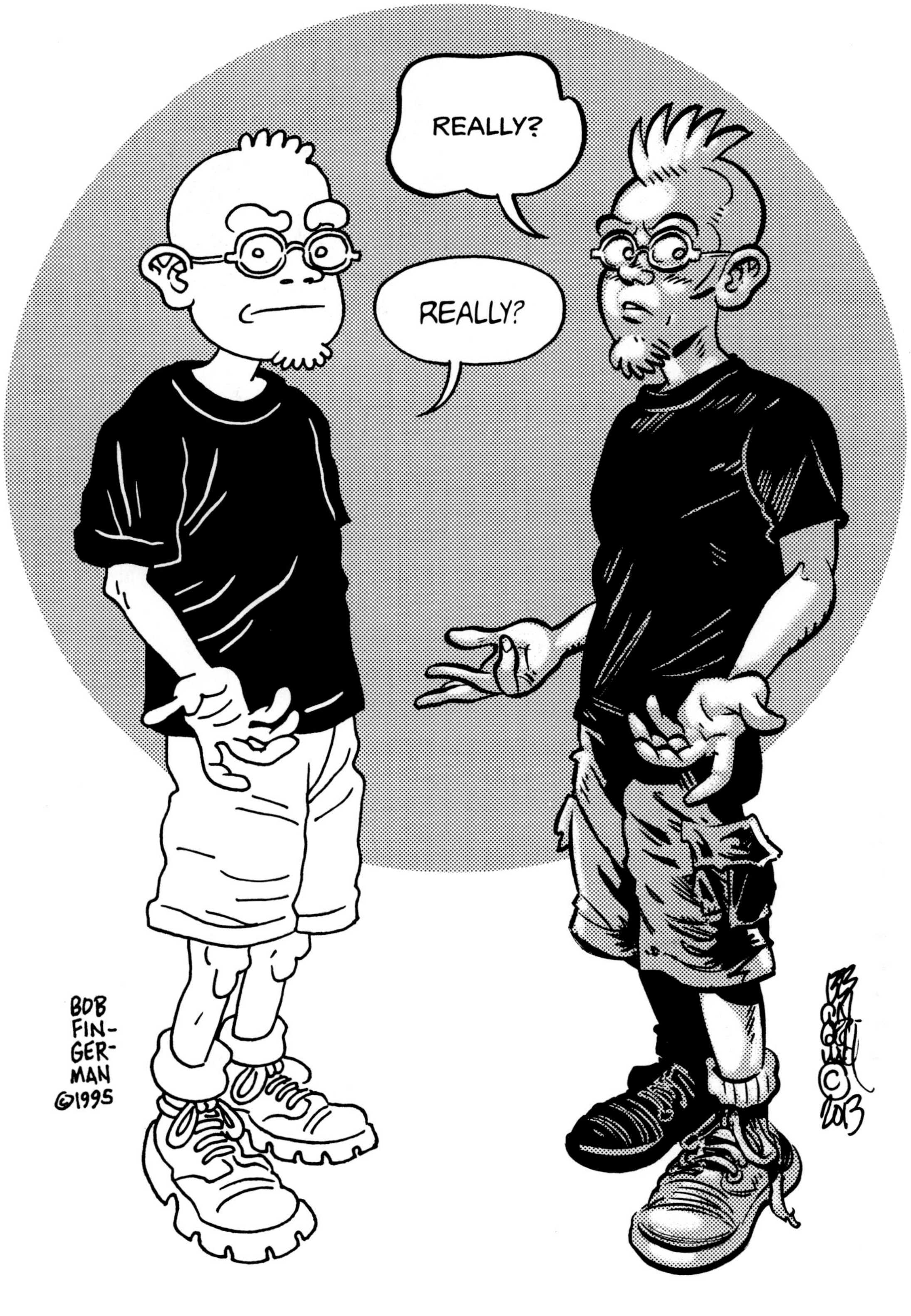
REALLY?
REALLY?
BOB FIN-GER-MAN ©1995